Professional Symbian Programming

Mobile Solutions on the EPOC Platform

Martin Tasker

**Jonathan Allin, Jonathan Dixon,
John Forrest, Mark Heath,
Tim Richardson, Mark Shackman**

Wrox Press Ltd. ®

Published by Wrox Press Ltd
Arden House, 1102 Warwick Road, Acock's Green, Birmingham B27 6BH, UK
Printed in USA
ISBN 1-861003-03-X

Trademark Acknowledgements

Wrox has endeavored to provide trademark information about all the companies and products mentioned in this book by the appropriate use of capitals. However, Wrox cannot guarantee the accuracy of this information.

Credits

For Symbian:

Principal Writer
Martin Tasker

Writers
Jonathan Allin
Jonathan Dixon
John Forrest (Purple Software)
Mark Heath
Tim Richardson
Mark Shackman

Project Manager
Andrew Margolis

Technical Illustrator
Trevor Coard

Additional Code
Steve Waddicor
Peter Ford

Code Review
Simon Chisholm
Keith de Mendonca
Andrew Thoelke

For Wrox:

Technical Editors
Tim Briggs
Jon Hill

Development Editor
Richard Collins

Project Manager
Chandima Nethisinghe

Managing Editor
James Hart

Index
Alessandro Ansa
Andrew Criddle

Design and Layout
Tom Bartlett
Mark Burdett
Jonathan Jones
John McNulty

Cover Design
Chris Morris

Cover Photography
Russell Meek

External Technical Reviewers
Evgenij Beresin, Richard Betts, Alastair Bradley, Ondra Cada, Mike Jipping, Vinay Kapoor, Tomi Koskinen, Sami Leppänen, John McAleely, Matt Millar, Will Powell, Eddie Pratt, Al Richey, Andrey Scherbakov, Andrew Schofield, Gavin Smyth, Erno Tuomainen, and Peter Wikström

To the engineers at Symbian who have created EPOC and are still creating it

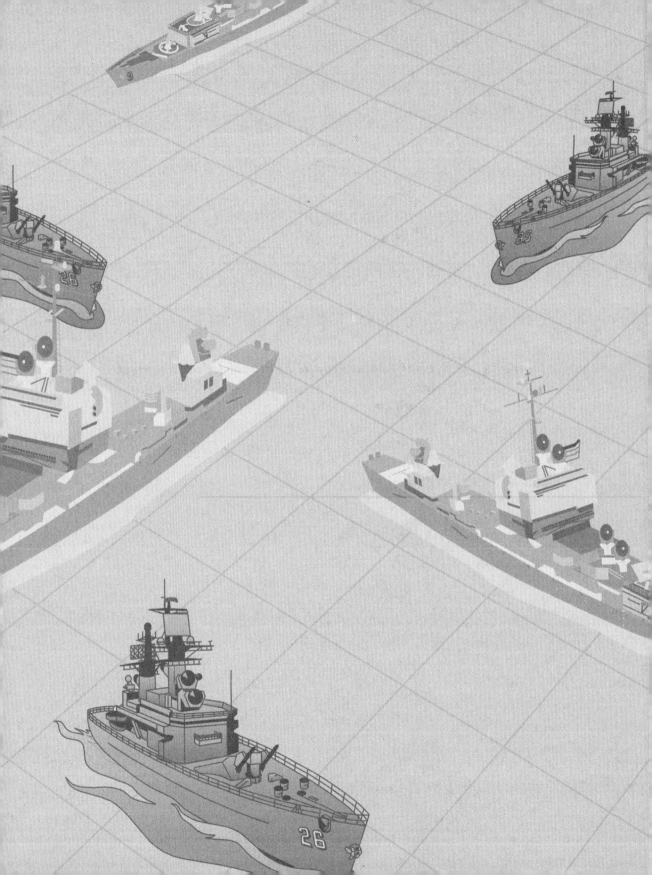

Table of Contents

Part One - EPOC Basics

Chapter 5: Strings and Descriptors · 133

Chapter 7: Streams, Stores, and File-based Applications 195

Chapter 8: Development Miscellany   239

Chapter 13: Finishing Touches   411

Chapter 14: Graphics in Practice   439

Part Three - Communications and Systems Programming

Chapter 16: Communications and Systems Programming 523

Chapter 17: The Transaction-oriented Games Stack 541

Chapter 18: Active Objects 575

Chapter 19: Client-server Framework   599

Chapter 20: The GSDP Server   627

Chapter 21: GDP Implementations   669

Chapter 22: Full Battleships   707

Part Four - A Full Platform

Chapter 23: Developing with Java   733

Chapter 24: The Wireless Application Protocol   787

Acknowledgements

It is a great privilege to work with experts. I've enjoyed that privilege in no small measure during my time at Psion and Symbian, and during this project with the whole editorial team at Wrox Press. I have learned a lot from all of them. Here, briefly, I record particular thanks to those who've worked to make this book what it is, and to those who have waited patiently for it to happen.

Firstly, and most of all, I'm indebted to the Protea project team who created the subject material for most of this book.

I've told the Protea story in Chapter 1, to give another perspective on why Symbian's EPOC technology is there as it is. Those I mention really did what I say they did – those I don't mention, and those I do, really did much more than is written there. If I've omitted details, and people, it's to keep it brief, to keep it to the point, to keep it readable, and to protect the innocent.

Next, the SDK team who worked with me to produce SDKs during and after the Protea project. I learned a lot from them as we worked together.

David Wood and Colly Myers were kind enough to release me from other responsibilities at Symbian in order to work full-time on the book. David's guidance, encouragement and support throughout the entire project have been invaluable.

Symbian staff who have contributed valuable comments at various stages of the book include Simon Chisholm, Keith de Mendonca, Mark Donohoe, Ralph Greenwell, David Knight, Phil Linttell, Bill Pinnell, Andrew Thoelke and many others. This is in addition to the huge peer review team assembled by Wrox Press. I have fielded over 2,000 comments with actions ranging from throwing whole chapters away, through restructuring, clarifying and wordsmithing, to doing nothing at all. But I've thought about every comment, and if anything has slipped through it's not for want of hawk-eyed vigilance on the part of the reviewers.

Acknowledgements

I'd like to thank Jonathan Dixon, Jonathan Allin, Mark Heath, John Forrest, Tim Richardson and Mark Shackman, the six writers whose contributions have ensured that Professional Symbian Programming covers the entire breadth of the Symbian platform, with the authority of experts in their field. Their contribution has in every case gone well beyond the call of duty. I'd like to express my thanks also to their managers and their loved ones, who for a short period might have seen less of them than they had been accustomed to.

Jonathan Dixon was responsible not only for the chapter that bears his name, but for the infrared and SMS implementations of Game Datagram Protocol that enable Battleships to function as a two-player game with long- and short-distance communication. It's been great working together on this project, and I am indebted both to Jonathan and his manager, Mal Minhas of the Personal Area Networking Group.

Thanks are due to Catriona Galbraith for looking after the contract from Symbian's end, Martin Owen for getting hold of the photos in Chapter 1, and Mark Shackman for his work on the CD-ROM.

Special thanks are due to all the figures in my life who have ever taught me anything about architecture or explanation. Among those not mentioned so far, Psion's Charles Davies is outstanding and I am grateful for particular information he has made available for the book. Other figures include Dr Martin Richards, Prof R M Needham, Dr S F Gull and Dr A C Norman who as supervisor and lecturers long ago taught me that some things are fun to hear about even if they're beyond my understanding, Finally Peter Gibbens who introduced me to physics, computers and radio communication, my Dad and Shirley Oakley for encouraging me, against the odds, to use my brain occasionally, and my Mum for keeping things going while I was using my brain.

As the senior technical editor on this project, Jon Hill of Wrox Press has kept me honest, has made sure I had *only* 2,000 review comments to handle by processing about twice as many himself, and has shaped the book in many ways. The entire team at Wrox Press has gone well beyond the call of duty: Jon's contribution has been outstanding. I'd also like to thank Tim Briggs, Richard Collins, James Hart, Victoria Hudgson and John Franklin for their contributions, patience and tact.

Many thanks are due to Filippe and Giuseppe of Addisons, that "darned fine coffee shop", whose legendary cappuccinos have stimulated much of the content of the book.

If a picture is worth a thousand words, then Trevor Coard is responsible for most of the content of the book! Only he will ever know how he deciphered the handwriting and hasty squiggles faxed in from seven engineers with inconvenient irregularity and constant urgency. Thanks Trevor.

Andrew Margolis has kept a department running in my absence, project managed the book, restrained my wilder plans, kept the whole team together, and battled with the CD production processes. Many thanks and much appreciation, to him, and to Caroline and Alex.

The last few months have unfairly stretched the patience of my family and friends. I'm grateful to my and my wife's families, the members of Grove Chapel, Camberwell, friends further afield, and especially to my parents-in-law for support and understanding.

Sarah has made more sacrifices than I have to finish this book. Anna Joy has remained bright and cheerful when Daddy relaxed again at weekends. I can only record here a small token of my thanks for their love, patience and support.

The Writing Team

Martin Tasker

Martin has an MA in Natural Sciences and Computer Science from Cambridge University. His interests have included communications and computers since high school: he qualified as a radio amateur in 1979, and started writing computer programs years before he had access to a computer. He was an early BBC Micro owner, for which he wrote and marketed a graphics package and a debugger in 6502 assembler – his first brush with ROM-based software.

During eight years at IBM Martin worked mainly in corporate network systems. From 1988 he participated in a four-person team that rewrote the 100,000-line System/370 assembler program that ran IBM's e-mail network – in better System/370 assembler.

From 1990 he worked for a year improving the network routing, with a 10,000 line C program and worldwide implementation project.

From 1993 Martin spent two years at Imperial College, London, using artificial intelligence to simulate route search, and object-oriented microsimulation to simulate route execution and congestion generation, in urban transportation networks, with novel techniques to model en route decision making. His main finding was that it was all very complicated.

In 1995 he got married, and joined Psion where he *really* began to learn about object orientation. He arrived toward the beginning of the Protea project, to which he made several architectural contributions, while running the SDK team that began the documentation of EPOC's C++ APIs, released the early SDKs, and kicked off the technical training program. He designed the HTML generation software used in Symbian's SDKs, and then re-used most of it for EPOC's help builder.

He is married to Sarah and they have a daughter, Anna Joy. Besides his family, he recalls that his interests include theology, languages, history and music, and is now looking forward to returning to some of them.

Jonathan Allin

Jonathan has a BSc in Electronics from Southampton University in the UK, and a DSc in Biomedical Engineering from the Technion in Israel. His first job was as a residential social worker with severely disabled children, which migrated into designing and building electronic and computerized aids for such children. He was with Acorn Computers for 8 years, helping to develop computers and software for schools and picking up an MBA on the way. He worked for Origin for three years, where he first became interested in Java, particularly in the role that it can play within the enterprise.

He now works for Symbian, talking about Java on EPOC, writing about Java on EPOC, and providing technical support for Java on EPOC. He is one of a number of people whose role is to ensure that EPOC provides the best Java platform for Wireless Information Devices.

Jonathan is married to Lauren. They have three children: Benjamin, Daniel, and Victoria. All three play rugby and music.

I would like to thank those who reviewed the material and who corrected my many technical and non-technical errors (any remaining errors are down to me), the Java development team under David Howell who suffered my innumerable questions, and Colin Turfus whose wide knowledge of EPOC and particular knowledge of JNI was invaluable.

Jonathan Dixon

Jonathan Dixon MEng A.C.G.I AMIEE has a degree in Information Systems Engineering from Imperial College, London. He has worked in the software industry for the last six years with a number of software houses. As well as developing communications software, he has worked on C++ testing tools and as a network administrator.

Since joining Symbian, he has developed the OBEX beaming software for use over IrDA, and is currently working on various technologies in the Personal Area Networking Team including Bluetooth.

Thanks to Mal Minhas, for handing me this project and allowing me the time to complete it. Also to all in the PAN team for their time and support throughout the project. Joe Fitzgerald, Chris Wilson, and the Telephony and Networking teams, for listening to my many and varied questions on subjects that don't concern me, and Martin, for not taking no for an answer. Emma, for all the sanity checks, even when they were a "fail". And finally, to Sir Walter Plinge.

John Forrest

John Forrest received a BA(Hons) in Computer Studies from the
University of Lancaster and a PhD in Computation from the University of
Manchester, both in the UK. He spent almost 15 years as a Lecturer at the
University of Manchester Institute of Science and Technology (UMIST),
teaching and researching in Systems Engineering. His teaching duties
were varied, ranging from hardware logic design to software engineering –
mostly directed at embedded, microprocessor-based systems. His research
was primarily in Hardware/Software Codesign – including how to
generate efficient hardware directly from C and C++ programs. He also
picked up some Unix systems-programming experience.

A desire for a change saw him leave academia to become an independent EPOC developer. He joined
Purple Software in 1999, where he specialises in EPOC applications programming.
John now lives in North London, and has interests including the cinema, walking and good food – not
necessarily in that order.

*I'd like to thank the other engineers at Purple Software for their input; in particular, John
Holloway for his technical advice, and Chris Scutt for checking through the example programs. I'd
also like to thank my partner Jane for her patience and general help in writing this chapter.*

Mark Heath

Mark has an MSc in Electronic System Design from Cranfield University,
and recently completed an MBA at the University of Surrey in the UK.
Mark's MBA thesis was quantitative research into the influence of new
product development practices on new product success in high-tech
companies. Mark started his career with Smiths Industries Aerospace and
Defence Systems, and then worked as a communication protocol software
engineer for five years at Datahouse Information Systems. Mark wrote
implementations of Internet protocols at a time when optimistic estimates
predicted that one day there would be 10,000 hosts on the net.

After Datahouse, Mark worked at Chase Research as project manager for ISDN terminal adapters,
product manager for ISDN technology (based in Boston, USA), and spent two years as Chase's
Engineering Manager at head office in Basingstoke, UK.

Mark joined Symbian in March 1999. As Engineering Manager for Communications Technology, Mark
runs a group composed of the networking, telephony, and personal area networking teams. He is a
member of the BCS and IEEE.

Since joining Symbian Mark has completed his MBA, got married to Irena, done an 850 mile cycle ride
for charity, bought a house, and become a father (to Esme). He commutes into central London in all
weathers on an unfeasibly large Triumph motorcycle.

*Thanks are due to Peter Ford who helped with the examples, the WAP Forum and all members of
the review team. Special thanks are due to Irena for letting me do most of the writing at home while
she held the baby!*

Tim Richardson

Tim Richardson graduated from Loughborough University of Technology in 1991 with a BEng (Hons) in Mathematical Engineering. From university he worked for British Telecom for seven years in Performance Engineering, then Verification, Validation and Testing, and finally in third line support for a prestigious BT platform. Tim joined Symbian's Developer Relations team, as the OPL specialist, at the start of 1999.

Tim's first experience of electronic PDAs was in the mid-80s, when he turned his programmable calculator into a PIM so he could remember to do his homework! Tim has not been without an electronic organizer since the early 90s.

While working for BT, Tim started his own company developing and selling an integrated contact and time manager for the Psion Series 5 (running EPOC). Due to the nature of his work for Symbian this business had to be passed on to someone else. He now spends his spare time split between Minis (a small car), digital photography and web site management.

I would like to thank Rick Andrews, Phil Spencer, Steve Waddicor and Howard Price for reviewing this chapter so thoroughly; Steve and Howard again for major contribution to sections of the chapter; and my wife, Melanie, for making sure it all made sense.

Mark Shackman

Mark Shackman BSc(Hons) MSc CertEd. graduated from South Bank University with a first class honours degree in Computing Studies. He then spent a further year at Brunel University completing his Masters degree in Digital Systems, with a specific focus on system software. Returning to his long-time interest in education, Mark trained as a teacher and then taught Mathematics & Information Technology at Hasmonean High School, London for 5 years before returning to the computer industry. After a spell at merchant bankers Morgan Stanley Dean Witter, Mark joined Psion Software in 1997 as a technical author, with particular emphasis on the Base and Connectivity documentation.

Since the formation of Symbian, Mark has had sole responsibility for the EPOC Connect SDK, subsequently transferring into the Connectivity Engineering Group. He currently works with third party developers, licensees and users of the various Connectivity newsgroups to provide help on and support for all aspects of Symbian's Connectivity solution, at the same time as writing SDK documentation & examples and acting as a PC installation program guru.

May I thank all those who reviewed the Connectivity chapter, in particular Joanne Stichbury for her very extensive comments, and David Spooner of Makesure Services Ltd., Adam Leach and David Kren for their observations and suggestions. Thanks are also due to Andrew Margolis for his Connectivity technical paper, SysDoc colleagues for support and encouragement when I joined the company, all the Connectivity team past and present in the Symbian "dungeon" for uncomplainingly providing answers to my constant questions, and finally to Hashem for everything else.

Foreword

In the early 1970s when I was programming mainframe computers, I worked on the introduction of a new 32-bit operating system. The new system was designed to replace an existing, very successful, operating system running on somewhat limited hardware. The new system was designed to do everything – including things that no-one had thought of yet. The result was overblown and unusable – actually less useful than the system it was intended to replace.

As a consequence I dreamed that one day I would write a new 32-bit operating system which would be tremendously effective by being very clearly focussed about what it had to achieve. Little did I imagine that I would have the privilege of carrying out my dream – on microprocessors which today are more powerful than the mainframes I was working on in the 1970s.

As we have faced the unique challenges of developing operating systems and application suites for the world's leading mobile devices, I and my colleagues have always remained committed to producing robust and reliable software. EPOC implements much of the latest thinking in the software world, but always in a way that adds value to the overall system without adding to its cost. This is the heart of good engineering. We developed many original and elegant constructs to make the development of robust and reliable software possible, such as EPOC's unique error handling framework, its event handling system based on active objects and a client-server architecture, and its powerful and flexible graphics architecture.

Professional Symbian Programming has been assembled by experts in the field with experience of real EPOC development. I would like to express my thanks to the whole team who through this book are helping to pass on the vision and knowledge that Symbian has used to create EPOC.

I hope you enjoy engineering with EPOC as much as I and my colleagues have enjoyed creating it. I have no doubt that EPOC will support you in producing well-engineered software – which is the first step in creating great products.

Colly Myers

Chief Executive Officer
Symbian Ltd.

Introduction

Symbian represents a unique proposition, in terms of its technology and its position in the world market for wireless information devices. Symbian's technology, encompassing an industrial strength operating system, a user-friendly application suite, PC-based data synchronization, and SDKs, covers the full spectrum of requirements for these devices.

This is a book by programmers, for programmers, covering the whole spectrum of Symbian development.

At the heart of Symbian's technology, EPOC is possibly the most exciting C++-based system in use today. A full OS is provided, with good object-oriented design from the ground up, and a very compact implementation. Power management is built right into the kernel, so you don't need to worry about it – and neither do end-users. Memory management, efficient event handling, files and documents, graphics and windowing, and many communications protocols are all provided through native C++ APIs. For porting standard C programs, a compatibility layer calls through to the native C++ code.

Professional Symbian Programming provides all you need to know to get started with EPOC programming, using Symbian's SDKs included in the book's CD-ROM, along with a suite of examples that have been developed specially for the book.

The chapters in the body of the book are organized into four major sections:

❑ **Introducing EPOC**: from Chapter 2 to Chapter 8, I introduce the main development tools and the really fundamental ideas you'll need in order to understand EPOC. Whatever your interest in EPOC, you'll need to read these chapters first.

❑ **Graphics and the EIKON GUI**: from Chapter 9 to Chapter 15, I describe EPOC's rich graphics programming environment, and the EIKON GUI which is the GUI for EPOC Release 5. I conclude these chapters with a look at the future, and how EPOC GUIs will evolve. If you're an application developer, or a GUI framework developer, these chapters will form a long-lasting starting point for access to detailed information in the SDKs.

❑ **Communications and System Programming**: from Chapter 16 to Chapter 22, I use a two-player game, Battleships, to motivate a description of EPOC's communications and systems programming architectures, including event-handling using active objects, and the client-server architecture. Jonathan Dixon, from Symbian's Personal Area Networking group, has contributed a chapter on infrared and SMS text messaging as used by Battleships. These chapters will make a good deal of sense, after Introducing EPOC, even if you skim over Graphics and the EIKON GUI.

❑ **A Full Platform**: from Chapter 23 onwards, a group of invited experts from Symbian and outside describe other major aspects of the Symbian platform, which build on the underlying robustness and power of EPOC. You can dip into these chapters in any order you like.

Altogether, these sections provide a total overview of the whole of Symbian's technology, viewed as a rich, industrial-strength development platform.

As a company, Symbian was launched by the world's major mobile phone handset manufacturers and Psion in June 1998. As a technology, EPOC was conceived in 1994 and delivered to first product in 1997. EPOC was Psion's fourth generation OS and application suite intended specifically for mobile devices, developed by a team that has now been working together for close to two decades. This combination of long experience with a modern system design make EPOC a great system to work with. I've had the privilege of being a member of that team for five years now. In Chapter 1, I'll describe how EPOC happened: what we aimed for, how we did it, and what we achieved. That'll establish a solid starting point for the rest of the book.

With EPOC alone, Symbian's technology would be incomplete. This book also includes expert chapters on

❑ **Java**: Jonathan Allin, of Symbian's Technical Consulting organization, describes EPOC's Java implementation, covering its history, development basics, porting Java applications from other platforms, writing Java applications specifically for EPOC, implementing native methods with the JNI, and a glance into the future

❑ **WAP**: Mark Heath, Symbian's Communications Technology Engineering Manager, describes this technology that is the key to the wireless Internet

❑ **Porting**: John Forrest, of Purple Software, describes the issues involved with porting code written in single-threaded or multi-threaded C to use EPOC's C standard library and C++ APIs. In the process, John gets to review the significance of some key aspects of EPOC's system design and how they affect your approach to porting projects.

❑ **OPL**: Tim Richardson, of Symbian's Developer Relations group, describes the Organiser Programming Language, a BASIC-like rapid application development language which has been evolving since Psion's second-generation Organiser II in 1986.

❑ **Connectivity**: Mark Shackman, of Symbian's Connectivity Engineering Group, describes the PC-based APIs provided by EPOC Connect, on which you can build custom data synchronization and connectivity applications in Visual Basic, Windows C++ and Delphi.

We cover the entire breadth of the Symbian programming experience. With over a quarter of a million words, nearly 300 illustrations and 44 example projects, we could also make some claims about depth.

In fact, this book is just a starting point for you to launch into development with the SDKs that are included on the CD-ROM. It puts everything in perspective: we tackle the big ideas, we do it in a logical order, and we provide lots of detail, hints and tips. But there is much more, even in EPOC Release 5, for which you'll need the SDK. Going forward, Symbian's technology platform will continue to expand – but this book is about the basics, and they'll remain.

Professional Symbian Programming complements Symbian's SDKs. The demanding pace of EPOC development has outstripped the supply of reference documentation, and the SDKs are still incomplete. Some important material is absent; some is so well hidden that it's not usually found until after it would have been useful; and some is based on perspectives which have matured with time. We have nearly three years experience of working with EPOC, since its first release in June 1997. We've trained hundreds of engineers within Symbian and in businesses throughout the world that are building on EPOC. This book reflects just some of that experience. We've plugged a couple of critical SDK gaps, especially on the client-server architecture; we've brought perspectives up to date; and in some places where the SDK is less than straightforward, we've aimed to be clear.

When you've put this book down, the SDKs will be your first resource for reference information on the central APIs in EPOC which we cover here. For reference documentation on more recent APIs, or on more specialized APIs, the SDKs are the only place to go. The SDKs contain valuable guide material, examples and source code, which together add up to an essential developer resource. We've pointed to these where they tie in with the book content. But as a general rule, look in the SDK anyway: you'll usually find additional information that takes things further than we could in this one book.

Who Is This Book For?

If you've programmed, at any level, in C++, it's for you. As a real and comprehensive system written in C++ from the ground up, and targeted at the high-growth area where computers and mobile communications converge, EPOC gives you opportunities in mass-market, enterprise and system programming that are unparalleled by any other system written in C++.

You'll no doubt find EPOC C++ different from other systems you've worked with. That doesn't mean EPOC C++ is hard. In general, we haven't exploited all the technical tricks offered by the C++ language: we've confined ourselves to relatively a safe set of programming practices that are easy to communicate and work with.

We do use a couple of C++ tricks here and there, but we get *much* more value in EPOC from good high-level design. Our design and thinking are entirely object-oriented, which has massive consequences for the way we approach software architecture, and massive consequences for our ability to re-use software. In turn, that enables us to make software systems compact and efficient. Design is hard to teach formally, and hard to learn formally. Experience is better. So I haven't wasted time on a dry and general design chapter: instead, I've let the explanations of EPOC's APIs, and my example projects, speak for themselves.

Besides C++ programmers, this book is interesting to other audiences:

❏ Java programmers

❏ any other programmer or manager looking to exploit the potential of mobile solutions with Symbian's technology

❏ consultants, trainers and authors thinking of basing their activity on Symbian's technology

❏ anyone with an interest in system design, since EPOC is a full and interesting example in its own right

There's lots to be done in all these areas, and we trust the book will help.

What You Need To Use This Book

As a C++ developer, I'm assuming you have a Windows-based PC and Microsoft Visual C++ 6.0 (or 5.0) – or, at least, that you can get hold of these when you need them, because this book is designed emphatically to be read from the comfort of your armchair, bed or bath, without a computer in sight. The EPOC SDKs provided on the CD which accompanies this book require Windows and Visual C++, and provide everything else you need to develop for EPOC. The PC-based emulator is all you'll need to build and run the supplied examples and to get started with EPOC development. Eventually, you'll probably want to buy an EPOC machine: models available as we went to press are listed in Appendix C.

To compile the Java code you'll need a version of the Java Development Kit between 1.1.4 and 1.1.8 – EPOC doesn't support Java 2, so you won't be able to use a JDK 1.2 compiler. Due to licencing restrictions, we are unable to include the web component in the SDKs shipping with this book, so you won't be able to test your applets within the EPOC emulator. However, you can download the necessary components from the Symbian Developer Network, after registering for free membership online at www.symbiandevnet.com.

To use the connectivity examples, you'll need a copy of EPOC Connect (or a proprietary version, such as PsiWin). This software is not included with the Connectivity SDK, but is distributed with all EPOC devices.

The Philosophy Of This Book

Writing is fun, challenging, and exhausting. I know someone who has just written a short book after 50 years in the same job, conveying some thoughts on the future of his profession: in the computer industry, we don't have that kind of luxury! My favourite book is 2000 years old, and still going strong: I doubt this one will last quite so long. We've done what needs to be done, as quickly as decently possible, and made the body of the book as long-lasting as we can safely predict.

In technical books, you can find several literary genres. Here are some of my favourites:

- ❏ the tour guide: you're on vacation and you have nothing to do, but you're ready for anything that's interesting. The guide walks you around, pointing out anything along the way, in no particular order except that it happened to be a convenient route. Later, over an ice cream or a coffee, you chat about anything that was interesting. Very leisurely, and not very structured: that's what vacations are for, after all.

- ❏ the dictionary: an alphabetically sorted and precise reference work. A short and informal dictionary can be like a tour guide, but real dictionaries are big, heavy, used for random access by most people, and read sequentially only by insomniacs.

- ❏ the detective novel: within a few pages of the beginning of the book, it becomes clear that there's a problem to be solved. A couple of hundred pages of excitement and suspense, false leads, incidental detail, and you believe you're getting close to a solution. Then the truth is revealed in a stunning climax.

- ❏ the pre-mission brief: a squad of commandos is about to set out on a dangerous mission. You're the briefing officer: you can give them purpose, highlight the expected difficulties, make sure they're properly equipped, and give them a map. That's all you can do: the rest is up to them. But you can make a big difference by briefing them properly.

You wouldn't expect this book to be like a vacation. I've tried to avoid suspense – though I haven't always succeeded. I've emphatically avoided the dictionary – that's the SDK's job. Where possible, I've opted for the pre-mission brief. I've given you the big ideas, the SDK is your equipment. Now it's over to you to execute the mission.

Conventions

To help you get the most from the text and keep track of what's happening, we've used a number of conventions throughout the book.

> **These boxes hold important, not-to-be forgotten information that is directly relevant to the surrounding text.**

While this style is used for asides to the current discussion.

We use several different fonts in the text of this book:

When we refer to word you use in your code, such as variables, classes and functions, or refer to the name of a file, we us this style: `iEikonEnv`, `ConstructL()`, or `e32base.h`

URLs are written like this: www.symbiandevnet.com

And when we list code, or the contents of files, we'll use the following convention:

```
Lines which show concepts directly related to the surrounding text are shown on a
gray background
But lines which do not introduce anything new, or which we have seen before, are
shown on a white background.
```

We show commands typed at the command line like this:

```
makmake battleships vc5
```

Tell Us What You Think

We've worked hard to make this book as useful to you as possible, so we'd like to know what you think. We're always keen to know what it is you want and need to know.

We appreciate feedback on our efforts and take both criticism and praise on board in our future editorial efforts. If you've anything to say, let us know on:

feedback@wrox.com
or
http://www.wrox.com

1

A New EPOC

In this chapter, I aim to give you the background you'll need to understand the context of developing with EPOC. I'll describe the Protea project that produced EPOC Release 1 and the Psion Series 5. You'll be able to understand the unique mix of design choices that governed EPOC's early evolution, and how those choices affect EPOC as it is today.

Leading up to Protea, there's some important pre-history about Psion and its earlier software systems that surfaces occasionally throughout later parts of the book. After Protea, I focus on Symbian, EPOC Release 5, and a brief look to the future.

Beginnings

In 1981 David Potter's new company released its first product. Potter, a physics lecturer at Imperial College London, had made good on the stock market and had quit his academic post to set up in business. He had initially titled his company Potter Scientific Investments, or PSI, but finding that name was already taken, he added another two letters to form **Psion**. To a physicist, "Psion" sounds exciting – like some newly discovered sub-atomic particle.

Within a few years, "Psion" was sounding exciting to consumers throughout Europe and further afield. In 1991, Psion's small and sophisticated personal organizers were in their third generation. With a keyboard suitable for touch-typing, a pocketable size, a sophisticated application suite, a power requirement low enough for a month of heavy use on two AA cells, and proper power management including instant on/off and a safe backup battery, Psion's invention was the clear world leader against competition from giants such as Apple, Sharp and HP.

In 1997, Psion launched its fourth-generation operating system, EPOC, at the heart of its new Series 5 model. The previous generations had given Psion's engineers more experience in this kind of software than any other team in the world. But EPOC was a total rewrite of the third-generation SIBO system that was by then reaching its limits – 16-bit architecture, C programming language, and close ties with the Intel x86 CPU architecture. SIBO had enjoyed a useful life of about 10 years, and total rewrites are expensive: EPOC was designed for useful life well into the new millennium.

Stepping back in time once again, 1981 also saw the first deployment of a modern mobile telephone system: the Nordic Mobile Telephone system, NMT. Developed jointly by Ericsson of Sweden and Nokia of Finland, it was launched in Saudi Arabia before being rolled out to its home countries later the same year. The equipment in use at the time was so heavy that pocket devices were out of the question – NMT was essentially a carphone system.

Throughout the 1980s and 1990s, equipment reduced in size, and became more personal and massively popular. New digital transmission standards were introduced throughout the world, bringing greater security and clarity, more effective use of the scarce radio spectrum, and the potential for reliable data transmission. High-end mobile phones began to evolve increasingly sophisticated software and, by the mid-1990s, the world's major handset manufacturers were looking for a suitable operating system with a sophisticated applications software suite that could be integrated conveniently into a mobile phone.

Symbian, formed in June 1998, is the result. Symbian is composed of the old software division of Psion, now spun out and owned jointly by Nokia, Ericsson, Motorola, Panasonic (Matsushita) and Psion. With headquarters and main development site in London, Symbian also has development sites at Cambridge, England and Ronneby, Sweden, and offices in Tokyo and Silicon Valley. To emphasize its move away from organizers and handheld computers into mobile phones and the like, Symbian calls products running EPOC, "Wireless Information Devices". A year after its formation, Symbian launched EPOC Release 5, a major upgrade incorporating a Java runtime, telephony APIs and other technology specifically for wireless devices.

1981 is widely known as the year in which IBM launched its revolutionary PC architecture. Less well known, 1981 was the launch year of a new British home computer, the BBC Micro, from Cambridge-based company Acorn. With an 8-bit 6502 CPU, 32k ROM and 32k RAM, the "Beeb" sold hundreds of thousands and was immensely popular with a generation of British computer enthusiasts – many of whom are at the core of the software engineering industry in Britain today. Astonishingly, in 1985, Acorn's engineers used a 128k version of the BBC Micro architecture as a CAD system on which they designed a revolutionary new CPU architecture, the Acorn RISC Machine or ARM. With only 22,000 transistors and a very simple instruction set, the ARM was built on radically different assumptions from those that were driving the desktop PC industry. The ARM was by far the most power-efficient chip available, as well as the cheapest, by the time Psion came to select a processor for its new EPOC-based product lines.

Nuclear physicists gave the world an even more spectacular technology boost. In 1993, Tim Berners-Lee worked at the European Centre for Nuclear Research (CERN) in Geneva, Switzerland. He invented HTML as a means for sharing information between members of the scientific research community in a new, inter-linked, World-Wide Web. Established systems required awkward and time-consuming commands to find information, and to transfer it from place to place using telnet, FTP, and curiosities such as gopher, veronica and wais. With a simple click to navigate anywhere on the Web, HTML unlocked an entirely new way of working.

The Web has created a new networked economy that has revolutionized publishing, media and commerce. So powerful are the resulting forces that they even threaten the meaningfulness of Microsoft's hegemony over desktop PC applications and operating systems. The resulting struggles between Microsoft, Netscape, Sun and the US Department of Justice are the fascination of the world.

Even more rapidly, a new wireless economy is beginning to emerge, as Internet and mobile phone technologies come together. Today, we are at the beginning of that revolution, in which Symbian and its EPOC technology is playing a central role, and which will within a few years dwarf even the scale of the Internet phenomenon. This book will equip you to be there too.

Psion

Potter had brought Charles Davies, a research assistant from Imperial College, and persuaded friends to join the new start-up too. Colly Myers, now chief executive officer of Symbian, was among the first. Working from a small office off the Edgware Road in Central London, they began with software distribution, and soon moved into software development.

Psion's first major software product was a flight simulator for the Sinclair ZX Spectrum, the third and most successful home computer produced by another British entrepreneur, Clive Sinclair. The flight simulator was a spectacular success: with over a million sales, the team was instantly rich, and the business was able to expand.

Sinclair introduced his next home computer, the QL, in 1984, and Psion bet again on its success. This time, they were wrong: the QL had technical problems with its in-built tape storage devices ("microdrives"), and it arrived on the market at a time when product expectations were being set by the IBM architecture. It was a flop, causing major difficulties for Potter and his team.

While they had been developing the software for the QL, there was a parallel development of a radical new concept: a database oriented pocket computer. After a short project, they released the Psion Organiser in 1984 and, building on the experience from this first model, the Organiser II in 1986. With a combined total of 32k ROM and RAM, the Organiser II range included consumer, professional and enterprise models, applications including diary, database, clock, alarms and calculator, solid-state disk drivers, peripherals including barcode and magnetic-card readers, and an in-built Organiser Programming Language (OPL) for rapid development of custom enterprise applications.

The Organiser was a huge success. Worldwide sales totaled well over a million by the time it was retired in the late 1990s.

By 1988, Psion had floated on the London Stock Exchange, and was again cash-rich and looking for new opportunities. Desktop PCs had become extremely powerful, and Psion sought to combine the power of the desktop PC with the portability of its organizer products. To do this would require a much more user-friendly set of applications than those available on the Organiser II, with a full screen and keyboard. In turn, these applications would require a new operating system. An ambitious project was initiated: **SIBO** ("sixteen-bit organiser" or "single-board", depending on whether you asked the software or hardware team) would build on the OS experience from the Organisers, and the office application experience from the old QL projects.

In 1990 the first SIBO machine was launched: the MC laptop. It sported a full-size keyboard, an LCD screen and a track-pad cursor. Inside was an Intel 186-compatible processor. The OS and applications occupied just 384k and included Diary, Alarms, Word, Personal Database, Calculator and others. Thanks to the power of SIBO and its GUI, the word processor required only 12k to support rich text editing. The operating system supported full multitasking: you could switch between running applications at the touch of a button. Everything ran in only 128k RAM (although 256k was available on a higher-specification model). In the PC world, OS/2 Version 2 and Windows 3.0 were to bring similar but slower capabilities to the desktop in 1991, for systems with 4MB as a practical minimum. And the MC would run for a week on just six AA alkaline cells.

Nevertheless, the MC was a flop. There were hardware issues: the track-pad was awkward, and the machine as a whole was notoriously prone to static. But the real killer was that, in the two years since the MC was conceived, PC miniaturization had resulted in practical laptops. The MC was simply too late.

The team was exhausted. Many had worked heroically, round the clock, to develop, debug, manufacture and release the MC. And now it was back to the drawing board - but not back to square one. The 16-bit operating system and application suite developed for the MC were flexible enough to be tailored for different hardware. As in 1984, Psion went for a smaller, more portable device.

The next machine they designed was a winner. The Series 3, released in 1991, was an easily pocketable device with a small but very usable QWERTY keyboard, an ingenious clamshell design, and improved versions of the MC applications. There was no hardware pointer, and no support for a pointer in the GUI software. Software development kits were issued: you could program SIBO in C, x86 assembler, or OPL. Uniquely for this class of machine, you could program without the assistance of a PC host, since the OPL editor, translator and interpreter were all built into the Series 3 itself.

The Series 3 was an instant success, and spawned a whole family of successful devices that led the world market for personal organizers for the next six years. Consumer variants included the Series 3a (1993) with a bigger display, a much improved Agenda schedule application, and a new built-in spreadsheet. Then there were the Series 3c (1996) with built-in infrared, the Siena (1996) with infrared, a calculator-like form factor, smaller screen and lower price, and the Series 3mx (1998) with three-times performance improvement over the 3c.

The WorkAbout, introduced in 1995, was an industrial variant designed to be held with one hand and used with the other. It included serious waterproofing, and was popular with more than one European forestry commission.

SIBO was an extremely valuable experience for Psion:

- SIBO machines succeeded in the marketplace because they were robust: they were very well designed and debugged. They almost never crashed, had to be rebooted, or lost the user's data.

- SIBO had effective power management. You could turn a SIBO machine on or off instantly. In the Series 3 range, two AA cells would last for over a month of heavy use. You could also change batteries without worry, thanks to a system with main battery, backup battery, and aggressively tested power management software that ensured the kernel handled power failure in every conceivable circumstance.

- SIBO's applications and GUI were extremely easy to use, especially for a device with no mouse or pen. The instruction manual was friendly, but more importantly the applications, graphic design and menus were self-explanatory. Machines functioned exactly as end users expected – including those who weren't very familiar with desktop PCs.

- The Series 3 machines all had a winning hardware combination: they were small enough to fit into your pocket, but had a reasonable keyboard on which you could touch type. Rival machines from this period did not share these features. HP and Sharp had poor keyboards, and Sharp's user interface was unintuitive. Rivals' power management could deliver nasty surprises, causing complete data loss. General Magic's GUI was so 'cool' that it entertained for a moment, but couldn't be used for anything useful. Other companies, including Microsoft, developed operating systems for handheld devices that were unusable in practice – and were wise enough not to release them. Apple's failure with the Newton was more complex, but characteristically its PR campaign had lasting effect: their term **Personal Digital Assistant** (PDA) still describes the product category.

- Psion learned later in SIBO's life that interoperability with other devices – especially desktop PCs – was vital for the success of their handheld products. People wanted to save their data to their PC for backup purposes. People wanted to be able to convert Word documents between PC and SIBO formats, for editing on their PC while in the office, or on their Psion while on the move. PIM products began to appear on PCs, and people wanted to synchronize their contact and schedule information between PC and Psion. In early 1995, Psion released PsiWin 1.0, a PC program whose GUI resembled Windows' File Manager, and which presented each drive on a connected SIBO machine as a disk similar to one on the PC. You could backup or restore from the menus, and you could drag-and-drop files easily between your PC and your SIBO machine. Series 3a sales were visibly boosted by the release of PsiWin.

These were the reasons why SIBO was very popular with consumers, but for developers and manufacturers, there are other forces behind successful products:

- SIBO delivered immense power to its applications through re-use of powerful system software components. The Word application in the MC was only a 12k program because SIBO included a component for manipulating rich text that was used not only by Word, but by many of the other applications too. The Series 3 ROM was only 384k. Even the final Series 3mx models needed only 1MB ROM, including spell-checking dictionaries.

- SIBO delivered power through object-oriented design and programming. Object orientation supports effective and manageable system design and evolution. Design is vital: you can't debug what you haven't designed in. Evolution is vital throughout a product's life. There were some initial worries about the efficiency of OO systems, but Psion soon learned OO programming patterns that optimized efficiency and good design.

❑ Finally, SIBO's applications were written in the form of engines that manipulated their data, and GUIs that interacted with the engines and the user. This allowed the same application engines to be used on the MC and the (quite different) Series 3 devices. The GUIs were flexible enough to be fine-tuned without rewriting them altogether, which allowed Psion to adapt SIBO for the different screen sizes of the Series 3, Series 3a, Siena and Work*About* models.

All of this experience was to prove vital when Psion's design team began work on EPOC.

Protea

By early 1994, Psion had considerable experience of working with SIBO. Like all systems, SIBO had limitations. It was becoming apparent, however, that these limitations were such that an entire rewrite would be needed to provide a platform for long-term future development.

Fundamentally, SIBO was a 16-bit system. 16-bit systems mean numbers and addresses no greater than 65,536 – 64k. So SIBO was full of 64k limits: on the size of DLLs, the size of documents, the size of a memory chunk, etc. The Intel-based PC world had invented cumbersome techniques for overcoming 64k limits, such as pairing up pointers into (segment:offset) combinations, but this uses program code and data bytes that are too scarce to waste on a handheld system. SIBO's original design didn't use it, and it would be cumbersome to graft it in.

With graphics, multimedia, longer documents, larger databases, and industry-standard communications all requiring 32-bit addressing, there was no real choice but to move on from the old 16-bit architecture. Thus, Psion had to travel the same road that IBM had traveled with OS/2 Version 2 in 1991, and Microsoft with Windows NT in 1993. It took Psion the 3 years until 1997 to deliver EPOC to production quality.

SIBO's GUI didn't support a pointing device – either pen or mouse. Support for a pointer would entail additions throughout the entire UI architecture, and the MC project had already shown that this would not be trivial.

SIBO was tied to the Intel x86 architecture. Large sections of the kernel were written in assembler, and porting it to another architecture would be difficult. And yet it was known that the Intel architecture was evolving in ways that were very far from the power and cost requirements of hand-portable devices.

SIBO was written in C. The object-oriented framework used by the GUI and higher-level system and application components was implemented ingeniously using the C preprocessor and proprietary tools such as a so-called "category translator". But to write a new system, and to attract the software engineers necessary to continue to develop that system, a modern standard language would be needed.

Psion needed to support not only Western European languages, but also worldwide markets. For this, support for 16-bit Unicode characters would be needed. But the characters in SIBO were encoded using such a mixture of schemes that it would be impossible to modify SIBO simply to build in support for Unicode characters.

What Next?

In mid-1994, Colly Myers was assigned to start designing what would become his fourth operating system, after the Organiser, the Organiser II, and SIBO. At the time, Psion had a flower theme for project code names, so Colly chose **Protea**, a large flower found mainly in South Africa.

Psion was again cash-rich, and the entire project would be funded from its own resources – as indeed every project had been, since its formation back in 1980. There was no serious competition around for the Series 3a at the time the project started, and Psion knew the lead times and technical issues involved in setting up a rival were non-trivial. Even so, serious competition *could* arrive at any time, and this gave conscious time-to-market pressure to the project leadership. It took three years to produce the Series 5, cost some £6 million, and involved at its peak a software team of around 70. For a major 32-bit operating system with application suite and software development kits, this was astonishingly fast and cheap.

Charles Davies, lead middleware architect on the project, identified two causes of failure in other software teams that Protea had to avoid. First, the Taligent team, a Florida-based alliance between Apple and IBM, had worked on a conceptually brilliant object-oriented OS, but had failed because their view of the end product was too vague. In short, they didn't know where they were heading, had no means to tell whether they had got there, and had no notion of whether there was a market for what they were doing. Protea learned much from Taligent's object-oriented wisdom – and determined to avoid their biggest mistake.

Second, a well-documented phenomenon in the computer industry is the 'second-system effect'. You have already done one system, you know its bugs and limitations, and you need to do a rewrite. The temptation is to fix everything, add vast numbers of improvements, and do something that is unquestionably better however you choose to measure it. But projects like that are always a year away from completion, because there is always more you could do.

Both these mistakes were avoided by a simple rule: the objective of Protea was to be better than a Series 3c. Yes, it was to be built on a brand new 32-bit architecture; yes, it would have greater longevity; yes, it would have a much improved GUI with pen support; yes, it would have much better built-in communications; yes, it would have better PC data synchronization. But there would be a limit: as the first product, Protea would be better than a Series 3c. Future improvements would deliver into future products.

In the end, EPOC Release 1, as found in the Psion Series 5, was *much* better than the Series 3c in almost every way – but it did also lack one or two features, and long-time Psion users missed them. And although Psion added *many* architectural features to EPOC that weren't present in SIBO, they were all there for definite reasons connected with the specific objective of releasing a machine that was simply "better than a Series 3c".

The Protea team's experience of 10 years and three previous operating systems gave it a great start on the project. Their use of C++, informed by Taligent and their own experience with OO in SIBO, enabled them to write a compact kernel, set of middleware libraries and GUI on which thin-but-powerful applications could be built.

Base and Tools

Colly's first task was to identify a development environment. SIBO had used an obscure DOS-based C compiler with a text mode debugger. Other handheld SDKs available at the time used DOS, Mac OS, or even two PCs – one for developing and one for running the target software. Colly knew his development team had to get ahead of the curve: he settled on Microsoft Windows NT as a robust and popular development platform, and Microsoft Visual C++ as the development environment. Its debugger was the best in the industry at the time.

The next task would be to design the low-level utility library that would provide services to all EPOC programs. Once this had been designed and implemented, higher-level components could be written above it, and the kernel, interfacing with real hardware, could be written below it.

Colly titled the low-level library **E32**, and it came to include the kernel, main device drivers and user library. The E stood for EPOC, and the 32 for 32 bits, in contrast to SIBO's 16. People have often asked what EPOC stands for, and various imaginative theories have arisen. The truth is simple: it's short for "epoch" – chosen because the devices that ran it would herald a new epoch in personal computing. EPOC had been used to refer to the SIBO kernel. In SIBO's 32-bit successor, it would come to mean the whole system.

It would be a long time, however, before real hardware, or even a compiler to generate code for it, would be available. Meanwhile, an emulator was written that provided exactly the right APIs to the user library, but implemented the kernel as a thin layer over Win32 APIs, and the screen as a window that could be moved around, like any other window, on the PC's screen.

The CPU

Mark Gretton, Psion's chief technologist, was assigned the job of choosing a CPU and designing an ASIC (application-specific integrated circuit) for the Protea.

He checked available designs and implementations from Intel, Motorola, Digital, Hitachi and SGI among others. In the end he settled on the ARM architecture. Acorn's design of the mid-1980s had matured into what was then an unusual business model in the semiconductor industry. The ARM architecture was licensed to scores of semiconductor companies who were free to incorporate it into any design they chose. As a result, there was good competition in the marketplace that, combined with the basic facts of a low transistor count, made ARM architecture parts available at very favorable prices. In terms of both MIPS/$ and MIPS/Watt, the ARM was the clear leader, and it was chosen for the Protea.

Gretton worked with ARM Ltd and Cirrus Logic to define an ASIC code-named EIGER (a mountain in Switzerland) that incorporated the ARM CPU core and all the peripherals needed by the Protea.

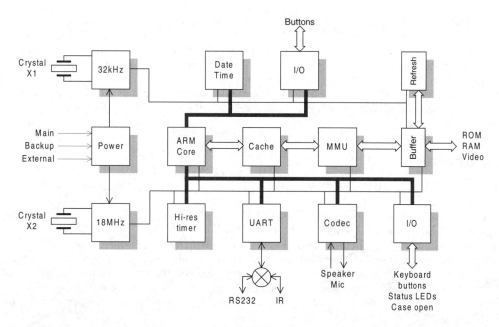

All possible steps were taken to conserve power. Static logic was used, so the chip retained its state without needing a constant clock. An 18MHz clock powered the CPU and high-speed logic. A 32kHz clock kept a date/time clock, RAM refresh logic and the interface with the on/off key going while the device was turned off. The MMU, a power-hungry part, was placed after the cache so that it needed to operate only on a cache miss. Three power inputs were supported – main battery, backup battery and external – with voltage detectors on the batteries to facilitate low-power warning. Non-maskable interrupt was reserved for rapid reaction to total loss of power – vital emergency power-down logic.

All the major devices were driven from the EIGER chip: keyboard, status LEDs, buttons for using the voice recorder while the Protea's case was closed, codec for sound recording and playback, LCD and digitizer controllers, real-time clock, date/time clock, and a single UART that could be used for either RS232 or infrared communication.

The 18MHz clock rate allowed the ARM core to deliver performance comparable with a 33MHz 486, at a fraction of the cost and power requirement. That was pretty good: at the time, the fastest desktop CPUs available were 90MHz Pentiums.

Initially, the Protea was specified to include only 1MB RAM, with a high-end 2MB model. This had been sufficient for the Series 3c but, as the project proceeded, it became clear that more RAM would be needed for a practical EPOC machine. Since RAM prices had begun to tumble in 1996, the specification was upped to 4MB for the entry model and 8MB for the higher-end machine.

SIBO had used static RAM, but dynamic RAM was much cheaper. EIGER included refresh logic that would still drain power even with the machine off – an idea that was hard to get used to. But the economics were compelling, and in any case the power drain was low: with AA cells, RAM contents would be retained for months with the machine turned off.

Having chosen the ARM CPU, one further issue remained: the compiler. Colly and Mark Gretton worked with Cygnus Inc. to add ARM support to the GNU C++ compiler, GCC. Using GCC had the significant advantage that it could be freely distributed with EPOC SDKs, and already supported Unix-style shared libraries. Psion funded Cygnus to convert its library support intoWindows-style DLLs and to add templates, which would be required by EPOC. At the time, GCC did not support C++ exception handling, and Psion didn't fund its development: it would be time-consuming, and EPOC's cleanup system, based on long SIBO experience, provided an alternative tailored specifically to EPOC's requirements.

The Machine

By mid-1995, the industrial design of the Protea had matured in all its major parameters.

Firstly, as a pen-based product, it would use an LCD screen with a digitizer for detecting pen taps and movement. The screen would have twice the area of the Series 3c's: 640x240 pixels, and either four or sixteen shades of gray. The choices involved in choosing a display are among the more difficult in handheld computer design. LCD contrast is low, and you can increase it significantly only by going to an active design that uses much more power. Add a digitizer over the LCD, and you reduce the contrast still further. Add a backlight, and you reduce it again. The Series 5's LCD proved to have significantly lower contrast than any Series 3 model's; one of the major improvements with the Series 5mx, released in 1999, was better display contrast.

It was immediately realized that using the pen on a design like the Series 3's would tip the device over. The Protea used an ingenious hinge design to avoid this problem that has proven immensely successful.

The Series 3 screen and keyboard had both had significant surrounds. It was decided to make the Protea screen fill the top half of the clamshell completely, while the keyboard completely filled the bottom half. At the time of writing, the Protea keyboard remains the best of in any product in its class, allowing very easy touch typing. The screen, already big for devices of this class, was made to look bigger still by extending it with application icons along the bottom, and common tasks (menu, clipboard, infrared beaming and zooming) along the left.

The Series 3 range had used flash-memory Solid-state Disks (SSDs) to store data, like diskettes on a PC. Each Series 3 model had two SSD slots. Eventually, the Series 5 settled on a single CF-card slot (Compact Flash, a subset of the PC-Card standard used for notebook peripherals). In practice, the only widely-supported type of CF card is the CF memory card, which functions like a disk in drive d:. For connecting to the outside world, the Protea design featured an RS232 connector supporting connection speeds up to 115kbps, and an infrared port for IrDA data beaming and printing.

Back to the Base

Meanwhile, Colly and his team continued with the base.

The distinctive features of the user library that will be familiar by the time you reach the end of this book – the descriptors used for text and binary data; the resource cleanup framework; the active objects used for asynchronous processing; the client-server framework used as the means to provide centralized services to EPOC threads, and to keep services out of the kernel – were all in place early on. The kernel was implemented as a special kind of server, and a true multitasking system began to emerge.

The base team also began to work on communications software: serial RS232 for the most basic communications, including that required for kernel debug logging, and sockets for higher-level protocols including a TCP/IP suite.

To run a real kernel, and real communications, you need real hardware. The EIGER chipset and adapted GCC compiler were not yet ready, so the base team used an ingenious alternative: they created the MX86 implementation of EPOC, which booted native on PC hardware. By this means, and using the sophisticated hardware debugging tools available for PCs, they were able to debug much of the kernel and device driver architecture before real ARM-based hardware arrived.

The GUI

The biggest challenge of the Protea project was the GUI. David Wood, chiefly responsible for the SIBO GUI implementation, was assigned the task of implementing the GUI for Protea. SIBO, as a personal organizer platform, had a GUI that was easy enough for anyone who was familiar with desktop-based windowing systems to use: there were views, dialogs and controls. The distinguishing feature of SIBO's GUI was not to choose a unique interaction metaphor, but to make the conventional windowing metaphor work really well for the small form factor and for non-technical users. Protea would continue this tradition: we briefly looked at GUIs such as Magic Cap, which took 'real-world' metaphors to extremes, and decided that they were unusable and indeed, after the initial novelty had worn off, seemed rather childish.

David knew what had to be done, and the necessity not to be carried away by the second-system effect, and got down to coding HCIL – the "human-computer interaction layer" – starting with the dialog framework, controls and central GUI utilities. He spent much of his time recruiting a team of bright engineers, nearly all of whom, like him, had backgrounds in hard sciences rather than software engineering. Evenings and even nights were spent merging in the code produced by his team, commenting on it, composing release notes for the rest of the Protea team, and feedback e-mails so that his team members could learn from their mistakes.

The standard controls included not just number and text editors, but calendars, date and time editors, latitude and longitude editors, and other components that may seem low on the list for general GUIs, but which are central to a personal organizer. The controls emerged quickly, but the dialog framework proved more complicated, and items such as scrollbars and list boxes more complicated still. Even so, a usable dialog framework quickly emerged.

Then came the first major rewrite.

It still wasn't certain whether the Protea product would include a pen (and a digitizer screen) or not. The GUI therefore had to be usable both with and without a pen. In the old days, when not every PC had a mouse, IBM and Microsoft designed the interaction metaphors used by Windows and OS/2 such that dialogs could be navigated using *Tab* and *Shift+Tab*, or a quick jump from control to control using *Alt* plus the control's accelerator key, which would be underlined in the dialog. The HCIL team duly set about implementing this behavior.

Some of the team began to point out, however, that most non-technical users have never used a PC without a mouse, and would never be able to guess the rules of the IBM/Microsoft dialog navigation system. People expect to use *arrows* to move around, not strange combinations of *Tab* and *Alt* keys. We would use arrows, or we would lose our non-technical users. The arrows vs. *Tab* debate brewed for a couple of months, raged for a couple of weeks, and was finally resolved in favor of arrows.

The result was radical change. Up and down arrows would be used to move between dialog controls. Left and right arrows would be used to move within controls. There was no mechanism for moving left and right *between* controls, which in turn meant that dialogs had to become one-dimensional: just a simple list of controls that would be formatted and laid out vertically. It also meant that *Tab* was available as a key within standard controls, and it was adopted to mean "pop out and display a fuller view" – a whole calendar, for example, or all the choices in a list.

This meant a complete re-specification and rewrite of the dialog framework, all controls, and all the applications that had been written to that date. After no fewer than 114 internal releases, HCIL was abandoned.

It was replaced by two new components: CONE (the "control environment"), and EIKON (pronounced "icon" – it's Greek for "appearance" or "form"), which was the new name for the GUI. CONE was responsible for the rectangular areas on the screen that could be used to place GUI components, and for ensuring that pointer and key events were offered to the right controls. CONE was *not* responsible for providing any real controls, or any look-and-feel. At a higher level, EIKON provided the look-and-feel specific to the Protea. If a different look-and-feel were ever required, EIKON could be replaced, but CONE would stay the same.

After some weeks of furious re-coding around the end of 1995, it was possible for most applications to change from HCIL to EIKON, and to get ready for the first big push to integrate the whole EPOC system.

Ironically, there was never a pen-less Protea, but EPOC's design was much better for this change, and EIKON is very easy to use without a pen. Future EPOC implementations without a pen *will* exist, and the ability to replace EIKON without replacing CONE has proved to be a crucial aspect of EPOC's adaptability in the demanding market for wireless information devices, a theme we'll cover in Chapter 15.

Middleware

Middleware is crucial. Without any middleware, each application must reinvent the same wheels, which costs time and ROM. It makes the applications inconsistent to use, and spreads the testing effort thinly across the ROM, rather than concentrating it on heavily re-used components. We had to have good middleware, to have a chance of fitting all the applications into the ROM budget – which was now projected at 6MB. With good middleware, it is very much easier to write software that is both compact and powerful.

But it is easy to go wrong with middleware:

❑   If you make a bad design decision in middleware, if affects *everyone*. You either have to rewrite the middleware, or have everyone live with the bad design, or face that fact that people will write their own rather than use a poor design.

❑   It is always tempting to add speculative generality to middleware – to provide APIs that do not only what you immediately want, but also 'other things' that you have a hunch will be important but you haven't time to do just yet. When it comes round to doing these other things, however, APIs designed with speculative generality can prove quite inappropriate – either because of a major design error, or because something minor was overlooked.

❑   Middleware is just as subject as anything else to the second-system effect.

There are ways to avoid these problems. There is an old cliché in object-oriented programming that software is not re-usable until it has been re-used. We went further: our philosophy was that software is not usable until it has been used. We developed the middleware at the same time as the applications, and iterated the two together, in order to make sure that the middleware was just right for its intended purpose.

Charles Davies led EPOC's middleware development team, building on experience from all Psion's previous software systems, and inspiration from Windows, X, Taligent and other systems.

They began with graphics: the GDI (graphics device interface), the fast bit-blitter, the font management system, the window server and the print system. The window server would be used to share the screen between all GUI applications: this server architecture was inspired by X, and had been used successfully on SIBO since 1988.

> *EPOC's graphic system has many unique aspects, including built-in zooming and on-screen print preview, that were designed in at a deep level based on previous experience with SIBO.*

Another SIBO component that was ported to EPOC (with improvements) was the rich text system. With one component to handle rich text content, another to handle its display, and an EIKON control to implement a full rich text editor, it was possible for relatively simple programs to use the full power of a text editor supporting any-length documents, a rich set of paragraph and character formatting, and embedded graphics.

SIBO's Agenda entries allowed you to attach a memo (which was in fact a full word processor document) that you could use, for instance, to take notes at meetings. This proved to be a fantastically useful feature, and Davies set about generalizing the idea so that EPOC rich text objects could embed any kind of data – word processor document, picture, or voice recording. The result was the embedded object system, lightweight and effective, built deep into EPOC's application architecture.

Underpinning all data storage in EPOC is a stream store that supports everything from the straightforward requirements of streaming and document embedding to the more demanding needs of persistent storage for databases. A relational DBMS, supporting multiple tables, was built on top of the stream store. Robust data management is hard: we put good brains on these components.

Applications

Protea's applications were developed at the same time as the base, middleware and GUI. With the relatively small teams in place, this allowed a good deal of iteration, and meant that the libraries were tailored to the requirements of the GUIs.

Nick Healey led the application suite development. He had an intuitive and lightning-fast grasp of what makes a good UI for non-technical people, and had been responsible for many of the best features of the SIBO Agenda, and for the PsiWin 1.0 project.

The application suite was a straight evolution of the SIBO applications: Agenda, Data, Word and Sheet would be the headliners. SIBO's separate Time and World applications would be merged into one, to save a taskbar button. A vector drawing application would show off the usefulness of a pen. Other applications included a calculator, a voice recorder, an old-style communications application, and a complete OPL development environment.

The applications were among the hardest of all the Protea projects. The constant releases of HCIL and EIKON caused frequent rewrites of parts of the application UIs, and unsurprisingly the complete change from HCIL to EIKON caused a major rewrite. The best application programmers were scarce, and were often moved from one project to another. The vagueness of the application specifications ("better than a Series 3c") gave very broad latitude to the software engineers.

But certain principles were clear from the beginning. First, the SIBO experience gave a good sense of what to aim for and, when over-ambitious ideas began to circulate – which often happened – it helped teams to reacquire reality. Second, the major applications were split into engine projects and UI projects, while those few that didn't have explicit engines, such as the world time clock, made such extensive use of EPOC middleware that in practice the middleware served as an engine.

> *In the event, the lull in activity caused by the HCIL to EIKON rewrite was put to good use: application specifications were reviewed, wilder enhancements were chopped out, and the robustness and usability of the remaining core were concentrated on.*

J-day

In mid-1995, the project end-date had been set to March 1996. Around October 1995, Potter did a *Sunday Times* interview promising a revolutionary new product in 1997 – to the great surprise of the development team. But even at that time, it was clear that March 1996 was not achievable, and in fact Psion's board still had nothing tangible to review.

Bill Batchelor had joined Psion in 1984. Having worked with Colly on the OS and applications of all Psion's major products, he was now Protea's project leader. He felt the pressure from the board and from his senior engineers to integrate the entire system and application suite. In January, he declared the first project milestone: May 31st 1996 would be J-Day – the day of judgement!

Protea would be integrated, would run on an EIGER test rack, and would be displayed to Psion's directors. The directors would then decide whether to release Protea, to can it, or to continue. One thing Batchelor was very clear about: this milestone date would not slip. It would be May 31st, whatever we had to show.

J-day gave the entire team something to focus on. When J-day was declared, we didn't even have test racks. All code outside the base team was written for the emulator. The base team had been running with MX86 for a while, but the so-called MARM build had never completed. The HCIL to EIKON rewrite had only just been finished, and the applications were still being rewritten. The application architecture that supported object embedding was in its infancy.

Astonishingly, we integrated Protea in time.

The racks, handmade by Psion's electronics workshop, began to arrive. The GCC compiler was debugged, and tools were written to construct ROM images and reproduce them on the racks. An arcane tool was hastily written to convert Visual C++ makefiles for the emulator into GCC makefiles for the MARM build. The drivers for the base were produced. The applications were polished off. GUIs and application views were improved to take account of the display contrast of the LCD – lower than it had been on the PC-based emulator. A rather basic system shell was adapted from the GUI test code. The first ROM including EIKON was built in early May 1996. David Wood built the J-day ROM at 8:05pm on 31st May, with only a few kilobytes to spare from 4MB.

Protea was shown to the directors. The project survived, but it was clearly nowhere near ready for release. It would be another year, constantly against the clock, before we were ready.

In June, all development stopped. Each team presented its achievement to the project core team. A J-day panel awarded points to each team, with the base team winning the magnum of champagne for their heroic work in getting the MARM port ready on time.

Tough decisions were made. The vector drawing application, brainchild of a Cambridge musician armed with a graphics textbook, was dropped in favor of a simpler pixel painting program. Features of various applications were assessed down to a fine level of detail. And it was decided to rewrite EIKON again.

The architecture adopted for CONE's controls had made a distinction in the class hierarchy between a window area that merely displayed things, and a control that could receive interactions. This proved to be an arbitrary and unhelpful distinction. On the other hand, a proper component architecture, in which controls could contain other controls, was essential. Improvements in the application architecture and object embedding system were also required. David Wood and Charles Davies went back to the drawing board and, on the third iteration, got it right. Meanwhile, the application teams went back to reconsider their specifications and, when the new EIKON came through in August, they knew what they had to do in order to re-code for the new architecture.

A Total Solution

To be better than the Series 3c, Protea needed to include not just the compelling application suite, great hardware and everything in between, but a complete solution for software development, and integration with PC-based data.

PsiWin 1.0 had been finished in May 1995, four years after the launch of the Series 3. It used a File Manager metaphor that was out of date within three months, as Windows 95, sporting the new Windows Explorer, launched in August of the same year. For Protea, PsiWin would be written simultaneously with what came to be known as the ROM-based EPOC components. Prior to J-day, work on PsiWin was mainly concerned with ensuring that where possible, EPOC's applications would use data structures in line with modern PC applications, to ease synchronization.

The main impact of this was a significant shift from the assumptions in the SIBO Agenda model, towards those being used on PC-based PIMs such as Microsoft Schedule+. Word already used formats inspired by PC-based RTF, and the other applications were easy enough to deal with. After J-day, a prototype Windows Explorer extension was written in Visual Basic: this was converted into a COM-based application framework into which the converters, written in-house or out-sourced to specialists such as DataViz Inc., could be slotted.

Like its SIBO predecessors, Protea would include an OPL development environment, so that software could be written on the machine without a PC, and so the many legacy applications already written in OPL could be upgraded. The OPL team enhanced the language to use 32-bit integers rather than 16-bit, added support for new EPOC features, removed the backdoor provided by old-fashioned software interrupts, and rewrote the OPL editor, translator, interpreter and utilities libraries.

The SDK team set about documenting the C++ APIs. The task was complicated by frequent API changes as the system developed and the ideas behind it changed, the total rewrites of EIKON, and a development organization small enough to do most things by verbal communication, and too busy to write things down. Much of the API documentation was reverse-engineered, and API coverage wasn't complete. Nonetheless, by launch, PC-based SDKs for both C++ and OPL were available.

One interesting part of the application suite was the spell checker. Licensed from Inso (now Lernout & Hauspie NV of Belgium), the code was written in C. But EPOC's APIs were all in C++ – there was a User::Alloc() function, but no malloc(). Thin layers over EPOC's C++ APIs were written so that the Inso code would build without too much modification, and the spell-check code was safely hidden in its own server. This was our first tussle with porting non-native code into EPOC, but it would not be the last.

In fact, the spell checker performs outstandingly well: the English dictionary contains over 100,000 words, which are checked quickly using a 250k .exe *and 500k of dictionary data.*

Beta Testing

Now the heat was on to deliver a product. Series 3c sales were showing signs of weakness, the Palm Pilot was making big inroads in the USA, and Microsoft fanfared a potential competitor in the shape of Windows CE during the summer. The Casio Cassiopeia, the first Windows CE machine, exhibited at Comdex Fall in 1996.

It was time to put the Protea project into beta phase and, once the applications had been rewritten for the (second) new EIKON, a succession of "B-days" was declared – beta ROMs. We knew we couldn't ship the beta ROMs, but they served as useful checkpoints. B-days were declared monthly, with B1 in September.

As the functionality of the applications was rounded out, Nick Healey and his team took a much harder look at usability. Now that they had a whole system to work with, they found innumerable issues ranging from user-hostile dialogs and cryptic messages to aesthetically displeasing pixel-level graphics. The issues were thrashed out with a "spec team" involving the application authors, Healey, Bill Batchelor, and representatives from Psion's product marketing department.

Psion was also beta testing its hardware. Yellow-cased machines with 4MB of re-programmable flash ROM were issued to the software team. They soon became known as "Bananas", and were the hardware platform for the B1 through B4 ROMs.

We hoped that B4, cut on December 20th, might be close to the final thing. We made many copies and showed it to Psion's whole product marketing department. They confirmed what we knew at heart anyway: that we still weren't ready to ship.

Christmas and New Year, another hardware revision and the B4 assessment delayed the B5 ROM to February. The new hardware betas had 6MB of flash ROM and, with their green cases, were predictably dubbed "Limes".

In March, we launched the product, confidentially, to Psion's developers and distributors. It was greeted with amazement. B6 SDKs and B6 Limes were made available, at nominal cost and under non-disclosure agreement, to prime the distributors and seed the independent developer market. It was only then that we learned the machine was to be called the Series 5. This took a lot of getting used to, and the word "Protea" still hasn't quite died out among the old-time developers.

Ship Mode

From January 1997, the Protea project went into functional freeze and final testing prior to shipping the new product. The team went into 'ship mode'. After March's B6 release, we retooled for quicker release cycles and built the first candidate release, C0, on 13th May. A candidate ROM was intended to be good enough to ship. After two weeks of testing and fixing, a go/no-go decision would be made, and we would either ship or the whole process would start again.

From the software perspective, the objectives of the ship mode phase were simple enough: make the applications and their UIs good enough to ship. Test the system aggressively and fix all showstopper bugs. That's all: no new APIs, and no new features except those absolutely required to make it good enough to ship. By C0 and C1, a bug had to be extremely serious – data loss or a machine reset – to count as a showstopper.

We had to get very real about dates. When you release a new consumer product, the hardware manufacturer (or OEM) orders parts ahead of time, with intent to start manufacturing on a certain day. The OEM's marketing people invite journalists to launch meetings on a certain day. The OEM informs its distributors and retailers that a new product is coming, so they can de-stock their channels of the old product and prepare for the new. The closer you get to the big day, the more expensive the results of a slip for everyone, right down to the distributors and retailers.

Psion was gearing up for a launch date of June 20th. On the critical path for the launch was the ROM masking time: it would take six weeks for the ROM image, built in London, to get burned into ROMs in Japan and shipped back to Psion's London factory to be assembled into the Series 5. That meant *we* had to release by May 9th. When we realized we were going to miss this deadline, Psion quickly substituted the masked ROM part with a programmable flash ROM that could be programmed in two weeks – thereby giving the software team another four weeks.

A candidate ROM is one that you think, before you build it, you could ship if you had to. So when you move from beta phase to candidate phase, you have to be pretty sure you have very few serious bugs left, and only fix those that really are showstoppers. After C0, director signoff was needed to fix any more bugs. After ten more days of extensive testing, a few more bugs were reported, even fewer bugs were fixed, and C1 was cut. Prizes were awarded to people who found the most showstoppers: Bill Batchelor was among the winners.

Finally, the Series 5 1.00 ROM was cut on 6th June: the image was sent to Psion's factory for immediate reprogramming into the flash-ROM Series 5s, and to Japan for masked ROMs in later production models. It was the 113th build of the ROM. Over 4,000 bugs had been reported since B5 alone.

Meanwhile, PsiWin 2.0 had gone through the same kind of process and shipped for CD manufacture on 24th May. The Series 5 was launched to the world on June 20th.

The Achievement

Protea was an extraordinary achievement. It was substantially better than a Series 3c. Its 32-bit software had no practical limits. The touch screen and new GUI were clearly a generation ahead of the old products. The keyboard was clearly the best in the world for this class of device. The applications delivered easy power.

In three years, we had produced from scratch a practical operating system in C++, spanning the entire realm from hardware to a full application suite. EPOC is still the only system in the world to have achieved this.

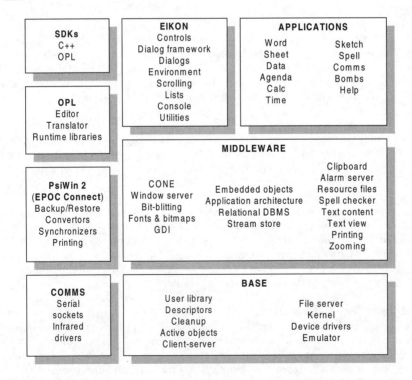

EPOC's ROM budget was only 6MB. It contained an entire suite of applications including a word processor, a spreadsheet, a database, a PIM, a calculator, a world time clock, a bitmap painting program, a voice recorder, a communications program, a development environment, a spell checker with 100,000-word dictionary, and a game written in OPL. The EIKON GUI, agenda and word processor were particularly rich in features. The object embedding system, allowing pictures in word processor documents, diary entries and the database, and memos or even sound recordings to be attached to diary entries, was unique.

EPOC is efficient. On the Series 5's 18MHz ARM CPU, the applications all run at a satisfactory pace. With only 4MB RAM, several instances of all applications may be active simultaneously, and task switching between them is virtually instantaneous. The applications scale well: diaries with thousands of entries and documents with scores of pages work with no more noticeable delay than near-empty ones.

Under the covers, EPOC was extremely robust. Memory management and cleanup technology developed early in the project had been applied rigorously throughout, so that EPOC was free from memory leaks not only during normal conditions, but also when memory was running short.

Testing was guided by three previous generations of products. Unit tests were carried out on each internal release of each component over the three years of the project — over 100 releases of the base, 300 of EIKON, and scores for every other component. J-day and the six beta ROMs gave over a year of integration testing. During ship mode, aggressive pinpoint testing for bizarre combinations of low-power conditions and failures in all kinds of software and devices gave further assurance to the robustness of the product.

As a result, user data loss in EPOC machines is very rare, and system resets almost unnecessary: it is not unusual to hear of Series 5 owners who haven't booted their machines for over a year. Colly and his team knew from the outset that these were key metrics for a personal device. They set out to achieve them, and they succeeded.

We had proved during development that EPOC was a truly portable OS. The MX86 port, used initially for testing prior to the arrival of the EIGER ASIC and the GCC toolchain, showed that we could boot natively on architecture quite different from the ARM's. At the time, we had no intention of ever running on a non-ARM architecture, but when a new architecture suitable for portable devices came along (as it did within a year in the shape of Motorola's M•CORE), EPOC would be ready.

EPOC is a great architectural achievement, conceived by great brains working together in a great team. During the project, we recruited and trained a first-class team of talented programmers and scientists: they were able to learn EPOC readily enough, and to contribute to its successful creation. Thousands, working in many companies on many continents, have joined them since in the creation of EPOC and EPOC-based products.

Perhaps the greatest achievement of all is that, although we started with a clean sheet, we were able to deliver something in just three years. Charles Davies had warned of the second-system effect. As project leader, Bill Batchelor sustained the pressure to release, and prevented us from 'gold-plating' in areas that didn't need it. We rewrote EIKON twice because its core architecture was important, but in other areas we stuck with what we had, even if it was painful to do so. We made tough decisions about what to omit, what to prioritize, and what not to improve because it was already working well enough.

For the software team, the whole experience was unforgettable, and probably never to be repeated. The team had tripled in size over the span of the project, to end at over 70. We had aimed at just one goal during all that period, and we achieved it. Working in Central London and commuting in by tube, bus and rail from all points of the compass, once in town we were like students. Most were under 30 – only two of the lead architects were over 40. Phenomenal brains were in good supply, and if our offices were a little shabby, it didn't matter much. Everything was debated, everyone with an opinion let it be known, and ideas were adopted on merit. There was a frontier atmosphere, combining a clear, shared vision with a kind of anarchy. We were clear about this as we recruited, and we attracted many very talented people. It didn't suit everyone: some quit to find an environment with more certainties. The months of ship mode were a visible strain, but the effort was sustained by the goal in view.

Post-project depression was inevitable. There was all too little time to celebrate, relax, and catch up on a few areas of research after the strain of ship mode. There would, in any case, never be such a project again. Some anticipated this, and quit even before the project completed.

Even as we celebrated the achievement, a few clouds were visible on the horizon. Windows CE faced EPOC in roughly the same product category. Palm's offering, much simpler than EPOC, was selling strongly. Psion experienced some manufacturing difficulties and couldn't keep up with demand for the Series 5. And after all the pressure of ship mode, we had probably released too early: it took another two impossible months of bug fixing to get the quality of the Series 5 ROM to an acceptable level, with the 1.01 ROM released in August and PsiWin 2.01 in September. This maintenance release became known as EPOC Release 2.

Now What Next?

After spending three years inventing something new, we now faced a long haul of catch-up. We would have to complete the e-mail, fax and web browser applications, and their underlying infrastructure (such as TCP/IP and dial-up networking). We had begun these long before Protea launched: we incorporated the fax engine into an EasyFax demonstration package and told customers we would have the Message Suite – a full fax, Internet e-mail and web browser package – "by autumn". We shipped it in November, with a PsiWin 2.1 release and updated SDKs by January 1998 – EPOC Release 3.

Psion also considered what to do next. It took them well over a year to agree on an answer, and to begin to broaden the product range beyond a single machine. With product cycles as they are, this meant no EPOC product releases for two years until the launch of the Series 5mx in June 1999. Only by late 1999 did Psion's new strategy for a broad consumer and enterprise product range begin to emerge into public view.

Meanwhile, the software team began to work with local companies on support for Far Eastern markets – particularly for Japanese and Chinese machines. The Unicode build of EPOC was resurrected, and they started on the technology needed for text input and formatting.

Java, developed by Sun independently during the same period as Protea, offers an attractive alternative as a programming language to C++ (powerful but technical) or OPL (popular but limited). A license was obtained, an expert team assembled and, even before the end of the Protea project, work began on EPOC's Java implementation.

Ultimately, however, EPOC's technical and commercial future was to be decided by the increasing demands for sophistication in the booming market for mobile phones.

Symbian

Successful British consumer technology companies are apparently so rare that people usually can't believe they will last. Journalists celebrate their success readily enough – and at the same time, just in case, they begin to draft obituaries ready for instant use.

So in the mid-1990s the journalists used to ask Potter, "Are you going to die like Apple, or are you going to die like IBM?" At the time, it seemed that IBM would die because it had ignored the PC – would Psion ignore the Palm Pilot? And it seemed that Apple would die because it had generated a cult following with its products, listened to its customers but no one else, and had not licensed MacOS to anyone but itself. Would Psion repeat the same mistakes?

Happily, both IBM and Apple are still with us, and showing every sign of health. But to Psion, the issues were serious. EPOC was designed from the beginning to be licensed to other manufacturers for use in their own devices.

SIBO was not really suitable for licensing. It would have been easy enough to license SIBO for OEMs to make devices that simply cloned Psion's. But since these OEMs would have been able to compete only on manufacturing economy, distribution and software bundles, that would have generated the same kind of low-margin market as seen in today's desktop PC industry.

EPOC was designed from the beginning to support a more attractive commercial model. EPOC would provide a substantial common core so that OEMs could gain real value by re-use. But EPOC would *also* provide flexibility. At the bottom, the base would port readily to different hardware configurations, including different CPU architectures. At the top, the EIKON GUI and the applications were structured so that they could be entirely replaced, whether merely to provide a different look and feel, or to address an entirely new class of machine, with different screen size, different input mechanisms and the like. Changing the UI is admittedly not simple, but EPOC makes it simpler than many other systems.

The flexibility supported by this design would allow EPOC to be licensed to OEMs that could then provide innovative products, far more than merely clones of the Psion Series 5.

To signal clearly its intentions to license EPOC, Psion placed the entire Protea software team, plus a tiny sales group, into a new company called Psion Software in June 1996. Psion Software's mission was to license EPOC to OEMs outside of the Psion Group. While EPOC was theoretically suitable for a wide range of applications (a director even talked to an elevator manufacturer on one occasion), it would in practice be better to focus in a well-defined area. The market they chose was the mobile phone industry.

By the mid-1990s, the mobile phone industry was a massive and revolutionary one. Psion had watched the markets develop: there were false starts everywhere, continued fragmentation in the USA, consolidation in Japan, and huge boosts in Europe and most of the rest of the world thanks to the adoption of the digital GSM standard.

It was clear that the communications and computing markets were converging in the mobile arena just as clearly as they had with the fixed Internet. Psion's first encounters with the phone industry were to talk about cables between SIBO devices and mobile phones, so the phones could be used as convenient modems. Psion investigated incorporating GSM into its own products – they even investigated buying a small phone manufacturer – but the deal came to nothing. For Psion Software, it was perhaps just as well: they remained free to license EPOC to non-Psion phone manufacturers without any obvious conflict of interest.

In late 1996, Nokia, renowned for its innovation, introduced the Nokia 9000 Communicator. It combined a GSM phone with a PDA running the GEOS system from Geoworks Inc. At first, this looked like bad news for Psion Software: Nokia had chosen a different software platform. But the cloud had a silver lining: it showed the world the potential of the product concept, and gave Psion Software an unexpected opportunity.

Nokia used GEOS to spare them the effort of writing all the PDA software – from the operating system to applications – in-house. Like SIBO, GEOS works very nicely on the models for which it was originally designed. But, like SIBO, GEOS has fundamental limits due to its 16-bit architecture that would make it difficult to adopt as a long-term platform.

Writing PDA software is complex. The high-end phone manufacturers all faced the same dilemma: to write their own software (expensive and risky), or to buy something off the shelf, having first checked that it would be a suitable long-term solution.

Psion Software's sales group had been making steady progress in licensing EPOC to the phone handset manufacturers. By early 1998, a new idea emerged: If Psion Software were an independent company, outside of the Psion Group, and owned by the handset manufacturers, then the latter would own a strong technology asset that would enable them to boost the entire market for communicator and smartphone devices. The handset manufacturers are fiercely competitive: EPOC was sufficiently adaptable to sustain their relentless innovation, and to allow them to compete by producing many different types of device.

Negotiations and due diligence began in early 1998. On June 24th, the new company and its business strategy were announced to the world. It would be called **Symbian**. Colly Myers would be its chief executive. Its owners would be Psion, Nokia and Ericsson. Motorola announced its intention to join the alliance, and did so formally from October. Japan's Matsushita, better known as Panasonic, joined in May 1999. Thus, Symbian is a global company, owned by Psion and the world's top four mobile phone manufacturers.

Symbian is no more a part of Psion than it is a part of its other four investor companies. The five investors contribute staff to a Supervisory Board that oversees the investment, but which does not get into details of individual licensee projects – a vital safeguard for customer confidentiality. Operational matters, including licensee projects, are handled by the Operational Board that was originally drawn from the executives of Psion Software. Symbian's EPOC licensees certainly include its investors, but there are also many more.

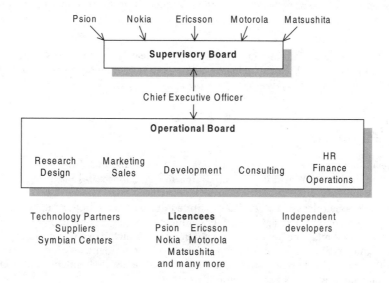

Symbian's main product is EPOC, which is licensed to phone manufacturers for inclusion in their own wireless information devices, which combine mobile phone and PDA functionality. **Communicators** are PDAs first, phones second. **Smartphones** are phones first, with added PDA-like sophistication. To ensure fairness, Symbian's royalty structure would be simple: $10 for a communicator license, $5 for a smartphone.

In addition to EPOC, Symbian would provide SDKs to enable software development and a technical consulting organization with a wide range of technical services to support licensees and developers. New drive was added to the development of EPOC technology to meet the requirements of wireless information devices:

❑ First, EPOC would become more communications-oriented. The e-mail and web browser applications took five months to arrive on the market after the Series 5 was announced: this delay would never happen again. Using the Email and Web applications felt like using a PC and a modem, only smaller and more portable: in future, messaging would be much better integrated, and would include options for phone-based text messaging as well as Internet e-mail.

❑ Second, the smartphone and communicator categories would be refined into a number of subcategories. Symbian's device family strategy slowly began to evolve, with two communicator designs code-named Crystal and Quartz, and a smartphone platform code-named Pearl. Crystal would be a logical evolution of the Series 5 into the product category defined by the Nokia 9000 communicator. Quartz would be a pen-based tablet device. Symbian would write the UIs for Crystal and Quartz, and ensure that licensees could add their own branding. Pearl, targeted at the smartphone sector where phone manufacturers demand greater product differentiation, would include EPOC's core technology but allow licensees much greater freedom to customize the applications and user interface.

❑ Third, EPOC would adopt key technologies such as Personal Java, JavaPhone, Bluetooth and WAP. Personal Java is a JDK 1.1.6-based Java implementation suitable for small-screen and small-memory devices. JavaPhone APIs provide access to contacts and schedule information in addition to phone features. Bluetooth is a short-range radio network offering the advantages of cable-free connection, without the line-of-sight requirements of infrared. WAP is a suite of networking and application protocols optimized for mobile wireless communication that will enable an entirely new generation of Internet-type applications in media, publishing and e-commerce.

In accord with this strategy, Symbian announced EPOC Release 5 in June 1999. It has much better integrated communications than earlier releases, and a Java implementation certified to JDK 1.1.4. Device families, Bluetooth and WAP are in the works.

EPOC Release 5

EPOC Release 5, on which the content of this book is based, is Symbian's first full release of EPOC. It was announced at the EPOC World developer conference in London in June 1999.

Compared with previous releases, EPOC R5's main feature was much better integration of personal information management and messaging. EPOC Connect – the new, generic, name for PsiWin – synchronizes contacts, e-mail and schedule information with equivalent PC-based programs. EPOC R5 includes a new Contacts application optimized for the real requirements of contacts handling, and for interchange with other PIMs based on the vCard standard. Previously, contacts had used a simple database table managed by the Data application.

EPOC R5 also includes a Java implementation. Specified to JDK 1.1.4 (although it includes a couple of fixes from later releases), it is smaller and faster than any competitive platform's Java implementation. It is certified Java Compatible and runs applications or applets compatible with JDK 1.1.4.

There is also some new architecture for telephony and messaging, and new Agenda and Contacts servers that allow PIM information to be shared effectively between multiple applications.

Finally, Symbian ensured that EPOC R5 was both 1999-ready, with the Euro symbol at 0x80 in the Windows Latin 1 code page, and 2000-ready, with a massive Y2K audit.

Applications

EPOC R5 makes the following applications available to the end user:

Category	Applications
Office	Word processor, spreadsheet, database, spell checker, jotter
PIM	Contacts manager, scheduler, world map and alarm clock
Communications	E-mail, fax and SMS, web browser, serial communications

Category	Applications
Utilities	Calculator, drawing package, voice notes
System	File/application browser; control panel with settings for time/date, sound, screen, power, keyboard, printer, modems, dialing, Internet service provider, locale, user information including password, Extras bar configuration tool, and program installer/uninstaller
Development	OPL program editor/translator
Game	Bombs
Data synchronization	PC-based EPOC Connect for data synchronization, file management, printing via PC, application installation from PC, and other utility functions

Software Development

Symbian supplies SDKs to write programs for EPOC Release 5 machines in three different languages:

- ❑ C++, optimized for EPOC system development and high-performance application programming

- ❑ Java, the industry-standard object-oriented language for applications, applets and APIs

- ❑ OPL, the BASIC-like rapid application development language whose roots go back to Psion's Organiser II

There is also an EPOC Connectivity SDK to exploit EPOC Connect's PC-based APIs for extra converters, synchronizers and other utility software. Most EPOC Connect APIs are delivered in COM format, allowing you to program in any compatible Windows-oriented language, such as Visual C++, Visual Basic or Delphi.

Devices

There are already several devices available running EPOC Release 5:

- ❑ Psion's Series 5mx was the first, and is my reference machine for this book.

- ❑ Psion Enterprise Computing's netBook is a very interesting machine, like a small, very lightweight, very long battery-life laptop. Enterprise computers have a lifetime measured in years, so this machine is a particularly interesting development target.

- ❑ Ericsson's MC218 is similar to the Psion Series 5, optimized for use with mobile phones.

- ❑ Psion's Series 7 is a consumer version of the netBook.

- ❑ Psion's Revo is the smallest available EPOC R5 machine, targeted specifically at consumers.

For further information on these machines, see the Appendices.

Beyond Release 5

Predicting the future is even harder than describing the past, but some aspects of Symbian's strategy are already emerging.

Better Communications Integration

EPOC will be built into much better-integrated communications products, and EPOC's communications APIs will become much easier to use from both C++ and Java.

This is going to make EPOC a truly communications-centric platform. There will always be room for good stand-alone applications that run entirely on a single EPOC machine, but as the integration of communications with EPOC continues, it will be more natural, and easier, to write communications-oriented applications. That's why we've devoted a good deal of this book to EPOC-based communications.

More Product Differentiation

EPOC products will differentiate into several categories aimed at different end users and end uses. The devices will share the same generic base, middleware, communications and application engine technology and APIs, but their user interfaces will be tailored to the physical requirements of the device in question.

We can already begin to see this with the variety of EPOC R5-based machines available. All share the same generic technology, and in the case of the EPOC R5 products, only minor modifications have been needed to the EIKON GUI and applications in order to implement machines with different screen sizes. In the case of future products, the distinctions will be more pronounced.

As stated above, Symbian has given the more data-centric products the name "communicators". The Crystal and Quartz communicator reference designs will make their way into products from 2000 onwards. Crystal will evolve EPOC R5 into the product category defined by the Nokia 9000, while Quartz is an entirely new design that will support a tablet-like form factor with stylus operation, handwriting recognition and powerful integrated wireless communications. Ericsson demonstrated a multimedia application on an early Quartz prototype in Geneva, in October 1999.

Smartphones are more voice-centric, and while Symbian provides the Pearl technology platform, licensees are free to provide their own user interfaces and specialist applications for particular smartphone products. The Ericsson R380, announced at CeBIT 99 for availability in 2000, uses a forerunner of Pearl. The recently announced cooperation between Symbian, Nokia and Palm will use Pearl.

Again, this has implications for developers:

❑   You will have to target your development to one or other of the platforms. This is essentially a commercial decision: each platform targets particular end users, and may be suitable for some purposes but not others. Think about the platform most suitable for your application, and develop for it.

❑ If you wish to target multiple EPOC platforms, you will have to use the same techniques as Symbian does in order to maximize technology re-use between one platform and another. Separate your middleware and application engines from anything to do with user interface. The middleware and application engines should be re-usable across all platforms; the user interfaces will need to be rewritten. The GUI frameworks will all have APIs *similar* to EIKON, which will make it easy enough to port your code without arbitrary rewriting, but you will need to make changes for the different screen sizes and input devices.

❑ Some products – particularly some smartphones – may be delivered as 'closed-box' devices that don't support end user installation of third-party applications. This reduces costs, security worries and product complexity – all vital for mass-market acceptance. You can't develop software for closed-box products using the same commercial model as for open-box products (such as making your software available on a web site for end users to download). But that doesn't mean there's no scope for EPOC software development on closed-box products: you just have to sell to the OEM or network operator rather than the end user.

EPOC Connect Improvements

EPOC Connect provides excellent data synchronization and many other facilities for users of EPOC machines and PC-based software from Microsoft, Lotus, Corel and others.

EPOC Connect is tightly integrated into the Windows Explorer on your PC. This makes it easy to drag and drop files from your PC to your EPOC machine, with automatic conversion if desired. It also makes it easy to explore your EPOC machine, and to open Word or Sheet files by simply double-clicking them from the Windows Explorer.

But for most other purposes, Windows Explorer is not a natural paradigm for the things you'd want to do with EPOC Connect. Power users have little difficulty with EPOC Connect's design, but non-technical end users can sometimes find it hard. So Symbian is redesigning EPOC Connect as a standard Windows application, with a UI designed to make *all* its functionality easily accessible to the average user.

EPOC device differentiation raises new questions for EPOC Connect. One is easily answered: *all application data formats will be identical* in EPOC Unicode builds, because all EPOC-based products will share the same generic technology for everything beneath their GUIs. So EPOC Connect will only ever need one set of converters, written by Symbian.

But device differentiation makes real differences in other cases. EPOC devices will include a **capabilities manager** that reports the capabilities of a device when connected to EPOC Connect. EPOC Connect will then be able to present an appropriate user interface: typically, this will be simpler for smartphone products, and more powerful for communicator products.

Looking forward further still, synchronization will move away from the PC focus to a network focus.

Worldwide Locale Support

Finally, EPOC will become truly international, adding support for worldwide locales including Chinese, Japanese, Korean, Thai, Arabic and Hebrew. This will require several new technology additions:

- ❑ General support for 16-bit Unicode characters (EPOC Release 5's narrow build supports only 8-bit characters mapped to the Windows Latin 1 character set)

- ❑ Support for advanced text input methods, using either keyboard or pen to enter characters in Kanji and other large character sets, and supporting the conventional methods already in use in the various locales that EPOC will target

- ❑ Additional sophistication in text formatting, to support the subtly different wrapping rules of Far Eastern text, and right-to-left writing for Arabic and Hebrew

For developers, the main thing to note here is that EPOC's Unicode build is source compatible with its narrow build. We'll cover the technical details in Chapter 5.

Part One

EPOC Basics

The next seven chapters are devoted to describing the basic APIs on which all EPOC programs are built.

To begin with, Chapter 2, Chapter 3 and Chapter 4 establish the context for the APIs: I describe the hardware facilities available on an EPOC machine, the base software that's needed to support programs on such hardware, how the privileged kernel supports applications and servers, and the conventions we use for writing C++ and getting the most out of object orientation.

Then, Chapter 5, Chapter 6 and Chapter 7 describe EPOC's most fundamental programming frameworks. Because they're fundamental, all the subsequent code in the book will be using the frameworks they describe. That gives you two options for reading them: you can either try to take in *everything* first time through, so you'll be in a commanding position to understand all the future examples; or you can take an impressionistic approach first time around: get a flavor of what's in the chapters, then read on through the book, see how this material is used, and come back later for reference.

This material is part guide, part tutorial. It's enough to get you through the rest of the book without looking at any reference material, enough for you to understand what EPOC's frameworks can do for you, and enough for you to understand at least the gist of any EPOC program that uses these frameworks. In a few cases, I'll guide you away from features you might see in the SDK, but which we're not as keen on now as when they were first designed. But most of the time, if you need more information, use the SDK.

The final chapter of this section contains additional pointers. Chapter 8 comprises a lightning tour of other basic EPOC APIs, and additional material about the software development tools, especially the emulator.

After this section, Part 2 leads you in to using the EIKON GUI and EPOC's graphics facilities. Alternatively, if you're more interested in communications and systems programming, you can skip right to Part 3, where I develop the Battleships application and transaction-oriented games stack (TOGS) to introduce EPOC's active objects and client-server frameworks, the design patterns involved in communications programming, and the implementation of two significant communications protocols.

2

Getting Started

It's time to do some real programming with EPOC. In this chapter, I'll introduce you to the emulator and the tools for building C++ programs. You can read this material – and the rest of the book – in one of two ways:

❑ Install the C++ SDK, the book CD-ROM and any other tools you need (such as Microsoft Visual C++), using the instructions in the appendices. Then you can read through the material at your desk, using a PC to walk through the examples.

❑ Read the book from the comfort of your armchair, take in what you see, and then come back to your PC later to walk through the examples and really get to grips with EPOC.

In this chapter, we won't get *too* involved in describing EPOC programming conventions, API functions, and so forth. Instead, we'll concentrate on the tools you need, and how to use them. Then in the next few chapters we'll go into specifics.

The first tool you need to know about is the **emulator**. Most EPOC software is developed first on the emulator and only then on real target hardware. The emulator also includes a complete EPOC application suite, and so mimics a real EPOC device almost exactly. We'll need to get familiar with the emulator, and we can use the opportunity to take a look at the applications and the distinctive features of EIKON, EPOC's GUI.

Then we'll get to the tools for creating programs. The easiest things to build are text mode console programs, so we'll start with a classic "Hello World" application, demonstrating how to compile it for either the emulator or a target EPOC machine, and how to launch and debug it using the Microsoft Visual C++ debugger.

Finally, because real programs on a user-friendly machine use a graphical interface, we'll conclude the chapter by building a GUI-based program. This will introduce another tool – the **resource compiler** – that defines basic GUI resources like toolbars, menus, shortcut keys, and dialogs, and allows you to write programs that can easily be adapted to non-English locales. We'll be using the GUI framework for most of the examples in the book, so it's crucial to know how to build GUI programs.

Using the Emulator

The emulator is a fundamental tool for all the EPOC SDKs, so it's vital that you get to know it and learn how to use it.

We'll do this from two points of view. If you've never seen EPOC before, the emulator offers an opportunity to get to know some EPOC basics from a user's perspective, and we'll look at these straight away. Later, we'll learn enough about how the emulator works so that you can begin to make effective use of it as a developer. If you're used to EPOC, then you may want to skip the next section and go straight to *Inside the Emulator* where we'll work through some examples.

Launching the Emulator

Once you've installed the EPOC C++ SDK, there are several ways of launching the emulator:

❑   From the Start menu: Start | Programs | EPOC Software | EPOC C++ SDK - EPOC Emulator ½ VGA

❑   From Windows Explorer: find directory \epoc32\release\wins\deb\ and launch epoc.exe

❑   From the command line: put \epoc32\release\wins\deb\ into your path, prefixed by the correct drive letter, launch a prompt, and just type epoc

We'll look at alternative initialization of the emulator in Chapter 8.

However you choose to start it, the first thing you'll see in the emulator is the System application – or, in programmer-speak, the **shell**. Also, you can see the main elements of the EPOC user interface around the edges of the screen.

The shell enables you to explore folders, select files and launch applications. Its menus allow you to view or change system settings, and it also has a control panel. It's very easy for end users to get to know the shell: you don't really need a manual. Just tap here and there, and you'll soon find out what it has to offer.

> *Use* F1 *on the PC keyboard, or tap on the triangle at the top of the left-hand sidebar, to launch the menus.*
>
> *On the emulator, you click with a mouse, but on a real EPOC machine you would tap with a pen. For reasons we'll discuss later, the difference is important, so I'll always say, 'tap', just to remind you.*

GUI Style

As you browse around the shell on the emulator, you'll begin to see how EIKON, EPOC's GUI, is optimized for the handheld form factor. Let's pause to notice a few things.

A Pen is not a Mouse

Go into the shell and tap (once) on a file that is not already selected (there should be some files in the Documents folder, by now, if you've toyed with opening EPOC's standard applications from the task bar). As you'd expect, your pen tap selects the file. Tap on the file again. This time, the file is opened.

> **This is an example of EPOC's 'select and open' principle, which is different from double-clicking in other GUIs, because a pen is not a mouse.**

When you double-click, the first click selects and the second click opens *if it occurs within a certain time after the first click*, and *if it's in the same place*. This is easy enough with a mouse, but quite difficult with a pen.

Double-tapping can be made to work with a pen: Windows CE's GUI, shoehorned down from the desktop, requires double-tap, and uses it just like the desktop versions of Windows. However, since EPOC was *designed* for pen use, it uses a more natural idiom. If you tap on an unselected item, it is selected. If you tap on a selected item, it is opened.

There are a number of other ways in which EPOC's GUI deals with the difference between a mouse and a pen:

❑ You can't hover with a pen. That rules out tooltips, so EPOC toolbar buttons are big enough to include text. Also, there's no pointer to change to a hand, an hourglass, or a crosshair, based on its position and the state of the program. That has a more subtle effect on the GUI and your application design.

❑ You can't right-click with a pen. Rather than using odd combinations such as *Alt*+tap to simulate a right click, EPOC simply doesn't use the metaphor.

❑ A pen isn't as accurate as a mouse, so pen-selectable items have to be bigger than mouse-selectable items, and it's useful to provide some reassurance about what has been selected: check out the behavior of buttons in dialogs (or menu items) that briefly animate as you select them. There is nothing you can do to unselect these items, but the animation at least confirms which item was selected.

It can be convenient to use your finger instead of a pen. (I use my finger on taskbar and sidebar keys, and the back of my fingernail on the screen, so as not to leave finger marks.) Where it's possible without compromising anything else, EPOC makes its GUI elements big enough to select with a finger.

So: a pen-based GUI is not a mouse-based GUI. EPOC's GUI is not a desktop GUI – it is different in ways that really matter. On the other hand, EPOC's GUI isn't different merely for the sake of it. Desktop GUIs are familiar to many people, and EPOC includes many familiar concepts. Some early handheld operating systems, such as Magic Cap, tried to be too different – and, as a result, they failed to gain mainstream acceptance.

Menu and Shortcut Keys

Have a close look at the menu in the shell. Again, the menu bar is different (but not too different) from menu bars in desktop GUIs. It remains hidden until needed, in order to save screen space.

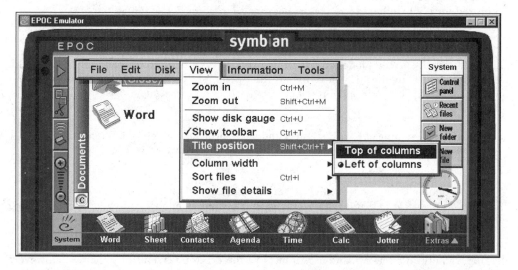

Cascaded menu items are used both to hide less common options, and to reduce the vertical space required by menu panes.

Use the menu with the pen (or your finger), and you'll see some interesting visual cues to confirm the option you selected: the option will flash very briefly before the menu disappears. It took a long time to get that effect just right!

As with all other elements of EPOC's GUI and applications, you can drive the menus with the keyboard as well as with the pen. You can use the arrow keys and *Enter* to select items or, for much quicker access, you can use the shortcut keys listed by most menu items to invoke the relevant function without going through the menus at all.

Toolbar

All EPOC applications have a toolbar, on the right-hand side of the display. At first sight, the toolbar is wasteful: it uses valuable screen space and, in any case, all of the toolbar functions are available through menu items or by other means. But there is good reason for the toolbar to be there (and besides, it can be switched on and off in all applications with *Ctrl+T*).

The toolbar is a great way for you to make your application easier to use, and perhaps to show off a couple of features that will really impress users. To get a feel for this, take a look through the toolbars in EPOC's standard applications. In the shell, for example, the top button is Control panel, providing easy access to configuration information, while Recent files advertises a feature that might have been missed altogether by many users. In Agenda, EPOC's PIM application, the top button allows you to switch between views (day, week, year, etc.), while the next two advertise nice features: Sketch says that you can insert a sketch as part of an entry, and Today takes you straight to today. (You can also use *Space*, but not a lot of people take the time to find that out in the help.)

> **All toolbars have the same format: a number of buttons, with a clock at the bottom and a filename area at the top.**

EIKON allows for any toolbar format, but the recommended one should be used unless there is a good reason not to. Quite late in the Protea project, people noticed that switching between applications was very ugly when toolbars changed arbitrarily from one application to another, and the rule that all toolbars should use the standard format was instituted.

Of course, there *are* exceptions when there are valid reasons to use a non-standard toolbar. Sketch, for instance, puts all its painting tools and palettes on the toolbar:

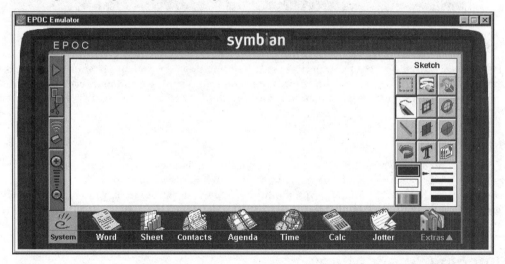

Many test applications also use a non-standard toolbar, but all other Symbian applications use the standard toolbar format. I'll use it for most of the examples in this book, and your commercial EPOC applications should use it too.

The Psion Revo has a smaller screen, which dictates a change to the standard toolbar format – there's only room for three buttons. The Psion netBook has a larger screen, which allows a larger toolbar – six buttons is standard.

As you would expect, toolbars are both keyboard- and pen-friendly. Toolbar functionality is *required* to be available through the keyboard (except in applications such as Sketch, which are pen-based for good reason).

Toolband

A couple of applications use a **toolband**, across the top of the screen, as well as a toolbar. The toolband provides a convenient way to access popular functions. It too can be switched on or off to save screen space, this time using *Shift+Ctrl+T*.

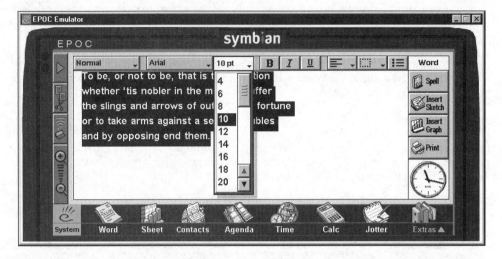

Sidebar

The sidebar is used by EIKON to perform standard functions for each application: displaying the menu, activating the clipboard (cut, copy, paste), infrared beaming (send and receive), and zooming (in and out). There are standard menu positions for all of these functions, and standard shortcut keys too.

Help

You can launch the system help file using *F2* from the emulator. On a real EPOC machine, there is a help key. The system help contains many topics for each application, and some general topics to help you use the EIKON GUI. Help is written in user-oriented, not programmer-oriented, language. If you write your own help, you should use the same kind of language. I'll show how to write your own help in *Adding Help* in Chapter 13.

Launching Applications

As you've probably already discovered, your starting point for launching applications is the **taskbar** – the row of buttons below the screen. There are seven icons for launching (or switching to) built-in applications. On the far left is the System icon, which is for switching to the shell itself. This is a bit like the taskbar used by all Windows platforms – even Windows CE – but screen size is limited on a handheld device, and EPOC doesn't waste space by showing the taskbar on the screen all the time.

What if there are more than seven built-in applications? And what about user applications like the ones we're going to write? Try clicking on the Extras icon on the right of the taskbar. You'll see extra rows of buttons slide up onto the screen, showing more applications. This means that you can launch any application you like with just two pen taps.

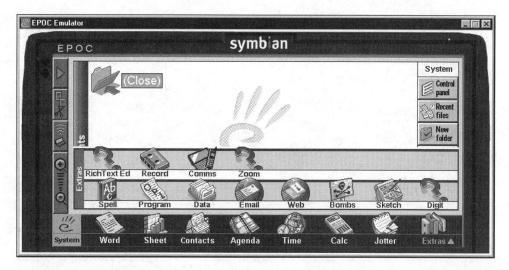

You can use the control panel to customize which applications appear on the Extras bar above the seven fixed taskbar icons. Tap on the Control panel button (top right) and open the Extras bar applet. You can set the Email application icon to appear above Word like this:

Then, you can *Ctrl*+tap on the Word icon, and Email will be launched without your having to tap on Extras at all.

The shell allows for four rows of 'extras' to appear on EPOC machines with this screen size, making for a total of thirty-two slots for applications. This is enough for most users, but power users and developers may require more. The shell provides for that by filling the thirty-second slot with a More icon that shows a list from which you can scroll and select:

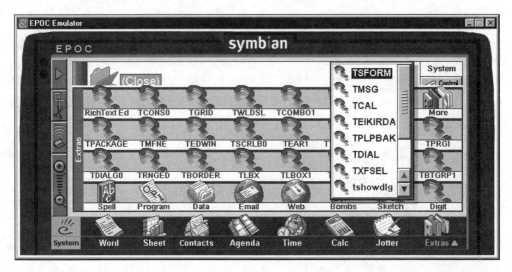

Moving on, you can use the **task list** to show which applications are open, and to switch between them or close them. Launch it by *Ctrl*+tapping on the System icon, or by tapping on the filename at the top right of any application screen containing a toolbar. You'll see something like this:

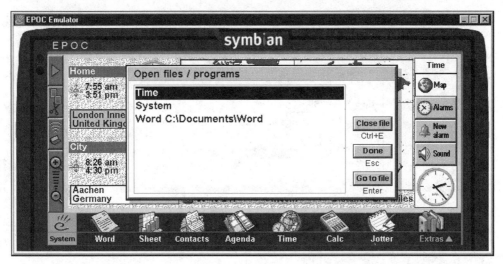

Some applications have associated files. Applications that are not file-based can be opened when you want to use them and closed when you've finished – there are no complications. With file-based applications, like Word and Sheet, you can create new files, embed one document in another, launch an application by opening its file rather than using the Extras bar, and so on. From the end user's perspective, these features are very easy to use.

As a developer *delivering* these facilities, you need to know the system in more detail. I'll cover this in Chapter 7 and chapters on the EIKON GUI (Chapters 9 to 15). The Battleships application, which I develop later in the book, uses a file to save the state of the game (I show how, in Chapter 18). It's not too hard to change an application to be file-based as you can get it working without files, and add load and save functions when you're ready.

Before we move on, you should take a couple of seconds to use the shell's Tools | Preferences... dialog, and ask the shell to show you hidden files and the System folder.

You've probably done the same thing with your PC's Windows Explorer settings. Hidden and system files may be frightening for end users, but they're the stuff of life for developers.

Inside the Emulator

We have used the emulator to see what EPOC looks like from a user's point of view, and hopefully that's whetted your appetite for the kinds of applications you can develop.

As a C++ developer, you build C++ code for the emulator and debug it by running it natively. You then have to rebuild it for the intended target machine. This has a few implications that you need to understand at this point.

The emulator maps features of the target machine onto features of your PC environment. For software development, it's particularly important to know how the emulator maps drives and directories onto your PC's filing system.

We'll explain these two topics next, and then we can move on to examining some code.

Source Compatibility

C++ is a platform-independent language that can be compiled to any instruction set. EPOC R5 machines use the ARM3 instruction set; future machines will support ARM4 and M•CORE – perhaps more. The PCs used to develop EPOC use the x86 instruction set.

So, a C++ program for the *emulator* is compiled to native x86 machine code. When a program has been debugged under the emulator, the same source code is simply recompiled to use the ARM instruction set, and transferred to an EPOC machine from which it can be run.

The following figure shows the steps involved in compiling for the two platforms. We'll introduce the details of this process later in this chapter.

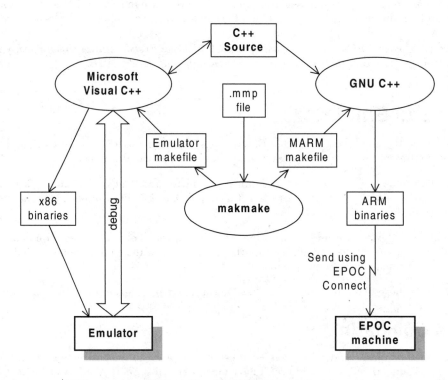

This **source compatibility** is achieved by delivering EPOC's base services to all user programs through the same APIs. On a real EPOC machine, the base services are implemented by the kernel, file server, and device drivers using the real machine's hardware. On the emulator, the base services use Win32 APIs, PC hardware, and the PC's file system. But the APIs are the same at source code level.

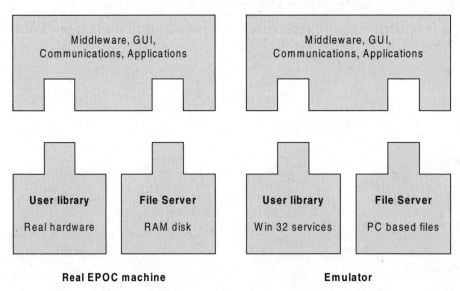

Source compatibility between the emulator and a real EPOC machine applies to the vast majority of EPOC. Only parts of the kernel, the file server, and device drivers need to be changed substantially. Applications, servers, and middleware libraries are completely source compatible, and need only a rebuild to transfer them from emulator to target machine. Some things don't even need to be rebuilt:

❑   Data files should be implementation independent. You can easily ensure this by using EPOC's stream and store APIs for saving data – don't just 'struct dump', because that puts internal formats into files, and internal formats may differ between EPOC implementations. A double, for example, has different internal formats on x86 and ARM. See Chapter 7 for more on data management in EPOC.

❑   Interpreted programs, such as those in pure Java or OPL, are just data as far as the emulator is concerned. You can transfer them freely from emulator to target machine without conversion. Java native methods and OPXs (their OPL equivalent) are really binary programs, and these clearly need to be rebuilt.

Drive Mapping

On a real EPOC machine, there are two important drives:

❑   z: is the ROM, which contains a bootstrap loader and all the .exe, .dll, and other files required to boot and run EPOC and its applications. All files on z: are read-only; program files are executed directly from the ROM rather than first being loaded into RAM.

❑   c: is the read/write drive that's allocated from system RAM. c: contains application data, application and system .ini files, and user-installed applications.

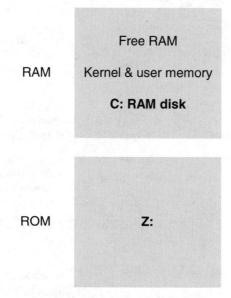

On the emulator, these drives are mapped onto subdirectories of the drive on which you installed the SDK. This is for safety, so that your EPOC programs can't write just anywhere on your Windows c: drive, and because most PC's don't have a z: drive anyway.

Because of Win32 technicalities, two other directories are involved, as shown below:

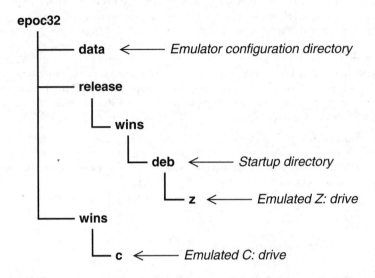

These are the directories and their uses:

Directory	Description	Contents
`\epoc32\data\`	Emulator configuration directory	`system.ini` (the initialization parameters for the emulator), `system.bmp` (the bitmap used as the fascia surround for the screen), and variants of the latter for screens of different sizes.
`\epoc32\release\wins\deb\`	Emulator startup directory	`epoc.exe`, the program you invoke from Windows to bring up the emulator, is in here. So are all the shared library DLLs.
`\epoc32\release\wins\deb\z\`	Emulated `z:` drive	Everything that the EPOC `z:` drive should contain, except shared library DLLs, which are in the parent directory.
`\epoc32\wins\c\`	Emulated `c:` drive	Any data and files. No compiled C++ programs – those should all be on `z:`. In the emulator, all compiled applications become part of the pseudo-ROM that is the emulated `z:` drive.

Why Those Long Names?

You might wonder why there are so many deeply nested directories. The directories categorize the EPOC SDK materials, as follows:

- ❑ \epoc32\ sets apart all EPOC SDK runtime software from anything else on the same drive
- ❑ release\ sets apart released code from documentation, temporary build files, configuration files, etc.
- ❑ wins\ sets apart the emulator from target machine builds
- ❑ deb\ sets apart the debug build from other builds
- ❑ z\ attempts to mirror the structure of z: on a real EPOC machine

An executable C++ program built for the emulator debug build won't run in any other execution environment, so the debug build is kept distinct from any other build.

It would be nice if \epoc32\release\wins\deb\z\ could contain the entire emulated z: drive. Unfortunately, it can't: .exes and shared library DLLs can't use EPOC's file structure, without impractical implications for the path environment in Win32. The only practical thing to do is place all .exes and shared library DLLs in the startup directory – \epoc32\release\wins\deb\.

Finally, data is independent of build, so c: is mapped to the \epoc32\wins\c\ directory and shared between all builds.

A limitation of the default scheme is that only a single emulator per PC drive is possible.

> *That's an awkward restriction. In Chapter 8, I describe a new directory-mapping scheme that can be used for delivering demonstration software in any directory, and for some other purposes. But it isn't supported by the C++ tools in EPOC Release 5, so you have to build using the default scheme.*

Hello World — Text Version

Now that you've started to get to grips with the emulator, it's time to get your first EPOC C++ program running. Even though EPOC is primarily a system for developing GUI applications, the simplest kind of programs use a text interface, so for our opening foray we'll learn how to build a program that writes "Hello world!" to a text console. That will introduce you to the tools required for building applications for both the emulator and a real machine, so that later on you'll be ready for a program with a GUI.

If you want to follow this chapter through at your desktop with the SDK, make sure that you've installed all the tools you need, and the example source for the book. See the appendices for more information.

The Program: `hellotext`

Here's the program we're going to build. It's your first example of EPOC C++ source code:

```cpp
// hellotext.cpp

#include <e32base.h>
#include <e32cons.h>

LOCAL_D CConsoleBase* console;

// Real main function
void MainL()
    {
    console->Printf(_L("Hello world!\n"));
    }

// Console harness
void ConsoleMainL()
    {
    // Get a console
    console = Console::NewL(_L("Hello Text"),
                           TSize(KConsFullScreen, KConsFullScreen));
    CleanupStack::PushL(console);

    // Call function
    MainL();

    // Wait for key
    console->Printf(_L("[ press any key ]"));
    console->Getch();                // Get and ignore character

    // Finished with console
    CleanupStack::PopAndDestroy(); // Console
    }

// Cleanup stack harness
GLDEF_C TInt E32Main()
    {
    __UHEAP_MARK;
    CTrapCleanup* cleanupStack = CTrapCleanup::New();
    TRAPD(error, ConsoleMainL());
    __ASSERT_ALWAYS(!error, User::Panic(_L("PEP"), error));
    delete cleanupStack;
    __UHEAP_MARKEND;
    return 0;
    }
```

It simply says "Hello world!" on the console, waits for you to press a key, and then exits. The output looks like this:

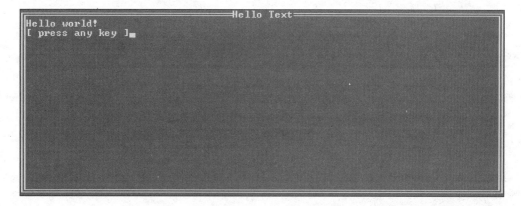

From now on, I'll include only the screen portion of the emulator in any screenshots, rather than the entire surround − unless of course there's something particularly interesting on the surround.

Our main purpose here is to understand EPOC's tool chain, but while we have the opportunity, let's notice a few things in the source code above. There are three functions:

❑ The actual "Hello world!" work is done in MainL()

❑ ConsoleMainL() allocates a console and calls MainL()

❑ E32Main() allocates a trap harness and then calls ConsoleMainL()

On first sight, this looks odd. Why have three functions to do what most programming systems can achieve in a single line? The answer is simple: real programs, even small ones, aren't one-liners. So there's no point in optimizing the system design to deliver a short, sub-minimal program. Instead, EPOC is optimized to meet the concerns of real-world programs − namely, to handle and recover from memory allocation failures, with minimal programming overhead. There's a second reason why this example is longer than you might expect: real programs on a user-friendly machine use a GUI framework rather than a raw console environment. If we want a console, we're on our own, and have to construct it ourselves, along with the error-handling framework that the GUI would have included for us.

Error handling is of fundamental importance in a machine, with limited memory and disk resources, such as those for which EPOC was designed. Errors are going to happen, and you can't afford not to handle them properly. I'll explain the error handling framework and its terminology, such as **trap harness**, **cleanup stack**, **leave**, **heap marking**, etc., in Chapter 6.

Every single program I write in this book is fully error-checked. EPOC's error-checking framework is easy to use, so the overheads for me are minimal. You might doubt that, judging by this example! After you've seen more realistic examples, you'll have better grounds for making a proper judgment.

Back to `hellotext`. The real work is done in `MainL()`:

```
// Real main function
void MainL()
    {
    console->Printf(_L("Hello world!\n"));
    }
```

The `printf()` that you would expect to find in a C "Hello World" program has become `console->Printf()` here. That's because EPOC is object-oriented: `Printf()` is a member of the `CConsoleBase` class.

The `_L()` macro turns a C-style string into an EPOC-style **descriptor**. We'll find out more about descriptors in Chapter 5.

EPOC always starts text programs with the `E32Main()` function. `E32Main()` and `ConsoleMainL()` build two pieces of infrastructure needed by `MainL()`: a **cleanup stack** and a **console**. Our code for `E32Main()` is:

```
// Cleanup stack harness
GLDEF_C TInt E32Main()
    {
    __UHEAP_MARK;
    CTrapCleanup* cleanupStack = CTrapCleanup::New();
    TRAPD(error, ConsoleMainL());
    __ASSERT_ALWAYS(!error, User::Panic(_L("PEP"), error));
    delete cleanupStack;
    __UHEAP_MARKEND;
    return 0;
    }
```

The declaration of `E32Main()` indicates that it is a global function. The `GLDEF_C` macro, which in practice is only used in this context, is defined as an empty macro in `E32def.h`. By marking a function `GLDEF_C`, you show that you have thought about it being exported from the object module. `E32Main()` returns an integer – a `TInt`. You could have written `int` instead of `TInt`, but since C++ compilers don't guarantee that `int` is a 32-bit signed integer, EPOC uses `typedefs` for standard types to make sure they are guaranteed to be the same across all EPOC implementations and compilers.

`E32Main()` sets up an error handling framework. It sets up a cleanup stack and then calls `ConsoleMainL()` under a trap harness. The trap harness catches errors – more precisely, it catches any functions that **leave**. If you're familiar with the exception handling in standard C++ or Java, `TRAP()` is like try and catch all in one, `User::Leave()` is like throw, and a function with `L` at the end of its name is like a function with `throws` in its prototype. It's very important to know what these functions are: the EPOC convention is to give them a name ending in `L()`.

Here's `ConsoleMainL()`:

```
// Console harness
void ConsoleMainL()
    {
    // Get a console
    console = Console::NewL(_L("Hello Text"),
                        TSize(KConsFullScreen, KConsFullScreen));
    CleanupStack::PushL(console);
```

```
// Call function
MainL();

// Wait for key
console->Printf(_L("[ press any key ]"));
console->Getch();              // Get and ignore character

// Finished with console
CleanupStack::PopAndDestroy(); // Console
}
```

This function allocates a console before calling `MainL()` to do the `Printf()`. After that, it waits for a key and then deletes the console again. There is no need to trap the call to `MainL()` because a leave would be handled by the `TRAP()` in `E32Main()`. The main purpose of the cleanup stack is to prevent memory leaks when a leave occurs. It does this by popping and destroying any object that has been pushed to it. So if `MainL()` leaves, the cleanup stack will ensure that the console is popped and destroyed. If `MainL()` doesn't leave, then the final statement in `ConsoleMainL()` will pop and destroy it anyway.

In fact, in this particular example, `MainL()` cannot leave, so the `L` isn't theoretically necessary. But this example is intended also as a starting point for other console mode programs, including programs that *do* leave. I've left the `L` there to remind you that it's acceptable for such programs to leave if necessary.

If you're curious, you can browse the headers: `e32base.h` contains some basic classes used in most EPOC programs, while `e32cons.h` is used for a console interface and therefore for text-mode programs – it wouldn't be necessary for GUI programs. You can find these headers (along with the headers for all EPOC APIs) in `\epoc32\include\` on your SDK installation drive.

Making Makefiles: `makmake`

We are going to build the program for two environments:

❑   The emulator

❑   A target machine

Like all C++ development under EPOC, we'll start by building the project to run under the emulator (that is, for an x86 instruction set) using Microsoft Visual C++. We use a debug build, so that we can see the symbolic debug information, and to get access to some useful memory-leak checking tools.

Later, we'll use the GNU C++ Compiler (GCC) to build the project for a target EPOC machine, using an ARM instruction set. At that stage we'll use the release build because EPOC doesn't presently support very effective target machine debugging – partly because the emulator is so good.

So, we will need to build the same source code twice. In fact, for demonstration purposes, we're going to build it three times, because Microsoft Visual C++ can compile the code from scratch on the command line, or can build it incrementally in the Visual Studio IDE.

Each build requires a different project file. Originally, EPOC developers started with a Microsoft Visual C++ project file and edited the settings using the dialog boxes. However, it was difficult to construct new projects, difficult when settings had to be changed for new Visual C++ releases, and difficult to convert the useful information in Visual C++ makefiles into a correct ARM makefile – although at one time a tool called `maktran` was used for this purpose.

A better solution was found: it is much simpler to put all the useful information into a single, quite simple, project specification file, and then to translate that file into the makefile or project file for the environment of choice. The C++ SDK supplies a tool called `makmake` to perform precisely this task: you edit your project specification (in a file that in this case is called `hellotext.mmp`), and then run `makmake` to convert it into an emulator command-line build (`wins` argument), emulator IDE build (`vc5` argument, for Visual C++ version 5, but also works with version 6), or ARM command-line build (`marm` argument).

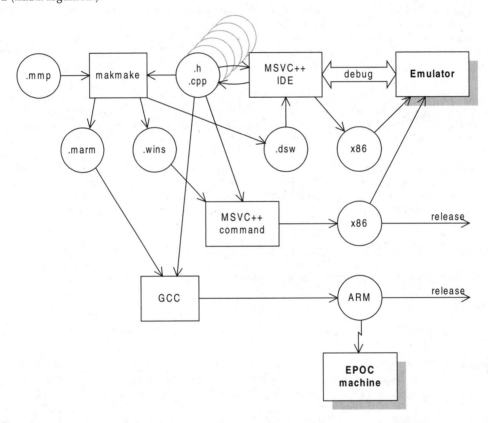

Here are the contents of `hellotext.mmp`:

```
// hellotext.mmp

TARGET        hellotext.exe
TARGETTYPE    exe
UID           0
UNICODEUID    0
```

```
PROJECT        pep
SUBPROJECT     hellotext
SOURCE         hellotext.cpp

USERINCLUDE    .
SYSTEMINCLUDE  \epoc32\include

LIBRARY        euser.lib
```

This is enough information to specify the entire project, enabling configuration files to be created for any platform or environment.

❑ The TARGET specifies the executable to be generated, and the TARGETTYPE confirms that it is a .exe

❑ The UID and UNICODEUID information are irrelevant for .exes, but I specify them explicitly as zero here, to suppress a makmake warning. I'll have more to say on UIDs later, since they are more important for GUI programs.

❑ PROJECT and SUBPROJECT specify the top-level and second-level directories that contain the source code for the example. This example must therefore reside in \pep\hellotext\ – if you move it, you have to change the .mmp file. All EPOC source code has to be two directory levels deep.

❑ SOURCE specifies the single source file within the subproject directory, namely hellotext.cpp (in later projects, we'll see that SOURCE can be used to specify multiple source files)

❑ USERINCLUDE and SYSTEMINCLUDE specify the directories to be searched for user (included with quotes; the SYSTEMINCLUDE path is searched as well) and system include files (included with angle brackets; only the SYSTEMINCLUDE path is searched). All EPOC projects should specify \epoc32\include\ for their SYSTEMINCLUDE path.

❑ LIBRARY specifies libraries to link to – these are the .lib files corresponding to the shared library DLLs whose functions you will be calling at runtime. In the case of this very simple program, all we need is the E32 user library, euser.lib.

makmake is there to ensure source code compatibility across all EPOC targets. You use the same .mmp file – which is really source code for the tool – to generate a makefile (or an IDE workspace) whose format depends on the EPOC target. makmake also ensures, through these makefiles and workspaces, that different directories are used to separate the intermediate files for each target.

Why does EPOC source code have to be two levels deep? Because the GNU tools used in the EPOC R5 (and earlier) SDKs have a very poor emulation of DOS directory path handling. As a result, tools built around them, such as makmake and the GCC toolchain, handle paths oddly too. The easiest thing was to fix source trees to two levels deep. We're all looking forward to the day when this restriction is lifted.

Building for the Emulator

Make sure you've installed the example projects from the book CD-ROM: see the appendices for how to do this.

To start the command-line build, open up a command prompt, change to your installation drive, and issue the following command to get into the source directory for this example:

```
cd \pep\hellotext
```

Next, you need to invoke makmake to make the makefile, and then nmake to build the project using Microsoft Visual C++'s command-line tools. To perform the first of these tasks, type:

```
makmake hellotext wins
```

After a short thinking time, this command will return – by default, makmake doesn't tell you anything. However, if you check the contents of the source directory, you'll notice two new files: hellotext.uid.cpp, which contains a UID for emulator use (see the *Getting a UID* section later for more on UIDs), and hellotext.wins, the makefile for emulator command-line builds.

Next, invoke nmake to use that makefile:

```
G:\pep\hellotext>nmake -f hellotext.wins

Microsoft (R) Program Maintenance Utility   Version 6.00.8168.0
Copyright (C) Microsoft Corp 1988-1998. All rights reserved.

        cl.exe  /MLd /Zi /Od /nologo /Zp4 /W4 /X /FR"\EPOC32\BUILD\PEP\WINS\DEB/
" /Fd"\EPOC32\RELEASE\WINS\DEB\HELLOTEXT.pdb" /D _DEBUG /D "__SYMBIAN32__" /D "_
_PSISOFT32__" /D "__VC32__" /D "__WINS__" /D "__EXE__"  /I "\PEP\HELLOTEXT" /I "
\EPOC32\INCLUDE" /Fo"\EPOC32\BUILD\PEP\WINS\DEB/" /c "..\..\PEP\HELLOTEXT\Hellot
ext.cpp"
Hellotext.cpp
        cl.exe  /MLd /Zi /Od /nologo /Zp4 /W4 /X /FR"\EPOC32\BUILD\PEP\WINS\DEB/
" /Fd"\EPOC32\RELEASE\WINS\DEB\HELLOTEXT.pdb" /D _DEBUG /D "__SYMBIAN32__" /D "_
_PSISOFT32__" /D "__VC32__" /D "__WINS__" /D "__EXE__"  /I "\PEP\HELLOTEXT" /I "
\EPOC32\INCLUDE" /Fo"\EPOC32\BUILD\PEP\WINS\DEB/" /c "..\..\PEP\HELLOTEXT\Hellot
ext.uid.cpp"
Hellotext.uid.cpp
        link.exe @C:\TEMP\nma00262.
EEXE.obj : warning LNK4099: PDB "eexe.pdb" was not found with "\EPOC32\RELEASE\W
INS\DEB\EEXE.obj" or at "G:\EPOC32\RELEASE\WINS\DEB\eexe.pdb"; linking object as
 if no debug info
        bscmake.exe @C:\TEMP\nmb00262.

G:\pep\hellotext>
```

From this output, you can see that nmake invokes four commands:

- The C++ compiler, cl.exe, gets invoked twice, to compile the main source module hellotext.cpp and the generated UID module hellotext.uid.cpp.

- The linker, link.exe, gets invoked with commands in a file; it actually generates \epoc32\release\wins\deb\hellotext.exe. A warning, which you can safely ignore, is issued during the link because there was no debug information for eexe.obj, a file that's linked into every EPOC .exe. It's good practice to aim for zero warnings during a build, but this one really doesn't matter.

- The browser information generator, bscmake.exe, is invoked to generate browser information for use while debugging.

The project is built into the emulator startup directory as \epoc32\release\wins\deb\hellotext.exe. To run the program, you can start it right from there, using either the command prompt or Windows Explorer. The emulator will boot, and you'll see Hello world! on the screen. Press any key and the emulator will close.

Why we didn't we type epoc.exe and then launch the program from the shell, as in the previous chapter? We'll explain more about that in Chapter 8. We'll also describe the role of eexe.obj, whose debugging information was missing above.

Building in the IDE

Now we know our tool chain is working, let's build the project from the IDE and debug through the example. First, you need to invoke makmake to generate the Visual C++ project file, so type:

```
makmake hellotext vc5
```

This makes a project file for Visual C++ version 5, which is also good for version 6. Open the workspace from within Visual Studio, and, if you're using version 6, confirm that you want to convert the workspace into version 6 format.

You should now be able to browse around the project. In the ClassView, you will see only functions and global data, because this project doesn't define any classes. In the FileView, you'll see two source files: hellotext.cpp, which is a real source file, and hellotext.uid.cpp, which was generated by makmake. You'll see no resource or header files.

Try building the project, using Build | Build hellotext.exe, or simply *F7*. This is what you'll get:

```
-----------------Configuration: HELLOTEXT - Win32 Uni Release-----------------
Compiling...
Hellotext.cpp
Hellotext.uid.cpp
Generating Code...
Linking...
LINK : fatal error LNK1181: cannot open input file
"\EPOC32\RELEASE\WINS\UREL\EEXE.OBJ"
Error executing link.exe.

HELLOTEXT.exe - 1 error(s), 0 warning(s)
```

> **The build failed because, by default, Visual C++ builds for Unicode release. However, you need to build for Win32 debug.**

Before you can build successfully, you need to change the active configuration of your project. Use Build | Set active configuration, and select Win32 Debug. You have to do this whenever you load a project into Visual C++ 6.0 for the first time. It would be nice if makmake did this for you, but cracking Microsoft's changing file formats isn't always straightforward, and the current active configuration is specified in a different file from the essentials of the .dsw which makmake constructs.

Now try building again (you may need to use Rebuild All, rather than simple Build): everything should be fine. As before, there will be the warning about eexe.pdb, but you already know that's nothing to worry about.

You can launch the emulator from the IDE using *Ctrl+F5*. Alternatively, you can debug through using any of the usual debug techniques – run to cursor, step over a whole line of code, step into each of the functions on a line, step out of the current function, run to breakpoint, etc.

If you're curious, you might want to try debugging through line-by-line. You'll begin to get a feel for what's worth doing and what's not, and it will give you some more insight into the system structure. On the other hand, there's no need to jump in this deep right now: I'll explain what you really need to know through the next few chapters. The main point to note just now is that Microsoft Visual C++ provides an excellent debugger, and as an EPOC developer you can take full advantage of it.

You can debug through the most important function calls using the source code and debugging information provided with the EPOC C++ SDK. Here are some tips:

❏   Don't try to debug any executive calls (Exec::Xxx()).

❏   Be careful when debugging traps – it's usually best to set a breakpoint on the target of the trap, and run to that.

❏   If you find yourself in a function for which the SDK doesn't provide the source, jump out of that function, hopefully back into your own code or some SDK-provided source code. Don't forget to reset the view to source.

Running on the Target Machine

The emulator is a good enough development environment on which to learn EPOC using only a PC and an EPOC C++ SDK. But if you're developing for a real EPOC machine, the emulator isn't your ultimate target: once you've built and debugged your application to a certain stage on the emulator, you'll want to start running it on the real machine also. This is a simple process: rebuild the same source code using the GCC compiler for ARM, and copy the resulting binaries to your EPOC machine.

Before we get too heavily involved in the building process, make sure that your machine is connected to your PC using EPOC Connect (or PsiWin). If you've set EPOC Connect to back up or synchronize on connection, let all that happen before you start using EPOC Connect to transfer the programs you have built.

Open Windows Explorer, check that your connection is functioning correctly, and navigate to your EPOC machine's `c:\system\` folder, like this:

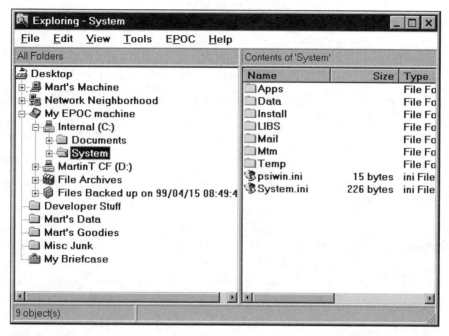

If you're going to be connected to the machine all day, you'll probably want to use mains power rather than batteries. In that case, you don't want your machine turning itself off just before you send it your new program build, so use the control panel's Switch on/off applet to set the automatic switch off mode to When no external power. Now you're ready.

For target machine builds, we have only command-line tools at our disposal. First, as usual, use makmake to make the makefile.

```
makmake hellotext marm
```

Then, build this using:

```
nmake -f hellotext.marm
```

This will invoke the GNU and EPOC toolchain to generate an incredible sequence of characters on your console:

```
G:\pep\hellotext>nmake -f hellotext.marm

Microsoft (R) Program Maintenance Utility   Version 6.00.8168.0
Copyright (C) Microsoft Corp 1988-1998. All rights reserved.

        gcc -s -fomit-frame-pointer -c -nostdinc -Wall -Wno-ctor-dtor-privacy -m
cpu-arm710 -mapcs-32  -mshort-load-bytes -msoft-float -O -fcheck-new -fvtable-th
unks -DNDEBUG -D__SYMBIAN32__ -D__PSISOFT32__ -D__GCC32__ -D__EPOC32__ -D__MARM_
_ -D__EXE__   -I "..\..\PEP\HELLOTEXT\" -I "..\..\PEP\HELLOTEXT" -I- -I "..\..\EP
OC32\INCLUDE" -o "..\..\EPOC32\BUILD\PEP\MARM\REL\HELLOTEXT.o" "..\..\PEP\HELLOT
EXT\Hellotext.cpp"
```

```
            if exist "..\..\EPOC32\BUILD\PEP\MARM\REL\HELLOTEXT.in" del "..\..\EPOC3
2\BUILD\PEP\MARM\REL\HELLOTEXT.in"
            cd "..\..\EPOC32\BUILD\PEP\MARM\REL"
            ar -M < C:\TEMP\nma00327.
""          ranlib "HELLOTEXT.in"
            cd "G:\pep\hellotext"
            ld -s -e _E32Startup  --base-file "..\..\EPOC32\BUILD\PEP\MARM\REL\HELLO
TEXT.bas"  -o "..\..\EPOC32\BUILD\PEP\MARM\REL\HELLOTEXT.EXE" "..\..\EPOC32\RELE
ASE\MARM\REL\EEXE.o"  --whole-archive "..\..\EPOC32\BUILD\PEP\MARM\REL\HELLOTEXT
.in"  --no-whole-archive "..\..\EPOC32\RELEASE\MARM\REL\EUSER.LIB"
            dlltool --output-exp "HELLOTEXT.exp"  --base-file "..\..\EPOC32\BUILD\PE
P\MARM\REL\HELLOTEXT.bas"  "..\..\EPOC32\RELEASE\MARM\REL\EEXE.o" "..\..\EPOC32\
BUILD\PEP\MARM\REL\HELLOTEXT.in"  "..\..\EPOC32\RELEASE\MARM\REL\EUSER.LIB"
            ld -s -e _E32Startup  -Map "..\..\EPOC32\RELEASE\MARM\REL\HELLOTEXT.map"
   -o "..\..\EPOC32\BUILD\PEP\MARM\REL\HELLOTEXT.EXE" "HELLOTEXT.exp"  "..\..\EPO
C32\RELEASE\MARM\REL\EEXE.o"  --whole-archive "..\..\EPOC32\BUILD\PEP\MARM\REL\H
ELLOTEXT.in"  --no-whole-archive "..\..\EPOC32\RELEASE\MARM\REL\EUSER.LIB"
            petran "..\..\EPOC32\BUILD\PEP\MARM\REL\HELLOTEXT.EXE" "..\..\EPOC32\REL
EASE\MARM\REL\HELLOTEXT.EXE"  -nocall -uid1 0x1000007a -uid2 0x00000000 -uid3 0x
00000000

PETRAN - PE file preprocessor V01.00 (Build 110)
Copyright (c) 1996-1999 Symbian Ltd.

            del "HELLOTEXT.exp"
            del "..\..\EPOC32\BUILD\PEP\MARM\REL\HELLOTEXT.EXE"

G:\pep\hellotext>
```

Here are the main commands:

- ❑ gcc compiles hellotext.cpp, the source file.

- ❑ A long sequence of GNU tools is invoked, ending in a second invocation of ld, which builds a GNU form of hellotext.exe in the (temporary) build directory.

- ❑ The EPOC-specific petran tool translates this form of hellotext.exe into a compact form suitable for loading at runtime by the EPOC loader.

The net result is that hellotext.exe is built into \epoc32\release\marm\rel\.

To get the program to run, you have to copy it to your EPOC machine and start it from there. The convention for .exe programs like this one is to copy them to c:\System\Programs\ and run them from there (though another directory will do just as well).

Go to the instance of Windows Explorer you opened up earlier, and create a Programs subdirectory in the c:\System directory on your EPOC machine.

Then navigate to \epoc32\release\marm\rel\, and copy hellotext.exe to the clipboard. Paste the file into the c:\System\Programs\ directory. EPOC Connect will analyze the file (in case it should apply a conversion to it), decide that this file doesn't need to be converted, and copy it straight over.

It doesn't take long to copy the program: it's only about 900 bytes! Compare this with the "Hello World" Win32 Console Application produced by Visual C++ 6.0's AppWizard, which is over 28k. The graphics "Hello World" program later in this chapter is less than 5k, and even when I add bitmapped buttons, zoomable application icon and built-in help in Chapter 13, it's still less than 20k.

After you've copied the file to your EPOC machine, navigate to `c:\System\Programs\`, and you'll see:

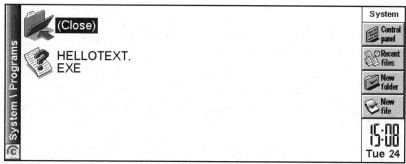

Open the program, and you'll see, in tiny print, the famous hello world message. *Congratulations!* You've got your first EPOC program working on both the EPOC emulator and a real EPOC machine.

Hello World — EIKON Version

Text mode programming is useful for testing and for learning, but production programs use a GUI. In this section, you'll learn how to build an application for the EIKON GUI.

It will take more time to learn how an EIKON GUI program works, and in this chapter we're not even going to try to explain the C++ code. There's nothing particularly difficult about it, but it will be easier to cover how EIKON uses C++ when we have seen more of how EPOC C++ works.

It's still worth getting to grips with the tools, though, because we'll be using GUI programs to show off some of the basics of EPOC in the next few chapters.

The Program

Our example program for this section is `helloeik`. Here's what it looks like.

You can see the world-famous text in the center of the screen. Round about, there are the usual EIKON resources – a toolbar, and a menu that happened to be popped up when I did the screenshot.

Despite the additions, the build process is similar to that for `hellotext`: we start with a `.mmp` file, turn it into the relevant makefile or project file, open up the IDE, build the program for the emulator and check that it works. Then we rebuild for MARM, copy to the target machine and run it there instead. There are, however, some important differences:

❏   EIKON programs must be built so that EPOC can recognize them and launch them from the **Extras** bar. To ensure this, a program called `helloeik` *must* be built into a path such as `\system\apps\helloeik\helloeik.app`.

❏   EIKON programs use EPOC's unique identifier (UID) scheme to verify that they *are* EIKON programs, and also to associate them, if necessary, with file types identified by the same UID.

❏   EIKON programs consist not only of the executable `.app` file, but also GUI data in a resource file.

In this example, we'll start by looking at the `makmake` project file for `helloeik.app`. We'll do a command-line build for the emulator, which generates `helloeik.app` together with its resource file, `helloeik.rsc`. Then we'll show how you can build the project from the IDE – including how to run EPOC's resource compiler, which is not directly supported by the Microsoft IDE. Finally, we'll build for MARM and transfer both files to a target machine using EPOC Connect.

The `makmake` Project File

Here is the project file for `helloeik`:

```
// helloeik.mmp

TARGET          helloeik.app
TARGETTYPE      app
UID             0x1000006c 0x10005401
UNICODEUID      0x1000006c 0
TARGETPATH      \system\apps\helloeik

PROJECT         pep
SUBPROJECT      helloeik
SOURCE          helloeik.cpp
RESOURCE        helloeik.rss

USERINCLUDE     .
SYSTEMINCLUDE   \epoc32\include

LIBRARY         euser.lib apparc.lib cone.lib eikon.lib
```

Compared with the `.mmp` file for `hellotext`, there are some interesting differences here:

❏   The `TARGET` is `helloeik.app`, and `TARGETTYPE` is `app` – that is, an application. `makmake` knows what to do to make the right kind of executable in the proper target directory.

❏   This time, the UIDs are non-zero. The first one you have to enter is `0x1000006c`, and in fact this is the same for all EIKON applications. The second should be obtained by you from EPOC World – I'll show how to do that shortly. I had to code the `UNICODEUID` statement to suppress a `makmake` warning, even though the EPOC Release 5 SDK doesn't support Unicode builds.

❑   The TARGETPATH specifies where helloeik.app will be generated. On the emulator, the emulated z: drive's path will be used as a prefix, so \epoc32\release\wins\deb\z\system\apps\helloeik\helloeik.app will be the path used for the emulator debug build.

❑   As well as a source file, a resource file – helloeik.rss – is included in the project.

❑   Many more .lib files are involved this time.

Getting a UID

Every EIKON application should have its own UID. This allows EPOC to distinguish files associated with that application from files associated with other applications. A UID is a 32-bit number which you get as you need from Symbian.

Microsoft uses 128-bit 'globally unique IDs', GUIDs. Programmers allocate their own, using a tool incorporating a random number generator and distinguishing numbers (such as network card ID and current date and time) to ensure uniqueness. EPOC uses 32-bit UIDs for compactness, but this rules out the random-number generation approach. That's why you have to apply for UIDs from Symbian.

Getting a UID is simple enough. Just send e-mail to uid@epocworld.com, titled 'UID request', and requesting clearly how many UIDs you want – ten is a reasonable first request. Assuming your e-mail includes your name and return e-mail address, that's all the information Symbian needs. Within 24 hours, you'll have your UIDs by return e-mail.

If you're impatient, or you want to do some experimentation before using real UIDs, you can allocate your own UIDs from a range that Symbian has reserved for this purpose: 0x01000000-0x0fffffff. However, you should never release any programs with UIDs in this range.

Don't build different EIKON applications with the same UID – even the same test UID – on your emulator or EPOC machine. If you do, the system will only recognize one of them, and you won't be able to launch the other.

Building the Application

To build from the command line, we follow the same steps as with hellotext:

```
makmake helloeik wins
nmake -f helloeik.wins
```

This time, we get a lot more output from the command-line build:

```
G:\pep\helloeik>nmake -f helloeik.wins

Microsoft (R) Program Maintenance Utility   Version 6.00.8168.0
Copyright (C) Microsoft Corp 1988-1998. All rights reserved.
```

```
        cpp -I "..\..\PEP\HELLOEIK\" -I "..\..\PEP\HELLOEIK" -I- -I "..\..\EPOC3
2\INCLUDE" -DLANGUAGE_SC < "..\..\PEP\HELLOEIK\HELLOEIK.RSS" > "..\..\PEP\HELLOE
IK\HELLOEIK.rpp"
        rcomp -o"\EPOC32\RELEASE\WINS\DEB\Z\SYSTEM\APPS\HELLOEIK\HELLOEIK.rSC" -
h"..\..\PEP\HELLOEIK\HELLOEIK.rs~" -i..\..\PEP\HELLOEIK\HELLOEIK.RSS -s"..\..\PE
P\HELLOEIK\HELLOEIK.rpp"

        del "..\..\PEP\HELLOEIK\HELLOEIK.rpp"
        call "MayRewriteHdr.bat"
        1 file(s) copied.
        del "..\..\PEP\HELLOEIK\HELLOEIK.rs~"
        cl.exe  /MDd /Zi /Od /nologo /Zp4 /W4 /X /FR"\EPOC32\BUILD\PEP\WINSD\DEB
/" /Fd"\EPOC32\RELEASE\WINS\DEB\HELLOEIK.pdb" /D _DEBUG /D "__SYMBIAN32__" /D "_
_PSISOFT32__" /D "__VC32__" /D "__WINS__" /D "__DLL__"  /I "\PEP\HELLOEIK" /I "\
EPOC32\INCLUDE" /Fo"\EPOC32\BUILD\PEP\WINSD\DEB/" /c "..\..\PEP\HELLOEIK\Helloei
k.cpp"
Helloeik.cpp
        cl.exe  /MDd /Zi /Od /nologo /Zp4 /W4 /X /FR"\EPOC32\BUILD\PEP\WINSD\DEB
/" /Fd"\EPOC32\RELEASE\WINS\DEB\HELLOEIK.pdb" /D _DEBUG /D "__SYMBIAN32__" /D "_
_PSISOFT32__" /D "__VC32__" /D "__WINS__" /D "__DLL__"  /I "\PEP\HELLOEIK" /I "\
EPOC32\INCLUDE" /Fo"\EPOC32\BUILD\PEP\WINSD\DEB/" /c "..\..\PEP\HELLOEIK\Helloei
k.uid.cpp"
Helloeik.uid.cpp
        link.exe @C:\TEMP\nma00344.
    Creating library \EPOC32\RELEASE\WINS\DEB\HELLOEIK.lib and object \EPOC32\REL
EASE\WINS\DEB\HELLOEIK.exp
        defmake /1?NewApplication@@YAPAVCApaApplication@@XZ "\EPOC32\BUILD\PEP\W
INSD\DEB\HELLOEIK.APP" "\EPOC32\BUILD\PEP\WINSD\DEB\HELLOEIK.def"

DEFMAKE - DLL processing utility V01.00 (Build 110)
Copyright (c) 1996-1999 Symbian Ltd.

Processing \EPOC32\BUILD\PEP\WINSD\DEB\HELLOEIK.APP to produce \EPOC32\BUILD\PEP
\WINSD\DEB\HELLOEIK.def
        lib.exe /nologo /machine:i386 /nodefaultlib /name:"HELLOEIK.APP" /def:"\
EPOC32\BUILD\PEP\WINSD\DEB\HELLOEIK.def" /out:"\EPOC32\RELEASE\WINS\DEB\HELLOEIK
.lib"
    Creating library \EPOC32\RELEASE\WINS\DEB\HELLOEIK.lib and object \EPOC32\REL
EASE\WINS\DEB\HELLOEIK.exp
        link.exe @C:\TEMP\nmb00344.
        del "\EPOC32\RELEASE\WINS\DEB\HELLOEIK.exp"
        del "\EPOC32\BUILD\PEP\WINSD\DEB\HELLOEIK.APP"
        bscmake.exe @C:\TEMP\nmc00344.

G:\pep\helloeik>
```

The sequence of processing here is:

❏   Firstly, the resource compiler rcomp is called to convert helloeik.rss into helloeik.rsc
(the resource file itself) and helloeik.rsg (a header file containing symbolic IDs for each
resource in helloeik.rsc). Prior to rcomp, the C++ preprocessor cpp is called to handle
includes. After rcomp, a test is made to see whether the newly generated header file is
different from the header file generated by a previous run of rcomp: if so, the old one is
replaced and, later in the build, any .cpp file that included the generated header will be
rebuilt. If no resource IDs have changed, however, it is desirable to avoid this rebuild, so the
old header file is not replaced by the new one.

- ❑ Then, cl.exe is called to compile the source file helloeik.cpp and the UID information in helloeik.uid.cpp.

- ❑ A much more complex sequence of link steps is then performed, which is standard for command-line builds that produce EPOC DLLs (even for the emulator).

- ❑ Finally, bscmake.exe is called to generate symbolic debug information.

When you've finished, the application will be in \epoc32\release\wins\deb\z\system\apps\helloeik\. In Windows Explorer, you'll see helloeik.app and helloeik.rsc, which are the real targets of the build. You'll also see helloeik.ilk, the incremental link database, and although this isn't needed at runtime, you should leave it in place because it speeds up rebuilds.

However, you can't launch the application directly by (say) double-clicking on helloeik.app from Windows Explorer. Instead, you have to launch the emulator using \epoc32\release\wins\deb\epoc.exe. You'll find that helloeik is on the **Extras** bar, and you can launch it from there.

Building in the IDE

The main phase of real application development is writing, building, and debugging from within the Visual Studio IDE – not the command line. To see how to build an EIKON program from the IDE, let's start with a clean sheet. If you tried out the command-line build above, issue,

```
nmake -f helloeik.wins clean
```

which will get rid of all files from the build. (This may also issue not-found messages as it tries to get rid of files that might have been produced, but weren't.)

You can then start by using·makmake to build the Visual C++ project file. Issue the following from the command line:

```
makmake helloeik vc5
```

Then, launch Visual Studio, open this project, confirm that you want to change it to Visual C++ 6 format, and set the active configuration to **Win32 Debug**.

The Source Code

In passing, note from the ClassView that there are four classes, two non-class functions, and a global constant. This is the minimum possible for a real EIKON application. Check the FileView, and you'll see there are three source files: helloeik.cpp, the main C++ source file; helloeik.uid.cpp, the source file generated by makmake to contain the UID information; and helloeik.rss, the resource file source text.

Our focus for the moment is on using the tools. We'll go into the C++ source, the four-class structure, and the resource file, in Chapter 9.

Building the Application

Let's try now to build the application. When I pressed *F7*, this is what happened:

```
--------------------Configuration: HELLOEIK - Win32 Debug--------------------
Compiling...
Helloeik.cpp
g:\pep\helloeik\helloeik.h(18) : fatal error C1083: Cannot open include file:
'helloeik.rsg': No such file or directory
Helloeik.uid.cpp
Generating Code...
Error executing cl.exe.

HELLOEIK.APP - 1 error(s), 0 warning(s)
```

The IDE could not build `helloeik.cpp` because it was unable to find a file called `helloeik.rsg`. This file is one of the two outputs from the resource compiler: it contains symbolic resource IDs.

> **When building an EIKON project from the IDE, you must first run the resource compiler. You also need to re-run it any time that you update the resource file, if that update would cause changes to symbolic IDs.**

The IDE doesn't include this step automatically in its build logic, so you have two options. You can either run the resource compiler from the command line and then build the C++ from the IDE, or you can customize Visual Studio so that the resource compiler can be run from an item on the **Tools** menu. Let's do both.

Invoking the Resource Compiler from the Command Line

In the build log above, we saw that the resource compiler `rcomp` required some setup (running the C++ preprocessor) and some tidying up (working out whether to update the `.rsg` header file with symbolic IDs). All of this is encapsulated in the `eikrs.bat` utility. Type:

```
eikrs helloeik sc
```

You'll get the cryptic response:

```
helloeik.RSG changed
```

This means the symbolic resource IDs were updated. If you run the command again, you will see that the IDs are *not* changed.

If you return to the IDE, you can now build the C++ project successfully. Here's what I got:

```
-------------------Configuration: HELLOEIK - Win32 Debug-------------------
Compiling...
Helloeik.cpp
Linking...
Helloeik.obj : warning LNK4197: export "?NewApplication@@YAPAVCApaApplication@@XZ"
specified multiple times; using first specification
   Creating library \EPOC32\RELEASE\WINS\DEB/HELLOEIK.lib and object
\EPOC32\RELEASE\WINS\DEB/HELLOEIK.exp

HELLOEIK.APP - 0 error(s), 1 warning(s)
```

Visual C++ generates a warning here because the incremental link database is missing. If you modify the program slightly and build again, this warning will disappear. If you rebuild too many times, the database is thrown away and Visual C++ does a full link. It would be nice to build without warnings, but we can live with this.

Invoking the Resource Compiler from the IDE

It's quite easy to customize the Visual Studio Tools menu so that the resource compiler can be invoked directly. To begin with, select the Tools | Customize... menu item. From the tabbed dialog that appears, select the Tools tab, and add EPOC Resource Comp&iler to the bottom of the list it contains:

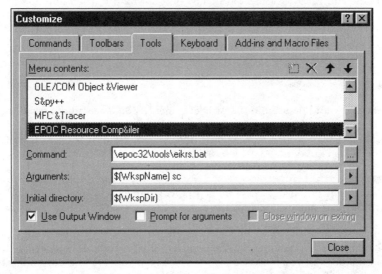

When you've entered the details above, close the dialog and check that the Tools menu now includes EPOC Resource Compiler. You should be able to invoke the new option with *Alt+T, I*. The new command will run the resource compiler eikrs.bat in the current workspace directory, with the current workspace name as its main argument. Provided that you have an EIKON project workspace open, this is exactly what you want.

If eikrs.bat *complains of being "Out of Environment space", add the following line to* c:\command.com:

/E:1024 /Cf:\epoc32\tools\eikrs.bat $(WkspName) sc

Launching the Program from the IDE

You can launch the program from the IDE by pressing *F5* (to debug) or *Ctrl+F5* (to run). However, since `helloeik.app` is a DLL, not a `.exe`, you will be asked which executable should be launched:

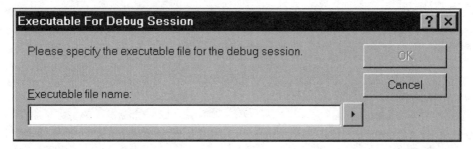

Enter `\epoc32\release\wins\deb\epoc.exe`, press *Return*, and the emulator will be launched. You can now launch `helloeik` from the **Extras** bar.

Rebuilding for a Target Machine

Let's finish this chapter by rebuilding `helloeik` for a target EPOC machine. The process is very simple: it's another command-line build, followed by a copy-over using EPOC Connect. Make sure that your machine and EPOC Connect are ready, just as you did when building `hellotext` for the target machine earlier on.

Now type,

```
makmake helloeik marm
nmake -f helloeik.marm
```

to make the makefile, and then build the project using it. You'll see all the usual tools being called — rcomp, gcc, petran, etc. Then, open an instance of Windows Explorer and go to `\epoc32\release\marm\rel\`, where you'll find `helloeik.app` and `helloeik.rsc`. Select them and copy them to the clipboard.

Go to My EPOC Machine, Internal (C:), `\system\apps\`, and create a new folder called `helloeik`. Paste the two files into this folder. EPOC Connect will copy them across, and once again it's very quick: the program and resource file amount to only 4.8K.

EPOC recognizes the application by its name, its presence in the `\system\apps\` directory tree, and its UID. Given that all these are correct, the application is considered installed as soon as you copy it across. Tap on **Extras**, and you'll see a question-mark icon with HELLOEIK underneath. Tap this, and you've launched your first GUI program on the EPOC machine.

The SDK and Technical Support

You've now seen how to use the SDK to build text and GUI programs for both the emulator and a real EPOC machine. Next, you need to start to learn about EPOC's APIs, and what you can use them for. I've written the book so that you can read it without looking at the SDK, but if you have the opportunity, you may wish to take time to have a quick look around it.

The majority of the SDK, comprising most of the tools, include files and the emulator, installs to the \epoc32\ directory tree on the installation drive. Example source code installs to other directories on the installation drive.

Here are some important locations on your SDK installation drive:

Location	Contents
\epoc32\include\	The most important directory for checking out EPOC APIs. Every EPOC header file is there – or, in a few special cases, in a subdirectory. When we write about headers like e32std.h, look for them in \epoc32\include\.
\sysdoc\index.html	Starting point for browsing the documentation.
\epoc32\tools\	The majority of the tools you'll use for building EPOC programs, including makmake and tools for bitmap conversion, icon building, making installable packages, etc.
\epoc32\gcc\bin\	The GNU C++ compiler, with ARM target.
\epoc32\release\wins\deb\	The debug-mode emulator's startup directory.
\epoc32ex\	C++ example projects, whose subdirectories correspond to EPOC APIs.
\boss\	The "Boss" Puzzle, a tutorial in EPOC and using the EIKON GUI.
\apparc\, \cone\, \e32\, \eikon\	Source code to go along with symbolic debugging information, which enables you to use the debugger with EPOC's most important application frameworks. The source code is also useful for browsing, picking up hints and tips, and making up for gaps in the documentation.
\word\, \wpeng\, \aiftool\	Source code designed to build EPOC Word, a full-scale EPOC application.
\aleppo\	Example files for aleppo, the EPOC help builder.
\eiktest\, \eikonex\	EIKON test programs that give total coverage of the EIKON GUI's APIs, and an EIKON miscellany of small test applications of dubious value.

For practical EPOC development, you need \epoc32\tools\, \epoc32\gcc\bin\ and \epoc32\release\wins\deb\ in your path, as well as the Microsoft Visual C++ command-line tools (including nmake).

The source code in \epoc32ex\ and \boss\ is accompanied by proper commentary in the SDK documentation. The other source code is undocumented and sparsely commented, but it's very useful if you feel like investigating.

The documentation is your main resource – apart from this book – for learning about EPOC. Like all large bodies of documentation, you have to know your way around in order to make maximum use of it.

The documentation is available in two forms: straight HTML, which you can find at `\sysdoc\index.html`, or an HTML help file, which you can find at `\sysdoc\htmlhelp\epoc.chm`. The straight HTML can be read by any web browser and, if your company has an intranet with a search facility, you can load the HTML onto your intranet and get full text search. If you haven't got this facility, the HTML help version is useful for searching – you'll need Microsoft Internet Explorer 4 or above to use it.

Here's a quick overview of the documentation structure:

Subject	Description
Getting started	Tells you about the SDK, but in reality tells you little about how to get started.
ER5 supplement	Tells you about newly documented APIs in EPOC Release 5.
C++ system documentation	Contains the most useful information in the SDK, including the best starting point:
	Programming EPOC: the real information on how to get started building programs and using the SDK
	SDK examples: inventory of the programs in `\epoc32ex\` and `\eiktest\`, along with the APIs illustrated by those programs
	EPOC reference: the most important guide and reference information for EPOC's central APIs
EPOC tools and utilities	Reference and guide to using the tools for building EPOC programs
The EPOC emulator	Reference information about the emulator
EPOC tutorial	A step-by-step guide through the Boss Puzzle tutorial
Technical papers	Index to the EPOC Release 5 technical papers that were available at the time the SDKs went for mastering – you can find a more up-to-date index at http://www.symbian.com/epoc/papers/papers.html

Symbian's technical support arrangements are changing from their old home on the EPOC World web site (http://developer.epocworld.com/) to a new home and new services on the Symbian Developer Network at http://www.symbiandevnet.com/.

By registering with the Symbian Developer Network, you get free access to all published SDKs, tools, and supporting knowledge bases. There is a library with all the on-line documentation, and a download area for SDK updates, new documentation, example code, patches and technology demonstrations. There are open newsgroups so you can network with other developers and share experience of working with EPOC technology. There's also news about events, training courses and industry developments.

Battleships

A lot of the code we'll develop during the course of the book will be part of Battleships, a substantial EPOC application. It shows how EPOC can do wireless communication at both short and long range, highlights many of the realities of communications programming, and is provided in a sufficiently flexible format that you can improve or adapt it for different games, communications protocols, or system programming purposes.

Because so much of the book looks forward to Battleships, it seems a good idea to introduce it here. Here's a screenshot of a game, halfway through:

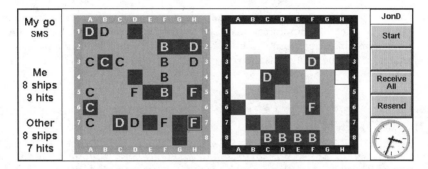

The classic game of battleships is played on paper or a wooden board, and works like this. Each player has an 8x8 game board, on which they lay a fleet comprising ten ships as follows:

❑   One battleship (B above), four squares long

❑   Two cruisers (C), each three squares long

❑   Three destroyers (D), each two squares long

❑   Four frigates (F), each one square

The ships can be aligned horizontally or vertically. Ships may not touch each other, even at the corners. Both players set up their boards independently, and neither player knows the layout of the ships on the other player's board.

The players agree who will go first, and then take turns. For each turn, one player calls a square to the other, say "B7". The other player responds with "Miss" if that square contained nothing; otherwise "Cruiser" (or another ship type) for a square that was hit. The player whose turn it is then marks the result on his version of the opponent's game board and also marks any squares that, because of the adjacency rules, cannot possibly contain a ship.

So, around the middle of the game, the screenshot above indicates that I have completely sunk two of my opponent's ships (a battleship and a frigate), and have also hit one square each on two destroyers. I've also marked squares that I don't need to try to hit as sea. My opponent has used a different policy, and perhaps had a little more luck: he has hit parts of six of my ships without sinking them, and has sunk two frigates. The winner, of course, is the person who is first to sink their opponent's fleet entirely.

I've built some interesting features into the version of Battleships in this book.

- ❏ You can play against someone in the same room, using infrared

- ❏ You can play against someone elsewhere, using SMS text messaging over GSM mobile phones

- ❏ You can play two games on a single EPOC machine, one against the other

- ❏ You can have many games going on simultaneously, all using different communications protocols

- ❏ You can save the state of a game in a file. Later, you can open that file and continue with the game. You can have as many files open as you want, and as many saved games as you want.

For you as a developer, Battleships presents many more opportunities. It's a moderately complex EIKON program, built on a communications stack called the transaction-oriented games stack (TOGS). So it's a good basis for learning about EIKON, and about EPOC communications and system programming. I'll be using it as the source of code snippets in many chapters throughout the book.

Example Projects

When you've installed the EPOC C++ SDK and the example code from the book's CD-ROM, you'll find many projects (besides `hellotext` and `helloeik`) in the `\pep\` directory. About half are independent example projects that I cover in association with various topics in the book. The remaining projects all build up to Battleships. Here are the independent projects:

Example	Purpose
`active`	Basic active objects example. See Chapter 18.
`buffers`	Dynamic buffers. See Chapter 8.
`cstring`	Strings in C. See Chapter 5.
`drawing`	Device independent drawing, with a reusable view and support for zooming. See Chapter 15.
`epocstring`	EPOC strings, using descriptors. See Chapter 5.
`helloeik`	Hello World, EIKON version. See this chapter for how to build, and Chapter 9 for a detailed look at its insides.
`helloeikfull`	Hello World, EIKON version, with finishing touches. See Chapter 13.
`helloeikhelp`	Help for `helloeikfull`: see Chapter 13.
`hellotext`	Hello World, text version. See this chapter. Code framework is used as a basis for `buffers` and `epocstring` examples.
`memorymagic`	How to allocate memory and clean it up again – and how not to. See Chapter 6.
`streams`	Using files and stream APIs to save and load data. See Chapter 7.

Here are the Battleships projects:

Example	Purpose
`battleships`	The full two-player Battleships game, which I introduce throughout the book, right up to the final full description in Chapter 22.
`bsaif`	The icon for Battleships.
`bships1`	Solo Ships, a single-player game, which I use as an example of an EIKON program supporting object embedding in Chapter 14.
`bsaif1`	The icon for Solo Ships.
`tpg`	A test version of the game, written before I wrote any of the communications code, which I briefly mention in Chapter 16.

And here are the TOGS projects, which are all needed for `battleships`, and which may also be used for other purposes:

Example	Purpose
`gdp`	Game Datagram Protocol (GDP) – the basic communications interface, plus three implementations (loopback, infrared and SMS). The interface specification is in Chapter 17, and the infrared and SMS implementations are described in Chapter 21.
`gdpchat`	Test chat program using GDP. See Chapter 17.
`gsdp`	Game Session Datagram Protocol (GSDP) – links packets into sessions, and distinguishes session types so that different games can be played. The interface specification is described in Chapter 17. GSDP uses an EPOC server, which I describe fully in Chapter 20.
`gsdpchat`	Test Chat program using GSDP. See Chapter 17.
`gsdpchataif`	Icon for Chat.
`rgcp`	Reliable Game Conversation Protocol (RGCP) – adds acknowledgements, re-sending, and piggy-backing to the GSDP session, so that an RGCP client can rely on the packet data it handles. See Chapter 17 and Chapter 22.
`rgcpchat`	Test Converse program using RGCP. See Chapter 17.
`rgcpchataif`	Icon for Converse.

Summary

In this chapter, we've not gone very heavily into code, but have instead focused on the tools that come with the SDK and how to use them to build and test two simple projects.

In this chapter we've looked at:

❑ How to use the Emulator

❑ Source compatibility between the Emulator and the target EPOC machine

❑ Quirks in the drive mapping from the EPOC device to the Emulator

❑ A hint as to what support EPOC offers to help you code safely

❑ How to make makefiles for different compilation targets, using makmake

❑ The basic structure of the project specification, the .mmp file

❑ Using and configuring Visual C++ IDE and command line tools

❑ Compiling and installing for the ARM platform

❑ The difference between a .exe and a .app file, how they're built and the directories in which they reside

❑ How to get UIDs for our EPOC applications, and what numbers to use in the meantime

❑ How to compile EPOC resources

❑ Some of the more important directories in the SDK

❑ The Battleships program, and other example projects, that we'll be using throughout the book

In the next chapter, we'll look at the concepts underlying the EPOC system – its constraints, architecture and the frameworks provided to the application developer.

3

System Structure

We've seen how to *build* programs for EPOC. Now we need some extra background information to understand how to *write* them.

In this chapter, we'll introduce as many issues as we need for the following chapters, without getting deeply involved in much C++ code. All these issues are fundamental for EPOC system design, and all will be essential background as we move to look at coding conventions, the user library, and other basic APIs in the next few chapters.

We'll start with by reviewing the hardware of a typical EPOC machine, from a developer's point of view. Hardware is more limited than that provided by a typical desktop computer, which on the one hand creates many new market opportunities, and on the other hand imposes many constraints on software and software development.

We'll look at the four types of software that need to run on EPOC:

❑ Applications

❑ Servers

❑ Engines

❑ Kernel

We'll cover the facilities provided by the EPOC base (the kernel plus lowest-level APIs) to support programming. Much of this is standard fare in system design, and will be familiar to anyone who's worked with an OS like Windows NT or Unix.

Then I'll introduce something that's quite unique to EPOC: its optimized event-handling system using active objects and the client-server framework. Although we won't be tackling the details of this framework until much later in the book, everything we do will use it, and its existence is a key enabler for EPOC's performance, compactness, and robustness.

I'll conclude the chapter with two sections on the big picture, to whet your appetite for the rest of the book. Firstly I'll summarize the EPOC R5 APIs that we'll be covering in the book. Then I'll do a quick tour through the application suite, so you can see how they use the APIs, and so get an idea for how you might use them yourself.

Hardware Resources

EPOC is intended to run on hand-portable, communications-oriented computers. This profoundly affects the design of its software system. So let's begin this section by looking at the hardware facilities more closely.

Here are the main aspects of hardware on an EPOC device:

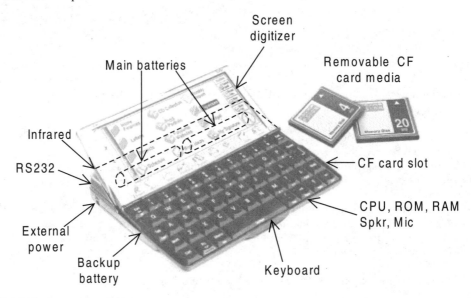

An EPOC-based system includes

❏ A CPU: EPOC is designed for 32-bit CPUs, running at lower speeds compared with CPUs in desktops or workstations. Available EPOC Release 5 systems are based on 36MHz ARM or 190MHz StrongARM CPUs. Future EPOC machines may use faster chips, and support for Motorola's M*CORE architecture is also planned.

❏ A ROM: the system ROM contains the OS and *all* the built-in middleware and applications. Compare this to a PC, in which only a small bootstrap loader and BIOS are built into ROM, with OS and applications loaded from hard disk. The system ROM is mapped as the z: drive. Everything in the ROM is accessible both as a file on z:, and directly by reading the data from ROM. So programs are executed in place, rather than being loaded into RAM and then executed, as PC programs are. EPOC Release 5 machines use around 12MB of ROM.

❑ System RAM: the system RAM is used for two purposes: RAM for use by active programs and the system kernel, and RAM used as 'disk' space accessed as the c: drive. The system uses as much as is needed for these purposes: you don't have to pre-allocate some RAM for one purpose and some for another. Usually there is also some free RAM. But since the total RAM on a typical machine is only around 8MB or 16MB, there is a real possibility that RAM may get exhausted, resulting in an out-of-memory error or (if the problem occurs when a file is being written) a disk full error.

❑ I/O devices, including a screen with 'digitizer' for pen input, a keyboard which may need to be even more compact than those found on laptops, a CF card slot for additional 'disks' accessed as d:, a serial port for RS232, dial-up TCP/IP, and connection to a PC; an infrared port for 'beaming' data between EPOC machines and others such as Palm or Nokia Communicators, or for convenient wireless access to data modems on a suitable mobile phone; and other devices.

❑ Power sources, including main batteries, backup battery and external power (from a mains adapter).

The Psion Series 5mx has 12MB ROM, 8MB or 16MB RAM, a 36MHz ARM CPU, one serial and one IR port, 640x240 pixel screen displaying either four or sixteen shades of gray, and a digitizer over the screen to support pen input (slightly extended to the left and below to support the sidebar and taskbar). Power is from main and backup batteries, and external (mains-derived) power.

EPOC OEMs have freedom to vary this basic specification quite widely. The Ericsson MC218 is very similar to the Psion Series 5mx. The Psion Revo has a smaller screen (480x160), and an in-built rechargeable battery instead of main and backup batteries; however, while it uses infrared for communication with other EPOC machines and compatible mobile phones, and a docking cradle for communication with PCs, the Revo has no CF card slot. The Psion netBook and Series 7 use a 190MHz StrongARM CPU, and have 640x480 color screens. The Geofox One, an EPOC Release 2-based machine no longer available, used a 640x320 screen without a digitizer: instead, it had a track pad pointer similar to those found on many laptop PCs.

OEMs also have flexibility in the way they manage the ROM and deliver built-in applications. Applications can be delivered on a CD-ROM with the device, to be installed into RAM if the user wants them, instead of being built into ROM – rather as you would bundle software with PCs. There's room for ingenuity in managing the ROM itself: the Psion netBook and Psion Series 5MX Pro have only a very small bootstrap loader in ROM. On cold boot, they load a ROM image from CF card into system RAM – using as much RAM as needed. After this, the RAM used is marked as read-only and behaves exactly like a ROM. This arrangement allows the ROM to be configurable by an enterprise IS department, or field replaced by the user.

We've put together information on machines available at the time of going to press, it's in the appendices.

EPOC supports this variability by essentially the same techniques used in the PC industry: it uses a device driver architecture, and offers an abstracted API for each device, to programs that use that device.

But EPOC is otherwise very different from the PC industry.

❑ Resources are constrained: the CPU is slower, and there is less memory

❑ There is no hard disk: we can't do disk-backed virtual memory, and we can't assume there is an infinite amount of room in which to place our program or data files

❑ Power management is critical: user data is often held on RAM disk, so power must *never* be lost, even when the machine is switched off, or the batteries are replaced. Data and machine state must be maintained in low-power conditions.

To summarize, you have to make software compact, and you have to tackle errors such as out-of-memory and others. You have to keep going, because EPOC systems virtually never reboot. EPOC is designed from the ground up to help you do this, but you must learn the disciplines this involves and implement them in the software you write.

Software Basics

The EPOC operating system and its applications can be divided into various types of component, with different types of boundary between them:

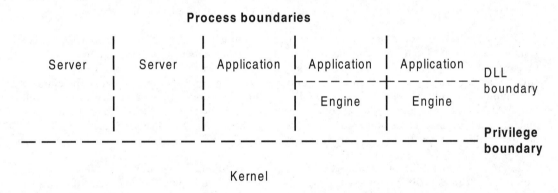

The **kernel** manages the machine's hardware resources such as system RAM and hardware devices. It provides and controls the way all other software component can access these resources. The kernel uses hardware-supported **privilege** to gain access to the resources. That is, the CPU will only perform certain privileged instructions for the kernel. It runs other programs – so-called **user-mode** programs – without privilege, so that they can only access system resources through the kernel APIs. The boundary between the kernel and all other components is a privilege boundary.

An **application** is a program with a user interface. Each application runs in a separate **process**, with its own virtual address space, so the boundary between one application and another is a process boundary. One application cannot accidentally overwrite another's data, because their address spaces are entirely separate.

A **server** is a program without a user interface. A server manages one or more resources. It provides an API so that **clients** can gain access to its services. A server's clients may be applications, or other servers. Each server generally runs in its own process, so that the boundary between a server and its clients is a process boundary. This provides a strong assurance of server integrity.

Actually, for performance reasons, certain closely related servers may run in the same process: we'll cover this in more detail below.

The isolation between a server and its clients is of the same order as the isolation between a kernel and user-mode programs – but servers are much easier to program and work with. EPOC uses servers to provide many services that, on other systems, are provided by the kernel or device drivers.

An **engine** is the part of an application that manipulates its data, rather than the part that interacts directly with the user. Often, you can easily divide an application into an engine part and a GUI part. Exactly where you draw this line is part of the art of software engineering. Most built-in EPOC applications, and the larger applications I'll be developing in this book, have engines of sufficient complexity that it's worth drawing the boundary explicitly. An application engine may be a separate source module, a separate DLL, or even a number of separate DLLs. The boundary between engine and application is a module or DLL boundary, whose main purpose is to promote good software design – in contrast to a process or privilege boundary, whose main purpose is to prevent unwanted interactions.

That gives us four component types, and three boundary types. DLL or module boundaries are very cheap to cross: they promote system integrity by modularization and encapsulation. The privilege boundary is a little more expensive to cross: it promotes system integrity by hiding the kernel and devices from user-mode code. Process boundaries are most expensive of all to cross: they promote integrity by isolating programs' private RAM from each other.

If you're an application programmer, you'll spend most of your time writing applications and – if your application is big enough – engines.

I use the word 'system programming' to refer to the art of writing server or kernel software. I'll be covering servers in this book, because they're important for communications programming. I'll give an overview of the kernel and what it does in this chapter, but I won't otherwise be covering how to program the kernel side of the privilege boundary.

Processes, Threads and Context Switching

The **process** is a fundamental unit of protection in EPOC. Each process has its own **address space**. The virtual addresses used by programs executing in that process are translated into physical addresses in the machine's ROM and RAM. The translation is managed by a **memory management unit** or MMU, so that read-only memory is shared, but the writable memory of one process is not accessible to the writable memory of another.

The **thread** is the fundamental unit of execution in EPOC. A process has one or more threads. Each thread executes independently of the others, but within the same address space. A thread can therefore change memory belonging to another thread in the same process – deliberately, or accidentally. Threads are not as well isolated from each other as processes.

Threads are **preemptively scheduled** by the EPOC kernel. The highest-priority thread that is eligible to run at a given time is run by the kernel. A thread that is ineligible is described as **suspended**. Threads may suspend to wait for events to happen and may **resume** when one of those events does happen. Whenever threads suspend or resume, the kernel checks which one is now the highest thread, and **schedules** it for execution. This can result in one thread being scheduled even while another one is running. The consequent interruption of the running thread by the higher priority thread is called **preemption**, and the possibility of preemption gives rise to the term **preemptive multitasking**.

The process of switching execution between one thread and another is **context switching**. Like any other system, EPOC's scheduler is written carefully to minimize the overheads involved with context switching.

Nevertheless, context switching is much more expensive than, say, a function call. The most expensive type of context switch is between a thread in one process and a thread in another, because a process switch also involves many changes to the MMU settings, and various hardware caches must be flushed. It's much cheaper to context switch between two threads in the same process.

Typically, each EPOC application uses its own process and just one thread. Each server also uses its own process and just one thread. But an application (or a server) is really a *thread* rather than a process. The decision to use a *separate* process for each application and server is merely one of convenience. In cases where servers are designed to cooperate closely together, they are sometimes packaged into a single process, so that context switching between them is cheaper. Thus all the major communications-related servers in EPOC – serial, sockets, and telephony – run in the same process.

How can an application or server run effectively in a single thread? Don't sophisticated applications need to perform background tasks? And shouldn't a server have a single thread for each client? EPOC implements sophisticated applications and servers using only a single thread, because it has a good event-handling system, based on **active objects**. I'll return to that, in the *Event Handling* section, below.

Executable Programs

As far as the CPU is concerned, a C++ program is just a series of instructions. But if we want to manage software effectively, we have to group code in more convenient packages. The packages EPOC uses are closely based on those used by Windows NT and similar systems. They are:

❑ A `.exe`, a program with a single main entry point `E32Main()`. When the system launches a new `.exe`, it first creates a new process and a main thread. The entry point is then called in the context of that thread.

❑ A **dynamic link library** or DLL, a library of program code with potentially many entry points. The system loads a DLL into the context of an existing thread (and therefore an existing process).

Both of these are **executables**. I'll use 'executable' when I mean either a `.exe` or a DLL. I'll never use just 'executable' if I mean a `.exe` specifically – I'll use '`.exe`'.

There are two important types of DLL:

❑ A **shared library DLL** provides a fixed API that can be used by one or more programs. Most shared library DLLs have the extension `.dll`. Executables are marked with the shared libraries they require and, when the system loads the executable at runtime, the required shared libraries are loaded automatically. This happens recursively, so any shared libraries needed by the shared libraries are also loaded, until everything required by the executable is ready.

❑ A **polymorphic DLL** implements an abstract API such as a printer driver, sockets protocol, or an EIKON application. Such DLLs typically use an extension other than `.dll` – `.prn`, `.prt`, or `.app`, for instance. In EPOC, polymorphic DLLs usually have a single entry point, which allocates and constructs a derived class of some base class associated with the DLL. Polymorphic DLLs are usually loaded explicitly by the program that requires them.

The Place of Execution

To be executed, an executable has to be **loaded**. This means that its program and data areas must be prepared for use. There are two cases here:

- ❑ The first case is an executable in ROM (drive z:). ROM-based executables are executed in-place. Loading is trivial for ROM-based executables.

- ❑ Executables not in ROM must first be loaded into RAM. This applies to executables on CF card removable media (drive d:), or in the system RAM disk (drive c:). This kind of loading involves more processing for EPOC.

Cutting Down the Size

EPOC optimizes the formats used for DLLs in order to make them as compact as possible in ROM and RAM.

- ❑ Most systems supporting DLLs or analogous concepts offer two options for identifying the entry points in them. You can refer to the entry points either by name, or by ordinal number. Names are potentially long, and wasteful of ROM and RAM. So EPOC uses link-by-ordinal exclusively.

- ❑ Loading into RAM can involve locating the executable at an address that cannot be determined until load time: this means that relocation information has to be included in the executable format. Loading into ROM happens effectively at build time. So EPOC's ROM-building tools perform the relocation and strip the DLLs of their relocation information to make them smaller still.

EPOC's link-by-ordinal scheme affects the disciplines used for binary compatibility (a future release of a DLL must use exactly the same ordinals as the previous release). The pre-loading scheme means among other things that you can't take an executable out of the ROM and deliver it in another package for RAM loading. These are largely matters for EPOC OEMs, and I shan't be describing them further in this book.

Loading and Sharing

Executables contain three types of binary data:

- ❑ Program code
- ❑ Read-only static data
- ❑ Read/write static data

EPOC handles .exes and DLLs differently.

.exes are not shared. If a .exe is loaded into RAM, it has its own areas for code, read-only data, and read/write data. If a second version of the same .exe is launched, new areas will be allocated for each of these. There is a small optimization: ROM-based .exes allocate a RAM area only for read/write data – the program code and read-only data are read directly from ROM.

DLLs are shared. When a DLL is first loaded into RAM, it is relocated to a particular address. When a second thread requires the same DLL, it doesn't have to load it – it merely **attaches** the copy already there. The DLL appears at the same address in all threads that use it. EPOC maintains reference counts, so that the DLL is only unloaded when no more threads are attached to it. ROM-based DLLs, like ROM-based .exes, are not actually loaded at all – they are simply used in-place in ROM.

Launching Applications and Servers

Most servers use their own `.exe` to generate their own process. For instance, `ewsrv.exe` is the window server, and `efsrv.exe` is the file server.

As we saw earlier, some servers piggyback into the process of others, to minimize context-switching overheads. The main server in such a group uses its own process – for instance, `c32exe.exe` launches the serial communications server. Other servers use a DLL and launch their own thread within the main server thread.

A console application, such as `hellotext.exe`, is built into its own `.exe`. A console application must create its own console, which it can then use to interact with the user.

Most GUI applications are EIKON applications like `helloeik.app`. EIKON applications are actually polymorphic DLLs whose main entry point, `NewApplication()`, creates and returns a `CEikApplication`-derived object. The application process is created by a small `.exe`, `apprun.exe`, to which the `.app` name is passed as a parameter. If the application wants to edit an embedded document, it can do so *without creating a new process* by loading the `.app` for the embedded document directly, in the same thread.

Other applications use similar techniques. Java applets are all run under a single shared JVM, owned by each web browser or `AppletViewer` application instance. Java applications are each launched under their own `java.exe` process.

Power Management

Power management is probably the single most important factor that makes the difference between a desktop system and a portable system:

❑ Power has to be used efficiently. Battery life – even with rechargeable batteries – makes a difference to how the user thinks of the device. So also does battery weight. EPOC needs to work effectively on lower-speed, lower-power, hardware than that used by desktop PCs.

❑ The machine should turn off instantly, and turn back on instantly as required – in the same state as it was when turned off.

❑ Certain parts of the system should still be able to run while the system is apparently off. For example, when an alarm is due, the machine should be turned on so that the alarm can sound.

❑ System boot should be avoided. Cold boot destroys the `c:` disk. Warm boot attempts to recover the `c:` disk, but even a warm boot takes several tens of seconds, and destroys the state of applications.

❑ Even if all power is removed suddenly, the system should do what it can to save critical information, so that there is a possibility of a warm boot when power returns (rather than a cold boot).

As an application or server programmer, your task is easier than that of the kernel. But you still get involved in power management. You have to write your programs efficiently, to make best use of an EPOC machine's scarce resources – this applies as much to power as to available RAM, CPU speed etc.

You have to be aware that power can be switched on and off at any time. If your display is animated, or if it depends on the time of day, then you have to make sure you request a power-on notification so that you can update your display when power is resumed.

The deeper you delve into the system, the more complicated power management becomes. For instance, as a device driver programmer, you can see that power management is more complex than simply machine on/off. The user thinks the machine is off if the display is turned off. But each hardware component is responsible for its own power management. A communications link driver should turn the physical device off if it's not needed. The kernel scheduler even turns the CPU off if all threads are waiting for an event. Every possible step is taken to save power and ensure that user data is retained even in the most difficult power-loss situations. I wish I could say the same about my laptop PC and its power management software!

The Kernel and E32

EPOC's most fundamental component is E32. E32 consists of the kernel, and user library. The kernel is entirely privileged. The user library, euser.dll, is the lowest-level user-mode code. It offers library functions to other user-mode code and controlled access to the kernel.

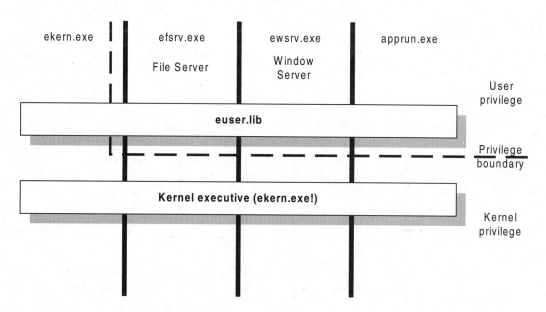

The kernel itself has two major components:

❏ The **kernel executive** runs privileged code in the context of a thread that usually executes in user mode. Executive code can therefore be preempted by higher-priority user-mode threads, or by the kernel server.

❏ The **kernel server** is the main thread of its own process and always runs privileged. The kernel server is the highest-priority thread in the system. It allocates and de-allocates kernel-side resources needed by the system and by user programs. It also performs functions on behalf of user-mode programs. The kernel server is a single thread: it handles user requests in sequence, non-preemptively.

We'll be describing `euser.dll`'s most important facilities in detail over the next few chapters. For now let's note that it offers three types of function:

- Functions that execute entirely user-side, such as most functions in the array and descriptor classes (descriptors are EPOC's version of strings)

- Functions that require privilege, and so cross into the executive, such as checking the time or locale settings

- Functions that require the services of the kernel server: these go through the user library, via the executive, to the server

The functions that operate entirely on the user-side can also be used safely by any kernel-side code. Kernel-side code that needs access to kernel facilities can (and must) use these facilities directly, rather than through the user library interface.

In this book, we'll be writing user-side code exclusively. So although the distinction between the types of function in the user library helps you to understand the system design, it's not essential for you to know all the possible circumstances in which kernel-side code might be called.

Device Drivers

System devices such as screen, keyboard, digitizer (for the pen), sound codec, status LEDs, power sensors, serial port, CF-card, etc. are all driven by low-level device drivers. It's possible to add devices and write drivers for them. EPOC OEMs usually do this: EPOC machines are not typically user-expandable in the same way that PCs are.

A device driver is implemented in several parts:

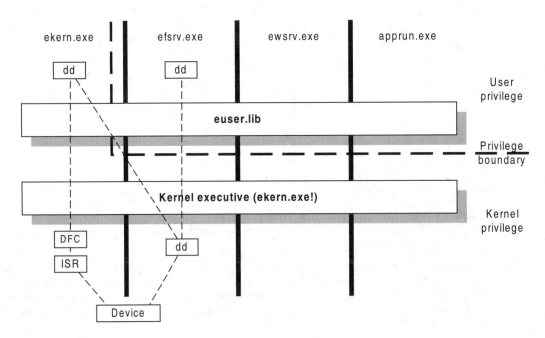

The kernel executive contains support for device drivers, so that a user program can issue a request to device driver code running kernel-side, in either the kernel executive or kernel server. Such requests typically initiate a device operation, or tell the driver that the requesting program is waiting for something to happen on the device.

Drivers also process device interrupts and then tell the user (or kernel) program that an earlier request is complete. Interrupt handling works at two levels.

❑   First-level handling is done by an **interrupt service routine** (ISR). ISRs must be short, and can't do very much, because they could occur at any time, even in the middle of a kernel server operation. Usually, they simply acknowledge the device that raised the interrupt and then set a flag to request the kernel to run a **delayed function call** (DFC) for second-level processing.

❑   The kernel schedules the DFC when it is in a more convenient state — immediately, if user-mode code was executing when the interrupt occurred; otherwise, when the kernel would have otherwise crossed the privilege boundary back to user code. DFCs can use most kernel APIs. DFCs typically do a small amount of processing and then post a user thread to indicate that an I/O request has completed.

If you're programming a device driver — or any part of the kernel — you need to be aware of the kernel environment, and of the interactions between the scheduler, interrupts, MMU etc. It's a specialist art, and beyond the scope of this book.

The user thread environment is much less restrictive, and much easier to work with. That's why EPOC does as much device-related programming as possible in user-mode servers.

Timers

The kernel supports a tick interrupt at 64Hz on ARM, and 10Hz on the PC-based emulator.

The tick interrupt is used to drive round robin scheduling of equal highest-priority threads. It can also be accessed (via User::After() and RTimer::After() function calls) by user programs. The tick interrupt suspends during power-off so that, if you request a timer to expire after 5 seconds, and then turn the machine off 2 seconds later, the timer event will occur 3 seconds after you turn the machine back on again — or even later, if you immediately turn the machine back off!

The kernel also supports a date/time clock, which you can access using User::At() and RTimer:At(). This timer expires at exactly the time requested. If the machine was turned off at the time, it is turned on. This is the kind of timer to use for alarms.

Memory

System memory is managed by the memory management unit (MMU).

ROM handling is easy. The ROM consists entirely of files, in a directory tree on drive z:, and is mapped to a fixed address, so that the data in every file can be accessed simply by reading it. Programs can be executed in place, and bitmaps and fonts can be used in place for on-screen blitting, without all the data going through the file server.

RAM management is more interesting. Physical RAM is divided into 4k pages by the MMU. Each physical page can be allocated to

❑ A user process's virtual address space: there may be many of these, as we have seen

❑ The kernel server process's virtual address space

❑ The RAM disk used as c:. Such RAM can only be accessed by the file server process

❑ DLLs loaded from a non-ROM filing system: RAM for DLLs is marked read-only after the DLL has been loaded. Each DLL appears at exactly the same virtual address for all threads that use it.

❑ Translation tables for the MMU: the MMU is carefully optimized to keep these small. But there is no practical limit on the number of processes and threads allowed in EPOC.

❑ The free list, of pages not yet allocated for any of the above purposes

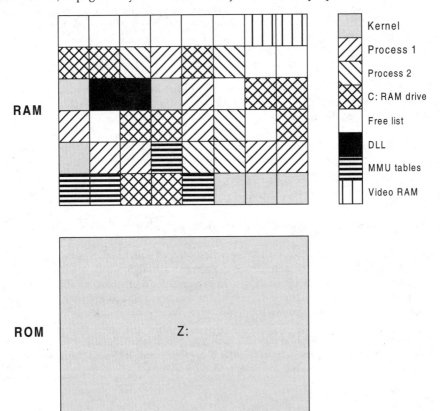

There is no virtual memory, backed up by a swap file on a large hard disk. So any page needed for user processes, the kernel or the RAM disk is taken from the free list. When the free list runs out, the next request for memory will cause an out-of-memory error – or a disk full error, if the request came from a file write.

Process and Thread Memory

When a .exe is launched, it creates a new process with a single main thread. During the lifetime of a process, other threads may also be created.

The process's address space includes regions for

❑ System-wide memory, such as the system ROM and RAM-loaded shared DLLs

❑ Process-wide memory, such as the .exe image and its writable static data

❑ Memory for each thread, for a very small stack and a default heap (which can grow up to a limit set by the EPOC OEM: it's 2MB on a Psion Series 5MX)

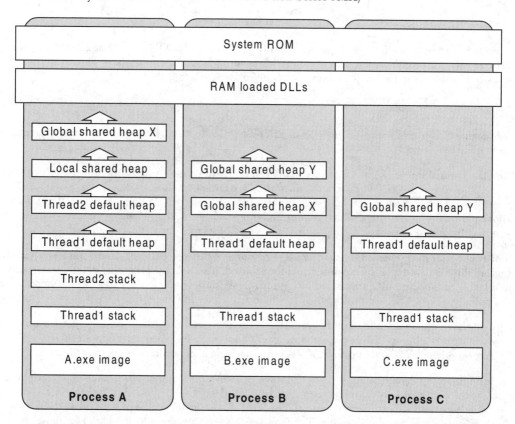

A thread's stack cannot grow after the thread has been launched. The thread will be panicked – terminated abruptly – if it overflows its stack. The usual initial stack size is 12k. The stack is used for C++ automatic variables in each function. So you have to avoid using large automatics. Instead, put all large variables on the heap.

A thread's default heap is used for all allocations using C++ operator new, and user library functions such as User::Alloc(). If possible, memory is allocated from existing pages committed to the heap. If that's not possible, the heap manager requests additional pages from the system free list. If the system free list has insufficient pages, the allocation will fail, giving an out-of-memory error.

Each thread has its own default heap, which is used for allocation by C++ operator `new` and de-allocation by `delete`. Because each thread makes allocations on its own non-shared heap allocation and de-allocation is very efficient. If an allocation can be satisfied without growing the heap, only a few instructions are required, no privilege boundaries need be crossed, and no synchronization with allocations by other threads is needed.

You can put small objects on the stack, such as integers or rectangles,

```
TInt x;
TRect region;
```

but most objects – especially larger ones – should go on the heap:

```
CEikDialog* dialog=new CGameSettingsDialog;
```

Objects whose class name begins with `C` can only go on the heap. Objects whose class name begins with `T`, however, can be either members of other classes, or automatics on the stack. Don't put them on the stack unless they're quite small. Beware especially of `TFileName`:

```
TFileName fileName;
```

A filename is 256 characters – 512 bytes in EPOC's Unicode build. There isn't room for too many of them on a 12k stack.

You can control the stack size in a `.exe`. This can apply to console programs, servers, or programs with no GUI – but not to EIKON programs, since they are launched with `apprun.exe`. You can also control the stack size when you launch a thread explicitly from within your program. If you have an application with an algorithm which requires a large stack, such as a heavily recursive game-tree search, you may have to encapsulate the algorithm in a `.exe` of its own, or a separate thread.

Since each user heap eats into a scarce system resource – the free page list – and since applications and servers run for months or years without being restarted, it's vital that programs detect heap failure due to a lack of memory, and it's vital that programs release unneeded memory as soon as possible. This is the domain of EPOC's cleanup framework, which will cover in Chapter 6.

Threads have independent default heaps in the sense that each thread always allocates from its own heap. But since all heaps are in the same process's address space, each thread in a process can access objects on other heaps in that process – provided suitable synchronization methods are used.

In addition to the default heap, threads can have other heaps. But these introduce new complications, so you should use them only if you have to. For any non-default heap, you must provide a specific C++ operator `new()` to allocate objects onto it. For local shared heaps – shared with other threads in the same process – you have to introduce synchronization using mutexes or the like. For global shared heaps – shared with threads in other processes – the heap is mapped to a different address in each process, so you have to introduce a smart reference system rather than straightforward pointers. All these things are possible if necessary – but they're rarely necessary. Usually, it's better to use a server to manage shared resources, rather than a shared heap. I give an overview of servers below, and cover them more thoroughly, including performance optimization, in Chapter 21.

A thread's non-shared heaps are allocated into a 256MB region of a process's virtual address space. By limiting the maximum size to 2MB (as on the Psion Series 5MX), there is an implied maximum of 128 threads per process.

No Writable Static in DLLs

> **EPOC DLLs do not support writable static data.**

DLLs only support read-only data, and program code. Writable static data is supported only by .exes.

This imposes some design disciplines on native EPOC code that, with object orientation, are actually very easy to live with. But it does make life more difficult when porting code, which often assumes the availability of writable static.

The easiest workaround is to use a .exe to contain the ported code. EPOC's spell check engine uses this technique. The .exe is packaged as an EPOC server, which allows it to be shared between multiple programs. By using a separate process, we also gain the benefit of isolation.

Here's why EPOC doesn't support writable static. Every DLL that supports writable static would require a separate chunk of RAM to be allocated, in every process that uses the DLL. There are about 100 DLLs in EPOC R5: perhaps the typical application uses 60 of them. Say I usually have about 20 applications running concurrently in my 12MB RAM machine, and there are about 10 system servers working on behalf of those applications. The smallest unit of physical memory allocation in conventional MMUs is 4k (and smaller wouldn't be at all sensible). If each DLL used even a single word of writable static, it would require 4k x (20 app processes + 10 server processes) x 60 DLLs each = 72MB of RAM just for the writable static!

I quite often have about 20 apps running on my PC too: 72MB on a PC isn't unacceptable – most of it is paged out to disk anyway – but for a handheld system this overhead, or anything approaching it, is out of the question.

You could argue that most DLLs wouldn't use writable static, so these figures are exaggerated. But EPOC's architects' response was that, if the facility were there, most people *would* use it, without even knowing that they were doing so. We would only find out at system integration time, and by then it would be too late to fix any problems. So writable static was not implemented by the EPOC loader.

EPOC R5 does provide a workaround for the writable static limitation, intended for system components only. Future releases of EPOC may further ease the restriction.

Even if the rules are loosened up, the underlying economics won't change: at least 4k of RAM will be consumed by each process that loads each DLL that requires writable static. Using writable static isn't environment-friendly. Don't do it without being aware of the consequences.

In fact EPOC associates a single machine word of writable static per thread with each DLL. This is **thread-local storage** or TLS. You can use the TLS word as an anchor for what would have been your writable static. There are no MMU granularities to worry about here – just a small performance implication, since getting the TLS pointer involves a system call which takes perhaps 20 or so instructions, rather than the single instruction required to get a normal pointer. Not all DLLs use TLS, but the system allocates the word anyway. In my scenario above, TLS would account for only 72k – which is perfectly acceptable.

Files

Let's summarize what we've already seen about files.

EPOC machines have no hard disk, as found on PCs. But EPOC always has two disks present, and may have more.

c:	RAM disk – full read/write file system. Contents are initialized to empty on a cold boot. Data is maintained as long as there is power to refresh the RAM. Data is recovered in a warm boot, unless it has been corrupted beyond recovery. Files can be extended indefinitely, so long as there are RAM pages to allocate to them from the system free list. RAM pages are subdivided into 512 byte sectors, so that small files are managed more efficiently.
z:	ROM – read-only file system. Contents are built by the EPOC OEM when building the device. Some machines, such as the Psion netBook or Series 5MX Pro, load a ROM image on cold boot, so that 'ROM' can be updated and replaced – by enterprise IS departments, distributors and so on.
d:	CF card – removable read/write media, supported by some EPOC machines. CF is **Compact Flash**, a non-volatile medium written using a higher-than-usual voltage 'flash'.
	Careful power management is used by EPOC's CF-card file system to ensure that 512 byte sector writes are **atomic** – they either complete fully, or don't even start. File formats such as those used by the persistent file store are written and extensively tested to assume, and support, atomic sector writing. These files can be recovered if failure occurs on any sector write. CF cards are slower than the RAM disk, but their non-volatility, and higher capacity – 20-200MB or so – makes them attractive.
	CF cards are an industry standard, slightly smaller than PC cards used on laptops. You can buy PC card to CF card adapters, to insert a CF card into a laptop and thus share data between your laptop and EPOC machine. CF cards are also used in other devices such as digital cameras. EPOC can share data with any other device that supports CF cards, provided it uses standard DOS partitions and the FAT (or VFAT) filing system.

The EPOC file server supports installable file systems that can be loaded at runtime without any kind of reboot. Additional drive letters, and additional media types, can also be supported, depending on system and user requirements.

I'll cover data management more extensively in Chapter 7.

Event Handling

> **Perhaps the most fundamental design decision in EPOC was to optimize the system for efficient event handling. Each native EPOC application or server is a single event-handling thread.** Active objects **are used to handle events non-preemptively.**

In the old days, programs were written with a `main()` that was in control: every so often the program would deign to check for user input, and would then process it.

With GUI systems, though, the user is in control. As programmers, we have had to get used to this change of viewpoint: to invert our programming mentality to event-driven programming. It took some time in the programming community for this to sink in: most of the change took place over about a decade, from 1985 to 1995.

Arguably, this change of mindset hasn't yet happened at the deeper levels of most operating systems. Most operating systems put a lot of effort into supporting processes and threads, along with their associated synchronization paraphernalia – but very little effort into event handling, and event-based system design paradigms. Even Java, a very recent system design, uses threads at the fundamental level rather than an event-handling framework.

But it so happens that, when the overwhelming majority of your code *is* event-based, a system design optimized for event handling is *much more efficient* than one optimized for conventional multitasking. We'll briefly review EPOC's fundamental building blocks for event-handling systems – active objects and the client-server architecture. You won't need to understand them in any more detail than this, until you need to write your own active objects and servers. I cover those topics, quite thoroughly, much later in the book – in Chapters 20 and 21.

Perspectives on Event Handling

Say you are using the EPOC Word application. If you press a key, a small cascade of events will occur, which are handled by at least three EPOC threads:

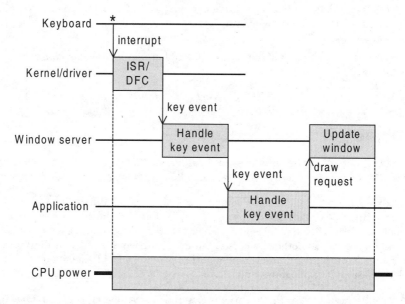

Let's look at this cascade from a couple of perspectives. First, from the whole-system point of view:

❑ The I/O device responsible for looking after the keyboard generates an interrupt

❑ The kernel handles the event. It interrogates the device, works out what ASCII key code to assign, and creates an event for whichever program is interested in raw key events – and in any real EPOC system, that's the window server.

- ❑ The window server then works out which application is currently receiving keystrokes, and sends the event to the application, in this case EPOC Word

- ❑ EPOC Word then handles the key – perhaps by adding text to the document, and then updating the display

- ❑ The window server updates the display, in response to the application's requests

From the power-management point of view, power is needed for the CPU only while it's doing something. Power is turned on to handle an interrupt, and turned off again when no more threads are eligible to run.

You can also look at the tasks in the diagram and ask, "What other events might this task have to handle?"

- ❑ The keyboard driver handles an interrupt, does minimal processing, and notifies a user-mode thread – in this case, the window server. The keyboard driver must also handle requests from the window server for key events. So the keyboard driver is an event-handling task that handles *two* types of event: requests from a user-mode thread and hardware events from the keyboard.

- ❑ The window server handles the key, does enough processing to identify the application that is currently taking keys, and then notifies the application. The window server, like the keyboard driver, also handles requests from the application for key presses. And the window server also performs screen drawing on behalf of all applications. So the window server is an event-handling task that handles these three event types (key events, requests to be notified about key events, and screen drawing) plus many more (for instance, pointer events, and requests to be notified about them).

- ❑ The application is an event-handling task that handles key events (and more, for instance pointer events).

So each task is an event handler. In EPOC, events are handled using active objects.

Active Objects

All native EPOC threads are essentially event handlers, with a single **active scheduler** per thread cooperating with one or more **active objects** to handle events from devices and other programs.

Each active object has a virtual member function called RunL(). RunL() gets called when the event happens for which the particular active object is responsible, and must be implemented to handle the event. Usually, it starts with some pre-processing to analyze the event. It may complete the handling of the event without calling any other functions. But in a framework, RunL() will usually call one or more virtual functions that the programmer implements to provide specific behavior. The most important frameworks are for GUI applications and servers:

- ❑ An application, such as the one in our example above, uses the CONE GUI framework. CONE analyzes input events, associates them with the correct control, and then calls virtual member functions such as OfferKeyEventL() to handle a key.

- ❑ A server, such as the window server above, uses the server framework to handle requests from client applications – including requests to draw on the screen, or to be notified about key events. Client requests are turned into messages that are sent to the server. The server framework analyzes these messages, associates them with the correct client, and calls ServiceL() on the server-side object representing the client, to handle the client's request.

A server also uses its own active objects to handle events other than client requests – for instance, key events from the kernel.

Active objects make life very easy for application programmers. All you have to do is to implement the correct framework function. Unless you need active objects for some other reason, you don't need to understand how they work. All you need to know is that your code must complete quickly (say, within a couple of seconds) so that your application is able to handle other events without undue delay.

You will eventually want to understand active objects, so I explain them fully later in the book, in Chapter 20. That's quite a lot later in the book, which proves my point: we don't need to get familiar with active objects until we get onto quite sophisticated programming.

Multitasking and Preemption

Threads implement **preemptive multitasking**, because one thread can preempt another if it has to handle an event – for instance, the window server can handle a key event while an application is running, by preempting the running application thread.

The ability of one thread to preempt another depends on their relative thread priorities. The most critical threads in the system are given the highest priorities – with the kernel, including device drivers, the highest priority of all.

EPOC implements multithreading so that it can run multiple applications and servers simultaneously.

Active objects implement **non-preemptive multitasking** within the context of a single thread, because each event must be completely handled by its RunL() before the next event on that thread can be handled.

Active objects, like threads, have priorities that affect their scheduling. But they affect it in quite a different way:

❑   With multithreading, the scheduling issue is "which thread should be running now?", to which the answer is always "the currently eligible-to-run thread with the highest priority". The question gets asked whenever thread priorities or eligibility are changed.

❑   With active objects, the scheduling issue only materializes when a RunL() has completed. The question for the active scheduler is then "which object's RunL() shall I run next?". The answer is "if there is just one object now eligible to run, then run it. If there is more than one eligible object, then choose the one with the highest priority. If there are no eligible objects, then wait for the next event and then decide what to do".

Some events are more important than others. It's much better to handle events in priority order than (say) first in, first out (FIFO). Events that control the thread (key events to an application, for example,) can be handled with higher priority than others (for instance, some kinds of animation). But once a RunL() has started – even for a low-priority event – it runs to completion. No other RunL() can be called until the current one has finished. That's ok, provided that all your event handlers are fairly quick – a couple of seconds at most, say, in an application, or a few milliseconds in a high-priority server.

Non-preemptive multitasking is surprisingly powerful. Actually, there should be no surprise about this: it's the natural paradigm to use for event handling. For instance, the window server handles key and pointer events, screen drawing, requests from every GUI-based application in the system, and animations including a flashing text cursor, sprites and self-updating clocks. It delivers all this sophistication using a single thread, with active-object-based multitasking.

And a sophisticated application such as EPOC Word uses active objects to handle status display update and text pagination at lower priority than more critical events – responding to editing events at and around the cursor position.

> **In many systems, the preferred way to multitask is to multithread. In EPOC, the preferred way to multitask is to use active objects.**

In a truly event-handling context, using active objects is pure win-win over using threads:

❑ You lose no functionality over threads, because preemption gains you nothing in a truly event-handled system

❑ You gain enormous convenience over threads, because you know you can't be preempted: you don't need to use mutexes, semaphores, critical sections or any kind of synchronization to protect against the activities of other active objects in your thread

Non-preemptive multitasking is not at all the same thing as **cooperative multitasking**. The 'cooperation' in cooperative multitasking is that one task has to say "I am now prepared for another task to run", for instance by using Yield() or a similar function. What this really means is "I am a long-running task, but I now wish to yield control to the system, so it can get any outstanding events handled if it needs to". This is a potentially messy way to mix event handling and non-event handling code: it often results in messy programs, and justifiably gives 'cooperative multitasking' a poor reputation. Active objects don't work like that: during RunL(), you have the system to yourself, and 'yield' occurs when your RunL() has finished.

> *Having said all that, EPOC does support a kind of yield. It's used exclusively for EIKON dialogs. It's dangerous to use it for any other purpose, since it's essential to guarantee that all yields nest correctly. In the case of dialogs, this is assured, since dialogs naturally nest. We'll see more of this in Chapter 20.*

All multitasking systems require a degree of cooperation, so that tasks can communicate with each other *where necessary*. Active objects require *less* cooperation than threads, because they are non-preemptively scheduled. And they can be just as independent as threads: a thread's active scheduler manages active objects independently of one another, just as the kernel scheduler manages threads independently of one another.

Servers

Most multithreaded programming in EPOC uses the client-server framework:

❑ A **server** thread is responsible for managing one or more related resources

❑ One or more **client** threads may use the server to perform functions which use those resources

EPOC's two most critical servers are the **file server**, which handles all files, and the **window server**, which handles user input and drawing to screen. A wide range of other servers is used to manage communications, databases, schedule, contacts, and the like. The kernel also acts as a kind of server. A client program may be either another server, or an application.

Client-server programming involves two potentially difficult issues:

❏ It involves multithreaded programming disciplines, which are difficult to get right

❏ It involves crossing process boundaries, which are a key guardian of system integrity

In order to minimize any difficulty associated with these issues, EPOC constrains the client/server interface to something that is small enough to maintain confidence in the usefulness of the process boundary, and built in such a way that you don't need to use thread synchronization as either the user or even the implementer of a server. The key elements of the interface are

❏ The **client interface**: each server provides an API to its clients – the client interface – which disguises all the client-server communications, so that clients can use the server easily without knowing the specifics of the client-server framework

❏ Kernel-supported **message passing**: if you're implementing a server (along with its client interface), this is the main method by which you pass requests from the client to the server, and handle them. The message-passing framework is powerful enough for the job – but no more complex than it needs to be.

❏ Kernel-supported **inter-thread read and write**: messages can't convey much information from client to server, and even less from server to client. To pass more information, a server can read from, or write to, a client's address space.

Most client classes that access server-based resources have names beginning with R. Two examples are RFile (a file, with functions such as Read(), Write(), Open() etc.) and RWindow (an on-screen window, with functions such as SetSize(), BeginRedraw() etc.). These client interface classes are implemented (by the server designer) using message passing and inter-thread read and write.

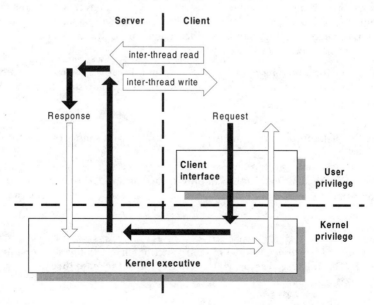

Clearly servers are event handlers. The central classes in any server are a single CServer-derived class to implement the behavior of the whole server and a number of CSession-derived classes to handle requests on behalf of each active client. CServer is an active object, whose RunL() interprets incoming messages, creates or destroys CSessions as needed, and calls their ServiceL() function to handle routine client requests. Most servers use more active objects to handle other events – such as key and pointer events, in the case of the window server, or disk-door-opened events, in the case of the file server.

The kernel server uses a similar framework. The RTimer class, and many other R classes in the user library, implement their APIs by message passing similar to that used by servers. The kernel server's framework is different from the standard server framework, to take account of the privilege-mode environment and the fact that there's only one kernel. But the principles are the same.

Device drivers also use a message passing system similar to that used by servers.

There's a lot more to say about servers. I cover this thoroughly in Chapter 21, which explains the message-passing framework in more detail, and also provides many tips for getting the best performance from servers.

Where Threads Matter

Most tasks are event handlers. So EPOC's design is optimized for event handling, with good results for ease of programming, system efficiency, and robustness.

But some tasks really are long-running threads. Game engine calculations, spreadsheet recalculation, background printing, and the like can be particularly long running. Status display updates, animations, and the like are only slightly less demanding.

EPOC has broadly two approaches to handling tasks that really are long-running threads.

- ❑ Simulate them using active objects, and chains of pseudo-events. Split the task into short increments, generate a low-priority pseudo-event that will be handled if no real events (such as user input) need handling; handle an increment and, if that doesn't complete the task, generate another pseudo-event.

- ❑ Really use multithreading. Launch a background thread and work out some scheme of communication between the application's (or server's) main thread and the background thread.

If it's possible, the first approach is strongly preferred, because it's more efficient.

In fact, the second approach is often impossible. EPOC servers have been designed to treat each client *thread* as a distinct entity. This means that an object, such as an RFile or RWindow, which was opened by one thread, cannot be used at all by any other thread – even a thread in the same process as the one that opened it.

> **So background threads are limited in their functionality to things that strictly don't require any sharing of server-provided resources with the main thread.**

There is an area of conflict where on the one hand your long-running task needs to share server-provided resources with the main application tasks, but on the other hand can't be cast into the incremental form that would enable you to drive it with active objects. It's not essentially difficult to write active-object-friendly code when starting from scratch, but this situation often arises when code is being ported to EPOC. It's an important situation, which John Forrest covers in detail in Chapter 28, and I cover to some extent in Chapter 20.

The sharing of server-based resources by different threads – in the same process – will also be implemented in the next release of EPOC. This will eliminate some EPOC-specific difficulties for multithreading.

Symbian's current Java implementation gives process-wide access to server-based resources by using an intermediate server thread (the design is given in Chapter 21). The new support for sharing will remove the need for this intermediate thread. This will speed up the Java implementation (which is already pretty good), and simplify the addition of future APIs, such as those required for JavaPhone.

APIs Covered in the Book

Now we've reviewed the type of hardware on which EPOC operates, the base facilities for constructing programs, and the event-handling system including the client-server framework.

EPOC's APIs divide into categories corresponding to those we used for types of program:

- ❑ The kernel exposes an API through the user library
- ❑ System servers expose APIs through their client interfaces
- ❑ Application engines expose APIs to the applications that use them
- ❑ Middleware components are APIs in perhaps the purest and simplest sense
- ❑ Other API types such as device drivers, sockets protocol implementations, printer drivers etc. are associated with particular system components

The major components in EPOC R5 are shown overleaf.

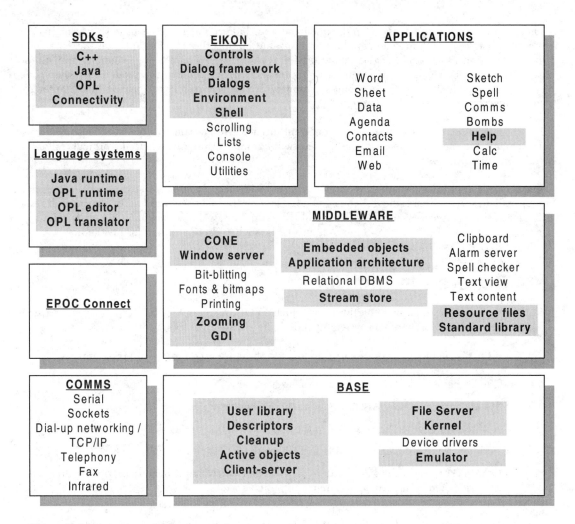

These divide into several broad groupings:

Group	Description
Base	Provides the fundamental APIs for all of EPOC, which I've described in this chapter.
Middleware	Graphics, data, and other components to support the GUI, engines, and applications.
EIKON	The system GUI framework including the Shell application
Applications	Application software can be divided into GUI parts (which use EIKON) and engines (which don't deal with graphics). Some applications are simply thin layers over middleware components: others have substantial engines.

Group	Description
Communications	Industry-standard communications protocols for serial and sockets-based communication, dial-up networking, TCP/IP, and infrared.
Language systems	The Java run-time environment, and the complete OPL development and run-time environment.
EPOC Connect	Communications protocols to connect to a PC, and services such as file format conversion, data synchronization for contacts, schedule entries and e-mail, clipboard synchronization, printing to a PC-based printer.

The table below shows the main C++/C APIs that we will be covering in the book. It introduces the issue of naming conventions for EPOC APIs – which, quite frankly, are not as clean as I would like. I've used

❑ A friendly title, which I'll normally use in the book, unless I need to be more precise

❑ The DLL name: add .dll to this for the DLL name to use at runtime, and add .lib for the import library that you must specify in your .mmp file at build time.

❑ The top-level project name in the source tree: this is the main system used internally by Symbian to refer to APIs, and often corresponds to the DLL name – though not always, since some projects produce more than one DLL, while others produce none at all. In any case only a very few components are shipped with source in the developer SDKs.

Throughout the book I'll use sometimes one form, sometimes another. You can always tell which form I'm using, because the presentation is different for each form. For good measure, I've included a category for each API (base, middleware etc.).

I've also included the header file naming convention. You'll find the corresponding header file(s) in \epoc32\include\, with the names indicated. In the case of the EPOC C standard library, the header files are isolated into their own directory – \epoc32\include\libc\.

Title	DLL	Source	Group	Headers	Description
User library	euser	E32	Base	e32def.h, e32std.h, e32base.h, e32*.h	Utility and kernel-object APIs. See Chapter 5 for strings and descriptors, Chapter 6 for resource cleanup, Chapter 20 for active objects, Chapter 21 for the principles behind client-server framework, Chapter 22 for an example server.

Table Continued on Following Page

Title	DLL	Source	Group	Headers	Description
File server	efsrv	F32	Base	f32file.h	File and device management. See Chapter 7.
GDI	gdi	GDI	Middleware	gdi.h	Abstract graphical device interface. See Chapter 11 for intro to drawing, Chapter 14 for other facilities with the emphasis on device independence.
Window server	ws32	WSERV	Middleware	w32std.h	Shares screen, keyboard and pointer between all applications. See Chapter 11 and Chapter 12 for details, along with coverage of CONE.
CONE	cone	CONE	Middleware	coe*.h	Control environment: works with window server to enable applications to use controls.
Stream store	estor	STORE	Middleware	s32*.h	Stream and store framework and main implementations. See Chapter 7.
C standard library	estlib	STDLIB	Middleware	libc*.h	Provides functions found in POSIX-compliant C programming environments, mostly as thin layers over base and sockets server APIs. See Chapter 28.
Resource files	bafl	BAFL	Middleware	ba*.h	Once grandly titled 'basic application framework library', its most useful aspect is resource files, though it also contains other APIs. See Chapter 2 and Chapter 9.

Title	DLL	Source	Group	Headers	Description
Application architecture	apparc	APPARC	Middleware	apa*.h	Governs file formats and application launching. Briefly mentioned in Chapter 7 and Chapter 9.
EIKON	eikon	EIKON	EIKON	eik*.h	The system GUI. See Chapter 9 and Chapter 15 for main write-up, and information throughout the book.
Sockets server	esock	ESOCK	Comms	es_*.h	Sockets-based comms using protocols such as TCP/IP, infrared and others. See Chapter 23.
Telephony server	etel	ETEL	Comms	etel*.h	Voice, data, address book etc. on landline or mobile phones and modems. See Chapter 23.

Some of the shaded boxes in the diagram of the components of EPOC R5 are parts of the corresponding API – for example, client-server etc. are provided by the user library, and zooming is provided by the GDI. Other shaded boxes aren't C++/C APIs – for example, the emulator, or Java language system.

I'll give you a good head start on the main APIs in this book. The SDK contains much additional valuable information on both the APIs I do cover, and those I don't.

How the Applications use the APIs

I'll end this chapter with a quick tour through the EPOC R5 application suite, showing how each application uses the EPOC APIs, to whet your appetite for the chapters that follow.

If you're interested in how many servers might be running in a live EPOC system, keep your eyes open as you read through the table. Most of the servers are mentioned there explicitly.

I've generally used the source tree naming convention for APIs used.

Office Applications

Word	Naturally, Word focuses on text APIs. ETEXT and FORM provide the re-usable rich text APIs – ETEXT for content, FORM for formatted views and printing. LEXICON (a server) is used for spell checking.
Sheet	Sheet is supported by two specialist components: GRID providing a spreadsheet grid view, and CHART, which draws its chart view.
Data	Data uses DBMS to provide underlying relational data management. Although DBMS supports relational data with multiple tables, the Data application is constrained to a single table, which makes the application easier to use, and easier to design and implement.
Spell	Spell re-uses the LEXICON engine, and provides a simple GUI.
Jotter	Jotter is a modified form of the Data application, using the same EPOC components.

Personal Information Management Applications

Contacts	The contacts application uses two important re-usable components. The CNTMODEL server manages the shared contacts database. CONTACUI provides EIKON-based user interface, which any application can use to select and manipulate contacts.
	Contacts are stored in a relational database, whose format is sufficiently flexible to allow for user-definable contacts attributes.
Agenda	Agenda uses the AGNMODEL server to manage shared agenda files. Agenda uses rich-text entries, managed by FORM and ETEXT. Agenda files use permanent file stores directly – not the relational database manager.
Time	TIME's underlying engine is EALWL, the alarm and world server. If you want to set an alarm, or find out city information, use EALWL.

Communications Applications

Email	For low-level communications, Email uses TCP/IP and other protocols provided by the sockets server ESOCK. Email integrates directly with the telephony server ETEL to pick up incoming SMS messages, and to send and receive faxes. Email integrates with dial-up networking and maintains a connection status display.
	A server is used to control all message store operations. Multiple clients may be simultaneously active. Incoming messages may be added to the store while client applications are running.
	Email uses so-called message transfer modules (MTMs) to provide flexibility in supporting new GUIs (other than EIKON), new message types (such as news) and new protocols (like IMAP).

Web	Web uses the same low-level communications technology as Email. The application architecture is used to launch non-HTML documents. A server implements a shared page and image cache.
Comms	The old-style Comms app uses an application engine including a general-purpose script interpreter. Comms uses the C32 communications server directly, without reference to the dial-up networking provided for TCP/IP and sockets protocols.

Summary

In this chapter we've surveyed the component parts of the EPOC system. W've seen:

- ❑ The impact of hardware on the design of EPOC and applications
- ❑ The four system component types – kernel, applications, servers, and engines
- ❑ Privilege, process, and DLL boundaries
- ❑ The difference between a .exe, a .dll, and .prn, .prt and .app files
- ❑ Using DLLs for EPOC applications allows multiple applications to run in one process for embedded documents
- ❑ DLL optimizations for EPOC – link by ordinal, address sharing, and lack of writable static
- ❑ Launching applications and servers using .exes
- ❑ Kernel and device driver overviews
- ❑ How EPOC handles memory
- ❑ Event handling is at the core of EPOC – using a combination of active objects and a client/server framework to allow non-preemptive multitasking
- ❑ Communications between client and server through messages and inter-thread read and write
- ❑ The main C/C++ APIs

In the next chapter, we'll look at EPOC's use of object-oriented techniques, the support that the C++ language provides, and that EPOC adds, to aid application development.

4

C++ and Object Orientation

In the previous two chapters, we've built some programs, and looked at the architecture of EPOC. In the next chapter, we'll be taking our first detailed look at some EPOC APIs. Before we do that, it's a good idea to take a look at how EPOC approaches aspects of design and programming in C++. That's the purpose of this chapter.

The use of C++ in EPOC is not exactly the same as C++ in other environments:

❑ C++ does more than EPOC requires – private inheritance, for instance, and full-blown multiple inheritance.

❑ C++ does less than EPOC requires – it doesn't insist on the number of bits used to represent basic types, and it doesn't know anything about DLLs.

❑ Different C++ communities do things differently, because their requirements are different. In EPOC, large-scale system design is combined with a focus on error handling and cleanup, and efficiency in terms of ROM and RAM budgets.

EPOC's fundamental design decisions were taken in 1994-95, and its toolchain for emulator and ARM builds was essentially stable by early 1996. Some differences between EPOC and other C++ cultures can be traced to the extent to which C++ facilities were supported on both the Microsoft Visual C++ and GNU C++ compilers available at that time.

Fundamental Types

Let's start with the basic types. e32def.h (in \epoc32\include\) contains definitions for 8-, 16-, and 32-bit integers and some other basic types that map onto underlying C++ types such as unsigned int, and which are guaranteed to be the same regardless of C++ implementation:

Signed Type	Unsigned Type	Description
TInt8	TUint8	Signed and unsigned 8-bit integers
TInt16	TUint16	Signed and unsigned 16-bit integers
TInt32	TUint32	Signed and unsigned 32-bit integers
TInt	TUint	Signed and unsigned integers: in practice, this means a 32-bit integer
TReal32	TReal64	Single- and double-precision IEEE 754 floating-point numbers (equated to float and double)
TReal		Equated to TReal64
TText8	TText16	Narrow and wide characters (equated to unsigned char and unsigned short int)
TBool		Boolean (equated to int, as required by the version of C++ supported by our old GCC (version 2.7.2))
TAny		Equated to void, and usually used as TAny* (a 'pointer to anything').

For integers, use TInt unless you have good reason not to. Use unsigned integer types only for flags, or unless you know exactly what you're doing with unsigned types in C++. Use specific integer widths when exchanging with external formats, or when space optimization is paramount.

A TInt64 is also available. Somewhat bizarrely, it's a class defined in e32std.h, rather than a typedef. However, TInt64 is rarely needed in practice, and there is no TUint64.

EPOC is designed for little-endian CPU architectures, and will probably never be ported to an exclusively big-endian architecture.

Don't use floating point unless you have to, because EPOC machines don't include hardware floating-point units. Most routine calculations in EPOC GUI or communications programs can be done using integers. If you're using floating point, use TReal for routine scientific calculations: conventional wisdom has it that TReal32 isn't precise enough for serious use. Use TReal32 when speed is of the essence, and when you know that it's sufficiently precise for your problem domain.

Use TBool to specify a Boolean return value from a function, rather than TInt. This conveys more information to anyone trying to read your code.

To represent Boolean values, don't use the TRUE and FALSE constants that are defined for historical reasons in e32def.h; rather, use ETrue and EFalse defined in e32std.h. Be aware, though, that ETrue is mapped to 1, but C++ interprets any integral value as 'true' if it is non-zero, so never compare a value with ETrue:

```
TBool b = something();
if(b == ETrue)              // Bad!
```

Instead, just rely on C++'s interpretation of Booleans:

```
if(b) { ... };
```

Always use the EPOC typedefs rather than native C++ types, to preserve compiler independence. The one exception to this rule is related to C++ void, which can mean either 'nothing' (as in void Foo()) or 'anything at all' (as in void* p). We use void for the 'nothing' case:

```
void Foo();                 // Returns no result
```

And TAny* for the 'pointer to anything' case:

```
TAny* p;                    // A pointer to anything
```

Fundamental types also include characters and text. We'll cover them in Chapter 5, along with descriptors, which are EPOC's version of strings.

Naming Conventions

Like any system, EPOC uses naming conventions to indicate what is important. The SDK and EPOC source code adhere completely to these conventions. Naming conventions are funny things: people tend either to love or hate them. Either way, I hope you'll find that the established naming conventions make understanding EPOC code much easier, and that, as these things go, they're not too burdensome.

The fundamental rule is, *use names to convey meaning.* Don't abbreviate too much (use real English), but don't make names too long and unwieldy. Another basic rule is that despite Symbian being UK-based, *APIs use American English spelling.* American English is the international language of APIs, so expect to see Color, Center, Gray and Synchronize rather than Colour, Centre, Grey and Synchronise.

Class Names

Classes use an initial letter to indicate the basic properties of the class. The main ones are:

Category	Examples	Description
T classes, types	TDesC, TPoint, TFileName	T classes don't have a destructor. They act like built-in types. That's why the typedefs for all built-in types begin with T. T classes can be allocated as automatics (if they're not too big), as members of other classes, or on the heap.
C classes	CConsoleBase, CActive, CBase	Any class derived from CBase. C classes are *always* allocated on the default heap. CBase's operator new() initializes all member data to zero when an object is allocated. CBase also includes a virtual destructor, so that by calling delete on a CBase* pointer any C object it points to is properly destroyed.
R classes	RFile, RTimer, RWriteStream, RWindow	Any class that owns resources other than on the default heap. Usually allocated as member variables or automatics: in a few cases, can be allocated on the default heap. Most R classes use Close() to free their associated resources.
M classes, interfaces	MGraphicsDeviceMap, MGameViewCmdHandler, MEikMenuObserver	An interface consisting of pure virtual functions and with no member data. A class implementing this interface should derive from it. M classes are the only approved use of multiple inheritance in EPOC: they act exactly as interfaces in Java. The old technical term was 'mixin', hence the use of M.
Static classes	User, Math, Mem, ConeUtils	A class consisting purely of static functions that can't be instantiated into an object. Such classes are useful containers of library functions.
Structs	SEikControlInfo	A C-style struct, without any member functions. There are only a few of these in EPOC: most later code uses T classes even for structs.

Some other prefixes are occasionally used for classes, in rare circumstances. The only one we'll encounter in this book is HBufC, for heap-based descriptors. Kernel-side programming uses D for kernel-side CBase-derived classes.

The distinction between T, C and R is very important in relation to cleanup properties, which I'll cover in detail in Chapter 6.

Lastly, always ensure that class names are nouns: classes are for objects, not actions

Data Names

These also use an initial letter, excepting automatics.

Category	Examples	Description
Enumerated constant	EMonday, ESolidBrush	Constants in an enumeration. If it has a name at all, the enumeration itself should have a T prefix, so that EMonday is a member of TDayOfWeek.
		When we cover EIKON resource files, we'll also find some #defined constants use an E prefix, in circumstances where the constants belong to a logically distinct set.
Constant	KMaxFileName, KRgbWhite	Constants of the #define type or const TInt type. KMax-type constants tend to be associated with length or size limits: KMaxFileName, for instance, is 256 (characters).
Member variable	iDevice, iX, iOppFleetView	Any non-static member variable should have an i prefix. The i refers to an 'instance' of a class.
Arguments	aDevice, aX, aOppFleetView	Any variable declared as an argument. The a stands for 'argument', not the English indefinite article. Don't use an for words that begin with a vowel!
Automatics	device, x, oppFleetView	Any variable declared as an automatic.

Static members aren't used in native EPOC code. Global variables, such as console, are sometimes used in .exes (though not in DLLs). Globals have no prefix. Some authors use initial capitals for globals, to distinguish them from automatics. I haven't got very strong views on the right way to do things here, preferring to avoid the issue by not using globals.

The i convention is important for cleanup. The C++ destructor takes care of member variables, so you can spot over-zealous cleanup code, such as CleanupStack::PushL(iMember) by using this naming convention.

As with class names, you should use nouns for value names, since they are objects, not functions.

Function Names

It's not the initial letter that matters so much here, as the final letter.

Category	Examples	Description
Non-leaving function	Foo(), Draw(), Intersects()	Use initial capital. Since functions do things, use a verb, rather than a noun.

Table Continued on Following Page

Category	Examples	Description
Leaving function	FooL(), CreateL(), AllocL(), NewL(), RunL()	Use final L. A leaving function may need to allocate memory, open a file, etc. – generally, to do some operation which might fail because there are insufficient resources or for other environment-related conditions (not programmer errors). When you call a leaving function, you must always consider what happens both when it succeeds, and when it leaves. You must ensure that both cases are handled. EPOC's cleanup framework is designed to allow you to do this. This is EPOC's most important naming convention.
LC functions	AllocLC(), CreateLC(), OpenLC() NewLC()	Allocate an object, and push it to the cleanup stack. If the function fails (which it might, since it involves allocation) then leave.
Simple getter	Size(), Device(), ComponentControl()	Get some property or member data of an object. Often getters are used when the member is private. Use a noun, corresponding with the member name.
Complex getter	GetTextL()	Get some property that requires more work, and perhaps even resource allocation. Resource-allocating getters should certainly use Get as a prefix; other than that the boundary between simple and complex getters is not hard-and-fast.
Setter	SetSize(), SetDevice(), SetCommandHandler(), SetCharFormatL()	Set some property. Some setters simply set a member. Some involve resource allocation, which may fail, and are therefore also an L function.

Macro Names

EPOC uses the usual conventions for C preprocessor macro names:

❑ Use only upper case, and split words with underscores, creating names like IMPORT_C, EXPORT_C, and STATIC_CAST.

❑ For build-dependent symbols, use two leading and trailing underscores (__VC32__, __GCC32__). The symbols _DEBUG and _UNICODE are notable exceptions to this rule.

Layout

It's not a naming issue, but all EPOC code also uses a common layout convention. I don't have to explain it: it's there throughout the book. Whatever layout convention you use for code in other environments, you'll find your EPOC code is easier to share if you use the EPOC convention.

Summary

Naming conventions are to some extent arbitrary: the only good thing you can say about most conventions is that life is better if everybody does the same thing.

But you'll probably have noticed that EPOC's naming convention does address one particular issue: cleanup. That's a key topic, which I'll cover in detail in Chapter 6. The distinction between C and T is fundamental to cleanup. R classes combine aspects of both C and T. The i prefix for members makes a fundamental distinction that is also cleanup-related. And the suffix L on leaving functions indicates functions that may require cleanup.

In other areas, EPOC's naming convention is probably neither worse nor better than anyone else's. All EPOC system and example code uses these conventions (with perhaps a couple of exceptions in the very oldest code), so your work will be made easier if you use them too.

Functions

Function prototypes in C++ header files can convey a lot of information, including:

- ❑ Whether it is imported from a DLL (indicated by IMPORT_C), inline and expanded from a header, or neither of these – that is, the function is private to a DLL

- ❑ Whether it is public, protected, or private in the C++ sense (you have to scan up the file to see this, but it's effectively part of the prototype even so)

- ❑ Whether it is virtual (you have to scan down the base classes to be sure about this, but it's part of the signature) – and, if virtual, whether it's pure virtual

- ❑ Whether it is static

- ❑ The return type (or void)

- ❑ The name – usually a good hint at what the function does

- ❑ Whether it can leave (L at the end of the name)

- ❑ The type and method of passing for all the arguments (with an optional name that hints at purpose, though the name is not formally part of the signature)

- ❑ Whether there are any optional arguments

- ❑ Whether it is const

If a function and its arguments (and class) have been named sensibly, and if the right type of parameter passing has been used, you can often guess what a function does just by looking at its prototype. For example, the function TInt RFile::Write(const TDesC8& aBuffer) is the basic function for writing data to a file – you can even guess that TDesC8 is a type suitable for data buffers by looking at this signature, though we won't encounter this class formally until the next chapter. The TInt return is an error code, while the aBuffer parameter is a descriptor containing the data and is not modified by the function.

Most of this is standard C++ fare. The exceptions are leaving functions, which we've already covered (and will explain it fully in Chapter 6), and the naming conventions associated with DLLs. These are very important and aren't covered by C++ standards: I'll cover the significance of IMPORT_C later in the chapter.

Function Parameters

Each parameter's declaration gives valuable information about whether that parameter is to be used for input or output, and a clue about whether the parameter is large or small. If a parameter is of basic type X, there are five possibilities for specifying it in a signature:

	By value	By & reference	By * reference
Input	X	const X&	const X*
Output		X&	X*

For 'input' parameters, there is a fundamental distinction between passing by value and passing by reference. When you pass by value, C++ copies the object into a new stack location before calling the function. You should pass by value only if you know the object is small – a built-in type, say, or something that will be shorter than two machine words (64 bits). If you pass by reference, only a 32-bit pointer is passed, regardless of the size of the data.

If you pass by reference, you have to choose between * and &. Usually, & is better. Use * if you have to, especially where a null value is possible, or you're transferring ownership of the object. It's more usual to pass C types with *, and R and T types directly or with &.

You have to use & for C++ copy constructors and assignment operators, but it's rare to need to code such things in EPOC. Some EPOC APIs use & for C types to indicate that a null value is not acceptable.

APIs

If you have a component X, then its API allows you to use X. In addition, the X's API lets you allow X to use you. In the old days, components were simple libraries. X would specify **library functions**, and you would call them to get X to do what you wanted.

Event-driven GUI systems are often associated with **frameworks**, which call your code to allow you to do things supported by the framework. For this, X specifies **framework functions**, and you implement them.

For a while, framework functions were called **callbacks**: the basic theory was that your code was really in control, but the library needed to call you back occasionally so you could complete a function for it. But the truth these days is that the framework is essentially in control, and it lets you do things. The framework functions are actually the main functions that allow you to do anything. 'Callback' is quite inappropriate for this. The word is not used for EPOC's major frameworks: only for a couple of situations where the old callback scenario really applies, or in relation to a couple of the oldest classes in EPOC.

We can loosely classify a class or even an entire API as either a **library API**, or a **framework API**. A library mainly contains functions that you call, while a framework consists mainly of functions that call you. Many APIs contain a good mixture of both: the GUI, for instance, calls you so that you can handle events, but provides functions that you call to draw graphics.

Types of Function

I've defined library functions and framework functions. But, throughout the book, I use other terms to describe the role of different types of function.

Of course, there's the **C++ constructor**. I almost always use the full term, including 'C++', because, as we'll see in Chapter 6, there's also a **second-phase constructor**, usually called `ConstructL()`, in many classes. There's only one **destructor**, though, so in that context I don't usually feel the need to say 'C++ destructor'.

Convenience functions are trivial wrappers for things that could otherwise be done with a smaller API. If a class contains two functions `Foo()` and `Bar()`,which do all that's required by the class, but you often find that code using your API contains sequences such as this:

```
x.Foo();
x.Bar();
```

Or this:

```
x.Foo(x.Bar());
y = (x.Foo() + x.Bar()) / 2;
```

Then you may wish to code some kind of convenience function `FooAndBar()` that represents the sequence. This will reduce code size, reduce mistakes, and make code easier to read.

The cost of convenience is another function to design and document, and the risk of being tempted to produce zillions of convenience functions which aren't really all that necessary or even convenient – and then being forced to maintain them for ever more, because people depend on them. This is a fine judgment call: sometimes we provide too few convenience functions, and sometimes too many.

DLLs and Other API Elements

An object-oriented system delivers APIs mainly as C++ **classes**, together with all their member functions and data. Classes that form part of an API are declared in header files, implemented in C++ source files, and delivered in DLLs.

Library APIs (or the library parts of a framework API) are delivered in shared library DLLs with a `.dll` file extension. The DLL's exported functions are made available in a `.lib` file to the linker at program build time.

Framework APIs are usually defined in terms of C++ classes containing virtual functions and an interface specification for a polymorphic DLL with an extension other than `.dll` (for instance, `.app` for a GUI application).

It's important to make sure that only the *interface* – not the implementation – is made available to programs that use the API. Classes that are not part of the API should not be declared in API header files, and their functions should not be exported from the DLLs that implement them. Functions and data that belong to the API classes, but which are not part of the API, should be marked `private`.

Besides classes, C++ APIs may contain enumerations, constants, template functions, and even non-member functions.

Exported Functions

For a non-virtual, non-inline member function to be part of an API, it must be:

❑ Declared public in a C++ class that appears in a public header file

❑ Exported from its DLL

You will see exported functions marked in their header files with IMPORT_C, like this:

```
class RTimer : public RHandleBase
    {
public:
    IMPORT_C TInt CreateLocal();
    IMPORT_C void Cancel();
    IMPORT_C void After(TRequestStatus& aStatus,
                        TTimeIntervalMicroSeconds32 anInterval);
    IMPORT_C void At(TRequestStatus& aStatus,
                     const TTime& aTime);
    IMPORT_C void Lock(TRequestStatus& aStatus,
                       TTimerLockSpec aLock);
    };
```

The IMPORT_C macro says that the function must be imported from a DLL by the user of that API. In the corresponding implementation, the function will be marked EXPORT_C, which means that it will be exported from the DLL. A function without IMPORT_C is not exported from its DLL, and cannot therefore be part of the public API.

These macros are defined in e32def.h. Their implementations are compiler-dependent, and differ between Visual C++ and GCC.

Virtual and inline functions don't need to be exported – they form a part of the API, even without IMPORT_C in the header file.

If you're writing an API to be delivered in a DLL for use by other DLLs, you'll need to mark your IMPORT_Cs and EXPORT_Cs carefully. I'll return to this topic in Chapter 22.

If you're not writing APIs – or you're not encapsulating them in DLLs for export – then you needn't worry about how to use IMPORT_C and EXPORT_C. It's enough to understand what they mean in the EPOC SDK's headers.

Virtual Functions and APIs

C++ isn't well designed for API delivery. There is no way to prevent further override of a virtual function, and there is no way to tell that a function is not virtual without looking down all the base classes to check for the virtual keyword.

C++'s access control specifiers aren't good for API delivery either. The meaning of public is clear enough, but protected makes a distinction between derived classes and other classes that doesn't put the boundary in the right place, since derivation is by no means the most important vehicle for code re-use in OO. private is not private when it comes to virtual functions: you can override private virtual functions whether or not this was intended by the designer of a base class.

C++ has no language support for packaging APIs except classes and header files. So we had to invent our own rules for DLLs.

Java is much better at all these things: it specifies them all in great detail, and in generally helpful ways.

These design issues are most awkward when it comes to virtual functions. Best practice in EPOC C++ includes the following guidelines:

- Declare a function virtual in the base class and in any derived class from which it is intended to further derive and override (or implement) this function.

- When declaring a virtual function in a derived class, include a comment such as `// from CCoeControl`, to indicate where the function was defined.

- Use `private` in a base class to indicate that your base class (or its friends) calls this function – this is usually the case for framework functions. If you don't like friends or the framework function is designed to be called from another class, then make it `public` in the base class.

- Use `private` in a derived class for a framework function that is implementing something in a framework base class

These guidelines are admittedly incomplete, and they're not always honored in EPOC code. But they're good for most cases.

Finally, there's another issue with virtual functions: if your class has virtual functions and you need to invoke the default C++ constructor from a DLL other than the one your class is delivered in, then you need to specify, and export, a default C++ constructor:

```
class CFoo : public CBase
    {
public:
    IMPORT_C CFoo();
    ...
    };
```

And then in the source code:

```
EXPORT_C CFoo::CFoo()
    {
    }
```

If you don't do this, a program that tries to create a default C++ constructor for your class won't be able to, because constructors need to create the virtual function table, and the information required is all inside your DLL. You'll get a link error.

Templates

EPOC uses C++ templates extensively, for collection classes, fixed-length buffers, and utility functions. EPOC's use of templates is optimized to minimize the size in 'expanded' template code – basically, by ensuring that templates never get expanded at all. The **thin template** pattern is the key to this.

EPOC also uses numeric arguments in templates to indicate string and buffer sizes.

The Thin Template Pattern

The thin template pattern uses templates to provide a type-safe wrapper round type-unsafe code. It works like this: code a generic base class, such as CArrayFixBase, which deals in 'unsafe' TAny* objects. This class is expanded into real code that goes in a DLL. Then, code a template class that derives from this one, and uses inline type-safe functions such as:

```
template <class T>
inline const T& CArrayFix<T>::operator[](TInt anIndex) const
    {
    return (*((const T*)CArrayFixBase::At(anIndex)));
    }
```

This returns the anIndexth item of type const T& in the CArrayFix<T> on which it is invoked. It acts as a type-safe wrapper around At() in the base class, which returns the anIndexth pointer of type TAny*.

This code looks pretty ugly, but the good news is that application programmers don't have to use it. They can simply use the template API:

```
CArrayFix<TFoo>* fooArray;
...
TFoo foo = (*fooArray)[4];
```

The template guarantees that this code is type-safe. The fact that the operator[]() is expanded inline means that no more code is generated when the template is used than if the type-unsafe base class had been used.

Numbers in Templates

Sometimes, the parameter to a template class is a number, rather than a type. Here's the declaration of TBuf, a buffer of variable length:

```
template <TInt S> class TBuf
    {
    ...
    };
```

You can then create a five-character buffer with:

```
TBuf<5> hello;
```

This uses the thin template pattern too: here's the inline constructor:

```
template <TInt S>
inline TBuf<S>::TBuf() : TDes(0,S)
    {
    }
```

It calls the TDes base class constructor, passing the right parameters, and then completes the default construction of a TBuf (a couple of extra instructions).

Casting

Casting is a necessary evil. Old-style C provides casting syntax that enables you to cast anything to anything. Over time, different casting patterns have emerged, including:

❑ Cast away const-ness (but don't change anything else)

❑ Cast to a related class (rather than an arbitrary cast)

❑ Reinterpret the bit pattern (effectively, old-style C casting)

As a (largely) standards-compliant compiler, Microsoft Visual C++ supports the casting keywords const_cast<>(), static_cast<>() and reinterpret_cast<>() that came into the C++ language to support these casting patterns. Unfortunately, the version of GNU C++ we use does not. So, in e32def.h, there are macros called CONST_CAST(), STATIC_CAST() and REINTERPRET_CAST() that are implemented as follows:

Macro name	Visual C++	GNU C++
CONST_CAST (type, exp)	(const_cast <type>(exp))	((type)(exp))
STATIC_CAST (type, exp)	(static_cast <type>(exp))	((type)(exp))
REINTERPRET_CAST (type, exp)	(reinterpret_cast <type>(exp))	((type)(exp))

By using these macros, you get the benefit of C++ cast checking on the emulator builds: GCC won't do C++ cast checking, but for user side code that has already been through Visual C++, this isn't an issue anyway.

Future EPOC C++ SDKs will use an updated GCC supporting C++-style casting, so that all code using these macros will pick up C++ cast checking.

Classes

As you'd expect, classes are used to represent objects, abstractions, and interfaces. Relationships between classes are used to represent relationships between objects or abstractions. The most important relationships between classes are:

- **uses-a**: if class A *uses-a* class B, then A has a member of type B, B&, const B&, B*, or const B*, or a function that can easily return a B in one of these guises. A can then use B's member functions and data.

- **has-a**: *has-a* is like *uses-a*, except that A takes responsibility for constructing and destroying the B as well as using it during its lifetime.

- **is-a**: if class A *is-a* class B, then B should be an abstraction of A. *is-a* relationships are usually represented in C++ using public derivation.

- **implements**: if class A implements an **interface** M, then it implements all M's pure virtual functions. Interface implementation is the only time multiple inheritance is used in EPOC.

A base class with unimplemented virtual functions is an **abstract class**. A derived class that has no unimplemented virtual functions is a **concrete** class. For example, a CCoeControl is an abstract control (a rectangular area on the screen supporting graphical user interaction), but a CEikEdwin is a concrete control (an EIKON edit window).

Sometimes, abstract/concrete notions are blurred. CEikDialog is concrete as far as its implementation of CCoeControl is concerned, but in fact CEikDialog is an abstract base class for user-specified dialogs or EIKON standard dialogs such as a CEikPrintPreviewDialog. Some abstract classes (such as both CCoeControl and CEikDialog) contain no pure virtual functions, but you need to implement at least one or two if you are to get meaningful behavior, so for practical purposes these classes are abstract.

Interfaces

EPOC makes quite extensive use of interface classes (originally called mixins). An interface is an abstract base class with no data and *only* pure virtual functions.

APIs that have both library and framework aspects often define their library aspect by means of a concrete class, and their framework by means of an interface class. To use such an API, you need to use the concrete class and implement the interface.

EPOC's PRINT API provides an example. In addition to library classes to start the print job, there are framework classes for printing part of a page, and for notifying the progress of the job to an application. MPrintProcessObserver is the interface for notifying progress:

```
class MPrintProcessObserver
    {
public:
    virtual void NotifyPrintStarted(
                TPrintParameters aPrintParams) = 0;

    virtual void NotifyBandPrinted(
                TInt aPercentageOfPagePrinted,
                TInt aCurrentPageNum,
                TInt aCurrentCopyNum) = 0;
    virtual void NotifyPrintEnded(TInt aErrorCode) = 0;
    };
```

This interface definition includes functions for reporting the beginning and end of a print job, and its progress at intervals throughout. The print process observer is implemented by EIKON, the GUI. EIKON's print progress dialog's definition starts:

```
class CEikPrintProgressDialog : public CEikDialog,
                                private MPrintProcessObserver
    {
    ...
```

You can read this as, "EIKON's print process dialog *is-a* dialog, and it *implements* the print process observer interface." You can see that this uses C++ multiple inheritance.

> **The only allowed use of multiple inheritance in EPOC is to implement interfaces. No other use is necessary.**

Java uses interfaces too: in Java, a class can have zero or one base class, and can implement zero, one, or more interfaces. Java has interface *and* implements *keywords, rather than a naming convention. Multiple inheritance isn't part of Java.*

Bad Practices

Many C++ features that look attractive at first sight are not used in EPOC – or, at least, they're not encouraged in anything other than very specific situations:

❑ Private inheritance. Inheritance should only be used for *is-a* relationships. Private inheritance (the default in C++) is used to mean *has-a*, so that the private base class effectively becomes a private data member.

❑ Multiple inheritance. Except in the case of interfaces, full-blown C++ multiple inheritance is more confusing than useful.

❑ Overriding non-trivial virtual functions. Base classes with virtual functions in them should either specify trivial behavior (doing nothing, for example), or leave them pure virtual. This helps you to be clear about the purpose of the virtual function.

❑ 'Just-in-case' tactics. Making functions virtual 'just in case' they should be overridden, or protected 'just in case' a derived class wishes to use them, is an excuse for unclear thinking. This kind of programming is always associated with muddy designs that are hard to use.

In a couple of instances, these practices are used for good reason. The thin template pattern is really a C++ technical trick, so it's fair game to use C++ technical tricks such as private inheritance to help implement it. But if you want your C++ to be a straightforward implementation of good object-oriented system design, you should use the object-oriented features of C++ rather than murky technical tricks.

Design Patterns

Object orientation supports good design, using the *uses-a*, *has-a*, *is-a*, and *implements* relationships.

Through good design, object orientation also supports good code re-use. That's particularly attractive for EPOC, since minimizing the amount of code you require to implement a particular system is a very important design goal.

But code re-use isn't the only form of re-use. Often, you find yourself doing the same thing again and again, but somehow you can't abstract it into an API – even using the full power of object-orientation and templates in C++. Or, you succeed in abstracting an API, but it's more difficult to use the API than it was to write the repeated code in the first place.

This is a good time to think in terms of re-using **design patterns**. Design patterns are ways of designing things, rather than objects or APIs that you can re-use or glue together.

EPOC contains many frequently used design patterns. EPOC's most characteristic design patterns relate to cleanup (see Chapter 6) and active objects (see Chapter 20). However, most of the patterns used in EPOC are standard patterns used elsewhere in the software industry.

Class Diagrams and UML

Object orientation is more about relationships than anything else. When you are working on understanding a software system you don't know, the key questions to ask are:

❑   What are the main classes – objects, abstractions, and interfaces?

❑   What are the intended relationships between them?

Only then is it worth asking anything about the functions and data members in individual classes.

Header files are very good at telling you what the functions and data members are, but pretty hopeless at telling you the relationships between classes (though you can sometimes work them out, with a little detective work). In other words, header files, even for well-designed APIs, aren't the place to get the broad picture.

UML is a visual notation that shows classes and their relationships very clearly. I've used it to illustrate the structure of many applications and EPOC APIs throughout the book. You can get good information on UML from Wrox's *Instant UML* book (Muller, 1997) or from the Rational website at http://www.rational.com.

You can use UML to convey detailed design information for the system visually (instead of, say, through header files). But that's not my purpose in this book. I have over 100 UML diagrams, but I don't believe you could construct a complete header file from any of them. Instead, I use UML to convey the main features of a system design, for the purposes of the current explanation. I omit functions if they're not relevant, and private and virtual specifiers if they can be guessed. I'm much more careful about relationships than I am about these details. If you want the details, go to the header file and the application code.

Here's a lightning tour of the main features of UML.

Describing APIs

UML can describe basic API relationships:

- ❑ The existence, name, and major classes in an API
- ❑ Whether and how one API uses another

For instance, you can read the following diagram as, "CONE uses WSERV. The main classes in CONE are CCoeEnv, CCoeControl, and CCoeAppUi. The main classes in WSERV are RWsSession, RWindow, and TWsEvent."

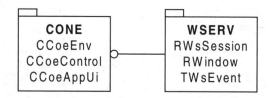

The open circle at the CONE end of the connection between the APIs shows that the CONE API uses the WSERV API.

Describing Classes

UML can describe classes and their content:

- ❑ The existence, name, major data members, and function members of a class
- ❑ Whether these are private or public (if that's interesting)

For instance, you can read the following diagram as, "CActive has private members called iStatus and iActive, a public Cancel() function, and a private RunL() function."

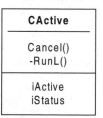

Describing Relationships Between Classes

UML can describe the relationships between classes:

- ❑ *has-a*: this uses a blob next to the class
- ❑ *uses-a*: this uses an open circle
- ❑ Whether the class on the other end of a *has-a* or *uses-a* relationship is intended to know anything about the class that has or uses it: if it's important to show that the class *doesn't* know anything, then an arrow is used to emphasize that the relationship is one-way

The following more complex diagram shows a few of these ideas:

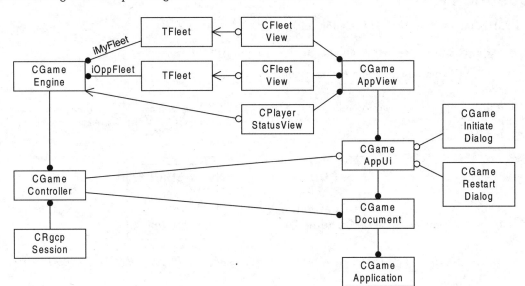

You can:

❑ Trace *has-a* relationships: the application *has-a* document, which *has-a* application user interface, which *has-a* application view. There are plenty of other *has-a* relationships in the rest of the diagram. Even if you don't know what the names mean yet, the relationships all sound very reasonable, and based on the names and relationships you can take a guess at their purpose that probably won't be too far wrong. I'll be explaining this diagram some more in Chapter 18, by which time it'll be very easy to understand.

❑ Trace major *uses-a* relationships, indicated by open circles. There may be other *uses-a* relationships besides those shown, but the ones we see highlighted are that the application UI uses the controller and a couple of dialogs, and that the various view classes use the various engine classes.

❑ Note when relationships are strictly one-way: I've used one-way arrows for the view-engine relationships to emphasize the point that the engine doesn't know anything about the views.

Describing Derivation

UML can convey derivation relationships:

❑ *is-a*: this is indicated by an open arrowhead

❑ *implements*: UML provides a dotted line with arrowhead for this purpose, You can also tell it's an *implements* relationship because the 'base' class name begins with M.

For instance, you can read the following diagram as, "The GSDP session *has-a* receive handler, which *is-a* active object. The receive handler *uses-a* GSDP packet handler interface. The client *has-a* GSDP session, and implements the GSDP handler interface."

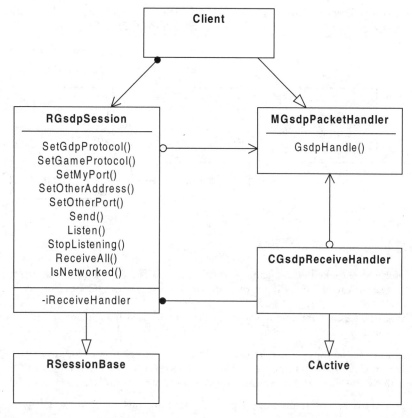

Incidentally, this is a standard version of the M class pattern I described earlier: the GSDP API provides a library class (`RGsdpSession`) and a framework class (`MGsdpReceiveHandler`). The client program uses the one and implements the other.

Cardinality

UML can convey **cardinality** – the number of objects expected at both ends of a relationship.

Unless otherwise stated, 1-to-1 cardinality is implied: this means that one of the using objects has exactly one of the used objects, perhaps as a member variable or a pointer.

If the cardinality is not 1-to-1, then you need to indicate its value with UML adornments. You usually write the number of objects intended, on one end of the UML connector. Common values are:

- ❑ 0..1: the object is optional – perhaps a pointer is used to refer to it

- ❑ 1..n, 0..n or simply n: an arbitrary number of objects is intended – a list, array, or other collection class may be used to contain them

- ❑ 10: exactly 10 objects are intended

For instance, you can read the following diagram as, "The engine's `iMyFleet` fleet always has 10 ships. The engine's `iOppFleet` fleet may have anything from 0 to 10 ships."

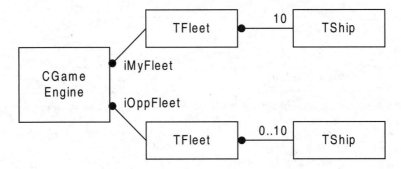

Summary

In this chapter, we've looked at the features of C++ that EPOC uses, those it avoids, and those it augments. We've also seen the coding standards that are used in EPOC. Specifically, we've seen:

- The use of EPOC fundamental types to guarantee consistent behavior between compilers and platforms.

- Naming conventions – the core ones help with cleanup. T, C, and R distinguish between different cleanup requirements for classes, i refers to member variables and L to leaving functions that may fail for reasons beyond the control of the programmer.

- M prefixes interfaces (consisting of pure virtual functions).

- Good design of function prototypes – how to code input and output parameters, and suggested use of references and pointers in EPOC.

- The difference between library and framework DLLs – the former provide functions that you call, the latter functions for you to implement that the framework will call.

- Exporting non-virtual, non-inline functions using the IMPORT_C and EXPORT_C macros.

- How to handle virtual functions.

- EPOC's use of templates and the thin template pattern to keep code size to a minimum.

- The four relationships between classes, and how to represent them in UML.

- The use of mixins to provide interfaces, and EPOC's only use of multiple inheritance.

In the next chapter, we'll start going through the EPOC APIs in earnest. We begin with descriptors, looking at how they're used to handle strings and binary data.

5

Strings and Descriptors

I once looked up the word 'computer' in a big dictionary in my high school library. It said, "one who computes." This view is somewhat old-fashioned: the truth is that most programmers expend far more effort on processing strings than they do computing with numbers, so it's a good idea to start getting to know EPOC's APIs by looking at its string handling facilities.

In C, string processing is inconvenient. You have an awkward choice of char*, char[], and malloc() with which to contend, just to allocate your strings. You get come help from such functions as strlen(), strcpy(), and strcat(), but little else. You have to pass around awkward maximum-length parameters to functions like strncpy() and strncat() that modify strings with an explicit length limit. You have to add one and subtract one for the trailing NUL at the end of every string. If you get your arithmetic slightly wrong, you overwrite memory and produce bugs that are hard to track down. It's not much fun.

In Java, life is much easier. There is a String class, with nice syntax such as a + operator for concatenating strings. Memory for strings looks after itself: new memory is allocated for new strings, and memory for old string values or intermediate results is garbage collected when no longer needed.

In standard C++, a similarly useful string class is also available, though it came along quite a while after the C++ language itself.

In EPOC, strings are implemented by **descriptors**. Descriptors provide a safe and consistent mechanism for dealing with both strings and general binary data regardless of the type of memory in which they reside.

Like the string classes in Java and standard C++, they're much more comfortable to work with than C strings. However, EPOC doesn't take the same approach as either Java or standard C++, because memory management is so important in EPOC. You have to be fully aware of the memory management issues when you're using descriptors.

I'll start this chapter off with a discussion of descriptors and memory management. Because C string handling gives you control of memory management, I'll compare descriptors and their memory management with C strings and theirs.

Then I'll move on to what you can do with descriptors. You need to know about both the concrete implementation classes and the two key abstract base classes, TDesC and TDes, which include a large number of convenience functions. TDesC is a two-word class (pointer and length), and its convenience functions are all const – that's what the C in TDesC stands for. TDes derives from TDesC, and adds an extra word (maximum length), and non-const convenience functions.

EPOC R5 is built to use 'narrow' characters – 8 bits, using Windows codepage 1252. Future releases of EPOC will use 'wide' characters – 16 bits, using Unicode. I'll explain the history of this, as well as the implications for writing your EPOC code today in such a way that it will build easily for wide EPOC.

Finally I'll look at descriptors' role in describing data – which is where they got their name. Descriptors are fundamental to many data-related APIs, such as the inter-thread reading and writing used by the client-server framework and reading and writing data to files.

Strings and Memory

To understand strings in any C or C++-based system, you have to understand memory management as it relates to strings. Essentially, there are three types of memory:

- ❑ Program binaries. In ROM, DLLs, and (for the most part) .exes, program binaries are constant and don't change. Literal strings that we build into our program go into program binaries.

- ❑ The stack (automatic objects). This is suitable for fixed-size objects whose lifetimes coincide with the function that creates them, and which aren't too big. Stack objects in EPOC shouldn't be too big, so they should only be used for *very small* strings – ten to twenty characters, say. It's quite acceptable to put pointers (and references) on the stack – even pointers to very large strings in program text or on the heap.

- ❑ The heap (dynamic objects). Memory is allocated from the default heap as and when required. It is used for objects (including strings) that are built or manipulated at runtime, and which can't go on the stack because they're too big, or because their lifetimes don't coincide with the function that created them.

Strings in C

So, in C, there are three ways to allocate a string, corresponding to whether they are held in program binaries, on the stack, or in heap memory.

A string in a program binary is represented thus:

```
static char hellorom[] = "hello";
```

You can get a *pointer* to this string, on the stack, simply by copying the address of the string data into an automatic:

```
const char* helloptr = hellorom;
```

You can put the string itself onto the stack, by declaring a character array of sufficient size on the stack, and then copying the string data into this array:

```
char hellostack[sizeof(hellorom)];
strcpy(hellostack, hellorom);
```

And you can put the string onto the heap, by allocating a heap cell of sufficient size, and then copying the string data:

```
char* helloheap = (char*)malloc(sizeof(hellorom));
strcpy(helloheap, hellorom);
```

You can find this code in \pep\cstring\ – the cstring project, which is a Visual C++ example project, builds into a Win32 console application. When the statements above have executed, the situation in memory – program binaries, heap, and stack – is:

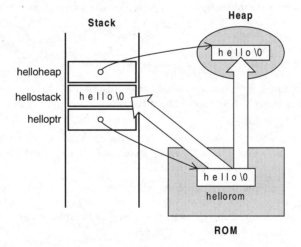

Strings in EPOC

Here's how EPOC does the same kind of thing. I'll go through the following program text more slowly. It's in \pep\epocstring\, an EPOC project with a text-mode program based on hellotext. Again, it's more interesting to run it from the debugger than to launch it from a console.

Build it using the same methods as you used to build hellotext in Chapter 2. As a reminder, that's:

```
cd \pep\epocstring
makmake epocstring vc5
```

Then go into the Visual Studio, open workspace, select epocstring.dsw from the relevant directory, confirm that you want to convert it to Visual C++ 6 format, change the active configuration to Win32 Debug, and you're ready. You can then build and step through the code.

To get a string into program binaries, use the _LIT macro (short for 'literal'):

```
_LIT(KHelloRom, "hello");
```

This puts a literal descriptor into your program binaries. The symbol for the descriptor is KHelloRom, and its value is "hello". You can get a pointer descriptor to this string, on the stack, using:

```
TPtrC helloPtr = KHelloRom;
```

TPtrC is a two-word object that includes both a pointer *and a length*. The statement above copies both of these into the helloPtr. With a pointer and a length, you can perform any const function on a string – anything that doesn't modify its data. That's the significance of the C in TPtrC.

You can get the string data itself into the stack, if you first create a buffer for it. Here's how:

```
TBufC<5> helloStack(KHelloRom);
```

TBufC<5> is a 5-character buffer descriptor. This object contains a single header word saying how long it is (in this case, 5 characters), followed by five bytes containing the data. As before, the C indicates that only const functions are allowed on a TBufC after its construction.

You can get the string data into a heap cell if you allocate a heap-based buffer and copy in the data:

```
HBufC* helloHeap = KHelloRom().AllocLC();
```

This statement is doing a lot of things. Let's take them in order:

- ❑ HBufC* is a pointer to a heap-based buffer descriptor. This is the only class in EPOC whose name begins with H. It's reasonable to have a unique name because, as we'll see, HBufC's properties are unique.

- ❑ By putting function brackets after KHelloRom(), I invoke an operator which turns it into the base class for all descriptors, TDesC. I need this because a literal descriptor is not derived from TDesC, for reasons I'll explain later.

- ❑ AllocLC(), on any descriptor class, allocates an HBufC of the required size on the default heap, and copies the (old) descriptor contents into the (new) HBufC. AllocLC() also pushes the HBufC* pointer to the cleanup stack, so that I can later delete the object using CleanupStack::PopAndDestroy().

In short, we create a new heap cell and copy the string text into it. Unlike my C program, this code is also fully error-checked and memory leak proof:

- ❑ If allocation fails, AllocLC() leaves. Everything is trapped and cleaned up by the cleanup mechanisms built into epocstring's startup code

- ❑ If a later function leaves, then the cleanup stack will cause the helloHeap object to be popped and destroyed

- ❑ If I forget to de-allocate this HBufC* and the one I allocate later in the example, the program panics on exit because of heap marking built into it

In the next chapter, I'll go into these issues more thoroughly. For now, it's enough to note that we didn't have to do much, given the framework that I just copied from `hellotext`, to make our program's cleanup safe. After this code has run, our program memory looks like this:

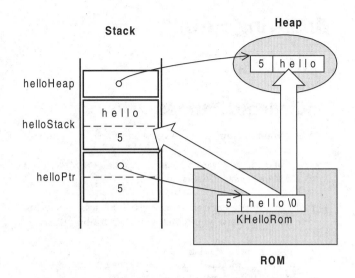

There are three descriptor types here, each corresponding to a different type of memory:

❑ A pointer descriptor, `TPtrC`, consisting of a length and a pointer to the data. This can be used where a `const char*` would be used in C.

❑ A buffer descriptor, `TBufC`, which contains the data itself and also its length. This can be used where a `char[]` would be used in C.

❑ A heap descriptor, always referred to by an `HBufC*` pointer, which is a heap cell containing the length and data (similar to a buffer). This is used where a `malloc()`'d cell would be used in C.

All these descriptor classes are derived from `TDesC`, which contains a `Length()` function to get the current length, and a `Ptr()` function to find the address of the data. The current data length is always the first machine word in a concrete descriptor class, so `TDesC::Length()` is implemented identically for all descriptor classes. In the case of a `TPtrC`, the address of the data is contained in the word after the length. For `HBufC` and `TBufC`, the address is simply the address of the object itself, plus 4 (for the length word).

With an address and a length, you have all you need for any `const` function on a string. `TDesC` provides those functions, and thus, so do the derived descriptor types.

On the face of it, `Ptr()` should be a virtual function, because it's an abstract interface that depends for its implementation on the concrete class. However, there is no need to use virtual functions, because there are only five descriptor classes and there will never be any more. Avoiding them means that we save one machine word – four bytes – from the size of every descriptor. Instead, the length word reserves four bits to indicate the concrete version of descriptor class and `TDesC::Ptr()` uses a switch statement to check these bits and calculate the data address correctly.

Of course, using four bits for a descriptor identifier leaves 'only' 28 bits for the length, and descriptor data is therefore constrained to around 250 million characters rather than 4 billion. This is not a serious restriction for EPOC.

Space efficiency matters in EPOC. Descriptors are space efficient, and they allow you to be.

Modifying Strings

Having compared the way C and EPOC handle constant strings, let's look at the support they provide for manipulating strings.

Modifying C Strings

When you add something to the end of a string, you have to have enough room for the new text.

Doing this in program binaries isn't an option: they can't be modified if they're in ROM or even in a RAM-loaded EPOC DLL.

You can allocate enough space on the stack by declaring an array big enough for both strings: you can save a byte because you won't need two trailing NULs:

```
static char worldrom[] = " world!";
char helloworldstack[sizeof(hellorom) + sizeof(worldrom) - 1];
strcpy(helloworldstack, hellorom);
strcat(helloworldstack, worldrom);
```

You can do a similar thing on the heap:

```
char* helloworldheap = (char*)malloc(strlen(hellorom) + strlen(worldrom) + 1);
strcpy(helloworldheap, hellorom);
strcat(helloworldheap, worldrom);
```

This time, I've used `strlen()` rather than `sizeof()`, to emphasize that heap-based allocation can evaluate lengths at runtime: I can't use `strlen()` to evaluate the size of my stack buffer. As a consequence, I have to add a byte rather than subtracting, because `strlen()` doesn't include the trailing NUL. In memory, the result of these operations looks like this:

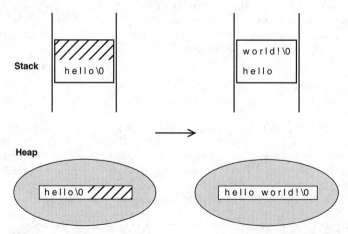

The issue here is that, had I got my array size wrong (for `helloworldstack`) or my heap cell size wrong (for `helloworldheap`), I might have overwritten the end of the string. It's not simply the irritation of having to add or subtract 1 for the trailing NUL – the real problem is that the string data might not fit into the memory allocated for it.

Modifying EPOC Strings

The `epocstring` example shows how to modify strings using descriptors. You can get a buffer suitable for appending one string to another by placing a `TBuf` on the stack:

```
_LIT(KWorldRom, " world!");
TBuf<12> helloWorldStack(KHelloRom);
helloWorldStack.Append(KWorldRom);
```

`TBuf<12>` is a modifiable buffer with a maximum length of 12 characters. After the constructor has completed, the data is initialized to `"hello"` and the current length is set to 5.

The code is somewhat unsatisfactory in that I have used a magic number, 12, for the size of the buffer, rather than calculating it. This is because you can't take the size of a `_LIT` constant. I could have avoided magic numbers, but it didn't seem worth it for this example.

`Append()` starts by checking the maximum length to ensure that there will be enough room for the final string. Then, assuming there is room, it appends the `" world!"` string, and adjusts the current length.

Here's how it looks in memory:

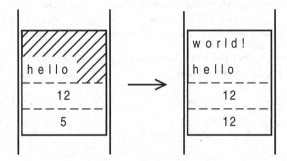

The processing of `Append()` illustrates two fundamental aspects of descriptors:

❑ The descriptor APIs do not perform memory allocation: you have to allocate a descriptor which is big enough.

❑ If you use the descriptor APIs, you can never overflow a buffer: if you try to do so, the system will panic your program. (That is, it will abort it with an error code. We'll look at panics in detail in the next chapter.)

C's string APIs are awkward because they don't perform memory allocation, unreliable because they allowed you to write beyond the end of memory allocated for strings, and doubly unreliable because, with all those trailing `NUL` calculations, you are quite likely to get it wrong occasionally anyway.

Java's `String` and standard C++'s `string` classes solve these problems, and also manage the memory for you. The cost of this functionality is more bytes for string objects, which doesn't matter as much in Java's and standard C++'s intended application areas as it does for EPOC.

EPOC is a kind of halfway house: you have to do your own memory management, but you can't overwrite memory beyond the end of a string and, if you try to, you'll find out about it very early in your debugging cycle. So descriptors contribute significantly to EPOC's compactness and robustness.

Modifying `HBufCs`

You might have thought there would be an `HBuf` class to make it easy for you to modify descriptors on the heap. But there isn't: if you want an `HBuf`, the best thing to do is allocate a `TBuf` of the right size, or use a `CBufBase`-derived class (see Chapter 8 for more on `CBufBase`).

You can modify an `HBufC`, by using the pointer descriptor `TPtr` to address the memory it contains:

```
HBufC* helloWorldHeap = HBufC::NewMaxLC(KHelloRom().Length() +
                        KWorldRom().Length());
TPtr helloWorldAppend = helloWorldHeap->Des();
helloWorldAppend = KHelloRom;
helloWorldAppend.Append(KWorldRom);
```

`HBufC::NewMaxLC()` allocates a heap cell of sufficient size to hold the requested number of bytes (12 in this case) plus a descriptor header. It sets the current length to 12, but doesn't set any data.

The `Des()` function returns a `TPtr` consisting of the address, current length, and heap cell length of the `HBufC` minus the length of its header. That means I can use the `TPtr` to change the `HBufC`'s content safely – though I can't change the `HBufC`'s current length through the `TPtr`.

Then I do the data copying: I set the `TPtr` content to contain `"hello"`, which sets its current length to 5, and then append `" world!"`, which sets its current length to 12.

In memory, it looks like this:

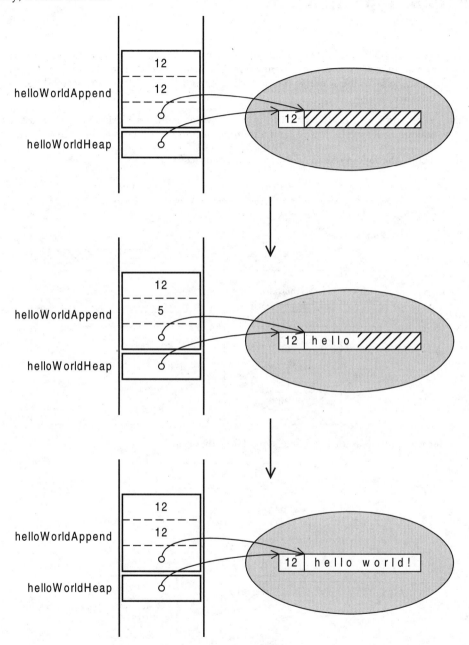

Admittedly, there is more code here than in the C case. But because the length and the maximum length are carried in the descriptors (rather than in an object that must be passed around separately), the code is just as safe as the TBuf code above.

Descriptor Type Summary

We have now seen five concrete descriptor types:

❑   `TPtrC`, `TBufC`, and `HBufC`, all derived from `TDesC`. All have a pointer and a current length, and all inherit `const` convenience functions from `TDesC`. The essential difference between these classes is the way they contain or refer to the string data. Also, they differ in how you initialize them.

❑   `TPtr` and `TBuf`, both derived from `TDes`, which is in turn derived from `TDesC`. `TDes` adds a maximum length to `TDesC`, and a number of non-const convenience functions.

We can picture the layout of each concrete descriptor as follows:

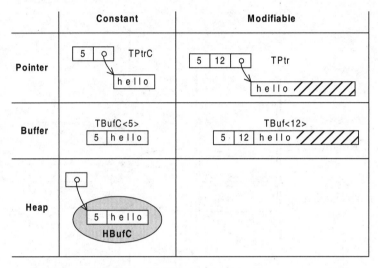

The other way to look at these classes is in a UML diagram:

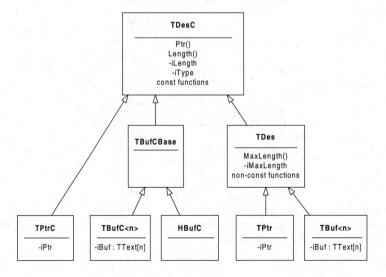

Using the Abstract Classes in Interfaces

TDesC and TDes are abstract classes, so you can never instantiate them. But in functions designed to manipulate strings, you should always use these base classes as the arguments. Use:

- ❑   const TDesC& to pass a descriptor for string data which you will read from, but not attempt to change

- ❑   TDes& to pass a descriptor for string data which you want to change

An example in epocstring is the greetEntity() global function:

```
void greetEntity(TDes& aGreeting, const TDesC& aEntity)
    {
    aGreeting.Append(aEntity);
    }
```

You pass one modifiable descriptor that contains the greeting text ("hello", perhaps), and you pass a non-modifiable descriptor that contains the entity to be greeted (the world, maybe). The function simply appends the entity onto the greeting. You can call this function using code like this:

```
TBuf<12> helloWorld(_L("hello"));
greetEntity(helloWorld, _L(" world!"));
```

I've used an alternative format for the literals used to initialize descriptors here: _L produces a TPtrC, which describes the text in the string. So greetEntity() gets called with TBuf<12> and TPtrC parameters, which suitably match its prototype requirements.

We saw when discussing TDesC how the current data length is always the first machine word of a concrete descriptor class, allowing the same Length() implementation in all classes. In TDes and its derived classes, the maximum allowed data length is always the second machine word, so TDes::MaxLength() is implemented identically for all modifiable descriptor classes.

The address of the first byte of data therefore varies depending on the concrete type of the descriptor class: sometimes it's the first byte after the length; sometimes it's the first byte after the maximum length; sometimes it's contained in a pointer after the length. This is why TDesC::Ptr() is implemented differently for each descriptor class.

Every other TDesC or TDes function depends only on Ptr(), Length(), and MaxLength(), so they can be implemented without any dependence on the concrete descriptor class.

Literals Again

We've now seen two kinds of literal descriptor:

- ❑   _LIT, which associates a symbol with a literal value and produces a TLitC, which is not derived from TDesC

- ❑   _L, which produces a TPtrC from a literal value and can be used without a name

At first sight, _L is more attractive, for precisely the two reasons I mentioned above. It was the only type of literal supported until EPOC R5, when _LIT was added. _L is now deprecated: let's see why.

Here's how _L works. It is defined as:

```
#define _L(string) TPtrC((const TText*) string)
```

So that this:

```
const TDesC& helloRef = _L("hello");
```

Does three things:

- ❑ When the program is built, the string, including the trailing NUL, is built into the program code. We can't avoid the trailing NUL, because we're using the C compiler's usual facilities to build the string.

- ❑ When the code is executed, a temporary TPtrC is constructed as an invisible automatic variable, with its pointer set to the address of the first byte of the string, and its length set to five.

- ❑ The address of this TPtrC temporary is then assigned to the const TDesC& reference, helloRef, a fully-fledged automatic variable.

This code works provided either that the reference is only used during the lifetime of the temporary – that is, during the lifetime of the function – or that the TPtrC pointer and length are copied if the descriptor is required outside this lifetime. This is usually OK, but you get the feeling that we're walking on eggshells.

Another issue we need to consider is that the second step above – constructing a TPtrC including the pointer, the length, and the four-bit descriptor class identifier – is always required. Code has to be built and run, wasting code bytes and execution time.

The _LIT macro tackles these issues as follows:

```
#define _LIT(name, s) const static TLitC<sizeof(s)> name = { sizeof(s) - 1, s }
```

The macro constructs, at compile time, a TLitC that builds into the program binary. It so happens that the binary format of a TLitC is exactly the same as that of a TBufC, since the four-bit type identifier used for TBufC is zero.

With this, if you code,

```
_LIT(KHelloRom, "hello");
```

and then use it like this,

```
const TDesC& helloDesC = KHelloRom;
```

then the TDesC& reference looks exactly like a reference to a TBufC. But no run-time temporary and no inline constructor code are generated, so ROM budget is significantly reduced for components that contain many string literals.

Here's a diagram to show the difference between _LIT and _L:

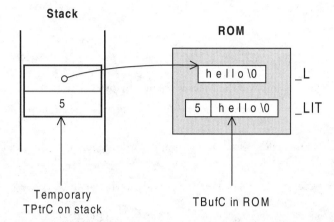

Most GUI programs use resource files to contain their language-dependent literal strings: we'll cover resource files in Chapter 9. But many system components require literals for system purposes, which don't get translated for different locales.

For those programs that do use literals, _L is now deprecated. Use _LIT instead.

Standard Descriptor Functions

I mentioned that descriptors contain many convenience functions – const functions in TDesC and both const and non-const functions in TDes. Here's a lightning tour to give you a taster. For more information, see the SDK. I also use many descriptor functions throughout the book.

If you wish, you can write your own descriptor functions: just put them into another class (or, exceptionally, no class at all) and pass descriptors to your functions as const TDesC& or TDes& parameters. EPOC itself provides utility classes that work this way; perhaps the most fundamental is TLex, which provides string-scanning functions and includes the code to convert a string into a number.

Basics

You can get at descriptor data using Ptr() to find its address, Length() to find out how many characters it is, and Size() to find out how many bytes of data it contains.

In narrow builds, Length() and Size() return the same result, but you should always use Length() when you're dealing with characters.

TDes provides MaxLength(), which says how many characters are allocated to the descriptor in total. Any manipulation function that would cause this to be exceeded will panic.

If you write your own string handling functions, you should usually construct them using the descriptor library functions as described here. In some circumstances you may wish to access descriptor contents directly and manipulate them using C pointers – Ptr() allows you to do that – but be careful. In particular, make sure you honor MaxLength() if you're modifying descriptor data, and make sure that any function you write panics if asked to do something that would overflow the allocated MaxLength().

Comparison

You can compare descriptors using:

- ❑   Compare(): this compares the bytes without any locale sensitivity
- ❑   CompareC(): this is sensitive to locale-specific collation position of each character in the strings
- ❑   CompareF(): this folds lower-case into upper-case, ignores accents, and takes account of locale-specific collation

The convenience operator<() and so on are provided, which call Compare() and return a TBool.

> *Collating is the process of removing any differences between characters so that they can be put in a sequence that allows for straightforward comparisons. **Folding** sets everything to upper case, and removes accents.*

Searching

TDesC's Locate() and Find() functions allow forward or reverse searching, with optional case insensitivity and accent insensitivity.

Extracting

TDesC's Left(), Right(), and Mid() functions can extract any part of a string.

Clearing And Setting

SetLength() allows the length to be specified to anything within range 0 to MaxLength(), and SetMax() sets the length to the maximum length.

Various Fill() functions allow a descriptor to be filled with data quickly.

Manipulating Data

TDes's Copy() function copies data to the descriptor, starting at the beginning, while Append() can copy additional data to the descriptor, starting where the existing data stops. There are variants of the Copy() function that perform case or accent folding.

Insert() inserts data into any position, pushing up subsequent characters toward the end of the string. Delete() deletes any sequence of characters, moving down subsequent characters to close the gap. Replace() overwrites characters in the middle of a string.

Letter Manipulation

TDes's Fold(), Collate(), LowerCase(), UpperCase(), and Capitalize() functions all manipulate characters in place.

> *It takes two to tango, and it also takes two to compare, so collating an individual string isn't very useful, and TDes::Collate() is therefore deprecated.*

Trimming and Justification

TDes's Trim() functions shave whitespace from either or both ends of a string. Justify() performs left, right, center, or no justification, and allows the fill character to be overridden. Various AppendJustify() functions append and justify simultaneously.

> *Justify() is not really very useful, since real text justification is done at the GUI level, not the individual string level.*

Formatting

TDes::AppendFormat() is a bit like C sprintf(): it takes a format string and a variable argument list, and appends the result to an existing descriptor. Functions such as Format() are implemented in terms of this one, as was CConsoleBase::Printf(), which we saw in hellotext and epocstring.

Many lower-level functions exist to support AppendFormat(): various Num() functions convert numbers into text, and corresponding AppendNum() functions append converted numbers onto an existing descriptor. For more information on TDes::AppendFormat(), see Chapter 8.

In C, scanning functions are provided by sscanf() and packaged variants such as scanf(), fscanf() etc. Similar functions are available in EPOC32, through TLex and associated classes, which scan data held in TDesCs. These functions are relatively specialized, and it was not thought appropriate to implement them directly in TDesC.

More Text APIs

EPOC uses descriptors for basic string handling. But a real GUI-based system needs more than strings; it needs classes for text that can be formatted conveniently into any size display area, edited conveniently, displayed using a full range of character and paragraph formatting, and include pictures. EPOC uses two sophisticated components, ETEXT (text content) and FORM (text views) to provide these functions, and convenient, re-usable, text editors in the EIKON GUI. Rich text also uses a more powerful memory management scheme than any of the descriptor classes: dynamic buffers, which are described in Chapter 8.

At the other end of the spectrum, an individual character has many attributes, such as upper case, alphabetic, whitespace, etc. The TChar class represents a single character, and includes functions to interrogate attributes. So you can write:

```
TBool u = TChar(_L("Hello")[4]).IsUpper();
```

This sets u to EFalse: change the 4 to a 0, and it will set u to ETrue.

TChar is defined in e32std.h. TLex functions use TChar to find character attributes. TChar character attributes involve kernel executive calls (albeit quite efficient ones), so don't use TChar or TLex where fast, locale-independent parsing is required: hard-code your own character and attribute tables instead.

Unicode

EPOC was designed from the beginning to support worldwide locales. Psion had been unable to address considerable interest from the Far East for its SIBO models, because characters were represented within SIBO by every conceivable means – C strings, arrays, integers, assembler symbols – all of which could be used to contain other data. It was not commercially feasible to modify SIBO to support 16-bit characters. EPOC would not repeat the same mistake, so its architects planned for 16-bit characters from the beginning.

> *When 8-bit characters are used, the values in the range 0-31 are used for control purposes, and 32-255 are mapped onto the Windows Latin 1 code page. With 16-bit characters, character values in the range 0-65535 are allowed. These are mapped onto the Unicode code page whose 256 lowest characters match those of the ISO Latin 1 code page, which in turn is (with a few exceptions) the same as Windows Latin 1. Unicode is big enough to provide code points for most of the characters used by practically all the world's living languages – and many of its dead languages too. In addition to providing code points for character glyphs in languages such as Chinese, Japanese, Korean, Thai, Hebrew, and Arabic, Unicode provides standards to support these languages' typesetting conventions, including cues for left-to-right and right-to-left changeovers.*

The technical foundation of EPOC's strategy was to define classes to represent text and to use them *everywhere* text was required, and *nowhere* else. By simply changing a compiler flag, it would then be possible to rebuild EPOC with 16-bit characters instead of 8-bit characters. Compiled code would be incompatible, and so would application data files, but there would be virtually no source code changes.

So symbols were assigned for all the critical text classes such as `TText` and `TDesC`. In the narrow build, these were equated to `TText8` and `TDesC8`. In the wide build, they were equated to `TText16` and `TDesC16`. The setting of the `_UNICODE` macro would be used to control which was which.

Other classes and macros included in this scheme are:

Symbol	Narrow	Wide	Meaning
TText	TText8	TText16	Character
_L	_L8	_L16	Literal (old-style)
_LIT	_LIT8	_LIT16	Literal (new-style)
TDesC	TDesC8	TDesC16	Non-modifiable descriptor
TDes	TDes8	TDes16	Modifiable descriptor
TPtrC	TPtrC8	TPtrC16	Non-modifiable pointer descriptor
TPtr	TPtr8	TPtr16	Modifiable pointer descriptor
TBufC	TBufC8	TBufC16	Non-modifiable buffer descriptor
TBuf	TBuf8	TBuf16	Modifiable buffer descriptor
HBufC	HBufC8	HBufC16	Heap descriptor
TLex	TLex8	TLex16	Lexer

You can find these definitions throughout `e32def.h`, `e32std.h`, `e32des8.h`, and `e32des16.h`.

In both builds, all the classes and types mentioned in the table above are present. But higher-level classes and types are build-specific: only in very rare cases do higher-level classes include narrow variants in the wide build or vice versa.

At first sight, this scheme grants a means to achieve 100% source compatibility:

❑ Code all your general-purpose text objects to use the neutral variants in the first column of the table above, for example, TText or TDesC.

❑ Where you are using descriptors to refer not to text, but to binary data, code specifically 8-bit classes, for example, TDesC8 – and use TInt8 or TUint8 rather than TText8, for an individual byte. Then, when the build variant changes to wide, your binary objects will stay eight-bit, but your text objects will change to 16-bit.

There are, however, several reasons why this scheme doesn't attain 100% source compatibility, even in Western locales:

❑ Some types of data are awkward, especially data in communications protocols that looks like a string, but is actually binary data that should always use eight-bit characters. Examples include the HELO used to log on to a POP post office, or the AT commands used for modems.

❑ You sometimes want to convert between binary and text data. In the narrow build, you can do this by assignment. In the wide build, you need to do some explicit conversion. You probably won't spot all cases when working with the narrow build alone, and even if you did, it isn't always obvious what to do about them.

❑ It's easy to forget, and accidentally code TDesC8 for character data – or, more likely, code TDesC for binary data. The narrow build won't spot the problem: it'll only bite when you start working seriously with the Unicode build.

When it comes to addressing a wider range of locales and Far Eastern requirements, including more interesting alphabets and character entry than those found in Western Europe, a host of new issues arises:

❑ The character attributes associated with the Unicode code page are far more complex than those associated with the CP1252 code page (for example, an LJ character can be upper case LJ, lower case lj or title case Lj: you need functions to detect all these and convert between them).

❑ You need to support more flexible typesetting than is supported by EPOC's current rich text system.

❑ You need to support established methods for handwriting recognition or keyboard text entry in Chinese, Japanese, Korean, and similar locales.

❑ You need genuinely scalable fonts, because while it's practical to store a 256-point character set in a variety of bitmapped sizes so you can scale by selecting a different bitmap, it's impractical to do this for huge alphabets.

So, in practice, supporting Unicode is about more than simply a wide character build. That's why Symbian isn't releasing a Unicode build of EPOC until mid 2000. At that time, you'll need to convert your programs to the wide build, and there will be SDKs that enable you to do so.

If your aim is simply to support Western markets, this will not be hard: you will only face the issues mentioned in the first list. If your aim is to support Far Eastern markets too, then you face a few more technical issues (but fewer than Symbian, because you'll be *using* EPOC's Far Eastern locale support, not *writing* it!) and many commercial issues (including localizing your applications and locale-specific marketing).

Symbian has already been through all this. During early EPOC development, we built and tested EPOC for about a year in both narrow and Unicode builds. We stopped building in Unicode in late 1995, in order to concentrate on the narrow build: RAM prices were very high at that time, so we didn't want to use Unicode for Western markets. And we also realized that we weren't going to be able to provide all the support for Far Eastern markets soon enough.

But we had run with the dual build system for long enough for all the programming practices to get well entrenched: that was good for us when we picked up the Unicode build again in early 1998, for EPOC R5 development. It wasn't too hard to convert every component to use the Unicode build. We dropped Unicode again, in early 1999, as we realized the Far Eastern support still wasn't industrial-strength, and the pressure to ship EPOC R5 mounted.

> *The results show. There's that annoying feature where* makmake *insists that you code a* UNICODEUID, *even though you can't build for Unicode. And a careful scan of the EPOC R5 SDKs reveals prototype front-end processors for Far Eastern input, and some fancy locale stuff here and there.*

Our experiences with Unicode so far make us reasonably confident that, if you follow the entrenched programming habits for choosing between character and binary data, and your application is not extremely sensitive to locale, then you should have little difficulty moving over to Unicode. When Unicode EPOC arrives, Symbian will issue detailed guidelines about the issues involved. Meanwhile the best strategy for preparation is:

- ❑ Get started with EPOC using EPOC R5, this book, the SDK, and the market opportunities offered by EPOC R5 machines
- ❑ Use the right types for binary and character data
- ❑ "Masterly inactivity" (to quote a Chinese phrase): don't try to tackle the awkward problems, because there aren't many of them, and it's better to expend that effort with a real SDK and the real guidelines, rather than trying to anticipate them in advance

Symbian now understands the space implications of Unicode reasonably well. RAM footprints for open documents are about 30-50% greater, depending on how text-intensive the application is. Files for saved documents are less than 2% bigger, if they contain only characters from the CP1252 character set, because Unicode's standard compression scheme is used for all text. Compiled programs are the same size within a couple of percent.

Binary Data

You can use descriptors just as well for data as you can for strings. The main reason you can do this is because descriptors include an explicit length, rather than using NUL as a terminator.

The data API and string API offered by descriptors are almost identical. The main things to watch out for are:

- ❑ Use TDesC8, TDes8, TBuf8, TPtr8, etc. rather than their equivalent TDesC, TDes, TBuf, and TPtr character classes.
- ❑ Use TUint8 or TInt8 for bytes, rather than TText.
- ❑ Locale-sensitive character-related functions, like FindF() and CompareF(), aren't useful for binary data.

❏ You can use Size() to give you the number of bytes in a descriptor, whether it's the 8-bit or 16-bit type. TDesC8::Size() gives the same answer as TDesC8::Length(). TDesC16::Size() is 2 * TDesC16::Length(). Generally, though, I always use Length(): I would only use Size() to find the number of bytes, of a text descriptor, so that I could turn it into binary.

APIs for writing and reading, or sending and receiving, are often specified in terms of binary data. Here, for example, is part of RFile's API:

```
class RFile : public RFsBase
    {
public:
    IMPORT_C TInt Open(RFs& aFs, const TDesC& aName, TUint aFileMode);
    IMPORT_C TInt Create(RFs& aFs, const TDesC& aName, TUint aFileMode);
    IMPORT_C TInt Replace(RFs& aFs, const TDesC& aName, TUint aFileMode);
    IMPORT_C TInt Temp(RFs& aFs, const TDesC& aPath,
                       TFileName& aName, TUint aFileMode);
    IMPORT_C TInt Write(const TDesC8& aDes);
    IMPORT_C TInt Write(const TDesC8& aDes, TInt aLength);
    IMPORT_C TInt Read(TDes8& aDes) const;
    IMPORT_C TInt Read(TDes8& aDes,TInt aLength) const;
    ...
    };
```

The Open(), Create(), Replace(), and Temp() functions take a filename, which is text, and is specified as a const TDesC&.

The Write() functions take a descriptor containing binary data to be written to the file. For binary data, these classes are specified as const TDesC8& – the '8' indicating that eight-bit bytes are intended, regardless of the size of a character. The version of Write() which takes only a descriptor writes its entire contents (up to Length() bytes) to the file. Many APIs use descriptors exactly like this, for sending binary data to another object.

There is another version of Write() here, which takes a length that is used to override the length in the descriptor. This is a simple convenience function. If it had not been provided in the API, and you wanted it, then instead of using file.Write(buffer,length), you could use file.Write(buffer.Left(length)). Left() returns a TPtrC with the same address as its argument, but its length shortened to the number of characters (or bytes) required.

Likewise, the Read() functions take a descriptor in which the data to be read will be put. These parameters are specified as TDes&types. Read()-like functions coded like this use one of three conventions:

❏ They fill the destination buffer to its MaxLength()

❏ They fill the destination buffer with a fixed amount of data, but truncate if that would exceed MaxLength()

❏ They fill the destination buffer with a fixed amount of data, but panic if the buffer isn't big enough

RFile usually fills the entire buffer – except when reading has reached the end of the file. Many servers and device drivers follow the third convention and expect the buffer to be big enough.

Communications protocols at the stream level behave like an RFile. Communications protocols at the packet level behave like a server or an I/O device.

In Chapter 16 and those that follow, we'll learn a lot more about binary descriptors, as we get to grips with packet-based communications and servers for the Battleships game.

Summary

In this chapter, I've introduced you to the way EPOC handles strings and other data, using descriptors. The main advantages of descriptors are:

❑ Descriptors can handle both string and binary data

❑ They provide a uniform API for dealing with data, whether it is part of a program binary, on the stack, or on the default heap

❑ They prevent buffer overflow errors, but otherwise don't hide memory management issues – preserving the balance between safety and efficiency that underlies EPOC

❑ Descriptors encapsulate the address and length of data

❑ The class structure allows source code to be re-targeted at Unicode with minimal changes

❑ 8-bit versions of descriptor classes allow binary data to be handled

In terms of the classes we've seen:

❑ For immutable strings and data, classes ending with C provide const functions, derived from TDesC

❑ When modifying strings or data, use classes derived from TDes, with its non-const functions

❑ The _LIT and _L macros, the difference between them and why _LIT is preferred

There are some topics that we'll return to later in the book – namely, how EPOC handles rich text (in Chapter 8) and more detail on handling binary data (in Chapter 16).

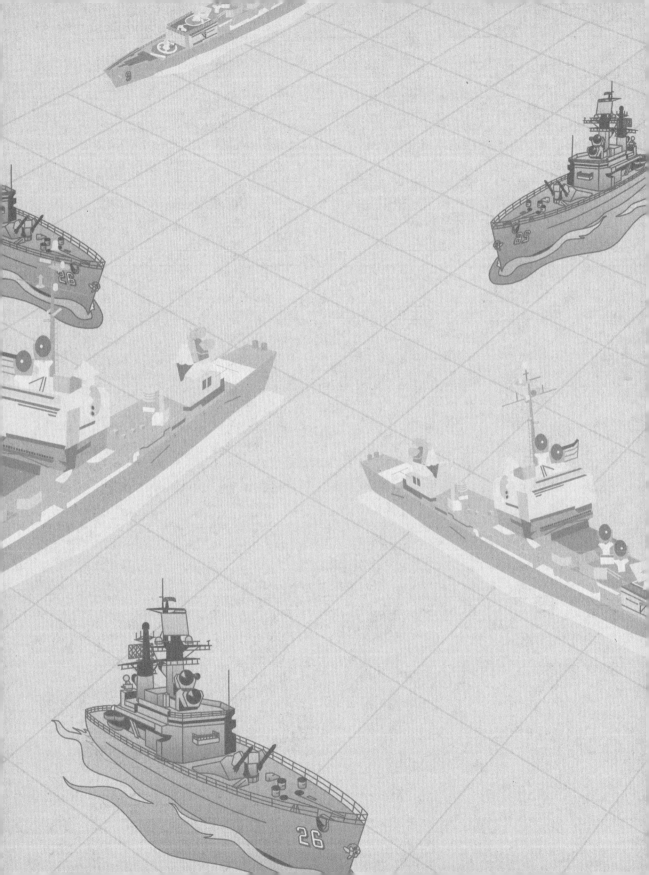

6

Error Handling and Cleanup

So far, we've seen two examples of EPOC code: hellotext, in Chapter 2, and epocstring, in Chapter 5. Both examples use the same copy-and-paste framework code that, as I said back Chapter 2, is there for handling errors and cleaning up. I didn't make much use of the framework in hellotext, but in epocstring I used it to handle out-of-memory errors when allocating HBufCs: I allocated them using AllocLC() and deleted them using CleanupStack::PopAndDestroy().

I also hinted in Chapter 4 that much of EPOC's naming convention is related to cleanup: C for heap-based classes, i for member variables, and L for functions that can leave.

In this chapter, I'm going to explain the error handling and cleanup framework. It's a vital part of EPOC, and you'll need to become familiar with it over the course of the book. Every line of code you write – or read – in EPOC will be influenced by thinking about cleanup. No other EPOC framework has that much impact: cleanup is fundamental in a very real sense.

Because of this, we've made sure that error handling and cleanup in EPOC is very effective, and very easy to do. My epocstring example was no more complicated than the C string example, and yet it was fully error checked. You'll see that repeatedly, throughout the book.

Having given the subject a big build-up, much of it won't become really useful until you've actually started programming in EPOC. Read this chapter at whatever pace suits you, and don't try to memorize everything! You'll see the patterns I describe here again and again, and you can always come back for reference if you need to.

Error handling is really about producing reliable programs. That's important for EPOC. Besides the cleanup framework (which deals with environment-related errors), this chapter includes a brief section on program errors, and also on testing in relation to finding and handling environment-related errors.

What Kinds of Error?

It's easiest to start this chapter by focusing on out-of-memory (OOM) errors.

These days, desktop PCs come with at least 64MB of RAM, virtual memory swapping out onto 6GB or more of hard disk, and users who expect to perform frequent reboots. In this environment, running out of memory is rare, so you can be quite cavalier about memory and resource management. You try *fairly* hard to release all the resources you can, but if you forget then it doesn't matter too much: things will get cleaned up when you close the application, or when you reboot. That's life in the desktop world.

By contrast, EPOC machines have as little as 4MB RAM, and usually no more than 16MB. The RAM contains the equivalent of a PC's RAM *and* hard disk: there is no disk-backed virtual memory. Your users consider their devices to be more like mobile phones or paper organizers than desktop PCs: they are *not* used to having to reboot frequently.

You have to face some key issues here – issues that don't trouble modern desktop software developers:

- ❑ You have to program efficiently, so that your programs don't use RAM unnecessarily. We've already begun to see how descriptors help with that.

- ❑ You have to release resources as soon as possible, because you can't afford for a running program to gobble up more and more RAM without ever releasing it.

- ❑ You have to cope with out-of-memory errors. In fact, you have to cope with potential out-of-memory in *every single operation* that can allocate memory, because an out-of-memory condition can arise in any such operation.

- ❑ When an out-of-memory situation arises that stops some operation from happening, you must not lose any user data, but must roll back to an acceptable and consistent state.

- ❑ When an out-of-memory situation occurs partway through an operation that involves the allocation of several resources, you must clean up all those resources as part of the process of rolling back.

> These considerations are fundamental to a successful handheld system. An operating system for handheld devices that doesn't provide the programmer with good support in these areas is doomed.

Here are some examples of where you might run out of memory when using a real handheld system.

When you launch a new application, resources are created first by the kernel (memory to hold information about the new process and thread used by the application), then by the application itself (the memory it requires), and then by various servers throughout the system. (The file server is constantly at-the-ready to load application resources, and the window server displays the application's graphics on-screen, and queues keyboard and pointer events to the application when it has focus.) At *any time* during this sequence, the attempt to allocate one of these resources may fail due to an out-of-memory condition. The whole application launch has to be called off, and the application, the kernel, and any servers that allocated resources during the aborted launch must then release them.

Application launch requires a lot of resources, so it's a good guess that the whole operation might fail if the system is running out of them. However, each of the resources required by the application is allocated *individually*, and potential failure must be detected in *each possible case*. Proper cleanup must occur wherever the failure occurred.

It's easy enough to clean up on application launch: you just kill everything and the application isn't launched. Nobody's data gets lost, and the user understands what has happened.

Other examples are more demanding. Imagine that you're typing into an EPOC Word document. Each key you press potentially expands the buffers used to store and format the rich text object that's at the heart of the Word application. If you press a key that requires the buffers to expand, but there is insufficient memory available, the operation will fail. In this case, it would clearly be quite wrong for the application to terminate – all your typing would be lost. Instead, the document must roll back to the state it was in before the key was processed, and any memory that was allocated successfully during the partially performed operation must be freed.

In fact, EPOC's error handling and cleanup framework is good for more than out-of-memory errors. Many operations can fail because of other environment conditions – reading and writing to files, opening files, sending and receiving over communications sessions. The error handling and cleanup framework can make it easier to deal with those kinds of error too.

Even user input errors can be handled using the cleanup framework: as an example, code that processes the OK button on a dialog can allocate many resources before finding that an error has occurred. Dialog code can use the cleanup framework to flag an error and free the resources with a single function call.

There's just one kind of error that the cleanup framework can't deal with: programming errors. If you write a program with an error, you have to fix it. The best service EPOC can do you (and your users) is to kill your program as soon as possible when the error is detected, with enough diagnostics to give you a chance to identify the error and fix it – hopefully, before you release the program. In EPOC, this is a **panic**. We've heard about panics already: in this chapter, I'll explain them.

Handling Out-of-memory Errors

For application programmers, the resources you use mostly consist of the memory in your own application. With that in mind, we'll introduce EPOC's cleanup tools in the context of dealing with out-of-memory conditions in your own application (or library) code. We'll get confident with out-of-memory handling, and then we'll look at handling cleanup with other kinds of resource.

EPOC's toolkit for handling out of memory, and for testing your out-of-memory handling, includes:

❑ The EIKON GUI framework's debug keys.

❑ Heap checking tools, which check that all resources that were allocated by a function are also freed.

❑ Proper use of the C++ destructor to destroy any owned objects.

❑ Heap failure tools, which produce deliberate out-of-memory errors for testing purposes.

- ❑ The leave mechanism, which is used to indicate an error. The fundamental function here is User::Leave(), which is at the heart of any L function. It does a job similar to C++'s and Java's throw.

- ❑ The **cleanup stack**: objects on the cleanup stack are deleted when a leave occurs.

- ❑ The **trap harness**: leave processing is caught by a trap. A leave aborts its function and any functions that called it, up to and excluding the first function that contains a trap harness. EPOC's trap harness does a similar job to C++'s and Java's try-catch mechanism.

- ❑ The **two-phase construction** pattern, necessary to ensure that C++ constructors never leave.

- ❑ The CBase class, the ultimate base class of all C classes, which is recognized by the cleanup stack, and includes a virtual C++ destructor, so that any C class can be cleaned up using the cleanup stack.

- ❑ Naming conventions that indicate class resource-allocation patterns, whether a function has the potential to leave, and other behavior important for cleanup. These conventions go together with some rules that make it easy to address cleanup requirements in the vast majority of cases.

The toolkit may look strange at first, even if you have used another error-handling framework. Actually it's quite easy to work with. It makes it possible to build very robust applications with only a few disciplines, and almost no programming overhead.

EIKON Debug Keys

Some of EPOC's memory management tools are quite conveniently accessible through debug builds of the EIKON GUI. Boot up the debug-mode emulator (\epoc32\release\wins\deb\epoc.exe) and start the EPOC Word application. Then type *Ctrl+Alt+Shift+C*. EIKON responds with 38 Window Server resources used.

> These *Ctrl+Alt+Shift*+key combinations are called the EIKON debug keys. **They are very useful for GUI application development, especially while you're getting used to EPOC.**

Back in Word, type *Ctrl+P*, for printing; a print dialog will appears. Press *Ctrl+Alt+Shift+C* again, and you'll see that another window server resource has been allocated: the Print dialog. When you dismiss the Print dialog by pressing *Esc*, the window server resource count will go back down to 38 again.

Three EIKON debug keys give resource counts like this one:

Ctrl+Alt+Shift+A	Heap cells in use
Ctrl+Alt+Shift+B	File server resources
Ctrl+Alt+Shift+C	Window server resources

Sadly, the most attractive key combination, Ctrl+Alt+Shift+A, which displays the number of heap cells allocated by this thread, fell victim to a low-level bug in the EPOC Release 5 emulator and can't be used. It will be back! Meanwhile, we'll work around it.

Next, try *Ctrl+Alt+Shift+P*. You should see a dialog that looks something like this:

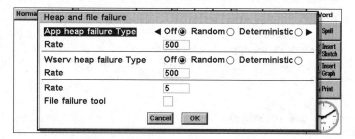

In the true spirit of debugging tools developed by engineers, this dialog isn't too pretty, but it's effective. To begin with, we'll use only the top part of the dialog, which controls the **heap failure tool**. There are three options here:

- ❑ **Off.** Allocations succeed unless there genuinely is insufficient memory.

- ❑ **Random.** Attempted allocations usually succeed (unless there really is insufficient memory), but randomly fail.

- ❑ **Deterministic.** You type in a number on the line below (say, 20). Then, allocations are guaranteed to fail on attempt number 20, 40, and so on. (They may also fail on other attempts, due to genuine out-of-memory.)

Try setting deterministic failure every 20 attempts, and then use the word processor to do some typing. Every two or three letters, you'll get an out-of-memory error, but you'll lose no data. This demonstrates that EPOC applications are written to handle out-of-memory conditions properly.

It also demonstrates that the rich text object that you're editing in Word is doing a lot of work for you, given that it's making around seven allocations per key. Most of these are unallocated again before the key press has been completely handled. Also, some allocations are connected with undo functionality.

If you like, you can try a few more experiments by setting the window server and file server failure modes as well. If you get stuck, use Ctrl+Alt+Shift+Q to reset all the failure modes to normal, so that operations fail only if there are genuine resource problems.

The debug keys are useful to have around. We'll see a few more, later in the book. Note that they only affect the operation of the main thread of the EIKON application in which you're currently working. So, you can't use debug keys to help with application launch, or with other threads. For that, you'll have to write your own code into the application you want to debug. It's not such a great restriction: native EPOC applications implement multitasking using active objects rather than multithreading, so usually, there won't be more than a single thread around.

The memorymagic Application

We're going to use EIKON's debug build facilities – including the debug key technology we introduced above – to demonstrate how EPOC's cleanup framework works at low levels. To show these off effectively, I've written an application called memorymagic. Although it's an EIKON application, all you need to understand about EIKON for the moment is how to build an EIKON application. As a reminder,

```
cd \pep\memorymagic
mkdir \epoc32\release\wins\deb\z\system\apps\memorymagic
eikrs memorymagic sc
makmake memorymagic vc5
```

You can then open the project in the Visual Studio, convert it to Visual C++ 6 format, change the build configuration to Win32 Debug, and build it.

You could actually also automate this whole thing from a command-line batch file I've provided:

```
cd \pep\memorymagic
bwins
makmake memorymagic vc5
```

But you have to open the project in the Visual Studio anyway, as you'll be reminded when you launch it. Here's the initial screen display:

This program is best appreciated from inside a debugger See chapter on cleanup for more information	Use 5 · Alloc Info Use 6 · New 1 Use 7 · Delete 1 Write File · New 2 Read File · Delete 2 Delete File · Use 3 Exit · Use 4

memorymagic is an EIKON application, but you don't need to be familiar with EIKON to understand this example. The important material is in the declarations of classes CX, CY, and CZ in memorymagic.h, and in the implementation of these classes in memorymagic.cpp. The main action in the program happens in the CExampleAppUi class: HandleCommandL() contains small functions that are invoked when you press toolbar buttons, and the destructor ~CExampleAppUi() is also important.

It's fun to play with memorymagic, but if you're in a hurry you can get what you need from this chapter without browsing the source code or running the application, since relevant screenshots and extracts are all included.

The Alloc Info button (or the *Shift+Ctrl+A* key, if it worked!) tells you how many heap cells have been allocated – 160 on my system, totaling 8028 bytes – immediately after the application has been launched. It should be pretty close to that on your system too.

Allocating, Destroying and Heap Balance

Let's use `memorymagic`'s New 1 and Delete 1 buttons to show some basic principles. If you check through the source code in the `.cpp` file, you'll see that New 1 is handled by the following code:

```
case EExampleCmdNew1:
    iObject1 = new CX;
    iEikonEnv->InfoMsg(_L("New 1"));
    break;
case EExampleCmdDelete1:
    delete iObject1;
    iEikonEnv->InfoMsg(_L("Delete 1"));
    break;
```

So, the New 1 button allocates and constructs a CX object (no need to worry, for now, what a CX is), and stores a pointer to it in `CExampleAppUi::iObject1`. The Delete 1 button destroys the object.

Both commands use EIKON's environment class, which includes a large function library, to display an info-message, so you know you've successfully invoked the function. The info-message flashes briefly in the top right corner of the screen.

Press New 1, and then check the number of heap cells allocated: it's up by one, as you'd expect. Press Delete 1, and then check the number of heap cells allocated again: it's down by one. Now close the application. Assuming you did nothing else, all will be well.

EPOC's Heap Balance Check

Launch `memorymagic` again, press New 1, and then close the application. This time, it's different. You get:

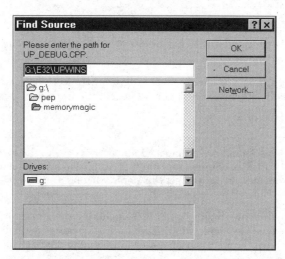

When you're debugging with the emulator, this is your first indication that a thread has panicked. Visual C++ is asking you for the source code that contains EPOC's panic function; unfortunately, it isn't shipped with the SDK, so all you can do is press *Escape*. You'll be told that a breakpoint occurred:

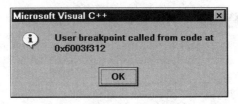

Press OK, and you'll then get a whole pile of disassembly in the main debugger window (because you didn't have the source). That's not too useful, so bring up the call stack (perhaps using *Alt+7*) and select the CCoeEnv destructor a few lines down:

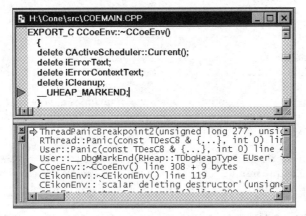

Remember that in the framework for hellotext, I included a __UHEAP_MARK macro at the beginning, and __UHEAP_MARKEND at the end? The GUI framework includes those macros for any GUI program, and the __UHEAP_MARKEND is called from its destructor, as you can see in the source code in the diagram above.

__UHEAP_MARKEND is there to check whether the heap is properly balanced. If the heap doesn't have the same number of cells allocated as when __UHEAP_MARK was called, your program gets panicked. In this case, we know why the heap isn't balanced: we allocated a cell and didn't delete it again.

All GUI programs benefit from this check. Your program may work perfectly satisfactorily until it exits, but if you forgot to delete any objects you allocated, the framework will panic your program on exit.

> **This ensures that heap imbalance gets picked up early in the development cycle, a great service to all EPOC programs. You don't even have to be careful about testing in order to benefit from this check: you get this panic whether you asked for it or not.**

This feature is built into all debug builds of EPOC – including the emulator, which is the normal development environment. It isn't built into release builds, because by then it isn't needed. Also, heap marking requires an otherwise unnecessary counter to be updated, which slows things down.

You can use __UHEAP_MARK and __UHEAP_MARKEND in your own code, and you can nest them.

Incidentally if you had impatiently started the emulator by running it (not debugging the application), then your first indication of a panic would be a dialog like this:

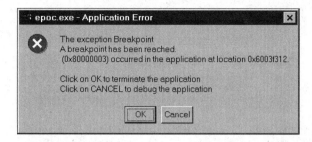

When you press Cancel to debug the application, the debugger will launch, and in due time it'll ask you for the same – missing – source file.

Use a Destructor

The solution to this problem is really pretty basic for C++ programmers:

> **Use a destructor to destroy objects you own.**

The right thing to correct the above problem would be to amend the destructor, `CExampleAppUi::~CExampleAppUi()`, to include:

```
delete iObject1;
```

We haven't included this line in `memorymagic` (although we do have `delete` statements for other objects that get created in other circumstances, as we'll see). You might wish to add this line yourself, and then re-run the scenario above. Press **New 1**, and then exit. The destructor should ensure heap balance, and the program will exit cleanly.

To summarize, you should only delete objects that you own – that is, objects with which you have a *has-a* relationship.

Don't Allocate Twice

Once you've added `delete iObject1` to `CExampleAppUi`'s destructor, rebuild `memorymagic` and start it again. Press **New 1** *twice*, and then exit. You'll get another panic.

The reason for this should be obvious. The second time through, we simply created a second `CX`, stored its address in `iObject1`, and forgot the address of the `CX` object we allocated previously. There was no way for the destructor – or any other part of the C++ system – to find this object, so it couldn't be deleted.

We could have solved this by coding:

```
case EExampleCmdNew1:
    delete iObject1;
    iObject1 = new CX;
    iEikonEnv->InfoMsg(_L("New 1"));
    break;
```

Here, we're taking advantage of the zero-checking service that C++ provides as part of `delete`. If the object has already been allocated, we delete it and allocate it again. If it hasn't yet been allocated, the `delete` statement will do nothing.

If you build this new line into `memorymagic`, you should find that it exits cleanly no matter how many times you press New 1.

Don't Delete Twice

If double allocation is a serious crime, then deleting twice is a capital offense. If you *allocate* something twice, the result is a heap cell that doesn't get destroyed, which gets picked up eventually by a `__UHEAP_MARKEND`. If you *delete* something twice, the effects can be more subtle.

`memorymagic` can demonstrate this effect too. Press New 1, and then press Delete 1 twice. In this case, I found that the application panics immediately, but in other situations I haven't always been so lucky: double deletion doesn't always cause an immediate crash, and sometimes it leaves side effects that only surface a long time after the real problem – the double delete – occurred. As a result, double deletes are very hard to debug.

On the other hand, double deletes are easy to avoid: just follow this little discipline:

> **C++ `delete` does not set the pointer to zero. If you delete any member object from outside its class's destructor, *you* must set the member pointer to zero.**

EPOC's `i` naming convention for class members makes it even easier to see when this is required. In our case, we need to amend the handler for the `EMagicCmdDelete1` command:

```
case EMagicCmdDelete1:
    delete iObject1;
    iObject1 = 0;
    iEikonEnv->InfoMsg(_L("New 1"));
    break;
```

We do not have to add a line like this to the destructor, because you know there that `iObject1` is never going to be used again.

Be clear about ownership. As I said above, your destructor should only delete objects that you own. This is fairly easy to control in the 99% of cases where ownership is not transferred. The majority of double-delete bugs probably arise from misunderstanding the consequences of ownership transfer: you just have to be careful.

Rely on Zeros

Just as C++ provides a zero-checking service as part of delete, EPOC provides a companion service as part of new, for any C class.

> **EPOC uses an overloaded `CBase::operator new()` to ensure that any object derived from `CBase` is zero initialized when first allocated with new. This means in particular that all pointers in any C class are zero initialized.**

This is a huge boon to EPOC C++ programmers. It means that you don't have to set pointers to zero yourself from the C++ constructor, just in case the objects pointed to are subsequently deleted. If you're used to initializing every member of every C++ object you create, it may be hard at first to trust EPOC to zero-initialize C objects, but in a context where every attempted allocation may fail, this feature is here to help you, as we'll see.

Finally, a word of warning: don't assume that this will happen to other objects that you allocate on the heap! R and T objects need proper construction. The only exception is if you can guarantee that all instances of an R or T class will be members of a C class.

And zero initialization wouldn't even happen to C objects if they were allocated on the stack. C objects are fundamentally not designed to go on the stack: they should always be allocated on the heap.

Heap Failure

I've labored the points about using C++ destructors properly, and relying on zero initialization in C classes. Now we can begin to tackle out-of-memory errors.

Leave if You Can't Allocate Memory

memorymagic has two buttons, New 2 and Delete 2, whose handlers are coded with all the lessons we learned earlier. In addition, we have an out-of-memory check. The command handlers look like this:

```
case EExampleCmdNew2:
    delete iObject2;
    iObject2 = new(ELeave) CX;
    iEikonEnv->InfoMsg(_L("New 2"));
    break;
case EExampleCmdDelete2:
    delete iObject2;
    iObject2 = 0;
    iEikonEnv->InfoMsg(_L("Delete 2"));
    break;
```

Also, as you saw earlier, the `CExampleAppUi` destructor includes `delete iObject2`. This line needs expanding:

```
iObject2 = new(ELeave) CX;
```

It's equivalent to:

```
{
CX* temp = ::new CX;
if(!temp)
    User::Leave(KErrNoMemory);
Mem::FillZ(temp, sizeof(CX));
iObject2 = temp;
}
```

In other words, if the allocation fails, the function leaves with an out-of-memory error. If it doesn't leave, it fills the `CX` with zeroes using `Mem::FillZ()`.

`new(ELeave)` uses some C++ magic. `operator new()` can be overridden to take a parameter that allows programmers to write their own memory allocator, something that EPOC exploits. There is an enumerated type called `TLeave` with a single constant, `ELeave`. `CBase::operator new(TLeave)` contains the code above. You invoke it by calling `new(ELeave) classname`; the value `ELeave` is thrown away, but its type is used to invoke the correct `operator new()`. The global `::operator new(TLeave)` is overridden in the same way — but it doesn't zero fill.

Try this in `memorymagic`. Start the program from the Visual C++ IDE, press *Ctrl+Alt+Shift+P*, and set the **App heap failure** mode to **Deterministic, 1**. Then press **New 2**. This should fail, and you'll see:

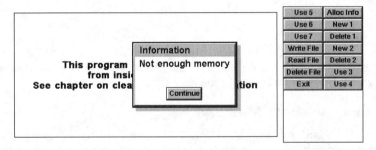

Reset the heap failure mode with *Ctrl+Alt+Shift+Q*, and then press any combination of **New 2** and **Delete 2** again. Exit the program. Everything should be clean.

The **Not enough memory** message was produced by the EIKON framework, which contains a trap for all functions that leave — in this case, the new operator function. This means that, without any programmer support, you can be sure that leaves are trapped, and an error message is displayed. Later, we'll see what a trap looks like.

> *You should always use* new(ELeave) *rather than plain* new. *Symbian considered making the default behavior for* new *to leave, but rejected this on the grounds that it would break compatibility for code being ported. This was perhaps an unfortunate choice: as in Standard C++ the default is now to throw an exception.*

Reallocate Properly

Now try another experiment with memorymagic. Start the program, press *Ctrl+Alt+Shift+P*, and set the App heap failure mode to Deterministic, 2.

Press New 2. Then press New 2 again. This will fail, and you'll see the Not enough memory message. Then, when you close the application, you'll get the panic dialog that means that you have heap imbalance. Why is this?

The answer is that the code for re-allocating iObject2 didn't anticipate failure. Here is the code again:

```
case EExampleCmdNew2:
    delete iObject2;
    iObject2 = new(ELeave) CX;
    iEikonEnv->InfoMsg(_L("New 2"));
    break;
```

If the new(ELeave) fails, then iObject2 is still pointing to the previously-allocated object, even though that object has been deleted. The result is going to be a double-deletion error, one way or another.

When re-allocating, you must always zero the pointer after delete and before new.

The code should have been:

```
case EExampleCmdNew2:
    delete iObject2;
    iObject2 = 0;
    iObject2 = new(ELeave) CX;
    iEikonEnv->InfoMsg(_L("New 2"));
    break;
```

Once again, there is no need to set pointers to zero after a delete in the destructor, because there is no chance that the pointer will ever be used again. But *at all other times*, if you delete something, you should zero its pointer immediately.

How Does Leave Work?

EPOC's User::Leave() function causes execution of the active function to terminate, and on through all calling functions, until the first function is found that contains a TRAP() or TRAPD() macro.

User::Leave() is defined in e32std.h; you pass a single 32-bit integer error code.

```
class User
    {
public:
    IMPORT_C static Leave(TInt aErrorCode);
    ...
    };
```

The TRAP() and TRAPD() macros are also defined in e32std.h; edited slightly, they look like this:

```
#define TRAP(_r,_s)    { \
                       TTrap __t; \
                       if(__t.Trap(_r) == 0) \
                           { \
                           _s; \
                           TTrap::UnTrap(); \
                           } \
                       }
#define TRAPD(_r,_s) TInt _r; \
                       { \
                       TTrap __t; \
                       if(__t.Trap(_r) == 0) \
                           { \
                           _s; \
                           TTrap::UnTrap(); \
                           } \
                       }
```

Macros like this aren't really meant to be understood, and the TTrap class isn't something you need to know about. The main point here is that TRAP() calls a function (its second parameter) and returns its leave code in a 32-bit integer (its first parameter). If the function returns normally, without leaving, then the leave code will be KErrNone (which is defined as zero). TRAPD() defines the leave code variable first, saving you a line of source code, and then essentially calls TRAP().

As we saw in Chapter 3, GUI applications are fundamentally event-driven. All code in an EIKON application runs under a RunL() function. If this leaves, the error is trapped by the active scheduler, using the following code:

```
TRAPD(r, pR->RunL());
if(r != KErrNone)
    pS->Error(r);
```

The active scheduler calls its Error() function, which is implemented by EIKON to run the one interesting piece of code which runs outside of a RunL() – its error dialog. The error dialog interprets all the standard error codes, and displays them in English – for instance, KErrNoMemory, which is -4, is displayed as Out of memory.

Error Codes

EPOC's approach to error codes is very simple. Standard error values are listed in e32std.h. Here are some of them:

```
const TInt KErrNone = 0;
const TInt KErrNotFound = (-1); // Must remain set to -1
const TInt KErrGeneral = (-2);
const TInt KErrCancel = (-3);
const TInt KErrNoMemory = (-4);
const TInt KErrNotSupported = (-5);
const TInt KErrArgument = (-6);
...
const TInt KErrBadPower = (-42);
const TInt KErrDirFull = (-43);
```

L Functions

> **It is very important to know whether a function might leave. Any function that could leave should have a name ending with L, so we get `RunL()`, `HandleCommandL()`, etc.**

If you're writing a function, and that function calls another one that might leave, then you should put an L in its name. This will remind you, your colleagues, or anyone else looking at your code, that this function might leave. Here are a few cases to think about:

❑   If you're writing a function that calls another, and the other is an L function, then your function must be an L function too (unless you trap the leave).

❑   If your function calls `new(ELeave)`, your function must also be an L function.

❑   If you're implementing a function provided by a framework, then it's important to know whether or not that framework function is an L function. If it is, you can allocate resources that can potentially leave. If not, your code must not leave – or, if it does, you must handle it privately. For example, `CEikAppUi::HandleCommandL()` allows you to leave, so user command handlers can allocate resources and potentially leave. `CCoeControl::Draw()` doesn't allow you to leave, so any drawing code you write must work with pre-allocated resources and not leave – or, if for its own reasons it can't pre-allocate resources, it must trap potential leaves and handle them privately.

❑   If you're specifying a framework function for others to implement, think very carefully about whether you will allow an implementer to leave. This is an essential aspect of your function. Don't just code it as an L function to allow the implementer to do what they want: code L if it's needed, and don't code it if it's not.

The L naming convention gives the same kind of message to the programmer as the `throws` clause in Java or standard C++. However, L is not checked by the compiler, so if you forget to include it in the name, the compiler will not complain. However, if someone else then uses your function and doesn't realize that it might leave, they may not take appropriate precautions.

> *In the C++ Knowledge Base on Symbian's web site, you'll find an L-correctness checking script that can be quite useful.*

Nested Traps

You don't often need to code your own traps, partly because the EIKON framework provides one for you, and partly because (as we'll see shortly) routine cleanup is handled by other means.

Sometimes, though, you'll need to perform a recovery action, in addition to some non-routine cleanup. Or you'll need to code a non-leaving function, such as `Draw()`, that allocates resources and draws successfully if possible, but otherwise traps any leaves and handles them internally. In these cases, you must code your own trap.

In a word processor, for example, processing a key press causes many things to happen – to name but two, there's the allocation of undo buffers, and the expansion of the document to take a new character. If anything like that goes wrong, you need to undo the operation completely. You could use code such as:

```
TRAPD(error, HandleKeyL());
if(error)
    {
    RevertUndoBuffer();

    // Any other special cleanup
    User::Leave(error);
    }
```

This performs some specialized cleanup, and then leaves anyway, so that the EIKON framework can post the error message.

While they will not normally need to allocate any resources, some Draw() functions are rather complicated and it may be appropriate to code them in such a way that they do make allocations. In this case, you have to hide the fact from the EIKON framework by trapping any failures yourself:

```
virtual void Draw(const TRect& aRect) const
    {
    TRAPD(error, MyPrivateDrawL(aRect));
    }
```

In this case, we choose to keep quiet if MyPrivateDrawL() failed. The failing draw code should take some graceful action, such as drawing in less detail, or blanking the entire rectangle, or not updating the previous display.

Don't use traps when you don't have to. Here's a particularly useless example:

```
TRAPD(error, FooL());
if(error)
    User::Leave(error);
```

The net effect of this code is precisely equivalent to:

```
FooL();
```

But it's more source code, more object code, and more processing time whether or not FooL() actually does leave.

The Cleanup Stack

Now we're ready to look at the cleanup stack. The cleanup stack addresses the problem of cleaning up objects that have been allocated on the heap, but to which the only pointer is an automatic variable. If the function that has allocated the objects leaves, the objects need to be cleaned up. Since EPOC doesn't use C++ exceptions, it needs to use its own mechanism to ensure that this happens.

In memorymagic, the Use 3 button is handled by the following code:

```
case EExampleCmdUse3:
    {
    CX* x = new(ELeave) CX;
    x->UseL();
    delete x;
    }
```

The UseL() function might leave. It's coded as:

```
void CX::UseL()
    {
    TInt* pi = new(ELeave) TInt;
    delete pi;
    }
```

You can invoke these functions from memorymagic by pressing Use 3, so go ahead and try it. When you exit the application, everything should be OK.

The code above could go wrong in two places. Firstly, the allocation of CX might fail – if so, the code leaves immediately with no harm done. You can try this in memorymagic too: set the heap to fail on the first allocation, press Use 3, and you'll see the Not enough memory message. Exit the application, and all will be well.

But what if the allocation of the TInt fails in UseL()? In this case, the CX, which is pointed to only by an automatic variable x in HandleCommandL(), can never be deleted. Try it: start memorymagic, set the heap to fail on the *second* allocation, press Use 3, see the Not enough memory message, and then exit the application. The heap check will find a memory leak, and panic the program.

Use the Cleanup Stack if You Need

What's actually happening here is that after this line has been executed:

```
CX* x = new(ELeave) CX;
```

The automatic x points to a cell on the heap. But after the leave, the stack frame containing x is abandoned without deleting x. That means the CX object is on the heap, but no pointer can reach it, and it will never get destroyed. That's why the heap check fails.

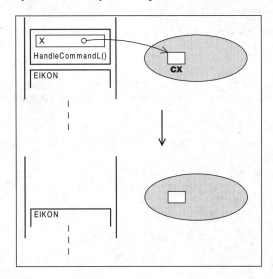

Conventionally, this is a 'memory leak'. Internally, Symbian uses the term 'alloc heaven': an allocated heap cell is in heaven, because it cannot be reached by pointers from any mortal program. Someone suggested the term 'alloc hell' to describe the horror caused by double deletion, but that term never caught on.

> **The** cleanup stack **can be used to hold a pointer to an object like this. Objects on the cleanup stack are destroyed when a leave occurs.**

Here's how we should have coded the handler for **Use 3**:

```
case EExampleCmdUse3:
    {
    CX* x = new(ELeave) CX;

    CleanupStack::PushL(x);
    x->UseL();
    CleanupStack::PopAndDestroy(); // x
    }
```

The cleanup stack class, `CleanupStack`, is defined in `e32base.h`. With these changes in place, here's what happens:

❑ Immediately after we have allocated the `CX` and stored its pointer in x, we also push a copy of this pointer to the cleanup stack.

❑ We then call `UseL()`.

❑ If this doesn't fail, our code pops the pointer from the cleanup stack and deletes the object. We could have used two lines of code for this (`CleanupStack::Pop()`, followed by `delete x`), but this is such a common pattern that EPOC provides a single function to do both.

❑ If `UseL()` *does* fail, then *as part of leave processing*, all objects on the cleanup stack are popped and destroyed anyway.

So our code works whether `UseL()` leaves or not. Change `memorymagic` to include this code, rebuild, set the heap to fail on the second allocation, invoke **Use 3**, and then exit the application. Once again, all will be well.

Of course, we could have done this without the aid of the cleanup stack by using code like this:

```
case EExampleCmdUse3:
    {
    CX* x = new(ELeave) CX;
    TRAPD(error, x->UseL());
    if(error)
        {
        delete x;
        User::Leave(error);
        }
    delete x;
    }
```

However, this is much less elegant. The cleanup stack works particularly well for a long sequence of operations, such as:

```
case EExampleCmdUse3:
    {
    CX* x = new(ELeave) CX;
    CleanupStack::PushL(x);
    x->UseL():
    x->UseL();
    x->UseL();
    CleanupStack::PopAndDestroy(); // x
    }
```

Any one of the calls to UseL() may fail, and it would begin to look very messy if we had to surround *every* L function with a trap harness just to address cleanup.

> *Notice that we used a comment to indicate the variable that we believe is being cleaned up by* CleanupStack::PopAndDestroy(). *It isn't strictly necessary, but it can prove reassuring in practice.*

C++'s native exception handling addresses the problem of automatics on the stack by calling their destructors explicitly, so that a separate cleanup stack isn't needed. C++ exception handling was not available at all on GCC, or reliably on Microsoft Visual C++, when EPOC was designed, so it wasn't an option to use it.

Don't Use the Cleanup Stack when you Don't Need It

You only need to use the cleanup stack to prevent an object's destructor from being bypassed. If the object's destructor is going to be called anyway, then you must not use the cleanup stack.

> **If an object is a member variable of another class (rather than an automatic like x above), then it will be destroyed by the class's destructor, so you should never push a member variable to the cleanup stack.**

Member variables are indicated in EPOC by an i prefix, so code like this is *always* wrong:

```
CleanupStack::PushL(iMember);
```

This is likely to produce a double deletion (once from the cleanup stack, once from the class's destructor).

What if CleanupStack::PushL() Fails?

Pushing to the cleanup stack may potentially allocate memory, and therefore may itself fail! You don't have to worry about this, because such a failure will be handled properly. But for reassurance, here's what happens under the covers.

EPOC addresses this possibility by always keeping at least one spare slot on the cleanup stack. When you do a PushL(), the object you are pushing is first placed on the cleanup stack (which is guaranteed to work, because there was a spare slot). Then, a new slot is allocated. If *that* fails, then the object you just pushed is popped and destroyed.

The cleanup stack actually allocates more than one slot at once, and doesn't throw away slots that have been allocated when they are popped. So pushing and popping from the cleanup stack are very efficient operations.

Since the cleanup stack is used to hold fairly temporary objects, or objects whose pointers haven't been stored as member pointers in their parent object during the parent object's construction, the number of cleanup stack slots ever needed by a practical program is not too high. More than ten would be very rare. So the cleanup stack itself is very unlikely to be a contributor to out-of-memory errors.

CBase and the Cleanup Stack

When we pushed x to the cleanup stack, we actually invoked the function CleanupStack::PushL(CBase* aPtr), because CX is derived from CBase.

When a subsequent PopAndDestroy() happens, this function can only call the destructor of a CBase-derived object. We have already noted that CBase::operator new() zero-initializes all member variables; now we meet CBase's second important property:

> **CBase's destructor is a virtual function.**

This means that any object derived from CBase can be pushed to the cleanup stack and, when it is popped and destroyed, its destructor is called (as you would expect).

> **The cleanup stack and C++ destructors make it very easy for an EPOC programmer to handle cleanup. Use the cleanup stack for objects pointed to only by C++ automatics. Use the destructor for objects pointed to by member variables. It just works. You very rarely need to use TRAP(). The resulting code is easy to write, compact, and efficient.**

Two-phase Construction

The cleanup stack can be used to hold pointers to heap-based objects so that they can be cleaned up if a leave occurs. This means you must have the opportunity to push objects to the cleanup stack. One key situation in which this would not be possible when using normal C++ conventions is in between the allocation performed by new, and the invocation of a C++ constructor that follows the allocation.

This problem requires us to invent a new rule: that C++ constructors cannot leave. We also need a work-around: two-phase construction.

C++ Constructors must not Leave

Let's see what happens if we allow C++ constructors to leave.

memorymagic has a class called CY that contains a member variable which points to a CX. Using conventional C++ techniques, we allocate the CX from the constructor:

```
class CY : public CBase
    {
public:
    CY();
    ~CY();
public:
    CX* iX;
    };
CY::CY()
    {
    iX = new(ELeave) CX;
    }
CY::~CY()
    {
    delete iX;
    }
```

memorymagic's **Use 4** button calls cleanup-friendly code, as follows:

```
case EExampleCmdUse4:
    {
    CY* y = new(ELeave) CY;
    CleanupStack::PushL(y);
    y->iX->UseL();
    CleanupStack::PopAndDestroy(); // y
    }
```

Looks good, doesn't it? We have used C++ constructors in the usual way, and we've used EPOC's cleanup stack properly too. Even so, this code *isn't* cleanup safe. It makes *three* allocations as it runs through:

❏   The command handler allocates the CY: if this fails, everything leaves and there's no problem.

❏   The CY constructor allocates the CX: if this fails, *the code leaves, but there is no CY on the cleanup stack*!

❏   CX::UseL() allocates a TInt: by this time, the CY *is* on the cleanup stack, and the CX will be looked after by CY's destructor, so if this allocation fails, everything gets cleaned up nicely.

Try running it through and setting the heap to fail after one, two, and then three allocations. You can verify that, if the second allocation fails, you get a memory leak. Needless to say, this is bad news. The trouble is that the C++ constructor is called at a time when no pointer to the object is accessible to the program. This code:

```
    CY* y = new(ELeave) CY;
```

Is effectively expanded by C++ to:

```
CY* y;
CY* temp = User::AllocL(sizeof(CY));   // Allocate memory
temp->CY::CY();                        // C++ constructor
y = temp;
```

The problem is that we get no opportunity to push the CY to the cleanup stack between the User::AllocL() function, which allocates the memory for the CY, and the C++ constructor, which might leave. And there's nothing we can do about this.

> **It's a fundamental rule in EPOC that no C++ constructor should contain any functions that can leave.**

Use `ConstructL()` for Construction that might Leave

We have to work around this restriction by providing a separate function to do any initialization that might leave. We call this function the **second-phase constructor** and, we usually name it ConstructL().

In memorymagic, we have at last coded a class correctly: CZ. This class is *like* CY, but it uses a second-phase constructor. Here's the class definition:

```
class CZ : public CBase
    {
public:
    static CZ* NewL();
    static CZ* NewLC();
    void ConstructL();
    ~CZ();
public:
    CX* iX;
    };
```

Here are the ConstructL() and destructor functions (we'll return to NewL() and NewLC() later):

```
void CZ::ConstructL()
    {
    iX = new(ELeave) CX;
    }
CZ::~CZ()
    {
    delete iX;
    }
```

So `CZ::constructL()` performs the same task as `CY::CY()`, but the leaving function `new(ELeave)` is now in a second-phase constructor, rather than the C++ constructor. Here's how we can use it:

```
case EExampleCmdUse5:
    {
    CZ* z = new(ELeave) CZ;
    CleanupStack::PushL(z);
    z->ConstructL();
    z->iX->UseL();
    CleanupStack::PopAndDestroy(); // z
    }
```

It's quite clear here that `ConstructL()` is cleanup-safe. You can try it out by running `memorymagic` and setting the heap to fail on the first, second, and third allocations.

First- and Second-phase Constructors

A class's initialization often involves:

❑ Copying some constructor arguments to class member variables

❑ Calling base class constructors

❑ Invoking some functions that cannot leave

❑ Invoking some functions that can leave

In C++, the rules are clear and basically simple (provided that you take a practical approach to software engineering – that is, you use only public single inheritance, and keep names distinct). With a second-phase constructor, you need to consider the following:

❑ Functions that can leave can *only* be called from the second-phase constructor

❑ Constructor arguments and member initialization can happen from either constructor, or even from both

❑ The base-class C++ constructors are automatically called by C++ in the usual way

❑ If base classes have `ConstructL()` functions, you must call them explicitly from your `ConstructL()` – preferably before you do anything else. You will have to use explicit scoping (`CMyBase::ConstructL()`, for example).

❑ If you're a base class with a second-phase constructor, you might want to give your second-phase constructor a distinctive name, so that it can be called by derived classes without the explicit scoping. `CEikAppUi`, for example, has a `BaseConstructL()` function that's called by derived classes.

It's good to do all the initialization you can from the C++ constructor, but you *must* initialize anything that could leave from the second-phase constructor.

When you use someone else's class, be sure to check whether you are required to perform single-phase or two-phase construction. There is no naming convention for classes as such: you have to check for `ConstructL()` or similarly named functions manually.

Throughout the book, and indeed in the EIKON programs we've seen already, we'll see examples of all these things happening.

Wrapping Up ConstructL(): NewL() and NewLC() Functions

Working with the two-phase constructor pattern can be a bit inconvenient, because the user of the class has to remember to call the second-phase constructor explicitly. This is less than the full support we are accustomed to from C++ constructors. A pattern that has emerged in EPOC to address this is the use of functions called NewL(). CZ has a static NewL() function that's coded as follows:

```
CZ* CZ::NewL()
    {
    CZ* self = new(ELeave) CZ;
    CleanupStack::PushL(self);
    self->ConstructL();
    CleanupStack::Pop();
    return self;
    }
```

Because CZ::NewL() is static, you can call it without any existing instance of CZ. The function allocates a CZ with new(ELeave) and then pushes it to the cleanup stack so that the second-phase constructor can safely be called. If the second-phase constructor fails then the object is popped and destroyed by the rules of the cleanup stack. Otherwise, the object is simply popped, and the pointer is returned. CZ::NewL() operates as a **factory function** – a static function that acts as a kind of constructor.

You can see how this is used in memorymagic's **Use 6** handler:

```
case EExampleCmdUse6:
    {
    iObject6 = CZ::NewL();
    iObject6->iX->UseL();
    delete iObject6;
    }
```

We didn't use the cleanup stack here because iObject6 is a member variable. The important thing about the code above is that nothing can leave between the CleanupStack::Pop(), and the assignment of the CZ* to iObject6.

If we want to refer to the new CZ from an automatic variable, then we need the cleanup stack throughout the lifetime of the CZ. We could use the NewL() above and then push the object to the cleanup stack on return, but that would be wasteful. Instead, we use a static NewLC() function that operates like NewL() but *doesn't* pop the object from the cleanup stack before returning:

```
CZ* CZ::NewLC()
    {
    CZ* self = new(ELeave) CZ;
    CleanupStack::PushL(self);
    self->ConstructL();
    return self;
    }
```

This allocates the new CZ and, if all goes well, leaves it on the cleanup stack – that's what the C in NewLC() stands for. If anything fails, the function leaves and everything is cleaned up.

This is used from **Use 7**, whose handler is:

```
case EExampleCmdUse7:
    {
    CZ* z = CZ::NewLC();
    z->iX->UseL();
    CleanupStack::PopAndDestroy(); // z
    }
```

This is very convenient, but it's not necessary to use NewL() and NewLC() in *every* class. If your class is a one-off class, designed for use only in your application, then it's a waste to code NewL()-type functions, and it's easy enough to code new followed by ConstructL() in the one place where your application constructs an instance of this class.

For classes designed for frequent re-use, the case for encapsulating construction in NewL()-type functions is more compelling.

For classes with more than one C++ constructor, such as application documents which may construct either a blank document, or a document loaded in from file, there is a very strong case to wrap up the various construction sequences in distinct NewL()-type functions.

During development, you sometimes change your mind about things like this, and equip a class with NewL()-type functions, or occasionally even remove them. The presence or absence of these convenience functions is not a fundamental property of a class, which is probably why it's not reflected in a naming convention.

CZ::NewL() was actually coded wastefully. If you're coding both a NewLC() and a NewL(), write the NewLC() first and then code NewL() as:

```
CZ* CZ::NewL()
    {
    CZ* self = CZ::NewLC();
    CleanupStack::Pop();
    return self;
    }
```

If you can push yourself to the cleanup stack from within NewL(), why not do it from the C++ constructor and allow leaves from within the constructor? Symbian considered this seriously, but for heavily derived classes there is no way to avoid repeatedly pushing and popping the class from the cleanup stack from all its base class constructors.

Summary of Cleanup Rules

We have used the `memorymagic` application and a few pages of commentary to explain the principles of memory management and cleanup in EPOC, and we could summarize all of it in a single rule:

❑ Whenever you see something that might leave, think about what happens (a) when it doesn't leave, and (b) when it does.

But thinking is hard! It's better to operate with a few safe patterns, so here's a more detailed summary of the rules we've seen:

❑ Always delete objects your class owns, from the class destructor

❑ Don't delete objects that you don't own (that is, those that you merely use)

❑ Don't allocate twice

❑ Don't delete twice

❑ When you delete outside of the destructor, immediately set the pointer to zero

❑ When you are reallocating, you must use the sequence "delete, set pointer to zero, allocate", just in case the allocate fails

❑ Use `new(ELeave)` rather than plain `new`

❑ Use `L` on the end of the name of any function that might leave

❑ When implementing virtual functions, don't allow them to leave if the virtual function name doesn't have an `L` on the end

❑ Use traps where you need to – for instance, when a function can't leave and must handle errors privately – and not where you don't

❑ Push an object to the cleanup stack if (a) that object is otherwise only referred to by an automatic pointer, and (b) you are going to call a function that might leave during that object's lifetime

❑ Never push a member variable to the cleanup stack – use the `iMember` naming convention for easy code review

❑ Give all heap-based objects a name beginning with C, and derive them from `CBase`. Trust `CBase` to zero-initialize all data, including all pointers. Exploit `CBase`'s virtual destructor for cleanup purposes.

❑ Never leave from a C++ constructor

❑ Put construction functions that might leave into a second-phase constructor such as `ConstructL()`

❑ Optionally, use `NewL()` and `NewLC()` to wrap up allocation and construction

In practice, it doesn't take long to get familiar with these rules and to work with them effectively. It's easy to trap many forms of misbehavior by using the debug keys provided by EIKON and the heap checking provided by CONE.

C and T classes

We've already seen that EPOC's naming convention for classes has been chosen to indicate their main cleanup properties. So far, I've described the cleanup-related properties of C classes. I'll briefly review them, and then re-introduce T classes, which are quite similar.

C classes are derived from CBase and allocated on the heap. They must therefore be cleaned up when they are no longer needed. Most C classes have a destructor.

C classes are referred to by pointer – a member variable of some class that owns it, a member variable of a class that uses it, or an automatic variable.

If a C class is referred to only by a single automatic, in a function that might leave, then the pointer should be pushed to the cleanup stack.

CBase offers just two things to any C class:

❑   Zero initialization, so that all member pointers and handles are initially zero, which is cleanup safe

❑   A virtual destructor, so that CBase-derived objects can be properly destroyed from the cleanup stack

By contrast, T types are *defined* as classes – or built-in types – that don't need a destructor. They don't need one, because they own no data. Examples of T types are:

❑   Any built-in type: these are given typedefs by EPOC, such as TInt for an unsigned integer.

❑   Any enumerated type, such as TAmPm, which indicates whether a formatted time-of-day is am or pm. All enumerations are Ts, though enumerated constants such as EAm or EPm begin with E.

❑   Class types that do not need a destructor, such as TBuf<40> (a buffer for a maximum of 40 characters) or TPtrC (a pointer to a string of any number of characters). TPtrC contains a pointer, but it only *uses* (rather than *has*) the characters it points to, and so it does not need a destructor.

> Ts do not own any data, so they don't need a destructor. However, Ts *may* have pointers, provided that these are *uses-a* pointers rather than *has-a* pointers, like TPtrC's string data pointer.

T types are normally allocated as automatics, or as member variables of any other kind of class.

It's possible (but rare) to allocate Ts explicitly on the heap. If so, you need to ensure that the heap cell is freed. You can push a T to the cleanup stack using code like this:

```
TDes* name = new(ELeave) TBuf<40>; // TDes is a base of TBuf
CleanupStack::PushL(name);
DoSomethingL();
CleanupStack::PopAndDestroy();      // name
```

This invokes `CleanupStack::PushL(TAny*)`. When something pushed as a `TAny*` is popped and destroyed, its memory is de-allocated, but no destructor is called.

> **If you forget to derive a C class from CBase, it will be pushed as a TAny*. The cleanup code will de-allocate the class's data, but won't call its destructor.**

A `T` can usually be assigned using a bit-wise copy. Therefore, `T` types do not need copy constructors or assignment operators (except in specialized cases, such as copying one `TBuf` to another, where the `TBuf`s' maximum lengths may differ).

Since `C` types reside on the heap and are referred to by pointers, `C` types are passed by reference — that is, by copying the pointer. Thus `C` types do not need a copy constructor or an assignment operator.

As a result, C++ copy constructors and assignment operators are extremely rare in EPOC.

R Classes

Many class names in EPOC begin with `R`, which stands for 'resource'. Usually, `R` objects contain a handle to a resource that's maintained elsewhere. Examples include `RFile` (maintained by the file server), `RWindow` (maintained by the window server), and `RTimer` (maintained by the kernel).

The `R` object itself is typically small (at a minimum, it contains only a handle). A function in an `R` class doesn't usually change the member data of the `R` class itself; rather, it sends a message to the real resource owner, which identifies the real object using the handle, performs the function, and sends back a result. Functions such as `Open()`, `Create()`, etc. allocate the resource and set the handle value. Typically, a `Close()` function frees the resource and sets the handle value to zero. A C++ constructor ensures that the handle is zero to begin with.

> *A few R classes do not obey the conventions described here. We will point out such classes as we encounter them.*

R classes are like `T` classes in some ways, and like `C` classes in other ways:

❑　Like `T` classes, they can be automatics or class members. Also like `T` classes, they can be copied (which just copies the handle), and the copy can be used like the original.

❑　As with `T` classes, it is very rare to refer to `R`s using pointers. They are usually passed by value or by reference.

❑　Like `C` classes, they own resources. Although `R` classes don't usually have a destructor, they do have a `Close()` function that has a similar effect (including setting the handle to zero, which is rather like zeroing the pointer to a `C` object). It's safe to call `Close()` twice — on an already closed `R` object it has no effect.

❏　Like C classes, they zero-initialize their handle value, so that functions can't be used until the handle is initialized. But the zero-initialization must be explicit, in a C++ constructor. There is no RBase corresponding to CBase.

memorymagic includes some functions that demonstrate various approaches to cleanup for R classes.

❏　Write file opens a file (c:\test.txt) and writes the text Hello world! into it

❏　Read file reads the text and prints it as an EIKON information message

❏　Delete file deletes the file

Each of these functions can be made to fail – you'll get a Not found error, for instance, if you delete the file when it hasn't been written, or it has already been deleted. You'll get Access denied if you write the file, set its properties to read only (using the shell), and then try to write to it again or delete it.

Without Error Checking

The simplest of these functions is Delete file. It could have been written, without error checking, as follows:

```
case EExampleCmdDeleteFile:
    {
    RFs fs;
    fs.Connect();
    fs.Delete(KTextFileName);
    fs.Close();
    }
```

The logic here is simple: you have to open a file server session (an RFs) before you can do anything, and close it afterwards. While the session is open, you can use it to perform file server operations, such as the Delete() function above. This open and close pattern is typical for R classes that communicate with servers.

Obviously, we don't recommend programming without error checking. Let's look at some approaches that will work *and* handle errors properly.

Rs as Member Variables

If the RFs were a member variable of CExampleAppUi, the code could have been written, with full error checking, as:

```
case EExampleCmdDeleteFile:
    {
    User::LeaveIfError(iFs.Connect());
    User::LeaveIfError(iFs.Delete(KTextFileName));
    iFs.Close();
    }
```

It's also important that CExampleAppUi's C++ destructor include a call to iFs.Close(), so that the RFs is closed even if the CExampleAppUI object is deleted.

Opening and closing server sessions is relatively expensive (approximately 300 microseconds for a file server session on a Psion Series 5mx), so it's better to keep server sessions open for a whole program, if you know you're going to need them a lot.

We could do this by including the User::LeaveIfError(iFs.Connect()) in the CExampleAppUi::ConstructL(). Then, the Delete file handler would become very simple indeed:

```
case EExampleCmdDeleteFile:
    {
    User::LeaveIfError(iFs.Delete(KTextFileName));
    }
```

This is a common pattern for using R objects. At the cost of a small amount of memory needed to maintain an open session throughout the lifetime of the application, we save having to open and close a session for every operation that uses one.

In fact, it's so common to need an RFs that the CONE environment provides one for you. I could have used:

```
case EExampleCmdDeleteFile:
    {
    User::LeaveIfError(
        iCoeEnv->FsSession().Delete(KTextFileName)
        );
    }
```

Then I wouldn't have needed to allocate my own RFs at all. It's a very good idea to re-use CONE's RFs, since an RFs object uses up significant amounts of memory.

Error Code Returns versus L Functions

RFs does not provide functions such as ConnectL() or DeleteL() that would leave with a TInt error code if an error were encountered. Instead, it provides Connect() and Delete(), which *return* a TInt error code (including KErrNone if the function returned successfully). This means you have to check errors explicitly using User::LeaveIfError(), which does nothing if its argument is KErrNone or a positive number, but leaves with the value of its argument if the argument is negative.

A few low-level EPOC APIs operate this way; their areas of application are a few important circumstances in which it would be inappropriate to leave:

❑   Many file or communications functions are called speculatively, to test whether a file is there or a link is up. It is information, not an error, if these functions return with 'not found' or a similar result.

❑   Symbian's implementation of the C Standard Library provides a thin layer over EPOC's native RFile and communications APIs that returns standard C-type error codes. It's much easier to handle errors directly than by trapping them. In any case, standard library programs don't have a cleanup stack.

Granted, leaves could have been trapped. But that was judged undesirably expensive. Instead, when you want a leave, you have to call `User::LeaveIfError()`. That's a little bit costly too, but not as expensive as trapping leaves.

Some truly ancient code in EPOC was written assuming that there might not be a cleanup stack at all. But this isn't a sensible assumption these days, and is certainly no justification for designing APIs that don't use L functions. All native EPOC code should ensure it has a cleanup stack, and design its APIs accordingly. The GUI application framework, and the server framework, provide you with a cleanup stack, so you only have to construct your own when you're writing a text console program.

> **If you are using components with `TInt` error codes, don't forget to use `User::LeaveIfError()` where you need it.**

Rs on the Cleanup Stack

Sometimes, you need to create and use an R object as an automatic variable rather than as a member of a C class. In this case, you need to be able to push to the cleanup stack. There are two options available to you:

❏   Use `CleanupClosePushL()`

❏   Do it directly: make a `TCleanupItem` consisting of a pointer to the R object, and a static function that will close it

A third option, the `TAutoClose<>` template, is now deprecated.

If you have an item with a `Close()` function, then `CleanupClosePushL()` (a global non-member function) will ensure that `Close()` is called when the item is popped-and-destroyed by the cleanup stack. C++ templates are used for this, so `Close()` does not have to be virtual.

The code below, taken from `memorymagic`, demonstrates how to use `CleanupClosePushL()`:

```
case EMagicCmdDeleteFile:
    {
    RFs fs;
    CleanupClosePushL(fs);
    User::LeaveIfError(fs.Connect());
    User::LeaveIfError(fs.Delete(KTextFileName));
    CleanupStack::PopAndDestroy(); // fs
    }
```

You just call `CleanupClosePushL()` after you've declared your object, and before you do anything that could leave. You can then use `CleanupStack::PopAndDestroy()` to close the object when you've finished with it.

185

You can look up the `TCleanupItem` class in `e32base.h`: it contains a pointer and a cleanup function. Anything pushed to the cleanup stack is actually a cleanup item. `CleanupStack::PushL(CBase*)`, `CleanupStack::PushL(TAny*)`, and `CleanupClosePushL()` simply create appropriate cleanup items and push them.

There are two other related functions:

❑ `CleanupReleasePushL()` works like `CleanupClosePushL()` except that it calls `Release()` instead of `Close()`.

❑ `CleanupDeletePushL()` is effectively the same as `CleanupStack::PushL(TAny*)`.

You can create your own `TCleanupItems` and push them if the cleanup functions offered by these facilities are insufficient.

User Errors

The cleanup framework is so good that you can use it to handle other types of error besides resource shortages.

One common case is handling errors in user input. The function in a dialog that processes the OK button (an overridden `CEikDialog::OkToExitL()`) must:

❑ Get each value from the dialog's controls

❑ Validate the values (the controls will have done basic validation, but you may need to do some more at this stage, taking the values of the whole dialog into account)

❑ Pass the values to a function that performs some action

A typical programming pattern for `OkToExitL()` is to use automatics to contain the T-type value, or to point to the C-type values, in each control.

If you find that something is invalid, at any stage in the `OkToExitL()` processing, you will need to:

❑ Display a message to the user indicating what the problem is

❑ Clean up all the values you have extracted from the dialog controls – that is, anything you have allocated on the heap

❑ Return

A great way to do this is to push all your control values, and any other temporary variables you need, to the cleanup stack, and then use `CEikonEnv`'s `LeaveWithInfoMsg()` function. This displays an info-message, and then leaves with `KErrLeaveNoAlert`. As part of standard leave processing, all the variables you have allocated will be cleaned up. EIKON's active scheduler traps the leave, as usual, but for this particular error code, instead of displaying a dialog with the error code in it, EIKON doesn't display anything.

Some people have realized independently that the framework is good for this, and tried to achieve the same effect by coding `User::Leave(KErrNone)`*. This appears to work, because you don't get the EIKON error message. But in fact the EIKON error handler isn't called at all, so you don't get some other useful things either. So use* `iEikonEnv->LeaveWithInfoMsg()` *or, if you don't need an info-message, use the same function but specify a resource ID of zero.*

In the next chapter, the `streams` program includes an example of this pattern.

More on Panics

So far, I've dealt with how you can respond to errors that are generated by the environment your program runs in – whether out-of-memory errors, files not being there, or bad user input.

One type of error that can't be handled this way is programming errors. These have to be fixed by rewriting the offending program. During development, that's usually your program (though, like the rest of us, you probably start by blaming the compiler!). The best thing EPOC can do for you here is to panic your program – to stop it from running as soon as the error has been detected, and to provide diagnostic information meaningful enough for you to use.

The basic function here is `User::Panic()`. Here's a panic function I use in my Battleships game, from `\pep\battleships\controller.cpp`:

```
static void Panic(TInt aPanic)
    {
    _LIT(KPanicCategory, "BSHIPS-CTRL");
    User::Panic(KPanicCategory, aPanic);
    }
```

`User::Panic()` takes a panic category string, which must be 16 characters or less (otherwise, the panic function gets panicked!), and a 32-bit error code.

On the emulator debug build, we've seen what this does: the kernel's panic function includes a `DEBUGGER()` macro that allows the debugger to be launched with the full context from the function that called panic. That gives you a reasonable chance of finding the bug.

On a release build, on a real EPOC machine, a panic simply displays a dialog titled Program closed, citing the process name, and the panic category and number you identified. Typically, it's real users who see this dialog, though you might be lucky enough to see it during development, before you release the program. To find bugs raised this way, you essentially have to guess the context from what the user was doing at the time, and the content of the Program closed dialog. You'll need inspiration and luck.

You can shorten the odds by being specific about the panic category and number, and by good design and testing before you release.

Although technically it's a thread that gets panicked, in fact EPOC will close the entire process. On a real machine, that means your application will get closed. On the emulator, there is only one Windows process, so the whole emulator is closed.

The standard practice for issuing panics is to use **assert macros**, of which there are two: __ASSERT_DEBUG and __ASSERT_ALWAYS. There are various schools of thought about which one to use when: as a general rule, put as many as you can into your debug code, and as few as you can into your release code. Do your own debugging: don't let your users do it for you.

Here's one of the many places where I might potentially call my Panic() function:

```
void CGameController::HandleRestartRequest()
    {
    __ASSERT_ALWAYS(IsFinished(),
        Panic(EHandleRestartReqNotFinished));

    // Transition to restarting
    SetState(ERestarting);
    }
```

The pattern here is __ASSERT_ALWAYS(*condition*, *expression*), where the *expression* is evaluated if the *condition* is not true. When the controller is asked to handle a restart request, I assert that the controller is in a finished state. If not, I panic with panic code EHandleRestartReqNotFinished. This gets handled by the Panic() function above, so that if this code were taken on a production machine, it would show Program closed with a category of BSHIPS-CTRL and a code of 12. The latter comes from an enumeration containing all my panic codes:

```
enum TPanic {
    EInitiateNotBlank,
    EListenNotBlank,
    ERestartNotFinished,
    ESetGdpNotBlank,
    ESetPrefBadState,
    EHitFleetNotMyTurn,
    EAbandonNotMyTurn,
    EResendBadState,
    EBindBadState,
    ESendStartNoPrefs,
    EHandleRequestBadOpcode,
    EHandleResponseBadOpcode,
    EHandleRestartReqNotFinished,
    EHandleStartReqNotAccepting,
    EHandleAbandondReqNotOppTurn,
    EHandleHitReqNotOppTurn,
    EHandleStartRespNotStarting,
    EHandleHitRespNotOppTurn,
    };
```

Incidentally, I considered it right to assert the IsFinished() condition, even in production code. The Battleships controller is a complex state machine, responding to events from systems outside my control, and responding to software that's difficult to debug even though it's within my control. I might not catch all the errors in it before I release, even if I test quite thoroughly. In this case, I want to be able to catch errors after release, so I use __ASSERT_ALWAYS instead of __ASSERT_DEBUG.

Testing Engines and Libraries

The EIKON framework includes a cleanup stack, a trap harness, and (in debug mode) heap balance checking and keys to control the heap failure mode. This makes it practically impossible for an EPOC developer to create a program with built-in heap imbalance under non-failure conditions, very easy to handle failures, and easy to test for correct operation – including heap balance – under failure conditions.

Lower- and intermediate-level EPOC APIs don't use the EIKON framework and therefore don't get these tools as part of their environment. To test these APIs, they must be driven either from an EIKON application, or from a test harness that constructs and manipulates the heap failure, heap balance checking, and other tools. Happily, this is quite easy, and test harnesses can be used to test engines very aggressively for proper resource management, even under failure conditions.

As an example of the kind of component for which you might wish to do this, take the engine for EPOC Sheet. The engine manipulates a grid of cells whose storage is highly optimized for compactness. Each cell contains an internal format representing the contents of that cell, perhaps including a formula that might be evaluated. The engine supports user operations on the sheet, such as entering new cells, deleting cells, or copying (including adjusting relative cell references). All of this is pure data manipulation – exactly the kind of thing that should be done with an engine module, rather than being tied to a GUI application. In this situation, you would want to test the engine firstly to verify the accuracy of its calculations, and secondly for its memory management, both under success conditions and failure due to memory shortage.

Firstly, you'd develop a test suite for testing the accuracy of calculations. The test suite would contain one or more programs of the following form:

❑ A command-line test program that loads the engine DLL but has no GUI. The test program will need to create its own cleanup stack and trap harness, like `hellotext`'s, because there's no GUI environment to give us these things for free.

❑ A test function that performs a potentially complex sequence of operations, and checks that their results are as expected. Think carefully, and aggressively, about the kinds of things you need to test.

❑ Heap check macros to ensure that the test function (and the engine it's driving) releases all memory that it allocates.

Secondly, you'd use that test suite during the entire lifetime of the development project – in early, pre-release testing, and post-release maintenance phases

❑ Every time you release your engine for other colleagues to use, run it through all tests. Diagnose *every* problem you find, before making a release. The earlier in the development cycle you pick up and solve problems, the better.

❑ If you add new functionality to the engine, but you have already released your engine for general use, then test the updated engine with the old test code. This will ensure that your enhancement (or fix) doesn't break any established, working function. This is **regression testing**.

Finally, you can combine a test function with the heap failure tools to perform high-stress, out-of-memory testing. A test harness might look like this:

```
for(TInt i = 1; i < KMaxHeapFailureTest; i++)
    {
    __UHEAP_MARK
    __UHEAP_SETFAIL(RHeap::EDeterministic, i);
    TRAPD(error, TestFunction());
    if(!error)
        break;
    __UHEAP_SETFAIL(RHeap::ENone,0)
    __UHEAP_MARKEND
    }
```

This loop runs the test function in such a way that each time through, one more successful heap allocation is allowed. It is guaranteed that there will be a KErrNoMemory error (if nothing else) that will cause a leave and cleanup. Any failure to clean up properly will be caught by the heap balance checks. The loop terminates either when the maximum number of iterations has completed, or when the test function completes without error.

Comparisons with Other Systems

EPOC's approach to resource management is a key part in fulfilling the requirements of handheld, resource-constrained computers.

We can see this if we compare EPOC to some other well-known systems, including its peers in the handheld sector. I'll briefly review the approaches taken by current Windows CE, Palm OS, C++ and Java.

Windows CE

From a programming perspective, Windows CE's greatest attraction is that is uses an extended subset of the Win32 APIs found in desktop versions of Windows. Experienced desktop Windows programmers can port their code (if it is written at a fairly basic Win32 level) to Windows CE without much adaptation.

But this attraction is also Windows CE's greatest weakness. The Win32 APIs were not designed to handle errors on every resource allocation, or to clean up properly. Nothing is done to reinforce good habits in Win32 programmers, especially in the desktop environment, which has become more and more forgiving. Programmers don't always check return codes, and don't always handle them well. To demonstrate what happens in a more hostile environment, try setting your PC's swap file size to only 1MB on an old-fashioned PC with less than about 64MB RAM. Boot up, open a random set of applications and large documents, and observe their failure modes. Do they fail cleanly? Is any of your work lost? It's not a pretty sight.

Because Windows CE is marketed to developers on the basic assumption that you don't have to change much in your existing Win32 code, there's no option to implement memory management that would alter every function call in existing source code. Instead, Windows CE's designers implemented a retrospective monitor/sweeper system. The CE system monitors available memory and, when it is running low, sweeps through all applications, asking them to release memory. This works with only loose cooperation between the system and applications – or, put another way, imposes only minimal requirements for change on existing Win32 programs.

When Windows CE's monitor detects that only a small amount of memory is still free (say, 256K or 64K), or when an allocation is about to fail due to an out-of-memory condition, the system sends a WM_HIBERNATE message to all applications. Each application must then try to free up some memory. The user may also be asked to close some applications. Ideally, this works fine, and the system continues on its way.

But if the applications *don't* free memory, or the user *doesn't* close some applications, the system takes more radical action: it may kill applications, with data loss. Applications are killed in reverse Z order – that is, the application that's furthest in the background is killed first. You can easily verify this by experimentation with a Windows CE device, and the only really safe way to deal with it is to save all application data when your application loses focus.

Windows CE's memory management is not tailored to the requirements of small systems, nor is it in any sense industrial strength. It is *possible* to write individual industrial-strength applications, libraries or servers for Windows CE, but the system provides little support for doing so, and in practice few applications take the necessary precautions.

Palm OS

Like EPOC, Palm OS was designed from the outset for small, memory-constrained environments. The APIs and system design convey this clearly, and every Palm programmer knows this from the outset.

Palm OS maintains a very small memory footprint by simple application design, and by closing applications when they are not in foreground. When an application is closed, it is *required* to save data. Most application data is stored in the Palm database manager, which handles saving as a routine part of the application.

Although Palm OS doesn't provide special cleanup support, cleanup comes at regular intervals anyway, because applications are so frequently closed. The Palm system design is very well suited to its task, though it would be difficult to scale this approach to a larger environment –for example, to support multitasking without closing down background applications, or to support a large number of active servers.

Windows CE can be compared quite usefully with Palm OS. Palm applications in the background are effectively in deep hibernation. Windows CE's shallow hibernation doesn't protect background applications from getting killed, so when Windows CE applications go into the background they have to save data – like Palm applications – in order to be truly safe. Palm OS's system design has the advantage of being fit for its intended purpose, but it's hard to scale up. Windows CE can clearly be scaled up (as you'd expect of a system that was initially scaled down!), but can only be made fit for its intended purpose by applications taking Palm-like precautions.

C++

The C++ language contains its own exception-handling system, using try, throw, and catch. Why does EPOC not use this system?

Historically, this system wasn't available when EPOC was designed. GCC didn't have any exception handling, and Microsoft Visual C++'s exception handling was considered insufficiently reliable, in 1995.

Additionally, EPOC doesn't use all the features of C++, support for which adds complexity to C++'s exception-handling. In particular, EPOC doesn't use multiple inheritance (except for interfaces), and the conventions for C and T classes are constrained compared with all the possibilities offered by the C++ language. EPOC also uses only a 32-bit integer for error codes, which most of the time works very well – a whole class hierarchy for exceptions is not needed. This means that the exception framework needed by EPOC is much simpler than that required by C++.

A regrettable consequence of EPOC's non-support for C++ exceptions is that standard C++ code, including code written with the C++ Standard Library, cannot easily be ported to EPOC. It is possible that updates to the EPOC tool chain – including an updated GCC compiler – may make this easier in future.

Java

Since Java is a popular programming environment, which also supports exceptions, it's interesting to compare EPOC's exception support with Java's.

As we have seen, cleanup requires firstly that you can throw exceptions, and secondly that you can deal with resources that are no longer needed. Java uses throw to raise exceptions, but unlike EPOC's User::Leave(), which uses only a 32-bit integer to indicate the type of exception, Java's throw creates an object of theoretically any class.

Superficially, Java's garbage collection is sufficient to deal with resources that are no longer needed. This is only true, however, in circumstances where EPOC would use pure T and C classes, for heap-based data. Where resources reside elsewhere (as for EPOC's R classes), simple garbage collection is not sufficient.

Java supports a finalize() method that works in a similar way to a C++ destructor or an EPOC R class's Close() function. The Java documentation cites file descriptors and graphics contexts as examples of classes that need to finalize() themselves by freeing associated server resources. finalize() can be called by the Java garbage collector when it gets around to cleaning up an object, or explicitly by user code if it is important to free the object at a specific time. If finalize() is called explicitly by user code, it may be called again by the Java garbage collector. For this reason, Java recommends that finalize() methods be coded defensively, so that nothing inappropriate happens when they are called twice.

Java's try-catch-finally syntax provides a mechanism akin to EPOC's cleanup stack, allowing code such as this:

```
try {
    open resource
    do something which might throw an exception
} catch (Exception e) {
    handle exception
} finally {
    close the resource (probably using finalize())
}
```

Java guarantees that the finally block will be executed, whether or not an exception occurs during the try block.

By using `finally` and `finalize()`, you can ensure that critical resources are properly freed as soon as you no longer need them.

Java's convenience comes at a price in terms of execution time and run-time RAM utilization, which are both less favorable than the requirements of EPOC C++. Even the best implementations of Java cannot avoid this. Nevertheless, Java does provide the language support that enables developers to implement proper resource management, even in relatively resource-constrained environments.

Summary

Memory and other resources are scarce in typical EPOC environments. Your programs *will* encounter resource shortages, and must be able to deal with them. You must avoid memory leaks, both under normal circumstances and when dealing with errors. EPOC provides an industrial-strength framework to support you, with very low programmer overhead, and very compact code.

In this chapter, we've seen:

❑ How the EIKON debug keys, and their simulated failures, and the heap-checking tools built into CONE, mean that testing your code is easy

❑ How EPOC's naming convention helps with error handling and cleanup

❑ Allocating and destroying objects on the heap – how to preserve heap balance, what to do if allocation fails, how to re-allocate safely

❑ How leaves work, the `TRAP()` and `TRAPD()` macros, and EPOC error codes

❑ How to spot an `L` function

❑ When to use your own traps

❑ When and how to use the cleanup stack

❑ Two-phase construction, using `ConstructL()` and the `NewL()` and `NewLC()` factory functions

❑ What `CBase` provides for any `C` class to help with cleanup

❑ Cleanup for `R` and `T` classes

❑ How to panic a program, and test engines and libraries

I've covered a lot of material in this chapter, and you could be forgiven for not taking it all in at once. Don't worry. If you only remember one thing from this chapter, remember that cleanup is vital. You'll see cleanup-related disciplines in all the code throughout the rest of the book, and you'll be able to come back here for reference when you need to.

7

Streams, Stores, and File-based Applications

In this chapter, we'll cover EPOC's file and data management in more detail. I'll introduce the main conventions for using files and the main APIs.

In Chapter 3, I introduced the file server and its services, including the c: RAM disk, z:, which maps all files in the ROM, and (in many EPOC machines) the d: removable CF card drive.

The conventions for using files, streams, and stores, including how to support embedded documents and where applications go, are dictated by the **application architecture**. We've already seen some of these conventions, such as the need to put applications in \System\apps*appname**appname*.app.

Because these conventions strongly influence EPOC's data management, I'll start the chapter by explaining them, before moving on to look at the file- and data-related APIs. The last part of the chapter provides an explanation of the various ways streams are written, stored, and read.

The Application Architecture

Psion's SIBO system included an Agenda application with a neat facility: you could attach a Word document to an agenda item. So, you could put a meeting in your agenda and then, when you went to the meeting, you could take notes in a memo attached to your agenda. Not just a trivial plain text memo either: you could use the full power of the word processor, with rich text, outline view, printing, and so on.

As a result, for many SIBO users, the agenda *was* their filing system: you could associate notes exactly with the event at which you took them, and you didn't have to invent filenames for every memo you created. The memo feature put a huge distance between SIBO and any rival systems on the market.

In EPOC, we obviously wanted to repeat this success. In fact, EPOC had to do better:

❑ We needed a better architecture than the kludge that had been used to attach memos to agenda items in SIBO

❑ There would be a much richer range of data types available in EPOC, and we wanted to embed anything in anything – memos in agenda, spreadsheets in Word documents, icons, sketches, and voice memos in text, photos in the contacts database, you name it

❑ We wanted the system to be open, so that developers could write new embeddable objects and new containers

❑ EPOC introduced serious graphics, so we wanted to be able not only to embed an object with a nice icon, but also to embed an object as a picture

And, as usual, we wanted to do this with maximum code re-use and compactness, and supreme ease-of-use.

If EPOC was going to meet the 'embed anything in anything' requirement, there would have to be a uniform overall structure for both applications and documents – where a **document** is an application's data.

There would also have to be conventions to detect installed applications and query their capabilities. As we've seen, an installed application must be in a directory of the form \system\apps*appname*\, and must be called *appname*.app.

In order to make C++ documents embed efficiently, EPOC requires that C++ applications must be DLLs. So when you launch an embedded document, a new DLL is loaded *in the same process as the embedding application's DLL* – in fact, the embedding application is run in the same thread as the embedded application. This is *much* more efficient than systems requiring inter-process communication, and because the design is simple, it's also more robust.

Virtually everything else in the resulting application architecture flows from these requirements. The application architecture:

❑ Specifies the association between document files and applications

❑ Says how to associate basic information with an application – including an icon, a caption, whether it is file-based, whether it can be embedded etc.

❑ Includes an API that you can interrogate to get lists of all installed applications, all embeddable applications, all running applications etc.

❑ Specifies the location of an application's .ini file

The two components in EPOC that really deal with applications closely are the shell (responsible for launching applications and for opening documents with the right application) and EIKON (the application framework). It follows that these two components are heavily dependent on the application architecture and its APIs.

File-based Applications

Document embedding isn't everything, and, in retrospect, we slightly over-emphasized it in the original application architecture as found in EPOC R1. In subsequent releases, the application architecture has been extended to include:

- ❑ Support for applications that don't use EPOC's native file format: this is done by associating a MIME type with a file according to industry standards so that, for instance, the type of an HTML file is text/html. You can launch an HTML file from the Shell and from within the EPOC web browser. In EPOC R1, you had to open non-native files from the application using File | Open.

- ❑ A better system for recognizing non-native files and application types, such as Java applications.

- ❑ Viewing attachments, such as those on e-mails.

There are two important types of file-based application:

- ❑ An application like Word, Sheet, Sketch, or Record is clearly file-based. You can save a Word document into a file, and load one from a file.

- ❑ An application like Agenda or Data is clearly file-based, but you don't load and save the whole file at once. Instead, you use the file as a database and you load and save individual *entries* at the same time. For efficiency, you also maintain some index data in RAM.

The following diagram illustrates the difference:

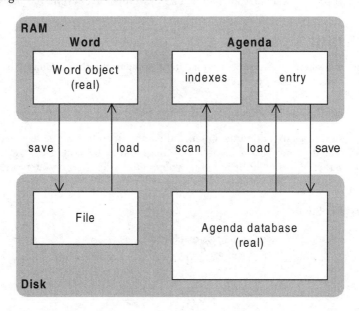

There are some similarities between these two types of file-based application: for instance, in either case, you can open the file by select-and-open from the shell.

But there are real differences also. In load/save type applications, we tend to think that the 'real' document is in RAM: the file is just a saved version of the real document. In database-type applications, we tend to think that the 'real' document is the database: each entry is just a RAM copy of something in the database. The disciplines for managing the documents as a whole are therefore quite different.

We decided that it was meaningful to make load/save type documents embeddable, but for database type documents it would be much harder and also less useful. So database type documents cannot be embedded (though they can certainly embed).

Finally, there are a few other ways an application handle files:

❏   An application like Calc is clearly *not* file-based (though you could make it so, if you wished!). It neither loads nor saves the state of its calculation.

❏   Similarly, there is no need for many test applications to be file-based.

❏   An application like Email clearly deals with files: it has several directories and files containing inbox, outbox, other folders, and all the messages. On the other hand, no sensible Email program – including those on the PC – would expose these directories and files to the user: it would be damaging for the user to try to manipulate them from the Shell (or Windows Explorer).

In all three cases, you can't open an application by opening a *file* belonging to that application from the shell.

So the idea of **file-based application** has a particular meaning in EPOC. Load/save applications like Word and so on are file-based and potentially embeddable. Database applications like Agenda are also file-based, but can't be embedded. Applications like Calc and Email aren't file-based.

Documents and Doors

The application architecture uses the word **document** to mean the thing you're editing, whether it's the main document or an embedded document.

When you launch a file from the shell, it opens the main document with the correct application.

If the application supports embedded documents, then you need to be able to create them, and you need to be able to see the ones you've created and to open them. At the user interface level, an embedded document is represented by a **door** – you open the door, and you go into the embedded document.

There are two types of door:

❏   Iconic: before it's opened, an icon is displayed

❏   Glass: before it's opened, you can see the content of the embedded object

You can see both types in the following screenshot:

The business of drawing glass doors is a graphics issue, which I'll briefly tackle in Chapter 15.

Document formats are a data issue. The document format is essentially the same whether an application is embedded or not. Even the way a document is associated with its application is essentially the same whether the document is embedded or not.

> **A key implication of this is that EPOC native documents are not recognized based on their file extension — because you don't get file names in embedded documents.**

So a file that's displayed on the EPOC shell view as Agenda has no hidden file extension, and file save dialogs don't add a default extension for you – as happens on Windows. If an Agenda icon appears next to the file, that's because its *internal* format indicates it's an Agenda file.

Strictly, documents are not the same as files. But it's easy to confuse them because file-based applications are very often called document-based applications in the EPOC literature.

User and System Files

From the user's perspective, there are just two types of file:

❑ Document files, which contain the end-user's own data

❑ System files, which contain frightening and mysterious things, which shouldn't be touched because it'll probably stop something working

For most end users, it's actually better to pretend that there's only *one* type of file – document files – and hide the system files altogether.

So, all system files are given a location in the \System\ folder – on whatever drive, z:, c:, or another. By default, the shell (and EIKON file-related dialogs) doesn't show the user the \System\ folder or any of its sub-folders. Your programs, your application's .ini files, and even the user data files maintained by programs like Email, should reside somewhere in the \System\ directory, so that end users can't find them using the shell.

As a developer, you need to get involved with system files. As I suggested in Chapter 2, you should use the shell's Tools | Preferences dialog to show system files.

The shell maintains a 'default folder' for end-user document files. The initial setting for this default is language-specific – on an English Psion Series 5 machine, it's c:\Documents\. You can change this to any drive and any folder you like. You can also store documents in folders other than the default – either subfolders of the default folder, or folders outside the default folder.

> *For many end users, any kind of file system is a source of unnecessary and worrisome choice. Future EPOC-based smartphone products will completely hide the file system from the user interface, with no option to expose it.*

> *System files are not indicated by the system attribute bit in the file's directory entry. That makes life too awkward when interchanging data with PCs. It's their location in the \System\ tree on some drive that counts.*

Application Information Files

If you create a GUI application and deliver it purely as, say, helloeik.app and helloeik.rsc – as we did in Chapter 2, then the application icon on the Extras bar is an ugly question-mark, and the application's caption is given as HELLOEIK. Furthermore, the application architecture makes default assumptions about the capabilities of the application – specifically, that it can't be embedded.

If you want a nice caption and a nice icon, or if you want to allow your application to be embedded, you have to code an **application information file** or AIF. In Chapter 13, I'll show how to create helloeik.aif to give an icon and captions to my GUI hello world application.

Summary of File Naming and Location Conventions

Here's a summary of the file types we've met so far, along with the folder and file naming conventions required by the application architecture:

Type	Name	Location
Application document files	Any name	Any folder on any read/write drive. \Documents\ is an initial default suggestion, in English-language locales
Non-document application files	Any name	In \System\ on any drive, according to requirements
Application program	*appname*.app	\System\Apps*appname*\ on any drive (including z: for built-in applications)
AIF	*appname*.aif	Same as .app
Resource file	*appname*.r??	Same as .app
.ini file	*appname*.ini	c:\System\Apps*appname*\ – only c: is allowed, so that the .ini file is (a) on a read/write drive and (b) always accessible to an application, even if removable media are changed

Type	Name	Location
Application-specific DLLs	`*.dll`	Same as `.app`
Shared DLLs	`*.dll`	`\System\Libs\`, ideally on same drive as `.app`
Shared `.exes`	`*.exe`	`\System\Programs\`, ideally on same drive as `.app`

Installing Software

To install software, you simply have to place the files in your application in the right directories. The application architecture is notified of changes in the file system, and updates its list of installed applications immediately, so that a new application and its icon appear immediately on the Extras bar.

There are three ways to install software:

- ❑ Manually copy each file using EPOC Connect, as we saw in Chapter 2. This method is suited only for developers and small applications.

- ❑ Installing from an installation package from your PC, using EPOC Connect

- ❑ Installing from an installation package on your EPOC machine, using Add/Remove programs on the control panel

These last two methods are friendlier for end users – you get to deal only with a single file, and you don't have to look at anything inside the `\System\` folder.

As a developer, you need to be able to produce installation packages. I'll explain how, in Chapter 13.

Introducing the APIs

Now that we've seen how the file system is used, it's time to look at the main file and data-related APIs. Here they are:

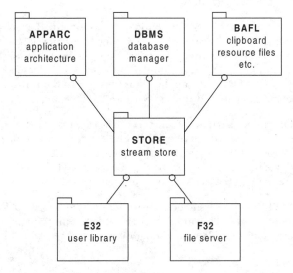

The file server provides fundamental file services such as drives, directories, and files, and installable file systems, for use by higher-level components. It also provides program-loading facilities required by E32 – which is why the file server is an integral part of EPOC's base.

Central to all native EPOC data handling is the **stream store**. Objects exchange data between RAM and streams using << and >> operators, or ExternalizeL() and InternalizeL() functions. Stores are just collections of streams. Native file and document formats use file stores and embedded stores. The APIs of the file server and the stream store will form the body of the material in the rest of this chapter.

I've introduced a lot of concepts here. As with the cleanup material, the main concepts will be reinforced throughout the body of the book, so don't feel you have to slow down and take everything in first time through.

I'll mention other aspects of the application architecture's APIs throughout the book. For example, resource files are important for GUI programs. I'll describe them in detail in Chapter 9.

Two features of EPOC's data management architecture that I won't be covering are its database management system, DBMS, and the clipboard.

The DBMS offers a relational database manager, including multiple tables in a single database, SQL or direct C++ APIs for both data definition and data manipulation, indexing, shared concurrent access, transactions with commit and revert, and incremental compaction of databases. The DBMS is documented in the EPOC C++ SDK and technical papers accessible from http://www.epocworld.com.

The clipboard API is specified in baclipb.h. It uses stream store technology and a single data file, clipbrd.dat, which is shared by all applications. This allows a copying program to put data on the clipboard in multiple formats, and a pasting program to select the best available format for its purposes. It is documented in the EPOC C++ SDK.

The File Server

The file server F32 offers a client API that allows user programs to manipulate drives, directories and files, and to read and write data in files.

F32 uses DOS-like conventions to offer up to 26 drives identified as a: to z:, a fully hierarchical directory structure, and long filenames incorporating almost any character – except those reserved by the file system itself. Directory names are separated by backslashes ('\', as in Windows), rather than by forward slashes ('/', as in UNIX). A period ('.') may be used to indicate an extension; although this has no special meaning to EPOC, some applications may assign their own meaning to them. A filename, *including* its drive and directory portion, may be up to 256 characters long.

Like Windows (and unlike UNIX), the file server is case preserving, but not case sensitive. In other words, if you create a file called My File, all EPOC directory operations will return the name My File with the original case. But if you search for My File, my file, MY file, or any other combination, the file My File will be returned. Clearly, this means that you can't have two files in the same directory whose names differ only in the cases of some of their letters.

The file server's API has been designed for easy mapping to POSIX APIs. The EPOC C standard library is built on top, using FILE and its associated functions to map to RFile and its member functions, and so on for other file-related operations.

The main classes in the file server API are:

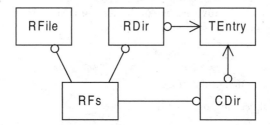

An `RFs` is a session from your program to the file server. You need a session for all file-related operations, and in order to be able to use other classes such as `RFile`, `RDir`, and `CDir` – whose purpose I'll explain below.

All these classes are defined in `f32file.h`.

File Server Sessions

All servers use session-based communication so that a client function such as `RFs::MkDir()` or `RFile::Write()` is converted into a message that's sent to the server. The requested function is performed in the server, and then any result is passed back to the client. It isn't necessary to understand how servers work in order to use them; all you need to know is that you can't do anything without a connected session – in the case of the file server, a connected `RFs`.

> *If you want to write a server, you need to understand them a lot more. I'll return to servers in Chapter 19.*

So the pattern for using the file server is:

- ❑ Connect an `RFs` to the file server
- ❑ Open a file, specifying which `RFs` to use
- ❑ Do what you want to do
- ❑ Close the file
- ❑ Close the `RFs` using `Close()`, since R objects don't have destructors

You can open any number of files or directories using a single `RFs`. You can carry an `RFs` as part of your application's object data, open it at the time you open your application, and close it when you finish. As we saw in the previous chapter, the CONE environment already has an open `RFs`, so you don't need to create one of your own from a GUI program: just use `iCoeEnv->FsSession()`.

> *`iCoeEnv` refers to `CCoeEnv`, the CONE environment. This in turn is the base class of `CEikonEnv`, the EIKON environment. We'll learn more about these classes in Chapter 9 and the following chapters.*

After you have closed the session, you won't be able to call any more member functions on objects that were opened using that session. You should make sure you close and clean up these objects – preferably before you close the session. In any case, when the session is closed, the server will clean up any server-side resources associated with the session.

RFs contains many useful file system-related operations:

- Manipulating the current directory
- Making, removing, and renaming directories
- Deleting and renaming files
- Changing directory and file attributes
- Notifying changes
- Manipulating drives and volumes
- Peeking at file data without opening the file (used by some file format recognizers)
- Adding and removing file systems
- System functions to control and check the status of the server

Check out the SDK for details.

The Current Directory

Most RFs-related functions are *stateless* – that is, the results of a function don't depend on any functions previously called. That's why you can share CONE's RFs with other DLLs used by your application.

RFs has just one item of state: its current directory. When you open an RFs, its current directory is set to c:\. You can use SetSessionPath() to change the current directory used by an open RFs. You can use SetDefaultPath() to change the initial current directory for all future RFs objects. The current directory includes the drive as well as directory names. So, unlike DOS, there is no concept of one current directory per drive.

The current directory is most useful for command-line tools written with the WINC build of EPOC. WINC *doesn't* set the current directory initially to c:\. Instead, it sets it to whatever the current directory was on the drive from which you started the WINC program. I'll explain WINC further in Chapter 8.

If you manipulate or rely on the current directory, make sure you use your own RFs rather than sharing one with other programs.

> *The current directory is irrelevant for most GUI programs, since EIKON file selector dialogs return full path and file names.*

Drives, File Systems, and Media

EPOC Release 5 supports three media formats:

❑ The ROM file system, which is assigned to z:, was built by the ROM builder, and is clearly read-only as far as EPOC programs are concerned.

❑ The RAM file system, which is assigned to c:, and shared with other users of RAM.

❑ CF card removable media: if present, the main CF drive is assigned to d:. CF (compact flash) requires little power to read, but rather more power to write. As battery power drains, it may become impossible to write to a CF drive. EPOC takes enormous care to ensure that a sector write is atomic (that is, it completes entirely, or it doesn't complete at all). In turn, higher-level components such as STORE and DBMS use formats and protocols that ensure failure to write CF media never results in a corrupt file.

The file server supports the addition of new file system drivers, either for networked drives or for new media types. Drivers may be added dynamically, without rebooting, and without interrupting any connected file server sessions.

The media configuration is an important variable of an EPOC machine. For example, the Psion Revo doesn't support removable media, and future EPOC-based smartphones won't even support conventional RAM-based c: – instead, they will use flash memory, so that c: data remains even when the machine's power is completely removed.

However, it's always safe to assume that an EPOC machine has a read-only z: drive and a read/write c: drive.

Files

An open file is represented by an RFile object. You can open a file with one of four RFile functions, each of which takes an RFs, so that the RFile has a session within which to communicate with the server. The 'open' functions are:

❑ Open(), which opens an existing file for either reading or writing

❑ Create(), which creates a new file for writing

❑ Replace(), which deletes an existing file and creates a new one for writing

❑ Temp(), which opens a temporary file and allocates a name to it

When you've opened a file, you can Read() from it into a TDes8, or Write() to it from a TDesC8. You can also Seek() to a position, and Flush() any server-side write buffers to the file.

Various access modes are supported: shared read, exclusive write, or shared write. Operations are blocked if they violate the access mode and existing sharing on the same file. You normally specify access mode when you open the file, although you can change it while the file is open using ChangeMode(). If you're using shared write access, you can use Lock() to claim temporary exclusive access to regions of the file, and then UnLock() later it.

While the file is open, you can change its name using Rename().

I'll be showing examples of opening, reading, and writing below. If you're interested in more details on the other functions, see the SDK.

205

Directories

A directory contains files and other directories, each of which is represented by a **directory entry** or simply, in file server API language, an **entry**.

The `RDir` class allows you to iterate through all the entries in a directory, while the `TEntry` type is used to contain a single entry.

It's expensive to call the file server once for each directory entry, so `RFs` provides high-level `GetDir()` functions that get more than one entry into a `CDir`.

You can change attributes of directory entries, including the hidden, system, read-only, and archive bits. The only bit with a really unambiguous meaning is read-only. If a file is specified as read-only, then you won't be able to write to it, or erase it.

Hidden files are optionally hidden by some higher-level components. System files are optionally hidden by some higher-level components. These attributes are supported for strict compatibility with VFAT, but usage conventions in the PC world are confused, and they aren't important in EPOC, so it's probably best not to use them. If you want to conceal files from average end users, use the `\System\` folder.

Directory entry timestamps are maintained by EPOC in UTC, not local time, so that backup programs – which are timestamp-based – don't get confused when there's a time zone change.

Cracking Filenames

Code that manipulates filenames is tricky. Potentially, a filename contains four parts:

❑   The drive (a single letter and a colon)

❑   The path (a list of directories starting and ending with a backslash)

❑   The filename (if an extension is specified, everything before the final dot; if not, everything after the final backslash)

❑   The extension (everything after the final dot (after the final backslash))

> Don't attempt to manipulate filenames yourself. Use EPOC's `TParseBase` classes to do it for you.

EPOC offers a small class hierarchy for manipulating filenames:

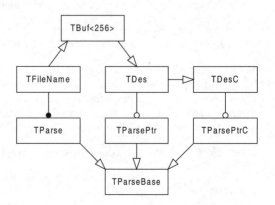

The base class for parsing is `TParseBase`. There are three implementations:

❑ `TParse`, which includes an entire filename and is therefore a large object

❑ `TParsePtr`, which functions like a `TPtr` in that it refers to a buffer outside itself that can be changed

❑ `TParsePtrC`, which functions like a `TPtrC` in that it refers to a buffer outside itself that cannot be changed

`TFileName` is simply `TBuf<256>`, a descriptor long enough to contain the longest possible file name.

> **TFileName is a big object — 268 bytes in a narrow build, and 524 bytes in a Unicode build. For this reason, you should never allocate or pass a TFileName on the stack. Where possible, use an HBufC* or some other descriptor type to contain the filename in as little space as possible.**

For instance, if you *know* that a certain filename is only 20 characters long, you could use a `TBuf<20>` to contain it.

The concrete `TParseXxx` classes allow you to query or manipulate a filename:

❑ `TParsePtrC` uses an existing filename referred to by a `const TDesC&`. It allows you to use all the query functions supported by the `TParseBase` class, which we'll examine shortly.

❑ `TParsePtr` uses an existing filename referred to by a `TDes&` parameter.

❑ `TParse` contains the filename as a `TFileName`. This is a big object, so don't use a `TParse` if a `TParsePtr` or `TParsePtrC` will do.

`TParseBase`'s query functions allow you to extract each element of a full filename: the drive, the path, the drive-and-path, the filename, the extension, the name-and-extension, or the full filename (which includes everything). You can ask whether the drive, path, filename, extension, or name-and-extension is present, and also whether the filename is in the root directory of a drive.

Wildcard matching using `'*'` for any string, and `'?'` for any individual character, is supported. You can ask whether the file specification contains any wildcards. Wildcard matching doesn't treat `'.'` as a special character (as it does on DOS).

If you're using `TParse` or `TParsePtr`, you can use `AddDir()` to add a single directory qualifier onto the end of the path, or `PopDir()` to take the final directory qualifier off the path.

`TParse`'s constructor allows you to pass three filenames that are parsed and stored in `TParse`'s internal `TFileName`. The drive, path, name of the file, and extension are taken from the first of the three filenames to specify them, respectively.

So you could pass `*.obj`, `hello.cpp` and `c:\projects\hello\`, and get `c:\projects\hello\hello.obj`. Not that EPOC is an ideal platform for running C++ compilers!

> **If you're specifying a directory name to any TParse-related class, you must include the trailing '\'.**

As usual in C++ source code, be careful to double all your '\' characters, as in _L("c:\\System\\"). For more details on all of this, see the SDK.

The streams Program

The streams program, in \pep\streams\, is an EIKON program that illustrates some aspects of the file server APIs we have mentioned above. It also displays some new EIKON techniques (how to use dialogs), and provides a very simple example of how to use the streams API, which I'll describe in the next section.

Here's a screenshot of the application in action:

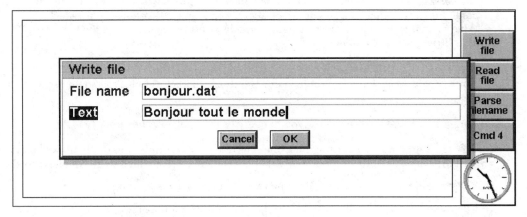

streams is based on helloeik. The toolbar (and menu, and hotkeys) provides three functions:

❑ **Write file** allows you to specify a filename and some text to write to it. The text is then displayed in the main application view.

❑ **Read file** allows you to specify a filename from which text will be read and displayed in the main application view.

❑ **Parse filename** uses a TParse object to crack the various components of the filename you specified.

The screenshot shows the **Write file** dialog. In a real EIKON program, you'd browse for a file using EIKON's file-selection dialogs, which offer much richer functionality. For the sake of this example, though, we're going down to basics and allowing the user to type in the filename directly. Here's the application structure:

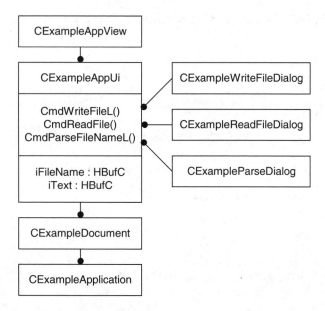

Compared with `helloeik`, this program has:

❏ Non-trivial command handling functions for its three main commands

❏ Dialogs that implement some of the handling of its three main commands

This is a well-structured EIKON program, and we'll describe its GUI-related aspects in more detail in Chapter 10.

> *It's well structured in the sense that it divides UI and non-UI parts well. It's not a conventional approach to loading and saving files in EIKON! We would normally do that by much better use of the application architecture, and EIKON's built-in dialogs.*

The main action is in `CExampleAppUi`'s `CmdXxxL()` functions, and the corresponding functions in their dialogs' post-processing functions, titled `OkToExitL()`.

Connecting to the File Server

Originally, I coded `streams` to include an `RFs` object which I opened from the app UI's second-phase constructor – in addition to initializing the `iFileName` and `iText` strings:

```
void CExampleAppUi::ConstructL()
    {
    ...
    iFileName = iEikonEnv->AllocReadResourceL(R_EXAMPLE_INITIAL_FILE);
    iText = iEikonEnv->AllocReadResourceL(R_EXAMPLE_TEXT_HELLO);
    User::LeaveIfError(iFs.Connect());
    }
```

I closed the `RFs` again in the app UI's C++ destructor – as well as freeing the `iFileName` and `iText` strings:

```
CExampleAppUi::~CExampleAppUi()
    {
    iFs.Close();
    delete iText;
    delete iFileName;
    ...
    }
```

But, as we saw earlier, CONE provides its own `RFs` that can normally be used by other components too. So I deleted the `iFs` member, deleted initialization and destruction code for it, and changed all references to use `iCoeEnv->FsSession()` instead.

Writing a File

The file writing command handler invokes `CExampleWriteFileDialog` and, after you press the OK button or the *Enter* key, its `OkToExitL()` function is called. It's quite a lump of code, so I'll take it a step at a time. First, I get the filename:

```
TBool CExampleWriteFileDialog::OkToExitL(TInt /* aKeycode */) // termination
    {
    // Get filename
    CEikEdwin* edwin = STATIC_CAST(CEikEdwin*,
                                    Control(EExampleControlIdFileName));
    HBufC* fileName = edwin->GetTextInHBufL();

    // Check it's even been specified
    if(!fileName)
        {
        TryChangeFocusToL(EExampleControlIdFileName);
        iEikonEnv->LeaveWithInfoMsg(R_EIK_TBUF_NO_FILENAME_SPECIFIED);
        }
    CleanupStack::PushL(fileName);
```

There's nothing obviously file-related in here, but there's some interesting descriptor and cleanup stack code. If this function succeeds, I have an `HBufC*` filename, which is pushed to the cleanup stack and contains a non-empty string. It can leave for numerous reasons, the most interesting of which is my call to `iEikonEnv->LeaveWithInfoMsg()`. This leaves, cleans up anything that needs cleaning up (nothing does, as it happens) and notifies the error to the user.

In fact, `iEikonEnv->LeaveWithInfoMsg()` reads its message from a resource file. To do this, a CONE function that uses CONE's built-in `RFs` is called. I'll also be using this in the next step, which is to check that the filename is valid:

```
    // Check it's a valid filename
    if(!iCoeEnv->FsSession().IsValidName(*fileName))
        {
        TryChangeFocusToL(EExampleControlIdFileName);
        iEikonEnv->LeaveWithInfoMsg(R_EIK_TBUF_INVALID_FILE_NAME);
        }
```

I just use `IsValidName()` to check whether it's valid: if not, I move the focus to the filename control and leave with an info-message. This time, I'm getting value from the cleanup stack. The `filename` will be popped and destroyed as part of this leave processing.

Now, I get the text to write to the file:

```
// Get the text string
edwin = STATIC_CAST(CEikEdwin*, Control(EExampleControlIdText));
HBufC* text = edwin->GetTextInHBufL();
if(!text)
    text = HBufC::NewL(0);
CleanupStack::PushL(text);
```

I don't really mind if it's blank this time but, for uniformity reasons, I allocate a zero-length string rather than using the zero pointer returned by this dialog API.

There's plenty of leaving code to follow, so I push the `text` to the cleanup stack before moving on to ensure that all the directories needed for the file exist:

```
// Ensure the directories etc. needed for the file exist
TInt err = iCoeEnv->FsSession().MkDirAll(*fileName);
if(err != KErrNone && err != KErrAlreadyExists)
    User::Leave(err);
```

The code makes a simple `MkDirAll()` call. This time you can see why RFs functions don't leave: I'm happy if either the directories didn't exist, and they were created successfully, or they did exist, and nothing happened. Otherwise I initiate a leave.

Now things get more delicate. I tentatively create the file, by opening it:

```
// Check whether it's going to be possible to create the file for writing
RFile file;
err = file.Create(iCoeEnv->FsSession(), *fileName, EFileWrite);
if(err != KErrNone && err != KErrAlreadyExists)
    User::Leave(err); // No need to close file, since it didn't open
```

`RFile::Create()` creates a new file if possible. If the file was already there, `err` contains `KErrAlreadyExists`: I want to know whether the user really wants to replace this file, and I'll check that in the next step. If the file wasn't there, but was created successfully by `RFile::Create()`, then `err` is set to `KErrNone`. In any other case, I leave.

If I had wanted to replace the file without checking with the user, I would have used `RFile::Replace()` to open the file. As it is, I want to check with the user:

```
// Check whether the user wants to replace the file, if it already exists
if(err == KErrAlreadyExists)
    {
    if(iEikonEnv->QueryWinL(R_EIK_TBUF_FILE_REPLACE_CONFIRM))
        User::LeaveIfError(file.Replace(iCoeEnv->FsSession(),
                                        *fileName,
                                        EFileWrite));
    else
        iEikonEnv->LeaveWithInfoMsg(0); // Let user try again
    }
```

If the attempt to create the file revealed that it already existed, I use an EIKON query dialog to confirm with the user. If the user insists, then I open the file again with `RFile::Replace()`. Any errors *this* time must be genuinely errors, so I don't have to check specific codes: I simply enclose the call with `User::LeaveIfError()`.

But if the user didn't want to replace the file, I leave silently with `iEikonEnv->LeaveWithInfoMsg(0)`. The leave helps to ensure that anything I've pushed to the cleanup stack is popped and destroyed. The 0 indicates that I'm not passing a resource ID of a message, because I don't want a message – none is needed, since the user knows exactly what has happened: they just replied No to a query.

Now I've done all the checks I need to make. I've verified user input, and I've verified that I can create the file for writing.

I prefer to separate UI code (like this) from engine code (which actually does things, like writing files), so I don't write the file from this function. Instead, I pass the parameters back to the app UI, which will process them when I return:

```
    file.Close();

    // Finished with user interaction: communicate parameters and return
    delete iAppUi->iFileName;
    iAppUi->iFileName = fileName;
    delete iAppUi->iText;
    iAppUi->iText = text;
    CleanupStack::Pop(2); // text, fileName
    return ETrue;
    }
```

I start by closing the file, because that's no longer needed here. I then set the `HBufC` pointers in the app UI to refer to the new strings, and make sure that whatever was there before is deleted. Finally, I pop both the new string pointers from the cleanup stack, because they are stored safely as member variables now.

The scene of processing now returns to my `WriteToFileL()` function:

```
    void CExampleAppUi::WriteFileL()
        {
        // Create a write stream on the file
        RFileWriteStream writer;
        writer.PushL();                    // Writer on cleanup stack
        User::LeaveIfError(writer.Replace(iCoeEnv->FsSession(),
                                          *iFileName,
                                          EFileWrite));

        // Write the text
        writer << *iText;
        writer.CommitL();

        // Finish
        CleanupStack::PopAndDestroy();     // Writer
        }
```

Having used an RFile to check that this file could be written, I *don't* use RFile::Write() to write it. Instead, I'm now using a higher-level class, RFileWriteStream, which is derived from RWriteStream. Every function you see in the code above, except the Replace() function I use to open the stream, is actually a member of the base class. RWriteStream provides a rich API including the insertion operator <<, which is used to write the text.

Before writing the text, I have to open the write stream — which in reality means opening the file and then initiating the stream for writing. And before I do that, I use PushL() so the write stream can push itself to the cleanup stack.

After writing, I commit the stream data using CommitL(), and then close the stream using CleanupStack::PopAndDestroy(). Committing to a write stream causes buffers to be flushed and sent to the file using RFile::Write(). This may fail, which is why CommitL() is a leaving function.

There are two good reasons for preferring to write this file through an RWriteStream rather than through an RFile:

❏ RFile::Write() is inconvenient to use and sometimes positively harmful. It's much safer to use the stream functions.

❏ RFile::Write() sends data *immediately* to the server, and RFile::Commit() flushes *server-side* buffers to the file. In contrast, RFileWriteStream keeps its buffers in memory on your thread's default heap. RFileWriteStream::CommitL() flushes *client-side* buffers by doing an RFile::Write(). If your pattern of writing activity consists of many operations that write small amounts of data, then writing to the file would involve significantly more client-server messages, which would severely impact performance.

RFileWriteStream includes a range of << functions for all EPOC's built-in types. As we'll see below, you can code an ExternalizeL() function on any class to allow it to be written out to any type of write stream using <<.

As usual, WriteFileL() is fully error checked. Every function that can leave is handled. Note that << can also leave, but doesn't have an L to indicate it!

WriteFileL() is extremely unlikely to fail in this case: only a few microseconds before calling it, I established that the conditions for writing were good, and I'm only writing a small amount of data. But it *could* fail, because conditions could change even in those few microseconds, and if I were writing a lot of data, it could easily fail with KErrDiskFull.

There is actually no way to ensure that WriteFileL() can't fail, so we have to handle failure in the calling function. This is one of those cases where the cleanup stack doesn't do what we want: we actually need a trap. Here's the code I use to invoke the dialog, and to call WriteFileL() under a trap:

```
void CExampleAppUi::CmdWriteFileL()
    {
    // Use a dialog to get parameters and verify them
    CEikDialog* dialog = new(ELeave) CExampleWriteFileDialog(this);
    if(!dialog->ExecuteLD(R_EXAMPLE_WRITE_FILE_DIALOG))
        return;
```

```
    // Write file under a trap
    TRAPD(err, WriteFileL());
    if(err)
        {
        delete iText;
        iText = 0;
        iCoeEnv->FsSession().Delete(*iFileName); // Don't check errors here!
        iAppView->DrawNow();
        User::Leave(err);
        }

    // Update view
    iAppView->DrawNow();
    }
```

The normal sequence of processing here is that I invoke the dialog (using a terse syntax that I'll cover in Chapter 10), write the file, and redraw the app view to reflect the new iText value (I'll cover drawing in Chapter 11).

If WriteFileL() leaves, I handle it by deleting iText and setting its pointer to 0. I also delete the file. Then I redraw the app view and use User::Leave() to propagate the error, so that EIKON can display an error message corresponding to the error code. Test this, if you like, by inserting User::Leave(KErrDiskFull) somewhere in WriteFileL().

My trap handler has one virtue: it lets the user know what's going on. It's still not good enough for serious application use, though, because this approach loses user and file data. It's a cardinal rule that EPOC shouldn't do that. A better approach would be to:

❑   Write the new data to a temporary file: if this fails, keep the user data in RAM, but delete the temporary file

❑   Delete the existing file: this is very unlikely to fail, but if it does, keep the user data in RAM, but delete the temporary file

❑   Rename the temporary file: this is very unlikely to fail, and if it does, we're in trouble. Keep the user data in RAM anyway

I would need to restructure my program to achieve this; the application architecture's framework for load/save and embeddable documents looks after these issues for you.

For database-type documents, you face these issues with *each entry* in the database. They are managed by the permanent file store class, which we'll encounter below.

Reading It Back

The code to read the data we have written is similar. Firstly, we read the filename from a dialog, and then use OkToExitL() to do some checking. This time, the code is much easier, and I'll present it in one segment:

```
TBool CExampleReadFileDialog::OkToExitL(TInt /* aKeycode */) // Termination
    {
    // Get filename
    CEikEdwin* edwin = STATIC_CAST(CEikEdwin*,
                                   Control(EExampleControlIdFileName));
    HBufC* fileName = edwin->GetTextInHBufL();

    // Check it's even been specified
    if(!fileName)
        {
        TryChangeFocusToL(EExampleControlIdFileName);
        iEikonEnv->LeaveWithInfoMsg(R_EIK_TBUF_NO_FILENAME_SPECIFIED);
        }
    CleanupStack::PushL(fileName);

    // Check it's a valid filename
    if(!iCoeEnv->FsSession().IsValidName(*fileName))
        {
        TryChangeFocusToL(EExampleControlIdFileName);
        iEikonEnv->LeaveWithInfoMsg(R_EIK_TBUF_INVALID_FILE_NAME);
        }

    // Check whether it's going to be possible to create the file for reading
    RFile file;
    User::LeaveIfError(file.Open(iCoeEnv->FsSession(), *fileName, EFileRead));
    file.Close();

    // Finished with user interaction: communicate parameters and return
    delete iAppUi->iFileName;
    iAppUi->iFileName = fileName;
    CleanupStack::Pop(); // fileName
    return ETrue;
    }
```

As before, the job of OkToExitL() is to check that the user's input is sensible. This function checks:

❑   That a filename has been specified

❑   That the filename is valid

❑   That it's going to be possible to read the file: I use RFile::Open() for this, and leave if there was any error

Assuming all is well, control returns to my command handler, which processes it using:

```
void CExampleAppUi::CmdReadFileL()
    {
    ...
    // Create a read stream on the file
    RFileReadStream reader;
    reader.PushL();                     // Reader on cleanup stack
    User::LeaveIfError(reader.Open(iCoeEnv->FsSession(),
                                   *iFileName,
                                   EFileRead));
```

```
    // Read the text
    HBufC* string = HBufC::NewL(reader, 10000);
    delete iText;
    iText = string;

    // Finish
    CleanupStack::PopAndDestroy();        // Reader
    ...
    }
```

The code is largely a mirror image of the code I used to write the data:

- ❑ I create an `RFileReadStream` object.

- ❑ Instead of using a `>>` operator to read the string that I wrote with `<<`, I use `HBufC::NewL(RReadStream&, TInt)`. This function takes a peek into the descriptor I wrote, checks how long it is, and allocates an `HBufC` that will be big enough to contain it (provided it's smaller than maximum length I also pass – in this case, `10000` characters). It then reads the data.

- ❑ I don't need to commit a read stream, because I've got all the data I want and I'm not writing anything. So I simply close with `CleanupStack::PopAndDestroy()`.

`RFileReadStream` is a mirror to `RFileWriteStream` and, as you might expect, it's derived from `RReadStream`. `RReadStream` contains many `>>` operators, and you can add support for reading to a class by coding `InternalizeL()`.

The only real issue in the code above was predicting how long the string would be. `HBufC::NewL(RReadStream&, TInt)` reads the descriptor that was written previously when `*iText` was written. Before allocating the `HBufC`, this function:

- ❑ Checks the length indicated in the stream

- ❑ Returns `KErrCorrupt` if the length is longer than the maximum I passed, or in various other circumstances where the length in the stream can't be valid

Parsing Filenames

The `streams` example shows how to use a `TParsePtrC` to crack a filename into its constituent parts. Here's some code to display all four parts of a filename in a dialog:

```
void CExampleParseDialog::PreLayoutDynInitL()
    {
    TParsePtrC parser(*iAppUi->iFileName);
    SetEdwinTextL(EExampleControlIdDrive, &parser.Drive());
    SetEdwinTextL(EExampleControlIdPath, &parser.Path());
    SetEdwinTextL(EExampleControlIdName, &parser.Name());
    SetEdwinTextL(EExampleControlIdExtension, &parser.Ext());
    }
```

The interesting thing here is that the `TParsePtr` constructor causes `TParsePtr` simply to store a reference to the filename string in `iFileName`. Because `TParsePtr` is essentially only a pointer, it uses very little space on the stack. I can then retrieve all its constituent parts using functions like `Drive()`.

For file manipulation, I need to use more space. Here's how I find the name of my help file, in the improved version of `helloeik` we'll be looking at in Chapter 13:

```
TFileName appFileName = Application()->AppFullName();
TParse fileNameParser;
fileNameParser.SetNoWild(_L(".hlp"), &appFileName, NULL);
TPtrC helpFileFullName = fileNameParser.FullName();
```

First, I get my application's full name into a `TFileName`. If I installed to `c:`, it's `c:\system\apps\helloeik\helloeik.app`. Then I set up a `TParse` to parse the name: its first argument is `.hlp`, second argument is my application name, and third argument null. Finally, I ask the `TParse` to return the full name of my help file, which is calculated as above by scanning each of the three parameters, so it's `c:\system\apps\helloeik\helloeik.hlp`.

This time, I had to change the data rather than simply pointing to it, so I couldn't use a `TParsePtr`. Having both a `TFileName` *and* a `TParse` on the stack uses a lot of room (over 1k in a Unicode build). You need to avoid this except where it's both necessary (as here) and safe (meaning you don't then call many more functions that are likely to have significant stack requirements).

Summary of the File APIs

EPOC's file APIs contain all the functions you would expect of a conventional file system. We use `RFs`, `TParse`, and `RFile` functions to manipulate the file system, files, and directories. We also use `RFs` to ensure our client program can communicate with the file server.

But we rarely use `RFile::Write()` or `RFile::Read()` for accessing file-based data. Instead, we usually use streams.

Streams

In the `streams` example, we got our first sight of EPOC's central classes for data management:

❑   `RWriteStream`, which **externalizes** objects to a stream

❑   `RReadStream`, which **internalizes** objects from a stream

External and Internal Formats

Data stored in program RAM is in **internal format**. Endian-ness, string representations, pointers between objects, padding between class members, and internally calculated values are all determined by the CPU type, C++ compiler, and program implementation.

Data stored in a file, or sent via a communications protocol, is in **external format**. The actual sequence of bits and bytes matters, including string representation and endian-ness. You can't have pointers – instead, you have to **serialize** an internal object network into an external stream, and **de-serialize** when you internalize again. Compression or encryption may also be used for the external format.

> You should distinguish carefully between internal and external formats. Never 'struct dump' (that is, never send your program's structs literally) when sending data to or over an external medium.

For reference, EPOC's emulator and ARM platform implementations have only a couple of internal format differences:

❑ 64-bit IEEE 754 double precision, floating-point numbers are stored with different endian-ness on ARM and x86 architectures.

❑ ARM requires that all 32-bit data be 32-bit aligned, whereas x86 does not. Therefore, ARM data structures potentially include padding that isn't present in their x86 equivalents.

The variety of internal formats will proliferate with future EPOC implementations, but the point about internal and external formats still stands: don't 'struct dump'. As we'll see, it's easy to write and use proper internalization and externalization functions that use EPOC's stream classes.

Ways to Externalize and Internalize Data

We mentioned two ways to externalize and, implicitly, three ways to internalize:

❑ You can use insertion and extraction operators: externalize with `stream << object`, and internalize with `stream >> object`

❑ You can externalize with `object.ExternalizeL(stream)`, and internalize with `object.InternalizeL(stream)`

❑ You can incorporate allocation, construction, and internalization into a single function of the form `object = class::NewL(stream)`

There are in fact many write stream and read stream classes that derive from `RWriteStream` and `RReadStream`, and access streams stored in different objects. These objects include:

❑ Files, as we have just seen

❑ Memory: a fixed area of memory that's described by a descriptor or a (pointer, length) pair; or an expandable area of memory described by a `CBufBase` (see Chapter 8)

❑ Stream stores, which I'll describe below

❑ Dictionary stores, which I'll also describe below

Some streams exist to perform pre-processing before writing to other streams. The most important example of this is REncryptStream, which encrypts data before writing it to a write stream, and RDecryptStream, which decrypts data just read from a read stream. Encryption is used, for example, to encrypt Word documents (check out the File | Password menu item). For more information on the encryption APIs, see the SDK.

To externalize, you always need an `RWriteStream`: in the code fragments below, `writer` could be an object of any class derived from `RWriteStream`.

To internalize, you always need an `RReadStream`: in the code fragments below, `reader` could be an object of any class derived from `RReadStream`.

<< and >> *Operators*

To externalize a built-in type, you can use <<:

```
TInt32 x;
writer << x;
TBufC<20> text = KText;
writer << text;
```

To internalize again, you can use >>:

```
TInt32 x;
reader >> x;
TBuf<20> text;
reader >> text;
```

However, you can't *always* use << and >>. The semantics of TInt specify only that it must be *at least* 32 bits; it may be longer. Furthermore, users may employ TInts to represent quantities that are known to require only, say, 8 bits in external format. As the application programmer, you know the right number of bits, and the EPOC stream doesn't try to second-guess you. If you write this:

```
TInt i;
writer << i;
```

The stream class doesn't know what to do. You will get an obscure compiler diagnostic. If you find yourself in this situation, you can either cast your TInt to the type you want to use, or use one of the specific write or read functions described below.

> **You cannot externalize a TInt using <<, or internalize it using >>. You must choose a function that specifies an external size for your data.**

The diagnostic is *incredibly* obscure: I got:

```
g:\epoc32\include\s32strm.inl(197) : error C2228: left of '.ExternalizeL' must
have class/struct/union type
g:\epoc32\include\s32strm.inl(240) : see reference to function template
instantiation 'void __cdecl DoExternalizeL(const int &,class RWriteStream &,class
Externalize::Member)' being compiled
```

There was no pointer into the offending line of my code at all! C++ compiler diagnostics for template-related problems still have a long way to go.

WriteXxxL() and ReadXxxL() Functions

If you want to be very specific about how your data is externalized, you can use the WriteXxxL() and ReadXxxL() member functions of RWriteStream and RReadStream. Here's some code:

```
TInt i = 53;
writer.WriteInt8L(i);
...
TInt j = reader.ReadInt8L();
```

By doing this, it's clear that you mean to use an 8-bit external format. Here's the complete set of `WriteXxxL()` and `ReadXxxL()` functions:

RWriteStream functions	RReadStream functions	<< type	External format
WriteL()	ReadL()		Data in internal format
WriteL(RReadStream&)	ReadL(RWriteStream&)		Transfer from other stream type
WriteInt8L()	ReadInt8L()	TInt8	8-bit signed integer
WriteInt16L()	ReadInt16L()	TInt16	16-bit signed integer, bytes stored little-endian
WriteInt32L()	ReadInt32L()	TInt32	32-bit signed integer, bytes stored little-endian
WriteUint8L()	ReadUint8L()	TUint8	8-bit unsigned integer
WriteUint16L()	ReadUint16L()	TUint16	16-bit unsigned integer, bytes stored little-endian
WriteUint32L()	ReadUint32L()	TUint32	32-bit unsigned integer, bytes stored little-endian
WriteReal32L()	ReadReal32L()	TReal32	32-bit IEEE754 single-precision floating point
WriteReal64L()	ReadReal64L()	TReal, TReal64	64-bit IEEE754 double-precision floating point

If you use `<<` and `>>` on built-in types, it will ultimately call these functions. The '`<<` type' column shows what EPOC data type will invoke these functions if used with the `<<` and `>>` operators.

Raw Data

The `WriteL()` and `ReadL()` functions for raw data deserve a closer look. Here are the `WriteL()` functions, as defined in the header file `S32strm.h`:

```
class RWriteStream
    {
public:
    ...
    IMPORT_C void WriteL(const TDesC8& aDes);
    IMPORT_C void WriteL(const TDesC8& aDes, TInt aLength);
    IMPORT_C void WriteL(const TUint8* aPtr, TInt aLength);
    ...
//
    IMPORT_C void WriteL(const TDesC16& aDes);
    IMPORT_C void WriteL(const TDesC16& aDes, TInt aLength);
    IMPORT_C void WriteL(const TUint16* aPtr, TInt aLength);
    ...
```

These functions simply write the data specified, according to the following rules:

❑ WriteL(const TDesC8& aDes, TInt aLength) writes aLength bytes from the beginning of the specified descriptor

❑ Without the aLength parameter, the whole descriptor is written

❑ The const TUint8* variant writes aLength bytes from the pointer specified

❑ The const TDesC16 and const TUint16* variants write Unicode characters (with little-endian byte order) instead of bytes

RReadStream comes with similar (though not precisely symmetrical) functions:

```
class RReadStream
    {
public:
    ...
    IMPORT_C void ReadL(TDes8& aDes);
    IMPORT_C void ReadL(TDes8& aDes, TInt aLength);
    IMPORT_C void ReadL(TDes8& aDes, TChar aDelim);
    IMPORT_C void ReadL(TUint8* aPtr, TInt aLength);
    IMPORT_C void ReadL(TInt aLength);
    ...
//
    IMPORT_C void ReadL(TDes16& aDes);
    IMPORT_C void ReadL(TDes16& aDes, TInt aLength);
    IMPORT_C void ReadL(TDes16& aDes, TChar aDelim);
    IMPORT_C void ReadL(TUint16* aPtr, TInt aLength);
    ...
```

The problem when reading is knowing when to stop. When you're writing, the descriptor length (or the aLength parameter) specifies the data length. When you're reading, the rules work like this:

❑ The TDes8& aDes format passes a descriptor whose MaxLength() bytes will be read

❑ If you specify aLength explicitly, then this number of bytes will be read

❑ If you specify a delimiter character, the stream will read up to *and including* that character. If the MaxLength() of the target descriptor is encountered before the delimiter character, reading stops after MaxLength() characters: nothing is read and thrown away.

Like all other ReadXxxL() functions, these functions will leave with KErrEof (end of file) if the end of file is encountered during the read operation.

You should use these raw data functions with great care. Any data that you externalize with WriteL() is effectively struct-dumped into the stream. This is fine provided that the data is already in external format. Be sure that it is!

When you internalize with ReadL(), you must always have a strategy for dealing with the anticipated maximum length of data. For example, you could decide that it would be unreasonable to have more than 10,000 bytes in a particular string, and so you check the length purportedly given, and if you find it's more than 10,000, you leave with KErrCorrupt. That's what HBufC::AllocL(RReadStream&, TInt) does.

Strings

You'll remember that I used this,

```
writer.iObj << *iText;
```

to externalize the content of the string in the **streams** program, where `iText` was an `HBufC*`. Now, this doesn't match against any of the basic types that are externalized using an `RWriteStream::WriteXxxL()` function. Instead, it uses C++ template magic to match against an **externalizer** for descriptors that writes a header and then the descriptor data.

To internalize a descriptor that has been externalized in this way, you have two choices. If the descriptor is short and of bounded length, you can use `>>` to internalize again:

```
TBuf<20> text;
reader.iObj >> text;
```

But if the length is variable, and you don't want to waste any space, you can internalize to a new `HBufC` of exactly the right length, which is the technique I used in `streams`:

```
iText = HBufC::NewL(reader.iObj, 10000);
```

In either case, C++ uses an **internalizer** for descriptors to re-internalize the data. The internalizer reads the header, which contains information about the descriptor's character width (8 or 16 bits) and length (in characters). You get panicked if the character width of the descriptor that was externalized doesn't match the descriptor type to which you're internalizing. The length is used to determine how much data to read.

It's possible to externalize strings using two `WriteL()` functions (one for the length of the data and another for the data itself), and then re-internalize them by reading the length and the data. But it's better to use the `<<` operator to externalize, and either `>>` or `HBufC::NewL(RReadStream&)` to internalize, for two reasons:

❑ The code is less difficult

❑ In future Unicode variants, you'll get standard Unicode compression (defined by the Unicode consortium) on data read and written this way

> *You* don't *get this compression when using* `WriteL(TDesC16&)`. *The standard Unicode compression scheme involves state, but* `WriteL()` *is of necessity stateless.*

ExternalizeL() and *InternalizeL()* Functions

We've now seen two methods for externalizing: using `<<`, and using `WriteXxxL()` functions. We also mentioned another method that I won't explain in detail: EPOC's use of an externalizer to make `<<` work in certain difficult cases. Furthermore, you've seen corresponding methods for internalizing.

If you have an object of class type, you need to write your own functions to enable that object to be externalized and internalized. These functions must have the following prototypes:

```
class Foo
    {
public:
    ...
    void ExternalizeL(RWriteStream& aStream) const;
    void InternalizeL(RReadStream& aStream);
    ...
    };
```

A general template for `operator<<()` ensures that you can externalize a Foo using either this:

```
Foo foo;
foo.ExternalizeL(writer);
```

Or this:

```
writer << foo;
```

A similar template exists for `operator>>()`.

The `ExternalizeL()` and `InternalizeL()` functions are not virtual, and there's no implication that Foo is derived from any particular base class, or that it has to be a C, T, or R class.

You then have to implement your own code to externalize and internalize the class. Here's some externalizing and internalizing code from my Battleships application:

```
void CGameController::ExternalizeL(RWriteStream& aStream) const
    {
    aStream.WriteUint8L(iState);
    aStream.WriteUint8L(iHaveFirstMovePref);
    aStream.WriteUint8L(iFirstMovePref);
    }

void CGameController::InternalizeL(RReadStream& aStream)
    {
    iState = (TState)aStream.ReadUint8L();
    iHaveFirstMovePref = aStream.ReadUint8L();
    iFirstMovePref = (TFirstMovePref)aStream.ReadUint8L();
    }
```

The patterns here are characteristic:

❑   The two functions mirror each other closely

❑   I know that all my data can be externalized into 8-bit unsigned integers, so I use `WriteUint8L()` to write, and the corresponding `ReadUint8L()` to read

❑   I don't use << and >>, because my internal format for all variables is a 32-bit integer – an enumeration for `iState` and `iFirstMovePref`, and a `TBool` for `iHaveFirstMovePref`

❑   I need some casting to convert integers back into enumerations when I read them in

If your object is more complicated, you can recursively externalize and internalize your member data.

ExternalizeL(), <<, or WriteXxxL()?

We have now seen *three* ways to externalize:

Technique	Application
writer << object	object may be a built-in integer (but not TInt), a real type, a descriptor, or any class with a properly-specified ExternalizeL() member function.
writer.WriteXxxL(object)	object must be a suitable built-in type, or descriptor whose contents are to be externalized as-is.
object.ExternalizeL(writer)	object is of class type, with a suitable ExternalizeL() function.

Which method should you use?

❏ If you want to externalize a descriptor *with its header*, then use <<.

❏ If you have to specify the exact length to use for a built-in type, and the internal format is either TInt or some length that's not what you want to use for the external format, then use a WriteXxxL() function.

❏ If you prefer to save typing, use << in preference to ExternalizeL() when dealing with a class type for which an ExternalizeL() exists.

❏ If you are writing a container class that's templated on some type T, you know whether T will be a built-in type or a class type. Use <<, and C++ will match against the right function.

This boils down to:

❏ Use << if you can

❏ Use specific WriteXxxL() functions if you have to

InternalizeL(), >>, ReadXxxL(), or NewL(RReadStream&)?

For the corresponding question about the best way to internalize, the basic rule is very simple: do the opposite of what you did when externalizing. Here's a trivial complication: when writing a 32-bit integer compactly to a write stream, you could use this:

```
writer << (TInt8)i;
```

But, when reading, you can't use this:

```
reader >> (TInt8)i;
```

For this reason (and because casts aren't nice anyway) it's better to use WriteInt8L() and ReadInt8L() in both cases, so you can easily check the symmetry of your InternalizeL() and ExternalizeL() functions.

Another complication is that you can think of internalizing as either an assignment or a construction. For a simple T class, assignment is OK:

```
reader >> iFoo;
```

But for a class of any complexity, or of variable length, it's better to think of internalizing as a constructor. If you're replacing an existing object, construct the new one by internalizing it, and then delete the old one and replace it:

```
CBar* bar = CBar::NewL(reader, other_parms);
delete iBar;
iBar = bar;
```

It uses more memory, but in many cases it's the only practical approach.

Types of Stream

The base RWriteStream and RReadStream interfaces are implemented by many interesting and useful derived classes that write to and read from streams in different media. Concrete stream types include:

Header file	Class names	Medium
s32file.h	RFileWriteStream, RFileReadStream	A file. Constructors specify either an open RFile, or a file server session and a filename.
s32mem.h	RDesWriteStream, RDesReadStream	Memory, identified by a descriptor.
s32mem.h	RMemWriteStream, RMemReadStream	Memory, identified by a pointer and length.
s32mem.h	RBufWriteStream, RBufReadStream	Memory, managed by a CBufBase-derived dynamic buffer (see Chapter 8). As new data is written through an RBufWriteStream, the destination CBufBase will be expanded as necessary.
s32std.h	RStoreWriteStream, RStoreReadStream	A stream store, of which more in the next section. RReadStream constructors specify a stream store and a stream ID. RWriteStream constructors for a new stream specify a stream store and return a stream ID. RWriteStream constructors for modifying an old stream specify a stream store and a stream ID.
s32stor.h	RDictionaryReadStream, RDictionaryWriteStream	A dictionary store. Constructors specify a dictionary store and a UID. See the section at the end of this chapter for more information.
s32crypt.h	REncryptStream, RDecryptStream	Another stream. Constructors specify the host stream, the CSecurityBase algorithm, and a string to initialize the CSecurityBase – effectively, a password.

Stores

At the beginning of this chapter, we saw that the major driver for many of EPOC's data APIs was the requirement for a consistent application file format, so that 'anything in anything' object embedding could be supported as far as applications would allow it.

Other systems provide stream APIs (such as Java and standard C), but EPOC goes further: streams do not exist in isolation. The stream store was designed from the outset with two important requirements in mind that lead us to the idea of a **store** as a collection of related streams:

❑ Embedded objects: an application document is a store, which can be implemented either as a file (for a main document), or as an embedded store (for an embedded document). It is highly desirable that, to an embedding application, an embedded document should appear as a collection of streams separate from those in the embedding document.

❑ Database management: EPOC's relational database uses streams for each table row, for each table header, and for database indexes. During the lifetime of a database, the store used always exists, but the streams within it are created, used, and deleted as required.

Direct File Stores

It's probably easiest to understand stores by means of an example. Let's consider the file format created by the Boss Puzzle, a sample application that's delivered with the EPOC SDK. The Boss Puzzle is a familiar single-player game in which you move the tiles around:

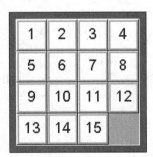
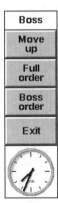

If you want to build and launch this yourself type the following at the command line, launch the emulator, and you'll find it on the Extras bar.

```
cd \boss\group
ebld eik7 wins deb
```

I closed the application after taking the screenshot above, than then looked at the document file in `c:\Documents\Boss`. In hex, it looks like this:

```
37000010  6d000010  53020010  75d06a32  ........  ........
31000000  01020304  05060708  090a0b0c  ........  ........
0d0e0f00  53020010  22424f53  532e6170  ........  .BOSS.ap
70045302  00101400  00008900  00102400  p.......  ........
0000                                      ..
```

This file consists of:

❏   A 16-byte header containing the file's UIDs and a checksum. The UIDs are 0x10000037 (for a direct file store), 0x1000006d (for an EIKON document), and 0x10000253 (for a Boss document). The header and checksum are generated by the file server.

❏   A 4-byte stream position indicating the beginning of a stream dictionary, which is 0x00000031

❏   The document data, which comprises 16 consecutive bytes containing the tile values in the Boss Puzzle. Since the puzzle has just been initialized, these 16 bytes simply contain increasing values 1, 2, 3, 4, ..., 15, 0 (the 0 represents the empty tile at the bottom right of the puzzle).

❏   An application header indicating the application's UID (four bytes), an externalized descriptor header byte 0x22, and the name of the application DLL BOSS.app.

❏   The stream dictionary, which starts with 0x04 to indicate four words of data – in reality, two associations. The first associates the application UID 0x10000253 with the document data at offset 0x00000014; the second associates the application identifier UID 0x10000089 with the application identifier stream at offset 0x00000024.

We can picture it like this:

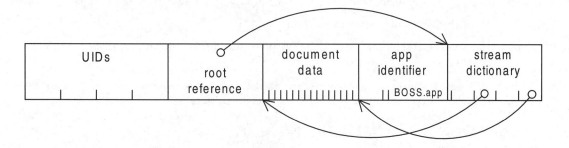

This type of file layout is frequently used, and found in many 'load/save' applications – applications that keep their data in RAM, and load and save the whole document only when necessary. The main features of this kind of layout are that seek positions are used to refer to data that has already been written – almost every reference in the file is backwards. The only exception is the reference to the root stream, which happens to be a forward reference from a fixed location early in the file.

In the language of the EPOC stream store, the document file is a **direct file store**, which is a kind of **persistent store**. The document has three streams, which we can picture like this:

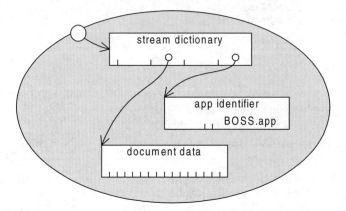

The **root stream** is accessible from the outside world. It contains a **stream dictionary**, which in turn points to two other streams. The **application identifier stream** contains information such as the application's DLL name, while the single **document data stream** contains the board layout. To write a file like this, we have to:

- ❑ Create a direct file store with the right name and UIDs. After this store is created, I don't need to know that it is a file store anymore: I just access it through persistent store functions

- ❑ Create a stream dictionary which will eventually be externalized onto the root stream

- ❑ Create, write, and close the document data stream: save its ID in the stream dictionary

- ❑ Create, write, and close the application identifier stream: save its ID in the stream dictionary

- ❑ Write the stream dictionary to a stream

- ❑ Close the persistent store, setting the stream containing the stream dictionary to be the root stream

The EPOC C++ SDK includes the \epoc32ex\docform\dfboswr2\ example that does just this. First, the file store is opened and remembered as a persistent store:

```
void CBossWriter::OpenStoreL(const TDesC& aFileName)
    {
    CFileStore* store = CDirectFileStore::CreateLC(iFs, aFileName, EFileWrite);
    store->SetTypeL(TUidType(KDirectFileStoreLayoutUid,
                             KUidAppDllDoc,
                             KUidBoss));
    CleanupStack::Pop();       // store
    iStore = store;            // iStore is a CPersistentStore*
    }
```

This creates a file with direct file store layout, and the right UIDs. It saves a pointer to the newly opened store in iStore, which is a CPersistentStore* (a base class of CDirectFileStore). Now that the file has been created, we need only use the more generic persistent store functions, as nothing is specific to CDirectFileStore.

Then we create the stream dictionary that will be written to the root stream:

```
void CBossWriter::OpenRootDictionaryL()
    {
    iRootDictionary = CStreamDictionary::NewL();
    }
```

Next, we call two functions in turn to write the data streams, and store their stream IDs in the stream dictionary:

```
void CBossWriter::WriteDocumentL()
    {
    TStreamId id = iPuzzle.StoreL(*iStore);
    iRootDictionary->AssignL(TUid::Uid(0x10000253), id);
    }

void CBossWriter::WriteAppIdentifierL()
    {
    TApaAppIdentifier ident(TUid::Uid(0x10000253), KTxtBossApp);
    RStoreWriteStream stream;
    TStreamId id = stream.CreateLC(*iStore);
    stream << ident;
    stream.CommitL();
    CleanupStack::PopAndDestroy(); // stream
    iRootDictionary->AssignL(KUidAppIdentifierStream, id);
    }
```

WriteDocumentL() calls the Boss engine's StoreL() function, which creates a stream, externalizes the engine data to the stream, closes the stream, and returns the stream ID. Then it stores that stream ID in the dictionary, associating it with the Boss Puzzle's UID.

WriteAppIdentifierL() shows how to create a stream: you use an RStoreWriteStream. Calling CreateLC(*iStore) creates it and gets its stream ID – and pushes it to the cleanup stack. The stream is then open, so you can write to it using <<. After writing, commit it using CommitL() and close it using CleanupStack::PopAndDestroy(). Finally, as before, we store the association between stream ID and UID in the stream dictionary.

Now we've written the two data streams, and we finish by writing the stream dictionary in a new·stream, setting that as the root stream of the store, and closing the store:

```
void CBossWriter::WriteRootDictionaryL()
    {
    RStoreWriteStream root;
    TStreamId id = root.CreateLC(*iStore);
    iRootDictionary->ExternalizeL(root);
    root.CommitL();
    CleanupStack::PopAndDestroy(); // root
    iStore->SetRootL(id);
    iStore->CommitL();
    }
```

We use the same technique as before to create the stream and get its ID. Then we externalize the dictionary and commit the stream. Finally we set the root stream ID, and commit the entire store. Shortly after this code, we call the C++ destructor on the `CPersistentStore`, which releases all the resources associated with the store.

While doing this commentary, I discovered a couple of oddities in the SDK source code. I've removed the oddities from the code reproduced in this book.

Embedded Stores

The code above was not specific to a direct file store. It would have worked equally well with any kind of persistent store.

The EPOC stream store provides an **embedded store** type that is intended specifically for object embedding. Imagine you have an EPOC Word document that embeds the Boss Puzzle (which you can do, as it happens). Here's what the store layout might look like, conceptually, with the Boss document inside the Word document:

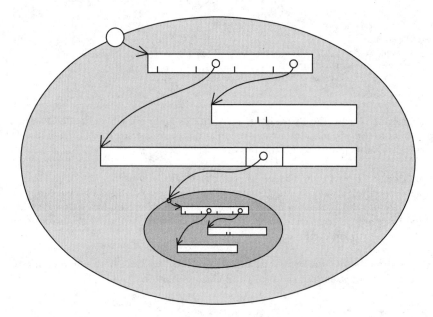

Actually, Word's store format is a bit more complicated than this, but the simplified version here is enough to explain our point.

The main document is a Word document, which uses a direct file store. As with the Boss Puzzle, the Word document has a root stream that is a stream dictionary referring to other streams. One of the streams will contain a stream ID that refers to a stream containing the embedded Boss Puzzle. From the point of view of the embedding store, this is a single stream.

From the point of view of the Boss Puzzle, though, this stream is an embedded store. The streams inside the embedded store are *exactly* as they were inside the direct file store.

The layout of an embedded store is *nearly* the same as a direct file store, but not quite. Embedded stores don't need the leading 16 bytes of UID information required by file stores, so these are omitted. The first four bytes of an embedded store contain the root stream ID. Stream IDs within an embedded store are *stream* seek positions relative to the stream in the embedding store, not file seek positions.

Permanent File Stores

We have now seen two types of store:

- ❏ Direct file stores
- ❏ Embedded stores

In these store types, the store adds little value above that of the medium containing it (the medium is either the containing file or the containing stream):

- ❏ Stream IDs are seek positions within the medium
- ❏ You can only refer to streams already created
- ❏ You cannot delete a stream after it has been created
- ❏ When you open a new stream, it is impossible to write anything else to any stream that was previously open
- ❏ When you close the store, you cannot later re-open it and change it (except under obscure conditions, and with additional constraints)

Despite – in fact, because of – these restrictions, the so-called direct-layout store types are simple to work with. They are well suited for load/save type applications, such as the Boss Puzzle or Word. For these applications, the 'real' document is in user RAM, and it's saved to file in entirety (or loaded from file) when necessary. When the document is saved, the old file is deleted and a new file is written again from the beginning.

For database-type applications, the 'real' document is the data in the database file. An application loads *some* information from the database into RAM to work with it, but it doesn't load the entire database into RAM at once. In fact, it loads and replaces information in the database a single entry at a time. In effect, for a database application, a *single entry* is like a load/save document, but the database as a whole is a permanent entity.

The stream store provides a store type for databases: the **permanent file store**. In a permanent file store:

- ❏ You can delete a stream after it has been created. You can also truncate it, and add to it in any way you like.
- ❏ You can keep as many streams open as you like, for either writing or reading. You can interleave writing to many streams (provided that you CommitL() between writing different streams' data).
- ❏ You can re-open the store after it has been closed, and do any manipulations you like.

However, this flexibility comes at a price. Most obviously, there is no correspondence between stream ID and seek position. This relationship is private to the implementation of the permanent file store. Furthermore, you can't guarantee that all data in a stream is contiguous.

You have to manage a permanent file store very carefully, just as you have to manage EPOC memory. You must avoid 'stream leaks' with the same vigilance as you avoid memory leaks. In fact, you must be even more vigilant, because permanent file stores survive even shutdown and restart of your applications, and of the EPOC machine as a whole. And you must do all this using techniques that are guaranteed, even under failure conditions.

The stream store provides a tool analogous to the cleanup stack for cleaning up write streams that have been half-written, due to an error occurring during the act of writing to a permanent file store. The central class is CStoreMap, which contains a list of open streams.

As you manipulate streams in a permanent file store, the store will gradually get larger and larger. The stream store provides incremental compaction APIs, so you can gradually compact a store, even while you're doing other work on it.

The permanent file store has been designed to be extremely robust. Robustness was prioritized even higher than space efficiency – though the format is still space-efficient.

The EPOC Agenda application uses the permanent file store directly. The DBMS component also uses the permanent file store; most other permanent file store users in EPOC are indirect users, through the DBMS. For more on using permanent file stores, CStoreMaps etc., see the SDK.

More on Embedding

Embedded stores are a useful convenience. Any application that uses a direct file store for its main document can also use an embedded store (and therefore be embedded) with relative ease. It follows that database-type applications, which use a permanent file store for their main document, cannot be embedded.

In theory, it would be possible to do document embedding without embedded stores. The naïve layout below, for example, could be used to embed Boss in Word without using an embedded store:

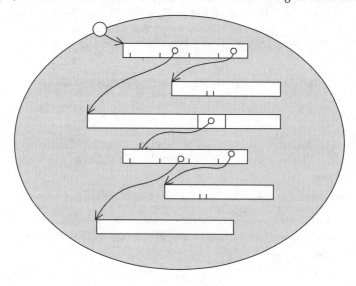

However, this creates a problem. Imagine that the Word object is itself embedded inside an Agenda entry. You select the entry, copy it to the clipboard, and then paste it into a different date.

With the naïve implementation above, you need to trace through the entire structure of the embedded Word and Boss documents in order to be able to copy the Agenda entry. Furthermore, if the Word document were encrypted, the user would need to enter the decryption password to decrypt it when loading, and then enter it again to encrypt it when saving.

This isn't good. By using an embedded store, the Agenda entry sees the Word document – and its embedded Boss document – as a single stream. Copying streams is trivially simple, and Agenda doesn't need to know anything at all about their content.

Types of Store

To summarize what we've seen so far:

- ❑ A load/save application uses a `CDirectFileStore` for its main document
- ❑ A load/save application uses a `CEmbeddedStore` when it is embedded
- ❑ A database application uses a `CPermanentFileStore` for its database

These three store types are part of a small hierarchy:

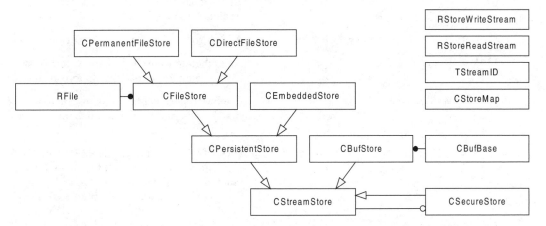

The base class for all stores is `CStreamStore`, whose API provides all the functionality needed to create, open, extend, and delete streams; to commit and revert (a kind of rollback) the entire store; and to reclaim and compact.

On top of `CStreamStore`, `CPersistentStore` provides one extra piece of functionality: you can designate á single stream as the root stream. This allows you to close the store and, later, open it again. Hence the store is **persistent**; like a file, its existence persists after a program has closed it, and even after the program itself has terminated.

The two file store types are derived from `CPersistentStore` via the `CFileStore` class. `CEmbeddedStore` is derived from `CPersistentStore` directly.

A `CBufStore` implements the `CStreamStore` interface in a dynamic buffer in RAM. Such a store is clearly *not* persistent: it cannot survive the destruction of its underlying buffer. `CBufStore` implements the full stream manipulation interface of `CStreamStore`. `CBufStores` are used for undo buffers in some apps, including Word.

Finally, `CSecureStore` allows an entire store to be encrypted or decrypted, just as `CSecureWriteStream` and `CSecureReadStream` support encryption and decryption of individual streams.

This class hierarchy uses a useful object-oriented pattern. Derivation in this class hierarchy is based on the distinction between non-persistent and persistent stores, and between file stores and other types. But the stream manipulation functionality cuts across the hierarchy – a full interface is supported by permanent file stores and buffer stores, while only a partial interface is supported by direct file stores and embedded stores. The only way to support this is to provide the full stream interface in the base class: derived classes implement these functions as appropriate, and return error codes when an unsupported function is called.

Here's a summary of the store types:

File	Name	Purpose
s32stor.h	CStreamStore	Base class, with extend, delete, commit, revert, reclaim, and compact functions – not all of which are available in all implementations.
s32stor.h	CPersistentStore	Adds a root stream to `CStreamStore`.
s32stor.h	CEmbeddedStore	An embedded store: open a new one on a write stream, or an old one on a read stream.
s32file.h	CFileStore	File-based persistent store. Constructors specify either an `RFs` and a filename, or an already-open `RFile`.
s32file.h	CDirectFileStore	Direct file store. Has a wide variety of constructors supporting all file-related open functions (open, create, replace, and temp). Can also be constructed from an already open `RFile`.
s32file.h	CPermanentFileStore	Permanent file store. Has a wide variety of constructors.
s32mem.h	CBufStore	Non-persistent store in a privately owned `CBufBase`. See Chapter 8 for more information on dynamic buffers.
s32crypt.h	CSecureStore	Secure store with encrypted streams and the like. Constructors specify host stream store, `CSecurityBase` encryption algorithm, and an initialization string.

Beware of the following sources of potential confusion:

❑ Don't get confused between a **persistent store** and a **permanent file store**. A persistent store has a root stream, and can persist after you've closed it. A permanent file store is the type of file store that's used by database applications; the database itself is permanent, although its *entries* may be saved, deleted, or replaced.

❑ Don't use file write streams and file read streams to access file stores; you use them to access files when the file is *not* a file store. *All* store types should be accessed with store write streams and store read streams – most often, you only need to use the write stream and read stream interfaces.

Dictionary Stores and `.ini` Files

A persistent stream store includes a stream network in which streams may contain stream IDs that refer to other streams, and which has a single root stream.

In contrast, a **dictionary store** contains a list of streams, each of which is accessed using a UID, rather than a stream ID:

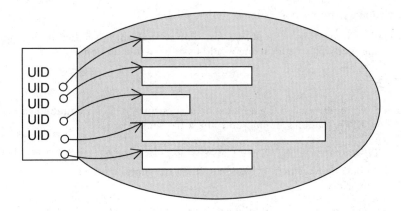

There is a small class hierarchy associated with dictionary stores:

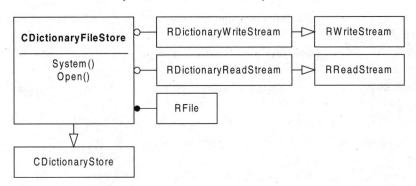

You write to a dictionary store using a dictionary write stream, which you construct specifying the dictionary store and a UID. You read from a dictionary store using a dictionary read stream, which you open specifying a dictionary store and a UID.

There is one concrete dictionary store class – the dictionary file store – which is used for .ini files. You can open the system .ini file, or a named .ini file for an application.

You should not keep dictionary stores permanently open. When you need to access a dictionary store:

❑ Open it: if this fails, wait a second or so and retry

❑ Open the stream you want

❑ Read or write the stream

❑ Close the store

To each application, the application architecture assigns a .ini file, which is a dictionary file store. Again, we need to beware the following sources of confusion:

❑ Dictionary stores have nothing to do with the stream dictionaries that we saw when looking at application document formats.

❑ A dictionary store is not a stream store at all.

❑ Therefore, a dictionary file store is not a file store at all: it is a dictionary store that happens to use a file. Perhaps a better name would have been 'file dictionary store'.

Summary

In this chapter, we've introduced the application architecture APIs for communicating with the file server, and how EPOC handles streams and stores. To summarize:

❑ The application architecture motivates the high-level view of data management in EPOC

❑ EPOC's data management is based around a conventional file system, accessed through the file server APIs

In practice, however, applications usually use streams and stores to read and write file data. The stream and store APIs support the application architecture, and deliver compactness in both code and data formats. More specifically, then, we've seen:

❑ How the application architecture finds applications, and how it uses UIDs to associate applications and their documents.

❑ The difference between load/save files that can embed or be embedded, and database applications that can embed load/save applications.

❑ A document has essentially the same structure whether it is embedded or not – and as such isn't identified by a file extension but by its internal UID.

❑ That an .aif file is needed for your application if it can be embedded.

❑ Where an application's .ini file is stored, and how it uses a dictionary store.

- ❑ The relationship between the file server, the stream store, and the application architecture.

- ❑ How to use an RFs object to get a session with the file server, how to use the CONE environment's RFs to save resources, and how RFs functions are stateless.

- ❑ Using an RFile, and navigating the EPOC file system in code.

- ❑ How to parse the path of a filename.

- ❑ Using the stream store APIs as a generic way to externalize and internalize data between streams and user RAM.

- ❑ When to use which function.

- ❑ Adding ExternalizeL() and InternalizeL() to your classes to support << and >> respectively.

- ❑ The structure of a persistent store, with a root stream containing a stream dictionary that points to the other streams of data in the application, and in consequence how an embedded store is just another stream.

- ❑ The difference between a direct file store and persistent store.

- ❑ How a dictionary store isn't a store at all.

In later chapters, especially as we tackle more complicated EIKON example programs, we will see how the application architecture works in practice.

8

Development Miscellany

We've now seen EPOC's basic development tools, the overall structure of the system, and the three most fundamental programming frameworks – for descriptors, cleanup, and data management.

Before we move on to graphics and the EIKON GUI, here's a miscellany of other useful information for developers: a few more useful APIs, information about the emulator, and building command-tools using EPOC's WINC build.

You'll find more reference information on some of these facilities in the SDK, and you'll find plenty of useful hints and tips on Symbian's EPOC World web site.

A Few Good APIs

We've seen the descriptor and cleanup APIs from the E32 user library. In later chapters (Chapter 18 and Chapter 19) I'll cover the user library's other two important frameworks – those for active objects and client-server programming.

Some other basic APIs, mostly from the user library, are also worth a mention – though I won't describe them in detail here.

User Class

`User` is a static class with over 70 functions in various categories. We've already seen `User::Leave()`, `User::LeaveIfError()`, and `User::Panic()`.

To support memory handling, use `User::Alloc()` which behaves like `malloc()` in C. `User::Free()` behaves like `free()`, while `User::Realloc()` behaves like `realloc()`. Leaving variants (`User::AllocL()`, `User::AllocLC()` etc) are also provided.

Two major functions suspend a thread until a timer expires:

❑ `User::After()` suspends until *after* a given number of microseconds has elapsed. `User::After()` uses the hardware tick interrupt and is designed for short-term timing, GUI time-outs etc.. The tick interrupt is turned off when the machine is turned off, so a `User::After()`'s completion is delayed until the machine is turned back on and the clock starts ticking again.

❑ `User::At()` suspends until a particular date and time. `At()` uses the date/time clock which is always running, even when the machine is turned off. When an `At()` timer completes, it will turn the machine on if necessary. `At()` timers are for alarms and other events for which an accurate date and time are essential.

These functions are defined in `e32std.h`:

```
class User : public UserHeap
    {
public:
    // Execution control
    IMPORT_C static void Exit(TInt aReason);
    IMPORT_C static void Panic(const TDesC& aCategory, TInt aReason);

    // Cleanup support
    IMPORT_C static void Leave(TInt aReason);
    IMPORT_C static void LeaveNoMemory();
    IMPORT_C static TInt LeaveIfError(TInt aReason);
    IMPORT_C static TAny* LeaveIfNull(TAny* aPtr);
    IMPORT_C static TAny* Alloc(TInt aSize);
    IMPORT_C static TAny* AllocL(TInt aSize);
    IMPORT_C static TAny* AllocLC(TInt aSize);
    IMPORT_C static void Free(TAny* aCell);
    IMPORT_C static TAny* ReAlloc(TAny* aCell,TInt aSize);
    IMPORT_C static TAny* ReAllocL(TAny* aCell,TInt aSize);

    // Synchronous timer services
    IMPORT_C static void After(TTimeIntervalMicroSeconds32 anInterval);
    IMPORT_C static TInt At(const TTime& aTime);
    ...
    };
```

Many other useful functions are provided. As usual, the SDK has the details.

The derivation of User *from* UserHeap, *another static class, betrays* User's *heritage as one of EPOC's oldest classes.*

Dynamic Buffers

CBufBase is an abstract base class for dynamic memory buffers, which store any number of bytes from zero upwards, and which can be expanded and contracted at will. You can read or write bytes from the buffer, insert bytes into the buffer, or delete them from it.

Here's the declaration of CBufBase, from e32base.h:

```
class CBufBase : public CBase
    {
public:
    IMPORT_C ~CBufBase();
    inline TInt Size() const;
    IMPORT_C void Reset();
    IMPORT_C void Read(TInt aPos, TDes8& aDes) const;
    IMPORT_C void Read(TInt aPos, TDes8& aDes, TInt aLength) const;
    IMPORT_C void Read(TInt aPos, TAny* aPtr, TInt aLength) const;
    IMPORT_C void Write(TInt aPos, const TDesC8& aDes);
    IMPORT_C void Write(TInt aPos, const TDesC8& aDes, TInt aLength);
    IMPORT_C void Write(TInt aPos, const TAny* aPtr, TInt aLength);
    IMPORT_C void InsertL(TInt aPos, const TDesC8& aDes);
    IMPORT_C void InsertL(TInt aPos, const TDesC8& aDes, TInt aLength);
    IMPORT_C void InsertL(TInt aPos, const TAny* aPtr, TInt aLength);
    IMPORT_C void ExpandL(TInt aPos, TInt aLength);
    IMPORT_C void ResizeL(TInt aSize);

    // Pure virtual
    virtual void Compress() = 0;
    virtual void Delete(TInt aPos, TInt aLength) = 0;
    virtual TPtr8 Ptr(TInt aPos) = 0;
    virtual TPtr8 BackPtr(TInt aPos) = 0;
private:
    virtual void DoInsertL(TInt aPos, const TAny* aPtr, TInt aLength) = 0;
protected:
    IMPORT_C CBufBase(TInt anExpandSize);
protected:
    TInt iSize;
    TInt iExpandSize;
    };
```

You can find out how many bytes are in a CBufBase using Size(). Bytes are indexed from 0. You insert using InsertL(), specifying a byte position from which to start inserting, and a pointer descriptor containing data (in fact, all InsertL() functions are convenience functions for the private DoInsertL()). You can delete data using Delete(); you can write data using Write() – this overwrites without inserting – and you can read using Read().

Two types of buffer are provided, both derived from CBufBase:

❑   CBufFlat, which puts all the bytes in a single heap cell. This means that access to any byte is quick (you just add the byte index to the beginning of the buffer). However, memory allocation can be inefficient (it might not be possible to expand the buffer when desired, even though there may be more than enough bytes of unused heap available).

❑ CBufSeg, which puts the bytes in multiple heap cells, each of which is a segment of the buffer. For large buffers which are constantly changing in size, and where insertions and deletions part-way through the buffer are frequent, segmented buffers are much more efficient than flat buffers. Finding a particular byte theoretically requires a walk of the entire segment structure: CBufSeg caches a reference to the last-used byte, which speeds up most operations.

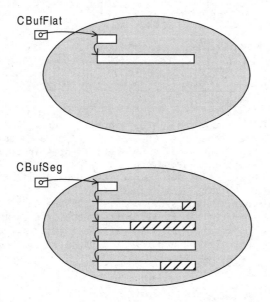

The buffers example illustrates the functions available. Here's the mainL() function:

```
void mainL()
    {
    CBufBase* buf = CBufSeg::NewL(4);
    CleanupStack::PushL(buf);
    //
    buf->InsertL(0, _L("hello!"));
    printBuffer(buf);
    buf->InsertL(5, _L(" world")); // "hello world!"
    printBuffer(buf);
    buf->Delete(2, 7); // "held!"
    printBuffer(buf);
    buf->Compress();
    printBuffer(buf);
    buf->ExpandL(2, 7); // "he.......ld!"
    printBuffer(buf);
    buf->Write(2, _L("llo wor"));
    printBuffer(buf);
    //
    CleanupStack::PopAndDestroy(); // buf
    }
```

This example is not Unicode correct. In a Unicode build, the descriptors used above would use 16-bit characters, but buffers *always* use 8-bit bytes. However, it does show the basics of insert, delete, compress, expand, and write with buffers.

The sample also shows how a CBufSeg is allocated. NewL() takes a granularity which is the maximum size of a segment. Oddly, there is no NewLC(), so I have to push the buffer explicitly onto the cleanup stack.

To scan all the data in a buffer, you need to know where the segment boundaries are. You can use the Ptr() function to get a TPtr descriptor for all the bytes from a given position, to the end of the segment that position is in. For a CBufFlat, that means all the data in the buffer. But for a CBufSeg, only the rest of the current segment is given.

printBuffer() in the example code shows how to do this:

```
void printBuffer(CBufBase* aBuffer)
    {
    console->Printf(_L("buffer="));
    TInt i = 0;
    TPtrC p = aBuffer->Ptr(i);
    while(p.Length() > 0)
        {
        console->Printf(_L("[%S]"), &p);
        i += p.Length();
        p.Set(aBuffer->Ptr(i));
        };
    console->Printf(_L("\n"));
    }
```

The result is:

```
buffer=[hell] [o!]
buffer=[hell] [o wo] [rld!]
buffer=[he] [ld!]
buffer=[held] [!]
buffer=[held] [ÌÌÌÌ] [!ld!]
buffer=[hell] [o wo] [rld!]
```

Because I specified a granularity of 4, the segments are all 4 bytes long.

When I delete the seven characters from the middle of the string, the segments are optimized for minimum data shuffling. After random operations on the buffer over a long period – say, operations controlled by a user typing and editing text in a word processor – the buffer can become very fragmented, with many segments containing less than the maximum amount of data. Compress() moves the data so that as few segments as possible are used.

ExpandL() and ResizeL() (which puts extra bytes at the end, if the new size is greater than the current size) are useful for making a sequence of InsertL() operations atomic and for improving their performance. Say you needed to insert six items: if you used six InsertL()s within your function InsertSixItemsL(), you would need to trap each one and, if it failed due to an out-of-memory error, you would need to delete all the items you had so far inserted. In addition, the use of repeated allocation for each InsertL() would impact performance and fragment the heap – especially for flat buffers. You can avoid all these problems by using ExpandL() or ResizeL(), and then a series of Write()s – which cannot leave.

If you're at your PC, replace the allocation of CBufSeg with a CBufFlat and run buffers again. You should have little difficulty predicting or explaining the results.

Dynamic buffers are used to store array elements in expandable arrays. Both flat and segmented arrays are provided, corresponding to the buffer types used to implement them. CArrayFixFlat<T> uses a flat buffer to store an array of T objects, while CArrayFixSeg<T> uses a segmented buffer. Ts are stored so that the nth T occupies sizeof(T) bytes from position n*sizeof(T) in the buffer. A CBufSeg granularity of a multiple of sizeof(T) is specified, so that a T never spans a segment boundary.

Dynamic buffers are also used to store rich text, derived from CEditableText, part of the ETEXT API defined in txt*.h headers. Segmented buffers are particularly efficient at handling the kind of operations required by intensive word processing. The rich text APIs include InsertL(), Write(), Read(), and Delete() with specifications similar to those of CBufBase. However, the position argument in all these functions is a *character* position, not a byte position: in Unicode builds, rich text uses two bytes per character. The SDK includes full documentation on rich text, and a pretty example project in \epoc32ex\form\.

Collections

The user library provides collection classes including arrays and lists ('queues', with Que in their name). They are an uninspiring lot, but they do the job. The SDK documents them thoroughly and has plenty of examples.

Locale

e32std.h includes many locale-related classes, covering time zones, formatting for time, date, and currency, measurement units for short distances (inches vs cm) and long distances (miles vs km). In a complete EPOC system, these settings are usually set through the control panel and used to control the settings of EIKON dialogs.

Locale settings depend on:

❑ The ROM locale: for instance a German machine will include German spell check dictionaries and a keyboard driver for the German QWERTZ layout

❑ The home city: controls the current time zone, and can be set through the control panel or the Time application. The home city default is ROM-locale dependent.

❑ Miscellaneous settings: other locale settings are entered by the user through the control panel, with ROM-locale dependent defaults.

Math

In e32math.h, the static class Math defines a range of standard IEEE 754 double-precision math functions, including a random number generator and all the usual log and trig functions.

EPOC C Standard Library

The STDLIB component delivers standard C functions, which are in general thin layers over corresponding EPOC functions.

This means, on the one hand, that you can use all your favorite C APIs, from `strlen()` and `malloc()` to `fopen()` and `quicksort()`, and on the other, that you can usually guess the behavior of functions such as `User::QuickSort()` because they're there to support standard library functions.

The EPOC C standard library was written to support the JVM port, which uses Sun's C source code for the JVM without alteration. By this measure alone, the standard library is well tested and powerful. It delivers POSIX-compliant C APIs layering over the EPOC user library, file server, and sockets server.

Prior to the JVM port, the only major in-house port was the spell check software from Lernout & Hauspie. Rather than writing a complete standard library, the EPOC developers wrote the most important functions – `strxxx()`, `malloc()`, `free()` etc. – in most cases, as simple `#define`s over the corresponding `User::` functions. The spell checker is heavily algorithmic, so this was enough to allow a relatively straightforward port without touching too much other code.

In Chapter 24, John Forrest of Purple Software explains how to use the C standard library to port standard C programs to EPOC. In Chapter 23, Jonathan Allin recounts the story of Symbian's Java implementation in more detail.

Variable Argument Lists

Variable argument lists are supported by macros in `e32def.h`. Their commonest use is in providing parameter lists to descriptor formatting functions such as `TDes::FormatList()`.

Here's how it's done in EIKON. `CEikonEnv::InfoMsg(TInt, ...)` takes a resource ID parameter and a variable list of formatting parameters. The resource ID is used to look up a format string, and the format parameters substitute into the string using (ultimately) a `TDes::AppendFormatList()` function.

To implement this version of `InfoMsg()`, EIKON uses a `VA_START` to get the start of the argument list, and a `VA_LIST` to pass a variable list to a lower-level version of `InfoMsg()`:

```
EXPORT_C void CEikonEnv::InfoMsg(TInt aResourceId, ...)
    {
    VA_LIST list;
    VA_START(list, aResourceId);
    InfoMsg(aResourceId, list);
    }
```

The lower-level version reads in the resource string, and does the real formatting, using `TDes::FormatList()`:

```
EXPORT_C void CEikonEnv::InfoMsg(TInt aResourceId, VA_LIST aList)
    {
    TEikInfoMsgBuf formatString;
    ReadResource(formatString, aResourceId);
```

```
      TEikInfoMsgBuf messageString;
      messageString.FormatList(formatString, aList);
      InfoMsg(messageString);
      }
```

In a function such as FormatList(), you would use VA_ARG(*list*, *n*) to get the *n*th argument from a VA_LIST.

VA_LIST requires that the parameter before the ... is a value parameter, not a reference parameter. So a function prototype of the form,

```
class CConsoleBase : public CBase
    {
public:
    IMPORT_C Printf(const TDesC& aFormat, ...);
    ...
```

wouldn't work, since the aFormat parameter is a reference. If you're coding format lists, you must use the TRefByValue class that implements the necessary C++ magic,

```
class CConsoleBase : public CBase
    {
public:
    IMPORT_C Printf(TRefByValue<const TDesC> aFormat, ...);
    ...
```

and the implementation of CConsoleBase::Printf() starts:

```
EXPORT_C CConsoleBase::Printf(TRefByValue<const TDesC> aFormat, ...)
    {
    VA_LIST(args, aFormat);
    ...
```

If you enjoy C++ puzzles, you will have fun with the definitions of the VA_ macros and TRefByValue<T>. You can find them in e32def.h and e32std.h, with descriptor-related overrides in e32des8.h and e32des16.h.

String Formatting

Although EPOC is a GUI system, Printf()-style formatting still has a useful role to play, and appears in a number of classes. We've already seen it in CConsoleBase::Printf() and CEikonEnv::InfoMsg(). There's another example of using it in buffers:

```
console->Printf(_L("[%S]"), &p);
```

As in C print formatting, the % character is followed by a format character, which interprets the corresponding argument for formatting. Here are the main format types:

Format	Argument type	Interpretation
%d	TInt	Decimal value of 32-bit signed integer
%e	TReal	Real in scientific notation
%g	TReal	Real in general format
%x	TUint	32-bit unsigned integer in hexadecimal
%s	TText*	String passed as the address of a NUL-terminated string, of either narrow characters (narrow build) or wide characters (Unicode build)
%S	TDesC*	String passed as the address of a descriptor

Beware of the difference between %s (for C strings) and %S (for descriptors). Also note that the descriptor version requires the argument to be a pointer to the descriptor.

The SDK documents the format characters along with its documentation for TDes::Format(). There are many more options, including width and precision specifiers.

RDebug **Class**

The RDebug class, defined in e32svr.h, includes a host of functions, of which the most interesting is Print(). If you're debugging under the emulator, RDebug::Print() prints to the debug output window. If you're debugging under real EPOC, RDebug::Print() uses an RS232 port, which you can connect to a PC and use a terminal emulator to view the debug output.

This kind of 'print debugging' is useful when a log of activity is handy, or when you have no access to the debugger. The trade-off is that you need an RS232 port spare on both your EPOC device and your PC. Jonathan Dixon's infrared and SMS communications drivers, which he describes in Chapter 21, use RDebug::Print() extensively. Logging gave him insight into some knotty issues during the development of the SMS driver.

The Emulator

As we've seen, the emulator is a vital tool in the EPOC software development process. For non-privileged code, the emulator is almost 100% source compatible with real EPOC machines. Many functions that used privileged code on other systems use servers on EPOC, so that for the system as a whole source compatibility is very high indeed.

The emulator uses Win32 APIs and services to emulate real-machine hardware and EPOC services, including:

❑ A Windows window to emulate the EPOC screen and surrounding machine fascia

❑ The Windows mouse to emulate the EPOC pointer

- ❑ The Windows keyboard to emulate the EPOC keyboard, plus some control functions

- ❑ Directories in the Windows file system to emulate standard EPOC drives

- ❑ Win32 threads to emulate EPOC threads

- ❑ A single Win32 process to emulate a single EPOC process containing *all* EPOC threads: this is an important difference between the emulator and a real EPOC machine, which I'll return to later in this chapter

- ❑ A single `.exe` to include EPOC startup code: this is `epoc.exe` in the case of any GUI program, or a custom `.exe` for any text console program

- ❑ Win32 DLLs to emulate EPOC DLLs, with Win32 DLL search order used instead of EPOC search order

- ❑ Win32 DLLs to emulate EPOC server `.exes`, with Win32 DLL search order used to find the Win32 DLL

- ❑ PC sound card to emulate EPOC sound codec

- ❑ PC communications ports to emulate EPOC communications ports

- ❑ The Visual Studio debug window, if active, for debug prints generated by `RDebug::Print()` (see `e32svr.h`)

For C++ development, the emulator's debug build is typically used. In addition to symbolic information for the Visual Studio debugger, the debug build contains useful facilities such as EIKON's debug keys, and heap balance checking in CONE.

For Java development, the emulator release build is used. See Chapter 23 for more information.

Key Mapping

The majority of the PC keyboard is mapped in a straightforward way to the EPOC keyboard. However, some special keys are available:

PC key	EPOC facility
Alt	*Fn* key
F1	*Menu* key
Alt+F2	*Help* key
Alt+F4	Close the emulator window
F5	Simulate disk door open
F6	Play button

Table Continued on Following Page

PC key	EPOC facility
F7	Rewind button
F8	Record button
F9	Power-off: minimizes emulator window. Maximize the window to emulate power-on again.
F10	Emergency shutdown: simulates critical battery-voltage condition
F11	Case close toggle: when case is closed, window title changes to indicate it, and emulated keyboard/pointer become inactive

Emulator Startup

The emulator uses only a single Win32 process. That means it uses only a single Windows `.exe`, which you launch somehow – from a command line, for example, or using Windows Explorer.

The `.exe` that you specify is the startup `.exe`, and it resides in the **startup directory**. I'll return to the topic of startup directories below. You have two choices for startup `.exe`:

❑ Build your own, like `hellotext.exe`, `epocstring.exe`, or `buffers.exe`

❑ Use `epoc.exe`, which starts the window server, EIKON environment, and Shell application, so that you can use the EPOC Shell to launch an EPOC application

Each EPOC `.exe` built for the emulator includes a stub file, `eexe.obj`. This file includes code to start up the emulated EPOC kernel and file server, and then call your `E32Main()` function. So in fact Windows starts by calling `eexe.obj`, and your code is called by `eexe.obj`.

As part of kernel startup, the emulator reads an initialization file and a fascia bitmap from its configuration directory. By default, the configuration directory is `\epoc32\data\`, the initialization file is `epoc.ini`, and the fascia bitmap is `epoc.bmp`.

`epoc.exe` uses exactly the same `eexe.obj` as any `.exe` you build yourself. In fact the source code for `epoc.exe` contains only a single line in its `E32Main()`, which starts the EPOC window server. The window server in turn starts the servers it needs (such as the font and bitmap server) and then reads its initialization data from the *emulated* `z:\system\data\wsini.ini`. By default, this `.ini` file contains instructions to the window server to start the Shell (`\system\apps\shell\shell.app`). The Shell launches the EIKON server and the application architecture server, scans through `\system\apps\` on every (emulated) drive to see what programs are installed, and finally displays the default documents folder.

That startup sequence begs two questions:

❑ What are the contents of the emulator's `.ini` file?

❑ What command-line arguments can I specify to override this?

I'll return to these questions after covering the emulator's use of PC directories.

Directories for the Emulator

There are three possibilities for the startup directory:

❑ For narrow debug builds, using the default scheme, the startup directory is
   `\epoc32\release\wins\deb\`

❑ For narrow release builds, using the default scheme, the startup directory is
   `\epoc32\release\wins\rel\`

❑ For any build using the new scheme in ER5, any directory is possible (but you should avoid potential clashes – so don't use any directory in the `\epoc32\release\` tree)

As we saw in Chapter 2, most SDK tools require the default scheme, so in practice you have to use it for software development. But once you've finished developing software, you can copy the emulator directories from their default-scheme locations (which are fixed) to new-scheme locations (which are all relative to the startup directory), and run your emulator package independently of the development environment, for demonstration purposes.

The Default Directory Scheme

Here's the default scheme:

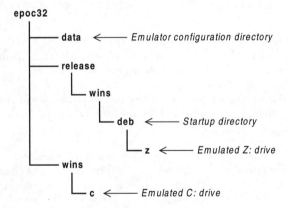

The directory tree is fixed relative to a drive. This is a major constraint on your flexibility in installing EPOC SDKs. These are the directories and their uses:

Directory	Description	Contents
`\epoc32\wins\c\`	Emulated `c:` drive	Any data, but no compiled C++ programs – those should all be on `z:`
`\epoc32\release\wins\deb\`	Startup directory	Startup `.exe`, and all shared library DLLs

Table Continued on Following Page

Directory	Description	Contents
\epoc32\release\wins\deb\z\	Emulated z: drive	Everything that the EPOC z: drive should contain, except shared library DLLs
\epoc32\data\	Configuration directory	Emulator .ini and fascia .bmp files

It would be nice if \epoc32\release\wins\deb\z\ could contain the entire emulated z: drive. Unfortunately, it can't: .exes and shared library DLLs can't use EPOC's file structure without impractical implications for the PATH environment in Win32. The only practical solution is to place all .exes and shared library DLLs in the startup directory – \epoc32\release\wins\deb\.

A limitation of the default scheme is that only a single emulator per PC drive is possible. If you want more emulators, you have to subst or network-map directories into new drives. That's why – unless the SDKs are all for exactly the same release of EPOC – you have to install different EPOC SDKs on different drives.

The New Directory Scheme

From EPOC Release 5, a new scheme was invented that allows you to start the emulator from whichever directory you choose – say, \mystuff\epoc\. The directories for emulated c: and z: drives, and emulator startup information, are subdirectories of the startup directory.

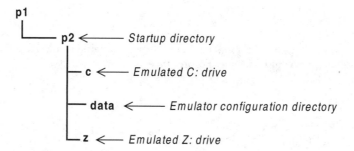

These are the rules that come into force if the startup directory is anything other than \epoc32\release\wins\buildtype\:

Directory	Description	Contents
startup\	Startup directory	Startup .exe and all shared library DLLs
startup\c\	Emulated c: drive	Data disk
startup\z\	Emulated z: drive	Program and program data disk for all files except shared libraries
startup\data\	Initialization	Emulator .ini and fascia .bmp files

Unfortunately, the other tools in the EPOC Release 5 SDKs were not changed, and so in practice you still have to build and debug in the default directory scheme.

Emulator Startup Parameters

You can control the emulator startup by parameters in epoc.ini. Here's the epoc.ini as supplied on the C++ SDK:

```
ScreenOffsetX 90
ScreenOffsetY 51
LedOffsetX 36
LedSize 14
```

This specifies the offset of the screen area from the top left of the fascia bitmap, and the position and size of the two emulated LEDs.

vga.ini specifies a VGA-sized screen region:

```
ScreenWidth 640
ScreenHeight 480
ScreenOffsetX 91
ScreenOffsetY 50
LedOffsetX 37
LedSize 14
```

The ScreenWidth and ScreenHeight parameters are specified explicitly here. If you want the emulator to use vga.ini, start it up with this (and yes, you really do need all those -- signs):

epoc -Mvga --

Besides c: and z:, you can make additional emulated drives available to EPOC programs under the emulator, by adding them to your .ini file. For instance,

```
_EPOC_DRIVE_D a:\
```

allows me to code a PC diskette drive as my EPOC d:, and therefore test the effects of removable media. Be careful to specify the _EPOC_DRIVE_D in upper case: the specification will be silently ignored if you don't.

You can override the emulated c: drive from the command line: use,

epoc -T --

to map the emulated c: drive to your PC's system temporary directory. This allows you to quickly boot up EPOC from a CD-ROM, which can be quite handy for demo purposes.

If you care about a specific emulated c:, use this:

epoc -C*pcpath* --

Note those two -- signs again!

Communications

On an EPOC R5 machine, all external communication is via a serial port – either using infrared, or RS232. This includes dial-up TCP/IP and IrDA communication. On the emulator, you use a PC's serial ports instead of real device hardware:

- ❑ You can test EPOC RS232 programs using PC RS232 ports

- ❑ You can use a PC-style serial cable, often available for data-capable mobile phones, to connect the EPOC emulator to a mobile phone

- ❑ You *can't* use your LAN for TCP/IP: instead, you have to use dial-up networking and a modem

- ❑ You can use an infrared pod, such as the JetEye pod described in Chapter 21, for IR beaming, or communication with an IR-enabled mobile phone

You have to get the settings right in the emulator control panel, to use the right port. See Chapter 21 for how we set up the JetEye pod to debug our IR driver for the transaction-oriented games stack (TOGS).

Some kinds of TCP/IP testing are much more convenient – not to say cheaper – if you can access TCP/IP services on your LAN, rather than using dial-up. If you need to do this, the best solution is to use RAS on Windows NT. You need a PC with two communications ports, connected to each other. Use one port for the emulator serial 'out', and another for RAS 'in'. Check out Symbian's developer web site, www.epocworld.com, for instructions on how to set up RAS on Windows NT for this purpose.

How Good is the Emulator?

The answer is, pretty good.

- ❑ Because the emulator uses straightforward mappings of EPOC facilities to Windows, there is relatively little fancy Win32 code at the bottom of the emulator, and therefore relatively little that can go wrong.

- ❑ The emulator runs in its own process. It's a process just like any other Windows process, so you can have multiple emulators all running on one machine for that conference demo.

- ❑ The emulator uses its own window. It's not resizable, but it can be dragged, and moved to front and back, just like any other window.

- ❑ The emulator uses files that you simply copy around on your PC directories. There's no special file pool that requires tools to check files in and out. If you copy a file to a directory used by the emulator for an emulated drive, it's instantly available for use.

There are a few things to watch out for, though.

Files copied to the emulator are instantly ready for use. But if you use the PC to copy a file, the emulator's F32 won't know that you've done this, and so no file-system notifications will trigger. So if the file is, say, a new application icon, the icon won't get refreshed automatically. You can force F32 to rescan by opening and closing the disk door, using *F5*.

For some reason, the emulator likes to keep application resource files open. So if you have the emulator running, you have used an application, and you want to update that application's resource file, you have to close the emulator – not just the application. This doesn't seem to apply to any other type of file – you can update the .app, for instance, without restarting the emulator.

The emulator is too fast. You can be deceived into thinking you have an application that performs well enough, especially if you use a super-fast PC for development work. And, of course, you *will* use a super-fast PC if you can, because C++ compilers use all the PC power you can throw at them.

PC screens and pointers aren't the same as EPOC machine screens and pointers. If an application looks good on a PC screen, and can be used effectively with a mouse, that doesn't mean it will also look good on a real device, with a real pointer (or your finger).

The emulator is only source compatible, not binary compatible. So you can't install compiled programs built for a real machine onto the emulator.

There are subtle incompatibilities in source code due to alignment restrictions on ARM, and the single-process restriction on the emulator.

The C++ dialect and warnings differ between Microsoft Visual C++ and GCC. Actually, the version of GCC used is a lot more limited. So, before you commit to a design that relies on too many C++ tricks, check out your ideas with GCC as well as with Microsoft Visual C++.

ARM data alignment rules are strict; x86 alignment rules are more relaxed. If you need alignment, copy potentially unaligned data byte by byte into an aligned area. For example:

```
TBuf8<200> buffer;
TInt index = 39; // not a multiple of 4!!
TInt* p = (TInt*)(buffer.Ptr() + index);
TInt i = *p;
```

The cast ought to be a warning of trouble: this code is platform dependent. It happens to work on x86, but not on ARM. You need to use code like:

```
TBuf8<200> buffer;
TInt index = 39; // not a multiple of 4!!
TInt i;
Mem::Copy(&i, buffer.Ptr() + index, 4);
```

On a target machine, each application and server is a separate process, with its own .exe. On the emulator, there is only one process, so applications use apprun.dll instead of apprun.exe, and most servers are delivered as DLLs. There are established patterns for working around these issues: they affect very few lines of EPOC code. For applications, the issue is addressed for you, so you don't need to worry. If you write a server, you'll need to copy one of the standard patterns, such as the one I use in Chapter 20.

On the emulator, all EPOC threads run in the same PC address space. So some very obscure and awkward bugs can result whereby code with random reads or writes appears to work under the emulator, but crashes quickly on a target machine. However, standard EPOC programming uses active objects and the client-server architecture, which means that *deliberate* use of shared memory is very rare. So very few programs are by nature difficult to debug because of differences between the emulator and target machines.

The emulator builds on top of Win32 APIs; real EPOC builds on a micro-kernel, hardware, and device drivers. If you're programming these, then the emulator won't help: you need the real hardware. Likewise, the emulator is of less help if you're working with communications, where there are always device-specific issues. You can go so far with the emulator, but ultimately you have to test on real hardware, and then you're into RDebug-type debugging.

On target machines, Symbian controls the executable image format, and has incorporated UIDs into it. On the emulator, Symbian clearly doesn't control the executable image format, so we use the stub .uid.cpp file to generate UIDs into the .E32_UID data segment. Files on the emulator are recognized as such by the application architecture, but aren't checked by the Windows loader as they are on a target machine.

For some projects, you can build for the emulator only, until the day before you ship. A simple rebuild, and you're up and running on the emulator and everything's fine. But it would be unwise to think all projects are like that, even all those that 'ought to be'. Any of the issues I mentioned above could be a factor in your project. The best way to tackle them is to see them a long way in advance. Build periodically for the real hardware. Check for obvious bugs, UI considerations, and performance. Take action early on, while you can still make a difference.

EIKON Debug Keys

In debug builds, the EIKON environment provides some useful keys – we already saw some of them in Chapter 6. All keys with the *Ctrl+Alt+Shift* modifiers are trapped by EIKON's debug key monitor. Here's a complete list of those that produce any effect:

Key	Description
A	Display allocation info-message, saying how many heap cells have been allocated by the current application's main thread – this key doesn't work on the EPOC R5 SDK
B	Display file server resource info-message, saying how many file server resources are allocated on behalf of the current application's built-in RFs
C	Display the window server resource info-message, saying how many window server resources are allocated on behalf of the current application's built-in window server session
F	Enable window server auto-flush for this application, so that each drawing command is immediately sent to the window server
H	Disable window server auto-flush for this application (the default state), so that drawing commands are batched together, and only sent to the window server when either the buffer is full, the application requests an explicit flush, or the application waits for another event
K	Not an EIKON debug key, but a window server hotkey also available in release builds. Causes the window server to kill the current application. Since the emulator is a single process, this key kills the entire emulator
M	Display Move me! dialog, which you can drag around the screen, causing your application to redraw in its wake
P	Display heap failure dialog, so you can specify systematic failures of heap allocations, file server allocations, and window server allocations

Table Continued on Following Page

Key	Description
Q	Cancel any heap failure mode settings, so that allocations only fail if the system is genuinely out of memory
R	Display and immediately remove a blank window, so that your application has to redraw its entire view
S	Not an EIKON debug key, but a window server hotkey that takes a screenshot
T	Display system task list – a handy alternative to the standard techniques, both of which require the pointer (I found this immensely useful for Battleships testing on the emulator)
V	Toggle display of verbose info-messages
Y	Mount simulated removable media device on x: – this key appears not to work on the EPOC R5 SDK
Z	Send keys ABCDEFGHIJ in rapid sequence to the application, to ensure it can handle rapid key events

WINC and Command-line Tools

Sometimes you want to write PC-hosted tools that use EPOC file formats. Three examples among Symbian's products are

- ❑ EPOC Connect accesses EPOC files so it can convert them into PC data formats
- ❑ aleppo, EPOC's help builder, writes a help database, which uses an EPOC file format
- ❑ aiftool, which builds application information files, also uses an EPOC file format

The easiest way to access file formats is through the APIs that produce those files – which, as we saw in the previous chapter, are tailored for easy re-use. EPOC's WINC build meets this need. WINC is a version of E32 and F32 that:

- ❑ Like the emulator, runs on Windows-hosted services
- ❑ Unlike the emulator, contains no support for graphics
- ❑ Offers exactly the same APIs, at binary level, to all higher-level EPOC executables, so that any non-graphics DLL built for the emulator can run on WINC unchanged
- ❑ Unlike the emulator, does not map filenames to emulated EPOC drives, but directly to the PC's file system
- ❑ Unlike the emulator, implements CConsoleBase consoles by sending their text output to stdout – that is, to a Win32 console if you launch a WINC program from the command line

The WINC components of EPOC Connect do not use a CConsoleBase console. Instead, they rely on the graphics components of EPOC Connect to use Windows' GUI for user interaction.

aiftool and aleppo use CConsoleBase to provide a log of their actions for the user, and WINC command-line parsing for command-line arguments.

To build a .exe for WINC, you have to specify the winc command-line argument to makmake. I used this technique to rebuild buffers for WINC and run it from the Windows NT command prompt:

```
G:\pep\buffers> \epoc32\release\winc\deb\buffers
buffer=[hell][o!]
buffer=[hell][o wo][rld!]
buffer=[he][ld!]
buffer=[held][!]
buffer=[held][ÏÏÏÏ][!ld!]
buffer=[hell][o wo][rld!]
[ press any key ]
G:\pep\buffers>
```

There's not much point in the 'press any key' prompt when running under WINC. That code is there on the emulator to prevent the emulator from disappearing before you see the output – but the NT command doesn't disappear when the WINC version of buffers has finished.

To get buffers running, I started with makmake, specifying the winc argument:

```
makmake buffers winc
```

This generates a suitable makefile that, as it happens, includes a version of eexe.obj that launches the WINC version of the EPOC kernel and file server. Then, I made the project:

```
nmake -f buffers.winc
```

Finally, I ran the program as above. Very simple! I could have generated a Visual C++ 5 project file for the WINC build, using,

```
makmake buffers vc5winc
```

and then opened the project from within the IDE, and debugged through it.

To deliver buffers as an independent program, you need to deliver buffers.exe and all associated DLLs in a single directory. The recommended way is to rebuild for release mode, and copy buffers.exe and the required DLLs from \epoc32\release\winc\rel\ into another directory.

If you are writing a command-line tool for use in the SDK, you will want it to be in your path. You can guarantee that \epoc32\tools\ will be in the path, but it is a bad idea to put the .exe and all DLLs into there because the DLLs delivered with one WINC tool may be incompatible with those delivered with another. It is recommended that you use \epoc32\tools\buffers\ as the run-time directory, and install a small stub batch file in \epoc32\tools\buffers.bat to launch it. The license agreement with the C++ SDK allows distribution of these DLLs for WINC tools: but do read the terms and conditions.

Command-line tools usually need to parse their command-line arguments. You will find useful functions for this in the CCommandLineArguments class in bacline.h. Here's its definition:

```
class CCommandLineArguments : public CBase
    {
public:
    // Construct/destruct
    IMPORT_C static CCommandLineArguments* NewLC();
    IMPORT_C static CCommandLineArguments* NewL();
    IMPORT_C ~CCommandLineArguments();

    // Extract
    IMPORT_C TPtrC Arg(TInt aArg) const;
    IMPORT_C TInt Count() const;
private:
    CCommandLineArguments();
    void ConstructL();
private:
    CArrayFixFlat<TPtrC>* iArgs;
    TCommand iCommandLine;
    TFileName iFileName;
    };
```

You create a CCommandLineArguments with NewL() or NewLC(), and then use Count() and Arg(TInt) as you would use argc and argv[] in a standard C program. Destroy the CCommandLineArguments object as soon as you can, because it uses quite a bit of heap memory.

> *In earlier releases of EPOC, WINC had an annoying bug: it used to force the initial current directory to* c:\. *This has been fixed in EPOC Release 5: the initial current directory is now the current directory when the command was invoked.*

Summary

This chapter finishes off the section of the book that introduces basic EPOC development techniques and APIs. In it, we've seen:

❑   Static functions from the User and Math classes. User library support for collections and locales.

❑   Dynamic buffers, flat and segmented, for arrays and rich text.

❑   EPOC's C standard library to support porting.

❑   How to support variable argument lists.

❑   Debugging with Printf()-style formatting of strings and the RDebug class.

❑   The emulator's key mappings, debug keys, startup settings, directory structures and setup for communications.

❑   Emulator gotchas – reasons to test your applications on target hardware well ahead of time.

❑   The WINC build of EPOC and its use for native file support on PCs.

In the next chapter, we return to the helloeik application, and look at the source code of a simple EIKON application.

Part Two

Graphics and the EIKON GUI

Any real application for the mass market needs an easy-to-use graphical interface. EIKON is EPOC Release 5's GUI framework, tailored for the needs of the form factor and market addressed by machines such as the Psion Series 5mx. Future Symbian device families will address different markets, and their GUI frameworks will differ in detail from EIKON, but the underlying graphics architecture, and the general spirit of the GUI, will be preserved.

So, in this section, I've concentrated on the following themes:

- ❏ In Chapter 9 and Chapter 10, a guide to and tour of EIKON's application framework, dialog framework, and concrete controls, which are the building blocks for any EIKON application you'll write

- ❏ In Chapter 11 and Chapter 12, a description of the graphics architecture in detail, especially those components that won't change (except for a gradual evolution) – namely the window server, CONE and the GDI

- ❏ In Chapter 13, the tools necessary to finish off a professional application, including icons, help and making an installable package

- ❏ In Chapter 14, a consolidation of the material in the previous three chapters, and a demonstration of how to make your applications embeddable and persistent.

- ❏ In Chapter 15, the main aspects of the graphics architecture that support device independence – and a discussion of the limits of device independence

With additional guidance and background detail, these chapters could easily swell to fill an entire book. As it is, some of the coverage here has the flavour of a whistle-stop tour: it isn't reference material. When you get down to detailed design and programming, you'll need to use the extra information that's provided by the APIs and source code in the SDK.

9

Getting Started with the EIKON GUI

Back in Chapter 2, we built both a text-mode and a GUI version of the "Hello World" program, and we made the point that no one really wants to run text-mode programs on a user-friendly system like EPOC.

At this stage in the book, we have seen enough of EPOC's fundamentals that we can start looking at real graphics and GUI programming with EIKON, the GUI environment in EPOC Release 5. EIKON is built on a sophisticated architecture for graphics and interaction that was inspired by many others, including X, SIBO, and Windows.

After a brief introduction to EPOC's graphics architecture, I'll spend the body of this chapter walking through `helloeik`, the GUI program we built in Chapter 2. I'll start by walking through the code, explaining how its design fits in with the EIKON framework. Then, I'll take you through a session with the debugger, which will reinforce the code design and also introduce some ideas about controls, pointer, and key event handling which we'll return to in Chapter 12. Finally I'll include a reference to the resource compiler, which is a key tool for GUI application development.

Introduction to the Graphics Architecture

The most important of EPOC's graphics and GUI components, and their main relationships, are shown in the diagram:

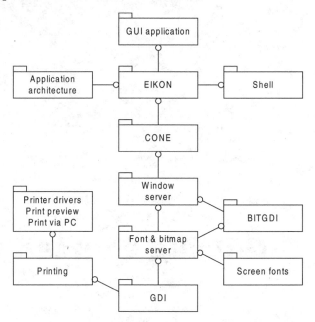

At the bottom is the GDI, which defines the drawing primitives and everything necessary to achieve device-independent drawing. The GDI is an entirely abstract component that has to be implemented in various contexts – for on-screen pixel graphics, for instance, or in a printer driver. I'll be covering the main drawing functions defined by the GDI in Chapter 11, and its support for device-independent drawing in Chapter 15.

The BITGDI handles optimized rasterizing and bit blitting for on-screen windows and off-screen bitmaps. The font and bitmap server (FBS) manages fonts and bitmaps – potentially large graphics entities – for optimal space efficiency.

Support for user interaction starts with the window server, which manages the screen, pointer, and keyboard on behalf of *all* GUI programs within the system. It shares these devices according to windowing conventions that are easily understood by the average end user. A standard window is represented in the client API by the RWindow class.

The window server is a single server process that provides a basic API for client applications to use. CONE, the control environment, runs in each application process and works with the window server's client-side API, to allow different parts of an application to share windows, the keyboard, and pointer events. A fundamental abstract class delivered by CONE is CCoeControl, a **control**, which is a unit of user interaction using any combination of screen, keyboard, and pointer. Many controls can share a single window. Concrete control types are derived from CCoeControl.

CONE doesn't provide any concrete controls: that's the job of EIKON, the system GUI, which defines look-and-feel. EIKON specifies a standard look-and-feel, and provides re-usable controls and other classes that implement that look-and-feel. For instance, EIKON applications usually have a toolbar, a menu bar, and shortcut keys; it's very easy to define these in the application's resource file, and EIKON manages them for you.

To the left of the central graphics components, I've included EPOC's printing components. Printer basics are defined in the GDI, while the PRINT component implements the GDI and defines a printer driver interface. Several printer drivers are delivered with EPOC R5, so that you can drive these printers directly from your EPOC machine. One catch-all driver, 'Print via PC', sends print commands to a PC's currently-installed printer driver via EPOC Connect, so that you can print to *any* printer model, provided it's attached to your PC. Print support also includes an on-screen preview, which is useful for checking basic page layout. Any application that can print can also preview without writing new drawing code.

Application Structure

In this chapter, we'll begin to understand how EIKON applications fit together, using the frameworks provided by EIKON and the application architecture. We'll start by looking closer at `helloeik.app`, which we first saw in Chapter 2. This time, we'll look at the source code in detail, and we'll go through it with the debugger to bring to life some of the ideas you've already learned, and to introduce what's to come.

On the screen, `helloeik` looks like this. It says Hello world!, and when you press any of the four toolbar buttons, it flashes a message in the top right corner that says which button you pressed:

To jog your memory, the source code in \pep\helloeik\ consists of the definitions and implementation of four classes – the minimum for an EIKON application – and a resource file. Here they are, set in context:

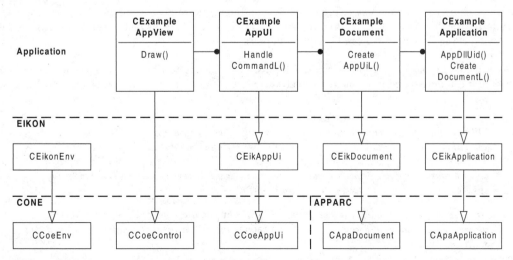

The figure shows the four classes (and their member functions) that you *have* to implement. Anything less than this, and you don't have an EIKON application. Right to left, the classes are:

❑ An **application**: in EIKON, the application class serves to define the *properties* of the application, and also to manufacture a new, blank, document. For a minimal application, you only have to define the application's UID.

❑ A **document**: a document represents the data model manipulated by the application. If the application is file-based, the document is responsible for storing and restoring the application's persistent data. Even if the application is not file-based, it must have a document class, even though that class doesn't do much apart from launch the app UI.

❑ An **app UI** (short for 'application user interface'). The most important function in the app UI is HandleCommandL(), which handles commands generated by menu items, toolbar buttons, and shortcut keys. The app UI itself is entirely invisible: it delegates drawing and screen-based interaction to the app view and other controls.

❑ An **app view**, which is, in fact, a concrete control. This displays the application data on screen and allows you to interact with it. An ultra-minimal control has only a Draw() function, but most controls also have HandlePointerEventL() and OfferKeyEventL() for input event handling.

Except for the app view, these classes are derived from base classes in EIKON. In turn, EIKON is based on two important frameworks:

❑ CONE, the **control environment**, is the framework for graphical interaction. I'll be describing CONE in detail in Chapter 11 and Chapter 12.

❑ APPARC, the **application architecture**, is the framework for applications and application data, as we saw in Chapter 7.

EIKON provides a library of useful functions in its environment class, CEikonEnv, which is in turn derived from CCoeEnv, the CONE environment, and I've shown these in the diagram as well. Fortunately, the application can use these functions without the need to write yet another derived class.

In addition to the four C++ classes, you have to define elements of your application's GUI – the menu, the toolbar, the shortcut keys, and any string resources you might want to use when localizing the application – in a **resource file**. We've used eikrs to build application resource files for helloeik and streams: we'll take a much closer look at resource files in this chapter.

Remember that this is a diagram for a *minimal* application. The application is free to use any other class it needs, and it can derive and implement more classes of its own, but no application can get smaller than this.

> *EPOC's stated design goal is to make real, potentially large, programs easier to write and understand. Compared with this aim, programming a minimal application really isn't very important. In consequence, the document class in non-file-based applications doesn't do much, and the idea that the app UI is there to 'edit the document' is a bit over-engineered. Thankfully, the application and document classes aren't hard to write.*

> *However, if you want to write a truly minimal application, you can get away with just three classes: an application, a document and a glass door – an application that can never be opened, but which can be embedded.*

Let's have a look at how the classes in `helloeik` implement the requirements of APPARC, EIKON, and CONE, and how the resource file is used to define the main elements of the GUI.

Application Architecture Support for Application and Document Classes

The application architecture's main contribution to EIKON applications is to provide a model for file-based applications and document embedding. `helloeik` doesn't use files or embedded documents, so it codes the application and document classes trivially. Here, I'll run through the APPARC-related code, and explain in passing what it's doing. Then I'll sum up some of APPARC's features, and give some pointers to more information in the book.

Here's the `helloeik` code that's responsible for implementing the requirements of the application architecture. You can find it at the bottom of `helloeik.cpp` in `\pep\helloeik\`.

```
// Document
CExampleDocument::CExampleDocument(CEikApplication& aApp) : CEikDocument(aApp)
    {
    }

CEikAppUi* CExampleDocument::CreateAppUiL()
    {
    return new(ELeave) CExampleAppUi;
    }

// Application
TUid CExampleApplication::AppDllUid() const
    {
    return KUidExample;
    }

CApaDocument* CExampleApplication::CreateDocumentL()
    {
    return new(ELeave) CExampleDocument(*this);
    }

// DLL interface code
EXPORT_C CApaApplication* NewApplication()
    {
    return new CExampleApplication;
    }

GLDEF_C TInt E32Dll(TDllReason)
    {
    return KErrNone;
    }
```

I've coded this file in reverse order, by which I mean that the calls into this code start at the bottom, with `E32Dll()`, and carry on up. In the next few sections, we'll follow the action, starting at the bottom.

DLL Startup Code

When you launch an application from the shell, the .exe that is launched is actually apprun.exe, with the application name and file name as command line parameters. apprun in turn uses the application architecture to load the correct application DLL.

> **Every EIKON application is a DLL.**

When you launch an application to edit an embedded document, *no* new process is created. The application architecture framework loads the application DLL – if it is not already loaded – into the same process as the main document's DLL (and indeed any other application DLLs that may be active, if there are multiple embedded documents).

Regardless of how the DLL gets loaded, however, the first important part of our code is the section that implements the DLL's interface. After loading it, the application architecture:

❑ Checks that its second UID is 0x1000006c

❑ Runs its first ordinal exported function to create an application object – that is, an object of a class derived from CApaApplication.

As we've already seen, makmake supports the generation of application DLLs. In order to understand those last two bullet points, let's take a closer look at the important features of a .mmp file for our application. helloeik.mmp starts:

```
TARGET helloeik.app
TARGETTYPE app
UID 0x1000006c 0x10005401
```

The app target type causes makmake to generate instructions that force NewApplication() to be exported as the first ordinal function from the helloeik.app DLL.

All EIKON applications specify a UID 0x1000006c, while UID 0x10005401 identifies my particular application helloeik.app. I allocated this UID from a block of 10 that were issued to me by EPOC World, as I described in Chapter 2.

> *I said above that 0x1000006c was the second UID for this application.* makmake *helpfully generates the first UID for you, a UID that indicates that the application is in fact a DLL.*

The main purpose of the DLL-related code in helloeik.cpp is to implement NewApplication():

```
// DLL interface code
EXPORT_C CApaApplication* NewApplication()
    {
    return new CExampleApplication;
    }

GLDEF_C TInt E32Dll(TDllReason)
    {
    return KErrNone;
    }
```

> You *must* code the prototype of `NewApplication()` exactly as shown, otherwise the
> C++ name mangling will be different from that expected by `makmake`'s first ordinal
> export specification, and your application won't link correctly.

My `NewApplication()` function returns my own application class, after first-phase construction. In the rather unlikely event that there isn't enough memory to allocate and C++-construct a `CExampleApplication` object, `NewApplication()` will return a null pointer and the application architecture loader will handle cleanup.

Note in passing that all EPOC DLLs *must* also code an `E32Dll()` function that *ought* to do nothing, as mine does above.

> *If it exists to do nothing, why is the function there and why does it take a parameter? In Windows terminology, this function is the DLL entry point, and it's called when the DLL is attached to or detached from a process or thread – at least, that's the theory, and we thought that would be useful for allocating DLL-specific data in the early days of EPOC development.*
>
> *In practice, however, it isn't called symmetrically in Windows, so it doesn't work under the emulator, and therefore is pretty useless for EPOC development. If you need to allocate DLL-specific memory, use the thread-local storage functions `Dll::Tls()` and `Dll::SetTls()`: call them from your main class's C++ constructor and destructor, and point to your class rather than some other ad hoc global variable structure. See `\cone\src\coemain.cpp` (along with `\cone\inc\coetls.h`) in the SDK for an example, and John Forrest's discussions on TLS in Chapter 24.*

The Application

Assuming that `NewApplication()` returned an application, the architecture then calls `AppDllUid()` to provide another check on the identity of the application DLL. That's all it needs to know about the application. It then calls `CreateDocumentL()`, which the application uses to create a default document. Both of these are virtual functions that I implement in my derived application class.

Here's the definition of `CExampleApplication` in `helloeik.h`:

```
class CExampleApplication : public CEikApplication
    {
private:                // From CApaApplication
    CApaDocument* CreateDocumentL();
    TUid AppDllUid() const;
    };
```

> *As the class diagram of the `helloeik` application shows, `CEikApplication` is itself derived from `CApaApplication`.*

And here's the implementation in `helloeik.cpp`:

```
// Application
TUid CExampleApplication::AppDllUid() const
    {
    return KUidExample;
    }

CApaDocument* CExampleApplication::CreateDocumentL()
    {
    return new(ELeave) CExampleDocument(*this);
    }
```

Given the explanation above, there's nothing too surprising here. I defined the UID in my `helloeik.h` file:

```
#ifdef _UNICODE
const TUid KUidExample = { 0 };
#else
const TUid KUidExample = { 0x10005401 };
#endif
```

I use the same UID here as in my `.mmp` file: the application architecture verifies that this is the same as my DLL UID, as a final check on the integrity of my application DLL.

> *When EPOC has Unicode support, I'll code a sensible UID in the Unicode case too. In the mean time, that code is just a placeholder.*

In the code above, then, you can see that the application class has two purposes:

❑ It conveys some information about the *capabilities* of the application, including its UID

❑ It acts as a factory for a default document

These are little things, but important. Pretty much every EIKON application contains these two functions coded just as I've implemented them here, changing only the class names and the UID from one application to the next.

The Document

The really interesting code starts with the document class. In a file-based application, the document essentially represents the data in the file. You can do several things with that data, each of which makes different demands: displaying it in a glass door, for example, or printing it, doesn't require an application – but editing it does. We'll see more of this in Chapter 15.

`CEikDocument` implements the `CApaDocument::EditL()` function by asking your derived document to create an application user interface (app UI), which is then used to 'edit' the document.

In a non-file-based application, you still have to code a function in the document class to create an app UI, since it's the app UI that does the real work. Apart from creating the app UI, then, the document class for such an application is trivial.

Here, then, is the declaration of CExampleDocument:

```
class CExampleDocument : public CEikDocument
    {
public:
    // Construct/destruct
    CExampleDocument(CEikApplication& aApp);

private:                  // From CEikDocument
    CEikAppUi* CreateAppUiL();
    };
```

And here's the implementation:

```
// Document
CExampleDocument::CExampleDocument(CEikApplication& aApp)
       : CEikDocument(aApp)
    {
    }

CEikAppUi* CExampleDocument::CreateAppUiL()
    {
    return new(ELeave) CExampleAppUi;
    }
```

We start with a C++ constructor that simply calls CEikDocument's constructor, passing in the application as an argument. Next, there's the virtual CreateAppUiL() function which, to nobody's surprise, returns a new app UI. Note carefully that CreateAppUiL() is responsible only for *first-phase* construction. We'll see the second phase shortly.

Summary

The application architecture's role in application launch is to:

- ❏ Load the DLL
- ❏ Call its first exported function to create a new 'application' – a CApaApplication-derived object
- ❏ Check the UID returned by the application object
- ❏ Ask the application to create a new default document
- ❏ Ask the document to edit itself, which EIKON implements by asking you to create an app UI

The application architecture's role in application launch is pretty trivial for applications like helloeik, which aren't file-based.

For file-based applications, you have to implement a less trivial document class, with one or more data members to contain (or point to) your document data, and StoreL() and RestoreL() functions to load and save. We'll see how that works for Battleships, in Chapter 22.

The App UI and Command Handling

The GUI action proper starts with the app UI, which has two main roles:

❑ A role defined by EIKON: to get **commands** to the application

❑ A role defined by CONE: to distribute keystrokes to controls, including the application's main view, which is owned by the app UI

A command is simply an instruction without any parameters, or any information about where it came from, which the program must execute. In any practical EIKON program, you implement `HandleCommandL(TInt aCommandId)` in your derived app UI class. The command ID is simply a 32-bit integer.

If that seems a vague definition, think of some places where commands can originate:

❑ From a menu: EIKON applications usually have menu trees, with File, Edit, View etc. panes, and commands such as File | Close, Edit | Paste etc., which are selected from an item on the menu pane.

❑ From a shortcut key: applications may assign a shortcut key to any command ID – whether or not it's on the menus. The conventional shortcut key for File | Close, for instance, is *Ctrl+E*.

❑ From a toolbar button: the toolbar makes common commands very prominent.

❑ From a sidebar button, such as the cut/copy/paste pop-up menu and IR beaming menu available from the sidebar, or the zoom in and zoom out icons on the sidebar.

A command such as 'zoom in' is available from all of these sources. It doesn't matter where it comes from, the app UI receives it as a 32-bit command ID in `HandleCommandL()` and simply executes the appropriate code to handle the command.

> In this chapter, I'll only show a trivial `HandleCommandL()` function. The main body of this chapter is dedicated to showing how to use resource files to specify the UI objects — menu, shortcut keys, toolbar — which can originate commands.

Some commands can be executed immediately, given only their ID. File | Close exits the application (we don't ask the user: we simply save their data. If the user didn't mean to exit, all they need to do is open the file again). View | Zoom in zooms the application view to the next highest zoom factor.

But other commands need further UI processing. A File | Open command needs a filename as a parameter. A File | Revert to saved command (which throws away any changes and re-loads the document from the last copy on file) should query the user to ask whether the user is sure. Handling such commands involves **dialogs**, which are the subject of the next chapter.

Not all input to applications comes from commands. If you type the letter X into a word processor while you're editing, it doesn't generate a command, but a key event. If you tap on a selected file in the shell, it doesn't generate a command, but a pointer event. Handling pointer and key events is the business of the app view and other controls in the application. After a chapter on drawing to controls (Chapter 11), I cover key and pointer interaction in Chapter 12.

Some key and pointer events are captured by controls in the EIKON framework, and turned into commands. Later this chapter, we'll get a glimpse into how EIKON's menu, toolbar, and shortcut key controls convert these basic UI events into commands.

Here's the declaration of CExampleAppUi in `helloeik.h`:

```
class CExampleAppUi : public CEikAppUi
    {
public:
    void ConstructL();
    ~CExampleAppUi();

private:                    // From CEikAppUi
    void HandleCommandL(TInt aCommand);

private:
    CExampleAppView* iAppView;
    };
```

As usual, the second-phase constructor and the destructor reveal who owns what:

```
void CExampleAppUi::ConstructL()
    {
    BaseConstructL();
    iAppView = new(ELeave) CExampleAppView;
    iAppView->ConstructL(ClientRect());
    }

CExampleAppUi::~CExampleAppUi()
    {
    delete iAppView;
    }
```

ConstructL() performs second-phase construction of the base class, CEikAppUi, using BaseConstructL(). It's this function that, among other things, reads the application's resource file and constructs the menu, shortcut keys, and toolbar for the application.

ConstructL() then constructs the main app view using a two-phase constructor. The ClientRect() passed as a parameter to the app view is the amount of screen left over after the toolbar and any other adornments set by CEikAppUi have been taken into account. Predictably, the destructor destroys the application view.

Here's the HandleCommandL() function:

```
void CExampleAppUi::HandleCommandL(TInt aCommand)
    {
    switch(aCommand)
        {
    case EExampleCmd1:
        iEikonEnv->InfoMsg(R_EXAMPLE_TEXT_CMD1);
        break;
```

```
        case EExampleCmd2:
            iEikonEnv->InfoMsg(R_EXAMPLE_TEXT_CMD2);
            break;
        case EExampleCmd3:
            iEikonEnv->InfoMsg(R_EXAMPLE_TEXT_CMD3);
            break;
        case EExampleCmd4:
            iEikonEnv->InfoMsg(R_EXAMPLE_TEXT_CMD4);
            break;
        case EEikCmdExit:
            Exit();
            }
        }
```

This function handles five commands. Four of these are defined by the application, and identified by the values EExampleCmd1 through EExampleCmd4; the other is defined by EIKON, and identified by EEikCmdExit.

EIKON's command constants are defined in eikcmds.hrh, which you can find in the \epoc32\include\ directory. .hrh files are designed to be included in both C++ programs (which need them, as above, for identifying commands to be handled) and resource scripts (which need them, as we'll see below, to indicate commands to be issued). EIKON's standard command definitions include many of the commonly found menu commands on the File, Edit and Help menus, and many others. All EPOC-defined command IDs are in the range 0x0100 to 0x01ff.

My command constants are defined in helloeik.hrh, as follows:

```
#define EExampleCmd1 0x1001
#define EExampleCmd2 0x1002
#define EExampleCmd3 0x1003
#define EExampleCmd4 0x1004
```

It's clearly important that the constants I choose should be unique with respect to EIKON's, so I started numbering them at 0x1000. That's standard practice, so you're safe if you do this too.

It's also standard practice to name these values with an E as if they were enumerated constants, but to #define them. This code works nicely with both C++ and the resource compiler. You might have expected to see enums, or otherwise K to identify constants. That's not the convention here, though enums are used to define many other EIKON constants for C++ and resource files.

To handle these commands, I call on EIKON:

❏   I deal with the EEikCmdExit command by calling Exit(). That resolves to CEikAppUi::Exit(), which terminates the EIKON environment.

❏   I deal with my own commands by calling CEikonEnv::InfoMsg() to display an **info-message** on the screen. InfoMsg() is just one of many useful functions in the EIKON environment; its argument is a resource ID that identifies a string to be displayed, for about three seconds, in the top right corner of the screen.

A more substantial application will have to handle *many* commands in its app UI's `HandleCommandL()` function. Normally, instead of handling them inline as I do here, you would code each case as a function call followed by `break`. Most EPOC applications (and my examples in this book) use a function named `CmdFoo()` or `CmdFooL()` to handle a command identified as `EExampleCmdFoo`.

The App View

Anything that can draw to the screen is a **control**. Controls can also (optionally) handle key and pointer events.

> *Note that controls don't have to be able to draw. They can be permanently invisible. But that's quite unusual: a permanently invisible control clearly can't handle pointer events, but it could handle keys, as we'll see in Chapter 12.*

The app UI is *not* a control. It owns one or more controls, including such obviously visible controls as the toolbar; we'll see a few others throughout the next few chapters.

In a typical EIKON application, you write one control yourself. You size it to the size of the **client rectangle**, the area of the screen remaining after the toolbar and so on have been taken into account. You then use that control to display your application data, and to handle key and pointer events (which are not commands).

`helloeik`'s application view is a control whose sole purpose is to draw the text "Hello world!" on the screen in a reasonably aesthetically pleasing manner. It doesn't handle key or pointer events.

Like all controls, `CExampleAppView` is derived from `CCoeControl`, which has virtual functions that you override to implement a particular control's functionality. In this case, the only function of interest is `Draw()`. Here's the definition:

```
class CExampleAppView : public CCoeControl
    {
public:
    ~CExampleAppView();
    void ConstructL(const TRect& aRect);

private:                    // From CCoeControl
    void Draw(const TRect&) const;
private:
    HBufC* iHelloWorld;
    };
```

Let's start with the implementation of the second-phase constructor and the destructor:

```
void CExampleAppView::ConstructL(const TRect& aRect)
    {
    CreateWindowL();
    SetRectL(aRect);
    ActivateL();
    iHelloWorld = iEikonEnv->AllocReadResourceL(R_EXAMPLE_TEXT_HELLO);
    }

CExampleAppView::~CExampleAppView()
    {
    delete iHelloWorld;
    }
```

ConstructL() uses CCoeControl() base-class library functions to create a window, set it to the rectangle offered, and activate it. It then reads the "Hello World!" text from a resource file into an HBufC, which is allocated the appropriate length. This is a common pattern in application programming. The memory for the HBufC is of course deleted in the destructor.

Here's the Draw() code:

```
void CExampleAppView::Draw(const TRect& /*aRect*/) const
    {
    CWindowGc& gc = SystemGc();
    TRect rect = Rect();
    rect.Shrink(10, 10);
    gc.DrawRect(rect);
    rect.Shrink(1, 1);
    const CFont* font = iEikonEnv->TitleFont();
    gc.UseFont(font);
    TInt baseline = rect.Height() / 2 - font->AscentInPixels() / 2;
    gc.DrawText(*iHelloWorld, rect, baseline, CGraphicsContext::ECenter);
    gc.DiscardFont();
    }
```

You can probably guess well enough what most of this code is doing. Note especially that the penultimate line is DrawText(), with the iHelloWorld string as an argument. It's *this* line that actually achieves our objective of saying hello to the watching world.

The purpose of this chapter, however, isn't to explain drawing or controls: I return to that in Chapter 11, where I'll cover this Draw() function and the functions called by ConstructL() thoroughly.

A Word about Header Files

I need to briefly mention the current EIKON header file culture. Here's the top of helloeik.cpp:

```
#include "helloeik.h"
#include <eikenv.h>
```

No problem there: I include the header files for my own application, and for the EIKON environment. What about `helloeik.h`? Here it is:

```
#ifndef __HELLOEIK_H
#define __HELLOEIK_H

#include <coecntrl.h>
#include <coeccntx.h>
#include <coemain.h>

#include <eikappui.h>
#include <eikapp.h>
#include <eikdoc.h>
#include <eikcmds.hrh>

#include <helloeik.rsg>
#include "helloeik.hrh"
...
#endif
```

This trivial EIKON program has to include not only its own `.rsg` and `.hrh` files (which are released to resource and command IDs, as we'll see shortly), but also three CONE headers and four EIKON headers. Frankly, It all seems a bit much. Why not just use,

```
#include <eikon.h>
```

and let it include anything else we're going to need?

This system arose early in the Protea project, when we were very sensitive about rebuild time. People included only the headers they needed for the classes they needed — not a bad software engineering principle, in a way. But with 130 headers in EPOC R5, each typically sporting only one or two classes, the experience of anyone who tries hard with 'minimal header inclusion' tends to run as follows:

- ❏ Start with `helloeik` or some minimal program from the SDK or a colleague
- ❏ Gradually add more functionality to it
- ❏ In the process, require more and more EIKON classes
- ❏ As a result, compilers complain because you haven't included the right header file for, say, `CEikToolbar`
- ❏ Using an inspired guess at the naming convention, or a quick search, you identify `eiktbar.h` as the relevant header file, and `#include` it

So far, so good. It's a nuisance when the build fails, but it's easily fixed and you move on, proud to be including only the minimal headers. Then you need to create another source file. What do you do? Copy an existing one. So you include all the headers it includes, whether or not you need them. Goodbye, minimal header inclusion.

The truth is that nobody wins with this fine-grained approach to headers: people who like minimalism don't achieve it, and people who don't care about minimalism don't like including scores of header files in their apps.

In the next releases of EPOC,

```
#include <eikon.h>
```

will include everything needed by EIKON in a source file, and,

```
#include <eikon.rh>
```

will include everything needed by EIKON in a resource file.

The Resource File

When we built `helloeik` back in Chapter 2, you also saw how to build a resource file, but we didn't look too deeply at the contents of that file, or how it tied in with the rest of the EIKON application.

This time we'll go through the resource file and I'll show in outline how the resources defined in it build up the app UI's menu etc.. This will give you a pretty good idea of how resource files work – good enough that you'll be able to read resource files and guess what they mean. But to use EIKON seriously, you need more than that, so I've included a mini-reference at the end of the chapter.

In the code we've examined so far, we've already references to things that must be implemented in the application's resource file:

❑ The strings R_EXAMPLE_TEXT_HELLO, R_EXAMPLE_TEXT_CMD1, etc.

❑ The enumerated constants EExampleCmd1, etc.

The other things we *haven't* seen in the code are the definitions necessary to construct some aspects of the application's GUI – the toolbar, the menu, and the shortcut keys. They're defined in the resource file too.

The Header

Let's look through the resource file, `helloeik.rss`, to see exactly what gets defined, and how. First up, there's some boilerplate material:

```
NAME HELO

#include <eikdef.rh>
#include <eikmenu.rh>
#include <eiktbar.rh>
#include <eikspace.rh>
#include <eikclock.rh>
#include <eikon.rsg>
```

The NAME allows one application to access multiple resource files. It has to be distinct from the names used by EIKON and one or two other system components. There's more to come on this subject later.

The `#include` statements load definitions of structures and constants that are used within the resource file.

```
#include "helloeik.hrh"
```

This particular `#include` refers to my own `.hrh` file. As you've already seen, this contains the enumerated constants for my application's commands. I need those commands in the C++ file so I can tell which command had been issued; I need them here so that I can associate the commands with the right GUI elements: menus, toolbar, shortcut keys, etc.

After the `NAME` and `#include` lines, every EIKON resource file begins with three unnamed resources as follows:

```
RESOURCE RSS_SIGNATURE { }

RESOURCE TBUF { buf=""; }

RESOURCE EIK_APP_INFO
    {
    menubar = r_example_menubar;
    hotkeys = r_example_hotkeys;
    toolbar = r_example_toolbar;
    }
```

The `RSS_SIGNATURE` allows me to specify version information, but I don't want to use this facility here. The `TBUF` allows me to specify a friendly name for my default file, but I don't want to use that either, since this isn't a file-based application.

Defining Menu, Shortcut Keys, and Toolbar Resources

Of more interest is the `EIK_APP_INFO` resource, which identifies the symbolic resource IDs of my menu, shortcut keys, and toolbar.

Next in the resource file comes a `TOOLBAR` resource, identified by the symbolic ID `r_example_toolbar`, which ties in with the symbolic ID given above in the `EIK_APP_INFO` resource.

Those upper and lower case letters can make you seasick. The reason for them is lost in the mists of time: the resource compiler predates EPOC by several years.

```
RESOURCE TOOLBAR r_example_toolbar
    {
    breadth = KEikStdToolBarWidth;
    controls=
        {
        TBAR_CTRL
            {
            type = EEikCtFileNameLabel;
            flags = EEikToolBarCtrlHasSetMinLength;
            length = KEikStdFileNameLabelHeight;
            },
```

```
        TBAR_BUTTON
            {
            id = EExampleCmd1;
            txt = "Cmd 1";
            flags = EEikToolBarCtrlHasSetMinLength;
            length = KEikStdToolBarButtonHeight;
            },
        TBAR_BUTTON
            {
            id = EExampleCmd2;
            txt = "Cmd 2";
            flags = EEikToolBarCtrlHasSetMinLength;
            length = KEikStdToolBarButtonHeight;
            },
        TBAR_BUTTON
            {
            id = EExampleCmd3;
            txt = "Cmd 3";
            flags = EEikToolBarCtrlHasSetMinLength;
            length = KEikStdToolBarButtonHeight;
            },
        TBAR_BUTTON
            {
            id = EExampleCmd4;
            txt = "Cmd 4";
            flags = EEikToolBarCtrlHasSetMinLength;
            length = KEikStdToolBarButtonHeight;
            },
        TBAR_CTRL
            {
            type=EEikCtSpacer;
            flags = EEikToolBarCtrlHasSetMinLength |
                    EEikToolBarCtrlIsStretchable;
            length = 0;
            control = SPACER;
            },
        TBAR_CTRL
            {
            type = EEikCtClock;
            control = CLOCK
                {
                digitalresourceid = R_EIK_DIGITAL_CLOCK;
                analogresourceid = R_EIK_ANALOG_CLOCK;
                };
            },
        TBAR_CTRL
            {
            type = EEikCtSpacer;
            flags = EEikToolBarCtrlHasSetMinLength;
            length = KEikStdGapBelowClock;
            control = SPACER;
            }
        };
    }
```

This rather overwhelming specification defines the standard appearance of a toolbar in EIKON. In order of appearance, there's a filename label, followed by a set of four buttons, and finally a clock, all suitably offset with spacers. Don't feel you have to analyze every last initialization value for each control: for a standard toolbar, you can copy and paste much of the code above.

I don't usually like copy-and-paste programming, but in this case it really is the right thing to do.

The Psion Revo has room for only three buttons of this type. On the Revo, EIKON makes an attempt to scale down your toolbar, and in any case omits the fourth button you specify in a resource like this. With some non-standard toolbars, the effects of the Revo's system may not be predictable, and you'll have to experiment to make things look nice.

The only parts of real interest are the sections of code for each button. The first one sets the pattern for the rest:

```
TBAR_BUTTON
    {
    id = EExampleCmd1;
    txt = "Cmd 1";
    flags = EEikToolBarCtrlHasSetMinLength;
    length = KEikStdToolBarButtonHeight;
    },
```

The important things here are that `EExampleCmd1` ties in with my enumerated command ID, and that Cmd 1 is the text that will appear on the button. The rest of this button definition – and in fact the entire toolbar resource – is a distraction unless we're doing something fancy.

The next section of the resource file contains my shortcut keys:

```
RESOURCE HOTKEYS r_example_hotkeys
    {
    control=
        {
        HOTKEY { command = EEikCmdExit; key = 'e'; }
        };
    }
```

The syntax is a bit bizarre (`control=` identifies all hotkeys identified by a *Ctrl+* key combination, so that `EEikCmdExit` is on *Ctrl+E*).

One essential point here, though, is that the resource definitions for shortcut keys *aren't* specified among the definitions for menu items. The menu knows about the shortcut key table, and displays the shortcut key associated with a menu item if their command IDs match – but you don't have to make this association yourself.

The style guide defines many standard assignments for commonly used program functions, which I list in Chapter 13. Don't use one of the standard assignments for a different purpose without very good reason. Use only `control=` and `shift_control=` assignments; the resource file also supports `plain=`, but that's for testing and shouldn't be used in real applications.

'Shortcut keys' is the style-guide-approved language for what most programmers call 'hotkeys'. We decided that 'hotkeys' was too ambiguous or frightening for end-users, so we chose a friendlier term to be used in the user interface, help text etc..

Here's the final resource that's promised by `EIK_APP_INFO`: the menu specification:

```
RESOURCE MENU_BAR r_example_menubar
    {
    titles =
        {
        MENU_TITLE
            {
            menu_pane = r_example_file_menu;
            txt = "File";
            },
        MENU_TITLE
            {
            menu_pane = r_example_other_menu;
            txt = "Other";
            }
        };
    }

RESOURCE MENU_PANE r_example_file_menu
    {
    items =
        {
        MENU_ITEM { command = EEikCmdExit; txt = "Close"; }
        };
    }

RESOURCE MENU_PANE r_example_other_menu
    {
    items =
        {
        MENU_ITEM { command = EExampleCmd1; txt = "Cmd 1"; },
        MENU_ITEM { command = EExampleCmd2; txt = "Cmd 2"; },
        MENU_ITEM { command = EExampleCmd3; txt = "Cmd 3"; },
        MENU_ITEM { command = EExampleCmd4; txt = "Cmd 4"; }
        };
    }
```

A menu bar has one or more menu panes, and a menu pane has one or more menu items. A menu item is associated with some text, and a command. More advanced menu trees have more options (cascading menus, check marks against options that are active, etc.), but I don't need them here.

EIKON's menus don't support the kind of shortcut keys found in Windows and other desktop systems that allow you to select File | Close using *Alt+F, C*. In EIKON, you either have to use the shortcut key (*Ctrl+E*) or navigate manually to the item.

We considered the Windows way seriously but rejected it on the grounds that it makes the menus look ugly, and most average Windows users don't understand what the underscores mean anyway. Displaying shortcuts as EIKON does advertises the facility in a way that anyone can understand, without a manual or training.

String Resources

Finally, there are the string resources, which are very simple indeed:

```
RESOURCE TBUF r_example_text_hello { buf = "Hello world!"; }

RESOURCE TBUF r_example_text_cmd1 { buf = "Command 1"; }
RESOURCE TBUF r_example_text_cmd2 { buf = "Command 2"; }
RESOURCE TBUF r_example_text_cmd3 { buf = "Command 3"; }
RESOURCE TBUF r_example_text_cmd4 { buf = "Command 4"; }
```

A properly constructed EIKON application should have *all* its translatable string resources in resource files, so that they can be translated without having to change the C++ code. This recommendation applies to string text within GUI elements (menu or toolbar items, for example) as well as those explicitly listed in TBUFs.

Summary

The resource file meets two major requirements for EIKON GUI programs:

❑ It allows the elements of the GUI to be defined in a format that's much more convenient than initializing everything using C++ program calls

❑ It allows strings to be defined externally to the C++ application, so they can be easily translated

Other systems use resource files to meet these requirements too, so EPOC is fairly conventional here.

It's often said that resource files save memory by removing the requirement to load things into RAM before they're needed. As you've seen, EPOC saves memory by many techniques, but resource files play only a minor role here. EIKON dialogs themselves are constructed dynamically from resources only when needed, while large objects such as bitmaps are not held in EPOC resource files, as they are on other systems.

Resource files in EPOC are plain text, and compiled using a tool analogous to a C++ compiler. I'll explain the format, and go into more detail about why EPOC does things this way, below.

Bringing It to Life

Now that you've seen how the different parts of the program fit together, let's bring it to life by running through the code with the Visual C++ debugger. Doing so will also shows us what debugging in the GUI environment is like – which, as a developer, is something you'll need to get used to anyway.

Start up Visual C++, and build the program according to the instructions in Chapter 2. Then you can begin debugging by pressing *F5*. As the debugger initializes and the emulator launches, you'll see all kinds of messages in the debug window about threads being launched and DLLs being loaded. In particular, you'll see which EPOC DLLs in the C++ SDK are supplied with debug information. At the end of the launch sequence, the shell will be running on the emulator.

Launching the Application

Don't launch helloeik *yet.* As you've seen on a number of occasions already, when you *do* launch the program, its functions will be called by the EIKON framework. For now, though, let's pretend that we don't know what will happen. A safe bet, then, is to put a breakpoint on every function in helloeik.cpp using the *F9* key. When you've done that, launch helloeik from the shell.

The first breakpoint to be hit is the one in E32Dll(), which gets called to attach a process, detach a process, and then attach a process again. This odd sequence is exactly why E32Dll() is a function best not used to do anything important.

Next, you'll see that NewApplication() is called, and the context in which this happens is interesting. If you take a look at the call stack (*Alt+7* gets you there quickly), you can confirm that NewApplication() is called by the application architecture, working on behalf of the EIKON program loader. The EPOC C++ SDK includes full source and debug information for these frameworks, so you can hunt around in the functions that call NewApplication() if you want.

```
Call Stack                                                                    ×
⇨ NewApplication() line 103
   CApaDll::CreateApplicationL(RFs & {...}, const TBuf<256> & {...}) line 313 + 3 bytes
   CApaProcess::AddAppDllL(const TDesC8 & {...}, TUid {...}) line 911
   CApaProcess::AddNewDocumentL(const TDesC8 & {...}, TUid {...}) line 610 + 16 bytes
   CEikonEnv::ConstructAppFromCommandLineL(const CApaCommandLine & {...}) line 970 + 39
   EikDll::RunAppInsideThread(CApaCommandLine * 0x0b2e2088) line 102 + 36 bytes
   AppThreadStartFunction(void * 0x0b2e2088) line 115 + 9 bytes
   User::StartThread(int (void *)* 0x40b0321f AppThreadStartFunction(void *), void * 0x0
   EKERN! 5b00d0b7()
   KERNEL32! bff88ef7()
```

After NewApplication(), you'll see all the other initialization functions in the application, document, app UI, and app view classes called in the correct sequence. Eventually, you'll see CExampleAppView::Draw() being called, and after that the emulator window is displayed.

Command and Event Handling

When you look at the code for HandleCommandL(), you might not think it's worth debugging through — after all, it's just a simple switch statement, and all the case handlers are one-liners. In fact, it's worthwhile for a number of reasons:

❑ There are three ways of getting commands to HandleCommandL(), and it's informative to look at the call stack in the debugger to see how commands that come from different starting points arrive in the same place

❑ Most of the case handlers display an info-message, and when that disappears your application view has to redraw itself. Because of this, your Draw() function gets called, with some surprises that we'll return to in Chapter 10.

❑ All calls to HandleCommandL() are generated as a result of some user-initiated event. As we saw in Chapter 3, this means active objects are involved in handling them. We can easily observe this by debugging through HandleCommandL().

❑ You begin to get a feel for many of the relationships between the window server, controls, and your application. These relationships are the stuff of life for GUI programming, and I'll be explaining them in the next few chapters.

In the next few sections, we'll invoke commands from the toolbar, menu, and shortcut keys, and I'll point out some of the interesting things revealed by the debugger.

Commands from the Toolbar

Starting with the first of these, use the pointer to press a toolbar button, say **Cmd 2**.

You'll see the debugger stop at the HandleCommandL() breakpoint, where the **Variables** window reveals the value of the aCommand parameter to be 4098, or 0x1002, which is EExampleCmd2. The **Call Stack** window is particularly revealing:

```
CExampleAppUi::HandleCommandL(int 4098) line 56
CEikAppUi::ProcessCommandL(int 4098) line 144
CEikToolBar::HandleControlEventL(CCoeControl * 0x0b7b4014,
    MCoeControlObserver::TCoeEvent EEventStateChanged) line 142
CCoeControl::ReportEventL(MCoeControlObserver::TCoeEvent EEventStateChanged) line
365
CEikButtonBase::HandlePointerEventL(const TPointerEvent & {...}) line 141
CCoeControl::ProcessPointerEventL(const TPointerEvent & {...}) line 330
CCoeControl::HandlePointerEventL(const TPointerEvent & {...}) line 359
CCoeControl::ProcessPointerEventL(const TPointerEvent & {...}) line 330
CCoeAppUi::HandleWsEventL(const TWsEvent & {...}, CCoeControl * 0x0b7b3d28) line
96
CCoeEnv::RunL() line 213
```

In Chapter 3, we saw that EPOC is fundamentally an event-handling system, and that events are handled by active objects in their RunL() member function. That's exactly what we've got here: a RunL() for the event from the window server.

The first thing to establish, in `CCoeAppUi::HandleWsEventL()`, is that this event is a pointer event. CONE's app UI then hands the event to the entire toolbar control, which in turn hands it to the button in which it took place. The button handles the pointer event using `CEikButtonBase::HandlePointerEventL()`.

In that function, the button reports an event to its observer, which happens to be the toolbar. The toolbar knows that the button is associated with command ID 4098, and so it calls `CEikAppUi::ProcessCommandL()` with that value.

Thankfully, as an application programmer, you don't have to worry about any of that: it's all looked after for you. The point is that you get to field a call to `HandleCommandL()` with command ID 4098 – 0x1002, or `EExampleCmd2`. If you debug through `HandleCommandL()`, you'll see how it's processed.

After `HandleCommandL()` completes processing, you'll see an info-message displayed on the emulator. When that has finished, your `CExampleAppView::Draw()` function will be called to redraw the part of the window that had been covered by the info-message.

> *Actually, the code you see in* `Draw()` *draws the whole screen. But the window server clips drawing to the invalid region that actually needed to be redrawn. For some controls, it's worth optimizing to avoid drawing outside the invalid region. We'll see more on this in Chapter 11.*

Commands from the Menu Bar

Next, use the *F1* on your PC keyboard to pop up the menu bar and to select Cmd 2 from the Other menu. As before, you hit the breakpoint in `HandleCommandL()`, but this time the call stack is different:

```
CExampleAppUi::HandleCommandL(int 4098) line 56
CEikAppUi::ProcessCommandL(int 4098) line 144
CEikMenuPane::ReportSelectionMadeL() line 762
CEikMenuPane::OfferKeyEventL(const TKeyEvent & {...}, TEventCode EEventKey, int 0)
line 987
CEikMenuBar::OfferKeyEventL(const TKeyEvent & {...}, TEventCode EEventKey) line
356 + 21 bytes
CCoeControlStack::OfferKeyL(const TKeyEvent & {...}, TEventCode EEventKey) line 36
+ 23 bytes
CCoeAppUi::HandleWsEventL(const TWsEvent & {...}, CCoeControl * 0x0b7b20fc) line
91 + 24 bytes
CCoeEnv::RunL() line 213
```

We have an event being handled by an active object's `RunL()` function, but this time the raw window server event is identified as a *key* event. The app UI delegates keystroke distribution to the control stack, which offers it to the menu bar, which in turn offers it to the menu pane. The menu pane reports that a selection has been made, which results in the menu being dismissed (in `CEikAppUi::ProcessCommandL()`), and the command being handled by `HandleCommandL()`.

We'll see the control stack, and its role in key handling, in Chapter 12.

This time, you'll see that the app view has to redraw twice: once to make up for the menu bar disappearing, and again to make up for the info-message disappearing.

Why didn't the app view redraw when you switched menu panes? The answer is that these panes (and their shadows) are handled using windows that maintain a backup copy of whatever is underneath them — so-called 'backed-up behind' windows. When the window moves or is dismissed, the window server replaces whatever was underneath from the backup copy, without asking for the application to redraw. Before this feature was implemented (prior to EPOC's first release), flipping between menu panes was very slow in all but the simplest applications.

Commands from Shortcut Keys

The final way into `HandleCommandL()` is via a shortcut key. You know that you can close the application with *Ctrl+E*; try this, and you'll get:

```
CExampleAppUi::HandleCommandL(int 256) line 56
CEikAppUi::ProcessCommandL(int 256) line 144
CEikMenuBar::OfferKeyEventL(const TKeyEvent & {...}, TEventCode EEventKey) line 280
CCoeControlStack::OfferKeyL(const TKeyEvent & {...}, TEventCode EEventKey) line 36 + 23 bytes
CCoeAppUi::HandleWsEventL(const TWsEvent & {...}, CCoeControl * 0x0b7b20fc) line 91 + 24 bytes
CCoeEnv::RunL() line 213
```

As before, `RunL()` handles the event, while `HandleWsEventL()` decides it's a key and gets it handled by the control stack. The control stack offers it to the menu bar, which recognizes shortcut keys and calls the application to process them.

Why are shortcut keys handled by the menu bar? Easy: the menu bar has to control the shortcut keys, because it has to be able to display them when the menu panes are showing. How did the key get to the menu bar when the menu bar wasn't showing? That's harder: I'll answer it fully when we cover key distribution and focus in Chapter 12.

Terminating the Application

By pressing *Ctrl+E*, we sealed the fate of our debugging session. As the application unwinds, you'll see the app UI's destructor, which explicitly calls the app view's destructor. You'll also see that `E32Dll()` is called for the final time before the application exits. You might as well end the debugging session by closing the emulator.

Summary

By doing a live demonstration, we've seen:

- ❑ How the application launches, handles commands, and exits
- ❑ Proof that all events in an EPOC application program are handled by an active object `RunL()` function
- ❑ Some insight into redrawing, which we'll cover in much more detail in Chapter 11
- ❑ Some insight into key and pointer handling, which we'll cover in much more detail in Chapter 12

Another interesting thing is that you get enough source code and debug information for the relevant application frameworks, so that you can dig very deep into what's happening in them. If you're in a tight corner, or the documentation has run out on you, this can be very handy.

Resource Files

We've now seen enough of resource files to understand how they're used to define the main elements required by an EIKON app UI. And, in the next chapter, we'll be using resource files to specify dialogs.

So this is a good place to review resource files, and the resource compiler, more closely. I highlight the main information you'll need: for a fuller reference, see the SDK – resource files are documented in all the EPOC SDKs.

An EIKON application such as `helloeik.app` uses a resource file to contain GUI element definitions and strings that are needed by the program at runtime. The runtime resource file for `helloeik.app` is `helloeik.rsc`, and it resides in the same directory as `helloeik.app`.

Resource files can contain up to 4095 resources that are accessed by ID. Each resource is simply binary data that's interpreted at runtime by whatever class or function uses it.

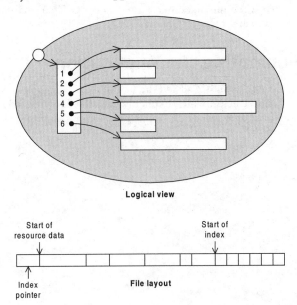

Logical view

File layout

Why is the index at the end of the file? The resource file is built by compiling the source one resource statement at a time. Only when the end of the source is reached can the resource compiler write the index.

To use a resource at runtime, a program must specify the correct ID *and* interpret the resource correctly. It's clearly vital that the resource ID you specify should refer to the binary resource data that you intended. Otherwise, your program may try to use data that contains the wrong value (or even the wrong data type) with disastrous results.

To prevent accidents, the resource file compiler packaged in `eikrs.bat` generates not only the resource file, but also a header file containing symbolic IDs for every resource contained in the file. The header file for `helloeik` is `helloeik.rsg`; it is written to the `\epoc32\include\` folder, and `#include`'d into `helloeik.cpp`. That's why you need to run the resource compiler *before* you run the C++ compiler when building an EIKON program.

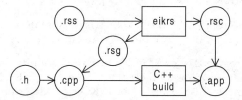

How is the data for an individual resource mapped into a structure that the application can use to read it? The resource compiler uses its built-in types, such as BYTE, DOUBLE, and TEXT, for the data members of a resource; it also uses a STRUCT statement to define aggregate types. (STRUCT definitions are packaged into `.rh` files in `\epoc32\include\`, where 'rh' stands for 'resource header'). EIKON provides many STRUCT definitions that you can use in your applications' resource files by `#include`'ing the relevant `eik*.rh` headers.

It's possible, but relatively unusual, for application programmers to write their own STRUCT statements. If you need to do this, the EPOC SDKs explain how.

How do you ensure that your resource script and C++ program use the same values for symbolic constants such as EExampleCmd1? As we've saw earlier, the resource compiler supports enum and #define definitions of constants, with a syntax similar to that used by C++. By convention, these definitions are contained in `.hrh` include files, which can be included in both C++ programs *and* resource scripts. 'hrh' stands for 'h' and 'rh' together.

Summary of Processing and File Types

Putting everything together, this is the picture we get of the files involved in building a GUI application:

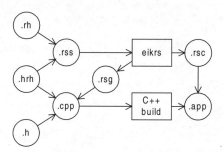

The resource-related files for `helloeik` are:

Filename	Description
`helloeik.rss`	Resource file script.
`helloeik.rsc`	Generated resource file.
`helloeik.rsg`	Generated header containing symbolic resource IDs that are included in the C++ program at build time.
`helloeik.hrh`	Header containing symbolic constants such as the command IDs, which are embedded into resources such as the menu bar, toolbar, and shortcut keys, and used in the C++ program in places such as `HandleCommandL()`.
`eik*.rh`	EIKON's standard STRUCTs for resources.
`eik*.hrh`	EIKON's standard symbolic IDs, such as the command ID for `EEikCmdExit`, and the flags used in various resource STRUCTs.
`eikon.rsg`	Resource IDs for EIKON's own resource file, which contains many useful resources. Most of these resources are for EIKON's internal use, although some are also available for EIKON programs to use.

EIKON has a vast treasury of `.rh` resource STRUCT definitions and specific resources (especially string resources) defined in `eikon.rsg`.

`helloeik` doesn't include any dialogs, but in most practical EIKON applications the greater part of the resource file is the section that defines this resource type. Other (less minimal) applications in the book *do* include dialog definitions, and we'll cover the topic more systematically in the next chapter.

Punctuation Rules

With a definition like this,

```
RESOURCE MENU_PANE r_example_other_menu
    {
    items =
        {
        MENU_ITEM { command = EExampleCmd1; txt = "Cmd 1"; },
        MENU_ITEM { command = EExampleCmd2; txt = "Cmd 2"; },
        MENU_ITEM { command = EExampleCmd3; txt = "Cmd 3"; },
        MENU_ITEM { command = EExampleCmd4; txt = "Cmd 4"; }
        };
    }
```

you could be forgiven for thinking that the punctuation character to use after a closing brace is arbitrary – should be it comma, a semicolon, or nothing at all? In fact, the rules are quite simple:

❑ If a closing brace is at the end of a member definition that started with something like items = { ... }, then put a semicolon after it

❑ If a closing brace separates two items in a list, such as the menu items in the items = member above, then put a comma after it

❑ Otherwise (that is, for the last item in a list, or at the end of a resource), don't put anything after a closing brace

Why an EPOC-specific Resource Compiler?

EPOC's resource compiler starts with a text source file and produces a binary data file that's delivered in parallel with the application's executable. Windows, on the other hand, uses a resource compiler that supports icons and graphics as well as text-based resources, and which builds the resources right into the application executable so that an application can be built as a single package. Furthermore, Windows programmers never see the text resource script nowadays, because Visual C++ includes powerful and convenient GUI-based editors.

So, why does EPOC have its own resource compiler, and how can an ordinary programmer survive without the graphical resource editing supported by modern Windows development environments? Basically, there are two reasons:

❑ Symbian wants to avoid unnecessary dependencies in the tool chain used for porting EPOC to new target platforms. It's easy to deliver resource files as a separate data file: it would be much harder to design them into the executable format for every platform supported by EPOC, including the emulator.

❑ EIKON lays out its own dialogs using a simple one-dimensional layout and, where possible, auto-sizes its controls. The pixel specifications needed for Windows dialog resources are not necessary in EPOC. That consideration alone removes Windows' pressing need for a graphical-based front end to its resource compiler.

Although the EPOC resource compiler looks somewhat old-fashioned on first sight, there are good reasons for it being as it is, and in reality it's not difficult to use.

Conservative .rsg Update

When you run eikrs on helloeik.rss, it generates both the binary resource file helloeik.rsc and the generated header file helloeik.rsg.

However, makmake correctly builds a dependency of helloeik.obj on helloeik.rsg, because helloeik.cpp includes helloeik.rsg. So, if helloeik.rsg is updated, the helloeik.app project needs rebuilding. Scale this up to a large application, and a change in its resource file-generated headers could cause lots of rebuilding.

eikrs avoids this potential problem by updating the `.rsg` file only when necessary – and it *isn't* necessary unless resource IDs have changed. Merely changing the text of a string won't cause the application's executable to go out of date.

This is why, when you run `eikrs`, you always get an indication of whether the `.rsg` file was changed or not.

Multiple Resource Files

A single resource file supports 4095 resources, but an EIKON application may use multiple resource files, each containing this number of resources. The application identifies each resource by a symbolic ID comprising two parts:

❏   A leading 20 bits (five hex digits) that identifies the resource file

❏   A trailing 12 bits (three hex digits) that identifies the resource

The leading 20 bits are generated from the four-character name that was specified in the NAME statement in the resource file. You can tell what the 20 bits are by looking at the `.rsg` file. Here, for example, is `helloeik.rsg`, which has the NAME HELO:

```
#define R_EXAMPLE_TOOLBAR        0x276a8004
#define R_EXAMPLE_HOTKEYS        0x276a8005
#define R_EXAMPLE_MENUBAR        0x276a8006
#define R_EXAMPLE_FILE_MENU      0x276a8007
#define R_EXAMPLE_OTHER_MENU     0x276a8008
#define R_EXAMPLE_TEXT_HELLO     0x276a8009
#define R_EXAMPLE_TEXT_CMD1      0x276a800a
#define R_EXAMPLE_TEXT_CMD2      0x276a800b
#define R_EXAMPLE_TEXT_CMD3      0x276a800c
#define R_EXAMPLE_TEXT_CMD4      0x276a800d
```

EIKON's resource file NAME is EIK, and its resource IDs begin with 0x00f3b. I'll list some interesting EIKON resources below.

You don't have to choose a NAME that's distinct from all other EPOC applications on your system – with only four letters, that could be tricky. The resource files available to your application are likely only to be EIKON's and your application's, so you simply have to avoid using EIK as a name. Avoid CONE, BAFL, and other EPOC component names as well, and you should be safe.

Quick Reference

This final section contains some very quick reference information on various aspects of the resource compiler. Using this, you will be able to do many basic tasks, and you'll know where to find out more from the SDK.

eikrs Command Line Syntax

You invoke `eikrs.bat` using the following syntax,

```
eikrs filename language [ variant [outdir]]
```

where:

Element	Description
filename	The filename of the resource file, whose extension must be `.rss`. Don't specify the extension; it will be added automatically.
language	The language ID of the generated resource file. The output file extension will be `.r`, followed by the language ID. Use `sc` for a language-neutral file, or `01`, `02`, etc. to select a language identified by the `TLanguage` enumeration in `e32std.h`. I don't document this further in this book.
variant	The variant you want to compile to – one of `rel`, `deb`, `urel`, or `udeb`. Defaults to `deb`.
outdir	The output directory for the `.rsc` file. If you specify this, then exactly what you specify will be used. If you don't, a default directory will be used, as described below.

The `.rsg` file is *always* generated to `\epoc32\include\`. If `eikrs` generates a `.rsg` file that's identical to the one already in `\epoc32\include\`, the existing one isn't updated.

The `.rsc` file is generated to the following directory:

❑ If an explicit directory is specified as the fourth parameter, it will be used.

❑ If the `\epoc32\release\wins\variant\z\system\apps\filename\` directory exists, then it will be used. (Here, *filename* is the first parameter to `eikrs`, and *variant* is the third parameter, or its default value `deb`.)

❑ Otherwise, the current directory is used.

Use an explicit output directory if you're generating a resource file for MARM specifically, or if you're generating a system resource file such as EIKON's, which resides in `\system\data\` on the emulated `z:` drive – that is, in `\epoc32\release\wins\variant\z\system\data\`.

eikrs and *rcomp*

`eikrs` is a convenience wrapper used for generating resource files from manual invocation, or from Visual C++'s tools menu. Its underlying engine is `rcomp.exe`.

`eikrs` adds the filename and directory conventions mentioned in the syntax chart above, and checks whether the `.rsg` file really needs updating. `eikrs` also runs the C preprocessor on a source file before invoking `rcomp`, in order to preprocess all #includes, #defines, and language-dependent #if statements.

rcomp is invoked directly by a makmake-generated command-line build script for either the emulator or a target machine. makmake generates effectively the same logic as eikrs, directly in the makefile.

Source File Syntax

Because processing starts with the C preprocessor, a resource file has the same lexical conventions as a C program, including source-file comments and C preprocessor directives. Legal statements in a resource file are:

Statement	Description
NAME	Defines the leading 20 bits of any resource ID. Must be specified prior to any RESOURCE statement.
STRUCT	Defines a named structure for use in building aggregate resources.
RESOURCE	Defines a resource, mapped using a certain STRUCT, and optionally given a name.
enum/ENUM	Defines an enumeration, and supports a syntax similar to C++'s.
CHARACTER_SET	Defines the character set for strings in the generated resource file. If not specified, cp1252 (the same character set used by Windows 9x and non-Unicode Windows NT) is the default.

The most important statement in an application resource file is RESOURCE. The statement must take the form,

```
RESOURCE struct_name [ id ] { member_initializer_list }
```

where:

Element	Description
struct_name	Refers to a previously-encountered STRUCT definition. In most application resource files, this means a STRUCT defined in a #included .rh file.
id	The symbolic resource ID (optional). If specified, this must be in lower-case, with optional underscores to separate words (for instance r_example_text_hello). Its upper-case equivalent will then be generated as a symbol in the .rsg file using a #define statement, as in #define R_EXAMPLE_TEXT_HELLO 0x276a8009.
member_initializer_list	A list of member initializers, separated by semicolons, and enclosed in braces { }. There is a sensible default system so that, if you don't specify members in the given STRUCT, they're usually set to numeric zero or an empty string.

A STRUCT is a sequence of named members that may be of built-in types, another STRUCT, or an array. The SDK's documentation on resource files covers all the possibilities. (In the C++ SDK, see EPOC Tools & Utilities\Application Resource Tools\Application Resource Tool Reference\Resource file format.) I can't add much of value to that documentation (the examples in the book aren't hard to follow without it). Besides reading the documentation, you can learn plenty by looking inside the .rh files in \epoc32\include\, together with the .rss files supplied in various projects in the SDK.

APIs for Reading Resources

BAFL provides the basic APIs for reading resources:

❑ The oddly named RResourceFile class, in barsc.h, is used for opening resource files, finding a numbered resource, and reading its data. (RResourceFile behaves more like a C class than an R class.)

❑ TResourceReader, in barsread.h, is a kind of stream-oriented reader for data in an individual resource. TResourceReader functions are provided that correspond to each of the resource compiler's built-in data types.

CONE builds on this to provide an environment in which multiple resource files may be loaded. A CONE (and hence an EIKON) program uses the following member functions of CCoeEnv to read resources:

Function	Description
AddResourceFileL(const TDesC& aFileName)	Adds a resource file, identified by its full path name, to the environment.
DeleteResourceFile(TInt aOffset)	Deletes the resource file, identified by its 20-bit leading offset, from the environment.

CreateResourceReaderLC(
     TResourceReader& aReader,
     TInt aResourceId)
	Creates and initializes an object of type TResourceReader to read the resource ID specified, from whichever resource file added to the CONE environment.

Other functions are built on these, including AllocReadResourceL() and AllocReadResourceLC(), which allocate an HBufC big enough for the resource and read it in. ReadResource() simply reads a resource into an existing descriptor (and panics if it can't).

EIKON's Resource File

EIKON's resource file, eikon.rsc, contains a plethora of useful resources that are available to any EIKON program. All you have to do is hunt through eikon.rss and its include files to find a suitable definition – or it can be quicker to hunt through eikon.rsg to find a symbolic constant with an interesting-looking name.

It's a great idea to re-use these resources if you can. Symbian has thought hard about the exact text in the strings used, and paid for translations into the other languages supported by EPOC. You can save yourself this thought and this localization effort, by re-using EIKON's resources.

`helloeik` just reuses EIKON's definitions of standard analog and digital clocks in its toolbar. All the other examples in this book (that involve a dialog) also reuse EIKON's standard dialog buttons, defined by R_EIK_BUTTONS_CANCEL_OK.

Summary

In this chapter, we've seen:

❑ How an EIKON application is put together and how it interacts with the frameworks provided by EIKON, CONE, and the application architecture

❑ That the EIKON app UI provides the framework for handling commands issued by the menu, toolbar, and shortcut keys

❑ Where commands come from, how to identify and handle them

❑ The structure of a resource file

❑ The sequence of calls in an EIKON application, during startup, when handling key and pointer events, when redrawing, and when closing down

❑ A quick tour of the resource compiler, which is a key tool for everyday EIKON programming.

`helloeik` is a rather bare EIKON application. I'll spend the next four chapters explaining dialogs, display graphics, interaction, and finishing touches needed for more serious applications so that, by Chapter 14, we're in a position to repeat the kind of walkthrough we did in this chapter, for a more sophisticated and useful program.

10

Dialogs and Concrete Controls

In the previous chapter, you saw how commands get to `HandleCommandL()` from the app UI's basic interaction resources: the toolbar, menus, and shortcut keys. In our simple `helloeik` application, we handled those commands pretty trivially – either by displaying an info-message, or by quitting the program.

In real applications, many commands are handled using a **dialog**: perhaps half of the effort required to program the GUI of a professional application is involved with dialog programming.

In this chapter, I'll introduce the design requirements for dialogs as seen by the user and (only just below the surface) by the programmer. I'll then move on to use some of the simple dialogs from example projects in this book to illustrate the essentials of dialog programming. Then, I'll do a lightning tour through the dialog framework's main APIs, the stock controls that EIKON provides for inclusion in dialogs, and some standard dialogs provided by EIKON.

Introducing Dialogs

I'll use four EIKON dialogs to show you the kinds of thing you can do with them.

I expect many readers are familiar with the way dialogs work on Windows, and have expectations about what dialogs ought to do, based on how they work in Windows. Windows and EIKON were designed for different types of hardware and different end-users however, so their dialog designs are different. I'll point out the differences as I go along, to help you understand where EIKON is coming from, and how to use it to deliver the best experience to the users of your applications.

A Query Dialog

Here's an EIKON query dialog:

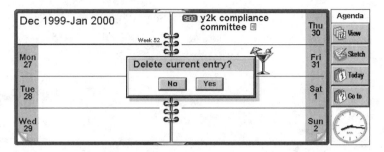

I got this by pressing *Delete* with the cursor on the y2k compliance meeting entry. The query is asking me "Delete current entry?" and I have to answer "No" or "Yes".

The most important point about this dialog is that it's a straightforward query, with a yes/no answer. Compare it with a similar dialog on Windows:

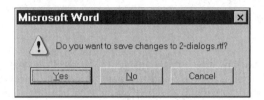

I got this by typing *Ctrl+F4* in Word (a shortcut for File | Close), as I was typing the previous paragraph. The question being asked here is, "Do you want to save changes to 2-dialogs.rtf?" I get three options. Consider how a new user would respond:

❑ Yes: that ought to save the changes – but it says nothing about exiting – in any case, the data is safe.

❑ No: if the user is a smart Windows user, they'll realize that 'no' means, "No, I don't want to save changes when closing the file." If they haven't used Windows before, they'll say, "No, I didn't ask for my file to be saved, I'll save it later when I've finished." They select 'no', and their document disappears! They have lost all their changes, even though that's not what they wanted.

❑ Cancel: a smart Windows user realizes that cancel means, "No, don't save changes, but keep the file open." If they're an average user, they won't understand how 'cancel' can be an answer to the question that was posed.

Almost every Windows user I know, who isn't a professional programmer, has lost data because of this Windows dialog.

This illustrates an important aspect of all EIKON UI programming: write for the inexperienced computer user, and make it clear what's going to happen when they select a menu or dialog option. The EIKON way is to ask a straight yes/no question in which the expectations and consequences of each possible answer are very clear.

If you're a Windows user, you'll notice a couple of other things about the EIKON query dialog:

❑ Yes and No are swapped around compared to the Windows way of doing things. Yes (and OK) buttons always go on the right of horizontal button lists, and the bottom of vertical button lists. Then most people can press these buttons without obscuring the rest of the dialog – all people operate from below the screen, and most people are right-handed.

❑ The dialog has a look-and-feel that might remind you of Windows 3.1 rather than Windows 9x or NT 4. That's because the high-contrast color scheme is important for the kind of screens for which EIKON is designed. Actually, if you look at the details, the design is considerably softer than the Windows 3.1 look-and-feel.

❑ Dialogs throw a shadow onto the window behind them.

❑ There's a title bar, which you can move around by dragging with the pen, just as you can with a Windows dialog.

❑ There's no notion of a currently focused button, and no underscored letters to indicate accelerator keys – more on that later.

A Single-page Dialog

Here's a conventional EIKON dialog with a single page:

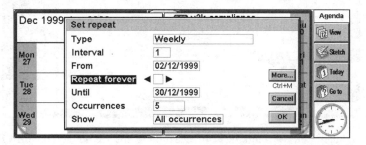

I got this by typing *Ctrl+R* on the entry, to set its repeat information, and then by changing a few fields.

One thing is immediately striking about this dialog: all its controls are in a vertical list. This is a key design decision for EIKON dialogs. It makes many things easier for both user and developer:

❏ Navigation from field to field is easy: just use the up and down arrows, or the pointer. No need for *Tab*, or for ugly underscores indicating accelerator keys.

❏ Dialog layout is easy: the only difficulty is establishing the width of the controls. The width of the vertical list is then determined by the widest control. In this case, that's the Type field – its width is governed by the longest item in the choice list, which happens to be Yearly by day of week, so you can repeat events on say the first Saturday in November each year.

❏ Because layout is so easy, you don't have to specify the pixel coordinates of each field in the dialog definition resource. In consequence, EIKON has no need of a GUI-based resource builder.

This dialog has the maximum possible number of controls – just seven. An eighth control would overflow the 240-pixel screen height. This has an important impact on EIKON dialog design:

❏ If you need more lines, you can use multi-page dialogs (see below).

❏ If you need more lines, you can use sub-dialogs, such as the one launched by More in the previous screenshot.

❏ Don't use either of these options if you don't need to. Don't create monster dialogs that offer a bewildering set of choices to the user. Experiment with a number of alternatives before committing a design to code – and even then, be prepared for further change.

Focus is indicated by a clear highlight – in this case, on the Repeat forever checkbox. If this is checked, as in the following screenshot, the Until and Occurrences fields are blanked out altogether:

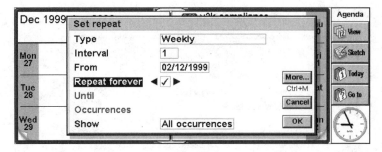

Both the focus highlight and the blanking of inaccessible fields are delivered with EIKON's usual high visual contrast.

Finally note that buttons can't be focused: OK is *always* on the *Enter* key, Cancel is *always* on *Escape*. Other buttons use a *Ctrl+* key combination, and are marked so the user can select them. Naturally, you can also select these buttons with a pointer.

A Multi-page Dialog

Here's a sample multi-page dialog:

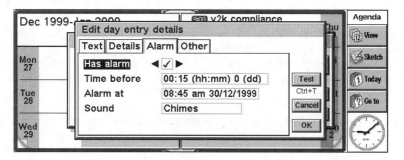

I got this dialog by pressing *Enter* to edit the Agenda entry: this allowed me to edit basic details – text, start time and date, duration, and entry type. However, there are *many* more details for each agenda item, including the alarms. So I pressed *Ctrl+A* for the Alarms/More button to produce the dialog above. Finally I pressed the right arrow to select the Has alarm check box. The dialog then produced the default settings – a chime, 15 minutes before the meeting.

This is a multi-page dialog. I can tap with the pointer on either of the page tabs, or I can use the up arrow from the top focused line, or the down arrow from the bottom line to get to the page tabs. I can then navigate the page tabs using the right and left arrow (or more pointer taps).

The button array, on the right, is associated with the entire dialog – not with each page. It's bad style to change it when the pages change.

Scrolling Dialogs

Finally, here's a scrolling dialog:

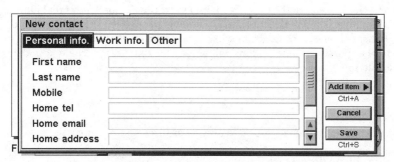

This is from the Contacts application. There are so many details associated with a new contact that they won't fit all on one screen. So the body of this dialog can scroll up or down. You can scroll using the scroll bar with the pointer, and using the keyboard; the dialog scrolls automatically if you move focus to a line that is off one end of the visible list.

Scrolling dialogs are designed for circumstances where you cannot know the number of fields that will be required. In EPOC's application suite, scrolling dialogs are used *only* for the Contacts application, and the general-purpose Data application.

Scrolling dialogs should *not* be used as an alternative to multi-page dialogs, sub-dialogs, or feature minimization, if the number of fields is actually within your control as a programmer.

Cue Text

You should make every effort to ensure that the meaning of the controls in your dialogs is transparently obvious to most users. Be prepared to work hard at this: you'll need to choose text and functionality with care, order lines and pages in your dialogs sensibly, and be particularly careful about options and initial setup. With some thought, you can often produce an application that needs little help text of any kind.

Sometimes, though, it's not possible – or perhaps not practical – to achieve this ideal. One useful tool when that happens is **cue text** in dialogs. Here's an example, from Battleships:

I count the need for this cue text as an indication that Battleships still has a way to go in terms of usability. Why should the *users* have to decide on such technicalities if their machines are already in infrared contact, say? Why can't we use some protocol to sort this out? In the case of the SMS protocol, it's much clearer that one person has to make the first call, and the other person has to receive it: why couldn't I have chosen words like Call and Wait for call that made that more obvious?

As a justification for needing this dialog, communications is generally complicated by nature, and communications setup is especially awkward. Ultimately, the end user pays real money for communications services, and makes choices about level of service. This means that they have to be able to control these choices – whether they like it or not. However hard we work to make these things as easy to control as possible, these options will always be with us, and cue text in dialogs will therefore always have a role somewhere.

Controls

Each line in a dialog is a captioned control with two or three components:

- ❑ A caption, to tell the user what the line is for
- ❑ A control, to allow something to be displayed and/or edited
- ❑ A tag, used by some controls to indicate measurement units, for example, inches or cm (see below)

Controls allow users to enter data. EIKON provides 56 stock controls that can be incorporated into dialogs. In the agenda and contacts dialogs above we've already seen text editors, date, time, time offset editors, check boxes, phone number editors, sound selectors, number editors, and choice lists. Knowing the controls available to you is a key aspect of dialog programming. You can also add your own controls.

> *Sometimes in this book I've used the word 'field' as a user-friendly synonym for 'control'. I'll always use 'control' when referring to programming.*

Dialog Processing

Dialogs should help the user to enter valid data and, if it's not valid, should point out the error as early and as helpfully as possible. This works in various ways:

❑ For some controls, you can specify validity criteria: for numeric editors, for instance, you can specify a range

❑ For some controls, you can't enter invalid data anyway: a checkbox can either be checked or unchecked

❑ After a control such as a choice list or check box has changed its value, you can override a dialog virtual function that responds by optionally changing the values of other controls. So, if a check box controlling whether an item has an alarm is changed, the fields specifying the alarm information are turned on or off.

❑ When focus moves from one line to another, you may also wish to do some validation and to change some other fields

❑ When OK or another button is selected, you can do whatever processing you like

Modality

Dialogs in EIKON are modal. While a dialog is being displayed, you can barely see the app view underneath, so there's no point in either allowing the user to do anything with the application while the dialog is active, or in reflecting the dialog-controlled changes instantly in app views.

Summary

EIKON dialogs are culturally similar to their cousins in other systems such as Windows. There are however many differences, designed to make life easier both for end-users and programmers.

In this chapter I'll be covering how to program dialogs in four stages:

❑ Simple dialog programming: getting to grips with the resource file and APIs for a simple dialog with just two text editor fields

❑ EIKON's stock controls: since dialog fields normally use stock controls provided by EIKON, the stock controls' resource file and C++ APIs are the most important, and certainly the biggest, set of APIs you'll need when programming with dialogs

❑ More of CEikDialog's API, showing the functions you can use for processing at the dialog level

❑ Some standard dialogs provided by EIKON, such as the query window

This chapter will form the barest introduction to dialog programming in EIKON. I'll highlight the major issues and take you quickly through the possibilities supported by the framework so that, simply by reading the book, you can get a good taster for what's possible.

A whole book could be written to cover the topics addressed by this chapter, and indeed the C++ SDK contains comprehensive documentation. If you want to program real projects, you'll need to use the SDK to get the information you need.

In the next two chapters, I'll explain how you can write your own controls. You'll also be able to see, as you read those chapters, how the architecture of CONE and the window server has been influenced by the requirements of dialogs.

Some Simple Dialogs

Although we didn't make much of it at the time, the streams application we employed in Chapter 7 used simple dialogs. Here's one of them in action:

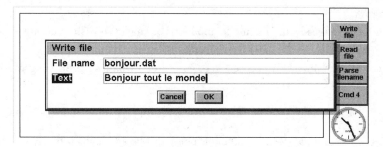

This shows the typical elements that comprise a single-page dialog:

❑ A title

❑ OK and Cancel buttons

❑ A vertical list of controls – in this case, two controls, each with a caption

The basic techniques involved in dialog programming are:

❑ Constructing the dialog: this is done using resource files

❑ Initializing each control when the dialog is first displayed

❑ Checking individual controls, and the dialog as a whole, for validity

❑ Getting information from each control, and kicking off some action when OK (or another button) is pressed

The good news is that you *don't* have to perform the complicated processing that could be required, say, for keyboard handling and character drawing within a text control. That's already done for you by EIKON's text editor control, which we'll study later on.

Here's the code from `streams.cpp` that launches the Write file dialog. It's a command handler function, `CmdWriteFileL()`, called directly from `HandleCommandL()` in the case for `EExampleCmdWriteFile`:

```
void CExampleAppUi::CmdWriteFileL()
    {
    // Use a dialog to get parameters and verify them
    CEikDialog* dialog = new(ELeave) CExampleWriteFileDialog(this);
    if(!dialog->ExecuteLD(R_EXAMPLE_WRITE_FILE_DIALOG))
        return;

    // Write file under a trap
    TRAPD(err, WriteFileL());
    if(err)
        {
        delete iText;
        iText = 0;

        // Don't check errors here!
        iCoeEnv->FsSession().Delete(*iFileName);
        iAppView->DrawNow();
        User::Leave(err);
        }

    // Update view
    iAppView->DrawNow();
    }
```

Processing is in three stages:

❑ A dialog is used to set up values for `iFileName` and `iText`

❑ Some code from the stream store API is used to open `iFileName` and write `iText` to it

❑ The application updates the view to reflect the data that has changed

This is a taste of **model-view-controller programming** (MVC), which I'll cover in more detail in the next chapter. For the moment, however, our interest is in the first lines of code in this function, which construct and run a dialog. Here they are again:

```
    CEikDialog* dialog = new(ELeave) CExampleWriteFileDialog(this);
    if(!dialog->ExecuteLD(R_EXAMPLE_WRITE_FILE_DIALOG))
        return;
```

This rather terse pattern is used to launch *every* EIKON dialog. First, a dialog object of type `CExampleWriteFileDialog` is allocated and C++-constructed. The app UI is passed as a parameter to the constructor, so that the dialog can later get at the app UI's data members – the whole point of the dialog is to update `iText` and `iFileName`.

Second, a single line is used to:

❑ Second-phase construct the dialog from a resource ID, in this case R_EXAMPLE_WRITE_FILE_DIALOG

❑ Run the dialog (that's what you'd expect something called ExecuteXxx() to do)

❑ Destroy the dialog after it's run (the D in ExecuteLD() means 'destroy when finished')

❑ Leave if there are any resource allocation problems or other environment errors (the L in ExecuteLD())

❑ Return ETrue if the user ended the dialog with OK

❑ Return EFalse if the user ended the dialog with Cancel

The if statement distinguishes between the return ETrue and return EFalse cases. If Cancel was pressed, then the return statement is taken, to prevent the rest of the WriteFileL() function being called to actually write the file.

As you program more dialogs, you'll soon come to appreciate the simplicity and regularity of these conventions.

Resource File Definition

The dialog was defined in a resource labeled R_EXAMPLE_WRITE_FILE_DIALOG. Here it is, from streams.rss:

```
RESOURCE DIALOG r_example_write_file_dialog
    {
    title = "Write file";
    buttons = R_EIK_BUTTONS_CANCEL_OK;
    flags = EEikDialogFlagWait;
    items =
        {
        DLG_LINE
            {
            type = EEikCtEdwin;
            prompt = "File name";
            id = EExampleControlIdFileName;
            control = EDWIN { width = 25; maxlength = 256; };
            },
        DLG_LINE
            {
            type = EEikCtEdwin;
            prompt = "Text";
            id = EExampleControlIdText;
            control = EDWIN { width = 25; maxlength = 256; };
            }
        };
    }
```

Simply put, the dialog has a title, standard OK and Cancel buttons, some flags, and some items. In keeping with EIKON's guidelines for positioning buttons, the Cancel/OK buttons are indicated by the resource name R_EIK_BUTTONS_CANCEL_OK.

Almost all dialogs should be coded with the line `flags = EEikDialogFlagWait`, which makes the dialog modal.

> *Regrettably, this is not the default. The default behavior is that your application can continue executing while the dialog is displayed. This isn't quite the same as a non-modal dialog. Non-waiting dialogs are typically used for activities like print progress monitoring, in which the application is printing while the dialog is being displayed. Because the application is printing, it doesn't accept user input, so a non-waiting dialog is effectively modal.*

The body of the dialog is a vertical list of controls, each of which has:

❑ A caption or prompt, such as File name

❑ An ID, such as EExampleControlIdFileName

❑ A type, such as EEikCtEdwin, and some initialization data of a format corresponding to the type, such as EDWIN { width = 25; maxlength = 256; }

Don't use more than seven controls. As far as C++ is concerned, there is no limit, but more than seven won't fit nicely onto a screen only 240 pixels high, and is also beginning to overwhelm users with too much choice. If you code too many controls, the dialog will overflow the screen, making it effectively unusable.

The prompt serves to identify the control's purpose to the user, while the ID identifies the control to the programmer. Later, we'll see that control IDs are used by C++ programs to specify the controls whose values they want to set or read. Like command IDs, control IDs are defined in the application's .hrh file, so they can be accessed both by resource file definitions and C++ programs.

The type of control used here, EEikCtEdwin, is an edit window; the EDWIN resource STRUCT is required to initialize such a control. In this example, I specify the size of the control (25 characters), which affects the dialog layout, and the maximum length of the data (256 characters).

Dialog Code

The base class for all dialogs is CEikDialog. Any dialog you write in your application will derive from CEikDialog, and it will typically implement at least two member functions – one for initializing the dialog, and one for processing the OK key.

'Read-only' dialogs, for displaying application data, need only implement the initialization function. Ultra-trivial dialogs, initialized entirely from resource files, needn't even implement the initialization function. More complex dialogs can implement many functions besides the two shown below: we'll return to this later on. All CEikDialog virtual functions have a do-nothing default implementation: you only override them if necessary.

Here's the declaration of `CExampleWriteFileDialog`, from `streams.cpp`:

> *That's right:* `streams.cpp`, *not* `streams.h`. *I've treated dialogs as being private to the app UI, so they were not given their own header.*

```
class CExampleWriteFileDialog : public CEikDialog
    {
public:
    CExampleWriteFileDialog(CExampleAppUi* aAppUi);

private:
    // From CEikDialog
    void PreLayoutDynInitL();          // Initialization
    TBool OkToExitL(TInt aKeycode);    // Termination

private:
    CExampleAppUi* iAppUi;
    };
```

The C++ constructor takes whatever parameter is necessary to connect the dialog to the outside world – in this case, my app UI, since it's this dialog's job to set its `iFileName` and `iText` members.

> *On reflection, this isn't actually a very good encapsulation of the interface: I should really have passed references to the* `iFileName` *and* `iText` *members, to make it clear that the dialog is intended to alter them and nothing else.*

Initialization is performed by `PreLayoutDynInitL()`. The 'pre-layout' part of the name means that the data you put into the dialog here will influence its layout – EIKON dialogs are laid out automatically to incorporate the optimum size of controls for the initialization data supplied.

Here's `PreLayoutDynInitL()`:

```
void CExampleWriteFileDialog::PreLayoutDynInitL()
    {
    SetEdwinTextL(EExampleControlIdFileName, iAppUi->iFileName);
    SetEdwinTextL(EExampleControlIdText, iAppUi->iText);
    }
```

This simply sets the edit windows to the existing values in `iFileName` and `iText`. Clearly, the `SetEdwinTextL()` function should only be used for controls that are actually edit windows. The control in such function calls is identified by its ID, as specified in the `id=` line in the resource file definition.

OK is handled by `OkToExitL()`. In fact, pressing any of the dialog buttons – *except* Cancel – will result in a call to this function. The function extracts values from the controls and, if everything is OK, returns `ETrue`, causing EIKON to dismiss the dialog. If there's a problem (if, say, the value for `iFileName` isn't actually a valid filename) then `OkToExitL()` may either leave or return `EFalse`, which will cause EIKON to continue with the dialog.

`OkToExitL()` is more complicated because it has to check the validity of the requested operation before returning control to the app UI:

```
TBool CExampleWriteFileDialog::OkToExitL(TInt /* aKeycode */) // termination
    {
    // Get file name
    CEikEdwin* edwin = STATIC_CAST(CEikEdwin*,
                                   Control(EExampleControlIdFileName));
    HBufC* fileName=edwin->GetTextInHBufL();

    // Check it's even been specified
    if(!fileName)
        {
        TryChangeFocusToL(EExampleControlIdFileName);
        iEikonEnv->LeaveWithInfoMsg(R_EIK_TBUF_NO_FILENAME_SPECIFIED);
        }
    CleanupStack::PushL(fileName);

    // Check it's a valid filename
    if(!iCoeEnv->FsSession().IsValidName(*fileName))
        {
        TryChangeFocusToL(EExampleControlIdFileName);
        iEikonEnv->LeaveWithInfoMsg(R_EIK_TBUF_INVALID_FILE_NAME);
        }

    // Get the text string
    edwin = STATIC_CAST(CEikEdwin*, Control(EExampleControlIdText));
    HBufC* text = edwin->GetTextInHBufL();
    if(!text)
        text = HBufC::NewL(0);
    CleanupStack::PushL(text);

    // Ensure the directories etc needed for the file exist
    TInt err = iCoeEnv->FsSession().MkDirAll(*fileName);
    if(err != KErrNone && err != KErrAlreadyExists)
        User::Leave(err);

    // Check whether it's going to be possible to create the file for writing
    RFile file;
    err = file.Create(iCoeEnv->FsSession(), *fileName, EFileWrite);
    if(err != KErrNone && err != KErrAlreadyExists)
        User::Leave(err); // No need to close file, since it didn't open

    // Check whether the user wants to replace the file, if it already exists
    if(err == KErrAlreadyExists)
        {
        if(iEikonEnv->QueryWinL(R_EIK_TBUF_FILE_REPLACE_CONFIRM))
            User::LeaveIfError(file.Replace(iCoeEnv->FsSession(),
                               *fileName, EFileWrite));
        else
            iEikonEnv->LeaveWithInfoMsg(0); // Let user try again
        }
    file.Close();
```

```
    // Finished with user interaction: communicate parameters and return
    delete iAppUi->iFileName;
    iAppUi->iFileName = fileName;
    delete iAppUi->iText;
    iAppUi->iText = text;
    CleanupStack::Pop(2); // text, fileName
    return ETrue;
    }
```

On a dialog with only Cancel and OK buttons, there's no point in checking the key code: it can only be the code for OK. For that reason, I've commented out the aKeyCode parameter name. On a dialog with other buttons, such as the buttons activated with *Ctrl+M* or *Ctrl+A* in the dialogs we saw earlier, you would also have to check for these key codes.

The processing sequence is:

❑ Get the filename: check that it's non-empty, and check that it's a valid filename

❑ Get the text: if it's empty, turn it into a zero-length string (rather than no string at all), because my file format requires that a string be written, even if it's an empty one

❑ Make sure the directory exists

❑ Check whether the user wants to overwrite an existing file

❑ Store the values from the dialog

❑ Return

Any of the checks or file operations in this sequence could fail, and the dialog is carefully coded to ensure that any such failure is entirely cleanup-safe. A User::Leave() from OkToExitL() is trapped by EIKON and ensures that the dialog doesn't exit. There are three types of leave from within this code:

❑ iEikonEnv->LeaveWithInfoMsg(*resource-id*): EIKON prints an info-message and then leaves with a special error code that causes no error message to be displayed. This is the recommended option for leaving when you detect an error in user input. Use the info-message to identify the error. Rely on cleanup to delete temporary variables such as fileName and text, which have been pushed to the cleanup stack.

❑ User::Leave() with a genuine error code, such as the error code from opening a file: EIKON will display the error message appropriate for that code.

❑ iEikonEnv->LeaveWithInfoMsg(0): this leaves without giving any message at all, but cleans up temporary variables. I use this variant when the user opts not to overwrite an existing file: it's obvious what the 'error' is at this point, so the user doesn't need to be told again.

The code above also shows how to use an EIKON query window. In this case I want to check whether the user wants to overwrite an existing file. iEikonEnv->QueryWinL() takes a resource ID indicating the question to ask, and returns ETrue for a Yes answer, EFalse for No.

Read-only Dialogs

The Battleships program also has some useful dialog examples. The settings display simply shows fields without allowing them to be edited. Here it is:

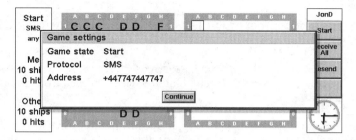

The phone number has been changed here, to protect the innocent.

The Continue button is deliberately ambiguous: you can use this button on a dialog that conveys either good news (in which OK would have been just as good) or bad news (where it would be an insult to the user to tell them that it was OK).

Here's the resource definition from \pep\battleships\battleships.rss:

```
RESOURCE DIALOG r_game_settings_dialog
    {
    title = "Game settings";
    buttons = R_EIK_BUTTONS_CONTINUE;
    flags = EEikDialogFlagWait;
    items =
        {
        DLG_LINE
            {
            type = EEikCtChoiceList;
            prompt = "Game state";
            id = EGameControlIdState;
            control = CHOICELIST { array_id = r_game_state; };
            itemflags = EEikDlgItemNoBorder | EEikDlgItemNonFocusing;
            },
        DLG_LINE
            {
            type = EEikCtChoiceList;
            prompt = "Protocol";
            id = EGameControlIdProtocol;
            control = CHOICELIST { array_id = r_game_gdp_protocols; };
            itemflags = EEikDlgItemNoBorder | EEikDlgItemNonFocusing;
            },
        DLG_LINE
            {
            type = EEikCtEdwin;
            prompt = "Address";
            id = EGameControlIdOtherAddress;
```

```
            control = EDWIN { width = 25; maxlength = 100; };
            itemflags = EEikDlgItemNoBorder | EEikDlgItemNonFocusing;
            }
        };
    }
```

The buttons = R_EIK_BUTTONS_CONTINUE line brings in the standard Continue button from the EIKON resource file.

Each DLG_LINE has itemflags = EEikDlgItemNoBorder | EEikDlgItemNonFocusing. Non-focusing lines can't be edited. There's not much point in having a border around something that can't be edited, so we turn that off too.

This dialog contains an editor (used simply to display a value, in this case) and two choice lists, indicated by type = EEikCtChoiceList, and a CHOICELIST struct to initialize the control. This specifies an array of text items, one for each choice. Here's r_game_gdp_protocols:

```
RESOURCE ARRAY r_game_gdp_protocols
    {
    items=
        {
        LBUF { txt = "Loopback"; },
        LBUF { txt = "Infrared"; },
        LBUF { txt = "SMS"; }
        };
    }
```

The C++ code for a display-only dialog doesn't need an OkToExitL() — just a PreLayoutDynInitL(). Here it is:

```
void CGameSettingsDialog::PreLayoutDynInitL()
    {
    // Game state
    SetChoiceListCurrentItem(EGameControlIdState, iController->State());

    // Protocol
    SetChoiceListCurrentItem(EGameControlIdProtocol,
                        iController->Gsdp().GetGdpProtocol() - 1);

    // Other address
    TBuf<KMaxGsdpAddress> address;
    iController->Gsdp().GetOtherAddress(address);
    SetEdwinTextL(EGameControlIdOtherAddress, &address);
    }
```

The calls to SetChoiceListCurrentItem() set an index into the array of items, which is assumed to be zero-based. That works well for the game state (which uses a zero-based enumeration) but not for the GDP protocol (which uses a one-based enumeration, with zero as an invalid value), so I have to subtract one from the GDP protocol enumeration value.

Simple Dialog Processing

The startup dialog in Battleships, which we saw earlier, includes a couple of other interesting features:

- ❑ Cue text, to indicate the purpose of the Start mode line
- ❑ The address field, which is displayed only if necessary – that is, only if you're initiating, and using a networked protocol which requires addresses

Here's the resource file definition:

```
RESOURCE DIALOG r_game_initiate_dialog
    {
    title = "Start first game";
    buttons = R_EIK_BUTTONS_CANCEL_OK;
    flags = EEikDialogFlagWait;
    items =
        {
        DLG_LINE
            {
            type = EEikCtChoiceList;
            prompt = "Protocol";
            id = EGameControlIdProtocol;
            control = CHOICELIST { array_id = r_game_gdp_protocols; };
            },
        DLG_LINE
            {
            type = EEikCtChoiceList;
            prompt = "Start mode";
            id = EGameControlIdStartMode;
            control = CHOICELIST { array_id = r_game_start_mode; };
            },
        DLG_LINE
            {
            type = EEikCtLabel;
            control = LABEL
                {
                standard_font = EEikLabelFontAnnotation;
                txt = "One player must Initiate, the other must Listen";
                };
            },
        DLG_LINE
            {
            type = EEikCtEdwin;
            prompt = "Address";
            id = EGameControlIdOtherAddress;
            control = EDWIN { width = 25; maxlength = 100; };
            },
        DLG_LINE
            {
            type = EEikCtChoiceList;
            prompt = "First move";
            id = EGameControlIdFirstMovePref;
```

```
            control = CHOICELIST { array_id = r_game_first_move; };
        }
    };
}
```

The cue text is indicated by:

```
        DLG_LINE
            {
            type = EEikCtLabel;
            control = LABEL
                {
                standard_font = EEikLabelFontAnnotation;
                txt = "One player must Initiate, the other must Listen";
                };
            },
```

This is a control without a prompt or control ID (neither are needed). The control is a label. You should always use the annotation font for cue text labels.

The other controls use an EDWIN and CHOICELISTs, which we've already met. The derived dialog class shows the functions we use to control the visibility of the address field:

```
    class CGameInitiateDialog : public CEikDialog
        {
    public:
        CGameInitiateDialog(CGameController* aController);
    private:
        // From CEikDialog
        void PreLayoutDynInitL();            // Settings on dialog launch
        TBool OkToExitL(TInt aKeycode);      // Action when OK pressed

        // Listen to changing selections
        void HandleControlStateChangeL(TInt aControlId);

        // Show only necessary controls
        void ShowRelevantControls();         // Called when needed
    private:
        CGameController* iController;
        };
```

As well as PreLayoutDynInitL() and OkToExitL(), I have implemented another CEikDialog framework function, HandleControlStateChangeL(), which gets called with the relevant control ID whenever the value of any of the choice list fields in the dialog is changed. I also have a function called ShowRelevantControls(), which I use to show or hide the address depending on the settings of other controls.

Here's the implementation of ShowRelevantControls():

```
    void CGameInitiateDialog::ShowRelevantControls()
        {
```

```
    // Get start mode: 1=listen, 0=initiate
    TInt listen = ChoiceListCurrentItem(EGameControlIdStartMode);

    // Get protocol
    RGsdpSession::TGdpProtocol protocol = (RGsdpSession::TGdpProtocol)
            (ChoiceListCurrentItem(EGameControlIdProtocol) + 1);

    // Show other address if mode=initiate, and protocol is networked
    TBool otherAddressNeeded = (!listen) && (protocol == RGsdpSession::EGdpSms);
    MakeLineVisible(EGameControlIdOtherAddress, otherAddressNeeded);
    }
```

The idea is to test the value of the GDP protocol and start mode choice lists, and work out whether another address is needed. I then call `MakeLineVisible()` — a `CEikDialog` library function — to make the address line visible only if it is needed.

> *There's one piece of dubious code above, though it's not to do with dialog processing. I know that SMS is the only networked GDP protocol, and hard-code this assumption into* `ShowRelevantControls()`. *It would be better to use an API to get this information.*

I call `ShowRelevantControls()` from two places — `PreLayoutDynInitL()` and `HandleControlStateChangeL()`. The first call is the last line of `PreLayoutDynInitL()`, after I've set up all the controls:

```
void CGameInitiateDialog::PreLayoutDynInitL()
    {
    // Protocol
    SetChoiceListCurrentItem(EGameControlIdProtocol,
                        iController->Gsdp().GetGdpProtocol() - 1);

    // Start mode;
    // Other address
    _LIT(KBlank,"");
    SetEdwinTextL(EGameControlIdOtherAddress, &KBlank);

    // First-move preferences
    // Show relevant controls
    ShowRelevantControls();
    }
```

`HandleControlStateChangeL()` calls `ShowRelevantControls()` only if it there was a change in the protocol or start mode lines:

```
void CGameInitiateDialog::HandleControlStateChangeL(TInt aControlId)
    {
    if(aControlId == EGameControlIdProtocol ||
       aControlId == EGameControlIdStartMode)
        ShowRelevantControls();
    }
```

`CEikDialog` provides other framework functions that you can implement to detect relevant events in the dialog and its controls. It also provides other library functions that you can implement to control the dialog.

Dialog APIs

The simple dialogs we've seen are enough to show us that `CEikDialog` offers a large range of framework functions, which you can override, and library functions, which you can use to provide specific dialog processing.

In this section, our lightning-quick tour of dialogs continues with an overview of these APIs.

Resource Specifications

Let's start with a closer look at the resource specification for dialogs. You define a dialog using the `DIALOG` resource `STRUCT`. Its members are:

Member	Description
`title = <string>`	The title of the dialog, displayed at the top
`flags = <bitmask>`	Optional bitmask of flags governing attributes of the dialog. Defaults to 0, but for nearly all dialogs you should specify `EEikDialogFlagsWait`.
`buttons = <resource>`	A resource defining the buttons to use in the dialog. Default is no buttons; many dialogs use `R_EIK_BUTTONS_CANCEL_OK`.
`items = <list>`	A comma-separated list of dialog items
`pages = <resource>`	A resource defining the pages in a multi-page dialog. Don't specify this if you only want a single-page dialog.

The flags for the dialog as a whole are specified in the `flags` member of the `DIALOG` structure. Flag bit values are defined by `EEikDialogFlagXxx` constants in `eikdialg.hrh`. Typical dialogs specify `EEikDialogFlagWait`; other flags control button positioning (right or bottom), whether there is a title, whether *Esc* is channeled through `OkToExitL()`, and several others.

The flags for a dialog *line* are specified in the `flags` member of the `DLG_ITEM` structure. Bit values for these flags are defined by `EEikDlgItemXxx` constants in `eikdialg.hrh`, and they allow you to specify that there should be a separator after this item, that the control doesn't take focus, that it has no border, etc.

Adding Buttons

If you want to code more buttons than the standard `R_EIK_BUTTONS_CANCEL_OK`, use code such as:

```
DLG_LINE { buttons = r_example_buttons_test_cancel_ok; ... }
```

```
RESOURCE DLG_BUTTONS r_example_buttons_test_cancel_ok
    {
    buttons=
        {
        DLG_BUTTON
            {
            id = EExampleBidTest;
            button = CMBUT { txt = "Test"; };
            hotkey = 'T';
            },
        DLG_BUTTON
            {
            id = EEikBidCancel;
            button = CMBUT { txt = "Cancel"; };
            hotkey = EEikBidCancel;
            },
        DLG_BUTTON
            {
            id = EEikBidOk;
            button = CMBUT { txt = "OK"; };
            hotkey = EEikBidOk;
            }
        };
    }
```

This causes a Test button marked with *Ctrl+T* to be included in the buttons for the dialog. You will need to test whether *Ctrl+T* or *Enter* has been pressed, in your `OkToExitL()` function.

If you want to display buttons horizontally across the bottom of the dialog, use dialog flag `EEikDialogFlagButtonsBelow`.

Basic Functions

`CEikDialog` provides a rich API for derived dialog classes. As usual, I'll summarize the functions here, and leave you to hunt around in the documentation and headers for more.

`CEikDialog` is derived from `CEikForm`, which is there to handle the commonality between regular dialogs and scrollable dialogs.

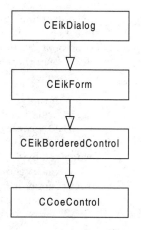

However, many CEikForm functions are overridden by CEikDialog, and the API to both classes is huge. I've presented the functions available to you as a CEikDialog user as if they were all present in CEikDialog itself, but for some of them you'll have to look in CEikForm.

In the next release of EPOC, CEikForm will no longer be a base class for CEikDialog.

That said, many of the functions in the dialog API are either convenience functions that add to the API's size without really adding to its complexity, or else they're for unusual requirements such as constructing dialogs dynamically without using a resource file. Leaving them aside, we get to a manageable set of framework and library functions. Here are some of the most important.

Framework Functions

The following virtual functions are called when various events happen during dialog processing. If you want to handle those events, override the default function provided by CEikDialog. In each case, the default function does nothing.

Function	Description
`virtual void PreLayoutDynInitL();`	Called prior to layout so you can initialize the dialog. Set control values here if you want them to influence sizing and layout.
`virtual void PostLayoutDynInitL();`	Called after layout so you can initialize the dialog. Set control values here if you *don't* want them to influence sizing and layout.
`virtual void SetInitialCurrentLine();`	Called during initialization to allow you to set the current line. Implement this if you want to override the default (which is the top line).
`virtual TBool OkToExitL(TInt aButtonId);`	Called when a button is pressed, but not for the Cancel button, unless you specify this in dialog flags. Return ETrue if it's OK to exit the dialog; EFalse otherwise. Leave if you want to report an error: this is interpreted as not being OK to exit.
`virtual void HandleControlStateChangeL( TInt aControlId);`	Called when the state of the given control changes, as reported by an EEventStateChanged event sent by the control to its observer. Certain controls, such as choice lists, call this when their state changes. Implement this function if you wish to change dialog settings – or those of other controls – in response to state changes.
`virtual SEikControlInfo CreateCustomControlL( TInt aControlType);`	Called during dialog construction when the control type indicated in the resource file is not recognized by the EIKON control factory. You must implement this if your dialog struct specifies a control type ID not recognized by the EIKON control factory – otherwise dialog construction will panic. SEikControlInfo is a struct containing a pointer to the new control, flags, and the resource ID of optional text after the control.

Sometimes, you want to do some processing when the user has finished working with one of the dialog's lines. For instance, when the user changes the 'duration' field of an event in the Agenda, dialog code should change the 'end time' field in sync. Changes in time and date editors don't get reported using `HandleControlStateChangeL()`, so you need to intercept the event when the user changes the focused line. This also applies to other multi-field numeric editors, MFNEs for short, which I'll list in the next section.

The solution is to override `PrepareForFocusTransitionL()`, which is virtual more-or-less by accident. It has a non-trivial default implementation, which doesn't include a parameter specifying which line is currently focused. Start your overridden function with:

```
CExampleMyDialog::PrepareForFocusTransitionL()
    {
    CEikDialog::PrepareForFocusTransitionL();
    TInt id = IdOfFocusControl();

    // Now do my stuff
    ...
    }
```

Call the base class implementation first: this will leave if the control with the current focus isn't valid, and so can't lose focus. Then call `IdOfFocusControl()` to get the control ID that's currently focused. Then decide what you need to do, and do it.

In the next release of EPOC, a `LineChangedL()` function will meet the basic requirement more cleanly.

Library Functions

You can call the following library functions from the framework functions listed above:

Function	Description
`CCoeControl*` `Control(TInt aControlId) const;`	Get a pointer to the control whose ID is specified: panic if the ID doesn't exist.
`CCoeControl*` `ControlOrNull(TInt aControlId) const;`	Get a pointer to the control whose ID is specified: return 0 if the ID doesn't exist.
`CEikLabel*` `ControlCaption(TInt aControlId) const;`	Get the caption associated with a control whose ID is specified.

`void`
`SetLineDimmedNow(TInt aControlId,`
`                 TBool aDimmed);`
	Dim or un-dim a line. Lines should be dimmed if it is not currently meaningful to select them.

`void`
`MakeLineVisible(TInt aControlId,`
`                TBool aVisible);`
	Make the control on a line visible or invisible (but don't change the visibility of its caption).

Function	Description

`void`
`MakeWholeLineVisible(TInt aControlId,`
`                TBool aVisible);`
	Make a whole line visible or invisible, both the caption and control.

`TInt` `IdOfFocusControl() const;`	Get the ID of the control with focus – that is, the control currently being used
`void` `TryChangeFocusToL(TInt aControlId);`	Calls `PrepareForFocusLossL()` on the currently-focused control and, if this doesn't leave, transfers focus to the control whose ID is specified. This is the way to change focus: the control with the focus should only refuse the request if its state is invalid.

EIKON's Stock Controls for Dialogs

From the dialog code above, we've seen that a basic part of dialog programming is using EIKON's stock controls in your dialogs. The general techniques for using stock controls are:

❑ Specify a control type in your DLG_LINE struct, using `type =`

❑ Specify initialization data for the control in your DLG_LINE struct, using `control=` and an appropriate resource STRUCT

❑ Do further control initialization from `PreLayoutDynInitL()` or `PostLayoutDynInitL()`

❑ Extract values from the control when needed, in `OkToExitL()` or other dialog processing functions

❑ Do other things, such as controlling the control's visibility, using dialog library functions

EIKON provides 56 stock controls that you can use in dialogs. In this section, I'll give a lightning-fast tour of those controls, including the resource STRUCTs you use to initialize them, and their C++ classes.

Here are the stock control classes, sorted by base class:

```
CEikCharMap              CEikBorderedControl        CEikBorderedControl
                         CEikButtonBase             CEikListBox
CEikCharEditor             CEikCheckBox               CEikDirContentsListBox
                           CEikOptionButton           CEikHierarchicalListBox
CEikHorOptionButtonList    CEikCommandButtonBase      CEikDirectoryTreeListBox
                             CEikTextButton           CEikTextListBox
CEikImageArray               CEikBitmapButton         CEikColumnListBox
                             CEikCommandButton      CEikMfne
CEikLabeledButton            CEikMenuButton           CEikNumberEditor
                         CEikControlGroup             CEikRangeEditor
CEikSpacer                 CEikDialogToolBar          CEikDurationEditor
                         CEikChoiceListBase           CEikTimeOffsetEditor
CEikAlignedControl         CEikGraySelector           CEikRangeRefEditor
  CEikImage                CEikChoiceList             CEikLatitudeEditor
  CEikLabel                  CEikFolderNameSelector   CEikLongitudeEditor
    CEikFontPreviewLabel     CEikDriveNameSelector  CEikTTimeEditor
                             CEikSoundSelector        CEikTimeEditor
CEikBorderedControl          CEikFileNameSelector     CEikDateEditor
  CEikBorderPreview            CEikUnifiedFileNameSelector  CEikTimeAndDateEditor
  CEikCalendar             CEikEdwin
  CEikClock                  CEikFloatingPointEditor
  CEikComboBox               CEikFixedPointEditor
  CEikFileBrowser            CEikTwipsEditor
  CEikFileNameLabel          CEikFileNameEditor
  CEikProgressInfo           CEikFolderNameEditor
  CEikPrintPreview           CEikTelephoneNumberEditor
  CEikSecretEditor           CEikGlobalTextEditor
  CEikWorldSelector          CEikRichTextEditor
```

All of these classes are derived ultimately from `CCoeControl`. The few classes at the beginning of the diagram, along with `CEikAlignedControl` and `CEikBorderedControl`, are derived directly, while all other controls on the diagram are derived indirectly.

The EPOC C++ SDK includes information, source code and examples for all the controls above, plus others that aren't intended for direct inclusion into dialogs.

To give you a very quick taster, here's a tour of the most important controls mentioned in the table above. You can either guess the function of the other controls based on their name, or look up the details in the SDK as and when you need them.

Buttons

```
CEikBorderedControl
CEikButtonBase
  CEikCheckBox
  CEikOptionButton
  CEikCommandButtonBase
    CEikTextButton
    CEikBitmapButton
    CEikCommandButton
      CEikMenuButton
```

A **command button** has text and/or graphics, and reports events to some observer. The toolbar uses command buttons.

A **menu button** pops up a menu pane when pressed: you can select an option from the menu pane either by releasing the command button and tapping on the pane, or by dragging across from button to menu item and then releasing.

Option buttons cooperate with each other to allow the user to choose from a small (up to four) number of options. In a dialog, option buttons should be combined in a **horizontal option button list**, so that all option buttons appear on a single line. In other systems, a horizontal option button list would be called a radio button group.

A **check box** allows you to enable or disable an option using a check mark.

Lists

```
CEikBorderedControl              CEikBorderedControl
  CEikChoiceListBase               CEikListBox
    CEikGraySelector                 CEikDirContentsListBox
    CEikChoiceList                   CEikHierarchicalListBox
      CEikFolderNameSelector           CEikDirectoryTreeListBox
      CEikDriveNameSelector          CEikTextListBox
      CEikSoundSelector              CEikColumnListBox
      CEikFileNameSelector
        CEikUnifiedFileNameSelector
```

Choice lists allow you to select from a large number of options. These controls are normally displayed in a small area that allows you to see one option at a time, and scroll between options using left and right arrows. If you tap on the control or press *Tab*, a vertically scrolling window pops up, that displays as many options as possible in the given screen size. Specific examples of choice lists include a basic selector for text items, a 'gray' selector (which can also select colors), and selectors for files, folders, drives, and sounds.

For some lists, the pop-up paradigm is inappropriate: it's better to display the whole list in its own (potentially large) area on the screen. EIKON uses **list boxes**, derived ultimately from CEikListBox, to do this. List boxes can display data in rows that scroll down, or they can produce a 'snaking' multi-column effect like the one used to show files on the System screen. Rows themselves can have multiple columns, and hierarchical lists that can be expanded and collapsed are also available.

The list box APIs are generalized to support any kind of data, although CEikTextListBox is a useful specialization for simple text lists. The other list classes have a reputation of being somewhat hard to use.

Editors

`CEikCharEditor`	`CEikBorderedControl`	`CEikBorderedControl`
`CEikBorderedControl`	`CEikEdwin`	`CEikMfne`
`CEikSecretEditor`	`CEikFloatingPointEditor`	`CEikNumberEditor`
	`CEikFixedPointEditor`	`CEikRangeEditor`
	`CEikTwipsEditor`	`CEikDurationEditor`
	`CEikFileNameEditor`	`CEikTimeOffsetEditor`
	`CEikFolderNameEditor`	`CEikRangeRefEditor`
	`CEikTelephoneNumberEditor`	`CEikLatitudeEditor`
	`CEikGlobalTextEditor`	`CEikLongitudeEditor`
	`CEikRichTextEditor`	`CEikTTimeEditor`
		`CEikTimeEditor`
		`CEikDateEditor`
		`CEikTimeAndDateEditor`

Integer numeric input is supported by **multi-field numeric editors** (MFNEs), whose base class is `CEikMfne`. An MFNE can edit one or more numbers, with checks on range, and separator characters between fields. A basic number editor edits a single number without any separators; more sophisticated ones edit number ranges, dates, times, time intervals, latitudes and longitudes, spreadsheet cell references etc. – everything you need for applications such as Agenda, Time/World, and Sheet.

Basic text input is supported by the **edit window** or **edwin**, which simply edits a string. A **combo box** is a hybrid editor and choice list: you can pick a pre-set value from the choice list, or enter a new value. Some more specialized editors are based on plain edwins, including editors for floating-point numbers, fixed-point numbers, and twips values.

> *A **twip** is 1/20 of a point, or 1/1440 of an inch – a basic unit of measurement for paper-based graphics. This is the fundamental unit of measurement for the EPOC GDI (and also for Windows graphics). A twips editor presents friendlier units – inches or centimeters – to the user, and returns a twips value to the program. See Chapter 15 for more on twips.*

Edwins edit plain text – just characters, without formatting. The derived global text editor adds support for global formatting – providing the same paragraph and character formatting for the whole text. The further derived rich text editor adds support for formatting paragraphs and characters individually, and support for embedded objects and pictures. These classes re-use EPOC's `CGlobalText` and `CRichText` classes, and they make it possible to deliver very sophisticated editing in a simple application. However, the APIs to these classes are wide, and the more sophisticated edwin classes also have a reputation of being hard to use.

Other editors include a **secret editor** (for passwords and the like), and a character editor intended for insert-symbol dialogs, where you can use a character map to select *any* character, regardless of whether it's available from the keyboard.

Using Controls in Dialogs

Now we've seen what stock controls can go into a dialog, we need to know how to specify them in a resource file `DLG_LINE` struct. `DLG_LINE` has the following members:

Member	Description
prompt = <string>	The caption for the control.
id = <number>	A numeric ID that can be used to retrieve the control. Use a constant defined in your application's .hrh file.
itemflags = <bitmask>	Optional bitmask of flags governing attributes of the line, such as whether to put a horizontal line below it. Defaults to 0.
type = <number>	A numeric ID indicating the control class to construct. See below for more information about this.
control = <struct>	Further initialization data, mapped by a STRUCT appropriate for the particular control type.
trailer = <string>	Optional trailer text, not usually specified. May be up to 40 characters.

The control in each dialog line is constructed by EIKON's **control factory**. The ID you specify to the `type` member of the `DLG_LINE` indicates to the control factory which control to construct. A new control is constructed, and its `ConstructFromResourceL()` function is then called to read the data specified by `control=` in order to initialize itself. (`ConstructFromResourceL()` is virtual in `CCoeControl`, and implemented by any derived class that can be constructed from resource-file data).

As a dialog programmer, then, you have to know the type IDs and resource STRUCTs associated with each control. The IDs are enumerated in `TEikStockControls` in `eikctrls.hrh`. Here's the complete list, in class hierarchy order:

Class	Header	ID	STRUCT
CEikCharMap	eikchmap.*	EEikCtCharMap	(none)
CEikCharEditor	eikchred.*	EEikCtCharEd	(none)
CEikHorOptionButtonList	eikhopbt.*	EEikCtHorOptionButList	HOROPBUT
CEikImageArray	eikimgar.*	EEikCtImageArray	IMAGE_ARRAY
CEikLabeledButton	eiklbbut.*	EEikCtLabeledButton	LBBUT
CEikSpacer	eikspace.*	EEikCtSpacer	SPACER
CEikImage	eikimage.*	EEikCtImage	IMAGE

Class	Header	ID	STRUCT
CEikLabel	eiklabel.*	EEikCtLabel	LABEL
CEikFontPreviewLabel	eikfprev.*	EEikCtFontPreview	FPREV
CEikBorderPreview	eikbprev.*	EEikCtBorderPreview	(none)
CEikCalendar	eikcal.*	EEikCtCalendar	CALENDAR
CEikClock	eikclock.*	EEikCtClock	CLOCK
CEikComboBox	eikcmbox.*	EEikCtComboBox	COMBOBOX
CEikFileBrowser	eikfbrow.*	EEikCtFileBrowser	FBROW
CEikFileNameLabel	eikfnlab.*	EEikCtFileNameLabel	(none)
CEikProgressInfo	eikprogi.*	EEikCtProgInfo	PROGRESSINFO
CEikPrintPreview	eikprtpv.*	EEikCtPrintPreview	PRTPREV
CEikSecretEditor	eikseced.*	EEikCtSecretEd	SECRETED
CEikWorldSelector	eikwsel.*	EEikCtWorldSelector	WORLD_SELECTOR
CEikCheckBox	eikchkbx.*	EEikCtCheckBox	(none)
CEikOptionButton	eikopbut.*	EEikCtOptionButton	(none)
CEikTextButton	eikcmbut.*	EEikCtTextButton	TXTBUT
CEikBitmapButton	eikcmbut.*	EEikCtBitmapButton	BMPBUT
CEikCommandButton	eikcmbut.*	EEikCtCommandButton	CMBUT
CEikMenuButton	eikmnbut.*	EEikCtMenuButton	MNBUT
CEikDialogToolBar	eikdlgtb.*	EEikCtDialogToolBar	DLG_TOOLBAR
CEikGraySelector	eikgysel.*	EEikCtGraySelector	GRAYSEL
CEikChoiceList	eikchlst.*	EEikCtChoiceList	CHOICELIST
CEikFolderNameSelector	eikfsel.*	EEikCtFolderNameSel	FOLDERNAMESELECTOR
CEikDriveNameSelector	eikfsel.*	EEikCtDriveNameSel	DRIVENAMESELECTOR
CEikSoundSelector	eiksndsl.*	EEikCtSoundSelector	(none)
CEikFileNameSelector	eikfsel.*	EEikCtFileNameSel	FILENAMESELECTOR
CEikUnifiedFileNameSelector	eikufsel.*	EEikCtUnifiedFileSel	UNIFIEDNAMESELECTOR
CEikEdwin	eikedwin.*	EEikCtEdwin	EDWIN
CEikFloatingPointEditor	eikfpne.*	EEikCtFlPtEd	FLPTED
CEikFixedPointEditor	eikfpne.*	EEikCtFxPtEd	FIXPTED
CEikTwipsEditor	eikfpne.*	EEikCtTwipsEd	TWIPSED
CEikFileNameEditor	eikfsel.*	EEikCtFileNameEd	FILENAMEEDITOR
CEikFolderNameEditor	eikfsel.*	EEikCtFolderNameEd	FOLDERNAMEEDITOR

Table Continued on Following Page

327

Class	Header	ID	STRUCT
CEikTelephoneNumberEditor	eikteled.*	EEikCtTelephoneNumberEditor	TELNUMBER
CEikGlobalTextEditor	eikgted.*	EEikCtGlobalTextEditor	GTXTED
CEikRichTextEditor	eikrted.*	EEikCtRichTextEditor	RTXTED
CEikDirContentsListBox	eikdclbx.*	EEikCtDirContentsListBox	DCLBOX
CEikDirectoryTreeListBox	eikdtlbx.*	EEikCtDirTreeListBox	DTLBOX
CEikTextListBox	eiktxlbx.*	EEikCtListBox	(none)
CEikColumnListBox	eikclb.*	EEikCtColListBox	(none)
CEikNumberEditor	eikmfne.*	EEikCtNumberEditor	NUMBER_EDITOR
CEikRangeEditor	eikmfne.*	EEikCtRangeEditor	RANGE_EDITOR
CEikDurationEditor	eikmfne.*	EEikCtDurationEditor	DURATION_EDITOR
CEikTimeOffsetEditor	eikmfne.*	EEikCtTimeOffsetEditor	TIME_OFFSET_EDITOR
CEikRangeRefEditor	eikrnged.*	EEikCtRangeRefEditor	CELL_RANGE_EDITOR
CEikLatitudeEditor	eikmfne.*	EEikCtLatitudeEditor	LATITUDE_EDITOR
CEikLongitudeEditor	eikmfne.*	EEikCtLongitudeEditor	LONGITUDE_EDITOR
CEikTimeEditor	eikmfne.*	EEikCtTimeEditor	TIME_EDITOR
CEikDateEditor	eikmfne.*	EEikCtDateEditor	DATE_EDITOR
CEikTimeAndDateEditor	eikmfne.*	EEikCtTimeAndDateEditor	TIME_AND_DATE_EDITOR

I've also listed the header files where you can find out more information. For example, if I specify eikmfne.*, then check out:

❑ eikmfne.h for the C++ API to the control

❑ eikmfne.rh for the resource STRUCT members you can use (almost all controls have initialization data that can be conveyed from a STRUCT)

❑ eikmfne.hrh for flag definitions (many controls support one or more flags)

In fact, you can almost always find the corresponding source code in \eikon\src*.cpp.

Convenience Functions

You can access any control in a dialog using the `Control()` function: specify the ID you use to identify the control in the resource file, and you will get a `CCoeControl*`. You can then cast this pointer to the type of control you know it really is, and access member functions such as getters, setters, and many others:

```
CEikEdwin* edwin = STATIC_CAST(CEikEdwin*,
                    Control(EExampleControlIdFileName));
HBufC* fileName = edwin->GetTextInHBufL();
```

This pattern would be *very* common in dialogs' `PreLayoutDynInitL()`, `HandleControlStateChangeL()`, and `OkToExit()` functions, except `CEikDialog` provides many convenience functions that allow you to achieve the same result with less code and no casting.

If my filename had been in a `TBuf` rather than an `HBufC`, I could have written the above using:

```
GetEdwinText(fileName, EExampleControlIdFileName);
```

As it is, I wanted it in an `HBufC` and there was no convenience function for that. I was unlucky. There are about 60 convenience functions in `CEikDialog` (and `CEikForm`), covering most get/set requirements for most of the standard controls I listed above. To list them, look in `Eikform.h` and `Eikdialg.h` in `\Eikon\inc`.

Custom Controls in Dialogs

EIKON dialogs aren't limited to using EIKON controls. You can add your own controls into a dialog as well. To do so, you'll first need to understand about writing controls – which is what the next two chapters are about.

Then, you'll need to do the following:

- ❏ For each dialog in which you want to include a custom control, implement its `CreateCustomControlL()` function

- ❏ In the resource file for the dialog, specify a `type=` that isn't used by the EIKON control factory

- ❏ In your `CreateCustomControlL()`, test for the relevant type, and construct an `SEikControlInfo` appropriate for your control

- ❏ Define a resource file `STRUCT` in a `.rh` file associated with your control, specifying the member names and types for the resource initialization data

- ❏ In your control, implement `ConstructFromResourceL()` to read in initialization data from a resource `STRUCT`

Have a look at the `\eiktest\` and `\epoc32ex\` example source code, which include several examples of creating custom controls. Also, check `ConstructFromResourceL()` source code for EIKON stock controls, in `\eikon\src\`.

Standard Dialogs

EIKON provides many convenient standard dialogs. Perhaps the most convenient are the alert and query dialogs.

Alerts

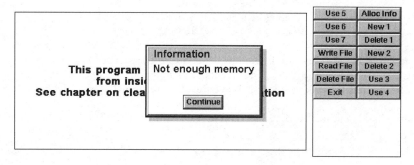

An **alert** displays a title saying Information, one or two lines of text, and a button labeled Continue. The EIKON environment constructs a ready-made alert dialog that you can invoke with `iEikonEnv->AlertWin()`, specifying either one or two string parameters (the second string, if specified, goes in the body of the dialog rather than its title). Because the dialog is pre-constructed, you can never run out of memory when using `AlertWin()`. Indeed, alert dialogs are used to indicate error conditions, including out-of-memory!

The Continue button is carefully chosen. How often have you seen error messages on your PC such as, "The system detected an unrecoverable error – OK"? This is a frequent source of user annoyance, so EIKON uses Continue, which is exactly what will happen when you press the button.

I don't know where the technical term 'alert' came from. Alerts pre-allocate their resources using a technique you can use yourself, if you want to – paradoxically, it's called **sleeping dialogs**. Check out the SDK for more information.

Queries

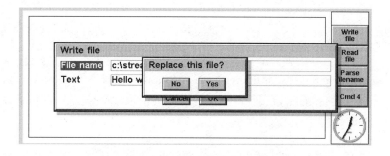

A query dialog enables a minimal form of interaction: you can use one to ask a simple yes/no question. As we saw earlier in this chapter, the streams application contains an example:

```
if(err == KErrAlreadyExists)
    {
    if(iEikonEnv->QueryWinL(R_EIK_TBUF_FILE_REPLACE_CONFIRM))
        User::LeaveIfError(file.Replace(iCoeEnv->FsSession(),
                            *fileName, EFileWrite));
    else
        iEikonEnv->LeaveWithInfoMsg(0); // Let user try again
    }
```

You run a query by specifying a string in a resource file that will be used as a question. I happened to be able to find an EIKON resource string, in eikon.rss, for this purpose: often, you'll need to write your own. The query dialog has a Yes button and a No button; iEikonEnv->QueryWinL() returns ETrue if Yes is pressed, or EFalse otherwise.

As I pointed out at the beginning of this chapter, the art is to ask truly yes/no questions – not to use the puzzling Windows-style yes/no/cancel.

Actually, the real art is to avoid queries altogether, if you can. The example above is not *really* the EIKON way: very few users want to throw away data. EIKON applications don't ask; they save and exit quietly. If you want to throw away your data, you have to invoke a special command, Revert to saved, which is buried in a cascaded menu because it's so rarely needed.

Note that query dialogs *aren't* sleeping dialogs, so the process of constructing and executing a query *can* leave. A query dialog is a special case of a CEikInfoDialog.

Other Standard Dialogs

EIKON provides many other standard dialogs. You can use them to:

- ❏ Open and save files, browse the file system, and create a new folder
- ❏ Choose a special character
- ❏ Dial a phone number
- ❏ Select a font, format, or display information on an embedded object, set text alignment, tabs, indent, paragraph spacing, or borders
- ❏ Perform page setup, print setup, and print preview
- ❏ Enter and change a password
- ❏ Set the current date and time

Additionally many of EIKON's more sophisticated controls include dialogs of their own – edwins, for example, include dialogs for find, replace, and options for replace; the infrared beaming system uses a dialog to display beaming progress information, and both printing and print preview include several of their own sub-dialogs.

Summary

In this chapter, I've introduced a lot of topics, answered the main questions, and left a *lot* of detail unanswered. You've now seen:

- ❏ What EIKON dialogs can do
- ❏ The basic shape of dialog programming, in both resource files and C++
- ❏ The framework, library and convenience functions in CEikDialog
- ❏ The stock controls offered by EIKON for inclusion in dialogs
- ❏ Some standard dialogs

There is much more information in the EPOC C++ SDK, including documentation, source code and examples about:

- ❏ EIKON stock controls
- ❏ Important CEikDialog functions
- ❏ How to implement custom controls for dialogs
- ❏ Programming multi-page dialogs

11

Graphics for Display

In the previous two chapters, we've begun to get familiar with the EIKON GUI, and we've got about as far as we can without actually doing any graphics. I passed over helloeik's app view's Draw() member without much comment, and all the other drawing has been done by EIKON's frameworks — toolbars, menus, dialogs, and standard controls.

Now it's time to get serious about graphics. In this chapter, I'll take you through the things you need to know for on-screen drawing, and in the next, the way that graphics support user interaction based on keyboard and pointer devices.

I'll start with drawing basics: how to get graphics on screen using the member functions of a fundamental class, CGraphicsContext. In addition to the basics, we'll need to look at how to update the screen without producing visible flicker.

A key concept for both drawing and interaction is the model-view-controller paradigm (MVC): I'll introduce this paradigm, which I'll be using for much of the rest of the book, and highlight its implications for drawing code.

Then I'll show how to share the screen using **windows** (RWindow) and **controls** (CCoeControl), and outline the implications of sharing on drawing code.

I'll conclude with a quick tour of the special effects that are supported by EPOC's graphics system.

Basics

GUIs present many more opportunities for displaying data than a console program. Even in a program as simple as "Hello World", you face these issues:

- ❑ What font should you use?
- ❑ What colors should you use for foreground and background?
- ❑ Where should you put the text?
- ❑ Should you set the text off in some kind of border or frame?
- ❑ How big is your screen, and how much of it do you get to draw the text?

Whichever way you look at it, you *have* to make these decisions, so the part of your program that says "hello world" will inevitably be bigger than the corresponding part of a text-mode program. Here, once again, is CExampleAppView::Draw() from helloeik:

```
void CExampleAppView::Draw(const TRect& /*aRect*/) const
    {
    CWindowGc& gc = SystemGc();
    TRect rect = Rect();
    rect.Shrink(10, 10);
    gc.DrawRect(rect);
    rect.Shrink(1, 1);
    const CFont* font = iEikonEnv->TitleFont();
    gc.UseFont(font);
    TInt baseline = rect.Height() / 2 + font->AscentInPixels() / 2;
    gc.DrawText(*iHelloWorld, rect, baseline, CGraphicsContext::ECenter);
    gc.DiscardFont();
    }
```

That's ten lines of code, where one would have been enough in hellotext. The good news, though, is that you are *able* to make decisions you need, and it's relatively easily to write the code to implement whatever you decide.

Controls

From the perspective of an EPOC application programmer, *all* drawing is done to a **control**. A control is a rectangular area of screen that occupies all or part of a **window**. The base class for all controls is CCoeControl, which is defined by EPOC's CONE component.

Here's the "Hello World" display:

As it happens, this screen includes two windows: the app view and the toolbar. The app view is a single control, while the toolbar comprises several controls:

❑ A **container** for the whole toolbar, which is a **compound control**

❑ **Component controls**, including the four buttons, the blank filename label above them, and the clock beneath them

In comparison, here's the view from the Battleships application that we'll develop in Chapter 22:

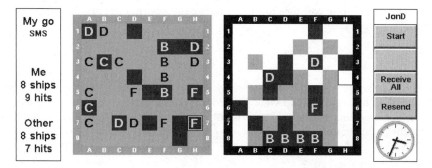

It may not look like it, but this screen contains two windows, as before: the app view and the toolbar. As before, the toolbar is a compound control. This time, though, the app view is also a compound control. Its component controls include:

❑ The player status view, on the left

❑ The view of my fleet, center left

❑ The view of my opponent's fleet, center right

These two applications already allow us to make some generalizations about controls:

❑ For an application, a control is the basic unit of GUI interaction: a control can do any sensible combination of drawing, pointer handling, and key handling

❑ For the system, a window is the basic unit of interaction: controls always use all or part of a window

❑ Controls can be compound: that is, they can contain component controls. A compound control is sometimes known as a container.

In this chapter, we'll see the role that controls (and windows) play in drawing. We'll continue to use the helloeik and Battleships applications as examples. In the next chapter, we'll look more closely at key- and pointer-based interaction.

Walking through `Draw()`

In EPOC, all drawing is done through a **graphics context** (GC), so it's no surprise that our `CExampleAppView::Draw()` function begins by getting hold of one using `SystemGc()`, a function in `CCoeControl`:

```
CWindowGc& gc = SystemGc();
```

All graphics context classes are derived from `CGraphicsContext`. Each derived class – such as `CWindowGc` here – is used for drawing on a particular graphics device (in our example, a window) and implements *all* the functionality specified by the base class, plus (and optionally) some extra functionality appropriate for the device in question.

> *Graphics contexts are a common notion in the world of computer graphics. Windows uses a 'device context'; Java uses a* `Graphics` *object.*

The next three lines of code conspire to draw a rectangular border ten pixels in from the edge of the app view's area on the screen:

```
TRect rect = Rect();
```

`CCoeControl::Rect()` gives the coordinates of the rectangle occupied by the control from within which it's called, in this case the app view. The coordinates are given relative to the window that the control uses. The coordinates used by `CWindowGc` drawing functions must also be relative to the window, so this is convenient.

```
rect.Shrink(10, 10);
```

This line makes the rectangle 10 pixels smaller than the control's rectangle on every side – top, right, bottom, and left. `TRect`, contains many utility functions like this, as we'll see below.

```
gc.DrawRect(rect);
```

This draws a rectangle using the default graphics context settings. These settings specify:

❑ That the pen creates a black, one-pixel wide, solid line: this causes the boundary of `rect` to be drawn in black

❑ That the brush is null, which means that the rectangle is not filled.

You can rely on the default GC configuration being set up prior to your `Draw()` function. Don't waste your time setting things that are guaranteed to be the default anyway.

Next, we are going to draw the text, centered in the rectangle. For good measure, we start by shrinking the rectangle by one pixel each side, so that we can afford to white it out without affecting the border we have just drawn:

```
rect.Shrink(1, 1);
```

Then, we get a font from the EIKON environment:

```
const CFont* font = iEikonEnv->TitleFont();
```

This is our first encounter with a `CFont *`. In Chapter 15, we'll have a careful look at how to get a font of a desired face, size, bold/italic attributes, etc. To avoid these issues right now, I just used a title font from the EIKON environment – it's the font used on the title bar of dialog boxes, and it's suitably bold and large.

It's not enough just to have a pointer to the font; we must also tell the graphics context to use it:

```
gc.UseFont(font);
```

This `UseFont()` lasts for all subsequent text drawing functions – until another `UseFont()` is issued, or until `DiscardFont()` is called.

Now we need to draw the text, centered in the `rect` rectangle:

```
TInt baseline = rect.Height() / 2 + font->AscentInPixels() / 2;
gc.DrawText(*iHelloWorld, rect, baseline, CGraphicsContext::ECenter);
```

This `DrawText()` function conveniently draws text with the GC's pen and font settings, and the entire rectangle area with the current brush settings. Horizontal justification is specified by its final parameter, which we specify here as `CGraphicsContext::ECenter`, to indicate that the text should be horizontally centered.

Oddly, `DrawText()` *doesn't* handle vertical justification for you, so you have to calculate the baseline yourself. Fortunately, the algorithm is simple and (unlike horizontal justification) it doesn't depend on the text of the string. You have to specify the baseline in pixels *down* from the top of the rectangle, so start with half the height of the rectangle (measured from its top downwards), and then add half the font's ascent.

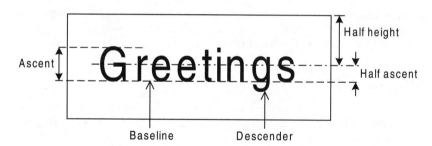

At this point, we've drawn the text, so we're finished with the font, and we can discard it:

```
gc.DiscardFont();
```

And there you have it. Our drawing code has drawn both graphics (a box) and text (a string in a box).

The `CGraphicsContext` API

As I stated above, all concrete graphics context classes are derived from `CGraphicsContext`, which offers a rich API for device-independent drawing. Let's pause briefly to describe this API. Its main features, in UML, are shown overleaf:

CGraphicsContext	TPoint	TSize
Set...() Draw...()	iX iY	iWidth iHeight

CGraphicsContext
pen brush fonts etc.

CFont	Region

TRect	
iTl : TPoint iBr : TPoint	
Move() Resize() Shrink() Grow() SetWidth() SetHeight()	IsEmpty() Contains(TPoint) Intersects(TRect) Intersection(TRect) BoundingRect(TRect) Center()

CGraphicsContext contains the main drawing functions, and is defined in gdi.h. All drawing is done using the current pen, brush, and font settings, and is clipped to the currently set clipping region. The pen, brush, font, and clipping region settings therefore provide context for graphics functions – hence the name of the class.

You can only set GC settings. There is no class for pen, brush etc., and you can't interrogate a GC to find out its current settings. You can keep a GC if you need to keep its settings, and you can reset a GC with a single function call if you need to throw all the settings away.

The drawing functions are illustrated by many examples throughout this book. CGraphicsContext is thoroughly documented in the EPOC C++ SDK, and a comprehensive example, \epoc32ex\graphics\grshell.mmp, illustrates all the functions covered below.

Coordinate Classes

Graphics are drawn to a device whose coordinate system is defined in pixels. Each point on the device has an (x, y) coordinate, measured from an origin at the top left of the device, with x coordinates increasing toward the right, and y coordinates increasing downwards.

In Chapter 15, we'll see how pixel coordinates are related to real-world units such as inches or centimeters. In this chapter, we'll concentrate on pixels and screen-oriented graphics.

2D supporting classes for points, rectangles, sizes, and regions are defined in e32std.h:

❑   TPoint contains iX and iY coordinates

❑   TRect contains two points, iTl for top left, and iBr for bottom right

❑   TSize contains iWidth and iHeight dimensions

These classes are equipped with a large range of constructors, operators, and functions to manipulate and combine them, but they make no attempt to encapsulate their members. You don't have to use get/set functions to access the (x, y) coordinates of a point, and so on. In truth, there would be very little point in doing so: the representations of these objects are genuinely public.

You have to get familiar with the exact definition of TRect. The top-left point is inside the rectangle, whereas the bottom-right point is just outside it:

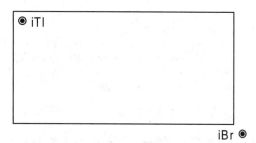

This definition makes some things easier (like calculating the size, because you simply subtract the x and y coordinates of the top-left from the bottom-right point) and some things harder (like rubber-banding calculations for interactively drawing a rectangle in EPOC Sketch, because you have to add $(1, 1)$ to the pointer coordinates to include the bottom-right corner correctly). If TRect had been defined to include its bottom-right corner, it would simply have made different things easier and different things harder.

Rectangles should be normalized, so that iTl coordinates are never greater than corresponding iBr coordinates. If you perform a calculation on a TRect that might violate this condition, call Normalize() to clear things up, by swapping the x coordinate values and/or y coordinate values as necessary.

Several region-related classes are also defined in e32std.h. These define a region of arbitrary shape as the union of several rectangles. The region classes are used extensively by the window server, but only in specialized application programs. It's worth noting in passing that a region can potentially have very many rectangles, so that the region classes in general may allocate resources on the heap (though they are heavily optimized so that, if only relatively few rectangles are needed to define the region, then no heap-based allocation is necessary). So, while points, rectangles, and sizes are simple T classes that are easy to allocate anywhere and pass around in client-server calls, regions require more careful management and, like C classes, need to be deleted or cleaned up when no longer required.

Context

CGraphicsContext holds several important items of context for drawing functions.

Pen

First, there's the **pen**, which defines draw modes (color and style) used for drawing lines, the outlines of filled shapes and text.

Draw mode options include Boolean operations on pixel color values – probably the only useful ones are solid (use the color specified), null (don't draw) and XOR with white (invert), which can be useful for cursor selection, rubber-banding etc.

Style options include solid, dotted, dashed etc., and also pen width. However, the BITGDI that draws screen graphics (which you saw in Chapter 9) doesn't support combinations of style and pen width – that is, it can't do thick dotted lines.

Use the `SetPenColor()`, `SetPenStyle()`, and `SetPenSize()` member functions to control the pen. By default, the pen is black, solid, and one pixel thick.

Brush

Next, there's the **brush**, which defines fill and background color or pattern. The brush can be null, solid, a hatching pattern, or a bitmap. For hatching and bitmaps, you can set an offset so that pattern fills on adjacent drawing primitives abut each other without odd edge effects. Use `SetBrushStyle()`, `SetBrushColor()`, `SetBrushOrigin()`, `SetBrushPattern()`, and `DiscardBrushPattern()` to control brush settings; defaults are null brush, zero origin.

Font

The **font** defines the font to be used for drawing text, and you specify it by passing a `CFont*` to `CGraphicsContext`. We'll cover fonts properly in Chapter 15, but for now you should note that the CONE environment has one font (`iCoeEnv->NormalFont()`), while the EIKON environment contains several (`iEikonEnv->TitleFont()`, `LegendFont()`, `SymbolFont()`, `AnnotationFont()`, and `DenseFont()`). Use `UseFont()` to set a font, `DiscardFont()` to say you no longer wish to use that font, and `SetUnderlineStyle()` and `SetStrikethroughStyle()` to set algorithmic enhancements to the font in use. By default, *no* font and *no* algorithmic enhancements are in use: you'll get panicked if you try to draw text without a font in use.

Current Position

Current position is set by `MoveTo()` and various `DrawXxxTo()` member functions, and moved by `MoveBy()` and corresponding `DrawXxxBy()` functions. It is also affected by `DrawPolyLine()`. The `XxxBy()` functions support relative moving and drawing. By default, the current position is at (0, 0).

Origin

The **origin** defines the offset from the device origin that will be used for drawing, and you can use `SetOrigin()` to control it. By default, the origin is (0, 0).

Clipping Region

The **clipping region** defines the region to which you want your graphics to be clipped. You can specify a simple rectangle, or a region that may be arbitrarily complex. Use `SetClippingRect()` to set a rectangular clipping region, and `CancelClippingRect()` to cancel it. By default, no clipping region (other than the device limits) applies.

Justification

Specialized **justification** settings for a variant of `DrawText()` can be set, although it's best not to call these directly from your own code. Instead, use EPOC's FORM component to create text views for you.

Use `Reset()` to set all context to default values.

Drawing Functions

Once you've set up the graphics context to your liking, there are numerous ways to draw to the screen. All GC functions are virtual, so they can be implemented in derived classes. Furthermore, all GC functions are designed to succeed, and so don't return anything (in C++ declarations, they return void). This requirement is so that multiple GC commands can be batched into a single message and sent to a server for execution: this would not be possible if any GC command had a return value.

Points and Lines

You can plot a single point, or draw an arc, a line, or a polyline. These functions all use the current pen; here are their declarations in gdi.h:

```
virtual void MoveTo(const TPoint& aPoint) = 0;
virtual void MoveBy(const TPoint& aVector) = 0;
virtual void Plot(const TPoint& aPoint) = 0;

virtual void DrawArc(const TRect& aRect,
                     const TPoint& aStart,
                     const TPoint& aEnd) = 0;
virtual void DrawLine(const TPoint& aPoint1,
                      const TPoint& aPoint2) = 0;
virtual void DrawLineTo(const TPoint& aPoint) = 0;
virtual void DrawLineBy(const TPoint& aVector) = 0;
virtual void DrawPolyLine(const CArrayFix<TPoint>* aPointList) = 0;
virtual void DrawPolyLine(const TPoint* aPointList,
                          TInt aNumPoints) = 0;
```

Note that line drawing (including arcs, and the last line in a polyline) excludes the last point of the line. As with the specification of TRect, this is a mixed blessing: sometimes it makes things easier, sometimes harder. If the last pixel were plotted automatically, it would be harder to un-plot it in the cases where this behavior were not desired. However it's easy enough to fix tricky cases by using Plot().

Check out the SDK for the interpretation of DrawArc() parameters.

DrawPolyLine() starts at the current cursor position set with MoveTo(), any XxxTo() or XxxBy() function, or DrawPolyLine(). Effectively, DrawPolyLine() uses DrawLineTo() to draw to every point specified.

Filled-Outline Shapes

You can draw several filled-outline shapes: a pie slice, ellipse, rectangle, rectangle with rounded corners, or a polygon. These functions use the pen and/or the brush. Use pen only to draw an outline. Use brush only to draw the shape. Use both to draw an outlined shape.

Here are the functions:

```
virtual void DrawPie(const TRect& aRect,
                     const TPoint& aStart,
                     const TPoint& aEnd) = 0;
virtual void DrawEllipse(const TRect& aRect) = 0;
virtual void DrawRect(const TRect& aRect) = 0;
```

```
        virtual void DrawRoundRect(const TRect& aRect,
                            const TSize& aCornerSize) = 0;
        virtual TInt DrawPolygon(const CArrayFix<TPoint>* aPointList,
                            TFillRule aFillRule = EAlternate) = 0;
        virtual TInt DrawPolygon(const TPoint* aPointList,
                            TInt aNumPoints,
                            TFillRule aFillRule = EAlternate) = 0;
```

The DrawPie() parameters are essentially the same as for DrawArc().

DrawPolygon() connects and fills all the points specified, and just as DrawLine(), no relative drawing is used or needed. Self-intersecting polygons may be drawn, in which case the fill rule parameter specifies the behavior for regions of even enclosure parity. Check the SDK and the grshell example for details.

Bitmaps

You can draw a bitmap either at scale of 1:1, or stretched to fit a rectangle you specify. Here are the functions:

```
        virtual void DrawBitmap(const TPoint& aTopLeft,
                            const CFbsBitmap* aSource) = 0;
        virtual void DrawBitmap(const TRect& aDestRect,
                            const CFbsBitmap* aSource) = 0;
        virtual void DrawBitmap(const TRect& aDestRect,
                            const CFbsBitmap* aSource,
                            const TRect& aSourceRect) = 0;
```

Use the same-size variant for high-performance blitting of GUI icons, and the stretch-blit variants for device-independent view code supporting on-screen zooming or printing.

See Chapter 15 for more on drawing bitmaps.

Text

You can draw text in the current font. Here are the functions for doing so:

```
        virtual void DrawText(const TDesC& aString,
                            const TPoint& aPosition) = 0;
        virtual void DrawText(const TDesC& aString,
                            const TRect& aBox,
                            TInt aBaselineOffset,
                            TTextAlign aHoriz = ELeft,
                            TInt aLeftMrg = 0) = 0;
```

The first (and apparently simpler) function uses the GC's justification settings, but you shouldn't call it yourself. Instead, use FORM if you need to handle properly laid out text. For general use, use the TRect variant that clips the text to the specified rectangle, and paints the rectangle background with the current brush.

> A graphics context has no default font, and if you call a text drawing function without a previous call to `UseFont()` in effect, you get a panic.

The panic is particularly ugly when you're drawing to a `CWindowGc` because all window-drawing functions are batched together and sent to the window to be executed later. The window server doesn't detect the absence of a `UseFont()` until the buffer is executed — by which time there is no context information about where the panic occurred.

Drawing and Redrawing

In a GUI program, all drawing is done by controls, which form all or part of a screen window. The derived control class's `Draw()` function is called when drawing is required. `Draw()` gets a graphics context using `SystemGc()` and draws into the area defined by its `Rect()` function, as we saw with helloeik's `CExampleAppView::Draw()`.

But it's a bit more complicated than that. Your control must not only **draw** its content, but must also **redraw** it when it changes, or when the system requires a redraw.

System-initiated redraws occur when:

❑   The window is first constructed

❑   The window, or part of it, is exposed after having been obscured by some other application or a dialog box

Application-initiated redraws occur when:

❑   The application changes the control's content, and wants these changes to be shown in an updated display

❑   The application changes the drawing parameters (such as color, scrolling, or zoom state), and wants these changes to be shown in an updated display

In addition, there are various other circumstances — partly system-initiated, partly application-initiated — in which redrawing must occur. For example, dismissing a dialog is application-initiated, but the redrawing of the controls underneath comes as a system-initiated request.

To understand redrawing properly, we have first to review the **model-view-controller** (MVC) paradigm. This is a good way to think about GUI systems, and using MVC concepts makes the following discussions much easier.

The Model, View, and Controller Pattern

On inspection, you'll notice that helloeik's `CExampleAppView::Draw()` function assumes the data we need is already available. It doesn't interrogate a database or ask the user for the string to draw — rather, it just uses the data that's already there in the `iHelloWorld` member of the control.

This is a standard paradigm in graphics: draw functions simply draw their model data: they don't change anything. If you want to change something, you use another function, and then call a draw function to reflect the update. In fact, this pattern is so common that it has a name: **model-view-controller**, often abbreviated simply to MVC:

❑ The **model** is the data that the program manipulates: in the case of "Hello World", it's the string text.

❑ The **view** is the view through which a user sees the model: in the case of "Hello World", it's the CExampleAppView class.

❑ The **controller** is the part of the program that updates the model and then requests the view to redraw in order to show the updates. In "Hello World", there are no updates and therefore there is no controller. When we come to the Battleships application, the controller will be quite sophisticated because updates may be generated either through user interaction or through events from the other player.

A strict MVC structure looks like this:

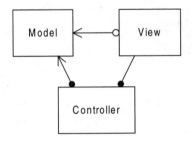

From the diagram:

❑ The model is an independent entity; if the program is file-based, the model very often corresponds with the program's persistent data

❑ The view *uses* the model, since its job is to draw it

❑ The controller's coordinates the model and view updates, so it *uses* both the model and the view

Depending on the program design, either of the *uses* relationships above may be upgraded into a stronger *has* relationship. The MVC pattern dictates the *uses* relationships, but doesn't force the *has* relationships specifically.

In some programs, the distinctions between model, view, and controller are cleanly reflected by boundaries between classes. But there are many reasons for the boundaries to become blurred in practice.

The "Hello World" program is so simple that there's no point in making such fine distinctions – its CExampleAppView contains both the model and the view, and there is no controller at all. Battleships, on the other hand, is complicated enough to use this structure, and greatly benefits from it. However, it turns out that the model (in the MVC sense) isn't the same as the CGameEngine engine class: it also includes some aspects of the CGameController. The view has to display things from both of these, so the boundary between MVC model and controller is not quite the same as that between the C++ engine and controller classes.

As you saw in the screenshot, Battleships has a compound app view that displays two fleets and the overall game status. The model for each part of this view is different. A sophisticated application uses the MVC pattern again and again – at the large scale for the whole application, and at a smaller scale for each interaction within it. You could say that even the toolbar has a model (defined by the resource file definitions that construct it) and a controller (somewhere in the EIKON application framework).

The MVC paradigm can become particularly blurred when giving feedback to some kinds of user interaction – navigation, cursor selection, animation, or drag-and-drop (which admittedly is rare in EPOC, though it does exist, for example when re-sizing grid columns in EPOC Sheet). Nonetheless, it remains extremely useful, and you can use it to think about the design of many EPOC controls and applications.

I should finish this section with a word on nomenclature. A 'control' in EPOC is not usually a 'controller' in the MVC sense, which is precisely why the word 'controller' is not used. An EPOC control does however usually contain pure MVC view functionality: its Draw() function draws a model without changing it.

In the EPOC literature, the word 'view' is used for a control or some drawing/interaction code, to highlight the fact that the 'view' is entirely separate from the 'model'. A good example would be ETEXT and FORM, EPOC's rich text components. ETEXT is a model without views; FORM provides views but has no model. We use 'app view' in this sense: while the model is often contained in the document class. In Battleships, I use 'fleet view' and 'player status view' as the names of my controls, because the fleet and player status 'model' data is kept in separate classes.

Often, in the EPOC literature, the word 'model' is used for application data that can be saved to file.

The Draw() Contract

EPOC controls use the Draw() function to implement MVC view functionality. CCoeControl::Draw() is defined in coecntrl.h as:

```
IMPORT_C virtual void Draw(const TRect& aRect) const;
```

A derived class will override this virtual function to draw – or redraw – its model. For the rare cases in which this function is not overridden, there's a default implementation that leaves the control blank.

> Because CCoeControl::Draw() is *strictly* an MVC view function, it should not update the model. It is therefore const, and non-leaving. Your Draw() implementation *must not leave*.

This is another reason why CGraphicsContext functions return void: if they could fail, Draw() could fail also.

System-initiated redraw handling starts in the window server, which detects when you need to redraw part of a window. In fact, it maintains an **invalid region** on the window, and sends an event to the application that owns the window, asking it to redraw the invalid region. CONE works out which controls intersect the invalid region and converts the event into a call to Draw() for all affected controls. A system-initiated redraw must redraw the model *exactly* as the previous draw.

Application-initiated redraw handling starts (by definition) in the application. If you update a model and need to redraw a control, you can simply call its DrawNow() function. DrawNow() is a non-virtual function in CCoeControl that:

❑ Tells the window server that the control is about to start redrawing

❑ Calls Draw()

❑ Tells the window server that the control has finished redrawing

In theory, then, you don't need to code any new functions in order to do an application-initiated redraw. You can simply call DrawNow(), so that your Draw() function is called in turn.

Where to Draw

It's possible that only a part of your control will need to be drawn (or redrawn). To understand this, you need to distinguish between the four regions shown below:

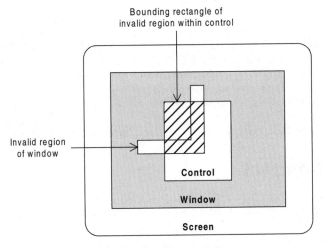

Your control is part of a window. The window server knows about the window, and knows which regions of the window are invalid – that is, the parts that need to be redrawn. Your Draw() function must draw the entire invalid region, but it must *not* draw outside the boundary of the control.

The window server will clip drawing to the invalid region – which is clearly bounded, in turn, by the boundary of the window itself.

> But if your control doesn't occupy the entire window, *you* are responsible for ensuring that your redraw doesn't spill beyond the boundaries of the control.

Often, this turns out not to be too onerous a responsibility: many controls, such as buttons and the various sections of the Battleships application screen, draw rectangles, lines, and text that are guaranteed to be inside the control's boundary in any case.

In the few cases where this doesn't happen, you can issue a `SetClippingRect()` call to the graphics context, which will ensure that future drawing is clipped to the control's rectangle. Here's an example, from the `drawing` example developed in Chapter 15:

```
aGc.SetClippingRect(aDeviceRect);
aGc.SetPenColor(KRgbDarkGray);
aGc.DrawRect(surround);
```

This was necessary because `surround` could have been bigger than `aDeviceRect`, which is the region of the control that this code is allowed to draw into. You can cancel this later, if you wish, with `CancelClippingRect()`, but since `CGraphicsContext::Reset()` does this anyway, and `Reset()` is called prior to each control's `Draw()`, you don't need to do this explicitly from a control.

How to Draw

Naturally, you should draw using the system GC and its member functions.

> **You can assume that the GC was reset before `Draw()` was called. Don't reset it yourself, and don't set colors and options that you don't need.**

Avoiding Wasteful Redraws

Drawing outside the invalid region is technically harmless (because such drawing will be clipped away by the window server whether it's inside your control's boundaries or not), but it's potentially wasteful. You may be able to save time by confining your drawing activity to the invalid region; the tradeoff is that you will have to do some testing to find out what you must draw, and what you do not need to draw.

That's the purpose of the `TRect` passed to your `Draw()` function: it is the bounding rectangle of the invalid region. If you wish, you can use this to draw (or redraw) only the part of the control within the passed `TRect`. It will be worth doing this if the cost of testing is outweighed by the savings from avoiding irrelevant drawing.

In practice, very few controls gain much by confining their redraw activity entirely to the bounding rectangle: it's simpler and not much slower to redraw the whole control. As a result, the majority of controls are coded to ignore the bounding rectangle that's passed. If you're writing a control that *does* use the `TRect`, remember that you still have to obey the contract to cover the entire invalid region within the boundary of your control, and nothing outside your control. You may still have to set a clipping region to ensure this – the system doesn't set one for you.

Early in the Protea project, we passed the invalid region (rather than its bounding rectangle) to `Draw()`. This turned out to be more trouble than it was worth. Regions are data structures of arbitrary size, which are much harder to pass around than TRects, but we had to pass them whether they were needed or not – and they usually weren't. As a compromise, we passed the bounding rectangle of the invalid region.

Breaking the `const` and Leave Rules

In quite rare circumstances, you may need to do some non-draw processing in `Draw()`. This could happen, for instance, if your view is very complicated and you're doing lazy initialization of some of the associated data structures in order to minimize memory usage.

In this case, you may need to allocate memory during `Draw()` to hold the results of your intermediate draw-related calculations, and this allocation could cause a leave. In addition, you'll want to use a pointer to refer to your newly allocated memory, perhaps in the control. This would require you to change the pointer value, which would violate the const-ness of `Draw()`.

The solutions here are to use casting to get rid of const-ness (for more information on the MUTABLE macros, see the SDK), and to put your resource-allocating code into a leaving function that gets called from a `TRAP()` within `Draw()`. You will also have to decide what to draw if your resource allocation fails.

Flicker-free Redraw

So far, we have suggested that you only need `Draw()` to do all your application's drawing. `Draw()` gets called when necessary for system-initiated redraws, and you can use `DrawNow()` to call `Draw()` for application-initiated redraws. However, there's a big problem with this simplistic approach: it makes applications impossible to use.

Firstly, it makes them slow, because you do too much redrawing in response to the most trivial updates. Secondly, it makes them ugly, because the draw-everything approach usually causes unacceptable flicker while the display is drawn and redrawn.

> The art of graphics in general is making it look pretty. The art of on-screen graphics is redrawing quickly and without flicker — and knowing when to stop optimizing.

We'll use the Battleships views to show the most important considerations involved here. Many EPOC applications are more complicated than Battleships, and take these considerations much further than I have done. In some cases, such as layout and updating rich text, the logic is hideously complicated. EPOC provides a single, reusable component for this purpose – FORM – so that application authors don't have to invent their own.

The most important cases for updating the views are as follows:

❑ When we start the game, bring the game to the foreground, or reload a game, we have to draw everything

❑ When most events take place in the game, we have to redraw the status view

❑ When something is hit, we have to reflect it in a fleet view – either my fleet, or the opponent's fleet

❑ When the cursor is moved (on the opponent's fleet view), we have to move the highlight quickly from the old cursor location to the new one

Let's examine each of these in turn.

Drawing Everything

The draw-everything situations are fairly easy. The status view is very quick to draw, and I don't need to do anything special. I had more trouble with the fleet view, pictured below:

I started out with code that looked something like this:

```
void CFleetView::Draw(const TRect&) const
    {
    DrawBoard();
    DrawBorders();
    DrawTiles();
    }
```

It:

❑   Draws a black square over the region of the board including both the border area and the sea area

❑   Draws the letters and numbers for the top, bottom, left, and right borders

❑   Draws the 64 tiles in the sea area

This is a classic flickery-draw function, in which the backgrounds are drawn first, and then over-painted by the foreground. It looks especially bad towards the bottom right of the sea area, because there is a significant delay between the first function call (which painted the whole board black) and the last one (which finally painted the 64th tile).

There is another problem, which I'll demonstrate in Chapter 15, because I had not whited out the background area between the board and the edge of the control. I could have tackled that easily enough using, say,

```
void CFleetView::Draw(const TRect&) const
    {
    ClearBackground();
    DrawBoard();
    DrawBorders();
    DrawTiles();
    }
```

but that would have made the flicker even worse.

> **The general solution to flicker problems is to avoid painting large areas twice.**

And so to my code in its present form:

```
void CFleetView::Draw(const TRect&) const
    {
    DrawOutside();
    DrawBorders();
    DrawTiles();
    }
```

This:

- ❏ Whites out the area of the control between the board rectangle and the border of the control — it doesn't touch the board area itself

- ❏ Draws the whole top, bottom, left, and right borders — without affecting the sea area

- ❏ Draws each of the 64 tiles in the sea area

My new draw-border code draws the border background and then over-paints it with the letters or numbers, which is a potential source of flicker. But the border is small, and the time interval between drawing the background and over-painting the eighth letter or number is too short to notice any flicker.

Likewise, the code I use to draw each tile starts by drawing the tile with its letter and then, if it's the cursor tile, over-paints the cursor. Again, this is OK: it happens so quickly that no one notices.

This emphasizes the point about the general rule for avoiding flicker: don't over-paint on a large scale. But, on a small scale, over-painting doesn't matter so much — and, in fact, avoiding over-painting on a small scale can become quite awkward to program.

In some circumstances, redraws need to be optimized much more than I've done here. You can use many techniques for optimizing drawing to eliminate flicker:

- ❏ Draw all the interesting content first — that is, draw the tiles, then the borders, and then the legend. This means that the things the user is interested in get drawn first.

- ❏ Optimize the drawing order so that the tile at the cursor position is drawn first. Again, this is what the user is most interested in.

- ❏ Draw subsequent tiles in order of increasing distance from the cursor tile, rather than scanning row-by-row and column-by-column

- ❏ Use active objects to allow view drawing to be mixed with user interaction — cursor movement or hit requests, for example — so that the application becomes responsive immediately

Each level of increased redraw optimization adds to program complexity. Fortunately none of this was necessary for the fleet view. In some EPOC application views, however these techniques make the difference between an application that is pleasant to use, and one that can barely be used at all. The Agenda year view, for instance, uses all the techniques mentioned above.

Status View Update

The status view update didn't need any optimization, even though the status view draw function appears to be quite complicated, with lots of detailed coordinate calculations, font selection, and string assembly.

The status view actually benefited from the buffering performed by the graphics system. As I mentioned above, drawing commands are buffered and only sent from the client application to the window server when necessary. They are then executed very rapidly indeed by the window server – typically, within a single screen refresh interval (1/70 second, which is 14 milliseconds, on the Psion Series 5mx). This is too fast for a user to notice any flicker.

The status view update uses only around 10 draw function calls, which probably all fit within a single buffer, and so are executed all together. If the status view had been more complicated (which it would have been, had I used a suitably professional graphic design), then it might have been more flicker-prone, and I would have had to take more precautions when redrawing it.

> **In any professional application, the aesthetics of a view are more important than the ease with which that view can be programmed.**

In this book, I've paid enough attention to aesthetics to make the points I need to make, but no more. I don't really think any of my graphics are satisfactory for serious use, and the status view is a prime example. In a real application it would have to be better, and if this meant the redraw code would need optimizing, then that would have to be done.

Good status views are particularly demanding. On the one hand, a rich status view conveys very useful information to the user. On the other hand, the user isn't looking at the status view all the time, and it *must not* compromise the application's responsiveness. For these reasons, status views are often updated using background active objects.

A good example of a status view from EPOC's standard application suite is the toolband at the top of a Word view. Of most interest to us here, is that it shows the font, paragraph formatting, and other information associated with the current cursor position. Its implementation is highly optimized using background active objects and a careful drawing order, so that document editing is not compromised at all.

Hit Reports

When a hit report comes in from the opponent's fleet, the fleet view is updated to show the affected tile. Calling DrawNow() would have done the job, but it would have involved drawing the board and its borders, which is slow and completely unnecessary – as these could not possibly have changed.

Looking for a better approach, I considered redrawing only the tiles that were affected by the hit. These are:

❑ The tile that was hit

❑ If that tile was a ship, then the squares diagonally adjacent to it (provided they're on the board, and provided they haven't already been hit), because we now know that these tiles must be sea

❑ If the tile was the final tile in a ship, then we know that *all* the tiles surrounding the ship must be sea, so we have to redraw them

It turns out that working out exactly which tiles are affected and doing a minimal redraw, is non-trivial – though we could do it if it was really necessary. Instead, I decided that I would redraw all the tiles. The code would be quick enough, and wouldn't cause perceived flicker because there would be no change to tiles that weren't affected. I wrote a `DrawTilesNow()` function to do this:

```
void CFleetView::DrawTilesNow() const
    {
    Window().Invalidate(iSeaArea);
    ActivateGc();
    Window().BeginRedraw(iSeaArea);
    DrawTiles();
    Window().EndRedraw();
    DeactivateGc();
    }
```

This function contains the logic needed to start and end the drawing operation and, in the middle, the same `DrawTiles()` function that I use to draw the board in the first place. During system-initiated redraw, the window server preparation is handled by the CONE framework. During application-initiated redraw, we have to do it ourselves before we can call `DrawTiles()`.

The DrawXxxNow() Pattern

> You can easily copy this `DrawXxxNow()` pattern for any selective redraws in your own applications.

It's useful to pause to note a few rules about application-initiated redraw here:

❑ Application-initiated redraw is usually done using a function whose name is `DrawXxxNow()`

❑ A `DrawXxx()` function (without the `Now`) expects to be called from within an activate-GC and begin-redraw bracket, and to draw to an area that was invalid

❑ A simple `DrawXxxNow()` will invalidate, activate-GC, begin-redraw, call `DrawXxx()`, and then end-redraw and deactivate-GC

❑ A more complex `DrawXxxNow()` function may need to call many `DrawXxx()` functions

❑ You should avoid calling multiple consecutive `DrawXxxNow()` functions if you can, because this involves (typically) wasteful invalidation, activate-GC, and begin-redraw brackets

❑ You *must* in any case avoid calling a `DrawXxxNow()` function from within an activate-GC/begin-redraw bracket, since it will cause a panic if you repeat these functions when a bracket is already active

Later, I'll explain what the activation and begin-redraw functions actually do.

Mixing Draw and Update Functions

> **Don't mix (view-related) draw functions with (model-related) update functions.**

For example, don't specify a function such as MoveCursor() to move the cursor *and* redraw the two affected squares. If you write all your model-update functions to update the view as well, you won't be able to issue a sequence of model updates without also causing many wasted view updates. The crime is compounded if your view update after, say, MoveCursor() is not optimized, so that it updates the whole view.

Instead, make MoveCursor() move the cursor *and nothing else.* You can call lots of model-update functions like this, calling an appropriate DrawXxxNow() function to update the view only when they have all executed. After a *really* complicated sequence of model updates, you might simply call DrawNow() to redraw the entire control.

If you *must* combine model updates with redrawing, make it clear in your function name that you're doing so – MoveCursorAndDrawNow(), for example. Then your users will know that such functions shouldn't be called during optimized update processing.

Cursor Movement

Cursor movement is highly interactive, and must perform supremely. When writing the application, I was prepared to optimize this seriously if necessary, and that would not have been difficult to do. When you move the cursor, by keyboard or pointer, at most two tiles are affected: the old and new cursor positions. It would have been easy to write a function to draw just the two affected tiles.

But it turned out to be unnecessary. Early in the development cycle, I experimented with DrawTilesNow(), which draws all 64 tiles. That turned out to be fast enough, and sufficiently flicker-free.

In more demanding applications, cursor movement can become very highly optimized. A common technique is to invert the affected pixels, so that no real drawing code is invoked at all – all you need to know is which region is affected, and use the logical operations of the GDI to invert the colors in the affected region. However, although this technique can be very fast, it needs careful attention to detail:

❑   Color inversion is good for black-and-white, but for color or more subtle shades of gray, it doesn't always produce visually acceptable results

❑   You still have to be able to handle system-initiated redraws, which means that you must be able to draw with the inverted color scheme on the affected region. It's insufficient simply to draw the view, and then to invert the cursor region. This would produce flicker precisely in the region where it is least acceptable. You must draw the view and cursor in one fell swoop.

❑   In fact, you have to combine system-initiated redraws with very high application responsiveness, so that the cursor can move even while a redraw is taking place. This simply amplifies the difficulties referred to above.

In general, cursor movement optimization is non-trivial. In almost every PC application I've used (including the word processor I'm using to write this book), I've noticed bugs associated with cursor redrawing. I have yet to notice such a bug in EPOC's built-in applications. I think the main reason for this is that the most demanding component, the FORM text view, is a single component that was written once and then re-used by all applications that need it, from Word to Agenda, Contacts, Data, and Sheet.

And I'm pretty confident my Battleships view is free of cursor redraw optimization bugs, because I haven't optimized it much! You can see the full code for CFleetView in Chapter 14.

It's the age-old lesson again: re-use existing code if you can, and don't optimize unless you have to. If you do have to optimize, choose your technique very carefully.

Sharing the Screen

Until now, I've covered the basics of drawing and, in many cases, I've had to tell you to do something without explaining why – for instance, the ActivateGc() and BeginRedraw() functions in DrawTilesNow().

Now it's time to be precise about how windows and controls work together to enable your application to share the screen with other applications, and to enable the different parts of your application to work together.

EPOC is a full multitasking system in which multiple applications may run concurrently. The screen is a single resource that must be shared among all these applications. EPOC implements this sharing using the **window server**. Each application draws to one or more **windows**; the window server manages the windows, ensuring that the correct window or windows are displayed, exposing and hiding windows as necessary, and managing overlaps.

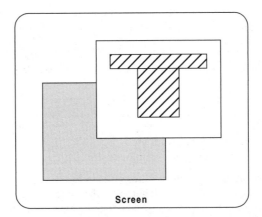

Screen

An application must also share the screen effectively between its own components. These components include the main application view, the toolbar, and other ornaments: dialogs, menus, and the like. An application uses **controls** for its components. Some controls – dialogs, for instance – use an entire window, but many others simply reside alongside other controls on an existing window. The buttons on a toolbar behave this way, as do the fleet views in the main application view of Battleships.

Every GUI client uses CONE, the control environment, to provide the basic framework for controls, and for communication with the window server:

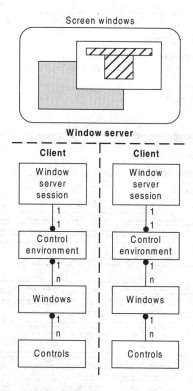

The window server maintains the windows used by all applications. It keeps track of their (x, y) positions and sizes, and also their front-to-back order, which is referred to as a z coordinate. As windows are moved and their z order changes, parts of them are exposed and need to be redrawn. For each window, the window server maintains an **invalid region**. When part of a window is invalid, the window server creates a redraw event, which is sent to the window's owning application so that the application can redraw it.

Every application is a client of the window server (we'll be describing the client-server framework in detail in Chapter 19). Happily, though, it's not necessary to understand the client-server framework in enormous detail for basic GUI programming, because the client interface is encapsulated by CONE.

CONE associates one or more controls with each window, and handles window server events. For instance, it handles a redraw event by calling the Draw() function for all controls that use the window indicated and fall within the bounding rectangle of the invalid region.

Window-owning and Lodger Controls

A control that requires a whole window is called a **window-owning control**. A control that requires only *part* of a window, on the other hand, is a **lodger control** or (more clumsily) a non-window-owning control.

A five-line dialog such as the Battleships Start first game dialog,

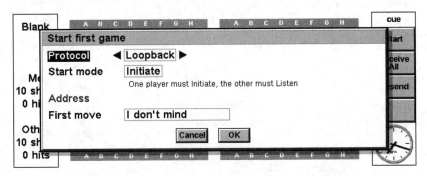

has a single window, but 21 controls (of which two happen to be invisible):

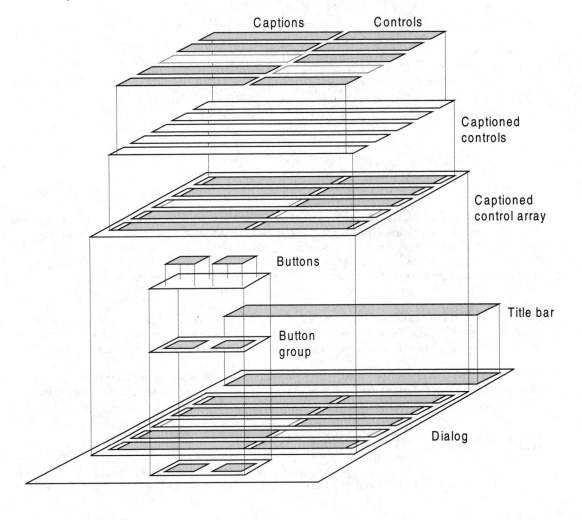

Although a window can have many controls, a control has only one window. Every control, whether it is window-owning or a lodger, ultimately occupies a rectangle on just one window, and the control draws to that rectangle on that window. A control's window is available via the `Window()` function in `CCoeControl`.

Lodgers vastly reduce the client-server traffic between an application and the window server. Only one client-server message is needed to create an entire dialog, since it includes only one window. Only one event is needed to redraw the whole dialog, no matter how many of its controls are affected. Dialogs are created and destroyed frequently in application use, so these optimizations make a significant difference.

Lodgers also reduce the overheads associated with complex entities such as a dialog, because controls are much more compact in memory than windows.

Finally, by their nature, lodgers have less demanding processing requirements. Windows may move, change z order, and overlap arbitrarily. Lodgers at peer level on the same window never intersect, and they only occupy a sub-region of their owning window or control. This makes the logic for detecting intersections much easier than that required for the arbitrarily complex regions managed by the window server.

All these factors improve the system efficiency of EPOC, compared to a scenario with no lodger controls. In order to take advantage of these features, most controls should be coded as lodgers, but there are a few circumstances in which you *need* a window:

❑ When there is no window to lodge in – this is the case for the application view.

❑ When you need shadows, as described later in this chapter. Shadows are used by dialogs, pop-up menus, pop-up list-boxes, menu panes, and the menu bar.

❑ When you need a backed-up window – we'll come back to these later.

❑ When you need to overlap peer controls in an arbitrary way – not according to lodger controls' stricter nesting rules.

❑ When you need the backup-behind property (see below), which is used by dialogs and menu panes to hold a bitmap of the window *behind* them.

Being window-owning is a fairly fundamental property of a control. There isn't much point in coding a control bi-modally – that is, to be *either* a lodger *or* window-owning. Decide which it should be, and commit to it.

On the other hand, only small parts of your control's code will be affected by the decision. So if you find out later that (for instance) your control that was previously a standalone app view now has a window to lodge in, then you should be able to modify your control quite easily.

For instance, in the drawing example in Chapter 15, the `CExampleHelloControl` class adapts helloeik's `CExampleAppView` to turn it into a lodger. The class declaration changes from,

```
class CExampleAppView : public CCoeControl
    {
public:
    ~CExampleAppView();
    void ConstructL(const TRect& aRect);
```

```
private: // From CCoeControl
    void Draw(const TRect&) const;

private:
    HBufC* iHelloWorld;
    };
```

to:

```
class CExampleHelloControl : public CCoeControl
    {
public:
    static CExampleHelloControl* NewL(const CCoeControl& aContainer,
                                      const TRect& aRect);
    ~CExampleHelloControl();

private:
    void ConstructL(const CCoeControl& aContainer, const TRect& aRect);

private: // From CCoeControl
    void Draw(const TRect&) const;
private:
    HBufC* iText;
    };
```

The essential change here is that I have to pass a CCoeControl& parameter to the control to tell it which CCoeControl to lodge in.

There are also two incidental changes. Firstly, I decided to provide CExampleHelloControl with a NewL() to encapsulate the two-phase construction. Secondly, I changed iHelloWorld to iText.

The construction changes from,

```
void CExampleAppView::ConstructL(const TRect& aRect)
    {
    CreateWindowL();
    SetRectL(aRect);
    ActivateL();
    iHelloWorld = iEikonEnv->AllocReadResourceL(R_EXAMPLE_TEXT_HELLO);
    }
```

to:

```
void CExampleHelloControl::ConstructL(const CCoeControl& aContainer,
                                      const TRect& aRect)
    {
    SetContainerWindowL(aContainer);
    SetRectL(aRect);
    iText = iEikonEnv->AllocReadResourceL(R_EXAMPLE_TEXT_HELLO_CONTROL);
    ActivateL();
    }
```

Instead of calling `CreateWindowL()` to create a window of the right size, I call `SetContainerWindowL()` to register myself as a lodger of a control on an existing window.

Compound Controls

There needs to be some structure in laying out lodger controls such as those in the Battleships Start first game dialog, or indeed in the Battleships app view. That discipline is obtained by using **compound controls**: a control is compound if it has one or more **component controls**, in addition to itself.

- ❑ A component control is contained entirely within the area of its owning control
- ❑ All components of a control must have non-overlapping rectangles
- ❑ A component control does not have to be a lodger: it can also be window-owning. In the majority of cases, however, a component control is a lodger

To indicate ownership of component controls to CONE's framework, a compound control must implement two virtual functions from `CCoeControl`:

- ❑ `CountComponentControls()` indicates how many components a control has – by default, it has zero, but you can override this
- ❑ `ComponentControl()` returns the *n*th component, with *n* from zero to the count of components minus one. By default this function panics (because it should never get called at all if there are zero components). If you override `CountComponentControls()`, you should also override this function to return a component for each possible value of *n*

Here's `CGameAppView`'s implementation of these functions, from the Battleships program:

```
TInt CGameAppView::CountComponentControls() const
    {
    return 3;
    }


CCoeControl* CGameAppView::ComponentControl(TInt aIndex) const
    {
    switch (aIndex)
        {
    case 0: return iMyFleetView;
    case 1: return iOppFleetView;
    case 2: return iStatusView;
        }
    return 0;
    }
```

The app view always has three components, so `CountComponentControls()` returns 3. The `ComponentControl()` function is a simple switch statement. The assignment of the controls to the three index values isn't really significant. I trust the CONE framework well enough not to call `ComponentControl()` with a bad index, so I don't bother to panic if the index is out of range.

A dialog is also a compound control, with typically only a single window. A dialog has an unpredictable number of component controls, so instead of hardcoding the answers to `CountComponentControls()` and `ComponentControl()` as I did above, `CEiKDialog` uses a variable-sized array to store dialog lines, and calculates the answers for these functions.

More on Drawing

Drawing to a window is easy for programs, but involves complex processing by EPOC:

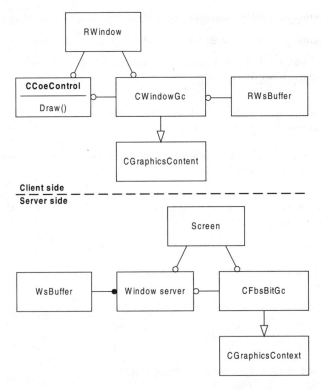

On the client side, an application uses a `CWindowGc` to draw to a window. `CWindowGc`'s functions are implemented by encoding and storing commands in the window server's client-side buffer. When the buffer is full, or when the client requests it, the instructions in the buffer are all sent to the window server, which decodes and executes them by drawing directly onto the screen, using a `CFbsBitGc` – a `CGraphicsContext`-derived class for drawing onto bitmapped devices. Prior to drawing, the window server sets up a clipping region to ensure that only the correct region of the correct window can be changed, whatever the current state of overlapping windows on the screen. The window server uses the BITGDI to 'rasterize' the drawing commands.

The client-side buffer, which wraps several window server commands into a single client-server transaction, significantly speeds up system graphics performance. The BITGDI plays an important role too: much of it is hand-optimized in ARM assembler.

The C++ code for the BITGDI is also maintained for the PC-hosted emulator (which runs on 300+MHz Pentiums and hardly needs optimizing), and as a starting point for ports to other CPU architectures (such as Motorola's M*Core).

We can now explain the `DrawTilesNow()` function that we saw earlier:

```
void CFleetView::DrawTilesNow() const
    {
    Window().Invalidate(iSeaArea);
    ActivateGc();
    Window().BeginRedraw(iSeaArea);
    DrawTiles();
    Window().EndRedraw();
    DeactivateGc();
    }
```

This is a member function of `CFleetView`, which is derived from `CCoeControl`. The central function is `DrawTiles()`, but this is bracketed by actions necessary to function correctly with the window server.

Invalidating

First, we use an `Invalidate()` function to invalidate the region we are about to draw.

Remember that the window server keeps track of all invalid regions on each window, and clips drawing to the total invalid region. So before you do an application-initiated redraw, you must invalidate the region you are about to redraw, otherwise nothing will appear (unless the region happened to be invalid for some other reason).

Activating the Graphics Context

Then, CONE's system graphics context must be activated. If you take a look in `coecntrl.cpp`, you'll find that `CCoeControl::ActivateGc()` is coded as:

```
EXPORT_C void CCoeControl::ActivateGc() const
    {
    CWindowGc& gc = iCoeEnv->SystemGc();
    if(iContext)
        iContext->ActivateContext(gc, *iWin);
    else
        gc.Activate(*iWin);
    }
```

The usual case just executes `gc.Activate()` on the control's window, telling the window server's client interface to use CONE's system GC to start drawing to it. The function also resets the window GC to use default settings. I'll explain the other case later on.

Beginning and Ending the Redraw

Immediately before drawing, we tell the window server we are about to begin redrawing a particular region. And immediately after redrawing, we tell the window server that we have finished. When the BeginRedraw() function is executed by the window server, it has two effects:

❑ The window server sets a clipping region to the intersection of the invalid region, the region specified by BeginRedraw(), and the region of the window that is visible on the screen.

❑ The window server then marks the region specified by BeginRedraw() as *valid* (or, more accurately, it subtracts the begin-redraw region from its current invalid region).

The application's draw code must then cover every pixel of the region specified by BeginRedraw(). If the application's draw code includes an explicit call to SetClippingRegion(), the region so specified is intersected with the clipping region calculated at BeginRedraw() time.

When the application has finished redrawing, it calls EndRedraw(). This enables the window server to delete the region object that it allocated during BeginRedraw() processing.

Concurrency

You're probably wondering why the window server marks the region as valid at *begin* redraw time rather than *end* redraw. The reason is that EPOC is a multitasking operating system. The following theoretical sequence of events shows why this protocol is needed:

❑ Application A issues begin-redraw. The affected region is marked valid on A's window

❑ A starts drawing

❑ Application B comes to the foreground, and its window overwrites A's

❑ B is terminated, so that A's window is again exposed

❑ Clearly, A's window is now invalid. The window server marks it as such.

❑ A continues redrawing, and issues end-redraw

At the end of this sequence, the region of the screen covered by the re-exposed region of A's window is in an arbitrary state. If the window server had marked A's window as valid at end-redraw time, the window server would not know that it still needs to be redrawn. Instead, the window server marks A's window as valid at begin-redraw time so that, by the end of a sequence like this, the window is correctly marked invalid, and can be redrawn.

You might think this sequence of events would be rare, but it *is* possible, so the system has to address it properly.

Redrawing

You should now find it pretty easy to understand how redrawing works. When the window server knows that a region of a window is invalid, it sends a redraw message to the window's owning application, specifying the bounding rectangle of the invalid region. This is picked up by CONE and handled using the following code:

```
EXPORT_C void CCoeControl::HandleRedrawEvent(const TRect& aRect) const
    {
    ActivateGc();
    Window().BeginRedraw(aRect);
    Draw(aRect);
    DrawComponents(aRect);
    Window().EndRedraw();
    DeactivateGc();
    }
```

This code has exact parallels to the code we saw in `DrawTilesNow()`: the activate and begin-redraw brackets are needed to set everything up correctly. However, CONE doesn't need to call `Invalidate()` here, because the whole point of the redraw is that a region is already known to be invalid. In fact, if CONE did call `Invalidate()` on the rectangle, it would potentially extend the invalid region, which would waste processing time.

Inside the activate and begin-redraw brackets, CONE draws the control using `Draw()` and passing the bounding rectangle. Then, CONE draws every component owned by this control using `DrawComponents()`, which is coded as follows:

```
void CCoeControl::DrawComponents(const TRect& aRect) const
    {
    const TInt count = CountComponentControls();
    for(TInt ii = 0; ii < count; ii++)
        {
        const CCoeControl* ctrl = ComponentControl(ii);
        if(!(ctrl->OwnsWindow()) && ctrl->IsVisible())
            {
            TRect rect;
            const TRect* pRect = (&aRect);
            if(!((ctrl->Flags()) & ECanDrawOutsideRect))
                {
                rect = ctrl->Rect();
                rect.Intersection(aRect);
                if(rect.IsEmpty())
                    continue;
                pRect = (&rect);
                }
            ResetGc();
            ctrl->Draw(*pRect);
            ctrl->DrawComponents(*pRect);
            }
        }
    }
```

CONE simply redraws every visible lodger component whose rectangle intersects the invalid rectangle, and then its components in turn. CONE adjusts the bounding invalid rectangle appropriately for each component control.

CONE also makes an allowance for a rare special case: controls that can potentially draw outside their own rectangle.

Default settings are assured here: the original call to `ActivateGc()` set default settings for the window-owning control that was drawn first; later calls to `ResetGc()` ensure that components are drawn with default settings also.

The loop above *doesn't* need to draw window-owning components of the window-owning control that received the original redraw request. This is because the window server will send a redraw message to such controls in any case, in due time.

You can see again here how lodger components promote system efficiency. For each component that is a lodger (instead of a window-owning control), you avoid the client-server message and the 'activate' and 'begin-redraw' brackets. All you need is a single `ResetGc()`, which occupies a single byte in the window server's client-side buffer.

Support for Flicker-free Drawing

As an application programmer, you should be aware of two aspects of the window server that promote flicker-free drawing.

Firstly, the window server clips drawing down to the intersection of the invalid region and the begin-redraw region, so if your drawing code tends to flicker, the effect will be confined to the area being necessarily redrawn.

You can exploit this in some draw-now situations. Imagine that I wanted to implement a cursor-movement function, but didn't want to alter my `DrawTiles()` function. I could write a `DrawTwoTilesNow()` function that accepted the (x, y) coordinates of two tiles to be drawn, enabling me to calculate and invalidate only those two rectangles. I could then activate a GC and begin-redraw the whole tiled area, calling `DrawTiles()` to do so. The window server would clip drawing activity to the two tiles affected, eliminating flicker anywhere else. It's a poor man's flicker-free solution, but in some cases it might just make the difference.

Secondly, the window server's client-side buffer provides useful flicker-free support. For a start, it improves overall system efficiency, so that everything works faster and flickers are therefore shorter. Also, it causes drawing commands to be batched up and executed rapidly by the window server using the BITGDI and a constant clipping region. In practice, this means that some sequences of draw commands are executed so fast that, even if your coding flickers by nature, no one will ever see the problem, especially on high-persistence LCD displays. The key here is to confine sequences that cause flicker to only a few consecutive draw commands, so that they all get executed as part of a single window-server buffer.

Finally, and most obviously, the use of lodger controls helps here too, because it means the window server buffer contains only a single `ResetGc()` command between controls, rather than a whole end bracket for redraw and GC deactivation, followed by a begin bracket for GC activation and redraw.

Backed-up Windows

In the window server, a standard window is represented by information about its position, size, visible region, and invalid region – and that's about all. In particular, no memory is set aside for the drawn content of the window, which is why the window server has to ask the application to redraw when a region is invalid.

But in some cases it's impractical for the application to redraw the window, for instance, if it's:

❑ An old-style program that's not structured for event handling, and so can't redraw

❑ An old-style program that's not structured in an MVC manner, has no model, and so can't redraw, even if it can handle events

❑ A program that takes so long to redraw that it's desirable to avoid redraws if at all possible

A program in an old-style interpreted language, such as OPL, is likely to suffer from all of these problems

In these cases, you can ask the window server to create a **backed-up window**: the window server creates a backup bitmap for the window, and handles redraws from the backup bitmap, without sending a redraw event to the client application.

The backup bitmap consumes more RAM than the object required to represent a standard window. If the system is running short on memory, it's more likely that creation of a backed-up window will fail, than creation of a standard window. If it does fail, the application will also fail, because requiring a backed-up window is a fairly fundamental property of a control. If you need backup, then you need it. If you can code proper redraw logic of sufficient performance, then you don't need backup.

Code that is designed for drawing to backed-up windows usually won't work with standard windows, because standard windows require redraws which code written for a backup window won't be able to handle.

On the other hand, code that is good for writing to a standard window is usually good for writing to a backed-up window: although the backed-up window won't call for redraws, there's no difference to the application-initiated draw code. The only technique that won't work for backed-up windows is to invalidate a window region in the hope of fielding a later redraw event – but this is a bad technique anyway.

Standard controls – such as the controls EIKON offers to application programmers – are usually lodger controls that are designed to work in standard windows. Such lodger controls will also work properly in backed-up windows, unless they use invalidation in the hope of fielding a later redraw. All EIKON stock controls are designed to work in both windows.

CCoeControl's DrawDeferred() function works, on a standard window, by invalidating the window region corresponding to the control. This causes a later redraw event. On a backed-up window, this won't work, so in that case DrawDeferred() simply calls DrawNow():

```
void CCoeControl::DrawDeferred() const
    {
    ...
    if(IsBackedUp())
        DrawNow();
    else
        Window().Invalidate(Rect());
    ...
    }
```

`CCoeControl`'s **Support for Drawing**

Now is a good time to summarize the drawing-related features of `CCoeControl` that we've seen so far.

First and foremost, a control is a rectangle that covers all or part of a window. All concrete controls are (ultimately) derived from the abstract base class `CCoeControl`. Various relationships exist between controls, other controls, and windows:

- ❏ A control can own a window, or be a lodger

- ❏ A control may have zero or more component controls: a control's components should not overlap, and should be contained entirely within the control's rectangle

- ❏ A control is associated with precisely one window, whether as the window-owning control, or as a lodger

- ❏ All lodgers are components of some control (ultimately, the component can be traced to a window-owning control)

- ❏ Component controls do not have to be lodgers; they can also be window-owning (say, for a small backed-up region)

Controls contain support for drawing, application-initiated redrawing, and system-initiated redrawing:

- ❏ Applications request controls to draw using the `DrawNow()` function

- ❏ The window server causes controls to draw when a region of the control's window becomes invalid

- ❏ In either case, `Draw()` is called to handle the drawing

- ❏ Functions exist to provide access to a GC for use on the control's window, to activate and deactivate that GC, and to reset it

Here are the main functions and data members associated with the above requirements.

Control Environment

Each control contains a pointer to the control environment, which any control can reach by specifying `iCoeEnv` (protected) or `ControlEnv()` (public):

```
class CCoeControl : public CBase
    {
public:
    ...
    inline CCoeEnv* ControlEnv() const;
    ...
protected:
    CCoeEnv* iCoeEnv;
    ...
    };
```

There are four ways in which you can access the control environment:

❑ From a derived control or app UI class, including your own application's app UI, you can use iCoeEnv to get at the CCoeEnv

❑ If you have a pointer to a control or app UI, you can use its public ControlEnv() function

❑ If you have access to neither of these things, you can use the static function CCoeEnv::Static(), which uses thread-local storage (TLS) to find the current environment

❑ Since TLS isn't particularly quick, you can also store a pointer somewhere in your object for faster access, if you need to do this frequently

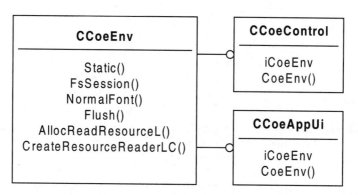

The control environment's facilities include:

❑ Access to the basic GUI resources: window server session, window group, screen device, and graphics context

❑ A permanently-available file server session, available via FsSession()

❑ A normal font for drawing to the screen (10-point Arial), available via NormalFont()

❑ A Flush() function to flush the window server buffer and optionally wait a short period

❑ Convenience functions for creating new graphics contexts and fonts on the screen device

❑ Support for multiple resource files, and many functions to read resources (see Chapter 9)

See the definition of CCoeEnv in coemain.h for the full list.

Window-owning and Lodging

A control may be either window-owning or a lodger. A window-owning control *has-a* window: a lodger simply *uses-a* window.

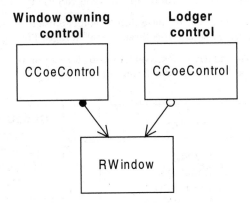

Either way, throughout the lifetime of a control, an `iWin` member points to a drawable window. The drawable window may be either standard (`RWindow`) or backed-up (`RBackedUpWindow`) — `RDrawableWindow` is a base class for both of these.

You can call a `CCoeControl` function from those listed below, during the second-phase constructor of a concrete control class, to indicate whether it's window-owning or a lodger.

The functions for specifying and testing the window are:

```
class CCoeControl : public CBase
    {
public:
    ...
    IMPORT_C virtual void SetContainerWindowL(const CCoeControl& aContainer);
    IMPORT_C void SetContainerWindow(RWindow& aWindow);
    IMPORT_C void SetContainerWindow(RBackedUpWindow& aWindow);

    ...
    inline RDrawableWindow* DrawableWindow() const;
    ...
    IMPORT_C TBool OwnsWindow() const;
    IMPORT_C TBool IsBackedUp() const;

    ...
protected:
    ...
    inline RWindow& Window() const;
    inline RBackedUpWindow& BackedUpWindow() const;
    IMPORT_C void CloseWindow();
    IMPORT_C void CreateWindowL();
    IMPORT_C void CreateWindowL(const CCoeControl* aParent);
    IMPORT_C void CreateWindowL(RWindowTreeNode& aParent);
    IMPORT_C void CreateWindowL(RWindowGroup* aParent);
```

```
        IMPORT_C void CreateBackedUpWindowL(RWindowTreeNode& aParent);
        IMPORT_C void CreateBackedUpWindowL(RWindowTreeNode& aParent,
                                            TDisplayMode aDisplayMode);
        ...
protected:
    CCoeEnv* iCoeEnv;
    ...
private:
    RDrawableWindow* iWin;
    ...
    };
```

The `CreateWindowL()` functions cause a new window – either standard, or backed-up – to be created.

The `SetContainerWindow()` functions tell the control to use an existing standard window or backed-up window. This should be used by controls that are themselves components of a control associated with the same window. `SetContainerWindowL()` tells the control to lodge in an existing control – and hence, ultimately, to use an existing window.

This function is both virtual and potentially leaving. That's not the best design in EPOC: really, it should be neither. You can guarantee that this function won't leave if it's not overridden, so try to think of this function as not having been designed to be overridden. A few classes in EIKON use it for purposes that could be achieved by other means.

Components

A control can have any number of component controls, from zero upwards. Here are the component-control functions:

```
class CCoeControl : public CBase
    {
public:
    ...
    IMPORT_C TInt Index(const CCoeControl* aControl) const;
    ...
    IMPORT_C virtual TInt CountComponentControls() const;
    IMPORT_C virtual CCoeControl* ComponentControl(TInt aIndex) const;
    ...
    };
```

If you want to implement a container control, you can store controls and using any data structure you want. You override `CountComponentControls()` to indicate how many controls you have, and `ComponentControl()` to return the control corresponding to each index value, starting from zero.

As we saw earlier, by default, `CountComponentControls()` returns zero, and `ComponentControl()` panics. These functions work as a pair: so make sure you override them both consistently.

`Index()` searches through the component controls one by one, to find one whose address matches the address passed. If none is found, `Index()` returns `KErrNotFound`, which is defined as -1.

> **The `CCoeControl` base class does not dictate how component controls should be stored in a container.**

If your container is a fixed-purpose container, such as the Battleships application view, which contains just three components, then you can use a pointer to address each component, hardcode `CountComponentControls()` to return 3, and use a switch statement in `ComponentControl()`.

On the other hand, if your container is a general-purpose container such as a dialog, you may wish to implement a general-purpose array to hold your component controls.

Position and Size

You can set a control's position and size. Here are the declarations related to position and size:

```
class CCoeControl : public CBase
    {
public:
    ...
    IMPORT_C void SetExtentL(const TPoint& aPosition, const TSize& aSize);
    IMPORT_C void SetSizeL(const TSize& aSize);
    IMPORT_C void SetPosition(const TPoint& aPosition);
    IMPORT_C void SetRectL(const TRect& aRect);
    IMPORT_C void SetExtentToWholeScreenL();

    ...
    IMPORT_C TSize Size() const;
    IMPORT_C TPoint Position() const;
    IMPORT_C TRect Rect() const;
    IMPORT_C TPoint PositionRelativeToScreen() const;

    ...
    IMPORT_C virtual void SizeChangedL();
    IMPORT_C virtual void PositionChanged();

    IMPORT_C void SetCornerAndSizeL(TCoeAlignment aCorner, const TSize& aSize);
    IMPORT_C void SetSizeWithoutNotificationL(const TSize& aSize);
    ...
protected:
    ...
    TPoint iPosition;
    TSize iSize;
    ...
    };
```

Position and size are stored in `iPosition` and `iSize`. You can interrogate them with `Position()`, `Size()`, or `Rect()`, and change them with `SetExtentL()`, `SetPosition()`, `SetSizeL()`, and `SetRectL()`.

Changing the size of a control could, in rare cases, cause memory to be allocated, which could fail – so all functions that change size are potentially leaving. SetPosition() does not change size, so cannot leave.

- ❑ When a control's size is changed, its virtual SizeChangedL() function is called

- ❑ A position change is notified by PositionChanged()

- ❑ SetExtentL() calls SizeChangedL() but not PositionChanged() – so think of SizeChangedL() as always notifying size change, and potentially notifying position change

- ❑ You can use SetSizeWithoutNotificationL() to prevent SizeChangedL() being called

- ❑ You can set and interrogate position relative to the owning window, and set the size to the whole screen. SetCornerAndSizeL() aligns a control's rectangle to one corner of the whole screen

This design isn't the best part of EPOC either. In future releases, leave will not be allowed from these functions. Merely resizing a control should not cause extra resources to be allocated, except in the rare kinds of control which might need to allocate resources in Draw(). In this case, you should take the same action: trap any leaves yourself.

Drawing

Functions relevant for drawing include:

```
class CCoeControl : public CBase
    {
public:
    ...
    IMPORT_C virtual void MakeVisible(TBool aVisible);
    ...
    IMPORT_C virtual void ActivateL();
    ...
    IMPORT_C void DrawNow() const;
    IMPORT_C void DrawDeferred() const;
    ...
    IMPORT_C TBool IsVisible() const;
    ...
protected:
    ...
    IMPORT_C void SetBlank();
    ...
    IMPORT_C CWindowGc& SystemGc() const;
    IMPORT_C void ActivateGc() const;
    IMPORT_C void ResetGc() const;
    IMPORT_C void DeactivateGc() const;
    IMPORT_C TBool IsReadyToDraw() const;
    IMPORT_C TBool IsActivated() const;
    IMPORT_C TBool IsBlank() const;
    ...
```

```
private:
    ...
    IMPORT_C virtual void Draw(const TRect& aRect) const;
    ...
    };
```

Use the functions as follows:

- ❑ You have to activate a control, using `ActivateL()`, as the final part of its second-phase construction. Assuming that, by the time `ActivateL()` is called, the control's extent is in place, and its model is fully initialized, this makes the control ready for drawing. You can use `IsActivated()` to test whether `ActivateL()` has been called.

- ❑ You can set a control to be visible or not – `Draw()` is not called for invisible controls

- ❑ `IsReadyToDraw()` returns `ETrue` if the control is both activated and visible

- ❑ `SetBlank()` is an obscure function that only affects controls which don't override `Draw()`. If you don't `SetBlank()`, then `CCoeControl::Draw()` does nothing. If you *do* `SetBlank()`, then `CCoeControl::Draw()` blanks the control.

- ❑ We have already seen that `Draw()` is the fundamental drawing function. `DrawNow()` initiates the correct drawing sequence to draw a control and all its components.

- ❑ `DrawDeferred()` simply invalidates the control's extent, so that the window server will send a redraw message, causing a redraw later. This guarantees a redraw will be called on the control at the earliest available opportunity, rather than forcing it now.

- ❑ `ActivateL()`, `MakeVisible()`, and `DrawNow()` recurse as appropriate through component controls

- ❑ `SystemGc()` returns a windowed graphics context for drawing. `ActivateGc()`, `ResetGc()`, and `DeactivateGc()` perform the GC preparation functions needed for redrawing.

> **Always use these functions, rather than directly calling `SystemGc.Activate(Window())`. It's more convenient, and it allows control contexts (see below) to be supported properly.**

Special Effects

The window server provides many useful special effects to application programs.

Shadows

Throughout the screenshots in the book, you'll have seen plenty of shadows – behind dialogs, behind menus, behind pop-up choice lists etc..

You have to specify that you want a window to cast a shadow, and say how 'high' the window is. The shadow actually falls on the window(s) behind the one which you specify casts shadows. To implement a shadow when it is cast, the window server asks the BITGDI to dim the region affected by the shadow. To maintain a shadow even when the window redraws, the window server executes the application's redraw command buffer twice: firstly, it uses a clipping region that *excludes* the shadowed part of the window and uses the BITGDI to draw using normal color mapping. Secondly, it uses a clipping region for only the shadowed parts, and puts the GC it uses for BITGDI drawing into shadow mode. This causes the BITGDI to 'darken' all colors used for drawing in the affected region. The net result is that the drawing appears with shadows very nicely – without affecting the application's drawing code at all.

Shadows are implemented in dialogs and the like by calling the `AddWindowShadow()` function in `CEikonEnv`:

```
void CEikonEnv::AddWindowShadow(CCoeControl* aWinArea)
    {
    aWinArea->DrawableWindow()->SetShadowHeight(3); // six pixels
    }
```

So the shadow is a fixed height in EIKON, but you can easily add it from your code.

Backing Up Behind

Backed-up-behind windows maintain a copy of the window *behind* them, so that when the backed-up-behind window is dismissed, the window behind can be redrawn by the window server without invoking application redraw code.

This effect is used for menu panes: it speeds up the process of flicking from one menu pane to another immensely. It's also used for dialogs, where it speeds up dialog dismissal.

When a backed-up-behind window is created, a big enough bitmap is allocated to back up the entire screen area that the window *and its shadow* are about to cover. The screen region is copied into this backup bitmap, and then the window is displayed. When the window is dismissed, the backup bitmap is copied back onto the screen. The net effect is that the application doesn't have to redraw at all, so that window dismissal is very quick.

The backup behind code is clever enough to update the backup bitmap when, for instance, a dialog is moved around the screen.

The backup behind code, however, is not an essential property of the window, but an optimization. So it gives up when it runs out of memory, when the window behind tries to redraw, or when another window with backup behind property is placed in front of the existing one. Then an application redraw is needed after all. This doesn't have any effect on application code – just on performance.

Incidentally, these rules imply that the menu *bar* cannot use backup behind, because that would violate the rule that only one window can have backup behind property. So when you dismiss the entire menu (either by canceling or choosing an option), you will notice that the top of your application view must do a redraw.

Animation

Sometimes, you want to do some drawing where timing is an essential feature of the visual effect. This isn't really something that fits well into the MVC paradigm, so we need special support for it.

One kind of animation is used to give reassuring cues in the GUI.

❑ If you select OK on a dialog – even using the keyboard – the OK button goes down for a short time (0.2 seconds, in fact) and then the action takes place

❑ If you select a menu item using the pointer, the item appears to flash briefly, in a subtle way, before the menu bar disappears and your command executes

In both cases, this animation reassures you that what you selected actually happened. Or, just as importantly, it alerts you to the possibility that something you *didn't* intend actually happened. Either way, animation is an extremely important cue: without it, EPOC's GUI would feel less easy to use.

As it happens, animation isn't the only potential clue that something happened Sound, such as key or digitizer clicks, can be useful too.

This animation is achieved very simply. In the case of the dialog button animation, for instance:

❑ Draw commands are issued to draw the button in a 'down' state

❑ The window server's client-side buffer is flushed, so that the draw commands are executed

❑ The application waits for 0.2 seconds

❑ The dialog is dismissed, and the relevant action takes place – in all probability, this will cause more drawing to occur

The key thing here is the flush-and-wait sequence. CONE provides a function to implement this, CCoeEnv::Flush(), which takes a time interval specified in microseconds. The following code therefore implements the flush and the wait:

```
iCoeEnv->Flush(200000);
```

The flush is vital. Without it, your draw commands might not get executed by the window server until the active scheduler is next called to wait for a new event – in other words, until the processing of the current key has finished. By that time, the dialog will have been dismissed, so that your draw commands will execute 'flicker-free' – just at the point when some flicker would have been useful!

Don't use this command to wait for longer than about 0.2 seconds: it will compromise the responsiveness of your application if you do so. The entire application thread, with all its active objects, is suspended during this 0.2-second wait. If you need animation to occur on a longer timescale, use an active object to handle the animation task. See Chapter 18 for a detailed description of active objects.

Even animation using active objects isn't good enough for some purposes, because active objects are scheduled non-preemptively and, particularly in application code, there is no guarantee about how long an active object event handler function may take to run. Some animations have to keep running, or else they look silly. Examples include the flashing text cursor, or the analog or digital clocks on the bottom of your application toolbar, or the EIKON busy message that appears when you program is running a particularly long event handler that (by definition) would prevent any other active object from running.

These animations run *as part of the window server* in a window server **animation DLL**. They are required to be good citizens of the window server, and to have *very* short-running active objects.

Conventional animations such as animated GIFs should be implemented by the active object technique unless there was compelling reason to use a window server animation DLL.

EIKON Debug Keys

As we saw in Chapter 6, debug builds of EIKON (in other words, on the emulator) allow you to use the following keys to control your program's drawing behavior:

Key	Effect
Ctrl+Alt+Shift+M	Creates a 'mover' window that you can move all around the screen, causing redraws underneath it
Ctrl+Alt+Shift+R	Causes the entire application view to redraw
Ctrl+Alt+Shift+F	Causes the window server client API to enable auto-flush, so that draw commands are sent to the window server as soon as they are issued, rather than waiting for the buffer to fill or a program-issued Flush() function.
	Try this and watch things slow down: it can be useful for naked-eye flicker testing.
	It's also handy for debugging redraws. You can step through drawing code and see every command produce an instant result on the emulator. You'll need a big monitor to see both the emulator and Visual Studio at the same time – but that's a hardware problem!
Ctrl+Alt+Shift+G	Disables auto-flush

Remember that these settings only apply to the current application's EIKON environment.

Control Context

The `ActivateGc()`, `DeactivateGc()`, and `ResetGc()` functions in a control normally pass directly through to window server functions: `gc.Activate(*iWin)`, `gc.Deactivate(*iWin)`, and `gc.Reset()`.

These functions, and the way that CONE calls them when recursing through component controls, guarantee that your GC is properly reset to default values before each control's `Draw()` function is called.

In some cases, you don't want your GC to reset to system default values: instead, you want to set the default values to something decided by the control. For this purpose, you can use a **control context**, an interface that overrides GC activate and reset behavior. See the SDK and examples for further details.

Scrolling

The window server supports scrolling: you can ask for a region of a window to be scrolled, up, down, left, or right. This results in:

❑ Some image data being lost

❑ The window server moving some image data in the requested direction

❑ An area of the window becoming invalid

The (new) invalid area is exactly the same size as the amount of (old) image data that was lost.

Scrolling is clearly always application-initiated. After a scroll, you should DrawXxxNow(): you don't need to invalidate the area that was invalidated by the scroll. You must ensure that the new drawing precisely abuts onto the old data, without any visible joins.

Summary

In this chapter I've concentrated on graphics for display – how to draw, and how to share the screen. More specifically, we've seen:

❑ How the work is shared between controls and windows.

❑ The use of compound controls to simplify layout.

❑ The difference between window-owning and lodger controls.

❑ The CGraphicsContext class and its API for drawing, getting position and bounding rectangles.

❑ The MVC pattern, which is the natural paradigm for most EPOC applications. MVC updates and redraws work well with standard RWindows. For non-MVC programs, or programs whose updates are particularly complex, backed-up windows may be more useful instead.

❑ Application- and system-initiated drawing

❑ Techniques for flicker-free drawing, and how CONE helps you achieve this.

❑ The activate-GC and begin-redraw brackets in DrawXxxNow()-type functions

❑ CCoeControl's functions for drawing.

❑ How to animate, cast a shadow, scroll, and back-up behind.

Graphics also provides the fundamental mechanism for user interaction, which is the subject of the next chapter.

12

Graphics for Interaction

In the last chapter, we saw the way that EPOC uses the MVC pattern, and how to draw in the context of controls and windows. In this chapter, I'll cover how to use controls for interaction with your programs.

In theory, it's easy. Just as controls provide a virtual `Draw()` function for drawing, they also provide two virtual functions for handling interaction: `HandlePointerEventL()` for handling pointer events, and `OfferKeyEventL()` for handling key events. You simply work out the coordinates of the pointer event, or the key code for the key event, and decide what to do.

Basic interaction handling does indeed involve knowing how to use these two functions, and I'll start the chapter by describing them. I'll also show that interaction is well suited to MVC: you turn key and pointer events into commands to update the model, and then let the model handle redrawing. However, this description of key and pointer event handling is really just the tip of the interaction iceberg. There are plenty of other issues to deal with:

❑ Key events are normally associated with a cursor location or the more general concept of **focus** – but not all key events go to the current focus location, and some key events cause focus to be changed

❑ A 'pointer down' event away from current focus usually causes focus to be changed. Sometimes, though, it's not good to change focus – perhaps because the currently focused control is not in a **valid** state, or because the control where the event occurred doesn't accept focus.

❑ Focus should be indicated by some visual effect (usually a highlight, or a cursor). Likewise, temporary inability to take focus should be indicated by a visual effect (usually some kind of dimming, or even making a control invisible altogether).

❑ The rules governing focus and focus transition should be easy to explain to users – better still, they shouldn't need to be explained at all. They should also be easy to explain to programmers.

The big issues in interaction are intimately related: namely drawing, pointer handling, key handling, model updates, component controls, focus, validity, temporary unavailability, ease of use, and ease of programming. You'll recall from Chapter 1 that we rewrote EIKON and CONE twice during EPOC's early development to get these things right – the first time for the users, the second time for the programmers.

Explaining these things is only slightly easier than designing them. Here goes, as smoothly as I can.

Key, Pointer, and Command Basics

As mentioned above, the basic functions that deal with interaction are `HandlePointerEventL()` and `OfferKeyEventL()`. To describe how they work, I'll start with the latter's implementation in `CFleetView`, the interactive heart of the Battleships app view.

Handling Key Events

Here's how `CFleetView` handles key events generated by an E32 device driver:

```
TKeyResponse CFleetView::OfferKeyEventL(const TKeyEvent& aKeyEvent,
                                        TEventCode aType)
    {
    if(aType != EEventKey)
        return EKeyWasNotConsumed;
    if(aKeyEvent.iCode == EKeyLeftArrow || aKeyEvent.iCode == EKeyRightArrow ||
       aKeyEvent.iCode == EKeyUpArrow   || aKeyEvent.iCode == EKeyDownArrow)
        {
        //Move cursor
        if(aKeyEvent.iCode == EKeyLeftArrow)
            MoveCursor(-1, 0);
        else if(aKeyEvent.iCode == EKeyRightArrow)
            MoveCursor(1, 0);
        else if(aKeyEvent.iCode == EKeyUpArrow)
            MoveCursor(0, -1);
        else if(aKeyEvent.iCode == EKeyDownArrow)
            MoveCursor(0, 1);

        // Redraw board
        DrawTilesNow();
        return EKeyWasConsumed;
        }
    else if(aKeyEvent.iCode == EKeySpace)
        {
        iCmdHandler->ViewCmdHitFleet(iCursorX, iCursorY);
        return EKeyWasConsumed;
        }
    return EKeyWasNotConsumed;
    }
```

`OfferKeyEventL()` is called on a control if the framework thinks that it ought to be offered (by the end of this chapter, you'll know what that means). If necessary, a control can indicate that it doesn't take keys: I do this elsewhere in the Battleships GUI, using methods that I'll explain later in this chapter.

We should note these points about the function:

- ❏ I don't have to check whether I should have been offered the key: I can rely on the framework offering it to me only if I am supposed to have it

- ❏ I don't have to 'consume' the key. I return a value (EKeyWasConsumed or EKeyWasNotConsumed) to indicate whether I consumed it

The function starts by determining the kind of key event. There are three possibilities: hardware key down, standard key, or hardware key up. I'm only interested in standard key events, indicated by the value EEventKey being passed in the second parameter of the function. I can handle the key in one of three ways:

- ❏ I can ignore it if it's not a key that I recognize or want to use at this time

- ❏ I can handle it entirely internally, within the control, by (say) moving the cursor or (if it were a numeric editor) changing the internal value and visual representation of the number being edited by the control

- ❏ I can generate some kind of command that will be handled outside the control, like the hit-fleet command that's generated when I press the space bar, or (if this were a choice list item in a dialog) an event saying that the value displayed in the choice list had been changed

For issuing commands from CFleetView, I call iCmdHandler->ViewCmdHitFleet(), specifying the coordinates of the tile to hit. iCmdHandler is of type MGameViewCmdHandler*, an interface class that I implement in CGameController. I'll show the definition of the interface below.

Those are the main issues in key event handling. But you also need to know some of the details about how to crack key events and key codes. The first parameter to OfferKeyEventL() is of type TKeyEvent&, a reference to a window server key event that's defined in w32std.h:

```
struct TKeyEvent
    {
    TUint iCode;
    TInt iScanCode;
    TUint iModifiers;    // State of modifier keys and pointing device
    TInt iRepeats;       // Count of auto repeats generated
    };
```

The legal values for iCode, iScanCode, and iModifiers are in e32keys.h.

- ❏ Use values from the TKeyCode enumeration to interpret iCode. The values are <0x20 for non-printing ASCII keys, 0x20-0xff for printing ASCII values, and >=0x1000 for the usual function, arrow, menu, etc. keys found on PC and EPOC keyboards.

- ❏ Use TStdScanCode and iScanCode for the extremely rare cases when scan codes are of interest. The scan codes are defined by the historical evolution of IBM PC keyboards since 1981: they originally represented the physical position of a key on the 81-key IBM PC keyboard, and have evolved since then to support new keyboards and preserve compatibility with older ones. Since EPOC keyboards are rather different, scan codes have limited value.

- ❏ Use TEventModifier to interpret the bits in iModifiers. This enables you to test explicitly for *Shift*, *Ctrl*, and other modifier keys. These are of particular interest in combination with navigation keys.

TEventCode is the type of window server event that is being handled; it can be one of EEventKey, EEventKeyDown, or EEventKeyUp. For ordinary event handling, most controls are interested in EEventKey.

If key-down *is* relevant to your application, then the auto-repeat count in the TKeyEvent might also be of interest. It tells you how many auto-repeats you have missed since you handled the last key event.

Handling Pointer Events

Here's how CFleetView handles pointer events:

```
void CFleetView::HandlePointerEventL(
        const TPointerEvent& aPointerEvent)
    {
    // Check whether we're interested
    if(aPointerEvent.iType == TPointerEvent::EButton1Down &&
        iSeaArea.Contains(aPointerEvent.iPosition))
        {
        // Identify the tile that was hit
        TInt x = (aPointerEvent.iPosition.iX - iSeaArea.iTl.iX) / iSeaRectSize;
        TInt y = (aPointerEvent.iPosition.iY - iSeaArea.iTl.iY) / iSeaRectSize;

        // Implement select and open semantics
        if(x == iCursorX && y == iCursorY) // Already there: hit it
            iCmdHandler->ViewCmdHitFleet(x, y);
        else                               // Not there: move there
            {
            SetCursor(x, y);
            DrawTilesNow();
            }
        }
    }
```

Like OfferKeyEventL(), HandlePointerEventL() is called on a control if the framework thinks the pointer event ought to be handled. Generally, that means the control is not dimmed or invisible, and it's the smallest area that surrounds the coordinates of the pointer event. Unlike OfferKeyEventL(), HandlePointerEventL() requires the control to handle the pointer event or ignore it: the event is not offered to be consumed optionally. That distinction is reflected in both the name (HandlePointerEventL()) and the return type (void).

As with keys, I can choose to handle the pointer event in one of three ways:

❑ I can ignore it: I do this if it's not a pointer-down event, or if the event occurs outside the sea area on the game board

❑ I can handle it internally, in this case by moving the cursor: I do this here if the pointer event happens in a tile that isn't already selected

❑ I can generate a command to be handled outside the control: I generate a hit-fleet command if the pointer event occurs in a tile that is already selected

I'm using the pointer events to generate exactly the same command as I was with the key events – a hit request. So, I handle these commands using the same MViewCmdHandler interface.

The TPointerEvent object passed to HandlePointerEventL() is defined in w32std.h as:

```
struct TPointerEvent
    {
    enum TType
        {
        EButton1Down,
        EButton1Up,
        EButton2Down,
        EButton2Up,
        EButton3Down,
        EButton3Up,
        EDrag,
        EMove,
        EButtonRepeat,
        ESwitchOn,
        };
    TType iType;              // Type of pointer event
    TUint iModifiers;         // State of pointing device and associated buttons
    TPoint iPosition;         // Window co-ordinates of mouse event
    TPoint iParentPosition;   // Position relative to parent window
    };
```

You can check for:

❑   Button 1 down (pen down)

❑   Button 1 up (pen up)

❑   Other buttons: you don't get these on pen-based devices

❑   Drag is rarely used in EPOC, but can be useful

❑   Move: you will *never* get this on pen-based devices. Devices supporting move also have to support a mouse cursor (which the window server does), control entry/exit notification, and changing the cursor to indicate what will happen if you press button 1. That's all hard work, and adds little value to EPOC devices.

❑   Button repeat: this is generated when a button is held down continuously in one place – it's just like keyboard repeat. It's most useful for controls such as scrollbar buttons or emulated on-screen keyboards.

❑   Switch-on: a useful event, though something of an artifice in the pointer event class

❑   Modifiers: state of all pointer buttons; also *Shift*, *Ctrl*, and *Alt* keys – using the same values as for key event modifiers

Turning Events into Commands

Whether I interact with the control using the keyboard or the pointer, I ultimately generate commands that should be handled by a different part of the program. For getting commands from one to the other, I use an interface class. Here it is:

```
class MGameViewCmdHandler
    {
public:
    virtual void ViewCmdHitFleet(TInt aX, TInt aY) = 0;
    };
```

```
class CFleetView : public CCoeControl
    {
public:
    // Construct/destruct/setup
    ~CFleetView();
    void ConstructL(const TRect& aRect, CCoeControl* aParent);
    void SetCmdHandler(MGameViewCmdHandler* aCmdHandler);
    void SetFleet(TFleet* aFleet);
    ...

    // Key handling - from CCoeControl
    TKeyResponse OfferKeyEventL(const TKeyEvent& aKeyEvent, TEventCode aType);
private:
    // From CCoeControl
    void Draw(const TRect&) const;
    void HandlePointerEventL(const TPointerEvent& aPointerEvent);
    ...
private:
    TFleet* iFleet;
    MGameViewCmdHandler* iCmdHandler;
    ...
    };
```

And here it is in UML:

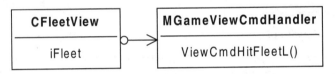

The interface class is a useful way of encapsulating the interaction that's happening between the control and the rest of the program. In the MVC sense, the rest of the program is the controller: the control doesn't care about its internal details provided that it handles the hit-fleet command correctly. Likewise, the controller doesn't care whether the command originated with a key event, a pointer event, or some other kind of event – it just wants to get called at the right time with the right parameters.

This pattern is repeated throughout the EPOC GUI, and it's a good one to adopt for your programs. As a further illustration, think about the way commands reach HandleCommandL(). The menu bar (which includes the shortcut key handler) uses an MEikMenuObserver for this, and doesn't otherwise care about the large API of the CEikAppUi class. The toolbar *also* uses the MEikMenuObserver interface. Similarly, command buttons use an MCoeControlObserver interface, which the toolbar implements by converting button events into application commands.

Interaction in Dialogs

From the preceding discussion, it should be apparent that it's not handling individual pointer and key events that makes programming an interactive graphics framework complex. Rather, it's handling the relationships between them, and the visual feedback you give in response, that can cause difficulty.

The dialog below, from EPOC Agenda, shows many of the issues involved. By studying it, we'll get some way to understanding how all of the separate aspects of interaction relate to one another. That will help you not only to make better use of the dialog framework, but also to write good app views, and to understand many aspects of the CCoeControl API.

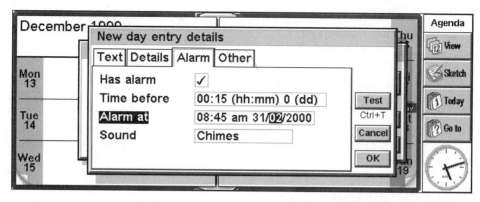

The first line is a checkbox that allows you to select whether there is an alarm at all. The remaining three lines are only visible if you want an alarm: they are a duration editor, a time-and-date editor, and a sound selector.

In the screenshot, the user is halfway through editing the date, which currently contains an impossible value: 31/02/2000 (31st February 2000, in UK locale).

User Requirements

Here are some user requirements, which I'll express in non-technical terms. (This is what you're supposed to do with user requirements: it helps you to see things clearly, and besides, users never give their requirements in technical terms.)

Firstly, the user needs to be able to understand what's going on. They can, because:

❑   The dialog where the action is taking place is in front of everything else

❑   The line where the action is taking place is highlighted

❑   The field where the action is taking place is highlighted

Secondly, the user should not be able to enter invalid data through the dialog. That means:

❑   If the user presses OK now, the dialog should complain that the date is invalid, and should not cause the usual action associated with OK (in this case, saving the Agenda item's settings) to happen. Instead, the dialog should stay active, with the highlight on the Alarm at field, so that the user can correct the date.

❑   If the user presses the up or down arrow to go to a different line in the dialog, the dialog should prevent it, because that would leave the date invalid. If the dialog allowed the current control to become invalid, there could be many invalid controls by the time the user pressed OK, and it would be difficult to know where to start asking the user for corrections.

❑   If the user tries to use the pointer to select a different dialog line, the dialog should prevent it for the same reasons.

❑   If the user presses the right or left arrow to edit another field in the date, then the dialog should allow it. Although the date is currently invalid, that's only a temporary situation: the user might be about to change the date to 31/03/2000, or 28/02/2000, which would be fine.

❑   If the user presses Cancel, the dialog should disappear without any validation.

❑ If the user corrects the date and *then* presses up or down, the highlight should move to the line above or below.

❑ If the user corrects the date and then selects any other line (or any other tab) on the dialog, then the highlight should move to that line (or tab).

❑ If the user changes the Alarm at value, then the Time before value should be changed in sync when the user moves away from the line on the dialog or presses OK. Similarly, if the user changes the Time before value, then the Alarm at value should change in sync.

❑ If the user un-checks the Has alarm box, then the remaining fields on this page should be dimmed or even disappear altogether, so that they can't be selected with either the pointer or the arrow keys.

Some Basic Abstractions

Based on this list of user requirements, you can see some abstractions beginning to take shape:

❑ The highlight is actually a visual indication of **focus**. The control that currently has focus receives the majority of key events; it therefore ought to know whether it has focus or not, and draw any necessary highlight accordingly. (Not all key events go to the control with focus: *Enter* usually causes OK to be pressed, rather than going to the highlighted control, and, if there's no active dialog, *Menu* activates the menu bar, even though it's invisible.)

❑ A control needs to be able to *refuse* interactions such as pointer events, or the ability to be selected with the up-and-down arrow keys. **Invisible** or **dimmed** controls should certainly refuse interactions. A control should know whether it is dimmed, and thereby draw itself in a suitable way.

❑ A control needs to be able to say whether it is in a **valid** state, and to respond to queries so that focus can be taken away from it.

❑ If a control's **state** changes, it needs to be able to report that to an **observer** such as the dialog, so that the dialog can handle any knock-on effects. (For example, if the checkbox changes to indicate no alarm, the dialog must make it impossible to select the other controls.)

The Test button highlights an interesting case of the need for a valid state: its purpose is to play the currently selected alarm sound. Does the date need to be valid for this? Strictly, it doesn't, but for consistency EIKON insists that it is. EIKON has no way to know that Test is related to alarm sounds: it might have been something to do with the date.

These are the user requirements. Throughout the rest of this chapter, I'll be describing how the GUI framework makes it possible for you meet them.

Programmer Requirements

If ease of use matters to end users, it certainly matters to programmers, who will have some requirements on the way all the ideas raised above should hang together:

❑ It should be possible to invent new dialogs with rich functionality, and to implement the validation rules, with sufficient ease that programmers will want to use these facilities to deliver helpful and usable dialogs.

❑ It should be possible to use *any* control in such dialogs – not only the stock controls provided by EIKON, but also any new control that you invent and wish to include in a dialog. (That's mot *all* controls, by the way: I don't see any need to include my fleet view in a dialog.)

❑ Given the number of different ideas here, it should be possible to write code that supports only the things you require for a particular control, without having to worry about implementing things that are unnecessary. Furthermore, you need to be confident that you've decided to include only those things that need including, and to exclude only those things that need excluding.

Compound Controls

I began to introduce the idea of compound controls in relation to drawing. It turns out that compounding also makes it very much easier to implement general-purpose containers such as dialogs. Returning once again to our alarm settings dialog, the visible controls on it are:

❑ A dialog, containing a title, a button group, a page selector, and a captioned control array

❑ A button group, containing three buttons and a label

❑ A captioned control array, containing four captioned controls

❑ Four captioned controls, each containing a label and a control

That's 21 controls altogether, all lodging in a single window.

For another example, see the Start new game dialog in Chapter 10, which had five captioned controls and two buttons, for a total of 20 controls.

It should be obvious that the dialog isn't the only container here. The captioned control array, and the captioned controls themselves, are also important containers with their own responsibilities, as we'll see. What we think of as 'the controls' in the dialog (the four lines we were talking about above) are more complicated than they appear, and account for only about a quarter of the controls actually on this dialog page.

Key Distribution and Focus

Here's a simplified account of how a dialog processes OfferKeyEventL() (for the full truth, check out CEikDialog::OfferKeyEventL() in the SDK). At any one time, precisely one of the controls in the captioned control array has focus. That means the line is highlighted, and is the scene of 'most' keyboard action. When the dialog is offered a key event, it handles some special cases itself, but otherwise it offers the key to the current control:

❑ *Enter*, *Escape* and any *Ctrl+* key are offered to the dialog buttons.

❑ Up and down arrows are initially offered to the general-purpose control in the currently focused captioned control: if this control doesn't consume them, the dialog processes them instead: it moves the focus up or down.

❑ Other keys are offered to the general-purpose control in the currently focused captioned control.

*A **general-purpose control** is one that can be used both in dialogs and app views. Incidentally to make a control intended for dialogs usable in app views isn't always difficult, and it's a good thing to aim for. But to make a control intended for app views usable in a dialog is rarely necessary, and you shouldn't try to do so without good reason.*

There are plenty of special cases (such as support for the page selector), but this description is enough to illustrate the role of focus, and also to begin to show why keys are offered, and why they are not always consumed.

It's important to give a clear visual indication of focus and all the components work together to achieve this:

❑ The dialog is the topmost window: it has focus merely by being there.

❑ The buttons and the title bar can never receive focus, so they don't need to change their drawing code in response to whether they're focused or not.

❑ When a captioned control is given focus, it sets both its label and its general-purpose control to be focused as well.

❑ The label draws itself in an inverse color scheme to indicate that it has focus (although, of course, it can never handle keys).

❑ The general-purpose control may or may not do something special to indicate that it has focus: if it does not, the user can tell from the caption which dialog line has focus. Many editors include some kind of cursor, or even the window server's flashing text cursor, to indicate they have focus.

To honor focus properly, then, a control designed to live in a dialog has to do nothing special *unless* it has its own cursor. Controls with a cursor should show it when focused, and not otherwise.

Dimming and Visibility

There are two ways to indicate that a control in a dialog cannot receive focus:

❑ Make it **invisible**. You can make the entire line – caption and control – invisible. CONE has full support for this action: invisible controls are omitted from redraw and pointer handling, and dialogs will not allow invisible lines to be given focus.

❑ **Dim** it. If you dim a control, it will be omitted from pointer handling. Dialogs will not allow a dimmed line to gain focus. However, CONE will not omit a dimmed control from redrawing; rather, the implementer of the control has to code Draw() to dim the control explicitly.

The good thing, supposedly, about dimming is that the user can still see the control and the value it contains – even though they can't change it. But actually, dimming is a nuisance: the writer of the control has to add support in Draw(), and it's not always obvious what to do. On an LCD screen with only four levels of gray, even non-dimmed controls have to be designed carefully for good visibility; designing dimmed-and-yet-still-visible controls is yet another design challenge. In any case, unavailable options might be entirely meaningless, in which case you don't want to dim the control, you want to hide it altogether.

EIKON dialogs use a cute compromise: when you call MakeLineVisible(EFalse), the dialog dims the captioned control (including its label), and makes the general-purpose control invisible. The user gets the right effect, the general-purpose control doesn't have to support dimming explicitly, and there's no attempt to display meaningless values.

The relevant functions for dimming are found in `CCoeControl`:

```
class CCoeControl : public CBase
    {
public:
    ...
    IMPORT_C virtual void SetDimmed(TBool aDimmed);
    ...
    IMPORT_C TBool IsDimmed() const;
    ...
    };
```

If you need to, honor `IsDimmed()` in your `Draw()` function.

Validation

While a control has focus and the user is editing it, it may (for good reasons) become temporarily invalid – the 31/02/2000 date in the above example is a good demonstration of this possibility. However, when focus is taken from a control – for a change in dialog line, or because OK was pressed – it's important that the control should be valid.

EIKON calls `PrepareForFocusLossL()` on any control from which it is about to remove focus. The default `CCoeControl` implementation of this function is empty: there is no need to override it for a control whose internal state can never be invalid (for example, a choice list, a button, a checkbox, or a text editor). If your control *could* be invalid, however, you should implement this function to check the current validity of the control. If it *is* invalid, you should:

❑   Issue some kind of message (such as an EIKON info-message) to inform the user that the control is invalid

❑   Leave, usually with error code `KErrNone`. This informs the dialog that the control is invalid, and prevents the dialog from changing the current line, continuing with OK button processing, etc.

As we saw in the `streams` example in Chapter 10, you can issue a single call to `iEikonEnv->LeaveWithInfoMsg()` to display an info-message and leave without displaying EIKON's standard error dialog.

Control Observers

Compounding produces a hierarchy of controls that's strictly related to coordinates. Components are contained within their container's extent, and peer controls don't overlap. As we've seen, that greatly simplifies drawing, and you can probably guess that it makes pointer event processing easier too.

Compounding defines a set of strictly hierarchical relationships, and draw and pointer event processing operate from top to bottom, that is from the dialog down to the controls.

Controls also report events, such as whether their state changed. Event reporting usually goes *up* the hierarchy – for instance, from a control contained in a dialog, to the dialog, so that you can handle the event with the dialog's `HandleStateChangeL()` function.

For this reason, many systems handle a chain of events by passing them up their window ownership hierarchy.

However, making the event reporting hierarchy the exact opposite of the compounding hierarchy turns out to be very awkward. We tried it with EPOC, and it ran into too much trouble: it was the fundamental reason for the second rewrite of EIKON in mid-1996, which I described in Chapter 1.

> **A key design decision in EPOC was to avoid fixing any association between the observer of an event, and the container control. The observer does not have to be the container control, or a control in the containment hierarchy; it doesn't even have to be a control at all.**

Object orientation highlighted the issue more strongly, and also provided a better way forward.

In EPOC, each control contains a member called iObserver that it can use to report various general-purpose events required by all controls that live in dialogs:

```
class CCoeControl : public CBase
    {
public:
    ...
    IMPORT_C void SetObserver(MCoeControlObserver* aObserver);
    inline MCoeControlObserver* Observer() const;
    ...
protected:
    ...
    IMPORT_C void ReportEventL(MCoeControlObserver::TCoeEvent aEvent);
    ...
private:
    ...
    MCoeControlObserver* iObserver;
    ...
    };
```

MCoeControlObserver is an interface that can be implemented by any class that wishes to observe controls. It is defined in coecobs.h, and has just one member function:

```
class MCoeControlObserver
    {
public:
    ...
    virtual void HandleControlEventL(CCoeControl* aControl,
                                     TCoeEvent aEventType) = 0;
    };
```

If you're writing a control, you can call ReportEventL() to report events to your observer (if you have one), which will give the observer an opportunity to do something about them.

The available event types are defined in MCoeControlObserver::TCoeEvent. They are:

```
enum TCoeEvent
    {
    EEventRequestExit,
    EEventRequestCancel,
    EEventRequestFocus,
    EEventPrepareFocusTransition,
    EEventStateChanged,
    EEventInteractionRefused
    };
```

We also saw this earlier in the chapter, with the `MGameViewCmdHandler` interface and `CFleetView` class.

State Changed

If you're implementing a general-purpose control, the only useful event here is `EEventStateChanged`. If you report this event from within a dialog, the dialog will call `HandleControlStateChangeL()`, which the dialog implementer can use to change the values or visibility of other controls on the dialog. That's the function the alarm settings dialog uses to make the settings visible or invisible in response to the checkbox changing. It's also the function I used in the Battleships initiate dialog, described in Chapter 10, to hide the other player's address when it wasn't needed.

For some controls, state-change reporting is optional. EIKON edit windows, for example, only report state changes if they're asked to – otherwise, every key press (except for navigation keys) would cause a state change.

You should certainly not report a state change until you have reached a valid state – it would be inappropriate to report a state change while the date is set to 31/02/2000. In fact, MFNEs (multi-field numeric editors, of which the time-and-date editor is an example) do not report state changes at all. That's because the states a number goes through when you're editing it are essentially random.

Container Behavior

If you're implementing a container such as a dialog, you should make yourself the observer of your contained controls, and handle the following three events, which are generated by CONE in specific circumstances:

Event Type	Description
EEventInteractionRefused	Pointer down on a dimmed control. EIKON dialogs handle this with the virtual function `HandleInteractionRefused()`, whose default implementation issues an info-message saying the control is not available. You can override this in a derived dialog to give a better-tailored message. ("You can't select this because you haven't installed x, y, z.")
EEventPrepareFocusTransition	Pointer down on a focusable control that is not focused. EIKON dialogs call `PrepareForFocusLossL()` on the currently focused control, so that that control can validate – and leave, if invalid. If the currently focused control leaves, processing of the pointer event will abort, so that focus is not transferred.

Table Continued on Following Page

Event Type	Description
EEventRequestFocus	A pointer event has been handled on a non-focused control, which now needs focus. Permission to change focus has been granted by the handler for the prepare-focus transition event above, so the container must now execute the focus change.
	EIKON dialogs handle this message by un-focusing the currently focused control, and focusing the control associated with the pointer event.

If you implement a general-purpose container, you should handle these three messages with semantics similar to those used by EIKON dialogs. The messages are all generated by CCoeControl::ProcessPointerEventL(), and you should not generate them yourself.

> *If the container is the observer, why not just say 'the container' and have an ownership hierarchy as in some other systems? Firstly, because controls can be used in containers which don't need to observe them. Secondly, because the dialog isn't actually the immediate container of, say, a choice list control – the dialog contains captioned controls, and in turn a captioned control contains the choice list. But the dialog is a direct observer of the choice list.*

Other Events

The MCoeControlObserver interface is designed for the general-purpose requirements of contained controls (reacting to changes in state) and containers (responding to interaction refused, prepare focus transition, and request focus events).

Special-purpose events should be handled by special-purpose interfaces, such as MGameViewCmdHandler from CFleetView, or MEikMenuObserver from EIKON menus and toolbars.

The 1D Paradigm

We've already seen that a fundamental EIKON design decision is to support only one-dimensional dialogs – that is, captioned controls on a dialog page are in a vertical column. Up and down arrow keys (rather than *Tab*) are used to navigate between dialog lines.

This has knock-on effects on the design of controls intended for dialogs: basically you should design them not to use up and down arrows. You will be offered all the arrow key events, but you should only consume them when necessary. Let's look at some specific cases to see how this works out.

In a single-line text editor, you don't need up and down arrows anyway: there's nowhere to go – though, clearly, horizontal arrows are useful.

In a multi-line text editor, you can use up and down arrows to navigate between lines of text. But when you're on the top line, up arrow takes you to the line above in the dialog. And when you're on the bottom line, down arrow takes you to the line below. So: only consume the arrow keys if you actually use them to change lines within the editor; don't consume them if you're already at the top (for up arrow) or bottom (for down arrow). By doing things this way, the *dialog* will be able to consume the events instead, to change the focused line.

EIKON choice lists use the right and left arrows to cycle through values, not up and down. Sometimes, though, up and down are more convenient, so you can press *Tab* to pop out a vertical (potentially scrolling) list of the items. The pop-out is modal: it captures the pointer and consumes all keys offered to it. You have to press *Enter* to select the item in the choice list, pop the list back in again – then you can use the rest of the dialog.

For instance, if you press *Tab* when focus is on a date control, you get a pop-up calendar for a whole month, which you can navigate without worrying about the dialog as a container. Only when you press *Enter* to select a date does the calendar pop back in again. Note, however, that both list boxes and date editors provide a way to work *without* tabbing out a pop-up. This is important: it saves keystrokes when the user knows what they want to do, and it avoids modality in the dialog.

MFNEs highlight a problem with this solution. If left and right arrows are used for navigating between fields, and up and down are used for navigating around the dialog, what about auto-nudging, so that you can (say) change 1999 into 2000 with one keystroke, not four? EIKON's answer is a compromise: the *M* key is used to nudge down by one, and . (period) to nudge up by one.

> *Yes, really! On a Psion Series 5 keyboard,* M *is just over the < sign, and . is near the > sign. Furthermore, you can use* Shift+ *to nudge by 10, so that* Shift+M *reduces the value by 10, and* Shift+. *increases it by 10. It sounds odd, and it even feels odd on the PC-based emulator, but it works well on a real machine.*
>
> *Incidentally, EIKON doesn't support pointer-based nudging at all, because it isn't really suitable for pen-based (or finger-based) operation. You would need such large nudgers that they would compromise other aspects of the UI.*

The upshot of this section is that we have four arrow-related design patterns for dialog-friendly controls:

❏ If they don't need to use the up or down arrow, then so much the better.

❏ If the up and down movement has limits within the control, then consume the arrow keys normally when in the control. If the user presses up when they are already at the top line within the control, or down when at the bottom line, don't consume the key: let the dialog have it instead, for navigating between lines.

❏ Use *Tab* to display a modal pop-up, during which you have complete freedom of movement (but do this sparingly, and allow a non-*Tab* alternative).

❏ If none of these approaches seems to work, think of another. The MFNE solution may not be terribly elegant, but it works, and it shows what sacrifices we're prepared to make in order to maximize usability of the system as a whole.

Containers

EIKON dialogs are just one example of a container: not every control you write needs to go into a dialog. Many controls will be designed for use in your app view instead, or perhaps for some other kind of container. Your container may be general purpose (like a dialog, which can contain an arbitrary number of controls of any type) or special purpose (like the Battleships app view, which contains just three controls: two fleet views and a status view).

If your container is general-purpose, you should use design patterns similar to those used by EIKON dialogs for handling validation, focus, changes of state, dimming, etc.. However, you don't need to use *every* pattern from EIKON dialogs – there's no reason, for instance, why an app view (or some general-purpose container) shouldn't use another scheme for navigating between controls. EIKON's standard dialogs and controls use up and down arrows, but yours need not do so provided that you can avoid surprising your users with an unnecessarily un-EIKON-like look and feel, and if interoperability with standard EIKON controls isn't an issue.

Key Processing Revisited

Now we've seen:

❑ What a simple control does with a key event in its `OfferKeyEventL()` member function.

❑ The idea of focus, which is where most key events go, and which is indicated visually by some kind of highlight.

❑ How, in a dialog, keys are handled either by the dialog itself, or by the currently focused control.

❑ How a control in a dialog may or may not consume a key offered to it. For instance, most controls don't consume up and down arrows: this allows the dialog to consume them instead, for navigation between controls.

This puts us in a better position to understand the full picture of key distribution, as handled by the window server and CONE together.

When a key is pressed, it is initially passed from E32's keyboard driver to the window server. If the key is a window server hotkey, then it causes an action associated with the hotkey, and it is not specifically routed to any application. Window server hotkeys include *Ctrl+Alt+Shift+K*, which kills the process associated with the foreground window.

However, the window server routes most key events to the application in the foreground, where they are detected by `CCoeEnv::RunL()` and passed on to `CCoeAppUi::HandleWsEventL()`, which identifies the event as a key event, and then `CCoeControlStack::OfferKeyL()`. CONE's **control stack** is responsible for offering keys to controls that can then handle them further.

In the EIKON environment, there are typically four types of control on the control stack:

❑ The EIKON debug keys control: this is an invisible control that consumes all *Ctrl+Alt+Shift+* keys and associates a particular action with most of them. For instance, *Ctrl+Alt+Shift+R* causes the current screen to be completely redrawn. If the debug keys control doesn't consume the key, it gets offered further down the stack.

❑ Any dialogs that might be active: the key is offered to the topmost active dialog, which will consume the key. Only if no dialog is active will the key be offered further down the stack.

❑ The menu bar: if the menu is invisible, it will only handle (and consume) the *Menu* key and any shortcut keys defined by the application. If the menu is visible, it will consume all keys offered to it. The fact that the menu bar is lower down in the control stack than *any* dialog prevents the menu from being invoked when a dialog is active.

❑ Any app views: an application view should usually ignore keys (and therefore not consume them) if it is invisible; otherwise it should handle and consume them.

For an application with three views (one of which is active), and two active nested dialogs, the control stack looks like this:

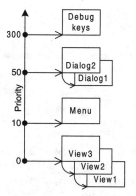

Key events are offered down the control stack firstly in order of priority (highest to lowest), and secondly in stack order (most recently added to least recently added, within each priority). The priorities shown above are defined in an enumeration in coeaui.h.

Using this stack structure, Symbian or an application programmer can insert something new into the GUI environment without having to re-write CONE or the existing GUI components.

Exactly how a control on the stack handles a key event depends on the control:

❑ Dialogs are general containers, and we've already seen how they offer keys around their component controls.

❑ App views are often also containers, and they will use their own logic, including at least some of the patterns used by dialogs, to offer keys to component controls.

❑ The EIKON debug keys control is a single control without any components: it either consumes a key, or it doesn't.

❑ The menu bar, when visible, includes at least two controls – the menu bar and a menu pane – and possibly more, since there may also be cascaded menus. The menu bar offers and handles keys among these controls to implement conventional menu navigation and item selection.

We can see again how focus and key handling are usually – but not always – related:

❑ The window server sends most keys to the application with focus – but not its own hotkeys.

❑ The control stack mechanism *usually* results in keys being handled by a control with focus: the topmost dialog, the menu if visible, or the application view. But keys are always offered to the debug keys control, which is always invisible, and if no dialog is showing, keys are always offered to the menu bar, even if it is invisible. In other words, these keys can be handled even though they're not associated with focus.

❑ Dialogs normally channel keys to the focused line, but navigation and button-related keys are handled differently.

❑ The menu bar maintains a focused pane and a focused item, and normally offers keys to them – but shortcut keys are handled independently of focus.

The Battleships app view can only ever send keys to the opponent's fleet view. It does this provided the fleet view can accept input events:

```
TKeyResponse CGameAppView::OfferKeyEventL(const TKeyEvent& aKeyEvent,
                                          TEventCode aType)
    {
    // Let the opponent-fleet view handle the key
    if(iOppFleetView->IsDimmed())
        return EKeyWasNotConsumed;
    else
        return iOppFleetView->OfferKeyEventL(aKeyEvent, aType);
    }
```

It might be a surprise that I test for whether the control is dimmed here, not whether it's focused. If the app view contained more than one interactive control, I would have to use focus, but as it is, focus is not the issue: it's whether the control can handle interaction right now, and that's indicated by the dimmed property. CONE recognizes dimmed, and doesn't pass pointer events to a dimmed control.

Clearly, a dimmed control can't have focus, but in situations where there is more than one non-dimmed control, focus must be used to distinguish between them.

Focus

Focus is supported throughout EPOC's graphics components. First, the window server associates focus with a **window group**. The window server routes keys to the application whose window group currently has focus. A window group owns all an applications windows, including app views, menus, dialogs, and any others. The window server sends focus-gained and focus-lost events to applications as their window groups gain and lose focus.

In response to window server focus-changed events, most EPOC applications do nothing. There is no point in redrawing their controls to indicate that they have lost focus, since unfocused apps can't be seen on the screen anyway.

CONE maintains the top focusable control on the control stack, and calls FocusChanged() on it to indicate when focus has changed. Similarly, container controls should also call a contained control's FocusChanged() function when they change the focus given to it.

A control should change its appearance depending on whether it has focus. If you need to indicate focus visually, use IsFocused() in your drawing code, to draw an appropriate highlight or cursor. Handle FocusChanged() to change between focus states (for example, to redraw, active, or deactivate the cursor). FocusChanged() includes a parameter TBool aRedrawNow to indicate whether an immediate redraw is needed.

You can control and interrogate focus with SetFocus(). This does *not* iterate through component controls: each container handles propagation of SetFocus() according to its own requirements.

You can use SetNonFocusing() and related functions to set whether a control allows itself to be focused. This can be a permanent state for some controls (they simply don't handle input), or a temporary state for others (this is analogous to dimming: see below).

To summarize, here are CCoeControl's focus-related functions:

```
class CCoeControl : public CBase
    {
public:
    ...
    IMPORT_C virtual void PrepareForFocusLossL();
    ...
    IMPORT_C void SetFocus(TBool aFocus, TDrawNow aDrawNow = ENoDrawNow);
    ...
    IMPORT_C TBool IsFocused() const;
    ...
    IMPORT_C void SetNonFocusing();
    IMPORT_C void SetFocusing(TBool aFocusing);
    IMPORT_C TBool IsNonFocusing() const;
    ...
protected:
    ...
    IMPORT_C virtual void FocusChanged(TDrawNow aDrawNow);
    ...
    };
```

The Text Cursor

Focus may be associated with a cursor. The window server provides a text cursor, and there may only be a single cursor on the screen at any one time. By convention, the text cursor must be in the focused control in the focused window. If your control uses the text cursor, you should be sure to implement FocusChanged() so that you can turn the cursor off when you lose focus, and on again when you regain it.

A control that uses the text cursor doesn't have to use it all the time. EIKON MFNEs, for instance, use a block cursor when the whole number is selected, and only use the flashing line cursor when needed.

Pointer Processing Revisited

The window server ensures that a pointer event gets to the right window, and the CONE framework ensures that it gets to the right control. The event can then be handled by HandlePointerEventL().

Interaction Paradigms

A control should interpret the entire pointer sequence. Two sequences in particular are very common.

Press-and-release is appropriate for many types of button:

❑ Pen down inside the button: provide visual feedback by making it obvious that the button is pressed down

❑ Pen may stay down, and/or be dragged, for an arbitrary period

❑ Pen up: if the pen is outside the button, release it, redraw it in its neutral state, and do nothing. If the pen is inside the button, release it, redraw it, and then do the action associated with the button.

Other, related, sequences are possible. For instance, EIKON supports buttons that activate as soon as they are pressed, whose state toggles, or which expand to show a drop-down list when pressed, so that you can drag and release on one of the items. There are many alternatives.

Select and open is appropriate in circumstances where other systems would use double-click:

❏ Pen down on an unselected item selects it

❏ Pen down on a selected item 'opens' it – in the case of CFleetView, 'open' means 'request a hit on'; in the case of the Shell, 'open' means open the file or application

Neither CONE nor EIKON supports double-click, and support for drag-and-drop isn't well developed. In both cases, you can roll your own if you need to.

Pick Correlation

Pick correlation means associating the right object with a pointer event. As we saw in HandlePointerEventL() for CFleetView at the start of the chapter, this was very easy to do:

❏ There is only one object type that could have been selected: a sea tile

❏ The object is rectangular

❏ The object is part of a simple grid

This meant that selecting the object was a matter of a simple bounds checking and division.

In more complicated cases (such as selecting text in a word processor, or an object in a vector graphics package), pick correlation can be an awkward business, and can involve even more optimization and complexity than is involved in drawing. However, you can use a few handy techniques to make life easier:

❏ Object orientation makes designing for pick correlation easier, just as it does most things

❏ Construct a pick list optimized for easy checking when a pointer event occurs

It so happens that you can often use the same code to handle both incremental redraw and pick correlation requirements. (You can see this happening quite clearly in CFleetView: the pre-calculated border and tile positions and sizes are used by both drawing and pick correlation.) The net effect is that your redraw and pick correlation code can be optimized together. Often, optimizing feels like inventing two solutions to solve one problem. In this case, one solution solves two problems, which is nice.

Grabbing the Pointer-down Control

When you drag outside a control – in, say, the press-and-release paradigm – you usually want all your pen events, including the release, to go to the control in which the pen went down. The framework therefore has to remember with which control the pen-down event was associated, and to channel all subsequent drags and the pen-up event to that control.

EPOC calls this **pointer grab**, and you'll see grab-related APIs in the window server and CONE to support it: the window server has to remember the right window, while CONE has to remember the right control. If you write a control that contains multiple press-and-release type objects, but for various reasons you don't want to implement those objects as component controls (perhaps they are not square), then you will also have to implement grab logic.

Capturing the Pointer

If an application launches an app-modal dialog (that is, most EPOC dialogs), then although the app view window is still visible around the dialog window, no pointer events should be allowed into the app view. This is **pointer capture**: the dialog captures the pointer.

You can use `CCoeControl::SetPointerCapture()` to capture all pointer events to a control. Clearly, the window server has to be involved also: displayable windows also support a pointer capture API.

Grab and capture can seem confusing. Grab means keeping pointer events associated with the control on which pointer-down event occurred. Capture means preventing pointer-downs being handled outside a particular control.

Getting High-resolution Pointer Events

The window server normally amalgamates drag events so that, after an application has handled the previous pointer event and asks the window server for another event, the window server only tells the application the coordinates to which the pointer has now been dragged.

This is the right thing to do when handling non-time-critical MVC-type interactions. But for time-critical applications, such as handwriting recognition, it's rather awkward. The client-server communication between the window server and application is too slow to handle events at the rate produced by handwriting. Without any special support, the system will effectively sample handwriting at too low a rate, with very poor results:

Some EPOC engineers refer to this affectionately as 'thruppenny-bitting', after the twelve-sided three-penny coin ('thruppenny bit') that went out of circulation in the UK in 1971. It is enough of a challenge to write a screen device driver that doesn't 'thruppenny-bit', let alone convey all this through the window server, client-server interfaces, handwriting recognition software for Western or Far Eastern alphabets, and finally to a mere application.

An application can ask the window server to buffer pointer events, and then receive the whole buffer in a single massive event. The window server will send the buffer when it is full, or immediately after the pen-up event, whichever is the sooner.

Controls handle a full pointer buffer with the `HandlePointerBufferReadyL()` function, which deals with the `EEventPointerBufferReady` event. The window server has corresponding supporting APIs.

Processing Pointer Events

We now have all the pieces of the puzzle, so let's run-through the processing of a pointer event from start to finish.

Pointer events are initially generated by E32's digitizer driver, and passed to the window server. The pointer event is usually associated with a window whose on-screen region includes the pointer event. However, as we've just seen, pointer grab may be in use to associate the event with the same window that was associated with pointer down, or pointer capture may be in use to reject the event altogether.

The window is a member of a window group, and the window group corresponds with an application. The window server sends the event to the relevant application. CONE's `CCoeEnv::RunL()` is called: it passes the event on to `CCoeAppUi::HandleWsEventL()`, which then identifies it as a pointer event associated with a particular window. This is the same process that's used for the key events, and is also what we saw in the Chapter 9 debugger run-through of `HelloEik`.

CONE finds the window-owning control associated with that window, and calls its (non-virtual) `ProcessPointerEventL()` function. `ProcessPointerEventL()` calls `HandlePointerEventL()` to handle the event. It also does some pre-processing, which I'll explain shortly.

`HandlePointerEventL()` is virtual: when implementing a simple control, you implement it to handle a pointer event, however you wish. If you don't implement this function, you get CONE's default implementation (in the `CCoeControl` class), which searches through all the visible, non-window-owning, component controls to find the one which includes the event coordinates, and then calls `ProcessPointerEventL()` on that control. This default implementation is good for compound controls, and you override it at your peril.

So, the pointer event is ultimately channeled to the right non-compound control, where you can handle it by overriding `HandlePointerEventL()`. Note, however, that the complications we've already seen in this section affect both `ProcessPointerEventL()` and `HandlePointerEventL()`:

❑ CONE's pointer-processing functions support pointer grab, so that once a pointer is grabbed, all subsequent events, to pointer-up, are channeled to the same control.

❑ CONE doesn't support pointer capture: you have to use windows (and window-owning controls) for that.

`ProcessPointerEventL()` implements the event reporting in the container needed for focus transfer between components: it generates interaction-refused events for dimmed controls, a prepare-focus-transition event for a focusable but non-focused control on pointer-down, and a request-focus *after* `HandlePointerEventL()` has been called, for controls that were not refused focus at prepare-focus-transition time.

If you use the pointer buffer to capture high-resolution pointer event sequences, CONE handles it with `ProcessPointerBufferL()`, and you have to handle it with `HandlePointerBufferL()`.

More on Window Server and CONE APIs

Now is a good time to review the classes provided by the window server and CONE, and how they affect the application framework.

Application to Window Server Communication

In every EPOC GUI application, four main system-provided framework classes are used to ensure that the application can communicate properly with the window server:

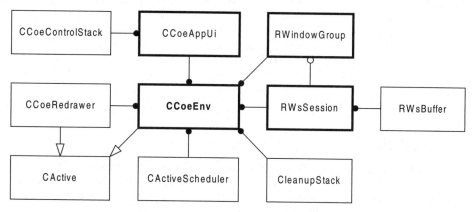

These classes are:

Class Name	Definition	Description
RWsSession	w32std.h	Window server session: this provides a client-server session from the application to the window server. All window server classes (window groups and windows) use this session for communication with the window server. The session also owns the application's client-side buffer, in which drawing and window manipulation commands are batched up before being sent to the server for execution.
RWindowGroup	w32std.h	A window group: this is the client-side version of the application's entire window hierarchy. A window group is associated with keyboard focus.
CCoeEnv	coemain.h	The control environment base class: this encapsulates the window server session in active objects whose RunL() member functions are invoked when events are received from the window server. These RunL()s analyze the events and call framework functions to handle them. The control environment sets up a cleanup stack for graphics programs. It also contains many useful utility functions.
CCoeAppUi	coeaui.h	The app UI base class. The essential purpose of CONE's app UI is to handle the control stack for first-level key event distribution. The app UI also performs some other, more incidental functions.

CONE provides some EPOC basics for cleanup handling (a cleanup stack) and event handling (an active scheduler). It wraps the window server session API in two active objects, to handle events generated by the window server. As we saw in Chapter 9, all event handling in a GUI program – keyboard, pointer, redraw, and others – takes place under an active-object RunL().

CONE actually uses *two* active objects: a higher-priority one for user-initiated events and a lower-priority one for redraw events. So if both a user-input and a redraw event occur while the previous user-input event is being handled, the framework will handle the user-input event first. Otherwise, the use of two active objects makes no difference at all to the application programmer.

> *There's some interesting design history here. Earlier in the Protea project, only a single active object was used. It seemed natural, then, to derive CCoeEnv directly from CActive. But then the redraw event stream was separated from the user-input event stream, creating a second active object. The result is that CCoeEnv is-a CActive (for user events), and has-a CActive (for redraw events). If we had designed this from scratch rather than making a late change, we would surely have said CCoeEnv has two active objects. This is a good case study for two of the guidelines I express elsewhere in this book: don't use inheritance where ownership will do, and hide active objects from your interfaces.*

Window Types

In the last chapter, we concentrated on the drawing-related interactions between CCoeControl and RWindow (and, occasionally, RBackedUpWindow). In this chapter, we've introduced key processing, which brings in RWindowGroup and CCoeAppUi. The window server classes involved here are part of a small window class hierarchy, defined in w32std.h, and illustrated below:

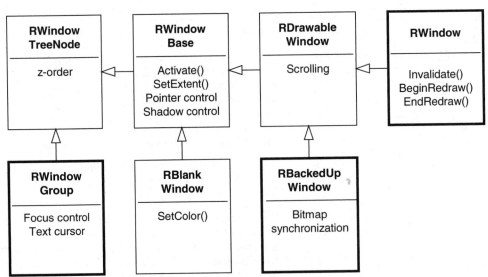

It's useful to understand these classes because, although for much of the time you can use their functions through CONE, CONE is not designed to encapsulate the window server (so that you don't have to understand it at all). Rather, CONE provides a convenience layer for lodger controls and compound controls, and for the window server's major functions such as drawing, pointer, and key event handling.

I won't be providing detailed information on these facilities: but I'll give enough of an overview that you can understand what's available, and find the information you need in the SDK.

Class Name	Description
RWindowTreeNode	Base class for all windows: a node in the tree that defines *z*-order
RWindowGroup	Unit of keyboard focus, and top-level owner of displayable windows
RWindowBase	Base class for all displayable windows
RBlankWindow	Entirely blank window
RDrawableWindow	Base class that defines windows which support drawing
RBackedUpWindow	Backed-up window: window server redraws invalid areas
RWindow	Standard window: application redraws invalid areas

For most application programming, the most important concrete classes are RWindow and RWindowGroup.

Because all displayable windows are ultimately owned by a window group, a window group is the top-level node in the tree that defines *z-order*. This means that all windows belonging to an application move back and forth in the *z-order as a group*. We can therefore use the terms "foreground application" and "application whose window group has focus" interchangeably.

The window server allows applications to have more than one window group, but CONE supports only a single window group per application, and this assumption is built into other EPOC components as well.

The window server provides other features that aren't supported by CONE, such as blank windows, and even non-rectangular windows whose shape is defined by a region.

Standard Window

A standard window has functionality inherited from the chain right up to RWindowTreeNode. However, the *interesting* functionality starts with RWindowBase, the base class for all displayable windows. RWindowBase includes:

❑ Activate(): you can use this function as the final step in a three-phase construction. (1) A default RWindow is just an empty client-side handle. (2) Use Construct() to connect the RWindow to an RWsSession and construct a server-side window. (3) After you have set all the window parameters, you need to use Activate() to display the window and enable it to receive events. In the case of an RWindow, the whole window will be invalid immediately after you activate it, so (unless you proceed immediately to redraw it) you'll get a redraw event.

❑ Position and size setting functions

❑ Pointer control

❑ Shadow control

❑ Backed-up behind

These functions can only be associated with a window that has a visible extent on the screen, so that's why they're introduced with RWindowBase. RWindowBase serves as a base class for blank windows, and also for RDrawableWindows. If you can draw a window, you can also scroll its contents, so scrolling functions are introduced here.

Finally, we get to RWindow. We have already seen the most important functions introduced here: Invalidate(), BeginRedraw(), and EndRedraw(). However, there are a few other interesting functions too:

❑ Construct() requires you to pass an RWindowTreeNode to serve as this window's parent. This can be another displayable window, or a window group. Window groups are the only kinds of windows that don't need a parent, so window groups are the top-level windows in the window tree – that is, in the *z*-order.

Construct() also requires you to pass a 32-bit handle. All events relating to this window include the handle. CONE passes the address of the window-owning control that owns this window: when CONE fields an event, it simply casts the handle to the address in order to associate it with the correct control.

❑ Easier-to-use variants of SetSize() and SetExtent() than those provided by RWindowBase.

❑ Two variants of SetBackgroundColor().

❑ GetInvalidRegion(): with this you can get the exact region that is invalid. If you have a particularly complex and well-optimized program, it enables you to improve on the bounding rectangle passed to a CONE Draw() function. You only need to invalidate and redraw the rectangles that comprise the invalid region, rather than their bounding rectangle, which is passed to CONE. Few programs are as demanding as this – but for those that are, the facility is there.

Window Group

The RWindowGroup class's primary role is to handle focus and key handling. Because window groups are the top-level nodes in the *z*-order, the only reasonable window group to grant focus is the foreground group.

Focus-related functions enable you to say that this window group can't take focus, or that it should automatically get focus (and foreground) when a pointer event occurs.

The window server supports a flashing text cursor, whose window, position, shape, etc. can be controlled through the window group. This is clearly the right place to do it, since the cursor is associated with focus.

One implication of this is that there can only be one text cursor per application. An application such as EPOC Word displays a flashing cursor in its app view when that view has focus in the CONE sense. But when a dialog is displayed, the view loses focus, and the app view must stop the cursor flashing. Moreover, it should relinquish control of it, so that it can be used for editing any text fields that might appear in the dialog.

GUI System Design

Now that we know about the display and interaction mechanisms delivered by CONE and the window server, we can recap how EIKON fits into an EPOC system.

An EIKON application runs in its own process. `apprun.exe` is used to launch the process, create three major frameworks, and load the application. The three major frameworks are

- ❏ CONE: the control environment, and link to the window server
- ❏ APPARC: the application architecture, which loads the application, handles its documents, ensures its name is displayed in the system task list etc.
- ❏ EIKON: uses both CONE and APPARC, provides standard GUI elements such as toolbar and menu, dialog framework, concrete controls, and many utility functions

In Chapter 9, I described the role of these components in launching an EIKON application, creating its application, document, app UI, and app view classes. In Chapter 14, I will describe a file-based application, which will demonstrate the role of the application architecture more clearly.

In addition to the on-screen application windows, the EIKON environment provides each EIKON application with a single off-screen window, which handles pointer events on the sidebar. Events on the sidebar window are reported to make the menu bar visible, pop up the edit menu, pop up the infrared beaming menu, or to zoom in or out.

The sidebar pop-ups generate `EEikCmdEditCut`, `EEikCmdEditCopy`, `EEikCmdEditPaste`, `EEikCmdIrdaSend`, `EEikCmdIrdaReceive`, `EEikCmdZoomIn`, and `EEikCmdZoomOut` commands. You don't have to specify these in your resource file – indeed, you cannot. If you want these commands, you have to implement them in your application's `HandleCommandL()`. I won't be covering the edit and infrared menus in this book, but in Chapter 14 and Chapter 15 I'll present code that implements zooming.

In any EIKON system, one special application and two servers are always active:

- ❏ The Shell ('System', in end user speak), which controls application launching and task switching.
- ❏ The EIKON server, which handles off-screen pointer events and also looks after other system-wide windows such as the password window.
- ❏ The application architecture server, which maintains lists of installed and active applications, and re-scans the file system and window group list when necessary in order to keep these lists up to date. The application architecture server maintains notify requests on the file system and the window server so it can rescan when necessary (and so it doesn't rescan when it's not necessary).

The Shell application works intimately with the application architecture server and EIKON server, which run as separate threads in the same process as the Shell. The Shell interprets events from the taskbar, and extends it with its Extras bar. The Extras bar is kept up to date by consulting the list of installed applications maintained by the application architecture server.

Summary

In this chapter I've covered the control and window server framework that supports GUI interaction, and shown how you should use this framework. Because everything is interlinked, it's probably the hardest chapter in the book. We've seen:

❑ The key and pointer event types

❑ How events are turned into commands

❑ How to handle focus, using window groups

❑ How the control stack for key event handling routes events to various destinations

❑ Dimming controls and validation

❑ Using observers to preserve the MVC pattern

❑ The difference between pointer-grab and pointer-capture

❑ The relationship between CONE and the window server

The next two chapters will be easier! Next, I'll cover finishing touches for EIKON applications. Then, in Chapter 14, I'll comment through an entire EIKON application, Solo Ships, a solitaire version of Battleships, which will demonstrate and reinforce many of the interaction principles I've introduced here.

13

Finishing Touches

After four heavy programming chapters, it's time to step back from the C++ and take a look at some of the softer, but equally important, aspects of producing a good EIKON application. I've titled this chapter *Finishing Touches*, but that's probably misleading; without these finishing touches, your application is a non-starter in the mass market.

I'll spend the major part of the chapter looking at additions to `helloeik`:

❏   Adding bitmaps to the toolbar buttons

❏   Adding an icon and a nice English-language caption for launching the application from the Shell

❏   Adding a help file, and a menu item to invoke it

❏   Wrapping up the whole program package into a single installable file, for easy delivery to end-users, and easy end-user installation

Along the way, I'll summarize the tools, and make a note about command-line building. Finally, I'll include a few notes from the EIKON style guide. We've already seen a few of its dictums (using genuine questions in query dialogs, for instance), which are designed to make life easier for the end user. The style guide is also there to help build consistency between EIKON applications from different authors.

Let's begin by adding the finishing touches to `helloeik`. You'll find the source code in `\pep\helloeikfull\`, though all source files are still named `helloeik.*`.

Adding Bitmaps

Here's a screenshot of the improved application we're working toward:

Like EPOC's built-in applications, there are now graphical icons on the toolbar. Compared with the version of helloeik in \pep\helloeik\, I needed to make two changes to get these icons:

❑ I created bitmaps and made them available to the program at runtime

❑ I changed the resource file text for the toolbar to include specifications for the bitmaps

❑ *I didn't have to modify the C++ program at all*

Creating the Bitmaps

EPOC has its own bitmap file format, the **multi-bitmap file**, or MBM. An MBM is constructed from several Windows .bmp files, using a tool called bmconv.

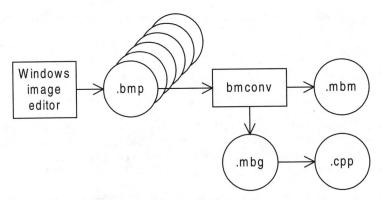

You can think of an MBM as an addition to the application's resource file, and a .mbg as an addition to the .rsg generated header, which contains symbolic IDs for the resources. Under Windows, bitmaps and other resources both go into resource files; EPOC treats them separately because the tools used to create MBMs and resource files are different.

I need two bitmaps for each toolbar button. First, there's the icon itself:

Second, there's a **mask**, which is black in the area of the icon I wish to select:

Only the regions of the bitmap corresponding to the black regions of the mask are copied onto the toolbar button. Everything else is ignored. So the white areas of the mask are effectively transparent, whatever the color in the corresponding parts of the data bitmap.

The selected region of the icon overlays the toolbar button underneath. The unselected region of the icon is ignored, so that the gray region of the toolbar button underneath is unchanged.

There's not much art in these bitmaps: I created them using Paint Shop Pro 5. I'm no graphic artist, and I didn't spend much time on the job. For real graphic art, get a real graphic artist. It's a different skill from programming in C++, and few programmers are any good at it.

The one thing it does have in common with programming, though, is that it takes a surprisingly long time to get good results.

I created four of these toolbar icons, and since they're all the same size, the same mask is good for all of them. Altogether, then, I created five bitmaps that I needed to turn into a single .mbm file, along with associated .mbg. Next, I used the following command:

```
bmconv /hhelloeik.mbg helloeik.mbm cmd1.bmp cmd1m.bmp cmd2.bmp cmd3.bmp cmd4.bmp
```

This gives a verbose log that you can choose to suppress by using the /q switch:

```
BMCONV version 50.
Compiling...
Multiple bitmap store type: File store
Epoc file: helloeik.mbm

Bitmap file 1    : Cmd1.bmp
Bitmap file 2    : Cmd1m.bmp
Bitmap file 3    : Cmd2.bmp
Bitmap file 4    : Cmd3.bmp
Bitmap file 5    : Cmd4.bmp
Success.
```

The result of this command is the production of `helloeik.mbm` in the same directory. Copy it to `\epoc32\release\wins\deb\z\system\apps\helloeik\`.

Because I've specified the /h switch, it also produces `helloeik.mbg`, the symbolic bitmap ID file, in the same directory. (Unlike a `.rsg` file, it's not copied into `\epoc32\include\`):

```
// helloeik.mbg
// Generated by BitmapCompiler
// Copyright (c) 1998 Symbian Lt//

enum TMbmHelloeik
    {
    EMbmHelloeikCmd1,
    EMbmHelloeikCmd1m,
    EMbmHelloeikCmd2,
    EMbmHelloeikCmd3,
    EMbmHelloeikCmd4
    };
```

The naming convention here is clear enough: there's an enumeration whose type name includes the MBM filename, and constants whose names are each made up from the MBM filename *and* the source bitmap filename.

I don't have to copy the `.mbg` into `\epoc32\include\` to be able to use it, but I do have to copy the `.mbm` into `\epoc32\release\wins\deb\z\system\apps\helloeik\`, and the command line to bmconv is already pretty complicated. So, I've written a quick batch file to do all this for me, `bmbm.bat` ('build MBM'), in `\pep\helloeikfull\`. If I update the `.bmp` files, I can run this quickly to update the `.mbm`:

```
bmconv /q /hhelloeik.mbg helloeik.mbm cmd1.bmp cmd1m.bmp cmd2.bmp cmd3.bmp
cmd4.bmp
if not exist \epoc32\release\wins\deb\z\system\apps\helloeik\nul mkdir
\epoc32\release\wins\deb\z\system\apps\helloeik
copy helloeik.mbm \epoc32\release\wins\deb\z\system\apps\helloeik
```

makmake doesn't include support for MBMs in its generated makefiles: you have to ensure that bmconv is called before running nmake or building from the IDE. In fact, you have to run bmconv even before you run makmake, because otherwise makmake won't be able to find the `.mbg` required by your program, and will flag an error.

Resource File Changes

The next step is to change the definition of each toolbar button in the resource file to add:

- The bitmap icon
- The bitmap mask
- The `.mbm` file from which to take them
- A specification about where to put the text in relation to the bitmap

This has essentially the same effect on all buttons. Button 1's definition is changed to:

```
TBAR_BUTTON
    {
    id = EExampleCmd1;
    bmpfile = "*";
    bmpid = EMbmHelloeikCmd1;
    bmpmask = EMbmHelloeikCmd1m;
    txt = "Cmd 1";
    layout = EEikCmdButTextRightPictureLeft |
            EEikCmdButDenseFont |
            EEikCmdButExcessToText;
    flags = EEikToolBarCtrlHasSetMinLength;
    length = KEikStdToolBarButtonHeight;
    },
```

The bitmap information is:

```
bmpfile = "*";
bmpid = EMbmHelloeikCmd1;
bmpmask = EMbmHelloeikCmd1m;
```

The asterisk specifies the application's own .mbm file, helloeik.mbm in the same directory as helloeik.app, and the symbolic IDs for the icon and mask, from the .mbg file.

It's quite possible to specify other .mbm files here, but you have to supply the full path in the bmpfile = parameter in order to do so. A potentially useful one is EIKON's own MBM, which is located in \system\data\eikon.mbm, and which has a symbolic ID file called \epoc32\include\eikon.mbg. EIKON's bitmap treasury includes the arrows used on scrollbars, bold/italic/underline icons, various other arrows, application icons, background textures, and the like.

The layout information is:

```
layout = EEikCmdButTextRightPictureLeft |
        EEikCmdButDenseFont |
        EEikCmdButExcessToText;
```

This specifies that the bitmap should be to the left of the text, that the text should be in a denser font, and that any extra space not required by the bitmap and text together should be considered as part of the text. This is the standard format for adding an icon to any toolbar.

Without using a dense font, it's hard to squeeze meaningful text alongside the bitmap. If you don't specify 'excess to text', the bitmap and text would be centered together, which usually looks odd. Better to fix the bitmap, and then let the text center in its own column.

Building the Application

After making these changes to the resource file, I rebuilt helloeik using:

```
makmake helloeik wins
nmake -f helloeik.wins clean
```

This cleans out any files that might have already been built from the old `helloeik`. Then, I can do:

```
nmake -f helloeik.wins
```

This invokes the resource compiler and the C++ compiler to rebuild the application. I can then launch the application in the usual way from the emulator.

More on `bmconv`

`bmconv` can also be used to turn `.mbms` back into `.bmps`, using the `/u` flag. One useful application of this facility is when you capture a screen on an EPOC machine using *Ctrl+Fn+Shift+S*, which results in a `.mbm` file with a single entry. You can transfer that to a PC using EPOC Connect, crack it using `bmconv`, and display and manipulate the resulting bitmap using an editor such as Paint Shop Pro. This is exactly the technique we used to get some of the screenshots in this book.

`bmconv` can construct bitmap files for ROM or non-ROM use. ROM-based bitmap files are not compressed; instead, they are stored in the normal display mode for the target device (which is known, since ROMs are device-specific). Of course, this makes ROM-based `.mbms` bigger, but because they use the intended display mode, bit-blitting to screen is very efficient. Bitmap files in ROM format cannot be mixed with those in application format: basically, you need to know which kind you are building.

> *Building a ROM is no trivial matter. Even `.exes` and DLLs are different in ROM: they are relocated to a definite address, and all relocation information is stripped out.*

Adding an Icon

Now that we've seen how to handle bitmap and resource conversion, we can generate an application icon and a better caption for the Extras bar and task list.

As we saw back in Chapter 7, the icon and caption, along with some other information about an application's capabilities, are contained in an **application information file** or **AIF**. Without an AIF, an application has a question-mark icon, a caption identical to its filename, and is assumed to be incapable of being embedded. The AIF has the same name as the application, and resides in the same directory. Unsurprisingly, its extension is `.aif`.

Our immediate concern is to give the application an icon. For that, we'll need an icon *and* a mask. In fact, we'll need *three* icons and masks, because the shell displays icons in three zoom states, and the realities of low-resolution graphics are that you have to hand-tailor bitmaps.

Here, for example, are the Agenda icons at the recommended resolutions: 24x24, 32x32 and 48x48 pixels:

For `helloeik`, I produced three sets of icons and masks at the required resolutions, using Paint Shop Pro and my limited artistic talent. Here they are:

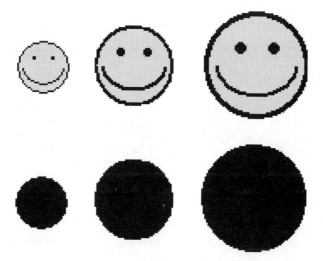

Each icon is a 16-colour bitmap. In `\pep\helloeikfull\`, you'll find these bitmaps with names such as `hello24.bmp` etc. I built them into a multi-bitmap file using:

```
bmconv /q helloaif.mbm /c4hello24.bmp hello24m.bmp /c4hello32.bmp hello32m.bmp
/c4hello48.bmp hello48m.bmp
```

I use the `/c4` switch before the color bitmaps to ensure that they are converted into sixteen-color EPOC bitmaps: without this switch, they are converted into four-gray bitmaps.

This time, I don't want a header file to be generated: so I omit the `/h` switch. The AIF format requires me to specify the bitmaps to `bmconv` in the right order, smallest first, with bitmaps before masks.

Now I have `helloaif.mbm`, which forms the graphical part of my AIF. The next job is to construct the AIF itself, and for that I need to introduce another tool, `aiftool`:

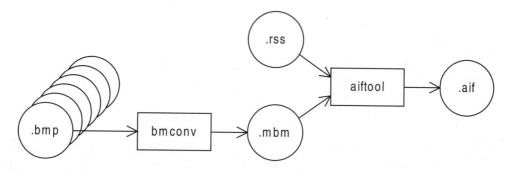

`aiftool` slightly overdoes re-use, and in doing so provides a convenient technology solution and a bizarre programming interface. You have to construct an MBM on the one hand, and a resource file on the other. From these, `aiftool` produces the AIF. Here's the resource file, `helloaif.rss`:

```
#include <aiftool.rh>

RESOURCE AIF_DATA
    {
    num_icons = 3;
    app_uid = 0x10005401;
    caption_list =
        {
        CAPTION { code = ELangEnglish; caption = "Hello!"; },
        CAPTION { code = ELangAmerican; caption = "Hello!"; },
        CAPTION { code = ELangGerman; caption = "Hallo!"; },
        CAPTION { code = ELangFrench; caption = "Bonjour!"; },
        CAPTION { code = ELangSwissFrench; caption = "Bonjour!"; },
        CAPTION { code = ELangItalian; caption = "Ciao!"; },
        CAPTION { code = ELangSpanish; caption = "Hola!"; }
        };
    }
```

This file specifies just three things:

❑   There are three icon sizes (with accompanying masks) in the bitmap file

❑   The application's UID

❑   The caption in various languages: in English, the caption is Hello!, which is going to look better on the Extras bar than HELLOEIK did

More oddness here: an AIF is good for multiple languages, whereas a resource file is good for only a single language.

Now we can run `aiftool`:

`aiftool helloaif helloaif.mbm`

Don't type the `.rss` extension on the resource file – you'll get a strange error if you do. Assuming that everything goes to plan, you'll see a rather verbose log:

```
AIF tool
Copyright (C) Symbian 1998
Compiling resource file

        1 file(s) copied.
Copying mbm
        1 file(s) copied.
Running AIF writer
Reading resource file...
Adding icons
Reading icons
Adding captions
Adding capability
Adding data types
Saving
        1 file(s) copied.
```

When this has finished, you'll see that `helloaif.aif` is in your current directory. Copy it to `\epoc32\release\wins\deb\z\system\apps\helloeik\`, and rename it to `helloeik.aif`.

> *Even more oddness! To avoid the rename, you can build your AIF in a separate directory, so that you can have an AIF specification file called `helloeik.rss`, which doesn't clash with the application's main resource file. I've taken that approach in other applications.*

I've incorporated all this logic into `baif.bat` ("build AIF"):

```
bmconv /q helloaif.mbm /c4hello64.bmp hello64m.bmp /c4hello32.bmp hello32m.bmp
/c4hello48.bmp hello48m.bmp
call aiftool helloaif helloaif.mbm
if not exist \epoc32\release\wins\deb\z\system\apps\helloeik\nul mkdir
\epoc32\release\wins\deb\z\system\apps\helloeik
copy helloaif.aif \epoc32\release\wins\deb\z\system\apps\helloeik\helloeik.aif
```

Now you can restart the emulator, tap on **Extras**, and you'll see the icon and nice caption:

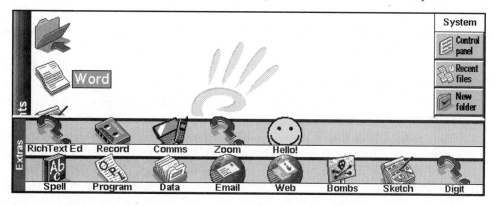

This is much cuter than the previous version.

Adding Help

A *proper* application should have help text. Your users probably don't need help for "Hello World" (if they do, then they need help!). In fact, you should take care to design your applications so that users don't need much help. But you may want to provide help text to provide a quick overview, to highlight some great features of your application that end users might not notice quickly, or to give a few real-world hints and tips.

EPOC's approach to help is quite distinctive. It is simple to program with, and simple to use. Above all, it's compact.

Help Facilities

Try pressing *Alt+F2* on the emulator (or the *Help* key on a real EPOC machine). Help for any of the built-in applications will be displayed in a format that looks remarkably like the EPOC Data application, and that's because it *is* the EPOC Data application, re-used for a different purpose.

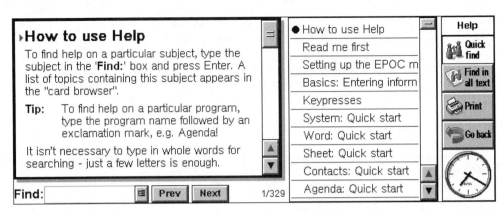

Here's what you can do with help:

❑ Each help topic is represented by a single database record

❑ You can see that each topic has a title, and rich text – which can include pictures

❑ You can search on any word in the topic or title: type link, for instance, to show all records with 'link' in (and press *Escape* if you want to return to all topics)

❑ Most topics are ordered alphabetically, but some important topics are specially brought to the front, for sequential reading

❑ You can search for all topics connected with a particular application by using an exclamation point, for example Agenda!

❑ You can't see it, but there's a synonym field that enables fast searches on user-friendly topic names, even if they're not the terminology normally used by EPOC (try schedule instead of agenda, for example)

❑ You can use the Tools | Switch 'Find' method menu item to swap between fast search (topic title and synonyms only – this is the default) and full search (include topic text)

EPOC provides a single built-in help database for its built-in applications, that's launched using the *Help* key – whatever application is currently running, even if it's not one of the built-in applications.

When you write help for your own application, you have to create a new help database, and provide a menu item so that users can launch it. It's recommended that you use Tools | Help, and shortcut key *Shift+Ctrl+H*, as shown in the full helloeik screenshot earlier.

Authoring Help

It's inconvenient to edit help databases directly. Instead, you author EPOC help using Microsoft Word, and then convert it into a database using another tool from the SDK, the bizarrely named aleppo.

In the mid-90s, there was a trend in the software industry to use Middle-Eastern cities as code names. Remember Cairo, Microsoft's code name for Windows NT 4.0? Symbian's first hypertext converter for its SDK documentation was titled Damascus, on the grounds that it had something to do with conversion, but it was architecturally unsound and got thrown away. A replacement called Samaria was written instead, which produces the HTML in all Symbian's published SDKs. Aleppo seemed a suitable name in this genre for the help builder.

`aleppo` takes a main input file in Microsoft Word RTF, and two control files. Its output is an EPOC Help database:

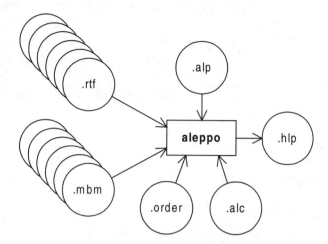

Go to `\pep\helloeikhelp\`, and you'll see the source and control files for `helloeikfull`'s help:

- ❑ `helloeik.rtf` is the source help text. Browse it using Microsoft Word, and you'll see the topics, synonyms, and text. The 'Hello world: quick start' topic has an underlined symbolic name after the titles, so it can be referred to by the order file.

- ❑ `helloeik.order`, the order file, which lists topics to sort in sequence at the top of the database (rather than alphabetically).

- ❑ `helloeik.alp`, a control file that specifies options for `aleppo`.

Here's a screenshot of the beginning of `helloeik.rtf` being edited in Microsoft Word 97:

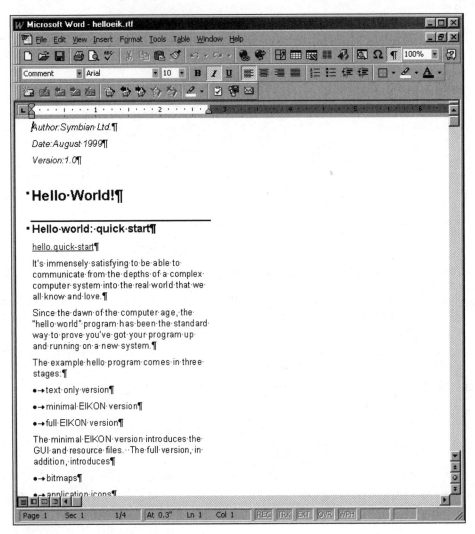

`helloeik.order` is very short indeed:

```
hello.quick-start
```

And here are the contents of `helloeik.alp`:

```
inputdirectory \pep\helloeikhelp\
outputdirectory \epoc32\wins\c\
outputfile helloeik.hlp
sourcefile helloeik
orderfile helloeik.order
workingdirectory \pep\helloeik\temp\
customizationfile \aleppo\projdir\uk.alc
```

You'll notice that the output directory is specified to generate the help file into the emulated `c:\`
directory, making it easy for me to test the generated help file, as we'll see shortly.

`aleppo` generates temporary files as it converts the source RTF into the target help database: the
directory to use for temporary files is specified in the control file.

`aleppo`'s operation can also be customized for various languages or required styles. This control file
specifies the customization file to use for UK English.

With these files, you can now run `aleppo` using:

```
aleppo -epoc helloeik.alp
```

You'll get:

```
Creating working directory...
Processing \pep\helloeikhelp\helloeik.rtf
Translating rtf to ptml
Translating ptml to cs-ptml
Translating cs-ptml to epochelp-sgml
Adding topics in helloeik to output file
Converting sgml to epochelp
```

This rather verbose log shows all the stages of the `aleppo` pipeline as it changes the source RTF into
the target database. You can test the target database by launching the emulator and using the shell to
browse to `c:\`. You'll see something like this:

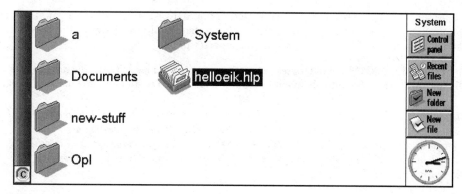

Open the help database, and you'll see:

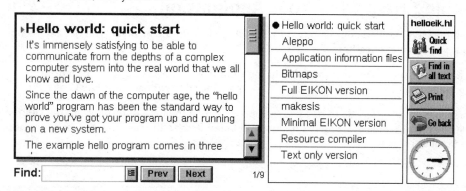

aleppo is documented in the C++ SDK, in the section on *EPOC Tools and Utilities*; for now, here are some key things to remember when authoring aleppo help.

aleppo source documents use **styled markup**. The purpose of a paragraph, or some characters within a paragraph, is indicated to aleppo by the named style of that paragraph – not by its formatting attributes.

The Microsoft RTF format supports named styles, and the epochelp.dot template supplied for editing with Microsoft Word defines sensible formatting attributes for the styles used by aleppo. Paragraph styles such as Normal, Heading 2, and List Bullet are standard in Microsoft Word, and are also used by aleppo. Character styles such as Key Name are included in the epochelp template, along with convenient keyboard shortcuts.

It's possible to include bitmaps in your help: you have to refer to them using an include directive from your help file source. For example, you can specify the following in Graphic Link style:

```
archive=pictures name=ordered-board
```

ordered-board.mbm is assumed to be a bitmap in the pictures\ subdirectory of a graphicsdirectory you specify in the .alp file.

In theory, any RTF editor can be used to produce the styled markup required by aleppo. I have experience of using Microsoft Word 95 and Microsoft Word 97 RTF. Word 2000 will probably work, but I haven't tested it. Other RTF-capable editors will only work if they preserve the style name information for paragraph and character styles.

The styles supported by aleppo are documented in the SDK. aleppo will warn you if you use an unsupported style, or if you do any manual formatting that should use a style – the only manual formatting allowed is bold, italic, subscript, and superscript.

Besides producing EPOC help databases, aleppo can also produce HTML. It's not great HTML, but it's OK for proofing in the unlikely event you don't have access to an emulator or real EPOC machine.

If you dig a little deeper into aleppo, you'll see that the interface to its final pipeline stage is also documented: it has an XML-like syntax. There's the possibility of an application here: you can convert e-texts into aleppo-compliant XML and then use aleppo to convert them into EPOC help databases, as a kind of electronic book. EPOC help databases are much more compact than corresponding HTML.

Launching Help from Your Application

When you have verified your help text by launching it from the browser, you need to be able to launch it from your own application.

The first thing to do is make it available in the right place: copy helloeik.hlp from \epoc32\wins\c\ to \epoc32\release\wins\deb\z\system\apps\helloeik\.

Then, you need to add code to helloeik.cpp to launch the help in response to the Help menu item or *Shift+Ctrl+ H* shortcut key. I added a hotkey and menu item to the resource file, in a format that should to be familiar by now.

I then changed the C++ code in two places: in `HandleCommandL()`, I added this:

```
case EEikCmdHelpContents:
    StartHelpL();
    break;
```

And in the app UI's destructor, I added this:

```
TRAPD(error, StopHelpL());
```

Unfortunately, `StartHelpL()` and `StopHelpL()` aren't standard application framework functions. I had to write them myself, and deal with the awkward cases explicitly:

- ❏ When I launch help, I have to test whether this particular help database has been launched already. If so, I don't launch it again: I just bring the existing application to the foreground.

- ❏ When I close the application, I test whether the help has been launched and, if so, close it.

This is system-level code, and as such it's quite interesting as you may be able to find other uses for it. Fortunately, the code is identical in all applications that need help, so you can certainly re-use it for that purpose. Here's the code for `StartHelpL()`:

```
void CExampleAppUi::StartHelpL()
    {
    // Get the help filename
    TFileName appFileName = Application()->AppFullName();
    TParse fileNameParser;
    fileNameParser.SetNoWild(_L(".hlp"), &appFileName, NULL);
    TPtrC helpFileFullName = fileNameParser.FullName();
    if(!ConeUtils::FileExists(helpFileFullName))
        User::Leave(KErrNotFound);
```

First, I get the filename, with the intention of replacing the `.app` on my application's DLL name with `.hlp`. I find my application's name from `Application()->AppFullName()`: at last, we can see some extra value from the application class that we've had to copy and tweak for all EIKON applications and which, so far, has simply returned its UID and acted as a document factory. I manipulate the filename using the recommended interface – the `TParse` classes – and then check whether it exists using the handy utility function `ConeUtils::FileExists()`. This last function uses CONE's built-in RFs, so I don't have to construct one of my own for the purpose of a quick check.

```
    // Scan through open programs
    TPtrC helpFileName = fileNameParser.Name();
    HBufC* matchString = HBufC::NewLC(2 + helpFileName.Length());
    matchString->Des().Format(_L("- %S"), &helpFileName);
    TApaTaskList taskList(iEikonEnv->WsSession());
    TInt numGroups = iEikonEnv->WsSession().NumWindowGroups(0);
```

Next I scan through the *open* applications to see whether my help database is already among them. I identify the help database using its application architecture task name, which will be Help - helloeik in an English locale. This is exactly the name on the task list display that you get by *Ctrl*+tapping on the System icon, or by tapping on the filename label at the top of any application toolbar. The Help part of this name is localizable, but I want my code to be language-independent, so I search for `"- helloeik"`. I construct the search string using `TDes::Format()`, and search using `TDesC::FindF()` (in the code that follows). The F indicates that characters are folded (to upper case, and without accents) before being compared.

```
for(TInt index = 0; index < numGroups; index++)
    {
    // Get task information
    TApaTask* task = new(ELeave) TApaTask(taskList.FindByPos(index));
    CleanupStack::PushL(task);
    CApaWindowGroupName* wgName= CApaWindowGroupName::NewLC(
                                 iEikonEnv->WsSession(), task->WgId());
    TUid uid = wgName->AppUid();
    TPtrC taskCaption = wgName->Caption();

    // Check it's a help app, and with the right caption
    TBool found = uid.iUid ==
        0x10000171 && taskCaption.FindF(*matchString) >= 0;

    // Bring to foreground if we found it
    if(found)
        {
        task->BringToForeground();
        CleanupStack::PopAndDestroy(3); // wgName, task, matchString
        return; // exit procedure
        }
    CleanupStack::PopAndDestroy(2); // wgName, task
    }

CleanupStack::PopAndDestroy(); // matchString

// If not found, then open the help database
EikDll::StartDocL(helpFileFullName);
User::After(1000000); // Pause 1s to give app time to start
}
```

I then search using the approved method for scanning through open programs: I use the TApaTaskList and TApaTask classes, and information from the window server (any application has a window group, by definition). If I find that the task is already open, it's very easy to bring it to the foreground, because the application architecture can do that for me: I simply use task->BringToForeground(). If the task isn't open, then I need to launch it myself. For that, I use a raw function in EikDll(), and then wait a suitable interval to give it chance to launch properly.

In unusual circumstances, this code may result in the same help file being launched twice. If this happens, the system will usually also close both help instances eventually, and even if it doesn't, the user will be able to close the unwanted help instance easily enough. When we consider server launch in Chapter 19 and Chapter 20, we'll see that the possibility of launching a server process twice is unacceptable: we need to take very careful measures to prevent it. For help launch, however, those measures aren't necessary

StopHelpL() involves almost exactly the same code, except that, if the task is found to be already running, I use task->EndTask() to stop it. If I don't find it running, I needn't do anything.

Helpful Applications and Unhelpful Help

Unlike PC-based help, EPOC's help doesn't include context sensitive help, nor does it include hyperlinks. Why is this?

- ❏ EPOC's help database search works well and, in practice, it's the only mechanism you need.

- ❏ Because EPOC's help facilities are relatively simple, it's easier to write help files.

❏   At runtime, EPOC's help databases and the application used to display them are both more compact than would be possible if they used more advanced features. This does mean, however, that when you're authoring EPOC help you have to think carefully about your topic titles, synonyms, and content, so that users can find items when searching.

On PCs, it can be a real chore to write context-sensitive help: as an EPOC developer, you should be glad that you are not required to do this. For example, Microsoft Word 95 has a Print dialog that's launched with focus on the Copies field. Press *F1* for help, and you'll see, "To specify the number of copies to print, enter a number in the Number of Copies box." Now ask yourself: does that information provide help to any user at all? If the dialog is designed well enough (which it is), the help isn't needed. If the dialog is designed badly, the dialog should be improved. If the user can't understand the dialog, they're not likely to understand the help either. But how much hassle was it for the developers to add that help to *every single control on every dialog* in this huge application? It all adds up to a vast amount of wasted effort that Microsoft might possibly be able to afford, but you probably can't.

Just occasionally, for about 0.1% of real fields in real dialogs in a real system, you might wish that you had context-sensitive help. Entering Internet Service Provider (ISP) settings, for example, is rather a technical business. The solution here is to provide a help topic that covers the whole topic of entering your ISP settings, and goes through the fields that are needed. You can encourage users to search for that help by providing a cue in the ISP settings dialog.

An even better approach is to provide an application-specific solution – in this case, that could be a means to install such complicated settings directly from a file. After some initial experience with EPOC Release 3's ISP settings dialogs, this is what Symbian did from EPOC Release 4 onwards: popular ISP settings are now available through Symbian's licensees' web sites (though advanced users can still type in their settings manually).

Make your *applications* truly helpful, and you won't need to provide help text that explains how to tackle bizarre difficulties that should never have been there in the first place. Don't design unhelpful applications, and don't waste time on help that isn't really helpful.

Making Your Application Installable

Up to this point, we've done everything in the emulator. It's time we rebuilt the application for MARM and installed it into a real EPOC machine. On the face of it, this is easy: we get a command line, change to \pep\helloeikfull\, and issue:

```
makmake helloeik marm
nmake -f helloeik.marm
```

This builds the .app for MARM, and we're ready to copy to the EPOC machine. But what do we copy? By now, our application consists of:

❏   A .app, in \epoc32\release\marm\rel\

❏   A .rsc, a .mbm, a .aif, and a .hlp, in
\epoc32\release\wins\deb\z\system\apps\helloeik\

427

To install this on the target machine, we need to copy all five files into c:\system\apps\helloeik\. As programmers, we could do this easily enough with EPOC Connect, as we did before, but this is unappealing for end users. If that weren't reason enough to want an installer, large programs such as Battleships need to be installed to more than one target directory on the EPOC machine.

EPOC's software installation suite enables you to package up all the release files for helloeik into a single distributable file, helloeik.sis. Your end users can then install this file to their EPOC machines either from a PC, or directly.

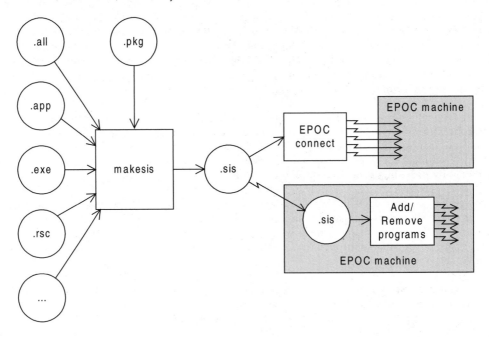

Using makesis

First, you have to produce the .sis file, for which purpose there's yet another EPOC tool: makesis. This application takes its instructions from a 'package file', which has one of the most obscure formats of any EPOC tool control file. Here is helloeik.pkg:

```
; helloeik.pkg
; Copyright (c) 1999 Symbian Ltd. All rights reserved
;
&EN
#{"Hello World application"},(0x10005401),1,0,0
"\epoc32\release\marm\rel\helloeik.app"-"!:\system\apps\helloeik\helloeik.app"
"\epoc32\release\wins\deb\z\system\apps\helloeik\helloeik.rsc"-
"!:\system\apps\helloeik\helloeik.rsc"
"\epoc32\release\wins\deb\z\system\apps\helloeik\helloeik.mbm"-
"!:\system\apps\helloeik\helloeik.mbm"
"\epoc32\release\wins\deb\z\system\apps\helloeik\helloeik.aif"-
"!:\system\apps\helloeik\helloeik.aif"
"\epoc32\wins\c\helloeik.hlp"-"!:\system\apps\helloeik\helloeik.hlp"
```

The body of this file should be obvious enough: source files on your PC that will be packed into the .sis file are specified, along with information about where they should be unpacked on installation. The '!' drive specifier means 'the chosen installation drive'. If you absolutely require a file to reside on the EPOC c: drive, for instance, you could have specified that instead – but this is rare, and should only be used if absolutely necessary.

> *One example is a pre-installed .ini file, since .ini files have to live on c:. Normally, applications should create their own defaults if a .ini file isn't available, so that pre-installation of .ini files is only necessary in specialized circumstances.*

The header is more interesting:

❑ The & line specifies the languages supported by this installation file: in this case, English only.

❑ The # line specifies the application's caption to be used at install time, its final UID, and its three-part version number – 1,0,0 is specified here, which will be displayed as 1.0(000), indicating major, minor and build.

This is the general form of a .pkg file for a basic, single-language application. In fact, the .pkg file format supports more options than this, including nested packages, multi-language installation files, and required dependencies. All of these are documented in the SDK, and in the next chapter we'll show you a .pkg file for a multi-language application.

You can run makesis from the \pep\helloeik\ directory by issuing this command:

```
makesis helloeik.pkg helloeik.sis
```

Installing Using EPOC Connect

It's then incredibly easy to install this to your EPOC machine: all you need to do is launch the .sis file! You can either double-click from Windows Explorer or even – in Windows NT – just type helloeik.sis on the command line. EPOC Connect will attempt to connect if necessary, and if your EPOC machine has more than one drive (A CF card for d: as well as the c: RAM disk, for example), you will be asked to which drive you want to install.

EPOC Connect will close all programs on your EPOC machine before installing the new program, and it won't reopen them afterwards. Programs that comply with EPOC style guidelines will close cleanly, with no loss of data.

The program is then copied over and installed. The installer asks you if you want to install another one – click Finish to indicate that you don't.

> *This is an unhelpfully helpful feature of EPOC Connect. It's very rare to want to install more programs.*

You can quickly verify this installation. On your EPOC machine, tap Extras; a smiley icon on the Extras bar indicates that your application – together with its AIF – has been installed. When you tap the icon, you'll see your toolbar with the bitmaps, which indicates that the MBM file was copied successfully. Finally, start Help to prove that your help file was also copied across.

Using Add/Remove

A more authoritative way to ensure that your program has installed successfully is to use the Add/remove icon in the EPOC machine's Control Panel. Bring this up, launch Add/remove, and you'll see something like this:

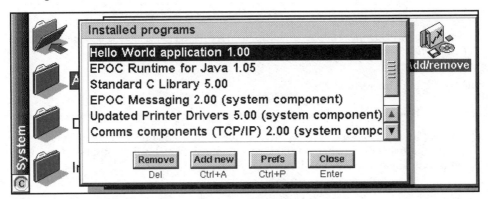

One of the benefits of installing using the `.sis` file format, rather than by copying files directly, is that you get an entry in this listing. You can use it to remove `helloeik`, if you like: just press *Del*, and then confirm. Tap **Extras**, and you'll see that it's gone.

Your end users can also use Add/remove to install a `.sis` file that they've downloaded to their EPOC machine without using a PC. You can simulate their download, say from a website, by copying the `.sis` file from your PC to your EPOC machine using EPOC Connect. On your PC, locate `helloeik.sis` using Windows Explorer and, instead of double-clicking to *install* from the PC, drag or paste `helloeik.sis` to *copy* from your PC to your EPOC machine's `c:\Documents\` directory.

Then invoke Add/remove again. Select Add new, and you'll see a dialog that allows you to select `helloeik.sis`. Choose this, and you'll find that it installs and gets listed with the other installed programs. Tap **Extras** and you'll see that it has returned.

The installation process optionally removes the `.sis` file from the `c:\Documents\` directory and places a slimmed-down version into `c:\System\Install\`. It is this slimmed-down version that contains uninstall information, and the information that's displayed by the Add/remove list.

> *The `.sis` file format, and Add/remove, are also available on the emulator. They can be useful for installing data, or pure Java or OPL programs. Don't even think about installing compiled C++ programs, Java with native methods, or OPL with OPXs using this method. Such programs will appear on the Extras bar, but they won't run, because they're built for ARM-based EPOC machines, not x86-based Windows PCs.*

Delivering Applications to End Users

I've now described how you can use `makesis` to make a `.sis` file, and how to install that file from either a PC (using EPOC Connect) or an EPOC machine (using Add/Remove). In reality the main customer of a `.sis` file is an end user. Think carefully about delivering applications:

❑ Make sure you replace test UIDs with releasable UIDs, allocated by Symbian

❑ Provide enough instructions to make it easy for end users to install and uninstall your software

The software installation suite was added to EPOC Release 3, with the Message Suite upgrade, in November 1997, and has been present on all releases since.

Support for installing .sis files was added to PsiWin 2.1, from January 1998, and has been present in all releases of EPOC Connect since then.

Summary of Tools

I've introduced four new tools in this chapter: bmconv, aiftool, aleppo, and makesis. Get to know them: they're an essential part of programming with EPOC GUIs, and they're also used by OPL and Java to implement the integration that they require with native EPOC.

To summarize:

❑   Bitmaps are built from Windows .bmps into EPOC .mbms and (optionally) a .mbg header file containing symbolic IDs. bmconv handles this conversion; it can also crack .mbms back into .bmps, and has specialist options for ROM building.

❑   Application information files (AIFs) contain icons, natural-language captions, and some other information about applications. They are constructed by aiftool, from a resource file and an MBM.

❑   Help files are edited in RTF and built by aleppo into an EPOC database with extension .hlp. A control file indicates all the processing required, and an order file specifies the initial topics to be placed in sequence at the top of the help file. All other topics are listed alphabetically below these initial ones.

❑   Installation uses a .sis file that is built by makesis from files specified in a .pkg file. The .sis file is then distributed to end users, and it can be installed from a PC using EPOC Connect, or from an EPOC machine by using the Add/remove icon in the Control Panel.

Command-line Building

As a developer, you will spend the majority of your time in the Microsoft Visual C++ IDE, editing and debugging programs. However, many aspects of EPOC program building can only effectively be done from the command-line – including, to begin with, running makmake to generate the IDE workspace file.

In this chapter, I've included plenty of examples of the raw commands that you need to use, for the tools I've described. In practice, you will probably want to write batch files, or more sophisticated makefile scripts, to automate building as much as possible.

I've written trivial batch files to do this: bmbm.bat to build MBMs, baif.bat to build AIFs, bhelp.bat to build help databases. I also provide bwins.bat to build an entire project for the emulator, and bmarm.bat to build for MARM, including making the .sis file.

Build systems are like other programs: they get bigger as your requirements get more sophisticated, and you find yourself doing the same thing over and over again. EPOC SDKs are provided with ebld.bat, the batch file used to build many programs internally by Symbian. ebld.bat is quite handy: you can build all the EIKON test code using a single command

```
cd \eiktest\group\
ebld all wins deb
```

My build .bat files are minimal, so you can easily understand them and see what's happening inside. Use whatever approach suits you best.

EIKON, Application Style, and Some General Rules

By now, you may feel that you're beginning to get used to the style of applications built using the EIKON GUI. Style here is not in the way you program, but in the way users see your programs. Good style (like good programming) is partly something provided and enabled by the system, and partly something you have to do yourself. EIKON's style guide was designed to take some fundamental things into account:

❑ End users who may not be very knowledgeable about computers – in fact, people who can be frightened by many kinds of technology, but who we want to feel comfortable with EPOC and its applications. If you've read this book so far, you're not one of them, so you have to think *hard* if you're going to deliver good applications to average end users.

❑ The physical parameters of the machine that first ran EIKON: the Psion Series 5, with its 53-key keyboard, LCD screen with 4 shades of not-very-clear gray, 640 x 240 screen size, digitizer and pointer, taskbar below, sidebar to the left.

❑ The requirements of the original application suite

All these factors change with time. In Chapter 15, I'll demonstrate how addressing the mass market requires us to take the realities of end users more seriously even than we did with EIKON. The different physical parameters of new devices dictate that Symbian and its licensees support several different user interfaces, and the changing application suite requirements will affect the things we consider important in a GUI. For the moment, however, I'll concentrate on EIKON as it is.

If I make comparisons here, it won't be with future EPOC GUIs, but with Microsoft Windows – simply because that's the best-understood starting point for most people. Originally, Windows was designed for people more computer-literate that most of its users are today. Windows and its applications have become ever more user-friendly, but the experience is *still* frightening for some end users. Even in 1991 when Windows 3.0 was released, the hardware you could assume was a color VGA display twice the height of a Psion Series 5's, a large keyboard, and a two-button mouse. By 1995 when Windows 95 arrived, the 'standard' display had moved to 800x600, with 1024x768 in many people's sights.

With smaller displays and less computer-oriented end users, the design parameters for EPOC's GUIs are radically different from those affecting desktop GUIs – just as constrained CPU power and memory make a big difference in EPOC system design.

The reference for EIKON style on 640x240 display machines is the *EIKON Application Style Guide*, which you can find on the EPOC C++ SDK in the *Technical Papers* section.

Here are some general rules:

- ❑ Every application should fill the screen. The screen is small enough as it is, and there's no point in making your user interface smaller than that.

  There are exceptions to this rule – in fact, there are good exception cases for most style guide rules. For instance, an application designed to add handwriting recognition to a device that doesn't build it in would need to use a window that floats above the current application. A full-screen window would be exactly the wrong *thing in this case. Arguably, the word 'application' is also wrong for such a program.*

- ❑ Each application should have a toolbar of the standard size and with the standard number of buttons, unless there's a very good reason not to (as in Sketch, for example). The toolbar can optionally be switched off.

- ❑ Good grayscale contrast (at least two shades) and a font of reasonable size should be used for all non-dimmed items in the user interface.

- ❑ The menu bar should not appear unless it's active.

- ❑ Make your application's main features easy to find out about (and easy to use) through the toolbar, the toolband, the menus, and the shortcut keys. Use cascaded menus to hide options that are used less often.

- ❑ Keep menu panes short (never more than eight items) and narrow (use few words, and don't repeat the wording on the menu bar or cascading menu item). Dim unavailable menu items, and use a variable check mark on constant text to indicate option selection status.

- ❑ When it's appropriate, use multi-page dialogs instead of monster menu hierarchies, because multi-page dialogs allow you to browse and change the available settings in a way that isn't possible by repeatedly hunting through menus.

- ❑ File-based applications must always have exactly one file open. If you don't want any files open, close the application. If you want many files open at once, open many instances of the application.

- ❑ Save files when the application closes, without asking the user first: this is what they want to happen 99.9% of the time. If possible, provide a "revert to saved" command that the user can use if they *really* don't want to save.

- ❑ Wording is very important. Use the standard vocabulary set by EIKON, its applications, and the style guide. Avoid ambiguity and programmer-centric vocabulary ("show the hidden window", "hotkey"); instead use user-centric vocabulary ("hide the game", "keyboard shortcut"). Take particular care over text that has to be short – on buttons, for example. Make sure that yes/no questions can *only* have those answers. Reassure the user: make it plain what actions will do.

- ❑ Remember that the pointer is a pen, not a mouse. Use pen-centric metaphors: use select-and-open rather than double-click, and avoid drag-and-drop.

- ❑ Don't forget the keyboard. Include keyboard shortcuts for menu commands, and include keyboard methods for interaction where possible. There is *very* little in the EPOC application suite that absolutely requires a pointer – confined mostly to the Sketch application, which is pretty much what you'd expect.

Standard Menu Items and Shortcut Keys

EIKON defines a standard layout for items that appear on menus a lot.

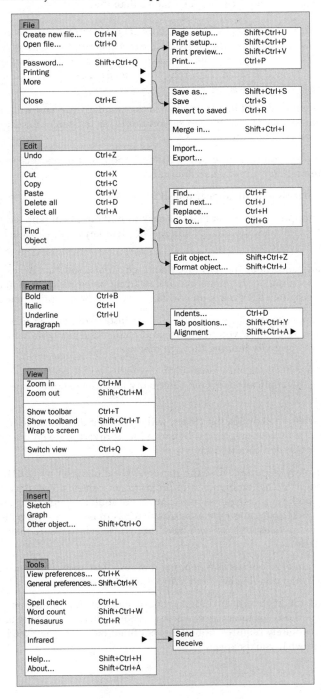

File

Create new file...	Ctrl+N
Open file...	Ctrl+O
Password...	Shift+Ctrl+Q
Printing	▶
More	▶
Close	Ctrl+E

Page setup...	Shift+Ctrl+U
Print setup...	Shift+Ctrl+P
Print preview...	Shift+Ctrl+V
Print...	Ctrl+P

Save as...	Shift+Ctrl+S
Save	Ctrl+S
Revert to saved	Ctrl+R
Merge in...	Shift+Ctrl+I
Import...	
Export...	

Edit

Undo	Ctrl+Z
Cut	Ctrl+X
Copy	Ctrl+C
Paste	Ctrl+V
Delete all	Ctrl+D
Select all	Ctrl+A
Find	▶
Object	▶

Find...	Ctrl+F
Find next...	Ctrl+J
Replace...	Ctrl+H
Go to...	Ctrl+G

Edit object...	Shift+Ctrl+Z
Format object...	Shift+Ctrl+J

Format

Bold	Ctrl+B
Italic	Ctrl+I
Underline	Ctrl+U
Paragraph	▶

Indents...	Ctrl+D
Tab positions...	Shift+Ctrl+Y
Alignment	Shift+Ctrl+A ▶

View

Zoom in	Ctrl+M
Zoom out	Shift+Ctrl+M
Show toolbar	Ctrl+T
Show toolband	Shift+Ctrl+T
Wrap to screen	Ctrl+W
Switch view	Ctrl+Q ▶

Insert

Sketch	
Graph	
Other object...	Shift+Ctrl+O

Tools

View preferences...	Ctrl+K
General preferences...	Shift+Ctrl+K
Spell check	Ctrl+L
Word count	Shift+Ctrl+W
Thesaurus	Ctrl+R
Infrared	▶
Help...	Shift+Ctrl+H
About...	Shift+Ctrl+A

Send
Receive

Clearly, not all applications feature all of these items on their menu trees. Equally clearly, most applications have their own items too. The style guide recommends you divide your application-specific menu items into major menu items (which have recommended positions high on the menu panes) and minor (which have recommended positions lower down, or cascaded).

The style guide also recommends standard shortcut keys for commonly used commands:

Key	Ctrl+key	Shift+Ctrl+key
A	Edit, Select all	Tools, About program
B	Format, Bold	
C	Edit, Copy	
D	Edit, Delete [all]	
E	File, Close	
F	Edit, Find	
G	Edit, Go to	
H	Edit, Find, Replace	Tools, Help on program
I	Format, Italic	File, More, Merge in
J	Edit, Find, Find next	Edit, Object, Format object
K	Tools, View preferences	Tools, General preferences
L	Tools, Spell check	Tools, Thesaurus
M	View, Zoom in	View, Zoom out
N	File, Create new file	
O	File, Open file	Insert, Other object
P	File, Print	File, Print, Print setup
Q	View, Switch view	File, Password
R	File, More, Revert to saved	
S	File, More, Save	File, Save as
T	View, Show toolbar	View, Show toolband
U	Format, Underline	File, Print, Page setup
V	Edit, Paste	File, Print, Print preview
W	View, Wrap to screen	Tools, Word count
X	Edit, Cut	
Y	Edit, Redo	
Z	Edit, Undo	Edit, Object, Edit object

As with the menus, these assignments are only a guide. Not every application implements all these functions, but most applications implement more functions for which shortcut keys are justified. Shortcut key assignments are a scarce resource, so if your application has more important functions than those listed here, conflicts may arise, and you may feel justified in overriding a standard shortcut key assignment with one specific to your application.

If you're writing an application and working out which shortcut keys to assign:

❏   Assign standard shortcut keys to standard functions.

❏   Use unassigned keys where possible.

❏   Re-use keys that your application can't possibly need, if you have to.

❏   Follow the practice of other EPOC applications, written since the style guide. If you need to re-use keys that are assigned by the style guide, don't re-use the most popular ones, many of which are shared with PC programs.

The most popular shortcut keys (in my opinion, not the style guide's) are the ones shared with PCs:

❏   *Ctrl+B, I, U* for bold, italic, underline

❏   *Ctrl+X, C, V* for cut, copy, paste

❏   *Ctrl+P* for printing

❏   *Ctrl+A* for select all

❏   *Ctrl+S* for save

❏   *Ctrl+Z, Y* for undo, redo

❏   *Ctrl+F* for find

Furthermore, there are two particular to EPOC:

❏   *Ctrl+E* for exiting the application

❏   *Ctrl+T* for toggling the toolbar

❏   *Shift+Ctrl+T* for toggling the toolband

Summary

If you're writing EPOC applications that you want to be widely used, style and finesse are essential.

It's worth taking time to study the behavior of the existing applications, and the style guide. You shouldn't follow every suggestion or every precedent without thinking about it; most applications depart from the style guide at one point or another. But if you can stay with the style guide where possible, it will help users get the hang of your applications very quickly.

In the next chapter, we'll put all we've learnt about EPOC graphics and UI into action in coding a one-player version of Battleships.

14

Graphics in Practice

In Chapter 9, I described a minimal EIKON application that simply showed how the EIKON framework and app UI fit together. After three heavy programming chapters and one on finishing touches, it's time to go through another application that builds on these ideas. Solo Ships is a single-player version of the Battleships game, ideally suited to this purpose.

This chapter is mostly about reinforcing the ideas we've seen in the previous few chapters: the MVC paradigm, controls and windows, in a more complex EIKON application structure.

I also take the opportunity to introduce two new ideas:

❏   Zooming, or size-independent graphics, which will lead us nicely into Chapter 15
❏   Persistence, or file-based applications with embedding, which at last builds on the promise of the stream store and application architecture that we introduced in Chapter 7. It also explains the role of the EIKON document class that we weren't able to exploit very much in Chapter 9.

Finally, this chapter is a foundation for understanding the Battleships application. I'll be introducing that application in the context of communications and system programming, and high-level design. In the Battleships chapters, I'll cover the GUI only in passing, so this chapter provides us with an opportunity to get all the GUI aspects together in one place.

Overview

Here's a screenshot of Solo Ships in action:

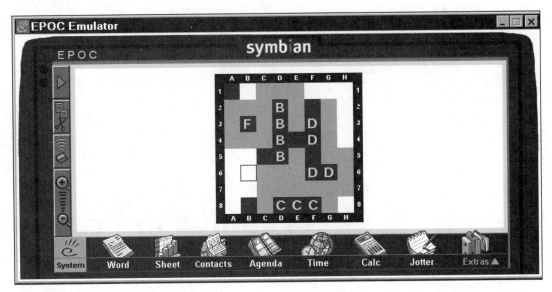

It's a pretty Spartan display, with no toolbar and no player status view – but that's all you need for this game.

You can embed a Solo Ships document in another document (once you've copied the `.aif` file from `bsaif1` to your application folder). Here's a Word document with three Solo Ships embedded objects:

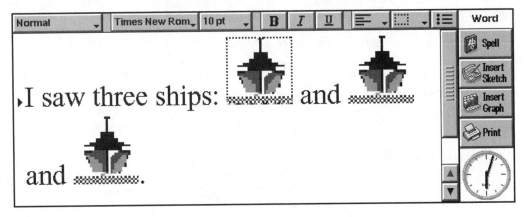

For fun, I've put the Word document in a high zoom state – 200%. The Solo Ships icon is stretched to a size appropriate for the zoom state. I supplied the icon in 24x24, 32x32, and 48x48 sizes: if I'd wanted a better effect at higher zoom states, I could have provided additional icons.

When you open any of the icons shown, you get a screen like the following:

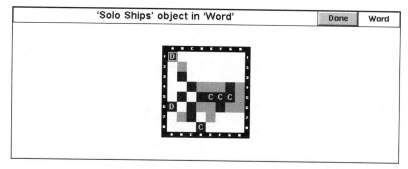

This shows an embedded version of the game. The embedding information bar at the top of the screen reduces the client area size – something you have to be careful about if you're writing an application designed for embedding.

The screenshot also shows another feature of Solo Ships that I'll be describing below: its view supports **zooming**, and in the screenshot above it's in a fairly small zoom state.

Embedding, remember, was one of the main motives for the EPOC application architecture, so it's good to see here how it's done. Zooming goes along with **size independent graphics**, which in turn leads to **device independent graphics** and also **device independent user interfaces** – important topics that I'll be covering in the next couple of chapters.

The other interesting feature of this application is that it's moderately complex: not just another "Hello World" application, it has 10 classes, a resource file, and an AIF; the classes include a total of 114 functions. That's small in comparison with the full Battleships program (76 classes) and tiny in comparison with EPOC as a whole. So as we approach Solo Ships, we'll begin to get an idea of the techniques we use to understand an object-oriented system at a higher level.

Program Structure

In Chapter 9, I introduced the structure of helloeik, which had four classes – the minimum for a practical EIKON program. bships1 (you'll find the code in \pep\bships1\) uses these four classes, and a further six, to build up a complete application:

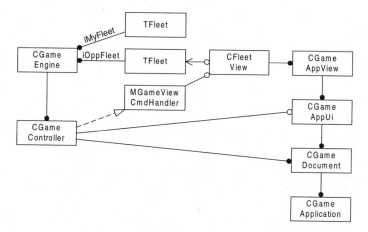

On the right, you can see the familiar EIKON classes – application, document, app UI, and app view.

On the left, you can see the classes that represent the application's persistent data: the controller and engine. The engine has two fleets: the opponent's fleet (which I have to destroy) and 'my' fleet which, in the full game, my opponent would destroy but, in the solo version of the game, serves a different purpose that I'll describe below. Each fleet has a number of ships in it, represented by TShip, a class not shown on the diagram.

The app view uses a single fleet view, with which we see the opponent's fleet (in the full game, it has a view for my fleet also). There is an interface class to handle hit requests from the view: this interface is implemented by the controller.

Two Important Boundaries

The *has-a* relationships and boundaries between classes in this diagram are significant. Two boundaries are particularly important:

- ❏ Objects representing persistent data, and objects that are part of the application framework. Ironically, the objects representing persistent data (CGameController and everything it *has*) are the least persistent objects in a running application – because, if a new file is opened, these objects are destroyed, and new ones are created to represent the new file.

- ❏ Objects holding persistent data, and those required to manipulate it through the GUI. The CGameAppUi (and everything it *has*) is used only to manipulate data through the GUI. When you finish editing an embedded object, the app UI (and everything it *has*) is destroyed, but the document (and everything it *has*, apart from the app UI) remains. The document class is used to save the embedded object data when the embedding application – Word, for example – is saved.

> **All this means you have to be very clear about where you can put your application's persistent data.**

In an application that supports embedding, persistent data *must* be in the document class and *must not* be in the app UI or views. You write your document class to contain all persistent data, and your app UI and views to *use* that data.

It's useful to write app UI and view classes that 'cache' values from the document model, so that drawing is quicker. But in a file-based application your app UI and view classes must be able to throw away all such cached information when the document changes. In a non-file-based application like helloeik, these considerations didn't matter. I kept the 'model' data in helloeik's CExampleAppView, as the iHelloText member.

If you are adding persistence to an application – that is, you're making it file-based – then your hardest task is likely to be ensuring that all document-related data is renewed in the views when the document changes.

If you are adding embedding to an application, the main thing to watch out for is persistent view-related data. You must store this in the document class. Depending on the nature of the application, this isn't likely to be very difficult.

I faced both these issues while developing Battleships:

❑ Originally, I wrote `tpg` (see Chapter 16) which had no persistence at all

❑ Battleships has persistence, so you can save a game played over a long period. Adding persistence created numerous issues, as I made sure the app UI and view could both accept a change in document.

❑ When I cut down Battleships into Solo Ships, and implemented embedding, there was no difficulty at all because the application was already structured properly and I had no persistent view data.

❑ When I decided to persist the zoom state, I had to move the master zoom value from the view to the controller.

The Engine

The Battleships engine represents the state of the game. The engine in Solo Ships is re-used, without any change at all, from the full Battleships game.

> 'Engine' is a synonym for 'model' in the MVC sense. Inside Symbian, these words are used interchangeably.

In full Battleships, the engine has two fleets whose purposes are obvious to a player of the game:

❑ My fleet: this is initialized by a random deal at the beginning of the game. I get to see it displayed in the left-hand fleet view. Each time my opponent hits a square on my fleet, the hit is registered in the engine's `iMyFleet` and on the corresponding view.

❑ The opponent's fleet: this is initialized to be entirely empty at the beginning of the game. I see it displayed in the right-hand fleet view. Each time I hit a square, I get a hit report back from the opponent that is used to update the information the engine has about the opponent's fleet. This is then reflected in the view. So, during the game, I get to know more and more about the opponent's fleet until – when I've sunk it entirely – I know everything about it.

In Solo Ships, I use the same objects, but not in the way they were originally intended:

❑ As in full Battleships, the opponent's fleet, and a view for it, are used for the fleet which I have to destroy

❑ The real information about the opponent's fleet is contained, not in the `iMyFleet` fleet on another machine, but in the `iMyFleet` fleet in the `CGameEngine` of the game that I am playing

That works fine. It shows quite nicely how, simply by re-plumbing the way objects are used by the program, I can re-use objects in different game designs.

The Controller

In the MVC paradigm, we saw that:

❑   The model contains the application data – in Solo Ships, most of the model is contained in the game engine, though the view's zoom state is also model data

❑   The view draws the model in a way which is meaningful to the human user

❑   The controller updates the model, and requests view redraws, in response to various kinds of event – including user interactions

The CGamecontroller class implements controller functionality. It owns the model (CGameEngine, and an iZoomFactor member). The controller ensures that the model state is saved to file (or embedded object). Finally, the controller handles all events that cause the model (and therefore the view) to change. In Solo Ships, there are two types of event:

❑   User interactions from the fleet view – handled by the controller as the implementer of the MGameViewCmdHandler interface

❑   Commands from the app UI – most app UI CmdXxxL() functions are pre-checked by the app UI, and then implemented by some controller function

For many applications, a separate controller class like this isn't needed. It's OK to put many of the controller functions inside the app UI or the model, provided that all the persistent data is inside the model.

But Solo Ships' application design is stripped down from the full Battleships application whose controller handled many functions that didn't originate in the app UI, but in incoming communications packets. In the full Battleships application, it's much easier to code the controller as its own separate class. Even in Solo Ships, the design is clear and easy to work with.

Engine Classes

We've seen about as much of the high-level view as we can realistically take in. Now it's time to get down to some more detail. Let's start with the engine, which is declared in engine.h and implemented in engine.cpp. The same source code – with no alterations at all – is used in full Battleships.

There are three classes:

Class	Description
CGameEngine	The engine itself, which includes two fleets (iMyFleet and iOppFleet), and some utility functions.
TFleet	A fleet. The same class is used to represent my fleet, and to represent my opponent's fleet.
TShip	A ship. My fleet is set up with 10 ships. My opponent's fleet initially has no ships, but I add information on new ships as they are discovered.

In UML, that's:

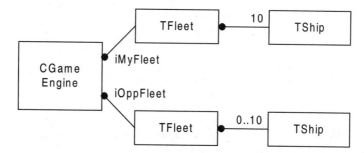

There's already an interesting design decision here. The two fleets are in some ways quite different:

❑ The engine know everything about my fleet: the only thing that changes throughout the game is the squares that have been hit by my opponent

❑ The engine initially knows nothing about my opponent's fleet: it finds out more throughout the game as it gets reports about the results of hits

Because of this, I wondered whether to use two different classes, one for each type of fleet, with a base class to represent their properties in common. But there is so much in common that eventually I decided not to do this. Each fleet object uses the same `TFleet` class, though some functions are intended only for use when it's my fleet, and others are intended only for the opponent's fleet.

Having functions that shouldn't be called seems like a messy design, but in this case a 'pure' design seemed even messier. I would need three fleet classes in the engine – and probably in the `CFleetView` too. For such a small application, it didn't seem worth it. Let's look at the individual engine classes more closely.

The Ship Class

The ship class is the most fundamental:

```
class TShip
    {
public:
    enum TShipType
        {
        EUnknown, ESea,
        EBattleship, ECruiser, EDestroyer, EFrigate
        };
public:
    TShip(); // Default constructor for no initialization
    TShip(TShipType aType);  // Initialize type, length, and remaining

    // Persistence
    void ExternalizeL(RWriteStream& aStream) const;
    void InternalizeL(RReadStream& aStream);
```

```
public:
    // Initialized members
    TShipType iType;          // Type
    TInt iLength;             // Length - determined from type
    TInt iRemaining;          // Remaining unit squares

    // Calculated members
    TInt iStartX, iStartY;    // Start position
    TInt iDx, iDy;            // Orientation vector
    };
```

A ship's first attribute is its type, iType, which may be battleship, cruiser, destroyer, or frigate. The type governs the length – 4, 3, 2, or 1 squares respectively.

The relationship between type and length is encapsulated in the TShip::TShip(TShipType) constructor: you specify a valid ship type, and the constructor sets the length. There's also a default constructor, needed so that arrays of TShips can be constructed in TFleet: the default constructor sets the ship type to unknown and the length to zero.

A ship has a starting square and a direction vector, for example, a battleship starting at (3,4) with a direction vector of (0, 1) will cover squares (3, 4), (3, 5), (3, 6), and (3, 7). Clearly the same battleship could also be described by a starting square of (3, 7) and a direction vector or (0, -1) – it doesn't matter.

The above information about ships is used during hit detection to work out whether a hit request affects a particular ship (in iMyFleet). When a hit is registered, I decrement the iRemaining count, which is initially set to the length of the ship. I can then tell when the ship has been entirely sunk.

The ship-type enumeration is worth a second look. TShip::TShipType is passed to, and returned from, many functions in the engine API. The ship type is an enumerated type, including constants not only for the four real ship types, but artificial values for unknown and sea. These are there to ensure that the ship type enumeration is compatible with the square states in TFleet.

> TShip::TShipType is represented in the engine's APIs and is used throughout the higher-level code that plays Solo Ships and, indeed, Battleships. The TFleet square states are private to TFleet. The requirement to keep TFleet's square states in sync with TShipType is a little awkward: initially I judged it tolerable in this small design, but on reflection I'm guilty of micro-optimization here – see the comment below.
>
> Another small-time design practice is that I don't hide the data members of TShip terribly well: in some contexts, I would have taken more trouble to make data members private, and to provide public accessors. Again, that didn't seem worth the trouble here.

There's nothing too difficult about TShip's implementation: check out engine.cpp for details.

The Fleet Class

A fleet is an 8x8 grid of squares containing up to 10 ships. Here's the declaration:

```
    class TFleet
        {
public:
    enum TSquareState // same as TShip::TShipType
        {
        EUnknown, ESea,
        EBattleship, ECruiser, EDestroyer, EFrigate,
        EHit=0x80
        };
public:
    // Setup
    TFleet();
    void SetupBlank();
    void SetupRandom();
    void SetMyFleet();
    void SetOppFleet();

    // Interrogators
    TBool IsMyFleet() const;
    TBool IsOppFleet() const;
    TBool IsShip(TInt aX, TInt aY) const;
    TShip::TShipType ShipType(TInt aX, TInt aY) const;
    TBool IsSea(TInt aX, TInt aY) const;
    TBool IsKnown(TInt aX, TInt aY) const;
    TBool IsHit(TInt aX, TInt aY) const;

    // Complicated interrogators
    TShip& ShipAt(TInt aX, TInt aY) const; // Use for my fleet only
    TShip* PossibleShipAt(TInt aX, TInt aY) const; // Use even if fleet unknown
    TInt RemainingSquares() const; // Fleet squares that haven't been destroyed
    TInt RemainingShips() const; // Ships that haven't been totally destroyed
    TInt SquaresHit() const; // Squares hit (sea or otherwise)

    // Change
    void SetSea(TInt aX, TInt aY); // Say a square is sea
    void SetShipType(TInt aX, TInt aY, TShip::TShipType aShipType);
    void SetHit(TInt aX, TInt aY); // Hit a square - must be known when it's hit
    void TestWholeShip(TInt aX, TInt aY); // Test whether hit has sunk a ship
    void SetSeaAroundHit(TInt aX, TInt aY); // Set sea around a hit square

    // Persistence
    void ExternalizeL(RWriteStream& aStream) const;
    void InternalizeL(RReadStream& aStream);
private:
    // Setup
    TBool TryPlaceShip(TInt aShipIndex, TShip::TShipType aShipType);
    void PlaceShip(TInt aShipIndex, TShip aShip);

    // Square accessors
    const TSquareState& Square(TInt aX, TInt aY) const;
    TSquareState& Square(TInt aX, TInt aY);
private:
    TSquareState iSquares[64];
    TBool iMyFleet; // Whether my fleet (which I know all about) or opponent's
(which I don't)
    TShip iShips[10]; // All the ships we know about
    TInt iKnownShips; // Number of ships known to be in fleet
    TInt iRemainingShips; // How many ships haven't been destroyed
    TInt iRemainingSquares; // How many squares haven't been destroyed
    TInt iSquaresHit; // How many squares (including sea) have been hit
    TInt64 iRandomSeed; // Seed for random-number generation during setup
    };
```

This is much more complex, and much more interesting.

You can think of a fleet as either an 8x8 grid of squares, each of which has something on it, or as a collection of ships, which happen to occupy squares. These two perspectives are both important for different purposes. I represent the squares perspective with iSquares and related counters, and the ships perspective with iShips and related counters.

We also noted above that the fleet supports different functions depending on whether it's my fleet, or the opponent's fleet.

Let's have a closer look the fleet class, from these different perspectives.

A Grid of Squares

The fleet is an 8x8 grid of squares, implemented by iSquares[64] and accessed by the private functions:

```
// Square accessors
const TSquareState& Square(TInt aX, TInt aY) const;
TSquareState& Square(TInt aX, TInt aY);
```

These implement the standard C++ pattern for getting and setting a value in a container. You can write,

```
Square(1, 3) = EBattleship;
```

which invokes the non-const version of Square() to set the state, or you can write,

```
state = Square(3, 5);
```

which invokes the double-const version of Square() to get the state.

The state of a square, represented by the TSquareState enumeration, is either unknown, sea, or one of the four ship types. This state can be ORed with a flag, 0x80, to indicate that the square has been hit.

> *As I said earlier, I'm guilty of micro-optimization here. On reflection, a better way to do this would be to have two squares arrays, one containing TShipTypes and the other containing TBools indicating whether the square had been hit. That would cost me 256 bytes of RAM per TFleet, would probably save me some bit-manipulation code in the TFleet member functions, and would make the square state show up nicely in the debugger as the enumerated constant values. It would be possible to re-arrange TFleet to do the right thing, and yet to change its internalizer and externalizers to preserve the same external format.*

In keeping with the way the fleet is coded, there are several functions which interrogate particular squares identified by (x, y) coordinate – ShipType(), IsSea(), IsKnown(), IsHit(), etc. There are also functions to change the state, such as SetHit(), SetSea(), and SetShipType().

A Collection of Ships

The second way to think about the fleet is as a collection of ships, implemented by iShips[10]. If the fleet is my fleet, these ships are initialized by SetupRandom(), from which point there are always ten ships. If the fleet is my opponent's fleet, these ships are cleared by SetupBlank() and then, as I hit complete ships in my opponent's fleet, this is detected and ships are added to iShips until, if I win the game, there are ten whole ships there.

In keeping with this way of thinking about the fleet, there are functions which place ships, detect the ship at a particular square, work out whether a particular square is part of a whole ship, etc.

My Fleet

When a TFleet represents my fleet, I must first set it up in preparation for a game, and then track the effects of my opponent's hits on it.

The functions to do this are:

Function	Description
TShip& ShipAt(TInt aX, TInt aY) const	Returns the ship at square (aX, aY), when it is known that there is a ship there
TShip* PossibleShipAt(TInt aX, TInt aY) const	Returns a pointer to the ship at square (aX, aY) if there is one, otherwise a null pointer
void SetupRandom()	Sets ships in a random configuration on the sea

PossibleShipAt() scans through iShips[] for each ship. For each ship, it walks from the starting square along the ship and tests whether the square is the one whose coordinates were passed to the function. If so, a pointer to the ship is returned. If no match is found, a null pointer is returned. ShipAt() simply calls PossibleShipAt(), asserts that the result is non-null, and returns the ship as a reference rather than a pointer.

SetupRandom() is an interesting function with some EPOC-specific code. The approach is takes is as follows:

❑ To place a ship, work out its starting coordinate and direction, and see if it can be placed on sea: if it does so, mark the ship squares appropriately, and mark all surrounding squares as sea, so that no ships can be place there. If it does not, (because there is already a ship there, or in adjacent squares) then try a different starting point and direction, up to 20 times.

❑ To place an entire fleet, try to place each of its 10 ships. If one of the ships could not be placed, even after 20 attempts, then judge the layout to be impossible and start again with the whole fleet. Try this up to 10,000 times.

This is a brute-force algorithm, but it works nicely enough in practice. The code for SetupRandom() shows how to seed and use random number generators in EPOC.

```
void TFleet::SetupRandom()
    {
    // Try to place each ship
    User::After(1);
    TTime now;
    now.HomeTime();
    iRandomSeed = now.Int64();
```

```
// Now try placing, up to 10,000 times
TInt shipsPlaced = 0;
for(TInt attempts = 0; attempts < 10000; attempts++)
    {
    SetupBlank();    // Blank everything
    shipsPlaced = 0; // No ships placed yet
    for(TInt ship = 0; ship < 10; ship++) // Try placing 10
        {
        TShip::TShipType shipType =
            ship < 1 ? TShip::EBattleship :
            ship < 3 ? TShip::ECruiser :
            ship < 6 ? TShip::EDestroyer :
            TShip::EFrigate;

        // If couldn't place, do another attempt
        if(!TryPlaceShip(ship,shipType)) break;

        shipsPlaced++; // One more ship placed
        }
    if(shipsPlaced == 10)
        break; // All ships placed - break
    }

// Check whether we placed all ships, or ran out of attempts
__ASSERT_ALWAYS(shipsPlaced == 10, Panic(EShipsNotAllPlaced));
iKnownShips = 10;

// Set remaining squares to sea
for(TInt x = 0; x < 8; x++)
    for(TInt y = 0; y < 8; y++)
        if(Square(x,y) == EUnknown)
            Square(x,y) = ESea;
}
```

The random number generator requires a 64-bit seed. The generator is seeded at the top of this code. As is conventional, we seed the generator by taking the latest value of the system timer:

```
User::After(1);
TTime now;
now.HomeTime();
iRandomSeed = now.Int64();
```

Incidentally, this is also the way to find out the current time in your local time zone. Check out the SDK for more details of TTime, and see EIKON's stock controls, including time-and-date editors and clocks, for ways to edit or display the time.

The first time I wrote this code, for the tpg version of the game, which lays out two fleets so that two players can use the same game program, I forgot to include the User::After(1) statement. As a result, the random number generators in both game engines picked up the same value of the system time as the initial seed, and therefore generated identical fleet layouts – which made for a fairly boring game!

User::After(1) is guaranteed to wait a single clock tick — 1/64 second on a real EPOC machine, 1/10 second on the emulator. So by coding User::After(1) before getting the seed time, I am guaranteed to get a seed value that has not been used before. The quality of these streams is easily good enough for applications such as Battleships layout.

TryPlaceShip() includes some code to use a random number:

```
// Select starting coordinates
TInt coord1 = TInt(Math::FRand(iRandomSeed)*(8 - ship.iLength)); // 0..8-length
TInt coord2 = TInt(Math::FRand(iRandomSeed)*8);                   // 0..7

// Sanity check in case Math::FRand() returned 1
if(coord1 + ship.iLength == 8 || coord2 == 8)
    continue;
```

This code uses Math::FRand() to produce a floating-point number between 0 and 1, and to update the seed for use next time Math::FRand() is called. It's not entirely clear from the SDK whether Math::FRand() can produce the value 1, so as a precaution I check this after generating the random number.

The approach I've taken to random number generation is good enough for Battleships, and many similar game-type applications.

You might want to think harder if random number generation were a really important feature of your game. Math::Rand() generates integer random numbers, which are more efficient than using floating-point. Math::Rand() and Math::FRand() use a linear congruential generator with well-chosen constants. Note that this won't be good enough for some applications (notably some types of encryption), but for Battleships, the facilities I've chosen are perfectly good enough.

The Opponent's Fleet

Here are some interesting TFleet functions relating to the opponent's fleet:

Functions	Description
void TestWholeShip (TInt aX, TInt aY)	Knowing that square (aX, aY) contains a ship and has just been hit, this function scans adjacent squares to see whether the whole ship has been hit and, if so, adds a new ship to the fleet's iShips[] array.
void SetSeaAroundHit (TInt aX, TInt aY)	Knowing that square (aX, aY) has just been hit and contains a ship, this function marks all adjacent squares as sea. Starts by marking diagonally adjacent squares. Then, if the entire ship has been found, marks all its surrounding squares.
void SetupBlank ()	Sets the 8 x 8 grid to contain blank squares.

The implementations of TestWholeShip() and SetSeaAroundHit() involve a lot of careful coding, but nothing very EPOC-specific. Check the source for details.

The Game Engine Class

The CGameEngine itself acts as a container for my fleet and the opponent's fleet, and contains query functions to indicate the state of play:

```
class CGameEngine : public CBase
    {
public:
    // Setup
    CGameEngine();

    // Reset
    void Reset();

    // Interrogate
    TBool IsWon() const;
    TBool IsLost() const;
    TBool IsStarted() const;
    TBool IsMyTurn() const;

    // Set up
    void SetFirstPlayer();
    void SetSecondPlayer();
public:
    TFleet iMyFleet;
    TFleet iOppFleet;
    TBool iFirstPlayer;
    };
```

CGameEngine doesn't require a ConstructL() because its members are all T objects, so construction cannot leave.

CGameEngine doesn't have a destructor either, so arguably it doesn't need to be a C class. I made it a C class, and have treated it as a C class throughout my code, so that the code works as a good basis for other classes without having to convert it from T to C and rethink everything related to cleanup. Using the C class is also useful to ensure zero initialization of all CGameEngine member data.

The View Classes

CGameAppView is a window-owning control with just one component – the CFleetView, which is coded as a lodger control.

This would be odd, if Solo Ships were the first application coded using these classes. In full Battleships, however, CGameAppView has three components – two fleet views, and a status view. So although I've changed the CGameAppView class for Solo Ships, the CFleetView hasn't changed at all.

You can find the declaration for CFleetView in view.h, and its source in view.cpp. CFleetView sends commands generated by key or pointer events to an MGameViewCmdHandler interface, also defined in view.h.

CGameAppView is declared in appview.h and implemented in appview.cpp. It's actually a pretty trivial class, as you might expect, given the description above. In order to understand the construction sequence in compound controls, and to give this section an easy start, I'll begin by describing CGameAppView.

The App View Container

Here's the declaration:

```
class CGameAppView : public CCoeControl
    {
public:
    ~CGameAppView();
    void ConstructL(const TRect& aRect);

    // Change controller
    void SetController(CGameController* aController);

    // Update
    void SetMyTurnAndDrawNow(TBool aMyTurn);
private:
    // From CCoeControl
    void Draw(const TRect&) const;
    TKeyResponse OfferKeyEventL(const TKeyEvent& aKeyEvent,TEventCode aType);
    TInt CountComponentControls() const;
    CCoeControl* ComponentControl(TInt aIndex) const;
private:
    // Uses-a - stuff elsewhere
    CGameController* iController;
    CGameEngine* iEngine;
public:
    // My stuff
    CFleetView* iOppFleetView;
    };
```

Library Functions

The main library functions in CGameAppView are:

Function	Description
void ConstructL (const TRect& aRect)	Constructs the app view, given a rectangle on the screen which is the app view's client area
void SetController (CGameController* aController)	Sets the game controller. A separate function is needed for this, because the game controller class is changed when a new document is loaded. A function like this will be needed for any app view in a file-based application.
void SetMyTurnAndDrawNow (TBool aMyTurn)	Called when the 'my turn' status changes. When it's my turn, the opponent fleet view is undimmed, so that I can navigate around it and hit a square. When it's not my turn, the opponent fleet view is dimmed, so I can't use it.

In full Battleships, the meaning of 'my turn' is fairly obvious. In Solo Ships, it's always my turn − unless the game has finished.

`ConstructL()` shows how to construct a window-owning control and then construct a component control:

```
void CGameAppView::ConstructL(const TRect& aRect)
    {
    CreateWindowL();
    SetRectL(aRect);

    // Set up fleet view
    TRect rect=Rect();
    rect.Shrink(10, 10);
    iOppFleetView=new(ELeave) CFleetView;
    iOppFleetView->ConstructL(rect, this);
    iOppFleetView->SetCursor(0, 0);
    iOppFleetView->SetDimmed(ETrue);

    // Activate
    ActivateL(); // Ready for drawing etc
    }
```

This begins by creating a new window, and then settings its rectangle (relative to the screen) to the client area rectangle passed as a parameter. From this point, I use `Rect()` to find coordinates *relative to the window*. This might be different from the aRect parameter: for instance, if Solo Ships is embedded, then the top of the screen contains a status bar.

I construct a `CFleetView` for the opponent's fleet, and dim it so that it cannot interact. I then activate the app view window, so that it will respond to redraw requests and `DrawNow()`.

`SetController()` just caches relevant information, and ensures that the fleet view also has this information:

```
void CGameAppView::SetController(CGameController* aController)
    {
    iController = aController;
    iEngine = iController->iEngine;
    iOppFleetView->SetFleet(&(iEngine->iOppFleet));
    iOppFleetView->SetCmdHandler(iController);
    iOppFleetView->SetDimmed(!iController->IsMyTurn());
    DrawNow();
    iController->SetAppView(this);
    }
```

The app view remembers the pointers to the controller and engine. It calls the `CFleetView` functions to tell the view which fleet to display, and sets command handling to the new controller. The `SetDimmed()` function sets the view to dimmed if it is not my turn, otherwise it is undimmed.

`DrawNow()` ensures that both the app view *and* its component controls get redrawn to reflect the model data in the new controller. Finally, the controller also has to know about its view, so this function calls `SetAppView()` to pass the information.

`SetMyTurnAndDrawNow()` is one of those functions which both changes status and does an incremental redraw. it is called by the controller whenever the state changes in a way which affects whether it is my turn or not.

Here it is:

```
void CGameAppView::SetMyTurnAndDrawNow(TBool aMyTurn)
    {
    iOppFleetView->SetDimmed(!aMyTurn);
    iOppFleetView->DrawBordersNow();
    }
```

This simply sets dimming according to whether it is (not) my turn, and then updates the borders on the view, which are used to convey the dimming effect.

Framework Functions

CGameAppView implements the framework functions required by CCoeControl. Here are the compounding functions:

```
TInt CGameAppView::CountComponentControls() const
    {
    return 1;
    }

CCoeControl* CGameAppView::ComponentControl(TInt aIndex) const
    {
    switch (aIndex)
        {
    case 0: return iOppFleetView;
        }
    return 0;
    }
```

As it stands, this looks slightly absurd. But in the full Battleships version, the app view has three components, so that there are a couple more cases in the switch statement. Draw() is equally uninteresting:

```
void CGameAppView::Draw(const TRect& /*aRect*/) const
    {
    }
```

Really, I needn't have coded this function at all!

OfferKeyEventL() is perhaps the most interesting framework function:

```
TKeyResponse CGameAppView::OfferKeyEventL(const TKeyEvent& aKeyEvent,
                                          TEventCode aType)
    {
    // Let the opponent-fleet view handle the key
    if(iOppFleetView->IsDimmed())
        return EKeyWasNotConsumed;
    else
        return iOppFleetView->OfferKeyEventL(aKeyEvent, aType);
    }
```

The key is offered to the opponent fleet view *if it is not dimmed*. Otherwise, the key is not consumed.

The Fleet View Class Declaration

The fleet view is a much more interesting control. Here is its declaration:

```
class CFleetView : public CCoeControl
    {
public:
    // Construct/destruct/setup
    ~CFleetView();
    void ConstructL(const TRect& aRect, CCoeControl* aParent);
    void SetCmdHandler(MGameViewCmdHandler* aCmdHandler);
    void SetFleet(TFleet* aFleet);

    // Zoom
    void SetZoomL(TInt aZoomFactor);
    TInt GetZoom() const;

    // Cursor
    void SetCursorOff();
    void SetCursor(TInt aX, TInt aY);
    TBool CursorOn() const;
    void GetCursor(TInt& aX, TInt& aY) const;

    // Incremental drawing
    void DrawTilesNow() const;
    void DrawBordersNow() const;

    // Key handling - from CCoeControl
    TKeyResponse OfferKeyEventL(const TKeyEvent& aKeyEvent, TEventCode aType);
private:
    // From CCoeControl
    void Draw(const TRect&) const;
    void HandlePointerEventL(const TPointerEvent& aPointerEvent);

    // Auxiliary draw functions
    void DrawOutside() const;
    void DrawBorders() const;
    void DrawHorizontalBorder(const TRect& aRect) const;
    void DrawVerticalBorder(const TRect& aRect) const;
    void DrawTiles() const;
    void DrawTile(TInt aX, TInt aY) const;

    // Cursor movement
    void MoveCursor(TInt aDx, TInt aDy);
private:
    TFleet* iFleet;
    MGameViewCmdHandler* iCmdHandler;

    // Cursor
    TBool iCursorOn;
    TInt iCursorX;
    TInt iCursorY;

    // Scale to use when calculating drawing stuff
    TInt iZoomFactor;
```

```
                    // Pre-calculated drawing stuff
            CFont* iBorderFont;
            CFont* iTileFont;
            TRect iBoardRect;       // Whole board
            TRect iTopBorder;       // All of top border
            TRect iBottomBorder;    // All bottom border
            TRect iLeftBorder;      // Left border, excluding top and bottom
            TRect iRightBorder;     // Right border, excluding top and bottom
            TRect iSeaArea;         // Sea area, inside board
            TInt iSeaRectSize;      // Side of sea tile (1/8th sea area)
            TInt iBorderSize;       // Size of border
            };
```

The really interesting member data here is:

```
            TFleet* iFleet;
            MGameViewCmdHandler* iCmdHandler;

            // Cursor
            TBool iCursorOn;
            TInt iCursorX;
            TInt iCursorY;

            // Scale to use when calculating drawing stuff
            TInt iZoomFactor;
```

iFleet is the model and iCmdHandler the controller in the MVC sense. So this control works as the V part of a well-structured MVC trio. The fleet view allows a cursor to be displayed, controlled by iCursorOn and (x, y) coordinates. Finally the view can be zoomed to a size that is (iZoomFactor / 1000) times the default size (more on this later).

Drawing the View

Many of the CFleetView data members contain sizes that are used for drawing the view. Shortly, I'll cover how those data members are initialized. First, though, I'll show the drawing code. The Draw() function draws the view in three stages:

```
    void CFleetView::Draw(const TRect&) const
        {
        DrawOutside();
        DrawBorders();
        DrawTiles();
        }
```

DrawOutside() whites out the region outside the board, so that – in accordance with the Draw() contract – the entire control is drawn.

DrawBorders() draws the top, bottom, left, and right border around the sea area:

```
    void CFleetView::DrawBorders() const
        {
        DrawHorizontalBorder(iTopBorder);
        DrawHorizontalBorder(iBottomBorder);
        DrawVerticalBorder(iLeftBorder);
        DrawVerticalBorder(iRightBorder);
        }
```

DrawTiles() simply draws all 64 tiles in the sea area: we'll take a closer look at it below.

Drawing Outside the Board

Here's `DrawOutside()`, which actually includes some drawing code:

```
void CFleetView::DrawOutside() const
    {
    CWindowGc& gc = SystemGc();

    // Brush settings
    gc.SetPenStyle(CGraphicsContext::ENullPen);
    gc.SetBrushStyle(CGraphicsContext::ESolidBrush);
    gc.SetBrushColor(KRgbWhite);

    // Top rectangle
    TRect top = Rect();
    top.iBr.iY = iBoardRect.iTl.iY;
    gc.DrawRect(top);

    // Bottom rectangle
    TRect bottom = Rect();
    bottom.iTl.iY = iBoardRect.iBr.iY;
    gc.DrawRect(bottom);

    // Right rectangle
    TRect right = Rect();
    right.iTl.iX = iBoardRect.iBr.iX;
    right.iTl.iY = iBoardRect.iTl.iY;
    right.iBr.iY = iBoardRect.iBr.iY;
    gc.DrawRect(right);

    // Left rectangle
    TRect left = Rect();
    left.iTl.iY = iBoardRect.iTl.iY;
    left.iBr.iX = iBoardRect.iTl.iX;
    left.iBr.iY = iBoardRect.iBr.iY;
    gc.DrawRect(left);
    }
```

This sets the brush to solid white, and the pen to null, and then draws four rectangles (some of which may be null) between the board and the control's boundaries. `iBoardRect` contains the board's rectangle, and `Rect()` the control's. Actually, this routine is longer than it needs to be. I could have just coded this to do the same thing:

```
void CFleetView::DrawOutside() const
    {
    CWindowGc& gc = SystemGc();

    // Brush settings
    gc.SetPenStyle(CGraphicsContext::ENullPen);
    gc.SetBrushStyle(CGraphicsContext::ESolidBrush);
    gc.SetBrushColor(KRgbWhite);

    // Top rectangle
    EikDrawUtils::DrawBetweenRects(gc, Rect(), iBoardRect);
    }
```

Clearing out the space between two rectangles is sufficiently common that this function is provided as a general utility.

Drawing the Borders

Here's `DrawHorizontalBorder()` – remember that this function gets called twice by `DrawBorders()`, once with the top border area as a parameter, and once with the bottom border area.

```
void CFleetView::DrawHorizontalBorder(const TRect& aRect) const
    {
    CWindowGc& gc = SystemGc();

    // Draw corners - in fact, whole border
    gc.SetBrushStyle(CGraphicsContext::ESolidBrush);
    gc.SetBrushColor(IsDimmed() ? KRgbGray : KRgbBlack);
    gc.SetPenStyle(CGraphicsContext::ENullPen);
    gc.DrawRect(aRect);

    // Draw letters
    gc.SetPenStyle(CGraphicsContext::ESolidPen);
    gc.SetPenColor(KRgbWhite);
    _LIT(KBorderLetters,"ABCDEFGH");
    gc.UseFont(iBorderFont);
    for(TInt i = 0; i < 8; i++)
        {
        TRect rect(
            aRect.iTl.iX + iBorderSize+i*iSeaRectSize,
              aRect.iTl.iY,
            aRect.iTl.iX + iBorderSize+(i+1)*iSeaRectSize,
              aRect.iBr.iY
            );
        TPtrC text = KBorderLetters().Mid(i, 1);
        TInt baseline = rect.Height()/2 + iBorderFont->AscentInPixels()/2;
        gc.DrawText(text, rect, baseline, CGraphicsContext::ECenter);
        }
    gc.DiscardFont();
    }
```

Firstly I set up the brush either to solid black or, if the control is dimmed, solid gray. I then draw the rectangle for the border. Then I draw the border letters.

Looking at it, this loop is less efficient than it might be. I could have set a null brush prior to the loop, to avoid re-painting the text. I could have saved some multiplication by initializing the rectangle for the A label and then using a simple addition to move along the X coordinates for each iteration, rather than doing the calculation from scratch each time. I have to admit, I wrote this code in a hurry. Then again, it's not the most critical code, so I'm not too worried.

It might also be better to get the label string out into a resource file, rather than hard-coded in the C++ code here. This one isn't an obvious localization issue: it's not clear that the ABCDEFGH string needs to be translated for other Latin-based alphabets, or even for non-Latin-based alphabets. I took the easy option here, for no better reason than that it was easy.

In fact, it wasn't initially obvious whether I should retain the lettered and numbered borders at all. You don't need them, technically, to play the game – as the computer looks after all the coordinates for you. It turns out that in practice it's useful to have them, because players like to talk about the state of the game and, without the numbers, they would have to invent their own coordinate system for this purpose.

The code for `DrawVerticalBorder()` is essentially the same as this.

Drawing the Tiles

`DrawTiles()` simply calls `DrawTile()` 64 times, once for each tile:

```
void CFleetView::DrawTiles() const
    {
    CWindowGc& gc = SystemGc();
    gc.UseFont(iTileFont);
    for(TInt x = 0; x < 8; x++)
        for(TInt y = 0; y < 8; y++)
            DrawTile(x, y);
    gc.DiscardFont();
    }
```

This sets up the font used to draw the tiles, and then draws each tile in turn. Originally, I put the `UseFont()` and `DiscardFont()` around each `DrawText()` call in my `DrawTile()` function below. This means that `UseFont()` and `DiscardFont()` are being called many times more than they need to be – a waste, because this is a surprisingly expensive call. When I took them out of the loop, as shown above, it speeded up redraw performance dramatically.

`DrawTile()` works in stages:

❑   First, determine the on-screen rectangle to use for the tile

❑   Then, determine the brush color, depending on whether the tile is unknown (white), known (blue), or hit (red)

❑   If the square is a ship (not sea or unknown), determine a character to use to represent it (depending on the ship type), a pen color to draw in (depending on whether it has been hit or not), and then draw the character in the square

❑   If the square is not a ship, then just draw the rectangle with the brush color and a null pen

❑   If the square is the cursor square, draw the cursor

Here it is: first, determine the rectangle:

```
void CFleetView::DrawTile(TInt aX, TInt aY) const
    {
    CWindowGc& gc = SystemGc();
    TRect rect(iSeaArea.iTl.iX + aX*iSeaRectSize,
               iSeaArea.iTl.iY + aY*iSeaRectSize,
               iSeaArea.iTl.iX + (aX + 1)*iSeaRectSize,
               iSeaArea.iTl.iY + (aY + 1)*iSeaRectSize);
```

This uses `iSeaArea` as the rectangle for the entire grid, and `iSeaRectSize` (a TInt) as the size of a tile. The calculation is simple.

Then, determine the brush color:

```
// Set background color depending on whether known, hit or otherwise
gc.SetBrushStyle(CGraphicsContext::ESolidBrush);
if(!iFleet->IsKnown(aX, aY))
    gc.SetBrushColor(KRgbWhite);
else if(iFleet->IsHit(aX, aY))
    gc.SetBrushColor(KRgbDarkRed);
else gc.SetBrushColor(KRgbCyan);
```

No problems here. Next, I decide whether I need to draw a letter (for part of a ship) or a blank square (for anything else):

```
// Draw either plain square or text
if(iFleet->IsShip(aX, aY))
    {
    // Set pen color depending on whether hit or not
    gc.SetPenStyle(CGraphicsContext::ESolidPen);
    if(iFleet->IsHit(aX, aY))
        gc.SetPenColor(KRgbYellow);
    else
        gc.SetPenColor(KRgbBlack);

    // Set character depending on ship and ship type
    TPtrC text;
    if(iFleet->IsShip(aX, aY))
        {
        _LIT(kShips,"BCDF");
        text.Set(kShips().Mid(iFleet->ShipType(aX, aY) -
                              TShip::EBattleship, 1));
        }
    else
        {
        text.Set(_L("?"));
        }

    // Draw the square
    TInt baseline=rect.Height()/2 + iTileFont->AscentInPixels()/2;
    gc.DrawText(text, rect, baseline, CGraphicsContext::ECenter);
    }
else // No ship
    {
    gc.SetPenStyle(CGraphicsContext::ENullPen);
    gc.DrawRect(rect);
    }
```

I was very keen to minimize waste here, so I don't use `DrawText()` where `DrawRect()` will do.

Just as with the borders, there is a localization issue here: I've chosen to use the string BCDF to represent Battleship, Cruiser, Destroyer, and Frigate. In other languages, these ships doubtless have different names, and perhaps the string should be localized. It's a pretty lousy representation, even in English.

Ideally, I would like to use a graphical representation rather than letters. But a graphical representation for a partial Battleship wouldn't look that good, unless it understood the position of the tile relative to the whole ship. And if that information were given away on the display, it would make the game too easy. So I've stuck with the BCDF string in the C++ source code. I can always change things if needed.

Finally I highlight the cursor square:

```
// Special border if it's the cursor square
if(iCursorOn && aX == iCursorX && aY == iCursorY)
    {
    gc.SetPenStyle(CGraphicsContext::ESolidPen);
```

```
        gc.SetBrushStyle(CGraphicsContext::ENullBrush);
        gc.SetPenColor(KRgbBlack);
        gc.DrawRect(rect);
        rect.Shrink(1,1);
        gc.SetPenColor(KRgbWhite);
        gc.DrawRect(rect);
        }
    }
```

The cursor is simply a black line around the outside of the tile, and a white line around the inside of that. The cursor had to look good whatever the color of the square underneath and around, whatever the contrast capabilities of the display, and at whatever zoom level. And yet the cursor should not altogether hide the square underneath.

It took me quite a few iterations to get a scheme that was acceptable. Unusually, the scheme I finally chose – for good aesthetic and functional reasons – was also very simple to execute in C++ code.

Redrawing the View

While developing this control it became evident that I needed two quick incremental redraw functions:

❑   DrawTilesNow() is called to update all tiles in the sea area, whenever anything changes – my own fleet view (in full Battleships) gets a hit, or the opponent's fleet view gets a hit report, or the cursor moves from one square to another.

❑   DrawBordersNow() is called to implement a change in dimmed status. This affects my view of the opponent's fleet, which is undimmed only when it's my turn to play.

DrawTilesNow() is a simple implementation of the application-initiated redraw protocol I described in Chapter 12:

```
    void CFleetView::DrawTilesNow() const
        {
        Window().Invalidate(iSeaArea);
        ActivateGc();
        Window().BeginRedraw(iSeaArea);
        DrawTiles();
        Window().EndRedraw();
        DeactivateGc();
        }
```

As I described in Chapter 11, I decided I didn't need a finer-control DrawXxxNow() function to update, say, only the two tiles affected by a cursor movement, or only the few tiles affected by a hit report. DrawBordersNow() is more complicated, because the region affected is not a simple square. Here it is:

```
    void CFleetView::DrawBordersNow() const
        {
        // Define the invalid region carefully
        Window().Invalidate(iTopBorder);
        Window().Invalidate(iBottomBorder);
        Window().Invalidate(iLeftBorder);
        Window().Invalidate(iRightBorder);
```

```
        // Redraw everything needed
        ActivateGc();
        Window().BeginRedraw(iTopBorder);
        DrawHorizontalBorder(iTopBorder);
        Window().EndRedraw();
        Window().BeginRedraw(iBottomBorder);
        DrawHorizontalBorder(iBottomBorder);
        Window().EndRedraw();
        Window().BeginRedraw(iLeftBorder);
        DrawVerticalBorder(iLeftBorder);
        Window().EndRedraw();
        Window().BeginRedraw(iRightBorder);
        DrawVerticalBorder(iRightBorder);
        Window().EndRedraw();
        DeactivateGc();
        }
```

First, I invalidate the total border region: all four border rectangles (the top and bottom borders also include the corners). Then I open an `ActivateGc()` bracket. Finally, for each border, I open a `BeginRedraw()` bracket, specifying the border as the region I am about to redraw.

Remember that `BeginRedraw()`:

❑   Sets a window server clipping region to the exposed, invalid region of the current window

❑   Marks the region specified as valid

❑   Expects me to paint every pixel of the `BeginRedraw()` region before I close the bracket with an `EndRedraw()` call

By the end of this sequence, I have redrawn all four borders.

This code looks a bit awkward: it would be nicer if the window server API allowed me to specify a whole region, rather than just a rectangle, to redraw. I did try to get away with a single redraw bracket, like this:

```
    void CFleetView::DrawBordersNow() const
        {
        // Define the invalid region carefully
        Window().Invalidate(iTopBorder);
        Window().Invalidate(iBottomBorder);
        Window().Invalidate(iLeftBorder);
        Window().Invalidate(iRightBorder);

        // Redraw everything needed
        ActivateGc();
        Window().BeginRedraw(iBoardRect);
        DrawHorizontalBorder(iTopBorder);
        DrawHorizontalBorder(iBottomBorder);
        DrawVerticalBorder(iLeftBorder);
        DrawVerticalBorder(iRightBorder);
        Window().EndRedraw();
        DeactivateGc();
        }
```

However:

- ❑ The window server would mark the sea area as valid at the beginning of the `BeginRedraw()` bracket

- ❑ I do nothing to paint the sea area during the bracket – a violation of the `BeginRedraw()` contract

So, if by some chance the sea area had been *invalid* before this bracket started, the window server would *believe* it to be valid afterwards, and would not therefore send a redraw event to the application to request that I update it. That's exactly the reason why `BeginRedraw()` expects me to paint every pixel mentioned in its parameter.

So, reluctantly, I discarded that idea.

Handling Events

I showed the key and pointer handling code in Chapter 12. The main interest here is not actually in how the events are handled, but in whether they are handled at all. It should be impossible to interact with the control when it is dimmed. This is not the responsibility of the control itself, but of the parts of the program that offer events.

Keys are offered to the fleet view by the app view. Above, we saw that the app view does not offer keys if the fleet view is dimmed.

Pointer events are also offered by the app view. The app view does not implement its own `HandlePointerEventL()`: rather, it picks up CONE's default implementation, which is designed for compound controls. This implementation includes a check for whether the control is dimmed.

A hit request event is offered to the rest of the program through the `MGameViewCmdHandler` interface, which is implemented by the `CGameController`.

Setup

The control's setup functions include `ConstructL()` and a C++ destructor. Here's `ConstructL()`:

```
void CFleetView::ConstructL(const TRect& aRect, CCoeControl* aParent)
    {
    SetContainerWindowL(*aParent);
    SetRectL(aRect);

    // Set zoom factor
    SetZoomL(1000);
    }
```

This time, the control is a lodger control, which specifies the app view (passed as a parameter) as its container, and sets its rectangle to the one passed.

`SetZoomL(1000)` sets the initial zoom factor to one-to-one, using code which we'll look at closely in the next section. This code calculates all the rectangles used for drawing (as we saw above) and pointer event handling (as we saw in Chapter 12).

The fleet view has a couple of other interesting functions. The destructor simply releases fonts that were allocated:

```
CFleetView::~CFleetView()
    {
    iCoeEnv->ReleaseScreenFont(iTileFont);
    iCoeEnv->ReleaseScreenFont(iBorderFont);
    }
```

GetZoom() returns the zoom factor last passed to SetZoomL():

```
TInt CFleetView::GetZoom() const
    {
    return iZoomFactor;
    }
```

Lastly, a couple of functions allow for the engine and command handler being changed when the application loads a new file:

```
void CFleetView::SetCmdHandler(MGameViewCmdHandler* aCmdHandler)
    {
    iCmdHandler = aCmdHandler;
    }

void CFleetView::SetFleet(TFleet* aFleet)
    {
    iFleet = aFleet;
    }
```

Scaling and Zooming

Now we've seen everything in CFleetView except SetZoomL(), which sets up all the pre-calculated rectangles, sizes, and fonts required to draw a fleet view – and also to redraw it, and to find the tile associated with a pointer event. Here are the relevant members of CFleetView:

```
CFont* iBorderFont;
CFont* iTileFont;
TRect iBoardRect;      // Whole board
TRect iTopBorder;      // All of top border
TRect iBottomBorder;   // All bottom border
TRect iLeftBorder;     // Left border, excluding top and bottom
TRect iRightBorder;    // Right border, excluding top and bottom
TRect iSeaArea;        // Sea area, inside board
TInt iSeaRectSize;     // Side of sea tile (1/8th sea area)
TInt iBorderSize;      // Size of border
```

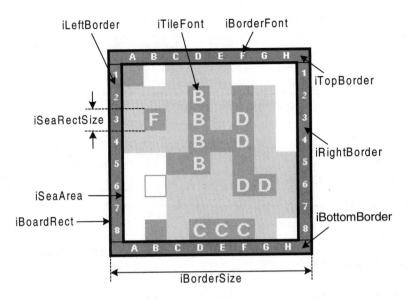

How do we calculate these? Well, firstly I have a concept of the board in my mind that says how big it should be:

❑   Each tile should be 1/3 inch high

❑   The border width should be 1/6 inch

❑   Therefore the total board size is 3 inches square (8 x 1/3 + 2 x 1/6)

I have encoded these definitions into some constant declarations toward the top of `view.cpp`:

```
const TInt KTileSizeInTwips = 480;                      // 1/3"
const TInt KBorderSizeInTwips = 240;                    // 1/6"
const TInt KIdealBoardSizeInTwips = 8 * KTileSizeInTwips +
                              2 * KBorderSizeInTwips;    // 3"
```

This introduces a new technical term: **twips**. A twip is one-*twen*ti*e*th of a *p*oint, and a point is 1/72 inch. There are therefore 1440 twips per inch. In `gdi.h`, you'll find this number as a constant: you'll also find twips per cm, and twips measurements for common paper sizes including Letter and A4.

Anyway, since the definition of a twip isn't likely to change anytime soon, I don't mind coding constants in the style above.

> *We have met twips before — EIKON's stock controls include a twips editor. The editor edits values*
> *in inches or cm, but internally its model uses twips.*

All programs that require an absolute unit of measurement, for paper-type distances, should use twips. A twip is small enough that you can express small distances in integers without much loss of precision. A twip is large enough that you can express quite large distances in a 32-bit signed integer — 37km, or over 130,000 sheets of Letter paper.

Drawing to graphics contexts is done in *pixels*, so I need to convert the board measurements from twips into pixels, taking into account:

- ❏ A scale factor which converts the 3 inches I need for the board, into the size, in inches, of the smallest dimension of the fleet view

- ❏ An amendment of this scale factor to take the view's zoom factor into account

I can then convert the size of the tile, and the border, again by converting inches into pixels. I can also work out the size of the fonts I'll need for the tiles (3/4 of the tile size) and the border (3/4 of the border width).

I do all these calculations in `SetZoomL()`. Let's have a look at the code: on the way we can see how to convert between pixels and inches, how to do zooming, and how to allocate fonts.

Firstly, I do nothing if the zoom factor hasn't changed:

```
void CFleetView::SetZoomL(TInt aZoomFactor)
    {
    // Check we're doing something useful
    if(iZoomFactor == aZoomFactor)
        return;
    iZoomFactor = aZoomFactor;
```

Then, I find the smallest board dimension, in pixels:

```
    // Find available size in pixels
    TInt boardSize = Rect().Width() < Rect().Height() ? Rect().Width() :
                                                        Rect().Height();
```

Then, I start converting into twips:

```
    // Calculate board size in twips, and hence scale factor
    TInt boardSizeInTwips =
        iCoeEnv->ScreenDevice()->HorizontalPixelsToTwips(boardSize);
    boardSizeInTwips = (boardSizeInTwips * iZoomFactor) / 1000; // Zoom
    TInt scaleFactor = (boardSizeInTwips * 1000) / KIdealBoardSizeInTwips;
    boardSize =
        iCoeEnv->ScreenDevice()->HorizontalTwipsToPixels(boardSizeInTwips);
```

The `HorizontalPixelsToTwips()` function converts a given number of twips into pixels. This is a device-specific thing: I use the screen device to give me the right answer. Then, I scale the board size (in twips) by the zoom factor to get the board size I will really be using.

Next, I calculate a scale factor: the ratio of the board size I will be using (in twips) to the ideal board size (in twips). I will be applying the same scale factor to the tiles and border, individually.

For both the scale factor and zoom factor, I use the number 1000 to indicate one-to-one. This means I can do a scaling calculation using code such as,

```
    scaled_number = (old_number * scale) / 1000;
```

with integer values. This is preferable to doing the calculations in floating-point numbers. This kind of 1000-based scaling is used elsewhere in EPOC graphics programming, as we'll see when we look at the `TZoomFactor` class, in the next chapter. Watch out, though, for two possible sources of error:

❑ Always multiply by the scale first, and then divide by one thousand – otherwise, you will lose precision

❑ Ensure that number to be scaled, combined with the scale factor, is less than the maximum possible integer – otherwise, you'll get overflow

The number 1000 was chosen to be sufficiently large to enable reasonable precision, but sufficiently small to reduce the risk of overflow. With a zoom factor of ten to one, and a twips value the size of a Letter paper, scaling calculations will reach 15,840 (twips high) x 10,000 (ten-to-one scale) = 158,400,000, which still leaves a good deal of room before you hit the 2.1 billion maximum signed integer value.

Finally I calculate a board size in pixels by calling the opposite function to the one I had before – `HorizontalTwipsToPixels()`.

I am assuming that pixels on the screen are square. This assumption is pretty safe.

Next, I calculate the real tile and border sizes, in twips, by applying the same scale factor as was used for the board (I'll be using these values later, to calculate the point sizes of fonts):

```
// Tile and border sizes also
TInt tileSizeInTwips = (KTileSizeInTwips*scaleFactor) / 1000;
TInt borderSizeInTwips = (KBorderSizeInTwips*scaleFactor) / 1000;
```

Then, I have to calculate the sizes, in pixels, of the tiles and border.

```
// Calculate tile and border sizes in pixels, ensuring even distribution
iBorderSize =
    iCoeEnv->ScreenDevice()->HorizontalTwipsToPixels(borderSizeInTwips);

iSeaRectSize = (boardSize-iBorderSize*2)/8; // 8th remaining, rounding down
TInt innerSize = iSeaRectSize*8; // Whole size of inner region
iBorderSize = (boardSize-innerSize) / 2; // Adjust border size again
boardSize = innerSize + iBorderSize*2; // Final board size
```

The algorithm I use here is carefully chosen:

❑ I get the border size in pixels using twips-to-pixels mapping

❑ I get the size of a tile (`iSeaRectSize`) by subtracting twice the border size from the whole-board size, and then dividing by eight

❑ It so happens that the tile-size calculation will probably introduce some kind of rounding error. As a result, when I multiply up the tile size by eight again to produce `innerSize`, I may be as many as seven pixels short of the inner size you would get if you subtracted twice the border size from the board size.

❑ I therefore re-calculate the border size, as half the remainder after subtracting the inner size from the board size – at worst, this gives me a one-pixel rounding error

❑ I finally re-calculate the board size, as the inner size plus twice the border size

This might seem like an odd sequence, but you have to take rounding errors in pixel calculations seriously, and this is the way to do it. Now I know the sizes of everything in pixels, it's easy (if tedious) to calculate the rectangles I'll need.

```
// Pre-calculate actual rectangles for everything
iBoardRect = TRect(0, 0, boardSize, boardSize);
iTopBorder = TRect(0, 0, boardSize, iBorderSize);
iBottomBorder = TRect(0, iBorderSize + innerSize, boardSize, boardSize);
iLeftBorder = TRect(0, iBorderSize, iBorderSize, iBorderSize + innerSize);
iRightBorder = TRect(iBorderSize + innerSize, iBorderSize,
                     boardSize, iBorderSize + innerSize);
iSeaArea = TRect(iBorderSize, iBorderSize,
                 iBorderSize + innerSize, iBorderSize + innerSize);

// Offset everything to center properly
TPoint offset(Rect().iTl.iX + (Rect().Width() - boardSize) / 2,
              Rect().iTl.iY + (Rect().Height() - boardSize) / 2)
iBoardRect.Move(offset);
iTopBorder.Move(offset);
iBottomBorder.Move(offset);
iLeftBorder.Move(offset);
iRightBorder.Move(offset);
iSeaArea.Move(offset);
```

Finally, I need to allocate fonts: an `iBorderFont` for the border, and an `iTileFile` for the sea area tiles. I use essentially the same algorithm in both cases:

```
// Get small font for drawing border
TFontSpec specBorder(_L("Arial"), (borderSizeInTwips * 3) / 4);
specBorder.iFontStyle.SetStrokeWeight(EStrokeWeightBold);
CFont* borderFont = iCoeEnv->CreateScreenFontL(specBorder);
if(iBorderFont)
    iCoeEnv->ReleaseScreenFont(iBorderFont);
iBorderFont = borderFont;

// Larger font for drawing tiles
TFontSpec specTile(_L("Arial"), (tileSizeInTwips*3) / 4);
specTile.iFontStyle.SetStrokeWeight(EStrokeWeightBold);
CFont* tileFont = iCoeEnv->CreateScreenFontL(specTile);
if(iTileFont)
    iCoeEnv->ReleaseScreenFont(iTileFont);
iTileFont = tileFont;
}
```

Firstly, I get a `TFontSpec`, in which I specify a font name (Arial in both cases) and size in twips (3/4 of the tile size or border width). I then set the font spec to include the bold attribute.

I call `CreateScreenFontL()` to ask the CONE environment to create a screen font for me, with those attributes – or to leave, if it cannot. Assuming this worked, I replace the previous font with the one I was allocated, and release the previous font using `ReleaseScreenFont()`.

This code has introduced us to many of the issues in size-independent on-screen graphics:

❑ Absolute units are measured in twips, 1/1440 of an inch

❑ You use a device to convert between pixels and twips. Although separate functions are provided for horizontal and vertical measurements, it's a fair bet that pixels, especially on screens, are square

❑ You can get at the screen device with `iCoeEnv->ScreenDevice()`

❑ In pixel calculations, rounding errors are real, so you have to calculate the sizes of elements in your view carefully to minimize the effects of rounding errors

❑ You can get a `CFont*`, needed for GC `UseFont()` functions, by creating a `TFontSpec` with a font name, size in twips, and any other attributes you need, and then using `iCoeEnv->CreateScreenFontL()` to allocate a font matching this as nearly as possible.

In the next chapter, I'll be explaining these issues in a lot more detail. For now, we have good proof that it works, because by zooming the view, or opening it inside an embedded object, you can see that it scales nicely to a wide variety of screen sizes.

The Controller

The controller is at the heart of Solo Ships and – in a much larger form – at the heart of Battleships also. Every update to the model goes through the controller – whether the update originated in the app UI, the app view, or (in the case of Battleships) in a packet coming in on a communications link.

In addition, the controller acts on the behalf of the EIKON/application-architecture document as the owner of the application's persistent data. That means that the controller can be changed throughout the lifetime of the application.

Here's the declaration of CGameController, in `controller.h`:

```
class CGameController : public CBase,
                        public MGameViewCmdHandler
    {
public:
    enum TState { EMyTurn, EFinished };
public:
    // Construct/destruct
    static CGameController* NewL();
    static CGameController* NewL(const CStreamStore& aStore,
                                 TStreamId aStreamId);
    void SetAppView(CGameAppView* aAppView);
    ~CGameController();

    // Persistence
    TStreamId StoreL(CStreamStore& aStore) const;

    // State
    inline TState State() const;
    inline TBool IsMyTurn() const;
    inline TBool IsFinished() const;
    void SetState(TState aState);
```

```
        // Game control
        void Reset();

        // Zooming
        void ZoomInL();
        void ZoomOutL();

    private:
        // Construct/restore
        void ConstructL();
        void RestoreL(const CStreamStore& aStore, TStreamId aStreamId);

        // Stream persistence
        void ExternalizeL(RWriteStream& aStream) const;
        void InternalizeL(RReadStream& aStream);

        // MGameViewCmdHandler stuff
        void ViewCmdHitFleet(TInt aX, TInt aY);
    public:
        CGameAppView* iAppView;
        CGameEngine* iEngine;

    private:
        // Cached pointers and values
        CEikonEnv* iEnv;

        // Private persistent state
        TState iState;

        // Zoom for internalizing
        TInt iZoomFactor;
        };
```

The controller knows the current game state: it's either my-turn, or finished (in Battleships, there are nine states). There are utility functions for interrogating the state, and for changing it.

Functions related to construction, destruction, and persistence are all provided. These allow you to create a new default document (NewL() on its own), or a new document restored from data on a stream store (NewL() with a stream store parameter). You can also store the document, or delete it.

We saw above that SetAppView() is called after the controller has been constructed, to link it in to the app view, which the controller updates after any model updates.

The controller implements three functions that are executed in response to app UI-originated commands: Reset() starts a new game, while ZoomInL() and ZoomOutL() cycle through zoom states. The controller implements one function in response to view originated commands: ViewCmdHitFleet().

We'll look at construction and persistence later. For now, let's look at how the controller implements commands originated in the app UI and view.

Accessing the EIKON Environment

The controller needs to use the EIKON environment for info-messages and suchlike. Its second-phase constructor includes the line,

```
iEnv = CEikonEnv::Static();
```

which gets the environment pointer from thread-local storage (TLS) and caches it in a handy pointer iEnv. Since TLS accesses are much slower than pointer accesses, this is normal practice for classes that use the EIKON environment.

You don't need to do this for CCoeControl- or CCoeAppUi-derived classes, since they already contain a pointer to the CONE environment (which is also the EIKON environment). The pointer is a protected member variable, iCoeEnv.

A handy #define in eikdef.h is provided to turn this into a pointer to the EIKON environment:

```
#define iEikonEnv (STATIC_CAST(CEikonEnv*, iCoeEnv))
```

This #define isn't exactly kosher C++. Among other undesirable effects of this definition, I *can't* call my own pointer to the EIKON environment iEikonEnv. That's why, following common practice, I chose to call it iEnv instead.

Zooming

Here's the code for ZoomInL():

```
void CGameController::ZoomInL()
    {
    TInt zoom = iZoomFactor;
    zoom =
        zoom < 250 ? 250 :
        zoom < 350 ? 350 :
        zoom < 500 ? 500 :
        zoom < 600 ? 600 :
        zoom < 750 ? 750 :
        zoom < 850 ? 850 :
        zoom < 1000 ? 1000 :
        250;
    iAppView->iOppFleetView->SetZoomL(zoom);
    iAppView->iOppFleetView->DrawNow();
    iZoomFactor = zoom;
    }
```

The controller supports seven levels of zoom here, all fairly arbitrarily chosen. The algorithm is easy to extend to any number of zoom states. Because I wanted to persist the zoom state, it must be a property of the controller: the zoom state in the app view is simply a cached version of the controller's value. I use iZoomFactor to cache the zoom state.

When I have calculated the new zoom state, I call SetZoomL() in the app view to implement the setting, and then DrawNow() to update the view. ZoomOutL() is handled in a similar way.

ViewCmdHitFleet() shows how the controller ties together the two fleets provided by the engine, so that the engine's iOppFleet is what I see on the screen, while the engine's iMyFleet is the real data for the 'opponent's' fleet.

```
void CGameController::ViewCmdHitFleet(TInt aX, TInt aY)
    {
    __ASSERT_ALWAYS(IsMyTurn(), Panic(EHitFleetNotMyTurn));

    // Check whether already known
    if(iEngine->iOppFleet.IsKnown(aX, aY))
        {
        iEnv->InfoMsg(R_GAME_ALREADY_KNOWN);
        return;
        }

    // Hit fleet
    iEngine->iOppFleet.SetShipType(aX, aY, iEngine->iMyFleet.ShipType(aX, aY));
    iEngine->iOppFleet.SetHit(aX,aY);

    // Update view
    iAppView->iOppFleetView->DrawTilesNow();

    // If game is won, transition to finished
    if(iEngine->IsWon())
        {
        SetState(EFinished);
        iEnv->InfoMsg(R_GAME_CONGRATULATIONS);
        }
    }
```

Firstly, the controller asserts that it has been called in the right circumstances. The view should be dimmed if it's not my turn to play, so it should be impossible for this function to be called. But just in case I forgot to dim the view, or just in case I didn't implement `OfferKeyEventL()` properly in `CGameAppView`, or because of some other problem I didn't think of – those are usually the worst kinds of problem! – I make this assertion so the program can quickly panic if it gets called in the wrong circumstances.

We'll see when we get to the Battleships version of the controller, with nine states and *many* functions that are only valid in certain states, that these assertions are extremely useful.

If the square I tried to hit is already known, then I issue an info-message and return: there is no point in taking this any further. Otherwise, I use two simple lines to transfer the knowledge of the real fleet from 'my fleet' to the opponent's fleet, and to say I hit that square:

```
iEngine->iOppFleet.SetShipType(aX, aY, iEngine->iMyFleet.ShipType(aX, aY));
iEngine->iOppFleet.SetHit(aX,aY);
```

If I hit a ship, the engine takes care of ensuring that surrounding squares, on the opponent's fleet, are marked as sea. After this, I update the opponent's fleet view using `DrawTilesNow()`.

Finally, I check whether this means I've won the game. If so, I write an EIKON info-message to say so, and set the state to finished. In real Battleships, the real complexity in the whole game arises from the fact that this line,

```
iEngine->iOppFleet.SetShipType(aX, aY, iEngine->iMyFleet.ShipType(aX, aY));
```

won't work. Instead of simply doing an object look-up, I have to send a message to the real opponent, wait for the response, and meanwhile allow the user of this game to close the file, temporarily or permanently abandon the game, re-send the message in case it got lost, etc.

Updating the State

The `SetState()` function includes the logic needed to dim (or un-dim) the opponent's fleet view, if necessary:

```
void CGameController::SetState(TState aState)
    {
    // Update app view, if needed, for change in 'my turn' status
    if(iAppView)
        {
        if(iState != EMyTurn && aState == EMyTurn)
            iAppView->SetMyTurnAndDrawNow(ETrue);
        else if(iState == EMyTurn && aState != EMyTurn)
            iAppView->SetMyTurnAndDrawNow(EFalse);
        }

    // Set state as requested
    iState = aState;
    }
```

This seems overkill in Solo Ships, but in Battleships the function is essentially the same: it ensures that the app view is kept up to date about whether or not it's my turn, however many states there are in the controller.

The App UI

Now we've reviewed the engine, view, and controller, we can return to the app UI. Back in Chapter 9, I described the app UI as if it was the main class in an EIKON application. In a way, that's true: the entire menu tree of any EIKON application is handled through the app UI, and in a typical large application, that amounts to a lot of commands.

But we now have another perspective on the app UI: it is just another source of events to be handled by the controller. This isn't an incompatible statement; it's just a different perspective. Here's the app UI declaration in `appui.h`:

```
class CGameAppUi : public CEikAppUi
    {
public:
    void ConstructL();
    ~CGameAppUi();
private:
    // From CEikAppUi
    void HandleCommandL(TInt aCommand);

    // Commands
    void CmdStartL();
    void CmdZoomInL();
    void CmdZoomOutL();

    // File-based app framework - from CEikAppUi
    TBool ProcessCommandParametersL(TApaCommand aCommand,
            TFileName& aDocumentName, const TDesC& /*aTail*/);
    void HandleModelChangeL();
```

```
private:
    // Uses
    CGameController* iController;

    // Has
    CGameAppView* iAppView;
    };
```

There are no surprises in the command-handling framework. CmdZoomInL() and CmdZoomOutL() are handled by passing them straight to the controller:

```
void CGameAppUi::CmdZoomInL()
    {
    iController->ZoomInL();
    }

void CGameAppUi::CmdZoomOutL()
    {
    iController->ZoomOutL();
    }
```

CmdStartL() checks to see if a game is already in progress, and queries you if so:

```
void CGameAppUi::CmdStartL()
    {
    // user-friendly check
    if(iController->IsMyTurn())
        {
        if(!iEikonEnv->QueryWinL(R_GAME_QUERY_ABANDON))
            return;
        }
    iController->Reset();
    iAppView->iOppFleetView->DrawTilesNow();
    }
```

If the game had finished anyway, or if the user confirmed that they really did want to start a new game, then the app UI asks the controller to reset, and gets the app view to redraw.

Back in Chapter 9, I introduced the resource file as being something quite heavily associated with the app UI. However, Solo Ships doesn't have a toolbar or any dialogs, so its resource file is not enormous. Here it is (minus #includes and suchlike):

```
NAME SHIP

...

RESOURCE RSS_SIGNATURE { }

RESOURCE TBUF { buf="Battleships"; }

RESOURCE EIK_APP_INFO
    {
    menubar=r_game_menubar;
    hotkeys=r_game_hotkeys;
    }
```

```
RESOURCE HOTKEYS r_game_hotkeys
    {
    control=
        {
        HOTKEY { command=EEikCmdExit; key='e'; },
        HOTKEY { command=EEikCmdZoomIn; key='m'; },
        HOTKEY { command=EGameCmdStart; key='n'; }
        };
    shift_control=
        {
        HOTKEY { command=EEikCmdZoomOut; key='m'; }
        };
    }

RESOURCE MENU_BAR r_game_menubar
    {
    titles=
        {
        MENU_TITLE { menu_pane=r_game_file_menu; txt="File"; }
        };
    }

RESOURCE MENU_PANE r_game_file_menu
    {
    items=
        {
        MENU_ITEM { command=EGameCmdStart; txt="New game"; },
        MENU_ITEM { command=EEikCmdExit; txt="Close program"; }
        };
    }

RESOURCE TBUF r_game_reset { buf="Starting new game"; }

RESOURCE TBUF r_game_already_known { buf="Square already known"; }
RESOURCE TBUF r_game_query_abandon { buf="Abandon game and start a new one?"; }
RESOURCE TBUF r_game_congratulations { buf="Congratulations!"; }
```

There are only four hotkeys (zoom in and out, new-game, and exit), and two menu options (new-game and exit). In addition, there are three strings for use in info-messages, and one for use in a query dialog. The hotkeys used here all follow style guide recommendations.

The zoom commands, `EEikCmdZoomIn` and `EEikCmdZoomOut`, are generated by the zoom in and zoom out icons on the sidebar, in addition to these hot keys. The style guide recommends menu items View | Zoom in and View | Zoom out, but I didn't think it was worth it for this application.

The other app UI functions are all related to persistence. I've been saving that topic up for a section of its own, so now's the time to tackle it.

Persistence

Before I go into the details of persistence, let's review the basics. Solo Ships is a **file-based application** in the sense I described in Chapter 7. That means that each instance of Solo Ships is associated with precisely one file, and that you can launch Solo Ships from the Shell by selecting and opening a Solo Ships file (as well as by selecting the application itself).

Not only is Solo Ships file-based, but it's capable of being **embedded**. That means that you can put a Solo Ships object inside, say, a word processor document. In this case, the Solo Ships document isn't loaded from file or saved to file: rather, it's loaded from or saved to an embedded store.

Because Solo Ships is file-based *and* embedding, it's usually more convenient to talk about its **document**-handling capabilities rather than file handling. Even so, the vocabulary is slightly overloaded; 'document' can mean the persistent data in either:

- ❑ An external form, in a direct file store or embedded store
- ❑ An internal form, in the application's document class

Solo Ships supports three document-related operations:

- ❑ Open application with new document
- ❑ Open application with existing document
- ❑ Exit application, and save data to document

The same three operations are required, whether the document is a main document (direct file store) or an embedded document (embedded store).

An EIKON application must have exactly one external document associated with it. Three familiar cases from the Windows world are impossible in EPOC:

- ❑ A blank document called, say, `Document1`, which isn't yet associated with a file. EPOC doesn't allow this, because it complicates the UI when closing the application.
- ❑ No document at all – just the File and Help menus. EPOC doesn't allow this, and doesn't really need it, because application startup is fast enough anyway.
- ❑ Multiple documents, which you can cycle around using the Window menu. If you want multiple documents, you open multiple instances of the application. (Windows itself is now moving away from multiple document applications back towards a single document interface.)

As a user, there are three ways to launch a file-based application from the Shell:

- ❑ From the Extras bar: this either switches to a running instance of the application, or opens a new instance if none is already open, or cycles to another instance of the application if one instance is already in foreground and multiple instances are active. If possible, the document that was previously being edited is launched. Otherwise, a new document is created.
- ❑ From the file browser, an existing file is launched: this either opens a new instance of the application, or causes the currently running instance of the application to save its data and switch files to the newly opened file.
- ❑ From the shell, you can ask to launch an application with a new file: this either opens a new instance of the application, or causes the currently-running instance of the application to save its data and switch files to the newly created file.

The switch-file behavior is designed for low-memory environments. From the perspective of most users, the only difference between an application switching files, and having multiple open instances of the same application, is a small difference in performance.

The net effect of the rules above is that creating files, and switching between them, is very intuitive on an EPOC machine, even for users who normally have difficulty with file systems.

Fortunately for the programmer, the Shell and application framework handle most of this. As an application programmer, you have to implement:

❑ Store and restore functions for your document

❑ New default document, new restored document, and a C++ destructor for your document

You also need to make sure you tackle the important boundaries mentioned above, so that:

❑ Your app UI can connect to a new document

❑ Your document can save and load without relying on the app UI

Store and Restore

A key motivator of the stream and store APIs introduced in Chapter 7 was to allow object embedding using the same code to save data both to main documents and embedded documents. The application architecture also dictates the form used for application stores. Here is the format we saw for the Boss puzzle:

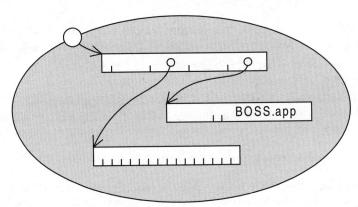

The store consists of a stream dictionary, in which UIDs are used to index an application identifier stream, and a stream containing application data. In the case of Solo Ships, we'll use a different application identifier, and different application data – but the principle is the same.

The application architecture and EIKON work together to call your document's StoreL() and RestoreL() functions when needed to store and restore documents from document stores. You have to supply code for storing the document data streams: the application architecture handles the app identifier stream for you.

Document Responsibilities

CGameDocument contains the basic functions you need to store and restore document data. Here's StoreL():

```
void CGameDocument::StoreL(CStreamStore& aStore,
                           CStreamDictionary& aStreamDict) const
    {
    TStreamId id = iController->StoreL(aStore);
    aStreamDict.AssignL(KUidExample,id);
    }
```

You get a stream store, which can be either an embedded store or a direct file store. This code uses `iController->StoreL()` to store the controller's data to the stream, and returns the stream ID of the stream so created. The next line associates the stream ID with a UID, in the document's stream dictionary. That's all you need to do.

There's also a corresponding `RestoreL()`:

```
void CGameDocument::RestoreL(const CStreamStore& aStore,
                             const CStreamDictionary& aStreamDict)
    {
    // New controller initialized from store
    TStreamId id = aStreamDict.At(KUidExample);
    CGameController* controller = CGameController::NewL(aStore, id);
    delete iController;
    iController = controller;
    }
```

This time, you look up the stream ID in the dictionary, and restore from it. There's a complication here, though. Instead of calling `iController->RestoreL()`, to overwrite the data in the controller, I construct an entirely new controller by using `CGameController::NewL(aStore, id)`. After I've constructed the new one successfully, I delete the old one, replacing it with the new controller.

As I observed in Chapter 7, this is a common pattern: for complicated objects, make the constructor semantics of `RestoreL()` explicit.

> *Applications may store more than one stream using the stream dictionary provided. Many applications use this to store different kinds of data.*

Storing the Controller Data

The document just passed the buck to the controller. Here's how the controller stores its data:

```
TStreamId CGameController::StoreL(CStreamStore& aStore) const
    {
    RStoreWriteStream stream;
    TStreamId id = stream.CreateLC(aStore);
    iEngine->ExternalizeL(stream);
    ExternalizeL(stream);
    stream.CommitL();
    CleanupStack::PopAndDestroy(); // stream
    return id;
    }
```

The idea here is to get a stream, externalize both the engine and any controller data to it, and then close the stream.

The engine's `ExternalizeL()` function looks like this:

```
void CGameEngine::ExternalizeL(RWriteStream& aStream) const
    {
    aStream << iMyFleet;
    aStream << iOppFleet;
    aStream.WriteUint8L(iFirstPlayer);
    }
```

This in turn calls the fleet's `ExternalizeL()`, twice:

```
void TFleet::ExternalizeL(RWriteStream& aStream) const
    {
    for(TInt i = 0; i < 64; i++)
        aStream.WriteUint8L(iSquares[i]);
    aStream.WriteUint8L(iMyFleet);
    for(i = 0; i < 10; i++)
        aStream << iShips[i];
    aStream.WriteInt8L(iKnownShips);
    aStream.WriteInt8L(iRemainingShips);
    aStream.WriteInt8L(iRemainingSquares);
    aStream.WriteInt8L(iSquaresHit);
    }
```

And this, in sequence, calls the ship's `ExternalizeL()`, ten times:

```
void TShip::ExternalizeL(RWriteStream& aStream) const
    {
    aStream.WriteUint8L(iType);
    aStream.WriteInt8L(iLength);
    aStream.WriteInt8L(iRemaining);
    aStream.WriteInt8L(iStartX);
    aStream.WriteInt8L(iStartY);
    aStream.WriteInt8L(iDx);
    aStream.WriteInt8L(iDy);
    }
```

Finally the controller itself externalizes some extra persistent data: namely, its state and the current zoom factor:

```
void CGameController::ExternalizeL(RWriteStream& aStream) const
    {
    aStream.WriteUint8L(iState);
    aStream.WriteInt32L(iZoomFactor);
    }
```

In all the code above, I use << stream insertion operators where I can. But I use `WriteXxxL()` operators where I have to, to specify the size of the integers and enumerations written to the stream — usually, 8 bits is sufficient.

EPOC allows me to optimize the external format to suit the properties of the data. So I am able to cut down what would otherwise have been quite a large file format to just 337 bytes.

Restoring the Controller Data

We saw that document's `RestoreL()` uses the controller's restoring `NewL()`, which is coded as follows:

```
CGameController* CGameController::NewL(const CStreamStore& aStore,
                                       TStreamId aStreamId)
    {
    CGameController* self = new(ELeave) CGameController;
    CleanupStack::PushL(self);
    self->RestoreL(aStore, aStreamId);
    CleanupStack::Pop();
    return self;
    }
```

`RestoreL()` is private, like `ConstructL()`, so that it can't be accidentally called by `CGameController`'s clients. Here it is:

```
void CGameController::RestoreL(const CStreamStore& aStore, TStreamId aStreamId)
    {
    iEnv = CEikonEnv::Static();
    RStoreReadStream stream;
    stream.OpenLC(aStore,aStreamId);
    iEngine = new(ELeave) CGameEngine;
    iEngine->InternalizeL(stream);
    InternalizeL(stream);
    CleanupStack::PopAndDestroy(); // stream
    }
```

The first task is to get an EIKON environment pointer. That's needed by the controller, whether it's constructing from scratch, or restoring from a document.

The engine is such a simple object that I haven't implemented a restoring constructor for it: instead, for the engine, I follow `new(ELeave)` by `InternalizeL()`.

The `InternalizeL()` functions are pretty-well the reverse of the `ExternalizeL()` functions we've already seen: they add little that's new, so I'll move quickly on.

Creating a Default Document

When the application is opened with a new file, it can't restore from anything, so instead it creates a new default document. That's an important responsibility of the application class:

```
CApaDocument* CGameApplication::CreateDocumentL()
    {
    CGameDocument* doc = new(ELeave) CGameDocument(*this);
    CleanupStack::PushL(doc);
    doc->ConstructL();
    CleanupStack::Pop();
    return doc;
    }
```

The document second-phase constructor creates a new controller:

```
void CGameDocument::ConstructL()
    {
    iController = CGameController::NewL();
    }
```

This uses the conventional NewL(), which constructs a default controller, rather than restoring one from file.

App UI Magic

Finally, we need some magic in the app UI to tie together file-based and embedding operations. Most importantly, the command handler for EEikCmdExit which, in all our applications until now, has just called Exit(), now includes SaveL():

```
void CGameAppUi::HandleCommandL(TInt aCommand)
    {
    switch (aCommand)
        {
    case EEikCmdExit:
        SaveL();
        Exit();
        break;
    ...
        }
    }
```

This calls CEikAppUi::SaveL(), which ensures that the framework saves the document data. In the app UI, you have to implement a HandleModelChangeL() function to update everything when the a new document is loaded and there is a consequent change in the MVC model:

```
void CGameAppUi::HandleModelChangeL()
    {
    // Change pointers to new objects
    iController = (STATIC_CAST(CGameDocument*, Document()))->iController;
    iAppView->SetController(iController);
#if 0
    // There's no toolbar, so no need for this standard copy-and-paste code
    // Update file name
    iEikonEnv->UpdateTaskNameL();
    CEikFileNameLabel* filenameLabel = STATIC_CAST(CEikFileNameLabel*,
            iToolBar->ControlById(EGameControlIdFileNameLabel));
    filenameLabel->UpdateL();
    filenameLabel->DrawNow();
#endif
    }
```

First, I use the document to find out my new controller, and then I pass on this information to the app view. Without this, you won't keep the app UI and app view up-to-date when the model changes.

I've #ifed out some code which appears in 99% of HandleModelChangeL() functions: if there is a toolbar, this code updates the file name label, at the top of the toolbar. Perhaps #if is a little brutal; a simple test of:

```
if(iToolBar) ...
```

would have been good enough for any application, including those that allow the toolbar to be turned on and off.

If your application is embedded, you have to inform the framework when your application exits. Here's the code you have to include, in the app UI's destructor:

```
CGameAppUi::~CGameAppUi()
    {
    delete iAppView;
    if(iDoorObserver)
        iDoorObserver->NotifyExit(MApaEmbeddedDocObserver::EKeepChanges);
    }
```

Finally, the framework specifies a virtual ProcessCommandParametersL() function and provides a default implementation for use in file-based applications. You have to code a trivial function to link these two together:

```
TBool CGameAppUi::ProcessCommandParametersL(TApaCommand aCommand,
                                            TFileName& aDocumentName,
                                            const TDesC& /*aTail*/)
    {
    return CEikAppUi::ProcessCommandParametersL(aCommand, aDocumentName);
    }
```

You don't need this function for non-file-based applications. For applications which process non-native EPOC formats, this function allows more tailored processing. However, for native applications, it always has this form.

AIF Specifications

Embeddable applications must have an AIF because, without one, applications are considered to be unembeddable.

You'll find the source materials for Solo Ships' AIF in \pep\bsaif1\. There are the usual bitmaps, a baif.bat file, and a resource script called bships1.rss – the same name as the application's resource script, which is why I put all the AIF material into a different directory. The resource script reads:

```
// bships1.rss
//
// Copyright (c) 2000 Symbian Ltd. All rights reserved.

#include <aiftool.rh>
```

```
RESOURCE AIF_DATA
    {
    num_icons = 3;
    app_uid = 0x10005cee;
    newfile = KAppSupportsNewFile;
    embeddability = KAppEmbeddable;
    caption_list =
        {
        CAPTION { code=ELangEnglish; caption="Solo Ships"; },
        CAPTION { code=ELangAmerican; caption="Solo Ships"; },
        CAPTION { code=ELangGerman; caption="Flotte 1"; },
        CAPTION { code=ELangItalian; caption="Flotta 1"; }
        };
    }
```

The interesting lines here are

❑ `newfile = KAppSupportsNewFile`, which says the application in built in such a way that it can switch files, when requested to do so by the shell, without closing down

❑ `embeddability = KAppEmbeddable` speaks for itself

Summary

In this chapter I've described a larger-scale EIKON application that shows some important aspects about writing real EIKON code:

❑ How to support persistence – for file-based and embedded applications

❑ How to provide a size independent view, and how to zoom it

❑ The value of the MVC paradigm for a larger application

Out of habit, and because of Symbian vocabulary that's been established for a long time, I've used 'engine' instead of model.

With this chapter, I've written all I'm going to on EIKON and file-based persistence. The SDK includes good examples of EIKON applications implementing more file-related operations: see `\epoc32ex\eikfile\` examples, and commentary.

The full version of Battleships will add to the framework established by Solo Ships. Battleships adds

❑ A little more EIKON functionality – in terms of dialogs whose code we've already seen, in Chapter 10

❑ A lot more communications and system programming, which is the subject of Chapter 16 thru Chapter 22 of this book

However, Battleships isn't going to add much more in terms of developing our understanding of EIKON.

In this chapter, I've introduced size-independent views, twips, font specs, and the screen device. In the next chapter, I'll move on to describe EPOC's device-independent graphics facilities in more detail.

15

The Quest for Device Independence

I have a piano arrangement of *Tubular Bells* by Mike Oldfield, which topped the British album charts throughout 1975-1976. It was originally produced on a vast range of instruments, all played by Oldfield himself, and electronically mixed. The piano arrangement uses only a single instrument, and it works reasonably well: it's easily recognizable as *Tubular Bells* and, like the original, it's hauntingly moving.

I don't know, on the other hand, whether anyone has yet tried to arrange Beethoven's Fifth Symphony for guitar. I suppose you could do *something* with it, but it would be impossible to play, and no one would get excited about the result. In any case, I can think of much better things to do with a guitar.

Musicians compose and arrange for instruments. Programmers write and port to devices and software systems. It's certainly worth trying to write code and applications in such a way that they can be ported widely, with as little code change as possible, preserving as much as possible of whatever it was that got people excited about the original. But it may not always be possible or even sensible: sometimes, new devices demand new applications, not just ports of old ones.

Attaining full portability and device independence is a Holy Grail of programming: no matter how long we remain on the quest, we never quite attain it. Sometimes, we think we're doing pretty well: we learn a few things along the way; we meet interesting fellow travelers; we make real achievements. But the journey continues.

In this chapter, I'll cover three types of device independence:

❑ Size-independent drawing: screens on different devices are different sizes, and it's nice to be able to re-size application views if possible. Size independence is closely related to zooming, which we saw how to do in the last chapter.

❑ Device-independent drawing: the screen isn't the only interesting device. Many applications need to be able to print. An embedded application with a glass door needs to be able to draw onto whatever device its embedding application is drawing – which may be either a screen or a printer. And there are many different types of printer.

❑ Device-independent user interfaces: a GUI requires not just on-screen drawing, but interaction as well. CONE's principles of pointer and key distribution, focus, and dimming, which I described in Chapter 12, can be used for any GUI. But the way EIKON builds on CONE is optimized for a particular device and its targeted end-users. It turns out that the design of the GUI, as a whole, is heavily dependent on device characteristics.

EPOC's graphics design inherited 10 years of experience of size-independent GUIs in SIBO, which had on the whole worked well. SIBO added printing late in the product cycle, with substantial changes to all components that supported printing: EPOC designed in device independence drawing from the beginning, so that components could be written to print or draw to screen.

Symbian's quest for device independence is now focused on device-independent GUIs. EIKON has been adapted for Psion's Revo (smaller than the 640x240 design size) and netBook (larger, and using a color screen). The forthcoming Quartz reference design has a 240x320 screen, a couple of buttons, but no keyboard: this is so different from EIKON's original design parameters that we have had to replace EIKON altogether.

The GUI as a whole is clearly device dependent: how much of an application, of the GUI system, and of the GUI itself, can we make device independent? That's a critical question, and I'll close this chapter by addressing it.

Device-independent Drawing

The main purpose of the drawing example is to demonstrate how to do device-independent drawing. Here's a screenshot:

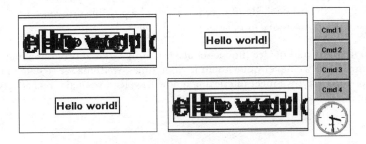

As you can see, this is based on the helloeik example. The screenshot also shows how *not* to do zooming – I'll come back to that later.

Here's the application structure:

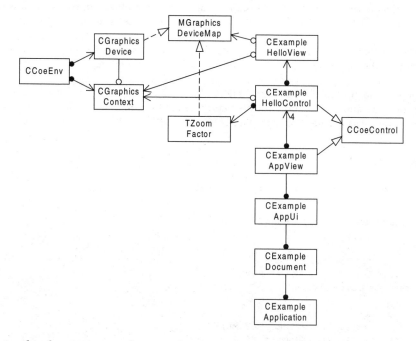

The app view has four instances of CExampleHelloControl, and in turn each control has its own CExampleHelloView, which does the drawing.

CExampleAppView and CExampleHelloControl are both controls – they are derived from CCoeControl. Controls are for on-screen interaction, so by definition they are device dependent. But there's no reason why a control shouldn't use a device-independent view to do its drawing. That's what happens here: CExampleHelloView is *not* a control, but is a class with drawing functions that just uses a graphics context (for drawing functions) and a graphics device map (for access to a graphics device's scaling functions).

The **graphics device map** is an interface that is implemented by two classes in EPOC: a graphics device itself, and a zoom factor. By coding device-independent classes to use a graphics device map, they get zooming for free.

The TZoomFactor is a bizarrely elegant class that both implements a graphics device map, and uses a class that implements a graphics device map:

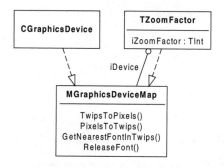

That means a TZoomFactor can use a graphics device, or it can use another zoom factor, multiplying the zooming effect of that zoom factor. This allows an embedded object, drawn as a glass door, to apply its own zoom factor, which scales along with the zoom factor of the embedding object.

CExampleHelloControl has a TZoomFactor, which uses the screen device. It passes this TZoomFactor as the device map parameter to the view's draw function.

You can find the code in \pep\drawing\. I'll assume by now that you're familiar enough with EIKON application structure and compound controls that I needn't describe the four main application classes in detail. Instead, I'll focus on the CExampleHelloView and CExampleHelloControl classes.

The View

The role of the view class is to draw the text to any device. Here is its declaration:

```
class CExampleHelloView : public CBase
    {
public:
    // Construct/destruct
    static CExampleHelloView* NewL();
    ~CExampleHelloView();

    // Settings
    void SetTextL(const TDesC& aText);
    void SetFullRedraw(TBool aFullRedraw);

    // Draw
    void DrawL(MGraphicsDeviceMap& aMap, CGraphicsContext& aGc,
               const TRect& aDeviceRect) const;
private:
    void ConstructL();
private:
    HBufC* iText;
    TBool iFullRedraw;
    };
```

Firstly, note that it's derived from CBase, not CCoeControl. No CCoeControl-derived class can be device-independent, because controls are heavily tied to the screen. Another hint at its intended device independence is the DrawL() function, which takes a device map, a graphics context, and a rectangle in which to draw. I'll explain the significance of these parameters shortly. The rest of the class consists of just a constructor, settings, and a destructor.

DrawL() is divided into four sections:

❑   Allocate a font for drawing text

❑   Draw the text

❑   Draw an outline

❑   Release the font

Device-independent and Device-dependent Line Drawing

However, it's easiest to start by looking at the part that draws an outline:

```
void CExampleHelloView::DrawL(MGraphicsDeviceMap& aMap,
                              CGraphicsContext& aGc,
                              const TRect& aDeviceRect) const
    {
    // Get font for drawing
    ...

    // Draw some text
    ...

    // Draw a surrounding rectangle
    TSize surroundSizeInTwips(1440,360);     // 1" x 1/4" surrounding box
    TSize surroundSize;
    surroundSize.iWidth =
        aMap.HorizontalTwipsToPixels(surroundSizeInTwips.iWidth);
    surroundSize.iHeight =
        aMap.VerticalTwipsToPixels(surroundSizeInTwips.iHeight);
    TRect surround(TPoint(aDeviceRect.Center().iX - surroundSize.iWidth / 2,
                   aDeviceRect.Center().iY - surroundSize.iHeight / 2),
                   surroundSize);
    aGc.SetBrushStyle(CGraphicsContext::ENullBrush);
    aGc.SetClippingRect(aDeviceRect);
    aGc.SetPenColor(KRgbDarkGray);
    aGc.DrawRect(surround);
    surround.Grow(1, 1);
    aGc.SetPenColor(KRgbBlack);
    aGc.DrawRect(surround);

    // Release the font
    ...
    }
```

The purpose of this code is to draw a box one-inch wide by one-quarter inch high. The box is slightly fancy: it is two pixels wide, dark gray on the 'inside' and black on the 'outside'.

All GC drawing functions are specified in pixels. So, before I can draw the rectangle, I have to convert the size I wanted, specified in twips, to a size in pixels. I do this using the twips-to-pixels functions of the device map. After some tedious centering arithmetic, I have a rectangle of the required size, centered in aDeviceRect.

Then I have a problem: I can't be sure that this surround rectangle is actually contained entirely within aDeviceRect, and I should not draw outside aDeviceRect. There is no guarantee, either on screen or another device, that drawing will be clipped to aDeviceRect. But because I need that guarantee here, I set up a clipping rectangle explicitly.

I draw the inner line and then use Grow(1, 1) to expand the rectangle by a single pixel in all directions, and draw the outer line.

Even device independent drawing code must take device realities into account.

In the previous chapter, we saw that we had to take rounding errors into account when sizing the grid for the Solo Ships fleet view.

Here, I am taking device realities into account in a different way. Although I calculate the size of the surround rectangle beginning with twips units, I do the expansion explicitly in pixels. Whatever display I draw this rectangle to, I want it to consist of a two pixel border: two lines spaced apart by a certain number of *twips* would overlap at small zoom states, and be spaced apart at large zoom states.

In general, taking device realities into account means you'll be careful about the order in which you calculate things, about how you address rounding errors, and about what you do in twips, and what you do in pixels.

Getting a Font

I wanted to draw the message in 12-point Arial bold text. '12-point Arial bold' is a device-independent way of specifying a font. What I needed to do was get a device-dependent font that meets this specification, taking into account the current device and zoom state.

Here's the code:

```
// Get font for drawing
TFontSpec fontSpec(_L("Arial"), 12 * 20);
fontSpec.iFontStyle =
    TFontStyle(EPostureUpright, EStrokeWeightBold, EPrintPosNormal);
CFont* font;
User::LeaveIfError(aMap.GetNearestFontInTwips(font, fontSpec));
```

The key function here is GetNearestFontInTwips(), a member function of MGraphicsDeviceMap. You pass a device-independent **font specification** (a TFontSpec) to this function, and you get back a pointer to device-dependent **font** (a CFont*).

This function usually finds a match but, in the unlikely case that it doesn't, it returns an error code: I trap this with User::LeaveIfError(), which is why the whole draw function can leave. We've already seen that CCoeControl::Draw() is non-leaving, so the prospect of calling a potentially-leaving DrawL() from Draw() should set alarm bells ringing. I'll return to that later.

The font specification uses the TFontSpec class, defined by the GDI, in gdi.h. Here's its declaration:

```
class TFontSpec
    {
public:
    IMPORT_C TFontSpec();
    IMPORT_C TFontSpec(const TDesC& aTypefaceName, TInt aHeight);
    IMPORT_C TBool operator==(const TFontSpec& aFontSpec) const;
    IMPORT_C void InternalizeL(RReadStream& aStream);
    IMPORT_C void ExternalizeL(RWriteStream& aStream) const;
public:
    TTypeface iTypeface;
    TInt iHeight;
    TFontStyle iFontStyle;
    };
```

A font specification consists of a typeface, a height, and a font style. The TTypeface class is also defined by the GDI. It has several attributes, of which the most important is the name.

When you use GetNearestFontInTwips(), the height is expected to be in twips: though some devices support a GetNearestFontInPixels() function that allows the height to be specified in pixels.

The font style covers **posture** (upright or italic), **stroke weight** (bold or normal), and **print position** (normal, subscript, or superscript).

> *Other font attributes, such as underline and strikethrough, aren't font attributes at all — they're drawing effects, and you can apply them using the CGraphicsContext functions.*

TFontSpec has a handy constructor that I used above for specifying 12-point Arial in a single statement. It also has a default constructor and assignment operator. Finally, TFontSpec has ExternalizeL() and InternalizeL() functions. These are important: a rich text object, for instance, may contain many TFontSpecs, and it must be able to externalize them when storing, and re-internalize them when restoring.

Drawing the Text

Originally, I used exactly the same code as I had used for helloeik (with aGc instead of gc, and aDeviceRect instead of rect):

```
// Draw some text
aGc.SetPenStyle(CGraphicsContext::ESolidPen);
aGc.SetPenColor(KRgbBlack);
aGc.UseFont(font);
TInt baseline = aDeviceRect.Height() / 2 + font->AscentInPixels() / 2;
aGc.DrawText(*iText, aDeviceRect, baseline, CGraphicsContext::ECenter);
aGc.DiscardFont();
```

This uses the device-dependent font we just allocated, and the version of DrawText() that specifies a rectangle, and guarantees that drawing will be clipped within that rectangle.

However, this code doesn't white out the background of aDeviceRect. So, if you change the zoom state and redraw the view, the text (and surrounding rectangle) from the previous zoom state are not overwritten. That's the reason for the confusion in the screenshot of our example.

So, before this text, I added the code:

```
if(iFullRedraw)
    {
    aGc.SetBrushStyle(CGraphicsContext::ESolidBrush);
    aGc.SetBrushColor(KRgbWhite);
    }
```

In a real program, this code would not be conditional! But I made it conditional here for fun, so you can easily see what happens if we forget full redraw.

Text and Device Independence

TFontSpec is a device-independent font specification whose format is completely exposed to you as an application programmer, and which you can save in your documents. CFont* refers to a device-dependent font, whose format you don't need to know and, for the majority of programmers, is not of much interest.

The mapping from TFontSpec to CFont* is ultimately handled by a graphics device (though the font specification may be zoomed by a zoom factor). Once you have a CFont*, you can only use it on the device that allocated it – more precisely, you can only use it for drawing through a GC to the device that allocated it.

When you no longer need a CFont*, you *must* ask the device to release it. So our DrawL() ends with

```
    // Release the font
    aMap.ReleaseFont(font);
```

If you forget to release a font, the effect will be the same as a memory leak: your program will get panicked on exit from emulator debug builds.

When you get a font through a device map, the device map chooses a pixel size for the font, and maps twips to pixels in just the same way as it would map twips to pixels with VerticalTwipsToPixels() (you specify a font's *height*, remember). So fonts and other graphics scale proportionately when you apply different zoom factors.

There's a problem with small fonts, though: they can't get smaller than one pixel! So at very low zoom factors, you'll see the following effect:

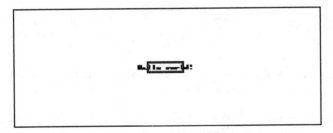

Again, we can see that device-independent code cannot escape the realities of real devices. EPOC's rich text view class understands small zoom factors and handles this case properly. EPOC's print preview effectively prints to the screen in extremely low zoom state. The print preview device understands that most characters at that zoom state are less than a single pixel. Most strings are a straight line whose length is best calculated by adding up the letter sizes in *twips*, and then translating into pixels, rather than using a single pixel per letter.

Using the View

CExampleHelloControl *has-a* CExampleHelloView, which it uses for drawing its model. Here's CExampleHelloControl::Draw():

```
void CExampleHelloControl::Draw(const TRect& /*aRect*/) const
    {
    CWindowGc& gc = SystemGc();
    TRect rect = Rect();
    rect.Shrink(10,10);
    gc.SetPenStyle(CGraphicsContext::ENullPen);
    gc.SetBrushStyle(CGraphicsContext::ESolidBrush);
    gc.SetBrushColor(KRgbWhite);
    EikDrawUtils::DrawBetweenRects(gc, Rect(), rect);
    gc.SetPenStyle(CGraphicsContext::ESolidPen);
    gc.SetPenColor(KRgbBlack);
    gc.SetBrushStyle(CGraphicsContext::ENullBrush);
    gc.DrawRect(rect);
    rect.Shrink(1,1);
    TRAPD(err, iView->DrawL(CONST_CAST(TZoomFactor&, iZoomFactor), gc, rect));
    }
```

First, CExampleHelloControl draws a surrounding 10-pixel border. This code is guaranteed to be on a screen, and the 10-pixel border is chosen independent of the zoom state (think about it: it would look silly if the border scales to honor the zoom state).

This time, I'm careful to draw every pixel: I use EikDrawUtils::DrawBetweenRects() to white out the region between the area painted by the view, and the border of the control. I then use the pen draw around the border, shrink by a pixel and offer the rectangle inside the pen outline to be drawn by the view.

It would be nice if I could simply call:

```
iView->Draw(iZoomFactor, gc, rect);
```

Instead, I have an ugly trap and a CONST_CAST():

```
TRAPD(err, iView->DrawL(CONST_CAST(TZoomFactor&, iZoomFactor), gc, rect));
```

This is necessary because GetNearestFontInTwips() and ReleaseFont() are non-const members of MGraphicsDeviceMap (from which TZoomFactor is derived), and because GetNearestFontInTwips() can potentially return an error, which I handle in DrawL() by leaving.

Ultimately, then, the reason for the ugliness in this function call is because I'm allocating resources while drawing. This is bad practice, which is why I have to trap and cast my way around the problems it causes.

> To make the code given in the drawing example truly suitable for large-scale use, I would have to pre-allocate a font on construction, change it if necessary on destruction, and change it when necessary in response to zoom state changes. This would introduce extra housekeeping.

But the fundamental point that this example does show is that you can implement drawing code that's completely independent of a control, and completely independent of the screen device.

Managing the Zoom Factor

We have already seen that:

❑   The view uses a device map to get fonts and do twips-to-pixels mappings

❑   The control passes a zoom factor to the view, as its device map

And we have already claimed that a device map ultimately uses a real device.

CExampleHelloControl shows how the zoom factor relates to the device. Here's the declaration of TZoomFactor in gdi.h:

```
class TZoomFactor : public MGraphicsDeviceMap
    {
public:
    IMPORT_C TZoomFactor();
    IMPORT_C ~TZoomFactor();
    inline TZoomFactor(const MGraphicsDeviceMap* aDevice);
    IMPORT_C TInt ZoomFactor() const;
    IMPORT_C void SetZoomFactor(TInt aZoomFactor);
    inline void SetGraphicsDeviceMap(const MGraphicsDeviceMap* aDevice);
    inline const MGraphicsDeviceMap* GraphicsDeviceMap() const;
    IMPORT_C void SetTwipToPixelMapping(const TSize& aSizeInPixels,
                                        const TSize& aSizeInTwips);
    IMPORT_C TInt HorizontalTwipsToPixels(TInt aTwipWidth) const;
    IMPORT_C TInt VerticalTwipsToPixels(TInt aTwipHeight) const;
    IMPORT_C TInt HorizontalPixelsToTwips(TInt aPixelWidth) const;
    IMPORT_C TInt VerticalPixelsToTwips(TInt aPixelHeight) const;
    IMPORT_C TInt GetNearestFontInTwips(CFont*& aFont,
                                        const TFontSpec& aFontSpec);
    IMPORT_C void ReleaseFont(CFont* aFont);
public:
    enum {EZoomOneToOne = 1000};
private:
    TInt iZoomFactor;
    const MGraphicsDeviceMap* iDevice;
    };
```

TZoomFactor both implements MGraphicsDeviceMap's interface, and uses a MGraphicsDeviceMap. TZoomFactor contains an integer, iZoomFactor, which is set to 1000 to indicate a one-to-one zoom, and proportionately for any other zoom factor.

In order to implement a function such as VerticalTwipsToPixels(), TZoomFactor uses code like this:

```
EXPORT_C TInt TZoomFactor::VerticalTwipsToPixels(TInt aTwipHeight) const
    {
    return iDevice->VerticalTwipsToPixels((aTwipHeight * iZoomFactor) / 1000);
    }
```

`TZoomFactor` scales the arguments before passing the function call on to its `MGraphicsDeviceMap`. Other functions combine the zoom and conversion between pixels and twips:

- ❑ A pixels-to-twips function scales *after* calling pixels-to-twips on the device map
- ❑ A get-nearest-font function scales the font's point size before calling get-nearest-font on the device map

The function names in `TZoomFactor` indicate several ways to set the zoom factor. The method I use in `CExampleHelloControl` is the most obvious one,

```
void CExampleHelloControl::SetZoom(TInt aZoomFactor)
    {
    iZoomFactor.SetZoomFactor(aZoomFactor);
    }
```

and `GetZoom()` works the other way round:

```
TInt CExampleHelloControl::GetZoom() const
    {
    return iZoomFactor.ZoomFactor();
    }
```

The `SetZoomIn()` function works like `CFleetView::SetZoomInL()` in the previous chapter:

```
void CExampleHelloControl::SetZoomIn()
    {
    TInt zoom = GetZoom();
    zoom =
        zoom < 250  ? 250  :
        zoom < 500  ? 500  :
        zoom < 1000 ? 1000 :
        zoom < 1500 ? 1500 :
        zoom < 2000 ? 2000 :
        zoom < 3000 ? 3000 :
        250;
    SetZoom(zoom);
    }
```

`SetZoomOut()` works the other way round. The rest of `CExampleHelloControl` is the usual kind of housekeeping that, by now, should hold few surprises. See the source code for the full details.

Views and Re-use

`CExampleHelloView` is a device-independent view: it contains no dependencies at all on any screen device. That means it can be re-used in some interesting contexts — especially glass doors and printing.

EPOC contains other views that are designed in a manner similar to `CExampleHelloView`. The best example of this is rich text views, delivered by the `CTextView` class in EPOC's FORM component.

Glass Doors

CExampleHelloView could be used in object embedding to implement a glass door. The GDI specifies a CPicture class (see gdi.h), from which any application's glass door must be derived. CPicture includes a key virtual function:

```
virtual void Draw(CGraphicsContext& aGc,
                  const TPoint& aTopLeft,
                  const TRect& aClipRect,
                  MGraphicsDeviceMap* aMap) const = 0;
```

In a derived class, you could implement this by calling this view's DrawL(), using code such as:

```
void CMyGlassDoor::Draw(CGraphicsContext& aGc, const TPoint& aTopLeft,
                        const TRect& /* aClipRect */, MGraphicsDeviceMap* aMap);
    {
    TSize size;
    GetOriginalSizeInTwips(size);
    size.iWidth = aMap->HorizontalTwipsToPixels(size.iWidth);
    size.iHeight = aMap->VerticalTwipsToPixels(size.iHeight);
    TRAPD(err, iView->DrawL(*aMap, aGc, TRect(aTopLeft, size)));
    }
```

In the C++ SDK, the Boss Puzzle provides example code that you can use to implement a complete glass door. See code in \boss\eik4\.

Printing

CExampleHelloView could also be used for printing and print preview, without any changes. The GDI specifies a conventional banded printing model that contains, at its heart, an interface class with a single virtual function:

```
class MPageRegionPrinter
    {
public:
    virtual void PrintBandL(CGraphicsDevice* aDevice,
                            TInt aPageNo
                            const TBandAttributes& aBandInPixels) = 0;
    };
```

TBandAttributes is defined as:

```
class TBandAttributes
    {
public:
    TRect iRect;
    TBool iTextIsIgnored;
    TBool iGraphicsIsIgnored;
    TBool iFirstBandOnPage;
    };
```

If you want your application to support printing, use EIKON dialogs to set up a print job and start printing. You need to write a class that implements `MPageRegionPrinter`, and then pass a pointer to it (an `MPageRegionPrinter*`) to the print job. The printer driver then calls your `PrintBandL()` as often as necessary to do the job.

The way in which a driver calls `PrintBandL()` depends on the characteristics of the printer. Clearly, the driver calls `PrintBandL()` at least once per page. Drivers may:

❑ Call `PrintBandL()` exactly once per page, specifying the page number and, in band attributes, a rectangle covering the whole page

❑ Save memory by covering the page in more than one band

❑ Work more efficiently by treating text and graphics separately so that, for instance, all text is covered in one band, while graphics are covered in several small bands.

As the implementer of `PrintBandL()`, you clearly have to honor the page number, so that you print the relevant text on every page.

Whether you take any notice of the band attributes is rather like whether you take any notice of the bounding rectangle passed to `CCoeControl::Draw()`: if you ignore these parameters, your code may work fine. But you may be able to substantially speed printing up by printing only what's necessary for each band.

Anyway, you could re-use the view code in `CExampleHelloView` to implement `PrintBandL()` for a single-page print:

```
void CMyApplication::PrintBandL(CGraphicsDevice* aDevice,
                                TInt /* aPageNo */
                                const TBandAttributes& /* aBandInPixels */)
    {
    CGraphicsContext* gc;
    User::LeaveIfError(aDevice->CreateContext(gc));
    TRect rectInTwips(2880, 2880, 2880, 1440);
    TRect rect(aDevice->HorizontalTwipsToPixels(rectInTwips.iTl.iX),
            aDevice->VerticalTwipsToPixels(rectInTwips.iTl.iY),
            aDevice->HorizontalTwipsToPixels(rectInTwips.iBr.iX),
            aDevice->VerticalTwipsToPixels(rectInTwips.iBr.iY));
    iView->DrawL(*aDevice, *gc, rect);
    delete gc;
    }
```

This prints the text in a rectangle 2x1 inches big, whose top left corner is 2 inches down, 2 inches right, from the edge of the paper – regardless of paper size and margins. More realistic print code would take account of the paper size and margins, which are set up by the EIKON dialogs. See \boss\eik9\ in the C++ SDK for a full example showing how this is done.

This time, it doesn't matter that `DrawL()` leaves, since `PrintBandL()` is allowed to leave too.

The `CGraphicsDevice::CreateContext()` function creates a GC suitable for drawing to the device. It is *the* way to create a graphics context. Calls such as `CCoeControl::SystemGc()` simply get a GC that has been created earlier by the CONE environment, using `iScreenDevice->CreateContext()`.

Rich Text and Other Views

Device-independent views are very powerful. You can use them in three important contexts:

❑ As the drawing code for all or part of a control

❑ As the drawing code for a glass door

❑ As the drawing code for printing – to any kind of printer supported by EPOC, including print preview and 'print via PC'

CExampleHelloView is a rather trivial example of the art. More complex examples are possible. More complex views have to tackle a couple of issues:

❑ They must support graphical interaction

❑ They should pre-allocate resources required for drawing, so that DrawL() can be changed to Draw()

Graphical interaction may require a cursor be maintained, a means to associate pointer events at an (x, y) coordinate with the correct object, and optimized view updates when the model is updated. The Boss Puzzle in the EPOC C++ SDK contains a view that supports graphical interaction, and that pre-allocates its resources so that Draw() cannot leave. See source code in \boss\view3\.

EPOC's own rich text view class is a powerful view, hiding extremely complex functionality underneath a moderately complex API. The CTextView class supports formatting and display of rich text (model objects derived from CEditableText), printing, editing, and very fast on-screen update – enough to allow high-speed typing in documents scores of pages long, even on an 18MHz ARM processor. In the MVC sense, CEditableText is a model, while CTextView is a view with utility functions for a controller. EIKON provides controls derived from CEikEdwin that act as an MVC controller as well as an EPOC control, which application programs can conveniently re-use to edit rich text objects.

Summary of Device-independent Drawing

In the previous chapter, I introduced size-independent drawing. In this section, we have looked at device-independent drawing, using device-independent views. In the MVC sense, the view provides MVC view functionality, and enough hooks for a controller. In the EPOC sense, the view can be used by a control to draw on-screen, but can also be used for other purposes such as glass doors and printing. A more sophisticated view will also support interaction.

The terminology is perhaps a little confused here. 'View' can mean device-independent drawing code, an MVC view, or just a control that happens to major on MVC view functionality, such as an app view or the Battleships fleet view.

It doesn't feel right to use the word 'view' to describe the EIKON debug keys, toolbar, dialog, or even menu, though these are all controls. These controls major on interaction or on MVC controller functionality.

We've also seen that the GDI provides a vital toolkit for device-independent drawing, including the MGraphicsDeviceMap class, graphics devices and zoom factors, and font specs and fonts:

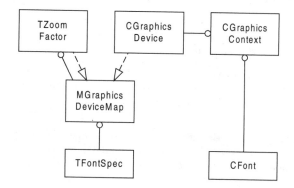

On the left of the figure, there are the device-independent classes, which allow you to operate in the twips domain when you need to:

Class	Description
CGraphicsDevice	The base class for any graphics device. Can manufacture a graphics context suitable for drawing to itself (using CreateContext()). Can manufacture fonts suitable for drawing to itself (using GetNearestFontInTwips() and similar functions). Includes twips-to-pixels mapping functions.
MGraphicsDeviceMap	Defines all the size-dependent functions in a graphics device, including twips-to-pixels conversions and font allocation/release. Used as the base class for both a real graphics device and a zoom factor, so that you can add zoom-friendly code to either, using this class to handle the zooming.
TZoomFactor	Implements MGraphicsDeviceMap. Manipulates the twips-to-pixels and font selection functions of another MGraphicsDeviceMap, to implement zooming.
TFontSpec	A device-independent font specification, supporting a name, point size, and style. In turn, the style includes italic/normal, bold/normal, and superscript/subscript/normal attributes. Other font-related attributes, such as color, underline, and strikethrough, are implemented algorithmically by drawing functions.

On the right hand side meanwhile, there are the device-dependent classes, which require you to operate in the pixel domain of the appropriate graphics device:

Class	Description
CGraphicsContext	The base class for all graphics contexts. Includes drawing state, and drawing functions. All drawing is specified in pixels of device-dependent size, and all text uses fonts with device-dependent size and representation.
CFont	A device-dependent font. Always accessed by CFont*. Most CFont functions, like AscentInPixels(), provide fast access to pixel sizes either for any character or a particular string.

Even device-independent drawing code cannot ignore the realities of devices: some things are calculated exclusively in the pixel domain, others are calculated in the twips domain and then converted to pixels. There is no general rule about which is best, though I'll offer some guidelines below.

Device independence is not an end in itself. Making your code device-independent involves some cost. But as a means to two important ends – printing, and glass door pictures for embedded objects – EPOC's facilities for device-independent drawing are excellent.

The GDI

Device-independent drawing is supported by EPOC's GDI – or graphics device interface. All graphics components, and all components that require a graphics object, such as text content, depend ultimately on the GDI.

The GDI defines:

❑ Basic units of measurement – pixels and twips – that are used by all drawing code

❑ Basic definitions for color

❑ Graphics devices and graphics contexts

❑ Fonts – including the paraphernalia of font specs that we saw above, and typeface stores that we'll see below

❑ Bitmapped graphics

❑ Device mapping and zooming

❑ Printing

The GDI is reasonably documented and well illustrated by examples in the EPOC C++ SDK. The catchall example program is \epoc32ex\grshell\grshell.mmp, which as its name suggests is a shell with several examples inside it, including the basic drawing functions supported by CGraphicsContext, bitmapped graphics, the CPicture class, zooming, off-screen bitmap manipulation, and the built-in fonts.

We've already seen most of the GDI. In this brief section, I'll review and develop a couple more themes:

- ❑ Introducing bitmap handling
- ❑ Some more on font management
- ❑ More on printing
- ❑ More on color and display modes

Blitting and Bitmaps

These days, displays are fundamentally bitmap-oriented. Graphics primitives such as `DrawLine()` have to **rasterize** or **render** the line – that is, they must determine which pixels should be drawn in order to create a bitmap image that looks like the desired line. Rasterizing in EPOC is the responsibility of the BITGDI, which implements all drawing functions specified by `CGraphicsContext` for drawing to on- and off-screen bitmaps.

Another approach to updating a bitmapped display is simply to **blit** to it: to copy a bitmap whose format is compatible with the format on the display. Blitting is extremely efficient, especially if the source and destination bitmaps are of identical format.

Any GUI worth its salt takes advantage of the efficiency of blitting to optimize certain operations:

- ❑ On-screen icons are not rendered using drawing primitives, but pre-constructed in a paint program and blitted to screen when required.
- ❑ Flicker-free screen updates are performed by rendering to an off-screen bitmap (potentially slow), and then blitting to the screen when needed (usually quick).
- ❑ Animation is a special case of flicker-free update that can be implemented using a sequence of blits, one for each image frame.
- ❑ Backed-up windows use off-screen bitmaps to maintain the backup: rendering is directed to window and/or backup bitmap as necessary, and redrawing is done entirely from the backup bitmap.
- ❑ Screen fonts are blitted from the font bitmaps onto the screen (or off-screen bitmap).

Blitting is great, but it isn't always the best thing to use:

- ❑ Bitmaps use a lot of memory, so if you can construct a picture from a short sequence of drawing primitives, it's often more compact than storing the picture as a bitmap.
- ❑ Bitmaps can't be scaled effectively: you lose information if you scale them down, and they look chunky if you scale them up. Also, scaling is generally slow, which eliminates one of the major advantages of using bitmaps.
- ❑ Bitmaps are fixed. You can only use them to store pre-drawn or pre-calculated pictures, or to cache calculated images for reuse over a short period of time.
- ❑ Bitmaps are highly efficient for screens, but highly inefficient for printers, because they involve large data transfers over relatively slow links. They also involve scaling, but usually that's acceptable on printers because the scaling is to a size similar to that which would have been used for the bitmap on screen anyway.

Here's a UML diagram of EPOC's bitmap support classes:

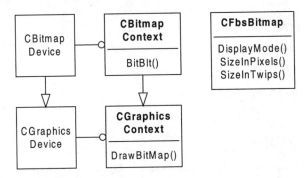

The base class for bitmaps is CFbsBitmap, which is defined in fbs.h. Key properties of a bitmap include:

❑ Its display mode – the number of bits per pixel, and color/gray encoding scheme. See the TDisplayMode enumeration in gdi.h, and the list below.

❑ Its size in pixels

❑ Its size in twips

❑ Its bitmap data, which you can get using GetScanLine() and similar functions

Functions are provided to set and access these properties, and also to internalize and externalize bitmaps using streams. CGraphicsContext requires that any graphics device (and hence any graphics context) can do four basic operations with any CFbsBitmap object. Here are CGraphicsContext's bitmap drawing functions:

❑ DrawBitmap() from the source bitmap to a region of the device, identified by its top-left corner. The bitmap is scaled according to its size in pixels, and the destination device's pixel size.

❑ DrawBitmap() from the source bitmap to a region of the device, identified by its bounding rectangle. The bitmap is stretched to fit.

❑ DrawBitmap() from a rectangular region of the source bitmap to a rectangular region of the device. The bitmap region is stretched to fit.

❑ Use of a bitmap in UseBrushPattern(), for background painting.

The GDI defines a bitmapped graphics device CBitmapDevice and, correspondingly, a bitmapped GC CBitmapContext. You can read pixels and scan lines from a CBitmapDevice, and create a CBitmapContext for drawing. You can clear, copy rectangles, blit, and 'blit under mask' to a CBitmapContext. (The blit-under-mask functions are used for drawing icons with transparent backgrounds.)

CBitmapContext::BitBlt() will always do one-for-one pixel blitting, regardless of pixel size. Compare this with CGraphicsContext::DrawBitmap(), which always scales if it needs to, even when copying from a bitmap to a bitmapped device.

Bitmaps are also managed by the font and bitmap server. Pre-built bitmaps are built into .mbm files, from Windows .bmps, using bmconv – usually, one per application, or one for subsystems such as EIKON. .mbms for can be built into ROM in a format corresponding to bitmap layout of the EPOC device's normal screen mode: this makes blitting from them particularly efficient. Bitmaps delivered with non-ROM components can be built into a compressed .mbm file from which bitmaps are loaded into the FBS's shared heap as needed, before being blitted elsewhere. Offscreen bitmaps may be allocated by applications: they reside in the FBS's shared heap.

The grshell example includes a comprehensive demonstration of bitmap-related functions.

More on Fonts

We have already seen the basics of handling fonts in your applications:

❏   You use a TFontSpec (and its supporting classes) to specify a font in a device-independent way.

❏   You use an MGraphicsDeviceMap, which ultimately leads to a CGraphicsDevice, to get a device-dependent font, using GetNearestFontInTwips() and the TFontSpec.

Each device has a private **typeface store**, implemented by CTypefaceStore, which stores a number of fonts in a range of sizes. You can interrogate the typeface store through the device: you can ask how many typefaces it has, and iterate through them all. For each typeface, you can ask about the available point sizes, and attributes.

EPOC Release 5's bitmap fonts for screen devices include:

❏   Standard fonts: Arial, Times New Roman, Courier New. These use Windows Latin 1 code page (CP1252) and are available in a wide range of pixel heights (24 each).

❏   Symbol fonts: Symbol, Calc, Eikon, Calcinv, Digital. These are specific to some EPOC applications and don't correspond to similarly named fonts on other systems.

The best way to get a preview of the symbol fonts is to use the grshell example in the SDK (\epoc32ex\graphics\grshell.mmp). This also shows how to use the typeface store API.

Printer devices usually have close equivalents to the standard fonts, so that high-quality printing is possible whether printing directly from EPOC, or through a PC using the 'Print via PC' driver.

Fonts for the screen (and off-screen bitmaps) are managed by the font and bitmap server (FBS). When you allocate a font, using GetNearestFont...() or similar functions, it creates a small client-side CFont* for the device, and also ensures that the bitmaps for the font are available for blitting to the screen (or off-screen bitmap). There are two cases here:

❏   For built-in fonts, the font bitmaps are in ROM. The CFont* acts as a handle to a ROM address. Getting a font is a low-cost operation for built-in fonts.

❏   For installable fonts, which may be delivered with an application, and may reside in RAM or on removable media, the font bitmaps are loaded into RAM and made accessible so that all programs can blit them efficiently from a shared heap. The CFont* acts as a handle to an address in this heap. Getting a font is expensive for installable fonts.

Releasing a font releases the client-side `CFont*` and, in the case of an installable font, decrements a usage count which will cause the font to be released when the usage count reaches zero.

Installable fonts are a main reason why `GetNearestFont...()` calls may fail (because of potential out-of-memory), and a strong incentive to `ReleaseFont()` as soon as possible.

Sometimes, you want a device-dependent font. For instance, you may want a font of a particular pixel size, without going through the trouble of mapping from pixels to twips and then back to pixels again. For this, you can use `GetNearestFontInPixels()` on most graphics devices: this uses a font spec but interprets its `iHeight` in pixels rather than twips. Or, you may want one of the symbol fonts listed above. For this, you can use `GetFontById()`, which requires you to specify a UID rather than a font spec.

Sometimes, even the device independence implied by a `TFontSpec` isn't device independent enough. You can rely on Arial, Times New Roman, and Courier being present on any Western-locale device, but future Unicode-based devices will use different fonts for Far Eastern character sets. In response, Symbian's EPOC applications usually contain font specification information in resource files, so that this aspect of an application can easily be localized. But don't over-generalize: text *layout* conventions are different for Far Eastern applications too, so you may have to change other things if you want to support Far Eastern locales. You don't need to make any special font-related changes to support Unicode-based Western-locale machines.

A more pressing issue, brought into sharp focus by the prospect of supporting large Far Eastern alphabets, is that of scalable fonts. EPOC Release 5 includes only bitmapped fonts, which are bit-blitted to the screen. The fonts in ROM are pre-rendered to various point sizes. For large point sizes, they are algorithmically scaled during blitting from ROM: it's useful for fonts that aren't needed often but the result isn't terribly elegant. You can easily tell by inspection that the 300% zoom version of Arial 12-point bold, used in `drawing` above, uses an algorithmically-scaled version of a smaller device font.

EPOC supports a so-called **open font system** that will be used to deliver fully scalable fonts in the next major release. This will enable fonts of arbitrary size to be produced. For Western locales, this is clearly useful, but for Far Eastern locales it's the difference between night and day, since the font information for even a single point size is enormous. By using scalable font technology, information is only *needed* for one size. Other sizes, and rasterization for printers, can be handled by the scalable font system.

For best performance, scalable fonts are rendered into an off-screen bitmap and blitted from there. Bitmaps for the fonts currently in use will be cached, and rasterization will be performed transparently as required. Needless to say, the system has been cunningly optimized to balance speed with RAM efficiency.

More on Printing

A comprehensive print model is built into the GDI, and implemented by higher-level components of EPOC. Print support includes:

❑ Support for a range of printer drivers

❑ Support for a 'print via PC' driver, which allows you to use EPOC Connect to print to the default printer on your PC

- Support for full color printing, and use of any available printer fonts to match `GetNearestFontInTwips()` calls. Potentially, printed output from EPOC is more accurate than screen output, if a document requires colors or fonts not supported by the screen device and its typeface store.

- On-screen print preview: this is just another graphics device, and is conveniently packaged for the use of EIKON programs

We've already seen that, at the heart of any print-enabled application, you have to implement `MPrintProcessObserver`'s `PrintBandL()` function.

You also need to implement the standard print functions, including:

- Page setup: supports paper size, margins, rich text for header and footer, and options for page numbering, header on first page, footer on first page.

- Print setup: the number of copies you want to print, and the driver you want to use. A variety of printers from HP, Canon, Epson, and Citizen are supported directly. General (text) printing is also supported. Fax is implemented as a printer model, for convenience (you can also use EPOC Email to send fax messages). The catchall driver is 'print via PC'.

- Print preview: a preview showing the layout on up to four pages, including options for setup.

- Print: starts an actual print job to the currently chosen printer, with the current settings.

- In your document model, you should externalize print settings.

This is all very easy to do, since the GDI defines all the base classes needed, EIKON provides standard dialogs that invoke the user interfaces required above, and the GDI classes include their own support for externalizing and internalizing. `\boss\eik9\` in the SDK includes full support for printing.

Color

The basic class for color is the `TRgb`: a red-green-blue color specification. A `TRgb` object is a 32-bit quantity, in which eight bits are each available for red (R), green (G), and blue (B). Eight bits are wasted.

> *What? Wasted memory in such a fundamental class in EPOC? Actually, the waste is small. First, it's hard to process 24-bit quantities efficiently in any processor architecture. More importantly, TRgbs don't exist in large numbers – unlike, say, the pixels on a screen or bitmap. Bitmaps are stored using only the minimum necessary number of bits.*

Constants are defined for the set of 16 EGA colors (so named after the IBM PC's 'Enhanced Graphics Adapter', which supported them and also introduced them into character set attributes). Here are the definitions in `gdi.h`, which also show how the R, G and B values are combined in a `TRgb`:

```
#define KRgbBlack       TRgb(0x000000)
#define KRgbDarkGray    TRgb(0x555555)
#define KRgbDarkRed     TRgb(0x000080)
#define KRgbDarkGreen   TRgb(0x008000)
#define KRgbDarkYellow  TRgb(0x008080)
#define KRgbDarkBlue    TRgb(0x800000)
```

```
#define KRgbDarkMagenta   TRgb(0x800080)
#define KRgbDarkCyan      TRgb(0x808000)
#define KRgbRed           TRgb(0x0000ff)
#define KRgbGreen         TRgb(0x00ff00)
#define KRgbYellow        TRgb(0x00ffff)
#define KRgbBlue          TRgb(0xff0000)
#define KRgbMagenta       TRgb(0xff00ff)
#define KRgbCyan          TRgb(0xffff00)
#define KRgbGray          TRgb(0xaaaaaa)
#define KRgbWhite         TRgb(0xffffff)
```

We use `#define` *rather than (say)* `const TRgb KRgbWhite = TRgb(0xffffff)` *because GCC 2.7.2 doesn't support build-time initialization of class constants. Initialization of any* `TRgb` *from one of these 'constants' is no more expensive than if 'proper'* `const TRgb`*s were used.*

> **All** `CGraphicsContext` **color specifications for pens and brushes use** `TRgb` **values.**
> **The graphics device then converts these into device-dependent color values internally.**

With measurement and fonts, you have to convert to device-dependent units (pixels and `CFont`s) before calling `CGraphicsContext` functions. The same approach could have been taken with colors but it wasn't, because the meaning of a color is less device-dependent than the size of a pixel or the bitmap for a font. You have to specify real colors when drawing to a `CGraphicsContext`; the key thing you have to know about a device is how many colors it supports.

Actually, the number of supported colors depends not only on the device, but also on the current display mode of the device. Some devices support multiple display modes: you can check the display modes supported by a window server screen device, and set your window to use a required display mode if it's supported. Some display modes consume more power than others, so the window server will change the display mode in use to the one with the minimum power requirement for any visible window.

You can create bitmaps with any display mode. When you blit them onto another bitmap, or a display them in a particular mode, the bitmap data is contracted or expanded as necessary to match the display mode of the target bitmap.

The display modes supported by EPOC are defined in the `TDisplayMode` enumeration in `gdi.h`. They are:

Mode	Bits	Type	Comment
ENone			A null value that shouldn't be present in any initialized `TDisplayMode` object.
EGray2	1	Grayscale	Black and white: displays `KRgbBlack` and `KRgbWhite`.
EGray4	2	Grayscale	Minimal grayscale: displays `KRgbBlack`, `KRgbDarkGray`, `KRgbGray`, and `KRgbWhite` exactly.

Mode	Bits	Type	Comment
EGray16	4	Grayscale	16 shades of gray.
EGray256	8	Grayscale	256 shades of gray.
EColor16	4	Color	Full EGA color set: displays all standard KRgbXxx values exactly.
EColor256	8	Color	Netscape color cube: exactly represents all 216 combinations of R, G, B in multiples of 0x33, plus all remaining 40 combinations of pure R in multiples of 0x11, pure G, pure B, and pure RGB gray likewise.
EColor64K	16	Color	High color: represents 5 bits of R, 6 bits of G, and 5 bits of B, so that 0xrrrrrrrr, 0xgggggggg, 0xbbbbbbbb will convert to TRgb(0xrrrrr000, 0xgggggg00, 0xbbbbb000), with the least significant bits of each color being dropped.
EColor16M	32	Color	8 bits each for R, G, and B. 8 bits wasted.
ERgb	32	Color	Like EColor16M
EColor4K	16	Color	Uses 4 bits each for R, G, and B. 4 bits are wasted.

Most devices have a preferred screen display mode: For the Psion Series 5 and similar devices, that's EGray4. For the Psion netBook and similar devices, it's EColor256.

The window server sets the screen's display mode to the most capable mode required by any currently visible window and supported by the hardware. So the 'preferred *screen* display mode' is actually implemented as a 'default *window* display mode'. On four-gray machines, sixteen-gray is also available, and you can create EGray16 windows if you need them. The tradeoff here is that color contrast is increased slightly, whereas total power consumption in the device is increased by about 30% – the extra power is needed to transfer twice as many bits per second from the system RAM to the display LCD controller.

On any EPOC machine, ROM bitmaps are generated in the preferred display mode, so that typically no bitmap transformations are required when blitting to screen.

If a color is passed to a CGraphicsContext function that is not supported exactly on the device, then the nearest supported color is used instead.

This nearest-color transformation is done before any other operation uses the color, including logical operations such as XOR. This can produce unexpected effects, but logical operations are in any case of dubious value on windowing systems – with the exception of XORing with KRgbWhite, which has its uses and will always work as expected.

You'll see mentions of 'palettes' in some of the GDI definitions; these were added to the design before support for any form of color display was implemented (in EPOC Release 5). When color display mode support was added, we decided not to use palettes to optimize (say) the shades available in a 256-colour display mode. Instead, we use the fixed Netscape color cube set, and that's it. This reduces the complexity of the API, loses no worthwhile features for devices in this class, and avoids the funnies you occasionally see (or remember seeing!) on Windows PCs when the palette was optimized for a foreground window while other visible windows' palettes went wild.

Colors raise their own issues of device dependence. As with measurement units, the uses of color by the EIKON GUI, applications, or parts of applications, break down into two categories:

❑　Those for which color is an essential part of the real-world model: for instance, photos taken by a digital camera, bitmaps being displayed through a web browser, or colors requested by the user of EPOC Word or EPOC Sketch.

❑　Those for which color is merely being used to highlight or set off some aspect of the UI, such as the colors used in menus, menu highlights, toolbar buttons, or window shadows.

We are quite used to having real-world colors mapped down onto black-and-white, or low-fidelity color. The best approach for real-world colors is simply to allow the `TDisplayMode` mappings to do their thing. You'll need to use device-dependent selector controls for applications like EPOC Word or EPOC Sketch: EIKON's historically named `CEikGraySelector` provides the necessary support.

UI color schemes are an art in themselves. Just as most desktop operating systems support color schemes that may be mapped, so does EPOC. However, EPOC does not support user selection: the choice belongs to the device OEM, with Symbian providing default schemes.

Prior to EPOC R5, EIKON and applications used hard-coded grayscale values for all their drawing. It's now recommended that UI color schemes be specified in terms of **logical colors** (for example, dialog title bar background) rather than RGB colors (light gray, dark cyan). EIKON then uses a kind of palette known as a **color list** to map logical colors into `TRgb` values. The color list:

❑　Supports logical-to-RGB color mappings loaded from resource files or specified programmatically

❑　Supports independent sections for EIKON and applications: a section is identified by application (or EIKON) UID, and a logical color by an enumerated constant

❑　Supports mappings for both four-gray and 256-color schemes: the 256-color scheme will be used, and will look good, if the screen mode supports 16 or more colors. Otherwise, the four-gray scheme will be used.

The color list is maintained by the EIKON environment, and is documented in the EPOC C++ SDK.

It's clearly right for the color list to belong to EIKON (rather than the GDI), since UI colors are a property of the GUI rather than the graphics system as a whole. Oddly, CCoeControl provides functions allowing colors determined by this scheme to be overridden: this is intended for Java and EPOC Web use, and should not be used by native applications.

The Developer's Quest for Device-independent Code

We noted above that device-independent drawing is not an end in itself, but a means to an end. Making your drawing code device independent is not without cost. Imagine, for instance, the changes you would have to make to CFleetView to make its drawing code device-independent.

So, when should you make your drawing code device-independent, and when don't you need to? There are two extreme cases in which the answer is quite clear:

❑ If your code is designed exclusively for a screen-based UI, then it should not be device-independent (though you may wish to build in some size independence)

❑ If your code is designed primarily for printing, with a screen-based UI for editing, then it should be device-independent

This means that an application toolbar can be highly device-dependent, as can the menu and the dialogs (though some size independence in the latter case would be useful). On the other hand, a text view intended for a word processor, should be highly device-independent; so too should a mapping program that might well be printer-oriented.

Real Devices Intrude

This answer is only a starting point, however, and there are many awkward, intermediate cases. You have to take the realities of the device into account, even when writing the most device-independent code.

The influence of target devices on your code is even greater when the devices are relatively limited in CPU power and display resolution. With high-resolution displays and near-infinite CPU power, you can render everything with no thought for rounding errors, scale etc. With small displays, slower CPUs, and no floating-point processor, you have to take much more care in both graphical design and programming.

The requirements for printing text efficiently, and for fast interactive editing of potentially enormous documents, are substantially different. EPOC's text view component contains much shared code, but also a lot of quite distinct code, for these two purposes. Less demanding applications will have a greater proportion of shared code.

In a map application, zooming introduces considerations not only of scaling, but also of visibility. In a high-level view of the map, you want to see any coastline, a few major cities, big rivers and any borders. In a zoomed-in view of a city, you want to see district names, underground train stations, public buildings, etc.

In the high-level view, you wouldn't try to draw these details at small scale: you would omit them altogether. And this omission is device-dependent: you can include more minor features in a printed view than in an on-screen view at the same zoom level, because most printers have higher resolution than a screen.

There are plenty of other complications with maps, such as aligning labels with features, and transverse scaling of linear elements such as roads – and many other applications share these considerations. Fortunately, you don't usually edit maps on a handheld device, so there isn't the need for very quick reformatting code that there is with word processors. As a result, there may actually be better code sharing between printer and screen views.

What is Real?

Sometimes, it's far from clear whether an application is a UI to an abstract object, or a representation of something real.

A game like Battleships could be considered as an abstract 8x8 grid that will only be drawn on screen, or it could be considered as a real board with a physical size, whose on-screen representation is just that: a representation, zoomed from the size of the real board. The graphics code will differ slightly depending on the decision you make here. Actually I changed from a pixel-based to a twips-based system without too much trouble, but then the Battleships fleet view is not very complicated.

Like its countless successors, the very first spreadsheet – VisiCalc – could be considered to be an abstract grid of cells, each containing text, numbers, or a formula. If you take that view, your drawing code can be pixel-oriented, and it won't be too difficult if you decide to support zooming. Even a simple spreadsheet like this has enormous value: it enables you to create displays and perform calculations that previously had to be programmed explicitly.

But as soon as people have these tools in their hands, they want to print them, including sensible page breaks and embedded charts. If you write a spreadsheet that supports all this, you need to design for printing from the beginning, and to optimize your on-screen views as representations of the printed page.

Mixtures and Muddles

A perverse consequence of trying to re-use code is that some interfaces are specified in a device-*independent* way when what you really want is quite device-*dependent*.

My first cut at the Battleships fleet view was specified in terms of pixels, but I used twips to get a 12-point Arial bold font for the ships, and 6-point Arial bold for the border legend. So although the grid and border would scale nicely, the tile sizes would not. You can see the historic code in \pep\tpg\view.cpp – the prototype I wrote before adding communications for Battleships, and then stripping down to Solo Ships.

Web browsing technology is very confused on this subject. It has evolved without clear distinctions between print and on-screen graphics. Text is specified in pseudo-device-independent form, while graphics are specified in pixels, which makes them shrink for high resolution on-screen displays, and forces an arbitrary decision about scaling when a view is printed. There is no clear relation between text sizes and graphics, which means they don't scale together on most browsers (though they do on EPOC's).

Web pages include forms-based controls such as buttons, text boxes, choice lists, and so on, which at first sight are interactive UI controls for on-screen use and whose size should therefore be in pixels, like other UI controls. But you have to be able to print them too, and perhaps also zoom them. With this architectural muddle, it's unsurprising that different browsers and different content publishers do things differently.

Theoretically, XML DTDs may improve the situation, but it's only likely to make a difference with the relatively few content providers who are smart enough to appreciate the issues and use the DTDs properly.

Summary

No system can survive radical changes in its underlying assumptions. The art of device-independent software development is to survive reasonable changes in underlying assumptions. That involves designing with flexible assumptions in mind – but not so much flexibility that the initial design becomes impossible to deliver:

- ❑ It's much easier to design for size independence than for device independence: you should make as many parts of your code size-independent as possible.

- ❑ Device independence has a cost associated with it, so you need to be able to assess when it's worth the cost. If you need to print, you should probably design in device independence from the beginning.

- ❑ All drawing should take into account the realities of devices. These don't matter much when what you're drawing is much bigger than, say, 20 pixels or more. But when what you're drawing is smaller, rounding errors are noticeable. Features smaller than about 3 pixels in size need special attention.

Getting this right can make a real difference to the functionality delivered in an application, its aesthetics, or the cost of development and maintenance. Fortunately there are many ways to get this more-or-less right, in the case of most applications, especially when the underlying system makes it easy for you to do the right thing.

Even so, for most of us, we're still working on getting the right degree of device independence into our programs: the quest continues.

Symbian's Quest

Symbian's task is not only to deliver size-independent and device-independent drawing code, but entire GUI systems, with their visual appearance and interaction mechanisms, put simply, their **look-and-feel** (LAF).

> **The GUI as a whole and applications that use the GUI are highly device-dependent, and highly dependent on their target markets.**

Put another way, if the device changes too much, or if the target markets change too much, then the GUI will have to change, as will the applications.

Symbian's EPOC design team has always known this, and has worked hard to control the implications for itself, its licensees, and for developers. This section is an account of Symbian's quest for the best way to evolve GUIs in line with changes in devices and market expectations. The general direction of this quest is becoming clearer, but while markets and technology continue to change, the journey's end is still a way away.

Right back in 1987, Psion faced these issues with the SIBO project. SIBO was conceived as a multi-platform operating system that would use the same system and application engines, but a different GUI (and different application GUIs) to support different devices. Within admittedly narrow parameters of variation, the concept worked for a range of quite distinct devices released between 1989 and 1997.

From the beginning, EPOC was designed with the same system structure. Most of the system would be consciously independent of the GUI. Application code would be carefully structured into engines (or models) that were also GUI independent. A replaceable GUI framework would define the system's look and feel, and applications' GUIs would be separate from their engines. If the GUI were replaced, only a small proportion of the total code in the system would need to be replaced along with it:

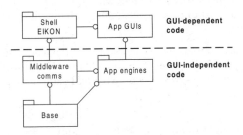

During early development of EPOC, we rewrote EIKON twice, but neither event had an impact on application engines: testimony to the effectiveness of the original split. The first rewrite factored the GUI (originally titled HCIL) into CONE (a key item of GUI infrastructure and yet completely independent of any specific GUI) and EIKON (the specific GUI intended for the Psion Series 5 and similar machines). This is why CONE is now the top component you'll see in the GUI-independent part of EPOC.

Tweaking EIKON

In late 1997, Geofox, an EPOC licensee, released its Geofox One. With a 640x320 display (somewhat taller than the 640x240 of the Psion Series 5) and a track pad (instead of an on-screen digitizer), Geofox needed to make only minor modifications to the GUI. A pointer cursor was added to the window server, and they needed a track pad driver as well. Physical buttons were also added to replace the pseudo-buttons on the Psion Series 5's taskbar and sidebar, and small modifications were made to the parts of EIKON that used off-screen windows in the Psion Series 5, to respond to the buttons instead.

That was that. All the applications scaled to fit the Geofox One's screen: they had been written with scalable views, and scaling *up* in size usually works without too many problems. The only thing that looked slightly odd on the Geofox One was the four-button toolbars, which left rather a lot of blank space below them.

Other relatively minor ports of EIKON and the applications have been made, too. The Psion netBook/Series 7 has a 640x480 color screen: it uses the EPOC Release 5 'color' color scheme (not the grayscale 'color' scheme used on say the Psion Series 5MX), and adds two extra buttons to each application toolbar to avoid obvious screen waste. The Psion Revo has scaled the applications down to a 480x160 display, with three-button toolbars, smaller fonts (measured in pixel size) and a few other tweaks.

What these ports show is actually quite unsurprising: EIKON can scale to a different form factor with only minor modifications to EIKON and its applications. Unfortunately, they also show that even a minor change in screen size makes some software look odd, or prevents it from running altogether unless the software is modified. My Battleships game's application view will look odd on a Psion netBook (acres of spare space above and below, and the player status view will look bizarre), and may not fit on a Revo at all (the status view might get be squashed too much). As I write, I haven't tried it on either machine, but I expect to have to perform a few minor tweaks when I do.

However, tweaking of this nature doesn't get you very far. If you want to run EPOC, and EPOC applications, on a *significantly* different device, you have to take a different approach.

Emulating EIKON

One approach we have never seriously considered is *emulation* of, say, the EIKON GUI on a device with a different screen size, or no keyboard.

The story of our Java port will illustrate why. In August 1998, Symbian attained 'Java Compatible' certification from Sun Microsystems for its Java implementation. To get that certification, we needed (among other things) to be able to run GUI applications and applets written in Java – often ones originally targeted at a much larger device.

We did that by adding some more tweaks to EIKON, and some support in the AWT implementation that links Java to EIKON. For instance, we added scrolling menu panes (which can include more items than will comfortably fit in a screen display), metaphors for emulating right-click, and scrolling app views. Altogether, that means that Java applications and applets can run without modification under EIKON. Very nice.

Nice for engineers, that is. It's fun just to be able to run a Java application or applet on an EPOC machine. But if a particular application uses menus and an app view that are too big to see all at once, and requires a contortionist to produce frequently-needed pointer gestures, it will appeal to few outside the technical community.

In Chapter 23, Jonathan Allin will show that Java applications ported to EPOC come into several categories:

- ❏ Those that are sufficiently undemanding to work acceptably without change

- ❏ Those that are *so* demanding on hardware resources that they simply won't run on EPOC at all

- ❏ Applications between these two extremes that work, but the emulation gets in the way and ruins their appeal to non-technical users

Only if you design Java applications with EPOC as the primary target can you guarantee a good fit when running on an EPOC machine.

Of course, these aren't really Java-specific issues: they apply to any kind of GUI porting. Emulation can work, but it can't be relied upon, and for mass-market appeal it's far from optimal.

Replacing EIKON

Symbian actually thought that EIKON (and application GUIs using EIKON) would be replaced altogether. Our first opportunity to do this was during 1997 and early 1998.

With Philips Consumer Communications, we produced an EPOC port for a new phone, the Ilium Accent. The product made it as far as market testing, but has not been generally released.

With a 640x200 display and no keyboard, the device parameters were radically different from those that drove EIKON. With an eye for mass-market users, Philips used specialist graphic design, resulting in different icons, round-edged buttons with illumination from the top right, and a completely different view architecture. A handwriting recognition system was included to make good the lack of a keyboard.

The result was a very fine new GUI, barely recognizable as anything to do with EIKON. Here's a screenshot from an emulator, showing an entry from my diary in February 1998:

To get this screenshot, all I did was copy my Agenda file to the Ilium Accent emulator's emulated c: drive and launch it: despite the change in GUI, there had been no change at all in the application engine or the data format.

The Accent was a big project that taught us a few things. One thing we learned was not to underestimate the cost or skills required to design an entirely new GUI – one that would not merely function, but would actually delight and enchant its end users.

Reference Designs

The experience of the Ilium Accent showed us clearly that EIKON *could* be replaced, but along with a couple of other projects that didn't even get as far as delivering a complete and usable GUI, it also demonstrated the costs and the risks involved.

As we began to realize this, in early 1999, Symbian announced a new strategy: it would support only about four **reference designs**, targeted at different types of hardware: two in the smartphone category, and two in the higher-end communicator category. The reference designs would be created with great care, using skills within Symbian and its investor companies, and would then be available to any Symbian licensee.

This was a step forward: by allowing different models to use the same reference design, we would achieve greater design re-use for both Symbian and independent software developers. That wouldn't have been possible with the previous, completely unconstrained, strategy. On the other hand, by creating more than one reference design, we would still achieve what we wanted: to make EPOC the system of choice across a wide range of different device types. Furthermore, multiple designs would spread risk: some would be more successful in the market than others, but we wouldn't necessarily know the winners in advance.

More and Less Flexibility

When we first envisaged reference designs, we thought in terms of a range of device parameters for each design, for example:

- ❑ Display in the range 320+ x 120+ pixels
- ❑ Optional pointer
- ❑ Keypad

But it soon became clear that this kind of flexibility leads to significant non-optimality in a design.

Let's say that you design a view for exactly 320x120 pixels: you go to all kinds of trouble to cram in text and abbreviate words; you use icons instead of text, pop-up displays, very simple views that sacrifice functionality, perfect alignment of various columns and icons, and so on. A display like this will break if you make it even a single pixel smaller, but *it will look equally odd if you make it larger:* users will wonder why you didn't use the extra space. Technical users won't mind much, and the effects aren't too bad when you go from large screens to larger screens. But with small screens, and non-technical users, it matters enormously. And that's the mass market.

To give another example, imagine that when you design, you take the view that there may or may not be a pointer. For devices without pointers, you introduce keyboard-driven ways of doing everything – on a phone with a keypad, that means ingenious combinations of arrow keys, Yes and No, and numeric/text entry using the 12-key pad. This is an awkward system that users really only accept because there is no alternative. If there *is* an alternative – if we deliver a design that is obviously optimized for pointer *as well as* keypad – users with only a keypad will consider it even more awkward. Worse still, we might forget to optimize the design sufficiently for the needs of keypad-only users. The lesson is the same as for screen sizes: you can just about pretend that the pointer is optional on the Psion Series 5, but on a small device, and with less technical users, you have to decide clearly one way or the other.

From this, we deduce that a GUI – especially at the smartphone end of the market – has to be quite *in*flexible in its design parameters. It must specify screen size and input devices exactly, and allow for no variation. A GUI for larger devices, on the other hand, can be more flexible.

Symbian will release its two communicator reference designs, codenamed Crystal and Quartz, into products from 2000 onwards. Crystal will evolve EPOC R5 into the product category defined by the Nokia 9000 communicator we saw in Chapter 1, while Quartz is an entirely new design that will support a tablet-like form factor with stylus operation, handwriting recognition and powerful integrated wireless communications. Ericsson demonstrated a multimedia application on an early Quartz prototype in October 1999.

Instead of providing complete reference designs for smartphones, Symbian now provides a technology platform codenamed Pearl, with licensees free to provide their own user interfaces and specialist applications for particular smartphone products.

The Ericsson R380, announced at CeBIT 99 for availability in 2000, will use a forerunner of Pearl. The cooperation between Symbian, Nokia, and Palm announced in October 1999, will use Pearl.

Look-and-feel Customization

If you change the look-and-feel of a GUI, it will be to provide more features, to cut irrelevant features out, or to change a few subtle effects (such as layout, fonts etc.):

❏ If you provide more features, you need to add APIs. Programs porting from the old GUI to the new will want to use these features, or they will look outdated.

❏ If you remove features, you'll need to remove their APIs. Programs porting from the old GUI to the new will have to remove any code that depends on these APIs, or they won't work.

❏ If you change layout, fonts, color schemes etc, then you may not change APIs, but programs porting from the old GUI to the new will, in general, have to change (though a few undemanding programs may not need to).

Many systems (including Java 2) provide 'LAF layers' that theoretically allow you to change the look-and-feel of a program's GUI without any change in the program code, in source or binary form. But there's only a limited number of things you can change without causing developers to want to rewrite their applications. For instance:

❏ If you change the font used in toolbar buttons to something larger, then some buttons will overflow.

❏ If you change the font used in toolbar buttons to something smaller, then some buttons for which you searched long and hard for short enough text, and eventually found a bad abbreviation, would now support longer text, and users will wonder why you chose such a bad text when a better one would have been easy to deliver.

❏ Most applications do some drawing that is based on the colors you expect the system to use. So if the system's color scheme changes, the application's aesthetics will be affected. This can be the case even if as much of the application's code as possible uses 'system palettes' for its drawing.

❏ If the style of buttons changes, then any custom controls in the application that have been written to look good with the old button style won't look good with the new button style

A thousand issues like these make the difference between an application that looks and feels good, and something that looks careless.

Symbian will support LAF customization in future GUIs, but the extent of allowed customization is likely to be limited, so that compatibility issues such as those above do not arise.

More Heritage

Look-and-feel customization is an attempt to preserve compatibility for basically similar GUIs. But the forces that create different device families are, by definition, more than a simple matter of look-and-feel customization.

Given this radical difference, it's obvious that APIs in general are going to change, the GUI needs to be rewritten, and applications based on the GUI need to be altered. Based on this observation, early EIKON replacements took the attitude that, if you were going to make changes, you might as well make big ones. Everything got changed, the very possibility of change increased the desire to change, and the effects on project costs, application rewrite costs etc. spiraled predictably out of control.

We now realize that you can change *many* aspects of a GUI without changing *all* of its programming interfaces. For instance, there is no good reason to change `HandleCommandL()` as a way of getting commands – however originated – to an app UI. Indeed, there is no strong reason to get rid of the app UI class, or to rename anything that doesn't need to be renamed.

So, future EPOC APIs will build consciously on the EIKON heritage: they will always maintain certain core classes, and the general `CEikXxx` naming convention. It's now a clearly stated objective to make it as easy as possible to port from one EPOC GUI to another.

Of course, you will be able to maintain heritage in your own code too. Despite the realities of device dependence, write as much of it as you think reasonable in a device-independent way. In particular, make it scalable, and re-colorable. Then, even if some effort is required to port to a different GUI, you can eliminate work that is really unnecessary.

Summary

The quest for device independence continues, both for Symbian, and for developers using Symbian technology.

I've outlined the story of Symbian's quest for device-independent code, so you can plan your own development strategy. While Symbian's strategy has been refined as it gains more experience, and no doubt will continue to be refined, our original position and vision have never been lost. So it's a safe bet that there will always be a range of EPOC devices on the market with quite different device parameters and, increasingly, with GUI systems other than EIKON.

At the technical level, Symbian is doing all it can to maximize your ability to re-use software. EPOC's base, middleware, and communications components don't depend on the GUI, and they won't change when EIKON is replaced. Parts of your application that depend on these components alone won't need to change from one GUI to another.

Even the changes being made in EPOC's GUIs are now being minimized, to preserve EIKON heritage where appropriate, and to change only parts that have genuine impact on look-and-feel. You will be able to re-use the code in your application that depends on EIKON, but isn't really dependent on look-and-feel.

You can also do all you can to minimize your dependence on a particular GUI by making as much as possible of your application design (but no more) device independent.

At the technical level, that leaves a minimized (but significant) body of device-dependent code in any serious application that will have to be changed when the application is ported from one GUI to another. How do you do this at reasonable cost? Ultimately, the choice here is not technical, but commercial.

For our part, Symbian will do all that is possible to minimize porting costs, by minimizing the differences between different EPOC GUIs, consistent with making them appropriate for their intended target device families and end users. Given this, the choice for a developer equates to choosing which device families are most suitable for the kind of application you wish to deploy, and then targeting them.

Part Three

Communications and Systems Programming

Symbian's technology platform is evolving towards ever-tighter integration of wireless communications. In the following chapters, I use the Battleships application to introduce system and communications programming in EPOC. In addition, through these chapters, you'll appreciate how object-oriented design makes a real difference when dealing with large programming systems.

In Chapter 16, I set the scene for what follows. After introducing EPOC R5's communications APIs, I describe the version of Battleships I first wrote, with no communications support at all. Based on the requirements of that program, I describe the purpose of the transaction-oriented games stack (TOGS), which we'll be developing throughout the next few chapters.

Chapter 17 is a fairly formal specification of TOGS. It's a tough read on the whole, and you can skim it if you like, but communications stacks don't happen by accident: they need to be designed. This *is* the design, which made it very easy to write the code. Use the chapter for reference in the book, or as a specification if you want to implement TOGS on non-EPOC platforms.

The next three chapters cover EPOC's key system programming frameworks: Chapter 18 covers active objects, which are how EPOC handles events, and how it implements multitasking in both application programs and servers. Chapter 19 covers the basics of client-server APIs and how the framework operates, while Chapter 20 covers the GSDP server at the heart of TOGS in detail.

In Chapter 21, Jonathan Dixon describes how he implemented GDP for infrared and SMS communication. As with the server chapters, this one is littered with good examples of how active objects are used in practice. Jonathan tackles real-world specifics, including the vagaries of SMS implementations.

Finally, in Chapter 22, I put all this together and describe the real Battleships application, from both a user perspective and the program design perspective. I show how the single function call that implemented a turn in Chapter 16 is turned into a sending a request, handling a request, sending a response, and handling a response, all in the context of a working TOGS stack. I conclude the chapter, and indeed the C++-oriented part of the book, with some ideas on how to take Battleships and TOGS forward.

16

Communications and Systems Programming

For the last six chapters, we've been learning about how to program GUI applications in EPOC. Now, we're going to move on to a new set of topics: communications and system programming. The attractiveness of EPOC as an application platform arises both from the portability of EPOC devices, and from their ability to use wireless communications at short range (via, say, Infrared or Bluetooth radio links) and long range (via mobile phones).

EPOC R5 offers a wide-ranging communications infrastructure: serial communications over RS232 and infrared, dial-up TCP/IP, IrDA, fax, and communication via GSM phones. Future EPOC releases will offer a much wider range of communications possibilities and, most importantly, will be tightly integrated with mobile phones.

Over the remaining C++-oriented chapters of the book, I'll be building the Battleships application, and its underlying transaction-oriented games stack (TOGS). Together, these demonstrate EPOC's ability with short- and long-range communication, and the power of its system programming frameworks — namely active objects and client-server. I'll also describe those frameworks in full.

I'll start this chapter with a brief review of EPOC Release 5's communications facilities. Then, I'll introduce the first version of the Battleships application, which I wrote without any communications support. Finally, I'll introduce the communications issues faced by Battleships and, indeed by any two-player turn-based game. This will serve to explain the design of TOGS, which will be the subject of the next four chapters. By Chapter 22, I'll be able to describe the Battleships application in full, and to suggest a few ways to take it forward.

If you're not already into communications programming, there are basically two ways you can approach the following chapters:

❑ Avoid communications: skip straight to Chapter 18 and Chapter 19, so you can learn about EPOC's active object and client-server frameworks, which are useful for all kinds of system programming tasks, whether or not they are communications-related.

❑ Take this as an opportunity to learn a few things about communications: you'll find parts of the next few chapters a heavy read, and you may need to refer to other communications literature for better explanations of some of the ideas. It will be worth the effort: communications programming opens up many opportunities on EPOC and in the whole modern networked economy.

You may wish to combine these approaches. Skim through until Chapter 18, read that in more detail, and then come back for the heavier communications material at your leisure.

Communications in EPOC R5

Here are EPOC's main communications facilities:

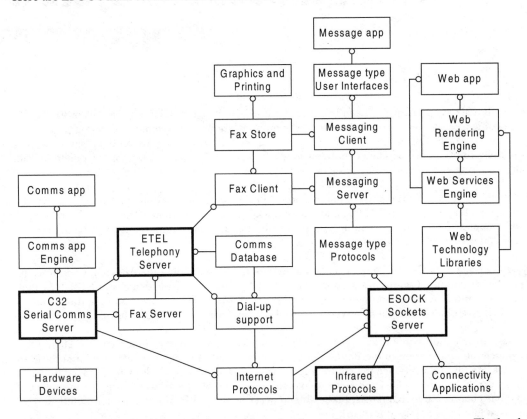

Communications in EPOC R5 centers around two hardware devices, and three servers. The hardware comprises two UARTs (hardware serial ports), one of which is connected to an RS232 cable, and the other to an infrared port.

The Psion Revo has infrared, but no serial cable. The Psion Series 5 (the original EPOC R1 machine) had a single UART that could be used for either the RS232 or the infrared port, but not both together.

The servers are:

❑ C32 – the serial communications server, which drives the communications ports and also runs serial-like protocols that use other communications services

❑ ESOCK – the sockets server, which provides a sockets-based API that's used for dial-up TCP/IP, IrDA via the infrared port, and the PLP protocol used by EPOC Connect

❑ ETEL – the telephony server, which is used to control phone-like devices including landline and mobile-phone modems, enabling them to make fax, data, and voice calls

These servers work closely together to offer communications facilities to higher-level programs, including the three communications applications included in EPOC R5:

❑ EPOC Email – provides fax send/receive, SMS send/receive, and Internet e-mail using dial-up TCP/IP for SMTP send, POP3/IMAP4 receive

❑ EPOC Web – web browser using dial-up TCP/IP

❑ EPOC Comms – an old-style communications application providing an RS232 terminal emulation, file transfer, and the like

Settings are a fact of life in communications. EPOC R5 includes a network database for modem and ISP (Internet Service Provider) settings. Settings are entered by the control panel and used for dial-up networking and ETEL operations.

Communications is clearly an essential prerequisite for connectivity and data synchronization with PCs, which Mark Shackman describes in Chapter 27.

Battleships uses two communications protocols:

❑ IrDA sockets, for short-range links

❑ SMS text messages, for long-range links – short message service, sent via a GSM mobile phone linked to the EPOC machine by cable or infrared

In Chapter 21, Jonathan Dixon describes how he used APIs from the diagram above to implement drivers for both these protocols. By reading that chapter, you'll gain specific insight into how EPOC's main communications components fit together.

You can also find good overview technical information on EPOC's communications facilities in technical papers on Symbian's web site, and detailed API reference in the C++ SDK.

Beyond EPOC R5

In future EPOC Releases, the communications suite will be considerably enhanced. Major improvements will include:

❑ Much tighter integration with mobile phones, with EPOC-based Communicator and Smartphone devices including both phone and handheld computer functionality.

❑ Better short links than those provided by IR: the Bluetooth radio protocol provides a link which doesn't require line-of-sight between two end-points, and which is good for a range up to 10m.

❑ More worldwide wireless telephony support including North American TDMA and third-generation W-CDMA, plus new GSM features such as GPRS (packet-based data which eliminates the wasteful 'modem simulation' needed to make a data call today).

❑ Support for WAP including its low-level components (analogous to TCP/IP) and high-level components (analogous to a web browser): in Chapter 24, Mark Heath introduces WAP.

❑ Support for phone-related APIs in other languages, such as the JavaPhone API, which (roughly) does for Java programmers what EPOC's ETEL and Contacts database do for C++ programmers today. Jonathan Allin introduces JavaPhone in Chapter 23.

For more information on the details and timing of these enhancements, you'll need to keep an eye on the Symbian web site.

Battleships Without Communications

The main problem with communications is that it's *complicated*. The final Battleships application has over 70 classes. There is simply no way to produce an application like that without planning carefully how to get from here to there.

My plan was to start with a version of Battleships that would demonstrate that the game could be played, but which wouldn't need communications at all. Then I could demonstrate my idea to a few people, and find someone to write the really hard communications code that I was pretty sure I wouldn't be able to write myself – at least, not while doing the rest of the book.

So I started by writing a two-player game, tpg for short, which you can find in the \pep\tpg\ example code directories. The purpose of tpg was to prove that the Battleships idea would work. It achieved that purpose – and then I stopped working on it and moved my attention to TOGS and the Battleships game itself.

So tpg contains 'old code', which is fine in most parts but, if you want a basis for your own programs, Battleships, Solo Ships or helloeik *would be better starting points.*

Here's a screenshot of a game that's just begun:

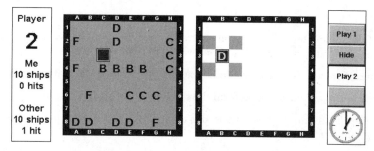

On the left, you have a status view that says it's player two's turn, and gives a few hit statistics. Then you have a view of 'my fleet' for player two (that's really player two's fleet), and of the 'opponent's fleet' for player two (that's really what player two thinks is player one's fleet). Finally, you have a toolbar, which shows more subtly that it's player two's board being shown.

You play this game as follows:

❑ Player one starts the game by launching it from the Extras bar. That shows player one's view, including 'my fleet' already laid out, and 'opponent's fleet' completely blank. Player one requests a hit on the 'opponent's fleet', and then presses the Hide button.

❑ Player one passes the game over to player 2.

❑ Player two then presses the Play 2 button, makes a move, and presses Hide again.

And so play continues. The hide system is good enough to make a playable game between friends, though it isn't really coded to stop determined cheats.

Here's the game design, in UML:

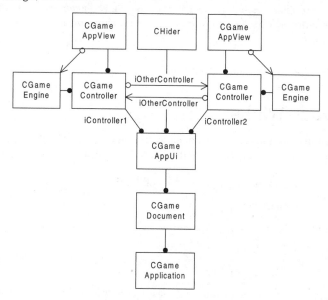

If you compare this with the Solo Ships design, which I described in Chapter 14, you'll notice that:

❑ There are *two* engines, views and controllers in tpg, one for each player

❑ Instead of the document owning the controller, and the app UI owning the view, the app UI owns the controller, and the controller owns the view

❑ The controllers are linked to each other, so that each has an idea of the 'other' player

❑ The engine and view classes perform the same function as in Solo Ships

❑ There are actually three app views in this application: the 'real' app views for player 1 and player 2, and the hider

In Chapter 14, we saw that, if you're going to implement persistence, the controller and engine have to be owned by the document – not the app UI. And the app view has to be owned by the app UI – not the controller. So the design of tpg wouldn't work for a file-based application.

The neat feature of tpg is that it contains two games in one program: there are two complete MVC systems here, one for each player. Each links to the other by the iOtherController pointer in each controller. This is just object-oriented plumbing, and it works really well: in principle I could have used exactly the same engine and view objects in tpg as are found in Solo Ships and Battleships.

There are two interesting aspects to this program:

❑ It does some interesting EIKON tricks: it has three app views, and it manipulates its toolbar buttons. It's useful to know this kind of trick, so we'll have a closer look at the code.

❑ It doesn't use communications to get information about the other player's fleet: instead, it uses object-oriented plumbing. We'll have a look at the code involved, and we'll explain why changing the ten or so lines of plumbing to support communications is going to carry us through five hard chapters before we get to a suitable replacement for them. Or, put another way, we'll understand why I wanted to take the tpg shortcut before doing all that communications work.

Let's look at these two things in turn.

View and Toolbar Tricks

Throughout the previous few chapters, we've been assuming that an EIKON application can have only a single view, but this is not so. Many of the built-in EPOC applications have more than one view:

❑ Agenda has day, week, month, year, to-do, and anniversary views

❑ Sheet has grid and chart views

❑ Data and Contacts have card and list views

❑ Time has world and clock views

❑ Calc has scientific and desktop views

❑ Email has folder, edit-message, and read-message views, and other views for SMS and fax messages

It's very easy to change views without changing the app UI, because the view is a quite distinct entity from the app UI.

The app UI has three members,

```
CGameController* iController1; // Controller for player 1
CGameController* iController2; // Controller for player 2
CHider* iHider;                // Hider view
```

and three corresponding flags that control whether they are visible. The Hide toolbar button calls CmdHideL() which is coded as:

```
void CGameAppUi::CmdHideL()
    {
    iDisplayPlayer1 = EFalse;
    iDisplayPlayer2 = EFalse;
    iDisplayHider = ETrue;
    UpdateDisplay();
    }
```

It simply sets the flags controlling the visibility of each view, and then calls UpdateDisplay(), which sets the views' visibility and updates the toolbar as follows:

```
void CGameAppUi::UpdateDisplay()
    {
    // View visibility
    iController1->iAppView->MakeVisible(iDisplayPlayer1);
    iController2->iAppView->MakeVisible(iDisplayPlayer2);
    iHider->MakeVisible(iDisplayHider);

    // Player 1
    CEikButtonBase* player1Button =
        STATIC_CAST(CEikButtonBase*, iToolBar->ControlById(EGameCmdPlayer1));
    if(iDisplayPlayer1)
        player1Button->SetState(CEikButtonBase::ESet);
    else
        player1Button->SetState(CEikButtonBase::EClear);

    // Player 2
    CEikButtonBase* player2Button =
        STATIC_CAST(CEikButtonBase*, iToolBar->ControlById(EGameCmdPlayer2));
    if(iDisplayPlayer2)
        player2Button->SetState(CEikButtonBase::ESet);
    else
        player2Button->SetState(CEikButtonBase::EClear);

    // Hider
    CEikButtonBase* hideButton =
        STATIC_CAST(CEikButtonBase*, iToolBar->ControlById(EGameCmdHide));
    if(iDisplayHider)
        hideButton->SetState(CEikButtonBase::ESet);
    else
        hideButton->SetState(CEikButtonBase::EClear);
```

```
    // Toolbar
    iToolBar->DrawNow();
    }
```

Controlling the visibility of each view is simple: `CCoeControl::MakeVisible()` is called on each view.

Controlling the visibility of toolbar buttons is more interesting. In the code above, you can see that I get each button individually and set or clear it, depending on the value of the corresponding flag. Finally, I issue `DrawNow()` for the whole toolbar.

Ideally I would have drawn only the buttons that changed. On a toolbar, `DrawNow()` can cause visible flicker. More general applications may change their toolbars or menus along with their views. In the C++ SDK, the example `\epoc32ex\eikmenu\im2view` shows how to code a two-view application that changes menu, toolbar, view, and toolband.

Object-oriented Plumbing

Here's part of the controller code that runs when the player using that controller requests a hit to a square on their opponent's fleet:

```
void CGameController::ViewCmdHitFleet(TInt aX, TInt aY)
    {
    ...
    // Get information from opponent's fleet
    TFleet& oppFleet = iOtherController->iGameEngine->iMyFleet;
    if(oppFleet.IsSea(aX,aY))
        fleet.SetSea(aX,aY);
    else
        fleet.SetShipType(aX, aY, oppFleet.ShipType(aX,aY));

    // Hit opponent's fleet
    oppFleet.SetHit(aX,aY);
    ...
    }
```

The purpose of this code is to:

❑   Find out what was on the opponent's fleet on that square

❑   Mark the information so found on my view of the opponent's fleet

❑   Mark the opponent's fleet as hit on that square

The code simply follows pointers to find the opponent's real fleet:

```
    TFleet& oppFleet = iOtherController->iGameEngine->iMyFleet;
```

Then, the code calls functions on both my view of the opponent's fleet, and on the opponent's fleet itself.

From a design point of view, this is all very elegant: I was able to re-use the same engine and view in Battleships, and testing them here just involved the plumbing above.

Communications is Different

But this implementation of `CGameController::ViewCmdHitFleet()` simply won't do in a real communications world. It uses a synchronous, reliable function call, with parameters in internal format, to find out the state of my opponent's fleet, and to inform my opponent that I have hit a square.

With real communications, I have to tackle some fundamental issues:

❑ Communications is asynchronous. I might have to wait an arbitrary time between sending the hit request, and receiving the response. While I'm waiting, I might change my mind and decide to abandon the game. So while I am waiting for the response from the other player, the game must be able to handle other kinds of input from me.

❑ Communications is unreliable. I need to use protocols which ensure that either my message gets to the other player, or that I am reliably informed that it has not got there for a reason that I can understand. I may need to be able to retry sending my message.

❑ Communications uses external formats. I will have to decide on the binary format that I use to communicate between the two games. I will have to change to external format when sending, and change back into internal format when receiving data. Furthermore, if I wish to play this game against an implementation running on a non-EPOC machine, I will have to publish these formats in sufficient detail that someone else will be able to reproduce them using a non-EPOC format.

❑ Communications is basically awkward for end users. It involves lots of fiddly setup, obscure error messages, and endless frustrations. Sometimes, there is no choice but to expose these things in the user interface of a communications-related application. But if at all possible, it's best to hide them.

❑ There are several forms of communications that would be attractive to the end user. Two that instantly spring to mind are playing the game between two machines in the same room, using the EPOC machines' infrared ports, and playing between players in different locations, using text messages between the players' mobile phones. I have to design the communications strategy to be able to work effectively with both.

❑ Finally, I will have to be able to get there from here. You can't just write thousands of lines of communications code and expect it to work. You have to test at each step of the way. That means you have to broadly envisage a reasonable scheme for each step along the way, before you set out along it.

TOGS

In the next few chapters, I'll be describing how we turned tpg into a real, playable, Battleships game with infrared and SMS text messaging communications.

The basic communications infrastructure is the **transaction-oriented games stack**, TOGS. I designed TOGS with the following objectives:

- ❏ It should support Battleships over infrared and SMS
- ❏ It should support other games, and other protocols
- ❏ It should take into account the realities of both SMS and IR as communications media, including the fact that text messaging is slow, expensive and unreliable
- ❏ It should allow an individual to play many games simultaneously with the same or different players
- ❏ It should support games played over a very long period (weeks, for instance)
- ❏ It should allow the machine to be backed up during the course of a game: since backup closes all applications, this means it should save the state of a game in a file and allow it to be restored again

I also had some objectives for the book:

- ❏ TOGS should be a good demonstration of EPOC's capabilities as a communications platform
- ❏ It should provide excellent example code for the EPOC client-server architecture, which isn't well covered in the SDK
- ❏ It should be fun

As I write, TOGS and Battleships together meet all these objectives. But even so, TOGS is a work in progress. It's not quite bug-free. There are design issues that I'll highlight along the way. And there's plenty of scope for future development of the stack and of its applications.

The Shape of TOGS

Just as in conventional programming, communications designers solve complex problems by breaking them into parts. Each part is called a **protocol**: a protocol is a set of conventions by which two sides can communicate.

It's customary to design protocols at various levels, and to layer one protocol on top of another. The result is a **stack** of protocols, in which data typically gets sent from an application down the stack to some physical transport medium, and then at the other end comes back up the stack to an application again.

Each layer in the stack is there for a definite purpose, and the layer above should assume that the layer below performs its purpose to its stated specification.

While you're developing the stack, you test each layer in turn, so that you can develop the whole stack gradually rather than writing everything and then trying to debug it all at once.

The stack I designed for Battleships has five layers. Here it is:

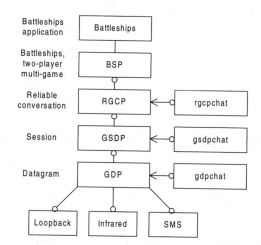

I'll be covering these layers in detail in the next chapter. Meanwhile, here's a very brief description of each layer.

Starting Points — Datagram and Conversation

It's best to start with GDP and RGCP.

❑ GDP, **game datagram protocol**, addresses the underlying realities of communications. With just about any real communications protocol, it's easy to send a datagram (a short packet of binary data). With just about any real communications protocol, the datagram may not arrive: datagrams may arrive out of sequence, may not arrive at all, or may even arrive more than once. The GDP specification allows all these things to happen, and is therefore very easy to implement for anyone with knowledge about specific real communications protocols.

❑ RGCP, **reliable game conversation protocol**, addresses the requirements of application programs. Firstly, two programs communicate to each other using a **session**: once the session is set up, there is simply an 'other' partner, and there's no need to choose who it is. Secondly, each party in the session takes it in turns to send a request, and receive a response – or, looked at the other way, to receive a request, and send a response. This is a **conversation**, and it's clearly a natural paradigm for a turn-based game. Finally programs want **reliable** behavior rather than the underlying unreliability of real communications systems.

'Reliability', in the communications sense, is a technical term with a precise definition. Clearly, 'reliable' doesn't mean that any packet you send is 100% certain to be received. You simply can't guarantee that: there could be network failures, or the recipient might have turned their machine off, lost it or even died. Reliable means that system behavior, as you perceive it, is consistent with what actually happened. So:

❑ If your request didn't get through, you can never receive a response, or another request from your opponent, and you cannot issue another request yourself – you get panicked by RGCP if you try, because that would violate the rules of conversation.

❑ If you receive a response, then that's an indication that your request did get through and was handled according to conversation rules by the other party. You can rely on that.

❑ If the packet you send arrives, then it's guaranteed to be the packet you sent.

❑ And so on: we could spell out many other particular cases.

In summary, GDP addresses the realities of communications, and RGCP meets the basic requirements of application programs.

GDP Implementations — IR, SMS, and Loopback

To implement GDP to deliver packets over a real communications protocol, you need real communications expertise. Jonathan Dixon was familiar with EPOC's communications APIs and wrote both the IrDA and SMS implementations of GDP. We've also discussed the GDP API on more than one occasion, and he recommended some design changes.

Jonathan is also familiar with the arts of real communications testing. He started by writing a loopback implementation of GDP, in which you simply receive whatever packet you send. He used this to test his test code, and then used his test code to test the infrared implementation and later the SMS implementation.

GDP loopback has also been very useful for testing the whole TOGS stack, and it enables you to play Battleships against another player on the same EPOC machine – or against yourself.

Jonathan describes the SMS and IR implementations of GDP in Chapter 21.

GSDP — Game Session Datagram Protocol

We could have written RGCP as a layer directly over GDP. Then, loopback would be useful simply for testing GDP test code, and real communication with, say, IR, would be used for playing a single game between two EPOC machines:

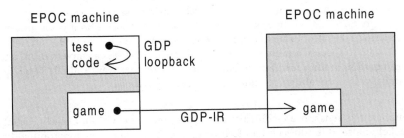

Admittedly you could play another game using another GDP protocol, say SMS. But having only one game on each EPOC machine per GDP protocol is too restrictive.

I wanted to be able to run more than one EPOC game on each machine, each using whatever protocol was really appropriate for it. And it would be quite nice to have a local facility, to play a game against another program on the same machine for test or demo purposes.

So I decided to run *all* GDP implementations inside a server. Contrast the previous diagram in which you can have only a single *application* per GDP protocol on each EPOC machine (which is a restriction), with the diagram below. There you can have only a single *server* on each EPOC machine, which shares GDP between all client applications (which is exactly the kind of thing that servers are there for).

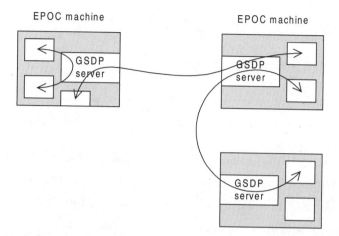

Given that a server can share GDP implementations, the question is, *how* should it share? It's easy enough to ensure that a client *sending* a datagram can get it to the right destination EPOC machine, but what happens when it reaches that machine? Which client should *receive* it?

The answer is that a session – a connection between two specific games – must be built in at this level in TOGS, instead of the RGCP level (which moves up the stack). Hence the name of this level: **game session datagram protocol** or GSDP. Each time a client program sends data using GSDP, the GSDP server adds session information into the GDP packet that is actually sent. When a GSDP server receives a packet, it interprets that session information to ensure that the packet is routed to the correct recipient. GSDP also includes the support for setting up a session.

GSDP is still unreliable: a datagram that is sent may not be received. GSDP also makes no assumptions about the order in which packets are sent. RGCP, the next layer up in the stack, adds reliability and conversation enforcement, which is useful for games like Battleships. GSDP could also be used as the basis of other protocols that add reliability in different ways for use by different types of application.

BSP — Battleships Protocol

Given that RGCP delivers reliable conversation facilities for use by games, the final task was to specify the protocols to be used by the Battleships game itself.

I called this protocol BSP. BSP allows you to set up an RGCP session, and play multiple Battleships games. It supports first-move arbitration, turns as hit-requests, abandoning a game midway through, starting a new game after the previous one was won, lost, or abandoned, and terminating a game including the RGCP session.

In fact, many of these requirements are generic, and BSP could be split into two layers – one for two-player multi-game sessions, and another for the Battleships game itself.

Test Programs

One of the reasons for splitting up a communications stack into layers is simply to be able to understand each layer, and to understand the stack as a whole.

Another compelling reason is to be able to build incrementally and test. Here's the order in which we developed TOGS and Battleships:

❑ Jonathan and I specified the GDP interface.

❑ Jonathan wrote the loopback implementation, and his own test harness. He was able to use the loopback implementation to verify that his test harness worked.

❑ Jonathan implemented GDP-IR, and tested it using the first test harness.

❑ I implemented gdpchat, an EIKON test program. I tested gdpchat in loopback mode, and then Jonathan's GDP-IR implementation, which worked for me the first time I built it.

❑ I implemented GSDP, and gsdpchat, which I used to test GSDP.

❑ I implemented RGCP, and rgcpchat, which I used to test RGCP.

❑ I implemented Battleships, relying firstly on the previous testing of RGCP, and secondly on the previous testing of Battleships' engines and views, so that hopefully I was mainly testing the Battleships controller at this stage, which is where Battleships implements BSP.

❑ Jonathan had by this time completed and tested GDP-SMS, and we made all the necessary changes up and down the stack to graft it in.

So, at each stage, we could rely on the tested aspects of our code being good, and concentrate debugging activity on the new aspects.

Of course, in real life, the progress down the list above isn't a one-way cascade. You don't catch *all* bugs in your test code, and you can never expect to. Even if you do, you make feature changes at previously tested levels of the stack. You have to go up and down the stack a few times, and maintain your test code along with the production code.

It's a fact of life that test code tends to take shortcuts, as you concentrate your efforts on the production code. There are plenty of engineers who enjoy gold-plating test code, and some applications – especially in communications or heavyweight data management – that demand extremely searching test suites. For production code in EPOC ROMs, Symbian takes these issues very seriously. My TOGS test code isn't gold-plated, but I've included it on the book's CD-ROM because it's an important aspect of the real-world development process.

Pattern Re-use

Re-use is good for software systems: it keeps them small and enhances their reliability. In Chapter 4, I made the point that sometimes you can't re-use *code*: you have to re-use *patterns* instead.

Communications is full of this kind of thing. TOGS includes patterns that are standard in the communications industry:

❑ An unreliable datagram protocol – like IP in TCP/IP

❑ The use of port IDs, in GSDP, to identify sessions – like TCP/IP and IrDA

❑ The use of a higher-level protocol, RGCP, to add reliability – like TCP in TCP/IP

Pattern re-use feels like re-inventing the wheel – a bad thing, if there was already a wheel around which you could have used. It turns out that, for all the cases above, there was no wheel already available:

❑ I couldn't use IP, because IP assumes bigger packets than would be supported, say, by SMS, and IP's addressing scheme isn't appropriate either for GDP-SMS (which uses phone numbers for an address), or GDP-IR (a point-to-point protocol which doesn't use any addresses at the GDP level)

❑ I couldn't even use sockets as provided by the ESOCK API, because although sockets are superficially attractive, the whole protocol is too heavyweight for the requirements of GDP, and I would still have had to write my own reliability layer for the specialist requirements of SMS. So I would have written more code to fit in with ESOCK than I would save by using it.

❑ I had to write the GSDP server instead of using, say, the address books associated with IrDA, because although IrDA can multiplex client sessions on one physical layer, other GDP protocols such as SMS cannot.

❑ I couldn't use TCP or even the same kind of approach that TCP uses, to deliver reliability, because it's far too heavyweight for the requirements of conversational games. Also, TCP makes assumptions about the cost of sending packets that aren't appropriate for SMS.

Although it sounds as if SMS is the villain of the piece here, causing all these rewrites, the same is true of the loopback protocol, and the same would be true of other possible GDP protocols such as Bluetooth, or WAP Wireless Datagram Protocol (WDP) datagrams.

Pattern re-use, where it is justified, can lead to substantial savings over code re-use. The DLLs to implement GSDP and RGCP total only 13,584 bytes.

If pattern re-use is justified, then the main issue isn't code bloat. What you really need to watch out for is that you re-use the right patterns. The patterns used in communications have been established over five decades of computer communication, two centuries of electronic communication, and three millennia of civilization. Good communications books don't date quickly, and are worth their weight in gold. Tanenbaum's *Computer Networks* (Prentice Hall, 3rd ed, 1996, ISBN 0133499456) is a particularly good read.

Building on TOGS

Like all the code supplied with the book, the TOGS code is delivered on the book's CD-ROM so you can use it as a starting point for your own projects. Unlike the other source code, there are some special licensing restrictions on TOGS, which you need to observe if you're modifying the TOGS code.

The restrictions are intended to prevent incompatible communications protocols appearing in the marketplace, so that players find they can't interoperate their Battleships game, or the GDP-SMS implementation. So, for instance, *any* implementation of BSP, identified by BSP's GSDP game protocol UID, must conform to the RGCP and BSP specifications in Chapter 17. And *any* implementation of GDP-SMS must conform to the specification in Chapter 21. You can write different games, different GDP drivers, or different ways of putting GDP onto SMS – just so long as you change the identifying features, so that existing implementations don't get confused.

The restrictions are *not* intended to prevent lots of activity, enterprise, and fun based on the TOGS source code. You can write new games, new servers – even servers not related to communications purposes – different reliability layers, and anything else you like, using the existing TOGS specification as a starting point. You can also write non-EPOC implementations of TOGS. I've written plenty of specific ideas, in Chapter 22.

The paragraphs above aren't the license agreement: for the full text, see the CD-ROM and the front material in the book.

Summary

We've now seen an overview of EPOC's communications facilities, the test version of Battleships without any communications at all, and the TOGS stack that is going to make programming Battleships and other applications easier.

For the next few chapters, we'll take you through the specification and implementation of TOGS, and EPOC's system programming frameworks that support this kind of activity.

17

The Transaction-oriented Games Stack

In the previous chapter, I introduced the transaction-oriented games stack (TOGS) that will be used as a foundation to build the Battleships game. In this chapter, I describe the main constituents of TOGS:

- ❑ GDP, providing unreliable datagram service
- ❑ GSDP, adding sessions
- ❑ RGCP, adding reliability and request/response conversation support
- ❑ BSP, implementing the processing for Battleships

I'll describe each of these protocols in the following way:

- ❑ Introduce it and say why it's there
- ❑ Describe the protocol in the abstract
- ❑ Outline the EPOC implementation
- ❑ Point out what future development is needed on this protocol

The material is all here in one chapter so that it forms a ready reference, and the chapter is included at this stage of the book because it shapes much of what follows. Even so, on a first read, you might find yourself wanting to skip some parts of this chapter, or wondering about some of the active object or client-server facilities to which I refer. Don't worry: they will be explained, and you can always come back and re-read.

I'll describe the Battleships game itself in Chapter 22. Jonathan Dixon describes his two implementations of GDP – GDP-IR and GDP-SMS – in Chapter 21.

GDP

GDP is the **Game Datagram Protocol**. Its purpose is to provide the simplest possible interface for sending and receiving packets of data. As a client, you call a SendL() function, specifying a to-address and some data – a datagram. A GDP implementation transfers this packet to the target address, where software executes a GdpHandleL() function whose parameters include the from-address and the data.

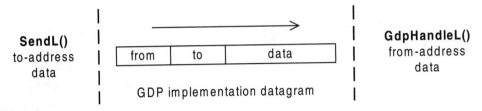

The address received by GdpHandleL() should be such that it can be used to generate a reply to the sender.

The address format is defined by the GDP implementation. A **networked** GDP implementation requires addresses. A **point-to-point** GDP implementation doesn't require addresses: it relies on physical connectivity to get a datagram to the other end-point. GDP-SMS is networked, and the address format is a phone number. GDP-IR is point-to-point, relying essentially on line-of-sight connection. Clearly, loopback is a point-to-point protocol.

GDP is not limited in its application to EPOC machines – a GDP implementation may communicate with non-EPOC machines as well. For this reason, a concrete GDP implementation should specify its physical data formats with sufficient precision for a non-EPOC system to be able to implement a corresponding GDP stack that connects to it.

GDP is unreliable. That means a request through SendL() is sent on a best-efforts basis, but it's not guaranteed to arrive precisely once – it may never arrive, or it may (in rare circumstances) arrive more than once. GDP is not responsible for taking recovery action, or for returning error codes for these events to its clients. However, GDP *should* make reasonable efforts, and it *should* be possible for the end user to understand its reason for failing. (The destination machine is turned off; a cable isn't connected; there is no visual path between infrared ports; the user made a mistake in the mechanics of sending a text message via SMS; etc.)

A GDP implementation should not fail due to timeouts in lower-level protocol stacks. GDP is designed for sending packets in games with a high concentration-to-action ratio, such as chess. The time between sending datagrams may be anything from several seconds to minutes, quarter-hours, days, or even weeks, and all the while both ends have a GDP session active. If a lower-level stack does have a timeout so it can't be kept open indefinitely, the GDP implementation should manage the lower-level stack in such a way as to hide this problem from the GDP client code. It could achieve this, for instance, by reopening the lower-level stack whenever a datagram is sent.

For receiving packets, GDP supports both **push** and **pull** protocols. GDP-IR is push: if an incoming GDP-IR packet arrives, GDP-IR will detect it and ask the client to handle it. GDP-SMS, in EPOC R5, is pull: you call a GDP function to request that the GDP-SMS implementation interrogates the phone for new messages. It is highly desirable to make protocols push-based, if at all possible.

EPOC Implementation

The EPOC implementation of GDP is in \pep\gdp\. It generates gdp.dll and gdp.lib, and exports gdp.h.

The GDP API consists of two interfaces. A client will use MGdpSession to send packets via the implementation, and implement MGdpPacketHandler to handle packets received from the implementation. A GDP implementation implements MGdpSession and uses MGdpPacketHandler. Here it is in UML:

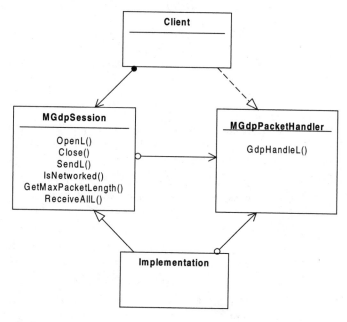

And here, in C++ declarations:

```
class MGdpPacketHandler
    {
public:
    virtual void GdpHandleL(const TDesC& aFromAddress, const TDesC8& aData) = 0;
    };
class MGdpSession
    {
public:
    virtual void OpenL(MGdpPacketHandler* aHandler) = 0;
    virtual void Close() = 0;
    virtual void SendL(const TDesC& aToAddress, const TDesC8& aData) = 0;
    virtual void ReceiveAllL() = 0;
    virtual TInt GetMaxPacketLength() = 0;
    virtual TBool IsNetworked() = 0;
    };
```

`MGdpSession` contains the following functions:

Function	Description
`OpenL()`	Constructs everything needed for the GDP implementation, and specifies the handler for received packets.
`Close()`	Destroys everything that the implementation has constructed. Finishes with `delete this`, so that the session is destroyed. Therefore, GDP sessions cannot be reopened after they have been closed.
`SendL()`	Makes best efforts to send a datagram. You need to specify a to-address (needed by networked implementations) and data. This function may leave if resources need to be reallocated (because, for instance, they have timed out since `OpenL()`). Returns synchronously, but may cause an asynchronous process to be initiated for sending the datagram: errors are not reported.
	An implementation must make a private copy of the aData that is to be sent. The caller may re-use the data buffer any time after calling `SendL()`.
`ReceiveAllL()`	Initiates an asynchronous process to cause any outstanding datagrams to be received. May leave if resources need to be reallocated (because, for instance, they have timed out since `OpenL()`).
`IsNetworked()`	Returns `ETrue` if the protocol is networked. In this case, a non-empty to-address is required for `SendL()` calls, and a non-empty from-address is passed to `GdpHandleL()`.
`GetMaxPacketLength()`	Returns the maximum length of a GDP datagram, excluding addresses, which can be transmitted by the protocol implementation.

`MGdpPacketHandler` contains the following function:

Function	Description
`GdpHandleL()`	Called to handle a packet that has been received, specifying the data and the from-address. For networked protocols, this enables you to reply to the sender.
	A handler should make a copy of the aData passed to it: the buffer may be re-used by a GDP implementation immediately after `GdpHandleL()` returns.

GDP Loopback Implementation

The loopback implementation of GDP is useful for testing, and also for local game play using the GSDP server. CGdpLoopback is declared in gdploop.h:

```
class CGdpLoopback : public CBase, public MGdpSession
    {
public:
    IMPORT_C CGdpLoopback();
    // From MGdpSession
    void OpenL(MGdpPacketHandler* aHandler); // Start up, and
                                             // set handler for packets received
    void Close();                            // Close and commit suicide
    void SendL(const TDesC& aToAddress, const TDesC8& aData);  // Send packet
    void ReceiveAllL();                      // Do a pull if necessary
    TInt GetMaxPacketLength();               // Max packet length
    TBool IsNetworked();   // If not point-to-point, then preserves addresses
private:
    MGdpPacketHandler* iHandler;
    };
```

It's simply a CBase class that implements the MGdpSession interface. It's implemented in gdploop.cpp. Here is the complete implementation:

```
EXPORT_C CGdpLoopback::CGdpLoopback()
    {
    }

void CGdpLoopback::OpenL(MGdpPacketHandler* aHandler)
    {
    iHandler = aHandler;
    }

void CGdpLoopback::Close() // close
    {
    delete this;
    }

void CGdpLoopback::SendL(const TDesC& /*aToAddress*/, const TDesC8& aData)
    {
    _LIT(KNullAddress, "");
    iHandler->GdpHandleL(KNullAddress, aData);
    }

void CGdpLoopback::ReceiveAllL() // do a pull if necessary
    {
    }

TInt CGdpLoopback::GetMaxPacketLength()
    {
    return KMaxTInt;
    }
```

```
TInt CGdpLoopback::IsNetworked()
    {
    return EFalse;
    }
```

The key function, SendL(), ignores the address given, and sends a packet which looks as though it has come from an empty origin address. Provided the receiver copies the data from the sender's buffer (which is required by the GdpHandleL() contract), SendL() fulfils its contract to not use the sender's data after SendL() has returned.

GDP Chat

gdpchat is a straightforward test program that enables you to use an EIKON dialog box to send text, and displays the last sent and last received message.

The version provided on the book's CD requires you to rebuild it to select a new GDP protocol, or to change the phone number when using GDP-SMS.

Taking GDP Forward

Since we wrote this specification, and integrated it into the GSDP server, we've realized that quite a few things need to be changed.

> **Most importantly, most of the Ls here are bogus. Only OpenL() should leave. SendL(), GdpHandleL(), and ReceiveAllL() should not.**

To change this now would have knock-on effects throughout the whole of TOGS. However, it's needed, because many of these functions are called from GSDP server contexts and, as I'll argue in Chapter 20, functions called from within a server should not leave unless they are processed directly in response to client requests.

> **Send() should be asynchronous.**

GDP should post a flag when it is capable of sending another datagram. With the present design, it isn't possible to implement a transmit queue in the GSDP server, which means that a datagram is bound to be lost if one is already in the process of being sent. While GDP is allowed to lose packets, this kind of unreliability is arbitrary, and can only be fixed by making Send() report when it has finished.

MGdpSession is a weird M class – the suicide semantics of Close() are rather un-EPOC-like. Better to make it a C class, equipped with an honest destructor.

GSDP

GSDP adds session capability to GSDP datagrams. On a single EPOC machine, all GDP implementations are run on a server. A client uses the GSDP client interface, not the GDP interface, to send data.

To the GDP datagram payload, GSDP adds:

- ❏ A from-port ID: this is the non-zero ID of a port used by the sending client

- ❏ A to-port ID: during an established session, this is a non-zero ID which identifies the client on the target EPOC machine (or other entity specified by a GDP address) which will receive the datagram

- ❏ A game protocol ID: this is used in session setup. When a client connects to the GSDP server on its machine, it specifies the game protocol it will use. If the client listens with its zero port ID, then an incoming packet with a zero port ID will be matched with a client's game protocol ID. Thus the game protocol ID ensures that the session is set up with a compatible partner.

These IDs are all 32-bit numbers. The from-port and to-port IDs are allocated by the GSDP server in ascending sequence. The game protocol ID is a UID. Theoretically, neither the game ID nor the from-port ID is needed throughout the session. But they provide a useful redundancy check.

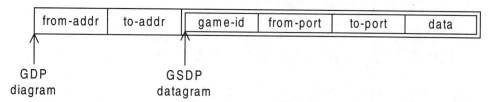

The GSDP datagram contents are passed as arguments to the GSDP send and handle functions. The session between the GSDP client and the GSDP server on the same machine carries the state required to set the non-data fields – from-port ID, to-address, to-port ID, and game protocol ID.

> *There is terminology confusion here: 'session' can be used to mean a GSDP session between two GSDP send-points, or a client-server session between an application and a server on an EPOC machine. The word 'session' is justified in both cases. I will try to be unambiguous.*

By using a GDP loopback implementation inside the GSDP server, two GSDP clients on the same machine may communicate with each other.

Although GSDP is session-based, it is *not* reliable. A GSDP send is no more reliable than a GDP send: it may result in zero, one, or more receives at the destination.

The GSDP client API allows you to specify the GDP implementation to be used for a GSDP session. GDP implementations are managed by the GSDP server. The GSDP server uses GDP implementations, as specified above, without any change.

For a packet to reach a particular GSDP client successfully, its sender must specify the correct address, port, and game protocol ID. There are two interesting cases here:

❑ The to-port is non-zero: a GSDP client must be listening with the correct port ID. This is used for communication after a session has been set up.

❑ The to-port is zero: a GSDP client must be listening with a zero port ID, and a matching game protocol ID. This is used for session setup.

These two possibilities allow a session between two partners to be set up and then maintained. The session is set up by the **initiating** partner, which sends a packet with a non-zero from-port, a game protocol ID, and a zero to-port. The session is accepted by a **listening** partner, which has a matching game protocol ID and a zero port ID. Once accepted, the listening partner allocates its own non-zero port ID, and sends back a packet to the initiating partner: this **binds** the session. Subsequent communication uses non-zero port IDs on both sides.

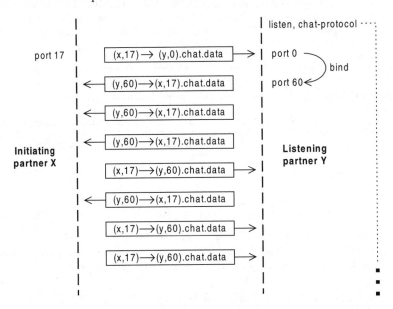

GSDP is intended to support two-player games with an arbitrarily long think time between moves. A GSDP session must persist even when the games are saved and closed at either or both ends. A client must save its GSDP state, including addresses and port IDs. The server provides functions that are able to support the client restoring its state. The server does not hold state information on clients' behalf, beyond client-server session termination.

The server queues incoming datagrams and holds them so that they can be received by a dormant client, or by a new client launched in listening mode. The queue is managed as follows:

❑ If an incoming datagram has a non-zero to-port ID, which matches the port ID of an active listening client, then that request is satisfied by the datagram – that is, the datagram is received.

❑   If the datagram has a zero to-port ID, and a game protocol ID that matches an active client with a zero port ID, a matching game protocol ID, and an outstanding receive request, then the request is satisfied and the datagram is received.

❑   If neither of these conditions is true, then the datagram is added to the queue.

❑   Whenever the game protocol ID or port ID of a client is changed, or a new receive request is issued, the queue is scanned to see if any datagrams in it match the rules above: if so, such datagrams are received.

❑   If a datagram is received by matching the above rules, but it doesn't match other sensible rules, then the datagram is dropped – that is, it's absorbed by the GSDP server and not sent to the client, and the client's receive request is not fulfilled. Examples of such 'sensible rules' include that the game protocol IDs must match when the port ID is non-zero, and the from-address should be as expected when the to-port ID is non-zero. These rules are based on redundant information in the GSDP packet, which allows a useful check to be performed.

❑   Packets on the queue may be expired according to rules at the discretion of the GSDP server implementer. If the queue is too large, then packets may not be accepted onto it when received by a GDP implementation. The present EPOC implementation expires packets only when the GSDP server is stopped – which happens when all its clients are stopped. The present EPOC implementation has a maximum queue length of 10: any additional packets are dropped.

❑   These awkward management issues notwithstanding, the queue is necessary because a client may not be started when an initiate request from a GSDP game on another EPOC machine arrives. Also, when a client's receive request is fulfilled, it doesn't issue a new one until it has handled the previous one, which causes a transient condition whereby the client is unable to receive.

GSDP specifies no formal mechanism for releasing a GSDP port ID, which means it's important that port IDs be allocated uniquely by a given GSDP server. The EPOC GSDP server maintains the last-allocated port ID in a file in c:\System\Data\: the port ID is incremented and re-stored every time a new session is initiated or accepted. This file persists across GSDP server invocations, and guarantees unique port ID allocation provided that all port IDs are dropped by the time wraparound occurs. In practice, this is sufficient: if one port ID were allocated per second, it would take over 143 years to wrap around.

EPOC Implementation — Client Side

On EPOC, the GSDP client API is defined in gsdp.h and delivered in gsdp.dll. The client API consists of two classes: a concrete RGsdpSession class to control the session and send packets, and an abstract MGsdpPacketHandler class that you should implement for handling received packets.

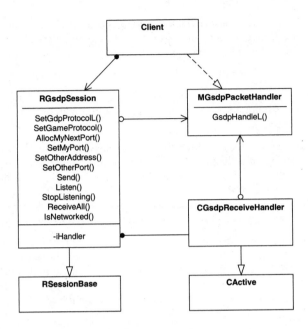

Additionally, a private, client-side active object, CGsdpReceiveHandler, turns the client listen function into a continuously renewed receive request. This removes any responsibility from the client to implement its own active object to handle or renew the request.

Here's RGsdpSession's declaration in C++, showing additional housekeeping and getter functions:

```cpp
class RGsdpSession : public RSessionBase
    {
public:
    enum TGdpProtocol
        {
        EGdpLoopback=1, EGdpIr, EGdpSms
        };
public:
    // Construct
    inline RGsdpSession() : iHandler(0) {};

    // Open/close
    IMPORT_C void ConnectL(MGsdpPacketHandler* aHandler);
    IMPORT_C void Close();

    // Load and get GDP protocol
    IMPORT_C void SetGdpProtocolL(TGdpProtocol aProtocol);
    IMPORT_C TGdpProtocol GetGdpProtocol() const;
    IMPORT_C TBool GdpIsNetworked() const;

    // Game protocol
    IMPORT_C void SetGameProtocol(TUint32 aProtocol);
    IMPORT_C TUint32 GetGameProtocol() const;
```

```
    // Set and get my address and port
    IMPORT_C void SetMyPort(TUint32 aPort);
    IMPORT_C TUint32 GetMyPort() const;
    IMPORT_C TUint32 AllocMyNextPort();

    // Set and get other address and port
    IMPORT_C void SetOtherAddress(const TDesC& aAddress);
    IMPORT_C void GetOtherAddress(TDes& aAddress) const;
    IMPORT_C void SetOtherPort(TUint32 aPort);
    IMPORT_C TUint32 GetOtherPort() const;

    // Main protocol functions
    IMPORT_C void Listen();
    IMPORT_C void StopListening();
    IMPORT_C void Send(const TDesC8& aData);

    // Initiate receive-all for "pull" protocols
    IMPORT_C void ReceiveAll() const;
private:
    friend class CGsdpReceiveHandler;
    void Receive(TDes8& aBuffer, TRequestStatus& aStatus);
    void CancelReceive();
    CGsdpReceiveHandler* iHandler;
    };
```

The functions of `RGsdpSession` include:

Function	Description
ConnectL()	Connects to the GSDP server, and specifies a GSDP packet handler. The server is launched if it is not already active.
Close()	Closes the session with the server. The server may choose to terminate if it has no more clients, but the client API does not mandate this.
SetGdpProtocolL()	Sets the GDP implementation to be used by the session. Will leave if the implementation is not available, or cannot be initialized.
GdpIsNetworked()	Indicates whether the GDP implementation is networked (requires valid addresses) or point-to-point (ignores addresses).
SetGameProtocol()	Sets the game protocol, specifying a 32-bit UID.
SetMyPort()	Sets my port ID, specifying the port ID as a 32-bit unsigned value. Use this function when restoring a session previously established.
AllocMyNextPort()	Allocates a unique port ID for me, and returns its value. Use this function when starting a new session.
SetOtherAddress()	Sets the address of the other partner in the communication, with a string. Used only by networked GDP implementations.

Function	Description
SetOtherPort()	Sets the port of the other partner in the communication, with a 32-bit unsigned value. Use this when setting up a session that has been previously established; set it to zero when starting a new session.
Listen()	Causes a Receive() request to be issued. When the request completes, the received datagram will be handled using MGsdpPacketHandler::GsdpHandleL(). The receive request will then be renewed so that, without client intervention, any number of packets can be received.
StopListening()	Cancels any outstanding receive request started by Listen(). You may issue this function even if no call to Listen() has been issued, or if it has already been canceled.
SendL()	Sends a datagram using whatever current address, port, GDP implementation, and game protocol ID are specified.
ReceiveAllL()	Causes the GDP implementation to do a ReceiveAllL(). This may result in received packets that need to be handled for *any* GSDP session that uses the same GDP implementation, not only the GSDP session that issued the ReceiveAllL().
GetXxx()	Getter functions for address, port, GDP implementation, and game protocol ID.

MGsdpPacketHandler is declared as,

```
class MGsdpPacketHandler
    {
public:
    virtual void GsdpHandleL(const TDesC8& aData) = 0;
    };
```

with the following function:

Function	Description
GsdpHandleL()	Handle a received packet. The server guarantees that the packet matches the game protocol and port numbers required by the protocol.

Server-side EPOC Implementation

The server is described in Chapter 20. It implements the requirements of the GSDP protocol's external behavior, and of the client interface.

GSDP Chat

GSDP chat is the test code for GSDP. You can find the C++ source in \pep\gsdpchat\, and the AIF source in \pep\gsdpchataif\. On the Extras bar, the caption in English is Chat.

GSDP chat uses GSDP to set up and continue a conversation. All GSDP chat packets use the distinguishing game protocol ID 0x10005405, which is also the third UID for tpgchat.app.

Partners to a chat session may be in one of four states:

State	Meaning
blank	Nothing happening, not even connected to GSDP.
bound	A session is bound and active.
initiating	The initiating partner has opened a session with the GSDP server, selected a GDP implementation, had a port ID allocated by the GSDP server, set the GSDP chat protocol ID to 0x10005405, and has sent a GSDP packet to a GDP address, specifying a zero port ID. The initiating partner is now waiting for a reply from that GDP address: the reply will cause the session to bind.
listening	A listening partner has opened a session with the GSDP server, selected a GDP implementation, is using a zero port ID, and has issued Listen(). The listening partner is expecting an incoming packet from any GDP address (using the same protocol), any GSDP port, and the GSDP chat protocol ID 0x10005405. When the packet comes in, the listening partner will accept it and bind the session.

A chat partner can only change to the bound state via listening or initiating. A bound session can only be established between two partners, one of which initiates while the other listens.

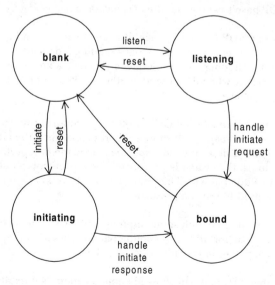

If two Chat users both try to initiate, or both just sit and listen, a session will not be set up. They must decide how to recover and start a session. A reset can be issued at any time, and will set the partner to the blank state.

Settings can be saved to file and later restored. When two chat users end their session, there is no formal way to tell GSDP of this fact. The partners simply cease to use their allocated port IDs.

The GSDP chat program provides the following user interface:

❏   Reset: reset everything and go into blank state

❏   Initiate: specify GDP implementation and my address (if appropriate), other partner's address, and initial message to send

❏   Listen: specify GDP implementation, and my address if appropriate

❏   Display settings: show GDP implementation, session state, my GDP address and GSDP port ID, and the other GDP address and GSDP port ID

❏   Send: send a datagram

❏   Receive All: initiate receive all on the GDP protocol in use

GSDP chat is a file-based application. You can create a new Chat file from the shell in order to launch the application. Session settings – along with the previously sent and received messages – will be persisted in the document file when the application is closed. You can then re-launch this file in order to carry on Chat over the same GSDP session.

Taking GSDP Forward

You'll notice that functions such as Send() and ReceiveAll() are coded without Ls in GSDP. I believe that to be correct; GDP hasn't yet got rid of its Ls, but should.

The most urgent requirement in GSDP is a send queue. If a client tries to send a datagram when the GDP implementation for that client session is already busy sending a datagram, then the later datagram is lost. This should be managed by adding a transmit queue. There is a knock-on effect: GDP Send() must be able to tell the GSDP server when it can send another packet, so that the GSDP transmit queue can know when to send the next packet.

The next most urgent requirement is to add full GDP protocol polymorphism, so that instead of defining supported protocols in an enum, and loading all supported protocols when the GSDP server initializes, SetGdpProtocolL() should take a descriptor that specifies the name of a protocol, and supporting functions should be provided to list the available protocols. Then, protocols would be loaded only as needed, and new ones could be added at will. This change would have knock-on effects on the code in any EIKON application that is used to select a protocol.

The receive queue management could do with some improvement. Two clients listening with the same game protocol ID should perhaps be forbidden. Incoming packets should perhaps be dropped instead of being held in a queue until an application is ready to receive them.

The port ID allocator has a subtle bug that will show in about a century's time: it doesn't prevent zero being allocated on ID wrap-around.

RGCP

TOGS is designed to support turn-based games, for which a reliable conversation protocol is the most suitable means of presenting the communications API to any game application. The role of RGCP is to present a reliable conversation protocol to applications.

Protocol Overview

After session setup, conversations follow a strict request-response sequence:

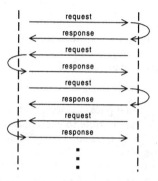

In order to save costs (a GSDP datagram using SMS has a financial cost to its sender), the response to the previous request by one partner shares a packet with the responding partner's next request, so that in terms of the lower-level GSDP communication, the picture is this:

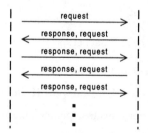

RGCP uses essentially the same methods as GSDP for session setup, but it adds reliability by allowing packets to be re-sent. RGCP also provides for normal session termination (rather than simply abandoning communications, which is the best you can do in GSDP).

Because RGCP is a conversation protocol, it is relatively easy to provide reliability. At most, one packet needs to be stored for potential re-sending (though in bad cases it may be re-sent many times). Contrast this with the kind of reliability mechanisms needed to implement FTP efficiently, in which **windowing** is used to send a potentially large number of outstanding packets before any acknowledgement is required – and all these outstanding packets may need to be re-sent. This means RGCP's job in adding reliability to GSDP is much easier than, say, TCP's job in adding reliability to IP.

The conversation protocol paradigm is clearly suitable for two-player, turn-based games. It can also be adapted for various situations that are not strictly conversational. For instance, a player may take multiple moves either by piggy-backing them into a single RGCP request, or by sending them in individual RGCP requests, with the other player acknowledging each one and sending a 'no-move' request in turn.

A single RGCP session may be used to play more than one game, if the request-response protocol for the game protocol ID supports it. The request-response protocol would then have to support not only game moves, but also game initialization, termination, and choosing who has the first move. BSP does this.

Re-send Management

Many reliable protocols manage re-sends by waiting a fixed time for an acknowledgement, and then re-sending if none is received. This approach is not open to RGCP, because thinking time between moves may be long, and the response, which serves as an acknowledgement, is not sent until the next move request.

Therefore, RGCP users must agree when a packet is lost, and re-send it manually. Since RGCP packets represent game moves – something quite tangible to each player – it is easy enough to determine when a packet has been lost, and easy enough to re-send. Thus, the manual intervention in a communications protocol has clear meaning for the user.

Although RGCP re-sends are manual, RGCP does provide reliability in the usual communications sense. RGCP will not allow either party in a conversation to send requests or responses *out of turn*, and will prevent any packet from being delivered to the RGCP receiver more than once, even if it is re-sent at the GSDP level.

Packet Structure

RGCP uses GSDP as a transport. An RGCP packet has the following structure:

- ❑ GDP header with from-address and to-address
- ❑ GSDP header with game protocol ID, from-port ID, and to-port ID
- ❑ RGCP sequence number (or zero for unsequenced packets)
- ❑ RGCP response packet
- ❑ RGCP request packet

The request and response packets have identical formats:

- ❑ One-byte length in range 0-127, giving the total length of opcode plus data
- ❑ One-byte opcode specifying the operation to be performed (if the length is 1 or greater)
- ❑ Data bytes, 0-126 bytes long

Certain opcodes are reserved for RGCP protocol functions. The meaning of all other opcodes depends on the particular type of conversation, as identified by the GSDP game protocol ID.

The minimum length of an RGCP datagram is 7 bytes, plus GSDP headers, plus GDP headers. The 7 bytes comprise four for the sequence number, one for a zero-length response, and two for the request (a length of one, and the request opcode).

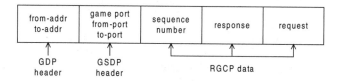

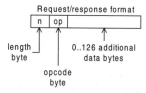

Sequencing and Re-sending

Once a GSDP session has been bound, only sequenced packets are accepted, with sequence numbers starting at 1 after session establishment. The receiver maintains a record of the last-received sequence number and drops packets whose sequence number is less than or equal to this, eliminating duplicates.

The RGCP transmitter maintains the last-sent packet, and re-sends it identically on request. The last-sent packet is deemed acknowledged when a corresponding response/request packet is received. The last-sent packet is deleted when it has been acknowledged, and cannot then be re-sent.

Session Setup

To set up a session, the initiating partner sends an 'initiate' request with a zero RGCP sequence number (and a zero GSDP to-port ID). This is received by a listening partner, who sends an 'initiate' response, any request, and sequence number one. The listening partner then considers itself bound in a session. When the initiating partner receives the 'initiate' response, it too considers itself bound in a session: the next response/request datagram it sends will be sequenced number one.

The listening partner sends the first sequenced packet. For the listening partner, receiving response n (from the initiating partner) acknowledges its request n. For the initiating partner, receiving response $n+1$ (from the listening partner) acknowledges its request n. The initiate-request and initiate-response datagrams may be re-sent using the usual RGCP re-send facility.

To terminate a session normally, the terminating partner sends a 'terminate' request. After sending a terminate request, the terminating partner is in the blank state: it does not expect to receive a response. The partner receiving a terminate request must therefore terminate without sending a response. A terminate request has a zero sequence number, because it can be sent at any time, without waiting for the terminating partner's turn in the conversation. A terminate request cannot be re-sent.

Although a terminate request has a zero sequence number, it is uniquely identified with a particular RGCP session because it specifies GSDP port numbers that are unique to that session.

Abnormal termination may occur through either partner in a session – or during session setup – simply ceasing to communicate. The other partner must realize by other means that this has happened, abandon their current session, and decide what further action to take.

Standard Opcodes

RGCP defines three request opcodes:

- ❑   0xff: initiate – also used to indicate initiate-response
- ❑   0xfe: terminate
- ❑   0x00: should not be used

Other opcodes may be defined by specific RGCP implementations.

Responses are uniquely associated with their corresponding requests, so a response opcode system is not strictly necessary. RGCP protocol designers may, however, find it convenient and/or safer to use the same opcodes for responses as they use for requests.

States and Transitions

As perceived by either endpoint, an RGCP session may have the following states:

State	Meaning
blank	No GSDP connection.
initiating	An initiate request has been sent, but no response has been received.
listening	Ready to receive an initiate request, but none has yet been received.
responding	The session has been bound, a request is being handled, and the partner must compose a response. This state lasts only for the duration of a single synchronous function call.
requesting	The session has been bound, and it is this partner's turn to compose and send a request.
waiting	The session has been bound, this party has sent a response/request, and is now waiting for its response and another request. Incoming responses are handled in waiting state.

Here are the allowable states, and all allowable transitions between them (except reset transitions, which have been omitted for clarity, but which are possible from any state to blank).

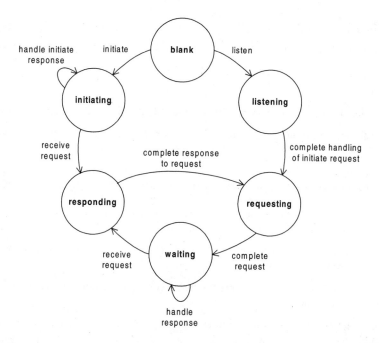

RGCP states correspond precisely to underlying GSDP states, with the distinction that GSDP's **bound** state is divided into two major states, **requesting** and **waiting**, that correspond to whether it's this partner's turn to 'talk' or not. That's natural: this is precisely what a conversation protocol is all about. The additional **responding** state is a brief transition state between **waiting** and **requesting**.

All of these states may be of arbitrary duration, except **responding**, which must complete in the duration of a single synchronous function call. This implies that an RGCP response should be a response to the request that contains *information* about the result of the other partner's move – not a responding *move*, which would take arbitrary time.

The following state transitions are possible:

❑ **blank** to **initiating** or **listening**: similar to GSDP

❑ **listening** or **initiating** to **blank**, by a simple reset

❑ **responding**, **requesting** or **waiting** to **blank**, by a terminate that's either called through this partner's API, or received from the other partner as a request

❑ **listening** to **requesting**, by handling an initiate request (the responding state that you might expect is handled internally by the RGCP stack)

❑ **initiating** to **responding**, by receiving an initiate response and handling the incoming request

❑ **waiting** to **responding**, by receiving a response and handling the incoming request

❑ **responding** to **requesting**, by completing the handling of an incoming request

❑ **requesting** to **waiting**, by completing the formulation of a request, and sending it

Packet Handling

RGCP's rules for handling incoming packets, delivered to it by GSDP, may be summarized as follows:

❏ [If the port IDs and game protocol ID don't match those for the session, incoming packets won't even be received.]

❏ If the packet's RGCP headers are malformed it is dropped.

❏ If the sequence number is zero, and it's a terminate request, then the RGCP session is immediately terminated: no response is sent.

❏ If the sequence number is zero, and it's an initiate request, and the current state is listening, then an initiate response is formulated accepting the initiate, the GSDP session is bound, and the RGCP state changes to requesting. The sending sequence number is incremented to 1 so that this becomes the first sequence number of an ordinary packet from the listening partner. In all other circumstances, a zero sequence number packet is dropped.

❏ If the sequence number is less than or equal to the last-received sequence number, then the packet is dropped.

❏ If the sequence number increments the last-received sequence number by more than one, then the packet is dropped.

❏ [We now assert that it is a normal in-session response/request datagram, so the state must be waiting.]

❏ The last-received packet sequence number is incremented.

❏ The response is handled, and then we check that the RGCP stack hasn't been terminated by higher-level function calls.

❏ The state is changed to responding; the request is handled, and we check again that the stack hasn't been terminated. If no response has been written, we produce a null response.

❏ [The response is not sent at this stage: rather, the partially-written send buffer is maintained until an RGCP request is sent. At that point, the response and request are sent in a GSDP datagram.]

❏ The state changes to requesting.

RGCP EPOC Implementation

The EPOC RGCP implementation is defined in `rgcp.h` and delivered in `rgcp.dll`.

The EPOC RGCP implementation operates entirely client-side, and builds on the GSDP client API. As usual, one concrete class (`CRgcpSession`) owns the session and handles sending, while another abstract class (`MRgcpHandler`) specifies virtual functions that should be implemented by the client.

Here is it in UML (omitting some housekeeping and getter functions):

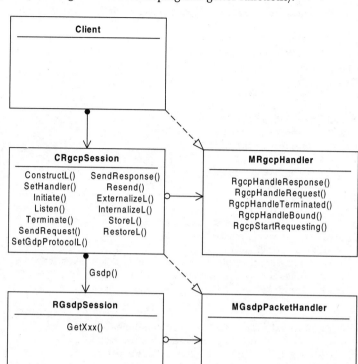

Here's `CRgcpSession`'s declaration in C++:

```
class CRgcpSession : public CBase, public MGsdpPacketHandler
    {
public:
    enum TState
        {
        EBlank, EListening, EInitiating, EResponding, ERequesting, EWaiting
        };
    enum TOpcode
        {
        EReserved=0,
        EInitiate=0xff,
        ETerminate=0xfe
        };
public:
    // Construct/destruct
    IMPORT_C CRgcpSession();
    IMPORT_C void ConstructL(TUint32 aGameProtocol);
    IMPORT_C ~CRgcpSession();
    IMPORT_C void SetHandler(MRgcpHandler* aHandler);
```

```
    // Initialization
    IMPORT_C void SetGdpProtocolL(RGsdpSession::TGdpProtocol aGdpProtocol);

    // State
    inline TState State() const;
    inline TBool IsBlank() const;
    inline TBool IsInitiating() const;
    inline TBool IsListening() const;
    inline TBool IsResponding() const;
    inline TBool IsRequesting() const;
    inline TBool IsWaiting() const;
    inline TBool IsBound() const;

    // State transition functions
    IMPORT_C void Initiate(const TDesC& aOtherAddress);
    IMPORT_C void Listen();
    IMPORT_C void Terminate();
    IMPORT_C void SendResponse(TInt aOpcode, const TDesC8& aData);
    IMPORT_C void SendResponse(TInt aOpcode);
    IMPORT_C void SendResponse();
    IMPORT_C void SendRequest(TInt aOpcode, const TDesC8& aData);
    IMPORT_C void SendRequest(TInt aOpcode);
    IMPORT_C void Resend();

    // Persistence
    IMPORT_C void ExternalizeL(RWriteStream& aStream) const;
    IMPORT_C void InternalizeL(RReadStream& aStream);
    IMPORT_C TStreamId StoreL(CStreamStore& aStore) const;
    IMPORT_C void RestoreL(const CStreamStore& aStore, TStreamId aStreamId);

    // Access to GSDP stuff
    inline const RGsdpSession& Gsdp() const;
private:
    // Help with sending
    void DoSendRequest(TInt aOpcode, const TDesC8& aData);
    void DoSendResponse(TInt aOpcode, const TDesC8& aData);
    void DoTerminate(TBool aClientInitiated);

    // Handle incoming datagrams
    void GsdpHandleL(const TDesC8& aData);
    void CrackPacketL(const TDesC8& aData, TInt& aSeqNo,
                      TInt& aResponseOpcode, TInt& aRequestOpcode);
    void HandlePacket(TInt aSeqNo,
                      TInt aResponseOpcode, TInt aRequestOpcode);
    void HandleTerminateRequest();
    void HandleInitiateRequest();
private:
    TState iState;
    RGsdpSession iGsdp;
    MRgcpHandler* iHandler;

    // Send apparatus
    TInt iNextSendSequenceNo;
```

```
    RDesWriteStream iSendWriter;
    TBuf8<KMaxGsdpData> iSendBuffer;

    // Receive apparatus
    TInt iLastReceivedSequenceNo;
    TBuf8<KMaxGsdpData> iReceiveBuffer;
    TBuf8<126> iResponse; // Rather wasteful
    TBuf8<126> iRequest;  // Rather wasteful
    };
```

The main functions are:

Function	Description
ConstructL()	Construct the session class, specifying a game protocol. Internally, the function constructs an RGsdpSession object for communicating down the stack.
SetHandler()	Sets a handler for incoming packets. Prior to setting the handler, you can store and restore state, but cannot invoke any communication functions. Specify 0 to unset the handler: communications functions will be stopped (without issuing a Terminate()). Specify a non-zero value to set a handler: if the state demands it, a GSDP Listen() will be issued.
SetGdpProtocolL()	Set the GDP protocol to be used.
State()	Get current state. A group of IsXxx() functions also allow you to test whether the session is in a particular state. IsBound() is included, to mean any of responding, requesting, or waiting.
Initiate()	Valid only from blank state. Specify the other address, and the state changes to initiating. An initiate request with zero sequence number is sent to the other address in a GSDP datagram (together with a null response). The datagram is held in the re-send buffer.
Listen()	Valid only from blank state. State changes to listening.
Terminate()	Valid from any state. From bound states, sends a terminate request to the other partner. State changes immediately to blank. The handler function RgcpTerminated() is called.
SendResponse()	Valid only from responding state. State changes to requesting. Specify an opcode and data up to 126 bytes in length. If specified, the opcode must *not* be one of those reserved by RGCP. An overload with no data parameter is provided: the data defaults to 0 bytes. A further overload with no opcode parameter can be used to generate a minimal response with no opcode.

Table Continued on Following Page

Function	Description
SendRequest()	Valid only from requesting state. State changes to waiting. Specify an opcode and data up to 126 bytes in length. The opcode must not be one of those reserved by RGCP. An overload with no data parameter is provided: the data defaults to 0 bytes. The previous response (and this request) is sent in a single GSDP datagram. The datagram is held in the re-send buffer.
Resend()	Valid only from initiating and waiting states. Re-sends the last GSDP datagram from the re-send buffer.
ExternalizeL()	Externalize state to stream, including all GSDP information and the re-send buffer.
InternalizeL()	Internalize state from stream, including all GSDP information and the re-send buffer.
StoreL()	Store state by creating a stream, externalizing, closing the stream, and returning its ID.
RestoreL()	Restore state by opening the specified stream, internalizing from it, and then closing the stream.
Gsdp()	Get a const version of the underlying GSDP session, so that GSDP settings can be interrogated.

Here's MRgcpHandler's declaration in C++:

```
class MRgcpHandler
    {
public:
    virtual void RgcpHandleResponse(TInt aOpcode, const TDesC8& aData) = 0;
    virtual void RgcpHandleRequest(TInt aOpcode, const TDesC8& aData) = 0;
    virtual void RgcpHandleTerminated(TBool aClientInitiated) = 0;
    virtual void RgcpHandleBound() = 0;
    virtual void RgcpStartRequesting() = 0;
    };
```

MRgcpHandler includes the following functions:

Function	Description
RgcpHandleResponse()	Handle response. Called in waiting state, this function takes opcode and data parameters. If the response was null, the opcode passed to this function is zero. After this function returns, state changes to responding (unless you called Terminate() to set the state to blank).

Function	Description
RgcpHandleRequest()	Handle request. Called in responding state, this function takes opcode and data parameters. You can call SendResponse() from within this function to send a response. If you do not call SendResponse(), then after this function returns, a default null response will be constructed. After this function returns, state changes to requesting (unless you called Terminate() to set the state to blank).
RgcpHandleTerminated()	Handle termination. Called in any state (except blank). Takes a parameter indicating whether the termination resulted from a client API call, or in response to a terminate request received from the other partner.
RgcpHandleBound()	Handle session binding. Called in initiating or listening states.
	If called in initiating state (because an initiate-response was received), then state afterwards changes to responding (unless you called Terminate() to set the state to blank). If called in listening state (because an initiate-request was received), then state afterwards changes to sending (unless you called Terminate() to set the state to blank).
RgcpStartRequesting()	Called when the state has changed to requesting. May be used to set an indicator to indicate the state transition. May be used to generate a synchronous request. You cannot generate such a request from RgcpHandleBound() or RgcpHandleRequest().

RGCP Converse

The Converse application is in \pep\rgcpchat\ and its AIF, which specifies a caption Converse in English, is in \pep\rgcpchataif\. It's not the most spectacular piece of test code and hasn't yet been updated to support SMS. For a better RGCP test application, see Battleships!

Taking RGCP Forward

RGCP's manual resend system and response piggybacking are tailored to the requirement of relatively expensive protocols, to avoid sending more datagrams than necessary.

For protocols such as infrared, which are fast and free, this is too heavyweight. It produces the oddity that, when playing Battleships over IR, you don't see a response to your move until the other player has decided what move to take. That's OK over SMS, but over infrared it feels odd.

It would be possible to add either another layer, or a fairly compatible modification, to RGCP:

❑ This could allow responses to be sent immediately, without waiting for a piggy-back packet

❑ Given the possibility of an immediate response, *require* an immediate response in some situations and, if one does not arrive, re-send automatically

I have provisionally called this protocol QRGCP (Q = quick), but haven't implemented it.

`CRgcpSession` could use better construction encapsulation. Rather than providing a C++ constructor to be followed by either `ConstructL()` or `RestoreL()`, it would be better to provide two public `NewL()`s, one with construct semantics, and the other with restore semantics.

The Battleships Protocol

BSP, the Battleships Protocol, builds on RGCP to allow players to play the two-player game. Within the span of a single conversation (or 'session'), multiple Battleships games may be played. Outside a session, you cannot play a game.

A session is set up by one partner initiating and the other listening. Partners specify whether they want to move first, or move second, or don't care. The decision is arbitrated in favor of the initiating partner (who will go first if they so requested, or if neither party cares, or if the other partner asked to go second).

Normal play consists of a sequence of move requests. The game may be finished by being won by one partner (and therefore lost by the other), or the player whose turn it is to move may abandon it. If the game is finished in either of these ways, the session remains active and another game can be started. This time, the player who lost or abandoned gets preference of first move.

The RGCP session may be terminated, at any time, which of course terminates any game currently in progress.

Protocol Overview

Here's a brief look at the details of BSP.

States

The possible states of a Battleships application are:

State	Meaning
blank	No conversation is established. The game is in an arbitrary state (either a neutral state if the program has just started, or the state at the end of the last game if a conversation has been terminated).
initiating	You have chosen whom to play against, and initiated a conversation with them. You have also specified your first-move preferences. The game is initialized to a neutral position.
listening	You have chosen to play and are waiting to accept a conversation initiated by someone else. You have also specified your first-move preferences. The game is initialized to a neutral position.

State	Meaning
starting	You are bound in a session and have sent a start request to the other player, specifying your first-move preferences. The game is initialized in a neutral position.
accepting	You are bound in a session and are expecting to receive a start request from the other player. You have specified your first-move preferences and the game is in a neutral position.
my-turn	A game is in progress, and it's your turn to move.
opp-turn	A game is in progress, and it's your opponent's turn to move.
finished	The game has been won, lost, or abandoned (which amount to sub-states of finished).
restarting	You are going to restart the game, but you don't yet have your first move preferences.

State Transitions

The transitions in the following diagram are described in more detail below:

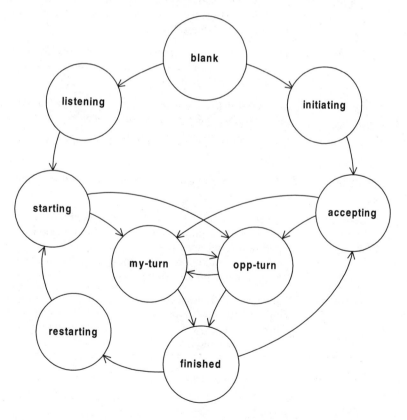

From	To	Occurs When
blank	initiating	Player specifies first-move preferences and the address of player to connect to. An RGCP initiate-request is sent.
blank	listening	Player specifies first-move preferences and starts RGCP listening.
listening	starting	RGCP initiate-request is received and a response sent, so that the RGCP session is bound. You send a start-request, specifying your first-move parameters.
initiating	accepting	RGCP initiate-response is received, so that the RGCP session is bound.
accepting	my-turn	You handle a start request from the other player. You arbitrate who has the first turn, and it's you. You send a start-response indicating this.
accepting	opp-turn	You handle a start request from the other player. You arbitrate who has the first turn, and it's the other player. You send a start-response indicating this, and then immediately send a no-operation request.
starting	my-turn	You receive a start response from the other player that indicates you have first turn: the next request from the other player will be a no-operation request.
starting	opp-turn	You receive a start-response from the other player that indicates the other player has first turn: the next request from the other player will be their move request.
my-turn	opp-turn	Through the GUI, you specify a move: this is composed as a move request and sent to the other player.
opp-turn	my-turn	You receive a move request from the other player, to which you respond.
my-turn	finished	You abandon the game: you send an abandon request to the other player.
opp-turn	finished	You receive a move request that causes you to lose the game (in which case you immediately send a move-response and a no-operation request, so the other player knows they have won); or you receive a move response indicating that you won the game; or you receive an abandon request.
finished	accepting	You are in BSP finished state and RGCP requesting state. This can happen because the other player abandoned, or you won. Through the UI, you specify your first-move preferences. You send a restart request with no parameters.

From	To	Occurs When
finished	restarting	You are in BSP finished state and RGCP waiting state. This can happen because you abandoned, or you lost. You receive a restart request from the other player, to which you respond.
restarting	starting	You have first-move parameters from the UI. You send a start request specifying your first-move parameters.
any	blank	You terminate the game, or you receive a terminate request from the other player to terminate it. If you terminated the game, you send an RGCP terminate request to the other player.

Some Scenarios

It's worth seeing how this works in a few scenarios. Here's how the game starts up, if the initiating player gets the first move:

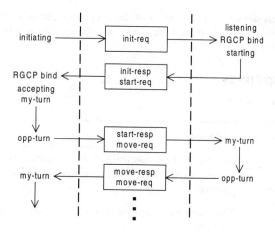

Here's how things work if the initiating player gets the second move:

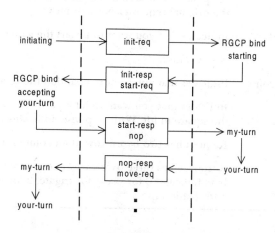

And here's what happens when one player wins the game:

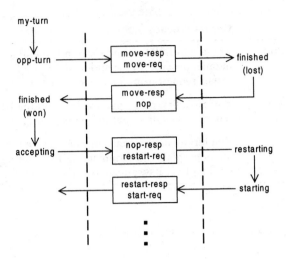

What happens after this depends on the result of the accepting player's arbitration. I haven't illustrated what happens when one player abandons the game, but the specifications and diagrams above should be sufficient to work it out.

Requests and Responses

The requests involved here are:

Opcode	Name	Details
1	start	Indicates that you want to start a game. With request, pass your first-move preference. With response, indicates who actually got first move.
		Request has one byte: 0 for don't-care, 1 for want-first, and 2 for want-second.
		Response has 0 to indicate the responder has first move, 1 to indicate the original requester has first move.
2	restart	Indicates that you want to restart the game.
3	nop	No operation.
4	abandon	Indicates that you want to abandon the current game.
10	hit	Indicates that you want to hit a particular square. With request, passes the square to hit. With response, indicates what was there.
		Request has two bytes: row, then column. Either may be in range 0-7.
		Response has three bytes: row and column as above, while a third byte indicates 0 for sea, 1 for frigate, 2 for destroyer, 3 for cruiser, and 4 for battleship.

First-move Arbitration

As we saw at the start of this section, the first move is arbitrated by the accepting player. At game setup, this is the initiating partner. At game restart, this is the partner who won the previous game, or the partner who did not abandon it.

Both players specify their first-move preference: want-first, don't-care, or want-second. The arbitrating player decides the first move when accepting the other player's start-request. In the event of a clash in preferences, the accepting player's preference overrides the starting player's preference. So the rules are:

❑ If the accepting player wants first move, they get it

❑ If the accepting player doesn't care, then they go first unless the starting player specified that they wanted to go first

❑ If the accepting player wants second move, then they go second

Game UI

The game UI needs to support the following functions, on top of the BSP protocol. The view displays:

❑ A status indicator

❑ My fleet

❑ My opponent's fleet

The commands are:

Command	Description
Start session	Starts game session. Valid in BSP blank state. Specify whether listening or initiating, and GDP protocol. If initiating, and using networked GDP, specify to-address. Specify first-move preference.
Move	Does a move. Valid in BSP my-turn state. Command initiated by pointer or spacebar from view of enemy fleet.
Abandon game	Abandons current game. Valid in BSP my-turn state.
Start new game	Starts new game when session already connected. Valid in BSP finished state. Specify first-move preference.
Terminate	Stops game session. Valid in any state.
Resend	Re-send last RGCP response/request packet. Valid in RGCP initiating or waiting states.
Receive all	Initiates receive of any packets. Valid in any state except BSP blank.

Program Structure

In the Battleships program, the CGameController handles all the BSP protocol, including functions called by the UI, and RGCP handler functions. The controller also implements all send-request and send-response functions implied by BSP, and maintains state transitions in accord with the design above.

A key aspect of the controller design is that every public function and many private functions assert the validity of the requested operation, given current BSP and RGCP states. The app UI and views are responsible for pre-checking user-initiated commands, so that no invalid command can be issued to the controller.

Taking BSP Forward

BSP combines a multi-game session protocol with the specifics of the Battleships game. It would be possible to separate out these aspects into two layers.

A truly general protocol may or may not be worthwhile: other games could re-use BSP's patterns without re-using its code. In any case, patterns differ between games. A game that can be tied, for instance (as opposed to only won or lost), may require a different approach.

It would be possible to improve on the first-move selection here, by changing only the UI, to select random first-move preferences. BSP itself would not have to be altered.

Summary

We've now seen TOGS components described in detail — with the exception of the GDP-IR and GDP-SMS implementations that are described in Chapter 21.

This chapter has been heavier and more precise than usual. I wrote it *before* I wrote most of the code it describes, and have not changed it substantially since — except that I've maintained some parts as the code has evolved. That's a healthy (if unusual!) software engineering practice. In this case, doing the documentation before the code saved me a *lot* of time.

Communications programming often involves state machines. It happens that state machines are peculiarly well suited to the style of programming encouraged in EPOC by active objects. And that's the subject of the next chapter.

18

Active Objects

Back in Chapter 3, we saw that EPOC's system design is optimized for event handling, and that all events are handled by active-object RunL() functions. We noted that the major frameworks in EPOC – CONE's application framework, and E32's server framework – are built as event handlers, so that typical applications and typical servers are just a single thread, using active objects to implement multitasking in response to events.

An event-handling thread has a single **active scheduler**, which is responsible for deciding the order in which events are handled. It also has one or more **active objects**, derived from CActive, which are responsible both for issuing requests (which will later result in an event happening), and for handling the event when the request completes. The active scheduler calls RunL() on the active object associated with the completed event.

CONE maintains an outstanding request to the window server for user input and other system events. When this request completes, it calls the right app UI and control functions to ensure that EIKON and, eventually, your application, handle the event properly. So, as we saw in Chapter 9, all application code is ultimately handled under the control of an active-object RunL().

It's because CONE provides this framework for you, that you can get started with EPOC application programming without knowing exactly how active objects work. But for more advanced GUI programming, and for anything to do with servers, we do need to know how they work in detail.

I'll tackle that in three stages:

❑ Firstly, I'll use the active example to show how a simple active object can request an event, and then handle it

❑ Then, I'll describe the active object framework

❑ Finally, I'll conclude with an overview of some well-established patterns for using active objects

As we cover servers in the next two chapters, there'll be plenty more opportunity to see how active objects work in practice.

A Simple Active Object

The \pep\active\ example demonstrates two active objects in use. It's derived from our first "Hello World" example from Chapter 2. Here's what it looks like when you launch it:

The Set Hello button triggers an EPOC timer. Three seconds later, that timer completes, causing an event. This event is handled by an active object, which puts an info-message saying Hello world! on the screen. During that three-second period, you can press Cancel to cancel the timer, so that the info-message never appears.

The Start flashing button starts the Hello world! text in the center of the display flashing, and Stop flashing stops it. The flashing is implemented by an active object that creates regular timer events and then handles them. Its event handling changes the visibility of the Hello World text, and redraws the view.

We'll start by looking at CDelayedHello, a derived active object class that implements Set Hello and its associated Cancel. Then I'll explain some of the underlying fundamentals, before taking a closer look at CFlashingHello (which implements Start flashing and Stop flashing) along with some other active object patterns.

```
class CDelayedHello : public CActive
    {
public:
    // Construct/destruct
    static CDelayedHello* NewL();
    ~CDelayedHello();

    // Request
    void SetHello(TTimeIntervalMicroSeconds32 aDelay);

private:
    // Construct/destruct
    CDelayedHello();
    void ConstructL(CEikonEnv* aEnv);
```

```
        // From CActive
        void RunL();
        void DoCancel();

    private:
        RTimer iTimer;        // Has
        CEikonEnv* iEnv;      // Uses
        };
```

From the class declaration, you can see that `CDelayedHello`:

- ❏ *Is-a* active object, derived from `CActive`
- ❏ *Has-a* event generator – an `RTimer`, whose API we'll see below
- ❏ Includes a **request function**, `SetHello()`, that requests an event from the `RTimer`
- ❏ Implements `RunL()`, to handle the event generated when the request completes
- ❏ Implements `DoCancel()`, to cancel any outstanding request

All active object classes share this pattern. They are derived from `CActive` and implement its `RunL()` and `DoCancel()` functions. They include an event generator, and at least one request function.

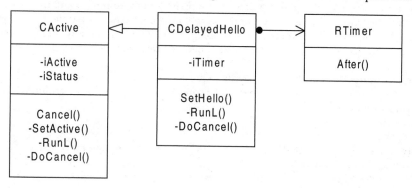

Construction and Destruction

Let's walk through the implementations of all the functions declared above. First, the easy bits: here are two of the members involved in construction and destruction.

```
CDelayedHello* CDelayedHello::NewL()
    {
    CDelayedHello* self = new(ELeave) CDelayedHello;
    CleanupStack::PushL(self);
    self->ConstructL();
    CleanupStack::Pop();
    return self;
    }

CDelayedHello::CDelayedHello() : CActive(0)
    {
    }
```

`NewL()` is a static function that follows the standard constructor-encapsulation pattern that we saw in Chapter 6.

The C++ constructor is required for any derived active object class: inside it, you call `CActive`'s constructor to specify the active object's **priority**, which is used for tie-breaking when more than one event occurs while another is being handled. You should specify zero here unless there are good reasons to specify something lower, or something higher. I'll cover those reasons below.

```
void CDelayedHello::ConstructL()
    {
    iEnv = CEikonEnv::Static();
    User::LeaveIfError(iTimer.CreateLocal());
    CActiveScheduler::Add(this);
    }

CDelayedHello::~CDelayedHello()
    {
    Cancel();
    iTimer.Close();
    }
```

The second-phase constructor gets a pointer to the EIKON environment, and then uses `iTimer.CreateLocal()` to request that the kernel create a kernel-side timer object, which we access through the `RTimer` handle. If there is any problem here, we leave. Finally, the new active object adds itself to the active scheduler, so that the active scheduler can include it in event handling.

The destructor starts by canceling any events requested by the active object. `Cancel()` is a standard `CActive` function that checks to see whether a request for an event is outstanding and, if so, calls `DoCancel()` to handle it.

> **Any active object class that implements a `DoCancel()` function must also call `Cancel()` in its destructor.**

The destructor closes the `RTimer` object, which destroys the corresponding kernel-side object. After this, the base `CActive` destructor will remove the active object from the active scheduler.

Requesting and Handling Events

`SetHello()` requests a timer event after a given delay:

```
void CDelayedHello::SetHello(TTimeIntervalMicroSeconds32 aDelay)
    {
    __ASSERT_ALWAYS(!IsActive(), User::Panic(_L("CDelayedHello"), 1));
    iTimer.After(iStatus, aDelay);
    SetActive();
    }
```

Every line in this function is important:

❑ First, we assert that no request is already outstanding (that is, that `IsActive()` is false). The client program must ensure that this is the case, either by refusing to issue another request when one is already outstanding, or by canceling the previous request.

❑ Then, we request the timer to generate an event after `aDelay` microseconds. The first parameter to `iTimer.After()` is a `TRequestStatus&` which refers to the `iStatus` member which we inherit from `CActive`. As I'll explain below, `TRequestStatus` plays a key role in event handling.

❑ Finally, we indicate that a request is outstanding by calling `SetActive()`.

This is the invariable pattern for active object request functions. Assert that no request is already active (or, in rare cases, cancel it). Then issue a request, passing your `iStatus` to some function that will later generate an event. Then call `SetActive()` to indicate that the request has been issued.

You can deduce from this that an active object can be responsible for only one outstanding request at a time. You can also deduce that all request functions take a `TRequestStatus&` parameter — or, put the other way round, any function you see with a `TRequestStatus&` parameter is a request function, which will complete asynchronously and generate an event.

Our EIKON program calls this function from `HandleCommandL()` using:

```
iDelayedHello->Cancel();            // Just in case
iDelayedHello->SetHello(3000000);   // 3-second delay
```

In other words, it cancels any request so that the assertion in `SetHello()` is guaranteed to succeed, and then requests a delayed info-message to appear after three seconds.

When the timer event occurs, it is handled by the active object framework, as we'll describe below, and results in `RunL()` being called:

```
void CDelayedHello::RunL()
    {
    iEnv->InfoMsg(R_EXAMPLE_TEXT_HELLO);
    }
```

Clearly, this code is very simple: it's a one-line function that produces an info-message with the usual greeting text.

> The degree of sophistication in an active object's `RunL()` function can vary enormously from one active object to another. CONE's `CCoeEnv::RunL()` function initiates an extremely sophisticated chain of processing: we have plenty of evidence for that from the debug session in Chapter 9. In contrast, the function above was a simple one-liner.

Canceling a Request

If your active object can issue requests, it *must* also be able to cancel them. CActive provides a Cancel() function that checks whether a request is active and, if so, calls DoCancel() to cancel it. As the implementer of the active object, you have to implement DoCancel():

```
void CDelayedHello::DoCancel()
    {
    iTimer.Cancel();
    }
```

There is no need for any checking here. Because CActive has already checked that a request is active, there is no need for you to check this, or to reset the active flag.

> **There is an obligation on any class with request functions, to provide corresponding cancel functions also.**

How It Works

It's time we looked beneath the surface to see how an event-handling thread, with an active scheduler and active objects, works. The general structure of such a thread is:

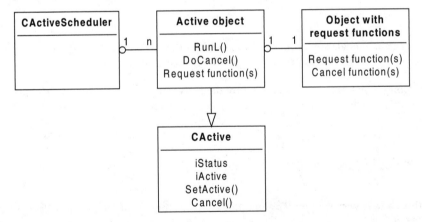

The thread may have many active objects. Each active object is associated with just one object that has request functions – functions taking a TRequestStatus& parameter. These request functions complete their requests asynchronously, resulting in an event. Because of this, objects with request functions are often referred to as **asynchronous service providers**.

> *Actually, we'll see below that this need not be a precisely one-to-one relationship. But it's easier to explain as if it were.*

When a program calls an active-object request function, the active object passes on the request to the asynchronous service provider. It passes its own iStatus as a TRequestStatus& parameter to the request function and, having called the request function, it immediately calls SetActive().

The TRequestStatus is a 32-bit object, intended to take a completion code. Before starting to execute the request function, the asynchronous service provider sets the value of the TRequestStatus to KRequestPending, which is defined as 0x80000001.

When the asynchronous service provider finishes processing the request, it generates an event. This means it signals the requesting thread's **request semaphore**, and *also* posts a completion code (such as KErrNone or any other standard error code – anything except KRequestPending is permissible) into the TRequestStatus.

The active scheduler is responsible for detecting the occurrence of an event, so as to associate it with the active object which requested it, and call RunL() on that active object.

The active scheduler calls User::WaitForAnyRequest() to detect an event. This function suspends the thread until one or more requests have completed. The active scheduler then scans through all its active objects, searching for one which has issued a request (iActive is set) and for which the request has completed (iStatus is some value *other* than KRequestPending). It clears that object's iActive and calls its RunL(). When the RunL() has completed, the scheduler issues User::WaitForAnyRequest() again.

So the scheduler handles precisely one event per User::WaitForAnyRequest(). If more than one event is outstanding, there's no problem: the next User::WaitForAnyRequest() will complete immediately without suspending the thread, and the scheduler will find the active object associated with the completed event.

If the scheduler can't find the active object associated with an event, this indicates a programming error known as **stray signal**. The active scheduler panics the thread.

Given the delicacy of this description, you might expect writing an active object to be difficult. In fact, as we've already seen with CDelayedHello, it's not. You simply have to:

❑ Issue request functions to an asynchronous service provider, remembering to call SetActive() after you have done so

❑ Handle completed requests with RunL()

❑ Be able to cancel requests with DoCancel()

❑ Set an appropriate priority

More on Canceling Requests

All asynchronous service providers must implement cancel functions corresponding to their request functions. All active objects which issue request functions must also provide a DoCancel() to cancel an outstanding request.

A cancel is actually a request for early completion. *Every* asynchronous request issued must complete precisely once – whether normally, or by a cancel. The cancel must return synchronously and quickly and, when it has returned, the original asynchronous request must have completed.

When a request is issued, it can complete in roughly four ways:

❑ The request can't even begin to execute, perhaps because there is no memory for the relevant resources, or there is a bad parameter. If this happens, the requesting function should not leave or return a non-zero error code. Instead, it should post its completion code into the request status, so that the request completes just once.

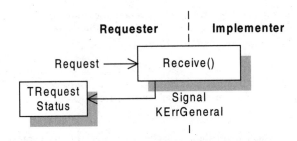

- The request is issued successfully, and completes successfully some time later. This is the normal case.

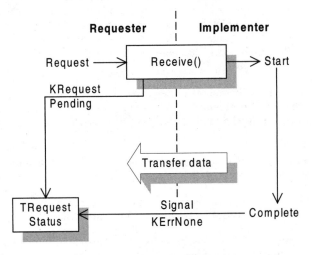

- The request is cancelled before it completes. As part of its cancel processing, the service provider posts the request complete with KErrCancel.

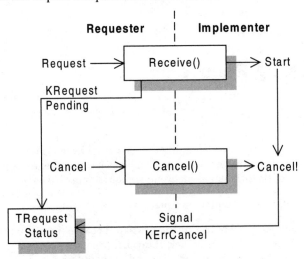

❏ The client issued a cancel, but the request completed normally before the service provider got to process the cancel. In this case, the service provider should ignore the cancel. In its turn, the client, through the `CActive::Cancel()` protocol, will ignore the normal completion. The client should be careful, however: normal completion might involve writing data to some buffers whose address was passed as part of the initial request. The client should be sure to issue `Cancel()` *before* destroying the buffers, just in case the request completes normally.

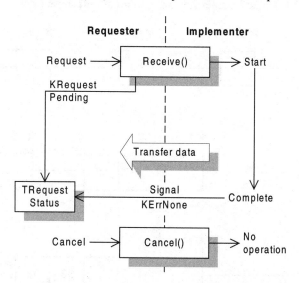

The GSDP server, which I describe in Chapter 20, provides asynchronous service. We'll see in that chapter how cancel looks from the service provider's side.

`CActive` implements the `Cancel()` function as follows:

❏ Check `iActive` to see whether there is an outstanding request. If not, nothing needs to be done.

❏ Call `DoCancel()` to cause the request to complete (if it hasn't completed already).

❏ Issue `User::WaitForRequest()`, specifying `iStatus`. This is guaranteed to complete immediately, but it also decrements the thread semaphore's value so that a subsequent call to `User::WaitForAnyRequest()` by the active scheduler will not falsely complete because of this cancelled request.

❏ Reset `iActive`, to indicate that there is no longer an outstanding request associated with this active object.

This logic is implemented in `CActive::Cancel()`; all you have to do, when you're writing a derived active object class, is implement `DoCancel()`. You don't have to — in fact, you must not — do any of the other things that `CActive::Cancel()` does.

How can a request still be outstanding, if it has already completed? Easy: the request has completed (in another thread), but it hasn't been handled by this thread. `iActive` indicates whether the request has been handled by this thread.

Non-preemption and Priority

Active objects in the same thread handle events non-preemptively. Only when one `RunL()` has completed is the active scheduler able to detect and handle another event.

The following picture shows some interesting scenarios: three events, e1, e2, and e3, occur in sequence. They are handled by h1, h2, and h3. Each handler takes a finite amount of time to execute.

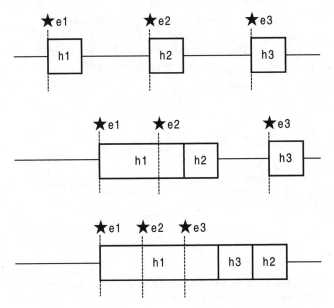

If events are widely spaced, as in the top line of the figure, then they are handled as soon as they occur.

If one event happens while a first event is being handled, as in the second line, then it is not handled until after the first handler has completed. This is non-preemptive event handling.

If *two* events happen while a first event is being handled, as in the third line, then when the first handler has completed, the thread can choose which of the two outstanding events to handle first. There is no obligation to handle events in the sequence in which they occurred. The active scheduler checks active objects in order of priority – highest priority first, lowest priority last, and calls `RunL()` on the first one it finds with a completed request. So if h3 has higher priority than h2, and if both e2 and e3 have happened by the time the active scheduler processes the completion of `User::WaitForAnyRequest()`, then h3 will be called first.

The priority of active objects is governed by a constructor parameter, which I set to zero in `CDelayedHello`. Awkwardly, there are two rival enumerations for active-object priorities. You would expect `CActive::TPriority` to be definitive – but it isn't. The CONE GUI framework defines `TACtivePriority` in `coemain.h`, which is used to set CONE's active object priorities. Since, as an application program, you'll be jostling with CONE active objects, there's a strong argument for this being the definitive definition, for application code at least.

In any case, zero is zero, and that's the priority you should use unless you have good reason. I'll cover such good reasons later in this chapter. In order to avoid the conflict generated above, I code zero explicitly in all my active objects, unless I have good reason not to.

Starting and Stopping the Scheduler

Application programmers never have to call CActiveScheduler::Start() and Stop(). The CONE framework does that for you.

The active scheduler's wait loop is started by issuing CActiveScheduler::Start(). Clearly, before this happens, at least one request function should be issued, so that the first User::WaitForAnyRequest() will actually complete. From that point on, any completed events will cause one of your active objects' RunL() functions to be called.

A RunL() function can stop the active scheduler by issuing CActiveScheduler::Stop(). When that RunL() returns, the function call to CActiveScheduler::Start() will complete.

Stopping the active scheduler will bring down the thread's event-handling framework, which is not something you should do lightly. Only do it if you are the main active object that controls the thread.

As a server programmer, you have to provide server bootstrap code that includes creating and starting the active scheduler for your server thread. I'll show you how to do that in Chapter 20.

The active scheduler offers a nesting facility, whereby you can issue CActiveScheduler::Start() from within a RunL() function. This is used to keep the active scheduler going while ostensibly handling a synchronous function. The end of the 'synchronous' function is indicated by a matching CActiveScheduler::Stop(). The net effect is like Yield() in some systems. This method is used by modal EIKON dialogs.

You shouldn't nest the active scheduler, however, unless you have thought carefully through the implications of doing so. In particular, you must ensure strict nesting of all CActiveScheduler::Start() and CActiveScheduler::Stop() functions – which is of course a natural property of modal dialogs.

Adding Functionality to the Active Scheduler

CActiveScheduler is a concrete class that can be used as-is. It also provides two virtual functions that can be used if you need them for additional purposes:

❑ If a RunL() called by the active scheduler leaves, Error(TInt) is called with the leave code. By default, this function does nothing.

❑ WaitForAnyRequest() may be used to perform some standard processing before issuing User::WaitForAnyRequest(). By default, this function simply issues User::WaitForAnyRequest(), and any override must also ensure that it calls User::WaitForAnyRequest().

The EIKON environment sets up an active scheduler whose Error() function displays a natural-language version of the KErrXxx error code with which RunL() left.

The CONE environment overrides CActiveScheduler::WaitForAnyRequest() to ensure that the window server's client-side buffer is flushed before issuing User::WaitForAnyRequest(). That means that any drawing done by the client during a RunL() is sent to the window server for execution so that, while waiting for the next user input, there is no outstanding drawing.

If you're implementing a server, it's useful to implement a scheduler with its own Error() function. We'll show how to do this in the GDSP server implementation, in Chapter 20.

Don't write over-elaborate overrides for CActiveScheduler::Error() and CActiveScheduler::WaitForAnyRequest(). If they're too elaborate, you create dependencies between your active objects and your active scheduler, which means that your active objects won't run in any other environment than (say) the server for which you designed them. That might be fine — just make sure you've thought about it.

Framework Summary

We can now understand all the functions in CActive and CActiveScheduler. Here they are, diagrammatically:

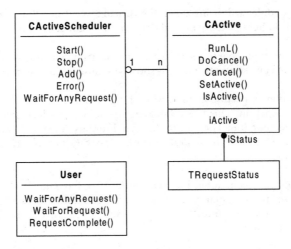

The CActive Class

Here's CActive's declaration, from e32base.h:

```
class CActive : public CBase
    {
public:
enum TPriority
    {
    EPriorityIdle=-100,
    EPriorityLow=-20,
    EPriorityStandard=0,
    EPriorityUserInput=10,
    EPriorityHigh=20,
    };
public:
    IMPORT_C ~CActive();
    IMPORT_C void Cancel();
    IMPORT_C void Deque();
    IMPORT_C void SetPriority(TInt aPriority);
    inline TBool IsActive() const;
    inline TBool IsAdded() const;
    inline TInt Priority() const;
```

```
protected:
    IMPORT_C CActive(TInt aPriority);
    IMPORT_C void SetActive();
// Pure virtual
    virtual void DoCancel() =0;
    virtual void RunL() =0;
public:
    TRequestStatus iStatus;
private:
    TBool iActive;
    TPriQueLink iLink;
    friend class CActiveScheduler;
    friend class CServer;
    };
```

Member functions here are:

Function	Description
~CActive()	Virtual destructor. Calls Deque() to de-queue the object from the active scheduler
Cancel()	Cancels a request. If a request is active, calls DoCancel(), waits synchronously for completion on iStatus, and sets the request as no longer active
SetPriority()	Change the priority after construction
Priority()	Returns the active object's priority
IsActive()	Indicates whether a request is outstanding
Deque()	Remove this object from the active scheduler
IsAdded()	Indicates whether the object has been added to the active scheduler
CActive()	C++ constructor: you must specify the active object's priority as a constructor parameter
SetActive()	Call this function after you have issued a request function, to indicate that a request is outstanding
DoCancel()	Implement this in a derived class to cancel a request issued to an asynchronous service provider. This function can only be called if a request is active. You must provide a way to cancel requests.
RunL()	Implement this in a derived class to handle the completion of a request that was issued

I've not yet met a case where Deque() or SetPriority() are necessary, or couldn't be handled by a different design approach. Bizarrely, although Deque() is a member of CActive, which enables you to remove an active object from the scheduler, you can only *add* an active object to the scheduler using a member function of CActiveScheduler (which is a friend class).

The *CActiveScheduler* Class

Here's CActiveScheduler's definition, from e32base.h:

```
class CActiveScheduler : public CBase
    {
public:
    IMPORT_C CActiveScheduler();
    IMPORT_C ~CActiveScheduler();
    IMPORT_C static void Install(CActiveScheduler* aScheduler);
    IMPORT_C static CActiveScheduler* Current();
    IMPORT_C static void Add(CActive* anActive);
    IMPORT_C static void Start();
    IMPORT_C static void Stop();
    IMPORT_C virtual void WaitForAnyRequest();
    IMPORT_C virtual void Error(TInt anError) const;
protected:
    inline TInt Level() const;
private:
    TInt iLevel;
    TPriQue<CActive> iActiveQ;
    };
```

Member functions here are:

Function	Description
CActiveScheduler()	Default C++ constructor, invoked when you create an active scheduler with new
~CActiveScheduler()	C++ destructor
Install()	Installs a pointer to the active scheduler specified in a privileged TLS location that is very fast to access – nearly as fast as a pointer. You can then access the active scheduler with the function CActiveScheduler::Current().
Current()	Returns a pointer to the currently installed active scheduler (or zero, if there isn't one)
Add()	Adds an active object to the scheduler. You should call this as part of the construction of all active objects, using CActiveScheduler::Add(this)
Start()	Starts the scheduler, or increase the scheduler nesting level. There should be at least one outstanding request on an active object, otherwise this will cause a thread to hang. This function includes the active scheduler's central wait loop handler. This function does not return until a corresponding Stop() has been issued.
Stop()	Decreases the nesting level. When the current RunL() or Error() has completed, this will cause the currently active Start() function to return.

Function	Description
WaitForAnyRequest()	Override this function if you want to perform special processing before calling user::WaitForAnyRequest()
Error()	Override this function to handle leaves from RunL() of any active object scheduled by the active scheduler. The TInt parameter is the leave code from RunL().

The declaration of CActive and CActiveScheduler are rather bizarre C++ and reflect, perhaps, the fact that these were among the earliest classes to be implemented in EPOC. However, in practice, this bizarreness doesn't get in the way of working with active objects, or of building well-engineered, large-scale, object-oriented systems with the active object framework.

The TRequestStatus Class

Here's the declaration of TRequestStatus, from e32std.h:

```
class TRequestStatus
    {
public:
    inline TRequestStatus();
    inline TRequestStatus(TInt aVal);
    inline TInt operator=(TInt aVal);
    inline TInt operator==(TInt aVal) const;
    inline TInt operator!=(TInt aVal) const;
    inline TInt operator>=(TInt aVal) const;
    inline TInt operator<=(TInt aVal) const;
    inline TInt operator>(TInt aVal) const;
    inline TInt operator<(TInt aVal) const;
    inline TInt Int() const;
private:
    TInt iStatus;
    };
```

A TRequestStatus is simply a well-encapsulated integer, which you can't do anything with except compare and assign.

Priority Enumerations

Here, again, is CActive's TPriority enumeration,

```
class CActive : public CBase
    {
public:
    enum TPriority
        {
        EPriorityIdle=-100,
        EPriorityLow=-20,
        EPriorityStandard=0,
        EPriorityUserInput=10,
        EPriorityHigh=20,
        };
...
```

And here's `TActivePriority` from `coemain.h`:

```
enum TActivePriority
    { // an alternative set to the TPriority in E32BASE.H
    EActivePriorityClockTimer=300,
    EActivePriorityIpcEventsHigh=200,
    EActivePriorityFepLoader=150,
    EActivePriorityWsEvents=100,
    EActivePriorityRedrawEvents=50,
    EActivePriorityDefault=0,
    EActivePriorityLogonA=-10
    };
```

In my opinion, the really important ones are:

Symbolic name	Value	Description
EActivePriorityWsEvents	100	User input events from the window server are handled at this priority
EActivePriorityRedrawEvents	50	Redraw events from the window server are handled at this priority
EActivePriorityDefault	0	Active objects should have this priority unless there is very good reason
EPriorityIdle	-100	Priority for background task active objects, which run in the idle time of all other active objects on the same thread

If you need to code non-zero priorities for your own active objects, you need to know the real (not just symbolic) values of the priorities above, so that you can ensure you fit in with them. `EPriorityHigh` and `EPriorityLow` would be good values to use if you want to be a little higher than zero, or a little lower. I'll cover priorities again below.

Active Object Patterns

`CDelayedHello` demonstrates the one-shot active object pattern. A single request is made through the API, and it's handled through the `RunL()` function. There are many other ways you can use active objects.

Maintaining an Outstanding Request

The `active` example shows the outstanding-request active object pattern, in which `RunL()` handles the completion of a previous request, and then issues a new request.

Here's the declaration of `CFlashingHello`:

```
class CFlashingHello : public CActive
    {
public:
    // Construct/destruct
    static CFlashingHello* NewL(CExampleAppView* aAppView);
    ~CFlashingHello();

    // Request
    void Start(TTimeIntervalMicroSeconds32 aHalfPeriod);

private:
    // Construct/destruct
    CFlashingHello();
    void ConstructL(CExampleAppView* aAppView);

    // From CActive
    void RunL();
    void DoCancel();

    // Utility
    void ShowText(TBool eShowText);

private:
    // Member variables
    RTimer iTimer;
    TTimeIntervalMicroSeconds32 iHalfPeriod;

    // Pointers elsewhere
    CExampleAppView* iAppView;
    };
```

And here's how it fits into the EIKON application program:

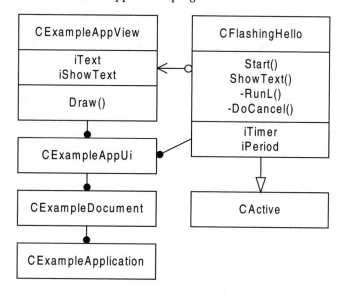

The Start(), RunL(), and DoCancel() functions of CFlashingHello show how to maintain an outstanding request. Here's Start():

```
void CFlashingHello::Start(TTimeIntervalMicroSeconds32 aHalfPeriod)
    {
    __ASSERT_ALWAYS(!IsActive(), User::Panic(_L("CFlashingHello"), 1));
    // Remember half-period
    iHalfPeriod=aHalfPeriod;

    // Hide the text, to begin with
    ShowText(EFalse);

    // Issue request
    iTimer.After(iStatus, iHalfPeriod);
    SetActive();
    }
```

Start() begins by asserting that a request is not already active, and ends by issuing a request – just as before. Because a whole series of requests will be issued, Start() doesn't merely pass the half-period parameter to the iTimer.After(), but stores is as a member variable for later use.

Start() also starts off the visible aspect of the flashing process, by immediately hiding the text (which is visible until Start() is called).

When the timer completes, RunL() is called:

```
void CFlashingHello::RunL()
    {
    // Change visibility of app view text
    ShowText(!iAppView->iShowText);

    // Reissue request
    iTimer.After(iStatus, iHalfPeriod);
    SetActive();
    }
```

RunL() changes the visibility of the text, to implement the flashing effect. Then, it simply renews the request to the timer with the same iHalfPeriod parameter as before. As always, the renewed request is followed by SetActive().

The only way to stop the flashing is to issue Cancel() which, as usual, checks whether a request is outstanding and, if so, calls our DoCancel() implementation:

```
void CFlashingHello::DoCancel()
    {
    // Ensure text is showing
    ShowText(ETrue);

    // Cancel timer
    iTimer.Cancel();
    }
```

We make sure the text is showing, and then cancel the timer.

`ShowText()` is the utility function that sets the visibility of the text; it simply changes the `iShowText` in the app view, and then redraws the app view.

```
void CFlashingHello::ShowText(TBool aShowText)
    {
    iAppView->iShowText = aShowText;
    iAppView->DrawNow();
    }
```

In summary, a continuously running active object is little harder to implement than a one-shot object.

Although this example looks simple enough, I experienced an unexpected half-hour of frustration with the debugger while testing it. Here's what I learned:

> Because the `DoCancel()` contains drawing code, it must be executed when there is still an environment in which drawing is possible. This means you must cancel or destroy the flashing hello *before* calling `CEikAppUi::Exit()`.

Here's my command handler for `EEikCmdExit`:

```
case EEikCmdExit:
    iFlashingHello->Cancel();
    Exit();
    break;
```

I just cancel the active object from here. I *destroy* it from its owning class's destructor – this is the right place to destroy it, since the destructor gets called in cleanup situations, while the command handler does not. Prior to coding this `Cancel()` explicitly in the exit command handling code, my `DoCancel()` was being called from the active object's destructor, and was trying to draw to an environment that, by then, had been destroyed.

You should always be careful about doing anything fancy from an active object's `DoCancel()`. Nothing in a `DoCancel()` should leave or allocate resources, and `DoCancel()` should complete very quickly. I got myself into trouble because I don't simply *stop* flashing when I cancel: instead, I restore the visibility state, which involves drawing. In fact, this is a good rule for any kind of cleanup or destructor: just clean up and destroy – don't do anything else.

Interfaces for Handling Completion

The `CDelayedHello` and `CFlashingHello` active objects are concrete classes that both define the requests and handle their completion. Often, though, active objects are used for implementing abstract interfaces. For instance, in a communications stack such as TOGS, you issue a request for some received data. When the data comes, you want a function to be called.

You know by now that, in EPOC, a requirement like this is going to be implemented with an active object that requests the received data using an asynchronous function, and then handles the completed receive with a `RunL()`. It's tempting to provide an interface that exposes this by including `CActive`-derived objects in your API, and inviting the client to implement a `RunL()` to handle the received data. For instance, you could use the following design:

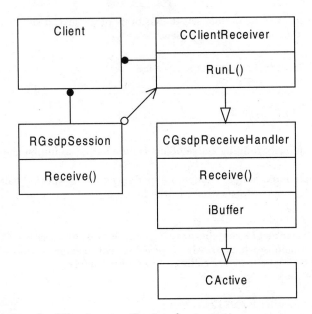

With this design, you write the following specification for RunL():

❑ "When implementing RunL(), the data requested by the client is in iBuffer. Handle this buffer according to the requirements of your protocol."

This works, but I don't like it. The client has to implement a derived active object, and has to use that object from the main client class. The API includes active objects, which cloud the real issues that the API is answering. And the design isn't portable to a non-EPOC system.

I prefer to hide active objects from APIs like this. Instead, I define an interface, such as MGsdpHandler, and use a hidden active object whose RunL() function calls MGsdpHandler::GsdpHandle() with the buffer reference passed as a parameter. In your API description, you can now say:

❑ "Your client class should implement the MGsdpHandler interface. The function MGsdpHandler::GsdpHandle(const TDesC8& aData) will be called to handle received data."

The GSDP client interface is structured as below:

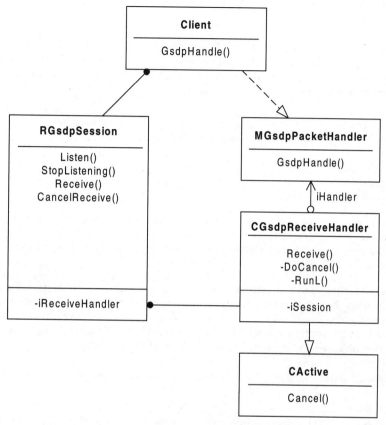

For good measure, the interface uses `Listen()` and `StopListening()` functions to maintain an outstanding request.

Long-running Tasks and Incremental Interfaces

Sometimes, you want to be able to implement a long-running task alongside your application's (or server's) main task. In non-EPOC systems, you might implement such a task with a 'background thread'. In EPOC, the best way to implement long-running tasks is with a low-priority active object that runs in the idle time of event-handling active objects. The paradigm for a long-running task is as follows:

- ❏ You write an active object that maintains an outstanding request

- ❏ In the `Start()` function for the outstanding request, you simply issue `SetActive()` and then `User::RequestComplete()` on your own `iStatus`, to make it *look* as if you issued a request, and to make it look as though that request has already completed

- ❏ You will therefore be eligible for `RunL()` next time control returns to the active scheduler

- ❏ When your `RunL()` is called, you should do some processing for the long-running task – say, about 100 millisecond's-worth of processing

❑ If your task is not complete, you then need to use the same technique as before to make it look as though you issued a request, and the request is completed

❑ If your task is complete, you simply stop and don't reissue your artificial request

❑ In DoCancel(), you may wish to destroy any intermediate data associated with the long-running task. You don't need to issue User::RequestComplete(), because you already did that from either Start() or RunL(). Remember: any request you issue should complete *precisely once*, so you don't need to complete it again.

Some EPOC APIs for long-running tasks are designed to be called from active objects in this way. For example, the DBMS provides compaction APIs whose specification is roughly:

```
void Start(parameters) ...;
TInt Step(TInt& aStep);
void Close();
```

Here, Start() starts off an operation, while Step() performs a single step, returns an error code, and sets its reference parameter to ETrue if the operation has finished, or EFalse otherwise. Close() releases all the resources associated with the incremental operation, so that it can be canceled even if it hasn't completed.

There are two advantages to providing a long-running task with an API like this. Firstly, it hides the active objects from the API and therefore prevents the active object paradigm from clouding your thinking about the real issue – namely, how to provide an incremental version of the function for your long-running task. Secondly, it allows the API to be used by code where there is no active scheduler and hence no active objects – for instance, from a native method in a Java thread.

> *In Chapter 25, John Forrest shows how to drive an engine from a long-running active object like this.*

In e32base.h, the CIdle class provides a ready-made (if near-trivial) wrapper for idle-time processing like this. Idle-time active objects should use a priority such as CActive::EPriorityIdle, which equates to -100. It's probably not a great idea to have too many idle-time active objects running in a single thread: if you want these objects to run together, you'll have to construct your own scheduling algorithm between the 'idle-time' objects.

Prioritizing and Maintaining Responsiveness

As we've seen, active objects specify a priority, which is passed as a parameter to their constructor, and is used to order the active objects on the active scheduler's queue. In turn, this governs the search order after a User::WaitForAnyRequest() completes: the higher the active object's priority, the earlier it will be checked by this scan. Therefore, if two or more active objects' requests complete while another request is being handled, it's the highest-priority object that will be handled first.

Normally, you should code your active objects so that priority doesn't matter. You should give most active objects a priority of zero. There can be good reasons to go higher or lower than this: some events really are more important than others. On a GUI thread, for instance, user responsiveness is critical. CONE's user input-handling active object therefore specifies a priority of 100. Keeping the view up to date is also important (though not as important as handling the events which might change the view). So CONE handles window-server redraw events at a priority of 50.

Any long-running tasks implemented by active objects are not really events at all, and should therefore be prioritized below anything that is an event. Long-running tasks should always have a negative priority: the recommended value is `CActive::EPriorityIdle`, which is -100.

In active objects, higher priority means simply that you get handled sooner than others, if your event completes along with several others during the handling of the previous `RunL()`. But active object priority does *not* cause pre-emption: if the previous `RunL()` takes a long time, nothing you can do with active object priority will get you scheduled sooner.

> **Make sure that you understand what active object priority means, and be sensible in allocating active object priorities.**

So, if you try to use an ultra-high-priority event to do something that requires a certain response time, it won't always work. An active object used to keep a sound channel going, say, could get held up behind a step in a long-running task doing printing or database compaction. In other words, you can't use high-priority active objects to achieve responses that *must* occur within a certain time of an event. For that, you need to use EPOC's pre-emptive thread system, appropriate buffering, and appropriate thread priorities.

Summary

EPOC has a highly responsive pre-emptive multi-threaded architecture. However, most application and server tasks are by nature event handlers, and active objects are a very suitable paradigm with which to handle events.

Because they are non-preemptive, it's very easy to program with active objects, because you don't need to code mutual exclusion with other threads trying to access the same resources.

Active objects also use fewer system resources than full-blown threads: thread overheads start around 4k kernel-side and 12k for user-side stack, whereas active objects need be only a few bytes in size. Additionally, switching between active objects is much cheaper than switching between threads, even in the same process.

This combination of ease of use and low resource requirement is a major factor in EPOC's overall system efficiency.

For some purposes, threads are necessary. In the next chapter, we'll include them as we discuss EPOC's client-server architecture. In Chapter 25, we introduce the considerations you'll meet when working with thread-based programs from other architectures.

19

Client-server Framework

Back in Chapter 3, we showed the process and privilege boundaries that EPOC uses to assure a high level of system integrity. We noted that EPOC's design is optimized for event handling and, in the last chapter, covered active objects in detail: active objects assure a high level of system integrity because they don't require the same kind of sharing disciplines as are needed in multithreaded systems.

The final major building block for EPOC's system integrity is the client-server framework, in which servers handle system resources on behalf of multiple clients. Examples of servers in EPOC include:

- ❑ The file server, which shares all file-related resources between all clients.

- ❑ The window server, which shares UI resources – keyboard, pointer, and screen – between all applications.

- ❑ The font and bitmap server, which manages shared, system-wide resources for fonts and bitmaps

- ❑ The database server, which is used to control database sharing where shared access is desired. The database server is optional: if a database is not intended to be shared between applications, you can drive it directly without using the server.

- ❑ The serial communications server, which shares the serial port and other virtual serial protocols between all client programs.

- ❑ The sockets server, which maintains sockets protocol resources and allows them to be shared between programs.

- ❑ Many other servers, associated with particular applications or subsystems such as messaging, web browsing, etc.

In this chapter, I'll describe the client-server framework's design in general terms, building on and reinforcing the treatment of active objects from the previous chapter. Specifically, I'll cover:

❑ The general design of the client-server framework

❑ Optimization for better performance, including examples taken from EPOC's standard servers

❑ The relationship between servers and preemptively-scheduled threads, including some recommendations on thread and active object priorities (and a little myth-busting into the bargain)

❑ Some reference information about the classes related to servers and threads

In the next chapter, we'll put the ideas from Chapter 17, Chapter 18, and this chapter together, as we describe the implementation of the GSDP server in detail.

Introduction

As we saw in Chapter 3, a server runs in a different thread – and usually a different process – from any of its clients. The kernel supports two ways to cross this thread boundary:

❑ Message passing – used in all client-server transactions

❑ Inter-thread data transfer – used, if necessary, to transfer more data between client and server

A client-server message consists of a 32-bit request code, and four 32-bit parameters. The result passed back from the server is a single 32-bit value. The 32 bits may be interpreted as a TInt, a TInt32, a TUint32, or any kind of pointer, depending on the needs of the particular message.

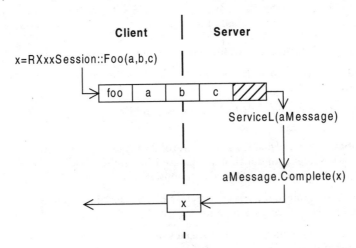

Some simple server transactions can be handled using message passing alone, but more complex transactions may need more data. In this case, the client should pass a pointer to a descriptor containing the data. Then, the server can use inter-thread read or write functions to transfer the data.

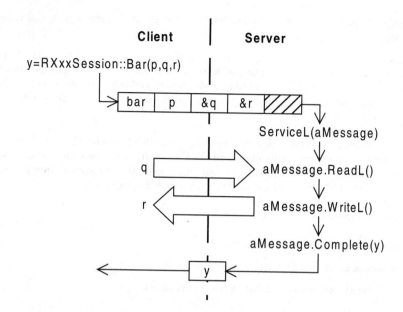

The **client-server framework** has to manage all this communication. In the remainder of this section, we'll look at several interesting aspects of that framework.

Handling Routine Requests

A routine message is passed from client to server over the client-server session:

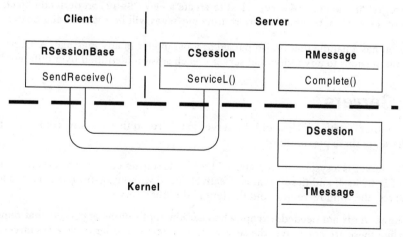

There are three parts to this session:

❑ A client-side class, derived from `RSessionBase`, which contains functions offered to the client. Each function is implemented by converting its parameters into suitable message parameters, and issuing a `SendReceive()` call to send the message to the server.

❏ A kernel-owned class, DSession, which links the client and the server, and is also used for cleanup.

❏ A server-side class, derived from CSession, which contains a ServiceL() function. The derived class uses this function to check the request code and call a handler function. The handler function interprets the message parameters and performs its service. When the handler has completed, it calls Complete() with a 32-bit return code that is returned to the client via the kernel.

You can find all the user-side classes for the client-server architecture in e32std.h and e32base.h. You don't get access to the kernel-side classes in the C++ SDK, and you don't need it. But as we'll see during the discussions that follow, the kernel's role in the client-server architecture is important, and it's helpful to understand that the kernel has an object representing the session.

The arts of handling routine requests are:

❏ To wrap up the parameters appropriately

❏ To minimize client-server communication

❏ To use inter-thread reads and writes where necessary

Setting up Sessions

One question you may be asking is, "How did a session for message-passing get there in the first place?"

When a client thread wishes to start using a server, it connects a client-server session to that server. The Connect() function (in RSessionBase) takes the name of the server. When it's called, the kernel creates a new session object. At that point, the server recognizes the connect message, and calls NewSessionL() in the derived server class to create a new CSession-derived object, representing the server end of the session, to which future routine messages will be routed using ServiceL().

A new session has a handle that is also passed as a parameter in any message. A single client thread may have multiple sessions to any individual server – each session identified by a different handle.

Starting Servers

That begs another question: "How did the server get there, so that sessions could be set up in the first place?" There are three possibilities:

❏ The server is a system server, started by EPOC startup code: such servers are essentially a part of EPOC itself and the system is effectively dead without them. Examples include the file server, the window server, and the font and bitmap server.

❏ The server is not needed, except when certain applications or servers that require it are active. When these are not active, the server can terminate in order to save resources. Such servers should be started from the client API prior to connecting a session, if they are not already active. They should terminate themselves if their last session is closed – perhaps after a short time-out period. Most servers are of this so-called **transient server** type, where startup and shutdown issues are particularly delicate. The GSDP server code in the next chapter shows how it's done.

❑ The server is not a shared system service at all, but a convenience for each instance of a running application. Examples include the POSIX and AWT servers in the EPOC Java implementation. In this case, the server should be started as part of application startup, and terminated as part of application shutdown.

When a server starts, it declares a name that must be used by all client connect messages. System servers should use a unique name, so that clients (through the client API) can easily find them and connect to them. Private servers should use a name that is private to the instance of the application that started them – for example, by including the application's main thread name in the server name.

After a session is connected, routine client-server communication uses the RSessionBase, DSession, and CSession objects in client, kernel, and server respectively, and the name isn't needed anymore.

Handling Asynchronous Requests

Servers are often associated with asynchronous request functions. As we saw in the last chapter, when examining the client API to a server, you can tell asynchronous request functions by their TRequestStatus& parameter. Asynchronous requests are handled by the client interface by using a form of RSessionBase::SendReceive() that also takes a TRequestStatus& parameter. The server keeps the message corresponding to the asynchronous request until that request has completed.

When the server completes the request, the kernel puts the completion code into the TRequestStatus passed by the client, and then signals the client's request semaphore to indicate that the request has completed.

In contrast, synchronous functions are sent as a message using a form of RSessionBase::SendReceive() that does *not* take a TRequestStatus& parameter. The message for a synchronous function must be completed synchronously by the server's handler function.

We saw in the previous chapter that any asynchronous request must be completed precisely once – whatever the circumstances. The kernel guarantees that, even if the server thread dies, an asynchronous request by a client is completed as part of the kernel's thread-death cleanup.

We also saw that any API that provides asynchronous request functions should also offer corresponding cancel functions: so cancel functions, too, are often present in servers' client APIs.

Ending a Session, and Cleanup after Client Death

When a client has finished with a client-server session, it should end it with RSessionBase::Close(). This sends a disconnect message to the server, which responds by simply destroying its end of the session: by calling the destructor of the CSession-derived object. Then, the kernel destroys its representation of the session. The handle of the client-side RSessionBase is set to zero.

It is safe for a client to call Close() on the RSessionBase again: when the handle is zero, Close() does nothing.

If the client thread dies, the kernel will perform thread-death cleanup and send a disconnect message to the server end of all the sessions for which it was a client thread. Thus, the server-side end of the session is destroyed, even if the client thread dies.

Servers must perform effective cleanup. When a CSession object is destroyed, any resources associated with it should also be destroyed. Usually, this is just standard C++ destructor processing.

Cleanup after Server Death

Servers should be written with the greatest care, so they do not terminate prematurely. But if a server does die, then the kernel gives the opportunity for clients to recover. Any outstanding messages from asynchronous requests will be completed with the KErrDied return code.

After a server has died, the client should clean up all RSessionBase objects relating to that server. Any SendReceive() issued on an RSessionBase to a dead server will result in a completion code of KErrServerTerminated. This will be the case even if a new instance of the server is started: old sessions will not be reconnected.

Handling Multiple Objects from One Session

A single client-server session may be used to handle multiple server-side objects.

EPOC provides a framework for this, consisting of RSubSessionBase on the client side (which uses the fourth message parameter as a sub-handle to the server-side object), and CObject and related classes on the server side.

The CObject classes are more complicated than is necessary for most requirements, and it's possible to use RSubSessionBase successfully without using CObjects. In any case, the idea is to route requests from the CServer::ServiceL() function to the particular server-side object that should handle the request.

The GSDP server doesn't use multiple objects in this way.

Performance

The fundamental means of communication between client and server is a transaction based on a message send, some optional inter-thread data transfer, and message completion. Compared with conventional multithreading, shared heaps, blocking I/O, mutex synchronization, and full-blown concurrent programming disciplines, this transaction-based model is less demanding for programmers and system resources. In itself, this is a significant boost to client-server performance and to EPOC's overall system performance.

However, when you implement a server – or even when, as a client, you use one – you should be aware of the performance issues that still exist, and what you can do to tackle them.

The issue that matters more than anything else is the frequency of transactions, and the cost of the main operations involved in a transaction:

❑ Context switching between processes is the most expensive operation – that is, sending a message to a server in a different process, or sending the response back from server to client

❑ Context switching between *threads*, when the client and server are in the same process, is much more efficient

❑ Inter-thread data transfers between processes are fairly expensive

❑ Inter-thread data transfers between threads in the same process are quite cheap

Compared with these costs, the difference between a small inter-thread data transfer and a large one is trivial.

Clearly, the actual cost of a client-server context switch depends on the specific EPOC hardware and on the present state of execution. You should think in terms of a few hundred microseconds – that is, around ten thousand cycles – expended largely on MMU manipulation or cache misses. The actual cost of a data transfer depends similarly on hardware specifics.

Bearing these costs in mind, some standard techniques have evolved to improve client-server performance. Some techniques are about server design (including the implementation of the client interface). Some are about sensible client programming. And some are down to EPOC system configuration. The main techniques are:

- ❏ Design the server and client interface to support client-side buffering and high-level transactions

- ❏ As a client programmer, cache server-side data. Some server support may be needed to keep the cache up-to-date.

- ❏ Configure the system so that related servers run in the same process

- ❏ As a last resort, design the server and its client interface to support shared memory

We will review these techniques in the following sections.

Client-side Buffering

The EPOC window server uses client-side buffering in order to minimize the number of transactions between the client and server. In a code sequence such as this:

```
CWindowGc& gc = SystemGc();
...
gc.SetPenStyle(CGraphicsContext::ESolidPen);
gc.SetBrushStyle(CGraphicsContext::ENullBrush);
gc.SetPenColor(KRgbBlack);
gc.DrawRect(rect);
rect.Shrink(1, 1);
gc.SetPenColor(KRgbWhite);
gc.DrawRect(rect);
```

A naïve server implementation would result in six client-server transactions, and cripplingly slow graphics. Instead of passing each function call to the server directly, the window server's client interface converts the call into an operating code with parameters that are stored in a client-side buffer. The above sequence requires only a few hundred machine instructions in the client thread, and a few hundred machine instructions in the server thread, plus one transaction that will also be used for other drawing.

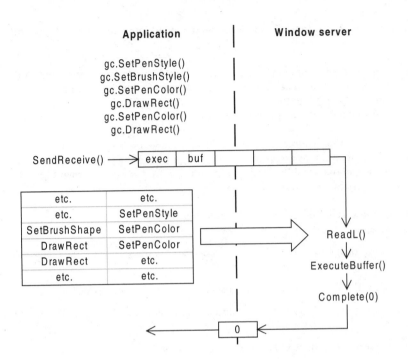

When the buffer is full, or when a function such as DrawPolyLine() (which requires large-scale data transfer) is invoked, the client interface 'flushes' the buffer — that is, it requests the window server to execute all operations stored in the buffer. The window server reads the buffer using an inter-thread read, and then executes all the drawing commands stored in it. The buffer is reasonably large, and its format has been optimized so that the above commands and more would easily fit inside one buffer.

> *Symbian has had two opportunities to see what happens if you don't do this kind of client-side buffering. Early during EPOC development, prior to implementing the window server buffer, graphics were very slow. During the Java implementation project, prior to implementing client-side buffering from Java programs to the AWT server, a similar thing happened. You can see the effects for yourself on the emulator by putting the window server client interface into 'auto-flush' mode, which empties the buffer after each command. Use Ctrl+Alt+Shift+F to turn on auto-flush, and Ctrl+Alt+Shift+G to turn it off again. The difference is noticeable — and bear in mind that your PC's clock is probably ten times faster than that of a Psion Series 5mx.*

Client-side buffering has some consequences in the API. First, the operations that are buffered cannot return a result. Second, you sometimes need to be able to force a buffer flush. With the window server, a Flush() function is available for this purpose. Flush() is called by EIKON's active scheduler prior to waiting for the next request, so there are relatively few circumstances in which you would need to call it yourself.

> *The stream store also implements client-side buffering. A write stream uses a buffer that is flushed to the destination file only when it is full, or when you call RWriteStream::CommitL(). A read stream uses a buffer that it pre-fills from the source file, and which it uses until another buffer of source data is needed.*

High-level Transactions

If the overheads of a transaction are high, then if possible you should specify the client API so that one transaction does a lot of work.

A good example of this is the capability and setup pattern used by the serial communications and other EPOC servers. Rather than providing many getter/setter functions to test and change the state of a communications port – speed, parity, data bits, stop bits, XON/XOFF, and the like – the communications server provides a single `struct` containing all the settings. You use a `Config()` call to get this `struct`; you can then change values in it, and use `SetConfig()` to send it back to the communications server.

Data Caching

Rather than read a data value from a server every time you need it, it's sometimes a good idea to cache the data value client-side. When they need it, your client programs can use this value without a client-server transaction. However, you must ensure that the cached value is updated when necessary.

For example, the Battleships status display shows the GDP protocol in use for the communication session. You can get this protocol from the GSDP server using a simple client API call, but that would require a client-server transaction every time the status view is drawn. It seemed simpler to cache the value in the status view, and to update it whenever the client changes the settings.

If the setting is updated by the server outside the client's control, then you need to use another method to update the client-side cache. For example, the system shell displays files in the current folder, and highlights any files that are currently open. Files may be deleted, and programs opened and closed, outside the shell's control. To keep the display up to date, the shell uses notification APIs in both the file server (which knows about all files) and the window server (which knows about all open GUI applications). The notification API generates an event when a relevant change occurs. The shell then responds to this event by asking the server for updated information. Thus there is no need for the shell to poll (which would waste power and time), or to require the user to refresh the display (which would be confusing).

> *On the emulator, you can alter a file visible to the shell by using the* Windows *shell rather than EPOC's. If you want EPOC to pick up this change and notify its shell, press and release F5. This simulates opening and closing the door on a real machine for a removable media device. In turn, this causes the file server to notify the shell of general changes, and the shell does a complete re-scan.*

Related Servers in the Same Process

Two key aspects of a client-server transaction are cheaper if the client and server are on different threads in the same process:

❑ Context switching is much cheaper, because no changes to the MMU are required

❑ Inter-thread data transfer is cheaper, because there is no need to map the relevant client's data space into the server's address space

These effects are particularly relevant in the hardware implementations used by most current available EPOC devices. Like the Psion Series 5, they use a post-cache MMU in order to save power (see Chapter 1). This means that the entire cache has to be flushed after a context switch, which slows things down.

There are several ways to ensure that a client-server call avoids these overheads.

Related servers can be run in the same process. EPOC Release 5, for example, runs the serial communications server, sockets server, and telephony server all in a single process. This process is isolated from clients, so that system integrity is maintained. But the many interactions between these servers are much lighter-weight than they would be if they were all in different processes.

EPOC Release 5 uses **fixed processes** to minimize the effects of context switching between the kernel, the four important server processes, and a client process (such as an application) that might be using them.

Conventional processes are mapped to different addresses depending on whether they're running or not. Fixed processes, and the kernel server, are always mapped to the same address. If context is switching between one conventional process, the kernel, and the fixed processes, then no MMU re-mapping or associated cache flushing needs to take place. This boosts overall system efficiency significantly.

The four important server processes are the communications server process (including all the communications-related servers), the file server, the window server, and the font and bitmap server. The diagram below shows the different types of servers and the processes in which they run:

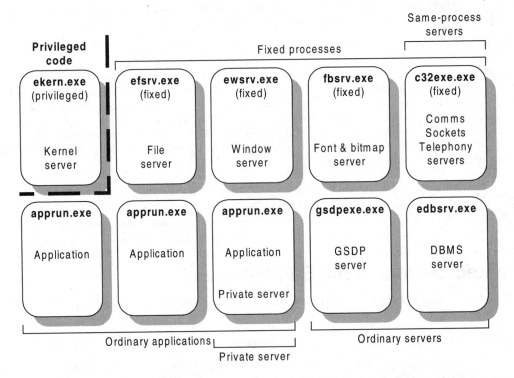

If you write a server for a specialist application, you may be able to run that server in the same process as the application that uses it. It's not always going to be possible, but where it *is* possible, it's easy enough to do.

Shared Memory

If the techniques outlined above don't deliver the performance you need, you can as a last resort use shared memory to avoid the transaction model of client-server communication altogether. You have to replace the transaction model with conventional mutex-type synchronization.

The font and bitmap server (FBS) uses this design, in conjunction with a client program and the window server.

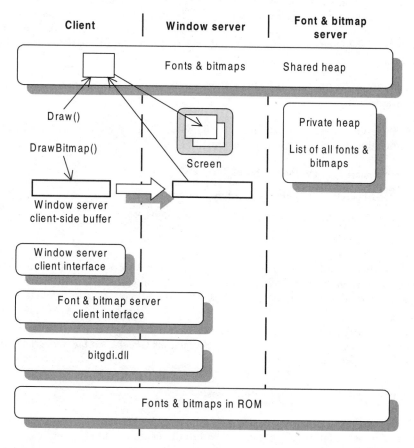

If EPOC had no FBS, then a client program that wanted to blit a bitmap to the screen would have two options:

❑ If the bitmap is already in ROM, the client can pass the address of the bitmap to the window server, and the window server can use the BITGDI to blit the bitmap from the ROM to the screen window.

❑ If the bitmap is created and drawn by the client in its own RAM, the client uses the BITGDI to draw the bitmap and then sends a message to the window server to draw the bitmap. The window server must then copy the bitmap from the client into its own memory, and use the BITGDI to blit it to screen. This would involve considerable inter-thread data transfer from client to window server, and also serious space allocation issues inside the window server.

To avoid the waste of both space and time involved in this kind of data transfer, the font and bitmap server mediates access to a shared heap that contains all RAM-based bitmaps. With the FBS:

- The usage patterns for ROM-based bitmaps are essentially unchanged

- To use a RAM-based bitmap, the client requests the FBS create the bitmap in its shared heap. The client uses the BITGDI to draw to the bitmap. The client locks the bitmap before it starts drawing, and unlocks it again when it has finished.

- When the client wants the window server to draw the bitmap to the screen, it sends a request specifying the bitmap's FBS-owned handle. The window server then uses this handle to identify the address of the bitmap in its address space (which may be different from the address in the client's). Finally, the window server uses the BITGDI to blit the bitmap to the screen.

This makes EPOC very efficient at handling bitmaps, which in turn contributes significantly to the speed of its graphics.

There is an interesting interaction between the FBS and the window server's client-side buffer. Imagine a client specifies the following sequence of events:

- Create a shared, RAM-loaded bitmap
- Use the BITGDI to initialize the bitmap contents
- Request the window server to draw the bitmap
- Delete the bitmap

By the time the client's buffer is flushed and executed by the window server (the third step above), the bitmap could have been deleted. To avoid this, the FBS client calls the window server client's Flush() function (through an interface function) before sending the FBS message to delete the bitmap.

> *As well as handling ROM- and RAM-resident bitmaps, the FBS also handles ROM- and RAM-resident fonts. The precise details are different from those for bitmaps, but the motivations for using a server to share font data are essentially the same.*

The shared memory technique is not without cost:

- The shared heap is mapped to different addresses in different processes. This means that conventional pointers cannot be used within the heap: a handle system has to be used instead.

- The shared heap is not the default heap for either client or server process. This means that the default operator new() and operator delete() don't work.

- For both the above reasons, objects designed for use in the default user heap cannot be placed onto a shared heap. New classes must be written specially for this purpose.

- You have to use mutex synchronization to control access to objects on the shared heap.

- You have to make sure that things stay in sync when you delete objects that are shared with other servers.

For the font and bitmap server, these costs are low, because the shared heap contains large-scale objects (fonts and bitmaps), and because the usage patterns of these objects minimize the difficulties of mutex-based sharing. In addition, the benefits of sharing are very high, because of:

❑   The intensity of operations involving bit-blitting

❑   The enormous difference the efficient implementation makes to users' perceptions of system efficiency

❑   The size of the objects that would have to be exchanged using client-server transactions if the shared heap were not available

Other shared-heap server designs have been implemented on EPOC, but in each case the design issues, and the cost/benefit analysis, have had to be thought through very carefully.

Servers and Threads

The session between a client and a server is owned by the kernel. The kernel specifies that the session is between the client *thread* and the server *thread*. This has simple, but profound, implications for any program that uses servers:

❑   Client-side resources representing server-side objects may only be used and destroyed by the client thread that created them.

❑   Server responsiveness to clients is governed by the duration of the longest possible RunL() of any active object running on the server thread.

Most of the time, these implications are not onerous. Most EPOC clients and servers are single-threaded, and the active object paradigm for event-handling threads is perfectly adequate. In a few cases, though, these implications raise issues for EPOC programmers and, as usual, some techniques have been developed to tackle them.

Sharing Client-side Objects

Many programs written for non-EPOC platforms are multithreaded: one thread might be used to handle user input, while another thread handles communication with a sockets protocol. The threads may communicate by means of a file, and either thread may wish to update the display. Naturally, the two threads synchronize using mutexes or semaphores.

> **This is not possible in EPOC because servers treat client sessions as being owned by a single client thread.**

Only the thread that opened an RFile may use it for reading and writing. When that thread terminates, the file server automatically cleans up the RFile. Likewise, only the thread that opened an RWsSession may use it and any window resources that it controls.

For pure EPOC programs, these restrictions don't matter. A pure EPOC program uses a single thread where other programs would use a process, and active objects where other programs would use threads.

The EPOC C Standard Library (STDLIB) demonstrates one way to tackle this resource ownership problem. STDLIB provides a POSIX-compliant `FILE` API that maps straight onto EPOC `RFile` member functions. While a single-threaded STDLIB program will call `RFile`'s member functions directly, a multithreaded STDLIB program starts a private server – the POSIX server – that is shared between all threads in the same process. The private server owns the EPOC `RFile`, and each thread's `FILE` functions are implemented by a thread-owned `RPosixFile` object that sends a message to the POSIX server's corresponding `RFile`.

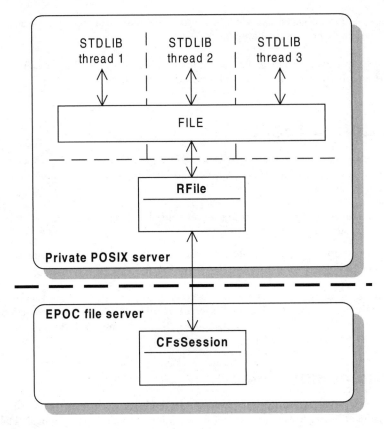

This allows EPOC resources to be shared by all threads in a process, but at some cost: a POSIX `FILE` operation involves *two* client-server transactions instead of one, and writing the interface layer for the `RPosixFile` is tedious.

The Java Virtual Machine (JVM) implementation in EPOC Release 5 uses POSIX threads and related objects such as files and sockets extensively. A JVM process therefore always includes a private POSIX server.

The JVM implementation also uses a GUI implemented using a similar pattern. All GUI functions in a JVM process are handled by another private server, the AWT server. The AWT server owns an EIKON environment, including a session with the EPOC window server. Thus, the EPOC resources have an exclusive owner. The cost of the AWT server is arguably less than the cost of the POSIX server, because the AWT server's operations are in any case complex and high-level, so that the server is providing significant value.

Even so, it is desirable that server-managed resources should be shared between client threads. In the next release of EPOC, new support in the kernel and server framework will allow servers to be changed so that they effectively support *process* ownership of resources, rather than *thread* ownership.

Multithreading in the Server

A server is implemented as a *single* event-handling thread. As usual in EPOC, the server thread implements event handling by using active objects.

In fact, the server itself is an active object: CServer::RunL() is coded to perform first-level handling of incoming requests, which usually results in a CSession::ServiceL() call to handle a message. CServer::NewSessionL() and CSession::~CSession() are also called in response to connect and disconnect messages.

The server may contain other active objects for handling input events, timeouts, and so on.

Time-critical Server Performance

For some time-critical applications, we can ask two very specific questions about server performance:

❑   What is the fastest guaranteed service time required to process a client message?

❑   What is the fastest guaranteed time needed to respond to an event on some I/O device owned by the server?

By 'fastest guaranteed time', I mean the time that would be required *in the worst possible circumstances.* Often, the service time or response time will be much better than this, but that can't be guaranteed because something else might be happening instead. It only takes a little thought to arrive at the following important conclusion:

> **The fastest guaranteed service time is limited by the duration of the longest-running RunL() of any active object in the server's main thread.**

This is because, when a client thread makes a request, the server thread may already be running a RunL() for another client request, or for some other activity within the server. The CServer::RunL() for the client request cannot pre-empt a RunL() that is already in progress. So the client will have to wait until the current RunL() has finished before its request even starts to be handled.

We can easily see that the same applies to responding to external events.

> **The fastest guaranteed response time to an external event is limited by the duration of the longest-running RunL() in the thread that drives a device.**

This has important implications for server design. If you are designing a high-performance server, you should not call long-running operations from *any* of your service functions. Furthermore, you should not perform long-running operations from *any* of the RunL()s of any other active object in your server's main thread.

If you need to deliver long-running operations to clients, or to perform long-running operations for internal reasons, you must run them on a different thread. The most obvious way to structure that thread would be as a server – clearly, a low-performance server. You might run the server as a private server in the main server's process. The low-performance server's 'client' API should deliver its long-running functions asynchronously, so that the high-performance server can kick them off quickly, and then handle their completion with an active object.

If your server specifies a server-side interface – for instance, one that allows plug-in protocol implementations – and if your server has any critical response time requirements, you should be very clear about the responsibilities of anyone implementing that interface.

Obviously, the kernel thread has the highest priority of any thread in the system. Device driver code – in interrupt service routines, device drivers, or delayed function calls (DFCs) – can block any other code. So device driver code, which is a special case of a plug-in API, should be particularly quick.

Thread Priorities

If you are interested in server performance, then you are probably also interested in thread priorities. The basic rule is simple.

> **A server with a shorter guaranteed response time should have a higher thread priority than a server with a longer guaranteed response time.**

Otherwise, a long-running RunL() in a low-performance server with a mistakenly high thread priority will block what might otherwise have been a short-running RunL() in a high-performance server whose priority has been sensibly chosen, but is lower than that of the misbehaved low-performance server.

> **Don't kid yourself about response times. Awarding a server a high thread priority doesn't necessarily give it a short guaranteed response time.**

To get short guaranteed response time, you must analyze *all* the RunL()s in your server's main thread. If any of them are longer than is justified by the thread priority you have awarded your server, then it's effectively a low-performance server and you're compromising the ability of any lower-priority server to deliver on its response time promise. That's antisocial behavior: don't do it.

Another rule about server thread priorities can be deduced from the rule above:

> **All system servers should have a priority that is higher than all applications.**

This is because an application might include arbitrarily long-running code. If it were allowed to run at higher priority than any server, the application would block the server from servicing any of its clients.

The Client-server APIs

It's now time for a brief review of the client-server APIs. I'll highlight the main features here, and in Chapter 20 I'll demonstrate how they're used in practice. The main classes are all defined in e32std.h and e32base.h. They are:

Class	Purpose
RThread	A thread
RHandleBase, RSessionBase	Client-side session classes
CServer, CSession, RMessage	Server-side server, session, and message classes
TPckg<T>, TPckgC<T>, TPckgBuf<T>	Type-safe buffer and pointer descriptors for any kind of data
RSubSessionBase	Client-side sub-session
CObject, CObjectCon, CObjectIx, CObjectConIx	Server-side classes related to sub-sessions

We will look at the main features of the most important classes. We won't deal with any of the sub-session classes.

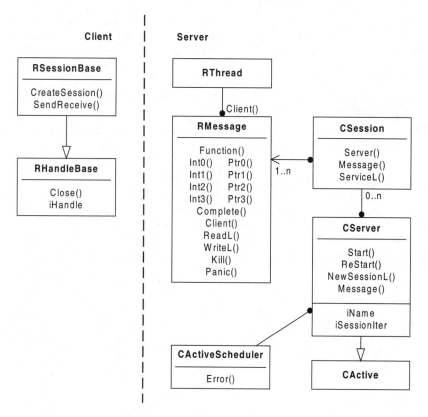

Thread Basics

Threads are basic for client-server programming, because the client and the server are separate threads, and must be able to refer to each other.

The RThread class enables one thread to create or refer to another, to manipulate the other thread, and to transfer data between itself and the other thread. RThread's default constructor is set up to create an RThread object for your own thread:

```
RThread me;
```

Usually, however, a program uses an RThread to refer to another thread. In the context of client-server programming, the server uses RThreads to refer to its clients. The server's client interface may use an RThread to create an instance of the server. It isn't usually necessary for client code to use RThreads directly.

The main things you can do with an RThread are:

❑   Create() a new thread. You specify a function where execution is to begin, and parameters to that function. The thread is created in suspended state, and you have to Resume() it to start it executing.

❑   Open() a handle to an existing thread

❑   Kill() and Panic() the thread. Killing is the normal way to end another thread; panicking indicates that the thread had a programming error. Servers use this to panic their client when the client passes a bad request.

❑   Set and query the thread's priority

❑   Cause an asynchronous request issued by that thread to complete, using RequestComplete()

❑   ReadL() data from a descriptor in the other thread's address space, or WriteL() data to a descriptor in the other thread's address space

The full RThread API is well documented in the C++ SDK.

Many RThread functions are mirrored in the User class's API. Functions such as Kill(), Panic(), and RequestComplete() affect the currently-running thread, so that,

```
User::Kill(KErrNone);
```

is equivalent to:

```
RThread me;
me.Kill(KErrNone);
```

Inter-thread Data Transfer and the Package Classes

> In the EPOC documentation, inter-thread data transfer is referred to as inter-thread communication, or ITC. I have used 'data transfer' rather than 'communication' here, because in reality communication is about much more than just data transfer.

All transfer of data between threads is based on six member functions of RThread (found in E32std.h):

```
TInt GetDesLength(const TAny* aPtr) const;
TInt GetDesMaxLength(const TAny* aPtr) const;
void ReadL(const TAny* aPtr, TDes8& aDes, TInt anOffset) const;
void ReadL(const TAny* aPtr, TDes16& aDes, TInt anOffset) const;
void WriteL(const TAny* aPtr, const TDesC8& aDes, TInt anOffset) const;
void WriteL(const TAny* aPtr, const TDesC16& aDes, TInt anOffset) const;
```

Inter-thread data transfer is performed from data buffers identified by a descriptor in both the currently running thread and the 'other' thread identified by the RThread object. The descriptor in the currently running thread is identified by a conventional descriptor reference (such as const TDesC8& for an 8-bit descriptor) from which an inter-thread write will take data. The descriptor in the other thread is identified by an address, passed as a const TAny*, which is the address of a descriptor *in the other thread's address space* (the address will probably have been passed from client to server, as one of the four 32-bit message parameters).

Bearing this in mind:

❑ GetDesLength(const TAny*) returns the Length() of the descriptor referred to in the other thread's address space.

❑ GetMaxDesLength(const TAny*) returns the MaxLength() of the descriptor referred to in the other thread's address space.

❑ ReadL(const TAny*, TDes8&, TInt) reads data from the other thread into a descriptor in this thread. Data is transferred from the anOffset'th byte of the source. The amount of data transferred is the smaller of the number of bytes between anOffset and GetDesLength() of the source descriptor in the other thread, and the MaxLength() of the destination descriptor in the current thread. There is also a 16-bit version of ReadL().

❑ WriteL(const TAny*, const TDesc8&, TInt) writes data from this thread into a descriptor in the other thread. A 16-bit variant is also provided.

If any of these functions is called with a TAny* that is not the address of a valid descriptor in the other thread, then a KErrBadDescriptor error results. GetMaxDesLength() and GetDesLength() return this as their result – you can distinguish it from a true descriptor length, because all EPOC error codes are negative. ReadL() and WriteL() leave with this as their error code.

> A bad descriptor almost certainly indicates a bad client program. Any server detecting KErrBadDescriptor should panic the offending client.

All inter-thread data transfer uses descriptors. This is appropriate, because descriptors contain an address and a length. If you wanted to transfer a floating-point number from a client to a server, you could use the following client code:

```
TInt p[4];                    // Message parameter array
TReal x = 3.1415926535;       // A 64-bit quantity
TPtrC8 xPtrC(&x, sizeof(x));  // Address and length in a descriptor
p[0] = &xPtrC;                // Pass address of descriptor as zeroth message parameter
```

And this code on the server side:

```
TReal x;
TPtr8 xPtr(&x, 0, sizeof(x));          // Address, length, max-length
Client().ReadL(Message.Ptr0(), &xPtr, 0);   // Transfer data
```

But this code isn't very type-safe, and it's not exactly straightforward either. The package classes offer a type-safe alternative. On the client side:

```
TInt p[4];                    // Message parameter array
TReal x = 3.1415926535;       // A 64-bit quantity
TPckgC<TReal> xPackage(x);    // Package into a descriptor
p[0] = &xPackage;             // Address of package
```

And the server side:

```
TReal x;
TPckg<TReal> xPackage(x);                        // Package it up
Client().ReadL(Message.Ptr0(), &xPackage, 0);   // Transfer data
```

The `TPckg<T>` and `TPckgC<T>` classes are simply type-safe, thin template wrappers around `TPtr8` and `TPtrC8`. A third package class, `TPckgBuf<T>`, performs a similar function for `TBuf8<sizeof(T)>`.

We can picture the APIs related to inter-thread data transfer, and other thread functions, as:

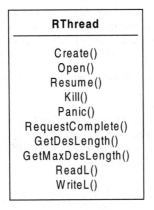

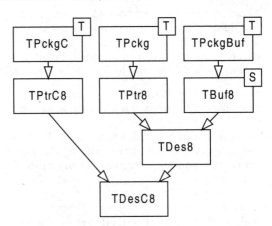

Client-side Objects

The main client-side object is RSessionBase, derived from RHandleBase. As a server provider, your client interface should include a class derived from RSessionBase that handles communications from client to server.

A *Client-side Handle for Server-side (and Kernel-side) Objects*

RHandleBase, which is defined in e32std.h, is the base class for client-side objects that refer to a number of kernel-side objects, and also for RSessionBase, which refers to server-side objects.

For our purposes, the only relevant aspects of the RHandleBase class declaration are:

```
class RHandleBase
    {
public:
    ...
    inline RHandleBase();
    IMPORT_C void Close();
    ...
    inline TInt Handle() const;
    ...
protected:
    TInt iHandle;
    };
```

In brief, an RHandleBase has a 32-bit handle that's used by the client to refer to a particular session with the server. From the server's perspective, the client's thread ID, combined with this handle, uniquely identifies a server-side session.

RSessionBase — *Client-side Session*

RSessionBase is the base class for any client-side session with a server. Here are the relevant parts of its declaration:

```
class RSessionBase : public RHandleBase
    {
protected:
    IMPORT_C TInt CreateSession(
        const TDesC& aServer,
        const TVersion& aVersion,
        TInt aMessageSlots,
        TTimeIntervalMicroSeconds32 aDelayTime = KSendDelayTime,
        TInt aRetryCount = KSendRetryCount);
    ...
    IMPORT_C void SendReceive(TInt aFunction, TAny* aPtr,
                            TRequestStatus& aStatus) const;
    IMPORT_C TInt SendReceive(TInt aFunction, TAny* aPtr) const;
    ...
private:
    TTimeIntervalMicroSeconds32 iDelayTime;
    TInt iRetryCount;
    ...
    };
```

You use CreateSession() to create a new session with the server. This allocates a handle in the base RHandleBase class. Normally your derived client class will call CreateSession() from a friendlier client function, such as Open(), Connect(), etc., as we saw with RFsSession in Chapter 7.

Use Close(), defined in the RHandleBase class, to close the session. After being closed, the handle is set to zero, so that the object can no longer be used. The handle is also set to zero by RHandleBase's inline constructor, prior to connecting the session.

Messages are sent using SendReceive(). The synchronous form of SendReceive() (the one that returns a TInt) is expected to complete immediately, by means of a synchronous ServiceL() function in the server. The asynchronous form may complete some time later.

RSessionBase is 12 bytes long: 4 bytes for the handle in the base class, and another 8 bytes for the iDelayTime and iRetryCount members. The send-receive functions use these values to try to re-send a message if, on the first attempt, the server was busy and could not service the request. It turns out, however, that these members are superfluous (because the server can never be busy at the time a message is sent): they will be removed in the next release of EPOC. Likewise, the aDelayTime and aRetryCount parameters to CreateSession() are superfluous: if you are writing a derived class, you can allow them to default.

Both forms of SendReceive() take a 32-bit TInt argument called aFunction that specifies the request code for the message. The TAny* aPtr argument should point to four 32-bit words containing pointers or 32-bit integers that carry the parameters of the message.

The synchronous form of SendReceive() is implemented (in private EPOC code) as:

```
TInt SendReceive(TInt aRequest, TAny* aPtr)
    {
    TRequestStatus status;
    SendReceive(aRequest, aPtr, status);
    User::WaitForRequest(status);
    return status.Int();
    }
```

The asynchronous version is the more fundamental. It causes a message to be sent containing:

❑   The request code
❑   Four 32-bit parameters
❑   The client's thread ID
❑   The handle from the RHandleBase
❑   The address, in the client's process, of the TRequestStatus to be used to complete the message

This is all wrapped up into a single message. When the server completes the message, it posts the 32-bit result back to the client's request status.

We can now explain the other two parameters to CreateSession().

The TInt aMessageSlots parameter tells the kernel how many messages to reserve for this client-server session. If the session supported only synchronous function calls, only one message slot could ever be used. If the session supports asynchronous requests, then one additional message is needed per asynchronous request that could possibly be outstanding. In most cases, that is one or two – very rarely are any more needed.

In the next release of EPOC, the kernel will allocate slots dynamically, so there will be no need to specify this parameter.

The TVersion contains three version numbers:

❑ Major, as in 5 for EPOC release 5

❑ Minor, indicating a minor feature release

❑ Build, indicating the build number – effectively a maintenance level

The TVersion is intended to ensure that the client API and the server implementation, which may be provided in separate DLLs, are at compatible levels.

Using TVersion is probably no more or less effective than using a host of other disciplines to make sure these programs are in sync. In the GSDP sample code, the same DLL is used to implement client interface and server, so we are happy to pass a TVersion(0, 0, 0) in our CreateSession().

Server-side Objects

The three main server-side objects are CServer, the base class for the entire server, CSession, the base class for a server-side object, and RMessage, which contains the message sent from a client.

There is just one CServer object per server, but there are as many CSession objects as there are RSessionBase objects currently in session with this server. There is one server-side RMessage object for each outstanding request: that means at most one RMessage for a request being handled synchronously from one client, and any number of RMessages for requests being handled asynchronously.

CServer — A Server

CServer is the active object that fields messages from all potential clients and channels them to the right CSession object to be interpreted and executed. Here are the relevant parts of the CServer declaration:

```
class CServer : public CActive
    {
    ...
public:
    IMPORT_C ~CServer();
    IMPORT_C TInt Start();
    IMPORT_C void StartL();
    IMPORT_C void ReStart();
    inline const RMessage& Message() const;
protected:
    ...
    IMPORT_C void DoCancel();
    IMPORT_C void RunL();
// Pure virtual
    virtual CSession* NewSessionL(RThread aClient,
                                  const TVersion& aVersion) const = 0;
    ...
protected:
    TSessionControl iControl;
    HBufC* iName;
```

```
    private:
        RServer iServer;
        TDblQue<CSession> iSessionQ;
        RMessage iMessage;
    protected:
        TDblQueIter<CSession> iSessionIter;
        };
```

The server *is-a* active object. It issues a request to the kernel for a message from any client. Its RunL() function (which should really be private) then handles the message, usually by finding the appropriate session and calling its ServiceL() function.

Bootstrap code for a server should create an active scheduler, a cleanup stack, and a server object; create a name for the server (stored in iName), and then issue Start() (or StartL()) to cause the server to issue its first request. The server name must be specified by any client wishing to connect to the server, as the aServer parameter to RSessionBase::CreateSession().

The server's RunL() function renews the request to the kernel automatically. However, It *doesn't* renew the request if (say) the client's ServiceL() function leaves. You have to handle this from the active scheduler's Error() function, and issue ReStart() to renew the request.

When the server handles a connect message, it invokes CreateSessionL() to create a new server-side CSession-derived object. Oddly that this function is const: you usually need to cast away const-ness when you implement this function, in order to be able to increment usage counts and do other housekeeping in your derived server class.

When the server handles a disconnect message, it simply deletes the affected session, which also causes its C++ destructor to be invoked.

The server stores the current message in iMessage. When you're handling a synchronous message, you can get at this using the Message() function. Usually, however, this isn't necessary, because the RMessage is passed as a parameter to CSession::ServiceL().

You can iterate through the sessions owned by the server, using the protected iSessionIter member.

CSession — *A Server-side Session*

CSession is the base class for the server-side end of a session. You implement its ServiceL() function to interpret and handle client requests. CSession also provides many convenience functions for accessing the client and the current message. The relevant parts of CSession are:

```
    class CSession : public CBase
        {
    public:
        IMPORT_C ~CSession();
        ...
        inline const CServer* Server() const;
        inline const RMessage& Message() const;
        ...
        virtual void ServiceL(const RMessage& aMessage) = 0;
    protected:
        IMPORT_C CSession(RThread aClient);
        ...
    private:
        TInt iResourceCountMark;
        RThread iClient;
```

```
    TDblQueLink iLink;
    const CServer* iServer;
    friend class CServer;
    };
```

Your derived class may include any kind of C++ constructor and second-phase constructor in order to initialize the session properly, with the proviso that the derived class's C++ constructor should pass the client thread's RThread to the protected CSession constructor.

You should implement ServiceL() to handle a message from the client. Interpret the request code and parameters in the RMessage from the client; when ServiceL() is complete, use aMessage.Complete() to pass a result back to the client. You can get at the server using Server().

The other functions provided by the CSession API are either for specialist use or deprecated, so I haven't described them here.

RMessage — A Server-side Message

When a client issues a message, it arrives at the server as an RMessage object. You can use the functions of RMessage to access the request code and message parameters. You also get a Client() function that returns an RThread for the client, and convenience functions to read from, write to, panic, terminate, or kill the client thread. You call Complete() to complete the handling of a message.

Here is the complete definition of RMessage:

```
class RMessage
    {
    friend class CServer;
public:
    enum TSessionMessages { EConnect = -1, EDisConnect = -2 };
public:
    IMPORT_C RMessage();
    IMPORT_C RMessage(const RMessage& aMessage);
    IMPORT_C RMessage& operator=(const RMessage& aMessage);
    IMPORT_C void Complete(TInt aReason) const;
    IMPORT_C void ReadL(const TAny* aPtr, TDes8& aDes) const;
    IMPORT_C void ReadL(const TAny* aPtr, TDes8& aDes, TInt anOffset) const;
    IMPORT_C void ReadL(const TAny* aPtr, TDes16& aDes) const;
    IMPORT_C void ReadL(const TAny* aPtr, TDes16& aDes, TInt anOffset) const;
    IMPORT_C void WriteL(const TAny* aPtr, const TDesC8& aDes) const;
    IMPORT_C void WriteL(const TAny* aPtr, const TDesC8& aDes,
                         TInt anOffset) const;
    IMPORT_C void WriteL(const TAny* aPtr, const TDesC16& aDes) const;
    IMPORT_C void WriteL(const TAny* aPtr, const TDesC16& aDes,
                         TInt anOffset) const;
    IMPORT_C void Panic(const TDesC& aCategory, TInt aReason) const;
    IMPORT_C void Kill(TInt aReason) const;
    IMPORT_C void Terminate(TInt aReason) const;
    inline TInt Function() const;
    inline const RThread& Client() const;
    inline TInt Int0() const;
    inline TInt Int1() const;
    inline TInt Int2() const;
    inline TInt Int3() const;
```

```
    inline const TAny* Ptr0() const;
    inline const TAny* Ptr1() const;
    inline const TAny* Ptr2() const;
    inline const TAny* Ptr3() const;
    inline const RMessagePtr MessagePtr() const;
protected:
    TInt iFunction;
    TInt iArgs[KMaxMessageArguments];
    RThread iClient;
    const TAny* iSessionPtr;
    const RMessage* iMessagePtr;
    };
```

The following are the most important functions you use when writing a server.

❑ Client() returns a const RThread& representing the client thread that sent the message.

❑ Function() returns the 32-bit request code for the function requested by the client.

❑ Int0(), Int1(), Int2(), and Int3() access the four message parameters, interpreting them as TInts. Ptr0(), Ptr1(), Ptr2(), and Ptr3() access the four parameters as well, interpreting them as TAny* pointers.

❑ When you have handled the function, you convey the 32-bit result to the client using Complete(). This causes the client's request status for the message to be posted with the completion code. The kernel also releases the kernel-side message slot.

❑ RMessage's ReadL() and WriteL() functions are convenience wrappers for corresponding RThread functions: they read and write from client's memory. Use these to communicate data that is too large to communicate within the operating code, parameters, and completion code. Likewise, RMessage's Panic(), Kill(), and Terminate() functions are convenience wrappers for corresponding RThread functions on the client thread.

> CSession has convenience functions corresponding to those in RMessage, but the CSession equivalents are deprecated: use the RMessage functions instead. That way, you'll respond to the client thread that sent the message, rather than the one that started the session. In the next version of EPOC, servers will support process ownership of resources, so this distinction will become important.

RMessage is not intended for derivation, so its protected members should really be private.

Summary

In this chapter, I've:

❑ Outlined the basic workings of servers

❑ Given some hints and tips for optimizing their performance

❑ Reviewed the API elements associated with servers

In the next chapter, we'll get practical: with the GSDP server, we can see all these facets of the client-server framework working together.

20

The GSDP Server

In the previous two chapters, I've described EPOC's active object and client-server frameworks – the foundations for system programming. I'm now in a position to describe the GSDP (Game Session Datagram Protocol) server we implemented for sharing GDP datagrams among multiple client games on a single EPOC machine. Along the way, we will encounter all the most important practical techniques needed to program an EPOC server.

We've already seen that the purpose of the GSDP server is to allow GDP drivers to be shared between multiple games on a single EPOC machine. To achieve this, the GSDP server:

❑   Runs the GDP implementations on behalf of all games on an EPOC machine

❑   Associates an origin, a destination address, a destination port number, and a game protocol with each client session, so that from the client's perspective, GSDP is a session protocol rather than a stateless datagram protocol

❑   When sending a packet, selects the right GDP implementation, and adds the correct port numbers and game protocol ID into the packet's datagram content

❑   When receiving a packet, uses the port number and protocol ID to select which client should receive it

This functionality is reflected in the server's client interface, and in its internal structure.

We've gained a lot of experience, both in writing servers and writing about them, since the server examples in the C++ SDK were written. The GSDP server, presented here, has its own specific task to perform, but in many ways it's typical, and I'll describe it in sufficient detail here that you can use it with confidence as a basis for implementing your own servers.

Software Structure

You can find the source code for the GSDP server and its client interface in \pep\gsdp\. Here's the structure of the server and its interfaces:

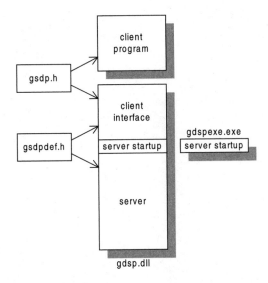

The server and its client interface are delivered in a single DLL, gsdp.dll. The client interface consists of a header file, gsdp.h, which we'll look at shortly, and corresponding functions exported from the DLL. Another header file, gsdpdef.h, includes definitions that tie the client interface and the server together – mainly the request codes passed in the various messages. All other header files are private to either the client alone, or the server alone.

The GSDP server is a **transient server**: it's started when a client needs it, and terminates itself when no more clients need it. The startup code launches the server as a new thread under the WINS emulator, or as a new process under MARM on target machines. The startup code for the emulator is *also* contained in gsdp.dll; for MARM, it's a separate, very small, .exe.

This design minimizes the differences between the two platforms. It follows the design of the EPOC DBMS server, which was written for EPOC Release 5. Among the useful aspects of this single-DLL design are that it eases debugging under the emulator, because there's only a single project, and it ensures that client and server code are in sync, because they're delivered in the same DLL.

Many EPOC servers use a separate DLL for the client interface, and a relatively large program for the server, delivered as a .exe for target machines, and a DLL for the emulator.

> *One reason which may compel server authors to use a .exe is if they cannot do anything to eliminate writable static in the server code, perhaps because they are porting code. Porting issues are sometimes the reason for using a client-server architecture in the first place: for example, EPOC's spell-check code, ported from source code licensed from Lernout & Hauspie, uses a server for this reason.*

The Client Interface

We saw a UML diagram representing the client interface in Chapter 17. Here is the code from gsdp.h:

```
// gsdp.h

#ifndef __GSDP_H
#define __GSDP_H

#include <e32base.h>

// Game session datagram protocol interface specification
class MGsdpPacketHandler
    {
public:
    virtual void GsdpHandleL(const TDesC8& aData) = 0;
    };

class CGsdpReceiveHandler;

class RGsdpSession : public RSessionBase
    {
public:
    enum TGdpProtocol { EGdpLoopback = 1, EGdpIr, EGdpSms };
public:
    // Construct
    inline RGsdpSession() : iHandler(0) {};

    // Open/close
    IMPORT_C void ConnectL(MGsdpPacketHandler* aHandler);
    IMPORT_C void Close();

    // Load and get GDP protocol
    IMPORT_C void SetGdpProtocolL(TGdpProtocol aProtocol);
    IMPORT_C TGdpProtocol GetGdpProtocol() const;
    IMPORT_C TBool GdpIsNetworked() const;

    // Game protocol
    IMPORT_C void SetGameProtocol(TUint32 aProtocol);
    IMPORT_C TUint32 GetGameProtocol() const;

    // Set and get my address and port
    IMPORT_C void SetMyPort(TUint32 aPort);
    IMPORT_C TUint32 GetMyPort() const;
    IMPORT_C TUint32 AllocMyNextPort();

    // Set and get other address and port
    IMPORT_C void SetOtherAddress(const TDesC& aAddress);
    IMPORT_C void GetOtherAddress(TDes& aAddress) const;
    IMPORT_C void SetOtherPort(TUint32 aPort);
    IMPORT_C TUint32 GetOtherPort() const;
```

```
    // Main protocol functions
    IMPORT_C void Listen();
    IMPORT_C void StopListening();
    IMPORT_C void Send(const TDesC8& aData);

    // Initiate receive-all for 'pull' protocols
    IMPORT_C void ReceiveAll() const;
private:
    friend class CGsdpReceiveHandler;
    void Receive(TDes8& aBuffer, TRequestStatus& aStatus);
    void CancelReceive();
    CGSdpReceiveHandler* iHandler;
    };

const TInt KMaxGsdpAddress=40;
const TInt KMaxGsdpData=100;

#endif
```

The interface follows the communications stack pattern that we've talked about before: requests are passed down the stack using functions of the RGsdpSession class, while data is passed up the stack by calling MGsdpPacketHandler::GsdpHandleL().

The client interface uses active objects, but hides them from the interface, so that:

❑   As a client, you do not have write a derived active object class – you just derive from MGSdpPacketHandler and implement GsdpHandleL()

❑   As a client, you can issue Listen() to receive any number of packets, and StopListening() to stop receiving them.

Internal to the client interface, there is a derived active object class – CGsdpReceiveHandler – that maintains the outstanding receive request, calling RGsdpSession's private, non-exported Receive() and CancelReceive() functions in order to do so.

Message-passing Functions

The majority of the client interface consists of message-passing functions that compose the parameters of the client interface function into a message, send the message, receive the response, and return the result to the client.

Here is a simple example:

```
EXPORT_C void RGsdpSession::SetGameProtocol(TUint32 aProtocol)
    {
    TInt p[4];
    p[0] = (TInt)aProtocol;
    SendReceive(EGsdpReqSetGameProtocol, p);
    }
```

The basic idea is to SendReceive() the request code, EGsdpReqSetGameProtocol, along with as many of the four 32-bit parameters as you actually need. In this case, we only need one: the game protocol.

EGsdpReqSetGameProtocol is defined symbolically in gsdpdef.h. This header file is included in the server so that the same constants are used when interpreting the request.

Oddly, there is no client-side equivalent of RMessage. You have to allocate your own array of four integers, store as many of the parameters as necessary, and then pass the array to SendReceive(). The number 4 is so heavily built into EPOC's architecture that I'm happy to use a literal here, contrary to the usual software engineering rules. If you really want a symbolic constant for this, you can use KMaxMessageArguments from e32std.h.

The corresponding getter function is:

```
EXPORT_C TUint32 RGsdpSession::GetGameProtocol() const
    {
    return SendReceive(EGsdpReqGetGameProtocol, 0);
    }
```

In this case, there's nothing to send, so we pass 0 to indicate that there's no message parameter array. The kernel will fill out the four parameters with undefined values – but this saves you having to waste code on them in your client interface.

You therefore have two choices about the message parameter array: if your request doesn't need any parameters, you don't need one, and can pass 0 (null) to SendReceive(). If you need any parameters, you must allocate an entire message array with all four slots, even if you don't need them all.

This time, we return a result – the game protocol ID. We simply return the 32-bit result that was passed back by the server as the return code of the message to the client.

Incidentally, it's fine to pass any 32-bit quantity back as the result of a synchronous message. The same pattern cannot be used for asynchronous messages because the active scheduler uses the special value KRequestPending to indicate that a request has not completed. So, if an asynchronous request completed with a value that just happened to be KRequestPending (0x80000001), the active scheduler would report a stray signal. An asynchronous version of the same function would have to use an inter-thread write to pass back any numeric value if there is the remotest possibility that the value might ever be KRequestPending.

Sometimes, the return value from SendReceive() is used as a genuine error code, like this:

```
EXPORT_C void RGsdpSession::SetGdpProtocolL(
                            RGsdpSession::TGdpProtocol aProtocol)
    {
    TInt p[4];
    p[0] = (TInt)aProtocol;
    TInt err = SendReceive(EGsdpReqSetGdpProtocol, p);
    User::LeaveIfError(err);
    }
```

In this case, we return normally if there is no error, otherwise we leave with the error code returned. This is most likely to be KErrNotFound or KErrNotSupported (try selecting the infrared protocol on the emulator to get KErrNotSupported).

For setting and getting the other machine's address, we have to pass the address of a descriptor:

```
EXPORT_C void RGsdpSession::SetOtherAddress(const TDesC& aAddress)
    {
    TInt p[4];
    p[0] = (TInt)&aAddress;
    SendReceive(EGsdpReqSetOtherAddress, p);
    }

EXPORT_C void RGsdpSession::GetOtherAddress(TDes& aAddress) const
    {
    TInt p[4];
    p[0] = (TInt)&aAddress;
    SendReceive(EGsdpReqGetOtherAddress, p);
    }
```

The setter function takes a const TDesC& parameter, and the getter a TDes&, so that from the client's perspective, the correct type-safe objects are passed. In either case, however, the client interface code simply passes a pointer to the descriptor as a message parameter. These pointers will eventually be used in calls to RThread::ReadL() and RThread::WriteL(), which we saw in the previous chapter.

Coding the message-passing functions is easy enough, if a little tedious for large client interface APIs. Inevitably, in practice, it involves a lot of copying-and-tweaking. Be very careful that you tweak *everything* you're supposed to. It's easy to copy to a new function name, change the parameter names a little, and then forget to change the request code. The results will be puzzling. A manual scan through your code first thing next morning is a good way to ensure you haven't done anything silly here. Good, full-coverage test code is also another useful weapon in your armory.

Listening and Receiving

The client interface for receiving data consists of two functions:

```
IMPORT_C void Listen();
IMPORT_C void StopListening();
```

RGsdpSession::Listen() makes the client interface start maintaining an outstanding receive request, using an outstanding-request pattern active object, like those we saw in Chapter 18. StopListening() tells the client interface to stop maintaining that request.

The corresponding active object is declared in the private header file gsdpcli.h as:

```
class CGsdpReceiveHandler : public CActive
    {
public:
    // Construct/destruct
    CGsdpReceiveHandler(MGsdpPacketHandler* aHandler, RGsdpSession& aSession);
    ~CGsdpReceiveHandler();

    // Operation
    void Receive();
private:
    // From CActive
    void RunL();
    void DoCancel();
private:
    RGsdpSession& iSession;
    MGsdpPacketHandler* iHandler;
    TBuf8<KMaxGsdpData> iBuffer;
    };
```

RGsdpSession::Listen() calls CGsdpReceiveHandler::Receive(),which is implemented as:

```
void CGsdpReceiveHandler::Receive()
    {
    iSession.Receive(iBuffer, iStatus);
    SetActive();
    }
```

In other words, the receive handler issues the initial request to receive data into its own receive buffer. When this first receive completes, the receive handler's RunL() is invoked:

```
void CGsdpReceiveHandler::RunL()
    {
    iHandler->GsdpHandleL(iBuffer);

    // Initiate next receive
    Receive();
    }
```

This calls the client's handler to pass the received data up the stack, and then issues another receive. If the client issues StopListening(), the client interface Cancel()s the receive handler active object, which in turn causes DoCancel() to be called:

```
void CGsdpReceiveHandler::DoCancel()
    {
    iSession.CancelReceive();
    }
```

This simply passes on the cancel to the server.

The receive message is the *only* asynchronous message supported by the client interface. It is implemented using the asynchronous version of SendReceive():

```
void RGsdpSession::Receive(TDes8& aBuffer, TRequestStatus& aStatus)
    {
    TInt p[4];
    p[0] = (TInt)&aBuffer;
    SendReceive(EGsdpReqReceive, p, aStatus);
    }
```

Every asynchronous request should have a corresponding cancel function. Here it is:

```
void RGsdpSession::CancelReceive()
    {
    SendReceive(EGsdpReqCancelReceive, 0);
    }
```

These functions are very simple on the client side. On the server side, however, their implementation is more interesting. Let's now begin to see how things look from that perspective.

Connecting and Disconnecting

The client interface and receive handler functions assume the server is already there, and that the client has already connected to it.

The client connects to the server using ConnectL(), which sets a handle value to associate with the session. The client disconnects using Close(), which zeroes the handle. As a precaution, the RGsdpSession's C++ constructor sets the handle value to zero, so that the session is clearly closed before ConnectL() is called. If you try to invoke any SendReceive() function on a zero-handle object, you'll get panicked.

If the GSDP server were a system server, guaranteed to be alive all the time (otherwise the system as a whole has effectively died), then all these functions would be very simple. This would do the trick for opening the session:

```
EXPORT_C void RGsdpSession::ConnectL(MGsdpPacketHandler* aHandler)
    {
    // Connect to server
    User::LeaveIfError(CreateSession(KGsdpServerName, TVersion(0,0,0), 2));

    // Create active object receive handler and add it to scheduler
    iHandler = new CGsdpReceiveHandler(aHandler, *this);
    if(!iHandler)
        {
        RSessionBase::Close();
        User::Leave(KErrNoMemory);
        }
    CActiveScheduler::Add(iHandler);
    }
```

And this would close it:

```
EXPORT_C void RGsdpSession::Close()
    {
    // Destroy receiver-handler
    delete iHandler;
    iHandler = 0;

    // Destroy server session
    RSessionBase::Close();
    }
```

Finally the inline constructor,

```
inline RGsdpSession() : iHandler(0) {};
```

would set the handle to zero before the session was first connected.

You can see that this logic is very simple. If I weren't using the hidden `iHandler` active object, this would all boil down to:

```
EXPORT_C void RGsdpSession::ConnectL(MGsdpPacketHandler* aHandler)
    {
    // Connect to server
    User::LeaveIfError(CreateSession(KGsdpServerName, TVersion(0,0,0), 2));
    }

EXPORT_C void RGsdpSession::Close()
    {
    RSessionBase::Close();
    }
```

To connect, I simply issue `CreateSession()`, specifying the name of the server (defined in `gsdpdef.h`):

```
#define KGsdpServerName _L("GSDP server")
```

The other parameters are a zeroed-out version struct (which I don't check, in the server, because I know the server code must be the same as the client's), and two message slots.

I need two message slots for the GSDP server:

❑   One for synchronous requests – the great majority of my client API calls

❑   One for the only asynchronous request supported by my client API, namely `Receive()`

If I added another possible outstanding asynchronous request (say, by adding an asynchronous `Send()` function) then I would have to increase the number of required message slots.

However, the GSDP server is not a system server. It's launched only when needed by clients, and it terminates itself when no longer needed. That creates special difficulties for ConnectL(). The *purpose* of ConnectL() is to connect reliably, in the communications sense of 'reliable', namely that:

❑ Either it succeeds in connecting to the GSDP server in such a way that there is exactly one GSDP server in the system, and the client is connected to it

❑ Or it fails to connect, and leaves, so that the client understands that connection has failed

It is *not* acceptable to:

❑ Accidentally launch a second instance of the GSDP server and connect to it

❑ Silently fail to connect, so that the client believes there is a connection, but there isn't one

The code that ensures reliable server connection is here in RGsdpSession::ConnectL(). It relies on code that ensures reliable server launch, running in the server itself: we'll look at that code below.

Here's the beginning of the real RGsdpSession::ConnectL(), as implemented in gsdpcli.cpp:

```
EXPORT_C void RGsdpSession::ConnectL(MGsdpPacketHandler* aHandler)
    {
    // Connect to server
    TInt err = KErrNone;
    for(TInt tries = 0; tries < 2; tries++)
        {
        err = CreateSession(KGsdpServerName, TVersion(0,0,0), 2);

        if(!err) break; // Connected to existing server - OK

        if(err != KErrNotFound && err != KErrServerTerminated)
            break; // Problems other than server not here - propagate error

        err = CGsdpScheduler::LaunchFromClient();

        if(!err) continue; // If server launched OK, try again to connect

        // If someone else got there first, try again to connect
        if(err == KErrAlreadyExists) continue;
        break; // Server not launched: don't cycle round again
        }
    User::LeaveIfError(err);
    ...
```

We try to connect the server, hoping it is already alive. If our original session returns with KErrNone, all's well.

We can deal with two possible error conditions – server not found, and server terminated – as we'll see shortly. If the attempt to connect to the server produced any other error, then we leave with the error code.

We can get KErrNotFound because the server hasn't been launched.

It may seem very unreasonable to get KErrServerTerminated when you're trying to connect — if the server has terminated, shouldn't we get KErrNotFound? The answer lies in the two-phase process for connection:

- ❑ Firstly, the kernel checks whether a server with the given name exists, and creates a DSession for it

- ❑ Then, the server sends a connect message to the server, which is handled by the CServer class and results in a NewSessionL() function call to create the server-side session

- ❑ The server returns the server-side handle to the new session, which the kernel stores in its DSession

- ❑ The kernel returns the relevant information to the connecting client

If, in the first step above, the kernel can't find the server, this process will return KErrNotFound. But if in the second step, the server happened to be in the process of terminating, it won't handle the message and you'll get KErrServerTerminated.

Whether the server wasn't found, or whether it was terminated, the response is the same: try to launch a new instance of the server, with the static CGsdpScheduler::LaunchFromClient(), which we'll look at below.

There are three potential outcomes to launching the server:

- ❑ We launched it successfully, and so received KErrNone

- ❑ Some other client tried to launch it, so we received KErrAlreadyExists

- ❑ Some other problem occurred

In the case of KErrNone and KErrAlreadyExists, we consider it a successful launch, and loop a second time to connect to the now-launched server.

In the case of another problem, we give up and leave with the error code.

Assuming, then, that CGsdpScheduler::LaunchFromClient() does its job, then RGsdpSession::ConnectL() connects reliably to the server — it either connects to precisely one server, or it fails to connect and lets the client know.

The Client API as a DLL

The GSDP server's client API is the first code we've looked at closely, which is delivered as a static interface DLL with exported functions. It's worth a quick break from the server theme to look at the DLL specifics here. Firstly, the .mmp file:

```
// gsdp.mmp

TARGET gsdp.dll
TARGETTYPE dll
UID 0x1000008d 0x10005407
UNICODEUID 0x1000008d 0
PROJECT pep
SUBPROJECT gsdp
SOURCE gsdpcli.cpp gsdpserv.cpp gsdpsess.cpp gsdpgdp.cpp gsdprxq.cpp gsdpport.cpp
USERINCLUDE . ..\gdp
SYSTEMINCLUDE \epoc32\include
LIBRARY euser.lib efsrv.lib estor.lib gdp.lib
```

The DLL specifics here are:

❏ TARGETTYPE dll, along with the .dll extension on the filename, which implies we want a static library DLL

❏ A second UID of 0x1000008d, which should be used for all static library DLLs (yes, the second UID: remember that the first one is specified implicitly by makmake)

As we saw with EIKON applications, every DLL has to have an E32Dll() function, even though this does nothing. Ours is in gsdpcli.cpp, right at the bottom:

```
EXPORT_C TInt E32Dll(TDllReason)
    {
    return 0;
    }
```

Functions that we wish to make available to clients of the DLL have to be exported from it. You mark them with IMPORT_C in header files, and EXPORT_C in source files.

Functions not exported from the DLL are effectively private, and so cannot be accessed by code not within the DLL. Thus no client can call RGsdpSession::Receive(), because it is private in the C++ sense, and is in any case not exported from the DLL.

There is no need to export the server-side functions to the client – in fact, it would be quite wrong to do so. Even if a client could get the header files, which have plenty of C++ public functions in them, the client shouldn't be able to call these functions directly.

gdp.dll and rgcp.dll are constructed similarly.

The Server Implementation

The server is *much* more complicated than the client, as you'll soon see by taking a look at its class definitions in gsdpserv.h. For a quick overview, here they are in UML:

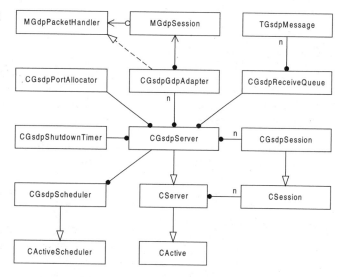

We're going to have to cover this one step at a time. The majority of the work for clients – including all the explicit message handling – is done in CGsdpSession, so we'll cover that class first.

GSDP datagrams are sent by simply wrapping them up and then using one of the GDP protocol implementations to send them. On receipt, the process is reversed. The server owns a list of CGsdpGdpAdapters, which both handle datagram wrapping and unwrapping, and own the specific GDP protocol implementations, so that there is one adapter for each GDP protocol. Adapters are shared between all sessions that use them. The server also uses a port number allocator to allocate unique port IDs to GSDP-initiating clients.

Receiving datagrams is more complicated than sending them, because an incoming datagram must be associated with the correct session. Incoming datagrams go onto a queue, and items are only taken off that queue when an appropriate client issues a receive request. Queue management can become complex and, when we look at this, we will be able to understand how asynchronous messages are handled server-side.

As you can see from the diagram, it's the server class, CGsdpServer, that holds everything together. Startup and shutdown are handled in conjunction with a derived active scheduler class, a shutdown timer, and some support from the CGsdpSession destructor. We'll end the description of the server with detailed coverage of startup and shutdown.

The patterns involved in this server are surprisingly common in other EPOC servers, like the window server and the serial communications server. Some of the important ones are:

- ❑ Client requests are handled by the CSession-derived class.

- ❑ A variety of protocol implementations are supported: the server has to maintain an adapter for each implementation, and associate each client with the correct one.

- ❑ Incoming events must be associated with a client, and must fulfill a receive request when one is outstanding. This requires that incoming events be managed by a queue.

Although the standard EPOC servers are often more sophisticated in their handling of these issues than the GSDP server, the latter provides a very solid foundation for building, and for adding extra sophistication where it is required.

Message Handling

When a client sends a message, the kernel gets it to the right server, and the server gets it to the right session. The session then handles the message using its `ServiceL()` function, which has to analyze the request code and parameters, decide which function to perform, and complete the message either synchronously or asynchronously.

`ServiceL()` is therefore a huge switch statement. Here is `CGsdpSession::ServiceL()`, edited to remove some repetition from the `case` clauses:

```
void CGsdpSession::ServiceL(const RMessage& aMessage)
    {
    switch (aMessage.Function())
        {
    case EGsdpReqSetGameProtocol: // TUint32 aProtocol
        SetGameProtocol(aMessage.Int0());
        aMessage.Complete(0);
        break;
    case EGsdpReqGetGameProtocol: // Returns TUint32
        aMessage.Complete(GetGameProtocol());
        break;
    case EGsdpReqSetGdpProtocol: // RGsdpSession::GdpProtocol aProtocol
        SetGdpProtocolL((RGsdpSession::TGdpProtocol)aMessage.Int0())
        aMessage.Complete(0);
        break;
    case EGsdpReqGetGdpProtocol: // Returns RGsdpSession::Protocol
        aMessage.Complete(GetGdpProtocol());
        break;
    case EGsdpReqGdpIsNetworked: // Returns TBool
        aMessage.Complete(GdpIsNetworked());
        break;
    ...
    case EGsdpReqSetOtherAddress: // const TAny& aAddress
        SetOtherAddress(aMessage.Ptr0());
        aMessage.Complete(0);
        break;
    case EGsdpReqGetOtherAddress: // TAny& aAddress
        GetOtherAddress(aMessage.Ptr0());
        aMessage.Complete(0);
        break;
    ...
    case EGsdpReqSend: // const TAny& aData
        aMessage.Complete(Send(aMessage.Ptr0()));
        break;
    ...
    case EGsdpReqReceive: // TAny& aBuffer - async
        Receive(aMessage.Ptr0());
        break;
```

```
        case EGsdpReqCancelReceive:
            CancelReceive();
            aMessage.Complete(0);
            break;
        default:
            iServer->PanicClient(EBadRequest);
            };
    }
```

I use four key functions of the RMessage class in this ServiceL() code:

- ❑ Function() gives me the request code
- ❑ Int0(), Int1(), Int2(), and Int3() return the message parameters as integers
- ❑ Ptr0(), Ptr1(), Ptr2(), and Ptr3() return the message parameters as TAny* pointers
- ❑ Complete() completes the message, returning the TInt completion code

My philosophy here is to get beyond the shaky, type-unsafe stage as soon as possible. So I contain all knowledge of RMessage parameter numbers and types within ServiceL(), and call second-level handler functions, specified with type-safe parameters, to do the real work. Most second-level functions don't then need to use any RMessage-related functions at all. Those that do can get the current RMessage by using the server's Message() function.

Error Handling

If the client request is malformed, we panic the client thread – just as we would panic our own thread if a conventional function call were made in error. The default case is handled by:

```
        iServer->PanicClient(EBadRequest);
```

This calls my CGsdpServer::PanicClient() function:

```
    void CGsdpServer::PanicClient(TInt aPanic) const
        {
        // Let's have a look before we panic the client
        __DEBUGGER()

        // OK, go for it
        ((RThread&)Message().Client()).Panic(_L("GSDP-Server"), aPanic);
        }
```

The heart of this function is the RThread::Panic() call to panic the client thread – that is, the client for the message currently being processed.

The cast to RThread& in the code above is really a CONST_CAST, needed because RMessage::Client() returns a const RThread& rather than an RThread&.

Until I put the __DEBUGGER() line in, it was impossible to analyze the cause of the panic under the emulator. The thread being panicked was in the middle of a send-receive function, somewhere in the kernel executive, and the corresponding debug information is not supplied in the SDK. However, the real cause of the panic is hidden inside the state of the *server*, so invoking the debugger from the server thread gives a much better clue about why the client thread was about to be panicked. The __DEBUGGER() macro only affects emulator debug builds, so I don't need to put any conditional compilation constructs around it.

The CGsdpServer::PanicClient() function should only be called when a client message is being processed. You should never need or want to panic a client thread at any other stage than when processing a message from it.

If the function servicing the client request leaves, then the active scheduler's Error() function is called:

```
void CGsdpScheduler::Error(TInt aError) const
    {
    // Panic if error didn't arise from server
    if(iServer->IsActive())
        PanicServer(EErrorFromNonClientObject);

    // If it's a bad descriptor, panic the client
    if(aError == KErrBadDescriptor)  // Client had bad descriptor
        {
        iServer->PanicClient(EBadDescriptor);
        }

    // Anyway, complete the outstanding message
    iServer->Message().Complete(aError);

    // Ready to roll again
    iServer->ReStart(); // Really means just continue reading client requests
    }
```

The scheduler's Error() function normally completes the message with the leave code, and then renews the server's request to the kernel for another message from some client. However, if the cause of the error was a bad descriptor passed from the client, this is deemed to be a programming error, and the client is panicked.

This Error() function should only be invoked when the server was processing a client request.

> As a corollary, the RunL() of any other active object in the server should *not* leave. Active objects that run in response to events other than client requests should pre-allocate their resources in response to a client message, so that future operations are guaranteed to succeed or, if the pre-allocation fails, the client is notified by the completion code of the pre-allocation message. In some cases, code inside RunL()s may legitimately leave: if this is so, you should trap such leaves so they don't get handled by the active scheduler.

Synchronous Message Handling

Once we're out of the type-unsafe territory of the ServiceL() switch statement, the message handler functions are usually quite straightforward. Here are the ones for setting and getting the game protocol:

```
void CGsdpSession::SetGameProtocol(TUint32 aProtocol)
    {
    // Set protocol
    iGameProtocol = aProtocol;

    // Check whether we can now receive anything
    if(iReceiveActive)
        iServer->iReceiveQueue->CheckPackets(this);
    }

TUint32 CGsdpSession::GetGameProtocol()
    {
    return iGameProtocol;
    }
```

Basically, the setter stores its argument in a member variable, while the getter returns the member variable as a result. The setter, though, includes some important code. If the game protocol supported by a session changes, then it's possible that a session in listening mode might be able to receive packets intended for the newly specified game protocol, so a function is called to check this. We'll return to that later.

The handlers for setting and getting the other partner's address involve inter-thread data transfer:

```
void CGsdpSession::SetOtherAddress(const TAny* aAddress)
    {
    Message().ReadL(aAddress, iOtherAddress);
    }

void CGsdpSession::GetOtherAddress(TAny* aAddress)
    {
    Message().WriteL(aAddress, iOtherAddress);
    }
```

It's that simple, thanks to the effectiveness of the ReadL() and WriteL() functions, and thanks to the error handling performed by CGsdpScheduler::Error().

Note here that we're using a TAny* as the address of a descriptor in *the other thread's* address space. I passed this address from the other thread as a message parameter. The ReadL() and WriteL() functions will check that the contents of the address look like a descriptor, and will leave with KErrBadDescriptor if they aren't convinced. The active scheduler Error() function we saw above will then panic the client.

The send handler does an inter-thread read to get the data to send, and then sends it using the correct GDP implementation:

```
TInt CGsdpSession::Send(const TAny* aData)
    {
    __ASSERT_ALWAYS(iMyPort != 0, iServer->PanicClient(ESendFromZeroPort));
    TBuf8<KMaxGsdpData> buffer;
    Client().ReadL(aData, buffer, 0);
    iGdpProtocol->SendL(iGameProtocol, iMyPort,
                        iOtherAddress, iOtherPort, buffer);
    return 0;
    }
```

As with all communications systems, a send may take a long time, and the success or otherwise of the send is only detected asynchronously. So, in most communications-related servers, send would be asynchronous.

The specification of GDP, however, makes send synchronous, and allows any datagrams that couldn't be sent to be dropped quietly. We'll cover the send process in a little more detail shortly, including the role of the GDP protocol adapters.

The Send() function above is L-inconsistent. Send() really ought to have an L because it calls ReadL() and WriteL(), which can leave with KErrBadDescriptor. At first, I thought this behavior was unreasonable: why should the server code leave, when the client is at fault? Aren't leaves for environment errors, rather than programming errors? In fact, a client's programming error is as good as a server environment error, so ReadL()'s and WriteL()'s leaving behaviour is correct – the server certainly can't go on to do more processing if the client's reads and writes fail. So Send() and other functions like it ought to have L on their name, so that I remember to take appropriate precautions with temporary heap-based objects when I call these functions.

Asynchronous Message Handling

The only asynchronous function available from the client-side session is Receive(). On the client side, this uses the asynchronous form of SendReceive(). On the server side, the case handler for this function omits the aMessage.Complete() that is present in all other case handlers, because the message will only complete when the receive completes. Here's some of that code from CGsdpSession::ServiceL() again:

```
case EGsdpReqSend: // const TAny& aData
    aMessage.Complete(Send(aMessage.Ptr0()));
    break;
    ...
case EGsdpReqReceive: // TAny& aBuffer - async
    Receive(aMessage.Ptr0());
    break;
case EGsdpReqCancelReceive:
    CancelReceive();
    aMessage.Complete(0);
    break;
```

The receive function is implemented as follows:

```
void CGsdpSession::Receive(const TAny* aBuffer)
    {
    __ASSERT_DEBUG(!iReceiveActive,
                    PanicServer(EReceiveReceiveAlreadyActive));

    // Remember receive request
    iReceiveMessage = Message();
    iReceiveBuffer = aBuffer;
    iReceiveActive = ETrue;

    // Check for immediate fulfillment
    iServer->iReceiveQueue->CheckPackets(this);
    }
```

The session indicates that a receive request has been issued, and stores the RMessage associated with the receive. It also stores the pointer to the client-side buffer, which is the destination for the received data.

Sometime later, the receive will complete. This will cause the data to be transferred to the client's buffer, using an inter-thread write, and the receive message will then complete. Then there are two possibilities:

❑ There is already data for this session to receive, waiting on the server's receive queue: in this case, the receive completes essentially synchronously from the CheckPackets() function shown above

❑ Some data arrives later and is handled by the RunL() of an active object other than the server. This completes the receive asynchronously.

As we saw in Chapter 18, any API providing an asynchronous request should also offer a corresponding cancel. Our server-side cancel code is:

```
void CGsdpSession::CancelReceive()
    {
    if (!iReceiveActive)
        return;
    iReceiveMessage.Complete(KErrCancel);
    iReceiveActive = EFalse;
    }
```

This is astonishingly simple, and yet fulfils the contract required by cancel:

❏ If no request has been issued, then no action needs to be taken. This could be the case if, say, the client thread issued a cancel just as an active object in the server thread was handling an incoming packet that satisfied the receive request. When the server gets to handle the cancel, it is executing the server's own RunL() and, by this time, the receive request is no longer active.

This could also happen in the much simpler case that no Receive() had been issued at all (although, thanks to the active object pattern I've used in the client API, that can't happen with this particular server: CancelReceive() is private in the client API, and is only issued if there was actually a request to cancel).

❏ Otherwise, the message is completed with KErrCancel, and the server-side flag is cleared, to indicate that a receive is no longer active.

❏ In either case, the client's cancel message completes synchronously.

❏ In either case, by the time the client's cancel message completes, the original receive message is guaranteed to have completed as well.

The details of receive queue handling are specific to receive-type requests: we'll look at that in more detail later in the chapter. However, all asynchronous messages, and their cancel requests, should be handled server-side by a pattern based on the one shown here.

Sending Datagrams

The purpose of the GSDP server is to send datagrams using a given GDP protocol, but wrapping them to include port IDs and game protocol ID. The diagram opposite shows the processing that happens to a GSDP datagram as it goes from client to the GDP medium:

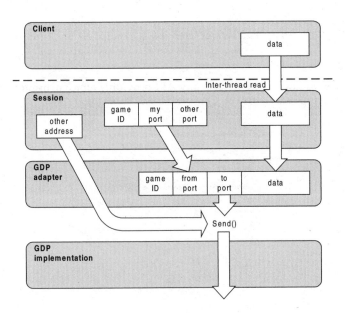

Before the processing in this figure takes place, the client has already done some setup using GSDP functions:

❑ The client has started a GSDP session

❑ The client has specified a GDP protocol, which causes the GSDP server to attach that protocol to the server-side session

❑ The client has specified a game protocol ID, its own port ID, and the other partner's address and port ID. The server simply stores these values in its `CGsdpSession` member variables

The client is then ready to send a GSDP datagram:

❑ The client calls `Send()`, which causes a `EGsdpReqSend` message to be sent to the server

❑ The server-side session uses an inter-thread read to get the data to send

❑ The data is then wrapped up to include the game protocol ID, my port ID as the from-port ID, and the other port ID as the to-port ID

❑ This datagram is then sent to the other address, using GDP send

The GDP implementation may then do any processing required to send the datagram. A loopback implementation will make a simple function call. A real implementation, such as the infrared implementation, will use a system of active objects to open the communications resources needed, send the datagram, and then close the communications resources again. However, GDP is not required to report the success of this operation back to the server. Provided the system of active objects used by the GDP implementation is reasonably well behaved, the implementation has no further effect on server design or performance.

Two parts of this sending process are worth discussing in more detail:

❑ Setting up the GDP protocol implementation required by the session: many servers implement some kind of polymorphism and, although we take some shortcuts in the GSDP server, we can highlight some of the standard issues.

❑ Manipulating the packet on its way from the session through the GDP adapter to the GDP `Send()` function.

Polymorphism

It's very common to want some kind of polymorphism in an interface, so that different drivers can be used. Printer drivers, serial communications protocols, sockets protocols, file systems, media drivers – all support the idea of a standard programming interface, but a range of implementations from which the client can select and use one at will.

In the GSDP server, we have a naïve form of this pattern:

❑ The client interface includes `SetGdpProtocolL()`, which sets the GDP protocol to be used for GSDP communications.

❑ The client interface identifies the possible GDP protocols using an enumeration, `RGsdpSession::TGdpProtocol`, which at present contains just three constants, `EGdpLoopback`, `EGdpIr`, and `EGdpSms`.

- ❏ The server, when it is started, initializes all three supported GDP protocol implementations. (Actually, under the emulator, the server doesn't try to load the infrared implementation because it doesn't work unless your PC has specialist equipment.)

- ❏ The server wraps up each GDP implementation in an adapter class, responsible for wrapping outgoing datagrams with the port and game protocol information, and for unwrapping incoming datagrams.

- ❏ When a client requests a particular GDP protocol, the server simply sets a pointer in the `CGsdpSession` to refer to the relevant GDP adapter.

There are serious problems with this naïve approach:

- ❏ It cannot be expanded without changing code in GSDP and any TOGS applications: to add the SMS implementation of GDP, for instance, I had to change the server, the client interface, and Battleships.

- ❏ It is wasteful: a protocol should not be loaded by the server unless it is needed by clients.

- ❏ It is error-prone: GDP-IR won't work on an emulator which isn't equipped with appropriate test hardware, so the GSDP server can't initialize on the emulator unless I comment out the call to initialize the GDP-IR adapter. `gdp.dll` won't even load on pre-EPOC R5 machines if it includes the GDP-SMS code, though the rest of Battleships will work fine. It's much better to load these protocols *when needed* – and therefore to block only the functionality that won't work anyway – than to require that the entire application be rebuilt to enable it to be deployed in different EPOC platforms.

After we've looked through the code as it stands, we'll discuss a couple of approaches to solving these problems.

The client interface for setting a GDP protocol is the `SetGdpProtocolL()` function in `RGsdpSession`. Server-side, this is implemented as:

```
CGsdpSession::SetGdpProtocolL(RGsdpSession::TGdpProtocol aProtocol)
    {
    switch (aProtocol)
        {
    case RGsdpSession::EGdpLoopback:
        iGdpProtocol=iServer->iGdpLoopback;
        break;
    case RGsdpSession::EGdpIr:
#ifdef __WINS__
        User::Leave(KErrNotSupported);
#endif
        iGdpProtocol=iServer->iGdpIr;
        break;
    case RGsdpSession::EGdpSms:
//#ifdef __WINS__
//      User::Leave(KErrNotSupported);
//#endif
        iGdpProtocol=iServer->iGdpSms;
        break;
```

```
        default:
          User::Leave(KErrNotFound);
          };
      }
```

There are signs of tinkering here, which proves the point I made about the evils of having to rebuild for different platforms. The code is simple enough, though: the protocol adapter is set to point to the correct adapter. I return `KErrNotSupported` if I don't believe the environment supports the protocol, and `KErrNotFound` if the requested protocol isn't one I know about.

Incidentally, `CGsdpSession::ConstructL()` contains the line

```
      iGdpProtocol = iServer->iGdpLoopback;
```

which sets the default protocol to loopback.

Sending a Datagram

When a packet is sent, the GDP adapter is used to send the client's datagram, along with the relevant game protocol and port information, to the GDP destination address:

```
TInt CGsdpSession::Send(const TAny* aData)
    {
    __ASSERT_ALWAYS(iMyPort != 0, iServer->PanicClient(ESendFromZeroPort));
    TBuf8<KMaxGsdpData> buffer;
    Client().ReadL(aData, buffer, 0);
    iGdpProtocol->SendL(iGameProtocol, iMyPort,
                   iOtherAddress, iOtherPort, buffer);
    return 0;
    }
```

The GDP adapter's `SendL()` function is implemented as follows:

```
void CGsdpGdpAdapter::SendL(TUint32 aGameProtocol,
                       TUint32 aFromPort,
                       const TDesC& aToAddress,
                       TUint32 aToPort,
                       const TDesC8& aData)
    {
    RDesWriteStream writer(iSendBuffer);
    writer << aGameProtocol;
    writer << aFromPort;
    writer << aToPort;
    writer << aData;
    writer.WriteL(aData);
    writer.CommitL();
    iGdpSession->SendL(aToAddress, iSendBuffer);
    }
```

This code works by forming a GDP datagram in the GDP adapter's `iSendBuffer`, containing the game protocol ID, from-port, to-port, and GSDP datagram data.

The `RDesWriteStream` class makes it convenient to write data to a buffer described by a descriptor. We simply write the data we need, and commit the stream. Because the stream store documents the external format of items written in this way, we can be confident about the external data format. For instance, the stream store guarantees that integers are written in little-endian byte order. We document this as the external format of a GSDP datagram.

When we look at what happens when a datagram is received, we will see this code in reverse.

Improving Polymorphism

The GSDP server's approach to GDP polymorphism is unexpandable and wasteful. Real EPOC servers that implement polymorphism do so in many well-established ways. Here's one approach that would work for the GSDP server.

Here's the client interface as it presently stands:

```
class RGsdpSession : public RSessionBase
    {
public:
    enum TGdpProtocol { EGdpLoopback = 1, EGdpIr, EGdpSms };
public:
    // Construct
    inline RGsdpSession() : iHandler(0) {};

    // Open/close
    IMPORT_C void ConnectL(MGsdpPacketHandler* aHandler);
    IMPORT_C void Close();

    // Load and get GDP protocol
    IMPORT_C void SetGdpProtocolL(TGdpProtocol aProtocol);
    IMPORT_C TGdpProtocol GetGdpProtocol() const;
    ...
    };
```

The fundamental change would be to replace `SetGdpProtocolL()`, and its enumerated parameter, with `LoadGdpProtocolL(const TDesC& aProtocol)`, where the string specifies the name of a GDP protocol DLL. The string would be interpreted by the server as the filename of a DLL resident in \system\libs\ on any drive, with file extension .gdp, and a given UID so that, for instance,

```
iGsdp.LoadProtocolL(_L("gdpir"));
```

would search for \system\libs\gdpir.gdp and load it if necessary.

This change would create two new requirements. On the client side, we would have to know what protocols are available. We'd need a function that allowed us to iterate through a list of available protocols, so we could offer this list to selection dialogs.

On the server side, we'd need to define the semantics of a .gdp DLL. It would have just a single function, whose prototype would be:

```
MGdpSession* NewSession();
```

This would create and return an uninitialized MGdpSession object – or return zero if the object could not be created.

Finally, on the server side, we'd adapt the CGsdpGdpAdapter class and the CSession::LoadProtocolL() handler functions to implement reference counting. We'd load the GDP implementation DLL only on the first request, and would increment its reference count when required by other sessions, and decrement it when these sessions either change to a different protocol, or are destroyed. When the reference count reached zero, we'd set a timer that, on expiry, would destroy the GDP adapter for that protocol.

Since the loopback implementation of GDP is both trivial and the default protocol, it would be appropriate to ensure that the loopback implementation was loaded permanently.

Receiving Datagrams

There are big differences between sending and receiving. Sending is initiated by the client, but receiving is initiated by something coming in from elsewhere. The client has to maintain an outstanding request to listen to incoming packets, and the server has to maintain a queue so that incoming packets don't get lost, just in case they arrive between the server-side completion of one receive message, and the client renewing the receive request.

Here's how receiving a packet is managed in the GSDP server:

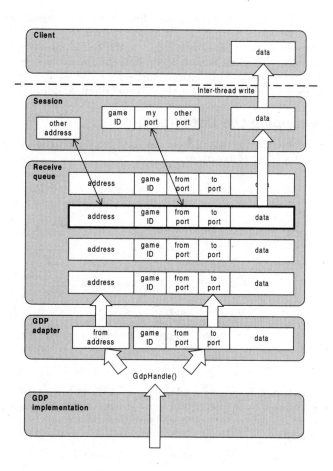

The steps in receiving a datagram are:

❑ The datagram arrives via a GDP implementation

❑ It is handled by the GDP adapter's GdpHandleL() function

❑ The GDP adapter parses the GSDP header information – game protocol ID, from-port, and to-port – and passes the datagram to the receive queue

❑ The receive queue allocates a slot for the incoming datagram, and adds it to the queue

❑ The receive queue then checks to see whether any session can receive the packet: this means the session must have an outstanding receive request, and either a matching port ID, or a zero port ID and a matching game protocol ID

❑ If a session can receive it, the message is sent to the client using inter-thread write, the receive message is completed, and the datagram slot is returned to the receive queue's free list

❑ On the client side, this will eventually cause the CGsdpReceiveHandler active object's RunL() to be scheduled, which calls the client's GsdpHandleL() function and then renews the receive request to the server

This is a classic 'receive' pattern that's used, with minor variations, by all servers that implement receive-type semantics. For instance, the window server's handling of input events uses a similar system: a raw event is received from the kernel, processed, and added to a queue. The client that should receive the event is identified, and the event is sent to the client as soon as possible. The most important differences between one server and another include the type of event that is handled, the means by which the target client is identified, and the queue management algorithms.

Unwrapping the Datagram

The datagram is passed from the GDP implementation to the GDP adapter and handled by its GdpHandleL() function:

```
void CGsdpGdpAdapter::GdpHandleL(const TDesC& aFromAddress,
                                 const TDesC8& aData)
    {
    TUint32 gameProtocol;
    TUint32 toPort;
    TUint32 fromPort;
    RDesReadStream reader(aData);
    gameProtocol = reader.ReadUint32L();
    reader >> fromPort;
    reader >> toPort;
    reader >> iReceiveBuffer;
    iServer->iReceiveQueue->Receive(gameProtocol, toPort,
                                    aFromAddress, fromPort, iReceiveBuffer);
    }
```

This uses a descriptor read stream to perform a series of read operations that exactly mirror those performed by the descriptor write stream in CGsdpGdpAdapter::SendL(). When the field values from the datagram have been identified, the datagram is sent to the receive queue's Receive() function.

The Receive Queue

The receive queue is a list of datagrams (referred to as 'packets' in its API) waiting to be received by clients. Packets are added to the list by the Receive() function. A packet just added to the list is offered to all sessions to see whether it can be received. When a session changes its settings or issues a receive, it checks the receive queue using CheckPackets() to see if there are any packets waiting for that session. By this means, a packet is delivered to a session as soon as possible.

Here is the definition:

```
class CGsdpReceiveQueue : public CBase
    {
public:
    enum TReceiveCheck { EAllowZero, EDontAllowZero };
public:
    // construct/destruct
    void ConstructL(CGsdpServer* aServer);
    ~CGsdpReceiveQueue();

    // functions
    void Receive(TUint32 aGameProtocol,
                 TUint32 aToPort,
                 const TDesC& aFromAddress,
                 TUint32 aFromPort,
                 const TDesC8& aData);
    void CheckPackets(CGsdpSession* aSession);
    void FreePacket(TGsdpPacket& aPacket);
private:
    CGsdpServer* iServer;
    TSglQue<TGsdpPacket> iPackets;
    TSglQue<TGsdpPacket> iSlots;
    };
```

When the receive queue is constructed, ten blank packets are added to the iSlots queue, and the iPackets queue is empty. When a packet is received, the following processing takes place:

```
void CGsdpReceiveQueue::Receive(TUint32 aGameProtocol,
                                TUint32 aToPort,
                                const TDesC& aFromAddress,
                                TUint32 aFromPort,
                                const TDesC8& aData)
    {
    // Get first free packet slot - drop packet if there isn't one
    TGsdpPacket* packet = iSlots.First();
    if(!packet)
        return;
    iSlots.Remove(*packet);

    // Plug in values
    packet->iGameProtocol = aGameProtocol;
    packet->iToPort = aToPort;
    packet->iFromAddress = aFromAddress;
    packet->iFromPort = aFromPort;
    packet->iData = aData;
```

```
    // Add to packet queue
    iPackets.AddLast(*packet);

    // See if it can be received
    CGsdpSession* session = iServer->SessionForPacket(*packet);
    if(!session)
        return;
    session->ReceivePacket(*packet);
    }
```

A slot is taken from the free list – if there are no slots, the incoming GDP packet is dropped. Then, the parameters to the function are stored in the packet, and the packet is added to the end of the iPackets queue.

The server is then asked to find a session that can receive the packet, using SessionForPacket(). This function is a member of the server class, because only the server class has access to the iterator for the server's CSession objects.

If the server can identify a session to receive the packet, the packet is received by calling the relevant session's ReceivePacket() function. Otherwise, the packet remains on the queue, and will hopefully be received later when a session changes its parameters or issues another receive request.

Here's how the server finds a session for the incoming packet:

```
CGsdpSession* CGsdpServer::SessionForPacket(const TGsdpPacket& aPacket)
    {
    CSession* session;
    // Iterate through sessions with non-zero port id
    iSessionIter.SetToFirst();
    for(session = iSessionIter++; session; session = iSessionIter++)
        {
        if(STATIC_CAST(CGsdpSession*, session)->GetMyPort() == 0)
            continue;
        if(STATIC_CAST(CGsdpSession*, session)->CanReceivePacket(aPacket))
            break;
        }

    if(session)
        return STATIC_CAST(CGsdpSession*, session);

    // Tterate through sessions with zero port id
    iSessionIter.SetToFirst();
    for(session = iSessionIter++; session; session = iSessionIter++)
        {
        if(STATIC_CAST(CGsdpSession*, session)->GetMyPort() != 0)
            continue;
        if(STATIC_CAST(CGsdpSession*, session)->CanReceivePacket(aPacket))
            break;
        }
    return STATIC_CAST(CGsdpSession*, session);
    }
```

The code is simple: it consists of two scans through all sessions. On the first scan, we *ignore* all sessions whose my-port ID is zero. On the second scan, we select *only* sessions whose my-port ID is zero. This means that packets with a non-zero to-port ID are matched against a specific session before being tried on a new listening session.

`CanReceivePacket()` tests whether a receive is active and, if so, whether the packet can be received according to other criteria:

```
TBool CGsdpSession::CanReceivePacket(const TGsdpPacket& aPacket) const
    {
    return iReceiveActive && (
        iMyPort == aPacket.iToPort && (
            iMyPort!=0 || // In session
            iMyPort==0 && iGameProtocol == aPacket.iGameProtocol // Listening
            )
        );
    }
```

If the packet can be received, the session receives it with `ReceivePacket()`, as follows:

```
void CGsdpSession::ReceivePacket(TGsdpPacket& aPacket)
    {
    // Decide whether to drop or to receive
    TBool drop = EFalse;
    if(aPacket.iGameProtocol != iGameProtocol)
        drop = ETrue;
    if(iOtherPort != 0 && (aPacket.iFromAddress != iOtherAddress ||
                           aPacket.iFromPort != iOtherPort))
        drop = ETrue;

    // Get remote's port and address information if we haven't already got it
    if(iOtherPort == 0)
        {
        iOtherPort = aPacket.iFromPort;
        iOtherAddress = aPacket.iFromAddress;
        }

    // Receive packet if we should
    if(!drop)
        {
        iReceiveMessage.WriteL(iReceiveBuffer, aPacket.iData);
        iReceiveMessage.Complete(KErrNone);
        iReceiveActive = EFalse;
        }

    // In any case, tell the receive queue to free the packet for future use
    iServer->iReceiveQueue->FreePacket(aPacket);
    }
```

This divides into three parts:

- ❏ We decide whether or not to drop the packet: this is just an interpretation of the rules laid down in the GSDP protocol specification

- ❏ If we are going to receive the packet, we write the data to the client, complete the session's outstanding receive request, and note that we no longer have a receive request active

- ❏ In any case, we tell the receive queue to free the packet slot so it can be used again for a new incoming packet

It's in this function that the client session's outstanding receive request is completed.

Most of the GDP packets received from a GDP implementation will be formed into a GSDP packet, placed on the receive queue, matched against a session with an outstanding receive request, and immediately received using `ReceivePacket()`.

If this were the process for *all* incoming packets, then there would be no need for a queue. But there are two reasons for maintaining a queue rather than simply offering the packet directly to the client.

First, the client could already be busy processing the previously received packet. In this case, the client will shortly renew its receive request, and it will then be possible to receive the packet. For this reason, the session's receive message handler function includes a check to see whether there are already any packets that this client can receive:

```
void CGsdpSession::Receive(const TAny* aBuffer)
    {
    __ASSERT_DEBUG(!iReceiveActive, PanicServer(EReceiveReceiveAlreadyActive));

    // Remember receive request
    iReceiveMessage = Message();
    iReceiveBuffer = aBuffer;
    iReceiveActive = ETrue;

    // Check for immediate fulfillment
    iServer->iReceiveQueue->CheckPackets(this);
    }
```

If the `CheckPackets()` function finds a packet that can be received, then the receive message handled by this function is immediately completed.

> **All servers that include receive-type processing will be affected in this way. Therefore all such servers must implement a queue to handle their incoming data.**

There is also a consideration unique to the design of the GSDP server. It's possible for the server to receive an incoming datagram for a session that has not yet been created, or whose settings have not yet been properly initialized. This allows the GSDP server to hold packets for:

❑   A new game that hasn't been started

❑   An existing game that has been closed temporarily and should be reopened

This applies until the game has been started, or re-opened.

Queue Management

The receive queue is a scarce resource – or, more precisely, the free slots on the receive queue are a scarce resource. They are pre-allocated so that a receive operation cannot fail due to an out-of-memory error. Precisely because they are pre-allocated, there are not many of them.

> **The receive queue should manage itself carefully to ensure that message slots are not allocated, and then never freed.**

This means that:

❑   Messages that cannot match any existing client should be dropped before they are added to the queue.

❑   When a client is terminated, any messages for that client should be deleted from the queue.

❑   If a client fails to clear a message after a reasonable period – say, 20 seconds or more – then the client is 'not responding' in the sense that users of Windows applications are familiar with. The server should drop packets for it, and should arguably panic the client.

The receive queue management in the GSDP server follows the specification of GSDP in Chapter 17 closely. But on reflection that specification is incomplete and may need to be improved, to support quicker deletion of non-received packets. The fact that the current specification is to keep received packets on the queue, before a game has started which can accept them, is the key item of contention here.

Startup and Shutdown

Earlier, we made the point that connection to a transient server was a delicate affair. We need to connect reliably in the sense that either we succeed in connecting to the one GSDP server, or we fail and report it to the client program. We mustn't fail silently, and we mustn't get into any situation where there are two GSDP servers. Part of the responsibility for this lies with the client interface, in `RGsdpSession::ConnectL()`: the remainder lies with the server startup code, which we'll now describe.

Additionally, server startup has to set up the server environment that will be used to deliver the GSDP server's services. That means, at a minimum:

❏ A new thread, with a cleanup stack, active scheduler, and `CServer` object ready to receive connection requests from clients via the kernel

❏ Anything specific that the server needs to do its job: in the case of the GSDP server, that means the receive queue, GDP adapters, port number allocator, shutdown timer, and so on

If the server can't construct all this, then launch is considered to have failed. If it *can* construct all this, then it's ready to receive client connect requests. Client connect requests may fail too – but that's a different matter from server launch.

Server startup is a kind of bootstrap process involving the following general steps:

❏ The client program launches a new thread (on the emulator) or process (on a real EPOC machine) running the server code

❏ The client then waits until the server has initialized

The server, for its part:

❏ Allocates a cleanup stack

❏ Allocates and constructs an active scheduler

❏ Allocates and constructs the server and all the objects the server owns

❏ Tells the client it has started – or, if any of the above operations fails, tells the client the return code indicating failure

❏ Starts the active scheduler, which enables the server to start handling requests

Like any other bootstrap process, the whole startup sequence is quite delicate. The following sections give a blow-by-blow commentary on the whole process.

You'll remember that the whole launch sequence is initiated by the following line in the client interface (`RGsdpSession::ConnectL()`, in fact) as part of session connect processing:

```
err = CGsdpScheduler::LaunchFromClient();
```

We have included many of the server launch functions as static members of `CGsdpScheduler`, which is defined as:

```
class CGsdpScheduler : public CActiveScheduler
    {
public:
    class TSignal
        {
    public:
        inline TSignal();
        inline TInt Set(const TDesC& aData);
```

```
                inline TSignal(TRequestStatus& aStatus);
                inline TPtrC Get() const;
                TRequestStatus* iStatus;
                TThreadId iId;
                };

        // Launch
        static TInt LaunchFromClient();

#ifdef __WINS__
        static TInt ThreadFunction(TAny* aThreadParms);
#endif

        IMPORT_C static TInt ThreadStart(TSignal& aSignal);
        static void ConstructL();
        ~CGsdpScheduler();
        void Error(TInt aError) const; // from CActiveScheduler
private:
        CGsdpServer* iServer;
        };
```

From Client Interface to Server Bootstrap

The LaunchFromClient() function is executed in the context of the client thread:

```
TInt CGsdpScheduler::LaunchFromClient()
    {
    // Set up waiting apparatus
    TRequestStatus status;
    TSignal signal(status);

    // Launch server thread (emulator) or process (EPOC)
#ifdef __WINS__
    RThread server;
    TInt err = server.Create(KGsdpServerName,ThreadFunction,
                        KDefaultStackSize * 2, KMinHeapSize,
                        100000, &signal, EOwnerProcess);
#else
    RProcess server;
    TInt err = server.Create(KGsdpServerExe,
                        signal.Get(),
                        TUidType(KNullUid, KNullUid, KNullUid),
                        EOwnerThread);
#endif

    if(err)
        return err;
    server.Resume();
    server.Close();

    // Wait for launch to complete
    User::WaitForRequest(status);
    return status.Int();
    }
```

Its main purpose is to launch a new thread (on the emulator) or process (on a real EPOC machine) in which the new server code will run. If the new thread or process cannot even be created, then LaunchFromClient() returns the error code. If the new thread or process was successfully created, then LaunchFromClient() waits for the server to initialize, and then passes the initialization error code (hopefully KErrNone!) back to the caller.

The synchronous wait at the end of this function means that the client process is unresponsive during server launch. In turn, that means server launch had better be quick in order to preserve application responsiveness. If you have a server whose launch takes a long time, you have three options:

❑ Settle for unresponsive applications during server launch

❑ Make the launch as quick as possible – for example, loading only the server framework – and then load any specific protocols you need from within the server, asynchronously, after launch

❑ Make the launch itself asynchronous, as far as the client is concerned: present this through an asynchronous Connect() function

I would prefer to keep launch-time asynchronicity inside the server.

Thread Launch on the Emulator

On the emulator, the new thread is given a name, stack size, minimum and maximum heap size, an entry point address, and an initial parameter, by the launching code above.

The EOwnerProcess indicates that the server thread is owned by the whole emulator process – not the launching client thread. The launching client thread may die while other clients are active, and would take the server thread down with it if we specified EOwnerThread.

If a server thread of the same name already exists (because another client was trying to launch it at the same time), then this call will return KErrAlreadyExists: server 'launch' will fail, but the client interface will simply try again to connect.

The thread function CGsdpScheduler::ThreadFunction() is a wrapper around CGsdpScheduler::ThreadStart():

```
#ifdef __WINS__
TInt CGsdpScheduler::ThreadFunction(TAny* aThreadParms)
    {
    // Get a handle to our code to prevent yank on client death
    RLibrary lib;
    lib.Load(_L("gsdp.dll")); // This ought to work, so no error handling

    // Go with the thread
    return ThreadStart(*REINTERPRET_CAST(TSignal*, aThreadParms));
    }
#endif
```

The main purpose of the code above is to act as a type-safe wrapper to ThreadStart(), which we'll see below.

The code that loads the gsdp.dll is there to ensure that this thread registers an interest in its own DLL code. We launched the thread by simply specifying a function address that happened to be around in RAM. But that function is part of gsdp.dll, which was loaded by the client application. If the client dies, it will decrement the usage count on gsdp.dll and (if it's the last client) Win32 will, quite correctly, unload the DLL. If the server's lifetime persists beyond that of the client (which it does, by two seconds) the server code will disappear while the server is still trying to use it, resulting in a horrible death for the server and indeed for the whole emulator. So, the server thread registers its long-term interest in gsdp.dll by loading it explicitly here. The RLibrary is deliberately not closed: it will be cleaned up, and the library unloaded, when the thread terminates after the server has finished and returned from ThreadStart().

Process Launch on EPOC

On real EPOC platforms, a process is launched from gsdpexe.exe, whose single function E32Main() is also designed to pass the parameter quickly to CGsdpScheduler::ThreadStart():

```
#include "gsdpserv.h"

TInt SetSignal(CGsdpScheduler::TSignal& aSignal);

GLDEF_C TInt E32Main()
    {
    CGsdpScheduler::TSignal signal;
    TInt err = SetSignal(signal);
    if(!err)
        err = CGsdpScheduler::ThreadStart(signal);
    return err;
    }


TInt SetSignal(CGsdpScheduler::TSignal& aSignal)
    {
    return aSignal.Set(RProcess().CommandLine());
    }
```

This deceptively simple function uses a lot of stack space that isn't needed throughout the lifetime of the server, which is why it's separate from E32Main().

The ingenious TSignal class is designed solely to allow the client thread to pass a TRequestStatus in such a way that it survives either the thread launch or the process launch above. Here, without further comment, is the implementation of CGsdpScheduler::TSignal:

```
inline CGsdpScheduler::TSignal::TSignal() {}
inline CGsdpScheduler::TSignal::TSignal(TRequestStatus& aStatus)
    : iStatus(&aStatus), iId(RThread().Id())
    { aStatus = KRequestPending; }
inline TPtrC CGsdpScheduler::TSignal::Get() const
    { return TPtrC((const TText*)this,sizeof(*this) / sizeof(TText)); }
inline TInt CGsdpScheduler::TSignal::Set(const TDesC& aData)
    { return aData.Size() != sizeof(*this) ? KErrGeneral :
      (Mem::Copy(this,aData.Ptr(),sizeof(*this)),KErrNone); }
```

It's unusual for EPOC code to differ between emulator and real EPOC. Server launch is one of the areas where the differences cut in. The design of the GSDP server minimizes those differences down to a couple of carefully controlled hotspots – which we've now dealt with.

Server Bootstrap

Whether on the emulator or a real EPOC machine, execution in the newly-launched server thread now begins in earnest with `CGsdpScheduler::ThreadStart()`:

```
EXPORT_C TInt CGsdpScheduler::ThreadStart(TSignal& aSignal)
    {
    __UHEAP_MARK;

    // Get thread that started us
    RThread starter;
    TInt err = starter.Open(aSignal.iId, EOwnerThread);
    if(!err)
        {
        // Get cleanup stack
        CTrapCleanup* cleanup = CTrapCleanup::New();

        // Initialize all up to and excluding starting scheduler
        if(cleanup)
            {
            TRAP(err, ConstructL());
            }
        else
            err = KErrNoMemory;

        // Tell starting thread we've started
        starter.RequestComplete(aSignal.iStatus, err);
        starter.Close();

        //  Start the active scheduler
        if(!err)
            CActiveScheduler::Start();

        // Close things down
        delete CActiveScheduler::Current();
        delete cleanup;
        }
    __UHEAP_MARKEND;
    return err;
    }
```

As we saw in Chapter 6, the bootstrap implements heap marking. If any server code is ever written that causes memory leaks, then the __UHEAP_MARKEND on server shutdown will cause a server panic. This means that sources of memory leak can be identified and fixed at the earliest point that they occur during development – a significant assurance of robustness in EPOC programs.

First, the server gets an RThread for the client thread that started it, so that it will later be able to signal the client that it has started. Assuming this worked as expected, the server constructs a cleanup stack. Then, it calls ConstructL() under a trap. If that's OK, construction is complete. The server signals the client thread that started it, and closes its RThread on the client thread because it won't need access to it again. Then the active scheduler is started, so that the server proper can start handling messages from clients.

When the server stops, the CActiveScheduler::Start() function will complete. The active scheduler deletes itself and deletes the cleanup stack, and can then return.

The final bootstrap function is CGsdpServer::ConstructL(). Remember that this is a static function.

```
void CGsdpScheduler::ConstructL()
    {
    // Nice roominess on cleanup stack
    for(TInt i = 0; i < 20; i++)
        CleanupStack::PushL((TAny*)0);
    CleanupStack::Pop(20);

    // Construct active scheduler
    CGsdpScheduler* self = new(ELeave) CGsdpScheduler;
    CActiveScheduler::Install(self);

    // Construct server
    self->iServer = new(ELeave) CGsdpServer;
    self->iServer->ConstructL();
    }
```

This function starts by pushing twenty items to the cleanup stack, and then popping them back off again. The motivation behind this odd-looking code is to prevent the cleanup stack growing during any code which might include heap balance checks (using __UHEAP_MARK and __UHEAP_MARKEND). PushL() potentially grows the cleanup stack, but Pop() doesn't shrink it, so growth of the cleanup stack during code being checked for heap imbalance will cause heap imbalance. This is a useful standard trick. Virtually no program will ever need more than twenty items on the cleanup stack.

Since the heap imbalance executes only in debug builds, the push/pop code should be bracketed in an #ifdef _DEBUG.

The next two lines construct a real active scheduler object (all the active scheduler functions we have been using so far have been static), and install it as the thread's current active scheduler. This effectively stores a pointer to the active scheduler using a special slot allocated by the kernel executive. If you need to, you can get at this pointer using CActiveScheduler::Current().

Finally, we construct the server and store a pointer to it in the newly constructed scheduler's iServer member variable.

Starting the Server

By the time we get to server construction, we are in normal C++ territory: we have a cleanup stack and active scheduler, we don't have to think about the thread that's launched us – in short, the code has lost the flavor of a bootstrap. `CGsdpServer`'s C++ constructor passes a zero active object priority down through the base `CServer` constructor:

```
CGsdpServer::CGsdpServer() : CServer(0)
    {
    }
```

This indicates that there is no special reason for the server to have higher or lower priority than any other active object in the thread. The main work of construction is handled by `ConstructL()`:

```
void CGsdpServer::ConstructL()
    {
    // Construct receive queue
    iReceiveQueue = new(ELeave) CGsdpReceiveQueue;
    iReceiveQueue->ConstructL(this);

    // Construct shutdown timer
    iShutdown = new(ELeave) CGsdpDelayedShutdown(this);
    iShutdown->ConstructL();

    // Construct port allocator
    iPortAllocator = new(ELeave) CGsdpPortAllocator;
    iPortAllocator->ConstructL();

    // Construct GDP protocol adapters
    iGdpLoopback = new(ELeave) CGsdpGdpAdapter;
    MGdpSession* gdpLoopback = new(ELeave) CGdpLoopback;
    iGdpLoopback->ConstructL(gdpLoopback, this);

#ifndef __WINS__
    iGdpIr = new(ELeave) CGsdpGdpAdapter;
    MGdpSession* gdpIr = new(ELeave) CGdpIrComms;
    iGdpIr->ConstructL(gdpIr, this);
    iGdpSms = new(ELeave) CGsdpGdpAdapter;
    MGdpSession* gdpSms = new(ELeave) CGdpSmsComms;
    iGdpSms->ConstructL(gdpSms, this);
#endif

    // Identify ourselves and open for service
    iName = KGsdpServerName.AllocL();
    StartL();

    // Initiate shut down unless we get client connections
    iShutdown->Start();
    }
```

`ConstructL()` constructs all the objects owned by the server, including its receive queue, shutdown timer, port number allocator, and protocol adapters (omitting the IR and SMS implementations under the emulator).

To start the server, `ConstructL()` allocates a name that matches the one used by the client to connect to the server – it doesn't have to be related to the thread name in any way. The final `StartL()` function issues a request to the kernel for the first message from a client.

Finally, `ConstructL()` initiates the shutdown timer, which will close the server unless a session is connected within two seconds.

Server Shutdown

The server shuts down two seconds after its last client session is closed. The server keeps a count of client sessions using `IncrementSessions()` and `DecrementSessions()`, which are called from `NewSessionL()` and from the session destructor:

```
void CGsdpServer::IncrementSessions()
    {
    iSessionCount++;
    iShutdown->Cancel();
    }

void CGsdpServer::DecrementSessions()
    {
    iSessionCount--;
    if(iSessionCount > 0)
        return;
    iShutdown->Start();
    }
```

So, the shutdown timer is started whenever there are no sessions (both when the server is constructed, and when the final session has ended), and is cancelled when a new session is created.

The shutdown timer class is a simple active object:

```
class CGsdpDelayedShutdown : public CActive
    {
public:
    CGsdpDelayedShutdown(CGsdpServer* aServer);
    void ConstructL();
    ~CGsdpDelayedShutdown();
    void Start();
private:
    void DoCancel();
    void RunL();
private:
    RTimer iTimer;
    CGsdpServer* iServer;
    };
```

The `Start()` function sets the timer:

```
void CGsdpDelayedShutdown::Start()
    {
    iTimer.After(iStatus, KGsdpShutdownInterval);
    SetActive();
    }
```

`KGsdpShutdownInterval` is defined, in `gsdpdef.h`, as,

```
const TInt KGsdpShutdownInterval=2000000;
```

or two seconds.

If the timer expires, `RunL()` initiates the shutdown:

```
void CGsdpDelayedShutdown::RunL()
    {
    CActiveScheduler::Stop();
    }
```

It simply stops the active scheduler, which causes the scheduler `Start()` function called from `CGsdpScheduler::ThreadStart()` to exit when `RunL()` has completed, which in turn causes `ThreadStart()`'s cleanup code to delete the active scheduler and the cleanup stack, and exit the thread. The active scheduler cleans up any active objects it owns, including the server.

Summary

In this chapter, we've walked through the most critical code in the GSDP server, and seen how a server hangs together in practice, and makes good use of the APIs and paradigms we discussed in the previous chapter. The book CD-ROM contains the entire source code for the GSDP server, in `\pep\gsdp\`.

Servers also demonstrate the power of active objects in routine server programming. Active objects are used for everything from the server, to the shutdown timer, to the GDP implementations themselves. Outside the server launch, we never had to think about concurrency issues, even for receive, send, and cancel processing.

There's plenty more work to be done with the design of GSDP server as it stands, including some extra L correctness, adding send queue management, better receive queue management, and better polymorphism for GDP protocol adapters. However, the GSDP server demonstrates the patterns used by many EPOC servers and is a useful example to copy from.

In the next chapter, Jonathan Dixon will take us through the development of the GDP IR and SMS protocols, which implement the communications functionality used by the real Battleships game. Then, in Chapter 22, I'll do a quick tour of the game itself, and make some more suggestions for taking this entire design forward.

21

GDP Implementations

In this book, we deal with three different GDP implementations. First, there's the loopback implementation, which has been mentioned on a number of occasions over the course of the last few chapters. This simply delivers packets back to the device sending them, by passing them straight back up through the GDP handle interface in its `SendL()` function. This is something that's very useful for testing client code, and provides the starting point for the two non-trivial implementations that we'll be looking at here:

❑   GDP-IR – communicates over the infrared medium, a point-to-point protocol

❑   GDP-SMS – uses the SMS text message medium, a networked protocol

Concrete GDP implementations provide the GDP services through the `M` class interfaces we defined in Chapter 17. They take the disparate services offered by the underlying communications medium and allow the protocol client (that is, the application using the protocol) to access them with minimal knowledge of that medium.

I will present these implementations in the order they were developed (infrared, then SMS), but first we need a bit of background in order to understand fully the framework used throughout the rest of the chapter.

I've tried my best to minimize the amount of communications-specific terminology used, and to give some clues to what's going on to readers from non-communications backgrounds when such terminology *is* necessary. If you wish to learn more about communications programming, there are many good textbooks (particularly those by Andrew Tanenbaum and William Stallings) that cover this area excellently.

Tasks, States and State Machines

Communications is asynchronous by its nature. In EPOC, communications services are provided by servers that present APIs through R (resource) objects, which in turn have asynchronous functions taking a TRequestStatus& parameter. As we saw in Chapter 18, the natural way to handle such functions is to encapsulate them in an active object framework.

A naïve GDP implementation would use a single active object to encapsulate every possible asynchronous function. This would result in a large and potentially uncontrollable system of active objects. Instead, we use the **state pattern**, which was also touched upon in Chapter 18. The state machine framework I present here provides a very robust method for developing state-machine based communications protocols. For one-off use, it could be considered rather heavyweight, but as I was able to re-use it through both the concrete implementations, particularly the more complex SMS case, it proved an invaluable benefit.

Typically, a **communications layer** provides a number of operations to clients using that layer. Internally, each operation (or **task**) may map to multiple sub-operations, each of which may be asynchronous. However, these operations must be carried out sequentially, which is where the state pattern comes in: it allows one active object effectively to change its class as it threads its way through the sub-operations (or **states**) required to carry out the task. Multiple tasks can (potentially) run in parallel, but within a task the states must be executed sequentially. So you can see how these tasks might map to threads in a traditional multithreaded system, but to active objects within EPOC.

From the GDP interface MGdpSession, it is clear that SMS and infrared have two principal tasks – sending and receiving – each of which maps to the various asynchronous operations that are required to achieve this communication through the relevant EPOC APIs. In addition, infrared has a further task concerned with resource management.

In order to simplify the development of the specific task implementations, I wrote a generalized GDP state machine class that provides a simple implementation of the state pattern appropriate to our needs. A specific task can be implemented by deriving from the CGdpStateMachine class, which in turn derives from CActive.

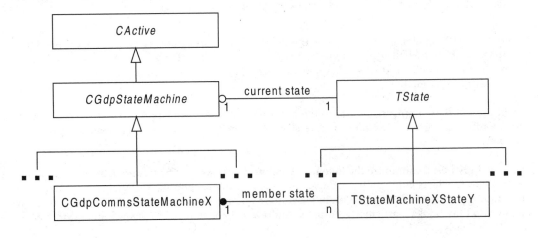

Each **state** of such a task is represented by a class derived from the TState base class, which is defined in gdpstatemc.h. Furthermore, each state has four virtual functions:

❑   EnterL(), which issues a request

❑   CompleteL(), which handles its completion (called from RunL() when the completion code is KErrNone)

❑   ErrorL(), which handles an error (called from RunL() when the completion code indicates an error)

❑   Cancel(), which is called if the task is cancelled by the user

There are also functions in CGdpStateMachine for transitioning between states.

To design a system using the state machine, you have to draw a state diagram, explain what the states are for, and determine the transitions between them.

GDP State Machines

Here's CGdpStateMachine, the abstract state machine class I used:

```
class CGdpStateMachine : public CActive
    {
public:
    ~CGdpStateMachine();

    class TState
        {
    public:
        virtual void EnterL() = 0;
        virtual TState* CompleteL() = 0;
        virtual TState* ErrorL(TInt aCode) = 0;
        virtual void Cancel() = 0;
        };

protected:
    CGdpStateMachine(TPriority aPriority);
    void ChangeState(TState* aNextState);
    inline TState* CurrentState();
    void SetNextState(TState* aNextState);
    void ReEnterCurrentState();

    // Methods to be implemented by concrete state machines
    virtual TState* ErrorOnStateEntry(TInt aError) = 0;
    virtual TState* ErrorOnStateExit(TInt aError) = 0;

private:
    // Overrides of CActive functions
    void RunL();
    void DoCancel();

private:
    TState* iState;        // Current state
    };
```

CGdpStateMachine derives from CActive and implements the pure virtual functions declared in that class – namely, RunL() and DoCancel(). This means that any concrete state machine can use the features provided by CActive without actually having to redefine these functions.

Derived concrete classes do however have to implement further abstract functions from CGdpStateMachine – namely, ErrorOnStateEntry() and ErrorOnStateExit(), which I will come to in a moment. In addition, the concrete state machine must provide appropriate means to interface with external objects.

The state base class, TState, is defined as a nested class within CGdpStateMachine. Each specific concrete state within a task must provide an instance of a class derived from this base. The iState member in CGdpStateMachine points to the current state – it is private, so derived classes must access it through the various getters and setters provided. This encapsulation is important, as it ensures we cannot inadvertently change state at an inappropriate time.

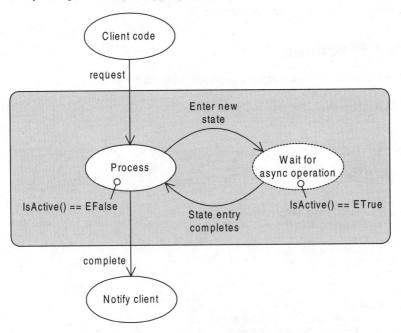

An initial state change occurs every time the task represented by the state machine is invoked. This may be through an external request (a 'send packet' request, for example) or just by opening the state machine. This can then cause a whole sequence of successive asynchronous requests, each with a corresponding state change. While these asynchronous operations are taking place, the task is 'active', meaning that no further external requests can be serviced until we're finished with this one. Finally, when no more asynchronous requests are required, the task returns to 'inactive' and the state machine is able to accept further client requests.

For every state change, there are two phases, as the figure above shows. First, we issue a request to enter the new state – which in turn will issue an asynchronous request – and second we complete the entry to the state, when the asynchronous request completes. At this point, there may be *another* state change – and further asynchronous request(s) – or the task may just complete. The latter case signifies the completion of the external request, and the machine moves back to its inactive mode waiting for another request.

The actual code to change state is as follows:

```
void CGdpStateMachine::ChangeState(CGdpStateMachine::TState* aNextState)
    {
    // Enter aNextState, and make it our current state.
    __ASSERT_ALWAYS(!IsActive(),
        GdpUtil::Panic(GdpUtil::EStateMachineStateError));
    TInt err;
    while(aNextState)
        {
        // State change required.
        iState = aNextState;
        TRAP(err, iState->EnterL());
        aNextState = err ? ErrorOnStateEntry(err) : NULL;
        }
    }
```

None of the state-changing functions (`ChangeState()`, `SetNextState()` and `ReEnterCurrentState()`) should be called while there are any outstanding asynchronous requests (that is, when we are halfway through a state change). The `__ASSERT_ALWAYS()` statement ensures that we don't ever break this invariant.

This function calls the `EnterL()` function of the state we wish to move to, which will issue any asynchronous requests required to move into that state. This code is run in a trap harness so that I can pass any leave errors to the concrete state machine's trap handler, `ErrorOnStateEntry()`. This trap handler can specify a new state to try to enter, allowing it to implement request retries, for example. I keep doing this until something succeeds, which I should point out because the concrete trap handler needs to be aware of the possibility of endless loops.

> **Generally, it is important that communications protocols never leave! This is because we do not own the active scheduler we are running in, and our internal state errors will mean little to the owner of the scheduler. Instead, we trap any potential leaves, and pass an error indication back to our client through an agreed interface if it's appropriate to do so.**

Trap harnesses do have a slight performance cost, so using a single trap harness, which passes any leaves to the implementation-specific error handler, removes the need for every individual state to have its own layer of harness and handler.

The state machine's `RunL()`, which handles the completion of state entry, is quite similar in essence:

```
void CGdpStateMachine::RunL()
    {
    __ASSERT_ALWAYS(iState != NULL,
        GdpUtil::Panic(GdpUtil::EStateMachineStateError));
    TState* nextState = NULL;
    TRAPD(err, nextState = iStatus.Int() ?
                        iState->ErrorL(iStatus.Int()) :
                        iState->CompleteL());
    if(err)
        {
        nextState = ErrorOnStateExit(err);
        }
    ChangeState(nextState);
    }
```

Here, I selectively call either the CompleteL() or ErrorL() members of the current state, depending on the outcome of the asynchronous request as returned by iStatus.Int(), inherited from CActive.

> *Both of these member functions indicate state entry asynchronous request completion. I've just separated them for implementation convenience within the concrete state classes.*

Again, this is run within a trap harness, and any errors are passed to the concrete state machine's ErrorOnStateExit() error handler.

Either one of the state completion functions, or (if it gets called) the error handler, may return a new state to try to enter next. If NULL is returned, we drop out of RunL() and revert to inactive mode.

Note that SetActive() is *never* called by the state machine. This is entirely the responsibility of the concrete state classes, whenever they make an asynchronous request.

The remaining state machine functions are fairly straightforward. The most interesting are DoCancel(), which simply calls the Cancel() member of the current state, and SetNextState(), which sets iState to the passed state, without actually going through the process of entering it. This is specifically so that any future calls to ReEnterCurrentState() will actually move to this new state, rather than the last one moved into. A more generic implementation would probably use a separate iNextState member to achieve this, but for our purposes I got away with using the iState variable to represent both current and next state, depending on the context in which it is used.

Infrared Implementation

The industry standard for infrared communications between computers and portable devices is known as **IrDA**, as defined by the Infrared Data Association (http://www.irda.org/). EPOC devices use these IrDA protocols for all infrared communications.

IrDA offers a rich protocol suite. It includes the ability to open and maintain a session, with suitable error recovery for reliability. It also includes a naming system for infrared devices and the services they provide.

First, we'll have a look at some of the key protocols in the IrDA protocol family, and then at how the programmer gains access to these protocols through EPOC's **ESOCK** API. Then I'll show you how our game protocol, GDP, will map onto IrDA, specifically using the **IrLMP** multiplexing protocol. I call this mapping, and the resulting implementation, GDP-IR. Finally, I'll present the code that makes up this concrete implementation as an example of how to use the ESOCK, and the IrDA protocol module within it.

The specific mapping of GDP onto the IrDA protocols is fundamental to the whole experience of using a GDP-IR-based game. With the mapping I have chosen, it is possible for the user to run multiple simultaneous games with a number of different parties, selecting which to communicate with by physically moving their machine to talk to the correct partner. But it also allows other applications to use IrDA while a game is in progress – to fetch e-mail between moves, for example. While there may be simpler ways of enabling infrared gaming, they all require a far more exclusive use of the IrDA stack, resulting in a far more limiting mode of operation for the user.

Although IrDA does have the concept of addresses for distinguishing devices from one another, we'll treat infrared as a point-to-point protocol at the GDP level. This is because the IrDA addresses are dynamically allocated, and might change during a game. We must be prepared to rediscover the address every time we wish to send a packet, using the IrDA discovery mechanism.

The IrDA Protocols

The assumption is often made that IrDA is simply, "RS232 serial communications over infrared," but this is not the case. In technical terms, it is more accurately described as a whole network stack running over infrared, even if the end result seen by the user is just an extra serial port. This is because IrDA actually defines a whole stack of protocols, in rather the same way as TCP, IP, and Ethernet are often used together in a stack.

IAS	IrLAN	OBEX	IrCOMM
	Tiny TP		
IrLMP			
IrLAP			
Physical Layer			

The reason for creating this stack is to provide a more sophisticated service to applications that use IrDA than that offered by a serial port, while also being optimized for mobile use. This includes extensive error detection and recovery, multiplexing of multiple applications onto a single physical link, and integral end-to-end flow control. When this is compared to a 'raw' serial port connection, the complexity of IrDA can soon be appreciated!

The IrDA stack is illustrated above. The white boxes are compulsory parts of an IrDA-compliant stack, and the gray boxes are optional. When the context is clear, the tendency is to drop the "Ir" from the protocol names, giving LAP, LMP, and IAS as the basic requirements – along with some physical device layer.

Error detection is carried out in the **Link Access Protocol**, LAP, which uses **Cyclic Redundancy Checks** (CRCs) to detect errors and negotiate a resend of any corrupt or lost frames.

Multiple sessions over a single link are supported through the **Link Management Protocol**, LMP, which multiplexes multiple virtual end-points called LSAPs (LMP **Service Access Point**) onto a single physical link. LMP is actually split into two parts: MUX, which does this multiplexing, and the **Information Access Service**, IAS. The latter facilitates multiple services by allowing a client to discover which SAP a particular required service is available on.

Optionally, flow control can be provided on a per-virtual connection (hence end-to-end) basis through the **Tiny Transport Protocol**, TinyTP.

The principle behind the IrDA standards is to support *ad-hoc* networking. It achieves this through two mechanisms: **device discovery**, and the previously mentioned IAS. Device discovery is carried out in the LAP layer. Simply put, it allows a device with no information about its environment to broadcast to any other device within optical range, and discover the address by which it can refer to any machines found. IAS then provides the means for it to ask individual devices if they support the required services, and how to get at those supported services. So in a typical example, a remote machine might be discovered, then – via IAS – the required service (such as printing, beaming, or even GDP) follows.

EPOC Support for IrDA

The natural place for the IrDA protocol family in the EPOC user library is as part of network communications, not serial communications. This means that all IrDA operations are carried out through ESOCK, which has its roots (at least conceptually) in the TCP/IP sockets interface that first appeared in BSD UNIX back in the 1980s. By using the sockets interface, far more control of the IrDA protocols is possible:

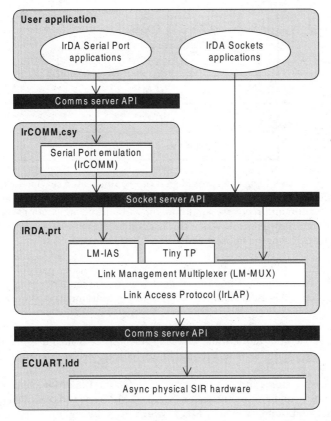

If you have experience of IrDA, you'll know that the specification includes "legacy application" support through a serial port emulation layer – **IrCOMM**. Indeed, this is also provided in EPOC in order to support legacy applications. The interface to it is provided through the comms server, which is responsible for serial port-style communications.

The problem with IrCOMM is that it pretty much kills the possibility of having multiple applications simultaneously using a single IrDA link, just as multiple applications cannot generally share a single physical serial port. While it might be possible to create multiple virtual IrCOMM serial ports in software, it is a far more complex case than that of multiple physical serial ports, where the user is easily able to see which pairs of ports are connected. With virtual ports, this is left to chance, and user frustration is the inevitable result.

The general recommendation is that any new application should use some form of IrDA-aware interface, rather than simply being written to work over a serial cable and letting IrCOMM do all the rest.

The GDP-IR Protocol Mapping

Upon further inspection of the IrDA stack, it became obvious that IrLMP provides almost all of the features I required for transporting GDP data over IrDA.

In IP, the end-to-end reliability is almost all provided by the transport layer (TCP, say) or higher levels. In IrDA, on the other hand, and apart from the necessarily complex issue of flow control, IrLMP is pretty reliable. This is because it operates directly over a point-to-point link that is itself flow-controlled and reliable. Packets cannot be delivered out of order, so in normal operation LMP should meet most of the requirements we set out. Packets are only lost if we have buffer overrun because the receiver can't consume packets as quickly as the sender produces them.

However, we *don't* require the extra complexity of the flow control and reliability provided by the TinyTP layer, because it is not of much use to our intended application. If we simply restrict ourselves to sending a single packet at a time – which is up to the client using the protocol to ensure – we gain nothing from TinyTP. Indeed, the GDP client interface has this implicit limitation built into it: there is no mechanism for the protocol to throttle back the client if it is getting carried away with sending packets for transmission. We have two choices: keep on buffering new packets indiscriminately until we run out of memory, or quietly assign them to the bit bucket. Our flow control is provided by the client only allowing one unacknowledged packet to be sent, or else being prepared for potential packet loss.

Another useful feature of IrLMP is that it fully preserves the packet framing information – that is, the delimiters at the start and end of packets – all the way to the client (in this case, GDP-IR). As illustrated in the figure below, this means that I don't have to mess around providing framing information for our PDU (**Protocol Data Unit**: what's passed between a protocol and the layer below it) by marking the start and end or length of each PDU so that it can be decoded at the receiving end. I simply shove it into an LMP SDU (**Service Data Unit:** the payload area used by the layer above), and let LMP do all this framing for us.

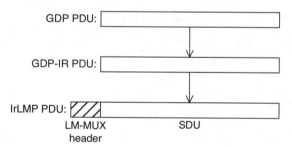

As shown in the figure, the result of all this is that we have an incredibly simple protocol! In fact, the GDP PDUs coming down from the protocol's client that are carried in our SDU are exactly equivalent to our PDUs: we need add no extra information. In other words, we can just send the chunks of data passed to SendL() directly in IrLMP packets.

On the theme of simplicity, we can design the datagram protocol to be simplex. This means that on any given GDP-IR channel (that is, an IrLMP connection), messages are only sent in one direction. In order to send datagrams in the opposite direction, a second channel must be opened. I achieve this by registering a custom IAS entry in every host that wants to be able to receive messages – in other words, any machine running GDP-IR. Then, when a host wants to send, it discovers other hosts in the neighborhood, and attempts the connection process using IAS.

One thing to remember when developing the GDP-IR code is that the LAP link might be (in fact, probably will be) broken between datagrams. This could happen when a player goes to lunch, or just fetches a coffee (taking their machine with them) while thinking about their next move. Due to the nature of IrDA, this means that the peer's hardware (IrLAP) device address might change between moves. This is the fundamental reason for not using IrDA addressing in the game. To get around this, we must be prepared to rediscover and IAS-query the peer machine before every turn – not just once per game. This is because the peer device's address might have changed, particularly if they have been promiscuously communicating with other devices between moves.

The GDP-IR Implementation

The structure of the infrared code is illustrated below. The main component from the client's point of view is the `CGdpIrComms` class shown in the center of the diagram. This implements the `MGdpSession` abstract interface, through which all client operations are performed (save for initially creating the object). This center class actually provides a simple, thin interface, or **façade**, into the various components used for infrared communications.

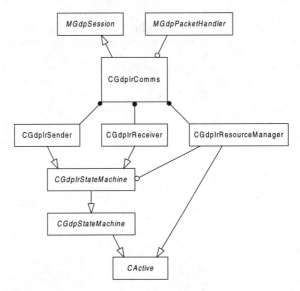

The three main sub-components, `CGdpIrSender`, `CGdpIrReceiver`, and `CGdpIrResourceManager`, actually carry out the three tasks required for the GDP session. You'll notice that the resource manager is not a state machine, however. This is simply because it only has one asynchronous operation, so it does not require the added complexity of internal states and transitions.

> *It is interesting to note that the session class, `CGdpIrComms`, has no state itself. This is because GDP-IR, along with all GDP implementations, is actually stateless. This may come as a surprise after all the talk about state machines, but it does make sense when you consider that GDP is a connectionless, best-efforts datagram protocol. All the state is concerned with is attempting to get a specific packet in or out of the machine – no significant state is held over between packet transmissions.*

Through the following sections, you'll see an in depth example of how to use the EPOC sockets API to communicate over infrared. For a programming reference for this API, and the specifics of the EPOC IrDA protocol implementation, please look up Comms and Networking in the EPOC C++ SDK.

Sender

The CGdpIrSender class handles the task of getting packets out over infrared. It comes to life whenever the client code calls the SendL() member of the GDP-IR session object, and continues asynchronous activity until the packet is successfully sent or it has completed a bound number of unsuccessful retries.

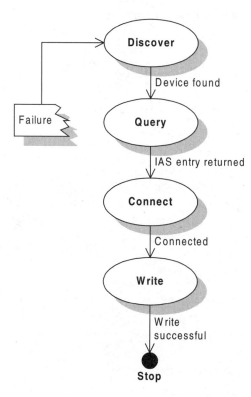

As the figure shows, up to four sequential operations are required to send GDP packets via infrared:

❑   Discovery: finding an IrDA machine in optical range to attempt to deliver the message to

❑   Query: connecting to the IAS server on the remote device located by discovery, asking if GDP is supported, and if so, what LSAP it is available on

❑   Connect: make an IrLMP socket connection to the remote LSAP found through IAS, where we know the GDP server should be listening

❑   Write: actually send the GDP packet to the peer across the connected socket

At any point in the sequence, an operation may fail. I deal with this by using the handler mechanism of the generic state machine to do a limited number of retries before giving up.

Each of the four operations identified are asynchronous in nature, so the CGdpIrSender task class is derived from CGdpIrStateMachine as follows (from gdpir.h):

```
class CGdpIrSender : public CGdpIrStateMachine
    {
    // State value declarations
    class TSenderState : public CGdpStateMachine::TState
        {
    public:
        TSenderState(CGdpIrSender& aSender);
        virtual TState* ErrorL(TInt aCode);
    protected:
        CGdpIrSender& iSender;
        };

    class TDiscoverState : public TSenderState
        {
    public:
        TDiscoverState(CGdpIrSender& aSender);
        void EnterL();
        TState* CompleteL();
        void Cancel();
    private:
        TNameEntry iNameEntry;
        };

    class TQueryState : public TSenderState
        {
    public:
        TQueryState(CGdpIrSender& aSender);
        void EnterL();
        TState* CompleteL();
        void Cancel();
    private:
        TIASResponse iIASResponse;
        };

    class TConnectState : public TSenderState
        {
    public:
        TConnectState(CGdpIrSender& aSender);
        void EnterL();
        TState* CompleteL();
        void Cancel();
        };

    class TWriteState : public TSenderState
        {
    public:
        TWriteState(CGdpIrSender& aSender);
        void EnterL();
        TState* CompleteL();
        void Cancel();
        };

    friend TDiscoverState;
    friend TQueryState;
    friend TConnectState;
    friend TWriteState;
public:
    CGdpIrSender(CGdpIrResourceManager& aResMan);
    void SendL(const TDesC& aAddress, const TDesC8& aData);
    ~CGdpIrSender();
    void OpenL();
    void Close();
```

```
protected:
    void Reset();

    // Overrides of CGdpStateMachine functions
    TState* ErrorOnStateEntry(TInt aError);
    TState* ErrorOnStateExit(TInt aError);

private:
    RSocket iSocket;
    TBuf8<KGdpIrMaxPacketLength> iPacket;
    TIrdaSockAddr iAddr;
    TInt iRetries;          // No. of (potential) remaining retries

    // States
    TDiscoverState iDiscoverState;
    TQueryState    iQueryState;
    TConnectState  iConnectState;
    TWriteState    iWriteState;
    };
```

As you can see, this class actually inherits from `CGdpIrStateMachine`, which is a very slightly specialized version of the abstract `CGdpStateMachine` class. I will introduce the facilities it adds when we discuss the resource manager later on.

The sender state machine defines several concrete state classes – `TDiscoverState`, `TQueryState`, `TConnectState` and `TWriteState` – along with one instance variable of each. These are the state objects that the current state pointer in the abstract state machine will point to. Each state class has a reference back to the sender object that it belongs to – this information is not automatically provided by the nesting construct, because it only affects the *class* relationship, not any specific *object* (or instance) relationship. I provide this reference variable in a generalized `TSenderState` class that all the concrete states derive from.

We'll now trace through the operation of sending a GDP-IR packet. The `OpenL()` function is called when the client code calls the corresponding function in `CGdpIrComms`. This puts it into an initial state, by calling `Reset()`, ready to accept requests to send packets.

The state machine gets kicked into life every time the `CGdpIrComms::SendL()` is called; this is the only point of contact with the GDP client in the whole process of sending.

```
void CGdpIrComms::SendL(const TDesC& aToAddress,
                        const TDesC8& aData)
    {
    __ASSERT_ALWAYS(iSender != NULL, GdpUtil::Fault(GdpUtil::EProtocolNotOpen));
    iSender->SendL(aToAddress, aData);
    }
```

This invokes the `SendL()` function within the sender class, which looks like this:

```
void CGdpIrSender::SendL(const TDesC& /*aAddress*/, const TDesC8& aData)
    {
    __ASSERT_ALWAYS(aData.Size() <= iPacket.MaxSize(),
                    GdpUtil::Fault(GdpUtil::EBadSendDescriptor));
    __ASSERT_DEBUG(CurrentState() != NULL,
                    GdpUtil::Panic(GdpUtil::ESenderNotReady));
```

```
    if(IsActive())
        return;                 // Don't leave - quietly drop the overflow packet
    iPacket.Copy(aData);        // Buffer packet until needed
    iRetries = KGdpIrSendRetries;
    ReEnterCurrentState();      // Kick us off again...
    }
```

As you can see, because GDP-IR isn't a networked protocol, we don't actually take up the offered destination address – we'll work this out for ourselves on a call-by-call basis, using the IrDA device discovery mechanism.

If we're already busy sending a packet, we simply give up on this new request and return – it is up to the client to ensure we're not given more packets than we can cope with.

We take a copy of the packet passed down, so that we can get at it later on once we're connected up and ready to send. We then set up how many times we're going to retry sending if the first attempt fails, and then set the state machine going.

You may wonder, with good reason, why we call ReEnterCurrentState() and not ChangeState(&iDiscoverState). This is a design decision in which either technique would actually work. My reasoning is that I decided not to put us back to discovery every time a new request comes in – only when an operation fails. This means that once we get a connection, we won't be distracted by any other IrDA devices that come into range – so long as *we* stay within connection range of the device we are communicating with. For example, if you're playing a game with your friend, and somebody else attempts to start up a session on a third machine nearby, you won't start delivering packets to them by mistake provided that you stay in contact with the friend. If the connection is lost, you'll have to make sure the correct device is found by physically obscuring any other device until the connection is re-established.

The first time a packet is sent, the current state (iState) will already be set to TDiscoverState, so ReEnterCurrentState() will cause us to enter that state:

```
void CGdpIrSender::TDiscoverState::EnterL()
    {
    CGdpIrResourceManager& resMan = iSender.iResMan;
    TProtocolDesc& desc = resMan.ProtocolDesc();

    iSender.iSocket.Close();
    resMan.ResetL();
    User::LeaveIfError(
        iSender.iSocket.Open(resMan.SocketServer(),
                             desc.iAddrFamily,
                             desc.iSockType,
                             desc.iProtocol));
    resMan.HostResolver().GetByName(KGdpIrDeviceSearchName,
                                    iNameEntry,
                                    iSender.iStatus);
    iSender.SetActive();
    }
```

To initiate a discovery, I first close various resources that might already be open (to ensure we are not connected to anybody), reopen them, and then issue the asynchronous request GetByName() on the host resolver resource. (The host resolver is a shared resource of type RHostResolver that I hold in the resource manager. It allows us to get access to the IrDA device discovery functionality through the sockets API.)

If this fails and leaves, the appropriate sender state machine error handler is invoked:

```
CGdpStateMachine::TState* CGdpIrSender::ErrorOnStateEntry(TInt /*aError*/)
    {
    Reset();
    return NULL; // Give up
    }
```

This just assumes that something fairly major has happened, and we may as well give up! In fact, it usually means that we were unable to open some resource needed for the send attempt, such as a socket or the host resolver. A more elegant solution would be to do a limited number of retries, backing-off for a (possibly incremental) period of time, before finally signaling a fatal error up to the client to let them know things have gone really badly. But for the example, this is adequate.

If the state entry completes successfully, however, the following code will be invoked by the RunL() implementation in the state machine framework, presented earlier:

```
CGdpStateMachine::TState* CGdpIrSender::TDiscoverState::CompleteL()
    {
    iSender.iAddr = iNameEntry().iAddr;
    return &(iSender.iQueryState);
    }
```

This simply stores the address of the remote machine discovered into the iAddr member of the sender state machine for future reference. Notice how we specify the next state to enter (query) now that the discovery has completed successfully.

If the discovery fails (typically, because no devices were found), the default ErrorL() function provided by our generalized TSenderState class is invoked:

```
CGdpStateMachine::TState* CGdpIrSender::TSenderState::ErrorL(TInt aCode)
    {
    User::Leave(aCode);
    return NULL;          // Never actually hit
    }
```

This simply passes the error code back up to the concrete state machine's ErrorOnStateExit() handler. If we wanted to, we could override this strategy in the TDiscoveryState class to provide more information on why the discovery failed, and perhaps take more appropriate action.

The sender state machine's error handler performs the following:

```
CGdpStateMachine::TState* CGdpIrSender::ErrorOnStateExit(TInt /*aError*/)
    {
    Reset();
    if(--iRetries < 0)
        return NULL;
    return CurrentState();   // Force re-entry to initial state
    }
```

As asynchronous errors often indicate a communications or remote device error (as opposed to synchronous (state entry) errors that are generally caused by local failure), we attempt to reset the state machine and do a limited number of retries.

If, for some reason, the operation is canceled while the discovery is taking place (generally because the user chose to quit, and hence `Close()` has been called), the following will be called:

```
void CGdpIrSender::TDiscoverState::Cancel()
    {
    iSender.iResMan.HostResolver().Cancel();
    }
```

The remaining three states are very similar to discovery, with implementations of at least `EnterL()`, `CompleteL()` and `Cancel()` as appropriate for the specific state events. In `TQueryState`, the IAS query is initiated like this:

```
TIASQuery query(KGdpIrClassName,
                KGdpIrAttributeName,
                iSender.iAddr.GetRemoteDevAddr());

iSender.iResMan.NetDatabase().Query(query,
                               iIASResponse,
                               iSender.iStatus);
iSender.SetActive();
```

Basically, a query record is made up and then passed to the network database API in ESOCK. `KGdpIrClassName` and `KGdpIrAttributeName` specify the unique IAS class and attribute that will be requested from the remote machine's information access database. This allows the GDP-IR receiver service to be located on that machine – so only machines supporting our GDP protocol should register an entry with this class.

> *We attempt to ensure the global uniqueness of this IAS entry by pre-pending part of a known unique string onto the front of the class name – I'm using our Internet DNS entry. This makes our full class name* com:symbian:psp:GDP. *There are still no guarantees that nobody else will use this same class name, but we've at least improved our odds of uniqueness!*

If the query completes successfully, we check the validity of the data returned, and if everything's OK we copy it into the port field of the destination address established through discovery:

```
TInt port = 0;
if(iIASResponse.Type() != EIASDataInteger ||
   iIASResponse.GetInteger(port) != KErrNone ||
   port <= 0 || port > 255)
     User::Leave(KErrNotFound); // IAS attribute was invalid

iSender.iAddr.SetPort(STATIC_CAST(TUint8, port));
```

This actually sets the remote **LSAP** that we will attempt to connect to (differentiating the incoming connection from, say, a file beam request) to the multiplexing layer – IrMUX. We can then attempt to connect to the remote service we've sought out.

You probably can guess by now that this is done in `TConnectState::EnterL()`:

```
iSender.iSocket.Connect(iSender.iAddr, iSender.iStatus);
iSender.SetActive();
```

I simply issue a connect operation on the socket, specifying the remote device address and LSAP. On successful completion, I instruct the state machine to move into the write state.

To enter write state, the following is performed:

```
iSender.iSocket.Write(iSender.iPacket, iSender.iStatus);
iSender.SetActive();
```

This simply requests an asynchronous write to the connected socket. While we are waiting for this to complete, we are conceptually "writing", and once it completes, we leave ourselves in the "written" state by simply returning NULL from the `TWriteState::CompleteL()` function. We are then ready to write more data on this connected socket, the next time `SendL()` is invoked. If the link is broken, this write will complete with the error code `KErrDisconnected`, and the default error handler will automatically reset the state and try again from discovery.

Receiver

Conceptually, the receiver is the mirror of the sender. However, the implementation is quite different because:

❑ Servicing discovery requests is handled automatically by the IrDA protocol, so we do not need to answer them explicitly

❑ Servicing IAS queries is also handled transparently, so long as we initially register our IAS database entry with the IrDA protocol

❑ The whole process of connection (that is, us accepting a connection) and reading is initiated by the remote machine – we must simply (and continuously) listen out for these incoming connections.

We do not need to do anything in our implementation of the `ReceiveAllL()` function provided by the `MGdpSession` interface, as we are always able to receive and handle data, the moment the remote machine chooses to give it to us. So, unlike the sender, which is brought to life only by a client request, the receiver can be activated at any time by an external event, which may culminate in a call up to the client code.

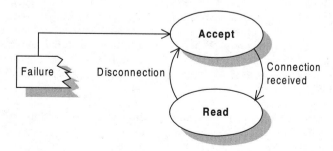

This all means that, as you can see, the state diagram for receive is very simple. The initial request is queued when the receiver is first opened, and no further calls by the client are required.

The class layout for the receiver is very similar to the sender, but it only has two state classes corresponding to objects for its states. When the protocol session is opened, the following is called:

```
void CGdpIrReceiver::OpenL(MGdpPacketHandler* aHandler)
    {
    __ASSERT_DEBUG(aHandler != NULL,
                    GdpUtil::Panic(GdpUtil::EReceiverBadHandle));
    __ASSERT_DEBUG(iHandler == NULL,
                    GdpUtil::Panic(GdpUtil::EReceiverInUse));
    iHandler = aHandler;
    TProtocolDesc& desc = iResMan.ProtocolDesc();

    User::LeaveIfError(iListenSocket.Open(iResMan.SocketServer(),
                                    desc.iAddrFamily,
                                    desc.iSockType,
                                    desc.iProtocol));

    TInt port = KGdpIrMinLsap - 1;
    TInt ret = KErrGeneral;
    while(port < KGdpIrMaxLsap && ret != KErrNone)
        {
        // Find a free port, if there is one available
        ++port;
        iAddr.SetPort(port);
        ret = iListenSocket.Bind(iAddr);
        }
    if(ret != KErrNone)
        User::Leave(KErrInUse);    // All ports are in use

    User::LeaveIfError(iListenSocket.Listen(4)); // Queue size 4

    iIASEntry.SetClassName(KGdpIrClassName);
    iIASEntry.SetAttributeName(KGdpIrAttributeName);
    iIASEntry.SetToInteger(iListenSocket.LocalPort());
    ret = iResMan.NetDatabase().Add(iIASEntry);
    if(ret != KErrNone && ret != KErrAlreadyExists)
        User::Leave(ret);

    ChangeState(&iAcceptState);
    }
```

As with the conventional (that is, BSD TCP/IP) sockets found in many systems, an incoming connection is received through the use of (at least) two sockets. First, you have a "listener" socket that you bind to the port you wish to listen on, and then you have an additional socket per concurrent connection that you accept individual connections onto. When binding, I do a sequential search from KGdpIrMinLsap to KGdpIrMaxLsap, for a free **LSAP** (or **port**) to listen on. It doesn't actually matter what the value of the LSAP is within this range, as long as it is this value that gets registered with IAS so that peer machines can find it.

Once we've found a free LSAP, you can see how the listener socket is set up. Initializing the listen is a synchronous call, so we do not need an extra state to do it in.

You can also see how the IAS entry is registered. This has to use exactly the same class and attribute name constants as for the query in the sender. The value of the attribute is loaded with the port that we bound our listener socket to.

Finally, we request an immediate state change to the accept state, so that right away we're ready to receive connection requests. This is carried out as follows:

```
void CGdpIrReceiver::TAcceptState::EnterL()
    {
    RSocket& readSock = iReceiver.iReadSocket;

    readSock.Close();
    User::LeaveIfError(readSock.Open(iReceiver.iResMan.SocketServer()));
    iReceiver.iListenSocket.Accept(readSock, iReceiver.iStatus);
    iReceiver.SetActive();
    }
```

I simply open up a socket to accept the connection on to, and then queue the asynchronous accept. If opening the socket fails, the receiver error handler simply instructs the state machine to retry the accept.

```
CGdpStateMachine::TState* CGdpIrReceiver::ErrorOnStateEntry(TInt /*aError*/)
    {
    return &iAcceptState;
    }
```

As with the sender, this indicates a fairly critical error. However, we must *try* to get back into the accept state if at all possible, or else we'll never receive any more incoming packets.

> *Again, a more intelligent and efficient approach might involve holding off in a third "delay retry" state or waiting for a* ReceiveAllL() *request before retrying, in order to pace the attempt to change the state back to accepting.*

When a remote machine attempts to make an LMP connection to our LSAP, the accept will complete, and the state machine is advanced to the read state. Note that on the server side, discovery and IAS requests are handled automatically for us by the stack, provided that we correctly register our IAS entry, as I showed back in OpenL().

We enter the read state as follows:

```
void CGdpIrReceiver::TReadState::EnterL()
    {
    iReceiver.iReadSocket.Read(iReceiver.iPacket, iReceiver.iStatus);
    iReceiver.SetActive();
    }
```

When some data arrives from the peer, this read will complete with the datagram sent being stored in iReceiver.iPacket. We pass it back up to the client like this:

```
CGdpStateMachine::TState* CGdpIrReceiver::TReadState::CompleteL()
    {
    _LIT(KNullAddress,"");
    iReceiver.iHandler->GdpHandleL(KNullAddress, iReceiver.iPacket);
    return this; // Queue another read, while the channel is open
    }
```

I return a pointer to the `this` object (the read state object), indicating that we should re-enter this state. This means that `EnterL()` is immediately called, and any more packets sent on this connection can be read.

As with the sender, if the connection is broken (by IrLAP going down), the read completes with the error code `KErrDisconnected`, and our default error handler will put us back into the waiting-for-connection state.

One thing worth mentioning is that if we have to cancel while in the accept state, we actually cancel on the listen socket that we *originally* invoked the `Accept()` on, and not the socket we *accepted* onto! That is,

```
iReceiver.iListenSocket.CancelAccept();
```

And *not*:

```
iReceiver.iReadSocket.CancelAccept();
```

Resource Manager

So far, I've just been using the resource manager, without actually explaining what it is. Basically, it's a convenient place to hold onto any resources that are shared between the sender and the receiver. Specifically, these are connections to the socket server, the host resolver, and the network database, which we have already seen used by the previous components. It also implements a bit of functionality in the form of `OpenL()`, `Close()` and `ResetL()` functions to set up and maintain these resources. Keeping this stuff out of the central `CGdpIrComms` class keeps the façade interface clean from any implementation detail, so minimizing the dependency of the GDP client on the implementations' internals.

I've also put a special task into the resource manager that does not fit neatly into either of the state machine objects. Its purpose is to look out for any disconnection of the LAP layer, and reset the resources if this occurs. This helps to ensure that any new discoveries will happen on a fresh LAP connection, without anything being left 'hanging around' from the previous failed link. This is done through a single, asynchronous `Ioctl()` call:

```
void CGdpIrResourceManager::DoIoctl()
    {
    iSocket.Ioctl(KDisconnectIndicationIoctl, iStatus, NULL, KIrdaAddrFamily);
    SetActive();
    }
```

In order to wait on this, the resource manager is derived from `CActive`, and every time its `RunL()` is hit, it knows the LAP link has gone down and we should reset:

```
void CGdpIrResourceManager::RunL()
    {
    ResetL();
    DoIoctl();
    }
```

No check is made of the completion code, as even if there was an error, we assume that the LAP layer has gone down so we may as well reset anyway! Again, more extensive analysis and checking could be done here.

GDP-IR Summary

We've now seen how the EPOC sockets server is used to connect, send and receive data over IrDA. This knowledge transfers very well to other protocols supported by the sockets server (such as TCP/IP), with differences only where absolutely dictated by the underlying specifications. As I indicated at the start of the chapter, comprehensive documentation of using these protocols is available in the EPOC SDK. In the future, many more protocols could become available through the sockets API – Bluetooth or WAP services, for example. The knowledge you've learned here will certainly be useful in accessing these future protocols.

There are many ways in which the code presented here could be extended to meet other requirements. For example:

❏ Performance tuning: a high-speed (more real-time) game using IrDA with reduced link turnaround times. This basically reduces the latency of communication, but with degradation of maximum throughput.

❏ Machine selection: rather than automatically sending packets to the first machine found by device discovery, a list of machines could be presented to the user for selection of a machine.

❏ Error handling: if sending fails, no feedback is given to the client application. A notify interface could be added to report this information.

SMS Implementation

SMS (short message service) is a great protocol, because with it you can play GDP games at a distance. The code I'll be presenting in this chapter, however, should be considered a concept implementation. It really works – in fact, it works about as well as it can in EPOC Release 5 – but it has a few loose ends due to the less-than-tight integration between EPOC R5 and telephones. And because it's SMS specific, it only addresses the GSM world. In future releases of EPOC, it will be possible – in fact, quite easy – to address both these issues.

Here's an overview of how the SMS implementation is intended to work with current EPOC devices. First, the scenario for sending a message:

❏ Sender gets ready with phone, putting it in contact with the EPOC device by cable or infrared as appropriate.

❏ Move made and immediately sent from EPOC device to phone.

❏ The phone zaps the SMS over the GSM network, to the receiver.

And then for receiving a message:

❏ Incoming message makes a bleep on receiving player's phone.

❏ Receiving player looks at message(s) on the phone (after all, there could be many, and they're not necessarily GDP messages). GDP messages are identified by GAME DATA: at the beginning, before they go into some form of coded data.

❑ If there are any GDP messages, the receiver tells their GDP game to receive them – again placing the phone in contact with the EPOC machine, by cable or infrared link.

❑ The GSDP server will channel the message(s) to the game session(s) for which they are intended. It will delete GDP messages from the phone. It will cause non-GDP messages to be marked "read", but not deleted.

GDP-SMS is a networked implementation: the "address" used to send a message is the other player's telephone number. However, because SMS behaves rather differently with different networks and handsets, an extra complication is added at this point. Some phones require you to specify a **Service Center Address** (SCA) to which messages are initially sent before being routed to their destination. The way SCAs are set depends on the phone and on the network. GDP-SMS uses knowledge about some phones and networks to get the SCA from the phone, but in some cases this can't be done, so the user is required to enter a long-form destination address of the form destination-number@sca-number.

SMS supports both seven and eight-bit data transport, but only 7-bit is universally implemented, so that's what I've chosen to use here. SMS supports a maximum message length of 160 7-bit characters. While the actual tasks of sending and receiving are very straightforward with SMS (compared to the issues we had to face with infrared), the formatting of data and messages before sending and after reception is a much greater concern.

The aim of my GDP-SMS implementation is to demonstrate GDP working over a large distance, and to provide you with a working example of how to use some of the telephony features within EPOC. Clearly, this is one area of EPOC that has huge scope for future additions and new development, but the fundamentals provided here should form an excellent base from which to explore these developments as they emerge.

ETEL, and EPOC Support for SMS

Within EPOC, SMS functionality (along with many other features) is provided through ETEL, the telephony server. ETEL is also used by TCP/IP and dial-up networking to establish PPP data connections, and by the fax server for contacting remote fax machines. It can also be used for accessing the phone books stored on GSM phones.

ETEL is configured through the control panel applets for Modems and Dialling, which must be set up for the particular modem and phone (in our case, this must be a GSM phone) we're using. If the EPOC Email/Messaging application can send and receive SMS messages, we know that there is a good chance our game applications will be able to do so as well.

In EPOC Release 5, ETEL operates in what we call a loosely coupled (or **two box**) world. This is where EPOC is hosted on a machine that only has occasional or temporally intermittent access to telephony devices. For example, a PDA only has telephony capability when connected – by wire or infrared – to a modem of some sort. Once disconnected, it loses this capability. This puts a limit on what can be done within EPOC, because at any point the telephony capability may go away, and possibly not come back for a considerable time.

Within GDP-SMS, the tangible result of this uncertainty is the Receive All button presented in the UI, and the corresponding function found in the GDP interface, through which we compensate for our temporal intermittence. In other words, we have to synchronize with the phone on contact to catch up with any changes (incoming messages) that happened while the two boxes were separated.

In the future, we will be able to find out about these changes *as they happen*, through use of the **one box** paradigm, where EPOC is hosted on the device with telephony capability. There is also the **virtual one box** paradigm, where traditionally separate EPOC and telephony devices are more tightly coupled through personal area networking technologies such as Bluetooth.

In EPOC Release 5, ETEL only provides access to the raw SMS messages sent to (and from) the phone, and from there to (and from) the network. This is called the **SMS PDU** (Protocol Data Unit) format, and it's defined as part of the GSM standards (GSM 03.40, available from http://www.etsi.org/). Formatting correct SMS PDUs to pass in and out of ETEL forms an important part of the GDP-SMS code. However, unless you need to alter or rewrite these routines for your purposes, you shouldn't need to reference these documents.

As the technologies evolve, future releases will provide more sophisticated, and ultimately GSM independent, forms of telephonic messaging.

The GDP-SMS Protocol Mapping

There are two requirements for formatting GDP-SMS messages before they can be placed inside an SMS PDU for sending to the phone. These are:

❑ Provide a means for multiplexing our messages in with any others on the user's phone, and recognizing them again at the receiving end

❑ Put the data into a 7-bit format, suitable for encoding into the 7-bit SMS PDU

These requirements mean that we must define our own internal message format that supports these features, which we call the GDP-SMS PDU, as shown in the figure below. As you can see, this is considerably more complex than its GDP-IR equivalent.

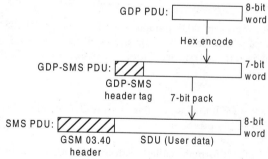

The data formats are as follows

❑ GDP PDU. This is the chunk of data that's passed down to our GDP implementation through the MGdpSession interface, along with protocol-specific addressing information.

❑ GDP-SMS PDU. Here, we've encoded the client data into a format suitable for transmission on the underlying carrier. In this example, we are encoding it so that it is 7-bit safe (that is, it only uses 7-bit data values), and we also put a unique header tag on the front so that we can spot our messages at the far end.

❑ SMS PDU. This is the protocol data unit that is actually passed out to the GSM network, via ETEL. This contains all the addressing and other header information that the mobile phone network (and particularly the SMS service center) requires to store and forward the message to its intended recipient.

The destination address passed down through the GDP interface is encoded directly into the SMS PDU, along with the SCA if present.

The GDP-SMS Implementation

The structure of GDP-SMS is intentionally very similar to that of GDP-IR, so I won't have to explain a whole new class structure. In particular, the SMS communications component has two `CGdpStateMachine`-derived classes called `CGdpSmsSender` and `CGdpSmsReceiver`, in much the same way that the infrared communications component did, for carrying out the basic sending and receiving tasks.

As I've hinted already, the big difference from GDP-IR is in holding and formatting messages between sending and receiving. In GDP-IR this was trivial, because no special formatting was needed – we just spat out the GDP data over IrLMP. With SMS, there are two far more complex stages required: creating GDP-SMS PDUs, and then wrapping these up into SMS PDUs. The former is an issue specific to GDP, whereas the latter is a general requirement for anything wishing to use ETEL for SMS messaging.

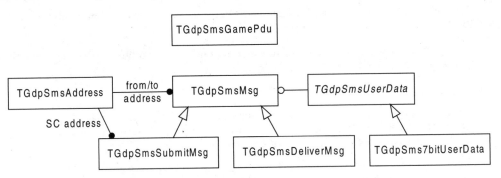

The set of classes we use to represent GDP data as it passes through GDP-SMS is shown above. An SMS PDU is represented by an object of class `TGdpSmsMsg`, and the GDP-SMS PDU is held in `TGdpSmsGamePdu`. To begin our analysis, we'll look at the lower layer SMS PDU.

SMS PDU Container

The first few container classes we'll look at are based around SMS PDUs, and their implementation is fairly independent of our example protocol.

There are two specific SMS PDU formats, called `TGdpSmsSubmitMsg` and `TGdpSmsDeliverMsg`, after the corresponding PDU types in the GSM 03.40 specification. They both derive from a single base message class that looks like this:

```
class TGdpSmsMsg
    {
public:
    TGdpSmsMsg(TGdpSmsUserData& aUserData);

protected:
    TGdpSmsAddress iFromToAddress;
    TGdpSmsUserData& iUd;
    };
```

As we saw in the class diagram, there are two main elements to the message: the user data element, and the 'from/to' address that's used to store either the destination address of an outgoing (submit) message, or the origin of an incoming (deliver) one. When the `TGdpSmsMsg` is constructed, it is initialized with a reference to an existing `TGdpSmsUserData` area, which it will use when required throughout its lifetime.

Most of the formatting functionality is provided by the two concrete subclasses.

```
class TGdpSmsSubmitMsg : public TGdpSmsMsg
    {
public:
    enum TValidity
        { // Refer to GSM 03.40 to extend these options
        EValidityOneHour = 11,
        EValidityOneDay = 167,
        EValidityOneWeek = 173
        };
    TGdpSmsSubmitMsg(TGdpSmsUserData& aUserData);
    inline TGdpSmsAddress& DestAddress();
    TGdpSmsAddress& ScAddress();

    void SetValidityPeriod(TValidity aValidity);
    TValidity ValidityPeriod() const;

    void EncodeL(TSms& aSms) const;

private:
    TGdpSmsAddress iScAddress;
    TValidity iValidityPeriod;
    };

class TGdpSmsDeliverMsg : public TGdpSmsMsg
    {
public:
    TGdpSmsDeliverMsg(TGdpSmsUserData& aUserData);
    inline TGdpSmsAddress& OriginAddress();

    TInt DecodeL(const TSms& aSms);
    };
```

The outgoing `TGdpSmsSubmitMsg` object contains two additional members: one for the SMS service center address, which is used when putting the message onto the network, and a validity period, for use by the network.

There is scope for many more members here, for all the other options available in SMS submit messages. I chose instead to 'hardwire' most of these to sensible common values, as they are not required to change in our example – but you might well find applications for them!

This hardwiring is done when the submit message is actually encoded into an ETEL `TSms` buffer object:

```
void TGdpSmsSubmitMsg::EncodeL(TSms& aSms) const
    {
    TSms::TPdu smsPdu;
    iScAddress.EncodeL(smsPdu);
    aSms.SetUseDefaultSca(EFalse);
    smsPdu.Append(0x11);      // SUBMIT, VPF = Integer
    smsPdu.Append(0x00);      // MR filled by phone
    iFromToAddress.EncodeL(smsPdu);
    smsPdu.Append(0x00);      // PID = non-interworking protocol
    smsPdu.Append(iUd.DataCodingScheme());
    smsPdu.Append(ValidityPeriod());
    iUd.EncodeL(smsPdu);
    aSms.SetPduL(smsPdu);
    }
```

If you want to know more about what these additional fields do, you should read the GSM 03.40 specification. Needless to say, blindly tweaking these fields will rarely result in success, as the phone and/or network will reject any ill-formatted or unsupported requests.

As you see, this function defers a lot of the work to the `EncodeL()` members of the various data items that make up the message, such as addresses and the user data area itself.

> *Notice how we place the SCA onto the front of the PDU. This is not part of the GSM 03.40 specification, but it is required by many modern phones. To this extent, ETEL virtually always expects it to be there, so I've made it a compulsory field in the SMS submit message.*

The decoding of messages, performed in `TGdpSmsDeliverMsg`, is pretty similar in format:

```
TInt TGdpSmsDeliverMsg::DecodeL(const TSms& aSms)
    {
    TPtrC8 smsPdu(aSms.PduL());

#define LEAVE_IF_DIFFERENT(octet, expval) \
        User::LeaveIfError((octet) == (expval) ? KErrNone : KErrNotFound)

    TInt extract = 0;

    LEAVE_IF_DIFFERENT(smsPdu[extract++] & (0x03 | 0x40), 0);
    extract += OriginAddress().DecodeL(smsPdu.Mid(extract));
    LEAVE_IF_DIFFERENT(smsPdu[extract++], 0);
    LEAVE_IF_DIFFERENT(smsPdu[extract++], iUd.DataCodingScheme());
    extract += 7;
    extract += iUd.DecodeL(smsPdu.Mid(extract));
    return extract;
    }
```

The main difference here is that I keep track of our current read position as we work through the message. As we come to each part of the message, we decode and store it in the appropriate member, or we ignore it, or we validate it against expected values. If at any point we come across something unexpected or invalid, we leave with `KErrNotFound`, meaning that we didn't find a message we can handle. These expected values are again hardwired, based on the values we send out in the `TGdpSmsSubmitMsg::EncodeL()` function. If you need to accept other values, you'll need to change this.

You might also notice that the service center address is not provided at the start of the message returned, so we don't have to pick it out first. This quirk is only apparent when sending a message.

The `TGdpSmsAddress` class is based on the ETEL `TGsmTelNumber` class, but provides a wrapper for reading and writing numbers as we require, and the `EncodeL()` and `DecodeL()` functions we've already seen invoked as part of the message encode and decode algorithms.

```
class TGdpSmsAddress
    {
public:
    void SetAddress(const TDesC& aAddress);
    void SetAddress(const TGsmTelNumber& aGsmNumber);
    void GetAddress(TDes& aAddress) const;
    void EncodeL(TDes8& aDest) const;
    TInt DecodeL(const TDesC8& aSrc);
protected:
    TGsmTelNumber iNumber;
    };
```

The telephone number can be set from a human readable string, and the function interprets it as appropriately as it can (for example, it takes "+44..." to mean "International number", "44...").

Slightly more interesting is the `TGdpSms7bitUserData` class:

```
class TGdpSms7bitUserData : public TGdpSmsUserData
    {
public:
    void EncodeL(TDes8& aDest) const;
    TInt DecodeL(const TDesC8& aSrc);
    TInt UserDataEncodedSize();
    TInt8 DataCodingScheme();
    };
```

All of its member functions are implementations of pure virtual functions declared in the base class, `TGdpSmsUserData`.

We don't have any user data setters or getters because the base class actually inherits from `TBuf<>`, so application code can write and retrieve its data using the expressive interface provided by EPOC descriptors.

This means it is the application code's responsibility to ensure it only puts in data that will be correctly encoded into the SMS PDU, according to the restrictions of the specific concrete class it uses. In our example, we only define and use `TGdpSms7bitUserData`, so each element of the descriptor must only use the least significant 7 bits, or else experience data loss!

The encoding algorithm in this class is quite intricate:

```
void TGdpSms7bitUserData::EncodeL(TDes8& aDest) const
    {
    aDest.Append(Length());
    TInt octet = 0;
    for(TInt i = 0; i < Length(); ++i)
        {
        TInt septet = (*this)[i] & 0x7F; // Clear MSB
        TInt rs = i%8;
        TInt ls = (8 - rs) % 8;

        octet |= (septet << ls) & 0xFF;
```

```
        if(ls > 0)
            { //We've just filled the current digit.
            aDest.Append(octet);
            octet = 0;
            if(ls > 1)
                { // Put left over bits into next octet
                octet = (septet >> rs);
                }
            }
        }
    if(Length() % 8 != 0)
        aDest.Append(octet); // Add any odd bits left over
    }
```

The first thing I do is to write out one byte containing the number of seven bit words in the rest of the user data area (this is actually the final byte of the GSM 03.40 header) before starting on the user data area.

The aim of the remaining code is to take the 7-bit (septet) data stored in the inherited descriptor area, and write it into the 8-bit (octet) destination buffer in a packed format, according to the SMS PDU specification. This packing operation uses every available bit of the octet buffer for storing data, rather than wasting the extra bits in every word, as we do in our source buffer.

The algorithm puts the first source septet straight into the first destination octet, along with 1 bit of the next source septet. It puts the remaining 6 bits of this second septet into the second destination octet, along with 2 bits of the third septet. The remaining 5 bits of this septet go into the following octet, and so on. i holds the index number of the current septet, while ls specifies how many bit-places we should shift the current septet left before adding it into the current octet. If this is greater than 0, we must have filled the current octet up, so we bolt it onto the end of our output buffer. If ls is also greater than 1, then some bits must not have fitted into this octet, so we do a right-shift of the remainder by rs bit-places, to put them into the next octet.

The total length of the resulting packed buffer is 7/8ths of our original length (in words), so UserDataEncodedSize() returns the following:

```
    return ((Length() + 1) * 7) / 8;
```

Why the extra 'plus one'? Well, that's because we want to round up the result, and adding one at the start achieves this, while only using integer arithmetic.

The 7-bit data-decoding algorithm is pretty much the same thing in reverse – take a look at the source files if you want to see more of this bit-twiddling stuff!

GDP-SMS PDU Containers

Now we can look at how to encode the data received through the GDP interface into our internal GDP-SMS PDU. The two stages needed here are to encode the 8-bit data passed down into a 7-bit safe format, and to add a unique tag onto the front of this so that we can spot SMS messages intended for us at the receiving end. This all happens within a `TGdpSmsGamePdu` object:

```
class TGdpSmsGamePdu
    {
public:
    TGdpSmsGamePdu(const TDesC& aTag);
    TPtrC Tag() const;
    void SetSdu(const TDesC8& aSdu);
    TPtrC8 Sdu() const;

    void EncodeL(TGdpSmsUserData& aSmsUd) const;
    TInt DecodeL(const TGdpSmsUserData& aSmsUd);
private:
    TBuf<KGdpSmsTagMaxSize> iTag;
    TBuf8<KGdpSmsSduMaxSize> iSdu;
    };
```

The tag is set for the lifetime of the object on construction, as it is necessary for both encoding and decoding. The other member of this object is a buffer for holding the 8-bit GDP data. Here's the encoding algorithm:

```
void TGdpSmsGamePdu::EncodeL(TGdpSmsUserData& aSmsUd) const
    {
    aSmsUd.Copy(iTag);
    for(TInt i = 0; i < iSdu.Length(); ++i)
        {
        TBuf<2> octet;
        octet.Format(_L("%02X"), iSdu[i]);
        aSmsUd.Append(octet);
        }
    }
```

As you can see, I just put the tag into the destination descriptor, and then write the 8-bit data in using the descriptor library's `Format()` function. The result is padded if necessary to take up exactly two 7-bit words per byte encoded. I'm assuming that each character produced by `FormatL()` fits into a 7 bit word – this is well founded, as by referring to the ASCII table you'll find that all possible hex characters are well within the 7 bit range.

So for every byte passed down from the GDP interface, we actually send two 7-bit words, one for each 4-bit nibble of the original byte. For example, 163 ($==$ 0xA3) is encoded as "A3" $==$ 0x41 0x33, which are both clearly 7 bit safe.

This is not a very efficient encoding scheme, as it takes 14 bits to transport 8 bits of GDP information. That's over 40% wasted! However, I chose this method for its simplicity, and its politeness to the user receiving the game data (it doesn't present an alien hieroglyphic message on the phone's display, just a bunch of hex characters). You're strongly encouraged to devise a more elaborate and efficient scheme, should you require it for some other purpose.

Decoding is, as always, the inverse of the encoding algorithm:

```
TInt TGdpSmsGamePdu::DecodeL(const TGdpSmsUserData& aSmsUd)
    {
    // Look for our "unique" tag...
    TInt gdpPduOffset = aSmsUd.Find(iTag);
    if(gdpPduOffset < 0)
        User::Leave(KErrNotFound);

    // We've got the gdpSdu now -- just need to 7-bit decode it
    TPtrC gdpEncSdu(aSmsUd.Mid(gdpPduOffset + iTag.Length()));

    // ASSERT gdpEncSdu.Length() is even
    if(gdpEncSdu.Length() % 2 != 0)
        User::Leave(KErrNotFound); // Not even no. of characters!

    // ASSERT gdpEncSdu.Length() <= KGdpSmsMaxDataLength * 2
    if(gdpEncSdu.Length() > KGdpSmsSduMaxSize * 2)
        User::Leave(KErrNotFound); // Too many characters!

    TInt octet = 0;
    for(TInt i = 0; i < gdpEncSdu.Length(); ++i)
        { //Rip out crude encoded data
        TInt nibble = gdpEncSdu[i];
        if(nibble >= '0' && nibble <= '9')
            octet |= (nibble - '0');
        else if(nibble >= 'A' && nibble <= 'F')
            octet |= ((nibble - 'A') + 10);
        else if(nibble >= 'a' && nibble <= 'f')
            octet |= ((nibble - 'a') + 10);
        else
            User::Leave(KErrNotFound); // Invalid character found!

        if(i % 2 == 0)
            {
            octet = octet << 4;
            }
        else
            {
            iSdu.Append(octet);
            octet = 0;
            }
        }
    return aSmsUd.Length(); // We consumed it all
    }
```

The implementation is a bit more involved than the encoding version, because:

❑   There might be no header tag, in which case we leave with KErrNotFound, informing the caller that this message wasn't for us.

❑   Even after establishing that it probably is for us, we may come across an invalid character at any point, or too many or not enough characters (half an encoded byte, perhaps). If this happens, we throw an error, and the calling code will assume the message wasn't for us after all.

❑   There is no convenient library function to decode ASCII-encoded hex, so we have to do this for ourselves.

Clearly, our so-called 'unique' tag does not actually guarantee that the packet is for us at all. Whatever string we choose to use, some other message could well have this string at the start. So if our decoding ever fails, we just assume that it wasn't for us at all. In fact, our highly redundant hex encoding actually helps increase our certainty that if a packet *is* correctly decoded, it *is* meant for us.

Note how this uniqueness issue is analogous to that of the IAS entry in GDP-IR. This is because in both cases, this is the token on which we multiplex our data in with other protocol connections/datagrams. There is no definitive solution to this, aside from everybody agreeing to use some centrally allocated unique identifier scheme (like DNS names or Ethernet addresses), or else use very long random identifiers to reduce the probability to near zero. Remember, this is not protection against malicious attacks – just a means of giving some chance of success!

Sender

Sending an SMS message through the ETEL interface is very straightforward. The only thing stopping us from directly invoking the RSmsMessaging::SendMessage() function with the SMS PDU we have labored to form, is that we may first need to find out what service center to use.

If the GDP client specified a service center as part of the SendL() address field, we just use that. But generally they won't, so we must retrieve it from the phone:

```
void CGdpSmsSender::TGetScaState::EnterL()
    {
    iSender.iResMan.iMessaging.GetDefaultSCAddress(iSender.iStatus, iFetchNum);
    iSender.SetActive();
    }
```

This is the EnterL() function for the first of our two sender states, TGetScaState. You can see that I just use the ETEL messaging API GetDefaultSCAddress() asynchronous function to do this. On success, I do this:

```
    iSender.iMsgSubmit.ScAddress().SetAddress(iFetchNum);
    iSender.iGotScAddress = ETrue;
    return &iSender.iSendMsgState;
```

Basically, this sets the TSmsGdpSubmit service center address with the result obtained, and moves on to sending:

```
void CGdpSmsSender::TSendMsgState::EnterL()
    {
    iSender.iMsgSubmit.EncodeL(iSmsMsg);
    iSender.iResMan.iMessaging.SendMessage(iSender.iStatus, iMsgRef, iSmsMsg);
    iSender.SetActive();
    }
```

This just encodes the submit SMS PDU up into our private TSms buffer, which gets passed into the message sending function. On failures, I do a bounded number of retries, as with the GDP-IR sender.

Receiver

Receiving SMS PDUs is very different from the equivalent in GDP-IR, and quite a bit more complex than sending an SMS PDU. Because we do not automatically know when a new SMS arrives, we rely on the client to issue a ReceiveAllL() to know that we should initiate the receive process.

On the first attempt, and on any unexplained error (which generally means the phone has been removed and then returned), we must (re)initialize the phone. This is done through the `Initialize()` asynchronous call within the ETEL `RPhone` interface.

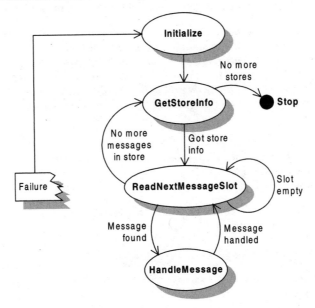

The next question is, where do we get the message from? As the message may or may not have been read already through the phone's own interface, we have no idea where the message will be stored on the phone, as different phones have a different number of SMS stores, and tend to use them for different purposes. The solution I chose was to search through all of the phone's message stores, including any in the SIM card in the phone.

So we iterate through all the stores on the phone, and within each store we iterate through all of the message slots (each slot can hold 0 or 1 messages), until we have found all the *used* slots. For each message found, we attempt to decode it, and if this succeeds, pass the GDP data up to the client, and delete it from the store.

This requires the following asynchronous requests:

❑ Get store information (once per store), to see how many slots it has, and how many are used

❑ Read message (once per message slot), and see if it's used

❑ Attempt to decode message (once per message found), and if successful, pass up to client and delete the original from the store

This directly tells us the states that are required, as shown in the state diagram above.

The process of rummaging through the phone's message store, looking for any messages addressed to us, is rather like rummaging through the pile of mail at the bottom of your stairs, seeing if any is for you. Except that we have several mailboxes' worth to rummage.

Getting store info works like this:

```
void CGdpSmsReceiver::TGetStoreInfoState::EnterL()
    {
    TInt totalStores;
    RSmsMessaging& messaging = iReceiver.iResMan.iMessaging;
    User::LeaveIfError(messaging.EnumerateMessageStores(totalStores));
    if(iReceiver.iNextStore >= totalStores)
        return;            // Stop
    messaging.GetMessageStoreInfo(iReceiver.iStatus,
                                  iReceiver.iNextStore,
                                  iReceiver.iStoreInfo);
    iReceiver.SetActive();
    }
```

First of all, I ask the ETEL messaging object how many stores the phone has, using RSmsMessaging::EnumerateMessageStores() – this way I can check if we've passed the last store. If so, we return without issuing a request, which moves the state machine into the inactive mode (that is, stop).

If there is another store, I issue the 'get store info' request, which on successful completion invokes the following:

```
CGdpStateMachine::TState* CGdpSmsReceiver::TGetStoreInfoState::CompleteL()
    {
    ++iReceiver.iNextStore;
    iReceiver.iMsgsFound = 0;
    iReceiver.iNextMsg = 1;
    iReceiver.iMsgStore.Close();
    iReceiver.iMsgStore.Open(iReceiver.iResMan.iMessaging,
                             iReceiver.iStoreInfo.iName);
    return &iReceiver.iReadMsgState;
    }
```

First, I update various pieces of state information, so I know which store to check next time round. Then I open up an RSmsStore object to access the store through (using the name provided in the store info just obtained), and finally I specify the read state as the next to be entered.

In the read state, we want to scan through all the message slots in the current store.

```
void CGdpSmsReceiver::TReadMsgState::EnterL()
    {
    if(iReceiver.iNextMsg > iReceiver.iStoreInfo.iTotal ||
        iReceiver.iMsgsFound >= iReceiver.iStoreInfo.iUsed)
        { // No more messages in this store
        TRequestStatus* req = &iReceiver.iStatus;
        User::RequestComplete(req, KErrCompletion);
        }
```

```
    else
        {
        iReceiver.iMsgStore.ReadSms(iReceiver.iStatus,
                                    iReceiver.iNextMsg,
                                    iReceiver.iStoreEntry);
        ++iReceiver.iNextMsg;
        }
    iReceiver.SetActive();
    }
```

If there are no more messages or message slots in this store, I complete the active object iStatus immediately, without actually issuing a request. This is done using the User::RequestComplete() function, and the code we pass in (KErrCompletion) will be held in the iStatus when the RunL() is next called. This is actually forcing an immediate change to another state when entering this one. If this pattern occurred more frequently, I'd have built it into the state machine architecture, by having EnterL() return a TState*, pointing to the new state required – if any.

If there are still unchecked slots remaining, I issue a read on the next message slot. If this completes successfully, iReceiver.iStoreEntry will hold a valid message, which I use later on in the handle message state.

```
CGdpStateMachine::TState* CGdpSmsReceiver::TReadMsgState::CompleteL()
    {
    ++iReceiver.iMsgsFound;
    return &iReceiver.iHandleMsgState;
    }
```

There are several reasons why the read might not complete successfully, which we handled in the ErrorL() member:

```
CGdpStateMachine::TState* CGdpSmsReceiver::TReadMsgState::ErrorL(TInt aCode)
    {
    switch(aCode)
        {
    case KErrGeneral:          // Message slot was empty
    case KErrNotFound:
        return this;
    case KErrCompletion:       // No more messages in this store
        return &iReceiver.iGetStoreInfoState;
        }
    User::Leave(aCode);
    return NULL;
    }
```

The cases are:

❑ Message slot was empty – proceed to next slot by re-entering the read state

❑ No more message slots in this store – go and look for the next store by returning to 'get store info' state

❑ Actual error in reading from the store – pass up error and retry if appropriate

Whenever a message is found, the handle message state is entered. First, we need to know if it's a GDP message, so I try to extract a game PDU from the raw SMS PDU returned from ETEL, in a separate member of the handle message state:

```
void CGdpSmsReceiver::THandleMsgState::ExtractGamePduL(
        TDes& aAddress, TGdpSmsGamePdu& aGamePdu)
    {
    RSmsStorage::TSmsMsgStoreEntry& entry = iReceiver.iStoreEntry;
    if(entry.iStatus != RSmsStorage::EStatusUnread &&
            entry.iStatus != RSmsStorage::EStatusRead)
        { // We've got a non-incoming message
        User::Leave(KErrNotFound);
        }
    TGdpSms7bitUserData userData;
    TGdpSmsDeliverMsg deliverMsg(userData);
    deliverMsg.DecodeL(entry.iMsg);
    deliverMsg.OriginAddress().GetAddress(aAddress);
    aGamePdu.DecodeL(userData);
    }
```

First, I test whether the message read is a delivery message, as opposed to an outgoing or status report message that might also exist in a phone's message store. If that's OK, I go on to decode the SMS PDU from the raw data held in `iReceiver.iStoreEntry`, into the `deliverMsg` object. If this succeeds, I then decode the user data section of this into the `aGamePdu` passed in. This holds the GDP data, ready for passing up to the client.

As you can see, this function can leave at any point if an error is encountered in decoding the SMS message. This may be because we've picked up a non-GDP message from the store, or that some other error was struck. The former is not a critical/fatal error, but we still leave (with code `KErrNotFound`) as a convenient way of throwing an exception, so as not to bother doing any further decoding.

```
void CGdpSmsReceiver::THandleMsgState::EnterL()
    {
    TGdpSmsGamePdu gamePdu(KGdpSmsHeaderTag);
    TBuf<KGsmMaxTelNumberSize> address;

    TRAPD(err, ExtractGamePduL(address, gamePdu));
    switch(err)
        {
    case KErrNone:
        // The message is for us! Delete from phone and pass up
        iReceiver.iMsgStore.Delete(iReceiver.iStatus, iReceiver.iNextMsg - 1);
        iReceiver.iHandler->GdpHandleL(address, gamePdu.Sdu());
        break;
    case KErrNotFound:
        { // Message not for us. Carry on to next message
        TRequestStatus* req = &iReceiver.iStatus;
        User::RequestComplete(req, KErrNotFound);
        break;
        }
    default:
        // Some other (unhandled) error. Pass it up.
        User::Leave(err);
        }
    iReceiver.SetActive();
    }
```

On entry to the handle message state, the first thing is to attempt to decode the message. This is run within a trap harness, so that I can check for the likely case that the message was not for GDP. If so, I do another forced state change, this time back to the read state, to look for more messages.

The interesting case, however, is where a GDP message *is* found. In this case, I issue an asynchronous delete request to ETEL, to get it to erase the GDP message from the phone, and pass up the decoded GDP data to the client application.

When the delete completes, we return back to read state to look for more messages:

```
CGdpStateMachine::TState* CGdpSmsReceiver::THandleMsgState::CompleteL()
    {
    return &iReceiver.iReadMsgState; // Go read the next message
    }
```

Resource Manager

As with GDP-IR, there is a resource manager in GDP-SMS – only it is significantly simpler, as it does not have any of the active management functionality that was present in GDP-IR. Put another way, it does not carry out any asynchronous task by itself, but simply acts as a single point of contact (or proxy) for resource access.

```
class CGdpSmsResourceManager : public CBase
    {
public:
    ~CGdpSmsResourceManager();
    void OpenL();
    void Close();
    void Initialize(TRequestStatus& aStatus);
    void InitializeCancel();

public:
    RCommServ       iCommServ;
    RTelServer      iTelServer;
    RBasicGsmPhone  iPhone;
    RSmsMessaging   iMessaging;
    };
```

As you can see, the resource manager is not `CActive` derived – it just holds the shared resources used by both the sender and receiver. These are all the `R` objects that we use to get access to the ETEL API.

It also has an `Initialize()` function, for initializing the phone. This request is routed through the resource manager, as it actually has global significance to both the sender and receiver. As it turns out, ETEL is very good at serializing any conflicting requests that are issued in parallel (for example, the receiver issuing an `Initialize()` while the sender is in the middle of a `SendMessage()`), so routing this request via the resource manager is purely a design point.

GDP-SMS Summary

In this section, we have seen how the EPOC ETEL server API is used to send and receive SMS messages via a GSM phone and network. In order to receive messages from a phone, retrieval and deletion of saved messages from the phone's store was presented.

ETEL is designed to provide a generic telephone interface, but is limited at this time by the realities of the hardware it is used with, specifically:

- ❏ It is used almost exclusively with either landline or GSM modems
- ❏ It is limited by the external interfaces provided by these modems, typically over the serial cable.

Nevertheless, this is a very useful example, as future EPOC releases will build on this basic functionality and augment it with more powerful and hardware independent messaging paradigms

Summary

I've already summarized the two major sections of this chapter above, and there seems little purpose in reiterating that information here. What remains, then, is to introduce the final chapter of this section, in which we'll examine and demonstrate the culmination of our efforts over the last few chapters: the Battleships game.

22

Full Battleships

In the last few chapters, we've seen how TOGS is designed, and the most important aspects of its implementation. That leaves only a little work left to describe Battleships. I'll provide brief tours of how the user uses the application, and of the program itself. I'll close with a few suggestions for improving Battleships and TOGS forward.

Using the Game

I explained the rules for Battleships right back in Chapter 1, and by now you'll have got used to them by playing Solo Ships.

The main issues with using Battleships are with connecting to the other player, and making sure that the communications works OK. Here, as a reminder, is what happens when you install Battleships, launch it from the Extras bar, and select Start game (*Ctrl+N*):

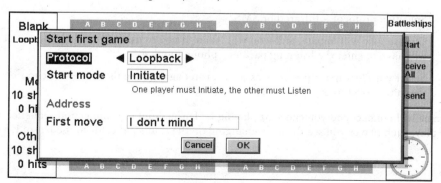

Your options here are related to the communications possibilities, and the way things work through the GSDP server:

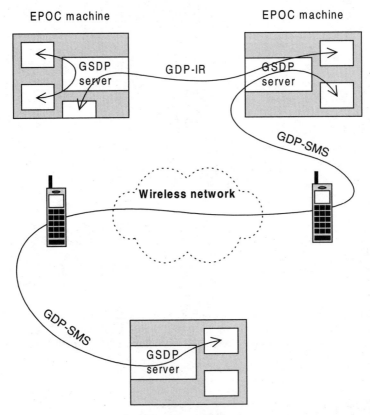

As this diagram shows, you can play for real using infrared or SMS, or for test purposes using loopback.

Playing for Real

If you are playing for real against someone else, with a real EPOC machine, then your easiest option is to:

❏   Specify a protocol – Infrared or SMS

❏   Choose who will initiate, and who will listen; if you're using SMS, then the initiating partner will have to enter the listening partner's phone number

❏   Select your first move preferences (if you can't agree, then the game will choose, in favor of the initiating partner's preference)

The game will connect and you can start playing it. Throughout the connection sequence and turn-based play, each player will see the state changing on the status indicator to the left of his or her screen.

Testing using Loopback

For testing the game using only a single machine – or the emulator – I find it best to use a different approach to launching the game. Instead of using the Extras bar to launch, go back to the Shell and select Create new file (*Ctrl+N*, or the fourth toolbar button).

❑   Enter a file name of Initiate, and a file type of Battleships, and select OK

❑   Start the game, select loopback protocol, and say you'll initiate

❑   Go back to the Shell, where you'll see the highlight is on your Initiate file. Go to the Extras bar, and select *Alt* (*Fn* on a real machine) and the Battleships application. This opens a new instance of Battleships.

❑   Start the second game, select loopback protocol, and say you'll listen

That will give you two games, one called Initiate, and the other which we'll call Listen to make the explanation easier. You can see their names in the file name area, at the top of the toolbar.

As soon as you press OK on the Listen game, you'll see a Connected to other player info-message, and the state will change from Blank to Start. Switch back to the Initiate game, and you'll see the status is My go, and the opponent fleet display on the right hand side has a black border instead of a gray one, indicating you can play. Select a square, hit it: the border will turn gray, and status will change to Other go. Flip back to the Listen game, notice where the Initiate game tried to hit, and play your turn. Carry on by flipping between the two games.

The loopback scenario shows how you can use file names to distinguish between different instances of the game. When playing against a real opponent on a different machine, I choose a filename corresponding to the player – so, some of the screenshots throughout the book are from a game I played against Jonathan Dixon, and you'll notice a JonD in the corner.

You can exit both games, and later start them again. Both games will get restored to the same state, including the correct current turn.

Reliability from RGCP

You can use the loopback function to demonstrate RGCP re-send, and packet dropping based on sequence numbers.

Say it's Initiate's turn to play: go into the Listen game and close it. Go into Initiate, and make a move. You know that the move is sent to the GSDP server, which can't deliver it immediately but, because of GSDP's present rules, it keeps the datagram in its receive queue. So close the Initiate game (and any other GSDP clients), wait for two seconds for the GSDP server to close itself down, and then launch both games – Initiate and Listen – again.

The net effect of these gymnastics is that you have sent a hit request from one game to the other, but it hasn't got through. You'll notice that both games think it's the other player's turn – Listen, because it sent a message that did get through, but it hasn't received the acknowledgement yet, and Initiate, because it sent a message that didn't get through.

You can re-send (*Ctrl+Y*, the standard shortcut key for Redo) from either application: a re-send from Listen will be ignored by Initiate (RGCP checks the sequence number and notes that the packet has already been received). A re-send from Initiate will be received by Listen and will cause Listen to change state to My turn.

If you like, you can run this code under the debugger: set breakpoints in RGCP code and you can see the packet dropping in action.

SMS and Receive-all

If you can arrange a game with SMS as a communications medium, you'll need to take care sending and receiving.

Each player will need an EPOC machine, a phone supporting both SMS text messaging and a data modem, and some means to connect the two devices together. In my testing, I've used an Ericsson SH888 with an IR data modem. Jonathan tested GDP on other phones from Ericsson, Nokia, and Motorola, on all four UK GSM networks.

The initiating player must specify the SMS protocol, and the other player's phone number. The listening player just specifies the SMS protocol.

When sending a message, each player must make sure the phone and EPOC machine are in IR contact. It's usually fairly obvious when you need to send a message – when starting a new game, or when sending a hit request. In a couple of cases, the game sends a message for you, but that's always immediately after receiving a message, so your machine and phone should be in IR contact anyway.

Depending on the phone, there may not be any visible indication that your message has sent successfully. Also, GDP doesn't have to indicate success. Finally, the performance of SMS text messaging in the UK networks that I've used is quite variable. Most networks are pretty good most of the time, but occasionally messages can get held up for a couple of hours, and this is more likely to happen when messages cross from one network to another.

All this adds up to a few reasons for uncertainty about whether a message sent over SMS has ever got to its destination. If you think a message may not have got through, you can re-send the last message by pressing Resend (*Ctrl+Y*).

When you want to receive messages onto the EPOC machine, you need to put the phone and EPOC machine in IR contact, press Receive All (*Ctrl+A*) on the Battleships game, and wait.

In the process of doing a receive-all for SMS:

❑ The GDP-SMS implementation looks at all messages stored in the phone. GDP messages are received by EPOC, and deleted from the phone. Non-GDP messages are marked 'read' on the phone: if they happen to be new messages, this has the potential for causing the user to miss a message – which is why the user ought always to do a manual scan of incoming messages before allowing a GDP receive-all.

❑ GSDP channels any messages received by GDP-SMS to the right game – that's not necessarily the game from which you issued Receive All.

Receive All is like checking for e-mail from a friend on your dial-up ISP. You have to go to the trouble of connecting, downloading messages, and disconnecting. There may or may not be a message from your friend. And whether there was or not, you've read in all the other messages.

The ability of GSDP to get the message to the right game is handy for a final test scenario as follows. Just as in the loopback case, you set up two games on the same EPOC machine. You put your own phone within IR contact of your EPOC machine. You then initiate one game, specifying your own phone number as the other player. Then, you can play a game against yourself! – remembering you're paying for the privilege of each move.

This is certainly useful for testing whether you've got the basic setup right, and I found it useful during development to test software functionality.

Using an Ericsson SH888 and the UK Vodafone network, I found that round-trip time from beginning to send a message to hearing the 'received' bleep on the phone was usually 8 seconds. A substantial part of this was EPOC-to-phone communication: you can tell that, because it takes about five seconds to do a receive-all.

This is the fastest way to send a message long-distance using EPOC R5. This whole 13-second round-trip time is shorter than it takes just to connect, via a mobile phone, to a dial-up ISP in order to send a TCP/IP message, and it costs less too.

It's pretty easy to set up connections for sending and receiving messages, but there are just enough things that can go wrong to make life potentially uncomfortable for some average users. Even so, the SMS implementation shows what can be done. I have some more detailed analysis of the issues here, and some suggestions for future work, at the end of the chapter.

From the Inside

Let's have a look at the design of Battleships, and some features of its implementation in C++. As a reminder, here is the class design for Solo Ships:

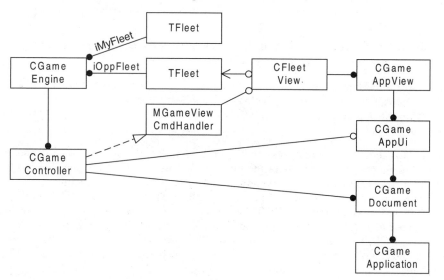

The controller contains the persistent document data required by EPOC's application architecture. The app view uses a single component control, the fleet view of the opponent's fleet. The fleet view uses an `MGameViewCmdHandler`, an interface implemented by the controller. The trick with Solo Ships was to use object-oriented plumbing to connect the opponent's fleet with the engine's `iMyFleet`.

Here's the design for Battleships:

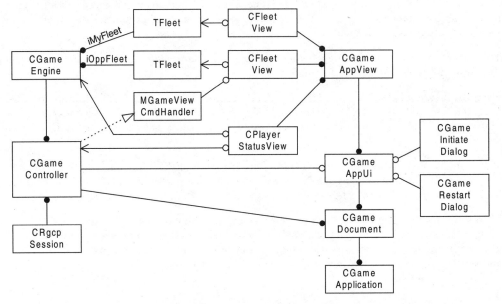

Compared with Solo Ships, the most important difference is that the controller now owns an RGCP stack, shown here by the `CRgcpSession` class. This implies three things:

❑   The controller uses `CRgcpSession` to send BSP requests and responses to the other player

❑   The controller implements `MRgcpHandler` to handle BSP requests and responses from the other player

❑   RGCP's persistent state is now included, along with the engine's persistent state, in the persistent state of the game as a whole

The next most important difference is that, this time, my fleet is my fleet for real, and I get a full and permanent view of it. The opponent's fleet is the opponent's fleet for real: I get a full, if empty, view for it. My view of the opponent's fleet can generate commands, which are handled as usual by the controller in my game.

The Battleships controller is somewhat more complicated than the Solo Ships controller, with 28 public and 23 private functions. It implements the full specification of BSP. The controller has been designed so that all function calls (except construction, destruction, persistence-related functions, and some `const` queries) correspond directly with an event in BSP. That includes events from the app UI, the view, and incoming data from the RGCP session. To assure system integrity, the controller asserts that all events occur in an allowed BSP state, and panics the program if it finds otherwise. It is the responsibility of the event source to pre-check validity – for instance, the opponent's fleet view should not issue a hit request unless the BSP state is my-turn: this particular condition is assured by dimming the view unless the BSP state is my-turn.

Finally the app UI uses two dialogs, to initiate a game (and RGCP communications session), and to start a new game (in the context of the same RGCP communications session).

You can find the code for Battleships in \pep\battleships\, including

Source files	Purpose
engine.cpp, engine.h	The engine: exactly as in Solo Ships
view.cpp, view.h	The fleet view, exactly as in Solo Ships
appview.cpp, appview.h	The app view and player status view
appui.cpp, appui.h	The EIKON application, document, and app UI classes, along with the initiate and new game dialogs
controller.cpp, controller.h	The controller
battleships.rss, battleships.hrh	Resource file and shared constants

You'll also find the AIF source code in \pep\bsaif\.

The Battleships project as a whole also uses TOGS APIs whose source is in \pep\gdp\, \pep\gsdp\ and \pep\rgcp\. If you've read through the walkthrough of Solo Ships in Chapter 14, and the description of BSP in Chapter 17, then the implementation of Battleships will contain few surprises.

I'll pause to look at a few representative functions, so you can get a flavor of how things hang together in a real TOGS game.

The Status View

Before we get involved in the communications code, let's look at the status view. There's not much to learn from its code, which you can read on the CD-ROM, but there are a couple of reminders of the realities of graphic design here.

I hastily wrote the status view for tpg, and spent the minimum possible time updating it for Battleships. Here it is, close up:

```
My go
 SMS


 Me
8 ships
 9 hits

Other
8 ships
 7 hits
```

It's not likely to win any design awards: it's not size independent, and it's not very pretty. It wasn't a very rewarding experience as a developer either: it took me longer to write than the Battleships engine.

The view is hard-coded to 72 pixels wide, to match the size of the toolbar. I had to think quite hard about the short words in this view, and I've stored all the text in Battleships' resource file so that, in theory, the application can be translated into a non-English language. But I'm nervous even about this: my strings are tight even in English, which is usually a good language for short words. In a language like German, it's likely that my strings will be too long, and ugly abbreviations may be necessary.

In fact, good status views are very hard to design. You have to spend a lot of time designing them, a lot of time programming them, and then be prepared for a few iterations. If the status is complicated and the application has to be supremely responsive (a word processor, for example), then you have to program the status view update as a background task using active objects. You need good graphics designers here, and programmers who are dedicated to getting the results right – not, as I was, someone hurrying along to complete a different task.

Handling Hit Requests

Remember that, in Solo Ships, the controller handled hit requests from the view using

```
void CGameController::ViewCmdHitFleet(TInt aX, TInt aY)
    {
    __ASSERT_ALWAYS(IsMyTurn(), Panic(EHitFleetNotMyTurn));

    // Check whether already known
    if(iEngine->iOppFleet.IsKnown(aX, aY))
        {
        iEnv->InfoMsg(R_GAME_ALREADY_KNOWN);
        return;
        }

    // Hit fleet
    iEngine->iOppFleet.SetShipType(aX, aY, iEngine->iMyFleet.ShipType(aX, aY));
    iEngine->iOppFleet.SetHit(aX, aY);

    // Update view
    iAppView->iOppFleetView->DrawTilesNow();

    // If game is won, transition to finished
    if(iEngine->IsWon())
        {
        SetState(EFinished);
        iEnv->InfoMsg(R_GAME_CONGRATULATIONS);
        }
    }
```

This code clearly won't work in a non-communications environment, because its most important two lines,

```
    // Hit fleet
    iEngine->iOppFleet.SetShipType(aX, aY, iEngine->iMyFleet.ShipType(aX, aY));
    iEngine->iOppFleet.SetHit(aX, aY);
```

use object-oriented plumbing, rather than communications, to find the state of the 'opponent's' fleet. In Battleships, the code reads simply:

```
void CGameController::ViewCmdHitFleet(TInt aX, TInt aY)
    {
    __ASSERT_ALWAYS(IsMyTurn(), Panic(EHitFleetNotMyTurn));
    SendHitRequest(aX, aY);
    SetState(EOppTurn);
    iAppView->DrawStatusNow();
    }
```

This code:

- ❏ Asserts that it is called only under the correct conditions – namely, that it's my turn
- ❏ Sends a hit request, using another controller function which, as we'll see shortly, calls an RGCP send
- ❏ Sets the state to the opponent's turn which, as we'll see shortly, has some side effects on the view
- ❏ Asks the app view to redraw the status view

This is classic controller programming in the MVC paradigm: to field an event, update the model, and then update the view.

Checking Conditions

Before any controller function is called, the caller should ensure the correct conditions. The controller itself asserts the correct conditions, and panics the application if they do not apply.

These assertions – which, because I use __ASSERT_ALWAYS, are built into release programs too – are vital aids to ensuring the quality of the released program.

There is a fine judgment call about whether to choose __ASSERT_DEBUG or __ASSERT_ALWAYS: asserts have a code space and runtime performance impact, and you should test code properly before releasing it. So if you can, it's better to use __ASSERT_DEBUG than __ASSERT_ALWAYS. I felt this code was complicated enough to warrant __ASSERT_ALWAYS.

If the choice between always and debug-only is finely balanced, the choice between using asserts and not using them at all is a no-brainer. You simply can't expect to debug state machine code like this effectively unless you use asserts extensively. Their role in ensuring quality is second only to taking care over the design – the kind of thinking that went into the specifications in Chapter 17.

So, the caller is responsible for making sure controller functions get called in the right conditions. There are three interesting cases here:

- ❏ The caller is the app UI: the user can issue commands at any time, so the app UI has to check whether the circumstances are valid and, if not, tell the user it can't execute the command and preferably also indicate why not
- ❏ The caller is the fleet view: the fleet view is prevented from issuing commands to the controller, by being dimmed when the controller is not in my-turn state
- ❏ The caller is RGCP, using one of its handler functions, in response to a datagram received from the other player. The rules of BSP should ensure that only good data gets sent from the other player, and the rules of GDP, GSDP and RGCP should ensure that only the data that was sent, over the intended session, is received. But for one reason or another this might not be the case, so the controller asserts the correct conditions on its RGCP handler functions.

We'll take a brief look at the code involved in the app UI and app view cases. We'll comment further on the RGCP case when we encounter it later.

App UI Checking

Here's an example of the app UI case. When it's my turn, I can choose instead of playing a turn to abandon the game. But I can't do that when it's not my turn. The app UI makes the check:

```
void CGameAppUi::CmdAbandonL()
    {
    // User-friendly check
    if(!iController->IsMyTurn())
        iEikonEnv->LeaveWithInfoMsg(R_GAME_NOT_YOUR_TURN);

    // Confirm with the user
    if(!iEikonEnv->QueryWinL(R_GAME_QUERY_ABANDON))
        return;

    // Do it
    iController->Abandon();
    }
```

The app UI also checks whether the user really wants to abandon the game, before calling the controller. So the controller's Abandon() function should only be called in the right circumstances, and asserts that this is the case:

```
void CGameController::Abandon()
    {
    __ASSERT_ALWAYS(IsMyTurn(), Panic(EAbandonNotMyTurn));
    SendAbandonRequest();
    SetState(EFinished);
    iEnv->InfoMsg(R_GAME_ABANDONED);
    iAppView->DrawStatusNow();
    }
```

Again, the MVC-style implementation of this function is very simple.

Dimming the View

The view is prevented from issuing commands at the wrong time by dimming it unless the state is my-turn. The controller includes support for this, in SetState():

```
void CGameController::SetState(TState aState)
    {
    // Update app view, if needed, for change in 'my turn' status
    if(iAppView)
        {
        if(iState != EMyTurn && aState == EMyTurn)
            iAppView->SetMyTurnAndDrawNow(ETrue);
        else if(iState == EMyTurn && aState != EMyTurn)
            iAppView->SetMyTurnAndDrawNow(EFalse);
        }

    // Set state as requested
    iState = aState;
    }
```

`CGameAppView::SetMyTurnAndDrawNow()` is implemented as:

```
void CGameAppView::SetMyTurnAndDrawNow(TBool aMyTurn)
    {
    iOppFleetView->SetDimmed(!aMyTurn);
    iOppFleetView->DrawBordersNow();
    }
```

CONE won't channel pointer events to a dimmed control.

Key processing is the responsibility of the app view:

```
TKeyResponse CGameAppView::OfferKeyEventL(const TKeyEvent& aKeyEvent,
                                          TEventCode aType)
    {
    // Let the opponent-fleet view handle the key
    if(iOppFleetView->IsDimmed())
        return EKeyWasNotConsumed;
    else
        return iOppFleetView->OfferKeyEventL(aKeyEvent, aType);
    }
```

So, pointer and key events can't go to the view except in the right circumstances. And, if I forgot to cater for every case in my app view programming, so that I can accidentally send a key event to the controller when it's not my turn, then the controller will pick this up with its assert.

I did forget a couple things during testing. For instance, I forgot to set the dimmed state correctly after restoring. I made that good in the following function,

```
void CGameAppView::SetController(CGameController* aController)
    {
    iController = aController;
    iEngine = iController->iEngine;
    iStatusView->SetController(iController);
    iMyFleetView->SetFleet(&(iEngine->iMyFleet));
    iOppFleetView->SetFleet(&(iEngine->iOppFleet));
    iOppFleetView->SetCmdHandler(iController);
    iOppFleetView->SetDimmed(!iController->IsMyTurn());
    DrawNow();
    iController->SetAppView(this);
    }
```

by inserting the line:

```
    iOppFleetView->SetDimmed(!iController->IsMyTurn());
```

The `SetController()` function is called from `HandleModelChangeL()` as part of the standard processing when a new model is loaded – that is, when the state of the game is restored from a file saved by a previous game.

It's easy to deduce a general rule for testing file-based applications from this. For each new feature you develop, you need to test at least twice, once in 'normal' circumstances, a second time after saving, closing the app, and reloading, and perhaps even a third time when you load a new file without closing the app.

Hit processing: the Full Story

We saw how the view command handler initiated hit request processing, in
`CGameController::ViewCmdHitFleet()`. The request now proceeds in four stages:

- ❑   I send a request using RGCP in my game
- ❑   The opponent receives the request using RGCP in their game
- ❑   The opponent sends a response using RGCP in their game
- ❑   I receive the response using RGCP in my game

Of course, the opponent's response doesn't actually get sent until the opponent makes their next
request. But the handling of my hit request doesn't depend on the opponent's next request, so we can
look at these four operations in isolation.

Sending the Request

Here's `SendHitRequest()`:

```
void CGameController::SendHitRequest(TInt aX, TInt aY)
    {
    TBuf8<10> buffer;
    RDesWriteStream writer(buffer);
    writer.WriteUint8L(aX);
    writer.WriteUint8L(aY);
    writer.CommitL();
    iRgcp->SendRequest(KGameOpcodeHit, buffer);
    }
```

I use a descriptor write stream to formulate a request, encoding the (x,y) coordinates I want to hit. I then
call RGCP `SendRequest()` specifying the hit-request opcode. The descriptor write stream is a
convenient API, and it enables me to guarantee the external format of the BSP hit request.

RGCP then sends the hit request (along with my previous response) using GSDP. The datagram arrives
at the other player's machine and is routed by GSDP to the correct game instance. RGCP cracks the
datagram into response and request, gets the previous response handled, and then calls code to handle
the current request.

If the GSDP datagram *didn't* get through, then I could re-send it. If I re-send but the datagram *did* get
through, then RGCP at the other player's end would drop the duplicate packet.

Either way, there is a guarantee that my request is handled only once.

Handling the Request

Here's how the request is handled. By implementing `MRgcpHandler`, the game controller in the other
player's game codes a first-level handler that calls a specific handler function depending on the request
opcode:

```
void CGameController::RgcpHandleRequest(TInt aOpcode, const TDesC8& aData)
    {
    switch(aOpcode)
        {
    case KGameOpcodeStart:
        HandleStartRequest(aData);
        break;
    case KGameOpcodeRestart:
        HandleRestartRequest();
        break;
    case KGameOpcodeNop:
        break;
    case KGameOpcodeAbandon:
        HandleAbandonRequest();
        break;
    case KGameOpcodeHit:
        HandleHitRequest(aData);
        break;
    default:
        Panic(EHandleRequestBadOpcode);
        }
    }
```

The hit request will be handled using the HandleHitRequest() function, which starts as follows:

```
void CGameController::HandleHitRequest(const TDesC8& aData)
    {
    __ASSERT_ALWAYS(IsOppTurn(), Panic(EHandleHitReqNotOppTurn));

    // Crack parameters
    RDesReadStream reader(aData);
    TInt x = reader.ReadUint8L();
    TInt y = reader.ReadUint8L();
```

This code begins by asserting that the hit request is being handled in BSP opp-turn state, and then uses a read-stream to get the function parameters.

This code will panic if the hit-request opcode is received at the wrong time, and will leave if the hit-request opcode comes at the right time but lacks the two further bytes in the request data. Downstream, the engine will panic in debug builds only if the (x, y) coordinates are outside the range 0..7.

This exemplifies a difficulty in communications programming: checking incoming data, and responding to problems in it:

❑ Should you panic (because there's nothing you can do, and there's no point in carrying on the game)?

❑ Should you drop the packet (say, leaving with KErrCorrupt) and issue a meaningful error dialog to the user? If so, how do you get really *meaningful* error information to the user?

❑ Should you drop the packet silently, so that the user, who is more interested in Battleships, a nice easy game, than the complexities of BSP and RGCP, doesn't get confused by communications-type error messages?

❑ Or should you trust that nothing will ever go wrong, and not implement any error checking at all?

Programmers are too fallible for it to be safe to assume that nothing will ever go wrong. We are technically fallible: our programs have bugs. We're morally fallible too – at least someone must be, because malicious programs keep on getting written. So it's a good idea to check incoming data, and so minimize exposure to all the things that could potentially be wrong with it. And it may not always be right to panic the user's program because of bad incoming data from another place.

Checks on incoming data should be made with the following goals in mind:

❑ Programming errors must be caught early – ideally, during debug phase, and in debug builds only

❑ Neither programming errors nor malicious acts should cause a program to lose truly personal data

❑ In cases where the *program* can't tell whether incoming data could cause personal data loss, the program should either reject the data out of hand, or give the *user* an opportunity to decide what to do, or should come with a general warning to the user to take precautions.

Battleships, along with the specifications of TOGS and GDP implementations, meets these criteria. If the program panics, the only thing that's lost is the state of the shared game between me and the person whose program caused the crash – not truly personal data. Admittedly Battleships meets the third criterion trivially, because the circumstances it caters for don't arise. In more complex situations (say, launching an executable e-mail attachment, which could be a virus) a user check *is* required.

Whole books could be written about this, but we'll move on to see what happens to the hit request. `HandleHitRequest()` continues:

```
// Hit the square
TFleet& fleet = iEngine->iMyFleet;
fleet.SetHit(x,y);
SendHitResponse(x, y, fleet.ShipType(x,y));
```

This is the code that ties together my hit request with the real state of the opponent's fleet, and sends the response back. We'll consider `SendHitResponse()` below.

BSP is designed so that the hit response contains a hit response – no more. So the code above was unconditional, and uncomplicated. However, after receiving a hit, the opponent has to analyze the consequences – whether it means the opponent has lost the game, for instance – and deal with them. `HandleHitRequest()` continues:

```
// Update view
iAppView->iMyFleetView->SetCursor(x,y);
iAppView->iMyFleetView->DrawTilesNow();

// If game is lost, issue a nop-request and transition to finished
if(iEngine->IsLost())
    {
    SendNopRequest();
    SetState(EFinished);
    }
else // Transition to my-turn
    SetState(EMyTurn);

// Update view
iAppView->DrawNow();
}
```

Firstly, there's an MVC view update: the other player updates 'my fleet' by setting the cursor to the hit location and redrawing its tiles.

If the game is lost, the other player's controller immediately sends a NOP request back to me. That flushes the buffer and causes the hit response to be sent immediately. That means I get to see the hit response, and to find out that I've won the game, without waiting for the other player to do anything. The state then changes, and the view is redrawn.

In the cold light of day, this looks like a bug. The final line should be
`iAppView->DrawStatusNow()`, *not* `DrawNow()`. *The bug is subtle, because it simply causes wasted redraws. You can tell what's happening, if you play the game on an emulator and are able to set up auto-flush so that redraw activity runs slow enough to see the unnecessary activity. That's not straightforward to do in loopback mode!*

Sending the Response

Here's the code used to send the hit response:

```
void CGameController::SendHitResponse(TInt aX, TInt aY,
                                      TShip::TShipType aShipType)
    {
    TBuf8<10> buffer;
    RDesWriteStream writer(buffer);
    writer.WriteUint8L(aX);
    writer.WriteUint8L(aY);
    writer.WriteUint8L(aShipType);
    writer.CommitL();
    iRgcp->SendResponse(KGameOpcodeHit, buffer);
    }
```

The code is pretty similar to the code for sending the hit request.

Handling the Response

When the response gets back to me, my controller handles it initially in `RgcpHandleResponse()`, which contains a switch statement identical in form to that in `RgcpHandleRequest()`. All being well, control then transfers to `HandleHitResponse()`:

```
void CGameController::HandleHitResponse(const TDesC8& aData)
    {
    __ASSERT_ALWAYS(IsOppTurn(), Panic(EHandleHitRespNotOppTurn));

    // Crack parameters
    RDesReadStream reader(aData);
    TInt x = reader.ReadUint8L();
    TInt y = reader.ReadUint8L();
    TShip::TShipType type = (TShip::TShipType)reader.ReadUint8L();

    // Update engine
    TFleet& fleet = iEngine->iOppFleet;
    if(type == TShip::ESea)
        fleet.SetSea(x, y);
    else
        fleet.SetShipType(x, y, type);
    fleet.SetHit(x, y);
```

```
        // Update view
        iAppView->iOppFleetView->SetCursor(x, y);
        iAppView->iOppFleetView->DrawTilesNow();

        // If you won the game, transition to finished
        if(iEngine->IsWon())
            SetState(EFinished);

        // Update view
        iAppView->DrawStatusNow();
        }
```

The code starts off similarly to the request handler. I assert the right condition, and crack the response data using a descriptor read stream.

Then I update my internal representation of the opponent's fleet, and my view of it. I check whether this means I've won and, if so, change state to finished. Finally, I update the status display – which will show either that it's my turn, or that I've won the game.

That completes the story of a hit request. What we could do with two lines of code in Solo Ships, and only a few lines in tpg, required the entire TOGS stack, and all the processing you've seen in the Battleships controller, to play a game against a different player.

Taking Battleships Further

We had a lot of fun developing Battleships as the flagship example program for the book. We aimed to deliver an example that would show EPOC's capabilities as a communications platform and provide lots of excellent code for you to use as a starting point for your own programs. With Battleships as it is, I think we've achieved that. But there's plenty more to do, so I'll conclude this chapter – indeed, the book's coverage of EPOC's C++ APIs – with some thoughts on taking Battleships and TOGS further.

The main categories of improvement are:

❑   Adding finesse on the Battleships game

❑   Other games

❑   Single-player games

❑   Improvements in EPOC and TOGS

Better Battleships

It's not hard to see how the Battleships game itself could be improved to increase its end-user appeal. Here are a few ideas.

Add Sound

Use the sound APIs documented in the EPOC SDK. See \boss\eik8\ for examples of the three sound APIs first provided in EPOC R1 and carried forward to EPOC R5.

Think about the user, and think about the user's friends. Don't build in too much sound and let the user turn it off as an option.

Better Status

As I commented earlier, the status view was written in haste. It could obviously be improved.

Integration with Address Book

Instead of requiring the user to type in the phone number manually, you could integrate with the Contacts Model API to allow you to select from people in your Contacts database who have a mobile phone number.

The Contacts Model documentation isn't available on the SDKs in the book's CD-ROM. Beta documentation has recently been published in the Professional Members' download area on the Symbian Developer Network website. This will eventually make its way into more public places.

User-controlled Layout

As it's presently implemented, Battleships is really two single-player games. The computer sets up both users' games, and the moves I make are largely independent of the moves of my opponent. Result: we're really playing two games against the clock, and the one who completes their game first is not really so much the winner, as the best (or luckiest) player. In fact if we took this view to an extreme, we could considerably save on the messaging involved in a game of Battleships.

In a real Battleships game, fleet layout is what really enables each player to test the psychology of the other. Adding an option for user-specified layout would make a good addition to the interest in playing the game. The code required to support this, in engine, app UI and view, would be non-trivial.

Random First-move Preferences

The first-move preference specification is awkward, and gives the users one more thing to think about. There's a strong argument for removing it from the UI and replacing it with a randomly set first-move preference. This could be done without changing BSP: the first-move calculation is still done from within the controller when the initiating player receives the listening player's initiate-response.

This is a good example of how to make a UI simpler, by removing choices that generate more confusion than flexibility.

To remove the choice about initiate/listen from the UI isn't possible with SMS, or even desirable. But the idea of making a call or sending a message is well enough understood. Perhaps the terminology could be better – Send First Message and Receive First Message – but this terminology doesn't suit protocols like IR.

With IR, it might be easier to remove the initiate/listen feature altogether, though any design would need to inspect the consequences up and down the TOGS stack.

Little things, maybe. But these are among the first UI features our end-users will see, and if they appear hard to use, some would-be users won't take a second look.

Chat Channel

BSP is sufficient to implement the rules of Battleships and to make the game playable. But a game of Battleships played between two players in a room, using old-style paper-and-pencil methods, wouldn't be simply a set of hit requests and responses. There would be comments, taunts, discussions about when to play the next game, etc. Chat adds to the psychology and interest of a real Battleships game, just as much as user-controlled fleet layout.

It would be nice to build in a chat channel to Battleships to support this kind of chat.

However, BSP is built on RGCP – a *conversational* protocol in which players take it in turn to send and receive messages. That's basically unsuitable for chat.

My favorite scheme to implement a chat channel would be to implement it at the GSDP level, so that the Battleships game has another connection to the GSDP server. That's easy – EPOC's client-server architecture supports multiple independent connections from any thread.

At the UI level, there would be no need to alter the start-new-game dialog (chat initiate/listen details are the same as for the game). The view would have to be altered to include chat data – or, as in tpg, a multi-view approach could be used. The persistent form of the game would have to be altered to include a log of chat – perhaps on a different stream from the main game data, so that chat could be added optionally without breaking the format of existing games.

With this scheme, each chat message would be a different GDP datagram from the datagram containing each BSP response/request pair. That's unfortunate, because of the real cost of a text message. There are many options for addressing this:

❑ Do nothing: the user pays the cost of each message, but no higher-level protocol needs to be altered

❑ Save datagrams at connection time: you don't need to send two initiate packets. In the BSP initiate packet, send the initiating partner's GSDP port ID allocated for chat, and in the BSP initiate-response, send the listening partner's GSDP port ID allocated for chat. This relies on GSDP's support for allocating a port ID without participating strictly in the initiate/listen protocol.

❑ Save datagrams at hit-request time: include an optional message with each hit request, and also with the initiate request.

❑ Low-level protocol piggy-backing: implement a completely different piggy-backing and reliability scheme than that supported by RGCP, which takes the chat requirement into account, and optimizes accordingly.

In my view, the first option isn't going far enough, while the final option is probably going too far. The middle two options require alterations to BSP, but not to the underlying TOGS protocols. If BSP is changed, then a different game protocol ID needs to be assigned, otherwise the changed BSP won't successfully interoperate with the existing BSP.

> *Incidentally the chat requirement – whether verbal or protocol-assisted – is a good reason for not removing the legend on the borders of the fleet view. At first I thought those legends were redundant. But having played the game with some humans, it quickly became apparent that without them it would be hard to talk about the game.*

Mid-game Protocol Change

It would be nice if the GDP protocol could be changed mid-game, so that a game could be played using long-range messaging (SMS) when the players are far apart, and short-range, free, messaging (IR) when they meet.

If the GDP protocol were changed, this would imply a change in the addressing information used by the players. However, the GSDP port IDs must not be changed: they are what define the game session.

This could probably be kludged without changing TOGS, but I suspect the optimal solution would involve changes at the GSDP level, if only for proper encapsulation.

Better Capability and State Support in TOGS

A characteristic of protocol stacks is that they don't represent complete encapsulation. For instance, it doesn't make much sense to use RGCP without being aware of the underlying realities of GSDP and GDP, even perhaps the realities of a particular GDP protocol. RGCP adds value to these layers, but doesn't entirely encapsulate them.

As a consequence, an RGCP application such as Battleships needs access to the underlying specifics. For instance, is the current GDP protocol networked, and does it require receive-all? What GDP protocols does the GSDP server support? How can I set, store, and restore a particular GDP and GSDP configuration?

At the moment, TOGS handles these issues with ad-hoc exposure and pass-through of getter and setter functions up and down the stack. A better system would be to use the capabilities pattern at each level:

❑   Define a struct that includes all capability and setting information for a given level

❑   Define getter and setter functions for this struct, which change its members

❑   Define getter and setter functions for a protocol level, which get a struct from the level's current settings, or set the settings from the values in a struct

Clearly, a different struct would be required for each level in the protocol stack.

The capabilities pattern is particularly worthwhile for a protocol layer with many capabilities, especially if that layer often resides towards the bottom of a stack.

Other Games

TOGS isn't designed for Battleships alone. Any turn-based game could be implemented on a TOGS stack, using GDP, GSDP, and RGCP unchanged, but replacing BSP and the Battleships game.

Suitable games would include Chess, Checkers (Draughts), Backgammon, Tic-Tac-Toe (Noughts and Crosses), Connect Four, Scrabble, and many other games, including two-player card games.

The developer investment required to produce a good game on top of TOGS is not high, since you don't have to build in the intelligence required for a human-versus-computer version of these games. You only have to specify and implement the protocols required to communicate moves, the rules needed to referee attempted moves, and a GUI.

Other games will probably use a variant of BSP. However, the details will be subtly different. Board games are based on a single shared game state (the board and pieces on it) that is public to both players. Battleships is a game of two halves, in which each player's initial fleet disposition is initially unshared, but as the game progresses it is selectively revealed to the other player.

Many games include some combination of shared state and unshared state. In Scrabble, for instance, the knowledge of your letters is private to you, the unused letter pool is unknown to anyone, and the board state is completely public. Many card games rely on guessing unshared state for much of the interest in the game. The whole intrigue in multi-player Diplomacy (though not the two-player version) arises from selective, and not always truthful, sharing of state between players.

The degree of shared state will have some effects on your game protocol. A key rule in gaming is to minimize disclosure – that is, don't share things at the protocol level and hide them at the UI level. For instance, in Battleships, it would be possible to exchange the entire state of each player's board at the beginning of the game, so that the response to hit requests could be instant. But then a knowledgeable player could find out the state of the opponent's game, and win in 20 moves.

Single-player Games

Solo Ships was an attractive and useful single-player version of Battleships – possible because Battleships is really two half-games.

Another single-player form of Battleships would involve the computer as a genuine opponent. The basic game design would use two `CGameEngines`, but only one `CGameAppView`. Instead of having an app view, the other engine would have a `CGameComputerPlayer`, which would make hit requests on behalf of the computer.

For a minimum level of skill, the computer player could make random hits on unknown squares. The engine includes some trivial logic to mark squares as sea, if they are diagonally adjacent to partial known ships, or directly adjacent to complete known ships, so random hits on unknown squares would not be a bad start for the computer player.

For a greater level of skill, the computer player could treat Battleships as a **constraint satisfaction problem** (CSP), a standard form of problem for which artificial intelligence research has developed many general methods. A little data from a few hits will generate enough constraints that a CSP approach can considerably improve on a purely random hit request. And a carefully chosen initial hit strategy will do better than a purely random initial hit strategy.

Many of the two-player games mentioned above could be improved by the addition of the option for a computer opponent. In the case of the more complex games, such as Chess, the barriers to entry are high, as engines suitable for deployment on EPOC already exist, and have in some cases been ported from bodies of code that have evolved over two or three decades.

Infrastructure Improvements

Besides improving the game – or using a different game – there are many things we could do to improve the facilities for games in general, as provided by both EPOC and the TOGS stack.

EPOC Release 5 and TOGS as they stand provide an attractive enough platform for turn-based games played at both short and long distance. Probably, the attraction of the long-distance option is limited by the trickiness involved in using GDP-SMS. In future EPOC releases, with much better integrated phones, SMS and other text messaging protocols will become transparently easy to use, which will boost the appeal of TOGS-based games enormously.

In forthcoming releases, EPOC will begin to use Unicode. TOGS has done all that is sensible to prepare for Unicode, but has taken the 'masterly inactivity' approach to converting between character- and byte-oriented data. That will need addressing for real Unicode builds.

TOGS is designed specifically for two-player turn-based games and can also support two-player chat. For multi-player games, or for real-time games, GDP and GSDP will still be useful, but alternatives to RGCP, tailored for multi-player or real-time requirements, will be needed. Some GDP implementations are clearly more suitable than others for real-time: any kind of pull protocol (such as receive-all for GDP-SMS) is clearly ruled out.

EPOC will also include a media system with better sound facilities and, eventually, support for an increasing range of graphics and video formats. This has obvious application to games. In the longer term, it's possible that many aspects of EPOC's architecture may evolve to support real-time games: this requires sound, graphics, and communications improvements, some of which will be delivered in software, some on silicon.

Here are some more ideas for taking TOGS forward with EPOC.

Better Long-distance Messaging

GDP-SMS provides a messaging transport that shows the viability and usefulness of long-range wireless messaging. It is the cheapest and fastest way to send a message to another EPOC machine, using only a mobile phone to access a communications network.

Ultimately, the UI behind this kind of messaging will be very simple, because the phone metaphors (initiate = send first message, listen = wait to receive first message, address = phone number) are well understood by end-users.

Presently, there are a couple of rough edges on GDP-SMS:

- ❑ The user has to pull messages, using Receive All, rather than having the network and system push them
- ❑ The user has to be careful to set up the phone and the EPOC machine so that GDP-SMS can link correctly to the phone, both for sending and receiving messages
- ❑ Receive All marks non-GDP messages as 'read'
- ❑ SMS is supported only on GSM networks

More tightly integrated telephony will address push, setup, and the distinction between GDP and other messages.

In the SMS world, Nokia has defined Smart Messaging protocols which could be exploited to deliver a much more satisfactory method of distinguishing between GDP messages, end-user text messages, and other types of Smart Message.

Smart Messaging is a solution for today. In the near future, WAP's wireless datagram protocol (WDP) is a better and more general solution. WDP, like all aspects of WAP, is bearer-independent, and so will support other bearers such as North America's TDMA. When EPOC includes WDP support, it will be an excellent basis for GDP.

EPOC will also deliver its own bearer-independent messaging infrastructure designed to ensure that an even wider generality of incoming messages are routed to the application that is intended to handle them.

Better Short-distance Messaging

The IR implementation of GDP works very well, and enables two players in the same room to have a good game of Battleships.

One oddity that end-users notice when playing Battleships over IR is that you don't get the hit response immediately – only when the other player takes a turn.

That makes sense in the case of SMS, where you're not in direct touch with the player and can't distinguish between time being used to send a message, and the time the other player needs in order to think about their next move.

But in IR, the economics and the game dynamics are different. This led me to propose, in my description of RGCP in Chapter 17, an enhancement which uses time-outs for acknowledgements, and doesn't piggy-back responses, for use when appropriate for the GDP protocol. I dubbed this enhancement QRGCP.

When EPOC supports Bluetooth short-range messaging, a GDP-BT driver would make a very nice addition to the suite.

We decided that GDP-IR was a point-to-point protocol, even though IrDA supports a kind of networking with addresses valid for a session. The decision for IR was easy: addresses are user-hostile, and the line-of-sight requirement has a clear end-user meaning in relation to a point-to-point connection.

With Bluetooth, the decision will be more difficult. The whole point of Bluetooth is to enable piconets to be setup up between multiple devices in sub-10-meter proximity but without line-of-sight communication. During the lifetime of a piconet, Bluetooth nodes enter and exit in arbitrary sequence. During the lifetime of a particular set of nodes in a piconet, each node has a fixed address – but that address has no lasting meaning, and is probably even more user-hostile than the addresses used in IrDA.

GDP-BT will probably need to be a networked GDP protocol, and will need to use a friendly form of EPOC machine address rather than the transient Bluetooth node address.

New EPOC Reference Designs

Symbian's new reference designs, in addition to including tighter integration with telephony, offer new opportunities.

Crystal has a GUI similar to EIKON. From the perspective of a game developer, the main features of Crystal will be Unicode, and the tighter integration of telephony already described.

Quartz, with its 240x320 portrait screen and pen-only design, will require new thinking about Battleships' UI: it won't make sense to put both fleet views on screen at once, and the player status view will need to be reworked. You can see, however, that the vast majority of Battleships code won't need to be altered, even for Quartz: the engine, fleet view, controller, and TOGS, which account for all of the difficult code except the status view, won't need to be touched at all.

Many Pearl machines will be 'closed' in the sense that they don't support the installation of software by end-users. However, there is room for direct marketing to OEMs and perhaps to distributors. The smaller screen sizes of many Pearl devices will present greater UI challenges in game design.

Other GDP Implementations, and Other Platforms

There's no need to wait for future generations of EPOC to do lots of interesting things with GDP, TOGS, and Battleships.

On EPOC R5, I thought of some other TOGS implementations – mostly of academic interest, but some could form the basis of a good commercial idea.

❑ The clipboard (see `baclipb.h`, the source code for Word application, and documentation in the SDK). Sending a datagram is equivalent to pasting to the clipboard. Clipboard text can be copied into an e-mail, sent to any internet e-mail address, received onto an EPOC machine, and copied from the e-mail to the clipboard. Receive all is equivalent to checking the clipboard for GDP data and copying it if some exists. The clipboard file could possibly be monitored so that explicit GDP receive-all isn't needed: if the clipboard is monitored, a system for preventing undesired immediate local loopback is needed.

❑ Serial cable: a direct serial connection between two machines, or between emulator and EPOC machine using the EPOC Connect cable, could be useful for testing.

❑ TCP/IP: this begs interesting questions, because EPOC R5 machines can only initiate sessions with a dial-up ISP (or private dial-up network), and they get their IP address allocated dynamically. So what destination address would you specify for a GDP datagram? One possibility here would be to use TCP/IP as the basis of playing against server-hosted games, in which a destination address could be of the form `games.some-company.com/battleships/martint:20`, including game protocol, user account, and optional port number information.

The TCP/IP idea isn't worth it for games between two EPOC machines: phone-based messaging is better. However, server-based facilities of one kind or another offer many interesting commercial ideas for TOGS-based games, and indeed for new game technology as it evolves. That could be an application for TCP/IP – or, in the very near future, for WAP protocols such as WDP.

The Palm III and later models include an IrDA stack that can be used to exchange contacts and schedule information with EPOC R5 machines. This stack could also be used to deliver a GDP-IR implementation. Along with a TOGS implementation on Palm, this would enable Battleships and other games to be played between EPOC and Palm machines.

GDP-SMS could be implemented on a PC, communicating with a phone via its IR port (available on most laptops) or a serial cable (available for many data-capable phones). Thus, TOGS could be implemented on a PC and used to play against EPOC-based TOGS games.

There is no reason why TOGS stacks couldn't be written in Java, especially on TCP/IP-based servers. A Java API to TOGS, using JNI over the C++ implementation, would also be possible on EPOC.

Summary

This is the end of the beginning.

In the book so far, we've concentrated on EPOC's C++ APIs and covered the basics, graphics and the EIKON GUI framework, communications and system programming. We've used Battleships to motivate much of this, especially the communications and system programming chapters.

You now have enough information to program EPOC C++ with confidence, and to find your way around the SDK for additional information, example code, and source code.

In the following final five chapters, we'll see what Symbian provides in addition to its C++ programming platform.

Part Four

A Full Platform

Symbian's technology platform is based on EPOC, a robust, compact and powerful system that spans from kernel to application suite, including communications, data management and graphics, designed using object-oriented techniques, and engineered in C++. That's a powerful platform for application and system delivery, and since it's specifically Symbian technology, we've dedicated the majority of the book to it.

But it's by no means the whole story. To paint the full picture, you need to include Symbian's implementations of industry-standard technologies such as Java and WAP, our additional programming systems for rapid application development and connectivity, and some guidance for porting valuable code written for other systems to work on EPOC. I've invited experts in these fields to contribute chapters on each of these subjects.

In Chapter 23, Jonathan Allin describes Symbian's Java implementation. On EPOC R5, we have an efficient Java Compatible implementation of JDK 1.1.4. In future EPOC releases, we will implement Personal Java and JavaPhone APIs with rich profiles.

In Chapter 24, Mark Heath describes WAP and its significance for future EPOC devices.

Symbian and other companies working with EPOC have now had plenty of opportunity to build up experience in porting code from standard C environments. John Forrest, of Purple Software, with wide academic and commercial experience of different development environments, contributes useful guidance in Chapter 25, including an introduction to the EPOC C standard library. Even if you're planning on writing native EPOC code from scratch, this chapter provides a useful angle on EPOC C++ programming, seen through the expectations generated by other software engineering backgrounds.

OPL is a rapid application development language with a long history on EPOC and its predecessors. Tim Richardson describes OPL in Chapter 26.

Last but not least, EPOC Connect is Symbian's solution for connectivity and data synchronization between EPOC machines and PCs. As well as a complete product, EPOC Connect includes APIs and an SDK that enables you to write powerful integration programs in any COM-aware language on the PC. In Chapter 27, Mark Shackman outlines this API, and provides examples in MFC C++ and Visual Basic.

23

Developing with Java

Symbian has made a strong commitment to Java. EPOC release 5 includes a Java virtual machine, supported by an EPOC SDK for Java that runs under Windows. Java is now a permanent part of the EPOC platform, and it is expected that every wireless information device, or WID, running EPOC will include a JVM. Java and C++ will be on an equal footing: they will have the same visibility, be of the same quality, and enjoy the same level of technical support. The Java implementation has driven (and continues to drive) changes in EPOC, in order to ensure that EPOC provides a first class Java platform.

This chapter provides an overview of Java on the EPOC platform. In it, we will:

❑   Review the EPOC Java implementation and the synergy between wireless information devices, Java, and EPOC

❑   Explore the EPOC SDK for Java, working through an example and making use of all the SDK tools as we go

❑   Look at how to use Java's native interface API (JNI) to access EPOC resources that are not directly accessible to Java applications

❑   Cover design issues that should be considered when writing Java applications for EPOC, or when adapting existing applications

❑   Take a look at the future of Java on EPOC

The first few sections can be read without a detailed knowledge of Java, while the later sections assume some level of Java expertise.

Java, Then and Now

On May 23, 1995, John Gage, director of the Science Office for Sun Microsystems, and Marc Andreessen, cofounder and executive vice president at Netscape, announced that Java technology was real, it was official, and it was going to be incorporated into Netscape Navigator.

Java technology was originally created as a programming tool – part of a small Sun project whose purpose was to anticipate and plan for the 'next wave' in computing. The project team's initial conclusion was that at least one significant trend would be the convergence of digitally controlled consumer devices and computers.

In the summer of 1992, the team emerged with a working demonstration: an interactive, handheld, home-entertainment device controller with an animated touch screen user interface. The device was called *7 ("StarSeven"), named after an "answer your phone from any extension" feature of the phone system in the team's office. In the demonstration, Duke, the now familiar Java technology mascot, was shown waving and doing cartwheels on the screen. The *7 device was able to control a wide range of entertainment platforms and appliances because it ran on an entirely new, processor-independent language. The new language was named 'Oak', after the tree outside the office window.

The *7 type of device was aimed at the TV set-top box and video-on-demand industries. Unfortunately, these industries were in their infancy and still trying to settle on viable business models. However, the technology was also right for the rapidly developing Internet. Oak became Java, and the first alpha release (version 1.0a2) was made available in March 1995, quickly capturing developer mind share. The agreement with Netscape gave the Java language credibility, and instant market access.

The first stable and really usable version of Java was the Java Development Kit 1.0.2, made available in 1996.

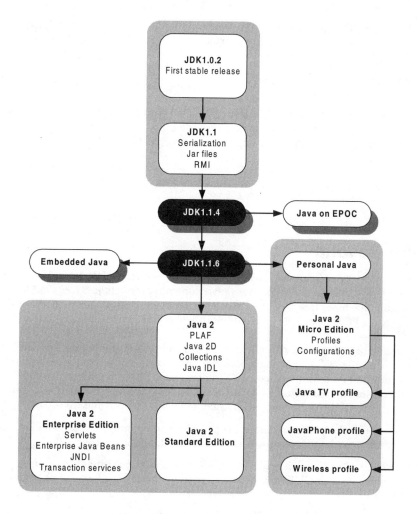

JDK 1.1

JDK 1.1 introduced a raft of new features, significantly widening Java's scope and usefulness. These are fully described in docs/relnotes/features.html, in your JDK 1.1 installation, but those of particular interest to WIDs include:

- ❏ Full internationalization, providing locales, collation services, and Unicode support.

- ❏ JAR (Java Archive) files, a file format that aggregates many files into a single file, and also supports compression. This makes transferring applications simpler and faster, particularly over HTTP. A JAR file can be digitally signed so that its point of origin can be authenticated and to ensure that it has not been tampered with.

- ❏ A security model that supports key management, certificate management, access control, and signed JAR files.

- ❏ Java Native Interface (JNI): a standard programming interface for accessing native methods from Java, and for embedding the Java virtual machine into native applications.

- ❏ Improved GUI facilities, including lightweight components, support for printing, clipboard, and a delegation-based event model.

JDK 1.1 went through a number of versions, from JDK 1.1.1 through to JDK 1.1.8. These were essentially bug fixes, though some new features were added. For instance, 1.1.6 allows RMI over IIOP, and added a JIT (Just In Time) compiler to improve run-time performance.

> **Symbian's current Java implementation is based on JDK 1.1.4.**

JDK 1.2 and Beyond

Java's horizons were extended again by JDK 1.2. In fact, the step from JDK 1.1 to JDK 1.2 was so great that Sun renamed JDK 1.2 as Java 2 (http://www.java.sun.com/products/jdk/1.2/java2.html). Java 2 is intended for desktop machines that have lots of processing power and memory, so although it's not of direct benefit to us as EPOC developers, the additions and enhancements are still interesting:

- ❏ The addition of Swing, a set of GUI components with a "pluggable look and feel", implemented in Java. The pluggable look and feel makes it straightforward to assign an OS-specific look and feel (Motif, Microsoft Windows, MacOS) or a uniform look and feel (Java Look & Feel) to an application, or to create a new look and feel. Swing also added a large number of new GUI components, such as tabbed panes, tables, and trees.

- ❏ Java 2D, a set of classes for advanced 2D graphics and imaging. These provide a single comprehensive model that encompasses line art, text, and images.

- ❏ The Accessibility API, which provides a clean interface to assisting technologies that interact and communicate with GUI components (for use by the disabled as well as the temporarily able-bodied).

- ❏ The Collections Framework, a unified framework for representing and manipulating collections.

- ❏ The Input Method Framework, enabling all text editing components to receive Japanese, Chinese, or Korean text input through input methods. An input method lets users enter thousands of different characters using keyboards with far fewer keys.

- ❏ The Java Sound API engine that replaced the JDK 1.1 sound engine, enabling playback of WAV, AIFF, AU, MIDI, and RMF files with much higher sound quality, both by applications and applets.

- ❏ The Java IDL API, which added CORBA capability to the Java platform.

- ❏ Security enhancements, allowing fine-grained access control for a particular resource.

- ❏ Enhancements to Java Beans, RMI, serialization, JAR, JNI, reflection, and JDBC.

- ❏ Faster memory allocation and garbage collection.

- ❏ Performance improvements to RMI and object serialization.

Of more interest to us is **Personal Java**. This is an offshoot from JDK 1.1 that's aimed at smaller devices with limited resources, and for creating networked applications for such devices for home, office and mobile use. It provides an improved class-loading model, resulting in significant savings in RAM compared to JDK 1.1. It also introduces a degree of choice of installation size, to allow tailoring to small devices. For instance, the `java.io.File` class can be omitted from devices with no accessible filing system. We'll discuss Personal Java in more detail later in the chapter.

Embedded Java, again based on JDK 1.1, is aimed at closed systems. Such systems generally have no user interface and are intended for a single application.

At JavaOne in 1999, Sun realigned its products into **editions**, principally to make it easier for developers to target Java applications for particular industries or device classes. Three editions are defined:

❑ Java 2 platform, standard edition (J2SE). This is Java 2.

❑ Java 2 platform, enterprise edition (J2EE). Aimed at developers who want to write distributed, multi-tier, transactional applications for the enterprise. Additions include Servlets, Enterprise Java Beans, Java's naming and directory interface, and transaction APIs.

❑ Java 2 platform, micro edition (J2ME). This is targeted at consumer electronics and embedded devices.

J2ME includes wireless information devices in its remit, so it's of great interest to us. It provides a process for defining **profiles** targeted at a particular industry or class of device. A profile consists of a subset of the standard Java classes, together with classes developed for the particular industry or device class in question. I'll have more to say about this later as well.

Why Java?

Before thinking about why we *should* use Java, let's ask ourselves, "Why not?" There are two particular problems to consider: Java can be slow, and Java applications do not have full access to a platform's resources.

Speed is not a problem on desktop machines. Lots of MIPS and lots of memory for JIT compilers mean that nowadays a Java application can feel as crisp as an application written in C++. However it *is* an issue on small devices, where memory is tight and CPU performance limited. Personal Java and Java 2ME attempt to address the speed issue, and we will take a brief look at these technologies later in the chapter.

Java has restricted access to a device's resources. A pure Java application running on EPOC will not have access to EIKON controls such as command buttons or date editors, or to EPOC data types such as Word, Sheet, DBMS and Agenda documents. In the near future, JavaPhone will provide part of the solution. Other areas can be addressed by design guidelines or classes provided by Symbian's developer support or by third parties. Some features, such as power management, can be accessed using JNI, but those EIKON controls that aren't also used by the AWT may be practically inaccessible.

But there are, of course, benefits to using Java:

❑ Java is a widely adopted standard that's driven by the Java community, while C++ (on EPOC) and OPL are proprietary. Providing Java on EPOC opens up the EPOC environment to millions of skilled Java developers and helps everything, from standardization processes to the availability of software engineers for critical projects.

❑ The learning curve is shallow. As this chapter will demonstrate, learning to use Java on EPOC is a much smaller task than going from C++ on Win32 to C++ on EPOC.

❑ It addresses the problems that native operating systems are struggling with, such as security, mobile code, internationalization, and pluggable look and feel.

❑ It's robust. EPOC devices are not switched off: *Ctrl+Alt+Del* is not an option, and robustness is therefore vital. Garbage collection means (almost) no memory leaks. The use of object references rather than pointers, and the availability of smart arrays, means no untraceable crashes. It also prevents deliberate programming misbehavior such as access to arbitrary data structures through misused pointers.

❑ Java provides a reasonably fast development environment. Perhaps not as instant as OPL, but certainly quicker than C++.

❑ Java solves a number of issues associated with C++ development. Java APIs are compact, and Java provides tools and processes that ensure they are well documented. C++ APIs can be hard to maintain and difficult to document and understand. This is not an EPOC-specific issue, but a feature of C++: we have to look after both header and implementation files; we need extra language constructs such as templates; we need additional coding to support memory management and smart arrays. (On the other hand, one can argue that C++ benefits from the provision of default parameters, and the ability to mark methods as const.)

The Benefits of Java on WIDs

What, then, does Java have to offer wireless information devices?

Java is designed for a connected world. Java's advantages of small code size and "from the ground up" security mean that the network operators can deploy executable content rapidly and safely, even over quite narrow bandwidth.

Java opens up opportunities for new services, especially those that are security related, such as mobile banking, remote ticket purchase, or wireless commerce. (Of course, secure applications *can* be written in C++; it's just a lot easier in Java.) Java applications are robust and can be developed rapidly, enabling the speedy introduction of such services by the service providers. Furthermore, Java's platform neutrality means that they can be deployed across a wide range of devices.

Java is succeeding in the corporate market (particularly in the financial and manufacturing sectors), where standards, rapid integration and rapid development are particularly important. Java applications can be deployed to a wide range of devices quickly and cheaply, minimizing cost of ownership. It is being used to extend the enterprise to more of its stakeholders, and to empower more of the organization's workforce. We can take advantage of Java's momentum in these areas to integrate WIDs into the enterprise computing environment, where they will become first-class corporate citizens.

Java technology provides secure and platform neutral support for disconnected network devices. These are devices that are not permanently connected to a network, like our desktops, nor standalone devices like simple PDAs, but devices that regularly connect to a network and need to synchronize with other machines on the network.

Because they are highly mobile, WIDs bring new opportunities: constant access to corporate data; information when it's required; remote connectivity; always being in touch. In the end, they are likely to overtake desktop PCs (see The Europe Company Limited's report on Psion, http://www.euroco.co.uk/), so if you're a Java programmer, learning how to use Java on a WID will allow you to address a bigger and potentially more dynamic market.

How will Java be used?

Within the WID market, we can sketch out four scenarios where Java might be considered:

- ❑ To run Java-based services
- ❑ As a platform for heavyweight desktop Java applications
- ❑ As an alternative to C++ and OPL in the developer community
- ❑ To develop flagship EPOC applications

The first scenario is about supporting "lowest common denominator" applications – that is, basic services, applets and applications that will run on any JVM, and more sophisticated services targeted at a particular wireless device or family of devices. This is almost certainly Java's primary role in the near term.

Large desktop Java applications, such as IDEs, word processors and Web browsers *can* run on the EPOC platform. However, there are installation and porting issues that need to be considered (discussed later on), and given the constrained CPU performance and memory footprint of wireless information devices, it's not clear how well such applications will run. Nor is it obvious that the need is there.

C++ and OPL are widely used by Symbian's developers and licensees. However, OPL is proprietary, and C++ on EPOC can present a daunting learning curve for the non-specialist developer. Java is an open standard and retains many of OPL's benefits, though OPL does have a couple of advantages:

- ❑ It is easier to give an OPL application an EPOC look and feel
- ❑ An OPL application can access most EPOC resources

If Java were usable by the developers as a replacement for C++, then it should also be possible to use Java to write flagship applications on EPOC. However, for the foreseeable future, there will always be a role for C++ in areas such as application engines and device drivers, which require full access to the platform's resources, a high level of tuning, and where performance must be maintained.

EPOC's Added Value

Where does EPOC fit in? If we are now convinced that Java is right for WIDs, and if the developers, licensees, and network operators are also convinced that they should be developing in Java, why should they then choose EPOC rather than any other platform running Java? The answer is in the benefits that EPOC provides:

❑ Robustness: Symbian's Java implementation is running on EPOC, which is designed to operate 24 hours a day, 7 days a week.

❑ Speed: The byte code interpreter loop is written in assembler, and EPOC in turn is very efficient.

❑ Tight footprint: The Java implementation takes advantages of EPOC's lean-and-mean philosophy.

❑ Support for the disconnected network model: EPOC's richness offers device intelligence in disconnected mode as well as in connected mode.

❑ Increasing integration with EPOC: application engines, EIKON controls and synchronization will all become more accessible.

EPOC and Java have much in common: for instance, C++ on EPOC takes tight control of memory management, uses a single inheritance model in which mixins (comparable to Java's interfaces) define a class's behavior, and makes wide use of dynamic libraries that reduce code size. The result is that Java on EPOC offers more opportunities than Java on other platforms.

Write Once, Run Anywhere

Sun's introduction of Java editions and profiles is recognition that Java's promise of "write once, run anywhere" was probably a bit optimistic. Porting a large application from a desktop PC to a PDA without changing anything is unrealistic, no matter what language it was written in.

However Java *is* designed for portability, which it achieves more convincingly and on a wider range of platforms than probably any other language. This is due to tight standardization of the behavior of built-in types, binary formats and VM specifications, and a full library that includes a GUI. As a consequence, simple Java applications and applets can often be run without any changes (and hence without having to recompile the class files) on most devices, including EPOC. Even porting more complex applications and applets is generally straightforward.

This section looks at the extent to which Java on EPOC can run unmodified Java applications and applets. Later, we'll look at installation issues and how we need to modify more typical Java applications to make them suitable for PDA-type devices.

The EPOC Web browser supports applets, so running an applet is just a question of pointing the browser at the correct URL. If the applet is local, it can also be run by double tapping on the relevant HTML file. The following screenshot shows the ArcTest example from Sun's JDK 1.1.8 (see demo\ArcTest\ in your JDK installation). The example was copied onto the EPOC device (a Psion netBook) as C:\Demos\ArcTest\, and then run by double tapping on the file example1.html.

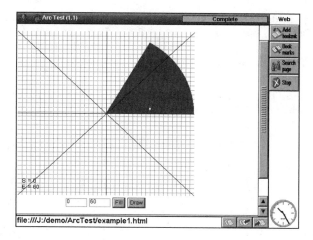

The application or applet must also be well behaved. For instance, the correct way to pass parameters to an applet from the HTML page is with the <PARAM> tag:

```
<APPLET CODE="MyApplet" WIDTH=400 HEIGHT=200>
    <PARAM NAME=temperature VALUE=8>
    <PARAM NAME=pressure VALUE=40>
</APPLET>
```

However, the following code works with Internet Explorer 4, but will fail with EPOC's web browser:

```
<APPLET CODE="MyApplet" WIDTH=400 HEIGHT=200 temperature=8 pressure=40>
</APPLET>
```

The EPOC emulator on the CD that comes with this book doesn't *include Web. Web is included in the EPOC SDK for Java that can be downloaded from the EPOC World web site (http://www.epocworld.com).*

The ArcTest example can also be run as an application. Instead of double tapping on the HTML file, double tap on the class file, ArcTest.class.

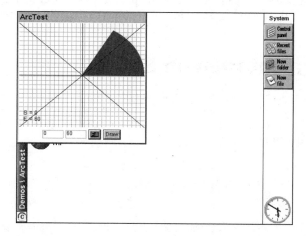

Alas, not everything in the garden is rosy. The screenshots below are of the DrawTest example (also from JDK 1.1.8). An EPOC radio button is much wider than a Windows radio button, and so there is not enough space for all the UI controls. Arguably, the error is with the application, because it has made non-portable assumptions about the size of the controls.

You might also have noticed that under EPOC the radio buttons don't have a colored background: this is a defect in the current EPOC implementation.

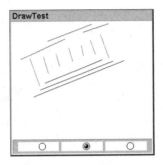

Closing an "off the shelf" Java application can also present problems. First, as can be seen from the DrawTest screenshot above, the `Frame` containing the Java application has no close icon. If the application has a button or menu entry to close it, fine. If not, it will have to be closed from EPOC's System dialog. However, even this will only work if the application has a suitable handler for the window-closing event – and the ArcTest and DrawTest demonstrations don't.

On a desktop PC, these and similar applications are generally launched from a command prompt and can be killed by using something like *Ctrl-C*. Such applications can be killed under EPOC from the System dialog by using *Ctrl-Shift-E*, but this really does kill the application, rather than shutting it down cleanly. This behavior is quite common under Windows, but it can cause memory leaks. Given that EPOC devices are predicated on robustness, this activity is not to be encouraged. Later on, we'll look at how to write a well-behaved Java application.

What about backward compatibility? By and large, any application written for JDK 1.0.2 will run on a later Java version. The exceptions to this are some of the J2ME profiles and embedded Java: because these can omit so many of the core Java 1.1 classes, there is no guarantee that the application will run. However, the introduction of profiles will encourage compatibility across an industry sector or class of device (such as WIDs), even if we cannot maintain compatibility across all Java platforms.

The Java Implementation on EPOC

Porting Java to EPOC began in February 1997. Symbian obtained a source license from Sun for JDK 1.1.2, which arrived in the form of 32MB of C and Java source code. Most of the code was a generic core, but there were platform-specific areas that required tailoring in the application layer, the standard C library, and the virtual machine.

The Mismatch Between EPOC and POSIX

The first hurdle to overcome was the mismatch between what was available on EPOC, and what Sun assumed was available. The source code was organized for ANSI C and POSIX, and assumed process-wide file handles usable by any thread, while EPOC file handles are thread-relative. There is no standard thread API, so inevitably work had to be done to match EPOC's thread APIs and its active scheduler model to a multithreaded model.

Overcoming these problems required a partial implementation of the standard C library (STDLIB), which drives the relevant EPOC C++ APIs, to handle the ANSI C and POSIX areas. It was also necessary to develop a `CPosixServer` thread to own the thread-relative file sessions (`RFs`) and `RFile` handles, a sockets API on top of ESOCK, a limited C++ API for asynchronous IOCTL, and a variation of the UNIX `select()` function to work on a single file descriptor. 64-bit integer arithmetic was handled by the GNU C++ compiler on EPOC hardware, and by Microsoft's Visual Studio for the emulator. Java monitors are implemented using a variation of the `RCriticalSection` class, which avoids the full cost of an `RSemaphore::Wait()` and `RSemaphore::Signal()` if the object is not currently locked. Further, the Java VM widely uses writable static data, which is not generally available to an EPOC DLL. This meant the build tools had to be modified so that the static data could be relocated at link time.

"Hello world" ran on 24 July 1997.

Implementing the AWT

Implementing the AWT was the second hurdle. Being pen based, the EPOC user interface is quite different to Windows and Motif. EPOC peer classes were written in Java, and an EPOC C++ layer wad developed to package up the arguments and pass the calls through to an AWT server. It is this server that does the real work: it has access to the CONE environment and all the necessary handles, and responsibility for converting input events into Java events.

The GraphLayout applet from Sun's JDK ran on 15 October 1997.

But there were still problems. The AWT server was originally 'known' to Java, but this could cause deadlocks during garbage collection, so it was redesigned as a secret thread. Problems with memory leaks and further problems with garbage collection also had to be overcome.

Optimization

Hurdle number three was also opportunity number one: optimization to ensure that EPOC's Java implementation performed well. The core of the byte code interpreter, a big switch statement in C code, was rewritten in ARM assembler. The more commonly used classes are pre-loaded: this reduces the RAM required and improves startup time, though it can increase the ROM needed too.

Finally, C++ classes and functions were written to generate the common assembler elements used by the byte code interpreter instructions. This makes it straightforward to try out new code or algorithms for these elements, and to take advantage of the optimizations that ARM assembler can provide.

Development moved from JDK 1.1.2 to JDK 1.1.4, and on 19 June 1998, the JDK 1.1.4 version of the GraphLayout applet ran successfully.

Certification

Obtaining certification was the fourth hurdle. The Java certification kit contains some 31,000 files and defines 6,000 individual tests. The validity of some of these tests had to be negotiated – those that made too generous assumptions about the amount of memory available, for instance. The test harness, written in Java, drove multiple slave machines. Typically, four machines were used, which allowed a test run to complete in about a day.

Java certification was obtained on 24 August 1998.

Integration

The final hurdle was integrating Java into EPOC. Java had to be integrated into Web to allow applets to be run and, because Java applications are generally started from a command line, an application launcher was required. Java applications on EPOC need a document UID, and class names or titles should appear in the task list. Tools to package Java applications for EPOC deployment were also developed.

The EPOC runtime for Java was included in EPOC release 5, which became available in May 1999. The EPOC SDK for Java was released at the EPOC World conference in June 1999.

Some Implementation Features

Here's a summary of the major features of EPOC's Java implementation:

- ❑ Based on JDK 1.1.4.

- ❑ One VM per EPOC process. The web browser runs multiple applets in the same VM, while each Java application runs in a separate EPOC process, and hence a separate VM.

- ❑ One EPOC thread per Java thread.

- ❑ Includes RMI, JavaBeans, and JDBC APIs. EPOC does not come with a JDBC driver for the EPOC DBMS databases, though Oracle and Sybase have both announced their intention to support deployment to the EPOC platform, and PointBase (http://www.pointbase.com) has targeted handheld devices, especially EPOC, with a pure Java, JDBC-compliant product.

- ❑ Includes Euro support

- ❑ Year 2000 compliant.

- ❑ Passes Sun's certification suite (the JCK).

- ❑ Integration with EPOC: Java applications appear automatically in the "Open files/programs" dialog, and a correctly installed Java application will appear on the Extras bar with its own icon.

Resource Requirements and Performance Issues

Running Java 1.1.4 on EPOC devices requires a minimum set of resources. In summary, these are:

❏ 32-bit CPU

❏ 36MHz clock or better. Small, simple applications can run on 18MHz, but an application with any complexity really needs 36MHz

❏ RAM requirement: under 2MB for a small Java application with a GUI

❏ ROM footprint: 2.7MB

The Need for Speed

Benchmarking PDA devices is problematic. There are no good benchmarks for PDA devices, and in the end the real test is running representative applications. However, the Caffeine benchmark has the benefit of being easy to apply, and the results are instructive.

Device	Processor	CaffeineMark 3 Result
Psion Series 5mx	36MHz ARM 710T	26
Psion netBook	190MHz StrongARM SA1100	141
HP Jornada 820	190MHz StrongARM SA1100	27-28
Desktop PC, NT4 SP4, 128MB – without JIT	366MHz Pentium II	500
Desktop PC, NT4 SP4, 128MB – with JIT	366MHz Pentium II	5,000

Comparing the second and third lines graphically illustrates the benefit of running Java on EPOC: a five-fold improvement in performance. In fact, the Jornada, with a 190MHz ARM processor, performs only marginally better than the Psion Series 5mx with its 36MHz ARM 710T.

Comparing PDAs with desktops is a bit like comparing apples with oranges, but it does raise two things:

❏ The dubiousness of benchmarks. In general, the desktop PC with JIT does not feel 35 times faster than the netBook.

❏ The realities associated with running Java on small machines. There is, and probably always will be, a large gulf between the performance of PDA-type devices and desktop machines.

However, Symbian's fast Java implementation is only half the story. The rest is down to you, the developer. Later on, we will look at the Dice Machine example, when we'll discuss a few ideas that might improve your code's performance.

Developing with the EPOC SDK for Java

We saw earlier that we didn't have to use the EPOC SDK for Java to install or run a Java application or applet. By the same token, we could develop our own Java application on whichever platform we choose and copy it to our EPOC device, without using the EPOC SDK for Java.

For practical applications, however, the SDK becomes essential. The emulator allows us to test and debug a Java application targeted for EPOC under Windows. With the SDK tools, we can make our application appear on the Extras bar so that it can be started like a C++ EPOC application, and we can give it its own icon. It can be packaged up to make it easy for the end user to install, and we can create help text for it. The SDK also provides tools and examples that allow us to write applications that can access native code using JNI.

What's in the EPOC SDK for Java (and what isn't)

The main components of the EPOC SDK for Java are:

- ❑ The EPOC emulator, which runs on Windows NT4/95/98
- ❑ Documentation in HTML format
- ❑ Examples and example code
- ❑ Tools that help develop, debug and deploy Java applications on EPOC
- ❑ Additional tools to support native method development using JNI

In addition, you will need a Java development kit. A suitable JDK can be downloaded free from the Java web site at http:// www.java.sun.com.

> **Use JDK 1.1.4 to 1.1.8. Do not use JDK 1.2 (Java on EPOC conforms to the JDK 1.1 standard).**

An IDE is useful, but not essential. Two to consider are NetBeans (again free from Sun, http://www.netbeans.com), and Kawa from Tek-Tools (http://www.tek-tools.com).

For JNI development, you will also need:

- ❑ Microsoft Visual C++ version 5 or 6
- ❑ The EPOC SDK for C++

Installation of the Java SDK creates the following directories:

- ❑ \sysdoc\: SDK help documents (launched from jindex.html or from Windows' Start menu). The documentation includes:
  - ❑ Getting Started, covering FAQs and troubleshooting

❑   Introduction: developing and customizing Java applications and applets

❑   Deployment: Deploying and running Java applications and Applets

❑   Developing native methods

❑   Command reference

❑   \erj\: classes.zip, JNI tools and examples, Sun's JDK demonstration applets

❑   \epoc32\: SDK tools are in \epoc32\tools\; Java-specific DLLs are in \epoc32\release\

The \erj\ folder will be mapped to drive j: on the emulator, using the technique you saw in Chapter 8, making it easier to access examples and demonstrations from within the emulator.

The Java virtual machine has to run as a thread in the emulator process, rather than running as a process in itself. This means that:

❑   Closing down the VM closes down the emulator.

❑   You can't run more than one instance of the VM in the emulator.

❑   When a Java application exits, the emulator will close down.

❑   Applets don't exit, so the VM won't be closed down. The emulator's web browser can therefore run multiple applets.

The Dice Machine Example

How many times have you wanted to play a board game, but not been able to find the dice? The Dice Machine rolls (up to 6) dice for you. It looks a bit like a one-armed bandit, but uses the numbers 1 to 6 instead of pictures of funny fruit.

This section works through the Dice Machine example (it's a more interesting application than the usual "Hello World", though a version of the latter can be found in the EPOC SDK for Java). We'll make use of all the tools provided in the EPOC SDK for Java, as well as looking at the use of packages and JAR files.

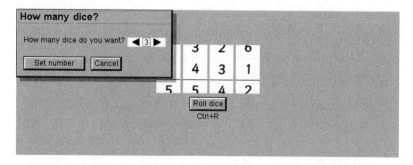

A die is represented by an image with the numbers 1 to 6 arranged vertically, so if you do want to turn the Dice Machine into a one-armed bandit, start by changing Dicenums.gif.

The general process for creating a Java application for EPOC is illustrated below. It's not strictly necessary to load the class files into a JAR file, but doing so means that the directory structure on the target device is much simpler, and that the application takes up less space because JAR files are compressed.

In general, three components need to be independently prepared:

❑ The application file (.app), which ensures that the application's icon appears on the Extras bar, and an associated .txt file that contains the command line to be passed to Java in order to run the application

❑ The Java class and JAR files (plus any DLLs required if JNI is being used).

❑ An Application Information File (.aif), which controls such details as the icon that will be displayed in the Extras bar

These three components in turn can be packaged into an installation, or .sis, file. A .sis file contains all the components needed by an application and can be easily installed on an EPOC device, making life much more straightforward for the end user of your application.

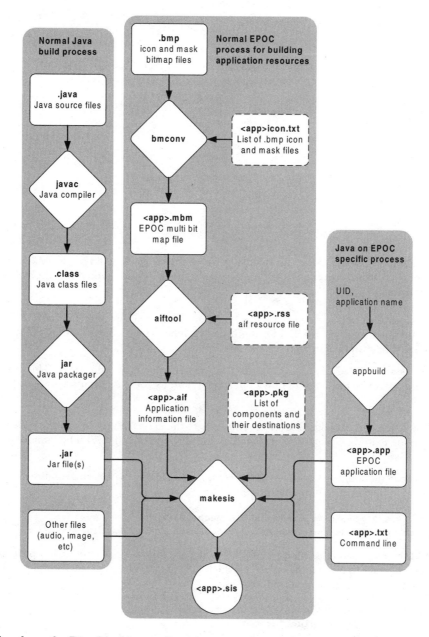

To build and run the Dice Machine application, we need to go through these steps:

❑ Copy the source code into `\epoc32\wins\c\system\apps\DiceMachine\` on the PC's drive into which you installed the SDK. The source code for this example can be found in `\Java Examples\DiceMachine\`. You should end up with a structure like this:

- ❏ Create the `DiceMachine.app` file. In general, the `.app` file will be created in the directory `\epoc32\wins\c\system\apps\<app>`, on the drive from which the `appbuild` command was run.

  Enter `appbuild DiceMachine 100052AE` at a command prompt. The second parameter is the unique identifier (or UID) for the Dice Machine, which is governed by the same rules that you saw back in Chapter 2.

- ❏ Create a file called `DiceMachine.txt` in the `DiceMachine\` directory. This contains the command to be passed to the Java interpreter, and its contents should be:

  `-cp DiceMachine.jar com.symbian.epoc.dicemachine.DiceMachine`
  The `-cp` argument adds `DiceMachine.jar` to the class path. If `-classpath` is used instead, then the existing class path is replaced, rather than appended to. (I'll have more to say about the class path shortly.)

- ❏ Compile the sources: Create a subdirectory `Code\` in the `DiceMachine` directory, then type in the following at a command prompt:

  ```
  cd \EPOC32\Wins\C\System\Apps\DiceMachine\Source
  javac -d ..\code com\symbian\epoc\dicemachine\DiceMachine.java
  ```

- ❏ Add the compiled classes into a JAR file: enter the following at a command prompt (note the JAR command's last parameter is ".", which tells the command to start adding files from the current directory, plus its subdirectories):

  ```
  cd \EPOC32\Wins\C\System\Apps\DiceMachine\Code
  jar -cfv ..\DiceMachine.jar .
  ```

- ❏ Start the emulator. A default icon for the Dice Machine (a question mark) will appear on the Extras bar, allowing it to be run like any other EPOC application

- ❏ Create the `.aif` file. This will give the application its own icon: the next section describes how to do this

- ❏ Install on an EPOC device: we could copy the application's files (`DiceMachine.txt`, `DiceMachine.app`, `DiceMachine.aif`, `DiceMachine.jar`, and `DiceNums.gif`) into `\System\Apps\DiceMachine\` on any drive on the EPOC device. Alternatively we can create an SIS installation file, as explained in the next section

Using the EPOC SDK for Java Tools

We will now see how to use the SDK tools to create an application information file (that is, a .aif file) and an installation file (a .sis file).

The .sis file is used by EPOC's installer technologies (either EPOC Install, which comes with EPOC Connect, or AppInst, which runs on the EPOC device itself) to install your application correctly onto an EPOC device.

The SDK tools require that the working folder is two folders beneath the root into which the SDKs were installed. For this example, create \Installation\DiceMachine\.

Creating the Dice Machine's Icon

> The pre-processor tool in \epoc32\gcc\bin\ folder\, which is needed by aiftool, was omitted from the EPOC SDK for Java. The necessary files can be downloaded from http://www.epocworld.com/downloads/patches.html#jtool. This download isn't required if you have already installed the EPOC SDK for C++.

EPOC's icons should consist of images of three different sizes: 48x48, 32x32, and 24x24 pixels. These correspond to the icon sizes in the current zoom levels of the EPOC Shell application. Each bitmap is accompanied by a mask that defines the transparent areas of the icon.

The required bitmaps can be found in \Java Examples\Installation\DiceMachine\; their self-evident names are dice24.bmp, mask24.bmp, dice32.bmp, mask32.bmp, dice48.bmp, and mask48.bmp. Copy these into the \Installation\DiceMachine\ directory you created.

The bitmap files now need to be compiled into the multi bitmap (or MBM) format used by EPOC. This is done with the bmconv.exe tool supplied with the Java SDK; to automate the process of building the icon file, it is possible to write a text file listing what needs to be processed. For the Dice Machine, create a file called DiceMachineIcon.txt whose contents are:

```
DiceMachineIcon.mbm
dice24.bmp
mask24.bmp
dice32.bmp
mask32.bmp
dice48.bmp
mask48.bmp
```

The first line specifies the name of the .mbm file to be generated, followed by the icons to be included. The sequence is smallest to largest, alternating between icon and mask.

Next, open up a command window, change directory to \Installation\DiceMachine\, and enter this:

```
bmconv DiceMachineIcon.txt
```

This will start bmconv, which will compile the .bmp files into a single EPOC bitmap file called DiceMachineIcon.mbm. This file in turn is needed to build the .aif file.

The .aif File

EPOC applications can have various different properties (they can be 'hidden' from view, they can be able to embed their documents in other programs, etc.) and also different captions, depending on the language of the machine they are running on. All this information is contained in the .aif file, which accompanies an application. However, most of these features only apply to C++ applications; for Java the most useful information supplied by a .aif file is the icon and its caption.

The Dice Machine's UID (0x100052AE) is needed for the .rss (resource) file, which is used by aiftool to construct the .aif file. The DiceMachine.rss file looks like this:

```
#include <aiftool.rh>

RESOURCE AIF_DATA
    {
    app_uid = 0x100052AE;
    caption_list =
        {
        CAPTION { code = ELangEnglish; caption = "Dice Machine"; },
        CAPTION { code = ELangFrench; caption = "Machine de Dés"; }
        };
    num_icons = 3;
    embeddability = KAppNotEmbeddable;
    }
```

caption_list heads up a list of captions for different languages (in this case English and French), while num_icons is the number of icon-mask pairs.

The format of .rss files is documented in the EPOC SDK for Java under /sysdoc/adk/DevTools/Tool_Guide_examples_aiftool.html.

You can now invoke aiftool with the .rss file. Launch a command window, go to the \Installation\DiceMachine\ folder, and then enter:

aiftool DiceMachine DiceMachineIcon.mbm

Note that you do not need to specify the extension for the file DiceMachine.rss.

aiftool will create a new file called DiceMachine.aif in \Installation\DiceMachine\. This should then be copied into the application directory, \epoc32\wins\c\system\apps\ DiceMachine\.

Starting the Dice Machine in the Emulator

At this point, you can start the emulator, and if all is well you will see the Dice Machine's icon on the Extras bar. Tap on it to start the application.

An application can also be started from a command window. Type in the following at the command prompt:

```
cd \Epoc32\Wins\C\System\Apps\DiceMachine
\epoc32\release\wins\rel\java -cp DiceMachine.jar com.symbian.epoc.dicemachine.DiceMachine
```

The `\rel\` element indicates that we will be running in the non-debug version of the emulator. The `-cp` switch modifies the class path, and is discussed in the next section.

Similarly, we can launch the EPOC applet viewer under the emulator. For the non-debug viewer, issue this command:

```
\epoc32\release\wins\rel\appletviewer.exe <URL>
```

No standard output?

If an application is launched from a command window under the emulator, standard output will be directed to that window. If the application was launched from the emulator's Extras bar, then a console will be created in the emulator and output directed to it.

On an EPOC device, the Java console is disabled by default. To enable it, create a file (of any type) called `console` in a folder `\system\java\` on any drive.

Writing to the console might make it appear as though your application won't shut down. If your application writes to the console, you will have to exit the console when you exit your application. When your application has finished, switch to the console window, which should be displaying the message "press any key to continue". Your application will exit when you follow this instruction. This behavior is provided so that developers have the chance to see console output before an application exits.

On the EPOC emulator, this behavior will only occur if the application writes to the EIKON console rather than to the Windows command prompt: this happens if you launch the Java application from the EPOC Extras bar, rather than the Windows command prompt.

Class Paths and the Current Directory on EPOC

> **EPOC has no concept of a system class path variable.**

The emulator's default class path includes:

- ❑ `\erj\lib\classes.zip`, which contains the Java classes
- ❑ `\erj\ext\`, where you should put any JAR files that are to be shared across applications
- ❑ `\erj\classes\`, where you should put classes that may be used by more than one application
- ❑ The current directory – that is, the directory from which the application was launched, or as set by the `-cd` switch

The class path on an EPOC device will be different. For the Psion Series 5mx, for example, it is:

- ❏ \System\Java\lib\classes.zip
- ❏ \System\Java\ext\ for shared JAR files
- ❏ \System\Java\classes\ for shared classes
- ❏ The current directory, specified as above

Use the -cp and -cd switches on the command line or in a .txt file to specify the class path and current directory respectively. The -cp switch is specific to EPOC's Java implementation, appending its argument to the existing class path. The Java -classpath switch can also be used, but it's less useful as it *replaces* the existing class path with the supplied class path.

> Speed hint: *The class path is searched in order, so put the classes, directories or JAR files that will be used most often earlier in the class path. If you are using the -cp switch, then the class loader will search in* classes.zip *before it looks in your own code.*
>
> *I will be highlighting a number of other ideas that can help improve an application's speed. For a small application like the Dice Machine, they will make little difference. In a larger application they can be significant, helping to overcome the relatively constrained CPU power available to the typical EPOC device.*

Packaging it all up

The only thing left is to install the application reliably on an EPOC device. This is taken care of with a .sis file, created by the makesis application.

You need to write a .pkg script, which makesis will use to create your installation file. The format of these files is described fully in the online documentation (/sysdoc/adk/Makesis-ref/Tool_Ref_makesis_pkg_ff.html). There are various flags and options that can be included: the .pkg file can be used to define how upgrades should be performed, how an application should be uninstalled, and to display a text file during installation. Looking at dicemachine.pkg, however, you will see that in this case we're just instructing the installer to put all of our 'deliverables' into \System\Apps\DiceMachine\ on the drive that the user will select at install time:

```
; Package file for the Dice Machine
&EN,FR
#{"Dice Machine", "Machine de Dés"},(0x100052AE),0,3,0
"\epoc32\wins\c\system\apps\DiceMachine\DiceMachine.app"-
                        "!:\system\apps\DiceMachine\DiceMachine.app"
"\epoc32\wins\c\system\apps\DiceMachine\DiceMachine.aif"-
                        "!:\system\apps\DiceMachine\DiceMachine.aif"
"\epoc32\wins\c\system\apps\DiceMachine\DiceMachine.txt"-
                        "!:\system\apps\DiceMachine\DiceMachine.txt"
"\epoc32\wins\c\system\apps\DiceMachine\DiceMachine.jar"-
                        "!:\system\apps\DiceMachine\DiceMachine.jar"
"\epoc32\wins\c\system\apps\DiceMachine\DiceNums.gif"-
                        "!:\system\apps\DiceMachine\DiceNums.gif"
```

Notes:

❑ Lines preceded by a semicolon are comments.

❑ The line preceded by an ampersand contains two-letter codes that indicate the languages supported by the application. In this case, English and French are supported; if the line is missing then English will be assumed.

❑ The line preceded by a hash specifies the name of the application, its UID (which must be the same as the UID specified when invoking the `appbuild` tool), the build version (major and minor, so 0.3 in this case) and the build variant (which is not used). The UID is used during installation to check for upgrades, and during uninstallation to identify which files belong to which application.

❑ The rest of the file specifies the files to be installed, and the destinations of those files on the target machine. The source and target filenames are separated by a hyphen.

❑ Replacing the target drive letter with an exclamation mark means that the user can specify the drive at installation time.

After creating the `.pkg` file, launch a command window, go to the `\Installation\DiceMachine\` directory, and then type:

```
makesis DiceMachine.pkg DiceMachine.sis
```

This will create the `DiceMachine.sis` file in the `\Installation\DiceMachine\` folder.

Once you have your `.sis` file, you are ready to install your application onto your EPOC device, or pass it on to other users to install on theirs.

A Closer Look at the Dice Machine

The Dice Machine is a fairly straightforward application, allowing us to concentrate on the EPOC-specific aspects of the code in our discussion. The diagram below shows its class structure:

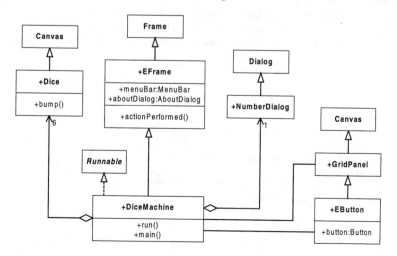

DiceMachine.java

DiceMachine.java contains the Dice Machine's main class. The application is created in the
com.symbian.epoc.dicemachine package, which is why the source, DiceMachine.java, is in the
directory com\symbian\epoc\dicemachine\. The header also imports the package
com.symbian.epoc.extension, which contains some useful support classes: EFrame, EButton, and
GridPanel:

```
package com.symbian.epoc.dicemachine;
    :
    :
import com.symbian.epoc.extension.*;
```

DiceMachine extends EFrame, part of our extension package. EFrame provides some support for an
EPOC look and feel, and in turn extends the Frame class. DiceMachine implements Runnable to
allow the dice to be 'rolled' in a separate thread:

```
public class DiceMachine extends EFrame implements ActionListener, Runnable {
```

diceImage references the GIF used to display the dice numbers; soundClip references the sound that
is played each time a dice stops rolling; dialogText is used by EFrame: it is the text displayed in the
application's About box:

```
Image diceImage;
java.applet.AudioClip soundClip;
String[] dialogText =
    { "--The EPOC Dice Machine--",
      "A Java demonstration",
      "that might also be of some use",
      "Version 0.03, 20 November 1999",
      "Jonathan Allin, Colin Turfus" };
```

DiceMachine adds two menu items to the menu bar provided by EFrame: rollItem and
numberItem. Both of these have keyboard shortcuts. rollB is an instance of our EButton class, and
performs the same action as the MenuItem object, rollItem. To conform to the EPOC style guide,
buttons should have matching menu entries, and the keyboard shortcut should appear beneath the
button. An EButton is just a button and a label in a GridPanel, with the label used to display the
button's keyboard shortcut (*Ctrl+R* in this case).

panel is an instance of our GridPanel helper class that's used to make laying out the UI components a
bit easier:

```
MenuItem rollItem = new MenuItem(
    "Roll dice", new MenuShortcut(KeyEvent.VK_R));
MenuItem numberItem = new MenuItem(
    "Number of dice", new MenuShortcut(KeyEvent.VK_N));
EButton rollB = new EButton("Roll dice", "Ctrl+R");
GridPanel panel = new GridPanel();
    :
    :
```

The constructor creates a new `Menu` called `controlMenu`, to which `numberItem` and `rollItem` are added. `controlMenu` is added in turn to `menuBar` (the menu bar provided by `EFrame`).

```java
public DiceMachine()
{
    :
    :
    Menu controlMenu = new Menu ("Control");
    controlMenu.add(numberItem);
    controlMenu.add(rollItem);
    numberItem.addActionListener(this);
    rollItem.addActionListener(this);
    menuBar.add(controlMenu);
```

Speed hint: *Create objects once, and re-use objects. This means we don't waste time recreating them, and means less work for the garbage collector when they are no longer needed. With this in mind, we create the dialog used to change the number of dice now, rather than creating it every time we want to show it, and we create all the dice we need now, rather than creating dice every time we change their number:*

```java
numberDialog = new NumberDialog(this, "How many dice?");

for(int i = 0; i < MAX_DICE_NUMBER; i++) {
    dice[i] = new Dice(diceImage, soundClip);
}
setNumberDice(4); // Add 4 dice to the panel
```

The next couple of lines show how `panel` (an instance of our `GridPanel` class) is used:

```java
panel.constraints.gridwidth = GridBagConstraints.REMAINDER;
panel.add(rollB.button, 0, 1);
rollB.button.addActionListener(this);
add(panel);
```

The last few lines set the title of the About dialog, and set the text it displays to `dialogText`:

```java
aboutDialog.setTitle("About the Dice Machine");
aboutDialog.text = dialogText;
show();
}
```

`actionPerformed()` picks up user events. Events generated when the user selects Roll dice or Set number of dice from the menu, or taps on the Roll button, are handled here. The last line ensures that events handled by `EFrame` are passed to it, namely `Exit` and `About`:

```java
public void actionPerformed(ActionEvent ae) {
    if((ae.getSource() == rollB.button) || (ae.getSource() == rollItem)) {
        :
        :
    } else if(ae.getSource() == numberItem) {
        numberDialog.show();
    } else super.actionPerformed(ae);
}
```

EFrame.java

EFrame is a simple Java class that provides some of the functionality needed to make a Java application look and behave like an EPOC C++ application. To use this functionality, a Java application can extend EFrame, rather than Frame. The class provides:

- ❑ A full screen

- ❑ A menu bar with Exit and About entries

- ❑ An About dialog, with methods aboutDialog.setTitle(String) and aboutDialog.setText(String[])

- ❑ A window-closing handler to ensure the application exits cleanly

Exit handling is particularly important. EPOC requires that each application can shut itself down safely, helping prevent memory leaks and orphaned processes.

EFrame is part of the com.symbian.epoc.extension package:

```
package com.symbian.epoc.extension;

import java.awt.*;
import java.awt.event.*;

public class EFrame extends Frame implements ActionListener {
```

Create a MenuBar, and add Tools and File menus. Create Close, About..., and Help submenus. (Note that \u2026 displays an ellipsis.):

```
public MenuBar menuBar = new MenuBar();
public Menu fileMenu = new Menu("File");
public MenuItem closeItem = new MenuItem(
    "Close", new MenuShortcut(KeyEvent.VK_E));
public Menu toolMenu = new Menu("Tools");
public MenuItem aboutItem = new MenuItem(
    "About\u2026", new MenuShortcut(KeyEvent.VK_A));
public MenuItem helpItem = new MenuItem(
    "Help", new MenuShortcut(KeyEvent.VK_H));

public AboutDialog aboutDialog;

static final int BORDER_WIDTH = 5;
static final int TITLE_HEIGHT = 25;

public EFrame() {
    this("");
}

public EFrame(String title) {
    super(title);
```

Under EPOC, our window-closing handler will be called when the user closes the application from EPOC's Open files/programs dialog:

```
WindowListener wl = new WindowAdapter() {
    public void windowClosing(WindowEvent we) {
        shutDown();
    }
};
addWindowListener(wl);

fileMenu.add(closeItem);
closeItem.addActionListener(this);

toolMenu.add(aboutItem);
aboutItem.addActionListener(this);
aboutDialog = new AboutDialog(this);

toolMenu.add(helpItem);
helpItem.addActionListener(this);

menuBar.add(fileMenu);
menuBar.add(toolMenu);
setMenuBar(menuBar);
```

Ensure that the application fills the available screen, and position the application so that the title bar is hidden off the top of the screen:

```
Dimension screenSize = getToolkit().getScreenSize();
setBounds(-BORDER_WIDTH, -TITLE_HEIGHT,
          screenSize.width + 2*BORDER_WIDTH,
          screenSize.height + TITLE_HEIGHT + BORDER_WIDTH);
}
```

A subclass of EFrame that implements actionPerformed() should call super.actionPeformed(ActionEvent e), to ensure that the actions handled by EFrame are not ignored.

```
public void actionPerformed(ActionEvent ae) {
    if(ae.getSource() == closeItem) {
        shutDown();
    } else if(ae.getSource() == aboutItem) {
        aboutDialog.setVisible(true);
```

EFrame is intended to make use of EPOC's help facility, but a fault in the current Java implementation means that Runtime.getRuntime().exec(<applicationName>) fails:

```
    } else if(ae.getSource() == helpItem) {
        try {
            Runtime.getRuntime().exec(
                "z:\\System\\Programs\\AppRun "
                "z:\\System\\Apps\\Data\\DATA.APP");
```

```
                    } catch(java.io.IOException ioe) {
                        ioe.printStackTrace();
                    }
                }
            }
```

AboutDialog is an inner class that provides the About dialog. The text for this is set by a subclass of EFrame (in this case, DiceMachine):

```
public class AboutDialog extends Dialog implements ActionListener {
    Button continueB = new Button("Continue");
    public String[] text = {""};
    final int WIDTH = 300;
    final int HEIGHT = 100;

    AboutDialog(Frame parent) {
        super(parent);
        setLayout(new FlowLayout());
        GridPanel panel = new GridPanel();
        Canvas canvas = new Canvas() {
            public void paint(Graphics g) {
                paintText(g);
            }
        };

        canvas.setSize(WIDTH, HEIGHT);
        panel.add(canvas, 0, 0);
        panel.add(continueB, 0, 1);
        continueB.addActionListener(this);
        add(panel);
        pack();
    }

    public void actionPerformed(ActionEvent ae) {
        if(ae.getSource() == continueB) setVisible(false);
    }
```

paintText() does most of the work. It lays out the String array with one String per line, working out the position of each line so that it's correctly centered and at the right height.

Speed hint: *Use temporary local variables inside loops. In the following, lineCount (and fm) could be replaced by resolving text.length and g.getFontMetric() each time through the loop. This would save two lines of code, but slow the loop down:*

```
public void paintText(Graphics g) {
    FontMetrics fm = g.getFontMetrics();
    int lineCount = text.length;
    for(int i = 0; i < lineCount; i++) {
        int xOffset = (WIDTH - fm.stringWidth(text[i])) / 2;
        g.drawString(text[i], xOffset, HEIGHT * (i + 1) / (lineCount+1));
    }
}
```

Override `shutDown()` for different or additional behavior when an application closes:

```
public void shutDown() {
        System.exit(0);
    }
}
```

GridPanel.java

The `GridPanel` class extends `Panel`, using a `GridBagLayout` for maximum flexibility when laying out components. It uses an instance of `GridBagConstraints` called `constraints`, which is made public so that the layout's flexibility is not lost:

```
package com.symbian.epoc.extension;

import java.awt.*;

public class GridPanel extends Panel {
    private GridBagLayout layout;
    public GridBagConstraints constraints;

    public GridPanel() {
        layout = new GridBagLayout();
        setLayout(layout);
        constraints = new GridBagConstraints();
        constraints.insets = new Insets(2, 2, 2, 2);
        constraints.anchor = GridBagConstraints.NORTH;
    }
```

`GridBagLayout` is the most complicated `LayoutManager`, but `GridPanel`'s `add()` method makes its use relatively straightforward:

```
public void add(Component item, int gridx, int gridy) {
        constraints.gridx = gridx;
        constraints.gridy = gridy;
        layout.setConstraints(item, constraints);
        add(item);
    }
}
```

EButton.java

`EButton` extends `GridPanel`, and contains a `Label` and a `Button`. The `Button` instance, `button`, is public. `EButton`'s constructor is used to set the text to be displayed in the `Button` and by the `Label`; the latter should be the keyboard shortcut:

```
package com.symbian.epoc.extension;
import java.awt.*;

public class EButton extends GridPanel {
    public Button button;
```

```
    public EButton(String label, String shortCut) {
        button = new Button(label);
        add(button, 0, 0);
        add(new Label(shortCut), 0, 1);
    }
}
```

Optimizing Your Code

Optimization is always important, but especially so on small devices. In the previous discussion, we highlighted a few ways in which we might be able to improve speed, but optimization is also about minimizing memory requirements. First, I can give you a few general rules:

❑   Optimize late, find out where you really need to optimize, and don't over-optimize.

❑   Optimization is often in conflict with code clarity and maintainability.

❑   Improving startup time and improving execution speed are often in conflict.

❑   Reducing code size, and hence memory, is often in conflict with improving speed.

❑   Performance is in the eye of the beholder, so let the user know that something is happening. You can use a status area to report on what your application is doing (but make it a comprehensible message!), and remember that the wait icon is generally not available.

❑   Use threads: loading or saving a file in a separate thread will let the user carry on with other work.

❑   Avoid using a loop that polls: use a blocking loop instead, or else use events. The following code fragment contains a loop that polls the keepRunning flag; running it increased battery consumption from 66mA to 163mA on my Psion Series 5mx. The battery consumption returned to 66mA when keepRunning was set to false:

```
Label status = new Label("Waiting");
boolean keepRunning = false;
    :
    :
public void run() {
    status.setText("Started");
    while(keepRunning) {
        status.setText("In loop");
    }
    status.setText("Stopped");
}
```

The directions above could usefully be applied to any development tool, but there are some Java-specific issues too:

❑   The browser has to create an HTTP request for each file transferred, so applet download time will be improved by putting all the required classes and resources into a single JAR file, and further improved because JAR files are compressed.

❑   Using JAR files for applications will save memory as well as improving performance a little, because the class loader has less searching to do.

❑ Concatenating `Strings` is easy, but slow. If you have lots of `Strings` to concatenate, use a `StringBuffer` instead. `StringBuffers` are mutable; `Strings` are not.

❑ Make invariant data ("constants") `static` and `final`.

❑ Mark methods as `final` wherever possible (this is also good design practice: in general, only expose the methods and variables that you know will be needed).

❑ Obfuscators, intended to make reverse compilation less useful, can reduce code size by removing unused data and symbolic names from compiled Java classes, and by replacing longer identifiers with shorter ones.

Debugging

Currently, debugging can only be carried out under the emulator: it is not possible to debug an application running on EPOC hardware. This will change with the next release of Java on EPOC, as I'll explain later.

We'll first look at how to debug using Sun's debugger, JDB, from the command line, and then show how an IDE such as Kawa can make life a little easier. We will use the Dice Machine as an example.

JDB from the Command Line

To debug a Java application, it must first be compiled with the `-g` flag, which creates the necessary debug tables within the class files. For the Dice Machine example, we have to return to the `Source\` directory and compile with:

```
javac -g -d ..\code com\symbian\epoc\dicemachine\DiceMachine.java
```

The EPOC SDK for Java does not include a version of JDB that starts up the emulator, so instead we have to start the emulator's Java interpreter with the `-debug` flag and attach to it remotely using JDB. (For further information about debugging using JDB, see the JDK documentation: `/docs/tooldocs/win32/jdb.html`.)

Start the emulator with the debug version of the JVM (`java_g.exe`) by entering the following at a Windows command prompt (note that this will run the application from the class files, not from the JAR file):

```
\epoc32\release\wins\rel\java_g.exe -debug -cd c:\system\apps\DiceMachine -cp Code
com.symbian.epoc.dicemachine.DiceMachine
```

This will start the Dice Machine in the emulator, and will also print an 'agent password' in the command window (56u3, for example) that can be used by JDB to link into this session. The use of a password prevents unauthorized linking to a running Java application.

Next, we need to start JDB and link into our running application. From another command window, enter:

```
jdb -host localhost -password 56u3
```

You can even run the emulator on one PC and debug from another, in which case the parameter for the `-host` argument would be the IP address or machine name of the PC running the emulator.

You can set a breakpoint in JDB by entering (say) `stop at DiceMachine:179` at the JDB prompt. If you haven't changed the source code, this should set a breakpoint at the start of the `Run()` method in the `DiceMachine` class, which should then be triggered when we press the Dice Machine's Roll button. We can then step through our code and inspect the values of local variables.

The Java compiler will not compile 'dead' code – that is, code that cannot be reached. This means that you can put debug statements in an `if(debug)` block, safe in the knowledge that if `debug` is `false`, the statements won't be compiled and therefore won't add to the class size:

```
boolean debug = false;

// The following statements won't be compiled
if(debug) {
    System.out.println("Debug information");
    System.out.println("Status: " + myClass);
}
```

Driving JDB from Kawa

Kawa is a straightforward IDE written specifically for use with Java applications. Local applications can be debugged using its own debugger, but it also provides a useful interface onto Sun's JDB. The former is the more powerful debugger (variables can be changed on the fly, for example), but it cannot be used for remote debugging.

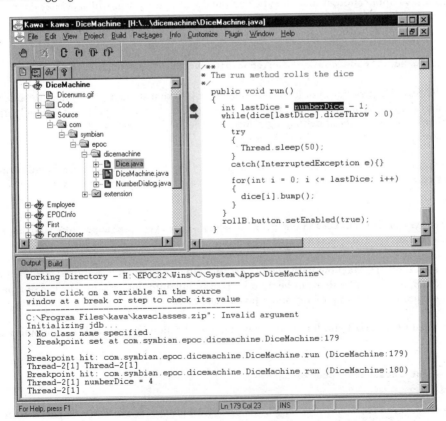

The above screenshot shows Kawa using JDB to debug the Dice Machine application remotely. Kawa's UI was used to start JDB, set a breakpoint, and step through the Run() method. We were then able to inspect the numberDice variable by double clicking on its value (which was 4, as can be seen in the Output window).

Targeting EPOC

We discussed earlier that it's not necessarily the case that a Java application or applet written for a desktop environment will run straightforwardly on EPOC. This isn't due to any limitations in EPOC, but due to the constraints (and opportunities) of wireless information devices.

In this section, we'll examine the problems of adapting a Java application to run on EPOC, and of writing a Java application specifically for EPOC.

Getting Closer to the EPOC Look and Feel

In general, we want a Java application to have the same look and feel as a standard EPOC application. The exception might be if we are targeting a wide range of devices, including non-EPOC devices, or if we are developing a vertical application.

Before we think about how to achieve our goal, we need to be clear what we mean by "the same look and feel". There are three areas to consider:

- ❑ Identical appearance and behavior of controls. This is achieved because Java UI controls use native peers (that is, they use existing EIKON controls).

- ❑ Identical appearance and behavior of applications. For example, applications should fill the screen, with no visible title bar.

- ❑ Java applications have access to the same resources as C++ applications, such as sound management.

Assistance in acquiring an EPOC look and feel can come from:

- ❑ Coding guidelines. These will describe how to code an application so that it shuts down cleanly, for example.

- ❑ Support from EPOC. If a Java application has a menu bar attached to a Frame, it will behave identically to a C++ application's menu bar. For instance, it will be hidden until the *Menu* key is pressed, saving screen real estate.

- ❑ Support classes. We have looked at how EFrame can provide some basic help, and we can look forward to classes that use JNI to access other useful EPOC resources.

In some cases, however, it may not be possible or practical to achieve all of our requirements: accessing EIKON controls that are not used by the AWT falls into this category.

Running Heavyweight Java Applications

This section explores the issues involved in installing and running larger Java applications, written for desktop machines, on EPOC. In particular, we'll look at Adobe Acrobat Viewer.

The first thing to say is that it's a testament to EPOC's Java implementation that such applications can be run at all. If you come across a *pure* Java application that *won't* run, it's likely to be through a lack of memory, disk space or processing power, or because it requires Java 2. Applications will also fail if they require the `javax.comm` package that gives access to a device's serial and parallel ports (`javax.comm` will be included in the next EPOC release). Finally, an application will be unusable if it has windows (that is, `Frames`) that need to be resized.

> **There is a bug in the emulator that means larger Java applications can only be launched from the command line (not from the emulator's Extras bar). This is not a problem on EPOC hardware.**

Installing and Running Adobe Acrobat Viewer

Adobe Acrobat Viewer is used to view Adobe PDF format files. It is a Java version of Acrobat Reader for use on platforms on which Acrobat Reader is not supported. It can be downloaded from http://www.adobe.com/products/acrviewer/main.html.

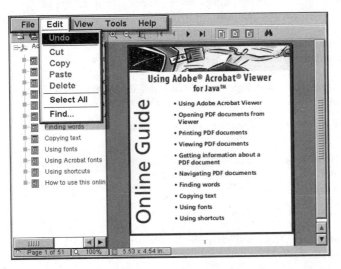

In terms of existing hardware, Acrobat Viewer can be run on a Psion Series 7 or Psion netBook. It won't work too well on a Psion Series 5mx because its initial window size is 640x480, which cannot be changed. (The Series 5mx's screen is 640 by 240 pixels.) The application also needs the extra processing power that the netBook and Series 7 provide.

Acrobat Viewer uses the AWT, and makes extensive use of lightweight components to achieve a pleasant appearance. It doesn't use Swing, which means that (a) the application will be smaller, and (b) it will use EPOC's menu bar, saving screen real estate.

Installation is relatively straightforward:

- ❑ Copy the JAR file `acrobat.jar` into `\Epoc32\wins\c\System\apps\Acrobat\` on the emulator.

- ❑ Create a `.app` file, `Acrobat.app`, so that an icon for the application will appear on the Extras bar. This can be achieved by entering `Appbuild Acrobat 100058A6` at a command prompt. (0x100058A6 is the UID assigned to Acrobat Viewer.)

- ❑ Create a file `Acrobat.txt` in the same directory. The contents of this should be:

```
-cp acrobat.jar com.adobe.acrobat.Viewer -d -console -v
```

   Here, the `-cp` parameter adds `acrobat.jar` to the existing class path, while `com.adobe.acrobat.Viewer` is the fully qualified name of the application's main class.

- ❑ The application can be launched from the emulator by entering the following at a command prompt:

```
\epoc32\release\wins\rel\java.exe -Mvga-- -cd c:\system\apps\Acrobat -cp
acrobat.jar com.adobe.acrobat.Viewer
```

   `-Mvga--` will start the emulator with a VGA screen size. (Note the bug that prevents the application from being launched from the emulator's Extras bar. This also means that the `.app` and `.txt` files won't be needed until we run on an EPOC device.)

To run on an EPOC device:

- ❑ Copy the `Acrobat\` directory and its contents into `\System\Apps\` on any drive.

- ❑ The application can then be run from the Extras bar (its icon will be a question mark, because we haven't created a special icon for it).

> **Although a Java application can be launched by double tapping on its class file, it's not possible to double tap on a JAR file to launch the Java application within it.**

Writing for EPOC

To achieve the best results when writing or porting Java applications for EPOC, we need to keep in mind the characteristics of the target device. This includes a small screen (which may be monochrome or color), pointer not mouse (or no pointer at all), relatively slow processor, and relatively little memory (the amount of available memory precludes just-in-time compilation). An EPOC application should be written so that it is possible (and straightforward) to drive it using the keyboard.

Furthermore, we can't depend on any of the following:

- ❑ Right-mouse clicks.

- ❑ Double-clicks. A double tap generates a double-click event, but this should be avoided as double tapping is not easy for a pen-based user. EPOC generally uses single tapping (tap once to select an item; tap again to activate it).

❑ Mouse drag (other than for, say, scroll bars). It's too easy to drop what you are dragging (a document, for example) in the wrong place.

❑ Mouse motion. This means there are quite a few UI features that won't work, including rollover icons (icons that change shape when the mouse pointer is moved over them), tool tips, and mouse pointers that change depending on the underlying component. (Imagine trying to resize a desktop window without the mouse pointer telling you when you are precisely over the few pixels of the frame used to adjust its size.)

❑ A wait icon will not always appear: generally, these are displayed instead of the mouse pointer, but a mouse pointer is usually not visible on a pen-based system. On EPOC, Java will only display the wait pointer (a small clock face) if a component has the focus and while the pen is in contact with that component. Native EPOC applications do not support the wait pointer at all.

❑ The ability to move or resize a window.

❑ Standard I/O. The console is not enabled by default, and it should only be used for development purposes

The figure below is a screen shot of the RemoteFiler application (the sources can be found in \Java Examples\RemoteFiler\). It was written specifically for the EPOC platform, though it will run on just about any machine with a JVM. The application is used to transfer files, create directories (either on the remote or local machine), and delete files and directories (again either on the remote or local machine). It uses TCP/IP to communicate with a matching server (written in Java) on the remote machine.

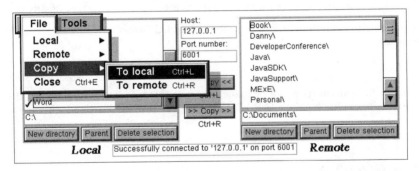

The application has been written to have an EPOC look and feel, and, perhaps more importantly, to be usable on a small device:

❑ The application adjusts its size to fill the screen, and has no visible title bar

❑ Menus are typical EPOC application menus

❑ The buttons have keyboard shortcuts to make it easier to drive the application from the keyboard, and buttons are matched with menu entries

❑ No dragging is required: files are transferred by selecting and copying

❑ The user interface is kept as simple as possible, and doesn't waste screen real estate

❑ Neither the application nor the user interface makes unrealistic demands on memory or CPU performance

In general, there will always be a gulf between desktop machines and PDA-type devices. Even though processing performance and available memory will increase on PDAs, the gap will remain as desktop performance also improves. You may also be writing for people who have not been indoctrinated with the standard windows paradigms.

Applications must therefore be written accordingly, taking advantage of the opportunities that PDA devices offer for mobile computing and wireless networking, but also being aware of the constraints that they impose.

Accessing EPOC Resources with JNI

The Java language is intended to be as platform-neutral as possible, and to achieve this it provides high-level support for most of the resources an application requires. However, there are times when it is necessary to gain access to unsupported EPOC resources. For instance, Java on EPOC release 5 does not include support for direct access to the RS232 or infrared ports.

JNI on EPOC can be used to:

- ❑ Access hardware-specific functionality
- ❑ Listen for and respond to EPOC system events
- ❑ Launch EIKON dialogs (such as Internet or modem settings)
- ❑ Access native EPOC data types, like DBMS
- ❑ Work around limitations and/or defects

However there are some parts of EPOC that even JNI can't reach. In particular, it is not possible to access EIKON controls that aren't known to the AWT server, such as date choosers, range selectors, or button bars.

> **The purpose of the section is to give a basic understanding in the use of JNI on EPOC. JNI is an intricate subject with plenty that can go wrong. For a full treatment of this subject, see *Essential JNI: Java Native Interface* (Prentice Hall, ISBN 0-13-679895-0). This chapter complements the JNI section in the EPOC SDK for Java, and assumes familiarity with it. It also assumes a basic knowledge of JNI.**

The EPOCInfo Example

EPOCInfo displays information about the EPOC device on which it is run. It is an extension of the PowerInfo example on the EPOC SDK for Java, and as well as showing the length of time on internal and external power, together with the current power source, it provides details of the available drives and adds a convenient GUI. It uses Java's native interface capability to access the native calls that provide this information.

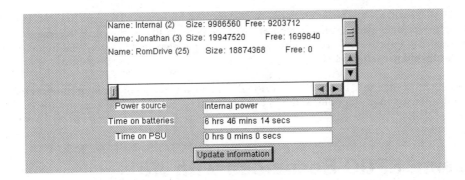

Summary of the Build Process

The table below lists the files and classes that make up the EPOCInfo example, and what each of them does. You will need to create the files, or adapt them from the PowerInfo example (\erj\examples\PowerInfo\).

File	Purpose
classes.mk	Lists the class files in the project, and those with native methods.
exports.def	Defines the lookup function needed by the native DLL that allows the library entry point to be resolved by name. Lists the native methods that the DLL exports.
EPOCInfoDll.cpp	Provides the E32Dll() entry point function that EPOC requires for all libraries.
runex.bat	Batch file that will launch EPOCInfo under the emulator.
Makefile	This is the makefile used to build the project.
EPOCInfo.app	Defines EPOCInfo's UIDs, so that its icon will appear on the Extras bar.
EPOCInfo.txt	Contains the command line used to launch EPOCInfo from the Extras bar.
EPOCInfo.java	Contains the main Java class, EPOCInfo.
EFrame.java	Provides some support for an EPOC look and feel.
GridPanel.java	Support class that helps with laying out UIs.
EPOCInfo.cpp	Implements the native methods.

The overall process for creating the EPOCInfo application looks like this:

❑   Start by copying across the PowerInfo example from \erj\examples\powerinfo\ into a new directory, erj\examples\EPOCInfo\.

❑   Edit makefile to replace all occurrences of the text "PowerInfo" (and its variants) with "EPOCInfo" (see below).

- ❏ Modify `classes.mk` (see below).

- ❏ Rename `powerinfodll.cpp` to `EPOCInfoDLL.cpp`.

- ❏ Modify `exports.def` (see below).

- ❏ Copy or create the source files (`EPOCInfo.cpp` and `EPOCInfo.java`) and the support classes (`EFrame.java` and `GridPanel.java`). The sources for this example can be found in `\Java Examples\EPOCInfo\`.

- ❏ Build and run.

The following sections describe this process, and how to make the necessary files, in detail. Fortunately, most of the work is handled by a make process. The diagram below shows what this does.

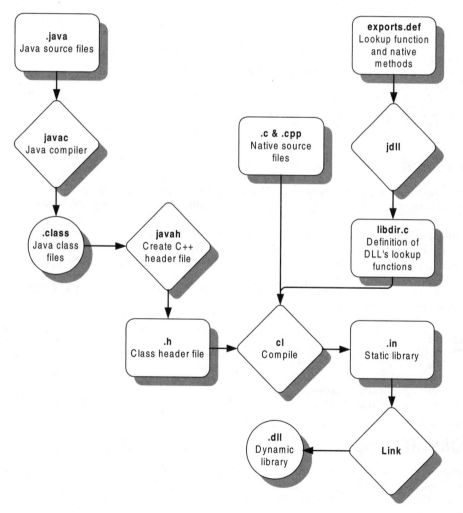

classes.mk

`classes.mk` lists the classes used by a project, and those with native methods:

❏   `FILES_class` is a list of all the classes in the project, regardless of whether they have native methods or not.

❏   `JNI_CLASSES` is a list of the classes that either have native methods, or have interfaces that need to be known to native code. The class names must include the package name if the classes are not in the default package.

`classes.mk` for the EPOCInfo application looks like this:

```
# classes-devkit.mk

FILES_class = EPOCInfo.class
JNI_CLASSES = EPOCInfo
CLASSPATH = .;$(CLASSES);$(LIBDIR)\classes.zip
.java.class :
    $(JAVAC) -classpath $(CLASSPATH) $<
clobber :: FORCE
    -@$(DEL) $(FILES_class)
```

exports.def

EPOC supports exporting functions from DLLs by ordinal rather than by name. This means that each native DLL must provide a lookup function that allows the library entry point to be resolved by name.

The build process will generate a file called `libdir.c` that contains the definition of this lookup function. For this to happen, you must provide the process with a `.def` (module definition) file. This is a text file that first identifies the lookup function, and then lists the native methods that the DLL exports.

By default, the build system expects the `.def` file to be called `exports.def`. The EPOCInfo `exports.def` file looks like this:

```
EXPORTS
    __epocinfo_lookup @ 1 NONAME
    Java_EPOCInfo_externalPowerPresent
    Java_EPOCInfo_timeOnPower
    Java_EPOCInfo_diskUsage
    Java_EPOCInfo_diskName
```

EPOCInfoDll.cpp

`EPOCInfoDll.cpp` is the EPOC DLL stub file. This provides the `E32Dll()` entry point function that EPOC requires for all libraries. Rename `PowerInfoDll.cpp` that you copied from the PowerInfo example. The contents can remain unchanged.

runex.bat

`runex.bat` is used to launch EPOCInfo from a command prompt. Its contents are:

```
\epoc32\release\wins\deb\java_g.exe -cd j:\examples\EPOCInfo EPOCInfo
```

The `deb\` element indicates that we are running the debug version of the emulator. This is because by default, the makefile creates a debug version of the EPOCInfo DLL for the Win32 build (that is, `epocinfo_g.dll`).

EPOCInfo.app

`EPOCInfo.app` defines EPOCInfo's UIDs, so that its icon will appear on the Extras bar. The ID that has been assigned to this application is 0x10005750. To create the file:

❑ Open a command window.

❑ Change to the drive containing the EPOC SDKs.

❑ Enter `appbuild EPOCInfo 10005750` at a command prompt.

❑ This will create the required file, unfortunately in the directory `\epoc32\wins\c\system\apps\EPOCInfo\`. Move the file from this directory to your `\erj\examples\EPOCInfo\` directory.

EPOCInfo.txt

`EPOCInfo.txt` contains the command that should be passed to the Java interpreter to launch EPOCInfo. Its contents are therefore simply:

```
EPOCInfo
```

Makefile

`Makefile` contains the instructions used to build the application. Use the version you copied from the PowerInfo example as a starting point. For this project, the contents should be:

```
binary = library
TOPDIR = ..\..
!include $(TOPDIR)\makefiles\make.defs
LIBRARY = epocinfo
EXTRA_LIBS = $(TRGDIR)\efsrv.lib
FILES_obj = $(OBJ)\epocinfo.$O $(OBJ)\epocinfodll.$O
!include $(TOPDIR)\makefiles\library.mk
```

❑ TOPDIR is the path from the project directory (that is, `\erj\examples\EPOCInfo\`) to the top-level directory into which this SDK was installed.

❑ LIBRARY = epocinfo sets the name of the DLL generated by the make process. The name of the DLL must be unique, and must be the same as the name used in the lookup function name in exports.def, described above.

❑ EXTRA_LIBS is a whitespace-separated list of additional libraries.

❑ FILES_obj is a list of the object files to which the native library is linked.

EPOCInfo.java

EPOCInfo.java contains the main Java class. The EPOCInfo class extends our EFrame class to help give the application an EPOC look and feel:

```
import java.awt.*;
import java.awt.event.*;

class EPOCInfo extends EFrame implements ActionListener {
```

Next, dialogText is displayed in the About dialog box provided by EFrame:

```
String[] dialogText =
    { "--The EPOC Information Console--",
      "A simple Java JNI demonstration",
      "Version 0.02, 21 October 1999",
      "Jonathan Allin" };

static final int FREE = 0;
static final int SIZE = 1;
static final int EXTERNAL = 0;
static final int INTERNAL = 1;

Button updateInfoB = new Button("Update information");
TextField timeIF = new TextField(25);
TextField timeEF = new TextField(25);
TextField sourceF = new TextField(25);
TextArea infoF = new TextArea(8, 45);
```

The four native methods are declared below (we will look at their implementation later). timeOnPower(int type) returns the time in microseconds that the device has been on external power (type equals 0) or internal power (type equals 1).

externalPowerPresent() returns true if the device is connected to an external device. Under the emulator, externalPowerPresent() will *always* return true, and timeOnPower() will return the elapsed time since the emulator was started.

diskUsage(int mode, int drive) returns the free space on drive if mode equals 0, and the size of the drive if mode equals 1. drive is an integer between 0 and 25. diskName(int drive) returns the name of the specified drive, or null if the drive is not present:

```
public native long timeOnPower(int type);
public native boolean externalPowerPresent();

// return of -18 = KErrNotReady, e.g. non-existent drive
public native long diskUsage(int mode, int drive);

// Returns a null String if there is an error
public native String diskName(int drive);
```

Load the native library containing the implementation of the native methods:

```
static { System.loadLibrary("epocinfo"); }
```

timeToString(long timeinms) is a utility method that returns the time in microseconds as a String suitable for printing:

```
public String timeToString(long timeinms) {
    final int MSINSECOND = 1000000;
    final int SECONDSINHOUR = 3600;
    final int SECONDSINMIN = 60;
    long seconds = timeinms / MSINSECOND;
    long hours = seconds / SECONDSINHOUR;
    long minutes = (seconds % SECONDSINHOUR) / SECONDSINMIN;
    seconds -= ((hours * SECONDSINHOUR) + (minutes * SECONDSINMIN));
    if(timeinms < 0) return "error";
    else return "" + hours + " hrs " +
            minutes + " mins " + seconds + " secs";
}
```

The constructor creates and positions all the UI controls, using our GridPanel class to make layout a bit easier. The last thing the constructor does is to call updateInfo(), which updates the user interface with information obtained using the native calls.

```
public EPOCInfo() {
    setTitle("The EPOC Information Console");
    GridPanel panel = new GridPanel();

    panel.constraints.gridwidth = 2;
    panel.add(infoF, 0, 0);
    panel.constraints.gridwidth = 1;
    panel.add(new Label("Power source"), 0, 1);
    panel.add(sourceF, 1, 1);
    panel.add(new Label("Time on batteries"), 0, 2);
    panel.add(timeIF, 1, 2);
    panel.add(new Label("Time on PSU"), 0, 3);
    panel.add(timeEF, 1, 3);
    panel.constraints.gridwidth = 2;
    panel.add(updateInfoB, 0, 4);
    updateInfoB.addActionListener(this);

    add(panel);
    aboutDialog.setTitle("About the EPOC Information Console");
```

```
        aboutDialog.text = dialogText;
        show();
        updateInfo();
    }
```

`updateInfo()` uses the native methods to gather information about the EPOC device, and then displays the results in the user interface:

```
    private void updateInfo() {
        if(externalPowerPresent()) sourceF.setText("External power");
        else sourceF.setText("Internal power");

        long result = timeOnPower(EXTERNAL);
        timeEF.setText(timeToString(result));

        result = timeOnPower(INTERNAL);
        timeIF.setText(timeToString(result));
```

Go through all the drives, only displaying information about drives the are present (`diskUsage()` returns a negative number if an error occurs, generally through trying to access a non-existent drive):

```
        infoF.setText("");
        for(int i = 0; i < 26; i++) {
            long free = diskUsage(FREE, i);
            if(free < 0) continue;
            infoF.append("Name: " + diskName(i) + " (" + i + ")\t");
            infoF.append("Size: " + diskUsage(SIZE, i) + "\t");
            infoF.append("Free: " + free + "\n");
        }
    }
```

Update the display when the `updateInfoB` button is pressed. Calling `super.actionPerformed()` ensures that any events not handled by this class are passed to the superclass, `EFrame`:

```
    public void actionPerformed(ActionEvent ae) {
        if(ae.getSource() == updateInfoB) updateInfo();
        else super.actionPerformed(ae);
    }
```

The `main()` method just creates an instance of the `EPOCInfo` class:

```
    public static void main(String[] argv) {
        new EPOCInfo();
    }
}
```

EFrame.java and GridPanel.java

`EFrame.java` and `GridPanel.java` are the same classes that we used in the Dice Machine application earlier, but for simplicity they have not been put into a package.

EPOCInfo.cpp

EPOCInfo.cpp contains the definition of the four native functions. The first two are also used in the PowerInfo example.

Include the header file, EPOCInfo.h, that was generated by javah during the make process:

```
#include <e32hal.h>
#include <f32file.h>
#include "EPOCInfo.h"
```

to_C() converts an EPOC TInt64 to a JNI jlong. This approach is necessary because EPOC stores a 64 bit integer as a structure:

```
inline jlong to_C (TInt64 a) {
    return *REINTERPRET_CAST(jlong*,&a);
}

enum { EExternalPower, EMainBattery };
```

The native implementation of timeOnPower() returns -1 if an error occurs:

```
JNIEXPORT jlong JNICALL Java_EPOCInfo_timeOnPower(
        JNIEnv* /*env*/,
        jobject /*obj*/,
        jint powersource) {
    TSupplyInfoV1Buf supply;
    jlong ret = 0;
    TInt err = UserHal::SupplyInfo(supply);
    if(err < 0) return -1;

    switch(powersource) {
        case EExternalPower:
            ret = to_C(supply().iExternalPowerInUseMicroSeconds.Int64());
            break;
        case EMainBattery:
            ret = to_C(supply().iMainBatteryInUseMicroSeconds.Int64());
            break;
    }
    return ret;
}
```

The native implementation of externalPowerPresent() returns true if the EPOC device is being powered from an external source (jboolean is an enumerated type that gets mapped to a Java boolean):

```
JNIEXPORT jboolean JNICALL Java_EPOCInfo_externalPowerPresent (
        JNIEnv* /*env*/,
        jobject /*obj*/) {
    TSupplyInfoV1Buf supply;
    TInt err = UserHal::SupplyInfo(supply);
```

```
        if((err == KErrNone) && supply().iExternalPowerPresent) {
            return JNI_TRUE;
        } else {
            return JNI_FALSE;
        }
    }
```

The native implementation of `diskUsage()` returns the drive's free space if `mode` equals 0, or the drive's size if `mode` equals 1:

```
JNIEXPORT jlong JNICALL Java_EPOCInfo_diskUsage (
        JNIEnv* /*env*/,
        jobject /*obj*/,
        jint mode,
        jint drive) {
    RFs fs;
    TVolumeInfo vi;
    TInt64 free = 0;
    TInt64 size = 0;
    TInt err;
    if(KErrNone == (err = fs.Connect())) {
        if(KErrNone == (err = fs.Volume(vi, drive))) {
            free = vi.iFree;
            size = vi.iSize;
            fs.Close();
            if(mode == 0) {
                return to_C(free);
            } else {
                return to_C(size);
            }
        }
    }
    fs.Close(); // Close() must always be called
    return err; // -18 = KErrNotReady, eg drive does not exist
}
```

The native implementation of `diskName()` returns the name of the drive specified by `drive` (an integer between 0 and 25). If the drive is not present, the call returns null (we could raise an exception, but (a) this would be slower, and (b) the absence of a drive is not an exceptional event). When running on the emulator, the method will return the name of the drive onto which the EPOC SDKs were installed:

```
JNIEXPORT jstring JNICALL Java_EPOCInfo_diskName (
        JNIEnv * jni,
        jobject /*obj*/,
        jint drive) {
    RFs fs;
    TVolumeInfo vi;
    if(KErrNone == fs.Connect()) {
        if(KErrNone == fs.Volume(vi, drive)) {
            fs.Close();
            TBuf<KMaxFileName + 1> name = vi.iName;
            const TText8* ptr = name.PtrZ();
```

```
            jstring str = jni->NewStringUTF(
                    REINTERPRET_CAST(const char*, ptr));
            return str;
        }
    }
    fs.Close();
    return NULL; // The calling Java class should check for a null String
}
```

Building and Running EPOCInfo Under the Emulator

To build the application to run under the emulator:

❑   Open a command window

❑   Change to the directory containing the EPOCInfo example

❑   Run vcvars32.bat

❑   Type nmake

nmake will do the following:

❑   Compile EPOCInfo.java, generating EPOCInfo.class and the other class files in the current directory

❑   Invoke javah, generating EPOCInfo.h in \erj\examples\EPOCInfo\CClassHeaders\ (PowerInfo.cpp #includes PowerInfo.h)

❑   Compile the native code (EPOCInfo.cpp and EPOCInfoDll.cpp)

❑   Build the native library epocinfo_g.dll into directory \epoc32\release\wins\deb\ (note the _g suffix to indicate that we have created a debug version of the DLL, which will therefore be placed in the deb\ directory)

To run the application, enter runex at the command prompt. This will launch the emulator, and then the EPOCInfo application.

Building, Installing, and Running EPOCInfo for an EPOC Device

To build for an EPOC device, type in nmake target=arm at the command prompt. This will build EPOCInfo.class and the other class files in the current directory, and the EPOC DLL, epocinfo.dll, in \erj\bin\arm\. These files are suitable for installing and running on an EPOC device.

To install the application:

❑   Copy epocinfo.dll into \system\libs\ on any drive on the EPOC device

❑   Create a directory called \system\apps\EPOCInfo\

❑   Copy EPOCInfo.txt, EPOCInfo.app, and the six class files into this directory

An icon representing the EPOCInfo application will then appear on the Extras bar, allowing EPOCInfo to be started like any other EPOC application.

Looking to the Future

We'll now take a look at some of the Java technologies that will affect Java on EPOC. These include Personal Java, JavaPhone, and Java 2 Micro Edition.

Personal Java and JavaPhone will form part of the next software release of EPOC. These technologies will address a number of issues with the current implementation: reduced ROM and RAM footprints, better access to underlying EPOC resources (reducing the need for JNI), and they're an opportunity to fix bugs.

We can also expect an optimized Java implementation for Motorola's M*Core: the EPOC port is expected to be running on development silicon early in 2000, with M*Core based products available in late 2000 or early 2001.

Personal Java

Personal Java is a configurable version of standard Java that's more appropriate for resource-limited devices. The full specification can be found at http://java.sun.com/products/personaljava/spec-1-1-3. It is based on JDK 1.1.6, which is essentially the same as JDK 1.1.4, though it includes some fixes and support for RMI over IIOP.

Personal Java requires less ROM and RAM. The ROM footprint on EPOC will vary from about 1.75MB to around 2.25MB, depending on the options chosen by a licensee (the current ROM footprint is around 2.7MB). The main gain, however, is in the reduced RAM requirement. A basic "Hello World" console application requires about 480KB, while a simple application that uses the AWT will require about 680KB. This is in contrast to the current RAM footprint, which is around 1.5MB to 2MB. Further details can be found at http://java.sun.com/products/personaljava/MemoryUsage.html.

Personal Java comes with an improved set of tools:

❑ JVMDI is the JVM debugger interface. This will allow any compliant debugging tool to debug Java applications running on EPOC hardware remotely.

❑ JVMPI is the JVM profiling interface. It will enable profiling tools to report on which code is being accessed, and to identify performance bottlenecks.

The JavaPhone APIs

JavaPhone provides APIs and interfaces to support the development of applications and information services for telephony devices. It's aimed at network operators and content providers to make it easier and quicker to develop robust, secure, and cross-platform services. Target devices are not just traditional handsets, but *any* device with telephony capability.

The APIs provide access to underlying EPOC functionality in a standard way from Java, considerably reducing the need for JNI programming. Further information can be obtained from Sun's web site at http://java.sun.com/products/javaphone.

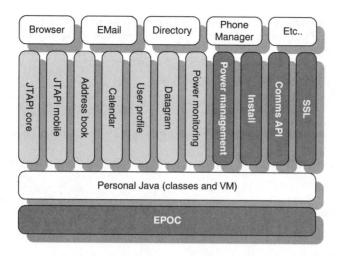

The diagram above illustrates JavaPhone's architecture. There are, in fact, two JavaPhone profiles: one for Internet screen phones, and one for mobile phones. It is the latter that's of interest to us, and which is illustrated in the diagram.

JavaPhone builds on Personal Java, so we still have all of Personal Java's capabilities. It is a composite of a number of APIs and interfaces: the required APIs are in light gray, while the optional APIs are in dark gray. End user applications sit on top of these APIs.

JTAPI core and JTAPI mobile provide access to ETEL (EPOC's telephony API). They provide the basic framework to model telephone calls, and for direct control of the basic telephone features:

❑   Making and tearing down calls, call forwarding, speed dialing

❑   Fine-grained state control of telephone calls: calls on hold, transferring telephone calls, setting up conferencing telephone calls

❑   JTAPI mobile provides support for multiple wireless networks, radio signal monitoring, switching the radio on and off, generating DTMF sequences

Sun's APIs for the Address book and Calendar were heavily influenced by Symbian's Contacts and Agenda APIs and closely mirror them, so we can take advantage of the optimized native support for these interfaces.

The User Profile package defines objects to get and set the current user contact information, which is returned in the same format as the Address book package.

The Comms APIs will be supported. This is the `javax.comm` package, which gives Java applications much-needed access to the serial, parallel, and infrared ports on an EPOC machine.

A JTAPI example

The following example illustrates how the JTAPI APIs can be used to establish a telephone call to "123456". (Note that it can't be run on the current EPOC Java implementation, but should it run on the next release.)

First, we import the provider's JTAPI package, which might be something like
`com.symbian.jtapi.telephony`. The provider is the 'window' through which JTAPI applications
see the telephony system:

```
import com.<provider>.jtapi.telephony.*;
import javax.telephony.*;

public class Example {
    public static final void main(String args[]) {
```

We create a provider by obtaining the default JTAPI implementation, and then the default provider for
that implementation:

```
Provider provider = null;
try {
    JtapiPeer peer = JtapiPeerFactory.getJtapiPeer(null);
    provider = peer.getProvider(null);
```

Of course, we need to catch the exception if something goes wrong. In this example, we are printing to
the console; in a real device we'd create an alert window.

```
} catch (Exception e) {
    System.out.println("Can't get provider: " +
                       e.toString());
    System.exit(0);
}
```

In the following section, an `Address` is a *logical* end point – a phone number, for example. A
`Terminal` is a *physical* end point, such as a phone set. One address can have more than one terminal,
and vice versa. For instance, an office might have two secretaries: both phones will ring if the secretarial
number is dialed (one address, two terminals), but in addition each secretary has their own personal
phone number (so each terminal has two addresses):

```
Address origaddr = null;
Terminal origterm = null;
try {
```

We need to get the address and terminal associated with the originating side of the telephone call
(potentially, the terminal from which the call is being made could have two numbers: one private, one
business):

```
origaddr = provider.getAddress("+447777876543");
```

We ask the `Address` for a list of `Terminals` on it, and arbitrarily choose the first one:

```
Terminal[] terminals = origaddr.getTerminals();
origterm = terminals[0];
} catch(Exception e) {
    System.out.println("Exception: "+e.toString());
    System.exit(0);
}
```

Finally, we create and place the telephone call:

```
.    Call call = null;
     try {
         call = provider.createCall();
         call.setState(javax.telephony.Call.ACTIVE);
         Connection c[] = call.connect(origterm, origaddr,"123456");
     } catch(Exception e) {
         System.out.println("Can't connect: " + e.toString());
         System.exit(0);
     }
   }
}
```

Java 2 Platform, Micro Edition

We saw earlier that Sun has organized its Java products into three editions. The smallest of these is the Java platform, micro edition. (See http://java.sun.com/products/kvm/wp/). In the mid term, it is expected that Symbian will align its Java implementation with the Mobile Information Device profile (discussed below) that is being defined as part of the J2ME process.

The Java 2 platform, micro edition, is targeted at consumer and embedded electronics, including cell phones, Internet screen phones, pagers, mobile point-of-sale terminals, and any other device constrained in processing power, memory, or graphical capability. It is driven by the needs of these small footprint devices, the conflicting requirements from different industries, and the recognition that one size *doesn't* fit all. To make this work, Sun will allow industry groups to define Java technology-based profiles specific to their industry. These profiles are collections of Java APIs built on top of a configuration that defines a Java technology-based platform suited to an industry or class of device. Profiles must be endorsed by Sun via the Java community process (http://java.sun.com/aboutJava/communityprocess).

J2ME consists of a virtual machine and a minimal layer of APIs that provide enough (and only enough) functionality to securely and safely download Java classes to a device and configure the Java environment. The set of core classes needed to achieve this is very limited: parts of java.lang, some error classes, some exception classes, and containers from java.util. The remaining JDK classes (or subsets of classes), including IO, graphics, and the AWT, are optional.

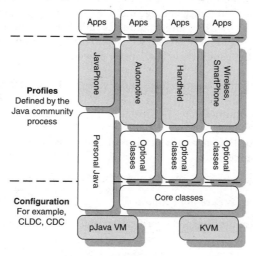

A **configuration** defines the VM (classic VM, Personal Java VM or KVM) and a set of optional classes taken from the JDK (that is, J2SE) core APIs. Two standard configurations are being defined for J2ME:

❑ **CDC**, or **Connected Device Configuration**: This is the larger configuration, employing a fully featured JVM, and which underlies the more capable profiles. It is this profile that will be of most interest to Symbian.

❑ **CLDC**, or **Connected, Limited Device Configuration**: Leaner configuration, employing the KVM. Underlies profiles targeted at feature phones and small devices. (Palm V, iMode, etc.)

JavaPhone is a profile that sits on top of Personal Java and, as we discussed earlier, is itself divided into two profiles: Internet smart phones and mobile phones. The Mobile Information Device profile (MIDP), currently under discussion, is aimed at the sort of small feature phone that would utilize the CLDC configuration. Symbian is on the MIDP, CDC, and CLDC experts group, and in particular are keen to ensure that CLDC is a subset of CDC. To achieve this, it is necessary that CLDC adopts a standard UI API. Symbian is also on the experts group for the Foundation Profile (http://web2.java.sun.com/aboutJava/communityprocess/accepted.html), aimed at devices that will operate within a rich variety of networks, and which don't require a standard user interface.

The KVM

The KVM (the Kilo virtual machine) is an aggressively optimized and scaled back VM, designed to fit on small devices such as smart phones and pagers, and as such underlies the CLDC configuration. It is not a cut-down version of an existing Java virtual machine, but was written from scratch in C. The KVM is about fitness for purpose: what it does, it does very well, but it is not intended to support a general purpose Java platform. It requires a specific programming model to handle code verification and garbage collection, and an application written for one KVM implementation is unlikely to work on another.

The KVM configuration has reduced memory requirements, at around 80 to 100KB. The KVM itself is about 48KB (EPOC's `javai.dll` compares well: it provides a full JDK 1.1 implementation in 128KB). The core libraries take a further 50KB or so, and Sun claim that useful applications can run on devices with as little as 128KB of memory.

Performance has been improved through a faster byte code interpreter, a single heap model with no memory management and fast thread switching, and a faster garbage collector. The garbage collector gains some of its performance by using direct addresses rather than indirect pointers. The downside is that data blocks on the heap cannot be moved, which will lead to memory fragmentation unless the code is carefully designed: the general rule is to create objects once and reuse them.

The net result is that target processors can be as small as a 16 bit, 16MHz devices.

The KVM is necessarily constrained:

❑ It has no support for JNI: any native calls required must be compiled into the KVM when it is built from Sun's source code

❑ Support for large data types (`long`, `float`, `double`) is optional

❑ Multidimensional arrays are not supported

❑ No class file verification. Bytecode verification must take place on the server

Configurations based on the KVM will be limited. There will be no standard UI library for the KVM; instead, graphics will be handled by native calls. (Espial is one company that has a lightweight graphics component set and corresponding API for KVM configurations.) This also means that emulating one device on another (such as emulating PalmPilot on EPOC) will require emulating an API layer.

Virtual machine functionality will be distributed between server and client:

❑   Class verification can be done by the server – that is, the client assumes any code it receives is trusted.

❑   Only the critical features are included in the client. Enhanced dynamic downloading capabilities will deliver new services to the client from the server as necessary, so for a device that doesn't contain all the Java libraries necessary to run a given application, the network server can determine the device's footprint, and deliver the application and additional libraries as a complete package.

By when?

The road map looks like this:

Now	EPOC v5	JDK 1.1.4
Q2 '00	EPOC v6	JavaPhone 1.0, pJava 3.01
Q1 '01	EPOC v7	JavaPhone 1.1, MIDP 1.0, CDC

Summary

This chapter has taken a look at Java on EPOC. In it, we have covered the strategic importance of Java to Symbian and the issues involved in running standard Java applications and applets. We have looked at writing Java applications and applets specifically for EPOC, how to achieve an EPOC look and feel, and how to use the Java native interface APIs to access native resource. Finally, we took a look at the Java technologies that will soon be available on EPOC.

24

The Wireless Application Protocol

WAP (**Wireless Application Protocol**) is a set of open standards whose job is to deliver Internet content to wireless devices. With WAP, wireless devices can gain access to the Internet using a **microbrowser**, which displays specially formatted web pages suitable for devices with tiny screens and no mouse. The WAP standards define:

❑ A programming model that, as you will see later, is based heavily on the existing WWW programming model, but is better suited to the requirements of wireless devices.

❑ A markup language called **WML** (**Wireless Markup Language**) that adheres to XML (eXtensible Markup Language) standards.

❑ A scripting language called **WMLScript** that complements WML and provides programmable functionality at the wireless device.

❑ A lightweight protocol stack that minimizes traffic, and hence bandwidth requirements. This stack can run over a wide range of international wireless bearers including circuit switched data calls and SMS (Short Message Service). This stack replaces the TCP/IP protocol stack used in the WWW model.

❑ A framework for **Wireless Telephony Applications** (**WTA**) that will give access to mobile telephony functionality from within WMLScript applets.

WAP is defined by the **WAP Forum** (http://www.wapforum.org), an industry association (formerly called Unwired Planet) that was formed by Nokia, Ericsson, Motorola, and Phone.com in 1997. Symbian became a member in 1998 and by the beginning of 2000 membership stood at over 250 organizations. The WAP Forum aims to provide interoperable standards that are open to all, and are independent of wireless network technology and devices. WAP is compatible with the existing digital wireless telephony networks, and future 3rd generation networks that will be much faster and offer enhanced multimedia support.

What Problems does WAP Solve?

Of course, technologies for delivering content to Internet users existed long before WAP. We are all familiar with browser-based Internet access on desktop PCs; the problem was that these technologies were not well suited to wireless information devices such as smart phones and communicators. The differences are in the characteristics of the network, the characteristics of the physical device, and the way the device is used.

The wireless network is different from a wired network, in that it offers mobility, but it does so at a cost; the trade-off is more constrained communication characteristics. In general, a wireless network has:

❑   Less bandwidth

❑   More latency (hidden transmission delays)

❑   Less reliable connections

❑   Less predictable availability

Wireless information devices also have more limited capabilities than desktop computers. They typically have:

❑   Less powerful CPUs

❑   Less memory (RAM, ROM), and no hard drive

❑   Restricted power consumption (limited by batteries)

❑   Smaller displays, with lower resolution, which are often monochrome

❑   Different input devices (no mouse and a limited keypad, but potentially voice input)

Finally, the users of wireless devices also have different needs to desktop users. They will:

❑   Have small specific tasks that need to be accomplished quickly

❑   Often use their devices while performing other tasks, or when they are on the move

❑   Not tolerate a long boot sequence, complicated menu structures or application crashes

There is a further issue that *existing* Internet content is formatted under the assumption of large, high-resolution displays, and that such content cannot easily be reformatted for small screens of diverse shapes and resolutions.

WAP attempts to solve all of the above problems, because the conditions we have just outlined are not likely to change soon. After all, wireless devices are designed to be more than simply portable (remember the first 'portable' PCs?) – they are designed to fit into the hand or pocket, and as such will be different from desktop devices for the foreseeable future.

WAP is not the only technology to enable wireless Internet; compact HTML (used in i-Mode phones) and HDML (Handheld Device Markup Language) both existed before WAP, along with other proprietary formats. In addition, SMS (Short Message Service) and paging allow the 'pushing' of content to mobile subscribers. However, WAP is likely to become the most popular solution, due to the support it has from the members of the WAP Forum.

The WAP Solution

WAP provides a user interface metaphor that is tailored for wireless information devices. Users navigate through a series of **cards** with scroll keys. In addition, context-dependent **soft keys** are presented on screen for specific operations or the selection of menu options. Navigation functions including Bookmarks, Back, and Home are inherited from the WWW browser model.

Another concept taken from the Web is the proxy model. WAP utilizes proxy technology to connect between the wireless domain and the WWW. The wireless device can offload tasks such as address resolution, caching, and protocol conversion to a device called a **WAP gateway** that's within the network connected to the Internet. This reduces the performance required from the wireless device.

The protocols used by WAP are similar in concept to those used by the Web, but are optimized for the low bandwidth, high latency characteristics of wireless networks. For example:

- **Wireless Transaction Protocol** (**WTP**) has less complexity than its opposite number, TCP, in the area of connection establishment and closure. A typical user session with three information requests from the client and three corresponding responses would require 7 packets to be sent in WAP, as opposed to 17 for web content over TCP/IP.

- WTP cuts out header overhead associated with the re-ordering of packets in TCP/IP. Unlike on the Internet, packets *cannot* become out of order between the WAP gateway and the client device. This reduction in complexity also removes the need for a complex and resource hungry TCP protocol implementation in the wireless device.

- The plain text headers of HTTP can be replaced with more compact binary headers. This increases speed and saves power by reducing the quantity of data that needs to be sent over the wireless link. The content, or payload, can also be compressed before being sent.

- Unlike TCP/IP, WAP includes a lightweight session suspension and re-establishment protocol. This allows sessions to be suspended to free up network resources and conserve battery energy.

- A WAP security model, which focuses on providing connection security between WAP client and server (WAP protocol endpoints). It uses a version of the TLS (Transport Layer Security) protocol that is normally used with TCP. This is called **WTLS** (**Wireless Transport Layer Security** protocol). The WAP gateway provides conversion between WTLS and TLS for accessing secure web applications. If security is required between a browser and origin server, they must use WAP protocols from end-to-end, or employ higher-level security mechanisms such as digital signatures and encryption.

WAP goes further than the web model to provide new wireless functionality in three key areas: 'push', location awareness, and the provision of a voice/data integration API called the **Wireless Telephony Application** (**WTA**).

- Push is useful in the wireless context for such tasks as e-mail notification. The ability to push information from the server (web site) to the client is not supported in the current web model, but provision has been made for this in WAP. At the time of writing, push is still work in progress at the WAP Forum. The proposed push specifications for WAP version 1.2 are available, along with the rest of the WAP specifications, from http://www.wapforum.org/what/technical.htm.

❑ Location awareness is possible because the WAP gateway can find out from the wireless network where the client is geographically, and could make this information available for location-sensitive content generation.

❑ WTA provides application developers with an interface from WML and WMLScript to a specific set of local, telephony-related functions in the wireless device, such as the ability to initiate phone calls from the device, and to respond to mobile network events as they occur.

Another current work in progress at the WAP Forum is the concept of user agent profiles (called **UAProf**). This helps deal with the diverse range of client devices by allowing the user agent to provide information about itself to the origin server or WAP gateway in the form of a URI. The origin server or gateway will then be able to modify responses based on characteristics of the user agent. The proposed UAProf specification is available for WAP version 1.2; it defines a set of components and attributes that WAP-enabled devices may convey.

UAProf may include (but is not limited to) hardware characteristics such as screen size, color capabilities, image capabilities, and manufacturer; software characteristics such as operating system vendor and version, support for MExE, and audio and video encoders; application/user preferences such as browser manufacturer and version, markup languages and versions supported, and scripting languages supported; WAP characteristics (WML script libraries, WAP version, WML deck size, etc.); and network characteristics such as latency and reliability. In summary, WAP has the following advantages over other technologies:

❑ It is optimized for low-bandwidth, high-latency networks, and client devices with limited functionality

❑ It will have support for location-dependent information (currently being planned)

❑ It will have the ability for content to be optimized for client device capabilities (currently being planned)

❑ It will offer support for telephony applications.

And if you have any doubt about its popularity, the WAP Forum predicts that by 2003, over 500 million WAP client devices may have been sold in the United States and Western Europe alone.

EPOC and WAP

The first EPOC device to deliver WAP (and one of the first WAP devices on the market) was the Ericsson MC218 mobile companion. The WAP browser supports WML version 1.1 and WMLScript version 1.1 on a browser area of at least 537x181 pixels.

The Ericsson R380 was the first EPOC phone to be announced with a built-in WAP browser. The R380 has a 360 x 120 pixel monochrome touch-screen, and text input is performed with an on-screen keyboard, or a character recognition screen. The WAP browser supports WML version 1.1 and WMLScript version 1.1 on a browser area of 310x100 pixels.

These and future EPOC devices will support existing and emerging WAP standards.

The WAP Programming Model

To see how the WAP programming model differs, look at the following diagram of the existing WWW programming model. The browser application in the client sends a series of requests for named data objects that are identified by a Uniform Resource Locator (URL). The server (web site) responds with the requested data in a standard content formats such as Hypertext Markup Language (HTML), GIF image files, PDF files, JavaScript, or others.

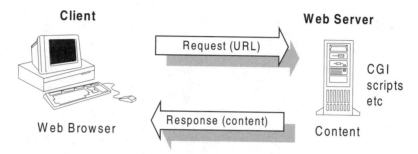

In contrast, the next diagram shows the WAP programming model, which is similar to the WWW programming model. A request for a URL is initiated at the client and sent (optionally in a compacted form) to the WAP gateway. The WAP gateway converts this request into standard Internet format and sends it to the server over TCP/IP. A response corresponding to the requested URL is generated at the server. This response is formatted in one of a set of well-known content formats (these are WML, WMLS, WBMP, vCard, or vCal, for WAP 1.1 and WAP 1.2). When this response is received by the WAP gateway it is encoded and passed on to the client using WAP protocols. The origin server may be a web server that is serving WML (this could be the WAP gateway itself), or a filter that is converting HTML into WML. (Push has been ignored for the purposes of this description.)

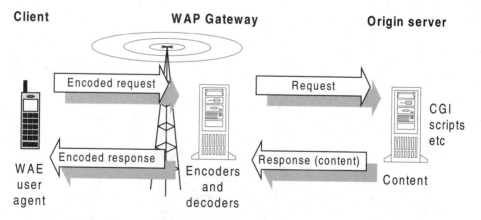

It is important to distinguish ownership of these devices: the requesting client exists within the handset or wireless information device, while the WAP gateway exists within the wireless network and is managed by the wireless network provider. Finally, the origin server, which provides the content, exists within the Internet domain and is managed by the owner of this Internet host. The following diagram shows the location of the various entities. It also shows a Wireless Telephony Application (WTA) server, which would also be owned by the network provider. In this example, the WTA server responds to the WAP client directly, and is used to provide WAP access to the features of the wireless network.

The underlying mechanisms for getting the packets of WAP information to the device are called **bearers**. Bearers for WAP are network dependent, and may be packet switched or circuit switched.

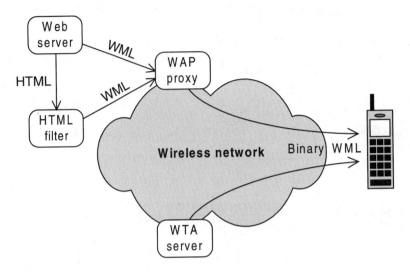

WAP Protocols

There are four layers of WAP protocols:

- ❑ Session Layer
- ❑ Transaction Layer
- ❑ Security Layer
- ❑ Datagram Layer

The following diagram shows the relationship between the layers, and compares this with the Internet protocol stack of the WWW model.

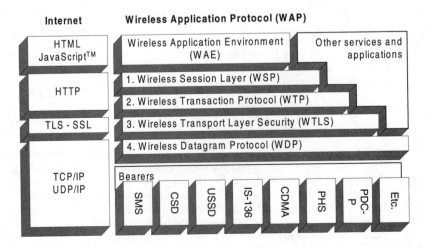

Wireless Application Environment

The **Wireless Application Environment** (**WAE**) is a general-purpose application environment based on a combination of WWW and mobile telephony technologies. It provides an application framework for wireless information devices that serves as a model for handset vendors, defining an application architecture and a general-purpose application programming model. It also defines what you, the programmer, can expect to find on a WAP-enabled client device that you are creating content for.

As we have seen in the earlier parts of this chapter, WAE closely follows the WWW model, using authoring and publishing methods from the WWW wherever possible. The WAE architecture permits content and services to be hosted on standard web servers, and all content is referred to by standard URLs. The major elements of the WAE model include:

- ❏ **WAE User Agents**. These are client-side software applications that provide specific functions such as displaying content. WAE requires user agents for the two main forms of WAP content: WML and WMLScript

- ❏ **Content Generators**. These are applications or services on origin servers that produce standard content formats in response to client side requests. It is expected that these will typically run on HTTP origin servers.

- ❏ **Standard Content Encoding**. Well-defined content allows a user agent (a microbrowser, for example) to display content and navigate through it. These content types include WML (compressed), WMLScript (bytecoded), standard image formats including WBMP, a multi-part container format (compacted MIME), and adopted business card (vCard) and calendar (vCal) formats.

- ❏ **Wireless Telephony Applications** (WTA). Some telephony specific extensions to provide you with call and feature control mechanisms for mobile network services, including making telephone calls.

Wireless Markup Language (WML)

WML is a tag-based document markup language, similar to HTML. WML is based on the eXtensible Markup Language (XML) and was developed specifically for narrowband wireless devices. In this environment, WML provides:

- ❏ Text and image support, with some formatting and layout commands

- ❏ WML **cards** grouped into **decks**. The deck is the unit of content transmission (as is an HTML page) and is identified by a URL. The deck is then split into one or more cards for display purposes, each identified using an `id` attribute.

- ❏ Support for managing navigation between cards and decks, including anchored links and commands for event handling. The commands can execute scripts, or be used for navigating.

- ❏ A mechanism for setting parameters for WML decks. Variables can be used in place of strings and substituted at runtime.

Cards and Decks

User interaction is described by a set of cards (grouped together in decks). Each card provides a specification for a particular user interaction. The user navigates to a card and reviews its contents. At this point, the user may enter requested information, or select an option before moving on to another card. Instructions within the cards may invoke services on the origin server, and further decks are retrieved from origin servers as required. As with HTML, WML decks may be stored as files on the origin server, or may be generated dynamically by a server application.

WML Features

WML provides the following:

- Support for text and images. As with HTML, WML provides the browser with a great deal of freedom to determine how the information should be displayed on the user interface. WML has a set of text markup elements, including those for emphasis (bold, italic, big, etc.), line break models (line wrapping and suppression), and tab columns.

- Support for user input. Requests for user input are made in abstract terms, allowing the user agent to implement *how* the user receives the input request at the user interface. WML includes a small set of input controls, including a text entry control for normal input and passwords. WML also supports validation of input at the client by allowing the programmer (WML author) to invoke scripts to check user input. You can also make sure that something is input, and that the input is in the right general form (letters or numbers) before you call a validation script, which saves network round trips.

- WML includes an **option selection** control that allows the programmer to present the user with a list of options that can set data, navigate among cards, or invoke scripts. WML also includes the task invocation controls go and prev. These initiate a navigation or a history management task respectively, such as popping the current card off the history stack. The browser (user agent) presents these controls, and is free to decide how to implement the user interface. For example, they could be associated with physical buttons, rendered onto a touch sensitive screen, or voice controlled.

- Navigation and history stack. Several navigation options are available using URLs, and, as with web browsers, WML uses a history stack mechanism.

- International support. WML's document character set is Unicode, providing for the display of most languages and dialects.

- Efficient use of bandwidth. WML has gone to great lengths to get the greatest use from narrow bandwidth. Multiple user interactions (taking the form of more than one card) can be specified in a single network transfer unit (by containing a group of cards in the same deck). Templates are available for use with multiple subsequent cards, and state management facilities are provided that minimize the need for server requests. WML cards can also introduce variables, which can be used to modify the contents of a parameterized card. These variables can be set by a call to the server and put results into a template card (that is, an element like <card> that has form but no content unless the variable is set). These variables have a lifetime that can be longer than a single deck, allowing them to be shared across multiple decks.

WML Specification

A full specification of WML is freely available on the Internet at the WAP Forum web site at http://www.wapforum.org/what/technical.htm#Approved.

WMLScript

WMLScript is a scripting language that provides application programmers with enhancements to WML. WMLScript adds more advanced user interface behavior, gives more intelligence to the wireless information device, provides access to device facilities, and makes certain message transactions with the server unnecessary. Overall, it adds the following capabilities:

❑ Validation of user input before it is sent to the server

❑ Direct interaction with the user (to display an error message or generate a dialog, for example), again reducing unnecessary server traffic

❑ Access to the services and facilities of the device

❑ Allows extensions to the device software and configuring a device after it has been deployed.

WMLScript also includes the following features:

❑ A scripting language similar to ECMAScript (and JavaScript), adapted to narrow-band operation

❑ Event-based script invocation

❑ Procedural logic for algorithms

❑ Tight integration with WML, including access to WML variables

❑ Strong class library support to get at browser info

WMLScript is weakly typed, and variable types can change over the lifecycle of the variable, depending on the data it contains.

Programmers are provided with operation support that includes assignment operations, arithmetic operations, logical operations and comparison operations. Functions are also supported. Available functions include those in standard libraries, those within the same script as the calling expression, and those in external scripts. WMLScript defines standard libraries for:

❑ The language core (such as abs(), min(), max(), isInt(), exit(), abort(), random(), seed())

❑ String handling (for example, length(), charAt(), subString(), find(), replace(), trim(), compare(), format())

❑ URL functions (such as isValid(), getHost(), getPort(), getReferer())

❑ Browser functions (including getVar(), setVar(), go(), prev(), and newContext())

❑ Floating point operations (pow(), round(), sqrt())

❑ Dialogs (prompt(), confirm(), alert()).

You *cannot* extend the available objects/functions with, say, plugins or Java, as you can with a normal web browser environment.

WMLScript Specification

As with WML, a full specification of WMLScript is freely available at the WAP Forum web site at http://www.wapforum.org/what/technical.htm#Approved. Rather than repeat this information here I shall instead provide and describe an example script, based on WMLScript version 1.1.

Starting WAP Programming

This section assumes that you have some familiarity with HTML. You don't need a WAP phone, or a wireless network subscription to start WAP programming. WAP toolkits that allow development on your desktop PC can be freely downloaded from a number of web sites, including Nokia's and Ericsson's. These toolkits typically provide:

❑ WML, WMLScript and WBMP (wireless bitmap) editors

❑ Encoders for bytecoding etc.

❑ Debugging support (variables can be set and displayed, for example)

❑ Simulated WAP clients with mobile phone type interfaces

❑ Documentation on the Toolkit and WAP standards

With these tools, WAP programs can be developed, debugged and tested on simulated clients. The tools also allow WML and WMLScript to be downloaded from the Internet, edited and tested on the simulated clients.

The following examples were developed on the Nokia WAP Toolkit, available from http://www.forum.nokia.com/developers/wap/wap.html.

Getting Going

Our first example introduces text display, button press response, navigation and comments. It consists of a WML deck with two cards. The text Welcome to... is displayed by the first card:

When the user presses the accept soft key (which in this case the user agent has put under an Options menu), the microbrowser (user agent) navigates to the second card and displays ... programming with WAP.

Here's the WML source code for this example, which you'll find has been installed on your machine as **\WAP Examples\example1.wml**:

```
<?xml version="1.0"?>
<!DOCTYPE wml PUBLIC "-//WAPFORUM//DTD WML 1.1//EN"
                 "http://www.wapforum.org/DTD/wml_1.1.xml">

<!-- Main body -->
<wml>                                      <!-- deck starts here -->
    <card id="Card_1" title="Card 1">      <!-- first card -->

        <!-- how to handle the accept button -->
        <do type="accept" label="Next">
            <go href="#Card_2"/>           <!-- navigate to Card_2 -->
        </do>

        <p>                                <!-- paragraph -->
        Welcome to...
        </p>
    </card>                                <!-- end of first card -->

    <card id="Card_2" title="Card 2">      <!-- second card -->
        <p>                                <!-- second paragraph -->
        ... programming with WAP
        </p>
    </card>                                <!-- end of second card -->
</wml>                                      <!-- end of deck -->
```

The first section, before the main body, identifies the document as XML marked up in WML; it must be included at the start of every WML deck.

```
<?xml version="1.0"?>
<!DOCTYPE wml PUBLIC "-//WAPFORUM//DTD WML 1.1//EN"
                 "http://www.wapforum.org/DTD/wml_1.1.xml">
```

WML comments follow the XML commenting style, which has syntax like this:

```
<!-- comment goes here -->
```

The main body shows the start of the deck. All WML decks must start with a `<wml>` tag, and end with `</wml>`.

```
<!-- Main body -->
<wml>                                    <!-- deck starts here -->

...

<wml>
```

This deck contains two cards, and the first card starts on the line with the first `<card>` tag. The content of the card sits between the start and end tags `<card>`, and `</card>`.

Cards are basically containers for text and input elements. They provide flexible presentation to a wide variety of devices with different display and input characteristics. Cards can span a number of physical display pages – indeed, they are likely to do so on small screen devices. `Fieldset` elements can be used to provide information to the user agent about suitable breaks to allow optimization of layout and navigation.

Most WML elements allow you to specify attributes; these are specified in the form `attribute=value`, where `attribute` is the attribute name (defined in WML) and `value` is the alphabetic or numeric value to be assigned. `id` is an attribute that can be assigned to any WML element, including cards, and provides elements with unique names within a deck. In this example the, `id` attribute of the second card is assigned the alphabetic value `Card_2`. This attribute is used for navigation to the second card.

Another attribute that can be assigned to cards is `title`. The purpose of the title attribute is to display advisory information to the user. In this example, the text Card 1 will be displayed as a title on the first card.

The third line of the main body (starting with `do`) defines an action:

```
<do type="accept" label="Next">
```

In this case, it tells the user agent what to do when the user presses a function key. The `accept` soft key is created by a pre-defined WAP element that the user agent must attempt to map to a physical user interface construct (such as a button, or a touch screen control). In this line, the WML instructs the browser to label the `accept` key Next.

The line following the `do` specifies what the user agent (browser) should do when the key is pressed:

```
<go href="#Card_2"/>                     <!-- navigate to Card_2 -->
```

The `href` attribute identifies the target URI; in this example, the card whose `id` is `Card_2`. WML has adopted fragment anchors from HTML. WML uses fragment anchors to identify individual cards within a deck. The format is the document (or deck) URL, followed by a hash mark (#) followed by a fragment identifier (in this case the card's `id` `Card_2`). If no document URL is specified, the current deck is used, and if no fragment identifier is specified the first card in the deck is used.

Templates, Timers and Images

The next example demonstrates the use of card templates, timer elements and the display of images. First, the text Select 'Picture' to see the photo is displayed.

When the user selects the Picture soft key, from the Options menu, a bitmap image (a photo of a baby's face) is displayed for a couple of seconds. When the timer expires, the text is redisplayed. This particular user agent puts all buttons in an options list associated with the left control key. Another browser we used drew a picture of a button on a touch sensitive screen. Note the scroll bar to the right of the image.

Templates, timers and images are all classed as elements, and as such can be assigned attributes.

❑ The <template> element declares a template for cards in the deck. Event bindings specified in a template (such as do or onevent) are applied to all cards in the deck, although individual cards may override those in the template.

❑ The <img> element allows images to be placed into the text flow, and images use the same layout as normal text. Attributes can be assigned for image elements. The src attribute specifies the URI for the image, and the alt attribute specifies an alternative textual representation, in case the image cannot be displayed.

❑ The <timer> element provides card timers:

    ❑ On card entry, the timer is initialized and started; on exit from the card it is stopped

    ❑ The value of the timer is specified in tenths of a second (although programmers should expect implementation of granularity to vary)

    ❑ When the counter decrements to zero, an ontimer event is sent to the card

    ❑ Each card can only have one timer

You'll find the source code for this example in the file \Wap Examples\example2.wml:

```
<?xml version="1.0"?>                           <!-- line 1 -->
<!DOCTYPE wml PUBLIC "-//WAPFORUM//DTD WML 1.1//EN"
                     "http://www.wapforum.org/DTD/wml_1.1.xml">


<wml>
    <!-- template for all cards in this deck -->
    <template>
        <do type="prev">                        <!-- when Prev is hit -->
            <noop/>                             <!-- do nothing -->
        </do>
    </template>

    <!-- first card displays text and waits for key press -->
    <card id="Card1" newcontext="true">

        <!-- label an options key "Picture" -->
        <do type="options" label="Picture">
            <!-- if pressed then navigate to URL -->
            <go href="#showpicture"/>
        </do>

        <!-- this paragraph gets centered -->
        <p align="center">
        Select 'Picture' to see the photo
        </p>
    </card>

    <!-- second card displays the image -->
    <card id="showpicture">

        <!-- back to previous card if timer expires -->
        <onevent type="ontimer">
            <prev/>
        </onevent>

        <!-- initialize timer to 25 tenths of a second -->
        <timer value="25"/>

        <!-- display the image, centralized -->
        <p align="center">
            <img src="baby.wbmp" alt="Just arrived"/>
        </p>                                    <!-- end of paragraph -->
    </card>                                     <!-- end of second card -->
</wml>                                          <!-- end of deck -->
```

The first part of the deck (after the `<wml>` tag) shows a template card:

```
<template>
    <do type="prev">              <!-- when Prev is hit -->
        <noop/>                   <!-- do nothing -->
    </do>
</template>
```

This template defines deck level characteristics that apply to both of the cards in the deck. In this case, the template defines a `<do>` element of type `prev`. `prev` is reserved in this context to refer to the user control that navigates backwards through history (similar to the Back control on a web browser). `<noop/>` means do nothing. This effectively disables the `prev` control for this deck.

The first card (`Card1`) sets the `newcontext` attribute to `true`.

```
<card id="Card1" newcontext="true">
```

This re-initializes the browser context upon entry, which includes clearing the navigational history state and any variables that are set. Next, a `<do>` element is set up of type `options`.

```
<do type="options" label="Picture">
```

WML recognizes the reserved `type` of `options` as a context sensitive request for options or additional operations. This creates the equivalent of a temporary soft button for this card with the programmer-defined label `Picture`.

As with the first example, the line following the `do` specifies what the user agent should do when the key is activated:

```
<go href="#showpicture"/>
```

The `href` attribute identifies the target URI; in this example the navigation target is the card whose `id` is `showpicture` (the second card).

In the first card, the `<p>` element sets central alignment for the text Select 'Picture' to see the photo.

```
<!-- this paragraph gets centered -->
<p align="center">
Select 'Picture' to see the photo
</p>
```

The second card in the deck has the value `showpicture` for its `id` attribute. This card uses a timer, and the first section of the card defines what to do when the timer expires (which is when the `ontimer` event is received).

```
<onevent type="ontimer">
    <prev/>
</onevent>
```

In this example the task `prev` is performed on timer expiry. In WML, `prev` performs a pop operation on the history stack (if history exists), removing the current URI from the stack. This automatically navigates the user back to the previous card, in this case `Card1`.

The next part of the second card is the timer initialization. Timers are initialized when a card is entered. This timer is set for 2.5 seconds.

```
<timer value="25"/>
```

The display of the image is left to the last item of the second card.

```
<p align="center">
    <img src="baby.wbmp" alt="Just arrived"/>
</p>
```

The wireless bitmap image `baby.wbmp` is displayed centered in the screen. Note that the mandatory `alt` attribute specifies what the browser should display if the image cannot be displayed for any reason.

User Input and WMLScript

This example demonstrates the use of user input, and the use of WMLScript to check the input. The example shows a word game. First, the rules of the game are explained on a scrolling screen. The OK button is user confirmation to proceed to the next screen (in this case it is actually mapped to the Options key by this user agent).

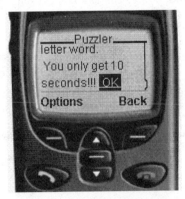

The user is then shown a word problem for 10 seconds:

After ten seconds, the user is moved onto the next card, where they can enter the answer. The solution to the problem is three letters that the user has to enter via the user-input device (probably the keypad):

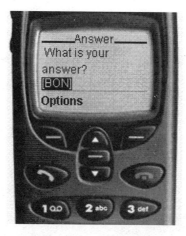

This user input is then checked against the correct answer using a function implemented in WMLScript (as WML itself cannot check user input). The user can then select the Display results option to see if they got the correct answer.

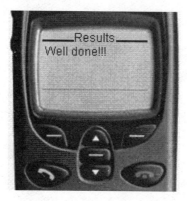

The source code for the final example in this chapter can be found in
\Wap Examples\example3.wml

```
<?xml version="1.0"?>
<!DOCTYPE wml PUBLIC "-//WAPFORUM//DTD WML 1.1//EN"
                    "http://www.wapforum.org/DTD/wml_1.1.xml">

<!-- Example devised and written by Peter Ford -->
<wml>
    <!-- First card -->
    <card id="card1" title="Puzzler">
        <p>
            Find the missing 3 letters that complete the first 6 letter
            word, and start the second 6 letter word.<br/>
            You only get 10 seconds!
```

```
                   <a href="#Question"> OK </a>
                   <do type="prev">
                       <prev/>
                   </do>
           </p>
       </card>

       <!-- Second card -->
       <card id="Question" ontimer="#Answer" title="Question" newcontext="true">
           <timer value="100"/>
           <p>
               <b> CAR --- NET </b>
           </p>
       </card>

       <!-- Third card -->
       <card id="Answer" title="Answer">
           <p>
               What is your answer?<br/>
               <input name="answer" size="3" maxlength="3"/>

               <do type="accept" label="Submit answer">
                   <go href="wordy.wmls#check('message', '$(answer)')"/>
               </do>

               <do type="options" label="Display results">

                   <!-- if pressed then navigate to URL -->
                   <go href="#result"/>
               </do>
           </p>
       </card>

       <!-- Fourth card -->
       <card id="result" title="Results">
           <p>
               $(message)<br/>
           </p>
       </card>

   </wml>
```

The first card displays the rules of the game. The anchor element:

```
    <a href="#Question"> OK </a>
```

is the forward navigational link to the next card: the user selects OK to proceed to the question card (second card).

The second card displays the word problem for 10 seconds, using a timer, so that the clue is only displayed to the user for a short period before being taken to the third card, called Answer, which allows them to enter their answer. The user's input is obtained by the line:

```
    <input name="answer" size="3" maxlength="3"/>
```

answer is the name of the variable that will store the input (note that this is the first time the variable is declared).

When the user has entered the solution, they can select **Submit answer**, which is created by an input control whose `type` is `accept`. The `label` attribute has a value of `Submit` answer, which is the text to display:

```
<do type="accept" label="Submit answer">
```

When the user selects this control, the WML line:

```
<go href="wordy.wmls#check('message', '$(answer)')"/>
```

passes the user's answer (in the variable `answer`) and a new string for the result message (called `message`) to the `check()` function within the WMLScript file `wordy.wmls`. The `check()` function sets the `message` variable to be either `Sorry, better luck next time`, or `Well done!`.

The user then has to select the **Display results** option, which is declared in the second input control (whose `type` is set to `option`), to see if their answer was correct. The fourth card simply displays the result message, which was set by the WMLScript function.

This next section shows the WMLScript that accompanies the above WML, and implements the check function. WML does not contain features for checking the user's answer; WMLScript is required to do this on the client device.

```
/*
 * File: wordy.wmls
 * Function: 'check' checks the user supplied answer
 * against the real answer (which is 'BON'), and sets
 * the message text accordingly
 *
 *@param varname the variable name to store the result
 *@param string1 the string entered by the user
 */
extern function check(varname, string1) {
    if(String.compare(string1, "BON")) {
        WMLBrowser.setVar(varname, "Sorry, better luck next time");
    } else {
        WMLBrowser.setVar(varname, "Well done!");
    }
}
```

The WMLScript starts with a comment. Notice the C-style commenting, which is different from WML. Then, the line:

```
extern function check(varname, string1) {
```

defines a function check with two variables. By using the `extern` keyword, we have enabled this function to be externally accessible. External functions can be called from outside the compilation unit in which they are defined.

WMLScript provides standard libraries, one of which is a string library. The check function uses the String.compare() function that is supplied with this library to compare the user answer with the correct answer (BON). The result of this compare is used to send the relevant result to the browser. The mechanism used to do this is the setVar function of the WMLBrowser library within WMLScript.

This example only scratches the surface of WMLScript. A good place to look for further information is the WAP Forum web site at http://www.wapforum.org/what/technical.htm.

Application Usability

There is one overriding guideline for designing WAP applications: *keep it simple*. Screen area is limited, memory is limited, and unlike a desktop browser the user may be performing other tasks when using your application.

Keep deck and image sizes down to a few kilobytes to reduce delays and conserve system resources. Also bear in mind the trade-off between putting many cards in each deck so that the user can navigate without waiting for new cards to be sent versus precisely the opposite – not putting too many cards in each deck so that the user doesn't have to wait a very long time to see the first page.

Try to keep text short by using short words and meaningful abbreviations. Use easily recognizable small images to complement common text items.

Keeping menu structures and levels as simple as possible will help prevent users becoming confused, and avoid them having to scroll through pages and pages of text.

Further Information

The above examples have demonstrated some of the features of WAP and WML, but as always in an area that's growing and changing quickly, it's important to stay up to date with new developments. To that end, the final section of this chapter consists of pointers to further information, and to sites run by early technology adopters.

WAP Standards

The specifications listed below are of interest to content developers and are available (with others) from the WAP Forum, at http://www.wapforum.org.

- ❑ Wireless Application Protocol Architecture Specification
- ❑ Wireless Application Environment Overview
- ❑ Wireless Application Environment Specification
- ❑ Wireless Markup Language Specification
- ❑ Binary XML Content Format Specification
- ❑ WMLScript Language Specification

❑   WMLScript Standard Libraries Specification

❑   WAP Caching Model Specification

❑   Wireless Transport Layer Security Specification

❑   Wireless Telephony Application Specification

Sample WAP Sites

Site	URL
BBC news	http://www.bbc.co.uk/mobile/mainmenu.wml
Ericsson business news	http://mobileinternet.ericsson.se/emi/default.asp
Wireless games	http://wirelessgames.com/index.wml
Stocksmart	http://agsub.stocksmart.com/ss.wml
Compuserve (WAP Portal in German)	http://wap.compuserve.de/index.wml
Manchester United Football Club	http://www.wapmanutd.com/menu.wml
Finnair	http://www.finnair.fi/wap/
Leo	http://dict.leo.org/wap
WAP Forum	http://www1.wapforum.org/wml/ho

The Gelon.net (http://www.gelon.net) and WAPLinks (http://www.waplinks.com) web sites maintain information on WAP resources, including WAP sites.

Other Useful References

❑   Standard ECMA-262: "ECMAScript Language Specification", ECMA, June 1997.

❑   "HTML 4.0 Specification, W3C Recommendation 18-December-1997, REC-HTML40-971218", D. Raggett, et al., September 17, 1997. URL: http://www.w3.org/TR/REC-html40.

❑   "Professional JavaScript", Andrea Chiarelli et al., Wrox Press, Inc., 1999.

❑   "JavaScript: The Definitive Guide", David Flanagan, O'Reilly & Associates, Inc. 1997.

❑   RFC1738 "Uniform Resource Locators (URL)", T. Berners-Lee, et al., December 1994. URL: ftp://ftp.isi.edu/in-notes/rfc1738.txt.

WAP Application Development Toolkits

WAP Application development toolkits are available for free download from Nokia http://www.forum.nokia.com/developers/wap/wap.html and Ericsson http://www.ericsson.com/WAP.

But remember that the wireless devices may not always support all the tags supported in the toolkit!

Design Guidelines

WAP application design guidelines for Ericsson EPOC products are available on the Ericsson web site. For example, http://www.ericsson.com/WAP/products/r380_design_guidelines_a.pdf.

Summary

WAP offers a practical way to offer Internet content and services to mobile users, solving problems imposed by wireless devices. With sales of mobile phones exceeding those of PCs, and with conservative estimates expecting the number of WAP-enabled devices in circulation by 2003 at over 500 million, we are going to see a boom in sites and services being made available to mobile users using this technology.

In this chapter, we have defined what WAP is, looked at the particular problems it solves, and described the techniques it employs to do so. We looked at the programming model and compared it with the World Wide Web, described the application environment, and covered what the programmer can expect to find on the target WAP device (the so-called 'user agent').

We also took a look at the Wireless Markup Language, the language used to present content and user interfaces on the limited size screens that are characteristic of mobile devices. We then developed some examples that introduced various aspects of wireless device programming with WML and WMLScript, from simple navigation between pages to an interactive puzzle game, which should put you in a position to start writing your own WAP applications.

25

Porting to EPOC

This chapter was written at our request by John Forrest of Purple Software, a leading independent software developer of advanced solutions for handheld computers. John has a wealth of expert knowledge and experience of porting existing software to EPOC devices.

The publication of this book should considerably ease the task of anyone contemplating porting. The disciplines of programming for resource-constrained devices that are never switched off, and which place a premium on efficient memory and CPU usage, are sometimes difficult to learn. Much of the key material about EPOC system architecture, active objects and communications is presented here for the first time. Together with this chapter, they should be regarded as essential reading for anyone approaching the task of moving existing code to EPOC.

This chapter is primarily concerned with porting to EPOC C and C++ programs that were originally written for other systems. In particular, it covers the following important activities:

❑ Porting C-language modules from other systems – particularly those written for a POSIX-like environment and using the standard C library.

❑ Overcoming some of the constraints of EPOC's C-language support, and in particular how to deal with global variables in the original source.

❑ Looking at how to link such modules into a standard EPOC C++ program, and how to make calls from the C modules back to the main C++ program.

❑ How to adapt the programs so that they are interactive, even when the processing is time consuming. Several approaches are described, since the 'best' method will depend very much on the original structure and how it was intended to work.

Introduction and Overview

This chapter is about **porting** – in other words, reusing code originally written for other platforms. During any software development, reuse of existing source code is almost always preferable to starting from scratch. On a relatively young platform such as EPOC, "reuse" will more often equate to "porting" than might be the case for more established systems with larger code libraries. The situations where porting might be used are various, but include existing applications, communications protocols, language interpreters and sub-modules that implement specific algorithms.

The fact that C++ is the primary development route for EPOC should mean that C and C++ code is readily portable to EPOC. There is a large library of C routines in particular, and the ability to run them easily on EPOC would be a distinct bonus. However, any examination of standard EPOC C++ programs will quickly show that they look rather different from those developed for other systems. Partly, this is a style issue, and relates to naming conventions. Nevertheless, EPOC does support its own C++ language dialect and its own set of libraries, and there are knock-on effects for C programs too. By and large, all the key differences result from the aims and objectives of EPOC itself.

The essential fact is that EPOC has different design aims from more familiar systems such as Microsoft Windows and UNIX. The system supports graphically rich, interactive programs on small-screened, battery-powered platforms with comparatively small memories and low processing power. Issues of efficiency in memory and battery usage are paramount. Certain simplifications in the supported language, such as not allowing global variables, have been made to help with this. Some other design decisions have helped to streamline the kernel, such as not allowing files to be directly shared between threads. Other 'restrictions' stem from the need to compile the same source for multiple target environments – to some extent, the need for custom type names and the leave mechanism can both be traced to this root.

On the other hand, compared with embedded-system environments, EPOC is very sophisticated; not only does it include the idea of a file store, but also advanced features like multi-processing, dynamic library linkage and client-server architectures. Servers are used for many functions, including window and file manipulation. One implication of this is that almost all of what would be system calls on other systems are implemented on EPOC as library calls, which may hide realities such as talking to servers.

Having said all this, porting *is* possible, and to a much greater extent than might at first seem the case. The general approach is not to attempt to port whole programs, but to port the essential parts of the code, grafting on some custom EPOC portions – in particular, the basis of any GUI will be EPOC-specific. The purpose of this chapter is to give some examples of the associated issues, and how they can be resolved. It is not intended to be exhaustive, as each porting project presents its own set of challenges, and requires its own solutions. However, there should be enough here to get you started.

> *It might be the case that you have jumped straight to this chapter because you've been given the task of porting a component. Perhaps the best advice that can be given is to gain some experience of the EPOC system itself, and how it is programmed, before starting the port itself. At the very least, read the main portions of this book!*

The chapter demonstrates how porting might be carried out using a number of examples: firstly a basic "Hello world", and then a slightly more complex filter example. Problems relating to global variables and the need for "concurrent" implementation are covered in some depth, together with suggested solutions. Some other useful topics are covered, such as how to make calls to C++ libraries from C. In addition, we will look at the aims of porting, and at why it is generally harder to port C++ than C code.

Hello World Example

We're going to start with a simple "Hello World" example that will be familiar to anyone who knows C:

```
#include <stdlib.h>
#include <stdio.h>

int main ()
    {
    printf("Hello world\n");
    return 0;
    }
```

The intended behavior of this code is obvious; the question is whether we can simply compile and execute this program on an EPOC target. In fact, it turns out that this is possible with no changes at all – although that might say more about the simplicity of the example than anything else. The only thing to add is the associated .mmp file, which contains the build instructions – or rather, contains the information from which the various makefiles are generated. The suggested .mmp file is as follows:

```
TARGET              hw.exe
TARGETTYPE          exe
UID                 0x01000a04 0
PROJECT             pephw
SUBPROJECT          hw
SOURCE              hw.c
SYSTEMINCLUDE       \epoc32\include \epoc32\include\libc
#if defined(MARM)
    LIBRARY         ecrt0.o
#else
    LIBRARY         ecrt0.obj
#endif
LIBRARY             estlib.lib euser.lib
```

The .mmp file contains instructions on how to build the file, in terms of what the source files are, the object files to link to, and the target file to be generated. By necessity, it contains the project and subproject names, which show where the code is to be maintained. However, .mmp files *don't* drive the compilation/linkage process. They contain lists of the source files and binary dependencies, but contain no information about how to build the source files. In this sense, .mmp files can be compared with **Imakefiles**, commonly used on UNIX projects as a sort of meta-makefile. To build an executable, we must first use the makmake utility to generate associated makefiles or equivalents.

This source compiles to a simple .exe program. If you wish to follow the example, you will find it in the Pephw directory, which should have been created on the same drive as your C++ SDK when you installed the code supplied with the book. To compile for the WINS emulator, go to the \pephw\hw folder and run this command:

```
makmake hw vc5
```

Load the resulting workspace into Visual C++, and compile. You can then run the program using the Go command from inside the IDE.

To compile for an EPOC target machine, you should return to the \pephw\hw folder and execute these commands:

```
makmake -makework hw marm
makmake hw marm
nmake -f hw.marm
```

This will generate a file hw.exe in the \epoc32\release\marm\rel folder, and as usual you'll need to install this in a folder on the target EPOC machine, using EPOC Connect. In addition, you may need to install the standard C library, if it is not already installed.

On both the emulator and the EPOC device, the behavior of the program is extremely predictable, and will result in the output shown below:

```
Hello world
Console closed - press any key
```

One thing that might capture your attention is that the system automatically waits for a key to be pressed. This behavior is specific to running C .exe programs – console-style EPOC C++ programs exit directly. This has advantages and disadvantages: it is useful in debugging, but you probably wouldn't want to see it in programs delivered to end users. Then again, for end users you will almost certainly want to deliver applications with GUIs – of which more below.

> Almost all of the examples in this section need the C run-time library, estdlib.dll. This is not shipped on all EPOC target machines, and you may need to install it. To do so, install the stdlib.sis file in folder \epoc32\release\marm\rel\ by double clicking on it from the Windows Explorer. If you need to generate a .sis file to distribute one of your own programs, then you should recursively include the stdlib.sis file. Under no circumstances should you copy the DLL file directly, as it can confuse the system — you may find it being deleted when uninstalling another program.
>
> The project and subproject names in the .mmp file correspond directly to the folder where the source files must be placed during compilation. If the SDK is installed on drive Z, the source files must be placed in folder z:\Project\SubProject\. There are no easy ways around this, and when porting projects it may require the original source organization to be changed.

It is important that you maintain .mmp files rather than hand-modifying the Visual C++ or makefile source. First, as a multiple-target system, this is the only way of ensuring that the build for the target proper corresponds to that for the emulator. Second, my experience is that upgrading to future versions of the EPOC C++ SDK will be smoother. Of course, that does mean that it's necessary to examine the makefile of the original program to create the .mmp files. Skipping this step by trying to generate your own project or makefiles, for example, is a major source of problems.

EPOC R5 does not support Unicode. For this reason, the supplied .mmp files do not include the UNICODEUID statements that give the UIDs used for Unicode builds. Although this leads to warnings when makmake is run, it is playing safe because the examples can't be built in a Unicode environment, for which they are not designed. In the future, Unicode versions of EPOC will appear – this will be a special case for source code compatibility. Expect Symbian to issue guidelines about using Unicode with STDLIB.

A More Complex Example

The "Hello world" example is not really very interesting. To look at the issues properly, we need a more complex example that's still reasonably compact. The running example that we will use in the rest of the chapter is that of a simple filter; the behavior of the basic program can be summarized as follows:

❑ The program reads one file and generates another.

❑ In the generated file, each byte corresponds to the average of the corresponding byte in the original file, together with the three bytes above and below it. Thus, for each output value, seven input values are averaged. This is illustrated in the figure below.

❑ There is obviously a problem with the first few and last few bytes in the file. The program acts as though there are several zero bytes below the first true value, and above the last.

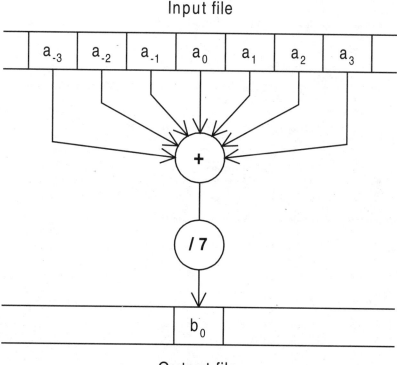

The original C program corresponds to example project peppcfilt, and the main source file is shown below. The file is reproduced almost in full so that you are absolutely clear about the issues – although even this small example looks rather long in print:

Note that in order to exercise some control on the length of an already-long chapter, comments have been removed from this and later source code listings. The source code on the CD retains these comments, and you are recommended to take a look at them.

```
#include <stdlib.h>
#include <stdio.h>
#include <string.h>

typedef signed char Value;
typedef signed short int ValueL;

#define FILTER_SIZE 3
#define BUFFER_LENGTH 128
#define LENGTH_OF_INPUT_BUFFER (BUFFER_LENGTH+FILTER_SIZE*2)

Value input_buffer[LENGTH_OF_INPUT_BUFFER];
Value output_buffer[BUFFER_LENGTH];

FILE* inFile;
FILE* outFile;

Value average(Value* value, int window_size)
    {
    ValueL total = 0;
    int index;

    for(index = -window_size; index <= window_size; index++)
        total = (ValueL)(total + value[index]);

    total = (ValueL)(total / (window_size * 2 + 1));
    return (Value)total;
    }

void filter_data(Value input[], Value output[], int num_values, int window_size)
    {
    int index;
    for(index = 0; index < num_values; index++)
        output[index] = average(&input[window_size + index], window_size);
    }

void filter(void)
    {
    int index, overflow_from_previous;

    for(index = 0; index < FILTER_SIZE; index++)
        input_buffer[LENGTH_OF_INPUT_BUFFER - FILTER_SIZE * 2 + index] = 0;

    fread(&input_buffer[LENGTH_OF_INPUT_BUFFER - FILTER_SIZE],
          sizeof(Value), FILTER_SIZE, inFile);
    overflow_from_previous = FILTER_SIZE;

    for(;;)
        {
        int num_to_filter, num_in_buffer, num_read;

        for(index = 0; index < FILTER_SIZE * 2; index++)
            input_buffer[index] = input_buffer[index + BUFFER_LENGTH];
```

```
            if(overflow_from_previous < FILTER_SIZE)
                num_read = 0;
            else
                num_read = fread(&input_buffer[FILTER_SIZE*2],
                                 sizeof(Value),
                                 BUFFER_LENGTH,
                                 inFile);

            for(index = num_read; index < BUFFER_LENGTH; index++)
                input_buffer[FILTER_SIZE * 2 + index] = 0;

            num_in_buffer = overflow_from_previous + num_read;
            if(num_in_buffer < BUFFER_LENGTH)
                num_to_filter = num_in_buffer;
            else
                num_to_filter = BUFFER_LENGTH;

            filter_data(input_buffer, output_buffer, num_to_filter, FILTER_SIZE);

            fwrite(output_buffer, sizeof(Value), num_to_filter, outFile);

            if(num_in_buffer < BUFFER_LENGTH)
                break;
            else
                overflow_from_previous = num_in_buffer - BUFFER_LENGTH;
            }
    }

int main(int argc, char *argv[])
    {
    int argn = argc - 1;
    char** args = &argv[1];
    char* output_file = NULL;
    char temp_output_file[128];
    char* input_file = NULL;

    if(argn == 0)
        {
        goto usage;
        }

    while(args[0][0] == '-')
        {
        char* p;

        for(p = &args[0][1]; *p; p++)
            switch(*p)
                {
                case 'o':
                    output_file = args[1];
                    args++; argn--;
                    break;
                default:
                    fprintf(stderr, "Unrecognised option -%c\n", *p);
                    goto usage;
                }
```

```
                args++; argn--;
            }
    if(argn == 0)
        {
        goto usage;
        }

    input_file = args[0];
    if((inFile = fopen(input_file, "rb")) == NULL)
        {
        fprintf(stderr, "Can't open %s\n", input_file);
        return -1;
        }

    if(output_file == NULL)
        {
        strcpy(temp_output_file, input_file);
        strcat(temp_output_file, "_out");

        output_file = temp_output_file;
        }

    if((outFile = fopen(output_file, "wb")) == NULL)
        {
        fprintf(stderr, "Can't create %s\n", output_file);
        return -1;
        }

    filter();
    fclose(inFile);
    fclose(outFile);

    return 0;

usage:
    fprintf(stderr, "Usage: %s [-o output] input\n", argv[0]);
    return -1;
    }
```

Compared with the skeletal description above, there are two things in particular to notice about this program.

❑   The program interface is UNIX-like, using command-line parameters:

    peppcfilt [-o outputfile] inputfile

    If the output filename is not given, then it is generated by adding _out to the end of the input filename.

❑   The program reads 128 bytes at a time, rather than working on single bytes. This is standard programming practice, but most of the complexity of the algorithm is due to it. In particular, the input buffer has to be 6 bytes longer than the output, to cater for the overspill top and bottom. At the beginning of each cycle, the top 6 bytes of the previous cycle are shifted down into the lower 6 bytes, and then the system tries to append 128 bytes. This is shown in the figure below.

The fact that it is 6 (not 3) bytes that are shifted down may seem counterintuitive. However, it should be remembered that the top 3 bytes of one cycle are really the first 3 bytes of the next, and that the 3 bytes below that are needed for overspill.

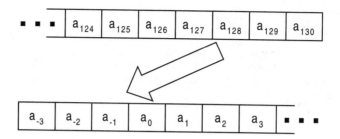

Phase A: Shift down

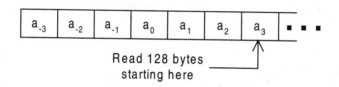

Read 128 bytes
starting here

Phase B: Read next block of data

As you might hope, we can compile and run this program under EPOC pretty much as it is, and this is demonstrated in example project `pepfilt1`. In addition to adding the `.mmp` file, though, we need to do something about the interface – that is, about the way files are specified. We cannot easily specify arguments when we run `.exe` files in an EPOC environment, and so it's necessary to rewrite the interface such that it will tolerate no arguments being supplied. The key to this is to write a new `do_filter()` function:

```
int do_filter(char* input_file_name, char* output_file_name)
    {
    char temp_output_file[128];

    if((inFile = fopen(input_file_name, "rb")) == NULL)
        {
        fprintf(stderr, "Can't open %s\n", input_file_name);
        return -1;
        }
```

```
        if(output_file_name == NULL)
            {
            strcpy(temp_output_file, input_file_name);
            strcat(temp_output_file, "_out");

            output_file_name = temp_output_file;
            }

        if((outFile = fopen(output_file_name, "wb")) == NULL)
            {
            fprintf(stderr, "Can't create %s\n", output_file_name);
            return -1;
            }

        filter();
        fclose(inFile);
        fclose(outFile);

        return 0;
        }
```

We also need to rework the main() function, so that if no arguments are supplied, the input filename is requested from the user. (The output filename is then generated by the default behavior.) In fact, with the do_filter() function in play, main() can be simplified significantly:

```
int main (int argc, char *argv[])
    {
    int argn = argc-1;
    char** args = &argv[1];
    char* output_file = NULL;
    char* input_file = NULL;

    if(argn == 0)
        {
        char input_file_name[128];

        printf("Enter filename : ");
        gets(input_file_name);

        return do_filter(input_file_name, NULL);
        }

    while(args[0][0] == '-')
        {

        ...

        }

    if(argn == 0)
        {
        goto usage;
        }
```

```
        input_file = args[0];
        return do_filter(input_file, output_file);

usage:
        fprintf(stderr, "Usage: %s [-o output] input\n", argv[0]);
        return -1;
        }
```

On a target machine, it is possible (although not necessarily convenient) to provide .exe programs with run-time arguments. The eshell.exe program, supplied with the SDK, provides a DOS-style command line interface instead of the standard graphical one. This can be useful during program development, and allows our example program to be run using its original syntax, but it is not suitable for typical end users. More details on how to install the eshell program are given in this project's readme file in the example code supplied with the book.

EPOC Limitations of C Programs

It is good that this program works virtually unchanged — and the changes we did make would be equally valid on UNIX or a PC. However, its style is obviously rather different from the programs that are typically run under EPOC, and the look and feel would not be suitable for a real application. Perhaps the major challenge of porting to EPOC is that the devices it runs on really *demand* programs with graphical front-ends, and it's this issue that we'll be dealing with in the following subsections.

One specific limitation you might come across is if the original program places large variables on the run-time stack — if it uses large arrays as local variables, for example. The standard EPOC C++ programming style is to use heap-based objects rather than local variables, and to reflect this the default stack is comparatively small at 8k. If you have large local variables, you may need to increase the stack size (which is an option to the .mmp file), but a much better solution would be to change the code so that heap memory is used instead. Heap memory associated with a program grows as required, so requesting too much stack is wasteful.

STDLIB: EPOC's Standard C Library

STDLIB is the EPOC implementation of the standard C library, including the C math library. It isn't supposed to be 100% complete implementation of all the POSIX standards; instead, it is a comparatively thin layer that runs on top of the various EPOC C++ libraries, but provides a standard C library interface. The objective is that a large proportion of C programs will run with little or no modification, at least in terms of the library calls they make. Symbian's biggest port with the standard library is the Java virtual machine: a big project, in which Symbian made practically no changes to Sun's source code.

Having the C library run on top of the C++ libraries is somewhat different to most systems — in fact, early C++ implementations were layered on C libraries — so it's worth a quick look at the reasons for this state of affairs. In practice, a large number of C library calls have direct equivalents in the EPOC C++ libraries, and all STDLIB needs to do is provide a simple wrapper function that calls the equivalent. malloc(), for example, equates to User::Alloc(), while sprintf() is functionally similar to TDes::Format(). Obviously, by implementing these as little more than calls to the C++ equivalent, STDLIB itself is kept as small as possible.

However, there is a much stronger reason for layering C libraries on C++. You may remember that EPOC does not really have *system calls* in the traditional sense – that is, a formal mechanism to invoke a function run with kernel privilege. Instead, it makes extensive use of client-server programming, with the client objects placed in C++ libraries that run as part of the application communicating with a server program that actually performs the action. For example, virtually all file operations are carried out by the file server, with which your application communicates using classes such as RFs and RFile – or more typically, using higher-level library functions that themselves use these lower-level classes. Thus, STDLIB *needs* to use these classes, either directly or indirectly, to perform file-based I/O. Replicating the behavior of RFile within STDLIB would involve having to rewrite large chunks of the C++ code in C, and really wasn't an option.

Thus, STDLIB is intended as a small, efficient, C-style interface to the EPOC libraries. As mentioned above, it is not 100% compliant, and there are no plans to make it so. All the issues relating to compliance stem from this layering on the C++ libraries:

❑ Some functions more closely resemble the equivalent C++ library functions than the standard C library behaviors. For example, the localization features associated with printf() don't work as such – they follow the equivalent TDes::Format() functionality.

❑ Some functions are not fully implemented, because there is no direct equivalent in the C++ libraries. Unfortunately, you might only discover this at runtime, while testing programs, because the library usually includes cut-down implementations that only partly work, or 'stub' versions that don't do anything but return an error. The most important of these are select(), signal(), exec(), and fork(), whose implementations are at odds with the EPOC run-time programming model. Some other things, such as directory entries and sockets, need to be handled differently – the details of the interface can vary.

❑ STDLIB uses threads in a special way – the way EPOC implements threads has side effects, although STDLIB does get around some of them. This is discussed below when we look at using EPOC threads in general.

In practice, the discrepancies between STDLIB and ANSI C are largely unimportant to your porting efforts. STDLIB ends up being used for the calculation/storage parts of an application, with the interactive modules written using EPOC-oriented C++. The vast majority of functions *do* work. Only if you try to port whole interactive or socket-based applications is your code likely to need significant rewriting, as these tend to use signal() and select() to control behavior. However, as we shall see in the next section, it is unlikely that you would want to do this.

In summary, the distinctly good news is that the STDLIB C library exists. The fact that it is not 100% compliant with ANSI C is not usually a problem in practice, unless you've got a program that uses select() or fork() and exec(). In the case of fork() and exec(), the solution generally involves replacing that part of the code with the EPOC equivalent, although there is no way for the called program to inherit open files from the parent – some redesign will be required if this is critical. There are usually ways around the lack of select(), and I'll have more to say on this subject below.

> Some C modules don't make any *library calls* – signal-processing functions, for example, often just read from and write to memory buffers that were supplied by main applications. In such circumstances, you don't have to link to the STDLIB library, which is only required if you make explicit library calls. In fact, if your program only uses a few basic STDLIB library calls, you may prefer to replace them with calls directly into the C++ libraries. This can be particularly useful if you are targeting programs at older EPOC machines, where the STDLIB library was not supplied in ROM. There may also be advantages if you are mixing C and C++ in the same module. In practice, those engines that don't perform their own I/O might just use malloc(), memcpy(), and not much else. The following shows how you can write code to bypass the standard calls.

```
// To go in .h file, included in the C source files:
#if __PSISOFT32__

#undef assert
#undef malloc
#undef free
#undef memset

#include <stddef.h> // for size_t

#ifdef NDEBUG
    #define assert(__cond)
#else NDEBUG
    extern void _Assert(int aCond);
    #define assert(__cond) _Assert(__cond)
#endif NDEBUG

extern void* _Malloc(size_t _size);
#define malloc(__count) _Malloc (__count)

extern void _Free(void *ptr);
#define free(__ptr) _Free(__ptr)

extern void _Memset(char* ptr, int value, size_t _size);
#define memset(__ptr,__value,__size) _Memset(__ptr,__value,__size)

#ifndef __GCC32__ // GCC has memcpy as an intrinsic
    #undef memcpy
    extern void* _Memcpy(void* dst, const void* src, size_t);
    #define memcpy _Memcpy
#endif

#endif __PSISOFT32__


// To go in a .cpp source file:
#if defined(_DEBUG)
extern "C" void _Assert(int aCond)
{
    ASSERT(aCond);
}
#endif (_DEBUG)

#include <stddef.h> // for size_t

extern "C" void* _Malloc(size_t aSize)
{
    return User::Alloc(aSize);
}

extern "C" void _Free(void *ptr)
{
    User::Free(ptr);
}
```

```
extern "C" void _Memset(char* ptr, int value, size_t _size)
{
    TUint8 *uPtr = REINTERPRET_CAST(TUint8*, ptr);
    TPtr8 des(uPtr, _size, _size);
    des.Fill(TChar(value));
}

#ifndef __GCC32__ // GCC has memcpy as an intrinsic
extern "C" void* _Memcpy(void* dst, const void* src, size_t _size)
{
    const TUint8 *source = STATIC_CAST(const TUint8*, src);
    TUint8 *destin = STATIC_CAST(TUint8*, dst);
    TPtrC8 srcDes(source, _size);
    TPtr8 dstDes(destin, _size);
    dstDes = srcDes;
    return dst;
}
#endif __GCC32__
```

> A further problem you may run into involves data types. Under C++, EPOC provides a whole range of predefined types such as TInt, TInt16, etc. Unfortunately, these are not available from C, as the e32def.h file includes C++ specific code. Where integer types are critical, most modules have a config.h file or similar, in which the types used can be given specifically. Copying the relevant parts from e32def.h is one possible approach.

Standard EPOC Applications

It's fairly obvious that the programs described so far do not appear to the users as standard EPOC applications. In particular, they do not have a graphical user interface, and do not appear on the Extras bar where users expect to find them.

One reason for this is that the executable code (let alone the source code) of these programs is quite different from that of 'normal' EPOC applications. We have produced .exe files, when EPOC applications are formed from sets of .app and .dll files. This seemingly minor difference has far reaching consequences:

❑   The rules of EPOC DLL file implementation state that you can't have global (or otherwise static) variables. There are ways around this, which we will look at, but they all involve some rewriting.

❑   .app files, which are the core DLL associated with each application, do not have a main() function. Instead, they require a NewApplication() function that returns a CApaApplication object – a bootstrap with which a CApaDocument is created. The usual CONE/EIKON run-time environment will want to create C...AppUi and C...AppView objects too. A typical NewApplication() function might look like this:

```
EXPORT_C CApaApplication* NewApplication()
    {
    return new CExampleApplication;
    }
```

❑   By definition, the application object classes must be written in C++, so it can already be seen that at least some C++ *must* be used to write the applications.

In reality, you will probably want to channel most of the GUI features of an application through the standard application classes, just as you would if you were writing an EPOC application from scratch – it's the way the libraries were designed to be used. Although you have some flexibility on how you actually do it, your program will have to process key, pointer and other events the way EPOC expects them to be handled.

Simple Rewrites of our Example as an EIKON Application

In order to make our example look and behave like a standard application, we have to change it somewhat. There is an apparent contradiction in this: we're porting a program, yet changing it. We will deal with this further below, but for now consider that the idea is to preserve as much of the original application as reasonably possible. What this means is that we will ditch that part of the program responsible for starting up, obtaining the relevant filenames, and then closing down, and replace it with a simple EIKON-based front end. We will replace the original main() function with a C++ class wrapper that is easily called from the user interface code.

As noted above, an EPOC application is actually formed from one .app DLL, and zero or more .dll DLLs. In our simple port, we are going to generate two DLL files:

❑   FiltUi.app: the main .app DLL, which controls the user interface

❑   FiltEng.dll: which will perform the filter function, and contains the C code

Creating the FiltUi.app DLL is fairly straightforward. To make it simple, we'll start with an existing example from the SDK, ikhello, in directory \epoc32ex\eikmin, and modify it. This sample contains simple instances of the main application classes, and is ideal for our purpose. The major change is the addition of a Filter file... command that links to a standard file open dialog, the result of which will be fed to the engine.

Porting the engine is a bit more complex, as we can't have global variables. In practice, there are two key approaches for dealing with this:

❑   Thread local storage (TLS)

❑   Explicit This

These two approaches yield rather different source code, so we will deal with them separately in the following sections.

This particular example is actually so simple that it could be rewritten without global variables at all. However, that is not typically true, so I'm going to ignore that technique.

Dealing with Global Variables using Thread Local Storage

Thread local storage is the closest thing there is to global variables in EPOC. For each DLL, it is possible to register a pointer to a dynamically created `struct` or `class` object, and then to look it up whenever it is required. The basis of the technique is that having done this, all global variables are re-mapped to data fields within the structure. In fact, this is on a per *thread*, per DLL basis, with each thread potentially having its own globals. (Indeed, this is how the STDLIB implements `errno` and other global variables so that each thread has its own `errno` copy.) If you use multithreading, you will have to be careful about this.

This particular version of the application is included as `pepfilt2` *in the example code supplied with the book.*

In this example, we introduce a new `.h` file, `globals.h`, which contains the declaration of this structure. The important part is as follows:

```
struct _Globals
    {
    Value input_buffer[LENGTH_OF_INPUT_BUFFER];
    Value output_buffer[BUFFER_LENGTH];

    FILE* inFile;
    FILE* outFile;
    };

typedef struct _Globals Globals;

extern Globals* TheGlobals();
```

Note that this is C, and that we have *not* followed standard EPOC programming conventions – if we had, there would be more to change. The key is that any reference to a global variable x has to be replaced by `globals->x`. Thus:

```
    input_buffer[index] = 0;
```

becomes:

```
    globals->input_buffer[index] = 0;
```

In addition, you need to include the following statement within each function that uses global variables:

```
Globals* globals = TheGlobals();
```

So far, so good. Next, we need to introduce code to create the globals object as required. In our example, the code to implement this is placed within the new `filteng.cpp` source file. The `TheGlobals()` function is relatively straightforward:

```
#if defined(__WINS__)
    Globals data;
    Globals* TheGlobals() { return &data; }
#else defined(__WINS__)
    Globals* TheGlobals()
        {
        return STATIC_CAST(Globals*, Dll::Tls());
        }
#endif
```

On a target machine, `TheGlobals()` calls `Dll::Tls()`, which returns the thread local storage pointer. The key requirement is then actually to create this block, which can be done as part of the `E32Dll()` function, as shown here:

```
#if defined(__MARM__)
    GLDEF_C TInt E32Dll(TDllReason aReason)
        {
        TInt res = KErrNone;
        Globals* pD;
        switch(aReason)
            {
        case EDllThreadAttach:
            pD = new Globals;
            if(pD == NULL)
                res = KErrNoMemory;
            else
                Dll::SetTls(pD);
            break;
        case EDllThreadDetach:
            delete Dll::Tls();
            Dll::SetTls(NULL);
            break;
        default:
            break;
            }
        return(res);
        }
#endif __MARM__

#if defined(__WINS__)
    GLDEF_C TInt E32Dll(TDllReason /*aReason*/)
        {
        return KErrNone;
        }
#endif __WINS__
```

The `E32Dll()` function is required for all EPOC DLLs, but it's usually a no-op. This example shows one of its uses: it's possible to tell when a thread is started and when it is stopped, and using this we can create or destroy the TLS data.

However, you can see that under the WINS emulator, very different code is used: we actually use a standard global variable, and then just return the pointer to it. It turns out that the parameters passed to `E32Dll()` under WINS are different from those on a target machine, so a different function would be required too. This is the behavior we saw back in Chapter 9.

> **This is a serious flaw: when the emulator and a real device require different code, a program can become impossible to debug because its behavior on the emulator is different from that on the target. The method used here only works because the WINS emulator is a single-process environment; it's strongly deprecated. However, it's worth discussing here, because it provides a relatively easy introduction to TLS.**

The next requirement is to extract all the error `printf()` statements from the original filter code: EPOC applications have no run-time console unless you implement one yourself. As an essentially graphical environment, EPOC uses **alerts** to notify the user about errors, so we're going to arrange for error values to be returned from the C code (instead of printing an error) and let the C++ code handle them. Thus, the original:

```
if((inFile = fopen(input_file_name, "rb")) == NULL)
    {
    fprintf(stderr, "Can't open %s\n", input_file_name);
    return -1;
    }
```

will become:

```
if((globals->inFile = fopen(input_file_name, "rb")) == NULL)
    {
    return -1;
    }
```

With these modifications to the original program, we can introduce the final requirement: a C++ class that wraps the original code so that we can call it from our new EIKON code. The definition of this class is as follows:

```
class FiltEng
    {
public:
    IMPORT_C static void FilterL(const TDesC& aFileName);
    IMPORT_C static void Close();
    };
```

This class has no data members, and all the function members are static, so I've not declared it as a C class. Indeed, it isn't *actually* necessary to use a class at all (global functions could be used instead), but doing so leads to fewer name clashes. The `FiltEng::FilterL()` function will invoke `do_filter()`, but it also needs to convert from the `TDes`-style strings used by the EPOC C++ libraries to the `char*`-style strings used within the C code. We also want it to leave if an error is returned by `do_filter()`, thus ensuring standard EPOC behavior. The implementation is as follows:

```
EXPORT_C void FiltEng::FilterL(const TDesC& aFileName)
    {
    char fileName[KMaxFileName];
    TPtr fileDes(REINTERPRET_CAST(TUint8*, fileName), KMaxFileName);

    fileDes = aFileName;
    fileDes.Append(TChar(0));
```

```
    TInt res = do_filter(fileName, NULL);

    if(res < 0)
        User::Leave(KErrGeneral);
    }
```

Here, `fileDes` is effectively a pointer to the `char` array `fileName`. Any changes we make to `fileDes` are actually made to `fileName`, but this way we can use the powerful EPOC C++ library functions to perform copies, rather than having to copy character-by-character into the array. We take a copy so we can append a zero byte without having to modify the original, which was passed as a `TDesC` and therefore should not be changed. Obviously, it's important to know that the `do_filter()` function doesn't modify the `fileName` parameter (you need to judge this case-by-case) – otherwise, we would need to implement a reverse action, and the argument to our C++ interface would have to be a modifiable `TDes` object.

Notice the key lines for handling errors:

```
    if(res < 0)
        User::Leave(KErrGeneral);
```

This is designed to link with the modified C code that returns -1 if it can't open input or output files, replacing the original code that printed out an error message. This essentially converts the error return into an EPOC leave that will be caught by the C++ library code resulting in an alert being displayed. This particular code is arguably too simplistic, as we've made no attempt to find out what the error was. If you wanted to be truly accurate, you could decode `errno` and generate a more accurate reason value. In practice, though, you will find that this code rarely fails: because we choose files using dialogs instead of typing in the filename, we know that the file exists when we get to this stage. You *may* see errors if your file has been opened by another program – the code should perhaps deal better with that scenario.

> *There is something of a mismatch between the EPOC approach to error messages and that of traditional C programs. Coupling a `printf()` statement with each `fopen()`, etc. means that you can have a unique message each time: "can't open", "can't create", and so forth. Under EPOC, the standard behavior just displays a message based on the error value, and ignores the context – if a module leaves, you don't necessarily know which library call caused the problem, and you're forced to use a generic message. There are no clear ways around this (unless you start using custom error values), but in practice it tends not to be a problem.*

Returning to the C++ interface, notice the `Close()` method of this class. The implementation of the function goes like this:

```
EXPORT_C void FiltEng::Close()
    {
    CloseSTDLIB();
    }
```

The purpose of this function is to call `CloseSTDLIB()` – a call to this function *must* be made before the program exits, so that any buffers will be deallocated. If you don't do this on the emulator, you'll get a panic, as happens whenever memory is not deallocated. (This may also happen if your C code doesn't recover any of the heap memory it has requested.) The `FiltEng::Close()` function is thus called from one of the destructors of the EIKON application objects; in this example I called it from the app UI, but it could equally have been the document.

There are several potential downsides to the TLS approach. Perhaps the most important is that all global and static variables have to be placed within the same object: you can only have one TLS object per DLL. For a large library, with several source files, this means that any localization is lost – in fact, the whole source organization tends to be broken up. In particular, if you have several static variables of the same name, you will have somehow to change their names to avoid clashes – which means changing the function bodies too. One area not illustrated by this example is what to do if you need to initialize any of the variables, but in that situation it makes sense to use one of the alternative solutions below, which have a clear constructor or OpenL() call. Even then, there is always the possibility that you may have to call static functions from outside their source file, because the initialization code has moved to another source file.

An additional issue with this approach is that of performance. The Dll::Tls() call takes a significantly longer time than a standard pointer lookup. Without changing the approach, the only way around this is to be careful about how frequently Dll::Tls() is called.

> Some programmers replace the global->x or equivalent with a macro called x, reducing the number of changes to the original program. If you do this, resist the temptation to use TheGlobals()->x, or similar, as the body. This will call Dll::Tls() for every global variable access, which has a distinct performance penalty.

> Notice the use of IMPORT_C/EXPORT_C in this example. This is required because we are calling the functions from another DLL. One advantage of using the wrapper class is that the original code is isolated from this change.

> On an EPOC machine with comparatively small memory, there is a greatly increased chance of getting a "disk full" event when writing. The filter example follows standard C programming practice by not checking that fwrite() succeeds; this isn't fatal here because the file is simply cut short if there are problems. In other circumstances, you may need to consider such effects. Similarly, it is more likely that malloc() will return 0, meaning out-of-memory, and you will need to check that your ported code does something sensible should this occur.

Improved TLS-based Schemes

As noted above, the use of TLS is the nearest thing that EPOC has to global variables in application. This is particularly true of the method described in the previous section – the variables exist from when the library is created, to when it ceases to exist. This can be a good style, especially if the original code is poorly structured, but we have already seen that it suffers from a serious flaw: different code is used in the emulator compared with the real device.

The generally recommended way of using TLS is to incorporate OpenL() and Close() functions, and then to call these as the program is created or shut down – typically from the document or app UI classes' constructors and destructors. The OpenL() and Close() functions are then responsible for creating and destroying the Globals object respectively. Possible implementations are as follows, which are shown in the example code supplied with the book as project pepfilt2a:

```
EXPORT_C void FiltEng::OpenL()
    {
    Globals *globals = STATIC_CAST(Globals*, Dll::Tls());
    if(globals == NULL)
        {
        globals = new(ELeave) Globals;
        Mem::FillZ(globals, sizeof(Globals));
        Dll::SetTls(globals);
        }
    globals->_count += 1;
    }

EXPORT_C void FiltEng::Close()
    {
    Globals *globals = STATIC_CAST(Globals*, Dll::Tls());
    if(globals == NULL)
        return;

    globals->_count -= 1;
    if(globals->_count == 0)
        {
        delete globals;
        Dll::SetTls(NULL);
        CloseSTDLIB();
        }
    }

Globals* TheGlobals()
    {
    return STATIC_CAST(Globals*, Dll::Tls());
    }
```

This particular implementation uses an additional field that is added to the Globals record: _count. The purpose of this is to allow nested OpenL()/Close() calls – the scheme is sometimes referred to as RegisterL()/Unregister() to reflect this. This is sometimes useful, particularly for unstructured code, or when you only want to create the Globals variable as required in order to save memory. In this particular example, this approach is probably overkill, and it could be replaced with a slightly simpler scheme that dispensed with _count – perhaps adding an assertion within OpenL() that globals is equal to 0.

Another possible TLS scheme is to change TheGlobals() so that the Globals object is created when Dll::Tls() returns 0 – obviously using Dll::SetTls() to store the new value. Although apparently simple, the downside of this technique is all the methods that call TheGlobals() need to handle out-of-memory events. Always creating from the same place is much simpler.

Dealing with Global Variables using Explicit This

It is quite likely that although they are used behind the scenes, the above examples were the first EPOC programs you've seen that use explicit TLS calls. The reason for this is fairly straightforward: in EPOC C++ programs, we almost always use data members instead of ordinary variables, with the significant advantage that within member functions, the this pointer is implicit.

With C programs, of course, this is not so straightforward: there is no implicit `this` pointer, and no method of directly associating functions and data structures. However, that does not stop us doing it explicitly: we can re-write our original C as "object-based C" by explicitly defining a `this` pointer. This technique is demonstrated in the `pepfilt3` example that accompanies the book.

The first requirement is to declare the `This` structure:

```
struct _This
    {
    Value input_buffer[LENGTH_OF_INPUT_BUFFER];
    Value output_buffer[BUFFER_LENGTH];

    FILE* inFile;
    FILE* outFile;
    };

typedef struct _This _This;
```

We no longer have a separate `globals.h` file — it makes sense to put the things it contained within the main header file, `filter.h`. With this change in place, the beginning of the `do_filter()` function now looks like:

```
int do_filter(_This *This, char* input_file_name, char* output_file_name)
    {
    char temp_output_file[128];

    if((This->inFile = fopen(input_file_name, "rb")) == NULL)
    {
        return -1;
    }

    ...
```

Notice that we've introduced an extra parameter, `This`, but that we no longer need to call `TheGlobals()` to reach the 'variables'.

This has obvious ramifications with the wrapper class: we store the `This` pointer as a data member, and therefore rewrite it as a standard C class, `CFiltEng`. This also has a knock-on effect on the EIKON user interface, as we must now create an 'engine' object before starting it up. You have a choice of placing the fairly trivial code to do this in the app UI object or the document object; I chose the latter for this example.

The explicit `This` method addresses most of the issues that relate to the TLS solution described above. First of all, there is no particular reason that the resulting performance of the code should be much worse than equivalent C++, where the `this` pointer is implicitly added to most calls. Perhaps more importantly, though, there is nothing to stop us from having more than one of these records within a file, so we no longer have to cut across any source organization.

About the only downside to this approach is that there are potentially more changes to be made: all the functions need to be passed the `This` pointer, except perhaps those that do not call other functions or access global variables. This means that almost all function declarations and calls have to be modified.

On balance, the facts that the original code structure can be largely retained, and that the TLS performance penalty is avoided, tip the balance toward explicit `This` as the preferred technique. However, there are exceptions, and the TLS method should not be dismissed out-of-hand.

It is perhaps worth noting that the explicit This *method uses no features exclusive to EPOC, so the resulting code will run unmodified on other systems. If required, you could modify the main version of the code so that it would also run on EPOC, rather than having to maintain separate EPOC code.*

Global Variables Master Class

At Purple Software, we commonly employ a variation of this approach: rather than mimic C++ using the explicit This field, we actually convert the source code to C++. In this technique, a 'master class' wraps all the C code within a module, so that the original C functions become member functions of this class, and the global variables become data members. In theory, not all C can be so converted, but this has seldom proved a real problem. There are probably more challenges if you are trying to maintain the source so that it can be compiled for multiple targets, but that isn't our goal.

Personal experience suggests that the number of changes required by this method are likely to be more than for the others we've considered – particularly as even functions that are local to a particular file have to be entered into the 'master class', unless they don't use global variables. However, if you bite the bullet and proceed with this technique, there are some distinct advantages. Not least, you can directly employ the predefined EPOC types, and you can more easily make calls to the C++ libraries if necessary. This chapter emphasizes the approaches that maintain the code as C, but much of the material applies equally if you convert the code to C++.

The pepfilt3 *example shows how to isolate the C code from the main C++ application by using a* TAny* *local field to hold the filter's* This *pointer, and using casts as appropriate.*

The CFiltEng class exhibits two-phase construction, as is common practice for EPOC C++. It is worth mentioning that if we were importing C++ code, we would have to be careful about conventional C++ constructors – if these allocate new memory, they should perhaps be replaced by the two-phase variety. I recommend that you always use the NewL()/NewLC() scheme, and declare the 'real' constructors and ConstructL() functions as protected. That way, the compiler will automatically show up most of the places where you need to change the interface.

In the example, the CFiltEng object is owned by the document object, not the app UI. Although placing it in the app UI would be simpler, the document is actually in existence for longer – in some applications, the document object can exist without an associated app UI. On balance, I think it's good practice to place 'engines' such as this within the document, that's not to say that I always follow this advice. In other examples in this chapter, the app UI becomes an 'observer' of the engine object in order to allow callbacks, and in those cases it's easier to make it responsible for creating the engine object too.

This example has split the code into two DLLs primarily for illustrative purposes. There are some advantages of using separate DLLs: one is required for each TLS structure, and it is possible to employ a separate test harness. There are also advantages in code structure. However, experience suggests that there are performance penalties, so in reality it would probably be best to merge the C module into the main .app *DLL.*

EPOC Structure from a Porting Viewpoint

So far, our examples have seemed to integrate well and cleanly into the main EPOC environment. In reality, it is almost certain that we will have to rewrite parts of the original program. Such rewriting may require the creation of custom libraries, or perhaps a modification of the way that code is called. All that can be said in general is that it is important to have a good grounding in the EPOC system and its architecture.

Without wanting to repeat material, it is perhaps reasonable to take a fresh look at some of the issues. To put it simply, the facilities and methods we use when porting are not necessarily those used when writing straight EPOC code. You have to be flexible when thinking of how to link the main system to your code.

To a large extent, EPOC is a modular operating system. The components that make it up, and the relationships between them, are shown in the figure below. The components are as follows:

❑ Core EPOC system: core types, descriptors (strings), exception/leave mechanism, processes, threads, files, streams, stores, etc.

❑ Active objects and Scheduler: C++ asynchronous processing handling.

❑ Bitmapped graphics: generic bitmap handling, and the ability to draw/print to real devices.

❑ Application infrastructure: launching, file association, etc.

❑ Comms protocol: communications and protocol support.

❑ CONE: graphical control structure – the ability to associate a part of a window with associated redraw and event-handling facilities. Includes useful features such as resource files.

❑ EIKON infrastructure: ranging from standard concepts such as buttons and dialogs, to particular instances of them. Also menus, toolbars, etc.

❑ Standard (EIKON) applications.

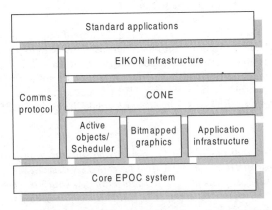

This is the set of layers that appear in machines like the Psion Series 5 and its successors. Other machines may have different components, especially at the higher layers. A number of extra facilities, such as specific communications protocols like TCP and IrDA, are actually provided via servers. They can be omitted from particular machines, or installed as options. One implication of this is that there is no single "EPOC system". You need to be careful about which facilities you require, and ensure that they are or will be installed on the machines you are targeting.

When writing EPOC applications from scratch, you will want to use the highest facilities possible. If you use the `CEikDialog` class as the basis for your dialogs, for example, much of the implementation is already done for you. When porting, different considerations apply: a program may already have its own dialog infrastructure, in which case porting the original structure may be more appropriate than porting to use that of EIKON.

MVC Program Design

It is also worth considering the way in which EPOC programs are typically designed: much stress is placed on the Model/View/Controller (MVC) methodology. Much more detail is given in Chapter 11, but essentially the technique divides each program module into three sub-modules:

- ❑ The **model**, sometimes also called an **engine**, is responsible for storing the data associated with the module, and for providing functions that manipulate it.
- ❑ The **view** is responsible for displaying the contents of the model, when required.
- ❑ The **controller** handles user interaction, typically by handling incoming user interface events. It is responsible for linking the model and the view, which generally act as slaves to the controller.

When porting, it's worth trying to divide the original program into the same categories. In practice, most porting work concerns models (engines), as is the case in our main example. Less commonly, it is possible to reuse view functions, but you'll almost certainly have to rewrite controllers to be EPOC specific. Just occasionally, it might be possible to use some of the code from other systems that performs the key controller task of linking views and models.

However it pans out, you can begin the process by trying to break down the original program into:

- ❑ Storage and data manipulation sub-modules: the model
- ❑ Graphical functions that read the data through the engine and display it: the view
- ❑ Interface functions that take incoming events and process them using the facilities of the model and the view: the controller

In summary, the majority of this chapter is really about porting basic engine functionality, which is generally perfectly feasible. The outstanding issues relate to concurrent programming, which is discussed in more depth below.

The Aims of Porting

So far, we've looked at porting without really assessing what we are trying to achieve. To understand the process completely, and to appreciate the issues involved, it is worth taking a step back. Consider the following assertions:

- ❑ When porting an application, we should not expect to create an exact EPOC version of the program.
- ❑ When porting an application, we should not expect to recreate the functionality and look of the original program perfectly.

The first of these statements is important: we are not expected to follow standard EPOC programming guidelines exactly, to utilize the EPOC library fully, or to follow the same methodologies that you would use for native EPOC programs. If you tried to do this, it wouldn't really be porting at all – it would be rewriting. That approach has its uses, but rewriting existing code is generally worth avoiding if you can.

The second point is probably more contentious, but what I want to emphasize is that in porting most applications we are trying to port the functionality, and a certain amount of the look. It is not usually appropriate to recreate the original perfectly, for various reasons:

- ❏ EPOC systems have limited memory and file space compared to larger machines. You may have to consider how efficiently files are stored by your applications.

- ❏ The screen is likely to be small, and may only show shades of gray. To make effective use of the screen available, you will need to consider at least some of the standard EPOC tricks, such as only displaying the menu when required, and making only sparing use of separate windows.

- ❏ To integrate properly with the rest of the EPOC system, you will have to mimic at least some of the functionality of the standard application interface. You will also rely on the facilities that EPOC provides.

A key question to ask is whether you intend your ported application to look more like a standard EPOC application or more like the original. If you follow standard EPOC look-and-feel guidelines and conventions, then your program should be easier to follow for end users that have experience in using the standard EPOC applications. On the other hand, if you try to preserve the original look-and-feel, your ported application should be more familiar to users who have experience of using the application on other platforms. At the end of the day, this is primarily a marketing decision, but it's important that you consider it from the outset: it has major implications for what you are going to port, and what is best written from scratch.

It is a matter of engineering compromise between what of the original can be maintained and what must be written anew. In principle, it is preferable to re-use code than to generate the equivalent from scratch. However, there comes a point when trying to adapt existing code to EPOC becomes more trouble than it is worth, or too many compromises in functionality are mandated. In such circumstances, it will be more appropriate to rewrite modules than to port them.

In practice, applications are made up of several key sub-modules, and some of these will be more portable than others. If you look within the sub-modules, some *parts* are likely to be more portable than others. The trick is being able to judge what of the original code can be ported and what cannot; judging what *functionality* is to be preserved is a separate (although not necessarily simpler) issue.

Unfortunately, there is no real substitute for experience in this matter, but I can try to give you some guidelines. The fact is that in most cases, like our simple example, the emphasis is placed on porting engine components. In some cases, this can be extended to look at graphics. As mentioned above, it is highly unlikely that controller code will be carried over – or at least, not the first-level handlers of incoming events. Of course, there may be further areas requiring attention if the source code uses library functions or system facilities that are not supported on EPOC.

The following sections will look at these issues in more detail, but don't forget that the aim of the exercise is always to produce applications with the required functionality, not necessarily to port 100% of the original program.

Graphics and Callbacks to C++

The primary output mechanism of most (if not all) EPOC devices is the display. With native EPOC C++ applications, drawing is performed by control or view objects. The question, then, is whether we can draw from imported C code. It's actually pretty unlikely that you will ever have to do this for real, but as part of the methodology I'll have to show you how to make calls from your imported C program back to C++ libraries, and that technique has many uses.

Before we do this, let's look at how graphical functions are normally organized in native EPOC applications. In general, you can divide drawing functions into two kinds:

❑ Application-initiated: functions that draw during normal processing

❑ System-initiated: functions that are called to refresh the contents of the screen, and can be called repeatedly to give the same effect

The key to standard EPOC functionality is that the window server can send redraw requests to any part of the screen, at any time. With EIKON applications, these requests are mapped to Draw() functions of the appropriate CONE control objects. The Draw() functions must somehow know what should be drawn on the screen, usually by examining the state of the stored data. If you want to draw a string somewhere on the screen, for example, you will typically store the string and font in object data fields, and possibly the position too. What you do not normally store is the bitmapped picture of the given string: storing the string, and not the bitmap, uses much less memory.

The biggest downside of relying exclusively on Draw() is that redrawing the whole screen to update a small part of it can be inefficient, and can lead to a flickering effect. Therefore, most EPOC programs include a second class of drawing function that works in an application-initiated manner, updating the screen as required. These are used to update the screen directly. However, in the EPOC scheme they are purely optimizations – correct behavior can be achieved just by calling Draw() functions. Indeed, it is essential that the application-initiated drawing functions produce exactly the same result as Draw() would.

If you want to port graphics-based code that follows the same scheme, there should be few problems. Indeed, it's worth trying to embed code like this into a CONE control, so that you can easily pick up the screen redraw request as a call to Draw(). However, not all programs follow this scheme – quite a few are intended to work primarily using application-initiated drawing functions. In this methodology, if you want to draw text on the screen, you do just that. Unless it is required for some other purpose, there is no need to store the strings being drawn. Generally, this suits a non-object-oriented, top-down programming style, and is therefore likely to be used by legacy code – often the sort of thing being ported.

Can we handle this kind of thing on EPOC? Actually, we can. The simplest method is to use **backed-up windows**, where a window has a 'shadow' bitmap of the same dimensions. When you draw to such a window, what actually happens is that the bitmap is modified, and then the modified area of the bitmap is copied to the screen. Whenever a redraw is required, the associated area of the bitmap is copied to the screen – there are no calls to Draw() functions.

Backed-up Windows

As an example, we're going to look at a modified version of our filter program that will draw starting and finished on the screen before and after the function being run. This string is going to come from the C code; the example is `pepfilt3a` from the source code supplied with the book. It is based on the previous version using explicit `This`.

The first modifications are to the constructor for the app view controller. Instead of the standard `CreateWindowL()` call, we use:

```
CreateBackedUpWindowL(iCoeEnv->RootWin(), EGray2);
```

To show the effect on the rest of the program, consider the code that actually draws the Hello World text. In the original, this was placed in `Draw()`. In the new organization, we introduce a new function, `DrawText()`:

```
void CExampleAppView::DrawText(const TDesC& aDes)
    {
    ActivateGc();
    CWindowGc& gc = SystemGc();

    TRect drawRect = Rect();
    drawRect.Shrink(10, 10);

    CFont* font = iExampleFont;
    TInt ascent = (drawRect.Height() -
                font->HeightInPixels()) / 2 +
                font->AscentInPixels();

    gc.UseFont(iExampleFont);
    gc.DrawText(aDes, drawRect, ascent,
             CGraphicsContext::ECenter, 0);

    DeactivateGc();
    }
```

Whenever you want to display a message on the screen, you call `DrawText()` with the string, so that to get the previous functionality we need to call:

```
DrawText(*iExampleText);
```

This is called from all the usual functions; in the sample it's called from `ActivateL()` (itself called at the end of the construction process), along with some additional instructions to draw a rectangle.

> If you use this style of code, be careful about `ActivateGc()`/`DeactivateGc()` calls. If you call `ActivateGc()` twice without calling `DeactiveGc()`, the system will panic. This particular way of coding, where these functions are called in the same routine as the drawing operations, is probably not the most appropriate: you could not call `DrawText()` from within another function that had itself called `ActivateGc()`.

So far, so good, but we don't seem to have solved our problem of getting the C program to draw text. To do this, we have to set up two linkages. First, we supply an observer class to the CFiltEng:

```
class MFiltEngObserver
    {
public:
    virtual void SupportDrawText(const TDesC& aString) = 0;
    };
```

We link this back to the app UI, so that a call to SupportDrawText() leads to a call to the DrawText() function described above. This involves the standard technique of saying that the App UI derives additionally from the MFiltEngObserver mixin class, and then passing it to the engine during construction.

Having done this, we need to use a similar mechanism for linking the C module back to its C++ wrapper. We add the following line to the _This declaration:

```
    void* engineSupport;
```

And the following function declaration:

```
    extern void SupportDrawText(void* aEngineSupport, char* aString);
```

engineSupport is actually a pointer back to the CFiltEng wrapper object: it is declared as void* so the C code does not need to see the C++ class declarations. Within the C++ code, we then add:

```
    extern "C" void SupportDrawText(void* aEngineSupport, char* aString)
        {
        TPtrC string(REINTERPRET_CAST(TUint8*, aString), strlen(aString));
        STATIC_CAST(CFiltEng*, aEngineSupport)->SupportDrawText(string);
        }

    void CFiltEng::SupportDrawText(const TDesC& aString)
        {
        iObserver->SupportDrawText(aString);
        }
```

Here, the primary SupportDrawText() routine first converts the C-style char* string to the TDesC style used in EPOC, and then invokes the wrapper's SupportDrawText() method. The conversion of char* strings is much simpler than the reverse process, because we don't need to modify the original data. The TPtrC object we create contains an extra field that is the length of the data, and we generate this at creation time – you may remember that for the reverse process, we had to take a copy in order to be able to append a null byte safely.

In this manner, the C call:

```
    SupportDrawText(This->engineSupport, "starting...");
```

will result in text being drawn directly on the screen. You can extend this approach to support additional callbacks by replicating the various calls. You don't need additional observer classes; just add additional pure virtual functions to MFiltEngObserver.

> In fact, this particular example doesn't quite work properly: nothing clears the screen
> before the text is drawn, and all strings are drawn on top of each other. It is left as an
> exercise to fix it, but this shows the problems of using backed-up windows, where it's
> not clear who is responsible for resetting the display.

A possible complexity in this arrangement is where the called C++ methods may leave – the point
being that C does not understand such a concept. It is therefore important to handle such possibilities
within your C++ code. Another feature of the pepfilt3a example is a second callback chain that
displays or cancels EIKON busy messages – flashing text in the bottom right-hand corner of the screen.
These are created using CEikonEnv::BusyMsgL(), which (as the L indicates) can leave, and canceled
using CEikonEnv::BusyMsgCancel(), which does not. The central routine in the app UI class that
we want to call from our C code is as follows:

```
void CExampleAppUi::SupportBusyMsgL(const TDesC& aString)
    {
    if(aString.Length() > 0)
        iEikonEnv->BusyMsgL(aString);
    else
        iEikonEnv->BusyMsgCancel();
    }
```

The interface code in the object is pretty similar to that above:

```
extern "C" void SupportBusyMsg(void* aEngineSupport, char* aString)
    {
    TPtrC string
    if(aString != NULL)
        string.Set(REINTERPRET_CAST(TUint8*, aString), strlen(aString));
    TRAPD(ignore,
        STATIC_CAST(CFiltEng*, aEngineSupport)->SupportBusyMsgL(string));
    }

void CFiltEng::SupportBusyMsgL(const TDesC& aString)
    {
    iObserver->SupportBusyMsgL(aString);
    }
```

There are two key differences between this scheme and the one for simply drawing text. The first is that
the TPtrC object is only set if the original parameter is not 0 – the default constructor for TPtrC creates
an object with zero length. The effect of this is that a call to:

```
SupportBusyMsg(This->engineSupport, "busy");
```

will result in CEikonEnv::BusyMsgL() being called with "busy" as the parameter, while the call:

```
SupportBusyMsg(This->engineSupport, NULL);
```

will end up in a call to `CEikonEnv::BusyMsgCancel()`. This gives a more C-like interface, although it's obviously not essential. The second difference is that we call the C++ code using a `TRAPD()` macro. If errors occur during processing and the called routines leave, then processing will fall back to this place and continue. In this particular example, not creating a busy message is not catastrophic, and we can just ignore the event. In other circumstances you may have to do something to correct the error, or return a 'failed' indication to the C program that could then do something more sensible.

This particular example is so simple that it would be a relatively straightforward matter to convert it into something that used a standard EPOC system-initiated drawing scheme. If this turns out to be the case, then it is recommended you do so.

*An alternative solution to using backed-up windows is to create an **off-screen bitmap** – that is, a bitmap object that exists on the window server but is not directly displayed. We can send draw commands to the bitmap, and then copy areas from the bitmap to a standard window in order to display them. This gives us more control over the redrawing, but the big advantage is that you can mix full application-initiated drawing with system-initiated: that is, some parts of the screen can be maintained one way, and some the other. It is also more memory efficient, as you only need screen copies for parts of the screen. The downside is the complexity, but with the extra control and efficiency gained, I recommend this approach.*

Model Design

The remaining part of this chapter is going to concentrate on various issues that arise specifically when porting standard engine code.

Porting C++ Code

You may be wondering why the porting examples I've shown have been based around C, when EPOC is at heart a C++ environment. The surprising truth is that although EPOC is based around C++, the dialect of the language supported is different enough from that used in other operating systems to make the porting of C programs more straightforward.

This is not to say that porting C++ programs is not feasible, but it's almost certainly going to be more complicated than porting programs written entirely in C. About the only advantage is that because of the availability of objects, it is easier to replace global variables. Some of the things you might have to deal with include:

❑   Restrictions on multiple inheritance

If a class has more than one parent class, only one of them is allowed to have data members. The remainder, mixin classes, can only possess member functions. Class hierarchies intended for other systems often break these constraints.

❑   C++ exceptions are not implemented

EPOC has its own rather different mechanism, based on leaves and the cleanup stack. The standard ISO mechanism is not implemented.

❏ Two-phase constructors

Unlike other C++ environments, EPOC uses a technique based around a two-phase construction process, where there are limits on what can be created by the constructor proper.

❏ Lack of standard C++ libraries

EPOC does not attempt to support standard C++ libraries – and considering all the above restrictions, they probably wouldn't port directly anyway. Instead, you have to use EPOC's own mechanisms. These often require changes to the way modules are organized; in particular, you will probably want to replace `iostream` usage with EPOC streams, and C++ `string` objects with EPOC descriptors.

❏ GCC 2.7.2 is not ISO compliant

It is important to realize that EPOC is a multi-target environment, where a properly written program will compile for and run on several platforms, without the source being changed. The problem with that is that the GCC compiler used to generate binaries for the MARM target understands an older version of the language than the Microsoft Visual C++ compiler used for the WINS emulator. To a certain extent, this can be massaged by the use of macros – the `STATIC_CAST()` macro, for example, maps to traditional casts for GCC and the standard C++ `static_cast<>()` construct on Visual C++. However, this obviously requires more changes when porting code, which may well have been written to the latest standard. There is no support for dynamic casts, or for the associated RTTI library.

These constraints suggest that it is unlikely you will find much C++ code that can be easily ported – except perhaps the sort of C++ code that uses no objects. Much more likely, if you have to port C++ model code, you will have to make significant changes before it will be valid under EPOC.

Asynchronous Programming and Long Loops

Interactive applications have to give the impression to the user that several things are going on concurrently. They have to be able to carry out background processing while ensuring that the screen is kept up to date, and that any pointer or key events are handled without delay. Inevitably, any program that involves some background programming, or which has to handle input from several sources, needs to be written using some kind of concurrent style.

EPOC offers three methods of generating concurrent programs:

❏ Processes. In the UNIX or Windows sense, each of these is a separate entity, running one or more threads of execution. Except for client-server arrangements, it is not normal EPOC practice to use more than one process to implement user applications – there are better ways of doing it.

❏ Threads. You can have more than one thread in each process, each with its own stack. The EPOC implementation of threads introduces its own problems, so we will leave them until the next section.

❏ Asynchronous processing. This is a traditional EPOC method. Many of the system calls have asynchronous versions, where instead of completing immediately, the calling function just issues a request that's completed later. On completion, a semaphore on the thread is signaled, and a status variable is set with the error code (or lack of it). The main program loop is to wait on the semaphore, find out which status variable has been set, and then call an appropriate handler. This is similar in outline, if not in detail, to the event-driven schemes used by some other systems.

Asynchronous processing forms the heart of most, if not all, EPOC applications. However, with C++ it is usually abstracted away using a concept known as **active objects** (AOs), which work together with an **active scheduler** (AS). AOs are covered in more detail Chapter 18, but they're such a useful and powerful tool that another quick look won't hurt. The basic scheme can be seen in this figure:

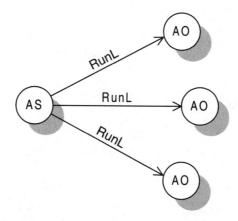

Essentially, AOs form an abstract C++ class that encapsulates asynchronous function calls: they contain a status variable, a flag to say they are waiting for action, and a RunL() function that's called to handle the completion of whatever 'system call' was issued – together with an extra function DoCancel() that's called to cancel an outstanding request. The other part of the system is the AS object, of which there is usually one per program (or one per thread). The AS performs the important job of waiting on the semaphore and calling the appropriate AOs.

To a large extent, this gives us a concurrent execution environment in which AOs are invoked when there is something to be done. The proviso is that it only works when RunL() commands do not enter long loops: it is essential that RunL() functions execute fairly quickly and return, because the program cannot perform any other functions while they are operating – this is the downside of their non-preemptive semantics.

The good news is that we can use AOs for background processing. Consider the following code sequence, which can be called from inside an AO:

```
TRequestStatus* status = &iStatus;
User::RequestComplete(status, KErrNone);
SetActive();
```

This construct bypasses the idea of a system call indicating completion of an asynchronous event – it's saying, "Run me as soon as possible." Using this sequence, you can get a very similar effect to using threads.

843

Turning again to our example, you might wonder why we would need to use background processing for the filter operation. The short answer is that if the file is large, the program effectively seizes up while the processing is carried out. In interactive applications, this is not usually tolerable: we want to filter in the background, so that the main application can still respond to events. The first attempt at this, `pepfilt4` in the example code supplied with the book, uses AOs. Obviously, it's not possible to integrate the AO class structure directly into C, so the first question to ask is how we will organize the system.

What we do is replace our `do_filter()` function with the following:

```
extern int open_filter(_This* This,
                        char* input_file_name, char* output_file_name);
extern int iterate_filter(_This* This);
extern void close_filter(_This* This);
```

We separate out the single function we had before into separate `open`, `iterate` and `close` functions. Note that the `iterate` function returns a value to indicate when the end of the processing has been reached.

Having done that, we modify the wrapper class so that `CFiltEng` is now an AO, and we introduce an observer class called `MFiltEngObserver` with a `FilterFinishedL()` function that we can call to tell the main application that the filter has finished. For completeness, we now have to spread the calls to the C code across the `CFiltEng` member functions. The `open_filter()` function is called from the kickoff function, now renamed `StartFilterL()` to reflect its changed behavior:

```
EXPORT_C void CFiltEng::StartFilterL(const TDesC& aFileName)
    {
    char fileName[KMaxFileName];
    TPtr fileDes(REINTERPRET_CAST(TUint8*, fileName), KMaxFileName);

    fileDes = aFileName;
    fileDes.Append(TChar(0));

    _This* This = STATIC_CAST(_This*, iFiltEngThis);

    TInt res = open_filter(This, fileName, NULL);
    TInt error = KErrNone;

    if(res < 0)
        error = KErrGeneral;
    else
        iProcessing = ETrue;

    TRequestStatus* status = &iStatus;
    User::RequestComplete(status, error);
    SetActive();
    }
```

Any errors are passed to `RunL()`, and then on to `FilterFinishedL()` – this leads to a clean interface. The `RunL()` function itself is fairly straightforward: after checking for errors on the previous cycle, we get the following:

```
        TInt moreToDo = iterate_filter(This);
        if(moreToDo)
            {
            TRequestStatus* status = &iStatus;
            User::RequestComplete(status, KErrNone);
            SetActive();
            }
        else
            {
            close_filter(This);
            iProcessing = EFalse;
            iObserver->FilterFinishedL(KErrNone);
            }
```

Depending on the result of `iterate_filter()`, we either request for the AO to be run again, or we finish off. About the only complexity is that we potentially have to promote some local variables from what was `do_filter()` to our `This` structure. We have to keep anything that is required from one iteration to the next, as the function is exited and all the variables are lost. On this occasion, it turns out that of the variables not already in `This`, only `overflow_from_previous` has to be moved.

> When programming with AOs, remember to be careful about priorities. It is important that the filter AO has a comparatively low priority, or it will stop any other AOs from running — these 'background processing' AOs are always runnable.
>
> Don't try to make explicit calls to `User::WaitForAnyRequest()` in any thread where you are using AOs (and therefore ASes). Active schedulers must also call this function, and will rapidly get confused and panic if something else has 'answered' the request. In any particular thread, you either use custom asynchronous event-handlers, or the AO/AS scheme. Since the CONE environment makes use of AOs, this means you must use AOs for asynchronous processing in the main thread of EIKON-based applications.

One possible problem with converting to the AO/AS scheme is if you want to wait for input on sockets, the console, or similar. If you use synchronous calls, which wait until any input is available, then these will block the whole thread – remember that you can only switch to another active object when you exit the current RunL() call. With C++ library calls, the solution would be to use the asynchronous version of the library call, but at face value there are no asynchronous implementations within STDLIB. To help with this, there are overloaded versions of the ioctl() call with an extra TRequestStatus& parameter. These can be used in a variation on a select() call, where you can be told when data is available on a single file descriptor, or when data has been written. For more information, see the STDLIB documentation.

EPOC Threads

The good news about threads is that EPOC has kernel-level support for running multiple threads within processes. The *really* good news, from the angle of porting, is that STDLIB has even better support for threads then the standard EPOC C++ libraries do – in particular, they support engines designed in a multithreaded manner. The only complication is that the threads are not POSIX compliant, meaning that some work may be required even in this case.

EPOC threads are centered on the RThread object that allows new threads to be created within the current process, each of which has its own stack and (usually) its own heap. Basic semaphores are implemented, so you can get mutual exclusion protection on shared variables, but you cannot share open files or sockets – in general, you can't share any system-level objects. This restriction was introduced so that the system doesn't have to deal with simultaneous accesses to an object from more than one thread, but it means that some redesign may be required in situations where threads are used to wait for incoming activity on sockets and other devices. There is a strong argument that this is not such a bad thing, as it is rather wasteful of memory.

Fortunately, STDLIB can be used in such a way that sockets and files *can* be shared between threads – as has already been mentioned in Chapter 22. Essentially, STDLIB runs quite differently depending on whether a CPosixServer object exists or not. If you need one of these, it must be created before you start to use STDLIB, or the system will get confused. If it exists, then all file and socket operations are redirected to the thread that owns the CPosixServer object. Because all files are owned by a single thread, EPOC is quite happy with this arrangement – indeed, it is essentially oblivious to the fact, as all it sees is the inter-thread communication. To create the CPosixServer object, you should use InstallPosixServerActiveObject() or SpawnPosixServerThread() – the latter creates a special thread for the server object, and is probably preferred. Once created, the server object is largely invisible to the program and works behind the scenes. On the other hand, if STDLIB is used without a CPosixServer object having been created, then all resources are owned by the thread that opened the file, socket, etc., and cannot be accessed by other threads.

The standard recommendation is that you always try to rewrite a thread-based program using the AO technique described in the previous section. Because AOs are non-preemptive, there are no problems with mutual exclusion, and no problems with objects being shared. Remember that the POSIX server approach only applies to STDLIB function calls, and you will need to do some extra work if your ported code calls back to the C++. However, removal of threads completely is not always so simple. Not all background functions are as easily adapted to this AO technique as our filter example. Some game-play engines are based on deep recursion, only exiting at the end of the run, and would need a complete rewrite to work with repeated AO calls. For such scenarios, EPOC threads are ideal. In practice, you will encounter two situations:

❑ The original program consisted of a sequential engine, with perhaps a second thread being used for interface work. In that case, it is generally more efficient *not* to create a CPosixServer and to use the STDLIB in 'direct' mode. Indeed, if you introduce several, separate engines into a program – CODECs for different sound formats, for example – then you still need not use a CPosixServer object, as the various engines won't be sharing files.

❑ If the original engine was designed in a multithreaded manner then you will almost certainly have to use a CPosixServer. Remember, though, that you can only share STDLIB objects, so you're totally dependent on the functionality it provides you.

One of the reasons for the development of STDLIB was the need to port the Java run-time engine to EPOC. Because Java itself uses threads, it was essential that the STDLIB supported multi-threaded usage. You may have similar requirements if you implement other language interpreters. However, if you can abstract the concept of threads away, you are likely to get more efficient code. Remember again that you can't share graphics contexts and other C++ based primitives between threads without deriving a similar scheme to the CPosixServer and writing it yourself. Obviously, this very much depends on the original code.

The obvious question, then, is how we might adapt our filter example so that the background processing uses a thread rather than the AO scheme – and I've provided a solution in example `pepfilt5`. Compared with the AO solution, the basic filter functionality is actually much simpler: with threads we can maintain the original `do_filter()` function call, but we are going to create a single, second thread in which the engine is run, while the user interface will continue to run in the original thread. Creating the thread is pretty simple too:

```
iEngineThread = new(ELeave) RThread;
TInt error = iEngineThread->Create(_L("Filter Engine"),
                                   EngineThreadEntryPoint,
                                   KDefaultStackSize,
                                   KMinHeapSize,
                                   0x1000000, this);
User::LeaveIfError(error);

iStatus = KRequestPending;
SetActive();

iEngineThread->Resume();
```

The entry point is a simple static function that eventually leads to a proper member function, `RunThread()`, being called. The tricky part is telling the main application when the thread has finished. We can't wait on a semaphore, because that would stop the active scheduler process. Instead, we need somehow to create an AO that will mimic the semaphore wait, because that will fit in with the AS/AO methodology.

I refer to the following scheme as 'remote AO signaling', because we are going to get the engine thread to set the value of an AO in the main thread, and then to signal the latter's semaphore as if it were the 'system'. Remember that each thread has its own semaphore anyway, used to indicate the completion of asynchronous system calls. To do this, we again make `CFiltEng` an AO – just like the background-processing AO scheme. However, the `RunL()` function is now much simpler:

```
void CFiltEng::RunL()
    {
    CloseDownEngineThread();
    iObserver->FilterFinishedL(iStatus.Int());
    }

void CFiltEng::CloseDownEngineThread()
    {
    if(iEngineThread)
        {
        iEngineThread->Kill(KErrNone);
        iEngineThread->Close();
        delete iEngineThread;
        iEngineThread = NULL;
        }
    }
```

Quite simply, this closes the thread down and calls the observer with the result. Note that the `CloseDownEngineThread()` function is designed to be called in `DoCancel()` and the destructor too, just in case the program is exited while calculation is still going on. You might have noticed that we use new to create the `iEngineThread` object and then call `delete` on it during closure. This style is recommended because you get a clear indication when the thread object has been created and destroyed. It helps you to deal with some seemingly strange features of `RThread` behavior. Consider the statement:

```
RThread sample;
```

This does not create a thread, but an `RThread` object. You might be thinking, "What's the difference?" Well, each `RThread` object can be thought of as a pointer: you can have more than one `RThread` object pointing to the same real thread, just as you can have more than one pointer variable pointing to the same object on the heap. If we have an `RThread` variable, we have to associate it with an actual threads: we can create a new one to point at, or we can point at an existing one − these actions are covered by the `Create()` and `Open()` methods respectively. For the same reason, `RThread::Close()` just closes the object; if you want to close the thread itself, you need to use `RThread::Kill()`. The final curious point about `RThread` is that the above declaration of `sample`, without any further function calls, sets it up as pointing to the current thread. The code to find the ID of the current thread is then as follows:

```
RThread myThread;
iMainThreadId = myThread.Id();
myThread.Close();
```

That just leaves two things to set up. First, in the original thread, we set the `CFiltEng` AO as pending:

```
iStatus = KRequestPending;
SetActive();
```

This tells the AS object that we are waiting for something − it doesn't need to know what. The more interesting code is called at the end of the engine thread:

```
RThread mainThread;
mainThread.Open(iMainThreadId);
TRequestStatus* status = &iStatus;
mainThread.RequestComplete(status, error);
mainThread.Close();
```

We are still inside the `CFiltEng` object, but we're running in a different thread. What we do here is to get a handle back to the main thread, so that we can use `RThread::RequestComplete()`, which performs the required behavior, signaling the semaphore of the main thread, and not the engine thread.

I hope this level of explanation has not put you off this technique. In itself, it does not fully address the issues raised by multithreaded EPOC programs, but I emphasize again that the background AO processing technique, described in the previous section, is more memory efficient, more predictable, and almost always preferred − assuming you have the choice.

> Depending on how you create them, most threads have their own heap. Although they can see objects in each other's heaps, beware of creating an object in one thread and deleting it in another. This will lead to problems. If you need this functionality, you will probably have to investigate shared heaps.

Instead of the 'remote AO signaling' approach being demonstrated here, we could have used `RThread::Logon()`, *which will asynchronously wait until the particular thread has exited. If that is all you want to do, it is far simpler to set up, and is generally recommended. However, the approach shown above is more generic, as it can be used for subsequent two-way communication between the threads – not just to indicate that the thread has reached the end.*

Polling, `select()` and other Concurrency Mechanisms

I've now shown you the major techniques used for implementing concurrent applications under EPOC. However, there are alternative strategies used in different systems, and you might come across these if you port related programs. Perhaps the most common are:

❏   `select()` – a traditional UNIX call. This is fed sets of file descriptors, and will wait until input is available on one of the inputs, or we can successfully write again to an output – or indeed, until a timeout occurs.

❏   Polling. A device is somehow dealt with behind the scenes, and we periodically check its status.

Let's look at polling for a moment. The problem with using structures like:

```
while(DataIsPresent())
    ProcessIt();
```

on any system is that it requires data to be processed behind the scenes. Typically, `DataIsPresent()` will be mapped to a system call, and the concurrency is provided by the system. Alternatively, the application has to mimic this behavior, making `DataIsPresent()` look like a system call but dealing with the concurrency in some other manner. I've seen several examples of porting where what was a system call in one system has to be simulated this way in another.

Let's go back to the pre-thread, pre-AO version of our filter example, where we were just using a long loop. The problem, as pointed out at the time, was that this tended to freeze the system while the processing was carried out. We introduced the AO and thread versions to solve this, but wouldn't it be nice if we could somehow say something like:

```
for(;;)
    {
    int num_to_filter, num_in_buffer, num_read;

    RunSystem(This->engineSupport);

    for(index = 0; index < FILTER_SIZE * 2; index++)
```

That is, we make a call to RunSystem() that should deal with any outstanding events and then let us carry on. Then the system would no longer freeze up.

It turns out that we *can* implement this behavior, at least to some extent. The situation we're in is illustrated in the figure below. The key is the ability to call the CActiveScheduler object recursively, using CActiveScheduler::Start(). If you do this, then what is effectively a new instance of the object is able to call any AOs, as required. At some stage, we need to get back to the original conditions, and we can do this using CActiveScheduler::Stop(), which says that when the current RunL() ends, this instance of the scheduler will exit.

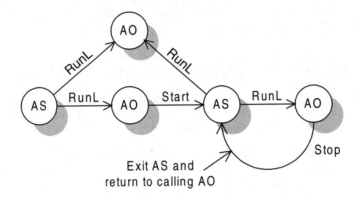

The question now is, "How?" We want to start the scheduler, run anything outstanding and then stop. The key to this is class CIdle, which calls a function when there is nothing more that can be processed – strictly speaking, nothing more of a higher priority than the value you give it. We can amend our CFiltEng wrapper object to take this into account: the source is given as project pepfilt6 in the example code supplied with the book, and the key changes are as follows:

```
void CFiltEng::RunSystemL()
    {
    TCallBack callback(StaticIdleCallback, this);
    iIdle->Start(callback);
    CActiveScheduler::Start();
    }

TInt CFiltEng::IdleCallback()
    {
    CActiveScheduler::Stop();
    return KErrNone;
    }
```

(I've omitted some static functions that are used to move between the C and C++.) The RunSystemL() call tells iIdle to call the callback function StaticIdleCallback(). This latter will itself call IdleCallback(), and then enter the AS. Any AOs waiting to be processed will be run at this point. When there is nothing else to do, IdleCallback() will be run, and the scheduler will stop. At this stage, control returns to RunSystemL(), and thus back to the filter routine.

There are lots of variations on this theme. If you wanted a polling-style mechanism for waiting for input on a socket, you could create an AO that waited for the input and set a flag to say that the input had arrived. Then, after (or perhaps before) running `RunSystemL()` you could check the flags and return appropriate values, as in:

```
TInt CXX..::DataIsPresent()
{
    RunSystem();
    return iDataFound;
}
```

Alternatively, you can create semantics similar to the UNIX `select()` statement: instead of using a `CIdle` object, arrange that the AO's monitoring I/O 'devices' exit the AS when they are activated. The algorithm of your "select" will be:

```
loop
    {
    check flags,
    CActiveScheduler::Start
    }
```

At this point, you might be thinking something along the lines of, "Why didn't he show us that to start with?" or, "That's exactly what I need!" Unfortunately, life is not so easy and there are problems with this method. First, there is a performance penalty, although it does not seem that unreasonable in practice. More interesting are the realities of the recursive implementation. Essentially, if you recurse, and then somebody else uses the same trick, you won't get control back until *they* exit. Standard EIKON dialogs, where the wait flag is set, actually use this trick during the call to `ExecuteLD()` – it allows screen redraws and event handling to continue. If your `RunSystem()` method recurses, and then a run AO starts a dialog, then no processing will continue until the dialog has finished. This is rarely acceptable. To get around this, you can use non-wait dialogs, although these are somewhat different.

> *This* `pepfilt6` *example on the CD has a number of minor flaws: it does nothing to prevent a file filter operation being executed while one is in progress, and it has particular problems if the exit command is given when it is busy. The program really needs modifying so that it handles the exit scenario cleanly – you might like to try this as an exercise.*

Miscellaneous Tricks and Tips

Porting is rather an open-ended subject. To a large extent, you will have to develop custom methodologies for each case. In addition to the standard techniques I've covered in this chapter, the following is a list of suggestions and pointers to act as a basis for exploring solutions:

❑ Document association

   If your program generates documents, it is quite likely that you'll want to associate them with your application, so that double clicking the document will automatically run your application and tell it to open the document. EPOC does this somewhat differently from other systems such as Windows. Standard EPOC documents include the UID of the associated application.

More than likely, you will continue to use file types developed for other systems, and not following the EPOC standards. To perform the association, you will need to create **recognizer objects**. These are called periodically by the system when it does not know the application associated with a given file, and are able to work out the type by the name or perhaps a quick read of the document.

❑ Implement engines as servers

I've shown you several ways of importing C code to form engines, and in particular concurrent engines, within EPOC applications. One alternative possibility that I've not touched is to implement your engine as a server. Apart from getting the concurrency for free (because it will run as a separate process), this has one major advantage over the techniques shown: servers are .exe programs, and thus are allowed global variables. For a reasonably sized module, there are likely to be fewer problems if you generate servers. But set against this are the overheads of inter-process communication.

❑ Use APPARC instead of EIKON

The main EIKON application classes are derived from a more basic set called APPARC. If the code you are porting includes the user-interface, and you want to preserve it, then it may be simpler to bypass EIKON and directly exploit the basic classes. Beware, though, that you will cease to be able to use lots of standard EIKON components, like dialogs and standard controls.

Porting from EPOC

In this chapter we've concentrated on what is the standard EPOC porting task: porting code from other systems to EPOC. However, there are also circumstances where you may need to port code designed for EPOC to other systems. For example, at Purple Software, we have chess programs that run on both EPOC and Windows CE platforms. Substantial amounts of the EPOC code is also used by the CE version — above and beyond modules that are standard C, and that were ported from elsewhere. As part of the port, we provide our own versions of EPOC libraries that work under CE. The key to this seems to be to focus on a relatively small subset of the EPOC run-time libraries, so that these libraries are relatively small. This means being very careful on the classes, and the functions within these classes, that we use. The fewer we use, the better. Of course, these restrictions are only applied to the code we wish to port.

Summary

In this chapter, we've looked at how we might port code, and especially C code, from other systems to EPOC. In general, most porting work emphasizes 'engines' — the modules that implement storage and the underlying functionality. For standard, top-down, sequential code, the main problems tend to relate to how we can execute the programs without freezing the application's handling of screen, pen, key, etc. events. In addition, we have problems with global variables, which cannot be implemented in the DLL binary modules we normally use. We've looked at several methods of solving these problems, and we looked at how we might link back to the main application, and also how we might port code based on alternative concurrent methods, like the UNIX select statement.

The main conclusion is that porting *is* possible, and in particular for C modules. However, we have to be very clear which parts of the original program should be ported, and which will need to be replaced by EPOC equivalents.

26

OPL

The **Organiser Programming Language**, or **OPL**, is similar to BASIC as seen in many other operating systems. An OPL program editor and translator is built into many EPOC devices, providing a programming environment that's available to the user while on the move, and away from a desktop development platform. OPL is also a very good rapid development (RAD) tool for testing out application ideas that you may later write in C++.

This chapter introduces OPL. It talks about the history of OPL, tells you about writing in OPL, and then guides you through a couple of examples: a simple "Hello world" program, and a fully event-driven (but still quite simple) OPL application. It then explains how to extend OPL with additional commands, guiding you through writing extensions in C++.

Assumptions

This chapter has been written with a few assumptions in mind.

- ❑ You have no prior knowledge of OPL, but you are already a competent developer in another computer language

- ❑ You have installed the ER5 OPL Software Development Kit (SDK)

- ❑ The keyboard language of any EPOC device you may be using is English (although the code will work on any language device)

A Simple OPL program: "Hello world!"

Before I tell you more about OPL, I will take you through writing and translating your first program. The following five-liner is about as simple as you can get: it just prints the phrase Hello world! on the screen (followed by [Press any key]), and then waits for you to press any key on the keyboard:

```
PROC HelloWorld:
  PRINT "Hello world!"
  PRINT "[Press any key]"
  GET
ENDP
```

All OPL procedures begin and end with PROC and ENDP. The PROC is always followed by a procedure name, which must be unique within the program. A colon must always follow the procedure name. Predictably, the second and third lines print text to the screen, while GET in the fourth line waits for any key press.

> **The first procedure in any OPL program is the first that will be executed when the program is run.**

Follow these steps to create and run your first OPL program:

- ❏ On the EPOC emulator (or EPOC device), move to the System view. Press the New file button, and a Create new file dialog will be displayed.

- ❏ Type a program name (HelloWorldSimple) in the Name field, and select Program in the Program option. Select OK.

- ❏ The program editor will open. You'll see that PROC : has already been entered on the first line, and ENDP on the third.

- ❏ You are now ready to start typing in the OPL program code shown above. You can use upper or lower case letters when entering OPL keywords; case is not important, although you will find that keeping a consistent case for keywords will help when you read through later.

- ❏ When you have finished typing in the code, press the Tran button on the toolbar to translate the program.

- ❏ When the program has been translated successfully, a prompt will appear asking whether the translated program should be run. Select Yes if you did not make any mistakes, or go back and check the code if there was an error. Try translating again.

- ❏ The program will run, displaying the Hello world! text and waiting for any key to be pressed.

When the program exits, you will be returned to the editor. In the System view, you'll find a file called `HelloWorldSimple.opo`. Selecting this file will run the program again.

About OPL

OPL first made its appearance on the Psion Organiser II in 1984. Before OPL, *all* programs for Psion's machines had to be written in assembler using a PC development kit, requiring the developer to have a good knowledge of programming.

By this time, the BASIC programming language was available for most home computers, making computer programming accessible to anyone who owned a computer. OPL was based on BASIC, but specialized for the Psion Organiser II. Users were able to write simple programs even if they didn't have an in-depth knowledge of computer programming.

OPL was *originally* designed as a database language to access or create databases shared with the Psion Organiser II's built-in Data application, but it has evolved with each new hardware device, always aiming to maintain good backward compatibility with previous versions. This helped developers to port existing OPL applications to a new device with the minimum of effort, while at the same time giving OPL applications the ability to have the same look and feel as the built-in applications. A key requirement for OPL was to make it possible to develop applications fully on the device itself.

> **The power of OPL has arisen from its extensibility. OPL has supported language extensions from the beginning, via 6301 assembler procedures on the Psion Organiser II, and now via C++ OPX procedures on devices running EPOC.**

On the Psion Organiser II, the OPL runtime was written in 6301 assembler. The main functionality included loops; conditionals; one-dimensional menus; database keywords; error handling; arithmetic operators; mathematical functions; language extensions written in assembler; and procedure files in a flat filing system. At this time, most of the applications were written for the corporate environment.

In the late 1980s, Psion launched the MC series of (laptop sized) devices. OPL was ported over to the 8086 CPU and had the broadly the same functionality as the Organiser – without menus, but with dynamically loadable modules, keywords to call OS services and input/output keywords (synchronous and asynchronous).

The Psion HC was again built around the 8086 chip, but it was more graphically based. In addition to the keywords added for the MC series, there were graphics keywords, the ability to call procedures by indirection, the concept of OPL applications that looked like built-in applications, event handling (for handling messages from the operating system such as switch files, close, etc.), and command-line support.

The Psion Series 3 (with the SIBO operating system) was released in 1991, and along with it came the first OPL Software Development Kit (SDK) giving many utilities and macros for nearly full access to the SIBO operating system services. Series 3 OPL added menus, dialogs, and the expression evaluator (used by the Calculator application).

When the Series 3a came out a few years later, OPL was again upgraded and remained almost unchanged for the rest of the SIBO range (Psion Series 3a, 3c, 3mx, Siena and Workabout series). It added allocator keywords, a cache with least-recently-used procedures flushed when necessary (for up to seven times speed improvement), and digital sound support.

In 1997, OPL was ported to C++ for the EPOC operating system, adding pen event handling, cascaded menus, popup menus, language extensions (using OPXs), constants and header files. Other enhancements included toolbar support and extremely powerful access to the EPOC database implementation. The EPOC OPL SDK was released shortly afterwards, allowing developers to develop OPL applications on a PC with the addition of a number of tools.

Release 5 of the EPOC operating system in 1999 added improved color support and file recognition thanks to MIME support, amongst many other minor improvements.

The Benefits of OPL

Since the Series 3, OPL has had an extremely enthusiastic and loyal third party development community on the Internet. One outcome of this is that the majority of Psion Series 3 and EPOC applications are written in OPL, including many commercial ones. The key points that developers like about OPL are:

❑ OPL is very easy to learn without any previous programming experience. The basics can be picked up within a day or two on the device itself; advanced OPL can be learnt within a few weeks. An OPL Help file is available for use on the EPOC machine.

❑ OPL applications can be developed on the device itself (so you can do it anywhere).

❑ The OPL editor with built-in translator is well suited to efficient and rapid application development.

❑ It's very quick and easy to develop high-quality programs that have the same look and feel as the built-in applications: toolbars, menus, dialogs, pen-event handling, asynchronous I/O support, etc. You can also develop applications without designing them completely first, which is very unlike C++.

❑ A mature OPL SDK provides good documentation and excellent support for OPL application development on the PC emulator, including the tools necessary to produce bitmaps and custom fonts.

❑   With OPX language extensions, it is possible to access most EPOC features available to C++ developers. Many OPXs have been developed by keen third party developers, and there are many core OPXs distributed by Symbian. These include improved access to the already powerful database; multi-page dialogs; access to the built-in Agenda file format; alarm setting; access to the built-in spell checker; and many more.

❑   As a tool, OPL is very useful for prototyping C++ applications.

❑   Enthusiastic and friendly support is provided by other OPL developers and via the various support resources provided through the Symbian Developer Network.

Implementation Architecture

There are two forms of OPL program: **applications** and **standalone programs**. OPL applications appear on the Extras bar, and can have files (or documents) associated with them. That is, their associated documents are displayed with the application icon, and can be selected from the System view to open the application. Apart from the occasional speed problem, OPL applications are practically indistinguishable from the built-in applications, which are almost all written in C++. And for many of the applications written in OPL, speed is not a concern.

A standalone OPL program will have the standard OPO icon, and will only run when it is selected from the System view or from another OPL or C++ program.

Writing and Translating OPL

The development paths are essentially the same whether you're using the program editor on the EPOC device itself, the one on the Windows emulator, or an ordinary text editor and the OPLTran tool. OPLTran is a PC-based program that can translate either plain text files or OPL program files from outside the emulator. The tool is documented in the OPL SDK.

> *In this chapter, it is assumed that you are using the program editor on either the EPOC device or the emulator.*

After deciding on a rough design for your application, the usual development process is that you:

❑   Write the program using the program editor.

❑   Translate the source code using the program editor. Translation converts OPL code into byte code that's interpreted at runtime by the OPL Runtime Application (which is roughly equivalent to the Java Virtual Machine). OPL programs are platform-independent: you can translate OPL programs on the emulator and transfer them to an EPOC device without any modification.

❑   Run the program. If an error occurs within code that you have not trapped with any of the OPL error trapping commands, you are taken to the line where the error happened.

Additional Steps for Developing Applications

OPL applications and programs can use **resource files** for all their text. Resource files enable you to change the text and hotkey codes without having to retranslate the application, since all the text and hotkeys for the application are held in a separate file. This is especially useful for creating multiple language versions of your application, with the text for each language being held in separate resource files.

Files can also be associated with OPL applications, so that the application will be run when the file is selected.

Lastly, If you're writing an application (as opposed to a program), you may want to design an icon that will appear on the Extras bar, and on each document created by the application.

More details on creating icons, using resource files, and file association, are given in the full DemoOPL application example below.

An Event-driven OPL Application

I have chosen to demonstrate OPL by writing a fully event-driven application that shows just how powerful it really can be.

I will take you through the application code, which has been split into four separate files, describing what's happening along the way. However, I won't describe each and every OPL keyword – you should turn to the OPL manual in the OPL SDK if you want to know more about individual commands.

Next, I'll show you how to generate the resource, graphic and help files, before finally demonstrating how to turn the translated code into a package that can be delivered to other EPOC users for them to install the application onto their devices. Please feel free to modify this code and use it as the basis for your own applications.

What the Application Does

As mentioned, this application is quite simple: it displays a single line of text in the middle of the screen. You may edit this text, zoom the text size in and out, save the text to a file, and open other DemoOPL format files via the toolbar, menus or hotkeys.

Once the application has been translated and run, you should see this:

The Application Code

This OPL application consists of a number of files containing the program code, the icon and bitmap graphics, the resource file, and the help file. Specifically, they are:

Code File Name	Contents
DemoOPL	The main application code
DemoOPLExternal.oph	Prototype declarations for all procedures used within the application
DemoOPLConst.oph	An OPL header file containing the constant declarations used within the main application
DemoOPLResource.oph	The language resource file constant declarations

I have used the following conventions within the code to make it easier to read:

❑ I have started all constants with the letter K. This is a common OPL convention.

❑ I have started all global variables with a capital G. Global variables in OPL are available to all procedures called *after* the variables have been declared. The global variables are destroyed once the declaring procedure has ended.

❑ OPL keywords are in upper case, except for graphic and dialog commands, which start with a small g and d respectively.

❑ Variables are in mixed case.

Support File Name	Contents
DemoOPL.icn	The application icon file
DemoOPL.mbm	Bitmaps used for the toolbar buttons
DemoOPL.hlp	The help file
DemoOPL.rss	The resource file (before compilation)
DemoOPL.pkg	'Application installation package' definition file

DemoOPL

All the code within this section should be entered into a single OPL program file called DemoOPL. Alternatively, you can find all the files on the accompanying CD. The program flow can be seen in the following diagram:

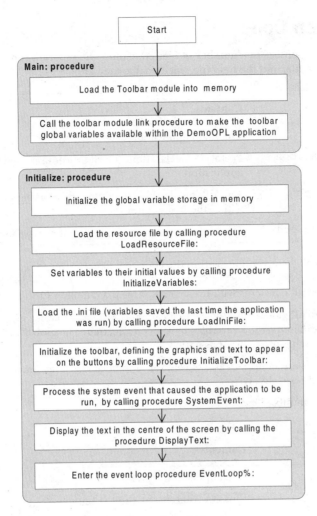

The DemoOPL application code follows in the sections below.

Including Code within Code

Here is the first block of code:

```
REM ********
REM Constants
REM ********
INCLUDE "DemoOPLConst.oph"

REM DECLARE EXTERNAL ensures that undeclared global variables
REM  and procedures are reported at translation time.
DECLARE EXTERNAL
INCLUDE "DemoOPLExternal.oph"
```

```
REM **************
REM Include headers
REM **************
INCLUDE "Const.oph"
INCLUDE "System.oxh"
INCLUDE "Printer.oxh"
INCLUDE "Bmp.oxh"
INCLUDE "Date.oxh"
INCLUDE "Toolbar.oph"

INCLUDE "DemoOPLResource.oph"
```

It's possible to split your application code into more than one file, and to 'include' that code within the main code, by using the INCLUDE keyword. However, there are a limited number of commands that can be inserted into another OPL program at translation time. The included file may contain CONST definitions, OPX procedure declarations, and OPL procedure declarations. The included file may not contain complete procedures themselves.

In this block, I have included a number of files. The first one is DemoOPLConst.oph, which includes constants used within the application. Next, I've used the DECLARE EXTERNAL command to tell the translator to check that all global variables and procedures in the code have been defined before use. This saves time when testing the application by cutting down the number of run-time errors. A separate OPL program file, DemoOPLExternal.oph, is used here to declare all the procedures.

Const.oph is another header file that defines many constants that can be used with OPL keywords. These constants make it much easier to write (and also to read) code, by replacing numbers with meaningful text.

Next, I have included a group of OPX header files (extension .oxh by convention). These are used to define OPX procedures and constants, and to load the OPX into memory at runtime. All the OPXs used in the DemoOPL application are held in the ROM of current EPOC devices: System.opx contains commands for controlling and interrogating the EPOC system; Printer.opx gives access to the standard EPOC printing facilities; Bmp.opx adds commands to load bitmaps into memory; Date.oxh adds date and time objects for use within OPL.

Standard EPOC applications use a toolbar down the right side of the screen displaying a number of buttons for quick access to common actions within applications, as well as a clock and a button to bring up a list of running programs. The toolbar in OPL is actually written in OPL. Toolbar.oph contains the procedure definitions and constants used by the toolbar, while the toolbar module itself is loaded later in the application.

Finally, DemoOPLResource.oph is the resource header file for this project. Creation and use of this file is discussed in a later section.

Defining an Application

```
REM ******************
REM Application Header
REM ******************
APP DemoOPL, KDemoOPLUID&
  ICON "DemoOPL.icn"
  CAPTION KAppNameEnglish$, KLangEnglish%
  FLAGS KFlagsAppFileBased%
ENDA
```

The APP..ENDA structure above is used to indicate that the OPL program is an application, as opposed to being simply an OPL program. Once translated, the OPL program will be put in the folder \System\Apps\DemoOPL\ and an application information file (.aif) will be created automatically. The .aif file contains the icons and other information about the application:

❑   ICON tells the translator where to get the application icons. The creation of the icon file, DemoOPL.icn, will be discussed in a later section.

❑   CAPTION defines the name of the application for a given language. You may use as many CAPTION lines as languages you translate the application text to.

❑   FLAGS tells the system what type of application is being written: whether it is file based, and whether its icon can be found in the Extras bar.

The First Procedure

```
REM *************************
REM Application Initialization
REM *************************
PROC Main:
   GLOBAL GScreenWidth%, GScreenHeight%

REM ESCAPE OFF should be remarked out
REM  until the application is bug free
   ESCAPE OFF

REM Get the original screen size. This should always be done
REM  before calling the Toolbar link procedure.
   gUSE KTextWindow%
   GScreenWidth% = gWIDTH
   GScreenHeight% = gHEIGHT

REM Load the Toolbar module, built into ROM
   LOADM File$:(KToolbar$)

REM Call the toolbar to link in the Toolbar Globals
   TBarLink:("Initialize")
ENDP
```

The first procedure in the code is *always* the first procedure to be called when the application is run. First, a couple of global variables are defined that are required when the toolbar is set up.

Next ESCAPE OFF is used to ensure that the keyboard shortcut *Ctrl+Esc* (*Alt+Esc* on the emulator) cannot be used to stop the application. Note that this should only be used once you are satisfied that your application is working correctly – you will not be able to stop your application if it gets into an infinite loop, for example.

Finally, this procedure loads in the Toolbar OPL module (which is held in the ROM of most EPOC devices) with the LOADM command, and then calls the TBarLink procedure from the toolbar module. TBarLink defines global variables that are then available from within the DemoOPL application. The parameter passed is the name of the next procedure to be run.

Initializing the Application

The next block of code is concerned with the initial setting up of the application – things like initializing variables and loading data and graphics from files.

```
REM ------------------------
REM Initialize the application
REM ------------------------
PROC Initialize:
   GLOBAL GDate&, GMenuPos%, GHelpThrdID&, GFont&(KZoomLevels%)
   GLOBAL GZoom%, GDemoOPLText$(KTextLen%), GTbVis%, GRsc&
   GLOBAL GDocumentName$(KMaxStringLen%), GChanged%
   GLOBAL GBitmaps&(KNumBitmaps%), GLastUsedFile$(KMaxStringLen%)

   LoadResourceFile:
   InitializeVariables:
   LoadIniFile:
   InitializeToolbar:

REM Parameters are passed in by the System.
REM These must be responded to before the first GETEVENT32.
   SystemEvent:(CMD$(KCmdUsedFile%), CMD$(KCmdLetter%))

REM Print the text in the window
   DisplayText:

REM Loop around the event loop endlessly
   DO
      EventLoop:
   UNTIL KFalse%
ENDP
```

`Initialize:` defines some global variables used in the application, and then calls various other procedures to set up the application.

`InitializeVariables:`, coming next, sets variables to initial values. Applications should use an initialization file (`.ini`) to store settings that are used every time the application is run – whether the user had the toolbar displayed the last time they ran the application, for example. The `.ini` file is read with `LoadIniFile:`.

```
REM ---------------------------------------------------
REM Initialize variables used within the application
REM ---------------------------------------------------
PROC InitializeVariables:
   EXTERNAL GDate&, GFont&(), GZoom%, GDemoOPLText$
   EXTERNAL GTbVis%, GChanged%

REM Create a new date/time object and set to the current date
   GDate& = DTNOW&:

REM Fonts at zoom levels. Constants from System.oxh
   GFont&(1) = KFontArialNormal13&
   GFont&(2) = KFontArialNormal22&
   GFont&(3) = KFontArialNormal32&
```

```
  REM The initial zoom
    GZoom% = 2

  REM The initial text
    GDemoOPLText$ = READRSC$:(RSC_HelloWorld&)

  REM True if the toolbar should be shown initially
    GTbVis% = KTrue%

  REM Flag to show if the text has been changed
    GChanged% = KFalse%
  ENDP


  REM -------------------------------------------------------
  REM Load graphics into memory from the multi-bitmap file
  REM -------------------------------------------------------
  PROC LoadGraphics:
    EXTERNAL GBitmaps&()
    LOCAL BmpFile$(KMaxStringLen%)

    BmpFile$ = File$:(KRoot$ + KBmpFile$)
    IF BmpFile$ = ""
      ALERT(KBmpFile$, ERR$:(KErrNotExists%))
      STOP
    ENDIF
    GBitmaps&(KMBMEdit%) = BITMAPLOAD&:(BmpFile$, KMBMEdit%-1)
    GBitmaps&(KMBMEditMask%) = BITMAPLOAD&:(BmpFile$, KMBMEditMask%-1)
    GBitmaps&(KMBMOpen%) = BITMAPLOAD&:(BmpFile$, KMBMOpen%-1)
    GBitmaps&(KMBMOpenMask%) = BITMAPLOAD&:(BmpFile$, KMBMOpenMask%-1)
    GBitmaps&(KMBMNew%) = BITMAPLOAD&:(BmpFile$, KMBMNew%-1)
    GBitmaps&(KMBMNewMask%) = BITMAPLOAD&:(BmpFile$, KMBMNewMask%-1)
    GBitmaps&(KMBMExit%) = BITMAPLOAD&:(BmpFile$, KMBMExit%-1)
    GBitmaps&(KMBMExitMask%) = BITMAPLOAD&:(BmpFile$, KMBMExitMask%-1)
  ENDP


  REM -------------------------
  REM Unload graphics from memory
  REM -------------------------
  PROC UnloadGraphics:
    EXTERNAL GBitmaps&()

    BITMAPUNLOAD:(GBitmaps&(KMBMEdit%))
    BITMAPUNLOAD:(GBitmaps&(KMBMEditMask%))
    BITMAPUNLOAD:(GBitmaps&(KMBMOpen%))
    BITMAPUNLOAD:(GBitmaps&(KMBMOpenMask%))
    BITMAPUNLOAD:(GBitmaps&(KMBMNew%))
    BITMAPUNLOAD:(GBitmaps&(KMBMNewMask%))
    BITMAPUNLOAD:(GBitmaps&(KMBMExit%))
    BITMAPUNLOAD:(GBitmaps&(KMBMExitMask%))
  ENDP
```

InitializeToolbar: sets up the toolbar with TBarInit:. TBarButt: then defines each of the buttons on the toolbar. The first parameter is the identity of a procedure that will be called when the button is pressed.

```
REM ---------------------
REM Initialize the toolbar
REM ---------------------
PROC InitializeToolbar:
  EXTERNAL GScreenWidth%, GScreenHeight%, GBitmaps&(), GTbVis%, TbVis%

  LoadGraphics:

REM Initialize the toolbar
  TBarInit:(READRSC$:(RSC_HelloWorld&), GScreenWidth%, GScreenHeight%)
REM The next four lines initialize the toolbar buttons
  TBarButt:("E", 1, READRSC$:(RSC_Edit&), 0, GBitmaps&(KMBMEdit%),
GBitmaps&(KMBMEditMask%), 0)
  TBarButt:("o", 2, READRSC$:(RSC_Open&), 0, GBitmaps&(KMBMOpen%),
GBitmaps&(KMBMOpenMask%), 0)
  TBarButt:("n", 3, READRSC$:(RSC_New&), 0, GBitmaps&(KMBMNew%),
GBitmaps&(KMBMNewMask%), 0)
  TBarButt:("e", 4, READRSC$:(RSC_Exit&), 0, GBitmaps&(KMBMExit%),
GBitmaps&(KMBMExitMask%), 0)

REM If the toolbar was visible the last time
REM DemoOPL was run, display it again
  TbVis% = NOT GTbVis%
  ToggleToolbar:
ENDP
```

LoadResourceFile: loads the resource file that contains all the text and hotkeys used in the application. Text is read from the resource file with the READRSC$: command; the parameter is the location of the string within the file, as defined in DemoOPLResource.oph.

```
REM --------------------------------
REM Load the resource file into memory
REM --------------------------------
PROC LoadResourceFile:
  EXTERNAL GRsc&
  LOCAL file$(KMaxStringLen%)

  file$ = File$:(KRoot$ + KResourceFile$)
  IF file$ = ""
    ALERT(KResourceFile$, ERR$(KErrNotExists%))
    STOP
  ENDIF
  GRsc& = LOADRSC&:(file$)
ENDP
```

Before the application flow is finally passed over to the event loop, the System event that started the application must be interpreted. This is done in SystemEvent:. The system passes a set of values to an OPL application when it is run, and these are examined using the system variable CMD$.

In many of the procedures, you will see an EXTERNAL list, which names all the global variables used in the procedure. It's used when checking that the global variables have been defined before use.

Displaying the Text

Next comes the procedure that prints text in the center of a bordered window.

```
REM ***************
REM Main Procedures
REM ***************
REM -------------------------
REM Display the text in a window
REM -------------------------
PROC DisplayText:
  EXTERNAL GDemoOPLText$, GFont&()
  EXTERNAL GZoom%, TbVis%, TbWidth%
  LOCAL inf&(48)

  gUSE KTextWindow%
  gCLS
  gFONT GFont&(GZoom%)
  gBORDER 0
  gINFO32 inf&()

REM Place the text in the middle of the window
  gAT 1, (gHEIGHT + inf&(KgInfo32FontHeight%)) / 2
  gPRINTB GDemoOPLText$, gWIDTH - 2, KgPrintBCentredAligned%
ENDP
```

The interesting things here are the graphics commands available in OPL. We are using a single window, but up to sixty-four independent windows can be used in an OPL procedure. They can be moved, hidden, resized and cleared.

The Event Loop

This is the main event-handling procedure from which the whole of the application is controlled. Most of the time the application is running will be spent in this loop. First, then, let's take a look at what events we will be checking for.

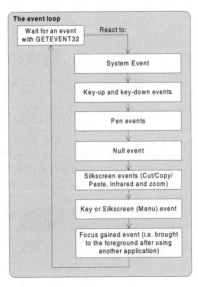

I have decided to detect only a subset of all the events I could have chosen. For example, I could have detected being moved to the background (that is, another application is used while leaving this application running in the background), or when the EPOC device is switched off and switched on. Those events could quite easily be added to the event loop too.

Also, I have chosen only to detect synchronous events. In other words, I am waiting for an event, doing nothing during that wait, and then interpreting what event occurred when it happens. An alternative is to use asynchronous events, but explaining how those work and how to deal with them in OPL is beyond the scope of this chapter.

Here is the event loop code; I will explain what's happening as we go along.

```
REM -------------
REM Handle events
REM -------------
PROC EventLoop:
    EXTERNAL GDate&
    LOCAL ev&(16), evType&, window%, x%, y%
    LOCAL command$(KMaxStringLen%), cmdLetter$(1)

    ONERR Error:: REM If an error occurs call the error handler.
                  REM REMark out this line during testing.
```

ONERR is one of OPL's error trapping commands. If an unexpected event occurs from this point until a matching ONERR OFF is used, procedure flow will commence at the point indicated by this command – that is, from the line beginning Error::. This line should be commented out until the code is working properly, otherwise the run-time error location doesn't work.

Here is the start of the event loop.

```
    WHILE KTrue%
        GETEVENT32 ev&()   REM Wait for an event

        evType& = ev&(KEvaType%)   REM Event type
```

We wait for an event to occur here, control only being returned to the application when an event has happened. The identity of the event and supporting information is returned in the elements of the ev&() array.

Once we have an event, we can interrogate it:

```
    REM Command from the System
        IF evType& = KEvCommand&
            REM String was passed by the system containing event info
            command$ = GETCMD$
            REM The command letter
            cmdLetter$ = LEFT$(command$, 1)
            REM Remainder of the command line
            command$ = RIGHT$(command$, LEN(command$)-1)
            REM Action the system event
            SystemEvent:(command$, cmdLetter$)
```

Here, we check whether the system has sent us an event. The system event type and filename (if any) is obtained with the GETCMD$ command. Note that the SystemEvent: procedure is being reused.

Next, we find out whether something happened at the keyboard:

```
REM A Key up or down event.
    ELSEIF (evType& = KEvKeyDown&) OR (evType& = KEvKeyUp&)
      CONTINUE
```

Pressing a key results in *at least* three events occurring:

- ❑ The first is a 'key down' event;
- ❑ Followed by the key that was pressed;
- ❑ And if the key is being held down, a number of repeat key events;
- ❑ Then a 'key-up' event.

In this application, the up and down key events are being ignored.

Next, we will handle pen events – that is, when the stylus comes into contact with the screen. The screen has been split into a number of areas, as shown in the figure below.

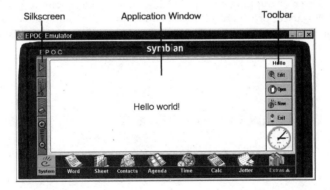

Here is the pen detection code:

```
REM Pen Event
    ELSEIF evType& = KEvPtr&
      REM Which window the pointer is in
      window% = ev&(KEvAPtrOplWindowId%)
      REM The x, y position in the window
      x% = ev&(KEvAPtrPositionX%)
      y% = ev&(KEvAPtrPositionY%)

REM Offer pen event to Toolbar handler
      IF TBarOffer%:(window%, ev&(KEvAPtrType%), x%, y%)
        CONTINUE
      ELSEIF ev&(KEvAPtrType%) = KEvPtrPenUp&
        PointerInWindow:(window%, x%, y%) REM Pen within a window
      ENDIF
```

Each 'button' on the silkscreen area is detected as its own separate event. Therefore, applications only need to detect where in the toolbar or application window the pen touched the screen. Fortunately, OPL helps you out here by knowing which window the pen is pointing to, and the position of the pen in the window.

This pen event should first be offered to the Toolbar handling procedure, TBarOffer%:, supplied in the toolbar module. This will see if the pen was on the toolbar, and if so, which part of the toolbar was pointed to. EPOC toolbars are intended to look and feel the same from application to application, so tapping on the clock will toggle the time view between an analog and a digital clock. Tapping on the area at the top of the toolbar will bring up a list of running applications where you may choose another application to bring to the foreground.

If one of the toolbar buttons was pressed, the procedure defined when the button was created will be called directly. If the pen was not pointing to the toolbar, you will need to handle the event yourself. Here, I have passed the event to the PointerInWindow: procedure.

The null event should not occur, but should be detected anyway, just in case.

```
REM No event occurred
    ELSEIF evType& = 0
        CONTINUE
```

As mentioned above, the silkscreen buttons around the screen are handled differently from normal pen events, returning event codes of their own. They are handled next:

```
REM Silkscreen buttons
    ELSEIF (evType& = KKeySidebarZoomIn%)
        ZoomOut:
    ELSEIF (evType& = KKeySidebarZoomOut%)
        ZoomIn:
    ELSEIF (evType& = KKeySidebarCutPaste%)
        ClipPopUp:
    ELSEIF (evType& = KKeySidebarIrDA%)
        IrDAPopUp:
```

The silkscreen Menu button should have the same effect as the keyboard *Menu* button, so they ought to be treated together. Here I am checking for the Menu silkscreen button and any key press, including the *Menu* key:

```
REM Sidebar Menu key OR Keypress
    ELSEIF (evType& = KKeySidebarMenu%) OR (evType& AND KEvNotKeyMask&) = 0
        IF (evType& <> KKeySidebarMenu%) AND (evType& <> KKeyMenu%) OR
(evType&=KKeyDial%)
            IF ProcessKeys%:(ev&(KEvAType%), (ev&(KEvAKMod%) AND KModifiers%),
ev&(KEvAKScanCode%))
                BREAK
            ENDIF
        ENDIF

REM Menu option Keycode Modifiers
        IF NOT OfferCommand%:(ev&(KEvaType%), ev&(KEvAKMod%))
            BREAK
        ENDIF
```

I am handling key presses with one of two procedures. `OfferCommand%:` is being used when one of the following conditions is true:

- ❏ The event came from a menu silkscreen button
- ❏ The event came from the *Menu* key
- ❏ The event was a key with one of the modifier keys: *Shift*, *Ctrl*, or *Fn*

Otherwise, the key event is passed to `ProcessKeys%:` for handling.

Lastly, the event loop can detect when the application is brought to the foreground, and perform some action when it happens. Here I have chosen to check whether the date has changed since the application was last used, but you can do anything you like here, such as ask for a password.

```
REM Focus gained
    ELSEIF evType& = KEvFocusGained&
      IF DifferentDay%: REM Date change
        GDate& = DTNOW&:
        gIPRINT READRSC$:(RSC_DateChange&), KBusyTopRight%
      ENDIF
    ENDIF
  ENDWH
  RETURN
```

If an error has happened somewhere within the event loop, the `HandleErrors:` procedure is called to handle it. Note that the application should not be allowed to crash and lose data. Your application should do everything it can to recover from any unexpected errors.

```
Error::
  ONERR OFF
  HandleErrors:
ENDP
```

Handling System Events

This `SystemEvent:` procedure reacts to an event passed to the application by the operating system.

```
REM --------------------
REM Action a system event
REM --------------------
PROC SystemEvent:(file$, cmdLetter$)
  IF cmdLetter$ = KGetCmdLetterCreate$        REM Create a new file
    CreateFile:(file$)
  ELSEIF cmdLetter$ = KGetCmdLetterOpen$      REM Open an existing file
    OpenFile:(file$)
  ELSEIF cmdLetter$ = KGetCmdLetterRestart$   REM Restart the application
    ResumeFile:
  ELSEIF cmdLetter$ = KGetCmdLetterExit$      REM Exit from the application
    Exit:
  ENDIF
ENDP
```

The four events are:

- ❑ Create a new file;
- ❑ Open a file;
- ❑ Restart the application with the previously used file; or
- ❑ Application shut down.

Handling the Keyboard

This procedure handles menu and hotkey events.

```
REM ------------------------------------------------------
REM Process command key presses (including Menu choices)
REM ------------------------------------------------------
PROC OfferCommand%:(key&, modif&)
  LOCAL hotK%, m%
  LOCAL Shift%, Control%, Fn%

REM Determine status of modifier keys
  IF modif& AND KKmodShift%
    Shift% = KTrue%
  ELSE
    Shift% = KFalse%
  ENDIF

  IF modif& AND KKmodControl%
    Control% = KTrue%
  ELSE
    Control% = KFalse%
  ENDIF

  IF modif& AND KKmodFn%
    Fn% = KTrue%
  ELSE
    Fn% = KFalse%
  ENDIF

  IF Fn%
    RETURN KFalse%
  ENDIF

REM Menu key OR Sidebar Menu
  IF ((key& = KKeyMenu%) OR (key& = KKeySidebarMenu%)) AND
      (NOT Control%) AND (NOT Shift%)
    m% = SHOWMENU%: REM Show Menu bar
```

If the menu silkscreen button or menu key has been pressed, a menu should be displayed. The result will be further interpreted:

```
REM Convert the menu chosen to a key code
    IF m%
        REM If a key is not attached to a menu item, then it is given a number
        IF m% <= 32
            MenuSpecial%:(m%)
            RETURN KTrue%
        ENDIF
```

Not all menu items need to have a shortcut key press. If they do not, they will be handled by `MenuSpecial%:`, which I'll show you shortly.

```
            Fn% = KFalse%
            Control% = KTrue%
            hotK% = m%

            IF hotK% <= %Z
                Shift% = KTrue%
                hotK% = hotK%+32
            ELSE
                Shift% = KFalse%
            ENDIF
        ELSE
            RETURN KTrue%
        ENDIF
    ELSE REM CTRL+(Shift)+Key pressed
        hotK% = key&-1+%a REM Control+a/A converts to 1
    ENDIF

REM ctrl+Key or Menu key
    IF Control% REM If Ctrl key is being held
        IF Shift% REM Shift is being pressed
            hotK% = hotK%-32
        ENDIF
```

The following code identifies which hotkey or menu choice has been used. The shortcut key values should be held in the resource file so that they can be changed along with the foreign language text.

```
REM Process the keys
    IF hotK% = READRSCLONG&:(RSC_KEYAbout&)
        About:
    ELSEIF hotK% = READRSCLONG&:(RSC_KEYExit&)
        Exit:
    ELSEIF hotK% = READRSCLONG&:(RSC_KEYHelp&)
        Help:
    ELSEIF hotK% = READRSCLONG&:(RSC_KEYShowToolbar&)
        ToggleToolbar:
    ELSEIF hotK% = READRSCLONG&:(RSC_KEYZoomIn&)
        ZoomIn:
```

```
        ELSEIF hotK% = READRSCLONG&:(RSC_KEYZoomOut&)
          ZoomOut:
        ELSEIF hotK% = (READRSCLONG&:(RSC_KEYPageSetup&)) OR
                       (hotK% = READRSCLONG&:(RSC_KEYPrintSetup&)) OR
                       (hotK% = READRSCLONG&:(RSC_KEYPrintPreview&)) OR
                       (hotK% = READRSCLONG&:(RSC_KEYPrint&))
          PrintOptions:(hotK%)
        ELSEIF hotK% = READRSCLONG&:(RSC_KEYEdit&)
          Edit:
        ELSEIF hotK% = READRSCLONG&:(RSC_KEYNew&)
          NewFile:
        ELSEIF hotK% = READRSCLONG&:(RSC_KEYOpen&)
          OpenExistingFile:
        ELSEIF hotK% = READRSCLONG&:(RSC_KEYSave&)
          SaveFile:(KReportSaved%)
        ELSEIF hotK% = READRSCLONG&:(RSC_KEYSaveAs&)
          SaveFileAs:
        ELSEIF hotK% = READRSCLONG&:(RSC_KEYRevertToSaved&)
          RevertToSaved:
        ENDIF
        RETURN KTrue%
      ENDIF
      RETURN KFalse%
    ENDP


    REM -------------------------------------------------
    REM Handle Menu choices that have no shortcut keys
    REM -------------------------------------------------
    PROC MenuSpecial%:(m%)
      IF m% = KMenuNoShortcut%
        gIPRINT READRSC$:(RSC_NoShortcut&)
      ENDIF
    ENDP
```

The other keyboard handling procedure is ProcessKeys%:. I am using it here to handle all the 'special' key events that are not menu key shortcuts – cursor keys, for example.

```
    REM --------------------------
    REM Process special Key Events
    REM --------------------------
    PROC ProcessKeys%:(key&, mod%, scancode%)
      LOCAL Shift%, Control%, Fn%

    REM Determine status of modifier keys
      IF Mod% AND KKmodShift%
        Shift% = KTrue%
      ELSE
        Shift% = KFalse%
      ENDIF

      IF Mod% AND KKmodControl%
        Control% = KTrue%
      ELSE
        Control% = KFalse%
      ENDIF
```

```
    IF Mod% AND KKmodFn% : Fn% = KTrue% : ELSE : Fn% = KFalse% : ENDIF

    IF Key& = KKeyPageDown32%                              REM PgDn
      gIPRINT READRSC$:(RSC_PgDn&), KBusyTopRight%
      RETURN KTrue%
    ELSEIF Key& = KKeyPageUp32%                            REM PgUp
      gIPRINT READRSC$:(RSC_PgUp&), KBusyTopRight%
      RETURN KTrue%
    ELSEIF Key& = KKeyPageRight32%                         REM End
      gIPRINT READRSC$:(RSC_PgRt&), KBusyTopRight%
      RETURN KTrue%
    ELSEIF Key& = KKeyPageLeft32%                          REM Home
      gIPRINT READRSC$:(RSC_PgLt&), KBusyTopRight%
      RETURN KTrue%
    ELSEIF Key& = KKeyDownArrow32%                         REM Down
      gIPRINT READRSC$:(RSC_Down&), KBusyTopRight%
      RETURN KTrue%
    ELSEIF Key& = KKeyUpArrow32%                           REM Up
      gIPRINT READRSC$:(RSC_Up&), KBusyTopRight%
      RETURN KTrue%
    ELSEIF Key& = KKeyRightArrow32%                        REM Right
      gIPRINT READRSC$:(RSC_Right&), KBusyTopRight%
      RETURN KTrue%
    ELSEIF Key& = KKeyLeftArrow32%                         REM Left
      gIPRINT READRSC$:(RSC_Left&), KBusyTopRight%
      RETURN KTrue%
    ELSEIF (Key& = KKeyDel%) AND (ScanCode% = 1)           REM Delete Key
      gIPRINT READRSC$:(RSC_Del&), KBusyTopRight%
      RETURN KTrue%
    ELSEIF Key& = KKeyEsc%                                 REM Escape key
      gIPRINT READRSC$:(RSC_Esc&), KBusyTopRight%
      RETURN KTrue%
    ELSEIF (Key& = KDButtonEnter%) AND (mod% = KNoModifiers%)  REM Enter
      gIPRINT READRSC$:(RSC_Ret&), KBusyTopRight%
      RETURN KTrue%
    ELSEIF ((Key& >= %a) AND (Key& <= %z)) AND Fn%
      gIPRINT READRSC$:(RSC_Fn&)+CHR$(Key&), KBusyTopRight%
      RETURN KTrue%
    ELSEIF ((Key& >= %A) AND (Key& <= %Z)) AND Fn%
      gIPRINT READRSC$:(RSC_FnSh&)+CHR$(Key&), KBusyTopRight%
      RETURN KTrue%
    ELSEIF (Key& = KKeyDial%) AND Fn%
      gIPRINT READRSC$:(RSC_Dial&), KBusyTopRight%
      RETURN KTrue%
    ELSEIF (Key& = KKeyTab%) AND (NOT Control%) REM Tab Key
      gIPRINT READRSC$:(RSC_Tab&), KBusyTopRight%
      RETURN KTrue%
    ENDIF
    RETURN KFalse%
ENDP
```

Handling Pen Events

Pen events are dealt with in this procedure:

```
REM ------------------------------
REM A pen event has been detected
REM ------------------------------
PROC PointerInWindow:(window%, x%, y%)
  gIPRINT READRSC$:(RSC_Pointer&) + NUM$(window%, 2) + READRSC$:(RSC_At&) +
                   NUM$(x%, 3) + "," + NUM$(y%, 3), KBusyTopRight%
ENDP
```

This code just flashes the position of the pen in the window, but you can use the pen-handing code of your choice here.

Zooming

In the DemoOPL application, I am using the zoom silkscreen buttons, menu options and hotkey presses as notification that I should change the size of the text.

```
REM -------
REM Zoom in
REM -------
PROC ZoomIn:
  EXTERNAL GZoom%

  GZoom% = GZoom% + 1
  IF GZoom% > KZoomLevels%
    GZoom% = 1
  ENDIF
  DisplayText:
ENDP

REM --------
REM Zoom Out
REM --------
PROC ZoomOut:
  EXTERNAL GZoom%

  GZoom% = GZoom% - 1
  IF GZoom% < 1
    GZoom% = KZoomLevels%
  ENDIF
  DisplayText:
ENDP
```

About...

Every application should have an 'About' box that gives the user information about the application, who wrote it, and (if applicable) how to get support.

```
REM --------------------
REM About the application
REM --------------------
PROC About:
  dINIT READRSC$:(RSC_AboutTitle&) + " v" + KVersion$
  dTEXT "", READRSC$:(RSC_Copyright&), KDTextCentre%
  dTEXT "", READRSC$:(RSC_About1&), KDTextCentre%
  dTEXT "", READRSC$:(RSC_About2&), KDTextCentre%
  dBUTTONS READRSC$:(RSC_Close&), KDButtonEnter% OR
                                  KDButtonNoLabel% OR
                                  KDButtonPlainKey%

  LOCK ON
    DIALOG
  LOCK OFF
ENDP
```

This procedure sees the appearance of the first dBUTTONS command in my application. The parameters warrant a little explanation, since it looks more complicated than it really is. dBUTTONS configures each button on the dialog. The parameters come in pairs: the text to appear on the button is first, followed by the button's keyboard shortcut and appearance. This button doesn't have a label shown below it (KDButtonNoLabel%), and *Ctrl* doesn't need to be pressed with the shortcut (KDButtonPlainKey%).

LOCK ON and LOCK OFF around a DIALOG keyword prevent the operating system from closing down an application that's displaying a dialog that requires user input.

Leaving the Application

There should be only one way out of the application, and the procedure that deals with it should handle the saving of files and writing to the initialization (.ini) file. It should also close the application's help if it is open, as well as unloading the resource file from memory and deleting any allocated memory.

```
REM --------------------
REM Exit the application
REM --------------------
PROC Exit:
  EXTERNAL GHelpThrdID&, GRsc&, GDate&

  SaveFile:(KNoReportSaved%) REM Save the current file
  CloseFile:  REM And close the file
  SaveIniFile: REM Save the current settings to the INI file

REM If a program help thread is running, close it
  IF GHelpThrdID& <> 0
    ONERR ExitAnyway::
    ENDTASK&:(GHelpThrdID&, 0)
  ENDIF

ExitAnyway::
  UNLOADRSC:(GRsc&) REM Unloads the resource file from memory
  UnloadGraphics:  REM Unload the bitmaps from memory
  UNLOADM File$:(KToolbar$) REM Unload the toolbar
  DTDeleteDateTime:(GDate&)
  STOP
ENDP
```

Helping the User

EPOC has a built in Help application that can be used to give the user help on using your application. As you saw in Chapter 13, the Help application is actually a special view of the built-in Data application.

```
    REM ------------------
    REM Open the Help file
    REM ------------------
    PROC Help:
      EXTERNAL GHelpThrdID&
      LOCAL HelpFile$(KDFileNameLen%)

      HelpFile$ = File$:(KRoot$+KHelpFile$)
      IF HelpFile$ <> ""
        IF GHelpThrdID& <> 0 REM help already running
          ONERR Notopen::  REM Just in case help is not running
          SETFOREGROUNDBYTHREAD&:(GHelpThrdID&, 0)  REM Bring help to foreground
        ELSE
Notopen::
          ONERR OFF
          REM Run the help application
          GHelpThrdID& = RUNAPP&:("Data", Helpfile$, "", 0)
        ENDIF
      ELSE
        gIPRINT READRSC$:(RSC_NoHelp&), KBusyTopRight%
      ENDIF
    ENDP
```

It is important to handle the help file correctly, and this is done by storing the thread identity of the Help application in a global variable, so that the application can return to it at a later date, or close it down when the application is exited.

Editing the Text

Editing text is easy in EPOC: you can just use the built-in dialog commands.

```
    REM -------------
    REM Edit the text
    REM -------------
    PROC Edit:
      EXTERNAL GDemoOPLText$, GChanged%

      dINIT READRSC$:(RSC_EditText&)
      dEDIT GDemoOPLText$, READRSC$:(RSC_Text&), 20
      dBUTTONS READRSC$:(RSC_Cancel&),
              KDButtonEsc% OR KDButtonNoLabel% OR KDButtonPlainKey%,
              READRSC$:(RSC_OK&),
              KDButtonEnter% OR KDButtonNoLabel% OR KDButtonPlainKey%
      LOCK ON
        IF NOT DIALOG
          GChanged% = KTrue%
          DisplayText:
        ENDIF
      LOCK OFF
    ENDP
```

dINIT initializes a dialog box; dEDIT adds a text edit line; and dBUTTONS, as you've already seen, adds a number of buttons to the bottom of the dialog. The dialog is displayed when the DIALOG command is called. It's that simple.

Printing from OPL

Printing from OPL is handled by the Printer OPX that's supplied in ROM.

```
REM ****************
REM Print Procedures
REM ****************
REM ----------------------------
REM Print the text to the printer
REM ----------------------------
PROC PrintOptions:(hotK%)
  ONERR error::
  IF hotK% = READRSCLONG&:(RSC_KEYPageSetup&)
    PageSetupDialog:
  ELSEIF hotK% = READRSCLONG&:(RSC_KEYPrintSetup&)
    PrintRangeDialog:
  ELSEIF hotK% = READRSCLONG&:(RSC_KEYPrintPreview&)
    Print:
    PrintPreviewDialog:
  ELSEIF hotK% = READRSCLONG&:(RSC_KEYPrint&)
    Print:
    PrintDialog:
  ENDIF
  GOTO end::

error::
  ALERT(ERR$(ERR))
end::
  ONERR OFF
ENDP
```

The above procedure simply handles the four printing-related options and calls a second procedure accordingly. In order, the four possibilities being checked for are:

❑   Page setup

❑   Printer setup

❑   Print preview

❑   Printing the document

The procedure that actually prints the text to a printer looks like this; the other procedures called by PrintOptions: are all built into OPL.

```
REM ----------------------------------
REM Print the text to the print buffer
REM ----------------------------------
PROC Print:
  EXTERNAL GDemoOPLText$
```

```
      ResetPrinting:                        REM Reset the printer buffer
      SetFontName:(KPrintFont$)             REM Change text font to KPrintFont$
      SetFontHeight:(KPrintFontSize%)       REM Font size is KPrintFontSize% twips
      SendStringToPrinter:(GDemoOPLText$)    REM Print the text
      SendNewParaToPrinter:                 REM Send the print buffer to the printer
   ENDP
```

Some more Toolbar Handling

This procedure is used to set the text at the top of the toolbar to the current filename:

```
   REM ******************
   REM Toolbar Procedures
   REM ******************
   PROC ToolBarTitle:(file$)
     EXTERNAL GDocumentName$
     LOCAL off%(6), filename$(KMaxStringLen%), title$(KMaxStringLen%)

     filename$=PARSE$(file$, GDocumentName$, off%())
     title$=MID$(filename$, off%(KParseAOffFilename%),
                off%(KParseAOffExt%) - off%(KParseAOffFilename%))
     TBarSetTitle:(title$)
   ENDP
```

It is usual to offer the user the choice of showing or hiding the toolbar:

```
   REM ----------------
   REM Hide/Show Toolbar
   REM ----------------
   PROC ToggleToolbar:
     EXTERNAL TbVis%, TbWidth%, GScreenWidth%, GScreenHeight%

     IF TbVis%
       TBARHIDE: REM Hide Toolbar
     ELSE
       TBARSHOW: REM Show toolbar
     ENDIF

   REM Resize the text window
     gUSE KTextWindow%
     gSETWIN 0, 0, GScreenWidth%+(TbVis%*TbWidth%), GScreenHeight%
     DisplayText:
   ENDP
```

Do you remember that when the toolbar was defined, we passed in a single letter to identify the procedure to be called if the button was pressed? Here are the procedures that are called. Their names are formed from the single letter added to the end of CMD, or CMDS if the letter is upper case.

```
   REM -------------------------------------------------
   REM Procedure called when first toolbar button is pressed
   REM -------------------------------------------------
   PROC cmdsE%:
     Edit:
   ENDP
```

```
REM ------------------------------------------------------------
REM Procedure called when second toolbar button is pressed
REM ------------------------------------------------------------
PROC cmdO%:
  OpenExistingFile:
ENDP

REM ------------------------------------------------------------
REM Procedure called when third toolbar button is pressed
REM ------------------------------------------------------------
PROC cmdN%:
  NewFile:
ENDP

REM ------------------------------------------------------------
REM Procedure called when fourth toolbar button is pressed
REM ------------------------------------------------------------
PROC cmdE%:
  Exit:
ENDP
```

Using Files

The file handling procedures in this application use the built-in OPL database keywords to create, read and write data files. It is important to handle files correctly, ensuring that a minimum amount of data is lost if an error occurs, or the EPOC device loses power. Using the procedures below as models for your own file handling procedures should help to ensure this.

The file handling procedures in a standard application should include the following facilities:

- ❑ Load a file
- ❑ Save a file
- ❑ Save a file with a new name
- ❑ Run the application using the last-used file
- ❑ Close the file

Here's the file handling code:

```
REM ***************
REM File Procedures
REM ***************
REM ----------------
REM Create a new file
REM ----------------
PROC CreateFile:(file$)
  EXTERNAL GLastUsedFile$, GDocumentName$
```

```
        SETDOC file$ REM Sets the icon for this file to the
                     REM globe icon, and sets the file which
                     REM appears in the task popup

    REM If the file already exists, delete it
      IF EXIST(file$)
        DELETE file$
      ENDIF

    REM Create a new file and save the contents
      CREATE " """+file$+""" FIELDS Text("+NUM$(KTextLen%, 3)+") TO Entries", A, F1$
```

Data files are created with the CREATE keyword, followed by a string defining the structure of the database. The grouping of quotes around file$ are required to include quotes in the CREATE string itself. One field, Text, is being created in the database table called Entries.

Databases are changed using a transaction paradigm. BEGINTRANS starts a database change; all subsequent database changes are then written to temporary records in the database.

```
    BEGINTRANS    REM Begin a new database transaction
```

INSERT creates a new entry in the database.

```
    INSERT        REM Modify the first record
```

Set the contents of the Text field.

```
    A.F1$ = READRSC$:(RSC_HelloWorld&)
```

Complete modifying the database record.

```
    PUT           REM Put the modified record back into the data file
```

Changes to the database are only actually *written* to the database when the COMMITTRANS keyword is used. Multiple changes may be made to the database between the BEGINTRANS and COMMITTRANS.

```
    COMMITTRANS   REM Commit the database transaction

    ToolBarTitle:(file$)
    GDocumentName$ = file$
    GLastUsedFile$ = file$
  ENDP


  REM --------------------------------
  REM Ask the user for a New file name
  REM --------------------------------
  PROC NewFile:
    EXTERNAL GLastUsedFile$, GDemoOPLText$
    LOCAL file$(KDFileNameLen%)
```

```
    LOCK ON
      file$ = CREATEFILEDIALOG$:("")
    LOCK OFF
    IF file$ <> ""
      SaveFile:(KNoReportSaved%) REM Save the current file
      CloseFile:
      GDemoOPLText$ = READRSC$:(RSC_HelloWorld&)
      DisplayText:
      CreateFile:(file$)
    ENDIF
ENDP


REM --------------------
REM Open an existing file
REM --------------------
PROC OpenExistingFile:
    EXTERNAL GLastUsedFile$
    LOCAL file$(KMaxStringLen%), path$(KMaxStringLen%), off%(6)

    path$ = LEFT$(PARSE$("", GLastUsedFile$, off%()), off%(KParseAOffFilename%)-1)
    LOCK ON
      file$ = OPENFILEDIALOG$:(path$, 0, KUidOplDoc&, KDemoOPLUID&)
    LOCK OFF
    IF file$ <> ""
      SaveFile:(KNoReportSaved%) REM Save the current file first
      CloseFile:
      OpenFile:(file$)
    ENDIF
ENDP


REM -----------
REM Open a file
REM -----------
PROC OpenFile:(file$)
    EXTERNAL GDemoOPLText$, GDocumentName$, GLastUsedFile$, GChanged%

    SETDOC file$ REM Sets the icon for this file to the globe icon

    BUSY READRSC$:(RSC_OpeningFile&), KBusyBottomRight%

    TRAP OPEN " """+file$+""" SELECT Text FROM Entries", A, F1$
    IF ERR
      ALERT(ERR$(ERR))
    ELSE
      USE A
      FIRST
      GDemoOPLText$ = A.F1$
      DisplayText:
      GChanged% = KFalse%
      GDocumentName$ = file$
      GLastUsedFile$ = file$
      ToolBarTitle:(file$)
    ENDIF
    BUSY OFF
ENDP
```

```
REM --------------------
REM Save the current file
REM --------------------
PROC SaveFile:(reportsave%)
  EXTERNAL GDemoOPLText$, GChanged%

  ONERR error::
  IF GChanged%
    IF reportsave%
      BUSY READRSC$:(RSC_Busy&), KBusyBottomRight%
    ENDIF
    USE A
    FIRST          REM Go to the first element
    BEGINTRANS     REM Begin a new database transaction
    MODIFY         REM Modify the first record
    A.F1$ = GDemoOPLText$
    PUT            REM Put the modified record back into the data file
    COMMITTRANS    REM Commit the database transaction

    GChanged% = KFalse%
    IF reportsave%
      BUSY OFF
      gIPRINT READRSC$:(RSC_Saved&), KBusyTopRight%
    ENDIF
  ELSE
    IF reportsave%
      gIPRINT READRSC$:(RSC_FileNotChanged&), KBusyTopRight%
    ENDIF
  ENDIF
  GOTO end::

error::
  gIPRINT READRSC$:(RSC_NotValidFile&)
end::
  ONERR OFF
ENDP


REM -------------------------------------------
REM Save the current file with a different name
REM -------------------------------------------
PROC SaveFileAs:
  EXTERNAL GDocumentName$, GChanged%
  LOCAL file$(KMaxStringLen%)

  file$ = GDocumentName$
  LOCK ON
    file$ = SAVEASFILEDIALOG$:(file$, #0)
  LOCK OFF
  IF file$ <> ""
    CloseFile:     REM The current file is not saved
    CreateFile:(file$) REM Create a new file
    GChanged% = KTrue%
    SaveFile:(KReportSaved%)
    GChanged% = KFalse%
  ENDIF
ENDP
```

```
REM ---------------------
REM Close the current file
REM ---------------------
PROC CloseFile:
  EXTERNAL GDocumentName$
  ONERR error::
  USE A
  CLOSE
  COMPACT GDocumentName$ REM Compact the database
error::
  ONERR OFF
ENDP


REM --------------
REM Revert to saved
REM --------------
PROC RevertToSaved:
  EXTERNAL GDocumentName$, GChanged%

  IF GChanged%
    dINIT READRSC$:(RSC_Revert1&)
    dTEXT "", READRSC$:(RSC_Revert2&)
    dBUTTONS READRSC$:(RSC_No&),
          -(READRSCLONG&:(RSC_KeyNo&) OR KDButtonNoLabel% OR KDButtonPlainKey%),
             READRSC$:(RSC_Yes&),
             READRSCLONG&:(RSC_KeyYes&) OR KDButtonNoLabel% OR KDButtonPlainKey%
    LOCK ON
      IF DIALOG
        CloseFile:
        OpenFile:(GDocumentName$)
        DisplayText:
        GChanged% = KFalse%
      ENDIF
    LOCK OFF
  ELSE
    gIPRINT READRSC$:(RSC_FileNotChanged&), KBusyTopRight%
  ENDIF
ENDP


REM -----------------------------
REM Resume with the last used file
REM -----------------------------
PROC ResumeFile:
  EXTERNAL GLastUsedFile$
  LOCAL file$(KMaxStringLen%)

  IF (GLastUsedFile$ = "") OR (NOT EXIST(GLastUsedFile$))
    file$ = CMD$(KCmdUsedFile%)
    IF EXIST(file$)
      OpenFile:(file$)
    ELSE
      CreateFile:(file$)
    ENDIF
  ELSE
    OpenFile:(GLastUsedFile$)
  ENDIF
ENDP
```

Menus

Whereas C++ uses resource files to define all menus and dialogs, OPL uses resource files only to hold strings and long integers. They are most often used to supply the text for menus and dialogs, and the hotkey codes.

The following procedure is used every time the menu is displayed. As you read through, you'll notice that the menus can be reconfigured from within the procedure.

```
REM **************
REM Menu Procedures
REM **************
REM ----------------
REM Show the menu bar
REM ----------------
PROC ShowMenu%:
    EXTERNAL TbVis%, GMenuPos%

    mINIT
```

Menus can cascade further menus; mCASC defines the cascading menus:

```
mCASC READRSC$:(RSC_Printing&), READRSC$:(RSC_PageSetup&),
      READRSCLONG&:(RSC_KEYPAGESETUP&), READRSC$:(RSC_PrintSetup&),
      READRSCLONG&:(RSC_KEYPRINTSETUP&), READRSC$:(RSC_PrintPreview&),
      READRSCLONG&:(RSC_KEYPRINTPREVIEW&), READRSC$:(RSC_Print&),
      READRSCLONG&:(RSC_KEYPrint&)
mCASC READRSC$:(RSC_More&), READRSC$:(RSC_SaveAs&),
      READRSCLONG&:(RSC_KEYSAVEAS&), READRSC$:(RSC_Save&),
      READRSCLONG&:(RSC_KEYSAVE&), READRSC$:(RSC_RevertToSaved&),
      READRSCLONG&:(RSC_KEYRevertToSaved&)
```

Next, the menus themselves are defined. Note that a minus sign before the menu shortcut key indicates that a line is to be drawn below the menu item.

```
mCARD READRSC$:(RSC_File&), READRSC$:(RSC_CreateNew&),
      READRSCLONG&:(RSC_KEYNEW&), READRSC$:(RSC_OpenExisting&),
      -READRSCLONG&:(RSC_KEYOPEN&), READRSC$:(RSC_Printing&)+">",
      16, READRSC$:(RSC_More&)+">", -17, READRSC$:(RSC_Close&),
      READRSCLONG&:(RSC_KEYExit&)
mCARD READRSC$:(RSC_Edit&), READRSC$:(RSC_EditTextMenu&),
      READRSCLONG&:(RSC_KEYEdit&), READRSC$:(RSC_NoShortcut&),
      KMenuNoShortcut%
```

The Show toolbar menu item has a check box beside it showing whether the toolbar is to be shown or not:

```
mCARD READRSC$:(RSC_View&), READRSC$:(RSC_ZoomIn&),
      READRSCLONG&:(RSC_KEYZoomIn&), READRSC$:(RSC_ZoomOut&),
      -READRSCLONG&:(RSC_KEYZoomOut&), READRSC$:(RSC_ShowToolbar&),
      READRSCLONG&:(RSC_KEYShowToolbar&) OR KMenuCheckBox% OR
                (KMenuSymbolOn%*(-TbVis%))
```

```
mCARD READRSC$:(RSC_Tools&), READRSC$:(RSC_About&),
        READRSCLONG&:(RSC_KEYAbout&), READRSC$:(RSC_Help&),
        READRSCLONG&:(RSC_KEYHelp&)
```

Finally, we display the menu and return the selection:

```
    RETURN MENU(GMenuPos%)
ENDP
```

Using Initialization Files

Initialization files (with the extension .ini) are used to store settings that are common to all files opened by an application. By convention, they are stored in internal memory (*not* an external memory card) in the application's folder; so for this application we would save initialization data in C:\System\Apps\DemoOPL\DemoOPL.ini.

The format of the file is up to you: it's quite possible to use a flat file or an OPL data file. On this occasion, I have chosen to use an OPL data file:

```
REM ********************
REM INI File Procedures
REM ********************
REM ------------------
REM Create the INI file
REM ------------------
PROC CreateIniFile:
  TRAP MKDIR "C:" + KRoot$
  TRAP DELETE "C:" + KRoot$+KINIFile$
  CREATE """C:" + KRoot$+KINIFile$ + """ FIELDS LastFile(255),
        Zoom, TBVis TO ini", A, F1$, F2%, F3%

  BEGINTRANS
  INSERT
  A.F1$ = ""
  A.F2% = 2
  A.F3% = KTrue%
  PUT
  COMMITTRANS
  CLOSE
ENDP


REM ----------------
REM Open the INI file
REM ----------------
PROC OpenIniFile:
  OPEN """C:" + KRoot$ + KINIFile$ + """ SELECT LastFile,
        Zoom, TBVis FROM INI", A, F1$, F2%, F3%
  FIRST
ENDP
```

```
REM -----------------
REM Load the INI file
REM -----------------
PROC LoadIniFile:
    EXTERNAL GLastUsedFile$, GZoom%, GTbVis%

    IF NOT EXIST("C:" + KRoot$ + KINIFile$)
        CreateIniFile:
        GLastUsedFile$ = ""
        GZoom% = 2
        GTbVis% = KTrue%
    ELSE
        OpenIniFile:
        GLastUsedFile$ = A.F1$
        GZoom% = A.F2%
        GTbVis% = A.F3%
        CLOSE
    ENDIF
ENDP

REM -----------------
REM Save the INI file
REM -----------------
PROC SaveIniFile:
    EXTERNAL GLastUsedFile$, GZoom%, TbVis%

    IF NOT EXIST("C:" + KRoot$ + KINIFile$)
        CreateIniFile:
    ENDIF

    OpenIniFile:
    BEGINTRANS
    MODIFY
    A.F1$ = GLastUsedFile$
    A.F2% = GZoom%
    A.F3% = TbVis%
    PUT
    COMMITTRANS
    CLOSE
    COMPACT "C:" + KRoot$ + KINIFile$
ENDP
```

Error Handling

Errors can occur in all but the simplest of programs. Sometimes it's because of errors in the application logic; at others it's because the user did something unexpected. However and wherever they occur though, the way you handle errors can make the difference between a good application and a bad one.

As mentioned in the section on the event loop above, we're using the ONERR command to trap any errors that occur in any code while the application is running. If one does occur, the following procedure is called to report the problem to the user:

```
REM ------------
REM Error Handler
REM ------------
PROC HandleErrors:
  dINIT READRSC$:(RSC_Error1&)
  dTEXT "", READRSC$:(RSC_Error2&)
  dTEXT "", READRSC$:(RSC_Error3&)
  dTEXT "", READRSC$:(RSC_Error4&), KDTextLineBelow%
  dTEXT "", READRSC$:(RSC_AppName&)+READRSC$:(RSC_Error5&)+KVersion$
  dTEXT "", READRSC$:(RSC_Error6&)+ERRX$
  dTEXT "", READRSC$:(RSC_Error7&)+ERR$(ERR)
  dBUTTONS READRSC$:(RSC_Continue&), KKeyEnter% OR KDButtonNoLabel% OR
                                     KDButtonPlainKey%

  LOCK ON
    DIALOG
  LOCK OFF
ENDP
```

Once the error has been reported, it is important to avoid just exiting the application, leaving the user to wonder what has happened to their data. Where possible, you should rescue what you can, and carry on with the application. How you do this, of course, is up to you in the context of your particular problem.

Miscellaneous other procedures

Here are a number of supporting procedures that are used by the application.

```
REM ----------------------------------
REM Checks whether the date has changed
REM ----------------------------------
PROC DifferentDay%:
  EXTERNAL GDate&
  LOCAL now&, ret%

  now& = DTNOW&:
  ret% = (DTDAYSDIFF&:(GDate&, now&) <> 0)
  DTDeleteDateTime:(now&)
  RETURN ret%
ENDP
```

To detect a date change, I have used a date object, provided by the Date OPX. In truth, this is a bit over the top, as all I really need to check is whether the *day* has changed. However, I've employed an object just to show that OPL can use them!

```
REM -------------------------------------
REM Return file position if the file exists
REM -------------------------------------
PROC File$:(F$)
  LOCAL i%

REM See whether the file is on any volatile memory first
  i% = %Y
  WHILE i% >= %A
    IF EXIST(CHR$(i%) + ":" + F$)
```

```
            RETURN CHR$(i%) + ":" + F$
        ENDIF
        i% = i%-1
    ENDWH
REM Then see whether the file is on the ROM (Z)
    IF EXIST("Z:" + F$)
        RETURN "Z:" + F$
    ENDIF

    RETURN "" REM File does not exist
ENDP
```

The above procedure searches all attached memory cards for the location of a particular file in the specified directory, starting from the last card (y:) and searching down to the first card (c:), and finally checking on the ROM (z:). Why check ROM last? This is so that newer versions of ROM files can be held in RAM and used instead.

```
REM -----------------------
REM The Cut/Copy/Paste popup
REM -----------------------
PROC ClipPopUp:
    LOCAL option%
    option% = mPOPUP(KClipPopupX%, KClipPopupY%, KMPopupPosTopLeft%,
            READRSC$:(RSC_Cut&), READRSCLONG&:(RSC_KEYCut&) OR KMenuDimmed%,
            READRSC$:(RSC_Copy&), READRSCLONG&:(RSC_KEYCopy&) OR KMenuDimmed%,
            READRSC$:(RSC_Paste&), READRSCLONG&:(RSC_KEYPaste&) OR KMenuDimmed%)
    REM Act on option here
ENDP

REM -----------------
REM The Infrared popup
REM -----------------
PROC IRDAPopUp:
    LOCAL option%
    option% = mPOPUP(KIRDAPopupX%, KIRDAPopupY%, KMPopupPosTopLeft%,
                READRSC$:(RSC_IRDASend&), 1 OR KMenuDimmed%,
                READRSC$:(RSC_IRDAReceive&), 2 OR KMenuDimmed%)
    REM Act on option here
ENDP
```

The above two procedures emulate the popup menus that appear when the Cut/Copy/Paste or infrared silkscreen buttons are touched. Currently, all the menu options are dimmed, as I have not written any code for them. By removing the OR KMenuDimmed% from each option and handling the value returned from mPOPUP, you can write procedures to handle cutting, copying, pasting and infrared beaming. Third party OPXs are available from the Internet and the Symbian Developer Network that provide access to the EPOC clipboard buffer and infrared functionality.

DemoOPLExternal.oph

The DemoOPLExternal.oph file lists the procedures in DemoOPL. The procedure parameter list is used at translation time to check that the correct number of parameters is being passed to the procedures, and that they are of the correct type (that is, you cannot use an integer where a float is expected, etc.).

DemoOPLConst.oph

The constants for the `DemoOPL` application have been split into a separate file simply to make the main file easier to use.

It is recommended that constants are used everywhere a 'magic number' would otherwise have to be used. Constants make the code much easier to read and understand, enable changes to these values to be made in only one place, and ensure that these values cannot be changed while the application is running.

```
REM --------------------
REM DemoOPL Constants List
REM --------------------

REM Application Information
CONST KDemoOPLUID& = &100042CB
CONST KAppNameEnglish$ = "DemoOPL"
CONST KVersion$ = "1.05"

REM Side bar button event values
CONST KKeySidebarCutPaste% = 10001
CONST KKeySidebarIrDA% = 10002
CONST KKeySidebarZoomOut% = 10003
CONST KKeySidebarZoomIn% = 10004

REM Event values
CONST KEvAKScanCode% = 3
CONST KKeyDial% = 4155
CONST KModifiers% = 255
CONST KNoModifiers% = 0

REM File locations and names
CONST KRoot$ = "\System\Apps\DemoOPL\"
CONST KBmpFile$ = "DemoOPL.mbm"
CONST KResourcefile$ = "DemoOPL.rsc"
CONST KHelpFile$ = "DemoOPL.hlp"
CONST KINIFile$ = "DemoOPL.ini"
CONST KToolbar$ = "\System\Opl\Toolbar.opo"
CONST KFirstDrive% = 67
CONST KLastDrive% = 90

REM Array sizes
CONST KTextLen% = 60
CONST KZoomLevels% = 3
CONST KNumBitmaps% = 8

REM Bitmap array locations
CONST KMBMEdit% = 1
CONST KMBMEditMask% = 2
CONST KMBMOpen% = 3
CONST KMBMOpenMask% = 4
CONST KMBMNew% = 5
CONST KMBMNewMask% = 6
CONST KMBMExit% = 7
CONST KMBMExitMask% = 8
```

```
REM Menu values
CONST KMenuNoShortcut% = 18

REM Screen positions
CONST KClipPopupX% = 0
CONST KClipPopupY% = 42
CONST KIrDAPopupX% = 0
CONST KIrDAPopupY% = 95

REM Print Constants
CONST KPrintFont$ = "Arial"
CONST KPrintFontSize%=200

REM Text Window
CONST KTextWindow%=1

REM Report file as saved
CONST KReportSaved% = -1
CONST KNoReportSaved% = 0

REM gINFO32 array locations
CONST KgInfo32FontHeight% = 3
```

Resource File

A resource file for an OPL application contains text and long integers for use within the application. This is most often used to support multiple languages without having to supply multiple versions of the application itself. Instead, multiple resource files are supplied that are much smaller than the application files.

Resource file scripts are plain text files, and you should create the following DemoOPL.rss resource script in a folder on the SDK installation disk of your PC.

The first three lines are mandatory. The NAME value may be up to four characters long, and is used to generate a unique ID so that more than one resource file can be used by the application.

```
// DemoOPL Resource file
// V1.05, 18 November 1999
NAME DEMO

#include <eikdef.rh>

RESOURCE RSS_SIGNATURE { }
```

The resource compiler allows **structures** to be defined. Here, a very simple structure is being defined that contains a single item: a long integer. This will hold a key value.

```
// Define new structures
STRUCT KEY
    {
    LONG key;
    }
```

The following lines define the text strings. RESOURCE TBUF tells the resource compiler that a text buffer is being defined. The third word is the name of the buffer (the name of the resource item used in application code), and this is followed by the buffer contents.

```
RESOURCE TBUF RSC_AppName { buf= "DemoOPL";}
RESOURCE TBUF RSC_HelloWorld { buf= "Hello world!";}
RESOURCE TBUF RSC_NotFound { buf= "cannot be found";}
RESOURCE TBUF RSC_Edit { buf= "Edit";}
RESOURCE TBUF RSC_Open { buf= "Open";}
RESOURCE TBUF RSC_New { buf= "New";}
RESOURCE TBUF RSC_Exit { buf= "Exit";}

...

RESOURCE TBUF RSC_RevertToSaved { buf="Revert to saved";}
RESOURCE TBUF RSC_Revert1 { buf="Revert to saved?";}
RESOURCE TBUF RSC_Revert2 { buf="All changes will be lost";}
RESOURCE TBUF RSC_OpeningFile { buf="Opening file"<KEllipsis>;}
RESOURCE TBUF RSC_Busy { buf="Busy";}
RESOURCE TBUF RSC_FileNotChanged { buf="File has not changed";}
```

Finally, the key codes are defined. As above, the first two words show the resource compiler that a key structure is being defined, while the values of the keys are the character codes used by EPOC (a list can be found in an appendix of the OPL SDK).

```
// Key codes
RESOURCE KEY RSC_KeyEdit { key= 69;}
RESOURCE KEY RSC_KeyOpen { key= 111;}
RESOURCE KEY RSC_KeyNew { key= 110;}

...

RESOURCE KEY RSC_KEYRevertToSaved { key= 114;}
```

To compile the resource file script into a resource file that's usable from OPL, you use the resource compiler, eikrs:

eikrs DemoOPL US

The third parameter is the language, used when the resource file contains multiple languages. You will need to use eikrs repeatedly, once for each language you wish to compile resources for.

A couple of files will be created: DemoOPL.RUK in \Epoc32\Release\Wins\Deb\Z\System\Data, and DemoOPL.RSG in \Epoc32\Include.

DemoOPL.RUK is the resource file itself, and should be copied to \System\Apps\DemoOPL\ and renamed to DemoOPL.rsc.

894

DemoOPL.RSG is a text file that defines the location of each resource within the resource file. The file is in a format suitable for a C++ program, and must be converted to a format usable by OPL.

Each line in the file is in the format:

```
#define RSC_Text              0x112ee002
```

However, they must all be converted to lines resembling:

```
CONST RSC_Text& = &112ee002
```

by replacing #define with CONST and 0x with & = &. Once converted, the text must be imported into an OPL program file called DemoOPLResource.oph.

Icon File

This application's icon file consists of six 'world' bitmaps, specifically:

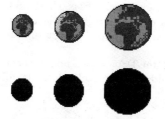

These icon images can be created in whatever package you usually use, but they must be saved in the standard Windows .bmp format. If EPOC Sketch was used, you can convert the files with EPOC Connect.

A bitmap conversion tool called bmconv is supplied with the EPOC SDKs. In order to use it, a new text file called icon.cnv should be created on the PC development platform in the same folder as the .bmp files. The contents of this file should be:

```
DemoOPL.icn Globe24.bmp Globe24m.bmp Globe32.bmp Globe32m.bmp Globe48.bmp
Globe48m.bmp
```

Next, to create the DemoOPL.icn file, use bmconv:

```
bmconv icon.cnv
```

This icon file does not need to be distributed with the rest of the application, since when the application is translated, the icons are included in the .aif file created by the translator.

Bitmap Files

The bitmap file, DemoOPL.mbm, is created in the same way as the icon file. Each of the images is to be used on the toolbar, and must be 24 by 24 pixels. The bmconv script file should be as follows:

```
DemoOPL.mbm edit.bmp editm.bmp open.bmp openm.bmp new.bmp newm.bmp exit.bmp
exitm.bmp
```

The following icons are used for this example:

Help File

It is usual for an application to have a help file that gives the user guidance in its operation. Help files are simply EPOC data files with the extension .hlp. They can therefore be created using the Data application on the EPOC device or emulator, or using the aleppo tool supplied with the EPOC SDKs that converts rich text format (.rtf) files created using a special template to help files.

If you've creating the help file with the Data application, it is conventional that the following data labels should be used, although you should allow yourself a little flexibility in order to make things as easy for the user as possible:

❑ Title – Text field giving the title of the help subject

❑ Body – Memo field with the text of the help subject. This may contain embedded objects.

❑ App name – Hidden text field with the name of the application

❑ Synonyms – Hidden text field that contains a list of words relating to the help subject that are used when the file is searched.

❑ Page – Hidden number field used for ordering the pages within the help file. The help file should be sorted on this field.

❑ ID – Hidden text field (5 characters) with the ID of the application. This field is not often used.

For this sample application, I created a one-record help file called DemoOPL.hlp, with the following contents:

Title	Demo OPL Application
Body	Example code written for Professional Symbian Programming.
	This is a 'framework' for an event-driven EPOC OPL application.
App name	DemoOPL
Synonyms	Help
Page	1
ID	

Packaging the Application for Installation

EPOC has a powerful tool for packaging files into a single installation file. This file is used to prepare and install an application to the right folders on the target device with little or no interaction from the user. The packaging tool, makesis, requires a script file; the DemoOPL.pkg example is listed below. You should note that installation files can be used to package multiple variants of the same application, to cope with different languages.

See Chapter 13 for more information about makesis.

```
; Create the SIS for the Demo OPL Application
; date: 11-11-1999
;
;language section
&EN


;
; installation header
#{"Demo OPL Application"},(0x100042CB),1,05,0
"DemoOPL.txt"-"",FT,TC
"\System\Apps\DemoOPL\DemoOPL.app"-"!:\System\Apps\DemoOPL\DemoOPL.app",FF
"\System\Apps\DemoOPL\DemoOPL.aif"-"!:\System\Apps\DemoOPL\DemoOPL.aif",FF
"\System\Apps\DemoOPL\DemoOPL.mbm"-"!:\System\Apps\DemoOPL\DemoOPL.mbm",FF
"\System\Apps\DemoOPL\DemoOPL.hlp"-"!:\System\Apps\DemoOPL\DemoOPL.hlp",FF
"\System\Apps\DemoOPL\DemoOPL.rsc"-"!:\System\Apps\DemoOPL\DemoOPL.rsc",FF
""-"C:\System\Apps\DemoOPL\DemoOPL.ini",FN
""-"C:\System\Apps\DemoOPL\",FN
```

You will notice some files mentioned in the above package file that I have not listed in the sections above:

❑ DemoOPL.txt is a plain text file that contains some text to be displayed before the application is installed. You can use it to give the user whatever information you need to.

❑ The last two lines are there to ensure that the initialization file and the directory it was in are removed when the application is uninstalled.

Extending OPL

OPL can be extended with OPL modules (OPMs) and OPL extensions (OPXs).

OPL Modules

OPL modules are OPL programs that are written and translated in exactly the same way as any other OPL program. They are loaded in by other OPL programs and applications using the OPL LOADM keyword. The procedures contained within the module can be called as though you had written them within your own program. They also have full access to your program's memory space, procedures, windows and global variables.

By convention, OPL Modules are known as 'OPM's. A number of OPMs can be downloaded from the Symbian Developers Network web site.

OPXs

OPXs extend OPL using a special form of the EPOC C++ dynamic linked libraries. As they are written in C++, they can give the same level of access to the EPOC operating system facilities as a C++ application. They also give the opportunity to code fast replacements for OPL procedures where speed is an issue.

An OPL author making use of your library will need you to provide two files: the OPX itself, and an 'OXH' file that declares the contents of the OPX. The remainder of this section describes an example OPX taken from the accompanying CD.

The OPL Header File: `simple.oxh`

An OXH is a header file that can be included by any OPL programmer wanting to make use of your OPX. It defines four things about an OPX:

❑   Its name

❑   Its unique identifier (UID)

❑   Its version number

❑   The procedures that it supplies, with arguments and return values

Here's the OXH file from the example:

```
rem SIMPLEOPX.OXH version 1.00
rem Header File for SIMPLEOPX.OPX
rem Copyright (c) 1999 Symbian Ltd. All Rights Reserved.

CONST KSimpleOpxUid&=&1000585D
CONST KSimpleOpxVersion%=$0100

CONST KReadOnly%=1
CONST KNotReadOnly%=0
```

```
DECLARE OPX SIMPLE,KSimpleOpxUid&,KSimpleOpxVersion%
  IsReadOnly&:(aFile$) : 1
  SetReadOnly:(aFile$,aState&) : 2
  Divide&:(aX&,aY&) : 100
END DECLARE
```

Note that the UID used here is one that has been allocated by Symbian. You'll need to apply for your own UIDs to use in your OPXs. The & at the beginning of the number indicates a long hexadecimal integer.

The version is given as a short integer, with the first two hex digits giving the major version number and the last two giving the minor. In human readable form, the major version is the part of the number in front of the decimal point, with the fractional part corresponding to the minor.

This OPX provides three procedures: IsReadOnly: and SetReadOnly: for testing and setting the 'read only' flags of files, and Divide: which divides one long integer by another. The & after IsReadOnly: and Divide: shows that the procedures return a long integer; the intention is for SetReadOnly: not to return any value. However, OPX procedures, just like OPL ones, default to returning a floating-point number if no other type is specified. We'll just return 0.0 as a dummy value.

The trailing numbers on each line are known as 'ordinals'. Communication between OPL and the OPX is via these ordinal numbers, rather than by procedure name.

The OPX Source Files

From the C++ point of view, all interaction with an OPX takes place through a single object derived from COpxBase (the OPX object). The OPX framework insures that no matter how many OPL modules access the OPX, there will only ever be one of these OPX objects. The object will be destroyed when the last module that uses it finishes. The OPX object may allocate resources for itself or create other objects to help perform its tasks, but it must ensure that when destroyed (when the last OPL client finishes) it frees the resources and deletes any objects it owns.

The OPL runtime executes a procedure by first pushing any arguments onto the OPL stack. It then calls the RunL() member function of the OPX object, passing the ordinal as a parameter. The OPX object is responsible for popping the arguments off the stack, pushing a result value onto the stack, and returning to the runtime.

Most OPXs are simple enough that they use a single .cpp file and a header file.

The C++ Header File: `simpleopx.h`

Here is the C++ header file:

```
// SIMPLEOPX.H

#if !defined(__SIMPLEOPX_H__)
#define __SIMPLEOPX_H__

// Include these standard header files for all OPXs
#include <opxapi.h>
#include <oplerr.h>
```

```
#include <opx.h>
#include <e32base.h>

// Additional files for this OPX
#include <f32file.h>
#include <opldb.h>

// Version number must be the same as the one in the OXH file.
const TInt KSimpleOpxVersion=0x0100;

// For ease of use and compatibility with previous versions, OPL uses -1
//  as the value of true. However C++ uses 1 as the value of true. To
//  be clear, define some constants.
const TInt32 KOplFalse=0;
const TInt32 KOplTrue=-1;

// This is the class definition for the OPX object.
class CSimpleOpx: public COpxBase
    {
private:
    enum TExtensions
        {
        // These enums must be the same values as are given in the OXH file
        EIsReadOnly = 1,
        ESetReadOnly,
        EDivide = 100
        };
public:
    // One function per OPL procedure
    void SetReadOnly();
    void IsReadOnly();
    void Divide();
public:
    static CSimpleOpx* NewLC(OplAPI& aOplAPI);
    ~CSimpleOpx();
    virtual void RunL(TInt aProcNum);
    virtual TInt CheckVersion(TInt aVersion);
private:
    CSimpleOpx(OplAPI& aOplAPI);
    void ConstructL();
    };

#endif
```

The C++ Source File: `simpleopx.cpp`

And here's the source code for the OPX, with a running commentary of what's going on. First up is RunL(), which is called every time one of the OPX procedures is called. The OPL runtime passes the ordinal number defined in the OXH file in aProcNum:

```
// SIMPLEOPX.CPP

#include "SimpleOPX.h"
```

```
void CSimpleOpx::RunL(TInt aProcNum)
    {
    switch (aProcNum)
        {
    case ESetReadOnly:
        SetReadOnly();
        break;
    case EIsReadOnly:
        IsReadOnly();
        break;
    case EDivide:
        Divide();
        break;
    default:
        User::Leave(KOplErrOpxProcNotFound);
        }
    }
```

If you were to write your own OPX, the above method is required. The three methods below are the ones that are available from OPL.

```
// OPX Procedure: readonly& = IsReadOnly&:(file$)
//
void CSimpleOpx::IsReadOnly()
    {
    // Get a pointer to file$ which on the OPL stack
    TPtrC8 aFile = iOplAPI.PopString8();

    // Use OPLs FileServerSession to save creating one here.
    RFs& fileServerSession = iOplAPI.DbManager()->FsSession();
    TUint attributeFlags;
    fileServerSession.Att(aFile,attributeFlags);
    if(attributeFlags & KEntryAttReadOnly)
        {
        // The OPL return value is pushed onto the stack.
        // Push() will take a TInt32, TInt16 or a descriptor,
        // depending on the procedure return type.
        iOplAPI.Push(KOplTrue);
        }
    else
        {
        iOplAPI.Push(KOplFalse);
        }
    }

// OPX procedure: SetReadOnly:(file$,state$)
//
void CSimpleOpx::SetReadOnly()
    {
    TInt32 aState = iOplAPI.PopInt32();
    TPtrC8 aFile = iOplAPI.PopString8();
    RFs& fileServerSession = iOplAPI.DbManager()->FsSession();
    if(aState)
        {
```

```
            // SetAtt parameters: (const TDesC& aName,
            // TUint aSetAttMask, TUint aClearAttMask);
            fileServerSession.SetAtt(aFile, KEntryAttReadOnly, 0);
            }
        else
            {
            fileServerSession.SetAtt(aFile, 0, KEntryAttReadOnly);
            }

        // The SetReadOnly procedure is not intended to return a
        // useful value. By default, all procedures must return a
        // floating point value on the stack, so make it a dummy value.
        iOplAPI.Push(0.0);
        }

// OPL call: result = Divide&:(x&,y&)
//
void CSimpleOpx::Divide()
    {
    TInt32 aY = iOplAPI.PopInt32();
    TInt32 aX = iOplAPI.PopInt32();
    if(aY == 0)
        {
        // Report an error to the OPL runtime - this may be trapped
        // using ONERR, otherwise it will be reported as an error.
        User::Leave(KOplErrDivideByZero);
        }
    TInt32 result = aX / aY;
    iOplAPI.Push(result);
    }
```

Everything beyond this point can be reused in your own OPXs. First, we have a function that checks whether this OPX version is compatible with the version the OPL program was created to use. An OPX with the same or greater major version number is OK; minor version numbers are not relevant. I'll have more to say about this later.

```
TBool CSimpleOpx::CheckVersion(TInt aVersion)
    {
    if((aVersion & 0xFF00) > (KSimpleOpxVersion & 0xFF00))
        {
        return EFalse;
        }
    else
        {
        return ETrue;
        }
    }

// Create a new OPX object, leaving a pointer to it on the cleanup stack.
//
CSimpleOpx* CSimpleOpx::NewLC(OplAPI& aOplAPI)
    {
    CSimpleOpx* This = new(ELeave) CSimpleOpx(aOplAPI);
```

```
    // Push "This" onto the cleanup stack, so that
    //  it'll be deleted again if a leave occurs
    CleanupStack::PushL(This);
    This->ConstructL();
    return This;
    }

CSimpleOpx::CSimpleOpx(OplAPI& aOplAPI)
    // Call the base class constructor
    : COpxBase(aOplAPI)
    {
    }
```

Any resources needed by the OPX may be allocated here, in the second-phase constructor. This gets called once during initialization of the first module that uses the OPX.

```
void CSimpleOpx::ConstructL()
    {
    }
```

And any resources allocated in ConstructL() should be deleted here in the destructor, which gets called once after the last module using the OPX has finished.

```
CSimpleOpx::~CSimpleOpx()
    {
    // Delete the single Thread Local Storage pointer to CSimpleOPX
    // that was created in the first call to NewOpxL()
    Dll::FreeTls();
    }
```

The OPL runtime calls this function at the start of every OPL module that uses this OPX:

```
EXPORT_C COpxBase* NewOpxL(OplAPI& aOplAPI)
    {
    CSimpleOpx* staticPointerToOpx = STATIC_CAST(CSimpleOpx*,Dll::Tls());

    // Pointer will be NULL if this is the first time this OPX has been loaded
    if(staticPointerToOpx == NULL)
        {
        // Only create a single instance of CSimpleOpx
        staticPointerToOpx = CSimpleOpx::NewLC(aOplAPI);
        User::LeaveIfError(Dll::SetTls(staticPointerToOpx));
        CleanupStack::Pop();  // staticPointerToOpx
        }

    // Give OPL a pointer to the single instance of CSimpleOpx
    return STATIC_CAST(COpxBase*,staticPointerToOpx);
    }
```

This exported function is provided so that a C++ program may query the OPX for its version number:

```
EXPORT_C TUint Version()
    {
    return KSimpleOpxVersion;
    }
```

And finally, although E32Dll() is not used by the OPX framework, it is mandatory for DLLs, so we just provide this minimal stub:

```
GLDEF_C TInt E32Dll(TDllReason /*aReason*/)
    {
    return(KErrNone);
    }
```

Compatibility between Different OPX Versions

OPXs tend to evolve over time, and different versions are released. This means that an OPL program that has been translated against one version of an OPX may end up being run against a different release. Given that a particular OPX is likely to be used by more than one application on a given machine, this is hard to avoid. To minimize problems caused in this area, there is a version numbering convention that you should follow.

- Simple bug fix releases of an OPX should keep the procedures, procedure ordinals, and procedure parameter declarations unchanged. The major version number should remain unchanged, and the minor version number should be increased. For example, v1.01 becomes v1.02.

- Releases that have extra procedures, but with existing procedure declarations unchanged, should have different major version numbers. For example, v2.05 should become v3.00.

- Releases where the declaration of existing procedures is changed should become new OPXs with a different OPX name and UID. For example, Agenda.OPX v1.05 becomes Agenda2.OPX v1.00.

Further Information

The Symbian support web site has a number of OPXs for download, and the SDK has full details of the OPX class COpxBase, and the utility functions available in OplAPI.

Summary

In summary, we have touched upon the following topics:

- I started by showing you a very simple OPL program
- I have told you a little about the history of OPL
- I then discussed the benefits of using OPL and how you can write it, including using the SDK
- The main part of this chapter took you through how to write a full, event-driven OPL application – right up to delivering it as an installable package

Lastly, I talked about extending OPL using OPL Modules (OPMs) and OPXs, written in C++

27

Connectivity

The ability to exchange files and synchronize data between an EPOC-based wireless information device (WID) and a desktop personal computer (PC) is an essential facility. In this chapter, I'll guide you through EPOC Connect, the PC connectivity software supplied as an integral part of the EPOC package. We'll examine its architecture, and the interfaces available to you as a developer for writing code that works with, and uses, its facilities.

About EPOC Connect

EPOC Connect is a generic Symbian product that provides a complete range of data synchronization and connectivity features. Running on the PC under Windows 95, Windows 98 or NT, it was originally developed as PsiWin for the Psion Series 5 machine – the very first EPOC system. This fact is reflected in the names of a number of internal components, as you'll see later in the chapter.

> *EPOC Connect is available to OEMs – Psion Computers ship it with their EPOC machines under the name PsiWin. Older versions of the product are usually available on Psion's web site (http://www.psion.com/downloads) for free download.*

EPOC Connect provides the following features that you can use:

- ❏ File management
- ❏ Backup and Restore
- ❏ Remote printing

- ❏ Document conversion
- ❏ Contacts and Agenda synchronization
- ❏ E-mail synchronization
- ❏ Application installation

File Management

EPOC Connect is completely integrated within Windows Explorer, so that the remote EPOC machine looks just like another device on the desktop. Drag-and-drop file and directory copying, and automatic conversion between local disks and the remote EPOC file system, function identically to similar operations performed entirely within the PC.

It is also possible to use Windows Explorer to open remote EPOC Word or EPOC Sheet files from the EPOC device on the PC. This automatically downloads the remote file and converts it for editing or viewing within a variety of standard PC products (such as Microsoft's Word and Excel, Lotus' SmartSuite, Corel's WordPerfect and Quattro Pro) or generic formats (rich text, comma separated variables, etc.). On being saved, the file is automatically converted back to the original EPOC format, and uploaded back to the attached EPOC device.

Backup and Restore

Backing up the data held on a mobile information device to a PC is one of the more important tasks handled by EPOC Connect. Users can back up data on demand, automatically on every connection, or at fixed intervals (daily, weekly, or monthly). There are also many options that can be used in conjunction with backup and restore operations, such as:

- ❏ Performing a full or an incremental backup/restore
- ❏ Archiving files that are deleted or have been updated
- ❏ Specifying a date range or a file extension filter of files to backup/restore
- ❏ Support for multiple mobile machines
- ❏ Individual file/directory backup/restore
- ❏ Format drives before restoring
- ❏ Error detection and handling facilities
- ❏ Automatic closing of programs before backup/restore, and automatic restarting of programs after backup/restore

These facilities are available to programmers via the **Backup Engine OLE Interface**, documented in the SDK, so you can do a backup or restore within your own code, without the user's intervention.

You don't have to worry about different machines, either: EPOC Connect recognizes an EPOC machine's unique ID, and can seamlessly manage multiple EPOC machines from a single PC. The backup data for each machine is stored in separate directory trees, with synchronization details and other settings also held separately. The appropriate information is automatically invoked on connection; no user input is required, as all the procedures for multiple machine management are totally transparent.

Remote Printing

When an EPOC device is connected to a PC, it is possible to print from the EPOC device to a printer attached to the PC simply by selecting 'Print via PC' as the printer device on the EPOC machine. EPOC Connect enables PCs and EPOC devices to communicate using multiple channels, so remote printing is available even while the remote link is being used for other purposes, such as synchronization.

Document Conversion

In order to provide document exchange between EPOC and Windows applications, EPOC Connect provides a series of converters between different formats on the two platforms. Using the converters, a Microsoft Word document in progress may be transferred from an office PC to a mobile EPOC device, where it can be opened in EPOC Word for continued editing. On return to base, the revised version of the document can simply be transferred back to the original PC in Microsoft Word format. All major Windows-based word processing and spreadsheet formats are supported: a list is currently held on Psion's web site at http://www.psion.com/computers/deskcomms_psiwintech.html.

Contacts and Agenda Synchronization

EPOC Connect allows the synchronization of personal information, such as contact details and diary files, between EPOC's own Contacts and Agenda applications and similar products on the PC platform. Address books, to-do lists and appointments kept in different programs on PC and EPOC platforms can be automatically coordinated, with updates performed in both directions with no user intervention. Most common PC Personal Information Managers (PIMs), such as Microsoft Schedule+, Microsoft Outlook, and Lotus Organizer are supported.

The EPOC Connect synchronizer is based around the internationally recognized Versit standard for calendar and contact management. The synchronization engine is licensed from Time Information Services of Godalming, England. Once again, the API for this engine is available in the SDK (under *Extending EPOC Connect*), so that you can write a plug-in to synchronize with your own products.

E-mail Synchronization

EPOC Messaging can also synchronize the inboxes and outboxes of the EPOC Email application with any PC e-mail client that supports either the MAPI or VIM standards for accessing messages.

Possibly the most obvious use for this technology is to enable mail to be read remotely at any time on a mobile WID, without compromising the role of the PC as the main archive for an e-mail message base. However, it also opens up new ways of working with electronic mail. For example, it is possible for a user to synchronize with their PC to download unread messages, use their EPOC machine to read and reply to mail, and then to re-synchronize with their PC, which then sends all the messages that they have written.

Application Installation

EPOC Connect allows applications to be installed on the EPOC device over a remote link simply by opening any EPOC .sis installation file on a PC. This feature is available from the PC's command line, as well as by double clicking from Windows Explorer. It makes it possible to install applications quickly and efficiently, since there is no need to copy the .sis file to the EPOC device.

Architecture

New products are continually coming to market, so EPOC Connect has been designed to allow for new converters to be added easily, and for synchronization of data with new software products. In order to facilitate this functionality, EPOC Connect has a layered architecture as follows:

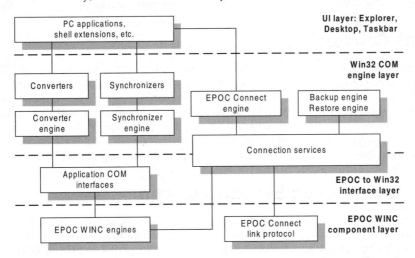

The diagram shows the structure of the EPOC Connect system, with the left-hand block detailing the standard conversion and synchronization paths. Data currently on the PC machine progresses from the relevant PC application at the top of the diagram, through the conversion or synchronization engines, finally passing via the EPOC-Win32 COM interfaces to the EPOC application engines. The process works similarly in reverse for EPOC data that is to be converted for a PC application.

The blocks on the right-hand side show how a PC application can access the EPOC Connect engine directly. This allows direct control of the EPOC file system by making a connection to the WID via the EPOC Connect link protocol component.

EPOC WINC Component Layer

At the bottom of the 'stack' lies the WINC layer. Essentially, WINC comprises the non-GUI parts of EPOC, allowing:

❑ EPOC application engines to be run from ordinary Win32 application programs in order to access EPOC application document files

❑ Any drive and directory in the PC's filing system to be accessed through the WINC F32 API – not just the emulated virtual drives

❑ Communication between a PC and an EPOC WID across a cable link

The WINC layer effectively contains the same engine code as the actual EPOC WID, but compiled for the PC. By using this same engine code on both the PC and the EPOC device, all the functionality of the EPOC engines is available to PC users, and identical data file formats are maintained on both platforms.

Also implemented at this level is the EPOC Connect Link Protocol for communications, which again runs the same code at both ends of the remote link cable, allowing data transfer between the PC and the EPOC device.

EPOC to Win32 Interface Layer

This layer provides a PC program with the means of communicating with the EPOC engines via COM interfaces, which allow access to:

- ❑ The EPOC Sheet engine
- ❑ The EPOC Word engine
- ❑ The EPOC Agenda model
- ❑ The EPOC Data model
- ❑ The EPOC Message Center engine

Most of the second part of this chapter explains the structure of these engines, and how you can access them from your own code.

The EPOC Connection Services component sits across both this layer and the one above, as it is more than just an interface to the link protocol component. It provides and maintains connection services across the link, in addition to implementing the functionality common to the EPOC Connect, Backup, and Restore engines.

Win32 COM Engine Layer

Within this layer are the main Win32 COM engines:

- ❑ The Converter engine
- ❑ The Synchronization engine
- ❑ The EPOC Connect engine
- ❑ The Backup and Restore engines

The Converter and Synchronization engines provide the basic facilities required to perform the functions that give them their names. Specific file format functionality is implemented by writing plug-ins, shown as **converters** and **synchronizers** on the diagram, so that synchronization and/or conversion functionality for your programs can be added easily. These would be accessible from whatever user interface has been implemented, while working seamlessly alongside those components supplied with the product.

The Backup and Restore and EPOC Connect engines also sit in this layer, and I'll discuss them later on. All of these are UI-independent Win32 components, allowing products with different user interfaces to employ the same engines.

User Interface Layer

The user interface integrates the EPOC file system into the Windows desktop, Explorer, and taskbar, and provides additional views onto EPOC data. It is not prescribed by the underlying levels and can be configured as required. Although the EPOC Connect interface conforms to Windows guidelines, this layer allows you the option of developing software to give a unique or brand-specific interface to EPOC Connect.

Programming using the EPOC Connect APIs

EPOC Connect provides access to its engines via a set of APIs. These are exposed as COM (Component Object Model) objects that can be used from a wide variety of Windows programming languages, such as Visual C++, Visual Basic and Delphi. The Connectivity SDK provides the necessary type library (.tlb) and component (.ocx) files that you'll need to allow COM-aware languages to access the EPOC Connect engines.

Installing the Connectivity SDK

Once you've installed the Connectivity SDK from the accompanying CD-ROM, you need to register the new components that were installed to the \epoc32\release\winc\rel directory. To do this, move all the files with extensions .tlb and .ocx into the same directory as you installed EPOC Connect 5 (usually \Program Files\Symbian\EPOC Connect) and register the ActiveX (.ocx) components by typing regsvr32 <component> for each one at a command line prompt.

Type libraries (.tlb files) contain details that allow your programs to access the classes and functions contained in the EPOC Connect .dll files. To use a type library in your Visual C++ environment, import it using the ClassWizard by clicking on the Add Class button, selecting the From a type library... option, and browsing for the required type library. In your Visual Basic environment, you can add a type library using the Project | References menu option, or add an ActiveX component to your toolbar using the Project | Components menu option.

Using the EPOC Connect Engines

To show you how easy it is to use EPOC Connect's engines in your own code, the following sections discuss each of them. I'll show you how the objects that comprise the engines fit together, and we'll take a look at some example code that demonstrates the basic functionality of each. Rather than sticking just to Visual C++ for these examples, I'll also use Visual Basic to demonstrate how the COM model works for EPOC Connect, and there's a Borland Delphi version of the EPOC Connect engine example on the CD-ROM as well.

Although I said earlier on that the code used on the EPOC WID is the same as that used in the WINC layer, there is one set of circumstances where this isn't entirely true. When running under a debugger, there is additional code to ensure that timings, memory management, process handling, etc. are sensibly dealt with. This means that (particularly in a non-C++ debugging environment) programs may cause exceptions when running under the debugger, but will operate correctly when executing normally.

Now let's have a look at those engines...

Remote Access using the EPOC Connect Engine

Basic access to a remote EPOC device is achieved using the EPOC Connect engine OLE interface, which provides a large variety of functions, including:

❑ Connecting the engine to the EPOC device

❑ Acquiring information about the attached EPOC device

❑ Reading information about EPOC device and PC drives, directories and files

❑ Copying, moving, renaming and deleting files on the EPOC device and PC

❑ Starting and stopping the programs on an EPOC device

❑ Synchronizing the PC and EPOC device clocks

An additional library, the EPOC Connect file browser, is also available using the `ecfile` ActiveX component. This provides very similar facilities to the standard Microsoft file open/save common dialog, and allows browsing and selection of files on the EPOC device.

Making a Connection

Three stages are required before you can actually access the EPOC device:

❑ Change to the EPOC Connect directory (or add it to your path) if you intend to use any of the application engines.

❑ Initialize the EPOC Connect engine. This is necessary to create the mechanism by which messages are passed back to your code.

❑ Connect to the EPOC device.

It's important to ensure that your applications run with the EPOC Connect directory set as the current directory, so that the software has access to all the underlying EPOC libraries (EKERN, etc.). You can do this either by changing the current directory once your application has started, or by adding the directory to your system's path. The EPOC Connect directory can be retrieved from the registry, as its location is usually stored in the `HKEY_LOCAL_MACHINE\Software\Psion\PsiWin32` key in the value `Installation Directory`, although this may vary on non-Psion machines.

Connecting in Visual Basic

The projects in the `\Connectivity Examples\` directory on the accompanying CD provide complete demonstrations of connecting with an EPOC device from Visual Basic, Delphi and Visual C++. You'll find that the code below is employed by all the Visual Basic projects that we'll discuss later in the chapter: it retrieves the location of your EPOC Connect installation:

```
Dim szBuffer As String, szBufferlen As Long
Dim res As Long, hKey As Long, opened As Long
Dim SA As SECURITY_ATTRIBUTES
Dim EPOCConnectInstallPath As String

szBuffer = Space(255)
szBufferlen = Len(szBuffer)
```

913

```
res = RegCreateKeyEx(HKEY_LOCAL_MACHINE, "Software\Psion\PsiWin32", _
                     0, "", 0, KEY_ALL_ACCESS, SA, hKey, opened)

If res = ERROR_SUCCESS Then
    res = RegQueryValueEx(hKey, "Installation Directory", _
                          0, REG_SZ, szBuffer, szBufferlen)
    If Len(Left(szBuffer, szBufferlen - 1)) > 0 Then
        EPOCConnectInstallPath = (Left(szBuffer, szBufferlen - 1))
    End If
Else
    MsgBox "**Failed access to registry; code " + Str$(res) + "**"
    End
End If
```

If this is successful, you can change to the directory with the following two lines of code:

```
ChDir EPOCConnectInstallPath
ChDrive Mid(EPOCConnectInstallPath, 1, 1)
```

Alternatively, you could add the EPOC Connect directory to the current environment's path like this:

```
envvar = "Path"
length = 2000
res = GetEnvironmentVariableA(envvar, path, length)

' Add EPOC Connect installation directory to the path
If InStr(path, EPOCConnectInstallPath) = 0 Then
    ' not already there, so need to insert it
    resstring = Left(path, InStr(path, Chr$(0)) - 1) + ";" + _
                    EPOCConnectInstallPath
    res = SetEnvironmentVariableA(envvar, resstring)
End If
```

The object that represents the connection to the is EPOC machine is called `PsiWinEng1` (it's housed in `pwengocx.ocx`), and it's now a simple step to initialize the engine and connect to it:

```
res = PsiWinEng1.Init
res = PsiWinEng1.Connect(20000) // Connect, giving 20 seconds as maximum wait
```

Obtaining Details of the EPOC Device

With a connection established, it's time to see what machine is sitting on the end of the wire or infrared port. This entails a call to `GetMachineOwnerInfo()`, which will retrieve the machine and the owner details. In Visual Basic, that looks like this:

```
Dim str As String
Dim Err As Long

' Public Const EPOC_MACHINE = 2
str = PsiWinEng1.GetMachineOwnerInfo(EPOC_MACHINE, Err)
```

To retrieve further details about the device, such as the battery status and free memory, you need to use the GetExtraMachineInfo() call to obtain the address of a pointer to a CPsiMachine interface; if the error code returned is 0, the interface can then be used. Rather than discuss this interface further, I've written a simple 'System Information' application to retrieve and display some details about the machine that's currently connected. It's only rudimentary, in that the error checking is minimal, but is easily understood.

First of all, here's the user interface; where a label is initially blank, I've put in the object name (as "lb_...") to indicate its position:

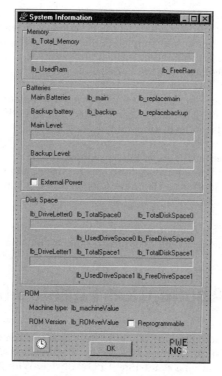

In essence, the program works by connecting to the device and setting up a timer. Whenever the timer's tick procedure is called, the machine information is updated. You'll find the complete source code for this example, in Visual Basic 6 and Delphi 5 versions, in the SysInfoVB and SysInfoD directories of the accompanying CD-ROM.

Going Further with the EPOC Connect Engine

Now that you've seen how to use the basic EPOC Connect engine, you can also use it to copy across files between the PC and the EPOC device. Just use the following call from Visual Basic:

```
result = PsiWinEng1.CopyFile(MACHINE_IS_EPOC, "c:\ecengtst", _
                   MACHINE_IS_PC, "u:\ECEngineTest", PSICOPY_OVERWRITE)
```

CopyFile() requires a machine type and filename for both the source file and the destination file (the filename can be changed during the copy operation). There's also a flags parameter, although at the moment there is only one flag defined: PSICOPY_OVERWRITE is used to indicate that the engine should overwrite the destination file if it already exists. If this flag is not present, an ERROR_ALREADY_EXISTS will occur.

To move the file, rather than copy it, use the MoveFile() function, which has the same parameters as CopyFile().

For all these functions, the EPOC Connect engine provides both an asynchronous and a synchronous interface. When using the asynchronous interface, the functions will send the request to the engine and return immediately. Once the request has completed, the engine will call the respective function (in C++, this is within your FileSystemInfo interface). For example, after a call to Init(), your OnInit() function will be called and an error code will be returned.

Functions under the synchronous interface wait until the request has completed before returning. To accommodate this, some functions have had parameters added, and others that are not required (such as OnInit() and OnCancel()) have been removed.

The EPOC Connect engine goes further than this, providing progress bar callbacks for longer operations, and information and manipulation functions for drives and files on the EPOC device. Full details are in the SDK (under Reference | Remote Access and Backup | EPOC Connect Engine OLE interface), included on the accompanying CD-ROM.

However, having opened up a connection, you now have access to the application engines that run on the EPOC device and, in the next section, we'll have a look at how to use them.

Using the EPOC Application Engines from a PC

Despite appearing to be a native Windows application, integrating seamlessly with Windows Explorer, EPOC Connect is in fact as much of an EPOC application as it is a Windows application. A lot of its internal workings are layered on top of the EPOC WINC code, which allows a PC to use exactly the same application engines that run on a standalone EPOC device. With these engines available to us even while running Windows, we have full programmatic access to all the data on the EPOC device.

In this section, I'm going to take a tour through the Word, Agenda, Data, Sheet, and Message Center application engines, to show how each builds up a document as a series of different objects. This will help you to identify which objects perform what operations, and which ones you need to use in your own applications. We'll illustrate how this works in practice with a series of code fragments that show how to manipulate your documents using Visual C++ and Visual Basic. The complete code is contained on the accompanying CD-ROM; within the book I'll intersperse the code with explanatory comments.

The Word Engine

The COM interface to the EPOC Word application, found in `psiword.dll`, has a top-level object called `ObjEpocWord`, from which you can obtain a document object, `ObjDocument`. This gives you access to the text contained in the document, stored within an `ObjRichText`. The Agenda and Sheet engines also use `ObjRichText` objects to store and format their data. You can see the hierarchy of Word objects in the figure below; `ObjParaFormat` and `ObjCharFormat` appear more than once to implement global and local formatting.

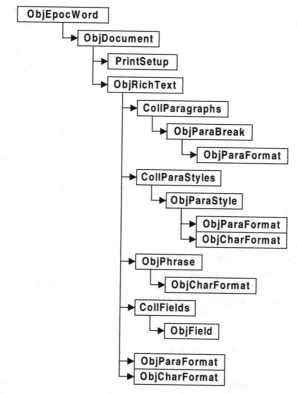

An `ObjRichText` object contains a stream of characters, with special characters to denote such things as page breaks, paragraph breaks, and embedded objects. The character stream consists of a series of paragraphs that themselves consist of phrases. Paragraphs are created by inserting paragraph breaks, and allow you to apply formatting to the phrase(s) that follow. (A phrase, by the way, may consist of both text and pictures.)

Text can be formatted in two ways:

❑ Paragraph formatting (via the `ObjParaFormat` object) is used to set attributes such as margin size, text alignment and justification, widow/orphan control and tab settings

❑ Character formatting (via the `ObjCharFormat` object) is used to change a character's color, height, language, font, etc.

To avoid having to set these attributes repeatedly, you can group a paragraph format object and a character format object together into a style object (ObjParaStyle), which can be named and then applied via a paragraph break object.

Each document has global character and paragraph formats, which are applied to all the text they contain. Once you've set the ObjRichText's initial formats, call the SetGlobalCharFormat() and SetGlobalParaFormat() methods to set the global styles. When you subsequently apply paragraph or character formatting, you are actually modifying the style that was applied to the previous paragraph break or, if no style was assigned, the global style.

To summarize all this, here's the recommended order of doing things when creating a new Word document from code:

- Set the ObjRichText object's paragraph and character format attributes (these will form the global style)
- Call the SetGlobalCharFormat() and SetGlobalParaFormat() functions to set the global style
- Set up all your other styles
- Create the first paragraph break using CreateParaBreak(), set its style and commit it
- Create a phrase using CreateText(), set its character format and commit it
- Continue adding paragraph breaks and phrases

There are a couple of additional paragraph formatting objects that aren't shown on the hierarchy diagram but may well be of interest to you. Tabs can be set up using the ObjTab object, which gives each tab a position and an alignment property, and all the tabs are accessed via the CollTabs collection object. Additionally, paragraph borders can be set using an ObjParaBorder object, or marked as being a bullet point by using an ObjParaBullet object.

Further details of these objects can be found in the SDK under Reference I OLE/COM Interfaces I EPOC WORD OLE Interface.

Let's move on to the example code, which you'll find in \Connectivity Examples\Word\. This program starts by creating a new document, writing some text in the (built-in) heading style, and following it with a couple of text phrases (the latter with some character formatting applied). The second procedure reopens the file, iterates through the global collections, printing out the data, and finally iterates through each paragraph, printing out the details of the phrases contained within. This should be sufficient to demonstrate how the objects fit together, so that you can use them (with a little more sophistication!) in your own code.

First, we declare the variables and open the file. Then, we create the document object and the rich text object that will contain the data.

```
Private Sub CreateFile_Click()

    ' Initialise main objects
    Dim oFile As New ObjEpocWord
    Dim oDoc As New ObjDocument
```

```
Dim oText As New ObjRichText
Dim oParaBreak As New ObjParaBreak
Dim oPhrase As New ObjPhrase
Dim oCharFormat As New ObjCharFormat

' Delete existing file
On Error Resume Next
Kill WRDFilename
On Error GoTo 0

' Open the file & get the text object
Set oDoc = oFile.Create(WRDFilename)
Set oText = oDoc.GetRichText
```

I've chosen not to define any global styles, instead just using the system defaults. The first paragraph contains the title of the document, so we create the paragraph break and assign it the (pre-defined) "Heading 1" style. This is all that's needed, so we can leave it here and commit the object.

```
Set oParaBreak = oText.CreateParaBreak
oParaBreak.StyleName = "Heading 1"
oParaBreak.Commit
Set oParaBreak = Nothing
```

The title itself is now required, so we create a phrase object and enter the text of the title before committing it.

```
Set oPhrase = oText.CreateText
oPhrase.Text = "Main Title Heading"
oPhrase.Commit
Set oPhrase = Nothing
```

The title is done, so we can start a new paragraph by creating a paragraph break and assigning it the required style. Here I've left it blank (so that it uses the global styles), but you may wish to define a "body text" here. Once the paragraph break has been committed, we can add another phrase with some text.

```
Set oParaBreak = oText.CreateParaBreak
oParaBreak.StyleName = ""
oParaBreak.Commit
Set oParaBreak = Nothing

Set oPhrase = oText.CreateText
oPhrase.Text = "Some normal text. "
oPhrase.Commit
Set oPhrase = Nothing
```

To illustrate how to apply character formatting, the final phrase will be in a bold font. Once the text has been added, we obtain the phrase's `CharFormat` object and set the bold attribute before committing:

```
Set oPhrase = oText.CreateText
oPhrase.Text = "Some bold text. "
Set oCharFormat = oPhrase.CharFormat
```

```
        oCharFormat.Bold = 1
        oPhrase.Commit
        Set oCharFormat = Nothing
        Set oPhrase = Nothing
```

Finally, we close the document object and the file.

```
        oDoc.Commit
        oFile.Close

        Status.Caption = "Word file created"

    End Sub
```

The second procedure – the one that reads this information back in – starts by opening the file and creating the document and rich text objects:

```
    Private Sub ExamineData_Click()

        Dim oFile As New ObjEpocWord
        Dim oDoc As New ObjDocument
        Dim oText As New ObjRichText

        Dim oStyleCollection As New CollParaStyles
        Dim oStyle As ObjParaStyle

        Dim oParaFormat As New ObjParaFormat
        Dim oCharFormat As New ObjCharFormat

        Dim oParagraphCollection As New CollParagraphs
        Dim oParagraph As New ObjParaBreak
        Dim oPhrase As New ObjPhrase

        Dim i As Integer

        Dim crlf As String
        crlf = Chr$(13) + Chr$(10)

        ' Open file & get text object (Fails if Word doesn't exist or is open)
        Set oDoc = oFile.Open(WRDFilename, 0)        ' read-only
        Set oText = oDoc.GetRichText
```

The first task is to retrieve the collection of global styles and display which ones have been defined. I don't actually display what attributes are set for each style – the Word sample in the SDK does this in great detail, and it's worth examining if you're interested.

```
        Output.Text = "**Global Styles:" + crlf

        Set oStyleCollection = oText.ParaStyles
        For Each oStyle In oStyleCollection
            Output.Text = Output.Text + "  Style: " + oStyle.Name + crlf
        Next
        Set oStyleCollection = Nothing
```

The global format objects are retrieved next, but again for clarity I've chosen not to show the settings.

```
Output.Text = Output.Text + crlf + "**Global Paragraph Format:" + crlf
Set oParaFormat = oText.ParaFormat

' Could now display all the global paragraph settings
Set oParaFormat = Nothing

Output.Text = Output.Text + crlf + "**Global Character Format:" + crlf
Set oCharFormat = oText.CharFormat

' Could now display all the global character settings
Set oCharFormat = Nothing
```

We now need to look at the textual contents of the file. The code iterates through each paragraph in the collection and displays some basic information about each phrase that it contains. The first step is to get the paragraph collection object:

```
Dim start As Integer, finish As Long
Dim someText, InfoText As String

Output.Text = Output.Text + crlf + "**Paragraphs:" + crlf

Set oParagraphCollection = oText.Paragraphs
```

At this point, we can display how many paragraphs the rich text object contains, and prepare to iterate through each paragraph.

```
Output.Text = Output.Text + "No of paragraphs: " + _
              Str$(oParagraphCollection.GetCount) + crlf

For i = 0 To (oParagraphCollection.GetCount - 1)
    Set oParagraph = oParagraphCollection.Item(i)
```

As the text within the rich text object is stored in a data stream, we display the start and end character position of the paragraph, and which style (if any) it uses.

```
start = oParagraph.ParagraphStart
finish = start + oParagraph.ParagraphLength
Output.Text = Output.Text + crlf + "**Paragraph " + Str$(i) + _
              " : (" + Str$(start) + " -"+ Str$(finish)+" )"

If(oParagraph.StyleName <> "") Then
    Output.Text = Output.Text + crlf + "Style : " + oParagraph.StyleName
End If
```

We can then iterate through all the phrases in the paragraph, printing out their positions in the text stream, and their contents.

```
    While(start < finish)
        ' Retrieve phrase object
        Set oPhrase = oText.GetText(start)
        ' Collect size information and text
        Output.Text = Output.Text + crlf + "**Phrase (" + Str$(start) + " -" + _
                    Str$(start+oPhrase.length)+" ) : " + oPhrase.Text
```

Just to demonstrate that the bold attribute was correctly set in the previous procedure, we retrieve the phrase's character format object and display the state of the bold attribute.

```
        Set oCharFormat = oPhrase.CharFormat

        ' Could now display all the phrase character settings, for example:
        Output.Text = Output.Text + crlf + "   Bold:" + Str$(oCharFormat.Bold)
        Set oCharFormat = Nothing
```

Finally, we update our record of the position in the current document and continue iterating, before eventually tidying up.

```
        start = start + oPhrase.length

        Set oPhrase = Nothing
    Wend

    Set oParagraph = Nothing
  Next

  oFile.Close

End Sub
```

Before moving on, two other print-related objects are worth mentioning. The `PrintSetup` object provides a list of the fonts that the printer supports; however, the document may contain additional fonts as a result of a paste from a document set up with a different printer driver. The `ObjFont` object contains information on how to render the font on a printer and on the screen, where the `FontName` property is the name of the printer font, and the remaining properties dictate how the font should be rendered on your EPOC machine.

The Agenda Engine

The Agenda engine model consists of a top-level object, `Epoc32ObjAgenda`, that creates, opens or closes an Agenda file. With the file open, an `Epoc32Agenda` object is used to create new entries in the Agenda, to create collections of entries, and to manage Agenda-wide facilities. The hierarchy of Agenda objects is shown on the next page.

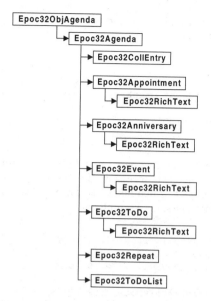

The sample code for the basic EPOC engines that we are looking at is in Visual Basic, as it's easily understood, but let's start this section by showing how to create the main object from the Microsoft Foundation Classes (MFC), as supplied with Visual C++.

Initially, we need to create an instance of the Agenda model (in `agnssync.dll`). This is done using the `COleDispatchDriver` method `CreateDispatch()`, passing it the ProgID of the component (in this case "AGNSERVERSYNC.OBJAGENDA"). For example:

```
Epoc32ObjAgenda theAgendaObj;

if(theAgendaObj.CreateDispatch("AGNSERVERSYNC.OBJAGENDA"))
    {
    ....
    }
else
    {
    // Error handling - cannot create the object
    }
```

We can then open the Agenda file with the `Open()` method, passing in the filename. This will return a new dispatch pointer to an `Epoc32Agenda` object. This can be achieved in two ways; you can do it like this:

```
LPDispatch pDis = theAgendaObj.Open("c:\\temp\\agnfile");
Epoc32Agenda theAgenda;
theAgenda.AttachDispatch(pDis);
```

Or you can use the constructor:

```
Epoc32Agenda theAgenda(theAgendaObj.Open("c:\\temp\\agnfile"));
```

Alternatively, using the `OpenExtended()` method, we could ensure that an existing file was opened and a valid dispatch pointer returned.

```
BOOL* bExists;
Epoc32Agenda theAgenda;
LPDispatch pDis = theAgendaObj.OpenExtended("c:\\temp\\agnfile", bExists);
if(bExists == TRUE)
    theAgenda.AttachDispatch(pDis);
...
```

It's important to set the **iteration period** (the date range to retrieve entries from) before any of the iterators (collections of Agenda objects) is accessed. This is done by using the `SetupDateIterator()` method of the `Epoc32Agenda` object, which takes a series of dates as parameters. These are best created using the `COleDateTime` class, for example:

```
COleDateTime startDate(1998, 1, 1, 0, 0, 0);
COleDateTime endDate(2000, 3, 1, 0, 0, 0);
COleDateTime lastSyncDate(1997, 1, 1, 0, 0, 0);

theAgenda.SetupDateIterator(startDate, startDate,
                            endDate, lastSyncDate, lastSyncDate);
```

Not only does the start date specify the beginning of the date range we're interested in, but I've also used it as the *second* parameter, so that I catch only repeating entries that first appear on or after my start date. Specifying an earlier date would allow me to look up repeating entries where the first repeat occurred *before* `StartDate` and a repeat instance actually falls in the specified period (from `StartDate` to `EndDate`). The last synchronization date is required so that an update is performed before the iteration list is constructed. This ensures that the garbage collection of de-referenced, deleted entries is efficient – that is entries that have been synchronized, deleted, and are now out of synchronization scope.

Now we can use the iterators to traverse through the entries within the Agenda file. These are all used in the same way: they pass back a **dispatch pointer** that is encompassed in the `Epoc32CollEntryList`, for example:

```
Epoc32CollEntryList theEvents(theAgenda.GetEventIterator());
```

The entry list can then be used to access the data:

```
// Get the number of entries in the collection
int noEntries = theEvents.GetCount();

// Get the entry in position 2
Epoc32Entry theEntry(theEvents.Item(2));
```

However, we 're getting ahead of ourselves: we can't use the iterators, because we haven't actually created any entries yet! An Agenda can contain four types of entries (anniversaries, appointments, events and ToDos), each of which can be created with the appropriate method:

```
// Create an Event
Epoc32Event theEvent(theAgenda.NewEvent());

// Create an anniversary
Epoc32Anniversary theAnniversary(theAgenda.NewAnniversary());

// Create an Appointment
Epoc32Appointment theAppointment(theAgenda.NewAppointment());

// Create a ToDo
Epoc32Todo theTodo(theAgenda.NewTodo());
```

Once the entry has been created, it can then be added to the Agenda with the `AddEntry()` method, or deleted with the `DeleteEntry()` method.

```
theAgenda.AddEntry(LPDISPATCH(theEvent));
theAgenda.DeleteEntry(LPDISPATCH(theEvent));
```

Having obtained an interface to an entry, we can read the contents by creating an interface to the entry's rich text object and calling its `GetNextChars()` method.

```
Epoc32RichText richText(theEvent.GetRichText());

BOOL bEmbedded;
BOOL bEnd;
CString contents = richText.GetNextChars(&bEmbedded, &bEnd);
```

The above code will read the next segment of text and place the text in the variable `contents`. If the bEnd variable is TRUE after the call, it shows that the end of the rich text object has been reached. If bEmbedded is TRUE, no text was available but an embedded object was available. Embedded objects can be retrieved using the `GetEmbeddedObject()` call, and the stream is manipulated in much the same way as discussed in the Word section above.

Entries can be set to repeat at certain intervals. Having created an entry, we use its `Epoc32Repeat` interface, obtained by calling the `GetRepeatData()` method, to set up the repeat pattern.

```
Epoc32Repeat repeat(theEvent.GetRepeatData());
```

There are six types of repeat that can be used (daily, weekly, monthly by date, monthly by days, yearly by date, yearly by day of week), and these are set by calling the `SetType()` method:

```
repeat.SetType("DAILY");           // Daily repeat
repeat.SetType("WEEKLY");          // Weekly repeat
repeat.SetType("MONTHLYBYDATES"); // Monthly by date repeats
repeat.SetType("MONTHLYBYDAYS");  // Monthly by days repeats
repeat.SetType("YEARLYBYDATE");   // Yearly by date repeat
repeat.SetType("YEARLYBYDAY");    // Yearly by day repeat
```

To exclude (or 'except') a certain date from a repeat, use exceptions. `AddException()` will add a certain date to the list of exceptions, while `RemoveException()` will remove one. To iterate through a list of exceptions, use `GetNoExceptions()` to find the total number of exceptions, and then `GetException()` to find the date of a specific exception.

Finally, before turning to our Visual Basic example, it's worth noting that the `Epoc32Agenda` object also provides additional information about the Agenda file.

```
// Number of deleted entries:
int noDel = theAgenda.GetNumberOfDeletions();

// Number of changed entries:
int noMod = theAgenda.GetNumberOfModifications();

// Number of dereferenced entries:
int noDer = theAgenda.GetNumberOfDereferences();

// Number of deleted todos:
int noDelTodos = theAgenda.GetNumberOfDeletedTodos();
```

So to the example: here's a simple Visual Basic program to open up an Agenda file from your EPOC device, display it on the PC, create a new entry and write it back to the EPOC device. The code is based on an example in the Connectivity SDK that contains a user interface based on that of a Psion Series 5; you'll find my version in `\Connectivity Examples\Agenda`. It's not an industrial-strength program, but it does show you the basic strategy for using Agenda in your own code.

The code essentially contains procedures to read in an Agenda file from the EPOC device and display it; and to write a new entry, with an embedded object, back out to the device. Let's look at the first of these:

```
Private Sub LoadAgenda()

    Dim oAgenda As Object
    Dim oEpoc32Agenda As Object
    Dim oEpoc32AppointmentCollection As Object
    Dim oEpoc32Appointment As Object
    Dim oRichText As Object
    Dim bEmbedded As Boolean
    Dim bAtEnd As Boolean
    Dim EndDate As Date
    Dim i As Integer

    Status.Caption = "Loading Agenda file " + AgendaFilename

    ' Creating object & reading data may be slow: change pointer to hourglass
    Screen.MousePointer = vbHourglass
```

Initially, we create the Agenda object, then open the file (the filename has already been obtained using the EPOC Connect File Browser control, in `OpenAgenda_Click()`).

```
Set oAgenda = CreateObject("AgnServerSync.ObjAgenda")

' If this fails, either agenda doesn't exist or is open
On Error GoTo openFailed
Set oEpoc32Agenda = oAgenda.Open(AgendaFilename)
On Error GoTo 0

' Clear the output display
OutputList.Clear
```

We then need to set up an iterator (the `FirstMonday` variable has already been initialized to midnight on the Monday of the current week) before the 'collection of appointments' object can be constructed.

```
' Set up iterator to end on Sunday at 23:59:59 (end of the week)
EndDate = Fix(FirstMonday + 6) + TimeValue("23:59:59")
oEpoc32Agenda.SetupDateIterator FirstMonday, FirstMonday, _
                        EndDate, "1/1/1980", "1/1/1980"

Set oEpoc32AppointmentCollection = oEpoc32Agenda.GetApptIterator
```

Having obtained a collection containing all our appointments this week, we iterate through each one, obtaining its rich text object and getting the first element of text.

```
For i = 0 To oEpoc32AppointmentCollection.GetCount - 1
    ' Enter appointment into list
    Set oEpoc32Appointment = oEpoc32AppointmentCollection.Item(i)
    Set oRichText = oEpoc32Appointment.GetRichText

    Dim Title As String
    oRichText.ResetToStart

    ' Get text of appointment
    Title = oRichText.GetNextChars(bEmbedded, bAtEnd)
```

Now let's check for any embedded data and, if we find any, display what type of object it is. I'm doing this twice, to ensure that I pick up any text that follows an embedded object, as the text wouldn't be retrieved on the first call to `GetNextChars()`.

```
    ' Test for embedded data
    If (bEmbedded) Then
        ' Add type descriptor to title
        Title = Title + " [" + oRichText.GetEmbeddedType + "]"
    End If

    ' If not at end, get second part of text of appointment
    If (bAtEnd) Then
    Else
        Title = Title + oRichText.GetNextChars(bEmbedded, bAtEnd)
        ' Test for embedded data
        If (bEmbedded) Then
            Title = Title + " [" + oRichText.GetEmbeddedType + "]"
        End If
    End If
    ' Ignore any further text objects
```

Having retrieved the entry, we need to add it to the display. I used a list box to show the appointments so that it would be possible to double-click a list box entry and extend the program's functionality.

```
            ' Add appointment to display array, with {A} to indicate appointment
            OutputList.AddItem Format(oEpoc32Appointment.StartDateTime, _
                        "mm/dd/yyyy  hh:mm") + " {A} " + Title + _
                        Format(oEpoc32Appointment.StartDateTime, "  hh:mm") + " - " + _
                        Format(oEpoc32Appointment.EndDateTime, "hh:mm")

            Set oRichText = Nothing

        Next i
```

I've used the date format mm/dd/yyyy here so that the entries display in date order. This would allow me to extend the example to retrieve events, anniversaries and ToDos – the code would be very similar, just creating the collections with the appropriate methods (GetEventIterator(), GetAnnivIterator() and GetTodoListIterator()) and iterating through all the entries in them.

Finally in this procedure, we need to close the Agenda object and generally tidy up:

```
        Set oEpoc32AppointmentCollection = Nothing

        oEpoc32Agenda.Close
        Set oEpoc32Agenda = Nothing
        Set oAgenda = Nothing

        ' Return mouse pointer to normal.
        Screen.MousePointer = vbDefault

    Exit Sub

    openFailed:
        Screen.MousePointer = vbDefault
        MsgBox "Error occurred opening file - make sure it's closed on EPOC device."

    End Sub
```

The second procedure, AddAppointment_Click(), writes an appointment back in to the Agenda. I've included an embedded object, to show how this is done.

```
    Private Sub AddAppointment_Click()
        Dim oAgenda As Object
        Dim oEpoc32Agenda As Object
        Dim oEpoc32Appointment As Object
        Dim oRichText As Object
        Dim EmbeddedObject As Object
        Dim EndDate As Date
        Dim Start As Date
        Dim Finish As Date
```

928

As before, we create the Agenda object, open the file, and set up the iterator:

```
    ' Ensure Agenda has been opened -  do so if not
    If AgendaFilename = "" Then OpenAgenda_Click

    ' Create the Agenda object
    Set oAgenda = CreateObject("AgnServerSync.ObjAgenda")

    ' If this fails, either agenda hasn't been opened, doesn't exist, or is open
    On Error GoTo openFailed
    Set oEpoc32Agenda = oAgenda.Open(AgendaFilename)
    On Error GoTo 0

    ' Set up iterator to end on Sunday at 23:59:59
    EndDate = Fix(FirstMonday + 6) + TimeValue("23:59:59")
    oEpoc32Agenda.SetupDateIterator FirstMonday, FirstMonday, _
                            EndDate, "1/1/1980", "1/1/1980"
```

Next, we create the new appointment object and give it a title, a start, and an end time.

```
    Set oEpoc32Appointment = oEpoc32Agenda.NewAppointment

    Set oRichText = oEpoc32Appointment.GetRichText
    oRichText.AddChars "This is an appointment"

    Start = Now
    Finish = Fix(Now) + TimeSerial(Hour(Start) + 1, Minute(Start), 0)
    oEpoc32Appointment.StartDateTime Start
    oEpoc32Appointment.EndDateTime Finish
```

Now we add in the embedded memo object. This consists of getting an `EmbeddedObject` using the `AddEmbeddedObject()` method, setting the contents of the memo, and finally adding the whole new appointment in to the Agenda.

```
    oRichText.AddChars " - Memo "
    Set EmbeddedObject = oRichText.AddEmbeddedObject()
    EmbeddedObject.AddChars ("This is a memo")

    oEpoc32Agenda.AddEntry oEpoc32Appointment
```

Finally, we again need to tidy up and do some error handling:

```
    oEpoc32Agenda.Close
    Set oEpoc32Agenda = Nothing
    Set oAgenda = Nothing

    ' Update Agenda
    LoadAgenda
Exit Sub
```

```
openFailed:
    Screen.MousePointer = vbDefault
    MsgBox "Error occurred opening file - make sure it is closed on EPOC device."

End Sub
```

Creating other types of entry objects is very similar: just call the appropriate method (NewAnniversary(), NewEvent(), or NewToDo()), fill in the required data, and add the entry to the Agenda.

The Data Engine

The Data engine model is accessible via the interface defined in psidato.dll. Through it, a database is considered as a set of records, and a record is defined in terms of fields. There is only one set of field definitions (that is, one table per database).

The top-level object is ObjEpocData, which allows a database to be created or opened. It returns another object, ObjDatabase, to reference this database. Once you have this object, you can access the collection of field definitions, CollFieldDefinitions, from which you can manipulate individual field definitions using the field definition object, ObjFieldDefinition.

In addition to the collection of field definitions, there is also an object containing the collection of records, CollRecords. This allows you to gain access to each record object, ObjRecord.

This hierarchy of objects in the Data interface is shown below.

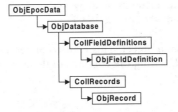

Turning straight to my example in \Connectivity Examples\Database\, let's first look at the Visual Basic procedure that creates an EPOC data file; it's so short that we can take it all in one go! Initially, we need to create the Data object and file, before setting up the field definitions (in this case, two fields named "Machine" and "Operating System"). Once the structure of the database has been assembled, we can commit it and close the file.

```
Private Sub CreateDB_Click()

    Dim oEPOCData As New ObjEpocData
    Dim oDatabase As New ObjDatabase
    Dim oField As New ObjFieldDefinition

    Set oDatabase = oEPOCData.Create(DBFilename)
```

```
    ' Create EPOC database fields & commit them
    Set oField = oDatabase.CreateFieldDefinition
    oField.Name = "Machine"
    oField.Commit
    Set oField = Nothing

    Set oField = oDatabase.CreateFieldDefinition
    oField.Name = "Op System"
    oField.Commit
    Set oField = Nothing

    oDatabase.Commit
    oEPOCData.Close

End Sub
```

Note that you *must* close the database once you've created it. To start populating it, re-open the file and add records.

Since the `SetValue` property requires an object of type `VARIANT`, I have to use the `CVar()` function to convert my data strings:

```
Private Sub AddData_Click()

    Dim oEPOCData As New ObjEpocData
    Dim oDatabase As New ObjDatabase
    Dim oRecord As New ObjRecord

    Set oDatabase = oEPOCData.Open(DBFilename)

    ' Create an EPOC database record, write data & commit it
    Set oRecord = oDatabase.CreateRecord
    oRecord.SetValue 0, CVar("Series 5")
    oRecord.SetValue 1, CVar("EPOC (ER3)")
    oRecord.Commit
    Set oRecord = Nothing

    ' Create another EPOC database record etc.
    Set oRecord = oDatabase.CreateRecord
    oRecord.SetValue 0, CVar("Series 3")
    oRecord.SetValue 1, CVar("SIBO")
    oRecord.Commit
    Set oRecord = Nothing

    oEPOCData.Close

End Sub
```

Our database is now complete. To access the records, just use the function `GetValue()` instead of `SetValue()`:

```
Private Sub DisplayData_Click()

    Dim oEPOCData As New ObjEpocData
    Dim oDatabase As New ObjDatabase
    Dim oCollRecords As Object
    Dim oCollFields As Object
    Dim oRecord As ObjRecord
```

We're going to print out all the fields in each record, so let's set up the record and field collection objects that will be needed, and initialize the record counter variable.

```
    Set oDatabase = oEPOCData.Open(DBFilename)
    Set oCollRecords = oDatabase.Records
    Set oCollFields = oDatabase.FieldDefinitions

    recordNo = 1
```

Now iterate through all the records, adding the record number to the display string.

```
    For Each oRecord In oCollRecords
        ' Display the record number
        Info = "Record:" + Str$(recordNo) + Chr$(10) + Chr$(13)
```

Then, for each field in the record, get the field title from the fields collection, and the field value from the record object, and add both to the display string.

```
        ' Loop through each field in record, get info
        For field = 0 To (oCollFields.Count() - 1)
            ' Build up field - show name and value
            Info = Info + "   " + oCollFields.Item(field).Name + _
                    " : " + oRecord.GetValue(field) + Chr$(10) + Chr$(13)
        Next field
```

Finally, print the display string for the record, continue iterating, and then close the database file.

```
        ' Display data for the record
        MsgBox Info

        ' Increment record number count
        recordNo = recordNo + 1
    Next oRecord

    oEPOCData.Close

End Sub
```

To amend a record, first call the record's `Update()` method, then use `SetValue()` to make the change, and finally call `Commit()` to save it.

```
Private Sub ChangeData_Click()

    Dim oEPOCData As New ObjEpocData
    Dim oDatabase As New ObjDatabase
    Dim oRecord As ObjRecord

Set oDatabase = oEPOCData.Open(DBFilename)

    ' Retrieve second record
    Set oRecord = oDatabase.Records.Item(1)

    ' Mark record for updating, change values & commit
    oRecord.Update
    oRecord.SetValue 0, CVar("Series 7")
    oRecord.SetValue 1, CVar("EPOC (ER5)")
    oRecord.Commit
    Set oRecord = Nothing

    oEPOCData.Close

End Sub
```

That's all there is to basic EPOC database manipulation! Once again, further details of the objects and functions can be found in the SDK.

The Sheet Engine

The EPOC Sheet engine can be found in `psisht.dll`, and has a top-level object called `ObjEpocSheet` to create or open files. Once opened, this returns an `ObjWorkBook` object, which contains a collection of worksheets, although multiple worksheets are not currently supported.

An `ObjWorkSheet` contains a collection of `ObjCells`, each of which can be formatted using `ObjNumFormat`, `ObjCharFormat` and `ObjParaFormat` objects. Each `ObjWorkSheet` also has an `ObjGrid` to specify the design of the worksheet.

A simplified version of the object hierarchy in the Sheet interface is shown below.

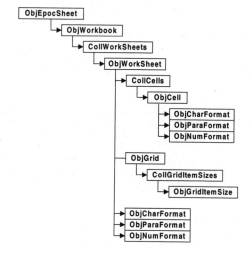

To create an EPOC sheet in the last of my productivity application samples
(`\Connectivity Examples\Spreadsheet\`), we use `ObjEpocSheet`'s `Create()` method to open a
new file and instantiate an `ObjWorkBook` object. This contains a collection of worksheets, and we want
to use the first one (at position 0 in the collection) for our data, as follows:

```
Private Sub CreateFile_Click()

    Dim oEpocSheet As New ObjEpocSheet
    Dim oWorkBook As Object
    Dim oWorkSheet As Object
    Dim oCell As Object
    Dim i As Integer
    Dim s As String

    Set oWorkBook = oEpocSheet.Create(SSFilename)

    ' Get first worksheet from collection & name it
    Set oWorkSheet = oWorkBook.WorkSheets.Item(0)
    oWorkSheet.Name = "Epoc Sheet 1"
```

Now we've got our worksheet, and we can start entering data. For the purposes of this sample, we'll
create a single column. The first cell will contain a numeric value, and the rest a simple formula that
adds 4 to the previous cell.

```
    ' Populate worksheet: col 0, cell 1 has value
    Set oCell = oWorkSheet.CreateCell
    oCell.Formula = CVar("=0")
    oCell.Row = 0
    oCell.Column = 0
    oCell.Commit
    Set oCell = Nothing

    ' Populate worksheet: rest of col 0 has formula
    For i = 1 To 100
        Set oCell = oWorkSheet.CreateCell
        s = "=A" & Format(i) & "+4"
        oCell.Formula = CVar(s)
        oCell.Row = i
        oCell.Column = 0
        oCell.Commit
        Set oCell = Nothing
    Next i
```

Finally, we'd better save all of our hard work.

```
    oWorkSheet.Commit
    oWorkBook.Commit
    oEpocSheet.Close
End Sub
```

We can now re-open our Sheet file to display the data it contains. I've used a standard Grid object with three columns: the first is fixed, the second (column A) contains the value of the cell and the third (column B) the formula that it contains.

Depending on the components you have installed on your machine, you may need to replace the Grid with a FlexGrid. In other words, you'll need to use `msflxgrd.ocx` *rather than* `grid32.ocx`. *With this modification in place, no further amendment is required to the project.*

```
Set oWorkBook = oEpocSheet.Open(SSFilename)
Set oCollCells = oWorkBook.WorkSheets.Item(0).Cells

Grid.Cols = 3   ' Only need a fixed and 2 writable columns
Grid.Rows = oCollCells.Count + 1
Grid.ColWidth(2) = Grid.ColWidth(1) * 2 ' Enlarge col B width for formulae
```

To display the cells, we can use Visual Basic's `For...Each` construct, which iterates through all the cells in the collection, allowing us easy access to the contents of the object:

```
For Each oCell In oCollCells
    ' Move to correct cell in col A
    Grid.Row = oCell.Row + 1
    Grid.Col = oCell.Column + 1

    ' Display value in col A
    Grid.Text = CStr(oCell.Value)

    ' Display formula in col B
    Grid.Col = Grid.Col + 1
    Grid.Text = CStr(oCell.Formula)
Next oCell
```

For completeness, here's the code to write the row and column headings, and to close the file.

```
For i = 1 To Grid.Rows - 1
    Grid.Col = 0
    Grid.Row = i
    Grid.Text = i
Next i

Grid.Row = 0
Grid.Col = 1
Grid.Text = "Value"
Grid.Col = 2
Grid.Text = "Formula"

oEpocSheet.Close
```

Complete worksheets and individual cells can have standard Rich Text Character and Paragraph formats. These are accessed from the rich text object interface supplied by the Word interface (in `psiword.dll`). It's quite easy to link the different object hierarchies together, as you can see in the following snippets, which manipulate a cell's character format. First, let's create a spreadsheet and set some properties.

```
        Dim oEpocSheet As New ObjEpocSheet
        Dim oWorkBook As Object
        Dim oWorkSheet As Object
        Dim oCell As Object
        Dim oCharFormat As Object
        Dim oFont As Object

        ' Create character format
        Set oWorkBook = oEpocSheet.Create(SSFilename)
        Set oWorkSheet = oWorkBook.WorkSheets.Item(0)
        Set oCell = oWorkSheet.CreateCell

        ' Got cell; now set value and format/font properties
        oCell.Value = "Hello People"
        Set oCharFormat = oCell.CharFormat
        oCharFormat.Bold = 1
        oCharFormat.Underline = enum_Underline.EWORD_U_On
        Set oFont = oCharFormat.Font
        oFont.FontName = "Times New Roman"

        ' Save data & close object
        oCell.Commit
        oWorkSheet.Commit
        oWorkBook.Commit
        oEpocSheet.Close
```

We can now reopen the file and test the various format properties to ensure they were set correctly:

```
        Set oWorkBook = oEpocSheet.Open(SSFilename)
        Set oWorkSheet = oWorkBook.WorkSheets.Item(0)
        Set oCell = oWorkSheet.Cells.Item(0)

        ' Got cell; now display value and format/font properties
        Debug.Print oCell.Value
        Set oCharFormat = oCell.CharFormat
        Debug.Print oCharFormat.Bold
        Set oFont = oCharFormat.Font
        Debug.Print oFont.FontName

        oEpocSheet.Close
```

The ease with which the bold and italic settings were applied above extends to a whole range of character and paragraph attributes. Characters can have their color, height, language and font changed; and paragraphs can have margin, alignment, widow/orphan control, justification and tab settings, as discussed in the earlier section on EPOC Word.

Message Center Interface

The EPOC Connect Message Center is a relatively new interface, providing a single point of access for all messaging types, such as e-mail, fax, SMS etc. Each type is implemented with a separate library that plugs into the Message Center interface, providing for future developments and alternative library implementations.

The top-level `IMessageCentre` object allows you to create `IMessageIndex` objects. These provide a directory tree structure (stored in a `CMIndex` object) within which messages can be held and manipulated. The `IIndexEntry` interface is used to traverse this message index directory tree. `IMessageIndex` objects also allow the creation of specific message-type interfaces (for example, an `IEmail` interface). Currently, only the e-mail message-type interface has been implemented.

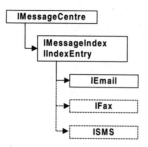

In showing you the following MFC-based example, I'm actually using the EPOC Message Center in the wrong way. It was designed for synchronization services, rather than for browsing, but this way I can take you through the interface without being too concerned with the intricacies of synchronization. I'm also going to extract C++ code fragments from all around the actual program, rather than just follow it through as with the previous examples. This is to show the various stages in the correct order, rather than being constrained by the program design. The full program is on the accompanying CD-ROM, so you can check out the complete code there.

To start with, we must obtain valid pointers to all the COM interfaces we wish to use, beginning with `IMessageCentre`:

```
if(FAILED(::CoCreateInstance(CLSID_MessageCentre,
                             NULL,
                             CLSCTX_INPROC_SERVER,
                             IID_IMessageCentre,
                             (void**)&m_pIMessageCentre)))
    {
    AfxMessageBox("Could not create EPOC Connect Message Centre");
    EndDialog(IDABORT);
    return true;
    }
```

We can now initialize the Message Center and specify the service ID that we want to use. The Service ID allows you to have sets of e-mails that need to be synchronized on different machines (a home PC and a work PC, for example). Setting the Service ID to zero on a new machine before calling `SetSyncService()` tells the Message Center to create and return a new Service ID, which you should store somewhere if you may need to use that specific ID in the future.

```
if(FAILED(m_pIMessageCentre->Initialise()))
    {
    AfxMessageBox("Could not initialise EPOC Connect Message Centre");
    EndDialog(IDABORT);
    return true;
    }
```

```
        // Now try to set the sync service
        if(FAILED(m_pIMessageCentre->SetSyncService(ServiceNameBSTR, &ServiceID)))
            {
            AfxMessageBox("Could not set required sync service");
            return false;
            }
```

Now that we've stipulated which service is to be used, an `IMessageIndex` interface can be obtained and initialized (and verified using `IndexLoaded()`).

```
        if(FAILED(m_pIMessageCentre->GetMessageIndexIF(
                                        (LPUNKNOWN*)&m_pIMessageIndex)))
            {
            AfxMessageBox("Could not get pointer to MessageIndex object");
            EndDialog(IDABORT);
            return true;
            }

        m_pIMessageIndex->AddRef();

        if(FAILED(m_pIMessageIndex->IndexLoaded()))
            {
            AfxMessageBox("Index not loaded");
            EndDialog(IDABORT);
            return true;
            }
```

The `IMessageIndex` interface is then queried to establish the existence of an `IIndexEntry` interface. Once a pointer to this latter interface has been successfully acquired, we will be able to access the various message-type objects — in this case, e-mail messages.

```
        if(FAILED(m_pIMessageIndex->QueryInterface(IID_IIndexEntry,
                                        (void**)&m_pIdx)))
            {
            AfxMessageBox("Could not find IndexEntry object");
            EndDialog(IDABORT);
            return true;
            }

        if(FAILED(m_pIMessageIndex->CreateEmailIF((LPUNKNOWN*)&m_pIEmail)))
            {
            AfxMessageBox("Could not get pointer to Email object") ;
            EndDialog(IDABORT);
            return true;
            }

        m_pIEmail->AddRef();
```

The Message Center is navigated via a tree structure. Having obtained the root (using `GetRoot()`), the objects that exist at the next level (usually Inbox, Outbox, etc.) can be retrieved by calling `GetChildrensUIDs()`. The contents of folders and other Message Center objects are accessed in a similar way, using `GetChildrensUIDs()` to move down and `GetParentsUID()` to move up a level, followed by `GetEntry()` to actually effect the move.

```
       VARIANT ChildrenList;
       VariantInit(&ChildrenList);

       if(FAILED(m_pIdx->GetChildrensUIDs(&ChildrenList)))
           {
           AfxMessageBox("Could not get children's UIDs");
           return false;
           }

       SAFEARRAY* pLstSA = ChildrenList.parray;
       if(pLstSA != NULL)
           {
           ...
```

We have now got a pointer to the array of child UIDs. Once we've selected the index of the required child's UID, and called `SafeArrayGetElement()` to read the actual UID, we can pass this to `GetEntry()` to actually move to the entry.

```
          if(FAILED(SafeArrayGetElement(pLstSA, &iter, &ChildUID)))
              {
              AfxMessageBox("Could not get element");
              return false;
              }

          m_pIdx->GetEntry(ChildUID);
```

Having loaded the entry, you can test its type attribute and, if it is a message, load the e-mail information (not included in the index) into the e-mail interface. All data is then cached locally in the PC (except for attachments).

```
       if(FAILED(m_pIEmail->GetEmail(messageUID)))
           {
           AfxMessageBox("Could not get email message");
           return false;
           }

       BSTR MsgBSTR;
       if(FAILED(m_pIEmail->GetText(&MsgBSTR)))
           {
           AfxMessageBox("Could not get email message text");
           return false;
           }

       CString Display = "";
       AfxBSTR2CString(&Display, MsgBSTR);
       AfxMessageBox(Display);
```

To update an existing e-mail, call `NewEmail()` first to initialize all the data structures, prior to calling `GetEmail()`. On completion of the changes, call `UpdateEmail()` to commit the changes to the Message Center. Adding a new e-mail is done similarly, but with a call to the `CommitNewEmail()` function as the final step, which will return the UID of the new email.

Synchronization and Conversion

Beyond access to the EPOC engines, the most important features provided by EPOC Connect are undoubtedly synchronization and document conversion. Because both are relatively complex topics, I'll give an overview of each so that you have a flavor of what enhancements to the basic EPOC Connect product are possible.

Synchronization Fundamentals

EPOC Connect supports synchronization of information between the EPOC-based Agenda and Contacts applications, and a wide variety of PC-based PIM applications. This ensures that users who keep information on both their EPOC device and their PCs don't have to maintain two independent sets of data, but can synchronize the data so that it's the same on both machines.

The actual synchronization process is performed by the Synchronization engine. This essentially involves comparing a set of data from the EPOC platform with one from the PC application, ensuring that the same data is maintained on both machines by making any changes required.

The Synchronization engine uses data that is closely based on the industry standard Versit formats. For contacts, this is the vCard format (version 2.1) and for calendar data such as appointments, events, anniversaries and tasks, the vCalendar format (version 1.0) is used (see http://www.imc.org for details). To handle e-mail messages, which cannot be placed under one of the existing Versit standards, Symbian have defined a vMail format. (This definition is neither produced nor endorsed by Versit, but is based on the standard principles of stream and property formatting used within the existing vCalendar and vCard standards.) The full specification is documented in the Connectivity SDK.

While the Synchronization engine does the work of reading, comparing and writing the streams of data, it requires a series of plug-ins, called ISyncApps, to convert the vCard/vCalendar/vEmail data into the PIM-specific data formats. (ISyncApps for the EPOC applications are provided with EPOC Connect.)

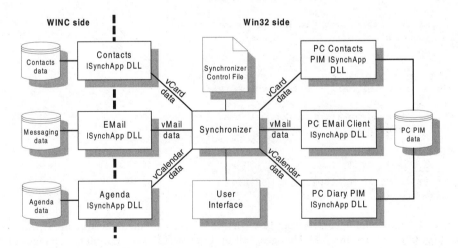

The only other addition that's required is a UI support DLL that integrates with the synchronization front-end program, allowing the user to select the synchronization options applicable to the application. This is normally implemented as a set of property pages, from which the synchronization set-up information is extracted and stored in a control file for later use.

Therefore, by writing a property page user interface and an `ISyncApp`, it is reasonably easy to integrate your own PC-based applications into EPOC Connect and have them work seamlessly alongside those already supported. Once again, full details with example code are contained in the SDK.

Conversion Fundamentals

Converters are required to export the data created by EPOC applications in a format that can be read by similar PC-based applications, and vice versa. Similarly to the synchronization process above, the Converter engine uses a series of DLL 'plug-ins' to provide converters for a range of different formats.

There are only a few steps required to write a new converter. To be accessible via the EPOC Connect COM interface, it must be written as an EPOC WINC DLL that:

❑ Provides one or more classes derived from `CConverterRepresentative`. These contain the actual converter code.

❑ Provides a class derived from `CConverterLibrary`, which allows the new converter to be added to the global list of converters.

❑ Exports an entry point at ordinal 2 that creates the newly derived class.

The converter should be put into the EPOC Connect directory together with any other WINC DLLs or resource files it requires, and added to a suitable converter control file. This control file contains a list of converter DLLs, and is used by the Converter engine when it is loading converters. A new control file can be created using the `ObjConverterLibraryInstaller` interface contained in the engine; alternatively, the DLL can be added to the default file, `control.1`, in the main EPOC Connect directory. The converter is now accessible to the Converter engine and therefore integrated into EPOC Connect.

The skeleton of a simple converter is explained more fully in the SDK, which also contains the source code for an EPOC fax-to-TIF converter as an example.

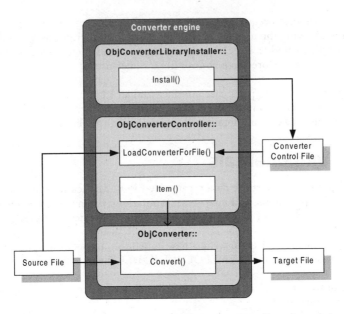

Once you've finished setting up the converter, it will be automatically selected during conversion (if appropriate), or it may be used by a program invoking the Converter engine directly. To initiate a conversion, use the engine's top-level object (ObjConverterController), which has four methods:

❑ LoadAllConverters() loads all converters contained in the DLLs specified in a control file

❑ LoadConverterForFile() loads the converters contained in the DLLs specified in a control file that can deal with a given data file

❑ Count() returns the number of suitable converters loaded

❑ Item() provides a COM object offering access to suitable converters

Using a converter involves first creating an ObjConverter object and selecting a specific converter using the COM object returned by ObjConverterController::Item().

This object contains a single Convert() method, which performs the file conversion. It also has three properties, which are passed to Convert() as parameters. They are the source file type, the target file type, and the target's default extension (such as .doc for Microsoft Word). Convert() can also take a suitable notification function as a callback if the progress of the conversion needs to be monitored.

The SDK example program, QuikView, shows how to accomplish this using Visual Basic. It selects the series of converters that can handle a specific source file, displays the available conversion options to the user, and then calls the Convert() function to perform the actual conversion.

Summary

This chapter has taken you through the facilities and engines provided by EPOC Connect for accessing EPOC WIDs and data formats, along with a brief glimpse into the more demanding areas of synchronization and conversion. What we've covered here is really only the basics of what's available to connectivity programmers, and the next port of call is the Connectivity SDK on the CD-ROM. This details how to use the backup/restore functionality of EPOC Connect, what's needed to integrate a new converter into EPOC Connect, how to perform synchronization, and the information you'll need to write custom servers, in addition to further analysis of the various engines.

EPOC Connect was designed with extensibility in mind, and I'd definitely recommend regular visits to the Symbian Developer Network web site (http://www.symbiandevnet.com) to see what's new in the world of EPOC Connect. In particular, the discussion.epoc.connect forum on the NNTP server news://publicnews.epocworld.com is a good source of support.

The knowledge you've gained in this chapter will give you a good grounding to make the most of new functionality in EPOC Connect as and when it becomes available; in the meantime, keep an eye on the web site for further details, investigate the SDK, and happy EPOC Connectivity programming!

The CD-ROM

Installation

The CD-ROM provided with Professional Symbian Programming contains all four EPOC Release 5 SDKs for Microsoft Windows NT/9x. You should realise that these SDKs were originally all produced as separate stand-alone products, and each one contains its own installation program and its own licence agreement. Each SDK was also designed to reside on its own logical drive, and not to coexist with other EPOC SDKs.

The SDKs on the CD are fundamentally the same as the ones that are available through Symbian's Developer Network, and it has not been possible to tailor them specially for this book. Consequently, we recommend that for the best and most reliable performance you do not install EPOC SDKs on top of each other. You should install each SDK on a separate logical drive. This is generally done by using the DOS subst command on a specific subdirectory from the command line before running any installation routines.

The following commands create a directory on the C drive and map it to the drive letter E.

```
c:
cd \
mkdir epocsdk1
subst e: epocsdk1
```

If you have multiple SDK installations, or if you wish to keep the EPOC SDKs apart from other things on your C drive, you might find this technique useful – you could, for example, run with drives E, F, G and H all dedicated to different EPOC SDKs. You can put the subst command into autoexec.bat (on Windows 9x) or into a .cmd file in your startup directory (on Windows NT), so that the E drive is always ready when your PC boots up.

An alternative technique, which works on Windows NT but can cause problems under Windows 9x, is to create a directory in the same manner as for subst, share it on the Windows network, and then map it as a network drive.

The example code projects specially written for this book and provided on the CD-ROM should likewise be installed to the logical drive containing the appropriate SDK, after the desired SDK has been installed.

> Should you decide to ignore this advice and install all the EPOC Release 5 SDKs on top of each other, you might get away with it, but it is not recommended. You may experience difficulty should you wish to uninstall one or other of the products, and you will almost certainly notice some instability in the EPOC emulator if features specific to one of the SDKs are accidentally invoked in an unsupported manner.

You should set up drive letters for each of the SDKs you wish to install before you begin the installation process.

The installer should start automatically when you insert the CD which accompanies this book. You will be presented with the option of installing an SDK or the sample code. You cannot install code unless you have a valid SDK installation.

The EPOC Emulator

The principal platform for all EPOC development is the Microsoft Windows-hosted EPOC Emulator. The Emulator uses the Win32 API to emulate the underlying hardware services required by EPOC devices. It implements all user-side EPOC APIs exactly as on an EPOC machine to provide a full emulation of a generic EPOC device.

The EPOC emulator is at the heart of the C++, OPL and Java SDKs. Native EPOC C++ software is built and debugged on the EPOC Emulator using Microsoft Visual C++, and then rebuilt for target machines using a customised GNU C++ Compiler implementation. Java and OPL are interpreted languages. Programs may be developed and debugged under the Emulator, and then transferred to an EPOC target machine without rebuilding.

The emulators provided on the accompanying CD have one difference from those supplied directly by Symbian: the EPOC Web browser is not included. However, the browser is available separately as a free download to anyone who registers with the Symbian Developer Network at http://www.symbiandevnet.com/.

C++ SDK

EPOC is written in C++. The C++ SDK provides access to all EPOC user-side APIs. EPOC is thoroughly object-oriented in its design, giving the compactness and re-use essential to produce efficient software for the device classes it targets.

The GNU C++ Compiler is required to allow compilation for native platforms (i.e. for deploying applications to EPOC devices), and is supplied with the C++ SDK. Microsoft Visual C++ (not supplied) is required for PC-based development. EPOC Connect (not supplied) is used to transfer binaries to the EPOC target machine.

System requirements

To install and run the EPOC Release 5 C++ SDK you will need:

- ❏ a PC running Windows NT 4.0, Windows 95 or Windows 98
- ❏ 300MB of free space
- ❏ Microsoft Visual C++ Version 5.0 or 6.0 (Version 6.0 requires a patch to be applied to some EPOC SDK components - this patch is included and applied by the installer program.)
- ❏ speed and RAM requirements as for Microsoft Visual C++ (133MHz, 64MB minimum recommended - but the more the better)

To browse the SDK documentation, you will need:

- ❏ a web browser which supports tables, for the HTML format
- ❏ a compatible browser, such as Microsoft Internet Explorer 4.0 or above, for the HTML Help

Tips

- ❏ During the installation, you should choose to install software (not browse the documentation).
- ❏ You needn't worry about shutting down much software!
- ❏ Remember that you will need to have a substed or otherwise mapped drive available.
- ❏ You should choose to install everything.
- ❏ In the unlikely event that you're using an old Windows 95 system with 32k blocks on your hard disk, watch out for disk full errors, as there are lots of small files in the SDK.
- ❏ You should always install Perl if you don't have a copy since much of EPOC toolchain requires it to be available.
- ❏ If you already have Symbian's version of GCC installed, you don't need to reinstall it: keep the one you have and just amend your path to suit.
- ❏ Don't forget to install the MSVC6 patch if you need it.
- ❏ Remember that you have to reboot before actually using the SDK.

> **Although the SDK will run happily on Windows 9x or NT 4.0, Symbian recommend that you consider using NT for serious development, as the platform is considerably more stable and suitable for heavy programming use.**

After installing and restarting, use the `path` command to ensure that the installer has properly amended your system path variable. It should contain `\epoc32\tools\`, `\epoc32\gcc\bin\` and `\epoc32\release\wins\deb\`, all on the drive where you installed the SDK, and also the path to the `Perl\bin` directory, wherever you installed that. If there is a problem (it sometimes happens under Windows 9x), make sure you change your `autoexec.bat` file to set the path correctly on startup.

Java SDK

The EPOC SDK for Java provides a Java Compatible VM and library for the EPOC platform, and supports implementation of Java applications and applets written using any standard Java development system. The EPOC Emulator is included, together with tools and utilities shared with other EPOC SDKs.

Native method development is also supported – note that this requires the EPOC C++ SDK.

System requirements are the same as for the C++ SDK. Many of the same tips apply.

OPL SDK

While OPL may be programmed directly on many EPOC devices, for convenience, the OPL SDK supports PC-based development using the EPOC Emulator and tools and utilities shared with other EPOC SDKs. OPL provides access to EPOC's most commonly-used APIs. Other APIs may be accessed using OPL extensions (known as OPXs) written in C++. OPXs may also be used to implement optimised library functions for OPL programs.

OPX development requires an EPOC C++ SDK.

System requirements are the same as for the C++ SDK. Many of the same tips apply.

Connectivity SDK

The EPOC Connectivity SDK supports conversion and synchronisation of EPOC data formats with a range of PC applications. Additionally, it supports remote control of EPOC devices from a PC. PC-based applications may be developed in either Windows C++, or Visual Basic. Together with the other EPOC SDKs, this provides an exceptionally flexible basis for rapid development of corporate connectivity applications.

The EPOC Connectivity SDK is the only SDK that doesn't mind residing on the same drive as any of the other SDKs. Similarly, they ignore its presence; there are no common files between this SDK and any of the others.

> **EPOC Connect itself is not provided with any of the SDKs and is not available on the book CD. It is, however, always provided with EPOC devices.**

The Code

The code installer can be run once you've installed the SDK or SDKs you're interested in. You'll be asked to identify which drives contain the SDKs, and the projects will be transferred to the correct directories.

Example Projects

This appendix details the projects described throughout the book which are included on the CD.

C++ Examples

Martin Tasker's C++ example projects can be copied to your local drive by the CD's installer program. This copies the \code\pep\ directory on the CD to a \pep\ directory on the same drive as your C++ SDK.

The \pep\ subdirectories usually contain one project each. About half are independent example projects, which are covered in association with various topics in the book. The remaining projects all build up to Battleships.

The Independent Projects:

Example	Purpose
active	Basic active objects example.
buffers	Dynamic buffers.
cstring	Strings in C.
drawing	Device independent drawing, with a re-usable view, and support for zooming.
epocstring	EPOC strings, using descriptors.
helloeik	Hello World, EIKON version.
helloeikfull	Hello World, EIKON version, with finishing touches.

Table Continued on Following Page

Example	Purpose
helloeikhelp	Help for `helloeikfull`.
hellotext	Hello World, text version. The code framework is used as a basis for the `buffers` and `epocstring` examples.
memorymagic	How to allocate memory and clean it up again – and how not to.
streams	Using files and stream APIs to save and load data.

The Battleships Projects:

Example	Purpose
battleships	The full two-player Battleships game.
bsaif	The icon for Battleships.
bships1	Solo Ships, a single-player game, used as an example of an EIKON program supporting object embedding.
bsaif1	The icon for Solo Ships.
tpg	A test version of the game.

The TOGS Projects

These are all needed for `battleships`, but may also be used for other purposes:

Example	Purpose
gdp	Game Datagram Protocol (GDP) – the basic comms interface, plus three implementations (loopback, IR and SMS).
gdpchat	Test chat program using GDP.
gsdp	Game Session Datagram Protocol (GSDP) – links packets into sessions, and distinguishes session types so that different games can be played.
gsdpchat	Test chat program using GSDP.
gsdpchataif	Icon for chat.
rgcp	Reliable Game Conversation Protocol (RGCP) – adds acknowledgements, re-sending, and piggy-backing to the GSDP session, so that an RGCP client can rely on the packet data it handles.
rgcpchat	Test Converse program using RGCP.
rgcpchataif	Icon for Converse.

Most of these examples have build scripts which you invoke with `bwins` (for building for the emulator) or `bmarm` (for building for an EPOC machine). Scripts such as `bmbm`, `baif` and `bhelp` are available for building MBMs, AIFs and help files.

Programs have been tested under the emulator on Windows NT and 98, and on a Psion Series 5mx Pro and 5mx.

Java

Jonathan Allin's Java examples are copied by the install program to a `\Java Examples\` directory on the same drive as your Java SDK.

The JNI examples require the C++ SDK to be installed.

Owing to licensing restrictions, it is not possible to include the Web Browser with any of the EPOC emulators provided on the CD. However, Java applets can still be tested with the Applet Viewer provided with the EPOC SDK for Java.

WAP

The WAP examples can be installed anywhere - they do not require an SDK.

OPL

Tim Richardson's OPL examples will be copied by the install program to the `\epoc32\wins\c\` directory on the same drive as your OPL SDK. This causes them to appear on the C: drive in the EPOC emulator.

However, if you choose to install them, Steve Waddicor's OPX examples will be installed to an `\opx\` directory on the same drive as your C++ SDK.

Connectivity

Mark Shackmans's connectivity examples will be installed to a `\Connectivity Examples\` directory on the same drive as your Connectivity SDK installation.

Porting

John Forrest's Porting examples will be installed to the directories `\pepfilt1\`, `\pepfilt2\`, `\pepfilt2a\`, `\pepfilt3\`, `\pepfilt3a\`, `\pepfilt4\`, `\pepfilt5\`, `\pepfilt6\`, `\pephw\`, `\peppcfilt\`, and `\peppchw\` directories on the same drive as your C++ SDK.

The examples are described in the book, but specific instructions on compiling and installing each example can be found in the `Readme.html` files in each example's folder. John Forrest offers the following general advice:

❑ Almost all the examples are EPOC source examples, and are intended to be compiled using the SDK. The exceptions are those whose name starts with the string `peppc`, eg. `peppchw`, which are shipped as DOS-style command line programs – although it should be possible to run them under UNIX.

❑ Where relevant the applications use temporary UIDs – by convention, UID values of less than 0x10000000 can be used for development purposes, but should be treated with care. In particular programs that use such UIDs must not be shipped to end-users. If you use these examples as the basis of real programs, it is essential that you obtain unique UIDs – instructions on how to do this are given in the SDK documentation.

❑ There are no `.sis` files generated by these projects, nor custom `.bat` build files. Purple Software's experience is that when learning it is better to "do it yourself", as it were.

❑ On an EPOC target machine, it is suggested that you install .exe files in folder C:\System\Programs\, although you will have to navigate to this folder yourself and thus enable the Show 'System' folder preference in the shell. Any .app files must be installed in the \System\Apps\ folder of the same name, so that FiltUi.app should be copied to folder C:\System\Apps\FiltUi\, which must be created if necessary. Don't forget to copy any associated .dll and .rsc files into the same folder – the .rsc files are best found using the Windows Explorer Find Files command. To copy files, use the drag and drop feature of EPOC Connect (PsiWin), but use the right-hand mouse button and select Copy instead of the standard Copy and Convert variant.

❑ In particular, most of the pepfilt examples generate both a FiltUi.app and an associated FiltEng.dll. However, the examples are totally incompatible – ensure that you run the appropriate .dll with the appropriate .app, or the effect will be unpredictable. As the same target filenames are used in several examples, you must remove any old binaries when returning to an earlier project. For the Visual C++ build, use either the "clean" or "Rebuild all" commands. For the MARM build, you should use the "clean" argument to the makefile, as in nmake -f pepfilt.marm clean. For both targets it is advisable to rebuild the resources using eikrs. (This requirement arises because we have a core example – the alternative, of using different example names for each variant, has its own problems.)

❑ Virtually all of the examples require the C run-time library (STDLIB) to be installed. This is already present on the WINS emulator, but not on all EPOC machines. To see if it is present, you can look at the Add/remove Control Panel where it will be shown as "Standard C Library" – any machine without such a control panel is unlikely to have the STDLIB installed. The library is installed as part of the Web program installation, but if you need to install it directly then install the stdlib.sis file in folder \epoc32\release\marm\rel\ – eg. by double clicking on it from the Windows Explorer.

❑ On real EPOC hardware it is sometimes useful to run eshell.exe, which gives a DOS-shell style command line environment. To install this, copy eshell.exe from folder \epoc32\release\marm\rel\ in your C++ SDK installation to somewhere convenient, eg. C:\ or C:\System\Programs\ on the target machine, using EPOC Connect (PsiWin).

Project	Description
Peppchw	Original DOS-style hello world program.
Pephw	Straight rework of Peppchw as an EPOC console program.
Peppcfilt	Original DOS-style version of the filter program.
Pepfilt1	Straight rework of Peppcfilt as an EPOC console program.
Pepfilt2	The filter example adapted to work as an EPOC application, with the filter code implemented as a separate DLL. This version uses thread local storage to get around the global variables problem.
Pepfilt3	Similar to Pepfilt2: an EPOC application with the filter code as a separate DLL. However, this version uses an explicit this record, instead of thread local storage.
Pepfilt3a	Variation of Pepfilt3 where the C performs graphics draws to the screen – involves using backed-up windows.
Pepfilt4	Rework of Pepfilt3 using Active Objects to provide background processing.
Pepfilt5	Rework of Pepfilt3 using threads to support background processing.
Pepfilt6	Rework of Pepfilt3 using a RunSystem call each iteration cycle from inside the C, which recursively calls the Active Scheduler.

C

EPOC machines

The first commercially available EPOC machine, launched in June 1997, was the **Series 5** from Psion Computers. Originally containing EPOC Release 1 (ROM 1.00), it was quickly followed in August 1997 by versions containing the maintenance release EPOC Release 2 (ROM 1.01). Both types of Series 5 were upgradeable to EPOC Release 3 by November 1997. EPOC Release 3 added an integrated Email and Fax application, together with a web browser.

Shortly after the release of the Series 5, Geofox released the **Geofox One** in October 1997. It had the same processor. The screen was bigger than the Series 5's half-VGA screen at 640x320 pixels, and it featured a glidepoint pad instead of touchscreen. It also had both Compact Flash and PCMCIA expansion slots.

The formation of Symbian in 1998 was followed soon after by Oregon Scientific's announcement of the **Osaris**. It featured an upgraded version of both the ARM processor and the operating system, and is the only machine to use EPOC Release 4.

The **Series 5mx** and **5mx Pro** were both launched by Psion Computers in June 1999. They are both twice the speed of the original Series 5, and used EPOC Release 5. Symbian's Java VM is provided on CD with all Series 5Mx devices.

Ericsson launched the **MC218** the following month. While also using EPOC Release 5, the MC218 has a12 MB ROM and includes Ericsson's own EPOC WAP browser and phone-specific applications.

The **netBook** was launched for the corporate market by Psion Enterprise Computing in June 1999, at the same time as the Series 5Mx. This is the first commercially available color EPOC machine and sports a full-size 640x480 VGA screen, a 190MHz StrongARM processor, and both Compact Flash and full PCMCIA expansion slots.

Psion Computers launched the **Series 7** in July 1999. This is a retail version of the netBook which comes with a 16MB EPOC Release 5 ROM. The 16MB RAM can be expanded to 32MB via two user accessible internal memory slots.

The most recent EPOC device, and the smallest to date, weighing only 200g, is the **Revo**, launched by Psion Computers in October 1999. It features a 480x160 screen and the same 36 MHz ARM710T processor as the Series 5Mx and the MC218. It has an 8MB EPOC Release 5 ROM and the same amount of RAM.

More hardware details on these machines are contained in the following tables.

Hardware Details

Psion Series 5	
Manufacturer	Psion Computers
EPOC Version	EPOC Release 1 / EPOC Release 2 / EPOC Release 3
	Note - After August 1997 these all contained EPOC Release 2 ROMs
Processor	ARM7110 18 MHz
ROM	6MB
RAM	4MB/8MB
Screen	640 x 240 16 grey scale
Ports	1 serial (either RS232 or IrDA)
Pointing Device	Pen
Expansion	Compact Flash
Power	2 x AA or 6V DC
Size	170 x 90 x 23 mm
Weight	354g

Geofox One	
Manufacturer	Geofox
EPOC Version	EPOC Release 2 / EPOC Release 3
Processor	ARM7110 18 MHz
ROM	8MB
RAM	4MB/16MB
Screen	640 x 320 16 grey scale
Ports	1 serial (either RS232 or IrDA) + PCMCIA
Pointing Device	Glidepoint
Expansion	Compact Flash and PCMCIA

Geofox One	
Power	2 x AA or 9V DC
Size	187 x 120 x 20 mm
Weight	390g

Osaris	
Manufacturer	Oregon Scientific
EPOC Version	EPOC Release 4
Processor	ARM7111 18 MHz
ROM	8MB
RAM	4MB/8MB
Screen	320 x 200 16 grey scale
Ports	2 serial (1 x RS232 1 x IrDA)
Pointing Device	Pen
Expansion	Compact Flash
Power	2 x AA or 4.5V DC
Size	170 x 90 x 23 mm
Weight	354g

Psion Series 5mx	
Manufacturer	Psion Computers
EPOC Version	EPOC Release 5
Processor	ARM710T 36 MHz
ROM	10MB
RAM	16MB
Screen	640 x 240 16 grey scale
Ports	2 serial (1 x RS232 1 x IrDA)
Pointing Device	Pen
Expansion	Compact Flash
Power	2 x AA or 6V DC
Size	170 x 90 x 23 mm
Weight	354g

Psion Series 5mx Pro	
Manufacturer	Psion Computers
EPOC Version	EPOC Release 5
	The operating system and custom application suites are loaded from CF card at system boot time
Processor	ARM710T 36 MHz
ROM	0MB
RAM	24MB
Screen	640 x 240 16 grey scale
Ports	2 serial (1 x RS232 1 x IrDA)
Pointing Device	Pen
Expansion	Compact Flash
Power	2 x AA or 6V DC
Size	170 x 90 x 23 mm
Weight	354g

Ericsson MC218	
Manufacturer	Ericsson
EPOC Version	EPOC Release 5
Processor	ARM710T 36 MHz
ROM	12MB
RAM	16MB
Screen	640 x 240 16 grey scale
Ports	2 serial (1 x RS232 1 x IrDA)
Pointing Device	Pen
Expansion	Compact Flash
Power	2 x AA or 6V DC
Size	170 x 90 x 23 mm
Weight	354g
Software	The MC218 includes Ericsson's WAP browser and phone apps

Psion netBook	
Manufacturer	Psion Enterprise Computing
EPOC Version	EPOC Release 5
	The operating system and custom application suites are loaded from CF card at system boot time
Processor	StrongARM1100 190 MHz
ROM	0MB
RAM	32/64MB
Screen	640 x 480 colour
Ports	2 serial (1 x RS232 1 x IrDA)
Pointing Device	Pen
Expansion	Compact Flash, Type I/II PCMCIA, IBM MicroDrive
Power	Removable Li-Ion rechargeable or 15.5V DC
Size	235 x 182 x 37 mm
Weight	1150g

Psion Series 7	
Manufacturer	Psion Computers
EPOC Version	EPOC Release 5
Processor	StrongARM1100 133 MHz
ROM	16MB
RAM	16MB (upgradable to 32 MB)
Screen	640 x 480 colour
Ports	2 serial (1 x RS232 1 x IrDA)
Pointing Device	Pen
Expansion	Compact Flash, Type I/II PCMCIA and 2 x Internal memory slots
Power	Removable Li-Ion rechargeable or 15.5V DC
Size	235 x 182 x 37 mm
Weight	1150g

Psion Revo	
Manufacturer	Psion Computers
EPOC Version	EPOC Release 5
Processor	ARM710T 36 MHz
ROM	8MB
RAM	8MB
Screen	480 x 160 16 grey scale
Ports	2 serial (1 x RS232 1 x IrDA)
Pointing Device	Pen
Expansion	None
Power	Inbuilt rechargeables or 6V DC
Size	157 x 79 x 18 mm
Weight	200g

D

Developer Resources

Whilst this book should have given you a thorough grounding in programming for the Symbian platform, the nature of mobile computing is that it is developing very fast. In order to keep up to date with technology changes, as well as polishing your EPOC code and programming techniques, there are a number of places you can turn to as a Symbian developer.

Symbian Developer Network

The best resource available is undoubtedly the technical support provided on-line by Symbian. This has moved from its old home on the EPOC World website (http://developer.epocworld.com/) to a new home, with new services, on the Symbian Developer Network at http://www.symbiandevnet.com/.

This gives registered members free access to all Symbian's published SDKs and tools, as well as the supporting knowledge bases. In addition, a fully comprehensive technical library and download area provide access to SDK updates, new documentation, sample code, patches and technology demos.

Most services are available through the web site http://www.symbiandevnet.com/, where industry, training, technical and event news is published regularly. Users are invited to join several targeted news groups and "Professional Members only" support forums giving every user access to the expertise available from the Symbian developer community world-wide. In addition, developers are updated on conferences and seminars hosted by the Symbian Developer Network in the United States, Europe and Asia-Pacific regions.

Developers wishing to have confidential and secured access to the support engineers at Symbian may access the Premium Support Programme from the web site. This is a paid service available to all Professional Members wishing to have a private line of communication to Symbian technical support staff.

Other on-line resources

The Web sites of EPOC licensees are fruitful places to start looking for technical information on specific hardware devices. For obvious historical reasons, Psion's web site at http://www.psion.com has the most information and the most links. Many of the third party Psion web sites have information which would be of interest to any EPOC developer. Third-party EPOC web sites are also beginning to appear: http://www.go32.com is an excellent example.

There are also a number of comp.sys.psion newsgroups which, while originally being devoted exclusively to Psion products, contain much that is useful to all EPOC developers. The Psion and Symbian conferences run by members of the British CIX conferencing system (http://www.cix.co.uk/subscribe/index.html) are also reliable places to look for independent discussion on all matters EPOC.

As comprehensive a list of Java URLs as you could hope to find is available from http://www.javalobby.org/. WAP developers will no doubt be aware of the Application development toolkits which are available for free download from Nokia http://www.forum.nokia.com/developers/wap/wap.html and Ericsson http://www.ericsson.com/WAP/.

Wrox Support

Wrox Press provides technical support for all its books via the website at http://www.wrox.com and via e-mail to support@wrox.com. The web site also features code download and errata sections, where you will be able to find updates and patches for the code featured in the book.

You'll also find information on Wrox's own Programmer to Programmer™ web sites and conferences, where you'll be able to keep up with the latest developments in the field.

When you email our support staff, make sure you include the title of the book, the last four digits of the ISBN (in the case of this book, that's 303X), and a page reference to the point in the book where you have a problem.

We will make every effort to answer any query you have which relates directly to technical issues and code included in the book, but we regret we can't offer assistance on topics beyond the book's scope. However, we now offer a service which allows our readers to get together to help one another out, via our website at http://p2p.wrox.com.

p2p.wrox.com

If you join the discussion lists with other readers at http://p2p.wrox.com, there'll be a chance to discuss specific issues raised by the book, as well as more general problems relating to Symbian development. The discussion lists at http://p2p.wrox.com are moderated by Wrox staff to ensure that there's no spam, and only useful, relevant discussion. You can receive the discussion lists via e-mail, or get a selected digest of the discussion, or simply browse the discussion archives online. The mailing list software ensures that your e-mail address is kept private so you don't need to worry about it falling into the wrong hands.

If you have any queries about this book, or Wrox books in general, or any comments, please don't hesitate to e-mail us at feedback@wrox.com.

E

CD Software Licenses

The following are the licenses that apply to the software included on the CD with this book. Please read the relevant license before installing any of the components from the CD.

Professional Symbian Programming Code License agreement

```
PLEASE READ THIS LICENCE AGREEMENT CAREFULLY:

This Licence Agreement ("AGREEMENT") is a legal agreement
between you (either an individual or an organisation such as
a company) and Symbian Ltd ("SYMBIAN"). This licence
agreement covers the use of any of the code ("CODE") included
either in the text of Professional Symbian Programming (the
"BOOK") or installed from the \pep\ directory and its
subdirectories on the CD-ROM accompanying the BOOK.

By copying installing or otherwise using the CODE, you agree
to be bound by the terms of this AGREEMENT. If you do not
agree to the terms of this AGREEMENT, SYMBIAN will not
license the CODE to you. In such event, you may not use or
copy the CODE, and you must destroy any copies of the CODE in
your possession.

This AGREEMENT constitutes the entire agreement and
understanding between the parties with respect to its subject
matter and replaces all previous written or oral agreements,
including all express or implied terms, and all
representations between, or undertakings by, the parties with
regard to such subject matter. This AGREEMENT cannot be
changed except by written agreement between the parties.
```

PRODUCT LICENCE

The CODE is protected by international copyright laws and treaty provisions, as well as other intellectual property laws and treaties. The CODE is licensed, not sold.

GRANT OF LICENCE

This AGREEMENT grants you the following rights:

a) The non-exclusive and limited right to use the CODE for learning about the SYMBIAN EPOC operating system ("EPOC") or for designing, developing and testing software products ("PRODUCTS") that

i) operate on devices that make use of EPOC as their primary operating system; or
ii) are a software development tool for EPOC; or
iii) utilise, or convert to or from, EPOC file formats.

b) The right to make a single back-up copy of the CODE. You may use the back-up copy solely for back-up and archival purposes.

DESCRIPTION OF LIMITATIONS ON THE USE OF SOURCE CODE FOR THE TRANSACTION-ORIENTED GAMES STACK ("TOGS CODE")

The TOGS CODE is defined by the contents of the \code\pep\cpp\gdp\, \code\pep\cpp\gsdp\, \code\pep\cpp\gsdpchat\, \code\pep\cpp\rgcp\, \code\pep\cpp\rgcpchat and \code\pep\cpp\battleships\ directories on the CD-ROM accompanying the BOOK.

a) You must not change the specification and behaviour of the TOGS CODE APIs, of the TOGS CODE communications protocols, or of the TOGS CODE file formats unless you also change the identifying feature of the component or components of TOGS CODE whose behaviour you have modified. In particular:

i) You may not change the APIs to the Game Datagram Protocol ("GDP") or the Game Session Datagram Protocol ("GSDP") without changing the name and Unique Identifier ("UID") of the associated DLL.
ii) You may not change the GSDP server behaviour without also changing the server name.
iii) You may not change the behaviour of the Infra-red ("IR") implementation of GDP without also changing the class name of its entry in the IR Link Management Protocol ("IrLMP") Information Access Service.
iv) You may not change the behaviour of the Short Message Service ("SMS") implementation of GDP without changing the tag used in its SMS message format.
v) You may not change the behaviour of GSDP unless you use different GDP implementations from those used in the TOGS CODE.
vi) You may not change the behaviour of GSDP chat without changing the GSDP game ID associated with it.
vii) You may not change the behaviour of RGCP chat without changing the GSDP game ID associated with it.
viii) You may not change the behaviour of the Battleships Protocol ("BSP") without changing the GSDP game ID associated with it.

ix) You may not change the behaviour of the Reliable Game Conversation Protocol ("RGCP").

b) You may not test GDP implementations except in isolation from other established uses of TOGS CODE-based applications.

DESCRIPTION OF OTHER RIGHTS AND LIMITATIONS

a)   Rental.   You may not rent or lease the CODE.
b)   Redistribution.   With the exception the components of the CODE covered by section c) below you must not distribute copies of the CODE in source form. You may distribute object code versions of the unmodified code provided that you comply with section f) below.
c)   Modification.   Subject to the limitations on the TOGS CODE source described above, you may modify the CODE for the purpose of learning about EPOC or for designing, developing and testing PRODUCTS and you may distribute source and object code versions of this modified code ("MODIFIED CODE"), provided that you comply with section f) below.
d)   Software Transfer.   You may not transfer any of your rights under this AGREEMENT.
e)   Termination.   The AGREEMENT lasts until you terminate it by destroying all copies of the CODE (including any printed materials and media). If you fail to comply with the conditions of the AGREEMENT, then SYMBIAN will terminate the AGREEMENT and you will be required, by the terms and conditions of the AGREEMENT, to destroy all copies of the CODE (including any printed materials and media).
f)   Redistribution.   You may distribute the MODIFIED CODE only as part of a software product ("APPLICATION") that adds significant functionality to that originally provided by the CODE provided that:

1.   Where the recipient of the APPLICATION is an end user you do not permit your end users further distribution of the MODIFIED CODE,
2.   Where the recipient of the APPLICATION is a distributor they may further distribute your APPLICATION including any MODIFIED CODE provided they comply with all the terms of this AGREEMENT and provided that such MODIFIED CODE is only distributed as part of your APPLICATION.
3.   You do not use SYMBIAN's trademarks, name or logos on or in relation to your Application or otherwise to market your APPLICATION,
4. You agree to indemnify and hold SYMBIAN harmless from and against any and all damages, losses, costs, claims, expenditure and liability arising out of or related to the use or distribution of your APPLICATION,
5.   You agree that SYMBIAN reserves all rights not expressly granted.
6.   You agree to include a copyright notice in the Application of equal prominence as any other copyright notice as follows: "This product includes software licensed from Symbian Ltd (c) Symbian Ltd 2000"

UPDATES

UPDATES may be made available by SYMBIAN or its publishers
from time to time. By installing or otherwise using such
UPDATES you agree to be bound by any ADDITIONAL TERMS that
may accompany such UPDATES. If you do not agree with such
ADDITIONAL TERMS you may not install, copy or otherwise use
such UPDATES.

COPYRIGHTS AND PATENTS

All title and copyrights in and to the CODE are owned by
SYMBIAN. All rights not specifically granted under this
AGREEMENT are reserved by SYMBIAN. All patent rights and
rights in inventions, in and to the CODE that are owned by
SYMBIAN are not licensed to you. SYMBIAN reserves its rights
to license these rights to you on commercial terms.
Commercial production and distribution of PRODUCTS may
infringe these rights. You agree to inform any recipient of
an Application of the limited scope of rights passed onto it.
Symbian reserves its rights to separately license these
rights to any recipient of an Application.

DISCLAIMER OF WARRANTY

SYMBIAN PROVIDES NO WARRANTY, TO THE EXTENT PERMITTED BY
APPLICABLE LAW. EXCEPT WHERE OTHERWISE STATED IN WRITING,
SYMBIAN PROVIDES THE CODE "AS IS" WITHOUT WARRANTY OF ANY
KIND, EITHER EXPRESSED OR IMPLIED, STATUTORY OR OTHERWISE,
INCLUDING, BUT NOT LIMITED TO, ANY IMPLIED WARRANTIES OF
MERCHANTABILITY AND FITNESS FOR A PARTICULAR PURPOSE. THIS
CODE IS LICENSED TO YOU WITHOUT FEE AND ACCORDINGLY YOU
ACCEPT THAT THE ENTIRE RISK AS TO THE QUALITY AND PERFORMANCE
OF THE CODE IS WITH YOU AND YOU AGREE NOT TO TAKE ANY
INCONSISTENT POSITION. SHOULD THE CODE PROVE DEFECTIVE, YOU
ASSUME THE COST OF ALL NECESSARY SERVICING, REPAIR OR
CORRECTION OF THE CODE AND OF ANY PRODUCT OR APPLICATION. IN
NO EVENT UNLESS REQUIRED BY APPLICABLE LAW WILL SYMBIAN BE
LIABLE TO YOU FOR DAMAGES (WHETHER ARISING IN CONTRACT, TORT,
NEGLIGENCE OR OTHERWISE), INCLUDING ANY LOST PROFITS, LOST
MONIES, LOST TIME, LOSSES ATTRIBUTABLE IN WHOLE OR PART TO
ANY DEFECTS IN THE DESIGN OR PERFORMANCE OF THE CODE OR ANY
PRODUCT OR APPLICATION, OR SPECIAL, INCIDENTAL OR
CONSEQUENTIAL DAMAGES ARISING OUT OF THE USE OR INABILITY TO
USE THE CODE, INCLUDING BUT NOT LIMITED TO LOSS OF DATA OR
DATA BEING RENDERED INACCURATE OR LOSSES SUSTAINED BY THIRD
PARTIES OR A FAILURE OF THE CODE TO OPERATE WITH PROGRAMS NOT
DISTRIBUTED BY SYMBIAN, EVEN IF SYMBIAN HAS BEEN ADVISED OF
THE POSSIBILITY OF SUCH DAMAGES, OR FOR ANY CLAIM BY ANY
OTHER PARTY. NOTHING IN THIS AGREEMENT LIMITS SYMBIAN'S
LIABILITY FOR DEATH OR PERSONAL INJURY CAUSED BY ITS
NEGLIGENCE.

Symbian EPOC Release 5 C++ SDK License Agreement

PLEASE READ THIS LICENCE AGREEMENT CAREFULLY:

This Licence Agreement ("AGREEMENT") is a legal agreement between you (either an individual or an organisation such as a company) and Symbian Ltd ("SYMBIAN"). This licence agreement covers the use of the Symbian EPOC Release 5 C++ Software Development Kit ("SDK"). The SDK includes "online" or electronic documentation, sample applications, development tools, utilities, computer software, and any printed materials. By installing or otherwise using the SDK, you agree to be bound by the terms of this AGREEMENT. If you do not agree to the terms of this AGREEMENT, SYMBIAN will not license the SDK to you. In such event, you may not use or copy the SDK, and you must destroy any copies of the SDK in your possession.

This AGREEMENT constitutes the entire agreement and understanding between the parties with respect to its subject matter and replaces all previous written or oral agreements, including all express or implied terms, and all representations between, or undertakings by, the parties with regard to such subject matter. This AGREEMENT cannot be changed except by written agreement between the parties.

PRODUCT LICENCE

The SDK is protected by international copyright laws and treaty provisions, as well as other intellectual property laws and treaties.
The SDK is licensed, not sold.

GRANT OF LICENCE

This AGREEMENT grants you the following rights:
a) The non-exclusive and limited right to use one copy of the SDK by you (if you are an individual) or by any employee (if you are an organisation) for designing, developing and testing software products ("PRODUCTS") that
i) operate on devices that make use of the SYMBIAN EPOC operating system ("EPOC") as their primary operating system; or
ii) are a software development tool for EPOC; or
iii) utilise, or convert to or from, EPOC file formats.
b) The right to make a single back-up copy of the SDK. You may use the back-up copy solely for back-up and archival purposes.
c) The non-exclusive and limited right to make a single copy of the electronic documentation contained in the SDK solely for the purpose of aiding you in the designing, developing and testing of PRODUCTS.

DESCRIPTION OF OTHER RIGHTS AND LIMITATIONS

a) Limitations on Reverse Engineering, Decompilation and Disassembly. You may not reverse engineer, decompile, or disassemble the SDK, except and only to the extent that such activity is expressly permitted by applicable law. Notwithstanding this limitation, Symbian will terminate this Agreement if you attempt or have attempted to reverse engineer, decompile, or disassemble the SDK in breach of this provision.

b) Rental. You may not rent or lease the SDK.

c) Redistribution. With the exception the components of the SDK covered by sections d) and e) below you must not distribute copies of the SDK, or any component of the SDK.

d) Example Code. You may use and modify the source code contained in the \epoc32ex\, \boss\, \wpeng\, \word\, \apparc\tsrc\, \apparc\tdata\ and \eikon\src\ directories of the SDK and their subdirectories ("EXAMPLE CODE"), but solely for the purpose of designing, developing and testing PRODUCTS and you may distribute source and object code versions of this modified EXAMPLE CODE ("MODIFIED CODE"), provided that you comply with section h) below.

e) Redistributable Components. You may distribute the object code components contained in the \epoc32\release\winc\deb\, \epoc32\release\winc\rel\, and \epoc32\tools\epocinst\ directories of the SDK ("REDISTRIBUTABLE COMPONENTS") provided that you comply with section h) below.

f) Software Transfer. You may not transfer any of your rights under this AGREEMENT.

g) Termination. The AGREEMENT lasts until you terminate it by destroying all copies of the SDK (including any printed materials and media). If you fail to comply with the conditions of the AGREEMENT, then SYMBIAN will terminate the AGREEMENT and you will be required, by the terms and conditions of the AGREEMENT, to destroy all copies of the SDK (including any printed materials and media).

h) Redistribution. You may distribute the MODIFIED CODE and REDISTRIBUTABLE COMPONENTS only as part of a software product ("APPLICATION") that adds significant functionality to the original functionality provided by the EXAMPLE CODE or REDISTRIBUTABLE COMPONENTS provided that:

1. Where the recipient of the APPLICATION is an end user you do not permit your end users further distribution of the MODIFIED CODE or REDISTRIBUTABLE COMPONENTS,

2. Where the recipient of the APPLICATION is a distributor they may further distribute your APPLICATION including any MODIFIED CODE or REDISTRIBUTABLE COMPONENTS provided they comply with all the terms of this AGREEMENT and provided that such MODIFIED CODE or REDISTRIBUTABLE COMPONENTS are only distributed as part of your APPLICATION.

3. You do not use SYMBIAN's trademarks, name or logos on or in relation to your Application or otherwise to market your APPLICATION,
4. You agree to indemnify and hold SYMBIAN harmless from and against any and all damages, losses, costs, claims, expenditure and liability arising out of or related to the use or distribution of your APPLICATION,
5. You agree that SYMBIAN reserves all rights not expressly granted.
6. You agree to include a copyright notice in the Application of equal prominence as any other copyright notice as follows: "This product includes software licensed from Symbian Ltd (c) Symbian Ltd 1998-9"

UPDATES

UPDATES may be made available by SYMBIAN from time to time. By installing or otherwise using such UPDATES you agree to be bound by any ADDITIONAL TERMS that may accompany such UPDATES. If you do not agree with such ADDITIONAL TERMS you may not install, copy or otherwise use such UPDATES.

COPYRIGHTS AND PATENTS

All title and copyrights in and to the SDK (including but not limited to any images, drawings, text and applications incorporated into the SDK), the accompanying printed materials, and any copies of the SDK, are variously owned by SYMBIAN and SYMBIAN suppliers. You may not copy any printed materials accompanying the SDK. All rights not specifically granted under this AGREEMENT are reserved by SYMBIAN. All patent rights and rights in inventions, in and to EPOC and in and to the SDK that are owned by SYMBIAN are not licensed to you. SYMBIAN reserves its rights to license these rights to you on commercial terms. Commercial production and distribution of PRODUCTS may infringe these rights. You agree to inform any recipient of an Application of the limited scope of rights passed onto it. Symbian reserves its rights to separately license these rights to any recipient of an Application.

DISCLAIMER OF WARRANTY

SYMBIAN PROVIDES NO WARRANTY, TO THE EXTENT PERMITTED BY APPLICABLE LAW. EXCEPT WHERE OTHERWISE STATED IN WRITING, SYMBIAN PROVIDES THE SDK "AS IS" WITHOUT WARRANTY OF ANY KIND, EITHER EXPRESSED OR IMPLIED, STATUTORY OR OTHERWISE, INCLUDING, BUT NOT LIMITED TO, ANY

IMPLIED WARRANTIES OF MERCHANTABILITY AND
FITNESS FOR A PARTICULAR PURPOSE. THIS SDK IS
LICENSED TO YOU WITHOUT FEE AND ACCORDINGLY
YOU ACCEPT THAT THE ENTIRE RISK AS TO THE QUALITY
AND PERFORMANCE OF THE SDK IS WITH YOU AND YOU
AGREE NOT TO TAKE ANY INCONSISTENT POSITION.
SHOULD THE SDK PROVE DEFECTIVE, YOU ASSUME THE
COST OF ALL NECESSARY SERVICING, REPAIR OR
CORRECTION OF THE SDK AND OF ANY PRODUCT OR
APPLICATION.

IN NO EVENT UNLESS REQUIRED BY APPLICABLE LAW
WILL SYMBIAN BE LIABLE TO YOU FOR DAMAGES
(WHETHER ARISING IN CONTRACT, TORT, NEGLIGENCE
OR OTHERWISE), INCLUDING ANY LOST PROFITS, LOST
MONIES, LOST TIME, LOSSES ATTRIBUTABLE IN WHOLE
OR PART TO ANY DEFECTS IN THE DESIGN OR
PERFORMANCE OF THE SDK OR ANY PRODUCT OR
APPLICATION, OR SPECIAL, INCIDENTAL OR
CONSEQUENTIAL DAMAGES ARISING OUT OF THE USE OR
INABILITY TO USE THE SDK, INCLUDING BUT NOT
LIMITED TO LOSS OF DATA OR DATA BEING RENDERED
INACCURATE OR LOSSES SUSTAINED BY THIRD ARTIES
OR A FAILURE OF THE SDK TO OPERATE WITH PROGRAMS
NOT DISTRIBUTED BY SYMBIAN, EVEN IF SYMBIAN HAS
BEEN ADVISED OF THE POSSIBILITY OF SUCH DAMAGES,
OR FOR ANY CLAIM BY ANY OTHER PARTY. NOTHING IN
THIS AGREEMENT LIMITS SYMBIAN'S LIABILITY FOR
DEATH OR PERSONAL INJURY CAUSED BY ITS
NEGLIGENCE.

Symbian EPOC Release 5 Java SDK License Agreement

PLEASE READ THIS LICENCE AGREEMENT CAREFULLY:

This Licence Agreement ("AGREEMENT") is a legal agreement
between you (either an individual or an organisation such
as a company) and Symbian Ltd ("SYMBIAN").
This licence agreement covers the use of the Symbian EPOC
Release 5 Software Development Kit for Java ("SDK"). The
SDK includes "online" or electronic documentation, sample
applications, development tools, utilities, computer
software, and any printed materials. By installing or
otherwise using the SDK, you agree to be bound by the
terms of this AGREEMENT.
If you do not agree to the terms of this AGREEMENT,
SYMBIAN will not license the SDK to you. In such event,
you may not use or copy the SDK, and you must destroy any
copies of the SDK in your possession.
The SDK is provided in the absence of any devices that
make use of EPOC as their primary operating system that
are capable of running Java software. The provision of this
SDK in no way obligates SYMBIAN or SYMBIAN's licensees to
make available such devices at any time in the future.

PRODUCT LICENCE

The SDK is protected by international copyright laws and
treaty provisions, as well as other intellectual property
laws and treaties. The SDK is licensed, not sold.

GRANT OF LICENCE

This AGREEMENT grants you the following rights:
a) The non-exclusive and limited right to use one copy of
the SDK by you (if you are an individual) or by any
employee (if you are an organisation) for the sole purpose
of designing, developing and testing software products
("PRODUCTS") that operate on devices that make use of the
SYMBIAN EPOC operating system ("EPOC") as their primary
operating system.
b) The right to make a single back-up copy of the SDK. You
may use the back-up copy solely for back-up and archival
purposes.
c) The non-exclusive and limited right to make a single
copy of the electronic documentation contained in the SDK
solely for the purpose of aiding you in the designing,
developing and testing of PRODUCTS.

DESCRIPTION OF OTHER RIGHTS AND LIMITATIONS

a) Limitations on Reverse Engineering, Decompilation and
Disassembly. You may not reverse engineer, decompile, or
disassemble the SDK, except and only to the extent that
such activity is expressly permitted by applicable law.
Notwithstanding this limitation, Symbian will terminate
this Agreement if you attempt or have attempted to reverse
engineer, decompile, or disassemble the SDK in breach of
this provision.
b) Rental. You may not rent or lease the SDK.
c) Redistribution. With the exception of the components
of the SDK covered by section d) below you must not
distribute copies of the SDK, or any component of the SDK.
d) Example Code. You may use and modify the source code
contained in the \examples\ directory of the SDK and its
subdirectories ("EXAMPLE CODE"), but solely for the
purpose of designing, developing and testing PRODUCTS and
you may distribute source and object code versions of this
modified EXAMPLE CODE ("MODIFIED CODE"), provided that you
comply with section g) below.
e) Software Transfer. You may not transfer any of your
rights under this AGREEMENT.
f) Termination. The AGREEMENT lasts until you terminate it
by destroying all copies of the SDK (including any printed
materials and media). If you fail to comply with the
conditions of the AGREEMENT, then SYMBIAN will terminate the
AGREEMENT and you will be required, by the terms and
conditions of the AGREEMENT, to destroy all copies of the
SDK (including any printed materials and media).
g) Redistribution. You may distribute the MODIFIED CODE
only as part of a software product ("APPLICATION") that
adds significant functionality to the original
functionality provided by the EXAMPLE CODE provided that:
1. Where the recipient of the APPLICATION is an end user you
do not permit your end users further distribution of the
MODIFIED CODE,
2. Where the recipient of the APPLICATION is a distributor
they may further distribute your APPLICATION including any
MODIFIED CODE provided they comply with all the terms of
this AGREEMENT and provided that such MODIFIED CODE is only
distributed as part of your APPLICATION.

3. You do not use SYMBIAN's trademarks, name or logos on or in relation to your Application or otherwise to market your APPLICATION,

4. You agree to indemnify and hold SYMBIAN harmless from and against any and all damages, losses, costs, claims, expenditure and liability arising out of or related to the use or distribution of your APPLICATION,

5. You agree that SYMBIAN reserves all rights not expressly granted.

6. You agree to include a copyright notice in the Application of equal prominence as any other copyright notice as follows: "This product includes software licensed from Symbian Ltd (c) Symbian Ltd 1998-9"

UPDATES

UPDATES may be made available by SYMBIAN from time to time. By installing or otherwise using such UPDATES you agree to be bound by any ADDITIONAL TERMS that may accompany such UPDATES. If you do not agree with such ADDITIONAL TERMS you may not install, copy or otherwise use such UPDATES. SYMBIAN is not obligated to provide upgrades or remedy any faults or problems with this SDK.

COPYRIGHTS AND PATENTS

All title and copyrights in and to the SDK (including but not limited to any images, drawings, text and applications incorporated into the SDK), the accompanying printed materials, and any copies of the SDK, are variously owned by SYMBIAN and SYMBIAN suppliers. You may not copy any printed materials accompanying the SDK. All rights not specifically granted under this AGREEMENT are reserved by SYMBIAN. All patent rights and rights in inventions, in and to EPOC and in and to the SDK that are owned by SYMBIAN are not licensed to you. SYMBIAN reserves its rights to license these rights to you on commercial terms. Commercial production and distribution of PRODUCTS may infringe these rights. You agree to inform any recipient of an Application of the limited scope of rights passed onto it. SYMBIAN reserves its rights to separately license these rights to any recipient of an Application.

DISCLAIMER OF WARRANTY

SYMBIAN PROVIDES NO WARRANTY, TO THE EXTENT PERMITTED BY APPLICABLE LAW. EXCEPT WHERE OTHERWISE STATED IN WRITING, SYMBIAN PROVIDES THE SDK "AS IS" WITHOUT WARRANTY OF ANY KIND, EITHER EXPRESSED OR IMPLIED, STATUTORY OR OTHERWISE, INCLUDING, BUT NOT LIMITED TO, ANY IMPLIED WARRANTIES OF MERCHANTABILITY AND FITNESS FOR A PARTICULAR PURPOSE. THIS SDK IS LICENSED TO YOU WITHOUT FEE AND ACCORDINGLY YOU ACCEPT THAT THE ENTIRE RISK AS TO THE QUALITY AND PERFORMANCE OF THE SDK IS WITH YOU AND YOU AGREE NOT TO TAKE ANY INCONSISTENT POSITION. SHOULD THE SDK PROVE DEFECTIVE, YOU ASSUME THE COST OF ALL NECESSARY SERVICING, REPAIR OR CORRECTION OF THE SDK AND OF ANY PRODUCT OR APPLICATION.

IN NO EVENT UNLESS REQUIRED BY APPLICABLE LAW WILL SYMBIAN BE LIABLE TO YOU FOR DAMAGES, (WHETHER ARISING IN CONTRACT, TORT, NEGLIGENCE OR OTHERWISE) INCLUDING ANY LOST PROFITS, LOST MONIES, LOST TIME, LOSSES ATTRIBUTABLE IN WHOLE OR PART TO ANY DEFECTS IN THE DESIGN OR PERFORMANCE OF THE SDK OR ANY PRODUCT OR APPLICATION OR SPECIAL, INCIDENTAL OR CONSEQUENTIAL DAMAGES ARISING OUT OF THE USE OR INABILITY TO USE THE SDK (INCLUDING BUT NOT LIMITED TO LOSS OF DATA OR DATA BEING RENDERED INACCURATE OR LOSSES SUSTAINED BY THIRD PARTIES OR A FAILURE OF THE SDK TO OPERATE WITH PROGRAMS NOT DISTRIBUTED BY SYMBIAN), EVEN IF SYMBIAN HAS BEEN ADVISED OF THE POSSIBILITY OF SUCH DAMAGES, OR FOR ANY CLAIM BY ANY OTHER PARTY. NOTHING IN THIS AGREEMENT LIMITS SYMBIAN'S LIABILITY FOR DEATH OR PERSONAL INJURY CAUSED BY ITS NEGLIGENCE.

Symbian EPOC Release 5 OPL SDK License agreement

Please ensure that you understand the terms and conditions of this Agreement before installing the software. You are reminded that this is a legal Agreement between you (either an individual or an organisation) and Symbian Ltd. If you wish to view this agreement after installation it can be found in the documentation under "Read This First", "License Agreement".

PLEASE READ THIS LICENCE AGREEMENT CAREFULLY:

This Licence Agreement ("AGREEMENT") is a legal agreement between you (either an individual or an organisation such as a company) and Symbian Ltd ("SYMBIAN").
This licence agreement covers the use of the Symbian EPOC OPL Software Development Kit ("SDK"). The SDK includes "online" or electronic documentation, sample applications, development tools, utilities, computer software, and any printed materials. By installing or otherwise using the SDK, you agree to be bound by the terms of this AGREEMENT. If you do not agree to the terms of this AGREEMENT, SYMBIAN will not license the SDK to you. In such event, you may not use or copy the SDK, and you must destroy any copies of the SDK in your possession.

This AGREEMENT constitutes the entire agreement and understanding between the parties with respect to its subject matter and replaces all previous written or oral agreements, including all express or implied terms, and all representations between, or undertakings by, the parties with regard to such subject matter. This AGREEMENT cannot be changed except by written agreement between the parties.

PRODUCT LICENCE

The SDK is protected by international copyright laws and treaty provisions, as well as other intellectual property laws and treaties. The SDK is licensed, not sold.

GRANT OF LICENCE

This AGREEMENT grants you the following rights:
a) The non-exclusive and limited right to use one copy of the SDK by you (if you are an individual) or by any employee (if you are an organisation) for the sole purpose of designing, developing and testing software products ("PRODUCTS") that
i) operate on devices that make use of the SYMBIAN EPOC operating system ("EPOC") as their primary operating system; or
ii) are a software development tool for EPOC; or
iii) utilise, or convert to or from, EPOC file formats.
b) The right to make a single back-up copy of the SDK. You may use the back-up copy solely for back-up and archival purposes.
c) The non-exclusive and limited right to make a single copy of the electronic documentation contained in the SDK solely for the purpose of aiding you in the designing, developing and testing of PRODUCTS.

DESCRIPTION OF OTHER RIGHTS AND LIMITATIONS

a) Limitations on Reverse Engineering, Decompilation and Disassembly. You may not reverse engineer, decompile, or disassemble the SDK, except and only to the extent that such activity is expressly permitted by applicable law. Notwithstanding this limitation, Symbian will terminate this Agreement if you attempt or have attempted to reverse engineer, decompile, or disassemble the SDK in breach of this provision.
b) Rental. You may not rent or lease the SDK.
c) Redistribution. With the exception of the components of the SDK covered by sections d) and e) below you must not distribute copies of the SDK, or any component of the SDK.
d) Example Code. You may use and modify the source code contained in the \epoc32\wins\c\opl\ directory of the SDK ("EXAMPLE CODE"), but solely for the purpose of designing, developing and testing PRODUCTS and you may distribute source and object code versions of this modified EXAMPLE CODE ("MODIFIED CODE"), provided that you comply with section h) below.
e) Redistributable Components. You may distribute the object code components contained in the \epoc32\release\marm\rel\ and \epoc32\tools\epocinst\ directories of the SDK ("REDISTRIBUTABLE COMPONENTS") provided that you comply with section h) below.
f) Software Transfer. You may not transfer any of your rights under this AGREEMENT.
g) Termination. The AGREEMENT lasts until you terminate it by destroying all copies of the SDK (including any printed materials and media). If you fail to comply with the conditions of the AGREEMENT, then SYMBIAN will terminate the AGREEMENT and you will be required, by the terms and conditions of the AGREEMENT, to destroy all copies of the SDK (including any printed materials and media).
h) Redistribution. You may distribute the MODIFIED CODE and REDISTRIBUTABLE COMPONENTS only as part of a software product ("APPLICATION") that adds significant functionality to the original functionality provided by the EXAMPLE CODE or REDISTRIBUTABLE COMPONENTS provided that:

1. Where the recipient of the APPLICATION is an end user
you do not permit your end users further distribution of
the MODIFIED CODE or REDISTRIBUTABLE COMPONENTS,
2. Where the recipient of the APPLICATION is a
distributor they may further distribute your APPLICATION
including any MODIFIED CODE or REDISTRIBUTABLE COMPONENTS
provided they comply with all the terms of this AGREEMENT
and provided that such MODIFIED CODE or REDISTRIBUTABLE
COMPONENTS are only distributed as part of your
APPLICATION.
3. You do not use SYMBIAN's trademarks, name or logos on
or in relation to your Application or otherwise to market
your APPLICATION,
4. You agree to indemnify and hold SYMBIAN harmless from
and against any and all damages, losses, costs, claims,
expenditure and liability arising out of or related to
the use or distribution of your APPLICATION,
5. You agree that SYMBIAN reserves all rights not
expressly granted.
6. You agree to include a copyright notice in the
Application of equal prominence as any other copyright
notice as follows: "This product includes software
licensed from Symbian Ltd (c) Symbian Ltd 1999"

UPDATES

UPDATES may be made available by SYMBIAN from time to
time. By installing or otherwise using such UPDATES you
agree to be bound by any ADDITIONAL TERMS that may
accompany such UPDATES. If you do not agree with such
ADDITIONAL TERMS you may not install, copy or otherwise
use such UPDATES.

COPYRIGHTS AND PATENTS

All title and copyrights in and to the SDK (including but
not limited to any images, drawings, text and
applications incorporated into the SDK), the accompanying
printed materials, and any copies of the SDK, are
variously owned by SYMBIAN and SYMBIAN suppliers. You may
not copy any printed materials accompanying the SDK. All
rights not specifically granted under this AGREEMENT are
reserved by SYMBIAN. All patent rights and rights in
inventions, in and to EPOC and in and to the SDK that are
owned by SYMBIAN are not licensed to you. SYMBIAN
reserves its rights to license these rights to you on
commercial terms. Commercial production and distribution
of PRODUCTS may infringe these rights. You agree to
inform any recipient of an Application of the limited
scope of rights passed onto it. Symbian reserves its
rights to separately license these rights to any
recipient of an Application.

DISCLAIMER OF WARRANTY

SYMBIAN PROVIDES NO WARRANTY, TO THE EXTENT PERMITTED BY
APPLICABLE LAW. EXCEPT WHERE OTHERWISE STATED IN WRITING,
SYMBIAN PROVIDES THE SDK "AS IS" WITHOUT WARRANTY OF ANY
KIND, EITHER EXPRESSED OR IMPLIED, STATUTORY OR
OTHERWISE, INCLUDING, BUT NOT LIMITED TO, ANY IMPLIED

WARRANTIES OF MERCHANTABILITY AND FITNESS FOR A
PARTICULAR PURPOSE. THIS SDK IS LICENSED TO YOU WITHOUT
FEE AND ACCORDINGLY YOU ACCEPT THAT THE ENTIRE RISK AS TO
THE QUALITY AND PERFORMANCE OF THE SDK IS WITH YOU AND
YOU AGREE NOT TO TAKE ANY INCONSISTENT POSITION. SHOULD
THE SDK PROVE DEFECTIVE, YOU ASSUME THE COST OF ALL
NECESSARY SERVICING, REPAIR OR CORRECTION OF THE SDK AND
OF ANY PRODUCT OR APPLICATION.

IN NO EVENT UNLESS REQUIRED BY APPLICABLE LAW WILL
SYMBIAN BE LIABLE TO YOU FOR DAMAGES, (WHETHER ARISING IN
CONTRACT, TORT, NEGLIGENCE OR OTHERWISE) INCLUDING ANY
LOST PROFITS, LOST MONIES, LOST TIME, LOSSES
ATTRIBUTABLE IN WHOLE OR PART TO ANY DEFECTS IN THE
DESIGN OR PERFORMANCE OF THE SDK OR ANY PRODUCT OR
APPLICATION, OR SPECIAL, INCIDENTAL OR CONSEQUENTIAL
DAMAGES ARISING OUT OF THE USE OR INABILITY TO USE THE
SDK (INCLUDING BUT NOT LIMITED TO LOSS OF DATA OR DATA
BEING RENDERED INACCURATE OR LOSSES SUSTAINED BY THIRD
PARTIES OR A FAILURE OF THE SDK TO OPERATE WITH PROGRAMS
NOT DISTRIBUTED BY SYMBIAN), EVEN IF SYMBIAN HAS BEEN
ADVISED OF THE POSSIBILITY OF SUCH DAMAGES, OR FOR ANY
CLAIM BY ANY OTHER PARTY. NOTHING IN THIS AGREEMENT
LIMITS SYMBIAN'S LIABILITY FOR DEATH OR PERSONAL INJURY
CAUSED BY ITS NEGLIGENCE.

Symbian EPOC Release 5 Connectivity SDK License agreement

Please ensure that you understand the terms and conditions
of this Agreement before installing the software.

You are reminded that this is a legal Agreement between you
(either an individual or an organisation) and Symbian Ltd.
If you wish to view this agreement after installation it can
be found in the documentation under "Introduction", "Read
This First", "Licence Agreement".

PLEASE READ THIS LICENCE AGREEMENT CAREFULLY:

This Licence Agreement ("AGREEMENT") is a legal agreement
between you (either an individual or an organisation such as
a company) and Symbian Ltd ("SYMBIAN"). This licence
agreement covers the use of the Symbian EPOC Connect Software
Development Kit ("SDK"). The SDK includes "online" or
electronic documentation, sample applications, development
tools, utilities, computer software, and any printed
materials. By installing or otherwise using the SDK, you
agree to be bound by the terms of this AGREEMENT. If you do
not agree to the terms of this AGREEMENT, SYMBIAN will not
license the SDK to you. In such event, you may not use or
copy the SDK, and you must destroy any copies of the SDK in
your possession.

This AGREEMENT constitutes the entire agreement and
understanding between the parties with respect to its subject
matter and replaces all previous written or oral agreements,
including all express or implied terms, and all
representations between, or undertakings by, the parties with
regard to such subject matter. This AGREEMENT cannot be
changed except by written agreement between the parties.

PRODUCT LICENCE

The SDK is protected by international copyright laws and treaty provisions, as well as other intellectual property laws and treaties. The SDK is licensed, not sold.

GRANT OF LICENCE

This AGREEMENT grants you the following rights:
a) The non-exclusive and limited right to use one copy of the SDK by you (if you are an individual) or by any employee (if you are an organisation) for the sole purpose of designing, developing and testing software products ("PRODUCTS") that inter-operate with SYMBIAN's EPOC Connect software (or branded versions thereof including but not limited to "PsiWin").
b) The right to make a single back-up copy of the SDK. You may usethe back-up copy solely for back-up and archival purposes.
c) The non-exclusive and limited right to make a single copy of the electronic documentation contained in the SDK solely for the purpose of aiding you in the designing, developing and testing of PRODUCTS.

DESCRIPTION OF OTHER RIGHTS AND LIMITATIONS

a) Limitations on Reverse Engineering, Decompilation and Disassembly. You may not reverse engineer, decompile, or disassemble the SDK, except and only to the extent that such activity is expressly permitted by applicable law. Notwithstanding this limitation, SYMBIAN will terminate this AGREEMENT if you attempt or have attempted to reverse engineer, decompile, or disassemble the SDK in breach of this provision.
b) Rental. You may not rent or lease the SDK.
c) Redistribution. With the exception of the components of the SDK covered by sections d) and e) below you must not distribute copies of the SDK, or any component of the SDK.
d) Example Code. You may use and modify the source code contained in the \ConnSDK directory of the SDK and its subdirectories ("EXAMPLE CODE"), but solely for the purpose of designing, developing and testing PRODUCTS and you may distribute source and object code versions of this modified EXAMPLE CODE ("MODIFIED CODE"), provided that you comply with section h) below.
e) Redistributable Components. You may use and redistribute the object code components contained in the \epoc32\release\winc\rel directory ("REDISTRIBUTABLE COMPONENTS") provided that you comply with section h) below.
f) Software Transfer. You may not transfer any of your rights under this AGREEMENT.
g) Termination. The AGREEMENT lasts until you terminate it by destroying all copies of the SDK (including any printed materials and media). If you fail to comply with the conditions of the AGREEMENT, then SYMBIAN will terminate the AGREEMENT and you will be required, by the terms and conditions of the AGREEMENT, to destroy all copies of the SDK (including any printed materials and media).

h) Redistribution. You may distribute the MODIFIED CODE and
REDISTRIBUTABLE COMPONENTS only as part of a software
product ("APPLICATION") that adds significant functionality
to the original functionality provided by the EXAMPLE CODE
or REDISTRIBUTABLE COMPONENTS provided that:
1. Where the recipient of the APPLICATION is an end user you
do not permit your end users further distribution of the
MODIFIED CODE or REDISTRIBUTABLE COMPONENTS,
2. Where the recipient of the APPLICATION is a distributor
they may further distribute your APPLICATION including any
MODIFIED CODE or REDISTRIBUTABLE COMPONENTS provided they
comply with all the terms of this AGREEMENT and provided
that such MODIFIED CODE or REDISTRIBUTABLE COMPONENTS are
only distributed as part of your APPLICATION.
3. You do not use SYMBIAN's trademarks, name or logos on or
in relation to your APPLICATION or otherwise to market your
APPLICATION,
4. You agree to indemnify and hold SYMBIAN harmless from and
against any and all damages, losses, costs, claims,
expenditure and liability arising out of or related to the
use or distribution of your APPLICATION,
5. You agree that SYMBIAN reserves all rights not expressly
granted.
6. You agree to include a copyright notice in the APPLICATION
of equal prominence as any other copyright notice as follows:
"This product includes software licensed from Symbian Ltd (c)
Symbian Ltd 1999"

UPDATES

UPDATES may be made available by SYMBIAN from time to time.
By installing or otherwise using such UPDATES you agree to
be bound by any ADDITIONAL TERMS that may accompany such
UPDATES. If you do not agree with such ADDITIONAL TERMS you
may not install, copy or otherwise use such UPDATES.

COPYRIGHTS AND PATENTS

All title and copyrights in and to the SDK (including but not
limited to any images, drawings, text and applications
incorporated into the SDK), the accompanying printed materials,
and any copies of the SDK, are variously owned by SYMBIAN and
SYMBIAN suppliers. You may not copy any printed materials
accompanying the SDK. All rights not specifically granted under
this AGREEMENT are reserved by SYMBIAN. All patent rights and
rights in inventions, in and to EPOC and in and to the SDK
that are owned by SYMBIAN are not licensed to you. SYMBIAN
reserves its rights to license these rights to you on
commercial terms. Commercial production and distribution of
PRODUCTS may infringe these rights. You agree to inform any
recipient of an APPLICATION of the limited scope of rights
passed on to it. SYMBIAN reserves its rights to separately
license these rights to any recipient of an APPLICATION.

DISCLAIMER OF WARRANTY

SYMBIAN PROVIDES NO WARRANTY, TO THE EXTENT PERMITTED BY
APPLICABLE LAW. EXCEPT WHERE OTHERWISE STATED IN WRITING,
SYMBIAN PROVIDES THE SDK "AS IS" WITHOUT WARRANTY OF ANY KIND,
EITHER EXPRESSED OR IMPLIED, STATUTORY OR OTHERWISE, INCLUDING,
BUT NOT LIMITED TO, ANY IMPLIED WARRANTIES OF MERCHANTABILITY
AND FITNESS FOR A PARTICULAR PURPOSE. THIS SDK IS LICENSED TO YOU
WITHOUT FEE AND ACCORDINGLY YOU ACCEPT THAT THE ENTIRE RISK AS TO
THE QUALITY AND PERFORMANCE OF THE SDK IS WITH YOU AND YOU AGREE
NOT TO TAKE ANY INCONSISTENT POSITION. SHOULD THE SDK PROVE
DEFECTIVE, YOU ASSUME THE COST OF ALL NECESSARY SERVICING, REPAIR
OR CORRECTION OF THE SDK AND OF ANY PRODUCT OR APPLICATION.

IN NO EVENT UNLESS REQUIRED BY APPLICABLE LAW WILL SYMBIAN BE
LIABLE TO YOU FOR DAMAGES (WHETHER ARISING IN CONTRACT, TORT,
NEGLIGENCE OR OTHERWISE), INCLUDING ANY LOST PROFITS, LOST MONIES,
LOST TIME, LOSSES ATTRIBUTABLE IN WHOLE OR PART TO ANY DEFECTS IN
THE DESIGN OR PERFORMANCE OF THE SDK OR ANY PRODUCT OR
APPLICATION, OR SPECIAL, INCIDENTAL OR CONSEQUENTIAL DAMAGES
ARISING OUT OF THE USE OR INABILITY TO USE THE SDK, INCLUDING BUT
NOT LIMITED TO LOSS OF DATA OR DATA BEING RENDERED INACCURATE OR
LOSSES SUSTAINED BY THIRD PARTIES OR A FAILURE OF THE SDK TO
OPERATE WITH PROGRAMS NOT DISTRIBUTED BY SYMBIAN), EVEN IF
SYMBIAN HAS BEEN ADVISED OF THE POSSIBILITY OF SUCH DAMAGES, OR
FOR ANY CLAIM BY ANY OTHER PARTY. NOTHING IN THIS AGREEMENT
LIMITS SYMBIAN'S LIABILITY FOR DEATH OR PERSONAL INJURY CAUSED BY
ITS NEGLIGENCE.

Index

Index

H

HandleCommandL() function, 272
app UI class, 266
from menu bar, 286
from shortcut keys, 287
from tool bar, 285
in helloeik example, 285
request functions, 579
HandleControlStateChangeL() function, 393
dialogs, 320
HandleHitRequest() function
Battleships program (example), 719
HandleHitResponse() function
hit responses (Battleships), 721
HandlePointerBufferReadyL() function, 401
HandlePointerEventL() function, 402
graphics interaction, 382
pick correlation, 400
pointer events, 384
HandleRedrawEvent() function
ActivateGc() function, 365
Draw() function, 365
DrawComponents() function, 365
redrawing, 364
HandleStateChange() function, 391
hardware
CPU, 82
EPOC devices, 82–84
EPOC R5, comms, 524
I/O devices, 83
power sources, 83
RAM, 83
ROM, 82
hardware serial ports
See UARTs
has-a class relationships, 124
Solo ships, 442
UML representation, 127
HBufC concrete descriptor, 136
modifying, 140
HCIL, 19
header files, 276
C++ header files, 899
OXHs, 898
resource files, 278
heap descriptors, 137
heap failure tool, 159
with test functions, 189
heaps
_UHEAP_MARK macro, 162
failure, 165–67
reallocating memory, 167
heap balance, 161–65

memory, 134
threads, 93
Hello World example
active objects, 576
CDelayedHello class, 576
functions, 577
CFlashingHello class, 591
device independence, 488
EIKON version, 65–74
application structure, 265
running with Visual C++ debugger, 284–88
porting, 813
SetHello() function, 578
text mode version, 53–65
view class, 490
using, 495
help facilities
authoring
aleppo help builder, 420
EPOC, 419
limitations, 426
help files, 46
adding, 419
DemoOPL example, 896
launching from application, 424
StartHelpL() function, 425
StopHelpL() function, 425
OPL, 879
history stacks, WML, 794
hit reports
DrawTilesNow() function, 354
flicker-free redraw, 353
horizontal option button lists, 324
HorizontalPixelsToTwips() function, 467
how to draw
Draw() function, 349
.hrh files, 290
#including, 277
control IDs, 309
resource scripts, 274
HTML, 10
producing, 424
human-computer interaction layer HCIL, 19

I

I/O devices
EPOC, 83
iActive
threads, 583
IAS
irDA, 675
LMP, 675
iCoeEnv

T

wrox
PROGRAMMER TO PROGRAMMER™

Wrox writes books for you. Any suggestions, or ideas about how you want information given in your ideal book will be studied by our team. Your comments are always valued at Wrox.

Free phone in USA 800-USE-WROX
Fax (312) 893 8001

UK Tel. (0121) 687 4100   Fax (0121) 687 4101

Professional Symbian Programming - Registration Card

Name _____

Address _____

_____

_____

_____

City_____ State/Region _____

Country_____ Postcode/Zip _____

E-mail _____

Occupation _____

How did you hear about this book? _____

☐ Book review (name) _____

☐ Advertisement (name) _____

☐ Recommendation _____

☐ Catalog _____

☐ Other _____

Where did you buy this book? _____

☐ Bookstore (name)_____ City _____

☐ Computer Store (name)_____

☐ Mail Order _____

☐ Other _____

What influenced you in the purchase of this book?

☐ Cover Design

☐ Contents

☐ Other (please specify) _____

How did you rate the overall contents of this book?

☐ Excellent   ☐ Good

☐ Average   ☐ Poor

What did you find most useful about this book? _____

What did you find least useful about this book? _____

Please add any additional comments. _____

What other subjects will you buy a computer book on soon? _____

What is the best computer book you have used this year?

_____

Note: This information will only be used to keep you updated about new Wrox Press titles and will not be used for any other purpose or passed to any other third party.

wrox
PROGRAMMER TO PROGRAMMER™

NB. If you post the bounce back card below in the UK, please send it to:

Wrox Press Ltd., Arden House, 1102 Warwick Road,
Acocks Green, Birmingham B27 6BH. UK.

——— *Computer Book Publishers* ———